Lecture Notes in Computer Science 9054

Commenced Publication in 1973
Founding and Former Series Editors:
Gerhard Goos, Juris Hartmanis, and Jan van Leeuwen

More information about this series at http://www.springer.com/series/7410

Gregor Leander (Ed.)

Fast
Software Encryption

22nd International Workshop, FSE 2015
Istanbul, Turkey, March 8–11, 2015
Revised Selected Papers

 Springer

Editor
Gregor Leander
Universität Bochum
Bochum
Germany

ISSN 0302-9743   ISSN 1611-3349 (electronic)
Lecture Notes in Computer Science
ISBN 978-3-662-48115-8   ISBN 978-3-662-48116-5 (eBook)
DOI 10.1007/978-3-662-48116-5

Library of Congress Control Number: 2015945331

LNCS Sublibrary: SL4 – Security and Cryptology

Springer Heidelberg New York Dordrecht London

Printed on acid-free paper

Springer-Verlag GmbH Berlin Heidelberg is part of Springer Science+Business Media
(www.springer.com)

Preface

The 22nd International Workshop on Fast Software Encryption (FSE 2015) was held in Istanbul, Turkey, March 8–11, 2015. The workshop was organized by TUBITAK - BILGEM with Hüseyin Demirci serving as the general chair and sponsored by the International Association for Cryptologic Research (IACR). The workshop had about 140 registered participants from 26 different countries.

FSE 2015 received 71 valid submissions. Each paper was reviewed by three reviewers and five reviewers in the case of a submission co-authored by members of the Program Committee. The entire double-blind review process took more than two months in which each paper was carefully taken into account. The Program Committee finally accepted 28 original articles to be presented at the workshop and published in these proceedings.

The Program Committee of FSE 2015 decided, in line with the tradition of previous years, to select a best paper. This year, the Program Committee awarded the contribution "GCM Security Bounds Reconsidered" by Yuichi Niwa, Keisuke Ohashi, Kazuhiko Minematsu, and Tetsu Iwata the best paper award of FSE 2015. This paper, along with the two contributions "Rotational Cryptanalysis of ARX Revisited" by Dmitry Khovratovich, Ivica Nikolić, Josef Pieprzyk, Przemysław Sokołowski, and Ron Steinfeld and "Meet-in-the-Middle Attacks and Structural Analysis of Round-Reduced PRINCE" by Patrick Derbezand and Léo Perrin, was furthermore solicited for the *Journal of Cryptology*.

FSE 2015 featured two invited talks, one by Meltem Sönmez Turan from the National Institute of Standards and Technology (NIST) about the NIST initiative on lightweight cryptography, and one by Jacob Appelbaum on NSA, mass surveillance, and its impact on society. The program of FSE 2015 also included a rump session with short talks on the latest results in the field. The rump session was chaired by Dan Bernstein and Tanja Lange.

The selection of papers would not have been possible without the enormous help of the Program Committee members and external reviewers. I am grateful for all their effort. It was great honor and good fun to work together with such an excellent committee.

For the local organization, I would like to express my gratitude to Hüseyin Demirci for the very professional and smooth organization of the workshop. Without him and his team, the event would not have been possible.

Finally, I hope that the reader enjoys these proceedings as much as I enjoyed the experiences of serving as program chair for FSE 2015.

May 2015   Gregor Leander

Organization

Program Committee

Elena Andreeva	KU Leuven, Belgium
Kazumaro Aoki	NTT Secure Platform Laboratories, Japan
Daniel Bernstein	University of Illinois at Chicago, USA, and TU/e, The Netherlands
Céline Blondeau	Aalto University, Finland
Andrey Bogdanov	Technical University of Denmark, Denmark
Anne Canteaut	Inria, France
Joan Daemen	STMicroelectronics, Belgium
Itai Dinur	Ecole Normale Superieure, Paris, France
Orr Dunkelman	University of Haifa, Israel
Tetsu Iwata	Nagoya University, Japan
Orhun Kara	TUBITAK - BILGEM, Turkey
Dmitry Khovratovich	University of Luxembourg, Luxembourg
Gaëtan Leurent	Inria, France
Stefan Lucks	Bauhaus-Universität Weimar, Germany
Amir Moradi	HGI, Ruhr University Bochum, Germany
María Naya-Plasencia	Inria, France
Svetla Nikova	KU Leuven, Belgium
Thomas Peyrin	Nanyang Technological University, Singapore
Vincent Rijmen	KU Leuven, Belgium
Martin Schläffer	Infineon Technologies, Austria
Tom Shrimpton	Portland State University, USA
Martijn Stam	University of Bristol, UK
François-Xavier Standaert	Université catholique de Louvain, Belgium
Vesselin Velichkov	University of Luxembourg, Luxembourg
Tolga Yalcin	UIST St. Paul the Apostle, Macedonia

External Reviewers

Farzaneh Abed	Claude Carlet	Christian Forler
Zahra Ahmadian	Hüseyin Demirci	Benedikt Gierlichs
Sedat Akleylek	Christoph Dobraunig	Vincent Grosso
Tomer Ashur	Maria Eichlseder	Benoît Gérard
Gilles Van Assche	Oğuzhan Ersoy	Mehmet Emin Gönen
Guido Bertoni	Muhammed Fethullah	Takanori Isobe
Begül Bilgin	Esgin	Arpan Jati
Christina Boura	Matthieu Finiasz	Jérémy Jean

Contents

Cryptanalysis of Authenticated Encryption Schemes

Proofs

Design

Lightweight

Cryptanalysis of Hash Functions and Stream Ciphers

Mass Surveillance

Block Cipher Cryptanalysis

Differential Analysis and Meet-in-the-Middle Attack Against Round-Reduced TWINE

Alex Biryukov, Patrick Derbez, and Léo Perrin$^{(\boxtimes)}$

SnT, University of Luxembourg, Luxembourg, Luxembourg
alex.biryukov@uni.lu, {patrick.derbez,leo.perrin}@uni.lu

Abstract. TWINE is a recent lightweight block cipher based on a Feistel structure. We first present two new attacks on TWINE-128 reduced to 25 rounds that have a slightly higher overall complexity than the 25-round attack presented by Wang and Wu at ACISP 2014, but a lower data complexity.

Then, we introduce alternative representations of both the round function of this block cipher and of a sequence of 4 rounds. LBlock, another lightweight block cipher, turns out to exhibit the same behaviour. Then, we illustrate how this alternative representation can shed new light on the security of TWINE by deriving high probability iterated truncated differential trails covering 4 rounds with probability 2^{-16}.

The importance of these is shown by combining different truncated differential trails to attack 23-rounds TWINE-128 and by giving a tighter lower bound on the high probability of some differentials by clustering differential characteristics following one of these truncated trails. A comparison between these high probability differentials and those recently found in a variant of LBlock by Leurent highlights the importance of considering the whole distribution of the coefficients in the difference distribution table of a S-Box and not only their maximum value.

Keywords: TWINE · LBlock · Meet-in-the-Middle · Truncated differential · Cryptanalysis

1 Introduction

Lightweightness is currently one of the most investigated topics in symmetric cryptography. As more and more appliances are expected to communicate with each other as well as over the internet, the need for primitives capable of running on low-power CPU's e.g. used in sensor networks as well as on small RFID tags is becoming more pressing. Many lightweight primitives intended to be usable in such constrained environment have been proposed during the last few years, a review of which can be found in [1].

A possible approach to design a lightweight primitive is to use many rounds with a simple structure. The Generalized Feistel Network (GFN), introduced

Patrick Derbez and Léo Perrin – Supported by the CORE ACRYPT project from the *Fond National de Recherche* (Luxembourg).

© International Association for Cryptologic Research 2015
G. Leander (Ed.): FSE 2015, LNCS 9054, pp. 3–27, 2015.
DOI: 10.1007/978-3-662-48116-5_1

by Nyberg in [2], is a modification of the regular Feistel Network which uses more than 2 branches. Having more branches allows the use of a simpler Feistel function, the branch permutation taking care of the diffusion, hence the suitability of this approach in a constrained context. However, the simple branch rotation used in most GFN with b branches requires b rounds to obtain full diffusion. To improve this number, more sophisticated permutations were introduced in [3] and one such permutation has been used by the authors of TWINE [4], a lightweight block cipher with a GFN structure: while TWINE uses 16 branches, only 8 rounds are necessary for full diffusion. TWINE is therefore both a good example of common trade-offs in lightweight cryptography, e.g. it has a simple round function iterated many times, and one of the only instances of a GFN with improved diffusion layer. A similar block cipher is LBlock [5], a lightweight block cipher which served as the basis for the design of LBlock-s, a variant with a different S-Box and key schedule used in the Lightweight Authenticated Cipher (LAC) submitted to the CAESAR competition by a related team [6]. While LBlock is described as a "regular" two-branched Feistel Network, the rotation used in its permutation layer and the simplicity of its Feistel function make it equivalent to a GFN similar to TWINE. The designers of TWINE pointed out this resemblance in [4].

In this paper, we focused our efforts on TWINE and tried different approaches to cryptanalyze it. First, we study Meet-in-the-Middle (MitM) attacks on TWINE-128 and describe an attack on 25 rounds[1]. It is based on the attack strategy proposed by Demirci and Selçuk at FSE 2008 [9] to attack both the 192 and 256-bit version of the AES reduced to 8 rounds and which is the starting point of the best attacks on the AES so far [10–12]. Then we study impossible differential attacks and show that thanks to the framework described by Boura *et al.* in [13] one can be mounted on 25 rounds with an overall complexity below the natural bound of the exhaustive search. Our 25-round attacks have a slightly higher time complexity than the 25-round attack presented by Wang and Wu [14] at ACISP 2014 but a lower data complexity. Interestingly, three different cryptanalysis techniques (meet-in-the-middle, impossible differential and zero-correlation linear) allow to break the same number of rounds with a similar overall complexity.

The particular permutation layer of TWINE implies, as we will see, an observable vulnerability of this block cipher against truncated differential cryptanalysis, an attack introduced by Knudsen [15]. Unlike "normal" differential cryptanalysis, this technique does not rely on studying fully specified trails where each bit of difference is supposed to have a particular value but instead on looking at more general patterns where some bit differences may take both values 0 and 1. In the case of word oriented cipher, we can restrict the investigation to trails where the differences are studied at the word level: either there is at least one difference over the whole word or there is none. Trails where some of the bits

---

[1] While a MitM attack on 25-round TWINE-128 is already in the literature [7], it has been shown in a note on eprint [8] that the complexity of this attack is actually higher than brute-force.

are not specified are often used when adding rounds on top and on the bottom of a differential distinguisher. However, using truncated differential covering all the rounds can also yield powerful attacks. For example, such an approach has been used recently by Lallemand et al. [16] to attack the lightweight block cipher KLEIN [17]. Truncated differential have also been used to enhance the search for high probability differentials. Two recent examples are the best attack on the block cipher PRINCE [18] and a differential forgery attack on the authenticated cipher LAC [19].

As we introduce new attacks on TWINE, we summarize the complexities of the best attacks against this cipher in the single-key model in Table 1.

Table 1. The best attacks on TWINE in the single-key model.

Description			Complexity		
Reference	Type	Version	Data	Time	Memory
[20]	Biclique	full TWINE-80	2^{60}	$2^{79.1}$	2^8
		full TWINE-128	2^{60}	$2^{126.82}$	2^8
[21]	Impossible diff.	23r TWINE-80	$2^{57.85}$	$2^{79.09}$	$2^{78.04}$
		24r TWINE-128	$2^{58.1}$	$2^{126.78}$	$2^{125.61}$
[14]	Zero-Cor. Linear	23r TWINE-80	$2^{62.1}$	$2^{72.15}$	2^{60}
		25r TWINE-128	$2^{62.1}$	$2^{122.12}$	2^{60}
Sect. 3.1	MitM	25r TWINE-128	2^{48}	$2^{124.7}$	2^{109}
Sect. 3.2	Impossible diff.	25r TWINE-128	$2^{59.1}$	$2^{124.5}$	$2^{78.1}$
Sect. 5.3	Truncated diff.	23r TWINE-128	2^{58}	$2^{126.78}$	2^{89}
			2^{62}	$2^{125.94}$	
			2^{64}	$2^{124.35}$	

Our Contributions. First, we describe in Sect. 3 our best attacks on TWINE-128, namely both a Meet-in-the-Middle attack and an Impossible Differential attack, leveraging the simplicity of the key schedule of this block cipher.

Then, we highlight in Sect. 4 a property of the permutation used in TWINE: rounds of encryption can be grouped into blocks of 4 rounds in such a way that two halves of the internal states of both ciphers evolve independently from one another during the first 3 rounds of the block and exchange information only during the fourth. We also discuss why LBlock and its simpler variant LBlock-s exhibit the same 4-round behaviour. As a consequence of this observation, we describe several high probability truncated differential trails for all these ciphers. We then leverage them in Sect. 5 to attack 23 rounds of TWINE-128 using comparatively low memory. Finally, we use these truncated trails to optimize a search for high probability differentials and show that the conservative choice of S-Box made by the designers of TWINE greatly limits the differential effect in this primitive — unlike in LBlock-s for instance.

2 Descriptions of TWINE, LBlock and LBlock-s

2.1 Description of TWINE

This block cipher uses 16 branches of 4-bits and has a very simple round function (see Fig. 1): the Feistel function consists in a xor of a sub-key and a call to a unique S-box based on the inverse function in $GF(2^4)$. Then, the branches are shuffled using a sophisticated nibble permutation ensuring faster diffusion than a simple shift [3]. One version of TWINE uses an 80 bits key, another uses a 128 bits key and we denote these versions TWINE-80 and TWINE-128. They only differ by their key-schedule and both have 36 rounds. Both key schedules are sparse GFN's using only 2 S-Box calls per round for TWINE-80 and 3 for TWINE-128. At each round, some fixed nibbles of the key-state are used as round keys for the block cipher. One round of TWINE is depicted on Fig. 1.

$$x_r[0..15]$$

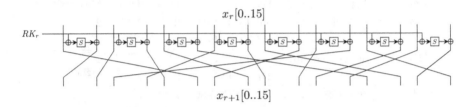

Fig. 1. The round function of TWINE.

Notations. Given a collection of messages $\{P^0, \ldots\}$, the nibble with index i taken at round r of message m is denoted $x_r^m[i]$. The master key is denoted K while the round key used at round r is denoted RK_r.

Keyschedule. The keyschedule produces the 36 round keys from the master key K. It is a variant of GFN with few Sboxes which is the same as the one used in the round function of TWINE. Two key lengths are available: 80 and 128 bits. In both cases, the subkey WK_0 is first initialized to K and then next subkeys are generated using round constants and the same round function: $WK_{i+1} = F(WK_i, CON^i)$, for $0 \leq i \leq 31$. Finally the round key RK_i is obtained by extracting 8 nibbles from WK_i. The function F used for 128-bit keys is depicted on Fig. 2. We refer the reader to [4] for the 80-bit version of the keyschedule.

2.2 Descriptions of LBlock and LBlock-s

LBlock [5] is a two-branched Feistel Network with a twist: a rotation is performed on the branch being xor-ed with the output of the Feistel function. This leads to a strong structural proximity with TWINE, as the authors of this cipher acknowledged.

The Feistel function of LBlock is made of a key addition, a S-box layer S made of 8 different 4-bits S-boxes and a nibble permutation P. In addition to the

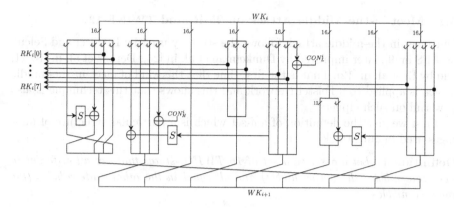

Fig. 2. Keyschedule of TWINE-128.

usual Feistel structure, there is a rotation by 8 bits to the left on the right branch before the xor. The complete round function is described in Fig. 3. LBlock only uses 80-bits keys. Its key-schedule is similar to that of PRESENT [22]: it relies on a rotation of the 80-bits register used to store the master key and on the application of two S-boxes. It uses 32 rounds to encrypt a plaintext.

LBlock-s, the block cipher used in the authenticated cipher LAC [6], is identical to LBlock except that the S-Box layer uses a unique S-Box instead of 8 different ones and that its key-schedule is closer to the one of TWINE-80. The S-Boxes of LBlock and that of LBlock-s all have similar differential properties.

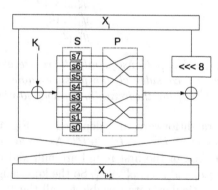

Fig. 3. The round function of LBlock

3   New Attacks on 25-Round TWINE-128

In this section we present two new attacks on 25-round TWINE, increasing by one the number of rounds broken if we omit biclique attacks.

3.1   Meet-in-the-Middle Attack on 25-Round TWINE-128

Our meet-in-the-middle attack follows the strategy used by Demirci and Selçuk on AES in [9], later improved by Dunkelman et al. in [23], Derbez et al. in [10,11] and by Li et al. in [12]. That is the first time that this kind of meet-in-the-middle attack is applied to a Feistel Network and this shows that this technique is also powerful on such ciphers.

First we give the definition of a δ-set which is a particular structure of messages used in our attack.

Definition 1. *Let a δ-set be a set of 16 TWINE-states that are all different in one state nibble (the active nibble) and all equal in the other state nibbles (the inactive nibbles).*

In the following we consider δ-sets such that the nibble 15 is the active one. For such a particular set we made the following observation which is the core of our new attack.

Observation 1. *Consider the encryption of a δ-set $\{P^0, P^1, \ldots, P^{15}\}$ through eleven full TWINE rounds. The ordered sequence*

$$[x_{11}^1[4] \oplus x_{11}^0[4], x_{11}^2[4] \oplus x_{11}^0[4], \ldots, x_{11}^{15}[4] \oplus x_{11}^0[4],$$
$$x_{11}^1[15] \oplus x_{11}^0[15], \ldots, x_{11}^{15}[15] \oplus x_{11}^0[15]]$$

is fully determined by the following 27 nibble parameters:

- $y_1^0[14]$
- $y_2^0[14]$
- $y_3^0[2, 14]$
- $y_4^0[2, 4, 14]$
- $y_5^0[0, 2, 4, 14]$

- $y_6^0[0, 2, 8, 12, 14]$
- $y_7^0[0, 4, 6, 10, 14]$
- $y_8^0[2, 8, 12]$
- $y_9^0[4, 10]$
- $y_{10}^0[2]$

where $y_r^m[2i] = x_r^m[2i] \oplus RK_r[i]$. Consequently, there are at most $2^{4 \times 27} = 2^{108}$ possible sequences when we consider all the possible choices of keys and δ-sets (out of the $2^{4 \times 2 \times 15} = 2^{120}$ of the theoretically possible 30-nibble sequences).

Proof. The proof is straightforward and depicted on Fig. 4. At the first step we know the differences $P^1 \oplus P^0, \ldots, P^{15} \oplus P^0$. As we are considering a δ-set, the differences in each sbox of the first round are null and thus we are able to compute the differences $x_1^1 \oplus x_1^0, \ldots, x_1^{15} \oplus x_1^0$. So the knowledge of $y_1^0[14]$ leads to the knowledge of this particular state variable for all the 16 messages and thus we know the differences in each sbox of this round and are able to compute the differences $x_2^1 \oplus x_2^0, \ldots, x_2^{15} \oplus x_2^0$. This procedure can be repeated until differences in both $x_{11}[4]$ and $x_{11}[15]$ are reached since at each step differences in sboxes are either null, not required or known.

Note that the actual value of the active nibble of P^0 does not affect the set of all the possible sequences since only differences are used. Thus the choice of P^0 is free but then the δ-set has to be ordered according to the difference in the active nibble.

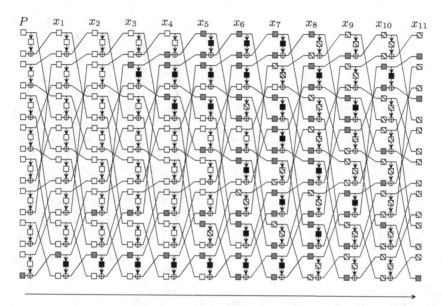

$P \quad x_1 \quad x_2 \quad x_3 \quad x_4 \quad x_5 \quad x_6 \quad x_7 \quad x_8 \quad x_9 \quad x_{10} \quad x_{11}$

Fig. 4. Encryption of a δ-set through 11 full TWINE rounds. Black nibbles are the parameters given in Observation 1. Differences in coloured nibbles are known. No difference in white nibbles.

This observation on 11-round TWINE is used to mount an attack on 25-round TWINE by adding 5 rounds at beginning and 9 at the end. The scenario of the attack is the following:

- **Offline phase.** Compute all the 2^{108} 120-bit sequences given in Observation 1, and store them in a hash table.
- **Online phase.**
  1. Pick a plaintext P^0.
  2. Guess the state variables required to identify a δ-set containing P^0.
  3. Ask for the corresponding ciphertexts.
  4. Guess the state variables required to compute differences in both $x_{11}[4]$ and $x_{11}[15]$ from the ciphertexts.
  5. Build the sequence and check if it belongs to the table.

Steps 2 and 4 are similar to the proof of Observation 1: first we propagate the differences from state x_5 to the plaintext and then we propagate differences from the ciphertexts to both $x_{11}[4]$ and $x_{11}[15]$. Thus 58 state nibbles are needed to perform the online phase as depicted on Fig. 5. Hopefully, the keyschedule equations reduce the amount of possible values from $2^{4 \cdot 58} = 2^{232}$ to 2^{124}. Indeed, knowing the full subkey WK_6 except nibble 26 leads to the knowledge of enough key material to partially encrypt and decrypt the plaintext and the ciphertext in order to obtain the value of the required state variables. This key material is depicted on Fig. 6.

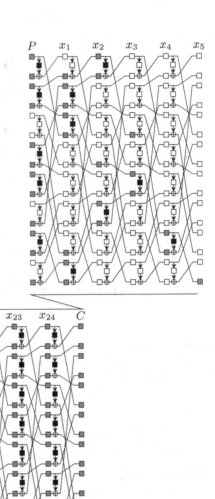

Fig. 5. Online phase of the 25-round attack. Black nibbles have to be known to compute differences in all coloured nibbles. No difference in white nibbles.

The data complexity of this attack is 2^{48} chosen plaintexts, the time complexity is $2^{124} \cdot 16$ partial encryptions/decryptions and the memory complexity is around 2^{108} 128-bit sequences. The probability for a false positive is approximately $2^{108} \cdot 2^{-120} = 2^{-12}$ and, as we try 2^{124} key guess, we expect that only 2^{116} remain after the last step. Thus, one can guess $WK_6[26]$ to fully recover the master key and then test it against two plaintext/ciphertext pairs.

Note that some minor improvements can be applied to the attack. First we can consider δ-set of 15 messages instead of 16 to save some memory and

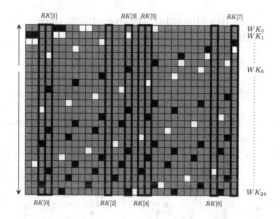

Fig. 6. Subkeys of 25-round TWINE. Gray (resp. colored) nibbles are computed from the full WK_6 except nibbles 15 and 26 (resp. except nibble 26).

time complexity while still providing enough filtering to retrieve the master key without increasing the overall complexity. Furthermore, knowing the subkey WK_6 except nibbles 15 and 26 provides enough key material (gray colored on Fig. 6) to compute all the state variables required by step 2 together with all the ones required by step 4 except 21 of them. Those ones are $y_{16}[14]$, $y_{17}[6, 10]$, $y_{18}[2, 8, 10]$, $y_{19}[0, 12]$, $y_{20}[2, 4, 6, 14]$, $y_{21}[2, 6, 8]$, $y_{22}[0, 2]$, $y_{23}[0, 4]$ and $y_{24}[6]$. Hence, we estimate the time complexity to be:

$$2^{120} \cdot 15 \cdot 37/200 + 2^{124} \cdot 15 \cdot 21/200 + 2 \cdot 2^{120} \approx 2^{124.7} \text{ encryptions,}$$

where 200 is the number of sboxes for one encryption. The memory complexity is approximately 2^{109} 64-bit blocks.

3.2 Impossible Differential Attack on 25-Round twine-128

Impossible differential cryptanalysis simultaneously introduced by Knudsen [24] and Biham *et al.* [25] is a powerful technique against a large variety of block ciphers. Recently, Boura *et al.* [13] proposed a generic vision of impossible differential attacks with the aim of simplifying and helping the construction and verification of this type of cryptanalysis. In particular, they provided a formula to compute the complexity of such an attack according to its parameters. To understand the formula we first briefly remain how an impossible differential attack is constructed. It starts by splitting the cipher in three parts: $E = E_3 \circ E_2 \circ E_1$ and by finding an impossible differential $(\Delta_X \nrightarrow \Delta_Y)$ through E_2. Then Δ_X (resp. Δ_Y) is propagated through E_1^{-1} (resp. E_3) with probability 1 to obtain Δ_{in} (resp. Δ_{out}). We denote by c_{in} and c_{out} the $\log_2$ of the probability of the transitions $\Delta_{in} \rightarrow \Delta_X$ and $\Delta_{out} \rightarrow \Delta_Y$ respectively. Finally we denote by k_{in} and k_{out} the key materials involved in those transitions. All in all the attack consists in discarding the keys k for which at least one pair follows the characteristic through E_1 and E_3 and in exhausting the remaining ones. The complexity of doing so is the following:

- **data:** C_{N_α}
- **memory:** N_α
- **time:** $C_{N_\alpha} + \left(1 + 2^{|k_{in} \cup k_{out}| - c_{in} - c_{out}}\right) N_\alpha C_{E'} + 2^{|k| - \alpha}$

where N_α is such that $(1 - 2^{-c_{in} - c_{out}})^{N_\alpha} < 2^{-\alpha}$, C_{N_α} is the number of chosen plaintexts required to generate N_α pairs satisfying $(\Delta_{in}, \Delta_{out})$, $|k|$ is the key size and $C_{E'}$ is the ratio of the cost of partial encryption to the full encryption.

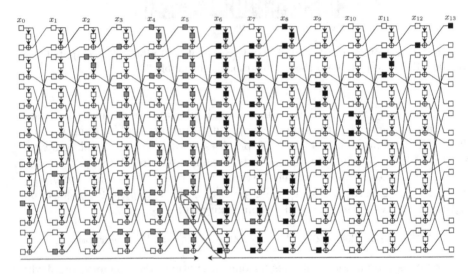

Fig. 7. Impossible truncated differential on 13 TWINE-rounds. No difference in white nibbles. Differences in black (resp. gray) nibbles are (resp. may be) non-zero.

We used this framework to mount an impossible differential attack on 25-round TWINE-128. First we found a truncated impossible characteristic through 13 rounds of TWINE which is described on Fig. 7. It was extended by 4 rounds at the start and by 8 rounds at the end in order to attack 25 rounds of the cipher. It can be seen in Fig. 8 that the difference in the plaintexts has to be zero in 11 nibbles such that $c_{in} + c_{out} = 16 + 60 = 76$. The key material $k_{in} \cup k_{out}$ is composed of $7 + 45 = 52$ round-key nibbles which can assume only 2^{124} thanks to the keyschedule of TWINE-128. Indeed, they all can be computed from the whole subkey WK_{24} except nibble 1 (see Fig. 9).

As a consequence, and according to the above formula, the complexity of our attack is $D = \alpha \cdot 2^{75.5 - 39} \cdot 2^{20} = \alpha \cdot 2^{56.5}$, $M = \alpha \cdot 2^{75.5}$ and $T \approx \alpha \cdot 2^{123.5} \cdot C_{E'} + 2^{128 - \alpha}$. As we estimate the ratio $C_{E'}$ to $52/200 \approx 2^{-1.9}$, the value of α minimizing the overall complexity is 5.87.

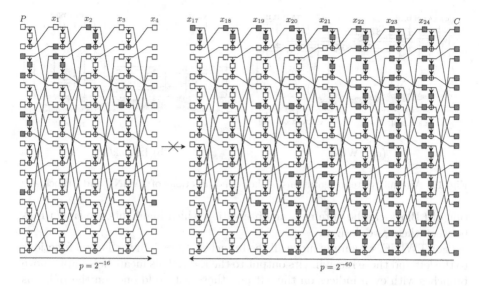

Fig. 8. Impossible differential attack on 25 rounds. No difference in white nibbles.

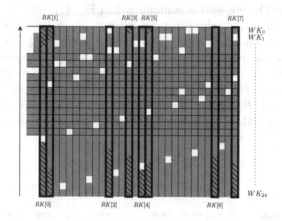

Fig. 9. Subkey nibbles obtained from WK_{24} except nibble 1. Hatched nibbles are the ones required in the impossible differential attack.

4   The 4-Round Structure of TWINE, LBlock and LBlock-s

4.1   Alternative Representation of the Round Functions

The round functions of TWINE can be described using an equivalent representation which allows a clearer representation of some differential paths. This alternative representation is given in Fig. 10a. Note that a similar representa-

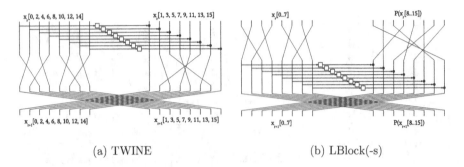

(a) TWINE   (b) LBlock(-s)

Fig. 10. Alternative representations of the round functions of TWINE and LBlock(-s).

tion of LBlock can be obtained, an observation which highlights the similarities between these two designs.

For TWINE, we simply move all the branches "going" in the Feistel functions to the left and those receiving its output to the right. This means we simply move branches with even indices on the left and those with odd ones on the right, as described in Fig. 10a.

The process leading to the alternative description of LBlock(-s) is more complicated than for TWINE and is summarized in Fig. 11. Since the S-boxes and the permutation layer P both operate on nibbles, $P \circ S$ is equivalent to $S' \circ P$ where S' is a reordered S-box layer. Then, instead of applying P within the Feistel function, we apply it before entering it and then apply the inverse $1/P$ of P on the same branch to compensate. Finally, we note that the rotation R and the inverse permutation $1/P$ are applied on the same data, so we combine them into one operation $R \circ (1/P)$. If we replace the two 32-bit words making the internal state of LBlock by eight 4-bit nibbles each, we obtain the representation given in Fig. 10b.

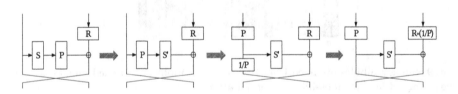

Fig. 11. How to obtain the alternative representation of LBlock(-s).

4.2   A 4-Round Cyclic Behavior

Using our alternative representation, we represent 4 rounds of TWINE easily (see left of Fig. 12). As we can see, the 16 branches can be grouped in two disjoint *components*, gray and black, such that branches from one component interact only with each other during 3 rounds out of 4. However, during the last round, branches from each component interact only with branches from the other component. Furthermore, these components are stable in the sense that such groups of 4 iterations can be plugged together to cover any number of rounds and remain separated for all rounds with index r with $r \not\equiv 3 \mod 4$. Indeed, in Fig. 12, the branches which are black at the output of the fourth round are exactly those which are gray at the input of the first round. If we draw these components separated from one another, we obtain another description of 4 rounds of TWINE given on the right of Fig. 12. The same can be done with LBlock(-s), see Fig. 13.

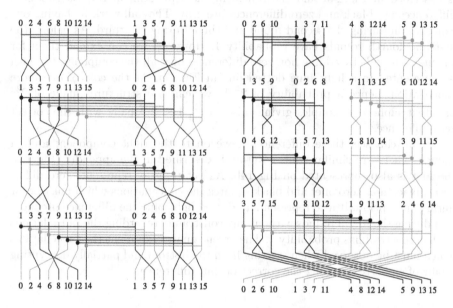

Fig. 12. Alternative representation of 4 rounds of TWINE. S-boxes are not shown and XOR's are represented by circles. On the left is the basic representation, on the right one which highlights the two components. Numbers correspond to nibble indices in the "regular" representation.

5 Truncated Differential Cryptanalysis of TWINE

5.1 Truncated Differentials over 4 Rounds

Because of the particular structure it has over 4 rounds, TWINE exhibits some truncated differential patterns with high probability. The simplest one implies 4 active branches in input and 4 active branches in the output of 4 rounds at the cost of 4 difference cancellations at round 3. Let $(x[0], x[2], x[6], x[10])$ have non zero differences. Then these differences will propagate to the full black component during the next two rounds. During round 3, if the differences in $(x[0], x[4], x[6], x[12])$ cancel themselves with the differences in $(x[1], x[5], x[7], x[13])$ after going through the key addition and the S-box layer, then the differences do not propagate to the red component. Hence, the differences remain contained in the black component for another 3 round with probability 1. Since 4 cancellations happen with probability 2^{-16} and since such truncated characteristics can be "plugged" so as to cover as many rounds as we want, we have a truncated differential covering $4r$ rounds with probability $2^{-16 \cdot r}$.

Other slightly different characteristics involve three active branches in the input and the output after 4 rounds in such a way that only 4 cancellations are necessary, meaning that they also have a probability of 2^{-16}. One of them is described in Fig. 14a and the others in the Appendix in Fig. 17. Non-zero differences are black and zero differences are gray. They all work by having one cancellation during the second round and three during the third. As before, the first and fourth rounds have probability 1. However, we can extend them for the first 4 rounds by adding non-zero differences over all the components (which is represented in a light blue dotted line in Fig. 17). At the cost of one more cancellation, hence a probability of 2^{-20}, we can use structures made of 2^{32} plaintext/ciphertext couples giving raise to $\binom{2^{32}}{2} \approx 2^{63}$ pairs with the correct zero-differences.

As we can see, these differences move on to the right component after 4 rounds. There are similar trails covering it described in the appendix (Fig. 18), the first is also represented on Fig. 14b. As before, gray represents zero differences, black non-zero ones and black squares the cancellations which must occur during encryption. It also represents in dotted light blue the difference propagation during the first 3 rounds without any constraints regarding the cancellations so that this trail has probability 1. The green squares represent the cancellations which must be observed when starting from the bottom and partially decrypting a pair of ciphertext having the correct output difference.

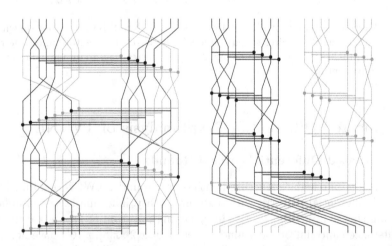

Fig. 13. Alternative representation of 4 rounds of LBlock(-s). S-boxes are not shown and XOR's are represented by circles. On the left is the basic representation, on the right one which highlights the two components.

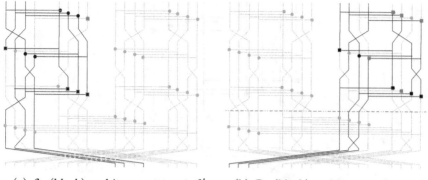

(a) $\mathcal{L}_1$ (black) and its counterpart $\mathcal{L}'_1$ (b) $\mathcal{R}_1$ (black) and its counterpart $\mathcal{R}'_1$

Fig. 14. 4-round truncated differentials for TWINE and their modified versions (Colored figure online).

It is therefore possible to cover as many rounds as we want using a characteristic $\mathcal{L}_i, \mathcal{R}_i, ..., \mathcal{L}_i, \mathcal{R}_i$ for any $i \in [1, 4]$. Such a trail would cover $4r$ rounds with probability $2^{-16 \cdot r}$. We also denote $\mathcal{L}'_i$ the trail $\mathcal{L}_i$ extended on top so as to have 8 non-zero input differences at the cost of one additional cancellation and $\mathcal{R}'_i$ the trail $\mathcal{R}_i$ reduced to 3 rounds and where no cancellations occur. Both $\mathcal{L}'_i$ and $\mathcal{R}'_i$ correspond to the case where the dotted light blue lines contain non-zero differences.

5.2 Efficient Key Recovery

The 4 cancellations (5 during the very first round) preventing the difference from spreading to the other component can be grouped into 2 sets each depending on a distinct set of 5 and 6 sub-keys. This phenomenon is illustrated on Fig. 15 where zero differences are in gray, the first sub-component is represented with a continuous line and the second with a dashed line. The cancellation during the first round of the iterated trail is only relevant during the very first round of encryption.

Starting from a pair of plaintexts separated by the correct input difference, it is easy to generate the set of all the sub-keys combinations which would lead to the trail we expect as follows:

1. Try all possible combinations of the sub-keys involved in the continuous (i.e. "not dashed") part of Fig. 15 and store only those leading to the correct cancellations. There are $2^{4 \cdot 5} = 2^{20}$ possibilities, out of which $2^{20-3 \cdot 4} = 2^8$ lead to the correct pattern.
2. Try all possible combinations of the sub-keys involved in the dashed part of Fig. 15 and store only those leading to the correct cancellations. There are $2^{4 \cdot 6} = 2^{24}$ possibilities, out of which $2^{20-2 \cdot 4} = 2^{16}$ lead to the correct pattern.
3. Combine the 2^8 and 2^{16} independent sub-candidates to obtain 2^{24} candidates of $4 \cdot (5 + 6) = 44$ bits each.

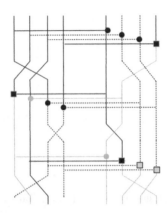

Fig. 15. Which S-boxes and sub-keys are involved in the 5 cancellations happening in $\mathcal{L}'_1$. Grey lines correspond to zero differences, squares to cancellations.

A very similar algorithm can be used to recover the candidates yielding the correct cancellations when partially decrypting the ciphertexts of the same pair. Doing so generates another 2^{24} candidates of 44 bits each.

5.3 Combining Truncated Differentials to Attack 23-Round TWINE-128

General Principle. The high level idea of this attack is to discard some combinations of values for the set made of the 12 sub-keys used to update the left component during the first 3 rounds and the 12 sub-keys used to update the right component during the last 3 rounds. These form of set of 24 nibbles, i.e. 96 bits. The first and last 4-round blocks of the truncated differential trails described in Fig. 16 all depend on the sub-keys in this set, although each of the trails only uses a different set of 88 bits out of the 96 bits available. It is therefore easy to combine the information deduced from each. A complete description of our attack follows.

Using the trails described in the previous Section, we can cover 23 rounds with probability $p = 2^{-84}$ in four different ways. The chaining of these different 4-round characteristics is described in Fig. 16 where a 0 means there is no difference on this nibble and a x means any non-zero difference. Note that they all require the same input truncated difference, all yield the same output truncated difference and once a branch has been "selected" during the third round by cancelling one of the difference, the truncated trail is fixed.

1. **Data Generation.** First of all, we need to generate the pairs from which we are going to extract information about the sub-keys. For this purpose, we use 2^s structures of 2^{32} plaintext/ciphertext couples each. In these structures, nibbles $x_0[0..3, 6, 7, 10, 11]$ take all possible values while the others are constant. We thus obtain 2^{s+63} pairs with the correct input difference at a cost

Round index

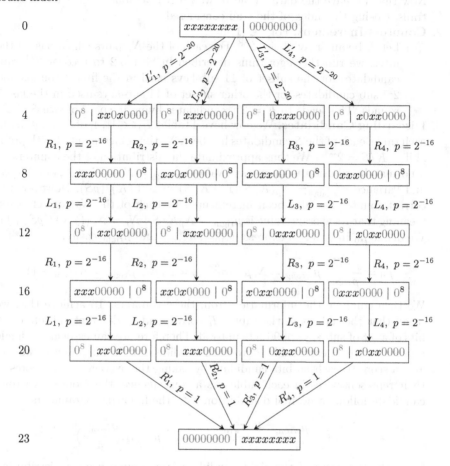

Fig. 16. The four distinct 23-round truncated differential trails we use to attack TWINE. The nibbles are ordered as in the left side of Fig. 12.

of $D = 2^{32+s}$ queries to an encryption oracle. We then obtain all the pairs which also have the correct output difference, namely[2] $0^8 x^8$, at the cost of 2^s sorting of arrays of 2^{32} ciphertexts. Since this output difference has probability $f = 2^{-32}$, this leaves $N_p = 2^{s+63} \cdot f = 2^{s+31}$ pairs with the correct input and output differences. Among these, there are $N_r = 2^{s+63} \cdot p = 2^{s-21}$ right pairs for each of the 4 truncated differential trails described in Fig. 16 — which means that s must be at least equal to 21. Note that $N_p = N_r f/p$ and $D = N_r/p$.

---

[2] The order of the nibbles in this difference corresponds to the order of the nibbles in our alternative representation.

Now that we have the data we need, we process as follows for each of the 4 trails, t being the index of the trail considered.

2. **Counters Increment.** For $t \in [1, 4]$

    (a) Let $\mathcal{T}_t$ be an array of size 2^{88}. For each of the N_p pairs which passed the filter, we run the algorithms described in Sect. 5.2 to recover 2^{24} sub-candidates for the subset of 11 sub-keys used in the first 3 rounds and 2^{24} sub-candidates for the other subset of 11 sub-keys used in the last 3 rounds. This leads to $K = 2^{48}$ candidates living in space of size $\mathcal{S} = 2^{88}$

3. **Discarding Candidates.** We now have 4 tables $\mathcal{T}_t, t \in [1, 4]$ of $\mathcal{S}$ counters. In each table, each of the $\mathcal{S}$ candidates has been N_p times incremented with probability $K/\mathcal{S} = 2^{-40}$. We thus approximate the distribution of the counters by a normal distribution with average value $\mu_{\text{wrong}} = N_p K/\mathcal{S} = N_r(fK)/(p\mathcal{S})$ and variance $\sigma^2_{\text{wrong}} = N_p(K/\mathcal{S})(1 - K/\mathcal{S}) \approx N_r(fK)/(p\mathcal{S})$. However, the correct counter has also been incremented by each of the N_r correct pairs, meaning that its average value is $\mu_{\text{right}} = N_p K/\mathcal{S} + N_r = N_r((fK)/(p\mathcal{S}) + 1)$. We define μ_0 in order to express μ_{wrong}, σ^2_{wrong} and μ_{right} easily:

$$\mu_0 = \frac{f \cdot K}{p \cdot \mathcal{S}}, \ \mu_{\text{wrong}} = N_r \mu_0, \ \sigma^2_{\text{wrong}} = N_r \mu_0, \ \mu_{\text{right}} = N_r(\mu_0 + 1).$$

We then combine the information from these counters. To achieve this, we recall that the indices in the tables $\mathcal{T}_t$ correspond to different subsets of 88 bits of a set of sub-keys of 96 bits in total. Therefore, we can associate a single representative in each table $\mathcal{T}_t$ to each candidate of 96 bits. Hence, we can give a score to each 96-bits candidate by taking the average of the scores of their representatives in each table. As a consequence, the score of a wrong candidate follows a normal distribution with the following parameters:

$$\mathcal{N}\left(\frac{4 \cdot \mu_{\text{wrong}}}{4}, \frac{4 \cdot \sigma^2_{\text{wrong}}}{4^2}\right) = \mathcal{N}\left(\mu_{\text{wrong}}, \frac{\sigma^2_{\text{wrong}}}{4}\right).$$

Similarly, the score of the right candidate is a sample from a distribution $\mathcal{N}\left(\mu_{\text{right}}, \sigma^2_{\text{right}}/4\right)$. If we want a probability of keeping the right candidate of about $1/2$, we need to discard all the candidates having a score below μ_{right}. We denote $\mathbb{P}_{\text{wrong}}$ the probability to keep a wrong candidate, i.e. the probability that a wrong candidate has a score greater than μ_{right}. It is given by:

$$\mathbb{P}_{\text{wrong}} = \frac{1}{2}\left[1 - \text{erf}\left(\frac{\mu_{\text{right}} - \mu_{\text{wrong}}}{\sqrt{2\sigma^2_{\text{wrong}}/4}}\right)\right] = \frac{1}{2}\left[1 - \text{erf}\left(\sqrt{\frac{2N_r}{\mu_0}}\right)\right]. \quad (1)$$

As we can see and unsurprisingly, the amount of wrong candidates discarded increases with the number N_r of right pairs for each trail. Table 2 gives the value of the probability $\mathbb{P}_{\text{wrong}}$ to keep a wrong candidate depending on the value of N_r as well as the corresponding data complexity knowing that $\mu_0 = 2^{-32+56+84-96} = 2^{12}$. Note also that the maximum value of N_r corresponds to the full code-book, i.e. when we query all 2^{32} possible structures, in which case, $N_r = 2^{32-21} = 2^{11}$.

Complexity Estimation. The memory complexity of the truncated differential attack described in the previous section is straight-forward to evaluate. We need to store at most 2^{63} plaintext/ciphertext pairs and 4 times 2^{88} counters. These counters are on average equal to $N_r \cdot 2^{12}$ with N_r equal to at most 2^{11}. Hence, 32 bits are more than enough for each of them. Storing the counters is clearly the dominating factor here, meaning that the memory complexity of this attack is $4 \cdot 2^{88} = 2^{90}$ counters of 32 bits or 2^{89} internal states.

We need $N_r \cdot 2^{53}$ plaintext/ciphertext pairs, meaning that the data complexity is $N_r \cdot 2^{53}$.

This also implies that we need at least the time taken to generate these. Furthermore, we also need to compute the possible candidates for each of the $N_r \cdot 2^{52}$ pairs which passed the filter. As seen in Sect. 5.2, this can be done in time 2^{48} for each pair. Hence, we also need to perform a counter increment $4 \cdot N_r \cdot 2^{52} \cdot 2^{48} = N_r \cdot 2^{102}$ times. Finally, for all the candidates with a high enough score, we need to brute-force the 32 remaining bits of the key. This requires $2^{128} \cdot \mathbb{P}_{\text{wrong}}$ encryptions. The complexities for different values of N_r are given in Table 2.

Table 2. Data, time and memory complexity of a truncated differential attack on TWINE-128.

N_r	$\mathbb{P}_{\text{wrong}}$	D	T	M
2^5	$2^{-1.22}$	2^{58}	$2^{126.78}$	2^{89}
2^7	$2^{-1.47}$	2^{60}	$2^{126.53}$	
2^9	$2^{-2.06}$	2^{62}	$2^{125.94}$	
2^{11}	$2^{-3.67}$	2^{64}	$2^{124.34}$	

6 Optimizing the Search for High Probability Differentials

While truncated differentials can be used directly to attack (round-reduced) block ciphers directly, they can also be used to optimize the search for high probability differentials. Indeed, by providing a "template" which differential characteristics should follow, it can reduce the size of the search space significantly and make the computation of a lower bound on a differential probability tighter. A similar approach was used in [18] to identify high probability differentials for PRINCE which were then used in a multiple differential attack which is the best attack on this cipher today. LAC [6], a lightweight candidate of the CAESAR competition based on a simplified version of LBlock called LBlock-s, has been the target of another high probability differential search in a note released online by Leurent [19].

In both cases, the method has been the same: first identify a high probability differential trail and then use a heuristic method to compute a lower bound on the probability of a differential by essentially clustering all characteristics following said truncated differential. Since we have iterated truncated trails covering any amount of rounds for TWINE, we apply this method on this cipher to identify high probability differentials.

For a truncated characteristic T covering r rounds, we denote $P_T[\delta \to \Delta]$ the probability of the differential $(\delta \to \Delta)$ obtained by summing the probabilities of all the differential trails mapping δ to Δ which follow the truncated trail. Using these probabilities, we build a matrix $M(C)$ such that $M(T)_{i,j} = P_T[i \to j]$. To obtain the distribution of Δ given δ, we simply multiply a vector made of zeroes everywhere except in position δ, where it is equal to 1, by $M(T)$. Note that the sum of the probabilities of the Δ's obtained in this fashion is not equal to 1 as the truncated trail itself does not have a probability of 1. Given $M(T)$, finding the differential with the highest probability can be done easily by finding the maximum coefficient in the matrix. The size of $M(T)$ is limited by only taking into account the values of δ and Δ which are coeherent with T.

In order to obtain the distribution of Δ after two iterations of the trail T, we multiply the same vector by the matrix $M(T) \times M(T)$, where "$\times$" denotes regular matrix multiplication. This construction can of course be iterated.

In the case of TWINE, we computed two matrices $M(\mathcal{L}_1)$ and $M(\mathcal{R}_1)$ corresponding to the truncated trails $\mathcal{L}_1$ and $\mathcal{R}_1$ described in Fig. 14a and b respectively. Both $M(\mathcal{L}_1)$ and $M(\mathcal{R}_1)$ are square matrices of size $2^{12} \times 2^{12}$ because both trails have only 3 non-zero nibbles as both their input and output. Using different multiplications of these, we found the high probability differentials given in Table 3.

Table 3. High probability differentials for round-reduced TWINE.

Rounds	Input difference	Output difference	Probability	# Active S-Boxes $\times 2^{-2}$
4	10 20 00 60 00 00 00 00	00 00 20 00 60 00 00 60	$2^{-17.496}$	2^{-18}
	60 20 00 60 00 00 00 00	00 00 20 00 60 00 00 10	$2^{-17.496}$	
	30 60 00 30 00 00 00 00	00 00 60 00 30 00 00 10	$2^{-17.759}$	
	10 60 00 30 00 00 00 00	00 00 60 00 30 00 00 30	$2^{-17.759}$	
8	10 20 00 60 00 00 00 00	60 20 00 10 00 00 00 00	$2^{-34.542}$	2^{-36}
	10 20 00 60 00 00 00 00	60 20 00 f0 00 00 00 00	$2^{-34.981}$	
	f0 20 00 60 00 00 00 00	60 20 00 10 00 00 00 00	$2^{-34.981}$	
	d0 f0 00 80 00 00 00 00	80 f0 00 d0 00 00 00 00	$2^{-34.994}$	
12	10 20 00 10 00 00 00 00	00 00 20 00 60 00 00 10	$2^{-52.083}$	2^{-54}
	10 20 00 60 00 00 00 00	00 00 20 00 10 00 00 10	$2^{-52.083}$	
	80 f0 00 80 00 00 00 00	00 00 f0 00 d0 00 00 80	$2^{-52.144}$	
	80 f0 00 d0 00 00 00 00	00 00 f0 00 80 00 00 80	$2^{-52.144}$	
16	60 20 00 60 00 00 00 00	60 20 00 60 00 00 00 00	$2^{-67.538}$	2^{-72}
	30 60 00 30 00 00 00 00	30 60 00 30 00 00 00 00	$2^{-67.595}$	
	90 30 00 90 00 00 00 00	90 30 00 90 00 00 00 00	$2^{-67.626}$	
	80 f0 00 80 00 00 00 00	80 f0 00 80 00 00 00 00	$2^{-67.762}$	

As we can see, the highest probability for a differential over 4 rounds is higher than we might expect. Indeed, 9 S-Boxes are involved in it and the maximum probability for a differential in the S-Box is 2^{-2}. Hence, the maximum probability of a characteristic is 2^{-18}, which is smaller than the value of $2^{-17.5}$ our model predicts and which we checked experimentally. The gain then increases as the number of rounds increases. For 12 rounds, we have 27 active S-Boxes which means that the probability of a characteristic cannot be higher than 2^{-54} and yet the highest differential probability is at least $2^{-52.1}$.

Leurent obtained more impressive results for LBlock-s (e.g. a lower bound of $2^{-29.8}$ for 8 rounds) which might be surprising at first glance since the linear layer of these two ciphers are very similar and both use S-Boxes with a maximum differential probability equal to 2^{-2}. However, the distribution of the coefficients in the difference distribution tables of the S-Boxes of these ciphers are different. For instance, with S_L and S_T denoting the S-Boxes of LBlock-s and TWINE respectively, we have $P[S_L(x + \delta) + S_L(x) = 4] = 2^{-2}$ for $\delta \in \{4, 5, 6, 7\}$ while there exists only one δ such that $P[S_T(x + \delta) + S_T(x) = \Delta] = 2^{-2}$ for any $\Delta \neq 0$. In other words, the distribution of the output differences is closer to being uniform in TWINE than in LBlock-s (and LBlock). To study the consequences of these variation in differential behaviour, we reiterated our differential search by replacing the S-box of TWINE by that of LBlock-s. We obtained four distinct differentials with probability at least $2^{-31.7}$ for 8 rounds.[3] This result is $2^{4.3}$ times better than what a wide-trail argument would give and 2^3 times higher than for the TWINE S-Box.

Our findings highlight both how large truncated differentials can be leveraged to prove tighter lower bounds on differential probabilities and how the distribution of the coefficients in the difference distribution table of a S-Box as a whole should be taken into account when designing a primitive in contrast to simply looking at the maximum coefficient, as is often the case when wide-trail arguments are used. For $n \times n$ S-Boxes affine equivalent to monomials of $GF(2^n)$, this distribution is fully described by the so-called *differential spectrum* [26] but, to the best of our knowledge, there is no generalization of this concept to arbitrary S-Boxes.

7 Conclusion

Suzaki et al. proposed a new type of permutation to be used in GFN's in [3] and later applied it to design TWINE. We presented two new attacks on 25 rounds out of 36 of this primitive which are, to the best of our knowledge, the best attacks in the single-key model. We then shed new light on the way information propagates in such a modified GFN and showed that the mixing actually operates in two phases: two halves of the internal state are mixed independently for three rounds and only exchange information during the fourth round. This behaviour is repeated *ad infinitum* and can also be observed in LBlock and its variant,

---

[3] Note that Leurent used a truncated differential with 17 active S-Boxes while our has 18. This difference is likely to account for the factor $2^{1.9}$ separating our results.

LBlock-s. We used this observation to find high probability truncated differential trails and then leveraged these results to both attack 23-rounds TWINE-128 and give a tighter lower bound on the high probability of some differentials, highlighting differences between TWINE and LBlock-s with regards to differential propagation in the process.

A   Appendix

A.1   Complete 4-Rounds Truncated Differential Characteristics for TWINE

In this Section, we present all the 4-rounds truncated differential trails we use to attack TWINE. Figure 17 describes trails on the left component and how they can be extended, at the cost of an additional cancellation, to have a larger input difference. Figure 18 describes trails on the right component and how they behave during the first 3 rounds if no cancellation occur.

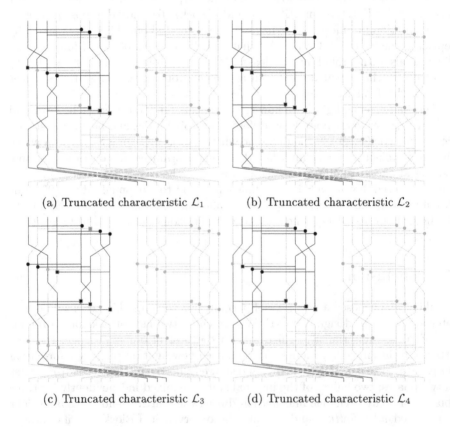

(a) Truncated characteristic $\mathcal{L}_1$ (b) Truncated characteristic $\mathcal{L}_2$

(c) Truncated characteristic $\mathcal{L}_3$ (d) Truncated characteristic $\mathcal{L}_4$

Fig. 17. Truncated differential characteristics on the left component of TWINE and their extensions towards the top. Zero differences are represented in black and squares correspond to places where cancellations are necessary (Colored figure online).

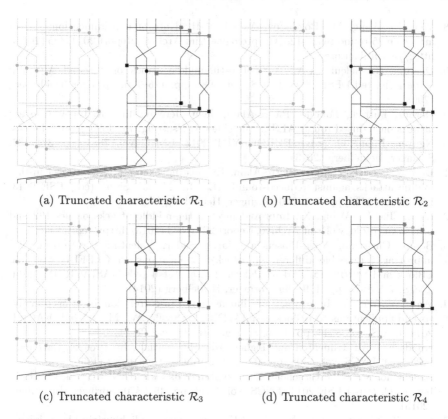

(a) Truncated characteristic $\mathcal{R}_1$ (b) Truncated characteristic $\mathcal{R}_2$

(c) Truncated characteristic $\mathcal{R}_3$ (d) Truncated characteristic $\mathcal{R}_4$

Fig. 18. Truncated differential characteristics on the right component of TWINE and their extensions towards the bottom.

References

1. Biryukov, A., Perrin, L.: State of the art in lightweight cryptography. http://cryptolux.org/index.php/Lightweight_Cryptography
2. Nyberg, K.: Generalized feistel networks. In: Kim, K., Matsumoto, T. (eds.) ASIACRYPT 1996. LNCS, vol. 1163, pp. 91–104. Springer, Heidelberg (1996)
3. Suzaki, T., Minematsu, K.: Improving the generalized feistel. In: Hong, S., Iwata, T. (eds.) FSE 2010. LNCS, vol. 6147, pp. 19–39. Springer, Heidelberg (2010)
4. Suzaki, Tomoyasu, Minematsu, Kazuhiko, Morioka, Sumio, Kobayashi, Eita: TWINE: a lightweight block cipher for multiple platforms. In: Knudsen, Lars R., Wu, Huapeng (eds.) SAC 2012. LNCS, vol. 7707, pp. 339–354. Springer, Heidelberg (2013)
5. Wu, W., Zhang, L.: LBlock: a lightweight block cipher. In: Lopez, J., Tsudik, G. (eds.) ACNS 2011. LNCS, vol. 6715, pp. 327–344. Springer, Heidelberg (2011)
6. Zhang, L., Wu, W., Wang, Y., Wu, S., Zhang, J.: Lac: A lightweight authenticated encryption cipher. Candidate for the CAESAR Competition (2014)
7. Boztas, Ö., Karakoç, F., Çoban, M.: Multidimensional meet-in-the-middle attacks on reduced-round TWINE-128. In: Avoine, G., Kara, O. (eds.) LightSec 2013. LNCS, vol. 8162, pp. 55–67. Springer, Heidelberg (2013)

8. Wen, L., Wang, M., Bogdanov, A., Chen, H.: Note of multidimensional mitm attack on 25-round twine-128. Cryptology ePrint Archive, Report 2014/425 (2014). http://eprint.iacr.org/

9. Demirci, H., Selçuk, A.A.: A meet-in-the-middle attack on 8-round AES. In: Nyberg, K. (ed.) FSE 2008. LNCS, vol. 5086, pp. 116–126. Springer, Heidelberg (2008)

10. Derbez, Patrick, Fouque, Pierre-Alain, Jean, Jérémy: Improved key recovery attacks on reduced-round AES in the single-key setting. In: Johansson, Thomas, Nguyen, Phong Q. (eds.) EUROCRYPT 2013. LNCS, vol. 7881, pp. 371–387. Springer, Heidelberg (2013)

11. Derbez, Patrick, Fouque, Pierre-Alain: Exhausting Demirci-Sel cuk meet-in-the-middle attacks against reduced-round AES. In: Moriai, Shiho (ed.) FSE 2013. LNCS, vol. 8424, pp. 541–560. Springer, Heidelberg (2014)

12. Li, L., Jia, K., Wang, X.: Improved meet-in-the-middle attacks on aes-192 and prince. Cryptology ePrint Archive, Report 2013/573 (2013). http://eprint.iacr.org/

13. Boura, Christina, Naya-Plasencia, María, Suder, Valentin: Scrutinizing and improving impossible differential attacks: applications to CLEFIA, camellia, LBlock and SIMON. In: Sarkar, Palash, Iwata, Tetsu (eds.) ASIACRYPT 2014. LNCS, vol. 8873, pp. 179–199. Springer, Heidelberg (2014)

14. Wang, Y., Wu, W.: Improved multidimensional zero-correlation linear cryptanalysis and applications to LBlock and TWINE. In: Susilo, W., Mu, Y. (eds.) ACISP 2014. LNCS, vol. 8544, pp. 1–16. Springer, Heidelberg (2014)

15. Knudsen, L.R.: Truncated and higher order differentials. In: Preneel, Bart (ed.) FSE 1994. LNCS, vol. 1008, pp. 196–211. Springer, Heidelberg (1995)

16. Lallemand, V., Naya-Plasencia, M.: Cryptanalysis of KLEIN. In: Cid, C., Rechberger, C. (eds.) FSE 2014. LNCS, vol. 8540, pp. 451–470. Springer, Heidelberg (2015)

17. Gong, Z., Nikova, S., Law, Y.W.: KLEIN: a new family of lightweight block ciphers. In: Juels, A., Paar, C. (eds.) RFIDSec 2011. LNCS, vol. 7055, pp. 1–18. Springer, Heidelberg (2012)

18. Canteaut, A., Fuhr, T., Gilbert, H., Naya-Plasencia, M., Reinhard, J.R.: Multiple differential cryptanalysis of round-reduced prince (full version). Cryptology ePrint Archive, Report 2014/089 (2014). http://eprint.iacr.org/

19. Leurent, G.: Differential forgery attack against LAC, July 2014. https://hal.inria.fr/hal-01017048

20. Çoban, M., Karakoç, F., Boztaş, Ö.: Biclique cryptanalysis of TWINE. In: Pieprzyk, J., Sadeghi, A.-R., Manulis, M. (eds.) CANS 2012. LNCS, vol. 7712, pp. 43–55. Springer, Heidelberg (2012)

21. Zheng, X., Jia, K.: Impossible differential attack on reduced-round TWINE. In: Lee, H.-S., Han, D.-G. (eds.) ICISC 2013. LNCS, vol. 8565, pp. 123–143. Springer, Heidelberg (2014)

22. Bogdanov, A.A., Knudsen, L.R., Leander, G., Paar, C., Poschmann, A., Robshaw, M., Seurin, Y., Vikkelsoe, C.: PRESENT: an ultra-lightweight block cipher. In: Paillier, P., Verbauwhede, I. (eds.) CHES 2007. LNCS, vol. 4727, pp. 450–466. Springer, Heidelberg (2007)

23. Dunkelman, O., Keller, N., Shamir, A.: Improved single-key attacks on 8-round AES-192 and AES-256. In: Abe, M. (ed.) ASIACRYPT 2010. LNCS, vol. 6477, pp. 158–176. Springer, Heidelberg (2010)

24. Knudsen, L.R.: Deal - a 128-bit block cipher. Technical report, Department of Informatics (1998)

25. Biham, E., Biryukov, A., Shamir, A.: Cryptanalysis of Skipjack reduced to 31 rounds using impossible differentials. In: Stern, J. (ed.) EUROCRYPT 1999. LNCS, vol. 1592, p. 12. Springer, Heidelberg (1999)
26. Blondeau, C., Canteaut, A., Charpin, P.: Differential properties of power functions. Int. J. Inf. Coding Theory 1(2), 149–170 (2010)

Improved Higher-Order Differential
Attacks on MISTY1

Achiya Bar-On[✉]

Department of Mathematics, Bar Ilan University,
52900 Ramat Gan, Israel
barona@macs.biu.ac.il

Abstract. MISTY1 is a block cipher designed by Matsui in 1997. It is widely deployed in Japan, and is recognized internationally as an European NESSIE-recommended cipher and an ISO standard. Since its introduction, MISTY1 was subjected to extensive cryptanalytic efforts, yet no attack significantly faster than exhaustive key search is known on its full version. The best currently known attack is a higher-order differential attack presented by Tsunoo et al. in 2012 which breaks a reduced variant of MISTY1 that contains 7 of the 8 rounds and 4 of the 5 FL layers in $2^{49.7}$ data and $2^{116.4}$ time.

In this paper, we present improved higher-order differential attacks on reduced-round MISTY1. Our attack on the variant considered by Tsunoo et al. requires roughly the same amount of data and only $2^{100.4}$ time (i.e., is 2^{16} times faster). Furthermore, we present the first attack on a MISTY1 variant with 7 rounds and all 5 FL layers, requiring $2^{51.4}$ data and 2^{121} time. To achieve our results, we use a new higher-order differential characteristic for 4-round MISTY1, as well as enhanced key recovery algorithms based on the *partial sums* technique.

1 Introduction

MISTY1 [10] is a 64-bit block cipher with 128-bit keys designed in 1997 by Matsui. In 2002, MISTY1 was selected by the Japanese government to be one of the CRYPTREC e-government ciphers, and since then, it became widely deployed in Japan. MISTY1 also gained recognition outside Japan, when it was selected to the portfolio of European NESSIE-recommended ciphers, and approved as an ISO standard in 2005. Furthermore, the block cipher KASUMI [1] designed as a slight modification of MISTY1 is used in the 3G cellular networks, which makes it one of the most widely used block ciphers today.

MISTY1 has an 8-round recursive Feistel structure, where the round function FO is in itself a 3-round Feistel construction, whose F-function FI is in turn a 3-round Feistel construction using 7-bit and 9-bit invertible S-boxes. The specific choice of S-boxes and the recursive structure ensure provable security against

A. Bar-On—This research was partially supported by the Israeli Ministry of Science, Technology and Space, and by the Check Point Institute for Information Security.

© International Association for Cryptologic Research 2015
G. Leander (Ed.): FSE 2015, LNCS 9054, pp. 28–47, 2015.
DOI: 10.1007/978-3-662-48116-5_2

differential and linear cryptanalysis. In order to thwart other types of attacks, after every two rounds an FL function is applied to each of the two halves independently. The FL functions are key-dependent linear functions which play the role of whitening layers.

Since its introduction, MISTY1 was subjected to extensive cryptanalytic efforts using a variety of techniques, which resulted in numerous attacks on its reduced variants. The best currently known attacks are the following:

- A higher-order differential (HOD) attack on 6-round MISTY1 with 4 of the 5 FL layers, with a semi-practical complexity of $2^{49.4}$ chosen plaintexts and time [13].
- An impossible differential attack on 7-round MISTY1 with 3 FL layers, that requires 2^{58} known plaintexts and $2^{124.4}$ time [5].
- A zero-correlation linear attack on 7-round MISTY1 with 4 FL layers, that requires $2^{62.9}$ known plaintexts and 2^{118} time [15].
- A HOD attack on 7-round MISTY1 with 4 of the 5 FL layers, that requires $2^{49.7}$ chosen plaintexts and $2^{116.4}$ encryptions [13].
- A related-key differential attack on the full MISTY1, that requires 2^{61} chosen ciphertexts and $2^{90.9}$ encryptions, and applies under a weak key class assumption [9].
- A meet-in-the-middle attack which allows to speed up exhaustive key search on the full MISTY1 [6] by a factor of between 2 and 4.

Examination of the best currently known attacks on MISTY1 suggests that up to date, the technique that provided the strongest results against reduced-round MISTY1 is the higher-order differential attack. In this paper, we examine the currently known HOD attacks on MISTY1 thoroughly and show that they can be improved, both in the exact characteristic used for the attack and in the key-recovery algorithm. The results we obtain are the following:

1. The 44-order differential characteristic for 4-round MISTY1 introduced and deployed in [13] can be replaced by more efficient 43-order differentials. This allows to reduce the data and time complexities of the attacks of [13] on 6-round MISTY1 from $2^{49.4}$ to 2^{47}. As we explain in Sect. 4, the order of the differential cannot be reduced further unless an entirely different characteristic is introduced.
2. The time complexity of the attack of [13] on 7-round MISTY1 can be reduced by a factor of 2^{16} by using the *partial sums* technique [4], along with optimizations exploiting the exact structure of MISTY1.
3. Despite the fact that 7-round MISTY1 with all 5 FL layers uses 64 additional subkey bits (compared to the variant attacked in [13]), we can break this variant in data $2^{51.4}$ and time 2^{121} using a complex key-recovery procedure based on the partial sums technique.

The latter result is the first known attack on 7-round MISTY1 with all 5 FL functions present. A comparison of our attacks with the best previously known attacks on reduced-round MISTY1 is presented in Table 1.

The paper is organized as follows. In Sect. 2 we describe the structure of MISTY1 and introduce some notations that will be used throughout the paper. Since our attack is based heavily on the HOD attacks of [13, 14], we describe these attacks briefly in Sect. 3. Our improved attack on 6-round MISTY1 is presented in Sect. 4. The attacks on 7-round MISTY1 with 4 and 5 FL layers are presented in Sects. 5 and 6, respectively. Finally, in Sect. 7 we summarize the paper.

Table 1. Summary of the best known single-key attacks on MISTY1

FO rounds	FL layers	Data complexity	Time complexity	Type
6	4	$2^{49.4}$	$2^{49.4}$	HOD attack [13]
6	4	2^{47}	2^{47}	HOD attack (Sect. 4)
7	3	2^{58} KP	$2^{124.4}$	ID attack [5]
7	4	$2^{62.9}$ KP	2^{118}	MZC attack [15]
7	4	$2^{49.7}$	$2^{116.4}$	HOD attack [13]
7	4	$2^{50.1}$	$2^{100.4}$	HOD attack (Sect. 5)
7	5	$2^{51.45}$	2^{121}	HOD attack (Sect. 6)

ID attack: Impossible Differential attack
HOD attack: Higher Order Differential attack
MZC attack: Multi-Dimensional Zero Correlation attack

2   Brief Description of MISTY1

MISTY1 is an 8-round Feistel construction, where the round function, FO, is in itself a variant of a 3-round Feistel construction, defined as follows. The input to FO is divided into two halves. The left one is XORed with a subkey, enters a keyed permutation FI, and the output is XORed with the right half. After the XOR, the two halves are swapped, and the same process (including the swap) is repeated two more times. After that, an additional swap and an XOR of the left half with a subkey is performed (see Fig. 1).

The FI function in itself also has a Feistel-like structure. Its 16-bit input is divided into two unequal parts – one of 9 bits, and the second of 7 bits. The left part (which contains 9 bits) enters an S-box, $S9$, and the output is XORed with the right 7-bit part (after padding the 7-bit value with two zeroes as the most significant bits). The two parts are swapped, the 7-bit part enters a different S-box, $S7$, and the output is XORed with 7 bits out of the 9 of the right part. The two parts are then XORed with a subkey, and swapped again. The 9-bit value again enters $S9$, and the output is XORed with the 7-bit part (after padding). The two parts are then swapped for the last time.

Every two rounds, starting before the first one, each of the two 32-bit halves enters an FL layer. The FL layer is a simple linear transformation. Its input is divided into two halves of 16 bits each, the AND of the left half with a subkey

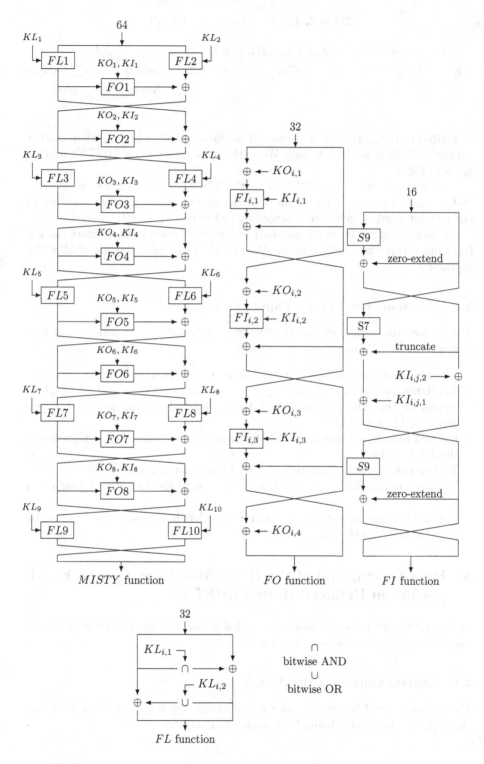

Fig. 1. Outline of MISTY1

Table 2. The key schedule of MISTY1

$KO_{i,1}$	$KO_{i,2}$	$KO_{i,3}$	$KO_{i,4}$	$KI_{i,1}$	$KI_{i,2}$	$KI_{i,3}$	$KL_{i,1}$	$KL_{i,2}$
K_i	K_{i+2}	K_{i+7}	K_{i+4}	K'_{i+5}	K'_{i+1}	K'_{i+3}	$K_{\frac{i+1}{2}}$ (odd i)	$K_{\frac{i+1}{2}+6}$ (odd i)
							$K_{\frac{i}{2}+4}$ (even i)	$K_{\frac{i}{2}+2}$ (even i)

is XORed to the right half, and the OR of the updated right half with another subkey is XORed to the left half. We outline the structure of MISTY1 and its parts in Fig. 1.

The key schedule of MISTY1 takes the 128-bit key, and treats it as eight 16-bit words $K_1, K_2, \ldots, K_8$. From this sequence of words, another sequence of eight 16-bit words is generated, according to the rule $K'_i = FI_{K_{i+1}}(K_i)$.

In each round, seven words are used as the round subkey, and each of the FL functions accepts two subkey words. We give the exact key schedule of MISTY1 in Table 2.

2.1 Notations Used in the Paper

Throughout the paper, we use the following notations for intermediate values during the MISTY1 encryption process.

- The plaintext and the ciphertext are denoted, as usual, by P and $C = E(P)$.
- The input of the i'th round ($1 \leq i \leq 8$) is denoted by X_i. If we want to emphasize that the intermediate value corresponds to the plaintext P, we denote it by $X_i(P)$.
- For odd rounds, we denote by X'_i the intermediate value after application of the FL functions.
- The output of the FO function of round i is denoted Out_i.
- For any intermediate value Z, $Z[k - l]$ denotes bits from k to l (inclusive) of Z.
- For any intermediate value Z, the right and left halves of Z are denoted by Z_R and Z_L, respectively.

3   Brief Description of the HOD Attacks of Tsunoo Et Al. [13,14] on Reduced-Round MISTY1

In this section we present a brief description of the attacks of Tsunoo et al. [13, 14], that serve as the basis for our results.

3.1 General Outline of the Attack

The higher order differential attack was presented by Knudsen [7] in 1994 (see also [8]). The basic idea behind the attack is as follows.

Let $f : \{0,1\}^n \to \{0,1\}$ be a Boolean function. Suppose that the degree of f (as a multivariate polynomial) is d and that $V \subseteq \{0,1\}^n$ is a vector subspace of dimension k. Then it is easy to show that Equation (1) holds, independently of x.

$$\bigoplus_{y \in V} f(x \oplus y) = \begin{cases} \text{const} & \text{if } k = d \\ 0 & \text{if } k > d. \end{cases} \tag{1}$$

Suppose now that for some block cipher E, the mapping from the plaintext to a single bit in some intermediate state, that is, $X_i[j]$, can be represented by a (key-dependent) Boolean function f_K of a low degree. Then by Eq. (1), we have

$$\bigoplus_{y \in V} X_i[j](x \oplus y) = \begin{cases} \text{const}(K) & \text{if } k = d \\ 0 & \text{if } k > d. \end{cases} \tag{2}$$

Note that $\text{const}(K)$ depends only on K and not on the choices of x and V. Equation (2) can be used to mount the following attack on E. Denote by E_1^{-1} the Boolean function that represents the mapping from the ciphertext of E to the intermediate state bit $X_i[j]$. Then Eq. (2) can be rewritten as

$$\bigoplus_{y \in V} E_1^{-1}(E(x \oplus y)) = \begin{cases} \text{const}(K) & \text{if } k = d \\ 0 & \text{if } k > d. \end{cases} \tag{3}$$

The adversary asks for the encryption of several structures of plaintexts of the form $\{x \oplus y | y \in V\}$, where x is arbitrary and V is an arbitrary vector subspace of degree d, partially decrypts the corresponding ciphertexts (by guessing the key material used in E_1^{-1}), and checks whether Eq. (3) holds. The dimension d of V is called *the order of the differential*.

As guessing the key material used in E_1^{-1} may be very time consuming, various other techniques are used to approach Eq. (3). The technique used in [13, 14] is linearization, which allows to exploit the low algebraic degree of a single MISTY1 round.

In the linearization method, we first express $X_i[j]$ as a multivariate polynomial $f'(C, K)$ in the ciphertext bits and the key bits, where ciphertext bits are treated as constants and key bits are treated as variables. This transforms Eq. (3) into a polynomial equation in the key bits. Then, we linearize the equation by replacing each non-linear expression in the key bits (e.g., $k_1 \cdot k_2$) with a new variable. In such a way, Eq. (3) for each structure of plaintexts contributes a linear equation, where the total amount m of variables is the number of non-linear terms in f'. If the equations we obtain are independent (which is usually the case), m equations are sufficient for obtaining a unique solution. Every extra equation can be used as a filtering condition. Hence, if the amount of key bits used in E_1^{-1} is s, then $m + s$ structures are sufficient for determining all of them.

In summary, the HOD attack of [13,14] on MISTY1 consists of three stages. The first stage is detecting a HOD of order as small as possible that "predicts" a bit as close as possible to the ciphertext. The second stage is to create a system of linear equations by linearization of the corresponding function E_1^{-1}. The third stage is solving the equation system.

Before presenting the three stages in some more detail, we introduce a notation that will be used throughout the paper to describe higher-order differentials of MISTY1.

Consider a partial encryption of MISTY1, which starts at the state X_j and ends at the state X_k, where we are interested only in the bits $X_k[\ell - m]$. Denote this encryption function by $E'_K : X_j \rightarrow X_k[\ell - m]$. We denote by $V^{(d)}_{X_j[i_1,\ldots i_d]} X_k[\ell - m]$ the d'th order differential that starts in X_j, where $V = span\{e_{i_1}, \ldots e_{i_d}\}$ is the vector subspace of $\{0,1\}^{64}$ spanned by the unit vectors $e_{i_1}, \ldots e_{i_d}$. In other words,

$$V^{(d)}_{X_j[i_1,\ldots i_d]} X_k[\ell - m] = \bigoplus_{y \in span\{e_{i_1},\ldots e_{i_n}\}} E'_K(x \oplus y).$$

3.2   A 44'th Order Differential for 4-round MISTY1

The 44'th order differential of 4-round MISTY1 found in [13] is a culmination of a series of observations.

The basic observation is a 7'th order differential of 3-round MISTY1 without FL functions discovered by Babbage and Frisch [2].

Theorem 1. *For any three consecutive rounds of MISTY1 without FL functions, the equation*

$$V^{(7)}_{X_i[0-6]} X_{i+3}[57 - 63] = 0x6d$$

holds, independently of the (fixed) value of the key and of the (constant) value of $X_i[7 - 63]$.

As noted in [2], the theorem fails for MISTY1 with FL layers. In order to overcome this obstacle, Tsunoo et al. [14] suggested the notion of *neighbor* bit positions.

Definition 2. *For any intermediate state Z of MISTY1, the neighbor of the bit position $Z[i]$ is the bit position $Z[i + 16]$.*

Tsunoo et al. showed that when we accompany each bit position in the 7'th order differential with its neighbor position, the resulting differential can bypass the FL layers.

Theorem 3. *For any three consecutive rounds of MISTY1 with FL functions that start at an even round $2j$, the equation*

$$V^{(14)}_{X_{2j}[0-6,16-22]} X'_{2j+3}[57 - 63] = 0$$

holds, independently of the (fixed) value of the key and of the (constant) value of $X_{2j}[7 - 15, 23 - 63]$.

Due to the Feistel structure of MISTY1, the 3-round 14'th order differential can be extended to a 4-round 46'th order differential by taking all the 2^{32} possible values in the previous round. We obtain:

Theorem 4. *For any four consecutive rounds of MISTY1 with FL functions that start at an odd round $2j + 1$, the equation*

$$V_{X_{2j+1}[0-31,32-38,48-54]}^{(46)} X'_{2j+5}[57-63] = 0$$

holds, independently of the (fixed) value of the key and of the (constant) value of $X_{2j+1}[39 - 47, 55 - 63]$.

The 7'th, 14'th and 46'th order differentials are illustrated in Fig. 2. The proof of the theorems can be found in [2,14].

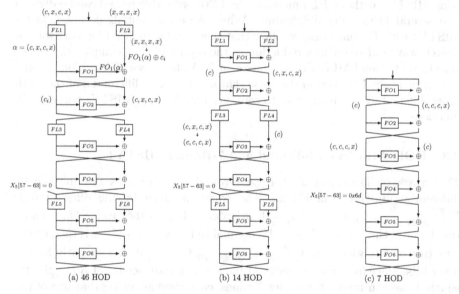

(a) 46 HOD   (b) 14 HOD   (c) 7 HOD

The form $(*, *, *, *)$ represents division of a 32-bit state into sets of $(9, 7, 9, 7)$ bits. The x's denote bit positions that are active in the differential. The c's denote "constant" bits. In Figure 2a, the symbol c_i, for $1 \le i \le 2^{32}$, denotes a 32-bit value that is constant for each sub-structure of size 2^{14}.

Fig. 2. Higher order differentials in MISTY1

The last observation, made by Tsunoo et al. in [13], is that each of the 14'th order differentials for 3-round MISTY1 presented above contains 28 12'th order differentials that also can be shown to sum up to zero (due to a non-maximal algebraic degree of the underlying function). These are all possible differentials obtained by taking any six of the 7 bits $X_{2j}[0 - 6]$, along with their neighbors. As some of these 12'th order differentials are linearly dependent, it turns out that only 22 of them can be used in parallel.

The observation of Tsunoo et al. in [13] allows to reduce the data and time complexities of the HOD attacks based on the 46'th round differential of 4-round MISTY1 by a factor of 22. Indeed, while in the previous attacks, each data structure of 2^{46} plaintexts contributes a single linear equation, Tsunoo et al.'s observation allows to use it to obtain 22 linearly independent equations (each coming from an extension by one round of a 12'th order differential). This obviously reduces the data complexity by a factor of 22, and if partial encryption/decryption of all the data is the most time consuming operation in the attack (as is the case for the attacks of [14], as we shall see below), the time complexity of the attacks is reduced by the same factor.

Given the progress in the size of HODs from paper to paper, it seems reasonable to check whether the differential can be improved yet another time by dividing the basic 12'th order differential to smaller ones. In this paper, we show that the answer is positive, to some extent. Namely, we show that when considering MISTY1 without FL functions, the 12'th order differential can be divided into several 11'th order differentials. While these differentials do not hold for MISTY1 with FL functions, we show that they can be applied in a more sophisticated way, and result in a reduction in the data and time complexities of the attacks on 6-round MISTY1 by a factor of 5. As far as we checked, our results cannot be pushed further, in the sense that no other sub-differential of the 12'th order differential of [14] sums up to zero, even for 3-round MISTY1 without FL functions.

3.3 HOD Attacks on 6-Round and 7-Round MISTY1

The attack of Tsunoo et al. [14] on 6-round MISTY1 uses the 46'th order differential illustrated in Fig. 2a. The equation given by the differential is $V_{P[0-31,32-38,48-54]}^{(46)} X_5[57-63] = 0$. In order to bypass the layer $FL5$, we note that if one of the bits in $KL_{5,2}[9-15]$ is equal to 1, say $KL_{5,2}[15] = 1$, then by the structure of FL, we obtain $V_{P[0-31,32-38,48-54]}^{(46)} X_5'[63] = 0$, and similarly for the other bits. Since for a vast majority of the keys, at least one bit of $KL_{5,2}[9-15]$ equals 1, we can repeat the attack 7 times, each time assuming that one of the bits equals 1, so that with an overwhelming probability the attack will succeed in one of the times.

Assume, w.l.o.g., that $KL_{5,2}[15] = 1$, and hence, we have the equation $V_{P[0-31,32-38,48-54]}^{(46)} X_5'[63] = 0$. By the Feistel structure, it follows that $V_{P[0-31,32-38,48-54]}^{(46)} X_6[31] = 0$. Note that $X_6[31] = FL7^{-1}(C)[63] \oplus Out_6[31]$. Since $FL7^{-1}$ acts as 16 parallel applications of a function from two bits to two bits, $FL7^{-1}(C)[63]$ for all ciphertexts can be computed easily given a guess of two key bits. Hence, all we need to do in order to check whether the differential is satisfied is to compute

$$\bigoplus_{y \in span\{e_0, e_1, \ldots, e_{38}, e_{48}, \ldots, e_{54}\}} Out_6[31](x \oplus y).$$

It turns out that when we represent the bit $Out_6[31]$ as a function of X_{6L}, its degree as a multilinear polynomial is only 3, and moreover, many of the possible second and third degree terms do not appear. As a result, after the linearization of this function we obtain only 189 variables.[1] Hence, 220 linear equations are sufficient to filter out all wrong suggestions of the subkey used in round 6. As each structure of size 2^{46} contributes 22 equations as described above, 10 structures, or $2^{49.4}$ chosen plaintexts are sufficient for the attack.

The time complexity of solving the equations (in all 7 attack attempts together) is at most $7 \cdot 220^3 = 2^{26.2}$ operations. As for the time required for creating the linear equation, the most naive way is to consider the ciphertexts one by one and check the contribution of each ciphertext to the equations. Even in this way, the time complexity of the attack is dominated by encrypting the plaintexts. (As we show in Sect. 4, this part can be performed very efficiently using the *partial sums* technique). Hence, the attack requires $2^{49.4}$ chosen plaintexts and its time complexity is $2^{49.4}$ encryptions.

The attack of Tsunoo et al. [14] on 7-round MISTY1 without the last FL layer is an easy extension of the 6-round attack. Most naively, one guesses all key material used in round 7, peels off the 7th round and applies the 6-round attack. As shown in [14], it is sufficient to guess 75 of the 96 key bits used in round 7, as the remaining key bits can be absorbed into the linear equations, at the price of slightly increasing the number of variables. In total, the data complexity is increased to $2^{49.7}$ chosen plaintexts, and the time complexity is $2^{49.4} \cdot 2^{75} = 2^{116.4}$ encryptions.

4   Improved Attack on 6-Round MISTY1 Using a 43'th Order Differential

In this section we show that the attack of Tsunoo et al. on 6-round MISTY1 can be improved by a factor of 5 in the data and time complexities, by using an improved higher-order differential, along with a refined key recovery technique.

In order to find out whether the differential of Tsunoo et al. can be improved, we first examined the simpler variant of MISTY1 without the FL functions and used an experimental approach. We considered the 12'th order differentials on 3-round MISTY1 used in [13], e.g., $V_{X_{2j}[0-5,16-21]}^{(12)} X'_{2j+3}[57-63]$, and checked whether replacing $V = span\{e_0, e_1, \ldots, e_5, e_{16}, \ldots, e_{21}\}$ with any of its subspaces of the form $V' = span\{e_{i_1}, \ldots e_{i_d}\}$ yields a higher-order differential. The experiment was performed for all the options of 6 out the 7 bits $X_{2j}[0-6]$ with their neighbors. For each such choice of a 12'th order differential, several random keys and random constants were taken.

The experiments showed the existence of 11'th order differentials, of the form $V_{X_{2j}[S,S']}^{(11)} X'_{2j+3}[57-63]$, where S is any subset of $[0-6]$ of size 6, and S' consists

---

[1] It should be noted that the number of variables depends on the exact bit in $X_6[25-31]$ that is analyzed. As each of the 7 bits is analyzed in one of the 7 applications of the attack, we use the maximal possible number of variables throughout the paper, as a worst-case assumption.

of 5 among the 6 neighbors of the elements of S. It turns out that all differentials of this form are indeed 11'th order differentials for 3-round MISTY1 without FL functions. On the other hand, the experiment showed that all other subspaces V' do not yield HODs, which implies that our improved differential cannot be improved further, unless entirely different HODs are used.

The obvious obstacle in exploiting the 11'th order differential is that it cannot bypass FL layers. However, it turns out that we can overcome this obstacle, using a careful key guessing procedure that exploits the exact structure of the FL's. We start with a 12'th order differential of 3-round MISTY1, like those used in [13] and show how to divide it into two 11'th order differentials. For sake of simplicity, we exemplify the process for the differential $V_{X_2[0-5,16-21]}^{(12)} X_5'[57-63]$.

It is clear that the only obstacle we have to bypass is the layer $FL3$. Our goal is to define the structure in X_2 (i.e., the input of the differential) in such a way that the corresponding structure after $FL3$ will be $V_{X_{3,L}'[0-5,16-20]}^{(11)}$. If this is achieved, the continuation of the differential will hold like in the differentials found for MISTY1 without the FL functions.

As FL acts like 16 2-bit to 2-bit invertible functions applied in parallel, it is clear that the structure in X_2 contains $V = span\{e_0, e_1, \ldots, e_4, e_{16}, \ldots, e_{20}\}$, and it is only left to determine which two of the four elements $0, e_5, e_{21}, e_5 \oplus e_{21}$ we should add. Now, we observe that there are only three possible pairs of elements (along with their complements), and one of them must lead to the desired form after the FL. Hence, it is sufficient to try 3 structures in X_2 to ensure that the HOD equation holds for one of them. Note that the structures we use are not standard HODs, as they do not correspond to an affine subspace.

In order to exploit all possible 11'th order differentials, we have to try 3 options for each of the 6 pairs of neighbor bit positions $(0, 16), (1, 17), \ldots, (5, 22)$, and thus, to repeat the attack 3^6 times. As we show below, all the steps of the attack can be performed very efficiently, such that even when they are repeated 3^6 times, the overall time complexity is still dominated by encrypting the plaintexts. We obtain 12 11'th order differentials, but due to linear dependence, we can use only 7 of them simultaneously. By using the same arguments (with $FL3 \circ FL1$ in place of $FL3$), we can divide the 44'th order differential of 4-round MISTY1 used in [13] into 12 43'th order differentials and use 7 of them simultaneously.

It is important to note that the "correct" structure in X_2 depends only on the secret key bits of the FL's, and hence, is common to *all* structures. We also note that an alternative way to overcome the FL layers is to guess the relevant subkey bits (e.g., bits $KL_{3,1}[5]$ and $KL_{3,2}[5]$ in the above example). However, such a guess for all 6 relevant pairs of neighbor positions requires to repeat the attack 4^6 times if the 12'th order differential is used, and 16^6 times if the 44'th order differential is used (as $FL3 \circ FL1$ has 4 key bits in each 2-bit to 2-bit function). Hence, our strategy of overcoming FL is significantly more efficient.

Now, we consider the time complexity of the improved attack. The stage of solving the linear equation system requires now at most $7 \cdot 220^3 \cdot 3^6 = 2^{35.6}$ operations, which is negligible compared to the time required for encrypting the plaintexts. We show now that the stage of constructing the linear equations can be also performed very efficiently, using the *partial sums* technique.

We observe that the 188 coefficients of the linear equations (except for the constant coefficient) can be divided into two groups of 130 and 58 coefficients, such that the first group depends only on bits $X_6[0-6]$ and their neighbors, and the second group depends only on bits $X_6[7-15]$ and their neighbors. Such a "separation" property of the MISTY1 round function was already used in [3,11,12]. As a result, we can compute these sets of coefficients separately.

Consider the computation of the 130 coefficients that depend only on $X_6[0-6, 16-22]$ for a single structure of size 2^{43}. The basic observation used in *partial-sum* techniques is that if for two ciphertexts, the corresponding values of $X_6[0-6, 16-22]$ are equal, then the contributions of these ciphertexts to $\displaystyle\bigoplus_{y \in span\{e_0, e_1, \ldots, e_{38}, e_{48}, \ldots, e_{54}\}} Out_6[31](x \oplus y)$ cancel each other. Hence, before computing the contribution of each ciphertext to the coefficients, we can reduce the structure into a list of size 2^{14} that represents the information on which of the 2^{14} possible values of $X_6[0-6, 16-22]$ appears an odd number of times in the structure. Furthermore, this reduction (or most of it, to be precise) can be performed before the guess of the exact structures in X_2, and hence it has to be performed only once for each structure. After the reduction is performed, we go over all 2^{14} values in the list and collect their contributions to the coefficients of the equations. (As shown in the next section, this part can also be performed more efficiently). The total time complexity of this step for each structure is

$$7 \cdot 3^6 \cdot (130 \cdot 2^{14} + 58 \cdot 2^{18}) \ll 2^{43},$$

and hence, the overall time complexity is dominated by the encryption of the plaintexts.

Summarizing the attack, the data and time complexities of the attack are 2^{47} chosen plaintexts and time, an improvement by a factor of 5 in both data and time complexities over the results of Tsunoo et al. (Note that the improvement is only by a factor of 5 and not by a factor of 7, since in order to exploit the structures optimally, we have to use "full" structures of size 2^{46}. Since a single structure is not sufficient, we must use two structures, and thus, the data complexity is 2^{47}.)

5   Improved Attack on 7-Round MISTY1 with 4 *FL* Layers

In this section we describe an attack on 7-round MISTY1 with all *FL* layers except the last layer $(FL9, FL10)$, that improves the attack presented in [14].

As the attack on 6-round MISTY1, our attack is based on the 46'th order differential $V_{P[0-31, 32-38, 48-54]}^{(46)} X_6[25-31] = 0$ and the attack equation derived from it:

$$\bigoplus_{y \in span\{e_0, e_1, \ldots, e_{38}, e_{48}, \ldots, e_{54}\}} Out_6[31](x \oplus y).$$

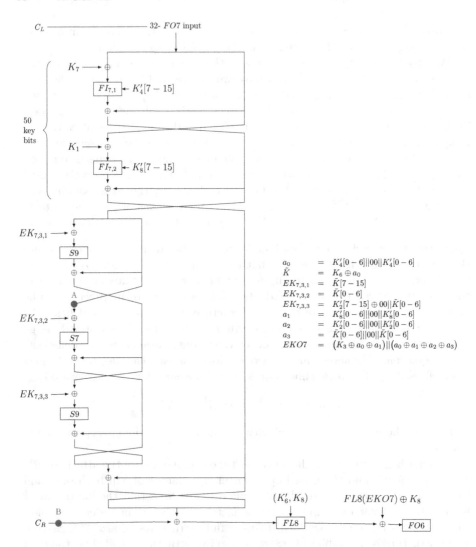

Fig. 3. Reference figure for the attack on 7-round MISTY1 without the last FL layer

However, in the case of the 7-round MISTY1 we have to guess some key material before creating the linear system. Since the attack procedure is a bit complex, we illustrate it in Fig. 3 which includes the order of the steps, as well as equivalent subkeys that we will use.

As noted in Sect. 4, the 188 coefficients of the linear equations (except for the constant coefficient) can be divided into two groups of 130 and 58 coefficients, that can be calculated separately. We describe the calculations for a single structure that corresponds to a 44'th order differential (recall that by [13], each 46'th round differential can be used to construct 22 such structures).

Calculation of the Coefficients Related to the Bits of $X_6[7-15]$. The procedure consists of several steps.

1. We guess the 50 key bits marked in the figure and decrypt all 2^{44} ciphertexts through the first two FI layers of round 7. At this stage, we note that if two intermediate values agree on 34 bit positions, which are the 16 bits of the input to $FI_{7,3}$ and the 18 bits $C_R[7-15, 23-31]$, then their contributions to the sum
$$\bigoplus_{y \in span\{e_0, e_1, \ldots, e_{38}, e_{48}, \ldots, e_{54}\}} Out_6[31](x \oplus y)$$ cancel each other. Hence, as in the 6-round attack, we can reduce the list of ciphertexts into a list of size 2^{34} that shows for each of the 2^{34} values of these 34 bits, whether it appears an odd number of times in the structure.

2. We guess 18 bits of $EK_{7,3,1}$, $EK_{7,3,3}$ and partially encrypt our list of 2^{34} values through $FI_{7,3}$. After this stage, we note that if two intermediate values agree on 25 bits positions (7 bits in the input to $S7$ of $FI_{7,3}$, marked by A, and 18 bits in C_R, marked by B), then their contributions to the sum cancel out. Hence, we can further reduce the list to 2^{25} values.

3. At this stage, when only one $S7$ (along with a 7-bit subkey) is left, we do not guess the remaining subkey, but rather represent the sum in the attack equation as a function of the current intermediate state and linearize this representation. The number of variables we obtain is $771 \approx 2^{9.6}$, and we can compute the coefficients efficiently using precomputed tables of size $2^{25} \cdot 771$ that store the contribution of each possible value of the 25 bits to the 771 coefficients.

4. We guess the 7 key bits of $EK_{7,3,2}$ and reduce the number of variables to 153. (Note that the number of variables is much higher than 58. This happens since when we guess part of the key after we constructed the equations, we cannot unify linearly dependent variables, and thus, the total number of variables is increased). This reduction can be performed by direct calculation in time complexity of $2^{9.6} \cdot 153$ for each key guess.

We note that guessing the key of the second $S9$ in $FI_{7,3}$ can be done in time complexity of 2^5 (instead of 2^9) by a somewhat complex procedure described in the full version of the paper. Combining all parts of the algorithm together, the time complexity of this part is

$$T_{X_6[7-15]} = 2^{50} \cdot 2^{44} + 2^{50+9} \cdot 2^{34} + 2^{50+9+5} \cdot 2^{34}$$
$$+ 2^{68} \cdot 2^{25} \cdot \frac{2^{9.6}}{2^6} \cdot 7 + 2^{75} \cdot 2^{9.5} \cdot 153$$
$$= 2^{94} + 2^{93} + 2^{98} + 2^{99.4} + 2^{92.3}$$
$$\approx 2^{99.9}$$

operations.

Calculation of the Coefficients Related to the Bits $X_6[0-6]$. In this case, the procedure is simpler:

1. We guess the 50 key bits marked in the figure and partially decrypt all 2^{44} ciphertexts through the first two FI functions of round 7 (like in the previous case). At this point, if two intermediate values agree on 30 bit positions, which are the 16 bits of the input to $FI_{7,3}$ and the 14 bits $C_R[0-6, 16-22]$, then their contributions to the sum cancel each other. Thus, we can reduce the data to a list of length 2^{30}.

2. We guess the 16 bits of $EK_{7,3,1}, EK_{7,3,2}$, and reduce the data list to a size of 2^{23}, and then guess the 9 bits of $EK_{7,3,3}$ and further reduce the list to only 2^{14} values.

3. We calculate the 130 coefficients of the linear equation using precomputed tables of size $2^{14} \cdot 130$.

The time complexity for this part is

$$
\begin{aligned}
T_{X_6[0-6]} &= 2^{50} \cdot 2^{44} + 2^{50+16} \cdot 2^{30} + 2^{66+9} \cdot 2^{23} + 2^{74} \cdot 2^{14} \cdot \frac{130}{2^6} \cdot 7 \\
&\approx 2^{94} + 2^{96} + 2^{98} + 2^{93.8} \approx 2^{98.5}
\end{aligned}
$$

operations.

Combining the Calculations. By combining the sets of coefficients computed in the two calculations described above, we create a system of linear equations. Since we guess 75 key bits overall, we have $7 \cdot 2^{75}$ linear systems to create and solve. The maximum number of variables for each system is $130 + 153 = 283$.

To filter out wrong keys and add a safety factor, we take $283 + 75 + 10 \approx 2^{8.55}$ structures of 44'th order differentials. As each structure corresponding to a 46'th order differential contains 22 structures of 44'th order differentials, we need $\frac{283+75+10}{22} \approx 17 \approx 2^{4.1}$ structures of 46'th order differentials to complete the attack. (Note that in this attack we cannot use our improved 43'th order differentials, since repeating the attack several times (as required for them) would increase the time complexity.) Thus, the total data complexity is $D = 2^{4.1} \cdot 2^{46} = 2^{50.1}$.

The time complexity is composed from encryption of the required data, creation of the linear systems and their solution. The time required for encryption of the data is negligible. The time of creation the linear systems is

$$
2^{8.55} \cdot (T_{X_6[7-15]} + T_{X_6[0-6]}) \approx 2^{8.55} \cdot 2^{100.3} = 2^{108.85}.
$$

The time of solving the 2^{75} linear systems is $2^{75} \cdot (2^{8.55})^3 \approx 2^{100.65}$ operations. Hence, the total time complexity of the attack is $T = 2^{108.85} + 2^{100.65} \approx 2^{108.85}$ simple operations. Assuming that each round of MISTY1 encryption is comparable to 50 simple operations like was assumed in [14], the time complexity is

$$
T = \frac{2^{108.85}}{7 \cdot 50} \approx 2^{100.4}
$$

7-round MISTY1 encryptions.

6 New Attack on 7-Round MISTY1 with All *FL* Layers Present

In this section we describe an attack on 7-round MISTY1 with all FL functions, which is the first attack on this variant that is significantly faster than exhaustive key search. The attack uses the same 44'th order differential and the same division into two types of linear coefficients like the attack presented in Sect. 5. However, in order to handle the 64 subkey bits that are added in this variant, we must perform a more careful procedure, that also takes into consideration the exact MISTY1 key schedule. As in the previous attack, we describe the calculations made for a single structure that corresponds to a 44'th order differential. The reference figure to this attack is Fig. 4.

Calculation of the Coefficients Related to the Bits of $X_6[7 - 15]$. The procedure consists of several steps.

1. We guess the 57 key bits of $K_1, K_7, K_8, K'_4[7 - 15]$ and partially decrypt all 2^{44} ciphertexts through $FL10$ and the first two FI functions of round 7. At this stage, we can reduce the data to a list of length 2^{43} (the 43 relevant bits correspond to 18 bits in C_R, 9 bits in the point B and the 16-bit input to $FI_{7,3}$).
2. We guess the 9 bits of $EK_{7,3,1}$. After this guess, the size of the list remains 2^{43} as before, but now the 43 bits correspond to 18 bits in C_R, 9 bits in B and all bits of A.
3. At this point, we perform linearization. Due to the amount of key material which we haven't guessed yet, the maximal possible number of variables is $2713 \approx 2^{11.4}$. Using directly a precomputed table for computing the coefficients requires a table of size $2^{43} \cdot 2^{11.4}$. Instead of this table, we will use three smaller tables. We note that out of the 2713 coefficients, there are 2269 coefficients in which only the bits of A, B and $C_R[7 - 15]$ are involved and 424 coefficients in which only the bits in A, B and $C_R[24 - 31]$ are involved. Only 20 variables are left which depend on all the 43 bits. Hence, we can use for the computation three smaller tables of sizes $2^{34} \cdot 2269, 2^{34} \cdot 424$, and $2^{43} \cdot 20$. Hence, the memory complexity required for the linearization is $2^{34} \cdot 2269 + 2^{34} \cdot 424 + 2^{43} \cdot 20 \approx 2^{47.66}$.
4. We guess the $16 + 9$ key bits of $EK_{7,3,2}, EK_{7,3,3}$ and $K'_3[7 - 15]$. Using the guessed key bits, and the fact that K_8 and KL_8 are known, we can reduce the number of variables. (As in Sect. 5, guessing the key at this point forces us to not unify linearly dependent variables.) The number of the new variables is only 213. This transformation is done by a direct calculation in time complexity of $2^{11.4} \cdot 213$ for each key guess (there is 2^{91} guesses at this point).

In total, the time complexity of this part is

$$T_{X_6[7-15]} = 2^{57} \cdot 2^{44} + 2^{57+9} \cdot 2^{43} + 2^{66} \cdot 2^{43} \cdot \frac{2^{11.4}}{2^6} \cdot 7 + 2^{91} \cdot 2^{11.4} \cdot 213$$

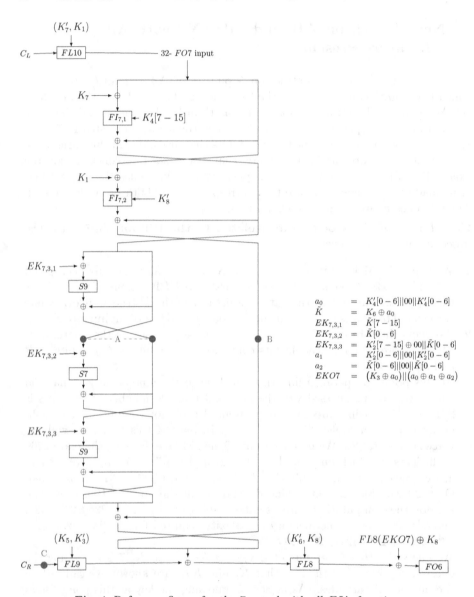

Fig. 4. Reference figure for the 7-round with all FL's functions

$$= 2^{101} + 2^{109} + 2^{117.2} + 2^{110.14}$$
$$\approx 2^{117.22}$$

operations.

Calculation of the Coefficients Related to the Bits $X_6[0-6]$. In this case, the procedure is simpler:

1. We guess the 57 key bits of $K_1, K_7, K_8, K_4'[7-15]$ and partially decrypt all the 2^{44} ciphertexts through $FL10$ and the first two FI layers of round 7. At this stage, the data can be reduced to a list of size 2^{37}, where the 37 bits are 14 bits of C_R, 7 bits in B and the input to $FI_{7,3}$.
2. We guess the 25 bits of $EK_{7,3,i}$ $i = 1, 2, 3$. After this guess, the size of the list is reduced to 2^{28}, which corresponds to 14 bits in C_R (after FL_9) and 14 bits before FL_9.
3. At this point we perform linearization. The maximum number of variables is $684 \approx 2^{9.42}$. We calculate them using a precomputed table of size $2^{28} \cdot 684$.

The time complexity for this part is

$$T_{X_6[0-6]} = 2^{57} \cdot 2^{44} + 2^{57+25} \cdot 2^{37} + 2^{82} \cdot 2^{28} \cdot \frac{2^{9.42}}{2^6} \cdot 7$$
$$\approx 2^{101} + 2^{119} + 2^{116.22} \approx 2^{119.2}$$

operations.

Combining the Calculations We create the system of linear equations using the two previous calculations. We have $7 \cdot 2^{91}$ linear systems to create and solve. The maximum number of variable for each system is $213 + 684 = 897$. (Note that this time, the number of variables is significantly larger than in the previous attacks, due to the amount of key material which we absorb into the equations.)

To filter out wrong keys and add a safety factor, we take $897 + 91 + 10 \approx 2^{9.97}$ structures that correspond to 44'th order differentials. Therefore, we need $\frac{897+91+10}{22} \approx 43.6 \approx 2^{5.45}$ structures of 46'th order differentials, which means that the total data complexity is

$$D = 2^{5.45} \cdot 2^{46} = 2^{51.45}.$$

The time complexity is composed from encryption of the required data, creation of linear systems and their solution. The time of data encryption is negligible. The time of creation the linear systems is $2^{9.97} \cdot (T_{X_6[7-15]} + T_{X_6[0-6]}) \approx 2^{9.97} \cdot 2^{119.56} = 2^{129.53}$ operations. The time of solving the 2^{91} linear systems is $2^{91} \cdot (2^{9.97})^3 \approx 2^{120.91}$ operations. The total time complexity is thus $T = 2^{129.53} + 2^{120.91} \approx 2^{129.53}$ simple operations. Assuming that each round of MISTY1 encryption is comparable to 50 simple operations, the time complexity is

$$T = \frac{2^{129.53}}{7 \cdot 50} \approx 2^{121}$$

7-round encryptions.

7   Summary and Conclusions

In this paper we investigated higher-order differential attacks on MISTY1. We improved the 44'th order differential used in the best previously known attack of

Tsunoo et al. [13] into a 43'th order differential, and used it to reduce the data and time complexities of the best known attack on 6-round MISTY1 from $2^{49.3}$ to $2^{46.5}$. We gave evidence that our 43'th order differential cannot be further improved using current techniques.

We also considered the best known higher-order differential attacks on 7-round MISTY1, also by Tsunoo et al. We showed that by using the partial sums technique and other techniques, the time complexity of the attack can be reduced from $2^{116.4}$ to $2^{100.4}$ – a reduction by a factor of 2^{16}. Finally, we presented an attack on 7-round MISTY with all FL functions present that requires $2^{51.5}$ chosen plaintexts and 2^{121} encryptions. This is the first known attack on a variant of MISTY1 with all FL layers.

As a problem for further research, it will be interesting to find out whether our techniques can be used also to improve higher-order differential attacks on KASUMI. It seems that the case of KASUMI will be harder, due to the higher algebraic degree of the modified FI function KASUMI uses.

References

1. 3rd Generation Partnership Project. Specification of the 3GPP Confidentiality and Integrity Algorithms - Document 2: KASUMI Specification (Release 6). Technical report 3GPP TS 35.202 V6.1.0 (2005–09), September 2005
2. Babbage, S., Frisch, L.: On MISTY1 higher order differential cryptanalysis. In: Won, D. (ed.) ICISC 2000. LNCS, vol. 2015, pp. 22–36. Springer, Heidelberg (2001)
3. Dunkelman, O., Keller, N.: Practical-time attacks against reduced variants of MISTY1. IACR Cryptol. ePrint Arch. **2013**, 431 (2013)
4. Ferguson, N., Kelsey, J., Lucks, S., Schneier, B., Stay, M., Wagner, D., Whiting, D.L.: Improved cryptanalysis of rijndael. In: Schneier, B. (ed.) FSE 2000. LNCS, vol. 1978, pp. 213–230. Springer, Heidelberg (2001)
5. Jia, K., Li, L.: Improved impossible differential attacks on reduced-round MISTY1. In: Lee, D.H., Yung, M. (eds.) WISA 2012. LNCS, vol. 7690, pp. 15–27. Springer, Heidelberg (2012). http://dblp.uni-trier.de/db/conf/wisa/wisa2012.html#JiaL12
6. Jia, K., Hongbo, Y., Wang, X.: A meet-in-the-middle attack on the full kasumi. IACR Cryptol. ePrint Arch. **2011**, 466 (2011)
7. Knudsen, L.R.: Truncated and higher order differentials. In: Preneel, B. (ed.) FSE 1994. LNCS, vol. 1008, pp. 196–211. Springer, Heidelberg (1995)
8. Lai, X.: Higher order derivatives and differential cryptanalysis. In: Blahut, R.E., Costello Jr., D.J., Maurer, U., Mittelholzer, T. (eds.) Communications and Cryptography. The International Series in Engineering and Computer Science, vol. 276, pp. 227–233. Springer, Heidelberg (1994)
9. Lu, J., Yap, W.-S., Wei, Y.: Weak keys of the full MISTY1 block cipher for related-key differential cryptanalysis. In: Dawson, E. (ed.) CT-RSA 2013. LNCS, vol. 7779, pp. 389–404. Springer, Heidelberg (2013)
10. Matsui, M.: New block encryption algorithm MISTY. In: Biham, E. (ed.) FSE 1997. LNCS, vol. 1267, pp. 54–68. Springer, Heidelberg (1997)
11. Sakurai, K., Zheng, Y.: On non-pseudorandomness from block ciphers with provable immunity against linear cryptanalysis. In: Proceedings of AAECC 1999. LNCS, vol. 1719, pp. 19–24. Springer (1999)

12. Sun, X., Lai, X.: Improved integral attacks on MISTY1. In: Jacobson Jr., M.J., Rijmen, V., Safavi-Naini, R. (eds.) SAC 2009. LNCS, vol. 5867, pp. 266–280. Springer, Heidelberg (2009)
13. Tsunoo, Y., Saito, T., Kawabata, T., Nakagawa, H.: Finding higher order differentials of MISTY1. IEICE Trans. **95–A**(6), 1049–1055 (2012)
14. Tsunoo, Y., Saito, T., Shigeri, M., Kawabata, T.: Higher order differential attacks on reduced-round MISTY1. In: Lee, P.J., Cheon, J.H. (eds.) ICISC 2008. LNCS, vol. 5461, pp. 415–431. Springer, Heidelberg (2009)
15. Yi, W., Chen, S.: Multidimensional zero-correlation linear attacks on reduced-round MISTY1. CoRR, abs/1410.4312 (2014)

Meet-in-the-Middle Technique for Truncated Differential and Its Applications to CLEFIA and Camellia

Leibo Li[1,3], Keting Jia[1], Xiaoyun Wang[2,3]([✉]), and Xiaoyang Dong[3]

[1] CCS, Department of Computer Science and Technology,
Tsinghua University, Beijing, China
lileibo@mail.sdu.edu.cn, ktjia@mail.tsinghua.edu.cn
[2] Institute for Advanced Study, Tsinghua University, Beijing, China
xiaoyunwang@tsinghua.edu.cn
[3] Key Laboratory of Cryptologic Technology and Information Security,
Ministry of Education, Shandong University, Jinan, China
dongxiaoyang@mail.sdu.edu.cn

Abstract. As one of the generalizations of differential cryptanalysis, the truncated differential cryptanalysis has become a powerful toolkit to evaluate the security of block ciphers. In this article, taking advantage of the meet-in-the-middle like technique, we introduce a new method to construct truncated differential characteristics of block ciphers. Based on the method, we propose 10-round and 8-round truncated differential characteristics for CLEFIA and Camellia, respectively, which are ISO standard block ciphers. Applying the 10-round truncated differential characteristic for CLEFIA, we launch attacks on 14/14/15-round CLEFIA-128/192/256 with 2^{108}, 2^{135} and 2^{203} encryptions, respectively. For Camellia, we utilize the 8-round truncated differential to attack 11/12-round Camellia-128/192 including the FL/FL^{-1} and whiten layers with $2^{121.3}$ and $2^{185.3}$ encryptions. As far as we know, most of the cases are the best results of these attacks on both ciphers.

Keywords: Block cipher · Cryptanalysis · Truncated differential · CLEFIA · Camellia

1 Introduction

Differential cryptanalysis is one of the principal attack methods on modern symmetric-key ciphers, which was firstly introduced by Biham and Shamir to analyze the block cipher DES in 1990 [3]. It exploits a differential trail $(\alpha \rightarrow \beta)$ with high probability, where α is the input difference, and β is the output difference. Based on the differential attack, many methods have been developed to evaluate the security of block ciphers, such as the related-key differential attack [4], truncated differential attack [16], high-order differential attack [17], impossible differential attack [2,15], multiple differential attack [6] and so forth.

© International Association for Cryptologic Research 2015
G. Leander (Ed.): FSE 2015, LNCS 9054, pp. 48–70, 2015.
DOI: 10.1007/978-3-662-48116-5_3

It is well known that the key point of the differential attack is to exploit the differential trial with high probability which covers as many rounds as possible. The traditional method is to find some short differential trials, and then connect these characteristics to form a long differential trial, such as the cryptanalysis of DES in [3]. Besides, evaluating the resistance of a block cipher against the differential attack has got a lot of attention from many cryptanalysts, which is usually carried out by calculating the minimum number of active S-boxes.

The truncated differential cryptanalysis was proposed by Knudsen in 1994 [16]. Different from the differential characteristic, the truncated differential includes a set of differential trails that have the same active S-boxes. Truncated differential attack has many similarities with differential attack, such as the method to construct the truncated differential, the complexity analysis and success rate evaluation.

Despite the fact that truncated differential cryptanalysis has been extensively employed, the tool to evaluate the security of block ciphers against the truncated differential cryptanalysis is worth further studying. Inspired by the impossible differential cryptanalysis, we introduce a new view to construct the truncated differential characteristics of block ciphers in this paper. In order to demonstrate the power of our method, we present its applications to the ISO standard block ciphers, CLEFIA and Camellia, and present the best results when compared with previous works. In detail, the contributions of our work are three-fold:

- **Meet-in-the-Middle Technique for Truncated Differentials.** We split the encryption E into two parts and $E = E_1 \circ E_0$, and consider the truncated differentials $(\Gamma_0 \xrightarrow{E_0} \Gamma_1)$ and $(\Gamma_2 \xrightarrow{E_1^{-1}} \Gamma_1)$. If the truncated differential $\mathcal{P}_r(\Gamma_0 \xrightarrow{E_0} \Gamma_1) = p$, and $\mathcal{P}_r(\Gamma_2 \xrightarrow{E_1^{-1}} \Gamma_1) = 1$, we prove that the probability of the truncated differential $\mathcal{P}_r(\Gamma_0 \xrightarrow{E} \Gamma_2) = p \times |\Gamma_2|/|\Gamma_1|$ under the assumption of Markov cipher. The method is available to many block ciphers, especially, for Feistel structure ciphers.

- **Truncated Differential Cryptanalysis of CLEFIA.** CLEFIA was proposed by Sony Corporation in 2007 [30], and was selected as an international standard by ISO/IEC 29192-2 in 2011 and e-Government recommended cipher by CRYPTREC project in 2013. The security of CLEFIA has attracted many attentions from worldwide cryptology researchers in previous years. Such as impossible differential cryptanalysis [8,26,32,34], improbable differential cryptanalysis [5,33], integral attacks [22,27,35] and zero-correlation cryptanalysis [7]. In this paper, we apply the meet-in-the-middle technique to construct a 10-round truncated differential characteristic of CLEFIA. And then we launch the key recovery attacks on 13/14/15-round CLEFIA-128/192/256, which cost 2^{99} encryptions with 2^{99} chosen plaintexts for CLEFIA-128, 2^{135} encryptions with 2^{100} chosen plaintexts for CLEFIA-192, and 2^{203} encryptions with 2^{100} chosen plaintexts for CLEFIA-256. Furthermore, combined with the function reduction technique [13] and the subkey relations, we firstly achieve the attack on 14-round CLEFIA-128 with 2^{100} chosen plaintexts and 2^{108} encryptions.

- **Truncated Differential Cryptanalysis of Camellia.** Camellia was proposed by NTT and Mitsubishi in 2000 [1], and was selected as an e-government recommended cipher by CRYPTREC in 2002, NESSIE block cipher portfolio in 2003 and international standard by ISO/IEC 18033-3 in 2005. Many methods of cryptanalysis were applied to attack reduced-round Camellia in previous years, such as higher order differential attack [12], linear and differential attacks [29], truncated differential attacks [14,19,31], collision attack [36], square attacks [20,21], impossible differential attacks [9,23,24,31,37], meet-in-the-middle attacks [10,11,25], and zero-correlation linear cryptanalysis [7]. In this paper, combining the new observations of FL functions and meet-in-the-middle technique, we introduce an 8-round truncated differential of Camellia for 99.2 % keys, and give the key recovery attacks on 11/12-round Camellia-128/192 with 2^{117} chosen plaintexts and $2^{121.3}$, $2^{185.3}$ encryptions, respectively. Both attacks are started from the first round and include the FL/FL^{-1} and whiten layers. Furthermore, using multiplied method proposed in [23], we extend the attacks to the full key space with 4 times of the time complexity.

Table 1 summarizes the major previously results of reduced-round CLEFIA and Camellia along with our results, where "†" means the attack works for 99.2 % keys. The cryptanalysis results on Camellia start from the first round and include whitening keys and FL/FL^{-1} layers.

The rest of this paper is organized as follows. Section 2 gives some notations used in this paper and brief descriptions of CLEFIA and Camellia. We introduce the meet-in-the-middle technique to find the truncated differential for block ciphers in Sect. 3. Section 4 presents the truncated differential cryptanalysis of round-reduced CLEFIA-128/192/256. The truncated differential attacks on 11/12-round Camellia-128/192 are given in Sect. 5. Finally, we make a conclusion of the paper in Sect. 6.

2   Preliminaries

This section lists some notations used throughout the paper, and presents brief descriptions of both block ciphers CLEFIA and Camellia.

2.1   Notations

The following notations are used in this paper:

$A_{r-1}, B_{r-1},$ the 4 input branches of the r-th round for CLEFIA
C_{r-1}, D_{r-1}

L_{r-1}, R_{r-1} the left and right 64-bit halves of the r-th round input for Camellia

$X^{[i]}$ the i-th byte of a bit string X, e.g., an $8l$-bit string $X = (X^{[0]}, \cdots, X^{[l-1]})$

$X^{\{i\}}$ the i-th bit of a bit string X, e.g., a l-bit string $X = X^{\{0\}} \| \cdots \| X^{\{l-1\}}$

Table 1. Summary of the attacks on reduced-round CLEFIA and Camellia

Cipher	Rounds	Attack type	Data	Time	Memory	Source
CLEFIA-128	12	Integral	2^{113}	$2^{116.7}$	N/A	[22]
	13	Impossible Diff	$2^{117.8}$	$2^{121.2}$	$2^{86.8}$	[26]
	13	Impossible Diff	$2^{116.16}$	$2^{114.58}$	$2^{83.16}$	[8]
	13	Truncated Diff	2^{99}	2^{99}	2^{80}	Section 4.2
	14	Truncated Diff	2^{100}	2^{108}	$2^{101.3}$	Section 4.4
CLEFIA-192	13	Impossible Diff	$2^{119.8}$	2^{146}	2^{120}	[34]
	13	Integral	2^{113}	$2^{180.5}$	N/A	[22]
	14	Multidim.ZC	$2^{127.5}$	$2^{180.2}$	2^{115}	[7]
	14	Truncated Diff	2^{100}	2^{135}	2^{131}	Section 4.3
CLEFIA-256	14	Impossible Diff	$2^{120.3}$	2^{212}	2^{121}	[34]
	14	Integral	2^{113}	$2^{244.5}$	N/A	[22]
	15	Multidim.ZC	$2^{127.5}$	$2^{244.2}$	2^{115}	[7]
	15	Truncated Diff	2^{100}	2^{203}	2^{139}	Section 4.5
Camellia-128	10	Impossible Diff	$2^{112.4}$	2^{120}	$2^{86.4}$	[23]
	11	ZC. FFT	$2^{125.3}$	$2^{124.8}$	2^{112}	[7]
	12	Impossible Diff	$2^{118.43}$	$2^{118.4}$	$2^{92.4}$	[8]
	11†	Truncated Diff	2^{117}	$2^{119.3}$	2^{119}	Section 5.2
	11	Truncated Diff	2^{117}	$2^{121.3}$	2^{119}	Section 5.2
Camellia-192	11	Impossible Diff	$2^{113.7}$	2^{184}	$2^{143.7}$	[23]
	12	ZC. FFT	$2^{125.7}$	$2^{188.8}$	2^{112}	[7]
	12	MITM	2^{113}	2^{180}	2^{158}	[11]
	12	Impossible Diff	$2^{119.7}$	$2^{161.06}$	$2^{150.7}$	[8]
	12†	Truncated Diff	2^{117}	$2^{183.3}$	2^{119}	Section 5.3
	12	Truncated Diff	2^{117}	$2^{185.3}$	2^{119}	Section 5.3

Γ	a set of differences
E	the encryption or partial encryption of a block cipher
M_0, M_1	the Maximum Distance Separable (MDS) matrixes used by CLEFIA
*, 0, ? ' * '	denotes the non-zero difference byte, '0' denotes the zero difference byte and '?' denotes the unknown byte
S_N	the signal-to-noise ratio
n_r	the number of rounds for a block cipher
$\mathcal{P}_r(X)$	the expected probability of the event X
ΔX	the difference of X and X'
$\oplus$, $\cap$, $\cup$	bitwise exclusive OR (XOR), AND, OR
$\|\Gamma\|$	the size of the set Γ
$x\|y$	bit string concatenation of x and y
$\lll l$	bit rotation to the left by l bits

2.2   Brief Description of CLEFIA

CLEFIA is a 128-bit block cipher with variable key lengths of 128, 192 and 256, which takes a 4-branch generalized Feistel network [30]. The number of rounds are 18/22/26 for CLEFIA-128/192/256, respectively. The procedure of encryption is described as follows.

A 128-bit plaintext P is split up into four 32-bit words P_0, P_1, P_2 and P_3. The input state of the first round $(A_0, B_0, C_0, D_0) = (P_0, P_1 \oplus kw_0, P_2, P_3 \oplus kw_1)$. For $r = 1$ to n_r, do the following steps:

$$A_r = B_{r-1} \oplus F_0(A_{r-1}, k_{2r-2}), \ B_r = C_{r-1},$$
$$C_r = D_{r-1} \oplus F_1(C_{r-1}, k_{2r-1}), \ D_r = A_{r-1}.$$

Finally, the 128-bit ciphertext C is computed as $C = (D_{n_r}, A_{n_r} \oplus kw_2, B_{n_r}, C_{n_r} \oplus kw_3)$.

The round function F_0 and F_1 take the SP structure (seen Fig. 1). There are two types of 8×8 S-boxes in substitution layer, and the order of s_0 and s_1 is different for both round functions. Specifically,

$$S_0(x_0, x_1, x_2, x_3) = (s_0(x_0), s_1(x_1), s_0(x_2), s_1(x_3)),$$
$$S_1(x_0, x_1, x_2, x_3) = (s_1(x_0), s_0(x_1), s_1(x_2), s_0(x_3)).$$

The diffusion layer uses two different Maximum Distance Separable (MDS) matrix, M_0 and M_1 in functions F_0 and F_1, respectively, and their branch number are both 5.

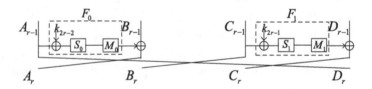

Fig. 1. The round function of CLEFIA

Key Schedule. For 128-bit key size, a 128-bit intermediate key K_L is generated by the master key K and a 10-round 4-branch generalized Feistel network $(GFN_{4,10})$. Then K and K_L are used to generate the whitening key and round keys with a linear transformation. For 192 and 256 key sizes, two 128-bit values K_L and K_R are generated from the main key K. After that, a 10-round 8-branch generalized Feistel network $(GFN_{8,10})$ is applied on (K_L, K_R) to generate a 256-bit intermediate key (K_A, K_B). Then the whitening keys and the round keys are derived from (K_L, K_R, K_A, K_B) by some linear transformations. For more detailed description of CLEFIA, please refer to [30].

2.3 Brief Description of Camellia

Camellia is a 128-bit block cipher with variable key lengths of 128, 192 and 256, which takes a balanced Feistel network. The number of rounds are 18/24/24 for Camellia-128/192/256, respectively. For Camellia-128, the encryption procedure is as follows.

Firstly, a 128-bit plaintext is $XORed$ with the whitening key (kw_0, kw_1) to get two 64-bit value L_0 and R_0. Then, for $r = 1$ to 18, except for $r = 6$ and 12, the following is carried out:

$$L_r = R_{r-1} \oplus F(L_{r-1}, k_{r-1}), \quad R_r = L_{r-1}.$$

For $r = 6$ and 12, do the following:

$$L'_r = R_{r-1} \oplus F(L_{r-1}, k_{r-1}), \quad R'_r = L_{r-1},$$
$$L_r = FL(L'_r, kf_{r/3-2}), \qquad R_r = FL^{-1}(R'_r, kf_{r/3-1}).$$

Lastly, the 128-bit ciphertext is $(R_{18} \oplus kw_2, L_{18} \oplus kw_3)$.

The round function F is composed of a key-addition layer, a substitution transformation S and a diffusion layer P. There are four types of 8×8 S-boxes s_1, s_2, s_3 and s_4 in the S transformation layer, and a 64-bit data is substituted as follows:

$$S(x_0, x_1, x_2, x_3, x_4, x_5, x_6, x_7) = (s_0(x_0), s_1(x_1), s_2(x_2), s_3(x_3), s_1(x_4), s_2(x_5), s_3(x_6), s_0(x_7)).$$

The linear transformation $P : (\{0,1\}^8)^8 \rightarrow (\{0,1\}^8)^8$ maps $(y_0, \cdots, y_7) \rightarrow (z_0, \cdots, z_7)$, this transformation and its inverse P^{-1} are defined as follows:

$$
\begin{aligned}
z_0 &= y_0 \oplus y_2 \oplus y_3 \oplus y_5 \oplus y_6 \oplus y_7, & y_0 &= z_1 \oplus z_2 \oplus z_3 \oplus z_5 \oplus z_6 \oplus z_7, \\
z_1 &= y_0 \oplus y_1 \oplus y_3 \oplus y_4 \oplus y_6 \oplus y_7, & y_1 &= z_0 \oplus z_2 \oplus z_3 \oplus z_4 \oplus z_6 \oplus z_7, \\
z_2 &= y_0 \oplus y_1 \oplus y_2 \oplus y_4 \oplus y_5 \oplus y_7, & y_2 &= z_0 \oplus z_1 \oplus z_3 \oplus z_4 \oplus z_5 \oplus z_7, \\
z_3 &= y_1 \oplus y_2 \oplus y_3 \oplus y_4 \oplus y_5 \oplus y_6, & y_3 &= z_0 \oplus z_1 \oplus z_2 \oplus z_4 \oplus z_5 \oplus z_6, \\
z_4 &= y_0 \oplus y_1 \oplus y_5 \oplus y_6 \oplus y_7, & y_4 &= z_0 \oplus z_1 \oplus z_4 \oplus z_6 \oplus z_7, \\
z_5 &= y_1 \oplus y_2 \oplus y_4 \oplus y_6 \oplus y_7, & y_5 &= z_1 \oplus z_2 \oplus z_4 \oplus z_5 \oplus z_7, \\
z_6 &= y_2 \oplus y_3 \oplus y_4 \oplus y_5 \oplus y_7, & y_6 &= z_2 \oplus z_3 \oplus z_4 \oplus z_5 \oplus z_6, \\
z_7 &= y_0 \oplus y_3 \oplus y_4 \oplus y_5 \oplus y_6, & y_7 &= z_0 \oplus z_3 \oplus z_5 \oplus z_6 \oplus z_7.
\end{aligned}
$$

The FL function is defined as $(X_L \| X_R, kf_L \| kf_R) \mapsto (Y_L \| Y_R)$, where

$$Y_R = ((X_L \cap kf_L) \lll 1) \oplus X_R, \quad Y_L = (Y_R \cup kf_R) \oplus X_L.$$

Similar to Camellia-128, Camellia-192/256 have 24-round Feistel structure, where the FL/FL^{-1} function layer are inserted in the 6-th, 12-th and 18-th rounds. Before the first round and after the last round, there are pre- and post-whitening layers as well. For details of Camellia, we refer to [1].

3 Meet-in-the-Middle Technique for Truncated Differential

The key part of truncated differential attack is to find a high-probability truncated differential characteristic covering as many rounds as possible for a block cipher. Here we introduce an interesting approach by applying meet-in-the-middle like technique to find the truncated differential of block ciphers. We first recall the definition of truncated differential.

Definition 1 [5]. *For the block cipher E with a parameter key K, the truncated differential characteristic $(\Gamma_{in} \xrightarrow{E} \Gamma_{out})$ is a set of differential trails, where Γ_{in} is a set of input differences, and Γ_{out} is a set of output differences. The expected probability of such truncated differential $(\Gamma_{in} \xrightarrow{E} \Gamma_{out})$ is defined by*

$$\mathcal{P}_r(\Gamma_{in} \xrightarrow{E} \Gamma_{out}) = \frac{1}{|\Gamma_{in}|} \sum_{a \in \Gamma_{in}} \mathcal{P}_r((E_K(X) \oplus E_K(X \oplus a)) \in \Gamma_{out})$$

$$= \frac{1}{|\Gamma_{in}|} \sum_{a \in \Gamma_{in}} \mathcal{P}_r(a \to \Gamma_{out}).$$

However, the average probability of the truncated differential characteristic for a random permutation is $\mathcal{P}_r(\Gamma_{in} \xrightarrow{E} \Gamma_{out}) = \frac{|\Gamma_{out}|}{2^n-1}$, where n is the block size. When a truncated differential characteristic with probability $\mathcal{P}_r(\Gamma_{in} \xrightarrow{E} \Gamma_{out}) = \frac{|\Gamma_{out}|}{2^n-1} + \varepsilon$ $(\varepsilon > 0)$, it is used to identify the secret key.

Here, we assume that E is a Markov cipher [18], that means the probability of a differential trail is often computed by multiplying the probabilities round by round. We apply the meet-in-the-middle technique to find the truncated differential characteristic. The block cipher is divided into two parts, i.e., $E = E_1 \circ E_0$, and there is a truncated differential characteristic with probability 1 for E_1^{-1}, i.e., $\mathcal{P}_r(\Gamma_2 \xrightarrow{E_1^{-1}} \Gamma_1) = 1$, depicted in Fig. 2. Then we know

$$\mathcal{P}_r(\Gamma_0 \xrightarrow{E} \Gamma_2) = \mathcal{P}_r(\Gamma_0 \xrightarrow{E_0} \Gamma_1) \times \mathcal{P}_r(\Gamma_1 \xrightarrow{E_1} \Gamma_2). \tag{1}$$

In order to compute the probability $\mathcal{P}_r(\Gamma_1 \xrightarrow{E_1} \Gamma_2)$, we introduce the following assumption.

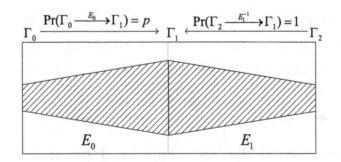

Fig. 2. Meet-in-the-middle technique for truncated differential

Assumption 1. *For the truncated differential $\Gamma_{in} \xrightarrow{E} \Gamma_{out}$, we assume that the expected probability of differential $\mathcal{P}_r(a \xrightarrow{E} b) = \mathcal{P}_r(b \xrightarrow{E^{-1}} a)$ when E is a Markov cipher for all $a \in \Gamma_{in}, b \in \Gamma_{out}$.*

Proposition 1. *Given a truncated differential $(\Gamma_2 \xrightarrow{E_1^{-1}} \Gamma_1)$ with probability 1, the expected probability of the truncated differential $(\Gamma_1 \xrightarrow{E_1} \Gamma_2)$ under Assumption 1 is*

$$\mathcal{P}_r(\Gamma_1 \xrightarrow{E_1} \Gamma_2) = \frac{|\Gamma_2|}{|\Gamma_1|},$$

where $|\Gamma_2| \leqslant |\Gamma_1|$.

Proof. Since $\mathcal{P}_r(\Gamma_2 \xrightarrow{E_1^{-1}} \Gamma_1) = 1$, then $\sum\limits_{a \in \Gamma_2} \mathcal{P}_r(a \xrightarrow{E_1^{-1}} \Gamma_1) = |\Gamma_2|$.

Furthermore, we deduce

$$\sum_{b \in \Gamma_1} \mathcal{P}_r(b \xrightarrow{E_1} \Gamma_2) = \sum_{b \in \Gamma_1} \sum_{a \in \Gamma_2} \mathcal{P}_r(b \xrightarrow{E_1} a)$$

$$= \sum_{a \in \Gamma_2} \sum_{b \in \Gamma_1} \mathcal{P}_r(a \xrightarrow{E_1^{-1}} b)$$

$$= \sum_{a \in \Gamma_2} \mathcal{P}_r(a \xrightarrow{E_1^{-1}} \Gamma_1) = |\Gamma_2|.$$

Therefore,

$$\mathcal{P}_r(\Gamma_1 \xrightarrow{E_1} \Gamma_2) = \frac{1}{|\Gamma_1|} \sum_{b \in \Gamma_1} \mathcal{P}_r(b \xrightarrow{E_1} \Gamma_2) = \frac{|\Gamma_2|}{|\Gamma_1|}.$$

Proposition 2. *For the block cipher $E = E_1 \circ E_0$, there are two truncated differential characteristics with high probability, i.e., $\mathcal{P}_r(\Gamma_0 \xrightarrow{E_0} \Gamma_1) = p$, and $\mathcal{P}_r(\Gamma_2 \xrightarrow{E_1^{-1}} \Gamma_1) = 1$, where Γ_0 is the input difference set of E, and Γ_1 and Γ_2 are the output difference sets of E_0 and E, respectively. Then the probability of the truncated differential $\Gamma_0 \xrightarrow{E} \Gamma_2$ is $p \times \frac{|\Gamma_2|}{|\Gamma_1|}$, where $|\Gamma_2| \leq |\Gamma_1|$.*

This proposition is easily obtained by the equation (1) and Proposition 1. It is obvious that when $\frac{p}{|\Gamma_1|} > 2^{-n}$, we can use Proposition 2 as distinguisher to recover the secret key. However, the impossible differential which exploits the differential characteristic of E_0 with probability zero, i.e., $\mathcal{P}_r(\Gamma_0 \xrightarrow{E_0} \Gamma_1) = 0$.

Proposition 3. *For the block cipher $E = E_1 \circ E_0$, there are two truncated differential characteristics with high probability, i.e., $\mathcal{P}_r(\Gamma_0 \xrightarrow{E_0} \Gamma_1) = p$, and $\mathcal{P}_r(\Gamma_2 \xrightarrow{E_1^{-1}} \Gamma_1) = q$. Then the probability of the truncated differential $\Gamma_0 \xrightarrow{E} \Gamma_2$ is larger than $pq \times \frac{|\Gamma_2|}{|\Gamma_1|}$, where $|\Gamma_2| \leq |\Gamma_1|$.*

This proposition is obviously deduced by Proposition 2. The truncated differential found by the meet-in-the-middle method may be also searched by the previous standard method, but this method is better for automation taking advantage of methods to find impossible differentials. Note that such feature could be discovered in many block ciphers, notably for Feistel structure block ciphers. We present the applications of our method to ISO standard block ciphers, CLEFIA and Camellia, for example.

4   Application to CLEFIA

In this section, we first construct a 10-round truncated differential of CLEFIA, then present the truncated differential cryptanalysis of reduced-round CLEFIA-128/192/256.

4.1   New Truncated Differentials of CLEFIA

Using the new method proposed in this paper, we introduce a 9-round truncated differential of CLEFIA, and then append one round to construct the 10-round truncated differential.

Proposition 4. *Let the input difference be $\Delta A_0 = \Delta C_0 = \Delta D_0 = (0,0,0,0)$ and $\Delta B_0 = (*,0,0,0)$, then after a 9-round encryption of CLEFIA, the probability of the output difference satisfying $\Delta B_9 = \Delta C_9 = \Delta D_9 = (0,0,0,0)$ and $\Delta A_9 = (*,0,0,0)$ is about 2^{-104}.*

Proof. As outlined in Fig. 3, we define the 9-round CLEFIA as E. The first five rounds of E is defined as E_0, the last four rounds as E_1. For the input differences

$$\Gamma_0 = (\Delta A_0, \Delta B_0, \Delta C_0, \Delta D_0) = (0,0,0,0,\ *,0,0,0,\ 0,0,0,0,\ 0,0,0,0),$$

the output differences after 5-round encryption satisfy

$$\Gamma_1 = (\Delta A_5, \Delta B_5, \Delta C_5, \Delta D_5) = (*,0,0,0,\ M_0(*,0,0,0) \oplus M_1(*,0,0,0),\ ?,?,?,?,\ ?,?,?,?)$$

with probability 2^{-24}. Similarly, for the differences

$$\Gamma_2 = (\Delta A_9, \Delta B_9, \Delta C_9, \Delta D_9) = (*,0,0,0,\ 0,0,0,0,\ 0,0,0,0,\ 0,0,0,0),$$

the corresponding output differences after 4-round decryption coincide to

$$\Gamma_1 = (\Delta A_5, \Delta B_5, \Delta C_5, \Delta D_5) = (*,0,0,0,\ M_0(*,0,0,0) \oplus M_1(*,0,0,0),\ ?,?,?,?,\ ?,?,?,?)$$

with probability 1.

Since $|\Gamma_1| = 2^{88}$, $|\Gamma_2| = 2^8$. Then, by the Proposition 2, the probability of truncated differential is

$$\mathcal{P}_r(\Gamma_0 \xrightarrow{E} \Gamma_2) = 2^{-24} \times 2^8/2^{88} = 2^{-104}.$$

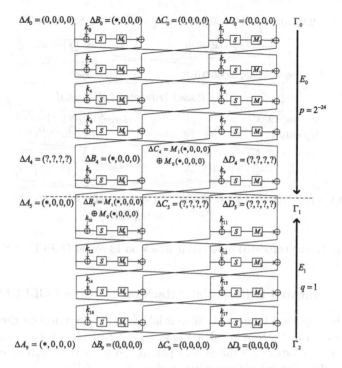

Fig. 3. The truncated differential of 9-round CLEFIA

$\square$

Here, if we change the output difference ΔA_9 as $(0, *, 0, 0)$, $(0, 0, *, 0)$ or $(0, 0, 0, *)$, the probability $\mathcal{P}_r(\Gamma_0 \xrightarrow{E_1} \Gamma_1) = 0$. As introduced in [34], $(\Gamma_0 \xrightarrow{E} \Gamma_2)$ is an impossible differential. Similarly, if the difference $\Delta A_9 = \Delta B_0$ in Proposition 4, $(\Gamma_0 \xrightarrow{E} \Gamma_2)$ is also an impossible differential [30].

Proposition 5. *Let the input difference be* $\Delta A_0 = \Delta C_0 = \Delta D_0 = (0, 0, 0, 0)$ *and* $\Delta B_0 = (*, 0, 0, 0)$, *then after 10-round encryption of CLEFIA, the probability of the output difference satisfying* $\Delta A_{10} = M_0(*, 0, 0, 0)$, $\Delta B_{10} = \Delta C_{10} = (0, 0, 0, 0)$ *and* $\Delta D_{10} = (*, 0, 0, 0)$ *is about* 2^{-104}, *which is greater than the uniform probability* 2^{-112}.

It is obviously for Proposition 5 that we append one round with probability 1 after 9-round truncated differential, and obtain the 10-round truncated differential.

Similarly, we get another 10-round truncated differential by swapping the values of ΔB_0 and ΔD_0, for example.

$$(0,0,0,0,\ 0,0,0,0,\ 0,0,0,0,\ *,0,0,0) \xrightarrow[2^{-104}]{10\ \text{rounds}} (0,0,0,0,\ *,0,0,0\ M_0(*,0,0,0),\ 0,0,0,0).$$

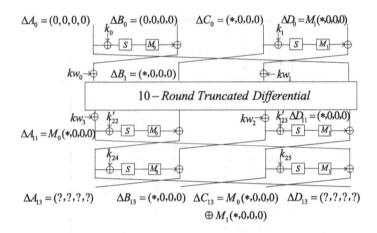

Fig. 4. The truncated differential attack on 13-round CLEFIA-128

4.2   The Truncated Differential Attack on 13-Round CLEFIA-128

Based on the 10-round truncated differential, we add one round on the top and two rounds on the bottom to attack 13-round CLEFIA-128 (see Fig. 4). We build a table T_1 to store 2^{16} differences $(M_0(b,0,0,0) \oplus M_1(a,0,0,0), a)$, where $a, b = 1, \ldots, 255$. The attack procedure is described as follows.

1. Choose 2^x structures of plaintexts, and each structure contains 2^{16} plaintexts with

$$A_0 = (x_0, x_1, x_2, x_3), \quad B_0 = (x_4, x_5, x_6, x_7),$$
$$C_0 = (\alpha_0, x_8, x_9, x_{10}), \quad D_0 = M_1(\alpha_1, x_{11}, x_{12}, x_{13}),$$

where $x_i(i = 0, \ldots, 13)$ is constant, while $\alpha_j(j = 0, 1)$ takes all possible values. Ask for the encryption of the plaintexts for each structure, and store them in a hash table H indexed by $B_{13}^{[1,2,3]}$. There are $2^{31+x} \times 2^{-24} = 2^{7+x}$ pairs on average which make $\Delta B_{13} = (*, 0, 0, 0)$. And then eliminate the pairs whose differences ΔC_{13} are not in T_1. There are about $2^{7+x} \times 2^{-16} = 2^{-9+x}$ pairs left.

2. Guess 24-bit subkey $k_{25}^{[1,2,3]}$, do the following substeps for every pair.
   (a) In the first round, deduce 8-bit subkey $k_1^{[0]}$ by the input and output differences of S-box.
   (b) In the 13-th round, get 32-bit subkey k_{24} by the input and output differences of S-boxes.
   (c) Deduce the subkey $k_{25}^{[0]}$, where the value of difference $M_1^{-1}(\Delta A_{11} \oplus \Delta C_{13})^{[0]}$ could be determined by the value of ΔC_{13}.
   (d) Compute A_{11} by partial encryption deduce the subkey k_{22}', where $k_{22}' = k_{22} \oplus kw_3$, and increase the corresponding counter of 80-bit subkey $(k_1^{[0]}, k_{22}', k_{24}, k_{25}^{[0]})$ by 1.

3. Choose the subkey whose count is the largest as the candidate of right key, then exhaustively search the rest unknown bits to obtain the master key.

Complexity Analysis. If we choose $x = 83$, the expected count of the right key is $\mu = 2^{x+31-8-104} = 4$. In step 1, we need $2^{x+16} = 2^{99}$ chosen plaintexts, which cost 2^{99} encryptions. The time complexity of step 2 is about $2^{x-9+24} \times 2/13 = 2^{95.3}$ encryptions. The memory complexity of the attack is about 2^{80} which is used to store key counters. By key schedule, we know the 72 subkeys $(k_{24}, k_{25}, k_1^{[0]})$ only depend on K_L. Then step 3 needs $2^{128-72+24} = 2^{80}$ encryptions to find the right key. Therefore, the time complexity is about 2^{99} encryptions. According to the definition of signal-to-noise ratio proposed in [3], the signal-to-noise ratio S_N is $2^{-104} \times 2^{-112} = 2^8$. According to [28], the success probability is

$$Ps = \int_{-\frac{\sqrt{\mu S_N} - \Phi^{-1}(1-2^{-a})}{\sqrt{S_N+1}}}^{\infty} \Phi(x)dx = 0.91,$$

where $a = 80$, for we choose the subkey with the largest count as the right key.

4.3 The Truncated Differential Attack on 14-Round CLEFIA-192

In this subsection, we give a truncated differential attack on 14-round CLEFIA-192 by prefixing one round on the top of the 13-round attack, illustrated in Fig. 6. In order to reduce the time complexity, we apply the partial function reduction technique proposed in [13].

Partial Function Reduction Technique. The partial function reduction technique is firstly proposed by Isobe and Shibutani at Asiacrypt 2013, which is used to reduce the guessed key involved in the attack for Feistel structure ciphers, of which the round function is composed of a S-box layer and a linear layer, such as Camellia and CLEFIA. For a group of chosen plaintexts, assume the left value is $L_0 = (\beta, y_0, y_1, y_2)$, where $y_i(i = 0, 1, 2)$ are fixed values and β is a variable. Since

$$M_0(s(k_0^{[0]} \oplus \beta), s(k_0^{[1]} \oplus y_0), s(k_0^{[2]} \oplus y_1), s(k_0^{[2]} \oplus y_2)$$
$$= M_0(0, s(k_0^{[1]} \oplus y_0), s(k_0^{[2]} \oplus y_1), s(k_0^{[3]} \oplus y_2)) \oplus M_0(s(k_0^{[0]} \oplus \beta), 0, 0, 0),$$

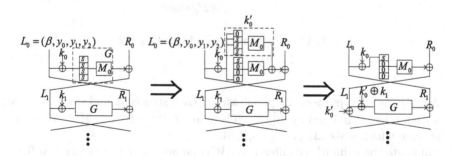

Fig. 5. Partial function reduction technique

then $k_0^{[1,2,3]}$ is treated as an equivalent key k_0', i.e., $k_0' = M_0(0, s(k_0^{[1]} \oplus y_0), s(k_0^{[2]} \oplus y_1), s(k_0^{[3]} \oplus y_2)$. As a result, only 40 bits of the 64-bit subkey (k_0, k_1) are involved in the key recovery attack, equivalent to $(k_0^{[0]}, k_0' \oplus k_1)$ (see Fig. 5).

The Attack on 14-Round CLEFIA-192. Utilizing the partial function reduction technique, we mount a 14-round attack by adding one round on the top of the 13-round attack. As illustrated in Fig. 6, we choose 2^x structures of plaintexts, and each structure contains 2^{48} plaintexts with

$$A_0 = M_1(\alpha_0, x_0, x_1, x_2), \quad B_0 = (\alpha_1, \alpha_2, \alpha_3, \alpha_4),$$
$$C_0 = (x_3, y_0, y_1, y_2), \quad D_0 = (\alpha_5, x_4, x_5, x_6),$$

where x_i and y_j are fixed values, α_i takes all possible values. In order to reduce the number of guessed subkey, let $y_j (j = 0, 1, 2)$ be constants for all structures, and then there are 2^{56} structures to be collected at most. According to partial function reduction technique, the equivalent key $k_1' = M_1(0, s_0(k_1^{[1]} \oplus y_0), s_1(k_0^{[2]} \oplus y_1), s_0(k_0^{[3]} \oplus y_2))$, and k_1' are equal for all structures. On the basic of this view, the attack on 14-round CLEFIA-192 is described as follows.

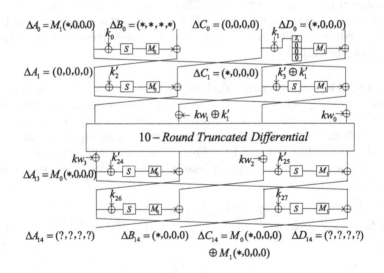

Fig. 6. The attack on 14-round CLEFIA-192

1. Ask for the encryption of the plaintexts for each structure, and store them in a hash table H indexed by $B_{14}^{[1,2,3]}$. There are $2^{95+x} \times 2^{-24} = 2^{71+x}$ pairs on average which make $\Delta B_{14} = (*, 0, 0, 0)$.
2. Eliminate the pairs whose differences ΔC_{14} do not conform to $M_0(*, 0, 0, 0) \oplus M_1(*, 0, 0, 0)$. There are about $2^{71+x} \times 2^{-16} = 2^{55+x}$ pairs left after this step.

3. Guess 8-bit subkey $k_1^{[0]}$, compute the difference ΔC_1 for every pair, then do the following substeps.

   (a) For a pair, compute 32-bit subkey k_0 by the input and output differences of S-boxes in the first round.

   (b) Deduce the input values C_1 by partial encryption, and get 8-bit equivalent key $(k_3' \oplus k_1')^{[0]}$ by the input and output differences of S-box, where k_3' is $k_3 \oplus kw_1$.

   (c) In the 14-th round, compute the 32-bit subkey k_{26} by the input and output difference of S-boxes.

   (d) Get the output difference of S-box by lookup table T_1 with ΔC_{14}, and then deduce 8-bit subkey $k_{27}^{[0]}$.

   (e) Guess 24-bit subkey $k_{27}^{[1,2,3]}$ to deduce 32-bit subkey k_{24}', where k_{24}' is $k_{24} \oplus kw_3$ by partial decryption.

   (f) Increase the corresponding counter of 136-bit subkey $(k_0, (k_3' \oplus k_1')^{[0]}, k_{24}', k_{26}, k_{27})$ by 1.

   (g) Choose the subkey whose counter is the largest as the candidate of the right key, then verify whether it is the master key by exhaustive search. If not, try the next guess of $k_1^{[0]}$.

Complexity Analysis. If we choose $x = 52$, the expected counter of the right key is $\mu = 2^{x+95-40} \times 2^{-104} = 8$, then the success probability is about 0.97. The data complexity of the attack is $2^{52+48} = 2^{100}$ chosen plaintexts. The time complexity of the attack is dominated by the Step 3. (e), which is equivalent to $2^{52+55+32} \times 2^{-4} = 2^{135}$ 14-round encryptions. The memory complexity of the attack is about $2^{52+55+24} = 2^{131}$ 136-bit words since the counters could be reused for every guess of $k_1^{[0]}$.

4.4   The Truncated Differential Attack on 14-Round CLEFIA-128

Considering the subkey relations, the 14-round attack could also be applied to CLEFIA-128. By the key schedule, we know the subkey $(k_0, k_1^{[0]}, k_{26}, k_{27})$ is determined by the following information:

$$k_0 : K_L^{\{0\sim31\}}, \quad k_{26} : K_L^{\{35\sim41\}} \| K_L^{\{28\sim34\}} \| K_L^{\{21\sim27\}} \| K_L^{\{14\sim20\}} \| K_L^{\{7\sim10\}},$$
$$k_1^{[0]} : K_L^{\{32\sim39\}}, \quad k_{27} : K_L^{\{11\sim13\}} \| K_L^{\{0\sim6\}} \| K_L^{\{64\sim85\}}.$$

It is obvious that there are 40 bits redundance, and the key involved in the attack is only 104 bits. The attack procedure is similar to the attack of 14-round CLEFIA-192.

1. Collect $2^{48+52} = 2^{100}$ plaintexts, then encrypt them and store the plaintext-ciphertext pairs in a table.

2. For every possible values of $k_{27}^{[0]}$, do the following substeps.

   (a) For each structure, compute the value $X = M_0^{-1}(M_1(s_1(B_{14}^{[0]} \oplus k_{27}^{[0]}), 0, 0, 0) \oplus C_{14})$, then restore the plaintext-ciphertext pairs indexed by 48-bit value $(B_{14}^{[1,2,3]}, X^{[1,2,3]})$. Thus, we can collect about $2^{52} \times 2^{95} \times 2^{-48} = 2^{99}$ pairs for each $k_{27}^{[0]}$, and each pair satisfies that $\Delta B_{14} = (*, 0, 0, 0)$ and ΔC_{14} belongs to the set $M_0(*, 0, 0, 0) \oplus M_1(*, 0, 0, 0)$.

  (b) Deduce 64-bit subkey (k_0, k_{26}) by partial encryption and decryption. Since these 72-bit subkey $(k_0, k_{26}, k_{27}^{[0]})$ only takes 42-bit information, then we filter more wrong pairs. There are about $2^{99} \times 2^{-30} = 2^{69}$ pairs remaining.

  (c) For every pair, deduce 8-bit equivalent key $(k_3' \oplus k_1')^{[0]}$, where 8-bit information of subkey $k_1^{[0]}$ have been deduced in the above step.

  (d) By subkey relations, guess 22-bit value $K_L^{\{64 \sim 85\}}$ instead of subkey $k_{27}^{[1,2,3]}$ to deduce 32-bit subkey k_{24}'.

  (e) Increase the corresponding counter of 104-bit information of subkey by 1.

3. After operations of all possible $k_{27}^{[0]}$, choose the subkey whose counter is the largest as the candidate of right key, and exhaustively search to obtain the master key.

Complexity Analysis. The data complexity of the attack is $2^{52+48} = 2^{100}$ chosen plaintexts. The time complexity of the attack is dominated by the Step 2. (a) and (b), which is equivalent to $2^{100} \times 2^8 = 2^{108}$ 14-round encryptions. The memory complexity of the attack is dominated by Step 1 and Step 2. (e) which is about $2^{100} \times 2 + 2^{99} = 2^{101.3}$ 128-bit words.

4.5   The Truncated Differential Attack on 15-Round CLEFIA-256

The attack on 15-round CLEFIA-256 is constructed by appending one round at the bottom of the 14-round attack. The attack procedure is similar to 14-round attack. We first choose 2^{52} structures of plaintexts and obtain the corresponding ciphertexts. Guess the subkey of last round function (k_{28}, k_{29}), then decrypt the ciphertexts to get the intermediate value $(A_{14}, B_{14}, C_{14}, D_{14})$ and store them in a hash table H indexed by $B_{14}^{[1,2,3]}$. For the collected pairs, filter the pairs whose differences ΔC_{14} don't belong to the set $M_0(*, 0, 0, 0) \oplus M_1(*, 0, 0, 0)$. After that, the number of remaining pairs is about 2^{107}. Then as described in the 14-round attack, we can obtain 2^{32} values of 144-bit subkey for each pair. Then choose the subkey whose counter is the largest under every 64-bit key guess, and verify whether it is the correct key. If not, try to the next key guess of (k_{28}, k_{29}). The data complexity of the attack is $2^{52+48} = 2^{100}$ chosen plaintexts. The time complexity of the attack is equivalent to $2^{107} \times 2^{64} \times 2^{32} = 2^{203}$ 15-round encryptions. The memory complexity of the attack is about 2^{139} 144-bit words.

5   Application to Camellia

In this section, we propose a 8-round truncated differential of Camellia, based on which, we introduce the truncated differential attack on reduced-round Camellia-128/192.

5.1 The Truncated Differential of Camellia

We first introduce a 7-round differential of Camellia for 99.2 % keys, based on which we give an 8-round truncated differential by appending one round at the bottom. The new differential is based on two interesting observations of FL function (Fig. 7).

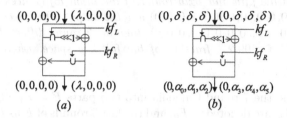

(a) (b)

Fig. 7. Observations of FL function

Observation 1. *Let the input difference of FL function be $(0,0,0,0,\lambda,0,0,0)$, where $\lambda = 2^{7-i}, i = 0,1,\ldots,7$. If the corresponding bit of inserted key $kf_R^{\{i\}} = 1$, then the output difference must be $(0,0,0,0,\lambda,0,0,0)$.*

For 8 values of λ whose hamming weight is 1, there are $2^{32} - 2^{24}$ values for kf_R (the hamming weight of $kf_R^{[0]}$ is not zero) keeping the output difference $(0,0,0,0,\lambda,0,0,0)$, which takes a fraction of $(1 - 2^{-8})$. The observation is available to FL^{-1} function.

Observation 2. *There are about 99.6 % values of (kf_L, kf_R) satisfying that if the input difference of FL function is $(0,\delta,\delta,\delta,0,\delta,\delta,\delta)$, then the probability that the output difference is $(0,\alpha_0,\alpha_1,\alpha_2,0,\alpha_3,\alpha_4,\alpha_5)$ is greater than 2^{-2}, where $\delta \neq 0$, $\alpha_i \neq 0$, and there exist at least a pair of (α_i,α_j) with $\alpha_i \neq \alpha_j$, $i,j = 0,1,\ldots,5, i \neq j$.*

We verify this observation by experiment on a PC. For a given key (kf_L, kf_R), we compute the output difference by traversing all the values of δ, and keep the δ which makes the output difference satisfying Observation 2. Let $S_\delta = \{\delta | (0,\alpha_0,\alpha_1,\alpha_2,0,\alpha_3,\alpha_4,\alpha_5) = FL(0,\delta,\delta,\delta,0,\delta,\delta,\delta), \alpha_i \neq 0, \exists 0 \leq i < j \leq 5, s.t. \alpha_i \neq \alpha_j\}$. Let $N_\delta = |S_\delta|$ be the set size. When $N_\delta > 64$, we denote the key as a weak key, vice versa. In our experiment, we choose 2^{32} values of (kf_L, kf_R) randomly, and exhaustive 255 values of input difference for each key to get the statistical result. On average, there are about 2^{24} values of (kf_L, kf_R) are not weak key. That means the fraction of weak key space is about $(1 - 2^{-8}) \approx 0.996$. In the following, we denote the full key space of FL function as K_{fl}, and the weak key space as $\widehat{K_{fl}}$. For the attacker, it is easy to obtain all the values of $\widehat{K_{fl}}$ by exhaustive search, the complexity is 2^{64} simple computations.

However, we list some examples of key which are not content with Observation 2. For instance, the key $kf_L^{\{i\}} = 0$, $kf_R^{\{i\}} = 1$ ($i = 0 \sim 31$), since the output difference would be $(0, \delta, \delta, \delta, 0, \delta, \delta, \delta)$ with probability 1 for any nonzero value δ in such case.

Based on the two observations, we build a 7-round differential for Camellia.

Proposition 6. *Given the 7-round Camellia encryption with a FL/FL^{-1} layer inserted between the fifth and sixth round, if the input differences of first round are $(0,0,0,0,0,0,0,0,\ 0,0,0,0,\lambda,0,0,0)$ and the output differences of 7-th round are $(0,0,0,0,\lambda,0,0,0,\ 0,0,0,0,0,0,0,0)$, then the 7-round differential holds with probability 2^{-114} for 99.2% fraction of the full key space, where $\lambda = 2^i$, $i = 0, 1, \ldots, 7$.*

Proof. We divide the 7-round Camellia into two parts $E = E_1 \circ E_0$, where the first 4 rounds of E are denoted as E_0, and the last 3 rounds of E as E_1, illustrated in Fig. 8. Let the output differences of E be

$$\Gamma_2 = (0,0,0,0,\lambda,0,0,0,0,0,0,0,0,0,0,0),$$

where $\lambda = 0 \times 80$. By Observation 1, we know $\Delta L_5' = (0,0,0,0,\lambda,0,0,0)$ when $kf_{0R}^{\{0\}} = 1$. By partial decryption, we get $\Delta R_5 = (0,\delta,\delta,\delta,0,\delta,\delta,\delta)$. By Observation 2, we know the output differences set S_δ with the size $N_\delta > 64$ hold with probability larger than 2^{-2} for a given weak key kf_1. Let $\Delta R_5' = S_\delta$.

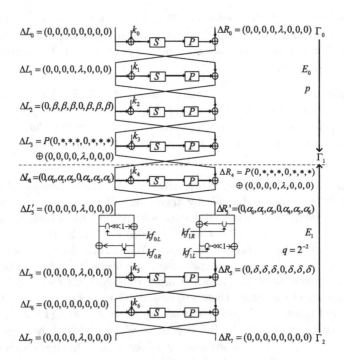

Fig. 8. Differential of 7-round Camellia

Then the output differences of E_1^{-1} are

$$\Gamma_1 = (\Delta R_5', \; P(0, *, *, *, 0, *, *, *) \oplus (0, 0, 0, 0, \lambda, 0, 0, 0)),$$

where there are N_δ values for $\Delta R_5'$. It is obviously $Pr(\Gamma_2 \xrightarrow{E_1^{-1}} \Gamma_1) = 2^{-2}$.

Let the input difference of E be $\Gamma_0 = (0, 0, 0, 0, 0, 0, 0, 0, \; 0, 0, 0, 0, \lambda, 0, 0, 0)$, and the output difference after E_0 be Γ_1. We know the probability $Pr(\Gamma_0 \xrightarrow{E_0} \Gamma_1) = N_\delta \times 2^{-64}$.

Since $|\Gamma_1| = 2^{48} \times N_\delta$, $|\Gamma_2| = 1$, the probability of the 7-round differential is

$$P_r(\Gamma_0 \xrightarrow{E} \Gamma_2) = 2^{-2} \times 2^{-64} \times N_\delta / (2^{48} \times N_\delta) = 2^{-114}.$$

according to Proposition 3.

Considering the FL/FL^{-1} functions, the 7-round differential holds only for the weak key (kf_0, kf_1) by Observations 1 and 2.

Similarly, the 7-round differentials of Camellia also hold with probability 2^{-114}, when $\lambda = 2^i, i = 0, 1, \ldots, 6$. Since the independent of the subkey kf_0 and kf_1, all the 8 7-round differentials of Camellia cover the key space is about $(1 - 2^{-8}) \times (1 - 2^{-8}) = 1 - 2^{-7} = 99.2\%$. □

Proposition 7. *Given the 8-round Camellia encryption with a FL/FL^{-1} layer inserted between the fifth and sixth round, if the input differences of first round are $(0, 0, 0, 0, 0, 0, 0, 0, \; 0, 0, 0, 0, \lambda, 0, 0, 0)$ and the output differences of 8-th round are $(0, \eta, \eta, \eta, 0, \eta, \eta, \eta, 0, 0, 0, 0, \lambda, 0, 0, 0)$, then the 8-round differential holds with probability 2^{-114} for a fraction of $(1 - 2^{-7})$ full key space, where $\lambda = 2^i, i = 0, 1, \ldots, 7$.*

Proof. On the basic of 7-round differential, we append one round after it with probability 1 and obtain the 8-round truncated differential. It is noted that the uniform probability of such truncated differential characteristic is 2^{-120}, which is smaller than 2^{-114}. □

Similarly, there are three other 8-round truncated differentials in the following.

$$(0, 0, 0, 0, 0, 0, 0, 0, \; 0, 0, 0, 0, \lambda, 0, 0) \xrightarrow[\;2^{-114}\;]{8 \text{ rounds}} (\eta, 0, \eta, \eta, \eta, 0, \eta, \eta, 0, 0, 0, 0, 0, \lambda, 0, 0),$$

$$(0, 0, 0, 0, 0, 0, 0, 0, \; 0, 0, 0, 0, 0, \lambda, 0) \xrightarrow[\;2^{-114}\;]{8 \text{ rounds}} (\eta, \eta, 0, \eta, \eta, \eta, 0, \eta, 0, 0, 0, 0, 0, 0, \lambda, 0),$$

$$(0, 0, 0, 0, 0, 0, 0, 0, \; 0, 0, 0, 0, 0, 0, \lambda) \xrightarrow[\;2^{-114}\;]{8 \text{ rounds}} (\eta, \eta, \eta, 0, \eta, \eta, \eta, 0, 0, 0, 0, 0, 0, 0, \lambda).$$

5.2   The Truncated Differential Attack on 11-Round Camellia-128

We first give an attack on 11-round Camellia-128 for weak key space, where we assume that the inserted key of FL/FL^{-1} layer (kf_1, kf_2) are weak key which takes a fraction of 99.2 %. Then we present the attack on the full key space by

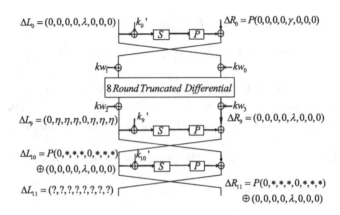

Fig. 9. The attack on 11-round Camellia-128

multiplied method given in [23]. The attack is mounted by adding one round on the top and two rounds on the bottom of the 8-round differential characteristic (see Fig. 9). The attack procedure is as follows.

1. Choose 2^n structures of plaintexts, and each structure contains 2^{16} plaintexts

$$(L_0, R_0) = (x_0, x_1, x_2, x_3, \alpha_0, x_4, x_5, x_6, P(x_7, x_8, x_9, x_{10}, \alpha_1, x_{11}, x_{12}, x_{13})),$$

where $x_i(i = 1, \ldots, 13)$ are fixed values in each structure, while $\alpha_i(i = 1, 2)$ take all the possible values.
2. Ask for the encryption of these plaintexts and store them in a table.
3. For $i = 32 \sim 39$, do the following substeps.
   (a) Restore 2^{n+16} plaintext-ciphertext pairs in a hash table H which is indexed by 15-bit value of ciphertext $(P^{-1}(R_{11})^{[0]}, P^{-1}(R_{11})^{\{32 \sim (i-1), (i+1) \sim 39\}})$. By birthday paradox, we get $2^{n+31} \times 2^{-15} = 2^{n+16}$ pairs whose differences satisfy $P^{-1}(\Delta R_{11}) = (0, *, *, *, 0, *, *, *) \oplus P^{-1}(0, 0, 0, 0, \lambda, 0, 0, 0)$, where "$\lambda$" denotes the nonzero differences with $\lambda^{\{j\}} = 0$ ($j \neq i - 32$).
   (b) Delete the pairs whose differences don't satisfy $\Delta L_0^{\{32 \sim (i-1), (i+1) \sim 39\}} \neq 0$. Then number of remaining pairs is about 2^{n+9}. After that, all pairs satisfy $(\Delta L_0, \Delta R_0) = (0, 0, 0, 0, \lambda, 0, 0, 0, P(0, 0, 0, 0, \gamma, 0, 0, 0))$ and $\Delta R_{11} = P(0, *, *, *, 0, *, *, *) \oplus (0, 0, 0, 0, \lambda, 0, 0, 0)$.
   (c) For each pair, deduce the equivalent key $k_0'^{[4]}$, where $k_0' = k_0 \oplus kw_0$.
   (d) For 2^8 possible values of η, do the following substeps.
      i. Deduce the equivalent key k_{10}', where $k_{10}' = k_{10} \oplus kw_3$.
      ii Deduce the equivalent key $k_9'^{[1,2,3,5,6,7]}$, where $k_9' = k_9 \oplus kw_2$.
   (e) Increase the corresponding counter of 120-bit information of subkey by 1.
   (f) After computations of all proper pairs, choose the subkey whose counter is the largest as the candidate of right key, and verify it by trivial test. If succeed, output the right key; otherwise, another value of i should be tried. It is noted that if $k f_{0R}^{\{i-32\}} = 1$, the attack should succeed for such i.

Complexity Analysis. If we choose $n = 101$, the expected counter of the right key is $\mu = 4$, and then the success probability is about 0.91. The data complexity of the attack is $2^{101+16} = 2^{117}$ chosen plaintexts. Step 2 needs about 2^{117} 11-round encryptions, which also needs 2^{118} 128-bit words to store all plaintext-ciphertext pairs. The time complexity of step 3 is equivalent to $2^3 \times 2^{118} \times 2^{-2} = 2^{119}$ 11-round encryptions. The memory requirement of step 3 is about 2^{118} 120-bit words since all counters could be reused for each value of i. In total, the time complexity of the attack is about $2^{119.3}$ 11-round encryptions and the memory complexity is about 2^{119}.

The Attack for the Full Key Space. For above attack, if the target key satisfies that (kf_{1L}, kf_{1R}) belongs to $\widehat{K_{fl}}$ and at least one bit of $kf_{0R}^{[0]}$ is 1, the attack would succeed. If failed, we conclude that $(kf_{1L}, kf_{1R}) \in K_{fl}/\widehat{K_{fl}}$ or $kf_{0R}^{[0]} = 0$. Thus, using this information, the attack could be extended to the full key space by multiplied method, which is as follows.

- **Phase 1.** Try to perform above truncated differential attack for weak key space. If success, obtain the correct key. Otherwise perform the next phase.
- **Phase 2.** Search the key set $K_{fl}/\widehat{K_{fl}}$. There are about 2^{56} values of (kf_{1L}, kf_{1R}) belong to this set. Then exhaustively search to get the master key. The time complexity of this step is about 2^{120}. If failed, perform the next phase.
- **Phase 3.** Announce the subkey $kf_{0R}^{[0]} = 0$, then exhaustively search for the remaining 120-bit value to obtain the master key.

The time complexity of the whole attack is about $2^{119.3} + 2^{120} + 2^{120} = 2^{121.3}$ 11-round encryptions. The data complexity is 2^{117} chosen plaintexts and the memory requirement is 2^{119} 128-bit words.

5.3 The Truncated Differential Attack on 12-Round Camellia-192

We add one round on the bottom of 11-round attack, and present a 12-round attack on Camellia-192 for the 99.2 % fraction of key space. The attack procedure is similar to the 11-round attack. First we choose 2^{117} plaintexts and encrypt the plaintexts to obtain the corresponding ciphertexts, then guess the 64-bit value k'_{11} and compute the intermediate value R_{11} for every plaintext-ciphertext pairs. After that, apply the 11-round attack to collect the proper pairs and deduce the equivalent key for every pair. The time complexity is equivalent to $2^{64} \times 2^{119.3} = 2^{183.3}$ 12-round encryptions. The memory could be reused in every guess of 64-bit value k'_{11}, which is about 2^{119} 128-bit words. The data complexity is about 2^{117} chosen plaintexts. Similarly, the time complexity of the attack for the full key space is about $2^{183.3} + 2^{184} + 2^{184} \approx 2^{185.3}$.

6 Conclusion

In this paper, inspired by the impossible differential attack, we find an interesting way to construct the truncated differential of block ciphers by the meet-in-the-middle like technique. Therefore, we present the truncated differential cryptanalysis of ISO standards CLEFIA and Camellia. For CLEFIA, we introduce a 10-round truncated differential characteristic to attack 14/14/15-round CLEFIA-128/192/256 with 2^{108}, 2^{135} and 2^{203} encryptions, respectively. For Camellia, we give an 8-round truncated differential to attack 11/12-round Camellia-128/192 including the FL/FL^{-1} and whiten layers with $2^{121.3}$ and $2^{185.3}$ encryptions. It is noted that the truncated differential introduced in our attack, in some cases, is very resembled to the impossible differential proposed in previous works. Nevertheless, the point focused on for the attacker is different in the two methods, one is the zero probability event but the other is the high probability event. It is also significant for us to study the more applications of the method. For example, the applications to Feistel block ciphers SMS4, TEA, XTEA, SIMON, etc.

Acknowledgments. We would like to thank anonymous reviewers for their very helpful comments on the paper. This work is supported by the National Natural Science Foundation of China (No. 61133013) and 973 Program (No.2013CB834205), and the National Natural Science Foundation of China (No. 61402256 and 61272035).

References

1. Aoki, K., Ichikawa, T., Kanda, M., Matsui, M., Moriai, S., Nakajima, J., Tokita, T.: Camellia: a 128-bit block cipher suitable for multiple platforms - design and analysis. In: Stinson, D.R., Tavares, S. (eds.) SAC 2000. LNCS, vol. 2012, pp. 39–56. Springer, Heidelberg (2001)
2. Biham, E., Biryukov, A., Shamir, A.: Cryptanalysis of skipjack reduced to 31 rounds using impossible differentials. In: Stern, J. (ed.) EUROCRYPT 1999. LNCS, vol. 1592, pp. 12–23. Springer, Heidelberg (1999)
3. Biham, E., Shamir, A.: Differential cryptanalysis of DES-like cryptosystems. In: Menezes, A., Vanstone, S.A. (eds.) CRYPTO 1990. LNCS, vol. 537, pp. 2–21. Springer, Heidelberg (1991)
4. Biham, E., Shamir, A.: New types of cryptanalytic attacks using related keys. J. Cryptol. **7**(4), 229–246 (1994)
5. Blondeau, C.: Improbable differential from impossible differential: on the validity of the model. In: Paul, G., Vaudenay, S. (eds.) INDOCRYPT 2013. LNCS, vol. 8250, pp. 149–160. Springer, Heidelberg (2013)
6. Blondeau, C., Gérard, B.: Multiple differential cryptanalysis: theory and practice. In: Joux, A. (ed.) FSE 2011. LNCS, vol. 6733, pp. 35–54. Springer, Heidelberg (2011)
7. Bogdanov, A., Geng, H., Wang, M., Wen, L., Collard, B.: Zero-correlation linear cryptanalysis with FFT and improved attacks on ISO standards camellia and CLEFIA. In: Lange, T., Lauter, K., Lisoněk, P. (eds.) SAC 2013. LNCS, vol. 8282, pp. 306–323. Springer, Heidelberg (2014)
8. Boura, C., Naya-Plasencia, M., Suder, V.: Scrutinizing and improving impossible differential attacks: applications to CLEFIA, Camellia, LBlock and SIMON. In: Sarkar, P., Iwata, T. (eds.) ASIACRYPT 2014. LNCS, vol. 8873, pp. 179–199. Springer, Heidelberg (2014)

9. Chen, J., Jia, K., Yu, H., Wang, X.: New impossible differential attacks of reduced-round Camellia-192 and Camellia-256. In: Parampalli, U., Hawkes, P. (eds.) ACISP 2011. LNCS, vol. 6812, pp. 16–33. Springer, Heidelberg (2011)

10. Chen, J., Li, L.: Low data complexity attack on reduced Camellia-256. In: Susilo, W., Mu, Y., Seberry, J. (eds.) ACISP 2012. LNCS, vol. 7372, pp. 101–114. Springer, Heidelberg (2012)

11. Dong, X., Li, L., Jia, K., Wang, X.: Improved attacks on reduced-round Camellia-128/192/256. In: Nyberg, K. (ed.) CT-RSA 2015. LNCS, vol. 9048, pp. 59–83. Springer, Heidelberg (2015)

12. Hatano, Y., Sekine, H., Kaneko, T.: Higher order differential attack of Camellia (II). In: Nyberg, K., Heys, H.M. (eds.) SAC 2002. LNCS, vol. 2595, pp. 129–146. Springer, Heidelberg (2003)

13. Isobe, T., Shibutani, K.: Generic key recovery attack on feistel scheme. In: Sako, K., Sarkar, P. (eds.) ASIACRYPT 2013, Part I. LNCS, vol. 8269, pp. 464–485. Springer, Heidelberg (2013)

14. Kanda, M., Matsumoto, T.: Security of Camellia against truncated differential cryptanalysis. In: Matsui, M. (ed.) FSE 2001. LNCS, vol. 2355, pp. 286–299. Springer, Heidelberg (2002)

15. Knudsen, L.: DEAL - a 128-bit block cipher. In: NIST AES Proposal (1998)

16. Knudsen, L.R.: Truncated and higher order differentials. In: Preneel, B. (ed.) FSE 1994. LNCS, vol. 1008, pp. 196–211. Springer, Heidelberg (1995)

17. Lai, X.: Higher order derivatives and differential cryptanalysis. In: Blahut, R., Costello Jr., D.J., Maurer, U., Mittelholzer, T. (eds.) Communications and Cryptography. The Springer International Series in Engineering and Computer Science, vol. 276, pp. 227–233. Springer, US (1994)

18. Lai, X., Massey, J.L.: Markov ciphers and differential cryptanalysis. In: Davies, D.W. (ed.) EUROCRYPT 1991. LNCS, vol. 547, pp. 17–38. Springer, Heidelberg (1991)

19. Lee, S., Hong, S.H., Lee, S.-J., Lim, J.-I., Yoon, S.H.: Truncated differential cryptanalysis of Camellia. In: Kim, K. (ed.) ICISC 2001. LNCS, vol. 2288, pp. 32–38. Springer, Heidelberg (2002)

20. Lei, D., Chao, L., Feng, K.: New observation on Camellia. In: Preneel, B., Tavares, S. (eds.) SAC 2005. LNCS, vol. 3897, pp. 51–64. Springer, Heidelberg (2006)

21. Duo, L., Li, C., Feng, K.: Square like attack on Camellia. In: Qing, S., Imai, H., Wang, G. (eds.) ICICS 2007. LNCS, vol. 4861, pp. 269–283. Springer, Heidelberg (2007)

22. Li, Y., Wu, W., Zhang, L.: Improved integral attacks on reduced-round CLEFIA block cipher. In: Jung, S., Yung, M. (eds.) WISA 2011. LNCS, vol. 7115, pp. 28–39. Springer, Heidelberg (2012)

23. Liu, Y., Li, L., Gu, D., Wang, X., Liu, Z., Chen, J., Li, W.: New observations on impossible differential cryptanalysis of reduced-round Camellia. In: Canteaut, A. (ed.) FSE 2012. LNCS, vol. 7549, pp. 90–109. Springer, Heidelberg (2012)

24. Lu, J., Kim, J.-S., Keller, N., Dunkelman, O.: Improving the efficiency of impossible differential cryptanalysis of reduced Camellia and MISTY1. In: Malkin, T. (ed.) CT-RSA 2008. LNCS, vol. 4964, pp. 370–386. Springer, Heidelberg (2008)

25. Lu, J., Wei, Y., Kim, J., Pasalic, E.: The higher-order meet-in-the-middle attack and its application to the Camellia block cipher. In: Galbraith, S., Nandi, M. (eds.) INDOCRYPT 2012. LNCS, vol. 7668, pp. 244–264. Springer, Heidelberg (2012)

26. Mala, H., Dakhilalian, M., Shakiba, M.: Impossible differential attacks on 13-round CLEFIA-128. J. Comput. Sci. Technol. **26**(4), 744–750 (2011)

27. Sasaki, Y., Wang, L.: Meet-in-the-middle technique for integral attacks against feistel ciphers. In: Knudsen, L.R., Wu, H. (eds.) SAC 2012. LNCS, vol. 7707, pp. 234–251. Springer, Heidelberg (2013)
28. Selçuk, A.A.: On probability of success in linear and differential cryptanalysis. J. Cryptol. **21**(1), 131–147 (2008)
29. Shirai, T.: Differential, linear, boomerang and rectangle cryptanalysis of reduced-round Camellia. In: The Third NESSIE Workshop (2002)
30. Shirai, T., Shibutani, K., Akishita, T., Moriai, S., Iwata, T.: The 128-bit block-cipher CLEFIA (extended abstract). In: Biryukov, A. (ed.) FSE 2007. LNCS, vol. 4593, pp. 181–195. Springer, Heidelberg (2007)
31. Sugita, M., Kobara, K., Imai, H.: Security of reduced version of the block cipher camellia against truncated and impossible differential cryptanalysis. In: Boyd, C. (ed.) ASIACRYPT 2001. LNCS, vol. 2248, pp. 193–207. Springer, Heidelberg (2001)
32. Tang, X., Sun, B., Li, R., Li, C.: Impossible differential cryptanalysis of 13-round CLEFIA-128. J. Syst. Softw. **84**(7), 1191–1196 (2011)
33. Tezcan, C.: The improbable differential attack: cryptanalysis of reduced round CLEFIA. In: Gong, G., Gupta, K.C. (eds.) INDOCRYPT 2010. LNCS, vol. 6498, pp. 197–209. Springer, Heidelberg (2010)
34. Tsunoo, Y., Tsujihara, E., Shigeri, M., Saito, T., Suzaki, T., Kubo, H.: Impossible differential cryptanalysis of CLEFIA. In: Nyberg, K. (ed.) FSE 2008. LNCS, vol. 5086, pp. 398–411. Springer, Heidelberg (2008)
35. Wang, W., Wang, X.: Saturation cryptanalysis of CLEFIA. J. Commun. **29**(10), 88–92 (2008)
36. Wenling, W., Dengguo, F., Hua, C.: Collision attack and pseudorandomness of reduced-round Camellia. In: Handschuh, H., Hasan, M.A. (eds.) SAC 2004. LNCS, vol. 3357, pp. 252–266. Springer, Heidelberg (2004)
37. Wu, W., Zhang, L., Zhang, W.: Improved impossible differential cryptanalysis of reduced-round Camellia. In: Avanzi, R.M., Keliher, L., Sica, F. (eds.) SAC 2008. LNCS, vol. 5381, pp. 442–456. Springer, Heidelberg (2009)

Understanding Attacks

Protecting Against Multidimensional Linear and Truncated Differential Cryptanalysis by Decorrelation

Céline Blondeau[1]([✉]), Aslı Bay[1,2], and Serge Vaudenay[2]

[1] Department of Computer Science, School of Science, Aalto University,
Espoo, Finland
celine.blondeau@aalto.fi
[2] EPFL, Lausanne, Switzerland

Abstract. The decorrelation theory provides a different point of view on the security of block cipher primitives. Results on some statistical attacks obtained in this context can support or provide new insight on the security of symmetric cryptographic primitives. In this paper, we study, for the first time, the multidimensional linear attacks as well as the truncated differential attacks in this context. We show that the cipher should be decorrelated of order two to be resistant against some multidimensional linear and truncated differential attacks. Previous results obtained with this theory for linear, differential, differential-linear and boomerang attacks are also resumed and improved in this paper.

Keywords: Decorrelation theory · Multidimensional linear cryptanalysis · Truncated differential cryptanalysis

1 Introduction

In the last 25 years many statistical attacks have been proposed and implemented on different symmetric key cryptographic primitives. Nowadays, new symmetric primitives are not considered secure until evaluation by the community. But it is often difficult to evaluate the security of a cipher due to the large number of known attacks.

In 1998, Vaudenay [18,21] introduced the decorrelation theory to prevent this long and tedious security evaluation. When a cipher is designed and proved secure up to a certain degree of decorrelation, it is secure against a wide range of statistical attacks. Among statistical attacks, differential cryptanalysis [8], linear cryptanalysis [17] and their generalizations have been prominent. For instance, we know that a cipher decorrelated of order two is resistant to the classical differential and linear cryptanalysis. Recently [7], it has been shown that the primitives should be decorrelated of order four to be protected against differential-linear [3,13] and boomerang [22] attacks.

Understanding the similitude of the different statistical attacks is of great importance to simplify the security analysis of the symmetric cryptographic

© International Association for Cryptologic Research 2015
G. Leander (Ed.): FSE 2015, LNCS 9054, pp. 73–91, 2015.
DOI: 10.1007/978-3-662-48116-5_4

primitives. While different works in that direction have been presented in the last couple of years [4,9,10,16], part of this unification can also be obtained by determining the order of decorrelation of the new presented attacks. However, the question of measuring the advantage of taking the information from different differentials or linear approximations has not yet been studied in the context of decorrelation theory. In this paper, we study the decorrelation order of the multidimensional linear and truncated differential attacks. In particular, we show that a cipher is protected against multidimensional linear attacks if it is decorrelated of order two. Some elements of the proof are related to the link between multidimensional linear attacks and truncated differential attacks which was discovered by Blondeau and Nyberg [9,10]. Using the result obtained for a special truncated differential distinguisher, we have been able to determine that the truncated differential attacks involving a large number of input differences are also decorrelated of order two. Using the decorrelation theory, in this paper, we provide for the first time an intuition on the power of truncated differential and multidimensional linear attacks as a function of the number of involved differential or linear approximations used in the attack.

Outline. In Sect. 2, we recall some basic definitions and previous works in the context of the decorrelation theory. In Sect. 3 we study the multidimensional linear attack in this context. In Sect. 4, we study the decorrelation order of the truncated differential attack. In Sect. 5, we provide some improvement of the previous results for the well known differential, linear, differential-linear and boomerang attacks. Section 6 concludes this paper.

2   Preliminaries

2.1   Statistical Attacks

We recall in this section some basic definitions related to the statistical attacks studied in this paper.

Linear cryptanalysis [17] uses a linear relation between bits from plaintexts, corresponding ciphertexts, and the encryption key. Given a permutation Enc over $\{0,1\}^\ell$, the strength of the linear relation is measured by its correlation. The *correlation* of a function $\mathsf{Enc} : \mathbb{F}_2^\ell \to \mathbb{F}_2^\ell$ at point $(\alpha, \beta) \in \mathbb{F}_2^\ell \times \mathbb{F}_2^\ell$ is defined as

$$\mathsf{cor}(\alpha, \beta) = 2^{-\ell}\Big[\# \left\{x \in \mathbb{F}_2^\ell | \alpha \cdot x \oplus \beta \cdot \mathsf{Enc}(x) = 0\right\} -$$
$$\# \left\{x \in \mathbb{F}_2^\ell | \alpha \cdot x \oplus \beta \cdot \mathsf{Enc}(x) = 1\right\}\Big],$$

where the quantity within brackets can be computed as the Walsh transform of $\alpha \cdot x \oplus \beta \cdot \mathsf{Enc}(x)$ evaluated at zero.

Through this paper, the square correlation at point $v = (\alpha, \beta) \in \mathbb{F}_2^{2\ell}$ will be denoted by $\mathsf{LP}^{\mathsf{Enc}}(v)$ and corresponds to $\mathsf{LP}^{\mathsf{Enc}}(v) = \mathsf{cor}^2(\alpha, \beta)$.

For the generalizations of linear cryptanalysis, such as multidimensional linear cryptanalysis [14], a quantity C, called *capacity*, is used for evaluating the non-uniformity of the set of linear approximations.

The capacity corresponds to the sum of the square correlations of the involved linear approximations. We let $V \subset \mathbb{F}_2^{2\ell}$ be the vector space spanned by different (α_j, β_j) masks. In the context of multidimensional linear attacks, we define the capacity

$$\mathsf{cap}_{\mathsf{Enc}}(V) = \sum_{v \in V, v \neq 0} \mathsf{LP}^{\mathsf{Enc}}(v).$$

In the following of this paper, we denote by k the dimension of V.

In differential cryptanalysis [8], the attacker is interested in finding and exploiting non-uniformity in occurrences of plaintext and ciphertext differences. Given the differences $\Delta \in \mathbb{F}_2^\ell$ and $\Gamma \in \mathbb{F}_2^\ell$, the probability $\mathsf{DP}^{\mathsf{Enc}}(\Delta, \Gamma)$ of the differential (Δ, Γ) is defined as

$$\mathsf{DP}^{\mathsf{Enc}}(\Delta, \Gamma) = 2^{-\ell} \#\{x \in \mathbb{F}_2^\ell \mid \mathsf{Enc}(x) \oplus \mathsf{Enc}(x \oplus \Delta) = \Gamma\}.$$

The power of the generalization of differential cryptanalysis involving multiple differentials is measured by a sum or average of these probabilities. For the truncated differential attacks [15] with differences (Δ, Γ) in the vector space $V^\perp \subset \mathbb{F}_2^{2\ell}$ we define

$$P_{\mathsf{Enc}}^{\mathsf{STD}}(V^\perp) = 2^{-2\ell} \#\{(x, x') \in \mathbb{F}_2^\ell \times \mathbb{F}_2^\ell \mid (x \oplus x', \mathsf{Enc}(x) \oplus \mathsf{Enc}(x')) \in V^\perp\}.$$

We can show that,

$$P_{\mathsf{Enc}}^{\mathsf{STD}}(V^\perp) = 2^{-\ell} \sum_{(\Delta, \Gamma) \in V^\perp} \mathsf{DP}^{\mathsf{Enc}}(\Delta, \Gamma).$$

Derived from the general link between differential probability and linear correlations [12], the authors of [10,11] show a general link between multidimensional linear attacks and truncated differential attacks. To derive in Sect. 3 the decorrelation order of a multidimensional linear attack, we will use this link. Using our notations, Theorem 1 of [11] corresponds to the following one.

Theorem 1. *Let $V^\perp$ be the set of all u such that $u \cdot v = 0$ for all $v \in V$. Using the previous notation, we obtain the following relation between $P_{\mathsf{Enc}}^{\mathsf{STD}}(V^\perp)$ and $\mathsf{cap}_{\mathsf{Enc}}(V)$:*

$$2^{-k} \mathsf{cap}_{\mathsf{Enc}}(V) = p_{\mathsf{Enc}}^{\mathsf{STD}}(V^\perp) - 2^{-k}.$$

Proof. We provide the proof with our settings. We have

$$1 + \mathsf{cap}_{\mathsf{Enc}}(V) = \sum_{v \in V} \mathsf{LP}^{\mathsf{Enc}}(v)$$

$$= \sum_{v \in V} 2^{-\ell} \sum_u (-1)^{u \cdot v} \mathsf{DP}^{\mathsf{Enc}}(u)$$

$$= 2^{-\ell} \sum_u \mathsf{DP}^{\mathsf{Enc}}(u) \sum_{v \in V} (-1)^{u \cdot v}.$$

Since $v \mapsto u \cdot v$ is a group homomorphism from V to $\mathbf{Z}_2$, either it is balanced, or identically equal to 0 (when $u \in V^\perp$, by definition). We have

$$1 + \mathsf{cap}_{\mathsf{Enc}}(V) = 2^{k-\ell} \sum_{u \in V^\perp} \mathsf{DP}^{\mathsf{Enc}}(u).$$

So, $p_{\mathsf{Enc}}^{\mathsf{STD}}(V^\perp) = 2^{-k} + 2^{-k}\mathsf{cap}_{\mathsf{Enc}}(V)$. $\qquad\qquad\square$

Splitting the space $V^\perp$ of involved differentials to the spaces $V_{\mathsf{in}}^\perp$ and $V_{\mathsf{out}}^\perp$ of input and output differences, we can define the truncated differential probability $P_{\mathsf{Enc}}^{\mathsf{TD}}$ as follows

$$P_{\mathsf{Enc}}^{\mathsf{TD}}(V^\perp) = 2^{-\ell} \frac{1}{|V_{\mathsf{in}}^\perp|} \sum_{\Delta \in V_{\mathsf{in}}^\perp} \#\{x \in \mathbb{F}_2^\ell \mid \mathsf{Enc}(x) \oplus \mathsf{Enc}(x \oplus \Delta) \in V_{\mathsf{out}}^\perp\}.$$

Differential-Linear Cryptanalysis. Differential and linear attacks were used together for the first time by Langford and Hellman [13]. This was *differential-linear cryptanalysis*. The basic idea is to split the cipher under consideration into a composition of two parts. The split should be such that, for the first part of the cipher there should exist a strong truncated differential with input difference Δ and for the second part there should exist a strongly biased linear approximation with output mask β. In [13], the particular case where the differential over the first part holds with probability one has been introduced. Later on, Biham et al. [3] generalized this attack using a probabilistic truncated differential on the first rounds of the distinguisher. In [11], Blondeau et al. presented a general model for this attack.

$$p_{\mathsf{Enc}}^{\mathsf{DL}}(\Delta, \beta) = 2^{-\ell} \# \left\{ x \mid \beta \cdot (\mathsf{Enc}(x) \oplus \mathsf{Enc}(x \oplus \Delta)) = 0 \right\}.$$

Boomerang Attack. In the boomerang attack, introduced in 1999 by Wagner [22], the advantage is taken from both the encryption and decryption. Given a difference Δ between two plaintexts x and x', the attacker is taking advantage of the probability

$$p_{\mathsf{Enc}}^{\mathsf{Boo}}(\Delta, \nabla) = 2^{-\ell} \# \left\{ x \mid \mathsf{Enc}^{-1}\left(\mathsf{Enc}(x) \oplus \nabla\right) \oplus \mathsf{Enc}^{-1}\left(\mathsf{Enc}(x \oplus \Delta) \oplus \nabla\right) = \Delta \right\},$$

where ∇ is a ciphertext difference.

2.2   The Decorrelation Theory

We consider a permutation Enc over $\{0,1\}^\ell$. Sometimes, Enc will be a random permutation with uniform distribution and will be denoted by C^*. Sometimes, it will be a permutation defined by a random key K and will be denoted by C_K.

Decorrelation was first presented in [18]. The non-adaptive (resp. adaptive) decorrelation of C_K of order d is denoted by $\|[C_K]^d - [C^*]^d\|_\infty$ (resp. $\|[C_K]^d - [C^*]^d\|_a$). It is the $\|\cdot\|_\infty$- (resp. $\|\cdot\|_a$-) distance between the matrices $[C_K]^d$ and $[C^*]^d$. Given a random Enc, we define $[\mathsf{Enc}]^d$, the d-wise distribution matrix by

$$[\mathsf{Enc}]^d_{(x_1,\ldots,x_d),(y_1,\ldots,y_d)} = \Pr[y_1 = \mathsf{Enc}(x_1),\ldots,y_d = \mathsf{Enc}(x_d)].$$

The $\| \cdot \|_\infty$-norm is defined by

$$\|M\|_\infty = \max_{x_1,\ldots,x_d} \sum_{y_1,\ldots,y_d} |M_{(x_1,\ldots,x_d),(y_1,\ldots,y_d)}|.$$

A random variable can be considered as a random function from a set of cardinality 1, so its d-wise distribution matrix is a row vector and the $\| \cdot \|_\infty$ matrix-norm corresponds to the $\| \cdot \|_1$ vector-norm. For distributions, the $\| \cdot \|_1$-distance is also called the *statistical distance*. The $\| \cdot \|_a$-norm was defined in [20] by

$$\|M\|_a = \max_{x_1} \sum_{y_1} \cdots \max_{x_d} \sum_{y_d} |M_{(x_1,\ldots,x_d),(y_1,\ldots,y_d)}|.$$

Here is the fundamental link between the best advantage of a distinguisher and decorrelation.

Theorem 2 (Best advantage and decorrelation, Theorem 10–11 of [21]). *The $\| \cdot \|_\infty$-decorrelation of order d of C_K, $\|[C_K]^d - [C^*]^d\|_\infty$, is twice the best advantage of a non-adaptive unbounded distinguisher between C_K and C^* which is allowed to make d encryption queries.*

The $\| \cdot \|_a$-decorrelation of order d of C_K, $\|[C_K]^d - [C^*]^d\|_a$, is twice the best advantage of an adaptive unbounded distinguisher between C_K and C^* which is allowed to make d encryption queries.

We say C_K is *decorrelated* if its decorrelation is small. We have *perfect decorrelation* when the decorrelation is 0. I.e., $[C_K]^d = [C^*]^d$, meaning

$$\Pr[y_1 = C_K(x_1),\ldots,y_d = C_K(x_d)] = \Pr[y_1 = C^*(x_1),\ldots,y_d = C^*(x_d)]$$

for all $x_1,\ldots,x_d,y_1,\ldots,y_d$.

For instance, decorrelation of order $d = 2$ corresponds to that $\Pr[y_1 = C_K(x_1), y_2 = C_K(x_2)]$ is always close to $\frac{1}{2^\ell(2^\ell-1)}$ for $x_1 \neq x_2$ and $y_1 \neq y_2$. This is the notion of *pairwise independence* by Wegman and Carter [23].

Given a permutation Enc over $\{0,1\}^\ell$, we define Q_{Enc}, a function from $\{0,1\} \times \{0,1\}^\ell$ to $\{0,1\}^\ell$ by

$$Q_{\mathsf{Enc}}(0,x) = \mathsf{Enc}(x) \quad \text{and} \quad Q_{\mathsf{Enc}}(1,y) = \mathsf{Enc}^{-1}(y).$$

To study distinguishers which can make encryption and decryption queries, we just consider the decorrelation of Q_{Enc} instead of the decorrelation of Enc. For this, we study the distance between $[Q_{C_K}]^d$ and $[Q_{C^*}]^d$.

We review some general security results below.

Non-adaptive iterated distinguisher of order d. Given an encryption function Enc, a *non-adaptive iterated distinguisher of order d* (Distinguisher Iter) is characterized by a distribution D and two Boolean functions T and f. With n iterations, it works as follows:

Distinguisher Iter:
1: **for** $i = 1$ to n **do**
2:     pick $(x_1, \ldots, x_d) \in (\{0,1\}^\ell)^d$ following distribution D
3:     set $y_j = \mathsf{Enc}(x_j)$ for $j = 1, \ldots, d$
4:     set $b_i = T(x_1, \ldots, x_d, y_1, \ldots, y_d)$
5: **end for**
6: output $f(b_1, \ldots, b_n)$

For such distinguisher, the following results have been derived in [19].

Theorem 3 (Advantage of Iter bounded by decorrelation [19], Theorem 18 of [21]). *For the Boolean function T, we have*

$$E(p_{C_K}^{\mathsf{Iter}}) - E(p_{C^*}^{\mathsf{Iter}}) \leq 5\sqrt[3]{n^2\left(2\delta + \frac{5d^2}{2 \times 2^\ell} + \frac{3}{2}\|[C_K]^{2d} - [C^*]^{2d}\|_\infty\right)} + n\|[C_K]^{2d} - [C^*]^{2d}\|_\infty$$

where δ is an upper bound on the probability that the distinguisher picks a plaintext in common between any two iterations. I.e., $\delta = \Pr[\exists i, j \quad x_i = x'_j : (x_1, \ldots, x_d) \leftarrow D, (x'_1, \ldots, x'_d) \leftarrow D]$.

Note that it was proven in [6,7] that we cannot have a general security result when δ is high or when we only have a decorrelation of order $2d - 1$.

Theorem 3 was generalized in [19] to the case where the range of T has s elements instead of 2:

Theorem 4 (Advantage of Iter bounded by decorrelation, Theorem 7 of [19]). *If T maps onto a set of s elements, we have*

$$E(p_{C_K}^{\mathsf{Iter}}) - E(p_{C^*}^{\mathsf{Iter}}) \leq 3s\sqrt[3]{n^2\left(2\delta + \frac{2d^2}{2^\ell} + \frac{d^3}{2^\ell(2^\ell - d)} + \frac{3}{2}\|[C_K]^{2d} - [C^*]^{2d}\|_\infty\right)} + \frac{ns}{2}\|[C_K]^{2d} - [C^*]^{2d}\|_\infty$$

where δ is an upper bound on the probability that the distinguisher picks a plaintext in common between any two iterations. I.e., $\delta = \Pr[\exists i, j \quad x_i = x'_j : (x_1, \ldots, x_d) \leftarrow D, (x'_1, \ldots, x'_d) \leftarrow D]$.

Adaptive iterated distinguisher of order d. Theorem 3 was generalized in [5,7] to adaptive plaintext-ciphertext iterated distinguishers (i.e., distinguishers which make in each iteration some adaptive queries and can also make chosen ciphertext queries): Given an encryption function Enc, an *adaptive plaintext-ciphertext iterated distinguisher of order d* (Distinguisher AIter) is characterized by $d - 1$ functions $q_1, \ldots, q_{d-1}$, and two Boolean functions T and f. With n iterations, it works as follows:

Distinguisher AIter:
1: **for** $i = 1$ to n **do**
2:    pick a uniformly distributed sequence ρ of random coins
3:    **for** $j = 1$ to d **do**
4:       set $z_j = q_j(Q_{\mathsf{Enc}}(z_1), \ldots, Q_{\mathsf{Enc}}(z_{j-1}); \rho)$
5:    **end for**
6:    set $b_i = T(Q_{\mathsf{Enc}}(z_1), \ldots, Q_{\mathsf{Enc}}(z_d); \rho)$
7: **end for**
8: output $f(b_1, \ldots, b_n)$

Theorem 5 (Advantage of AIter bounded by decorrelation [5], Theorem 5 of [7]). *We have*

$$E(p_{C_K}^{\mathsf{Alter}}) - E(p_{C^*}^{\mathsf{Alter}}) \leq 5\sqrt[3]{n^2 \left(2\delta + e^{8d^2 2^{-\ell}} + \frac{2d^2}{2^\ell} + \frac{3}{2}\|[Q_{C_K}]^{2d} - [Q_{C^*}]^{2d}\|_\infty\right)}$$
$$+ n\|[Q_{C_K}]^{2d} - [Q_{C^*}]^{2d}\|_\infty$$

where δ is an upper bound on the probability that the distinguisher picks a query in common between any two iterations.

In what follows we give tighter results for specific classes of iterated attacks for which we can get rid of δ and sometimes rely on a lower decorrelation order.

2.3   Previous Results in the Context of Decorrelation Theory

To obtain the decorrelation order as well as the order of the different statistical attacks we have to describe the distinguishers we are working with. In this section, we describe the differential, linear, differential-linear and boomerang attacks, and recall the different results obtained for these distinguishers. A comparison with the results obtained for the multidimensional linear and truncated differential attacks will be presented later in this paper.

Differential Cryptanalysis. Given an encryption function Enc, a *differential distinguisher* (Distinguisher DC) is characterized by two differences Δ and Γ and a Boolean function f. With n iterations, it works as follows:

Distinguisher DC:
1: **for** $i = 1$ to n **do**
2:    pick $x \in \{0,1\}^\ell$ uniformly
3:    set $x' = x \oplus \Delta$
4:    set $y = \mathsf{Enc}(x)$ and $y' = \mathsf{Enc}(x')$
5:    set $b_i = 1_{y \oplus y' = \Gamma}$
6: **end for**
7: output $f(b_1, \ldots, b_n)$

This is a non-adaptive iterated attack of order 2.

Theorem 6 (Advantage of DC bounded by decorrelation, Theorem 13 of [21]). *For the function* $f(b_1, \ldots, b_n) = \max_i b_i$, *we have*

$$E(p_{C_K}^{DC}) - E(p_{C^*}^{DC}) \leq \frac{n}{2^\ell - 1} + \frac{n}{2}\|[C_K]^2 - [C^*]^2\|_\infty.$$

Linear Cryptanalysis. Given an encryption function Enc, a *linear distinguisher* (Distinguisher LC) is characterized by two masks α and β, and a Boolean function f. With n iterations, it works as follows:

Distinguisher LC:
1: **for** $i = 1$ to n **do**
2:    pick $x \in \{0,1\}^\ell$ uniformly
3:    set $y = \text{Enc}(x)$
4:    set $b_i = \alpha \cdot x \oplus \beta \cdot y$
5: **end for**
6: output $f(b_1, \ldots, b_n)$

This is a non-adaptive iterated attack of order 1.

Theorem 7 (Advantage of LC bounded by decorrelation, Theorem 17 of [21]). *We have*

$$E(p_{C_K}^{LC}) - E(p_{C^*}^{LC}) \leq 3\sqrt[3]{n\|[C_K]^2 - [C^*]^2\|_\infty + \frac{n}{2^\ell - 1}} + 3\sqrt[3]{\frac{n}{2^\ell - 1}}.$$

Differential-Linear Cryptanalysis. Given a function Enc, a *differential-linear distinguisher* is characterized by a difference Δ, a mask β, and a Boolean function f. With n iterations, it works as follows:

Distinguisher DL:
1: **for** $i = 1$ to n **do**
2:    pick $x_1 \in \{0,1\}^\ell$ uniformly
3:    set $x_2 = x_1 \oplus \Delta$
4:    set $y_1 = \text{Enc}(x_1)$ and $y_2 = \text{Enc}(x_2)$
5:    set $b_i = \beta \cdot (y_1 \oplus y_2)$
6: **end for**
7: output $f(b_1, \ldots, b_n)$

This is a non-adaptive iterated attack of order 2.

Theorem 8 (Advantage of DL bounded by decorrelation, Theorem 7 of [7]). *We have*

$$E(p_{C_K}^{DL}) - E(p_{C^*}^{DL}) \leq 3\sqrt[3]{n\|[C_K]^4 - [C^*]^4\|_\infty + n\frac{2 \times 2^\ell - 5}{(2^\ell - 1)(2^\ell - 3)}} +$$

$$3\sqrt[3]{n\frac{2 \times 2^\ell - 5}{(2^\ell - 1)(2^\ell - 3)}}.$$

This results say that if a cipher is decorrelation to the order 4, it is protected against differential- linear cryptanalysis. It was further proven in [1, pp. 77–78] that some ciphers decorrelated to the order 3 can have a high advantage with DL. Which means that the decorrelation of order 4 is really what is needed.

Remark 9. The result from [7] was stated for a function f based on a counter $b_1 + \cdots + b_n$ but it is easy to see that the proof holds for a more general f as it is very similar to that of Theorem 7.

Boomerang Cryptanalysis. Given an encryption function Enc, a *boomerang distinguisher* is characterized by two differences Δ and ∇ and a Boolean function f. With n iterations, it works as follows:

Distinguisher Boo:
1: **for** $i = 1$ to n **do**
2:   pick $x_1 \in \{0,1\}^\ell$ uniformly
3:   set $x_2 = x_1 \oplus \Delta$
4:   set $y_1 = \mathsf{Enc}(x_1)$ and $y_2 = \mathsf{Enc}(x_2)$
5:   set $y_3 = y_1 \oplus \nabla$ and $y_4 = y_2 \oplus \nabla$
6:   set $x_3 = \mathsf{Enc}^{-1}(y_3)$ and $x_4 = \mathsf{Enc}^{-1}(y_4)$
7:   set $b_i = 1_{x_3 \oplus x_4 = \Delta}$
8: **end for**
9: output $f(b_1, \ldots, b_n)$

This is an *adaptive plaintext-ciphertext* iterated attack of order 4.

Theorem 10 (Advantage of Boo bounded by decorrelation, Theorem 8 of [7]). *For the function* $f(b_1, \ldots, b_n) = \max_i b_i$, *we have*

$$E(p_{C_K}^{\mathsf{Boo}}) - E(p_{C^*}^{\mathsf{Boo}}) \leq n \frac{2 \times 2^\ell - 5}{(2^\ell - 1)(2^\ell - 3)} + \frac{n}{2} \|[C_K]^4 - [C^*]^4\|_a.$$

It was further proven in [1, pp. 79–80] that some ciphers decorrelated to the order 3 can have a high advantage with Boo. We deduce that decorrelation of order 4 is really what is needed.

A summary of the results presented in this section (and new ones) is given in Table 1.

3   Multidimensional Linear Cryptanalysis

In this section we study the multidimensional linear (ML) attack. To do so we consider the following multidimensional linear distinguisher (Distinguisher ML):

Distinguisher ML:
1: **for** $i = 1$ to n **do**
2:     pick a random $x \in \{0,1\}^{\ell}$
3:     set $y = \mathsf{Enc}(x)$
4:     **for** $j = 1$ to k **do**
5:         set $b_{i,j} = (\alpha_j \cdot x) \oplus (\beta_j \cdot y)$
6:     **end for**
7:     set $b_i = (b_{i,1}, \dots, b_{i,k})$
8: **end for**
9: output $f(b_1, \dots, b_n)$

I.e., we look at the observed distribution of the bits $(b_{1,1}, \dots, b_{n,k})$ and we take a decision by following a function f. According to this algorithm, this attack looks like a non-adaptive iterated attack of order 1, except that a vector b_i is kept instead of a bit at each iteration. We want to bound the advantage of this distinguisher for any function f. We let $p_{\mathsf{Enc}}^{\mathsf{ML}}$ be the probability (over the selection of the random x's) to output 1 by using the fixed function Enc. We want to bound

$$E(p_{C_K}^{\mathsf{ML}}) - E(p_{C^*}^{\mathsf{ML}})$$

where K is a random key, C_K is the encryption under the key K, and $E(p_{C_K}^{\mathsf{ML}})$ is the expected value over the distribution of K, and where C^* is a uniformly distributed random permutation and $E(p_{C^*}^{\mathsf{ML}})$ is the expected value over the distribution of C^*.

For Enc fixed, all vectors b_i are independent and identically distributed. We let D_{Enc} be the distribution of the vector b_i.

We let V be the vector space spanned by the (α_j, β_j) masks. We recall that k denotes the dimension of V.

We could apply Theorem 4 with $d = 1$, $s = 2^k$, $\delta = 2^{-\ell}$, and obtain

$$E(p_{C_K}^{\mathsf{ML}}) - E(p_{C^*}^{\mathsf{ML}}) \leq 3 \times 2^k \sqrt[3]{n^2 \left(\frac{4}{2^{\ell}} + \frac{1}{2^{\ell}(2^{\ell} - 1)} + \frac{3}{2} \| [C_K]^2 - [C^*]^2 \|_{\infty} \right)}$$
$$+ \frac{n 2^k}{2} \| [C_K]^2 - [C^*]^2 \|_{\infty}.$$

With a negligible decorrelation, we would obtain a security for a data complexity n up to approximately $2^{\frac{\ell}{2} - 3k}$. Nevertheless, this is meaningless when the dimension k of V is such that $k > \frac{\ell}{6}$. With the technique to develop in this section, we aim at $n \approx 2^{\frac{\ell - k}{2}}$. This makes sense until k is close to ℓ.

We note that if $k > \ell$, there exists a Boolean function $\mathsf{bit}(y)$ on the ciphertext and a mapping from $b_i = (b_{i,1}, \dots, b_{i,k})$ to $(x, \mathsf{bit}(y))$. For n relatively small, the vectors $(b_1, \dots, b_n)$ uniquely identify the key K. So, there exists a function f (maybe with high complexity) leading to a very high advantage. Hence, we cannot prove any security without assuming any complexity on f.

For $k = \ell - \mathsf{cste}$, we could have cases in which there is a mapping from b_i to $(x_1, \dots, x_{k-1}, \mathsf{bit}(y))$ so $2^{\mathsf{cste}+1}$ possible values for x. We can eliminate keys for which none of these x lead to bit(y). This eliminates a fraction $2^{-2^{\text{cste}+1}}$ of the keys. So, for n within the order of magnitude of $2^{2^{\text{cste}+1}}$, we uniquely determine the key. So, no information-theoretic security is feasible for these values of n.

Remark 11 (Relation with [14] and [10,11]). In [14], the function f used to evaluate the multidimensional linear approximation is based on LLR or χ^2 statistical test. In [10,11], where the relation between the truncated differential and multidimensional linear key-recovery attacks is derived, the function f is based on the χ^2 test.

To provide a bound on $p_{\text{Enc}}^{\text{ML}} - p_{\text{Enc}^*}^{\text{ML}}$, we consider the following distinguisher, which is a special truncated differential (STD) distinguisher:

Distinguisher STD:
1: pick two plaintexts x and x' at random
2: set $y = \mathsf{Enc}(x)$ and $y' = \mathsf{Enc}(x')$
3: output $1_{(x'-x,\mathsf{Enc}(x')-\mathsf{Enc}(x))\in V^\perp}$

This distinguisher is a known plaintext truncated differential distinguisher using only one pair of samples. It corresponds to a non-adaptive attack using two queries.

Let $p_{\text{Enc}}^{\text{STD}}$ be the probability that the output is 1 with Enc fixed. Clearly, as given in Sect. 2.1, we have

$$p_{\text{Enc}}^{\text{STD}} = \sum_{(\Delta,\Gamma)\in V^\perp} 2^{-\ell}\mathsf{DP}^{\mathsf{Enc}}(\Delta,\Gamma).$$

Lemma 12 (Euclidean distance vs. capacity). *We let U be the uniform distribution. We have*

$$\|D_{\mathsf{Enc}} - U\|_2^2 = 2^{-k}\mathsf{cap}_{\mathsf{Enc}}(V).$$

Proof If $v \in V$, we can write $v = \sum_j \lambda_j(\alpha_j, \beta_j)$. Then,

$$\mathsf{LP}^{\mathsf{Enc}}(v) = \left(E\left((-1)^{v\cdot(x,\mathsf{Enc}(x))}\right)\right)^2$$
$$= \left(E\left((-1)^{\sum_j \lambda_j(\alpha_j,\beta_j)\cdot(x,\mathsf{Enc}(x))}\right)\right)^2$$
$$= \left(E\left((-1)^{\sum_j \lambda_j b_j}\right)\right)^2$$
$$= E\left((-1)^{\sum_j \lambda_j(b_j+b'_j)}\right)$$

so,

$$\sum_{v\in V} \mathsf{LP}^{\mathsf{Enc}}(v) = 2^k \Pr[b_1 = b'_1, \ldots, b_k = b'_k] = 2^k \sum_{b_1,\ldots,b_k} \Pr[b_1,\ldots,b_k]^2$$

from which we deduce

$$\sum_{v \in V, v \neq 0} \mathsf{LP}^{\mathsf{Enc}}(v) = 2^k \|D_{\mathsf{Enc}} - U\|_2^2.$$

$\square$

Lemma 13 (Statistical distance of iterated distribution). *Let n be an integer and D_β be a probability distribution for $\beta \in \{0,1\}$. Let $D_\beta^{\otimes n}$ be the distributions of vectors of n independent samples following D_β. We have*

$$\|D_0^{\otimes n} - D_1^{\otimes n}\|_1 \leq n\|D_0 - D_1\|_1.$$

Proof. We use

$$aa' - bb' = (a - b)\frac{a' + b'}{2} + (a' - b')\frac{a + b}{2}.$$

We have

$$\|D_0^{\otimes n} - D_1^{\otimes n}\|_1 = \frac{1}{2}\sum_{u,v}|D_0(u)D_0^{\otimes(n-1)}(v) - D_1(u)D_1^{\otimes(n-1)}(v)|$$

$$\leq \frac{1}{2}\sum_u |D_0(u) - D_1(u)|\sum_v \frac{D_0^{\otimes(n-1)}(v) + D_1^{\otimes(n-1)}(v)}{2} +$$

$$\frac{1}{2}\sum_v |D_0^{\otimes(n-1)}(v) - D_1^{\otimes(n-1)}(v)|\sum_u \frac{D_0(u) + D_1(u)}{2}$$

$$= \|D_0 - D_1\|_1 + \|D_0^{\otimes(n-1)} - D_1^{\otimes(n-1)}\|_1.$$

We conclude by proving the result by induction. $\square$

Lemma 14 (Advantage of ML vs. Euclidean distance). *For any fixed* Enc *and* Enc*, *we have*

$$p_{\mathsf{Enc}}^{\mathsf{ML}} - p_{\mathsf{Enc}^*}^{\mathsf{ML}} \leq \frac{n2^{\frac{k}{2}}}{2}\|D_{\mathsf{Enc}} - D_{\mathsf{Enc}^*}\|_2.$$

Proof. Thanks to Theorem 2, we have $p_{\mathsf{Enc}}^{\mathsf{ML}} - p_{\mathsf{Enc}^*}^{\mathsf{ML}} \leq \frac{1}{2}\|D_{\mathsf{Enc}}^{\otimes n} - D_{\mathsf{Enc}^*}^{\otimes n}\|_1$. Then, we have $\|D_{\mathsf{Enc}}^{\otimes n} - D_{\mathsf{Enc}^*}^{\otimes n}\|_1 \leq n\|D_{\mathsf{Enc}} - D_{\mathsf{Enc}^*}\|_1$ due to Lemma 13. Next, we use $\|D_{\mathsf{Enc}} - D_{\mathsf{Enc}^*}\|_1 \leq 2^{\frac{k}{2}}\|D_{\mathsf{Enc}} - D_{\mathsf{Enc}^*}\|_2$ due to the Cauchy-Schwarz Inequality. $\square$

Remark 15. For $k = 1$ (linear cryptanalysis), we have $\mathsf{cap}_{\mathsf{Enc}}(V) = \mathsf{LP}^{\mathsf{Enc}}(\alpha_1, \beta_1)$. From Lemma 12 and Lemma 14, we obtain

$$|p_{\mathsf{Enc}}^{\mathsf{ML}} - p_{\mathsf{Enc}^*}^{\mathsf{ML}}| \leq \frac{n}{2}\sqrt{\mathsf{LP}^{\mathsf{Enc}}(\alpha_1, \beta_1)} + \frac{n}{2}\sqrt{\mathsf{LP}^{\mathsf{Enc}^*}(\alpha_1, \beta_1)}$$

for any fixed Enc and Enc*. From [21, Lemma 15], we know that there is a constant p_0 such that for any fixed Enc, we have $|p_{\mathsf{Enc}}^{\mathsf{ML}} - p_0| \leq 2\sqrt{n\mathsf{LP}^{\mathsf{Enc}}(\alpha_1, \beta_1)}$. So,

$$|p_{\mathsf{Enc}}^{\mathsf{ML}} - p_{\mathsf{Enc}^*}^{\mathsf{ML}}| \leq 2\sqrt{n\mathsf{LP}^{\mathsf{Enc}}(\alpha_1, \beta_1)} + 2\sqrt{n\mathsf{LP}^{\mathsf{Enc}^*}(\alpha_1, \beta_1)}.$$

As we can see, the bound obtained from Lemma 14 is not tight in the case where $k = 1$. We are loosing a factor $\sqrt{n}$. The loss comes from Lemma 13 which is far from being tight.

Lemma 16 (Link between ML and STD). *For any fixed* Enc *and* Enc*, *we have*

$$p_{\mathsf{Enc}}^{\mathsf{ML}} - p_{\mathsf{Enc}^*}^{\mathsf{ML}} \leq \frac{n2^{\frac{k}{2}}}{2}\sqrt{p_{\mathsf{Enc}}^{\mathsf{STD}} - 2^{-k}} + \frac{n2^{\frac{k}{2}}}{2}\sqrt{p_{\mathsf{Enc}^*}^{\mathsf{STD}} - 2^{-k}}.$$

Proof. We apply Theorem 1, Lemma 12, Lemma 14, and the triangular inequality $\|D_{\mathsf{Enc}} - D_{\mathsf{Enc}^*}\|_2 \leq \|D_{\mathsf{Enc}} - U\|_2 + \|D_{\mathsf{Enc}^*} - U\|_2$. □

Lemma 17. (Using decorrelation in STD). *We have*

$$E(p_{C_K}^{\mathsf{STD}}) \leq E(p_{C^*}^{\mathsf{STD}}) + \frac{1}{2}\|[C_K]^2 - [C^*]^2\|_\infty.$$

Proof. $E(p_{C_K}^{\mathsf{STD}}) - E(p_{C^*}^{\mathsf{STD}})$ expresses as the advantage of STD, a non-adaptive distinguisher limited to two queries. We conclude by using Theorem 2. □

Lemma 18 (The ideal case in STD). *We have*

$$E(p_{C^*}^{\mathsf{STD}} - 2^{-k}) \leq 2^{-\ell}\frac{1 - 2^{-k}}{1 - 2^{-\ell}}.$$

Assuming that all α_j are linearly independent and that all β_j are linearly independent, we further have

$$E(p_{C^*}^{\mathsf{STD}} - 2^{-k}) = 2^{-\ell}\frac{1 - 2^{-k}}{1 - 2^{-\ell}}.$$

Proof. From Theorem 1, we have

$$p_{\mathsf{Enc}}^{\mathsf{STD}} = 2^{-k} + 2^{-k}\sum_{v \in V, v \neq 0}\mathsf{LP}^{\mathsf{Enc}}(v).$$

There are exactly $2^k - 1$ vectors v which are non-zero. When all α_j resp. all β_j are linearly independent, neither the left half nor the right half of v is zero. Based on [21, Lemma 14], we deduce $E(\mathsf{LP}^{C^*}(v)) = \frac{1}{2^\ell - 1}$ and obtain

$$E(p_{C^*}^{\mathsf{STD}}) = 2^{-k} + 2^{-k}\frac{2^k - 1}{2^\ell - 1}.$$

Without the assumption of independence, there are some of the vectors $v \neq 0$ such that either the left half or the right half is zero but not both. Therefore, we have $\mathsf{LP}^{C^*}(v) = 0$. Since this satisfies $E(\mathsf{LP}^{C^*}(v)) \leq \frac{1}{2^\ell - 1}$, we still have

$$E(p_{C^*}^{\mathsf{STD}}) \leq 2^{-k} + 2^{-k}\frac{2^k - 1}{2^\ell - 1}.$$

□

Theorem 19 (Advantage of ML bounded by decorrelation). *We have*

$$E(p_{C_K}^{\mathsf{ML}}) - E(p_{C^*}^{\mathsf{ML}}) \leq n\sqrt{2^{k-\ell} + 2^{k-1}\|[C_K]^2 - [C^*]^2\|_\infty}.$$

Proof. We first apply Lemma 16. Then, since $\sqrt{\cdot}$ is concave, the Jensen inequality says that

$$E\left(\sqrt{p_{\mathsf{Enc}}^{\mathsf{STD}} - 2^{-k}}\right) \leq \sqrt{E(p_{\mathsf{Enc}}^{\mathsf{STD}} - 2^{-k})}.$$

By using Lemma 17 and Lemma 18, we obtain

$$E(p_{C_K}^{\mathsf{ML}}) - E(p_{C^*}^{\mathsf{ML}}) \leq n\sqrt{2^{k-\ell}\frac{1 - 2^{-k}}{1 - 2^{-\ell}} + 2^{k-1}\|[C_K]^2 - [C^*]^2\|_\infty}.$$

The bound in Theorem 19 is trivial for $k > \ell$. For $k \leq \ell$, we bound $\frac{1-2^{-k}}{1-2^{-\ell}} \leq 1$ and conclude. □

4   Truncated Differential Attack

As in [10,11], we restrict to V of form $V_{\mathsf{in}} \times V_{\mathsf{out}}$ with V_{in} and V_{out} subspaces of $\{0,1\}^\ell$ of dimension s and q, respectively. We have $V^\perp = V_{\mathsf{in}}^\perp \times V_{\mathsf{out}}^\perp$. The dimension of $V^\perp$ is $2\ell - k = \ell - s + \ell - q$. We consider the following distinguisher:

Distinguisher TD:
  1: **for** $i = 1$ to n **do**
  2:    pick $(x, x') \in (\{0,1\}^\ell)^2$ uniformly such that $x \oplus x' \in V_{\mathsf{in}}^\perp$
  3:    set $y = \mathsf{Enc}(x)$ and $y' = \mathsf{Enc}(x')$
  4:    set $b_i = 1_{((x,y)\oplus(x',y'))\in V^\perp}$
  5: **end for**
  6: output $f(b_1, \ldots, b_n)$

The function f which computes the output depending on the vector b is left arbitrary. For instance, with $f(b_1, \ldots, b_n) = b_1 \cdots b_n$, this captures *impossible differentials* [2]. This is a non-adaptive iterated attack of order 2.

Lemma 20 (Link between TD and STD). *For any fixed* Enc *and* Enc^*, *we have*

$$|p_{\mathsf{Enc}}^{\mathsf{TD}} - p_{\mathsf{Enc}^*}^{\mathsf{TD}}| \leq n2^s|p_{\mathsf{Enc}}^{\mathsf{STD}} - p_{\mathsf{Enc}^*}^{\mathsf{STD}}|.$$

Proof. We let p^1 denote the best distinguisher with same D and $n = 1$. We apply Lemma 13 and we obtain

$$|p_{\mathsf{Enc}}^{\mathsf{TD}} - p_{\mathsf{Enc}^*}^{\mathsf{TD}}| \leq n|p_{\mathsf{Enc}}^1 - p_{\mathsf{Enc}^*}^1|.$$

Clearly, depending on the sign of $p_{\mathsf{Enc}}^1 - p_{\mathsf{Enc}^*}^1$, either p^1 is the probability that a differential is found, or it is the probability that it is not found. In any case, we have $2^{-s}|p_{\mathsf{Enc}}^1 - p_{\mathsf{Enc}^*}^1| = |p_{\mathsf{Enc}}^{\mathsf{STD}} - p_{\mathsf{Enc}^*}^{\mathsf{STD}}|$, and we obtain the result. □

Theorem 21 (Advantage of TD bounded by decorrelation). *For the TD differential distinguisher described in this section, we have*

$$E(p_{C_K}^{\mathsf{TD}}) - E(p_{C^*}^{\mathsf{TD}}) \leq n2^{1+s-\ell}\frac{1-2^{-k}}{1-2^{-\ell}} + n2^{s-1}\|[C_K]^2 - [C^*]^2\|_\infty.$$

Proof. Due to Lemma 20, we have

$$p_{\mathsf{Enc}}^{\mathsf{TD}} - p_{\mathsf{Enc}^*}^{\mathsf{TD}} \leq n2^s|p_{\mathsf{Enc}}^{\mathsf{STD}} - 2^{-k}| + n2^s|p_{\mathsf{Enc}^*}^{\mathsf{STD}} - 2^{-k}|$$
$$= n2^s\left(p_{\mathsf{Enc}}^{\mathsf{STD}} - 2^{-k}\right) + n2^s\left(p_{\mathsf{Enc}^*}^{\mathsf{STD}} - 2^{-k}\right)$$

since we know from Theorem 1 that $p_{\mathsf{Enc}}^{\mathsf{STD}} - 2^{-k}$ is positive. Based on Lemma 17, we have, $E(p_{C_K}^{\mathsf{STD}}) - E(p_{C^*}^{\mathsf{STD}}) \leq \frac{1}{2}\|[C_K]^2 - [C^*]^2\|_\infty$. So,

$$E(p_{C_K}^{\mathsf{TD}}) - E(p_{C^*}^{\mathsf{TD}}) \leq 2n2^s\left(E(p_{C^*}^{\mathsf{STD}}) - 2^{-k}\right) + n2^{s-1}\|[C_K]^2 - [C^*]^2\|_\infty.$$

Due to Lemma 18, we obtain the result.   □

Remark 22. The critical term for ML in Theorem 19 is $n^2 2^{k-1}\|[C_K]^2 - [C^*]^2\|_\infty$. The one for TD in Theorem 21 is $n2^{s-1}\|[C_K]^2 - [C^*]^2\|_\infty$. Presumably, we have lost a factor n in Theorem 19 and the difference between ML and TD should only be k vs. s, the dimension of V vs. the one of V_{in}.

Remark 23. For $s = \ell - 1$ and $q = 1$, $V_{\mathsf{in}}^\perp$ has a single non-zero vector (which can be seen as a difference vector Δ) and V_{out} has a single non-zero vector (which can be seen as a mask Γ). However, our bound is useless in that case since $2^{1+s-\ell} = 1$. Here, we used again the loose bound of Lemma 13, but changing n into $\sqrt{n}$ would not change this fact. Actually, TD becomes equivalent to DL in this case, and it is known that 4-decorrelation is needed to protect against DL [1]. Since our TD-security results uses 2-decorrelation, improving this bound to get a more useful one in the case of DL would require to use 4-decorrelation. Except for the equivalence to DL, these observations extend to all values of q.

5   Improvement of Previous Results

5.1   Improvement in the Linear and Differential-Linear Contexts

If $\|[C_K]^2 - [C^*]^2\|_\infty \approx 2^{-\ell}$, the bound derived in Theorem 7, for linear attacks, is approximately equal to $3(1 + \sqrt[3]{2})\sqrt[3]{n2^{-\ell}}$ and is useful only if the attacker can take advantage of up to $2^\ell/311$ plaintext-ciphertext pairs. For a 64-bit cipher, it would corresponds to attacks with data complexity less than $2^{55.71}$. In this section we provide a new bound, for linear attacks, useful for n up to $2^\ell/24$ which is $2^{59.42}$.

Theorem 7, which is given in Sect. 2.1, has been originally derived in 2003 [21]. The following result consists of an improvement of the upper bound of $E(p_{C_K}^{\mathsf{LC}}) - E(p_{C^*}^{\mathsf{LC}})$. This improvement is obtained thanks to the Jensen equality.

Theorem 24 (Advantage of LC bounded by decorrelation, improvement of Theorem 7). *For the linear distinguisher of Sect. 2.3, we have*

$$E(p_{C_K}^{\mathsf{LC}}) - E(p_{C^*}^{\mathsf{LC}}) \leq 2\sqrt{n\|[C_K]^2 - [C^*]^2\|_\infty} + \frac{n}{2^\ell - 1} + 2\sqrt{\frac{n}{2^\ell - 1}}.$$

Proof. Based on [21, Lemma 15], we know that there is some p_0 such that for every Enc, we have $|p^{\mathsf{Enc}} - p_0| \leq 2\sqrt{n\mathsf{LP}^{\mathsf{Enc}}(a,b)}$.

To prove Theorem 7, the method used in [21] consisted in getting for any A that[1] $E(p_{\mathsf{Enc}}^{\mathsf{LC}}) - p_0 \leq 2 \cdot A\sqrt{n} + \frac{1}{A^2}E(\mathsf{LP}^{\mathsf{Enc}}(\alpha,\beta))$ and then in minimizing the sum in terms of A. In [21], $A = n^{-\frac{1}{6}}\sqrt[3]{E(\mathsf{LP}^{\mathsf{Enc}}(\alpha,\beta))}$ was taken, to get $E(p_{\mathsf{Enc}}^{\mathsf{LC}}) - p_0 \leq 3\sqrt[3]{nE(\mathsf{LP}^{\mathsf{Enc}}(\alpha,\beta))}$.

To derive the improved bound, instead, we use the Jensen inequality to obtain $|E(p^{\mathsf{Enc}}) - p_0| \leq 2\sqrt{nE(\mathsf{LP}^{\mathsf{Enc}}(\alpha,\beta))}$.

We consider the elementary non-adaptive distinguisher picking x and x' and checking if $\alpha \cdot (x \oplus x') = \beta \cdot (\mathsf{Enc}(x) \oplus \mathsf{Enc}(x'))$. The probability of the equality is $p^2 + (1-p)^2 = \frac{1}{2}(2p-1)^2 + \frac{1}{2}$ where $p = \Pr[\alpha \cdot x = \beta \cdot \mathsf{Enc}(x)]$. Therefore, it is $\frac{1}{2}\mathsf{LP}^{\mathsf{Enc}}(\alpha,\beta) + \frac{1}{2}$ and $\mathsf{LP}^{\mathsf{Enc}}(\alpha,\beta)$ expresses the advantage of a non-adaptive distinguisher using two queries. From Theorem 2, we have $E(\mathsf{LP}^{C_K}(\alpha,\beta)) \leq E(\mathsf{LP}^{C^*}(\alpha,\beta)) + \|[C_K]^2 - [C^*]^2\|_\infty$. From [21, Lemma 14] we obtain that

$$E(\mathsf{LP}^{C^*}(\alpha,\beta)) = \frac{1}{2^\ell - 1}.$$

$\square$

In the same way the bound derived for the differential-linear attack, in Theorem 8 is approximately equal to $3(\sqrt[3]{3} + \sqrt[3]{2})\sqrt[3]{n2^{-\ell}}$ and is useful for an attacker which can take advantage to up to $2^\ell/532$ plaintext-ciphertext pairs. Using the same technique, meaning the Jensen inequality, we can improve Theorem 8 and derive a new bound in the differential-linear context which is valid for any attack using up to $2^\ell/39$ plaintext-ciphertext pairs.

Theorem 25 (Advantage of DL bounded by decorrelation, improvement of Theorem 8). *For the differential-linear distinguisher of Sect. 2.3, we have*

$$E(p_{C_K}^{\mathsf{DL}}) - E(p_{C^*}^{\mathsf{DL}}) \leq 2\sqrt{n\|[C_K]^4 - [C^*]^4\|_\infty + n\frac{2 \times 2^\ell - 5}{(2^\ell - 1)(2^\ell - 3)}} +$$

$$2\sqrt{n\frac{2 \times 2^\ell - 5}{(2^\ell - 1)(2^\ell - 3)}}.$$

---

[1] The last term bounds the probability that $\mathsf{LP}^{\mathsf{Enc}}(\alpha,\beta)$ exceeds A^2 and the first is a consequence of [21, Lemma 15].

5.2   In the Context of Differential and Boomerang Attacks, Extension of Theorems 6 and 10

Before providing, in this section, an extension of Theorem 6 and 10, we present an extension of [21, Lemma 15] for the following iterative distinguisher:

Distinguisher Dist:
1: **for** $i = 1$ to n **do**
2:     pick a bit b_i with expected value p_{Enc}
3: **end for**
4: output $f(b_1, \ldots, b_n)$

Lemma 26. *Let p_{Enc} be a probability depending on a cipher* Enc. *We have* $|E(p_{C_K}^{\mathsf{Dist}}) - E(p_{C^*}^{\mathsf{Dist}})| \leq n . \max(E(p_{C_K}), E(p_{C^*}))$.

Proof. If $f(0, \ldots, 0) = 0$, then $p_{\mathsf{Enc}}^{\mathsf{Dist}} \leq n p_{\mathsf{Enc}}$ and $E(p_{C_K}^{\mathsf{Dist}}) - E(p_{C^*}^{\mathsf{Dist}}) \leq E(p_{C_K}^{\mathsf{Dist}}) \leq nE(p_{C_K})$. Similarly, we have $E(p_{C^*}^{\mathsf{Dist}}) - E(p_{C_K}^{\mathsf{Dist}}) \leq E(p_{C^*}^{\mathsf{Dist}}) \leq nE(p_{C^*})$, and the result holds in this case.

If $f(0, \ldots, 0) = 1$, we change f to $1 - f$ without changing $|E(p_{C^*}^{\mathsf{Dist}}) - E(p_{C_K}^{\mathsf{Dist}})|$ and go back to the previous case.   □

Differential Distinguisher. In Sect. 2.1, the differential distinguisher is defined for a given Boolean function f corresponding to $f(b_1, \cdots b_n) = \max_i b_i$. In practice, for many differential attacks more than one valid pair is necessary to distinguish the cipher from a random permutation. In this section we generalize this distinguisher to any Boolean function f.

Theorem 27 (Advantage of DC bounded by decorrelation, improved Theorem 6). *For the distinguisher DC, we have*

$$E(p_{C_K}^{\mathsf{DC}}) - E(p_{C^*}^{\mathsf{DC}}) \leq \frac{n}{2^\ell - 1} + \frac{n}{2} \| [C_K]^2 - [C^*]^2 \|_\infty.$$

Proof. The proof is similar to the proof of Theorem 6 which can be found in [21, Theorem 13]. The difference is that we use Lemma 26 to get rid of the arbitrary f.

Boomerang Distinguisher. In the same way, we can improve the boomerang distinguisher by considering any Boolean function f. As for Theorem 10, we can prove the following result.

Theorem 28 (Advantage of Boo bounded by decorrelation, improved Theorem 10). *For the distinguisher Boo, we have*

$$E(p_{C_K}^{\mathsf{Boo}}) - E(p_{C^*}^{\mathsf{Boo}}) \leq n \frac{2 \times 2^\ell - 5}{(2^\ell - 1)(2^\ell - 3)} + \frac{n}{2} \| [C_K]^4 - [C^*]^4 \|_a.$$

Table 1. The decorrelation order of some statistical attacks.

Attack	Decorrelation order	Type of attack	Attack order	Maximal n
Linear LC	2	iterative	1	2^ℓ
Differential DC	2	iterative	2	2^ℓ
Differential-linear DL	4	iterative	2	$2^{\ell-1}$
Boomerang Boo	4	adaptive, iterative	4	$2^{\ell-1}$
Multidimensional linear ML	2	vector-iterative	1	$2^{\frac{\ell-k}{2}}$
Truncated differential TD	2	iterative	2	$2^{\ell-s-1}$

6   Conclusion

In this paper, we studied the multidimensional linear and truncated differential attacks in the context of the decorrelation theory. We showed that these attacks are non-adaptive iterated attacks of order 2. Table 1 summarizes the considered attacks. In particular, we obtained three types of results:

- we improved the bounds for the linear and differential-linear distinguishers (Theorems 7 and 8 are improved by Theorems 24 and 25, respectively);
- we generalized the differential and boomerang distinguishers to allow an arbitrary function f (Theorems 6 and 10 are improved by Theorems 27 and 28, respectively);
- we proved the security for multidimensional linear and truncated differential with decorrelation (Theorems 19 and 21).

We let as open problems the seek for an improved Lemma 13 with $\sqrt{n}$ instead of n as suggested in Remark 15. This would allow for better bounds in Theorem 19 and 21. We shall also find better bounds based on a higher order of decorrelation, in particular to link Theorem 21 to Theorem 25 (see Remark 23).

References

1. A. Bay. Provable Security of Block Ciphers and Cryptanalysis. PhD thesis no. 6220, EPFL (2014) http://library.epfl.ch/theses/?nr=6220
2. Biham, E., Biryukov, A., Shamir, A.: Cryptanalysis of Skipjack reduced to 31 rounds using impossible differentials. In: Stern, J. (ed.) EUROCRYPT 1999. LNCS, vol. 1592, pp. 12–23. Springer, Heidelberg (1999)
3. Biham, E., Dunkelman, O., Keller, N.: Enhancing differential-linear cryptanalysis. In: Zheng, Y. (ed.) ASIACRYPT 2002. LNCS, vol. 2501, pp. 254–266. Springer, Heidelberg (2002)
4. Bogdanov, A., Leander, G., Nyberg, K., Wang, M.: Integral and multidimensional linear distinguishers with correlation zero. In: Wang, X., Sako, K. (eds.) ASIACRYPT 2012. LNCS, vol. 7658, pp. 244–261. Springer, Heidelberg (2012)

5. Bay, A., Mashatan, A., Vaudenay, S.: Resistance against adaptive plaintext-ciphertext iterated distinguishers. In: Galbraith, S., Nandi, M. (eds.) INDOCRYPT 2012. LNCS, vol. 7668, pp. 528–544. Springer, Heidelberg (2012)

6. Bay, A., Mashatan, A., Vaudenay, S.: Resistance against iterated attacks by decorrelation revisited. In: Safavi-Naini, R., Canetti, R. (eds.) CRYPTO 2012. LNCS, vol. 7417, pp. 741–757. Springer, Heidelberg (2012)

7. Bay, A., Mashatan, A., Vaudenay, S.: Revisiting iterated attacks in the context of decorrelation. Crypt. Commun. **6**, 279–311 (2014)

8. Biham, E., Shamir, A.: Differential cryptanalysis of DES-like cryptosystems. In: Menezes, A., Vanstone, S.A. (eds.) CRYPTO 1990. LNCS, vol. 537, pp. 2–21. Springer, Heidelberg (1991)

9. Blondeau, C., Nyberg, K.: New links between differential and linear cryptanalysis. In: Johansson, T., Nguyen, P.Q. (eds.) EUROCRYPT 2013. LNCS, vol. 7881, pp. 388–404. Springer, Heidelberg (2013)

10. Blondeau, C., Nyberg, K.: Links between truncated differential and multidimensional linear properties of block ciphers and underlying attack complexities. In: Nguyen, P.Q., Oswald, E. (eds.) EUROCRYPT 2014. LNCS, vol. 8441, pp. 165–182. Springer, Heidelberg (2014)

11. Blondeau, C., Leander, G., Nyberg, K.: Differential-linear cryptanalysis revisited. In: Cid, C., Rechberger, C. (eds.) FSE 2014. LNCS, vol. 8540, pp. 411–430. Springer, Heidelberg (2015)

12. Chabaud, F., Vaudenay, S.: Links between differential and linear cryptanalysis. In: De Santis, A. (ed.) EUROCRYPT 1994. LNCS, vol. 950, pp. 356–365. Springer, Heidelberg (1995)

13. Langford, S.K., Hellman, M.E.: Differential-linear cryptanalysis. In: Desmedt, Y.G. (ed.) CRYPTO 1994. LNCS, vol. 839, pp. 17–25. Springer, Heidelberg (1994)

14. Hermelin, M., Cho, J.Y., Nyberg, K.: Multidimensional extension of Matsui's algorithm 2. In: Dunkelman, O. (ed.) FSE 2009. LNCS, vol. 5665, pp. 209–227. Springer, Heidelberg (2009)

15. Knudsen, L.R.: Truncated and higher order differentials. In: Preneel, B. (ed.) FSE 1994. LNCS, vol. 1008. Springer, Heidelberg (1995)

16. Leander, G.: On linear hulls, statistical saturation attacks, PRESENT and a cryptanalysis of PUFFIN. In: Paterson, K.G. (ed.) EUROCRYPT 2011. LNCS, vol. 6632, pp. 303–322. Springer, Heidelberg (2011)

17. Matsui, M.: Linear cryptanalysis method for DES cipher. In: Helleseth, T. (ed.) EUROCRYPT 1993. LNCS, vol. 765, pp. 386–397. Springer, Heidelberg (1994)

18. Vaudenay, S.: Provable security for block ciphers by decorrelation. In: Morvan, M., Meinel, C., Krob, D. (eds.) STACS 1998. LNCS, vol. 1373. Springer, Heidelberg (1998)

19. Vaudenay, S.: Resistance against general iterated attacks. In: Stern, J. (ed.) EUROCRYPT 1999. LNCS, vol. 1592, pp. 255–271. Springer, Heidelberg (1999)

20. Vaudenay, S.: Adaptive-attack norm for decorrelation and super-pseudorandomness. In: Heys, H.M., Adams, C.M. (eds.) SAC 1999. LNCS, vol. 1758, pp. 49–61. Springer, Heidelberg (2000)

21. Vaudenay, S.: Decorrelation: a theory for block cipher security. J. Crypt. **16**(4), 249–286 (2003)

22. Wagner, D.: The boomerang attack. In: Knudsen, L.R. (ed.) FSE 1999. LNCS, vol. 1636, p. 156. Springer, Heidelberg (1999)

23. Wegman, M.N., Carter, J.L.: New hash functions and their use in authentication and set equality. J. Comput. Syst. Sci. **22**, 265–279 (1981)

Analysis of Impossible, Integral and Zero-Correlation Attacks on Type-II Generalized Feistel Networks Using the Matrix Method

Céline Blondeau[1][(✉)] and Marine Minier[2]

[1] Department of Computer Science, School of Science, Aalto University,
Espoo, Finland
celine.blondeau@aalto.fi
[2] Université de Lyon, INRIA, INSA-Lyon, CITI, Villeurbanne, France
marine.minier@insa-lyon.fr

Abstract. While recent publications have shown strong relations between impossible differential and zero-correlation distinguishers as well as between zero-correlation and integral distinguishers, we analyze in this paper some relations between the underlying key-recovery attacks against Type-II Feistel networks. The results of this paper are build on the relation presented at ACNS 2014. In particular, using a matrix representation of the round function, we show that we can not only find impossible, integral and multidimensional zero-correlation distinguishers but also find the key-words involved in the underlined key-recovery attacks. Based on this representation, for matrix-method-derived strongly-related zero-correlation and impossible distinguishers, we show that the key-words involved in the zero-correlation attack is a subset of the key-words involved in the impossible differential attack. Other relations between the key-words involved in zero-correlation, impossible and integral attacks are also extracted. Also we show that in this context the data complexity of the multidimensional zero-correlation attack is larger than that of the other two attacks.

Keywords: Block ciphers · Feistel like ciphers · Impossible differential · Zero-correlation · Integral · Key-recovery attacks · Matrix method

1 Introduction

Impossible differential (ID) [2,20], integral (INT) [21] and multidimensional zero-correlation (ZC) [10] attacks are efficient attacks for word-oriented block ciphers such as Feistel-like ciphers.

Classically, *ID distinguishers* take advantage of differentials which never occur for the studied permutations. The security of word-oriented block ciphers is evaluated with respect to this attack. As early as in 2003, based on a matrix representation of the round function, automated methods to find IDs have been proposed [19].

© International Association for Cryptologic Research 2015
G. Leander (Ed.): FSE 2015, LNCS 9054, pp. 92–113, 2015.
DOI: 10.1007/978-3-662-48116-5_5

In *ZC cryptanalysis*, the attacker rather takes advantage of linear approximations that have probability $1/2$ to hold. This relatively new attack, which can be seen as a multidimensional linear attack with capacity equal to zero [9], has also been applied to many word-oriented block ciphers [8,9,11,26,30,31]. The published attacks, which improve upon the state-of-the-art cryptanalysis, can either cover more rounds than the ID attacks, or perform in less time than the ID attacks on the same number of rounds.

In *INT attacks*, attackers look for particular subsets of chosen plaintexts where some parts of the input are equal to constant whereas the other parts take all possible values. The interesting subsets are the ones such that the sum taken on all the input values after a certain number of rounds is equal to a known value, to another sum or to zero at some particular locations. This attack, also known as saturation or square attack was originally proposed by Knudsen as a dedicated attack against Square [16].

Recently, mathematical and structural relations between the underlying distinguishers have been discussed in the literature. In 2012, Bogdanov et al. [9] showed that the existence of a particular type of integral distinguisher, called zero-correlation integral distinguisher, implies the existence of a zero-correlation distinguisher. Among other relations, in [6,7] it is shown that in some particular cases, ZC distinguishers and ID distinguishers are mathematically equivalent. While this condition is not often verified in practice, it is shown in [3] that for many Feistel-type ciphers, ID and ZC distinguishers which are build using a matrix method can be derived from each other. The results of [3] are derived from a matrix representation of the cipher [1] and from the fact that ID and ZC distinguishers can be derived from this representation using the so-called $\mathcal{U}$-method [19].

Motivation. In practice, the security regarding these three attacks is often analyzed independently and key-recovery attacks in the ID, ZC and INT contexts are part of different publications. As illustrated in Table 1 usually the number of attacked rounds in all these contexts is similar. When the attacks cover the same number of rounds, it often seems that the relation between these attacks can be seen as a kind of data/time/memory trade-off. While depending of the cipher, different tricks can be used to improve the time and memory complexity of the attacks, we observe that the number of key-words involved in the attack is usually independent of the method used to perform the key-recovery attack.

Our Contributions. *Relation between ZC and INT distinguishers.* From the preliminary link between ZC and integral ZC distinguishers presented in [9], we derive a general relation between ZC and INT distinguishers. In particular we discuss cases where matrix-method-derived INT distinguishers cover less or more rounds than matrix-method-derived ZC distinguishers.

Relation between the data complexities of ID, ZC and INT attacks. When the distinguishers are matrix-method-related the same number of differential and linear approximations are involved in the attack. In such a case, we can compare the data complexity of ID and ZC. In particular we show that the data

Table 1. Best attacks on some well known ciphers.

Cipher	Attacked Rounds	Rounds Dist	Type	Data	Time	Memory	Ref
HIGHT	27	16 (10–25)	ID	2^{58} CP	$2^{126.6}$	2^{120}	[15]
HIGHT	27	16 (10–25)	ZC	$2^{62.79}$ DKP	$2^{120.78}$	2^{43}	[31]
Camellia-128	11	8 (2–8)	ID	$2^{118.4}$CP	$2^{118.43}$	$2^{92.4}$	[14]
Camellia-128	11	7 (3–8)	ZC	$2^{125.3}$KP	$2^{125.8}$	2^{112}	[8]
SIMON-32/64	19	11 (5–15)	ID	2^{32} CP	$2^{62.56}$	2^{44}	[14]
SIMON-32/64	20	11 (6–16)	ZC	2^{32} KP	$2^{56.96}$	$2^{41.42}$	[29]
SIMON-32/64	21	15 (1–15)	INT	2^{31} CP	2^{63}	2^{54}	[29]
LBlock	22	15 (1–14)	INT	2^{61}CP	$2^{70.00}$	2^{63}	[24]
LBlock	22	14 (5–18)	ID[a]	2^{58}CP	$2^{79.28}$	2^{68}	[18]
LBlock	22	14 (5–18)	ZC[b]	2^{64} DKP	$2^{70.54}$	2^{64}	[26]
LBlock	22	14 (5–18)	ID[b]	2^{60} CP	$2^{71.53}$	2^{59}	[13]
LBlock	23	14 (6–19)	ID[b]	2^{59} CP	$2^{75.36}$	2^{74}	[13]
LBlock	23	14 (6–19)	ZC	$2^{63.87}$ DKP	**$2^{73.94}$**	**2^{60}**	this paper

[a]In [26], it is mentioned that the attack applies to an old version of the cipher.
[b]parameters provided in the original article for the lowest time complexity.
CP: Chosen plaintexts.
KP: Known plaintexts.
DKP: Distinct known plaintexts.

complexity of a ZC attack is in that case larger than that of an ID attack. A similar comparison with INT attacks is also studied.

Relation between the key-words involved in ID, ZC, and INT attacks. Illustrated by the ID, INT and ZC attacks on LBlock [32], we show that there exists a strong relation between the key-words involved in the different key-recovery attacks. In particular, we show that when the matrix-method-derived distinguishers are strongly related then the key-words involved in a ZC attack on a Type-II GFN correspond to a subset of the key-words involved in an ID attack.

Attack on LBlock. For illustration purposes, we present a ZC attack on 23 rounds of LBlock. The time and memory complexities of this attack are smaller than those of the recent ID attack [13] on this cipher.

Outline. Some preliminary notations are defined in Sect. 2. In Sect. 3, we describe how the matrix method can be used to find ID, ZC and INT distinguishers on Feistel ciphers and recall the relations between these different distinguishers. In Sect. 4, we compare the data complexity of these attacks and illustrate on LBlock the strong relation between the key-words involved in the different attacks. In Sect. 5, we explain how we can use the matrix method to determine the key-words involved in the key-recovery part of the attack. In Sect. 6, we present an attack on LBlock. Section 7 concludes this paper.

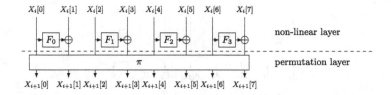

Fig. 1. One round of a Type-II GFN with $b = 8$ blocks.

2   Preliminaries

The structural link between ID and ZC distinguishers described in [3] is relevant for Feistel-like ciphers commonly referred as Generalized Feistel Network (GFN) [27]. More precisely, the round $i + 1$ of a GFN inputs a block X_i of n bits divided in $b \geq 2$ blocks of c bits each and outputs a block X_{i+1}. We denote by $X_i[0], \cdots, X_i[b-1]$ the b input blocks of a GFN round and by $X_{i+1}[0], \cdots, X_{i+1}[b-1]$ the corresponding output blocks. A GFN can be separated into two successive layers, as done in [1,27]: a non-linear layer and a permutation layer, as shown in Fig. 1. The non-linear layer is made of key-dependent functions F_i which input some blocks of size c bits and where the corresponding outputs are added (usually Xor-ed) to some other blocks. The permutation layer is a block-wise permutation of the b blocks denoted by π. For example, for the classical Type-II GFN, the permutation is the circular shift.

A generic method that uses a matrix representation and captures the previous definition of GFNs is presented in [1]. This representation could be useful to find ID, ZC and INT distinguishers as well as to show some links between them as began in [3]. Definition 1 sums up this approach for the Type-II GFNs.

Definition 1. *Omitting key and constant addition, the round function of a Type-II GFN with b branches, b even, can be matricially represented as a combination of two $b \times b$ matrices $\mathcal{F}$, $\mathcal{P}$ with coefficients $\{0, 1, F_i\}$ where the $\{F_i\}_{i \leq b/2}$ denote the internal non-linear functions.*

- *Representing the non-linear layer (F-layer), the non-zero coefficients of the matrix $\mathcal{F}$ are equal to 1 in the diagonal and have coefficient F_i in row j and column ℓ if the input of the function F_i is given by the ℓ-th branch and the output is Xor-ed to the j-th branch. Meaning that, for a Type-II GFN, $\mathcal{F}$ have one F_i on each even row and even column.*
- *Representing the permutation of the branches (P-layer), the matrix $\mathcal{P}$ is a permutation matrix with only one non-zero coefficient per line and column. From these two matrices, a Type-II GFN round function can be represented by a $b \times b$ matrix $\mathcal{R}$ as $\mathcal{R} = \mathcal{P} \cdot \mathcal{F}$, the inverse of the round function is $\mathcal{R}^{-1} = \mathcal{F} \cdot \mathcal{P}^{-1}$.*

As observed in [27], optimal diffusion block permutations have the property that any input block with an even number is mapped to a block with an odd number, and vice versa. A Feistel cipher with this property is called *alternating Type-II*

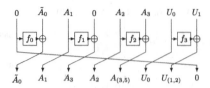

Fig. 2. An example of passing one round of a classical Type-II GFN in the ID context using the previous notations and the rules of Table 3.

GFN (AGFN). Some of the results of this paper assume alternating Type-II GFNs.

In [3,26], another matrix representation is used to find ZC distinguishers on Feistel-like ciphers. The $\mathcal{U}$-method used to find ZC distinguishers relies on the mirror representation of the round function.

Definition 2. *For a Feistel-like cipher given the matrix representation of the round function* $\mathcal{R} = \mathcal{P} \cdot \mathcal{F}$, *we call mirror function the round function described by the matrix* $\mathcal{M} = \mathcal{P} \cdot \mathcal{F}^T$, *where* $\mathcal{F}^T$ *denotes the transposition of the matrix* $\mathcal{F}$.

3 Distinguishers

The matrix method, which is defined in [19,23,26,33] is used to find respectively ID, INT and ZC distinguishers. For these three attacks, different quantities are involved. For instance, ID distinguishers are derived from an inconsistency between partial differences and ZC distinguishers are derived from an inconsistency between partial linear masks. To show the similarities between ID, ZC and INT attacks, the same notations will be used in the different contexts. These notations are summed up in Table 2. For instance, for a given a value, the quantity A_a denotes respectively a non-zero difference in the ID context, a non-zero mask in the ZC context and symbolizes a permutation of the elements of $\mathbb{F}_2^c$ in the INT context. While for type-1 distinguishers (see Definition 3 in Sect. 3.2) $\tilde{A}_a$ does not have to be differentiated from A_a, such distinction is necessary to find type-2 and type-3 distinguishers. Using these notations, the state of a b-branches GFN can be represented as a vector of b elements of the form given in Table 2. When necessary, this b-word vector will be denoted by V_i^{ID}, V_i^{ZC} or V_i^{INT}. For example, in Fig. 2 we have : $V_{i-1}^{ID} = (0, \tilde{A}_0, A_1, 0, A_2, A_3, U_0, U_1)$. The vector V_i^{ID} is computed using the rules given in Table 3.

3.1 The Matrix Method on GFNs

ID Distinguisher. In [19,23], the matrix method which allows to efficiently find ID distinguishers for Feistel-type ciphers is described. The algorithm mainly implements the rules given in Table 3 to propagate a partial difference through the rounds of a cipher. The values a and u are arbitrary values starting at 0. As explained in [33], these indexes allow simplifications of type $A_a \oplus A_a = 0$.

Table 2. General notations representing a partial-state. a and u are some counters.

	ID	ZC	INT
0	Zero difference	Zero mask	Constant value[a]
$\tilde{A}_a$	Known non-zero difference	Known non-zero mask	Known permutation
A_a	Non-zero difference	Non-zero mask	Permutation
U_u	Unknown difference	Unknown mask	Unknown
$A_a \oplus A_{a'} = U_u$		$= U_u$	Known sum

[a]: Usually denoted by C in the INT context.

Table 3. Propagation rules in the ID, ZC and INT context when using the matrix method.

Rules to pass an F function

F	0	$\tilde{A}_i$	A_i	U_j or $A_i \oplus A_j$
	0	$A_{(\max_a)+1}$	$A_{(\max_a)+1}$	$U_{(\max_u)+1}$

Rules to pass a $\oplus$

$\oplus$	0	$\tilde{A}_i$	A_i	U_i
0	0	$\tilde{A}_i$	A_i	U_i
A_j	A_j	$\tilde{A}_i \oplus A_j$	$A_i \oplus A_j$	$A_j \oplus U_i$
$\tilde{A}_j$	$\tilde{A}_j$	$\tilde{A}_i \oplus \tilde{A}_j$	$A_i \oplus A_j$	$A_j \oplus U_i$
U_j	U_j	$\tilde{A}_i \oplus U_j$	$A_i \oplus U_j$	$U_j \oplus U_i$

Using the matrix representation of the round function, we can derive an ID distinguisher on a GFN.

Proposition 1. *Given V_0^{ID} and W_0^{ID} a representation of the input and output differences, we have an ID distinguisher (V_0^{ID}, W_0^{ID}) on $s_0 + s_1$ rounds if we have an inconsistency between $X = \mathcal{R}^{s_0} \cdot V_0^{ID}$ and $Y = \mathcal{R}^{-s_1} \cdot W_0^{ID}$.*

More details on inconsistencies in the ID and ZC contexts are provided later in this section.

ZC Distinguisher. In [26], the matrix method to find ZC distinguishers is presented. The main difference with the method used in the ID context comes from the fact that the mirror matrix $\mathcal{M}$ (see Definition 2) must be used instead of the round function matrix $\mathcal{R}$.

Proposition 2. *Given V_0^{ZC} and W_0^{ZC} a representation of the input and output linear masks, we have a ZC distinguisher (V_0^{ZC}, W_0^{ZC}) on $s_0 + s_1$ rounds if we have an inconsistency between $\mathcal{M}^{s_0} \cdot V_0^{ZC}$ and $\mathcal{M}^{-s_1} \cdot W_0^{ZC}$.*

INT Distinguisher. In [33], the authors proposed an algorithm to automatically find INT distinguishers. The algorithm uses the same rules and the same matrix representation $\mathcal{R}$ as in the ID context, only the termination rules differ. For Type-II GFNs, these rules can be expressed as follows.

Corollary 1. *Given a representative vector Z^{INT}, for a GFN as given in Definition 1, we have an INT distinguisher on $s_0 + s_1$ rounds if the following rules are fulfilled:*

- *Termination at the end of an INT distinguisher: If $W_0^{INT} = \mathcal{R}^{s_1} \cdot Z^{INT}$ is such that there exists $i < b$ and a set J with $W_0^{INT}[i] = \oplus_{j \in J} A_j$ and for $\tilde{W} = \mathcal{R}^{s_1+1} \cdot Z^{INT}$, for all i and J, we have $\tilde{W}[i] \neq \oplus_{j \in J} A_j$.*
- *Termination at the beginning of an INT distinguisher: If $V_0^{INT} = \mathcal{R}^{-s_0} \cdot Z^{INT}$ is such that $\exists\ i \in \{0, \cdots, (b-1)\}$ with $V_0^{INT}[i] = 0$ (with classical notation $= C$).*

Throughout this paper, we assume that the ID, ZC and INT distinguishers are derived from the matrix method.

3.2 Equivalence Between Matrix-Method-Derived ID and ZC Distinguishers

In [3], a condition of equivalence between matrix-method-derived ID and ZC distinguishers is given.

Theorem 1 ([3]). *Let $\mathcal{R}$ be the matrix representation of the round function of a GFN and $\mathcal{M}$ be the matrix representation of its mirror function as given in Sect. 2. If there exists a $b \times b$ permutation matrix $\mathcal{Q}$ such that*

$$\mathcal{R} = \mathcal{Q} \cdot \mathcal{M} \cdot \mathcal{Q}^{-1} \text{ or } \mathcal{R} = \mathcal{Q} \cdot \mathcal{M}^{-1} \cdot \mathcal{Q}^{-1}, \tag{1}$$

we deduce that: an impossible differential distinguisher on r rounds involving a number of differentials equal to M exists if and only if a zero-correlation linear distinguisher on r rounds involving M linear masks exists.

As shown in [3], most of the Feistel networks verify this condition. In the remainder of this paper, we say that a Feistel-like cipher has matrix-method-derived *related ID and ZC distinguishers* when the relation is derived from the previous property.

Lemma 1. *Given the matrices $\mathcal{R} = \mathcal{P} \cdot \mathcal{F}$ and $\mathcal{M} = \mathcal{P} \cdot \mathcal{F}^T$,*

- *If the condition $\mathcal{R} = \mathcal{Q} \cdot \mathcal{M} \cdot \mathcal{Q}^{-1}$ of (1) is fulfilled and $\mathcal{P} \cdot \mathcal{Q} = \mathcal{Q} \cdot \mathcal{P}$ we have $\mathcal{F} = \mathcal{Q} \cdot \mathcal{F}^T \cdot \mathcal{Q}^{-1}$.*
- *If the condition $\mathcal{R} = \mathcal{Q} \cdot \mathcal{M}^{-1} \cdot \mathcal{Q}^{-1}$ of (1) is fulfilled we have $\mathcal{F} = \mathcal{Q}_1 \cdot \mathcal{F}^T \cdot \mathcal{Q}_2$ with $\mathcal{Q}_1 = \mathcal{P}^{-1} \cdot \mathcal{Q}$ and $\mathcal{Q}_2 = \mathcal{P}^{-1} \cdot \mathcal{Q}^{-1}$.*

Remark 1. For a Type-II GFN as given in Definition 1, there always exists a permutation matrix $\mathcal{Q}$ such that $\mathcal{F}^T = \mathcal{Q} \cdot \mathcal{F} \cdot \mathcal{Q}^{-1}$. This matrix $\mathcal{Q}$ corresponds to the permutation $\sigma : (0, \cdots, (b-1)) \rightarrow (1, 0, 3, 2, \cdots, (b-1), (b-2))$.

While in [12] improved ID distinguishers are presented, using the matrix method for Type-II GFNs we can observe three types of ID and ZC distinguishers [23].

Definition 3. *Given $X = \mathcal{R}^{s_0} \cdot V_0^{ID}$ and $Y = \mathcal{R}^{-s_1} \cdot W_0^{ID}$ or $X = \mathcal{M}^{s_0} \cdot V_0^{ZC}$ and $Y = \mathcal{M}^{-s_1} \cdot W_0^{ZC}$. Following the work of [12,23], for a Type-II GFN, we define three types of distinguishers. Let $p \in \{0, \cdots, (b-1)\}$ denote the index of the studied state Y and $Y[p]$ the status of this p-th word.*

- An ID (resp. ZC) distinguisher of type-1 denoted by ID1 (resp. ZC1) is a distinguisher with independent input and output differences (resp. masks). For these distinguishers, the inconsistency is usually:

$$\exists\, p \in \{0, \cdots, (b-1)\} \mid (Y[p] = 0 \text{ and } X[p] = A_a) \text{ or } (Y[p] = A_a \text{ and } X[p] = 0).$$

- An ID (resp. ZC) distinguisher of type-2 denoted by ID2 (resp. ZC2) is a distinguisher where a non-zero output-difference word (resp. output-mask word) should be different from an input one. Given $\tilde{A}_{a_0}$ a word of V_0 and W_0, the inconsistency is:

$$\exists\, p \in \{0, \cdots, (b-1)\} \mid Y[p] = X[p] = \tilde{A}_a.$$

- An ID (resp. ZC) distinguisher of type-3 is a distinguisher where non-zero input- and output-difference words (resp. output-mask words) should be equal. Given $\tilde{A}_{a_0}$ a word of V_0 and W_0, we have an ID distinguisher of type-3 (ID3) on $s_0 + s_1 + 1$ rounds if:

$$\exists\, p \in \{0, \cdots, (b-1)\} \mid (\mathcal{F} \cdot X)[p] = \tilde{A}_{a_0} \oplus A_{a_1} \text{ and } (\mathcal{P}^{-1} \cdot Y)[p] = \tilde{A}_{a_0}. \quad (2)$$

Replacing $\mathcal{F}$ by $\mathcal{F}^T$ in (2) we obtain a ZC distinguisher of type-3 (ZC3).

Clearly, our matrix method captures the distinguishers found using the matrix method described in [23] as in the rules given in Table 3 used to define the transitions of our matrix method, we have: $F(\tilde{A}_i) = A_{(\max_a)+1}$ and $\tilde{A}_i \oplus A_j$ is kept as $\tilde{A}_i \oplus A_j$ when crossing a xor operation. For example, the ID distinguisher presented in [23] on 16-round of Gen-Skipkack is of type ID2 and the ID distinguisher on 19-round of Gen-CAST256 is of type ID3. The link between ZC and ID distinguishers thus depends of Theorem 1. However, our matrix method does not capture the distinguishers of [12] which depend on differential transition properties of the involved S-boxes.

3.3 Comparison with INT Distinguishers

A zero-correlation integral distinguisher is defined in [9] as an integral distinguisher with balanced output words. In Sect. 3 of [9] a direct relation between zero-correlation integral distinguisher and ZC distinguisher of type-1 is extracted.

As a zero-correlation integral distinguisher is stronger than a general integral distinguisher with sum over an output word equal to zero, we can see that in general, one more round could be added to the zero-correlation integral distinguisher to transform it into an INT distinguisher because if the partial outputs of the zero-correlation integral distinguisher occur equally often, the last linear transformation maps it into an integral distinguisher. More precisely for Type-II GFNs, we deduce that the number of rounds on which an INT distinguisher applies, is greater than or equal to the number of rounds on which a ZC distinguisher of type-1 applies. More precisely for an alternating Type-II GFN, we can show the following results which are proved in the extended version [5].

Table 4. GFNs of [27] with $b = 8$. For these ciphers based on the results of [3], we can show that $s^{ID} = s^{ZC}$. π defines the permutation of the branches.

Name	π	s^{ID}	s^{INT}
Type-II	$\{7, 0, 1, 2, 3, 4, 5, 6\}$	17	16
Nyberg	$\{2, 0, 4, 1, 6, 3, 7, 5\}$	14	15
No.1	$\{3, 0, 1, 4, 7, 2, 5, 6\}$	11	11
No.2	$\{3, 0, 7, 4, 5, 6, 1, 2\}$	10	11

Lemma 2. *For an alternating GFN of Type-II, given $s_{\max}^{ZC1}$ (resp. $s_{\max}^{INT}$) the maximum number of rounds on which a matrix-method-derived ZC distinguisher of type-1 (resp. an INT distinguisher) applied, we have $s_{\max}^{ZC1} = s_{\max}^{INT}$ or $s_{\max}^{ZC1} = s_{\max}^{INT} - 1$.*

Remark 2. In practice, for the Type-II GFNs of [27], we observed (see for instance Table 4) and proved[1], that the number of rounds on which matrix-method-derived INT and ID distinguishers apply is $s^{INT} = s^{ID}$, $s^{INT} = s^{ID} - 1$ or $s^{INT} = s^{ID} + 1$. This relation follows by the relation between the ZC and ID distinguishers.

Remark 3. According to Proposition 1 and Corollary 1, the same matrix representation is used to derive ID and INT distinguishers. Given Z^{INT} as in Cor. 1, we denote by $\tilde{X} = \mathcal{R}^{s_0} \cdot Z^{INT}$ and $\tilde{Y} = \mathcal{R}^{-s_1} \cdot Z^{INT}$. Now for a Type-II alternating GFN, we can find the different types of impossible differential distinguishers by analyzing the different inconsistency cases between $\tilde{X}$ and $\tilde{Y}$ or a permutation of $\tilde{Y}$.

4   The Key-Recovery: Notations and Examples

The time and memory complexities of ID, ZC and INT key-recovery attacks are dependent on the number of key-words involved in the attacks. In ID attacks, a distinction is classically made between the key-words which lead to a reduction of the number of pairs and the key-words which are just helping in the partial encryption/decryption without reducing the number of involved pairs ([13], Fig. 2). While the first ones are usually called *sieving key-words* leading to a so called *sieving step*, we called *guessed key-words* the latter ones. The *involved key-words* correspond to the sieving key-words and guessed key-words.

Similar concepts can be observed in ZC and INT attacks, where most of the involved key-words lead to a reduction of the size of the table storing the partial distribution. To simplify the description and the comparison, the same terminology will be used in these three contexts. In the ZC and INT contexts, a sieving key-word corresponds to a key-word leading to a reduction of the

---
[1] These cases can be derived from the proofs given page 15–16 of [27].

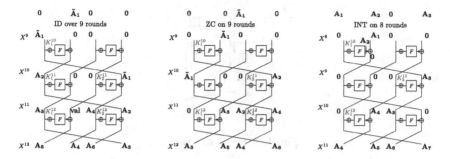

Fig. 3. Key-recovery in the ID and ZC context and the first partial sum in the INT context. The key-words in red are sieving key-words, the blue ones are guessed key-words.

size of the stored distributions. The number of key-words involved in a key-recovery attack on $s + r$ rounds is denoted by $|\mathcal{K}|$. The number of key-words leading to a sieving step is denoted by $|\mathcal{S}|$ and the number of guessed key-words is denoted by $|\mathcal{G}|$. To compute the complexity of a key-recovery attack we denote by $HW(V)$, the weight of a b-word vector V as $HW(V) = b - |\{\ell \in \{0 \cdots (b-1)\}|V[\ell] = 0\}|$.

To illustrate this concept, we discuss the examples of ID, ZC and INT attacks on a 4 branches Feistel as well as on LBlock [32].

4.1 Example of Attacks on a 4 Branches Feistel Network

In Fig. 3, we illustrate ID, ZC and INT key-recovery attacks on the last three rounds of a classical type-II GFN with 4 branches. While some of the notations will be defined later, we illustrate the meaning of guessed and sieving key-words in the ID and ZC context by providing some steps of the key-recovery algorithms. For instance some steps of the generic ZC attack on this structure could be:

- Store the distribution of $[X^0[2], X^{10}[0, 1, 2, 3]]$ (5 words)
- Try the sieving key K_1^{10} and compute the distribution of $[X^0[2], X^{11}[1], X^{12}[1, 2]]$ (4 words)
- Try the guessed key K_2^{10} and compute the distribution of $[X^0[2], X^9[1, 2, 3]]$ (4 words)

The last step consists at studying the distribution of $[X^0[2], X^7[1]]$.

4.2 Relation Between the Involved Key-Words on LBlock

LBlock is a new lightweight block cipher designed by Wu and Zhang in 2011 [32]. It uses 80-bit keys and 64-bit blocks seen at nibble level and is based on a modified 32-round Feistel structure. We denote by $P = L_0 \| R_0$ the 64-bit plaintext, where L_0 and R_0 are 32-bit vectors. The encryption process is as follows: $R_i = L_{i-1}$ and $L_i = F(L_{i-1}, K_i) \oplus (R_{i-1} \lll 8)$ where the F function could

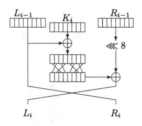

Fig. 4. A round of LBlock.

be divided into three steps (see Fig. 4). First, the 32-bit subkey K_i is added to L_{i-1} by a simple XOR. Then, a nonlinear layer applies to the result. This nonlinear layer consists of the application nibble by nibble of eight different 4-bit Sboxes $S_0, \ldots, S_7$ (see [32] for a complete description of the S-boxes). Finally, the resulting nibbles are permuted as shown on Fig. 4.

The key-schedule takes as input a master key K seen as a key register denoted at bit level as $K = K_{79}K_{78} \cdots K_0$ and outputs round-subkeys k_i of 32 bits. It repeats the following steps for $i = 1$ to 31 knowing that k_1 is initialized with the 32 leftmost bits of the key register K:

1. $K \lll 29$
2. $[K_{79}K_{78}K_{77}K_{76}] = S_9[K_{79}K_{78}K_{77}K_{76}]$ where S_9 is the tenth S-box.
3. $[K_{75}K_{74}K_{73}K_{72}] = S_8[K_{75}K_{74}K_{73}K_{72}]$ where S_8 is the ninth S-box.
4. $[K_{50}K_{49}K_{48}K_{47}] = [K_{50}K_{49}K_{48}K_{47}] \oplus [i]_2$
5. k_{i+1} is selected as the leftmost 32 bits of the key register K.

For this cipher which can be seen, as described in [26], as a Type-II GFN, ID and ZC distinguishers can be derived from each other [3] and can be applied on 14 rounds [32]. INT distinguishers reach 15 rounds [32].

Derived from these distinguishers, ID and ZC attacks on 22 rounds [13, 18, 26] as well as ID attacks on 23 rounds [13, 14] have been performed. An INT attack on 22 rounds has also been presented [24]. For the illustration purpose of this section, we assume that the round-keys are independent. As the attacks of [13, 18, 24, 26] depend on the key-schedule more details on these attacks will only be presented in Sect. 6. In this example represented in Fig. 5 and in Fig. 6, we observe a strong relation between the key-words involved in the different attacks, when the distinguishers are, what we will call, *strongly related* (the same key-words are involved in a key-recovery attack on $1 + s + 1$ rounds). For this illustration we use as reference the ID attack of [13] derived from the ID distinguisher: $[((0,0,0,0,0,0,0,0), (0,0,0,0,*,0,0,0)) \nrightarrow ((0,0,0,0,0,0,*,0,0), (0,0,0,0,0,0,0,0))]$.

For the ZC distinguisher we use: $[((0,0,0,0,0,0,*,0), (0,0,0,0,0,0,0,0)) \nrightarrow ((0,0,0,0,0,0,0,0), (0,0,0,0,0,0,*,0))]$.

The keys $K_5[3]$ and $K_{20}[2]$ are involved in both attacks, meaning that the chosen ID and ZC distinguishers are strongly related. We also observe that in that case, as for the classical type-II GFN given in Fig. 3, the key-words involved

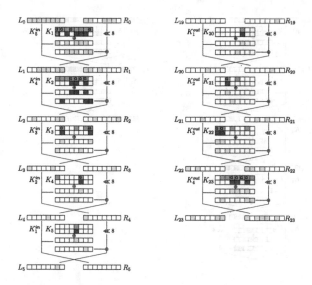

In blue (bottom): the key-words involved in the ZC attack
In green (top): the key-words involved in the ID attack
G: a guessed key-word (non-sieving key-word)
In yellow: the state-words involved in the ZC attack

Fig. 5. The key-recovery part of ID, ZC attacks on LBlock.

in the ZC attack corresponds to a subset of the key-words involved in the ID attack. We also compare this attack, with an INT attack derived from the following INT distinguisher on 15 rounds:

$[((A, A, A, A, A, A, C, A), (A, A, A, A, A, A, A, A)) \rightarrow ((*, *, *, *, *, *, *, *), (*, *, *, *, *, *, A \oplus A, *))]$. Before providing in Sect. 5 a proof regarding the relations between the different involved key-words, we analyze in the next section, relations between the data complexities of these different attacks.

4.3 Data Complexity of a Key-Recovery Attack

ZC Attack. We denote by M the number of linear approximations which have correlation zero and which are evaluated in the attack. Improving the estimate of [9], it has been proven in [8] that the data complexity N^{ZC} of a distinct-known-plaintext ZC key-recovery attack is

$$N^{ZC} \approx \frac{(2^n - 1)[z_{1-\alpha} + z_{1-\beta}]}{\sqrt{M/2} + z_{1-\alpha}} + 1, \tag{3}$$

where z_x is obtained from the inverse of the cumulative distribution function Φ of the normal distribution: $z_x = \Phi^{-1}(x)$, $1 - \alpha$ corresponds to the success probability of the attack and $-\log_2(\beta)$ to the advantage of the attack. As the manipulation of the normal distribution makes the comparison between attacks difficult,

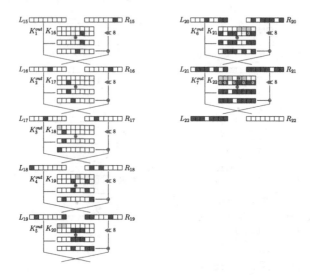

In dark blue (bottom): the key-words involved in the first partial sum
In light blue (top): the key-words involved in the second partial sum
G: a guessed key-word (non-sieving key-word)
In dark blue: the state-words involved in the first partial sum

Fig. 6. The key-recovery part of an INT attack on LBlock.

in the remainder of this paper we use an approximation of it. In particular, we can show (see for instance [28]) that for $\beta < 2^{-5}$, $z_{1-\beta} = \Phi^{-1}(1-\beta) \approx \sqrt{-2\log(\beta)}$. While an approximation of $z_{1-\alpha}$ can also be used, in many ZC attacks, the success probability is fixed to $1 - \alpha = 1 - 2^{-2.7} \approx 0.85$ such that $z_{1-\alpha} \approx 1.02$. Using this approximation, the data complexity of a ZC key-recovery attack becomes

$$N^{ZC} \approx \frac{2^n \left[z_{1-\alpha} + \sqrt{2 \cdot \log(1/\beta)} \right]}{\sqrt{(M-1)/2} + z_{1-\alpha}} + 1. \tag{4}$$

ID Attack. For most of the attacks in the differential context, the data complexity of an ID key-recovery attack is computed as a function of the structure of the input and output differences but also of the different sieves performed during the attack. In an ID attack, if at least one key remains at the end of the key-recovery part we are certain that the correct key is among them. In statistical terms [4], this particularity means that the success probability $1 - \alpha$ of the attack is equal to 1. Given structures of size 2^t and given 2^m structures used in an ID attack, the data complexity is $N^{ID} = 2^{m+t}$.

In the ID cryptanalysis context [2,14], it is commonly assumed that the false alarm probability, denoted β in this paper is determined by $\beta = (1 - 2^{-q})^{2^{m+2t-1-p}} \approx e^{2^{m+2t-p-q-1}}$, where 2^{-p} corresponds to the product probabilities discarding plaintext-pairs and 2^q corresponds to the probability of discarding a key. Thus, we have

$$N^{ID} \approx 2^{p+q-t} \cdot 2 \cdot \log(1/\beta). \tag{5}$$

When the data complexity is smaller than the maximal size of a structure or if the ID attack can be done in the known plaintext model, we have $N^{ID} = \sqrt{2^{p+q-1} \log(1/\beta)}$. If we have M differentials involved in our ID distinguisher, we can show that $2^{p+q+n-t} = 2^{2n}/M$, where n is the size of the encrypted blocks. In the case where more than one structure is used, we have

$$N^{ID} \approx \frac{2^n}{M} \cdot 2 \cdot \log(1/\beta). \tag{6}$$

From a direct comparison between (4) and (6) we deduce that:

Lemma 3. *Given two related ID and ZC distinguishers, involving M differentials or linear approximations, if the success probability of the ZC attack is 50 % ($z_{1-\alpha} = 0$), we have $N^{ID} \leq N^{ZC}$ as long as $\log(1/\beta) \leq M$. This relation remains true, for larger success probabilities since the data complexity of the ZC attack will, in that case, be larger too.*

INT Attack. Given V_0^{INT} as defined in Corollary 1, the data complexity of an INT attack is proportional to the number v of active words in V_0^{INT}: $N^{INT} = \mathcal{O}(2^{c \cdot v})$. For this attack, false alarm occurs when the sum on a word is randomly equal to 0. As this event occurs with probability 2^{-c}, we can derive in a time/memory trade-off way, the success of an INT attack with $\beta = (1 - 2^{-c})^{2^{c|\mathcal{K}|}}$ where $|\mathcal{K}|$ is the number of key-words involved in the key-recovery part of the attack. The overall data complexity of an INT attack is:

$$N^{INT} \approx 2^{c \cdot v} \cdot 2 \cdot \log(1/\beta). \tag{7}$$

Remark 4. For many Feistel-like ciphers, the number M of differences involved in an ID distinguisher of type-1, is $M = 2^{2 \cdot c}$ (see examples in [23]) and the weight v of V_0^{INT} is $b - 1$. In this case, a comparison between (7) and (5) gives $N^{ID1} = N^{INT}/2^c$.

This relation stays about to be true in the case of an ID distinguisher of type-2 (in this case, $M = (2^c - 1)^2$). When comparing an ID distinguisher of type-3 with $M = 2^c$ to an INT distinguisher with $v = b - 1$ we obtain that $N^{INT} = N^{ID3}$.

Remark 5. Assuming as in many attacks that $HW(V_0^{ZC1}) = HW(W_0^{ZC1})$ and $HW(V_0^{INT}) = b - HW(V_0^{ZC1})$ and given a success probability $1 - \alpha$ of 50 % in the ZC context, we obtain that $N^{INT}/N^{ZC1} \approx \sqrt{2 \log(1/\beta)}$. Thus, the data complexity of an INT attack is greater than the one of a ZC1 attack. For larger success probability, this is no more true and in general $N^{INT} \leq N^{ZC}$.

After the analysis of the data complexities, some questions arise. In particular we could wonder what is the benefit of a ZC attack if its data complexity is larger than the one of an INT or ID attack. In the next section, using a matrix representation of the round function, we study the relation between the key-words involved in the different attacks and show that for matrix-method-derived related distinguishers the number of key-words involved in a ZC key-recovery attack is smaller than the number of key-words involved in a ID attack on the same number of rounds.

5   Key-Words Involved in a Key-Recovery Attack

From a matrix representation of Type-II GFN ciphers, we analyze in this section the key-recovery part of these attacks. This analysis is done for *related* and *strongly related* matrix-method-derived ID, ZC and INT distinguishers.

We say that the *ZC and INT distinguishers are strongly related* if the same key-words are involved in a key-recovery attack over one round of partial decryption. In this section, strongly related INT and ZC distinguishers do not necessary apply on the same number of rounds.

We say that the *ZC and ID distinguishers are strongly related* if the same key-words are involved in a key-recovery attack over one round of partial encryption and one round of partial decryption.

For instance, for the Nyberg constructions, the matrix-method derived ID and ZC distinguishers are related but are not strongly related. This can be proven by observing that for this non-alternating cipher, $\mathcal{P} \cdot \mathcal{Q} \neq \mathcal{Q} \cdot \mathcal{P}$ for $\mathcal{Q}$ defined as in Remark 1. But, for this cipher, the distinguishers are related in the sense of Theorem 1.

5.1   A Matrix Representation for Analyzing Key-Recovery Attacks

In the same way, we can derive ID, ZC and INT distinguishers of a Feistel cipher using a matrix representation of the round function, we show in this section how we can find the key-words involved in the attack using a matrix method. In this section, the vectors V_0 and W_0 represent respectively the input and output of the distinguishers. The vectors V_i and W_j represent the state when $i \leq r_{\text{in}}$ rounds are added at the beginning of a distinguisher and $j \leq r_{\text{out}}$ rounds are added at the end of this distinguisher. The knowledge of the value of the vectors $\{V_i\}_{i<r_{\text{in}}}$ and $\{W_j\}_{j<r_{\text{out}}}$ will be necessary to compute the number of attacked rounds in the ID, ZC and INT contexts. The operations on these vectors correspond to those given in Sect. 3.

In that case, the vectors $V_i, W_j \in \{(0, \tilde{A}_a, A_a, val)\}^b$ where $A_i, \tilde{A}_i$ denote a difference-word or a state-word which has to be computed and 0 denote words with no difference or a state-word with value unnecessary for the attack. We use the following arithmetic similar to the one given in Table 2: $0 \oplus A_a = A_a$, $A_a \oplus A_{a'} = A_{a''}$, $F(0) = 0$ and $F(A_a) = A_{a'}$. The description of *val* is given later in this section and is only used in the ID context. As explained in Sect. 3, the notation $\tilde{A}_a$ is necessary for the type-2 and type-3 ID and ZC distinguishers, which hold when the input and output differences (masks) should be respectively strictly different or strictly equal.

In an INT attack, using the partial sum technique introduced in [25] and described in Fig. 7, the key-recovery attack could be divided in two searching paths reducing the overall time complexity. The computational time required by the second path is marginal as it usually allows to gain at least one round for free. More sophisticated attacks such as meet in the middle attacks could be mount using INT distinguishers (see for example [22]). For comparison purposes, we do not integrate those tricks in our study of the key-words involved in the attack. In all the cases, considering only the primary branch of the partial sum technique, we show that the number of involved key-words in the INT context is always lower than the number of key-words involved in the ZC context and in the ID context considering only the r_{out} direction.

Moreover, as all the INT distinguishers obtained using the matrix method are in fact higher order integral distinguishers with $b - 1$ or $b - 2$ active words in input, the computational cost to pay when trying to add one round at the beginning of this distinguisher is really high (except when some particular tricks such as the ones described in [17] could be considered which is not always the case) and to stay as generic as possible, we only consider a key-recovery attack on r_{out} rounds at the end of the INT distinguisher.

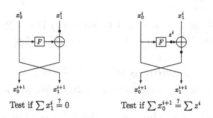

Fig. 7. On the left, the test to perform without the partial sum. On the right, the test to perform with the partial sum divides the computations into two steps.

Illustrated by the example provided in Fig. 3, when V_0 and W_0 are in dependant, the sieving and guessed key-words can be found as follows.

Lemma 4. *In the ZC context,*

- *Given the vector V_{i-1}. Let $V_A = \mathcal{P}^{-1} \cdot V_{i-1}$.*
  - *The key-word $K_i[p]$ is a sieving key-word if $V_A[2p+1] \neq 0$ and $V_A[2p] = 0$.*
  - *The key-word $K_i[p]$ is a guessed key-word if $V_A[2p+1] \neq 0$ and $V_A[2p] \neq 0$.*
  - *The vector V_i is computed as $V_i = \mathcal{F}^T \cdot V_A = \mathcal{F}^T \cdot \mathcal{P}^{-1} \cdot V_{i-1}$.*
  - *The number of active words corresponds to the weight of V_i.*
- *Given the vector W_{j-1}.*
  - *The key-word $K_j[p]$ is a sieving key-word if $W_{j-1}[2p + 1] \neq 0$ and $W_{j-1}[2p] = 0$.*

- *The key-word $K_j[p]$ is a guessed key-word if $W_{j-1}[2p+1] \neq 0$ and $W_{j-1}[2p] \neq 0$.*
- *The vector W_j is computed as $W_j = \mathcal{M} \cdot W_{j-1} = \mathcal{P} \cdot \mathcal{F}^T \cdot W_{j-1}$.*
- *The number of active words corresponds to the weight of W_j.*

Usually in the ID context the matrix method allows us to only study the propagation of the differences. However, in the partial encryption/decryption process there are cases where even if the difference is equal to 0, the knowledge of the value is necessary to complete the key-recovery. We introduce the notation *val*, to represent such a word with difference 0. The weight of a vector V corresponds to the number of non-zero differences.

Lemma 5. *In the ID context,*

- *Given the vector V_{i-1} and $V_A = \mathcal{P}^{-1} \cdot V_{i-1}$.*
  - *The key-word $K_i[p]$ is a sieving key-word if $V_A[2p] \neq 0$ and $V_A[2p+1] = 0$ or val.*
  - *The key-word $K_i[p]$ is a guessed key-word if $V_A[2p+1] \neq 0$.*
  - *In the case where $V_A[2p+1] \neq 0$ and $V_A[2p] = 0$, update $V_A[2p]$ to val.*
  - *The vector V_i is computed as $V_i = \mathcal{F} \cdot V_A$.*
  - *The number of active words corresponds to the weight of $\mathcal{F} \cdot V_A$.*
- *Given the vector W_{j-1}.*
  - *The key-word $K_j[p]$ is a sieving key-word if $W_{j-1}[2p] \neq 0$ and $W_{j-1}[2p+1] = 0$ or val.*
  - *The key-word $K_j[p]$ is a guessed key-word if $W_{j-1}[2p+1] \neq 0$.*
  - *In the case where $W_{j-1}[2p+1] \neq 0$ and $W_{j-1}[2p] = 0$, update $W_{j-1}[2p]$ to val.*
  - *The vector W_j is computed as $W_j = \mathcal{P} \cdot \mathcal{F} \cdot W_{j-1}$.*
  - *The number of active words corresponds to the weight of $\mathcal{P} \cdot \mathcal{F} \cdot W_{j-1}$.*

Proof. The proof is similar to the one in the ZC case but the reasoning is done with differentials instead of with the state-values. The difficult case corresponds to the third point. Indeed, when $V_A[2p+1] \neq 0$ and $V_A[2p] = 0$, it means that the value $V_A[2p]$ needs to be known even if the difference is 0 and thus for that purpose, we decide to use the *val* notation.

Lemma 6. *In the INT context, only the output direction on r_{out} rounds is considered. Given the distinguisher (V_0^{INT}, Y_0^{INT}) we define W_0^{INT} such that $W_0^{INT}[p] = 0$ if $Y_0^{INT}[p] = U_u$ and $W_0^{INT}[p] = A_a$ if $Y_0^{INT}[p] = A_a$ or $Y_0^{INT}[p] = \oplus_i A_i$.*

- *The key recovery is similar to the one in the ZC context, starting from the vector W_0^{INT}.*
- *The partial sum technique, can be applied from writing $W_1^{INT} = W_{1,1}^{INT} + W_{1,2}^{INT}$ and splitting the key recovery for the two vectors $W_{1,1}^{INT}$ and $W_{1,2}^{INT}$.*

5.2 Relations Between the Key-Words of the Different Attacks

From the rules expressed in the previous section, we can derive the following relations between the key-words involved in the different attacks for related and strongly related matrix-method-derived distinguishers.

Lemma 7. *For a Type-II GFN, given a matrix-method-derived ZC distinguisher and its strongly related ID distinguisher, the key-words involved in a ZC key-recovery attack is a subset of the key-words involved in an ID key-recovery attack. The number of sieving key-words is identical.*

Proof. In this proof, we define the matrix $\mathcal{Q}$ such that $\mathcal{F}^T = \mathcal{Q} \cdot \mathcal{F} \cdot \mathcal{Q}^{-1}$ (see Remark 1). According to the hypothesis made in the beginning of this section in order to have the same key-words involved in attacks on $1+1$ rounds, the vectors V_0^{ID} and V_0^{ZC} are such that $V_0^{ZC} = \mathcal{Q} \cdot V_0^{ID}$. We denote by $\tilde{V}_i^{ZC} = \mathcal{Q} \cdot V_i^{ZC}$. In this case the first part of Lemma 4 can be rewritten as:

- The key-word $K_i[p]$ is a sieving key-word if $\tilde{V}_A^{ZC}[2p] \neq 0$ and $\tilde{V}_A^{ZC}[2p+1] = 0$.
- The key-word $K_i[p]$ is a guessed key-word if $\tilde{V}_A^{ZC}[2p] \neq 0$ and $\tilde{V}_A^{ZC}[2p+1] \neq 0$.
- The vector V_i is computed as $V_i = \mathcal{F}^T \cdot V_A = \mathcal{Q} \cdot \mathcal{F} \cdot \tilde{V}_A^{ZC}$.

From the relation $V_0^{ZC} = \mathcal{Q} \cdot V_0^{ID}$ and the previous observations, we deduce that the number of sieving key-words among the key K_1^{in} is the same in both ZC and ID attacks. The same observation can be done on W_0^{ZC} and W_0^{ID}.

Note that if $V_i^{ZC} = \mathcal{Q} \cdot V_i^{ID}$ then the number of guessed key-words in the ID context is larger than in the ZC context since the rule to determine if a key is a guessed key in the ZC context are more restrictive than the one in the ID context. Remain to analyze the general relation between V_i^{ZC} and V_i^{ID}. Assume that $V_{i-1}^{ZC} = \mathcal{Q} \cdot V_{i-1}^{ID}$ (this is true for $i = 1$), meaning that $\tilde{V}_A^{ZC} = V_A^{ID}$ before update of this one. According to the third bullet of Lemma 5, after update of V_A^{ID}, we have $\tilde{V}_A^{ZC} = V_A^{ID} + V'$ where V' is a vector of b elements all equal to 0 or *val*. We conclude from the fact that operations on the matrix are additive.

Lemma 8. *For Type-II GFNs fulfilling one of the conditions given in Theorem 1 and for related ZC and ID distinguishers, the key-words involved in the encryption (resp. decryption) side of the ZC attack correspond to a subset of the key-words involved in the encryption (resp. decryption) side of the ID attack.*

Proof. The proof is similar to the one of Lemma 7 using the tools of the proof of Theorem 1.

The proof of the following results can be found in the extended version [5].

Lemma 9. *Given a ZC distinguisher and a strongly related INT distinguisher, without the partial sum technique, the key-words involved in the two attacks on r_{out} rounds added at the end of the distinguisher $\mathcal{K}_{r_{\text{out}}}^{ZC}$ and $\mathcal{K}_{r_{\text{out}}}^{INT}$ are, modulo the round index, the same. For an alternating Type-II GFN, when considering the dominant part of the partial sum PS technique, we have:* $|\mathcal{K}_{r_{\text{out}}+1}^{INT_{PS}}| = |\mathcal{K}_{r_{\text{out}}}^{INT}| + 1$.

Table 5. Data/Time trade-offs: comparison of the complexities of the ID attack of [13] and of the new ZC attack. M is the number of linear masks involved in the attack. a denotes the advantage of the attack, meaning that $\beta = 2^{-a}$.

ID on 23 rounds from [13]			ZC on 23 rounds				
Data	Time	Memory	Data	Time	Memory	a	M
2^{57}	$2^{78.58}$	2^{72}	$2^{61.90}$	$2^{76.78}$	2^{60}	5	2^8
2^{59}	$2^{75.36}$	2^{74}	$2^{62.16}$	$2^{76.47}$	2^{60}	7	2^8
2^{61}	$2^{76.48}$	2^{76}	$2^{62.61}$	$2^{75.95}$	2^{59}	7	2^7
2^{63}	$2^{78.48}$	2^{78}	$2^{63.87}$	$2^{76.51}$	$\mathbf{2^{56}}$	7	2^4
			$2^{63.87}$	$\mathbf{2^{73.94}}$	2^{60}	7	2^4

Lemma 10. *Given a ZC distinguisher, for an alternating Type-II GFN, denoting by $|\mathcal{K}_i^{ZC_{in}}|$ (resp. $|\mathcal{K}_j^{ZC_{out}}|$) the number of key-words involved in the i first rounds (resp. in the j last rounds) of the attack we have $|\mathcal{K}_{r_{out}}^{ZC_{out}}| \geq |\mathcal{K}_i^{ZC_{in}}| + |\mathcal{K}_j^{ZC_{out}}|$ with $i + j = r_{out}$. If $HW(W_0^{INT}) = HW(W_0^{ZC}) = 1$, for $r_{out} \geq 3$, we have $|\mathcal{K}_{r_{out}+1}^{INT_{PS}}| \geq |\mathcal{K}_i^{ZC}| + |\mathcal{K}_j^{ZC}|$.*

6   A ZC Attack on LBlock

In Sect. 4 we show a relation between the key-words involved in a key-recovery attack on LBlock. In this section we present a ZC attack on 23 rounds of this cipher when taking into consideration the key-schedule of this cipher.

In the INT attack of [24], 69 key-bits are involved and among them, 55 are sieving key-bits. The ZC attack of [26] requires to guess $2^{4\cdot14} = 2^{56}$ keys. Complexities of the best attacks on LBlock are resumed in Table 1.

In the analysis provided in [13], using a different ID distinguisher leads to only guess 71 key-bits in the attack on 22 rounds. A similar analysis shows that only 2 extra bits need to be guessed in the attack on 23 rounds. As done in [13] and [24] in the ID and INT context, from an analysis of the key-schedule we can derive a ZC attack on 23 rounds of LBlock.

The description of the attack is given in the extended version of this paper [5].

In Table 5, we provide the complexity for a number M of linear approximations between 2^4 and 2^8. The results show that even if the key-dependency is stronger in the ID context we can also take advantage of this key-dependency in a ZC attack to obtain an attack with a better time complexity. Due to the use of tricks to reduce the time complexity, the memory complexity of the ID attack of [13] is larger than the one of the ZC attack.

7   Conclusion

In this paper, we show how we can use the matrix method to analyse the key-recovery of Feistel-like ciphers. Based on a matrix representation of the round function we determine the key-words involved in ID, ZC or INT key-recovery attacks. In particular we illustate, that in many cases, when the matrix-method-derived distinguishers are related the number of involved key-words is smaller in the ZC and INT context than in the ID context. Nevertheless, our analysis also show that when the same number of differential and linear approximations are used, the data complexity of a ZC attack is larger than the one of a related ID attack.

While most of the results of this paper are dedicated to Type-II GFN, similar results can be obtained for other ciphers. For example, ID and ZC attacks behave similarly against the Feistel-like ciphers, HIGHT [15,31] and SIMON [29] (see Table 1) which contain modular additions, AND and rotation operations. Whereas the INT distinguisher is less efficient for HIGHT than ZC and ID distinguishers, it is more efficient, at bit level, in the case of SIMON.

Acknowledgment. The authors would like to thank the anonymous referees for their helpful comments. We also wish to thank the Aalto Science Institute (AScI) for funding the research visit of Marine Minier at Aalto University.

References

1. Berger, T.P., Minier, M., Thomas, G.: Extended generalized Feistel networks using matrix representation. In: Lange, T., Lauter, K., Lisoněk, P. (eds.) SAC 2013. LNCS, vol. 8282, pp. 289–305. Springer, Heidelberg (2014)
2. Biham, E., Biryukov, A., Shamir, A.: Cryptanalysis of Skipjack reduced to 31 rounds using impossible differentials. In: Stern, J. (ed.) EUROCRYPT 1999. LNCS, vol. 1592, p. 12. Springer, Heidelberg (1999)
3. Blondeau, C., Bogdanov, A., Wang, M.: On the (in)equivalence of impossible differential and zero-correlation distinguishers for Feistel- and Skipjack-type ciphers. In: Boureanu, I., Owesarski, P., Vaudenay, S. (eds.) ACNS 2014. LNCS, vol. 8479, pp. 271–288. Springer, Heidelberg (2014)
4. Blondeau, C., Gérard, B., Tillich, J.-P.: Accurate estimates of the data complexity and success probability for various cryptanalyses. Des. Codes Crypt. 59(1–3), 3–34 (2011)
5. Blondeau, C., Minier, M.: Relations between impossible, integral and zero-correlation key-recovery attacks (extended version). Cryptology ePrint Archive, Report 2015/141 (2015). http://eprint.iacr.org/
6. Blondeau, C., Nyberg, K.: New links between differential and linear cryptanalysis. In: Johansson, T., Nguyen, P.Q. (eds.) EUROCRYPT 2013. LNCS, vol. 7881, pp. 388–404. Springer, Heidelberg (2013)
7. Blondeau, C., Nyberg, K.: Links between truncated differential and multidimensional linear properties of block ciphers and underlying attack complexities. In: Nguyen, P.Q., Oswald, E. (eds.) EUROCRYPT 2014. LNCS, vol. 8441, pp. 165–182. Springer, Heidelberg (2014)
8. Bogdanov, A., Geng, H., Wang, M., Wen, L., Collard, B.: Zero-correlation linear cryptanalysis with FFT and improved attacks on ISO standards Camellia and CLEFIA. In: Lange, T., Lauter, K., Lisoněk, P. (eds.) SAC 2013. LNCS, vol. 8282, pp. 306–323. Springer, Heidelberg (2014)

9. Bogdanov, A., Leander, G., Nyberg, K., Wang, M.: Integral and multidimensional linear distinguishers with correlation zero. In: Wang, X., Sako, K. (eds.) ASIACRYPT 2012. LNCS, vol. 7658, pp. 244–261. Springer, Heidelberg (2012)
10. Bogdanov, A., Rijmen, V.: Zero-correlation linear cryptanalysis of block ciphers. IACR Cryptology, p. 123 (2011) ePrint Archive 2011
11. Bogdanov, A., Wang, M.: Zero correlation linear cryptanalysis with reduced data complexity. In: Canteaut, A. (ed.) FSE 2012. LNCS, vol. 7549, pp. 29–48. Springer, Heidelberg (2012)
12. Bouillaguet, C., Dunkelman, O., Fouque, P.-A., Leurent, G.: New insights on impossible differential cryptanalysis. In: Miri, A., Vaudenay, S. (eds.) SAC 2011. LNCS, vol. 7118, pp. 243–259. Springer, Heidelberg (2012)
13. Boura, C., Minier, M., Naya-Plasencia, M., Suder, V.: Improved impossible differential attacks against round-reduced LBlock. Cryptology ePrint Archive, Report 2014/279 (2014). http://eprint.iacr.org/
14. Boura, C., Naya-Plasencia, M., Suder, V.: Scrutinizing and improving impossible differential attacks: applications to CLEFIA, Camellia, LBlock and SIMON. In: Sarkar, P., Iwata, T. (eds.) ASIACRYPT 2014. LNCS, vol. 8873, pp. 179–199. Springer, Heidelberg (2014)
15. Chen, J., Wang, M., Preneel, B.: Impossible differential cryptanalysis of the lightweight block ciphers TEA, XTEA and HIGHT. In: Mitrokotsa, A., Vaudenay, S. (eds.) AFRICACRYPT 2012. LNCS, vol. 7374, pp. 117–137. Springer, Heidelberg (2012)
16. Daemen, J., Knudsen, L.R., Rijmen, V.: The block cipher SQUARE. In: Biham, E. (ed.) FSE 1997. LNCS, vol. 1267, pp. 149–165. Springer, Heidelberg (1997)
17. Ferguson, N., Kelsey, J., Lucks, S., Schneier, B., Stay, M., Wagner, D., Whiting, D.L.: Improved cryptanalysis of Rijndael. In: Schneier, B. (ed.) FSE 2000. LNCS, vol. 1978, pp. 213–230. Springer, Heidelberg (2001)
18. Karakoç, F., Demirci, H., Harmancı, A.E.: Impossible differential cryptanalysis of reduced-round LBlock. In: Askoxylakis, I., Pöhls, H.C., Posegga, J. (eds.) WISTP 2012. LNCS, vol. 7322, pp. 179–188. Springer, Heidelberg (2012)
19. Kim, J.-S., Hong, S.H., Sung, J., Lee, S.-J., Lim, J.-I., Sung, S.H.: Impossible differential cryptanalysis for block cipher structures. In: Johansson, T., Maitra, S. (eds.) INDOCRYPT 2003. LNCS, vol. 2904, pp. 82–96. Springer, Heidelberg (2003)
20. Knudsen, L.: DEAL-a 128-bit block cipher. complexity, vol. 258, no. 2 (1998)
21. Knudsen, L.R., Wagner, D.: Integral Cryptanalysis. In: Daemen, J., Rijmen, V. (eds.) FSE 2002. LNCS, vol. 2365, pp. 112–127. Springer, Heidelberg (2002)
22. Lu, J., Wei, Y., Kim, J., Pasalic, E.: The higher-order meet-in-the-middle attack and its application to the Camellia block cipher. Theor. Comput. Sci. **527**, 102–122 (2014)
23. Luo, Y., Lai, X., Wu, Z., Gong, G.: A unified method for finding impossible differentials of block cipher structures. Inf. Sci. **263**, 211–220 (2014)
24. Sasaki, Y., Wang, L.: Comprehensive study of integral analysis on 22-round LBlock. In: Kwon, T., Lee, M.-K., Kwon, D. (eds.) ICISC 2012. LNCS, vol. 7839, pp. 156–169. Springer, Heidelberg (2013)
25. Sasaki, Y., Wang, L.: Meet-in-the-middle technique for integral attacks against Feistel ciphers. In: Knudsen, L.R., Wu, H. (eds.) SAC 2012. LNCS, vol. 7707, pp. 234–251. Springer, Heidelberg (2013)
26. Soleimany, H., Nyberg, K.: Zero-correlation linear cryptanalysis of reduced-round LBlock. Des. Codes Crypt. **73**(2), 683–698 (2014)

27. Suzaki, T., Minematsu, K.: Improving the generalized Feistel. In: Hong, S., Iwata, T. (eds.) FSE 2010. LNCS, vol. 6147, pp. 19–39. Springer, Heidelberg (2010)
28. Voutier, P.M.: A new approximation to the normal distribution quantile function (2010). ArXiv e-prints, February 2010
29. Wang, Q., Liu, Z., Varici, K., Sasaki, Y., Rijmen, V., Todo, Y.: Cryptanalysis of Reduced-round SIMON32 and SIMON48. Cryptology ePrint Archive, Report 2014/761 (2014). http://eprint.iacr.org/
30. Wen, L., Wang, M., Bogdanov, A.: Multidimensional zero-correlation linear cryptanalysis of E2. In: Pointcheval, D., Vergnaud, D. (eds.) AFRICACRYPT. LNCS, vol. 8469, pp. 147–164. Springer, Heidelberg (2014)
31. Wen, L., Wang, M., Bogdanov, A., Chena, H.: Multidimensional zero-correlation attacks on lightweight block cipher HIGHT: improved cryptanalysis of an ISO standard. Inf. Process. Lett. **114**(6), 322–330 (2014)
32. Wu, W., Zhang, L.: LBlock: a lightweight block cipher. In: Lopez, J., Tsudik, G. (eds.) ACNS 2011. LNCS, vol. 6715, pp. 327–344. Springer, Heidelberg (2011)
33. Zhang, W., Su, B., Wu, W., Feng, D., Wu, C.: Extending higher-order integral: an efficient unified algorithm of constructing integral distinguishers for block ciphers. In: Bao, F., Samarati, P., Zhou, J. (eds.) ACNS 2012. LNCS, vol. 7341, pp. 117–134. Springer, Heidelberg (2012)

Implementation Issues

Simpler and More Efficient Rank Estimation for Side-Channel Security Assessment

Cezary Glowacz[1], Vincent Grosso[2], Romain Poussier[2], Joachim Schüth[1], and François-Xavier Standaert[2](✉)

[1] Security Consulting and Engineering, T-Systems GEI GmbH, Bonn, Germany
[2] ICTEAM/ELEN/Crypto Group, Université catholique de Louvain, Louvain-la-neuve, Belgium
fstandae@uclouvain.be

Abstract. Rank estimation algorithms allow analyzing the computational security of cryptographic keys for which adversaries have obtained partial information thanks to leakage or cryptanalysis. They are particularly useful in side-channel security evaluations, where the key is known by the evaluator but not reachable with exhaustive search. A first instance of such algorithms has been proposed at Eurocrypt 2013. In this paper, we propose a new tool for rank estimation that is conceptually simpler and much more efficient than this previous proposal. It allows approximating the key rank of (128-bit, 256-bit) symmetric keys with very tight bounds (i.e. with less than one bit of error), almost instantaneously and with limited memory. It also scales nicely to larger (e.g. 1024-bit) key sizes, for which the previous algorithm was hardly applicable.

1 Introduction

Despite progresses in the analysis and understanding of side-channel attacks, empirical evaluations remain an essential ingredient in the security assessment of leaking devices. The main reason for this fact is that the leakage of cryptographic implementations is highly device-specific. This implies that the actual security level provided by ad hoc countermeasures such as masking (e.g. [2,13] and related works) or shuffling (e.g. [7,19] and related works) may depend on the underlying technology on which they are running (e.g. glitches in integrated circuits are an illustration of this concern [11]). In fact, even in leakage-resilient primitives that aim to prevent/mitigate side-channel attacks by cryptographic design, the need to bound/quantify the leakages in a rigorous way is an important ingredient for connecting formal analysis with concrete security levels (e.g. [5,16]).

In this context, the usual strategy for an evaluation laboratory is to launch a set of popular attacks, and to determine whether the adversary can break the implementation (i.e. recover the key). The vast majority of these popular attacks are "divide-and-conquer" ones[1], where different pieces of a master key

---

[1] Including but not limited to Kocher et al.'s seminal Differential Power Analysis (DPA) [8], Brier et al.'s Correlation Power Analysis (CPA) [1], Chari et al.'s Template Attacks (TA) [3], Gierlichs et al.'s Mutual Information Analysis (MIA) [6] and Schindler et al.'s stochastic approach based on Linear Regression (LR) [14]. Following [10], we will use the term "standard DPAs" for those attacks.

© International Association for Cryptologic Research 2015
G. Leander (Ed.): FSE 2015, LNCS 9054, pp. 117–129, 2015.
DOI: 10.1007/978-3-662-48116-5_6

are recovered independently, and then recombined via enumeration [12,17]. But as recently observed by Veyrat-Charvillon, Gérard and Standaert at Eurocrypt 2013, such security evaluations are limited to the computational power of the evaluator [18]. This is typically a worrying situation since it sets a hard limit to the decision whether an implementation is "practically secure". For example, one could decide we have a practically secure AES implementation as soon as the number of keys to enumerate is beyond 2^{50}, but this does not provide any hint whether the concrete security level is 2^{51} or 2^{120}. The latter makes a significant difference in practice, especially in view of the possibility of improved measurement setups, signal processing, information extraction, ..., that usually has to be taken into account for any physical security evaluation, e.g. via larger security margins. As a consequence, the main contribution in [18] was to introduce a rank estimation algorithm which enables evaluators to (quite efficiently) approximate the security level of any implementation, by approximating the position of the master key in the list of 2^{128} possible ones provided by an attack (even if it is beyond enumeration power). This allowed, for the first time, to compute all the security metrics introduced in [15] and to summarize them into "security graphs" (i.e. plots of the adversary's success probability in function of the number of side-channel measurement and enumeration power).

Technically, the Eurocrypt 2013 algorithm essentially results from the time vs. memory tradeoff between depth-first and breadth-first search in a large data structure representing the key space. More precisely, since depth-first exploration of the key space is too computationally intensive, it rather exploits breadth-first search up to the memory limits of the computing device on which rank estimation is performed. This allows the algorithm to rapidly converge towards reasonably accurate bounds on the key rank. But of course, it implies that refining the bounds becomes exponentially difficult at some point, which may lead to limited accuracies in certain contexts (e.g. large key sizes, typically). Concretely, the representation of a side-channel attack's results also has a strong impact on the efficiency of the Eurocrypt 2013 rank estimation. For example in the AES case, representing a DPA outcome as 8 lists of size 2^{16} leads to more (time) efficient rank estimation than representing it as 16 lists of size 2^8. Using a (more memory consuming) representation with 5 lists of 2^{24} elements and one list of 2^8 elements typically allowed bounds with approximately 10 bits of tightness[2] within seconds of computation, and bounds with approximately 5 bits of tightness within minutes of computation, for a 128-bit key leading to a post side-channel attack security level of 80 bits. Note that the time complexity of the latter rank estimation algorithm is dependent of the estimated security level (and 80-bit was the experimental worst-case in the 128-bit example of [18]). Summarizing, the Eurocrypt 2013 algorithm provides satisfying estimations of the key rank as long as the key size is limited (to symmetric key sizes, typically) and the tightness required by the evaluators can be left to a couple of bits.

In this paper, we provide an alternative rank estimation algorithm that enjoys simplicity and (much) improved (time and memory) efficiency. The algorithm

---

[2] Measured with the log of the ratio between the upper and lower bounds.

essentially works in four steps. First, we express the DPA outcome with lists of log probabilities (each list corresponding to a piece of key). Second, we compute the histograms of these log probabilities for all the lists, with a sufficient number of equally-sized bins. Third, we recursively compute the convolution between these histograms. Eventually, we approximate the security level from the last histogram as the number of keys having larger log probabilities than the correct one (that is known by the evaluator). Bounds can additionally be obtained by tracking the quantization errors (depending on the bins' width). Besides its simplicity, this algorithm leads to bounds with less than one bit of tightness within seconds of computation (using the same computing platform as for the previous estimates). Furthermore, and contrary to the Eurocrypt 2013 algorithm, it nicely scales to larger key sizes and leads to rank estimations with good tightness for key sizes up to 1024-bit in our experiments (probably larger if needed).

We finally recall that the proposed algorithm is not limited to physical security evaluations, and is potentially useful in any cryptanalysis context where experiments are needed to validate an hypothetical attack model as well.

Related Works. In [9], Lange et al. adapt the problem of enumeration and rank estimation to the asymmetric setting, where the pieces of key are typically not independent. Ye et al. propose an alternative approach to quantify the computational security left after a side-channel attack, based on the (probabilistic) leakage models derived during such attacks [21]. It can potentially be applied without knowledge of the master key, which comes at the cost of possible biases if the models are imperfect. Eventually, the recent work in [4] describes a solution to bound the security of a leaking implementation based on (simpler to estimate) information theoretic metrics, which borrows from our following results.

2 Background

2.1 Side-Channel Cryptanalysis

Details on how divide-and-conquer side-channel attacks actually extract information about the master key are not necessary for describing the rank estimation problem. For the rest of the paper, we only need to specify the DPA outcomes as follows. Say we target an n-bit master key k and cut it into $N_p = \frac{n}{b}$ pieces of b bits, next denoted as subkeys k_i (for simplicity, we assume that b divides n). The side-channel adversary uses the leakages corresponding to a set of q inputs $\mathcal{X}_q$ leading to a set of q leakages $\mathcal{L}_q$. As a result of the attack, he obtains N_p lists of probabilities $\Pr[k_i^* | \mathcal{X}_q, \mathcal{L}_q]$, where $i \in [1 : N_p]$ and k_i^* denotes a subkey candidate among the $N_k = 2^b$ possible ones. Note that TA and LR-based attacks indeed output such probabilities directly. For other (typically non-profiled) attacks such as DPA or CPA, a Bayesian extension can be used for this purpose [17].

2.2   Rank Estimation

Concretely, each of the N_p lists of probabilities obtained by the divide-and-conquer adversary is typically small (i.e. easy to enumerate). So one can straightforwardly compute the rank of each subkey. The rank estimation problem is simply defined as the problem of estimating the master key rank based on the N_p lists $\Pr[k_i^*|\mathcal{X}_q, \mathcal{L}_q]$. Quite naturally, the problem is trivial when the attack is directly successful (i.e. when the master key is rated first). But it becomes tricky whenever this rank becomes larger. The solution in [18] was to organize the keys by sorting their subkeys according to the posterior probabilities provided by DPA, and to represent them as a high-dimensional dataspace (with N_p dimensions). The full key space can then be partitioned in two volumes: one defined by the key candidates with probability higher than the correct key, one defined by the key candidates with probability lower than the correct key. Using this geometrical representation, the rank estimation problem can be stated as the one of finding bounds for these "higher" and "lower" volumes. It essentially works by carving volumes representing key candidates on each side of their boundary, in order to progressively refine the (lower and upper) bounds on the key rank. As mentioned in introduction, this approach is efficient as long as the carved volumes are large enough, and becomes computationally intensive afterwards.

3   Simpler and More Efficient Rank Estimation

3.1   Algorithm Specification

We denote the DPA outcomes as lists of log probabilities $LP_i = \log(\Pr[k_i^*|\mathcal{X}_q, \mathcal{L}_q])$, and the histograms (with N_{bin} equally-sized bins) corresponding to these lists as $H_i = \text{hist}(LP_i, \text{bins})$, where bins is the (same) set of bins used for all histograms. We further denote the convolution between two histograms as $\text{conv}(H_i, H_j)$. From these notations, our rank estimation proposal is specified by Algorithm 1.

The algorithm exploits the property that for two multisets of numbers $\mathcal{S}_1$ and $\mathcal{S}_2$ of which the distribution is described by the histograms H_1, H_2, the distribution of the numbers in the multiset $\mathcal{S} = \mathcal{S}_1 + \mathcal{S}_2 := \{x_1 + x_2 | x_1 \in \mathcal{S}_1, x_2 \in \mathcal{S}_2\}$ can be approximated by a convolution of the histograms H_1 and H_2, *if the histograms use the same binsize*. That is if the histograms H_1 and H_2 describe the frequencies of numbers in the multisets $\mathcal{S}_1$ and $\mathcal{S}_2$, such that $H_1(x)$ gives the number of elements in $\mathcal{S}_1$ that equal x and $H_2(y)$ gives the number of elements in $\mathcal{S}_2$ that equal y, then the frequencies of numbers in the multiset $\mathcal{S}$ of all possible sums is approximated by the histogram H with $H(z) \approx \sum_{x+y=z} H_1(x) \times H_2(y) = \sum_x H_1(x) \times H_2(z-x)$. If $\mathcal{S}_1$ and $\mathcal{S}_2$ contain only integers, this is the convolution of the histograms H_1 and H_2 (considered as vectors). Similarly, if there is no quantization error (i.e. the log probabilities exactly equal the mid values of their respective bins), this property holds as well, provided that the bin widths of both histograms are equal. Thus, assuming that the quantization error are small

---

Algorithm 1. Rank estimation.

Input: The key log probability $\log(\Pr[k|\mathcal{X}_q, \mathcal{L}_q])$ and the histograms H_i.
Output: An approximation of k's rank.

initialization: $H_{\text{curr}} = H_1$;

histograms convolution:
for $i = 2 : N_p$
    $H_{\text{curr}} = \text{conv}(H_{\text{curr}}, H_i)$;
end

rank estimation:

$$\text{estimated\_rank} \approx \sum_{i=\text{bins}(\log(\Pr[k|\mathcal{X}_q, \mathcal{L}_q]))}^{N_p \cdot N_{\text{bin}} - (N_p - 1)} H_{\text{curr}}(i).$$

---

enough, the histogram of all possible sums of two log probability lists can be approximated by the convolution of the two corresponding histograms.

Note that the (log) probability of the correct key has to be known by the evaluator – as in [18]. Note also that the number of bins of the current histogram H_{curr} increases linearly with the number of convolutions executed N_p. Overall, the accuracy of the approximated rank essentially depends on the number of bins N_{bin} and number of pieces N_p, leading to the simple tightness vs. time complexity tradeoff discussed in the next sections. And the memory complexity is roughly $N_p \times N_{bin}$, which is easily managable in practice (see Sect. 4.1).

3.2 Bounding the Error

Let us assume two log probabilities $LP_1^{(j)}$ and $LP_2^{(j)}$ corresponding to the jth candidates in the lists LP_1 and LP_2. They are associated with two bins of central value $m_1^{(j)}$ and $m_2^{(j)}$ in the histograms H_1 and H_2. Whenever summing those log probabilities (as required to combine two lists of probabilities), it may happen that the central value of the bin corresponding to $LP_1^{(j)} + LP_2^{(j)}$ is different than $m_1^{(j)} + m_2^{(j)}$ (which corresponds to the approximated sum of log probabilities obtained from the convolution in Algorithm 1). This typically occurs if the distance between the log probabilities $LP_1^{(j)}, LP_2^{(j)}$ and their bins' central values $m_1^{(j)}, m_2^{(j)}$ is too large, as illustrated by the following numerical example.

Example 1. Take two lists $LP_1 = \{0, 0.02, 0.07, 0.11, 0.14, 0.16, 0.19, 0.3\}$ and $LP_2 = \{0.02, 0.02, 0.036, 0.04, 0.12, 0.19, 0.24, 0.29\}$. For $N_{\text{bin}} = 3$, it leads to a common binsize of $S_{\text{bin}} = 0.1$, and central values $\{0.05, 0.15, 0.25\}$. Hence, we obtain $H_1 = \{3, 4, 1\}$ and $H_2 = \{4, 2, 2\}$. The convolution $H_3 = \text{conv}(H_1, H_2)$ is a histogram with $N_{\text{bin}} = 5$ and central values $\{0.1, 0.2, 0.3, 0.4, 0.5\}$, given by $H_3 = \{12, 22, 18, 10, 2\}$. As a result, the sum of log probabilities $LP_1^{(7)} + LP_2^{(8)}$ equals $0.19 + 0.29 = 0.48$ and should be placed in the bin with central value 0.5.

Yet, since their corresponding central values are 0.15 and 0.25, the convolution approximates their sum within the bin of central value $0.15 + 0.25 = 0.4$.

In other words, the rank estimation accuracy is limited by quantization errors (of one bin in our example). Fortunately, we can bound the number of bins between the result of the convolution and the real sum of log probabilities as follows.

Proposition 1. *Let* $\{LP_i\}_{i=1}^{N_p}$ *be* N_p *lists of log probabilities with their* j*th elements denoted as* $LP_i^{(j)}$ *and set in the bins of central values* $m_i^{(j)}$ *of the corresponding histograms* $\{H_i\}_{i=1}^{N_p}$. *The quantization error (in bins) between* $\sum_{i=1}^{N_p} LP_i^{(j)}$ *(i.e. the actual sum of log probabilities) and* $\sum_{i=1}^{N_p} m_i^{(j)}$ *(i.e. the sum of the bins' central values corresponding to these log probabilities) is at most* $N_p/2$.

Proof. If S_{bin} is the binsize, the equation $\left| LP_i^{(j)} - m_i^{(j)} \right| \leq \dfrac{S_{\mathrm{bin}}}{2}$ holds for each $i \in [1 : N_p]$. Hence, by summing over all the pieces, we obtain:

$$-\frac{S_{\mathrm{bin}}}{2} \times N_p \leq \sum_{i=1}^{N_p} (LP_i^{(j)} - m_i^{(j)}) \leq \frac{S_{\mathrm{bin}}}{2} \times N_p.$$

Hence, we also have:

$$\left| \sum_{i=1}^{N_p} LP_i^{(j)} - \sum_{i=1}^{N_p} m_i^{(j)} \right| \leq \frac{N_p}{2} \times S_{\mathrm{bin}},$$

which limits the distance between $\sum_{i=1}^{N_p} LP_i^{(j)}$ and $\sum_{i=1}^{N_p} m_i^{(j)}$ to $\dfrac{N_p}{2}$ bins.   □

Following, we can directly bound the estimated rank in Algorithm 1 with:

$$\mathrm{rank\_lower\_bound} = \sum_{i=\mathrm{bin}(\log(\Pr[k|\mathcal{X}_q,\mathcal{L}_q]))+N_p}^{N_p \cdot N_{\mathrm{bin}} - (N_p - 1)} H_{\mathrm{curr}}(i),$$

and:

$$\mathrm{rank\_upper\_bound} = \sum_{i=\mathrm{bin}(\log(\Pr[k|\mathcal{X}_q,\mathcal{L}_q]))-N_p}^{N_p \cdot N_{\mathrm{bin}} - (N_p - 1)} H_{\mathrm{curr}}(i),$$

where the N_p (vs. $N_p/2$) value comes from the fact that the distance limit holds for each list of log probabilities independently. Hence, a triangle inequality with $\sum_{i=1}^{N_p} m_i^{(j)}$ as origin gives us an interval of size $2 \times N_p$ bins around $\sum_{i=1}^{N_p} LP_i^{(j)}$.

4   Performance Evaluation

In this section, we analyze the performance of Algorithm 1. For comparison purposes, we first use the same AES experimental setup as Veyrat-Charvillon et al. We then extend our experiments to larger key sizes. In the latter case, we only run our new algorithm as comparisons can only become more favorable in this context. Indeed, the carving phase of the proposal in [18] is quite sensitive to an increase of the number of dimensions. In order to keep their algorithm (time) efficient, the authors therefore start their rank estimation by merging some dimensions, which is quite memory intensive. Note that the functional correctness of our algorithm derives from the previous section. Yet, we tested its implementation by comparing our results with the ones obtained by enumeration for key ranks up to 2^{32}, and made sure that these results were consistent with the ones obtained using the open source code of the Eurocrypt 2013 paper.

4.1   AES-128 Case Study

As in [18], we considered simulated attacks where the adversary is provided with 16 leakage samples of the shape $l_i = \mathsf{HW}(\mathsf{S}(x_i \oplus k_i)) + n_i$ for $i \in [1 : 16]$, where HW is the Hamming weight function, S is the AES S-box, k_i and x_i are the previously defined subkeys and corresponding plaintext bytes, and n_i is a Gaussian-distributed random noise. We then performed classical TAs using the noise variance and number of plaintexts as parameters, so that the adversary computes 16 lists of 256 posterior probabilities. As in the previous paper as well, the efficiency of the rank estimation algorithms was quite independent of the type of leakage exploited: the only influencing factor in our performance evaluations was the rank of the correct key candidate. For this purpose, we started by reproducing an experiment where we launched many independent attacks, with different security levels and increasing time complexities, and plotted the resulting bounds' tightness (defined in Footnote 2). The left (resp. right) part of Fig. 1 contains the results of this experiment for the Eurocrypt 2013 algorithm[3] (resp. Algorithm 1). In both cases, they were obtained on a desktop computer with an Intel i7 core, without any parallelization effort (details on the implementation of Algorithm 1 are in Appendix B). Two clear observations can be extracted from this figure. First, the security levels leading to the most complex rank estimations differ for the two algorithms (i.e. key ranks around 2^{80} are most challenging with the Eurocrypt 2013 algorithm, enumerable key ranks are the most challenging with ours). Second and most importantly, the new bounds are much tighter (less than one bit of distance between the bounds) and obtained much faster (in less than a second). Note that the experiments with 0.05 s, 0.5 s and 5 s of computations in the right part of the figure respectively correspond to 5K, 50K and 500 K starting bins in the initial histograms. The latter case corresponds to 64 MB of memory using doubling point precision.

---

[3] Using 8 lists of size 2^{16} for illustration.

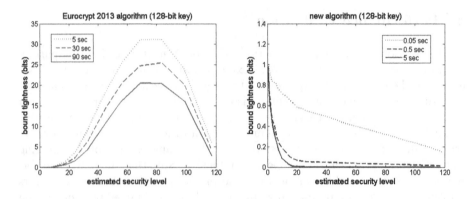

Fig. 1. Rank estimation tightness in function of the security level.

In order to make the comparison even more explicit, we additionally provide the "convergence graphs" where the upper and lower bounds on the key rank are plotted in function of the time complexity. As clear from Fig. 2, the convergence is incomparably faster with the histogram-based approach than with the Eurocrypt 2013 one. Additional results for other relevant security levels (namely ≈ 60-bit and ≈ 100-bit) are provided in Appendix, Figs. 5 and 6. For completeness, we also provide a zoom of Fig. 2 (right) and its companion where the X axis is expressed in number of starting bins in Appendix, Fig. 7.

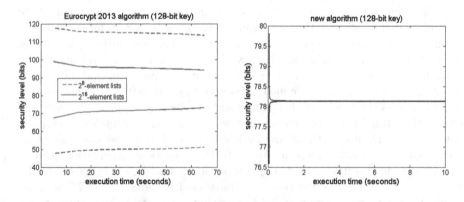

Fig. 2. Rank estimation convergence for an ≈ 80-bit security level.

4.2   Larger Key Sizes

In order to analyze situations with larger key sizes, we simply extended our AES simulated setting to more 8-bit pieces. Namely, we considered key sizes of 256, 512 and 1024 bits (i.e. $N_p = 32, 64, 128$). We omit the figure corresponding to the 256-bit case because it is extremely close to the 128-bit one, and represent the convergence graphs of the two latter cases in Fig. 3. While the application of the Eurocrypt 2013 method hardly provides useful results on this context, the figure clearly exhibits that Algorithm 1 produces tight bounds within seconds of computation, even in this challenging case. As expected, the increase of execution time in the 1024-bit example mainly corresponds to the convolutions' cost that becomes significant as the number of bins increases (in $N_{\text{bin}} \log(N_{\text{bin}})$). This trends remains observed as long as the memory requirements of Algorithm 1 can fit in RAM, which was always the case in our experiments.

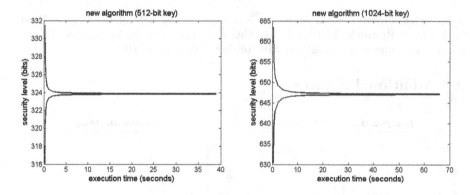

Fig. 3. Rank estimation convergence for 512- and 1024-bit keys.

Eventually, we additionally provide graphs representing the bounds' tightness in function of the security level for these 512- and 1024-bit cases in Fig. 4. They essentially confirm the observation already made in Fig. 1 that the most challenging key ranks to estimate (with our new algorithm) are the lower ones. Note that in these latter cases, the experiments with 0.1 s (resp. 0.5) and 1 (resp. 5) were performed with respectively 2 K and 20K starting bins.

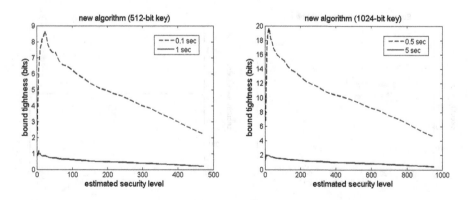

Fig. 4. Rank estimation tightness in function of the security level.

5 Conclusions

This paper provides a surprisingly simple alternative of rank estimation algorithm, that significantly outperforms the previous proposal from Eurocrypt 2013. It has natural applications in the field of side-channel cryptanalysis and is a tool of choice for evaluation laboratories willing to quantify the security level of a leaking implementation in a rigorous manner. More generally, it can also be useful in the evaluation of any cryptanalytic technique where the advantage gained is not sufficient for key recovery and not predictable by analytical means.

Acknowledgements. F.-X. Standaert is a research associate of the Belgian Fund for Scientific Research (FNRS-F.R.S.). This work has been funded in parts by the European Commission through the ERC project 280141 (CRASH).

A Additional Figures

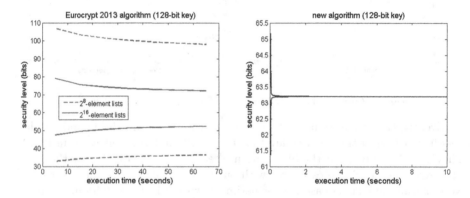

Fig. 5. Rank estimation convergence for an ≈ 60-bit security level.

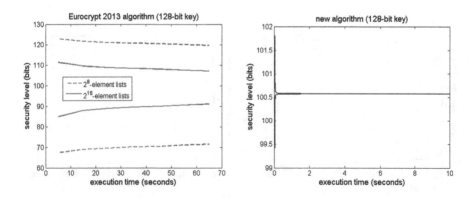

Fig. 6. Rank estimation convergence for an ≈ 100-bit security level.

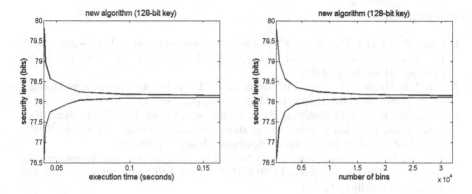

Fig. 7. Rank estimation convergence for an ≈ 80-bit security level (zoom).

B Implementation Details

One additional advantage of Algorithm 1 is that is it straightforward to implement, in particular if efficient convolution algorithms for vectors of arbitrary precision integers are available out of the box, as in a number of mathematical programming languages. Our experiments were performed with Matlab scripts, which turn out to be sufficiently efficient for all the case studies we considered. Yet, we mention that if efficient convolutions algorithms are not available out of the box, they can easily be implemented using more readily available primitives. One possible approach is to use a mixture of floating point arithmetic and representation of large numbers according to the Chinese Remainder Theorem. For example, a set of moderately sized primes, like the 20 largest primes below 10000, is chosen, and each histogram is converted into a CRT representation by using the 20 integer vectors that are obtained by modular reduction with each of the 20 chosen primes. This particular choice of primes is suitable to represent numbers of up to 265 bits (i.e. for rank estimation of 256-bit keys). In this example, when two histograms are to be convoluted, 20 regular convolutions are computed, each one modulo the corresponding prime base. To speed up the computation, each of these 20 convolutions can be performed by multiplication in Fourier space with regular double precision floating point arithmetic, i.e. two FFTs, one element-wise multiplication of two complex vectors, and one inverse FFT. Since the exact result is known to consist of integer values, computational inaccuracies can unambiguously be removed by rounding to the nearest integers. In the CRT representation, the input values are bounded by the prime bases, and this sufficiently limits the requirements on floating point precision. After rounding to integer values, modular reductions to the corresponding prime bases are performed to obtain the CRT representation of the convolution result. The result can be left in CRT representation until all histograms (i.e. the histograms for all subkeys) have been convoluted. Only a single CRT back transform to large integers is required after all the histograms have been convoluted.

References

1. Brier, E., Clavier, C., Olivier, F.: Correlation power analysis with a leakage model. In: Joye, M., Quisquater, J.-J. (eds.) CHES 2004. LNCS, vol. 3156, pp. 16–29. Springer, Heidelberg (2004)
2. Chari, S., Jutla, C.S., Rao, J.R., Rohatgi, P.: Towards sound approaches to counteract power-analysis attacks. In: Wiener [20], pp. 398–412
3. Chari, S., Rao, J.R., Rohatgi, P.: Template attacks. In: Kaliski Jr., B.S., Koç, Ç.K., Paar, C. (eds.) Cryptographic Hardware and Embedded Systems - CHES 2002. LNCS, vol. 2523, pp. 13–28. Springer, Heidelberg (2002)
4. Duc, A., Faust, S., Standaert, F.-X.: Making masking security proofs concrete. In: Oswald, E., Fischlin, M. (eds.) EUROCRYPT 2015. LNCS, vol. 9056, pp. 401–429. Springer, Heidelberg (2015)
5. Dziembowski, S., Pietrzak, K.: Leakage-resilient cryptography. In: 49th Annual IEEE Symposium on Foundations of Computer Science, FOCS 2008, 25–28 October 2008, Philadelphia, PA, USA, pp. 293–302. IEEE Computer Society (2008)
6. Gierlichs, B., Batina, L., Tuyls, P., Preneel, B.: Mutual information analysis. In: Oswald, E., Rohatgi, P. (eds.) CHES 2008. LNCS, vol. 5154, pp. 426–442. Springer, Heidelberg (2008)
7. Herbst, C., Oswald, E., Mangard, S.: An AES smart card implementation resistant to power analysis attacks. In: Zhou, J., Yung, M., Bao, F. (eds.) ACNS 2006. LNCS, vol. 3989, pp. 239–252. Springer, Heidelberg (2006)
8. Kocher, P.C., Jaffe, J., Jun, B.: Differential power analysis. In: Wiener [20], pp. 388–397
9. Lange, T., van Vredendaal, C., Wakker, M.: Kangaroos in side-channel attacks. In: Joye, M., Moradi, A. (eds.) CARDIS 2014. LNCS, vol. 8968, pp. 104–121. Springer, Heidelberg (2015)
10. Mangard, S., Oswald, E., Standaert, F.-X.: One for all - all for one: unifying standard differential power analysis attacks. IET Inf. Secur. 5(2), 100–110 (2011)
11. Mangard, S., Popp, T., Gammel, B.M.: Side-channel leakage of masked CMOS gates. In: Menezes, A. (ed.) CT-RSA 2005. LNCS, vol. 3376, pp. 351–365. Springer, Heidelberg (2005)
12. Pan, J., van Woudenberg, J.G.J., den Hartog, J.I., Witteman, M.F.: Improving DPA by peak distribution analysis. In: Biryukov, A., Gong, G., Stinson, D.R. (eds.) SAC 2010. LNCS, vol. 6544, pp. 241–261. Springer, Heidelberg (2011)
13. Rivain, M., Prouff, E.: Provably secure higher-order masking of AES. In: Mangard, S., Standaert, F.-X. (eds.) CHES 2010. LNCS, vol. 6225, pp. 413–427. Springer, Heidelberg (2010)
14. Schindler, W., Lemke, K., Paar, C.: A stochastic model for differential side channel cryptanalysis. In: Rao, J.R., Sunar, B. (eds.) CHES 2005. LNCS, vol. 3659, pp. 30–46. Springer, Heidelberg (2005)
15. Standaert, F.-X., Malkin, T.G., Yung, M.: A unified framework for the analysis of side-channel key recovery attacks. In: Joux, A. (ed.) EUROCRYPT 2009. LNCS, vol. 5479, pp. 443–461. Springer, Heidelberg (2009)
16. Standaert, F.-X., Pereira, O., Yu, Y.: Leakage-resilient symmetric cryptography under empirically verifiable assumptions. In: Canetti, R., Garay, J.A. (eds.) CRYPTO 2013, Part I. LNCS, vol. 8042, pp. 335–352. Springer, Heidelberg (2013)
17. Veyrat-Charvillon, N., Gérard, B., Renauld, M., Standaert, F.-X.: An optimal key enumeration algorithm and its application to side-channel attacks. In: Knudsen, L.R., Wu, H. (eds.) SAC 2012. LNCS, vol. 7707, pp. 390–406. Springer, Heidelberg (2013)

18. Veyrat-Charvillon, N., Gérard, B., Standaert, F.-X.: Security evaluations beyond computing power. In: Johansson, T., Nguyen, P.Q. (eds.) EUROCRYPT 2013. LNCS, vol. 7881, pp. 126–141. Springer, Heidelberg (2013)
19. Veyrat-Charvillon, N., Medwed, M., Kerckhof, S., Standaert, F.-X.: Shuffling against side-channel attacks: a comprehensive study with cautionary note. In: Wang, X., Sako, K. (eds.) ASIACRYPT 2012. LNCS, vol. 7658, pp. 740–757. Springer, Heidelberg (2012)
20. Wiener, M.J. (ed.): CRYPTO '99. LNCS, vol. 1666. Springer, Heidelberg (1999)
21. Ye, X., Eisenbarth, T., Martin, W.: Bounded, yet sufficient? How to determine whether limited side channel information enables key recovery. In: Joye, M., Moradi, A. (eds.) CARDIS 2014. LNCS, vol. 8968, pp. 215–232. Springer, Heidelberg (2015)

Conversion from Arithmetic to Boolean Masking with Logarithmic Complexity

Jean-Sébastien Coron[1]($\boxtimes$), Johann Großschädl[1], Mehdi Tibouchi[2], and Praveen Kumar Vadnala[1]

[1] University of Luxembourg, Luxembourg, Luxembourg
{jean-sebastien.coron,johann.groszschaedl,praveen.vadnala}@uni.lu
[2] NTT Secure Platform Laboratories, Tokyo, Japan
tibouchi.mehdi@lab.ntt.co.jp

Abstract. A general technique to protect a cryptographic algorithm against side-channel attacks consists in masking all intermediate variables with a random value. For cryptographic algorithms combining Boolean operations with arithmetic operations, one must then perform conversions between Boolean masking and arithmetic masking. At CHES 2001, Goubin described a very elegant algorithm for converting from Boolean masking to arithmetic masking, with only a *constant* number of operations. Goubin also described an algorithm for converting from arithmetic to Boolean masking, but with $\mathcal{O}(k)$ operations where k is the addition bit size. In this paper we describe an improved algorithm with time complexity $\mathcal{O}(\log k)$ only. Our new algorithm is based on the Kogge-Stone carry look-ahead adder, which computes the carry signal in $\mathcal{O}(\log k)$ instead of $\mathcal{O}(k)$ for the classical ripple carry adder. We also describe an algorithm for performing arithmetic addition modulo 2^k directly on Boolean shares, with the same complexity $\mathcal{O}(\log k)$ instead of $\mathcal{O}(k)$. We prove the security of our new algorithm against first-order attacks. Our algorithm performs well in practice, as for $k = 64$ we obtain a 23 % improvement compared to Goubin's algorithm.

1   Introduction

Side-Channel Attacks. Side-channel attacks belong to the genre of implementation attacks and exploit the fact thaevice performing a cryptographic algorithm leaks information related to the secret key through certain physical phenomena such as execution time, power consumption, EM radiation, etc. Depending on the source of the information leakage and the required post-processing, one can distinguish different categories of side-channel attacks, e.g. timing attacks, Simple Power Analysis (SPA) attacks, and Differential Power Analysis (DPA) attacks [KJJ99]. The former uses data-dependent (i.e. plaintext-dependent) variations in the execution time of a cryptographic algorithm to deduce information about the secret key involved in the computation of the ciphertext. In contrast, power analysis attacks require the attacker to measure the power consumption of a device while it executes a cryptographic algorithm [PMO07]. To perform an SPA

© International Association for Cryptologic Research 2015
G. Leander (Ed.): FSE 2015, LNCS 9054, pp. 130–149, 2015.
DOI: 10.1007/978-3-662-48116-5_7

attack, the attacker typically collects only one (or very few) power trace(s) and attempts to recover the secret key by focusing on differences between patterns within a trace. A DPA attack, on the other hand, requires many power traces and employs sophisticated statistical techniques to analyze differences between the traces [MOP07].

Even though DPA was first described using the DES algorithm as an example, it became soon clear that power analysis attacks can also be applied to break other secret-key algorithms, e.g. AES as well as public-key algorithms, e.g. RSA. A DPA attack normally exploits the principle of divide and conquer, which is possible since most block ciphers use the secret key only partially at a given point of time. Hence, the attacker can recover one part of the key at a time by studying the relationship between the actual power consumption and estimated power values derived from a theoretical model of the device. During the past 15 years, dozens of papers about successful DPA attacks on different implementations (hardware, software) of numerous secret-key cryptosystems (block ciphers, stream ciphers, keyed-hash message authentication codes) have been published. The experiments described in these papers confirm the real-world impact of DPA attacks in the sense that unprotected (or insufficiently protected) implementations of cryptographic algorithms can be broken in relatively short time using relatively cheap equipment.

The vast number of successful DPA attacks reported in the literature has initiated a large body of research on countermeasures. From a high-level point of view, countermeasures against DPA attacks can be divided into *hiding* (i.e. decreasing the signal-to-noise ratio) and *masking* (i.e. randomizing all the sensitive data) [MOP07]. Approaches to hiding-style countermeasures attempt to "equalize" the power consumption profile (i.e. making the power consumption invariant for all possible values of the secret key) or to randomize the power consumption so that a profile can no longer be correlated to any secret information. Masking, on the other hand, conceals every key-dependent intermediate result with a random value, the so-called mask, in order to break the dependency between the sensitive variable (*i.e.* involving the secret key) and the power consumption.

The Masking Countermeasure. Though masking is often considered to be less efficient (in terms of execution time) than hiding, it provides the key benefit that one can formally prove its security under certain assumptions on the device leakage model and the attacker's capabilities. The way masking is applied depends on the concrete operations executed by a cipher. In general, logical operations (e.g. XOR, Shift, etc.) are protected using Boolean masking, whereas additions/subtractions and multiplications require arithmetic and multiplicative masking, respectively. When a cryptographic algorithm involves a combination of these operations, it becomes necessary to convert the masks from one form to the other in order to get the correct result. Examples of algorithms that perform both arithmetic (e.g. modular addition) and logical operations include two SHA-3 finalists (namely Blake and Skein) as well as all four stream ciphers in the eSTREAM software portfolio. Also, ARX-based block ciphers (e.g. XTEA [NW97] and Threefish) and the hash functions SHA-1 and SHA-2 fall into this category. From a design point of view, modular addition gives essential non-linearity with increased throughput and hence is used in several lightweight block ciphers e.g. SPECK [BSS+13]. Therefore, techniques for conversion between Boolean and arithmetic masks are of significant practical importance.

Conversion Between Boolean and Arithmetic Masking. At CHES 2001, Goubin described a very elegant algorithm for converting from Boolean masking to arithmetic masking, with only a *constant* number of operations, independent of the addition bit size k. Goubin also described an algorithm for converting from arithmetic to Boolean masking, but with $\mathcal{O}(k)$ operations. A different arithmetic to Boolean conversion algorithm was later described in [CT03], based on pre-computed tables; an extension was described in [NP04] to reduce the memory consumption. At CHES 2012, Debraize described a modification of the table-based conversion in [CT03], correcting a bug and improving time performances, still with asymptotic complexity $\mathcal{O}(k)$.

Karroumi et al. recently noticed in [KRJ14] that Goubin's recursion formula for converting from arithmetic to Boolean masking can also be used to compute an arithmetic addition $z = x + y \bmod 2^k$ directly with masked shares $x = x_1 \oplus x_2$ and $y = y_1 \oplus y_2$. The advantage of this method is that one doesn't need to follow the three step process, i.e. converting x and y from Boolean to arithmetic masking, then performing the addition with arithmetic masks and then converting back from arithmetic to Boolean masks. The authors showed that this can lead to better performances in practice for the block cipher XTEA. However, as their algorithm is based on Goubin's recursion formula, its complexity is still $\mathcal{O}(k)$.

Conversion algorithms have recently been extended to higher-order counter-measure in [CGV14], based on Goubin's conversion method. For security against any attack of order t, their solution has time complexity $\mathcal{O}(n^2 \cdot k)$ for $n = 2t + 1$ shares.

New Algorithms with Logarithmic Complexity. In this paper we describe a new algorithm for converting from arithmetic to Boolean masking with complexity $\mathcal{O}(\log k)$ instead of $\mathcal{O}(k)$. Our algorithm is based on the Kogge-Stone carry look-ahead adder [KS73], which computes the carry signal in $\mathcal{O}(\log k)$ instead of $\mathcal{O}(k)$ for the classical ripple carry adder. Following [BN05] and [KRJ14] we also describe a variant algorithm for performing arithmetic addition modulo 2^k directly on Boolean shares, with complexity $\mathcal{O}(\log k)$ instead of $\mathcal{O}(k)$. We prove the security of our new algorithms against first-order attacks.

We also provide implementation results for our algorithms along with existing algorithms on a 32-bit microcontroller. Our results show that the new algorithms perform better than Goubin's algorithm for $k \geq 32$, as we obtain 14 % improvement in execution time for $k = 32$, and 23 % improvement for $k = 64$. We also describe our results for first-order secure implementations of HMAC-SHA-1 ($k = 32$) and of the SPECK block-cipher ($k = 64$).

2   Goubin's Algorithms

In this section we first recall Goubin's algorithm for converting from Boolean masking to arithmetic masking and conversely [Gou01], secure against first-order attacks. Given a k-bit variable x, for Boolean masking we write:

$$x = x' \oplus r$$

where x' is the masked variable and $r \leftarrow \{0,1\}^k$. Similarly for arithmetic masking we write

$$x = A + r \bmod 2^k$$

In the following all additions and subtractions are done modulo 2^k, for some parameter k.

The goal of the paper is to describe efficient conversion algorithms between Boolean and arithmetic masking, secure against first-order attacks. Given x' and r, one should compute the arithmetic mask $A = (x' \oplus r) - r \bmod 2^k$ without leaking information about $x = x' \oplus r$; this implies that one cannot compute $A = (x' \oplus r) - r \bmod 2^k$ directly, as this would leak information about the sensitive variable $x = x' \oplus r$; instead all intermediate variables should be properly randomized so that no information is leaked about x. Similarly given A and r one must compute the Boolean mask $x' = (A + r) \oplus r$ without leaking information about $x = A + r$.

2.1   Boolean to Arithmetic Conversion

We first recall the Boolean to arithmetic conversion algorithm from Goubin [Gou01]. One considers the following function $\Psi_{x'}(r) : \mathbb{F}_{2^k} \to \mathbb{F}_{2^k}$:

$$\Psi_{x'}(r) = (x' \oplus r) - r$$

Theorem 1 (Goubin [Gou01]). *The function $\Psi_{x'}(r) = (x' \oplus r) - r$ is affine over $\mathbb{F}_2$.*

Using this affine property, the conversion from Boolean to arithmetic masking is straightforward. Given $x', r \in \mathbb{F}_{2^k}$ we must compute A such that $x' \oplus r = A + r$. From the affine property of $\Psi_{x'}(r)$ we can write:

$$A = (x' \oplus r) - r = \Psi_{x'}(r) = \Psi_{x'}(r \oplus r_2) \oplus \big(\Psi_{x'}(r_2) \oplus \Psi_{x'}(0)\big)$$

for any $r_2 \in \mathbb{F}_{2^k}$. Therefore the technique consists in first generating a uniformly distributed random r_2 in $\mathbb{F}_{2^k}$, then computing $\Psi_{x'}(r \oplus r_2)$ and $\Psi_{x'}(r_2) \oplus \Psi_{x'}(0)$ separately, and finally performing XOR operation on these two to get A. The technique is clearly secure against first-order attacks; namely the left term $\Psi_{x'}(r \oplus r_2)$ is independent from r and therefore from $x = x' \oplus r$, and the right term $\Psi_{x'}(r_2) \oplus \Psi_{x'}(0)$ is also independent from r and therefore from x. Note that the technique is very efficient as it requires only a constant number of operations (independent of k).

2.2   From Arithmetic to Boolean Masking

Goubin also described in [Gou01] a technique for converting from arithmetic to Boolean masking, secure against first-order attacks. However it is more complex than from Boolean to arithmetic masking; its complexity is $\mathcal{O}(k)$ for additions modulo 2^k. It is based on the following theorem.

Theorem 2 (Goubin [Gou01]). *If we denote* $x' = (A + r) \oplus r$, *we also have* $x' = A \oplus u_{k-1}$, *where* u_{k-1} *is obtained from the following recursion formula:*

$$\begin{cases} u_0 = 0 \\ \forall k \geq 0, u_{k+1} = 2[u_k \wedge (A \oplus r) \oplus (A \wedge r)] \end{cases} \quad (1)$$

Since the iterative computation of u_i contains only XOR and AND operations, it can easily be protected against first-order attacks. We refer to Appendix A for the full conversion algorithm.

3   A New Recursive Formula Based on Kogge-Stone Adder

Our new conversion algorithm is based on the Kogge-Stone adder [KS73], a carry look-ahead adder that generates the carry signal in $\mathcal{O}(\log k)$ time, when addition is performed modulo 2^k. In this section we first recall the classical ripple-carry adder, which generates the carry signal in $\mathcal{O}(k)$ time, and we show how Goubin's recursion formula (1) can be derived from it. The derivation of our new recursion formula from the Kogge-Stone adder will proceed similarly.

3.1   The Ripple-Carry Adder and Goubin's Recursion Formula

We first recall the classical ripple-carry adder. Given three bits x, y and c, the carry c' for $x + y + c$ can be computed as $c' = (x \wedge y) \oplus (x \wedge c) \oplus (y \wedge c)$. Therefore, the modular addition of two k-bit variables x and y can be defined recursively as follows:

$$(x + y)^{(i)} = x^{(i)} \oplus y^{(i)} \oplus c^{(i)} \quad (2)$$

for $0 \leq i < k$, where

$$\begin{cases} c^{(0)} = 0 \\ \forall i \geq 1, c^{(i)} = (x^{(i-1)} \wedge y^{(i-1)}) \oplus (x^{(i-1)} \wedge c^{(i-1)}) \oplus (c^{(i-1)} \wedge y^{(i-1)}) \end{cases} \quad (3)$$

where $x^{(i)}$ represents the ith bit of the variable x, with $x^{(0)}$ being the least significant bit.

In the following, we show how recursion (3) can be computed directly with k-bit values instead of bits, which enables us to recover Goubin's recursion (1). For this, we define the sequences x_j, y_j and v_j whose $j + 1$ least significant bits are the same as x, y and c respectively:

$$x_j = \bigoplus_{i=0}^{j} 2^i x^{(i)}, \quad y_j = \bigoplus_{i=0}^{j} 2^i y^{(i)}, \quad v_j = \bigoplus_{i=0}^{j} 2^i c^{(i)} \quad (4)$$

for $0 \leq j \leq k - 1$. Since $c^{(0)} = 0$ we can actually start the summation for v_j at $i = 1$; we get from (3):

$$v_{j+1} = \bigoplus_{i=1}^{j+1} 2^i c^{(i)}$$

$$v_{j+1} = \bigoplus_{i=1}^{j+1} 2^i \left((x^{(i-1)} \wedge y^{(i-1)}) \oplus (x^{(i-1)} \wedge c^{(i-1)}) \oplus (c^{(i-1)} \wedge y^{(i-1)}) \right)$$

$$v_{j+1} = 2 \bigoplus_{i=0}^{j} 2^i \left((x^{(i)} \wedge y^{(i)}) \oplus (x^{(i)} \wedge c^{(i)}) \oplus (c^{(i)} \wedge y^{(i)}) \right)$$

$$v_{j+1} = 2((x_j \wedge y_j) \oplus (x_j \wedge v_j) \oplus (y_j \wedge v_j))$$

which gives the recursive equation:

$$
\begin{cases}
v_0 = 0 \\
\forall j \geq 0, \ v_{j+1} = 2 \left(v_j \wedge (x_j \oplus y_j) \oplus (x_j \wedge y_j) \right)
\end{cases}
\tag{5}
$$

Therefore we have obtained a recursion similar to (3), but with k-bit values instead of single bits. Note that from the definition of v_j in (4) the variables v_j and v_{j+1} have the same least significant bits from bit 0 to bit j, which is not immediately obvious when considering only recursion (5). Combining (2) and (4) we obtain $x_j + y_j = x_j \oplus y_j \oplus v_j$ for all $0 \leq j \leq k - 1$. For k-bit values x and y, we have $x = x_{k-1}$ and $y = y_{k-1}$, which gives:

$$x + y = x \oplus y \oplus v_{k-1}$$

We now define the same recursion as (5), but with constant x, y instead of x_j, y_j. That is, we let

$$
\begin{cases}
u_0 = 0 \\
\forall j \geq 0, \ u_{j+1} = 2 \left(u_j \wedge (x \oplus y) \oplus (x \wedge y) \right)
\end{cases}
\tag{6}
$$

which is exactly the same recursion as Goubin's recursion (1). It is easy to show inductively that the variables u_j and v_j have the same least significant bits, from bit 0 to bit j. Let us assume that this is true for u_j and v_j. From recursions (5) and (6) we have that the least significant bits of v_{j+1} and u_{j+1} from bit 0 to bit $j + 1$ only depend on the least significant bits from bit 0 to bit j of v_j, x_j and y_j, and of u_j, x and y respectively. Since these are the same, the induction is proved.

Eventually for k-bit registers we have $u_{k-1} = v_{k-1}$, which proves Goubin's recursion formula (1), namely:

$$x + y = x \oplus y \oplus u_{k-1}$$

As mentioned previously, this recursion formula requires $k - 1$ iterations on k-bit registers. In the following, we describe an improved recursion based on the Kogge-Stone carry look-ahead adder, requiring only $\log_2 k$ iterations.

3.2   The Kogge-Stone Carry Look-Ahead Adder

In this section we first recall the general solution from [KS73] for first-order recurrence equations; the Kogge-Stone carry look-ahead adder is a direct application.

General First-Order Recurrence Equation. We consider the following recurrence equation:

$$\begin{cases} z_0 = b_0 \\ \forall i \geq 1, \ z_i = a_i z_{i-1} + b_i \end{cases} \tag{7}$$

We define the function $Q(m, n)$ for $m \geq n$:

$$Q(m, n) = \sum_{j=n}^{m} \left(\prod_{i=j+1}^{m} a_i \right) b_j \tag{8}$$

We have $Q(0,0) = b_0 = z_0$, $Q(1,0) = a_1 b_0 + b_1 = z_1$, and more generally:

$$Q(m, 0) = \sum_{j=0}^{m-1} \left(\prod_{i=j+1}^{m} a_i \right) b_j + b_m$$

$$= a_m \sum_{j=0}^{m-1} \left(\prod_{i=j+1}^{m-1} a_i \right) b_j + b_m = a_m Q(m-1, 0) + b_m$$

Therefore the sequence $Q(m, 0)$ satisfies the same recurrence as z_m, which implies $Q(m, 0) = z_m$ for all $m \geq 0$. Moreover we have:

$$Q(2m-1, 0) = \sum_{j=0}^{2m-1} \left(\prod_{i=j+1}^{2m-1} a_i \right) b_j$$

$$= \left(\prod_{j=m}^{2m-1} a_j \right) \sum_{j=0}^{m-1} \left(\prod_{i=j+1}^{m-1} a_i \right) b_j + \sum_{j=m}^{2m-1} \left(\prod_{i=j+1}^{2m-1} a_i \right) b_j$$

which gives the recursive doubling equation:

$$Q(2m-1, 0) = \left(\prod_{j=m}^{2m-1} a_j \right) Q(m-1, 0) + Q(2m-1, m)$$

where each term $Q(m-1, 0)$ and $Q(2m-1, m)$ contain only m terms a_i and b_i, instead of $2m$ in $Q(2m-1, 0)$. Therefore the two terms can be computed in parallel. This is also the case for the product $\prod_{j=m}^{2m-1} a_j$ which can be computed with a product tree. Therefore by recursive splitting with N processors, the sequence element z_N can be computed in time $\mathcal{O}(\log_2 N)$, instead of $\mathcal{O}(N)$ with a single processor.

The Kogge-Stone Carry Look-Ahead Adder. The Kogge-Stone carry look-ahead adder [KS73] is a direct application of the previous technique. Namely writing $c_i = c^{(i)}$, $a_i = x^{(i)} \oplus y^{(i)}$ and $b_i = x^{(i)} \wedge y^{(i)}$ for all $i \geq 0$, we obtain from (3) the recurrence relation for the carry signal c_i:

$$\begin{cases} c_0 = 0 \\ \forall i \geq 1, \ c_i = (a_{i-1} \wedge c_{i-1}) \oplus b_{i-1} \end{cases}$$

which is similar to (7), where $\wedge$ is the multiplication and $\oplus$ the addition. We can therefore compute the carry signal c_i for $0 \leq i < k$ in time $\mathcal{O}(\log k)$ instead of $\mathcal{O}(k)$.

More precisely, the Kogge-Stone carry look-ahead adder can be defined as follows. For all $0 \leq j < k$ one defines the sequence of bits:

$$P_{0,j} = x^{(j)} \oplus y^{(j)}, \quad G_{0,j} = x^{(j)} \wedge y^{(j)} \tag{9}$$

and the following recursive equations:

$$\begin{cases} P_{i,j} = P_{i-1,j} \wedge P_{i-1,j-2^{i-1}} \\ [.1cm]G_{i,j} = (P_{i-1,j} \wedge G_{i-1,j-2^{i-1}}) \oplus G_{i-1,j} \end{cases} \tag{10}$$

for $2^{i-1} \leq j < k$, and $P_{i,j} = P_{i-1,j}$ and $G_{i,j} = G_{i-1,j}$ for $0 \leq j < 2^{i-1}$. The following lemma shows that the carry signal c_j can be computed from the sequence $G_{i,j}$.

Lemma 1. *We have $(x+y)^{(j)} = x^{(j)} \oplus y^{(j)} \oplus c_j$ for all $0 \leq j < k$ where the carry signal c_j is computed as $c_0 = 0$, $c_1 = G_{0,0}$ and $c_{j+1} = G_{i,j}$ for $2^{i-1} \leq j < 2^i$.*

To compute the carry signal up to c_{k-1}, one must therefore compute the sequences $P_{i,j}$ and $G_{i,j}$ up to $i = \lceil \log_2(k-1) \rceil$. For completeness we provide the proof of Lemma 1 in Appendix B.

3.3   Our New Recursive Algorithm

We now derive a recursion formula with k-bit variables instead of single bits; we proceed as in Sect. 3.1, using the more efficient Kogge-Stone carry look-ahead algorithm, instead of the classical ripple-carry adder for Goubin's recursion. We prove the following theorem, analogous to Theorem 2, but with complexity $\mathcal{O}(\log k)$ instead of $\mathcal{O}(k)$. Given a variable x, we denote by $x \ll \ell$ the variable x left-shifted by ℓ bits, keeping only k bits in total.

Theorem 3. *Let $x, y \in \{0,1\}^k$ and $n = \lceil \log_2(k-1) \rceil$. Define the sequence of k-bit variables P_i and G_i, with $P_0 = x \oplus y$ and $G_0 = x \wedge y$, and*

$$\begin{cases} P_i = P_{i-1} \wedge (P_{i-1} \ll 2^{i-1}) \\ G_i = (P_{i-1} \wedge (G_{i-1} \ll 2^{i-1})) \oplus G_{i-1} \end{cases} \tag{11}$$

for $1 \leq i \leq n$. Then $x + y = x \oplus y \oplus (2G_n)$.

Proof. We start from the sequences $P_{i,j}$ and $G_{i,j}$ defined in Sect. 3.2 corresponding to the Kogge-Stone carry look-ahead adder, and we proceed as in Sect. 3.1. We define the variables:

$$P_i := \sum_{j=2^i-1}^{k-1} 2^j P_{i,j} \quad G_i := \sum_{j=0}^{k-1} 2^j G_{i,j}$$

which from (9) gives the initial condition $P_0 = x \oplus y$ and $G_0 = x \wedge y$, and using (10):

$$P_i = \sum_{j=2^i-1}^{k-1} 2^j P_{i,j} = \sum_{j=2^i-1}^{k-1} 2^j (P_{i-1,j} \wedge P_{i-1,j-2^{i-1}})$$

$$= \left(\sum_{j=2^i-1}^{k-1} 2^j P_{i-1,j} \right) \wedge \left(\sum_{j=2^i-1}^{k-1} 2^j P_{i-1,j-2^{i-1}} \right)$$

We can start the summation of the $P_{i,j}$ bits with $j = 2^{i-1} - 1$ instead of $2^i - 1$, because the other summation still starts with $j = 2^i - 1$, hence the corresponding bits are ANDed with 0. This gives:

$$P_i = \left(\sum_{j=2^{i-1}-1}^{k-1} 2^j P_{i-1,j} \right) \wedge \left(\sum_{j=2^i-1}^{k-1} 2^j P_{i-1,j-2^{i-1}} \right)$$

$$= P_{i-1} \wedge \left(\sum_{j=2^{i-1}-1}^{k-1-2^{i-1}} 2^{j+2^{i-1}} P_{i-1,j} \right) = P_{i-1} \wedge (P_{i-1} \ll 2^{i-1})$$

Hence we get the same recursion formula for P_i as in (11). Similarly we have using (10):

$$G_i = \sum_{j=0}^{k-1} 2^j G_{i,j} = \sum_{j=2^i-1}^{k-1} 2^j \left((P_{i-1,j} \wedge G_{i-1,j-2^{i-1}}) \oplus G_{i-1,j} \right) + \sum_{j=0}^{2^{i-1}-1} 2^j G_{i-1,j}$$

$$= \left(\sum_{j=2^i-1}^{k-1} 2^j \left(P_{i-1,j} \wedge G_{i-1,j-2^{i-1}} \right) \right) \oplus G_{i-1}$$

$$= \left(P_{i-1} \wedge (G_{i-1} \ll 2^{i-1}) \right) \oplus G_{i-1}$$

Therefore we obtain the same recurrence for P_i and G_i as (11). Since from Lemma 1 we have that $c_{j+1} = G_{i,j}$ for all $2^{i-1} \leq j < 2^i$, and $G_{i,j} = G_{i-1,j}$ for $0 \leq j < 2^{i-1}$, we obtain $c_{j+1} = G_{i,j}$ for all $0 \leq j < 2^i$. Taking $i = n = \lceil \log_2(k-1) \rceil$, we obtain $c_{j+1} = G_{n,j}$ for all $0 \leq j \leq k - 2 < k - 1 \leq 2^n$. This implies:

$$\sum_{j=0}^{k-1} 2^j c_j = \sum_{j=1}^{k-1} 2^j c_j = 2 \sum_{j=0}^{k-2} 2^j c_{j+1} = 2 \sum_{j=0}^{k-2} 2^j G_{n,j} = 2 G_n$$

Since from Lemma 1 we have $(x + y)^{(j)} = x^{(j)} \oplus y^{(j)} \oplus c_j$ for all $0 \leq j < k$, this implies $x + y = x \oplus y \oplus (2G_n)$ as required. $\square$

The complexity of the previous recursion is only $\mathcal{O}(\log k)$, as opposed to $\mathcal{O}(k)$ with Goubin's recursion. The sequence can be computed using the algorithm below; note that we do not compute the last element P_n since it is not used in the computation of G_n. Note also that the algorithm below could be used as a $\mathcal{O}(\log k)$ implementation of arithmetic addition $z = x + y \bmod 2^k$ for processors having only Boolean operations.

Algorithm 1. Kogge-Stone Adder

Require: $x, y \in \{0, 1\}^k$, and $n = \max(\lceil \log_2(k - 1) \rceil, 1)$.
Ensure: $z = x + y \bmod 2^k$
1: $P \leftarrow x \oplus y$
2: $G \leftarrow x \wedge y$
3: **for** $i := 1$ to $n - 1$ **do**
4:     $G \leftarrow (P \wedge (G \ll 2^{i-1})) \oplus G$
5:     $P \leftarrow P \wedge (P \ll 2^{i-1})$
6: **end for**
7: $G \leftarrow (P \wedge (G \ll 2^{n-1})) \oplus G$
8: **return** $x \oplus y \oplus (2G)$

---

4   Our New Conversion Algorithm

Our new conversion algorithm from arithmetic to Boolean masking is a direct application of the Kogge-Stone adder in Algorithm 1. We are given as input two arithmetic shares A, r of $x = A + r \bmod 2^k$, and we must compute x' such that $x = x' \oplus r$, without leaking information about x.

Since Algorithm 1 only contains Boolean operations, it is easy to protect against first-order attacks. Assume that we give as input the two arithmetic shares A and r to Algorithm 1; the algorithm first computes $P = A \oplus r$ and $G = A \wedge r$, and after n iterations outputs $x = A + r = A \oplus r \oplus (2G)$. Obviously one cannot compute $P = A \oplus r$ and $G = A \wedge r$ directly since that would reveal information about the sensitive variable $x = A + r$. Instead we protect all intermediate variables with a random mask s using standard techniques, that is we only work with $P' = P \oplus s$ and $G' = G \oplus s$. Eventually we obtain a masked $x' = x \oplus s$ as required, in time $\mathcal{O}(\log k)$ instead of $\mathcal{O}(k)$.

4.1   Secure Computation of AND

Since Algorithm 1 contains AND operations, we first show how to secure the AND operation against first-order attacks. The technique is essentially the same as in [ISW03]. With $x = x' \oplus s$ and $y = y' \oplus t$ for two independent random masks s and t, we have for any u:

$$(x \wedge y) \oplus u = ((x' \oplus s) \wedge (y' \oplus t)) \oplus u = (x' \wedge y') \oplus (x' \wedge t) \oplus (s \wedge y') \oplus (s \wedge t) \oplus u$$

Algorithm 2. SecAnd

Require: x', y', s, t, u such that $x' = x \oplus s$ and $y' = y \oplus t$.
Ensure: z' such that $z' = (x \wedge y) \oplus u$.
1: $z' \leftarrow u \oplus (x' \wedge y')$
2: $z' \leftarrow z' \oplus (x' \wedge t)$
3: $z' \leftarrow z' \oplus (s \wedge y')$
4: $z' \leftarrow z' \oplus (s \wedge t)$
5: **return** z'

We see that the SecAnd algorithm requires 8 Boolean operations. The following Lemma shows that the SecAnd algorithm is secure against first-order attacks.

Lemma 2. *When s, t and u are uniformly and independently distributed in $\mathbb{F}_{2^k}$, all intermediate variables in the SecAnd algorithm have a distribution independent from x and y.*

Proof. Since s and t are uniformly and independently distributed in $\mathbb{F}_{2^k}$, the variables $x' = x \oplus s$ and $y' = y \oplus t$ are also uniformly and independently distributed in $\mathbb{F}_{2^k}$. Therefore the distribution of $x' \wedge y'$ is independent from x and y. The same holds for the variables $x' \wedge t$, $s \wedge y'$ and $s \wedge t$. Moreover since u is uniformly distributed in $\mathbb{F}_{2^k}$, the distribution of z' from Line 1 to Line 4 is uniform in $\mathbb{F}_{2^k}$; hence its distribution is also independent from x and y.   □

4.2   Secure Computation of XOR

Similarly we show how to secure the XOR computation of Algorithm 1. With $x = x' \oplus s$ and $y = y' \oplus u$ where s and u are two independent masks, we have:

$$(x \oplus y) \oplus s = x' \oplus s \oplus y' \oplus u \oplus s = x' \oplus y' \oplus u$$

Algorithm 3. SecXor

Require: x', y', u, such that $x' = x \oplus s$, and $y' = y \oplus u$.
Ensure: z' such that $z' = (x \oplus y) \oplus s$.
1: $z' \leftarrow x' \oplus y'$
2: $z' \leftarrow z' \oplus u$
3: **return** z'

We see that the SecXor algorithm requires 2 Boolean operations. The following Lemma shows that the SecXor algorithm is secure against first-order attacks. It is easy to see that all the intermediate variables in the algorithm are uniformly distributed in $\mathbb{F}_{2^k}$, and hence the proof is straightforward.

Lemma 3. *When s and u are uniformly and independently distributed in $\mathbb{F}_{2^k}$, all intermediate variables in the SecXor algorithm have a distribution independent from x and y.*

4.3   Secure Computation of Shift

Finally we show how to secure the Shift operation in Algorithm 1 against first-order attacks. With $x = x' \oplus s$, we have for any t:

$$(x \ll j) \oplus t = ((x' \oplus s) \ll j) \oplus t = (x' \ll j) \oplus (s \ll j) \oplus t$$

This gives the following algorithm.

Algorithm 4. SecShift

Require: x', s, t and j such that $x' = x \oplus s$ and $j > 0$.
Ensure: y' such that $y' = (x \ll j) \oplus t$.
1: $y' \leftarrow t \oplus (x' \ll j)$
2: $y' \leftarrow y' \oplus (s \ll j)$
3: **return** y'

We see that the SecShift algorithm requires 4 Boolean operations. The following Lemma shows that the SecShift algorithm is secure against first-order attacks. The proof is straightforward so we omit it.

Lemma 4. *When s and t are uniformly and independently distributed in $\mathbb{F}_{2^k}$, all intermediate variables in the SecShift algorithm have a distribution independent from x.*

4.4   Our New Conversion Algorithm

Finally we can convert Algorithm 1 into a first-order secure algorithm by protecting all intermediate variables with a random mask; see Algorithm 5 below.

Since the SecAnd subroutine requires 8 operations, the SecXor subroutine requires 2 operations, and the SecShift subroutine requires 4 operations, lines 7 to 11 require $2 \cdot 8 + 2 \cdot 4 + 2 + 2 = 28$ operations, hence $28 \cdot (n-1)$ operations for the main loop. The total number of operations is then $7 + 28 \cdot (n-1) + 4 + 8 + 2 + 4 = 28 \cdot n - 3$. In summary, for a register size $k = 2^n$ the number of operations is $28 \cdot \log_2 k - 3$, in addition to the generation of 3 random numbers. Note that the same random numbers s, t and u can actually be used for all executions of the conversion algorithm in a given execution. The following Lemma proves the security of our new conversion algorithm against first-order attacks.

Lemma 5. *When r is uniformly distributed in $\mathbb{F}_{2^k}$, any intermediate variable in Algorithm 5 has a distribution independent from $x = A + r \mod 2^k$.*

Proof. The proof is based on the previous lemma for SecAnd, SecXor and SecShift, and also the fact that all intermediate variables from Line 2 to 5 and in lines 12, 13, 18, and 19 have a distribution independent from x. Namely $(A \oplus t) \wedge r$ and $t \wedge r$ have a distribution independent from x, and the other intermediate variables have the uniform distribution. $\square$

Algorithm 5. Kogge-Stone Arithmetic to Boolean Conversion

Require: $A, r \in \{0,1\}^k$ and $n = \max(\lceil \log_2(k-1) \rceil, 1)$
Ensure: x' such that $x' \oplus r = A + r \bmod 2^k$.

1: Let $s \leftarrow \{0,1\}^k$, $t \leftarrow \{0,1\}^k$, $u \leftarrow \{0,1\}^k$.
2: $P' \leftarrow A \oplus s$
3: $P' \leftarrow P' \oplus r$ $\triangleright P' = (A \oplus r) \oplus s = P \oplus s$
4: $G' \leftarrow s \oplus ((A \oplus t) \wedge r)$
5: $G' \leftarrow G' \oplus (t \wedge r)$ $\triangleright G' = (A \wedge r) \oplus s = G \oplus s$
6: **for** $i := 1$ to $n-1$ **do**
7:     $H \leftarrow \mathsf{SecShift}(G', s, t, 2^{i-1})$ $\triangleright H = (G \ll 2^{i-1}) \oplus t$
8:     $U \leftarrow \mathsf{SecAnd}(P', H, s, t, u)$ $\triangleright U = (P \wedge (G \ll 2^{i-1})) \oplus u$
9:     $G' \leftarrow \mathsf{SecXor}(G', U, u)$ $\triangleright G' = ((P \wedge (G \ll 2^{i-1})) \oplus G) \oplus s$
10:    $H \leftarrow \mathsf{SecShift}(P', s, t, 2^{i-1})$ $\triangleright H = (P \ll 2^{i-1}) \oplus t$
11:    $P' \leftarrow \mathsf{SecAnd}(P', H, s, t, u)$ $\triangleright P' = (P \wedge (P \ll 2^{i-1})) \oplus u$
12:    $P' \leftarrow P' \oplus s$
13:    $P' \leftarrow P' \oplus u$ $\triangleright P' = (P \wedge (P \ll 2^{i-1})) \oplus s$
14: **end for**
15: $H \leftarrow \mathsf{SecShift}(G', s, t, 2^{n-1})$ $\triangleright H = (G \ll 2^{n-1}) \oplus t$
16: $U \leftarrow \mathsf{SecAnd}(P', H, s, t, u)$ $\triangleright U = (P \wedge (G \ll 2^{n-1})) \oplus u$
17: $G' \leftarrow \mathsf{SecXor}(G', U, u)$ $\triangleright G' = ((P \wedge (G \ll 2^{n-1})) \oplus G) \oplus s$
18: $x' \leftarrow A \oplus 2G'$ $\triangleright x' = (A + r) \oplus r \oplus 2s$
19: $x' \leftarrow x' \oplus 2s$ $\triangleright x' = (A + r) \oplus r$
20: **return** x'

---

5   Addition Without Conversion

Beak and Noh proposed a method to mask the ripple carry adder in [BN05]. Similarly, Karroumi et al. [KRJ14] used Goubin's recursion formula (1) to compute an arithmetic addition $z = x + y \bmod 2^k$ directly with masked shares $x' = x \oplus s$ and $y' = y \oplus r$, that is without first converting x and y from Boolean to arithmetic masking, then performing the addition with arithmetic masks, and then converting back from arithmetic to Boolean masks. They showed that this can lead to better performances in practice for the block cipher XTEA.

In this section we describe an analogous algorithm for performing addition directly on the masked shares, based on the Kogge-Stone adder instead of Goubin's formula, to get $\mathcal{O}(\log k)$ complexity instead of $\mathcal{O}(k)$. More precisely, we receive as input the shares x', y' such that $x' = x \oplus s$ and $y' = y \oplus r$, and the goal is to compute z' such that $z' = (x + y) \oplus r$. For this it suffices to perform the addition $z = x + y \bmod 2^k$ as in Algorithm 1, but with the masked variables $x' = x \oplus s$ and $y' = y \oplus r$ instead of x, y, while protecting all intermediate variables with a Boolean mask; this is straightforward since Algorithm 1 contains only Boolean operations; see Algorithm 6 below.

Algorithm 6. Kogge-Stone Masked Addition

Require: $x', y', r, s \in \{0,1\}^k$ and $n = \max(\lceil \log_2(k-1) \rceil, 1)$.
Ensure: z' such that $z' = (x+y) \oplus r$, where $x = x' \oplus s$ and $y = y' \oplus r$
 1: Let $t \leftarrow \{0,1\}^k$, $u \leftarrow \{0,1\}^k$.
 2: $P' \leftarrow \mathsf{SecXor}(x', y', r)$ $\triangleright P' = (x \oplus y) \oplus s = P \oplus s$
 3: $G' \leftarrow \mathsf{SecAnd}(x', y', s, r, u)$ $\triangleright G' = (x \wedge y) \oplus u = G \oplus u$
 4: $G' \leftarrow G' \oplus s$
 5: $G' \leftarrow G' \oplus u$ $\triangleright G' = (x \wedge y) \oplus s = G \oplus s$
 6: **for** $i := 1$ to $n-1$ **do**
 7:   $H \leftarrow \mathsf{SecShift}(G', s, t, 2^{i-1})$ $\triangleright H = (G \ll 2^{i-1}) \oplus t$
 8:   $U \leftarrow \mathsf{SecAnd}(P', H, s, t, u)$ $\triangleright U = \left(P \wedge (G \ll 2^{i-1})\right) \oplus u$
 9:   $G' \leftarrow \mathsf{SecXor}(G', U, u)$ $\triangleright G' = \left((P \wedge (G \ll 2^{i-1})) \oplus G\right) \oplus s$
10:   $H \leftarrow \mathsf{SecShift}(P', s, t, 2^{i-1})$ $\triangleright H = (P \ll 2^{i-1}) \oplus t$
11:   $P' \leftarrow \mathsf{SecAnd}(P', H, s, t, u)$ $\triangleright P' = \left(P \wedge (P \ll 2^{i-1})\right) \oplus u$
12:   $P' \leftarrow P' \oplus s$
13:   $P' \leftarrow P' \oplus u$ $\triangleright P' = \left(P \wedge (P \ll 2^{i-1})\right) \oplus s$
14: **end for**
15: $H \leftarrow \mathsf{SecShift}(G', s, t, 2^{n-1})$ $\triangleright H = (G \ll 2^{n-1}) \oplus t$
16: $U \leftarrow \mathsf{SecAnd}(P', H, s, t, u)$ $\triangleright U = \left(P \wedge (G \ll 2^{n-1})\right) \oplus u$
17: $G' \leftarrow \mathsf{SecXor}(G', U, u)$ $\triangleright G' = \left((P \wedge (G \ll 2^{n-1})) \oplus G\right) \oplus s$
18: $z' \leftarrow \mathsf{SecXor}(y', x', s)$ $\triangleright z' = (x \oplus y) \oplus r$
19: $z' \leftarrow z' \oplus (2G')$ $\triangleright z' = (x+y) \oplus 2s \oplus r$
20: $z' \leftarrow z' \oplus 2s$ $\triangleright z' = (x+y) \oplus r$
21: **return** z'

As previously the main loop requires $28 \cdot (n-1)$ operations. The total number of operations is then $12 + 28 \cdot (n-1) + 20 = 28 \cdot n + 4$. In summary, for a register size $k = 2^n$ the number of operations is $28 \cdot \log_2 k + 4$, with additionally the generation of 2 random numbers; as previously those 2 random numbers along with r and s can be reused for subsequent additions within the same execution. The following Lemma proves the security of Algorithm 6 against first-order attacks. The proof is similar to the proof of Lemma 5 and is therefore omitted.

Lemma 6. *For a uniformly and independently distributed randoms $r \in \{0,1\}^k$ and $s \in \{0,1\}^k$, any intermediate variable in the Kogge-Stone Masked Addition has the uniform distribution.*

6 Analysis and Implementation

6.1 Comparison with Existing Algorithms

We compare in Table 1 the complexity of our new algorithms with Goubin's algorithms and Debraize's algorithms for various addition bit sizes k.[1] We give the number of random numbers required for each of the algorithms as well as the

---

[1] For Debraize's algorithm the operation count does not involve the precomputation phase. In case of $k = 8$ and $\ell = 8$ the result can be obtained by a single table look-up.

Table 1. Number of randoms (rand) and elementary operations required for Goubin's algorithms, Debraize's algorithm and our new algorithms for various values of k.

Algorithm	rand	$k = 8$	$k = 16$	$k = 32$	$k = 64$	k
Goubin's A→B conversion	1	41	81	161	321	$5k + 1$
Debraize's A→B conversion ($\ell = 4$)	2	36	74	150	302	$19(k/4) - 2$
Debraize's A→B conversion ($\ell = 8$)	2	-	36	74	150	$19(k/8) - 2$
New A→B conversion	3	81	109	137	165	$28 \log_2 k - 3$
Goubin's addition [KRJ14]	1	48	88	168	328	$5k + 8$
New addition	2	88	116	144	172	$28 \log_2 k + 4$

number of elementary operations. Goubin's original conversion algorithm from arithmetic to Boolean masking required $5k + 5$ operations and a single random generation. This was recently improved by Karroumi et al. down to $5k + 1$ operations [KRJ14]. The authors also provided an algorithm to compute first-order secure addition on Boolean shares using Goubin's recursion formula, requiring $5k + 8$ operations and a single random generation. See Appendix A for more details. On the other hand Debraize's algorithm requires $19(k/\ell) - 2$ operations with a lookup table of size 2^ℓ and the generation of two randoms.

We see that our algorithms outperform Goubin's algorithms for $k \geq 32$ but are slower than Debraize's algorithm with $\ell = 8$ (without taking into account its pre-computation phase). In practice, most cryptographic constructions performing arithmetic operations use addition modulo 2^{32}; for example HMAC-SHA-1 [NIS95] and XTEA [NW97]. There also exists cryptographic constructions with additions modulo 2^{64}, for example Threefish used in the hash function Skein, a SHA-3 finalist, and the SPECK block-cipher (see Sect. 6.3).

6.2   Practical Implementation

We have implemented our new algorithms along with Goubin's algorithms; we have also implemented the table-based arithmetic to Boolean conversion algorithm described by Debraize in [Deb12]. For Debraize's algorithm, we considered two possibilities for the partition of the data, with word length $\ell = 4$ and $\ell = 8$. Our implementations were done on a 32-bit AVR microcontroller *AT32UC3A0512*, based on RISC microprocessor architecture. It can run at frequencies up to 66 MHZ and has SRAM of size 64 KB along with a flash of 512 KB. We used the C programming language and the machine code was produced using the AVR-GCC compiler with further optimization (*e.g.* loop unrolling). For the generation of random numbers we used a pseudorandom number generator based on linear feedback shift registers.[2]

The results are summarized in Table 2. We can see that our new algorithms perform better than Goubin's algorithms from $k = 32$ onward. When $k = 32$, our algorithms perform roughly 14 % better than Goubin's algorithms. Moreover,

---

[2] Note that the reported results have strong dependency on the RNG and hence can change if a different RNG is used.

Table 2. Number of clock cycles on a 32-bit processor required for Goubin's conversion algorithm, Debraize's conversion algorithm, our new conversion algorithm, Goubin's addition from [KRJ14], and our new addition, for various arithmetic sizes k. The last two columns denote the precomputation time and the table size (in bytes) required for Debraize's algorithm.

	$k = 8$	$k = 16$	$k = 32$	$k = 64$	Prep	Mem.
Goubin's A→B conversion	180	312	543	1672	-	-
Debraize's A→B conversion ($\ell = 4$)	149	285	505	1573	1221	32
Debraize's A→B conversion ($\ell = 8$)	-	193	316	846	18024	1024
New A→B conversion	301	386	467	1284	-	-
Goubin's addition [KRJ14]	235	350	582	1789	-	-
New addition	344	429	513	1340	-	-

our conversion algorithm performs 7 % better than Debraize's algorithm ($\ell = 4$). For $k = 64$, we can see even better improvement i.e., 23 % faster than Goubin's algorithm and 22 % better than Debraize's algorithm ($\ell = 4$). On the other hand, Debraize's algorithm performs better than our algorithms for $\ell = 8$; however as opposed to Debraize's algorithm our conversion algorithm requires neither preprocessing nor extra memory.

6.3   Application to HMAC-SHA-1 and SPECK

We have implemented HMAC-SHA-1 [NIS95] using the technique above to protect against first-order attacks, on the same microcontroller as in Sect. 6.2. To convert from arithmetic to Boolean masking, we used one of the following: Goubin's algorithm, Debraize's algorithm or our new algorithm. The results for computing HMAC-SHA-1 of a single message block are summarized in Table 3. For Debraize's algorithm, the timings also include the precomputation time required for creating the tables. Our algorithms give better performances than Goubin and Debraize ($\ell = 4$), but Debraize with $\ell = 8$ is still slightly better; however as opposed to Debraize, our algorithms do not require extra memory. For the masked addition (instead of conversions), the new algorithm performs 10 % better than Goubin's algorithm.

SPECK is a family of lightweight block ciphers proposed by NSA, which provides high throughput for application in software [BSS+13]. The SPECK family includes various ciphers based on ARX (Addition, Rotation, XOR) design with different block and key sizes. To verify the performance results of our algorithms for $k = 64$, we used SPECK 128/128, where block and key sizes both equal to 128 and additions are performed modulo 2^{64}. We summarize the performance of all the algorithms in Table 4.

As we can see our algorithms outperform Goubin and Debraize's algorithm ($\ell = 4$), but not Debraize's algorithm for $\ell = 8$, as for HMAC-SHA-1.

Table 3. Running time in thousands of clock-cycles and penalty factor for HMAC-SHA-1 on a 32-bit processor. The last column denotes the table size (in bytes) required for Debraize's algorithm.

	Time	Penalty Factor	Mem.
HMAC-SHA-1 unmasked	128	1	-
HMAC-SHA-1 with Goubin's conversion	423	3.3	-
HMAC-SHA-1 with Debraize's conversion ($\ell = 4$)	418	3.26	32
HMAC-SHA-1 with Debraize's conversion ($\ell = 8$)	402	3.1	1024
HMAC-SHA-1 with new conversion	410	3.2	-
HMAC-SHA-1 with Goubin's addition [KRJ14]	1022	8	-
HMAC-SHA-1 with new addition	933	7.2	-

Table 4. Running time in clock-cycles and penalty factor for SPECK on a 32-bit processor. The last column denotes the table size (in bytes) required for Debraize's algorithm.

	Time	Penalty Factor	Memory
SPECK unmasked	2047	1	-
SPECK with Goubin's conversion	63550	31	-
SPECK with Debraize's conversion ($\ell = 4$)	61603	30	32
SPECK with Debraize's conversion ($\ell = 8$)	37718	18	1024
SPECK with new conversion	51134	24	-
SPECK with Goubin's addition [KRJ14]	62942	30	-
SPECK with new addition	48574	23	-

A   Goubin's Arithmetic-to-Boolean Conversion

From Theorem 2, one obtains the following corollary.

Corollary 1 ([Gou01]). *For any random $\gamma \in \mathbb{F}_{2^k}$, if we assume $x' = (A+r)\oplus r$, we also have $x' = A \oplus 2\gamma \oplus t_{k-1}$, where t_{k-1} can be obtained from the following recursion formula:*

$$\begin{cases} t_0 = 2\gamma \\ \forall i \geq 0, t_{i+1} = 2[t_i \wedge (A \oplus r) \oplus \omega] \end{cases} \tag{12}$$

where $\omega = \gamma \oplus (2\gamma) \wedge (A \oplus r) \oplus A \wedge r$.

Since the iterative computation of t_i contains only XOR and AND operations, it can easily be protected against first-order attacks. This gives the algorithm below.

Algorithm 7. Goubin A→B Conversion

Require: A, r such that $x = A + r$
Ensure: x', r such that $x' = x \oplus r$
 1: $\gamma \leftarrow rand(k)$
 2: $T \leftarrow 2\gamma$
 3: $x' \leftarrow \gamma \oplus r$
 4: $\Omega \leftarrow \gamma \wedge x'$
 5: $x' \leftarrow T \oplus A$
 6: $\gamma \leftarrow \gamma \oplus x'$
 7: $\gamma \leftarrow \gamma \wedge r$
 8: $\Omega \leftarrow \Omega \oplus \gamma$
 9: $\gamma \leftarrow T \wedge A$
10: $\Omega \leftarrow \Omega \oplus \gamma$
11: **for** $j := 1$ to $k - 1$ **do**
12:      $\gamma \leftarrow T \wedge r$
13:      $\gamma \leftarrow \gamma \oplus \Omega$
14:      $T \leftarrow T \wedge A$
15:      $\gamma \leftarrow \gamma \oplus T$
16:      $T \leftarrow 2\gamma$
17: **end for**
18: $x' \leftarrow x' \oplus T$

We can see that the total number of operations in the above algorithm is $5k + 5$, in addition to one random number generation. Karroumi *et al.* recently improved Goubin's conversion scheme down to $5k + 1$ operations [KRJ14]. More precisely they start the loop in (12) from $i = 2$ instead of $i = 1$, and compute t_1 directly with a single operation, which decreases the number of operations by 4.

Karroumi *et al.* also provided an algorithm to compute first-order secure addition on Boolean shares using Goubin's recursion formula, requiring $5k + 8$ operations and a single random generation. More precisely, given two sensitive variables x and y masked as $x = x' \oplus s$ and $y = y' \oplus r$, their algorithm computes two shares $z_1 = (x + y) \oplus r \oplus s$, $z_2 = r \oplus s$ using Goubin's recursion formula (1); we refer to [KRJ14] for more details.

B   Proof of Lemma 1

We consider again recursion (7):

$$\begin{cases} z_0 = b_0 \\ \forall i \geq 1, \ z_i = a_i z_{i-1} + b_i \end{cases}$$

The recursion for c_i is similar when we denote the AND operation by a multiplication, and the XOR operation by an addition:

$$\begin{cases} c_0 = 0 \\ \forall i \geq 1, \ c_i = a_{i-1} c_{i-1} + b_{i-1} \end{cases}$$

Therefore we obtain $c_{i+1} = z_i$ for all $i \geq 0$. From the $Q(m,n)$ function given in (8) we define the sequences:

$$G_{i,j} := Q\big(j, \max(j - 2^i + 1, 0)\big)$$

$$P_{i,j} := \prod_{v=\max(j-2^i+1,0)}^{j} a_v$$

We show that these sequences satisfy the same recurrence (10) from Sect. 3.2. From (8) we have the recurrence for $j \geq 2^{i-1}$:

$$
\begin{aligned}
G_{i,j} &= \sum_{u=\max(j-2^i+1,0)}^{j} \left(\prod_{v=u+1}^{j} a_v\right) b_u \\
&= \sum_{u=\max(j-2^i+1,0)}^{j-2^{i-1}} \left(\prod_{v=u+1}^{j} a_v\right) b_u + \sum_{u=j-2^{i-1}+1}^{j} \left(\prod_{v=u+1}^{j} a_v\right) b_u \\
&= \left(\prod_{v=j-2^{i-1}+1}^{j} a_v\right) \sum_{u=\max(j-2^i+1,0)}^{j-2^{i-1}} \left(\prod_{v=u+1}^{j-2^{i-1}} a_v\right) b_u + Q(j, j - 2^{i-1} + 1) \\
&= P_{i-1,j} \cdot Q\big(j - 2^{i-1}, \max(j - 2^i + 1, 0)\big) + G_{i-1,j} \\
&= P_{i-1,j} \cdot G_{i-1,j-2^{i-1}} + G_{i-1,j}
\end{aligned}
$$

We obtain a similar recurrence for $P_{i,j}$ when $j \geq 2^{i-1}$:

$$
\begin{aligned}
P_{i,j} &= \prod_{v=\max(j-2^i+1,0)}^{j} a_v \\
&= \left(\prod_{v=\max(j-2^i+1,0)}^{j-2^{i-1}} a_v\right) \cdot \left(\prod_{v=j-2^{i-1}+1}^{j} a_v\right) = P_{i-1,j-2^{i-1}} \cdot P_{i-1,j}
\end{aligned}
$$

In summary we obtain for $j \geq 2^{i-1}$ the relations:

$$
\begin{cases}
G_{i,j} = P_{i-1,j} \cdot G_{i-1,j-2^{i-1}} + G_{i-1,j} \\
[.1cm] P_{i,j} = P_{i-1,j} \cdot P_{i-1,j-2^{i-1}}
\end{cases}
$$

which are exactly the same as (10) from Sect. 3.2. Moreover for $0 \leq j < 2^{i-1}$, as in Sect. 3.2, we have $G_{i,j} = Q(j,0) = G_{i-1,j}$ and $P_{i,j} = P_{i-1,j}$. Finally we have the same initial conditions $G_{0,j} = Q(j,j) = b_j = x^{(j)} \wedge y^{(j)}$ and $P_{0,j} = a_j = x^{(j)} \oplus y^{(j)}$. This proves that the sequence $G_{i,j}$ defined by (10) in Sect. 3.2 is such that:

$$G_{i,j} = Q\big(j, \max(j - 2^i + 1, 0)\big)$$

This implies that we have $G_{0,0} = Q(0,0) = z_0$ and $G_{i,j} = Q(j,0) = z_j$ for all $2^{i-1} \leq j < 2^i$. Moreover as noted initially we have $c_{j+1} = z_j$ for all $j \geq 0$. Therefore the recurrence from Sect. 3.2 indeed computes the carry signal c_j, with $c_0 = 0$, $c_1 = G_{0,0}$ and $c_{j+1} = G_{i,j}$ for $2^{i-1} \leq j < 2^i$. This terminates the proof of Lemma 1. $\qquad\square$

References

[BN05] Beak, Y., Noh, M.-J.: Differential power attack and masking method. Trends Math. **8**, 1–15 (2005)

[BSS+13] Beaulieu, R., Shors, D., Smith, J., Treatman-Clark, S., Weeks, B., Wingers, L.: The SIMON and SPECK families of lightweight block ciphers. IACR Cryptology ePrint Archive, 2013:404 (2013)

[CGV14] Coron, J.-S., Großschädl, J., Vadnala, P.K.: Secure conversion between boolean and arithmetic masking of any order. In: Batina, L., Robshaw, M. (eds.) CHES 2014. LNCS, vol. 8731, pp. 188–205. Springer, Heidelberg (2014)

[CT03] Coron, J.-S., Tchulkine, A.: A new algorithm for switching from arithmetic to boolean masking. In: Walter, C.D., Koç, Ç.K., Paar, C. (eds.) CHES 2003. LNCS, vol. 2779, pp. 89–97. Springer, Heidelberg (2003)

[Deb12] Debraize, B.: Efficient and provably secure methods for switching from arithmetic to boolean masking. In: Prouff, E., Schaumont, P. (eds.) CHES 2012. LNCS, vol. 7428, pp. 107–121. Springer, Heidelberg (2012)

[Gou01] Goubin, L.: A sound method for switching between boolean and arithmetic masking. In: Koç, Ç.K., Naccache, D., Paar, C. (eds.) CHES 2001. LNCS, vol. 2162, pp. 3–15. Springer, Heidelberg (2001)

[ISW03] Ishai, Y., Sahai, A., Wagner, D.: Private circuits: securing hardware against probing attacks. In: Boneh, D. (ed.) CRYPTO 2003. LNCS, vol. 2729, pp. 463–481. Springer, Heidelberg (2003)

[KJJ99] Kocher, P.C., Jaffe, J., Jun, B.: Differential power analysis. In: Wiener, M. (ed.) CRYPTO 1999. LNCS, vol. 1666, pp. 388–397. Springer, Heidelberg (1999)

[KRJ14] Karroumi, M., Richard, B., Joye, M.: Addition with blinded operands. In: Prouff, E. (ed.) COSADE 2014. LNCS, vol. 8622, pp. 41–55. Springer, Heidelberg (2014)

[KS73] Kogge, P.M., Stone, H.S.: A parallel algorithm for the efficient solution of a general class of recurrence equations. IEEE Trans. Comput. **100**(8), 786–793 (1973)

[MOP07] Mangard, S., Oswald, E., Popp, T.: Power Analysis Attacks - Revealing the Secrets Of Smart Cards. Springer, US (2007)

[NIS95] NIST. Secure hash standard. In Federal Information Processing Standard, FIPA-180-1 (1995)

[NP04] Neiße, O., Pulkus, J.: Switching blindings with a view towards IDEA. In: Joye, M., Quisquater, J.-J. (eds.) CHES 2004. LNCS, vol. 3156, pp. 230–239. Springer, Heidelberg (2004)

[NW97] Needham, R.M. Wheeler, D.J.: Tea extentions. Technical report, Computer Laboratory, University of Cambridge (1997)

[PMO07] Popp, T., Mangard, S., Oswald, E.: Power analysis attacks and countermeasures. IEEE Design Test Comput. **24**(6), 535–543 (2007)

Comb to Pipeline: Fast Software Encryption Revisited

Andrey Bogdanov[✉], Martin M. Lauridsen, and Elmar Tischhauser

DTU Compute, Technical University of Denmark, Kgs. Lyngby, Denmark
{anbog,mmeh,ewti}@dtu.dk

Abstract. AES-NI, or Advanced Encryption Standard New Instructions, is an extension of the x86 architecture proposed by Intel in 2008. With a pipelined implementation utilizing AES-NI, parallelizable modes such as AES-CTR become extremely efficient. However, out of the four non-trivial NIST-recommended encryption modes, three are inherently sequential: CBC, CFB, and OFB. This inhibits the advantage of using AES-NI significantly. Similar observations apply to CMAC, CCM and a great deal of other modes. We address this issue by proposing the *comb scheduler* – a fast scheduling algorithm based on an efficient look-ahead strategy, featuring a low overhead – with which sequential modes profit from the AES-NI pipeline in real-world settings by filling it with multiple, independent messages.

We apply the comb scheduler to implementations on Haswell, Intel's latest microarchitecture, for a wide range of modes. We observe a *drastic speed-up of factor 5 for NIST's CBC, CFB, OFB and CMAC* performing around 0.88 cpb. Surprisingly, contrary to the entire body of previous performance analysis, the *throughput of the authenticated encryption (AE) mode CCM gets very close to that of GCM and OCB3*, with about 1.64 cpb (vs. 1.63 cpb and 1.51 cpb, resp.), despite Haswell's heavily improved binary field multiplication. This suggests CCM as an AE mode of choice as it is NIST-recommended, does not have any weak-key issues like GCM, and is royalty-free as opposed to OCB3. Among the CAESAR contestants, the comb scheduler significantly speeds up CLOC/SILC, JAMBU, and POET, with the mostly sequential nonce-misuse resistant design of POET, performing at 2.14 cpb, becoming faster than the well-parallelizable COPA.

Finally, this paper provides the first optimized AES-NI implementations for the novel AE modes OTR, CLOC/SILC, COBRA, POET, McOE-G, and Julius.

Keywords: AES-NI · pclmulqdq · Haswell · Authenticated encryption · CAESAR · CBC · OFB · CFB · CMAC · CCM · GCM · OCB3 · OTR · CLOC · COBRA · JAMBU · SILC · McOE-G · COPA · POET · Julius

1 Introduction

With the introduction of AES-NI, Advanced Encryption Standard New Instructions, on Intel's microarchitectures starting from Westmere and later as well as

© International Association for Cryptologic Research 2015
G. Leander (Ed.): FSE 2015, LNCS 9054, pp. 150–171, 2015.
DOI: 10.1007/978-3-662-48116-5_8

on a variety of AMD CPUs, AES received a sigfinicant speed-up in standard software, going well below 1 cycle per byte (cpb) and possessing a constant running time, which also thwarts cache-timing attacks. Important applications for AES-NI include OpenSSL, Microsoft's BitLocker, Apple's FileVault, TrueCrypt, PGP and many more. In a nutshell, AES-NI provides dedicated instructions for AES encryption and decryption. On Haswell, Intel's newest architecture, the latency of these instructions is 7 clock cycles (cc) and the throughput is 1 cc. That is, AES-NI has a pipeline of length 7 and one can issue one instruction per clock cycle. This pipeline can be naturally exploited by parallel AES modes such as CTR in the encryption domain, PMAC in the message authentication domain as well as GCM and OCB in the authenticated encryption domain.

However, numerous AES modes of operation – both standardized and novel such as CAESAR[1] submissions – are essentially sequential by design. Indeed, NIST-standardized CBC, CFB, OFB and CMAC [10] as well as CLOC and POET from FSE 2014 and McOE-G from FSE 2012 are essentially sequential, which limits their performance on state-of-the-art servers and desktops significantly, as the pipeline cannot be filled entirely, having a severe performance penalty as a consequence.

In this paper, we aim to address this gap and propose an *efficient look-ahead comb scheduler for real-world Internet packets*. Its application can change the landscape of AES modes of operation in terms of their practical throughput. Our contributions are as follows:

Novel Comb Scheduler. Communication devices of high-speed links are likely to process many messages at the same time. Indeed, on the Internet, the bulk of data is transmitted in packets of sizes between 1 and 2 KB, following a bimodal distribution. While most previous implementations of block cipher modes consider processing a single message, we propose to process several messages in parallel, which reflects this reality. This is particularly beneficial when using an inherently sequential mode. In this work, for the first time, we deal with AES modes of operation in this setting (see Sect. 3). More specifically, as our main contribution, we propose an efficient look-ahead comb scheduler. For real-world packet lengths on the Internet, this algorithm allows us to fill the pipeline of AES-NI and attain significant speed-ups for many popular modes. After covering some background in Sect. 2, we present our comb scheduler and its analysis in Sect. 3.

Speed-Up of Factor 5 for NIST's CBC, OFB, CFB and CMAC. When applied to the NIST-recommended encryption and MAC modes, our comb scheduler delivers a performance gain of factor 5 with the real-world packet sizes. The modes get as fast as 0.88 cpb compared to around 4.5 cpb in the sequential message processing setting. These results are provided in Sect. 4.

Change of Landscape for AE. When our comb scheduler is applied to AE modes of operation, a high performance improvement is attained as well with

---

[1] Competition for Authenticated Encryption: Security, Applicability, and Robustness.

the real-world message size distribution. CCM, having a sequential CBC-based MAC inside, gets as fast as GCM and OCB which are inherently parallel. Being royalty-free, NIST-recommended and weak-key free, CCM becomes an attractive AE mode of operation in this setting.

In the context of the ongoing CAESAR competition, in the domain of nonce-misuse resistant modes, the essentially sequential POET gets a significant speed-up of factor 2.7 down to 2.14 cpb. Its rival CAESAR contestant COPA runs as 2.68 cpb, while being insecure under release of unverified plaintext. This is somewhat surprising, considering that POET uses 3 AES calls per block vs. 2 AES calls per block for COPA.

Section 5 also contains first-time comprehensive performance evaluations of further AES-based modes in the CAESAR competition and beyond, both in the sequential and comb-scheduled implementations, including OTR, CLOC/SILC, JAMBU, COBRA, McOE-G and Julius.

Faster $GF(2^{128})$ Multiplications on Haswell. Section 6 focuses on the technical implementation tricks on Haswell that we used to obtain our results and contains a detailed study of improved $GF(2^{128})$ multiplications on the architecture.

2   Background

In this paper, we consider AES-based symmetric primitives, that is, algorithms that make use of the (full) AES block cipher in a black-box fashion. In particular, this includes block cipher modes of operation, block cipher based message authentication codes, and authentication encryption (AE) modes.

NIST-recommended Modes. In its special publications SP-800-38A-D [10], NIST recommends the following modes of operation: ECB, CBC, CFB, OFB and CTR as basic encryption modes; CMAC as authentication mode; and CCM and GCM as authenticated encryption modes.

Authenticated Encryption Modes and CAESAR. Besides the widely employed and standardized modes CCM and GCM, a great number of modes for authenticated encryption have been proposed, many of them being contestants in the currently ongoing CAESAR competition. We give a brief overview of the AE modes we will consider in this study.

We split up our consideration into two categories: (i) *nonce-misuse resistant* AE modes, by which we mean modes that maintain authenticity and privacy up to a common message prefix even when the nonce is repeated (also called OAE security) and (ii) *nonce-based* AE modes which either lose authenticity, privacy or both when nonces are repeated. The modes we consider in the former camp are McOE-G, COPA, POET and Julius, while the nonce-based modes considered are CCM, GCM, OCB3, OTR, CLOC, COBRA, JAMBU and SILC. Table 1 gives a comparison of the modes considered in this work. The price to pay for a mode to be nonce-misuse resistant includes extra computation, a higher serialization degree, or both. One of the fundamental questions we answer in this

Table 1. Overview of the AE modes considered in this paper. The ∥ column indicates parallelizability; the "IF" column indicates whether a mode needs the inverse of the underlying block cipher in decryption/verification; the "E" and "M" columns give the number of calls, per message block, to the underlying block cipher and multiplications in $GF(2^n)$, respectively.

	Ref.	Year	∥	IF	E	M	Description
Nonce-based AE modes							
CCM	[37]	2002	–	yes	2	–	CTR encryption, CBC-MAC authentication
GCM	[31]	2004	yes	yes	1	1	CTR mode with chain of multiplications
OCB3	[26]	2010	yes	–	1	–	Gray code-based xor-encrypt-xor (XEX)
OTR	[33]	2013	yes	yes	1	–	Two-block Feistel structure
CLOC	[21]	2014	–	yes	1	–	CFB mode with low overhead
COBRA	[5]	2014	yes	yes	1	1	Combining OTR with chain of multiplications
JAMBU	[38]	2014	–	yes	1	–	AES in stream mode, lightweight
SILC	[22]	2014	–	yes	1	–	CLOC with smaller hardware footprint
Nonce-misuse resistant AE modes							
McOE-G	[11]	2011	–	–	1	1	Serial multiplication-encryption chain
COPA	[4]	2013	yes	–	2	–	Two-round XEX
POET	[1]	2014	yes	–	3	–	XEX with two AXU (full AES-128 call) chains
Julius	[7]	2014	–	–	1	2	SIV with polynomial hashing

work is how much one has to pay, in terms of performance, to maintain this level of security when repeating nonces.

For the specifications of the AE modes considered, we refer to the relevant references listed in Table 1. We clarify that for COBRA we refer to the FSE 2014 version with its reduced security claims (compared to the withdrawn CAESAR candidate); with POET we refer to the version where the universal hashing is implemented as full AES-128 (since using four rounds would not comprise a mode of operation); and with Julius, we mean the CAESAR candidate regular Julius-ECB.

The AES-NI Instruction Set. Proposed in 2008 and implemented as of their 2010 Westmere microarchitecture, Intel developed special instructions for fast AES encryption and decryption [15], called the *AES New Instruction Set (AES-NI)*. It provides instructions for computing one AES round `aesenc`, `aesenclast`, its inverse `aesdec`, `aesdeclast`, and auxiliary instructions for key scheduling. The instructions do not only offer better performance, but security as well, since they are leaking no timing information. AES-NI is supported in a subset of Westmere, Sandy Bridge, Ivy Bridge and Haswell microarchitectures. A range of AMD processors also support the instructions under the name *AES Instructions*, including processors in the Bulldozer, Piledriver and Jaguar series [19].

Pipelining. Instruction pipelines allow CPUs to execute the same instruction for data-independent instances in an overlapping fashion. This is done by subdividing the instruction into steps called *pipeline stages*, with each stage processing its part of one instruction at a time. The performance of a pipelined instruction is characterized by its latency L (number of cycles to complete one instruction) and throughput T (the number of cycles to wait between issuing instructions). For instance, on the original Westmere architecture, the AES-NI `aesenc` instruction has a latency of 6 cycles and a throughput of 2, meaning that one instruction can be issued every two cycles.

Previous Work. Matsui and Fukuda at FSE 2005 [29] and Matsui [28] at FSE 2006 pioneered comprehensive studys on how to optimize symmetric primitives on the then-contemporary generation of Intel microprocessors. One year later, Matsui and Nakajima [30] demonstrated that the vector instruction units of the Core 2 architecture lends itself to very fast bitsliced implementations of block ciphers. For the AES, on a variety of platforms, Bernstein and Schwabe [8] developed various micro-optimizations yielding vastly improved performance. Intel's AES instructions were introduced to the symmetric community by Shay Gueron's tutorial [14] at FSE 2009. In the same year, Käsper and Schwabe announced new records for bitsliced AES-CTR and AES-GCM performance [25]. At FSE 2010, Osvik et al. [35] explored fast AES implementations on AVR and GPU platforms. Finally, a study of the performance of CCM, GCM, OCB3 and CTR modes was presented by Krovetz and Rogaway [26] at FSE 2011.

3   Comb Scheduler: An Efficient Look-Ahead Strategy

3.1   Motivation

A substantial number of block cipher modes of operation for (authenticated) encryption are inherently sequential in nature. Among the NIST-recommended modes, this includes the classic CBC, OFB, CFB and CCM modes as well as CBC derivatives such as CMAC. Also, more recent designs essentially owe their sequential nature to design goals, e.g allowing lightweight implementations or achieving stricter notions of security, for instance not requiring a nonce for security (or allowing its reuse). Examples include ALE [9], APE [3], CLOC [21] the McOE family of algorithms [11,12], and some variants of POET [1].

While being able to perform well in other environments, such algorithms cannot benefit from the available pipelining opportunities on contemporary general-purpose CPUs. For instance, as detailed in Sect. 6, the AES-NI encryption instructions on Intel's recent Haswell architecture feature a high throughput of 1, but a relatively high latency of 7 cycles. Modes of operation that need to process data sequentially will invariably be penalized in such environments.

Furthermore, even if designed with parallelizability in mind, (authenticated) modes of operation for block ciphers typically achieve their best performance when operating on somewhat longer messages, often due to the simple fact that these diminish the impact of potentially costly initialization phases and tag generation. Equally importantly, only longer messages allow high-performance software implementations to make full use of the available pipelining opportunities [2,16,26,32].

In practice, however, one rarely encounters messages which allow to achieve the maximum performance of an algorithm. Recent studies on packet sizes on the Internet demonstrate that they basically follow a bimodal distribution [24,34,36]: 44 % of packets are between 40 and 100 bytes long; 37 % are between 1400 and 1500 bytes in size; the remaining 19 % are somewhere in between. Throughout the paper, we refer to this as the *realistic* distribution of message lengths. This emphasizes the importance of good performance for messages up to around 2 KB, as opposed to longer messages. Second, when looking at the weighted distribution, this implies that the vast majority of data is actually transmitted in packets of medium size between 1 and 2 KB. Considering the first mode of the distribution, we observe that many of the very small packets of Internet traffic comprise TCP ACKs (which are typically not encrypted), and that the use of authentication and encryption layers such as TLS or IPsec incurs overhead significant enough to blow up a payload of 1 byte to a 124 byte packet [20]. It is therefore this range of message sizes (128 to 2048 bytes) that authenticated modes of encryption should excel at processing, when employed for encryption of Internet traffic.

3.2   Filling the Pipeline: Multiple Messages

It follows from the above discussion that the standard approach of considering one message at a time, while arguably optimizing message processing latency, can not always generate optimal throughput in high-performance software implementations in most practically relevant scenarios. This is not surprising for the inherently sequential modes, but even when employing a parallelizable design, the prevailing distribution of message lengths makes it hard to achieve the best performance.

In order to remedy this, we propose to consider the scheduling of multiple messages in parallel *already in the implementation of the algorithm itself*, as opposed to considering it as a (single-message) black box to the message scheduler. This opens up possibilities of increasing the performance in the cases of both sequential modes and the availability of multiple shorter or medium-sized messages. In the first case, the performance penalty of sequential execution can potentially be hidden by filling the pipeline with a sufficient number of operations on independent data. In the second case, there is a potential of increasing performance by keeping the pipeline filled also for the overhead operations such as block cipher or multiplication calls during initialization or tag generation.

Note that while in this paper we consider the processing of multiple messages on a single core, the multiple message approach naturally extends to multi-core settings.

Conceptually, the transition of a sequential to a multiple message implementation can be viewed as similar to the transition from a straightforward to a bit-sliced implementation approach.

We note that an idealistic view of multiple-message processing was given in [9] for dedicated authenticated encryption algorithm ALE. This consideration was rather rudimentary, did not involve real-world packet size distributions, and did not treat any modes of operation.

It is also important to note that while multiple message processing has the potential to increase the throughput of an implementation, it can also increase its latency (see also Sect. 3.4). The degree of parallelism therefore has to be chosen carefully and with the required application profile in mind.

3.3   Message Scheduling with a Comb

Consider the scenario where a number of messages of varying lengths need to be processed by a sequential encryption algorithm. As outlined before, blocks from multiple messages have to be processed in an interleaved fashion in order to make use of the available inter-message parallelism. Having messages of different lengths implies that generally the pipeline cannot always be filled completely. At the same time, the goal to schedule the message blocks such that pipeline usage is maximized has to be weighed against the computational cost of making such scheduling decisions: in particular, every conditional statement during the processing of the bulk data results in a pipeline stall.

In order to reconcile the goal of exploiting multi-message parallelism for sequential algorithms with the need for low-overhead scheduling, we propose *comb scheduling*.

Comb scheduling is based on the observation that ideally, messages processed in parallel have the same length, so given a desired (maximum) parallelism degree P and a list of message lengths $\ell_1, \ldots, \ell_k$, we can subdivide the computation in a number of *windows*, in each of which we process as many consecutive message blocks as we can for as many independent messages as possible according to the restrictions based on the given message lengths.

Since our scheduling problem exhibits optimal substructure, this greedy approach yields an optimal solution. Furthermore, the scheduling decisions of how many blocks are to be processed at which parallelism level can be precomputed once the ℓ_i are known. This implies that instead of making each processing step conditional, we only have conditional statements whenever we proceed from one window to the next.

The comb scheduling method is outlined in Algorithms 1 and 2. In order to simplify the combing, the messages are pre-sorted by decreasing length[2]. This sorting step can be implemented via an optimal sorting network for the constant value of P chosen by the implementation. Alternatively, a low-overhead algorithm like Insertion Sort can be used.

---

[2] Note that this can be implemented by pointer swapping only, without copying of data blocks.

Algorithm 1. COMBSCHEDULER

Input : k messages $M_1, \ldots, M_k$ of lengths $\ell_1, \ldots, \ell_k$ blocks
Input : Parallelism degree P

1   $L \leftarrow$ list of tuples (M_j, ℓ_j) sorted by decreasing ℓ_j
2   Denote by $L[i] = (M_i, \ell_i)$ the i-th tuple in L
3   **while** $|L| > 0$ **do**
4      $r \leftarrow \min\{P, |L|\}$
5   Perform initialization for messages $M_1, \ldots, M_r$
6      $\mathcal{P}, \mathcal{B} \leftarrow$ PRECOMPUTEWINDOWS$(\ell_1, \ldots, \ell_r)$
7      $completedBlocks \leftarrow 0$
8   **for** $w = 1, \ldots, |\mathcal{P}|$ **do**   // *Loop over windows*
9   **for** $i = 1, \ldots, \mathcal{B}[w]$ **do**   // *Loop over blocks in window*
10   **for** $j = 1, \ldots, \mathcal{P}[w]$ **do**   // *Loop over messages in window*
11   Process block $(completedBlocks + i)$ of message M_j
12   **end**
13   **end**
14         $completedBlocks \leftarrow completedBlocks + \mathcal{B}[w]$
15   **end**
16   Perform finalization for messages $M_1, \ldots, M_r$
17   Remove the r first elements from L
18   **end**

Algorithm 2. PRECOMPUTEWINDOWS$(\ell_1, \ldots, \ell_r)$

Input : r message lengths $\ell_1, \ldots, \ell_r$ in blocks, s.t.
         $\forall i = 1, \ldots, r - 1 : \ell_i \geq \ell_{i+1}$
Output: List $\mathcal{P}$ with $\mathcal{P}[w]$ the number of messages to process in parallel
         in window w
Output: List $\mathcal{B}$ with $\mathcal{B}[w]$ the number of blocks to process in window w

1   $\mathcal{P} \leftarrow []$, $\mathcal{B} \leftarrow []$ // *Initialize to empty lists*
2   $w \leftarrow 1$, $q_{last} \leftarrow 0$, $i \leftarrow r$
3   **while** $i > 1$ **do**   // *Scan windows right to left*
4      $q \leftarrow \ell_i$, $j \leftarrow i - 1$
5   **while** $j \geq 1$ and $\ell_j = \ell_i$ **do** $j \leftarrow j - 1$;   // *Left-extend while lengths equal*
6      $\mathcal{P}[w] \leftarrow i$
7      $\mathcal{B}[w] \leftarrow q - q_{last}$
8      $q_{last} \leftarrow q$, $i \leftarrow j$, $w \leftarrow w + 1$
9   **end**
10   **if** $i = 1$ **then**   // *Leftover message*
11      $\mathcal{P}[w] \leftarrow 1$
12      $\mathcal{B}[w] \leftarrow \ell_1 - q_{last}$
13   **end**
14   **return** $\mathcal{P}, \mathcal{B}$

The sorted messages are then processed in groups of P. Inside each group, the processing is window by window according to the precomputed parallelism levels $\mathcal{P}$ and window lengths $\mathcal{B}$: In window w, the same $\mathcal{P}[w]$ messages of the current message group are processed $\mathcal{B}[w]$ blocks further. In the next window, at least one message will be exhausted, and the parallelism level decreases by at least one.

As comb scheduling is processing the blocks by common (sub-)length from left to right, our method can be considered a symmetric-key variant of the well-known comb method for (multi-)exponentiation [27].

Choice of the Parallelism Degree. In order to make optimal use of the pipeline, the parallelism degree P should be chosen according to

$$P = L \cdot T,$$

with L denoting the latency (in cycles) and T the throughput (in instructions/cycles) of the pipelined instruction. For AES-NI, the latency and throughput of the `aesenc` instruction vary from platform to platform. A summary for the Haswell microarchitecture is given in Table 7 in Sect. 6.2, suggesting $P = 7$ for this platform.

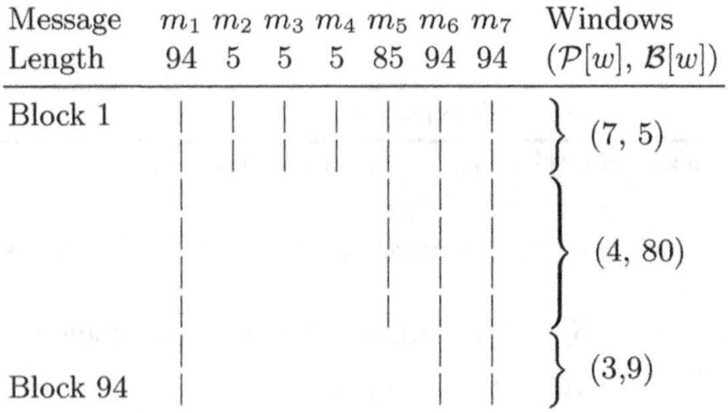

Message	m_1	m_2	m_3	m_4	m_5	m_6	m_7	Windows
Length	94	5	5	5	85	94	94	$(\mathcal{P}[w], \mathcal{B}[w])$

Block 1 ... (7, 5)

(4, 80)

Block 94 ... (3,9)

Fig. 1. Comb scheduling example for 7 messages of lengths $(94, 5, 5, 5, 85, 94, 94)$ blocks

An Example. We illustrate comb scheduling in Fig. 1 with an example where $P = k = 7$: The precomputation determines that all 7 messages can be processed in a pipelined fashion for the first 5 blocks; four of the 7 messages can be processed further for the next 80 blocks; and finally three remaining messages are processed for another 9 blocks.

3.4   Latency Vs Throughput

A point worth discussing is the latency increase one has to pay when using multiple message processing. Since the speed-up is limited by the parallelization level, one can at most hope for the same latency as in the sequential processing case.

We illustrate this by the example of CBC mode when implemented in the multiple message setting with comb scheduling. We consider two distributions for message lenghts: One where all messages are 2048 bytes long, and one realistic distribution of Internet traffic. The performance data is given in Table 2.

Table 2. Performance of CBC encryption (cpb) and relative speed-up for comb scheduling with different parallelization levels for fixed lengths of 2048 bytes (top) and realistic message lengths (bottom).

	Sequential	Parallelization level P						
		2	3	4	5	6	7	8
2 K messages	4.38	2.19	1.47	1.11	0.91	0.76	0.66	0.65
Relative speed-up	×1.00	×2.00	×2.98	×3.95	×4.81	×5.76	×6.64	×6.74
Realistic distribution	4.38	2.42	1.73	1.37	1.08	0.98	0.87	0.85
Relative speed-up	×1.00	×1.81	×2.53	×3.20	×4.06	×4.47	×5.03	×5.15

Table 2 shows that for identical message lengths, the ideal linear speed-up is actually achieved for 2 to 4 parallel messages: Setting $|M| = 2048$, instead of waiting $4.38 \cdot |M|$ cycles in the sequential case, one has a latency of either $2.19 \cdot 2 = 4.38 \cdot |M|$, $1.47 \cdot 3 = 4.41 \cdot |M|$ or $1.11 \cdot 4 = 4.44 \cdot |M|$ cycles, respectively. Starting from 5 messages, the latency slightly increases with the throughput, however remaining at a manageable level even for 7 messages, where it is only around 5 % higher than in the sequential case, while achieving a 6.64 times speed-up in throughput. For realistic message lengths, using 7 multiple messages, we see an average increase in latency of 39 % which has to be contrasted (and, depending on the application, weighed against) the significant 5.03 times speed-up in throughput.

4 Pipelined NIST Encryption Modes

In this section, we present the results of our performance study of the NIST-recommended encryption modes when instantiated with AES as the block cipher and implemented with AES-NI and AVX vector instructions. We remark that we only measure encryption. Some modes covered, such as CBC and CFB, are sequential in encryption but parallel in decryption.

Experimental Setting. All measurements were taken on a single core of an Intel Core i5-4300U CPU (Haswell) at 1900 MHz. For each combination of parameters, the performance was determined as the median of 91 averaged timings of 200 measurements each. This method has also been used by Krovetz and Rogaway in their benchmarking of authenticated encryption modes in [26]. The measurements are taken over samples from the realistic distribution on message lengths.

Out of the basic NIST modes, ECB and CTR are inherently parallelizable and already achieve good performance with trivial sequential message scheduling. Three other modes, CBC, OFB and CFB, however, are inherently sequential and therefore need to make use of inter-message parallelism to benefit from the available pipelining. The same holds for the NIST-recommended CMAC message authentication code. We therefore measure the performance of all modes with sequential processing, and additionally the performance of the sequential modes with comb message scheduling.

Table 3. Performance comparison (in cpb) of NIST encryption modes with trivial sequential processing and comb scheduling. Message lengths are sampled from the realistic Internet traffic distribution.

Mode	Sequential processing	**Comb scheduling**	Speed-up
AES-ECB	0.65	—	—
AES-CTR	0.78	—	—
AES-CBC	4.47	**0.87**	×5.14
AES-OFB	4.48	**0.88**	×5.09
AES-CFB	4.45	**0.89**	×5.00
CMAC-AES	4.29	**0.84**	×5.10

Discussion. Our performance results for pipelined implementations of NIST encryption modes are presented in Table 3. It is apparent that the parallel processing of multiple messages using comb scheduling speeds up encryption performance by a factor of around 5, bringing the sequential modes within about 10 % of CTR mode performance. The results also indicate that the overhead induced by the comb scheduling algorithm itself can be considered negligible compared to the AES calls.

Due to their simple structure with almost no overhead, it comes as no surprise that CBC, OFB and CFB performance are virtually identical. That CMAC performs slightly better despite additional initialization overhead can be explained by the fact that there are no ciphertext blocks to be stored to memory.

5   Pipelined Authenticated Encryption

We now turn our attention to the AES-NI software performance of authenticated encryption modes. We consider the well-established modes CCM, GCM and OCB3 as well as a number of more recent proposals, many of them being contestants in the ongoing CAESAR competition.

Experimental Setting. The same experimental setup as for the encryption modes applies. For our performance measurements, we are interested in the performance of the various AE modes of operation during their *bulk processing* of message blocks, i.e. during the encryption phase. To that end, we *do not* measure the time spent on processing associated data. As some schemes can have a significant overhead when computing authentication tags (finalization) for short messages, we *do* include this phase in the measurements as well.

5.1 Performance in the Real World

Out of the AE modes in consideration, GCM, OCB3, OTR, COBRA, COPA and Julius are parallelizable designs. We therefore only measure their performance with sequential message processing. On the other hand, CCM, CLOC, SILC, JAMBU, McOE-G and POET are sequential designs and as such will also be measured in combination with comb scheduling. In all cases, we again measure the performance using the message lengths sampled from the realistic bimodal distribution of typical Internet traffic.

Table 4 lists the results of the performance measurements. For the sequential modes where comb scheduling was implemented, the relative speed-up compared to normal sequential processing is indicated in the last column. In this table, the nonce-based AE modes are listed separately from those offering nonce-misuse resistance in order to provide a better estimation of the performance penalty one has to pay for achieving a stricter notion of security.

Table 4. Performance comparison (in cpb) of AES-based AE modes with trivial sequential processing and comb scheduling. Message lengths are sampled from the realistic Internet traffic distribution. CAESAR candidates are marked using a * after their name.

(a) Nonce-based AE modes

Mode	Sequential	**Comb**	Speed-up
CCM	5.22	**1.64**	×3.18
GCM	1.63	—	—
OCB3*	1.51	—	—
OTR*	1.91	—	—
COBRA	3.56	—	—
CLOC*	4.47	**1.45**	×3.08
JAMBU*	9.12	**2.05**	×4.45
SILC*	4.53	**1.49**	×3.04

(b) Nonce-misuse resistant AE modes

Mode	Sequential	**Comb**	Speed-up
McOE-G	7.41	**1.79**	×4.14
COPA*	2.68	—	—
POET*	5.85	**2.14**	×2.73
Julius*	3.73	—	—

Discussion. The performance data demonstrates that comb scheduling of multiple messages consistently provides a speed-up of factors between 3 and 4 compared to normal sequential processing. For typical Internet packet sizes, comb scheduling enables sequential AE modes to run with performance comparable to the parallelizable designs, in some cases even outperforming them. This can be attributed to the fact that AE modes typically have heavier initialization and finalization than normal encryption modes, both implying a penalty for short message performance. By using comb scheduling, however, also the initial and final AES calls can be (at least partially) parallelized between different messages. The relative speed-up for this will typically reduce with the message length. The surprisingly good performance of McOE-G is due to the fact that it basically benefits doubly from multiple message processing, since not only the AES calls, but also its sequential finite field multiplications can now be pipelined. For the comb scheduling implementation of CCM, which is two-pass, it is worth noting that all scheduling precomputations only need to be done once, since exactly the same processing windows can be used for both passes.

Best Performance Characteristics. From Table 4, it is apparent that for encryption of typical Internet packets, the difference, with respect to performance, between sequential and parallelizable modes somewhat blurs when comb scheduling is employed. This is especially true for the nonce-based setting, where CLOC, SILC, CCM, GCM and OCB3 all perform on a very comparable level. For the nonce-misuse resistant modes, our results surprisingly even show better performance of the two sequential modes for this application scenario. This can be attributed to the fact that the additional processing needed for achieving nonce-misuse resistance hampers performance on short messages, which can be mitigated to some extent by comb scheduling.

5.2   Traditional Approach: Sequential Messages of Fixed Lengths

While the previous section analyzed the performance of the various AE modes using a model for a realistic message lengths, we provide some more detail on the exact performance exhibited by these modes for a range of (fixed) message lengths in this section. To this end, we provide performance measurements for specific message lengths between 128 and 2048 bytes. The results are summarized in Table 5.

Table 5. Performance comparison (in cpb) of AE modes for processing a single message of various, fixed message lengths.

(a) Nonce-based AE modes

Mode	Message length (bytes)				
	128	256	512	1024	2048
CCM	5.35	5.19	5.14	5.11	5.10
GCM	2.09	1.61	1.34	1.20	1.14
OCB3	2.19	1.43	1.06	0.87	0.81
OTR	2.97	1.34	1.13	1.02	0.96
CLOC	4.50	4.46	4.44	4.46	4.44
COBRA	4.41	3.21	2.96	2.83	2.77
JAMBU	9.33	9.09	8.97	8.94	8.88
SILC	4.57	4.54	4.52	4.51	4.50

(b) Nonce-misuse resistant AE modes

Mode	Message length (bytes)				
	128	256	512	1024	2048
McOE-G	7.77	7.36	7.17	7.07	7.02
COPA	3.37	2.64	2.27	2.08	1.88
POET	6.89	5.74	5.17	4.88	4.74
Julius	4.18	4.69	3.24	3.08	3.03

Table 6. Performance comparison (in cpb) of sequential AE modes when comb scheduling is used for various fixed message lengths.

(a) Nonce-based AE modes

Mode	Message length (bytes)				
	128	256	512	1024	2048
CCM	1.51	1.44	1.40	1.38	1.37
CLOC	1.40	1.31	1.26	1.24	1.23
JAMBU	2.14	1.98	1.89	1.85	1.82
SILC	1.43	1.33	1.28	1.25	1.24

(b) Nonce-misuse resistant AE modes

Mode	Message length (bytes)				
	128	256	512	1024	2048
McOE-G	1.91	1.76	1.68	1.64	1.62
POET	2.56	2.23	2.06	1.97	1.93

Discussion. The performance data clearly shows the expected difference between sequential and parallelizable modes when no use of multiple parallel messages can be made. Only initialization-heavy sequential modes like McOE-G and POET show significant performance differences between shorter and longer messages, while this effect is usually very pronounced for the parallelizable modes such as OCB3 and COPA. It can be seen from Table 5, that in the nonce-based setting, the best performance is generally offered by OCB3, although OTR and GCM (on Haswell) provide quite similar performance. Among the nonce-misuse resistant modes, COPA performs best for all message sizes.

5.3   Exploring the Limits: Upper Bounding the Comb Scheduler Advantage

Having seen the performance data with comb scheduling for realistic message lengths, it is natural to consider the question what the performance of the various modes would be for the ideal scenario where the scheduler is given only messages of a fixed length. In this case, the comb precomputation would result in only one processing window, so essentially no scheduler-induced branches are needed during the processing of the messages. In a sense, this constitutes an *upper bound* for the multi-message performance with comb scheduling for the various encryption algorithms.

Table 6 summarizes the performance of the previously considered sequential AE modes when comb scheduling is combined with fixed message lengths (i.e. message lengths sampled from a deterministic distribution).

Discussion. It can be seen that for all modes considered, the performance for longer messages at least slightly improves compared to the realistic message length mix of Table 4, though the differences are quite small and do not exceed around 0.2 cpb. For smaller lengths, the difference can be more pronounced for a mode with heavy initialization such as POET. Overall, this shows that comb scheduling for a realistic distribution provides a performance which is very comparable to that of comb scheduling of messages with an idealized distribution.

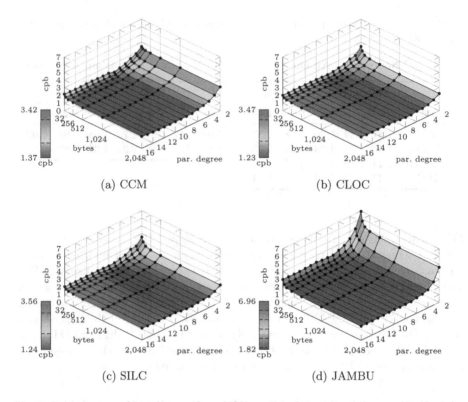

(a) CCM   (b) CLOC

(c) SILC   (d) JAMBU

Fig. 2. Performance of serial nonce-based AE modes of operation when comb scheduling is used with different parallelization levels for various fixed message lengths (Color figure online)

Exploring the Parameter Space. Besides the distribution of the message lengths, the parallelization degree influences the performance of the comb scheduler. Even though $P = 7$ is optimal for Haswell, applications might choose a lower value if typically only few messages are available simultaneously, in order to avoid a latency blowup. The dependency of the performance on both individual parameters is further detailed in Figs. 2 and 3, where the comb scheduling performance is shown for a range of fixed message lengths $(32, \ldots, 2048)$ and parallelization degrees $(2, \ldots, 16)$. The horizontal lines in the color key of both figures indicate the integer values in the interval.

Impact of Working Set Sizes. It can be seen from the plots that, as expected, most modes achieve their best speed-up in the multiple messages scenario for a parallelization level of around 7 messages. It is worth noting, however, that for each of these messages, a complete working set (internal state of the algorithm) has to be maintained. Since only 16 128-bit XMM registers are available, even a working set of three 128-bit words (for instance cipher state, tweak mask, checksum) for 7 simultaneously processed messages will already exceed the number of

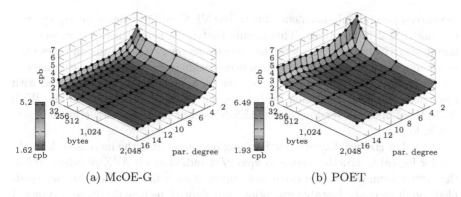

(a) McOE-G   (b) POET

Fig. 3. Performance of serial nonce-misuse resistant AE modes of operation when comb scheduling is used with different parallelization levels for various fixed message lengths (Color figure online)

available registers. As the parallelization degree P increases, this becomes more and more a factor. This can be especially seen for POET, which has a larger internal state per instance. By contrast, CCM, JAMBU and McOE-G suffer a lot less from this effect.

The experimental results also confirm the intuition of Sect. 6.1 that Haswell's improved memory interface can handle fairly large working set sizes efficiently by hiding the stack access latency between the cryptographic operations. This allows more multiple messages to be processed faster despite the increased register pressure, basically until the number of moves exceeds the latency of the other operations, or ultimately the limits of the Level-1 cache are reached.

6   Haswell Tricks: Towards Faster Code

In this section, we describe some of the optimization techniques and architecture features that were used for our implementations on Haswell.

6.1   General Considerations: AVX and AVX2 Instructions

In our Haswell-optimized AE scheme implementations we make heavy use of Intel Advanced Vector Extensions (AVX) which has been present in Intel processors since Sandy Bridge. AVX can be considered as an extension of the SSE+[3] streaming SIMD instructions operating on 128-bit xmm0 through xmm15 registers.

While AVX and AVX2, the latter which appears first on Intel's Haswell processor, brings mainly support for 256-bit wide registers to the table, this is not immediately useful in implementing an AES-based AE scheme, as the AES-NI instructions as well as the pclmulqdq instruction support only the use of 128-bit xmm registers. However, a feature of AVX that we use extensively is

---
[3] i.e. SSE, SSE2, etc.

the three-operand enhancement, due to the VEX coding scheme, of legacy two-operand SSE2 instructions. This means that, in a single instruction, one can non-destructively perform vector bit operations on two operands and store the result in a third operand, rather than overwriting one of the inputs, e.g. one can do $c = a \oplus b$ rather than $a = a \oplus b$. This eliminates overhead associated with mov operations required when overwriting an operand is not acceptable. With AVX, three-operand versions of the AES-NI and pclmulqdq instructions are also available.

A further Haswell feature worth taking into account is the increased throughput for logical instructions such as vpxor/vpand/vpor on AVX registers: While the latency remains at one cycle, now up to 3 such instructions can be scheduled simultaneously. Notable exceptions are algorithms heavily relying on mixed 64/128 bit logical operations such as JAMBU, for which the inclusion of a fourth 64-bit ALU implies that such algorithms will actually benefit from frequent conversion to 64-bit arithmetic via vpextrq/vpinsrq rather than artificial extension of 64-bit operands to 128 bits for operation on the AVX registers.

On Haswell, the improved memory controller allows two simultaneous 16-byte aligned moves vmovdqa from registers to memory, with a latency of one cycle. This implies that on Haswell, the comparatively large latency of cryptographic instructions such as vaesenc or pclmulqdq allows the implementer to "hide" more memory accesses to the stack when larger internal state of the algorithm leads to register shortage. This also benefits the generally larger working sets induced by the multiple message strategy described in Sect. 3.

6.2 Improved AES Instructions

In Haswell, the AES-NI encryption and decryption instructions had their latency improved from 8 cycles on Sandy and Ivy Bridge[4], down to 7 cycles [18]. This is especially beneficial for sequential implementations such as AES-CBC, CCM, McOE-G, CLOC, SILC and JAMBU. Furthermore, the throughput has been slightly optimized, allowing for better performance in parallel. Table 7 gives an overview of the latencies and inverse throughputs measured on our test machine (Core i5-4300U). The data was obtained using the test suite of Fog [13].

Table 7. Experimental latency (L) and inverse throughput (T^{-1}) of AES-NI and pclmulqdq instructions on Intel's Haswell microarchitecture

Instruction	L	T^{-1}	Instruction	L	T^{-1}
aesenc	7	1	aesimc	14	2
aesdec	7	1	aeskeygenassist	10	8
aesenclast	7	1	pclmulqdq	7	2
aesdeclast	7	1			

---

[4] We remark that Fog reports a latency of 4 cycles for aesenc on Ivy Bridge [13].

6.3 Improvements for Multiplication in $GF(2^{128})$

The pclmulqdq instruction was introduced by Intel along with the AES-NI instructions [17], but is not part of AES-NI itself. The instruction takes two 128-bit inputs and a byte input imm8, and performs carry-less multiplication of a combination of one 64-bit half of each operand. The choice of halves of the two operands to be multiplied is determined by the value of bits 4 and 0 of imm8.

Most practically used AE modes using multiplication in a finite field use block lengths of 128 bits. As a consequence, multiplications are in the field $GF(2^{128})$. As the particular choice of finite field does not influence the security proofs, modes use the tried-and-true GCM finite field. For our performance study, we have used two different implementation approaches for finite field multiplication (gfmul). The first implementation, which we refer to as the *classical method*, was introduced in Intel's white paper [17]. It applies pclmulqdq three times in a carry-less Karatsuba multiplication followed by modular reduction. The second implementation variant, which we refer to as the *Haswell-optimized method*, was proposed by Gueron [16] with the goal of leveraging the much improved pclmulqdq performance on Haswell to trade many shifts and XORs for one more multiplication. This is motivated by the improvements in both latency (7 vs. 14 cycles) and inverse throughput (2 vs. 8 cycles) on Haswell [18].

In modes where the output of a multiplication over $GF(2^{128})$ is not directly used, other than as a part of a chain combined using addition, the aggregated reduction method by Jankowski and Laurent [23] can be used to gain speed-ups. This method uses the inductive definitions of chaining values combined with the distributivity law for the finite field to postpone modular reduction at the cost of storing powers of an operand. Among the modes we benchmark in this work, the aggregated reduction method is applicable only to GCM and Julius. We therefore use this approach for those two modes, but apply the general gfmul implementations to the other modes.

6.4 Classical Vs. Haswell $GF(2^{128})$ Multiplication

Here we compare the classical and Haswell-optimized methods of multiplication in $GF(2^{128})$. We compare the performance of those AE modes that use full $GF(2^{128})$ multiplications (as opposed to aggregated reduction): McOE-G and COBRA, when instantiated using the two different multiplication algorithms. Figure 4 shows that when processing a single message, the classical implementation of gfmul performs better than the Haswell-optimized method, while the situation is reversed when processing multiple messages in parallel.

Given the speed-up of pclmulqdq on Haswell, this may seem somewhat counter-intuitive at first. We observe, however, that McOE-G and COBRA basically make sequential use of multiplications, which precludes utilizing the pipeline for sequential implementations. In this case, the still substantial latency of pclmulqdq is enough to offset the gains by replacing several other instructions for the reduction. This is different in the multiple message case, where the availability of independent data allows our implementations to make more efficient use of the pipeline, leading to superior results over the classical multiplication method.

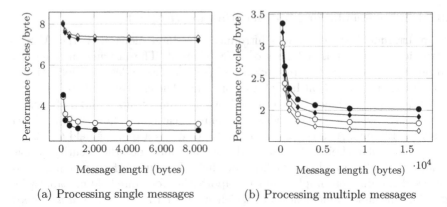

(a) Processing single messages   (b) Processing multiple messages

Fig. 4. Performance of McOE-G (diamond mark) and COBRA (circle mark) with single messages (left) and 8 multiple messages of equal length (right). Data points with hollow marks are for classical multiplication while filled marks are for Haswell-optimization multiplication.

6.5   Haswell-Optimized Doubling in $GF(2^{128})$

The doubling operation in $GF(2^{128})$ is commonly used in AE schemes [6], and indeed among the schemes we benchmark, it is used by OCB3, OTR, COBRA, COPA and POET. Doubling in this field consists of left shifting the input by one bit and doing a conditional XOR of a reduction polynomial if the MSB of the input equals one. Neither SSE+ nor AVX provide an instruction to shift a whole xmm register bitwise nor to directly test just its MSB. Thus, these functions have to be emulated with other operations, opening up a number of implementation choices.

We emulate a left shift by one bit by the following procedure, which is optimal with regard to the number of instructions and cycles: Given an input v, the value $2v \in GF(2^{128})$ is computed as in Listing. Consider $v = (v_L \| v_R)$ where v_L and v_R are 64-bit values. In line 3 we set $v_1 = (v_L \ll 1 \| v_R \ll 1)$ and lines 4 and 5 set first $v_2 = (v_R \| 0)$ and then $v_2 = ((v_R \gg 63) \| 0)$. As such, we have $v \ll 1 = v_1 \mid v_2$. This leaves us with a number of possibilities when implementing the branching of line 6, which can be categorized as (i) extracting parts from v and testing, (ii) AVX variants of the test instruction, (iii) extracting a mask with the MSB of each part of v and (iv) comparing against $10 \cdots 0_2$ (called MSB_MASK in Listing and RP is the reduction constant) and then extracting from the comparison result. Some of these approaches again leave several possibilities regarding the number of bits extracted, etc.

Interestingly, the approach taken to check the MSB of v has a great impact on the doubling performance. This is illustrated by Table 5 where we give performance of the doubling operation using various combinations of approaches. The numbers are obtained by averaging over 10^8 experiments. Surprisingly, we see that there is a significant speed-up, about a factor $\times 3$, when using comparison with MSB_MASK combined with extraction, over the other methods. Thus, we suggest to use this approach, where line 6 can be implemented as

if (_mm_extract_epi8(_mm_cmpgt_epi8(MSB_MASK, v), 15) == 0).

Listing (1.1) Doubling in $GF(2^{128})$

```
1  __m128i xtime(__m128i v) {
2    __m128i v1,v2;
3    v1 = _mm_slli_epi64(v,1);
4    v2 = _mm_slli_si128(v,8);
5    v2 = _mm_srli_epi64(v2,63);
6    if (msb of v == 1)
7      return _mm_xor_si128(_mm_or_si128(
          v1,v2),RP);
8    else
9      return _mm_or_si128(v1,v2);
10 }
```

(a) Performance of doubling with different approaches to MSB testing

Approach	Cycles
(i) Extraction	15.4
(ii) Test	15.4
(iii) MSB mask	16.7
(iv) Compare + extract	5.6

7 Conclusions

In this paper, we have discussed the performance of various block cipher-based symmetric primitives when instantiated with the AES on Intel's recent Haswell architecture.

As a general technique to speed up both inherently sequential modes and to deal with the typical scenario of having many shorter messages, we proposed our *comb scheduler*, an efficient algorithm for the scheduling of multiple simultaneous messages which is based on a look-ahead strategy within a certain window size. This leads to significant speed-ups for essentially all sequential modes, even when taking realistic Internet traffic distributions into account. Applied to the NIST-recommended modes CBC, CFB, OFB and CMAC, comb scheduling attains a significant speed-up of factor at least 5, resulting in a performance of around 0.88 cpb, which is within about 10 % of the performance of the parallelizable CTR mode on the same message distribution.

Applying comb scheduling to authenticated encryption modes (which typically feature higher initialization and finalization overhead, thus penalizing performance on the frequently occurring short messages), our technique speeds up the inherently sequential AE modes CCM, CLOC, SILC, JAMBU, McOE-G and POET by factors between 3 and 4.5. This particularly results in a CCM performance comparable to GCM or OCB3, without being afflicted by issues with weak-key classes or encumbered by patents.

Our study also establishes that for practitioners wishing to use a nonce-misuse resistant AE mode, the POET design with comb scheduling attains better performance than the completely parallelizable mode COPA. Since POET furthermore offers ciphertext-misuse resistance, this suggests that users do not have to choose between good performance or stricter notions of security.

References

1. Abed, F., Fluhrer, S., Forler, C., List, E., Lucks, S., McGrew, D., Wenzel, J.: Pipelineable on-line encryption. In: Cid, C., Rechberger, C. (eds.) FSE 2014. LNCS, vol. 8540, pp. 205–223. Springer, Heidelberg (2015)

2. Akdemir, K., Dixon, M., Feghali, W., Fay, P., Gopal, V., Guilford, J., Ozturk, E., Wolrich, G., Zohar, R.: Breakthrough AES Performance with Intel AES New Instructions. Intel Corporation (2010)
3. Andreeva, E., Bilgin, B., Bogdanov, A., Luykx, A., Mennink, B., Mouha, N., Yasuda, K.: APE: authenticated permutation-based encryption for lightweight cryptography. In: Cid, C., Rechberger, C. (eds.) FSE 2014. LNCS, vol. 8540, pp. 168–186. Springer, Heidelberg (2015)
4. Andreeva, E., Bogdanov, A., Luykx, A., Mennink, B., Tischhauser, E., Yasuda, K.: Parallelizable and authenticated online ciphers. In: Sako, K., Sarkar, P. (eds.) ASIACRYPT 2013, Part I. LNCS, vol. 8269, pp. 424–443. Springer, Heidelberg (2013)
5. Andreeva, E., Luykx, A., Mennink, B., Yasuda, K.: COBRA: a parallelizable authenticated online cipher without block cipher inverse. In: Cid, C., Rechberger, C. (eds.) FSE 2014. LNCS, vol. 8540, pp. 187–203. Springer, Heidelberg (2015)
6. Aoki, K., Iwata, T., Yasuda, K.: How fast can a two-pass mode go? a parallel deterministic authenticated encryption mode for AES-NI. In: DIAC 2012: Directions in Authenticated Ciphers (2012)
7. Bahack, L.: Julius: Secure Mode of Operation for Authenticated Encryption Based on ECB and Finite Field Multiplications. CAESAR competition proposal
8. Bernstein, D.J., Schwabe, P.: New AES software speed records. In: Chowdhury, D.R., Rijmen, V., Das, A. (eds.) INDOCRYPT 2008. LNCS, vol. 5365, pp. 322–336. Springer, Heidelberg (2008)
9. Bogdanov, A., Mendel, F., Regazzoni, F., Rijmen, V., Tischhauser, E.: ALE: AES-based lightweight authenticated encryption. In: Moriai, S. (ed.) FSE 2013. LNCS, vol. 8424, pp. 447–466. Springer, Heidelberg (2014)
10. Dworkin, M.J.: SP 800-38D. Recommendation for Block Cipher Modes of Operation: Galois/Counter Mode (GCM) and GMAC. Technical report, Gaithersburg, MD, USA (2007)
11. Fleischmann, E., Forler, C., Lucks, S.: McOE: a family of almost foolproof on-line authenticated encryption schemes. In: Canteaut, A. (ed.) FSE 2012. LNCS, vol. 7549, pp. 196–215. Springer, Heidelberg (2012)
12. Fleischmann, E., Forler, C., Lucks, S., Wenzel, J.: McOE: A Family of Almost Foolproof On-Line Authenticated Encryption Schemes. Cryptology ePrint Archive, Report 2011/644 (2011). http://eprint.iacr.org/
13. Fog, A.: Software Optimization Resources, February 2014. http://www.agner.org/optimize/. Accessed 17 February 2014
14. Gueron, S.: Intel's new AES Instructions for enhanced performance and security. In: Dunkelman, O. (ed.) FSE 2009. LNCS, vol. 5665, pp. 51–66. Springer, Heidelberg (2009)
15. Gueron, S.: Intel Advanced Encryption Standard (AES) New Instructions Set. Intel Corporation (2010)
16. Gueron, S.: AES-GCM software performance on the current high end CPUs as a performance baseline for CAESAR. In: DIAC 2013: Directions in Authenticated Ciphers (2013)
17. Gueron, S., Kounavis, M.E.: Intel Carry-Less Multiplication Instruction and its Usage for Computing the GCM Mode. Intel Corporation (2010)
18. Gulley, S., Gopal, V.: Haswell Cryptographic Performance. Intel Corporation (2013)
19. Hollingsworth, V.: New "Bulldozer" and "Piledriver" Instructions. Advanced Micro Devices Inc. (2012)

20. Iveson, S.: IPSec Bandwidth Overhead Using AES, October 2013. http://packetpushers.net/ipsec-bandwidth-overhead-using-aes/. Accessed 17 February 2014

21. Iwata, T., Minematsu, K., Guo, J., Morioka, S.: CLOC: authenticated encryption for short input. In: Cid, C., Rechberger, C. (eds.) FSE 2014. LNCS, vol. 8540, pp. 149–167. Springer, Heidelberg (2015)

22. Iwata, T., Minematsu, K., Guo, J., Morioka, S., Kobayashi, E.: SILC: Simple Lightweight CFB. CAESAR competition proposal

23. Jankowski, K., Laurent, P.: Packed AES-GCM Algorithm Suitable for AES/P-CLMULQDQ Instructions, pp. 135–138 (2011)

24. John, W., Tafvelin, S.: Analysis of internet backbone traffic and header anomalies observed. In: Internet Measurement Conference, pp. 111–116 (2007)

25. Käsper, E., Schwabe, P.: Faster and Timing-Attack Resistant AES-GCM. In: Clavier, C., Gaj, K. (eds.) CHES 2009. LNCS, vol. 5747, pp. 1–17. Springer, Heidelberg (2009)

26. Krovetz, T., Rogaway, P.: The software performance of authenticated-encryption modes. In: Joux, A. (ed.) FSE 2011. LNCS, vol. 6733, pp. 306–327. Springer, Heidelberg (2011)

27. Lim, C.H., Lee, P.J.: More Flexible Exponentiation with Precomputation. In: Desmedt, Y.G. (ed.) CRYPTO 1994. LNCS, vol. 839, pp. 95–107. Springer, Heidelberg (1994)

28. Matsui, M.: How far can we go on the x64 processors? In: Robshaw, M. (ed.) FSE 2006. LNCS, vol. 4047, pp. 341–358. Springer, Heidelberg (2006)

29. Matsui, M., Fukuda, S.: How to maximize software performance of symmetric primitives on Pentium III and 4 processors. In: Gilbert, H., Handschuh, H. (eds.) FSE 2005. LNCS, vol. 3557, pp. 398–412. Springer, Heidelberg (2005)

30. Matsui, M., Nakajima, J.: On the power of bitslice implementation on intel core2 processor. In: Paillier, P., Verbauwhede, I. (eds.) CHES 2007. LNCS, vol. 4727, pp. 121–134. Springer, Heidelberg (2007)

31. Dworkin, M.J.: SP 800-38D. Recommendation for Block Cipher Modes of Operation: Galois/Counter Mode (GCM) and GMAC. Technical report, National Institute of Standards & Technology, Gaithersburg, MD, USA (2007)

32. McGrew, D.A., Viega, J.: The security and performance of the Galois/Counter Mode (GCM) of operation. In: Canteaut, A., Viswanathan, K. (eds.) INDOCRYPT 2004. LNCS, vol. 3348, pp. 343–355. Springer, Heidelberg (2004)

33. Minematsu, K.: Parallelizable rate-1 authenticated encryption from pseudorandom functions. In: Nguyen, P.Q., Oswald, E. (eds.) EUROCRYPT 2014. LNCS, vol. 8441, pp. 275–292. Springer, Heidelberg (2014)

34. Murray, D., Koziniec, T.: The state of enterprise network traffic in 2012. In: 2012 18th Asia-Pacific Conference on Communications (APCC), pp. 179–184. IEEE (2012)

35. Osvik, D.A., Bos, J.W., Stefan, D., Canright, D.: Fast software AES encryption. In: Hong, S., Iwata, T. (eds.) FSE 2010. LNCS, vol. 6147, pp. 75–93. Springer, Heidelberg (2010)

36. Pentikousis, K., Badr, H.G.: Quantifying the deployment of TCP options - a comparative study, pp. 647–649 (2004)

37. Whiting, D., Housley, R., Ferguson, N.: Counter with CBC-MAC (CCM) (2003)

38. Wu, H., Huang, T.: JAMBU Lightweight Authenticated Encryption Mode and AES-JAMBU. CAESAR competition proposal

More Block Cipher Cryptanalysis

Security of the AES with a Secret S-Box

Tyge Tiessen[✉], Lars R. Knudsen, Stefan Kölbl, and Martin M. Lauridsen

DTU Compute, Technical University of Denmark, Kgs. Lyngby, Denmark
{tyti,lrkn,stek,mmeh}@dtu.dk

Abstract. How does the security of the AES change when the S-box is replaced by a secret S-box, about which the adversary has no knowledge? Would it be safe to reduce the number of encryption rounds?

In this paper, we demonstrate attacks based on integral cryptanalysis which allow to recover both the secret key and the secret S-box for respectively four, five, and six rounds of the AES. Despite the significantly larger amount of secret information which an adversary needs to recover, the attacks are very efficient with time/data complexities of $2^{17}/2^{16}$, $2^{38}/2^{40}$ and $2^{90}/2^{64}$, respectively.

Another interesting aspect of our attack is that it works both as chosen plaintext and as chosen ciphertext attack. Surprisingly, the chosen ciphertext variant has a significantly lower time complexity in the attacks on four and five round, compared to the respective chosen plaintext attacks.

Keywords: AES · Integral cryptanalysis · Secret S-box

1 Introduction

The Advanced Encryption Standard (AES) [10] is an iterated block cipher using 10, 12, or 14 rounds depending on the key size of 128, 192, or 256 bits. These variants are named AES-128, AES-192, and AES-256.

In this paper we consider the cipher that is derived from the AES by replacing the S-box with a secret 8-bit S-box while keeping everything else unchanged. If the choice of S-box is made uniformly at random from all 8-bit S-boxes, the size of the secret information increases from 128–256 bits, the key size in the AES, to 1812–1940 bits. Clearly the security level of such a cipher could be very high, thus the question is: Could the number of rounds of this cipher be reduced to fewer than 10 rounds (as in AES-128)?

The AES was designed in order to achieve good resistance against differential and linear cryptanalysis, and this includes the choice of the S-box. Nonetheless a randomly chosen S-box is very likely to be highly resistant against these attacks as well.

The method that is most successful in attacking AES for up to 6 rounds is integral cryptanalysis. Somewhat surprisingly, a variant of this attack also applies to the AES variant with a secret S-box with up to 6 rounds, and although the complexity of the attack is larger than for the attack on the original AES, the time complexity is still less than exhaustive search of a 128-bit key.

© International Association for Cryptologic Research 2015
G. Leander (Ed.): FSE 2015, LNCS 9054, pp. 175–189, 2015.
DOI: 10.1007/978-3-662-48116-5_9

Related Work. The idea of integral cryptanalysis was conceived as a dedicated attack against the block cipher SQUARE [3]. This attack is able to break up to six rounds of AES-128. Biryukov and Shamir applied integral cryptanalysis to a generalised SPN structure denoted SASAS [1], which consists of three substitution layers separated by two affine layers. In their paper, the attacker is assumed not to have any knowledge about the linear layer or the S-boxes which are all allowed to be chosen independently at random. The SASAS attack recovers an equivalent representation of this SPN and thus allows decryption of any ciphertext. The attack allows to break the equivalent of three rounds of AES. It does *not*, however, recover neither the key nor the S-box.

The case of the AES with a secret S-box, which we consider in this paper, lies in between two cases: The original SQUARE attack on one hand can not be directly applied to the case with the secret S-box as it requires knowledge of the S-box to peel off the last layer after guessing some key bits. The SASAS attack, on the other hand, can be used to attack three rounds of this cipher. However, it is not very effective, as the extra knowledge of the linear layer and the equality of all S-boxes remains unused.

The security of PRESENT with a secret S-box was studied by Borghoff et al. in [2] and allows an attack on 28 out of 31 rounds using slightly less than 2^{64} plaintexts. This attack was further improved by Liu et al. in [8]. As the attack depends on the weakness of some randomly chosen 4-bit S-boxes, it seems hard to apply it to the 8-bit S-boxes used in the AES.

Furthermore there are various block cipher designs based on using a secret, key-dependent substitutions like Khufu [9], Blowfish [14], Twofish [15] or Maya [7]. The attack also bears some resemblance to so-called SCARE (Side-Channel Analysis for Reverse Engineering) attacks in which side-channel information is used to recover unknown parts of cipher implementations (see for example [13]).

Our Contributions. We demonstrate that despite the increased size of the secret information in the cipher, we are able to recover both the secret key and the S-box for the 4-round, 5-round and 6-round versions of AES-128 by building up on techniques from integral cryptanalysis. Our attacks on four and five rounds are practical and achieve almost the same complexity as previous attacks which do not need to recover a secret S-box. The 6-round attack has a complexity of 2^{90} which is already much less than exhaustive search of the key, let alone of the S-box.

Table 1 compares the complexities for our attacks with those of previous integral attacks on AES-128 and the SASAS attack. Interestingly, the time complexities of the 4-round and 5-round attacks are lower by a factor of 2^{11} and 2^{16} respectively in the chosen ciphertext variant as compared to the chosen plaintext variant.

Organisation. This paper is organised as follows. In sect. 2 the notation and a specification of the AES is given. In sect. 3 we analyse the security of the AES

Table 1. Results of integral cryptanalysis on AES-128 with a secret S-box, AES-128 and SASAS with AES-like parameters. The time complexity is given in encryption equivalents, the data complexity is given in number of plaintexts/ciphertexts (16 bytes), the memory complexity is given in bytes. We assume that one round of encryption corresponds to 2^5 table lookups.

Cipher	Rounds	Complexity			Reference
		Time	Data	Memory	
SASAS	3	2^{21}	2^{16}	2^{20}	[1]
AES-128 (secret S-box)	4	2^{17}	2^{16}	2^{16}	*This work*
AES-128	4	2^{14}	2^9	–	[4]
AES-128 (secret S-box)	5	2^{38}	2^{40}	2^{40}	*This work*
AES-128	5	2^{38}	2^{33}	–	[4]
AES-128 (secret S-box)	6	2^{90}	2^{64}	2^{69}	*This work*
AES-128	6	2^{44}	2^{34}	2^{36}	[6]

with a secret S-box with respect to statistical and integral attacks. Section 4 holds the concluding remarks.

2   AES Specification

The AES [10] is an iterated block cipher that operates on 128-bit blocks and comes in three variants: AES-128, AES-192, and AES-256, which have key sizes of 128, 192 and 256 bits, respectively. The number of rounds T is 10, 12, and 14 respectively. The AES uses the four operations SubBytes, ShiftRows, MixColumns, and AddRoundKey which are detailed below. We use R_i, $1 \leq i \leq T$, to denote the round function which takes a 128-bit block as input and provides a 128-bit block as output. The ith round is defined as

$$R_i = \begin{cases} \texttt{AddRoundKey}_i \circ \texttt{MixColumns} \circ \texttt{ShiftRows} \circ \texttt{SubBytes} & , i < T \\ \texttt{AddRoundKey}_i \circ \texttt{ShiftRows} \circ \texttt{SubBytes} & , i = T \end{cases}.$$

Before the first round, a pre-whitening key is used in a step AddRoundKey$_0$, so the T-round encryption with master key K is denoted as

$$E_K = R_T \circ \cdots \circ R_1 \circ \texttt{AddRoundKey}_0.$$

Each of the four operations operate on a 128-bit block arranged in a 4×4 byte matrix:

$$\begin{pmatrix} s_0 & s_4 & s_8 & s_{12} \\ s_1 & s_5 & s_9 & s_{13} \\ s_2 & s_6 & s_{10} & s_{14} \\ s_3 & s_7 & s_{11} & s_{15} \end{pmatrix}.$$

The bytes are regarded as elements of what is called the *Rijndael finite field* $\mathbb{F}_{256} = \mathbb{F}_2[x]/(x^8 + x^4 + x^3 + x + 1)$. In the Rijndael finite field, an element is represented by a single byte $a = (a_7 a_6 \cdots a_1 a_0)$ with $a_i \in \mathbb{F}_2$, which in turn represents the field element

$$a(x) = a_7 x^7 + a_6 x^6 + \cdots + a_1 x + a_0.$$

We use hexadecimal notation in typewriter font to write byte values. As such $a = 01$ represents $a(x) = 1$, $a = 02$ represents $a(x) = x$, and so on. In the following, we briefly describe the four operations used in AES.

2.1   SubBytes

In the SubBytes operation, each of the 16 bytes in the state matrix is replaced by another value according to an 8-bit S-box. In the standard AES, the AES S-box is used whose full description is available to the adversary. However, in our analysis we will assume that the S-box is secret and thus unknown to the adversary.

2.2   ShiftRows

In the ShiftRows step, the ith row of the state, $0 \le i \le 3$, is rotated to the left by i positions. As such,

$$\text{ShiftRows} \left(\begin{pmatrix} s_0 & s_4 & s_8 & s_{12} \\ s_1 & s_5 & s_9 & s_{13} \\ s_2 & s_6 & s_{10} & s_{14} \\ s_3 & s_7 & s_{11} & s_{15} \end{pmatrix} \right) = \left(\begin{pmatrix} s_0 & s_4 & s_8 & s_{12} \\ s_5 & s_9 & s_{13} & s_1 \\ s_{10} & s_{14} & s_2 & s_6 \\ s_{15} & s_3 & s_7 & s_{11} \end{pmatrix} \right).$$

2.3   MixColumns

In this step, each of the four columns of the state matrix are multiplied from the right onto an invertible matrix M over the Rijndael finite field. The matrix M and its inverse are

$$M = \begin{pmatrix} 02 & 03 & 01 & 01 \\ 01 & 02 & 03 & 01 \\ 01 & 01 & 02 & 03 \\ 03 & 01 & 01 & 02 \end{pmatrix} \quad \text{and} \quad M^{-1} = \begin{pmatrix} 0e & 0b & 0d & 09 \\ 09 & 0e & 0b & 0d \\ 0d & 09 & 0e & 0b \\ 0b & 0d & 09 & 0e \end{pmatrix}.$$

2.4   AddRoundKey

In this step, a 128-bit round key is added to the state using the XOR operation. The $T + 1$ round keys, denoted $RK_0, \ldots, RK_T$ are generated using the AES key schedule. A brief description of the AES key schedule can be found in Appendix A.

3   Cryptanalysis of the AES with a Secret S-Box

3.1   Differential and Linear Cryptanalysis

First, we consider the security of the AES with a secret S-box which is chosen uniformly at random against the two most commonly used attacks vectors for block ciphers: differential cryptanalysis and linear cryptanalysis. The original AES was designed to resist these two attacks.

It has been shown that for mappings chosen uniformly at random from the set of all m-bit bijective mappings, the expected value of the highest probability of a (non-trivial) differential characteristic is at most $\frac{2m}{2^m}$ [11]. In our case where $m = 8$, this means that for a randomly chosen 8-bit S-box the expected maximum probability of a differential characteristic is $\frac{16}{2^8} = 2^{-4}$.

Since the number of active S-boxes for four rounds of the AES is at least 25 [4], one has an upper bound of the probability for any 4-round differential characteristic of 2^{-100}, and thus an upper bound for any 8-round differential characteristic of 2^{-200}. This is sufficient to conclude that differential cryptanalysis will not pose a threat to variants of the AES where the S-box is replaced by a randomly chosen 8-bit S-box.

It is possible to prove a similar result for linear cryptanalysis using the bounds of linear characteristics from [12].

3.2   Integral Cryptanalysis on Four Rounds

Summary. Before we go into the details of the attack, let us summarize it shortly. The attack splits the task of determining the secret S-box into consecutive steps that find increasingly better approximations of the secret S-box.

First we use the fact that we can create balanced sets of intermediate texts right after the first SubBytes step in round 1 by applying the SQUARE attack as a chosen ciphertext attack[1]. These balanced sets can be used to set up a system of linear equations which can be used to determine the secret S-box up to affine equivalence over $\mathbb{F}_2^8$ as is similarly done in the SASAS attack [1]. A representative from this equivalence class is already sufficient to determine the whitening key up to 256 variants.

The knowledge about the whitening key and the representative of the S-box equivalence class allow us now to determine the intermediate texts right before the MixColumns step in round 1 up to affine equivalence over $\mathbb{F}_2^8$. As a result of the SQUARE attack, the intermediate texts *after* the MixColumns step should take on each byte value in each byte position exactly once. This can be used to determine the secret S-box up to affine equivalence over $\mathbb{F}_{256}$. Finally, the secret S-box can be determined using knowledge of the key schedule.

---

[1] The reason for using a chosen ciphertext instead of a chosen plaintext attack will be explained later.

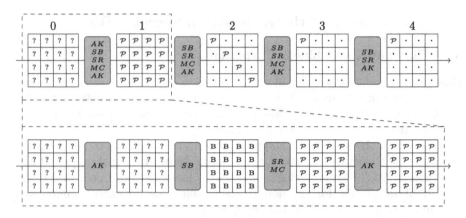

Fig. 1. Outline of the 4-round integral attack. The following notation is used: $\mathcal{P}$ takes each of the 256 values once, · is constant, B is balanced and the values ? are unknown.

Prerequisites. Before we start with the attack, let us clarify the notation. We assume that the last round, the fourth in this case, does not contain a MixColumns operation, as is the case for the last round of standard AES.

By a Λ-set, we mean a set of 256 messages that differ only in one byte but take for this byte all possible 256 values. Just as in the standard SQUARE [3] attack, when we decrypt a Λ-set with 4-round AES, we get intermediate texts right after the SubBytes step of round 1 that are balanced, i.e. the sum of all texts is equal to the text containing only zeroes, In particular, this set of messages is balanced in every byte.

Finding an Affine Equivalent of the Secret S-Box over $\mathbb{F}_2^8$. Let $p_i, 0 \leq i < 256$, be the list of the first bytes of the 256 plaintexts, generated from the Λ-set of ciphertexts. Let k_0 be the first byte of the whitening key. We can now write the fact that the intermediate texts are balanced right after the first SubBytes step as

$$\bigoplus_{i=0}^{255} S(p_i \oplus k_0) = 0$$

where S is the secret S-box. Let $z_i := S(k_0 \oplus i)$. The above equation is then linear in the z_{p_i} and can be written as

$$z_{p_0} \oplus z_{p_1} \oplus \cdots \oplus z_{p_{255}} = 0. \tag{1}$$

As duplicate values in the p_i values will cancel out, only those p_i need to be taken into account that appear an odd number of times in the list.

Taking different Λ-sets of ciphertexts, we can now try to generate enough linear equations to be able to determine S uniquely. Unfortunately, we encounter two problems now. Firstly, we do not know the value of k_0. We can thus only hope to determine $S(k_0 \oplus \cdot)$. Secondly, the above equations are invariant under affine transformations: Let A be an affine transformation from $\mathbb{F}_2^8$ to $\mathbb{F}_2^8$. Then

$$A(z_{p_0}) \oplus A(z_{p_1}) \oplus \cdots \oplus A(z_{c_{255}}) = 0$$

is also true for any set of p_i that fulfills equation (1) and has an even number of summands. We can thus at best determine $S(k_0 \oplus \cdot)$ up to 2^{72} affine equivalent variants. Using the fact that the affine mapping needs to be invertible, we can thus at best determine the set

$$\{A \circ S(k_0 \oplus \cdot) \mid A : \mathbb{F}_2^8 \to \mathbb{F}_2^8 \text{ is invertible}\}$$

which is of size $2^{70.2}$.

As each linear equation like Eq. 1 gives us one byte of information and as we can only determine the S-box up to $2^{72} = 2^{9\cdot8}$ variants, there can at most be $256 - 9 = 247$ linearly independent equations like equation (1). We found that using 256 different Λ-sets suffices in most cases to generate a set of equations with rank 247.

Given such a set of equations, it is now easy to determine one representative from the set of affine equivalents to $S(k_0 \oplus \cdot)$. Let this representative be denoted as S', i.e. $S' = A \circ S(k_0 \oplus \cdot)$ for some invertible affine $A : \mathbb{F}_2^8 \to \mathbb{F}_2^8$ and unknown k_0.

Determining the Whitening Key. Let now $p_{i,j}$ with $0 \leq i < 256$ and $0 \leq j < 8$ be byte j of the plaintext i in one of the Λ-sets and let k_j be byte j of the whitening key. We then have for $a \in \mathbb{F}_2^8$:

$$a = k_j \quad \Rightarrow \quad 0 = \bigoplus_{i=0}^{255} S(a \oplus p_{i,j}),$$

which is generally not true for $a \neq k_j$, a fact the standard SQUARE attack is based on as well. For invertible affine $A : \mathbb{F}_2^8 \to \mathbb{F}_2^8$, we also have the equivalence

$$0 = \bigoplus_{i=0}^{255} S(a \oplus p_{i,j}) \quad \Leftrightarrow \quad 0 = \bigoplus_{i=0}^{255} A \circ S(a \oplus p_{i,j}).$$

We can thus for each byte j with $1 \leq j < 8$ find $k_j \oplus k_0$ by trying out for which of the 256 possible values of a we have

$$\bigoplus_{i=0}^{255} S'(a \oplus p_{i,j}) = 0$$

for all Λ-sets. This allows us to determine the whitening key up to 256 variants, depending on the value of k_0. Let us set $k' = (0, k_1 \oplus k_0, k_2 \oplus k_0, \ldots, k_{15} \oplus k_0)$. Then when using k' as the whitening key and S' as the S-box for encryption, the intermediate texts after the ShiftRows step in round 1 will correspond to the correct intermediate texts up to a fixed affine transformation on each byte.

Finding an Affine Equivalent of the Secret S-Box over $\mathbb{F}_{256}$. When we decrypt a Λ-set, the set of intermediate texts that we get after the MixColumns step in round 1 will take all 256 possible values in each of the 16 state bytes (see Fig. 1). The key idea here is to use this property to filter out wrong candidates for the secret S-box.

For a set of 256 bytes, we say that it has the $\mathcal{P}$ property if it contains every possible value exactly once. Let V be a set of 256 byte vectors. We will likewise say that V has the $\mathcal{P}$ property if V has this property in every byte position.

If V is now the set of intermediate texts after the MixColumns operation in round 1, that is the result of the decryption of a Λ-set, we know from the SQUARE attack that V has the $\mathcal{P}$ property. Let now D be the corresponding set of intermediate texts directly before the MixColumns step. We can test our candidate S' for S, by constructing the corresponding candidate set D' for the intermediate texts after the ShiftRows step in round 1 with our acquired knowledge of the whitening key, and applying the MixColumns operation on this set D' to see whether we obtain a set with the $\mathcal{P}$ property.

For how many of the 2^{72} candidates for S' do we expect this to hold? Let A be the affine transformation by which S' deviates from S. Then the byte vectors in D' also deviate by this transformation from the true set D. Clearly, if A consists only of an addition, the $\mathcal{P}$ property of MD' is preserved where M is the MixColumns matrix. We can thus restrict A to linear transformations.

In the case, that A corresponds to an invertible linear mapping over $\mathbb{F}_{256}$, i.e. a multiplication with some element from $\mathbb{F}_{256}^*$, the set of intermediate texts after the MixColumns step will still have the $\mathcal{P}$ property as well since the linear transformation commutes with the multiplication within the MixColumns matrix M and the application of the invertible linear transformation A on the set MD leaves the $\mathcal{P}$ property untouched:

$$MD' = MAD = AMD.$$

Opposed to this, when A does not commute with the multiplication in $\mathbb{F}_{256}$, the $\mathcal{P}$ property of MD' is in general not preserved. As is shown in Appendix B, if A commutes with a primitive element of $\mathbb{F}_{256}$, A corresponds to multiplication with an element of $\mathbb{F}_{256}$. As 03 is a primitive element of the Rijndael field and is an entry in every row and column of M, the only class of affine transformations that preserve the $\mathcal{P}$ property of MD' is exactly the affine transformations over $\mathbb{F}_{256}$.

Checking whether the $\mathcal{P}$ property holds for MD' allows us thus to find the correct S up to affine transformations over $\mathbb{F}_{256}$. Nevertheless, still $2^{72-16} = 2^{56}$ candidates need to be tested.

Complexity Reduction: Finding the Affine Equivalent over $\mathbb{F}_{256}$. The specific structure of the MixColumns matrix M allows us to reduce the computational complexity of finding the correct affine representative amongst the 2^{56} possible candidates.

Let us define that a set of $2l$ vectors over $\mathbb{F}_2^n$ has the $\mathcal{R}$ property if both 1 and 0 appear in every bit position exactly l times. Note that the $\mathcal{P}$ property implies the $\mathcal{R}$ property and that the $\mathcal{R}$ property implies that the set of vectors is balanced but the opposite direction of implications is in generally false. As the $\mathcal{R}$ property, like the $\mathcal{P}$ property, is not preserved by the MixColumns layer, we still expect to find the correct representative by testing for the $\mathcal{R}$ property instead of the $\mathcal{P}$ property[2].

Let us take a closer look at the specific form of matrix M. When written as a linear function from F_{256}^4 to F_{256}^4, it has the form

$$M = \begin{pmatrix} 02\ 03\ 01\ 01 \\ 01\ 02\ 03\ 01 \\ 01\ 01\ 02\ 03 \\ 03\ 01\ 01\ 02 \end{pmatrix}. \tag{2}$$

If we associate the multiplication with 01, 02, and 03 with their respective linear mappings from $\mathbb{F}_2^8$ to $\mathbb{F}_2^8$, we get the following representations:

$$01 = \begin{pmatrix} 1\,0\,0\,0\,0\,0\,0\,0 \\ 0\,1\,0\,0\,0\,0\,0\,0 \\ 0\,0\,1\,0\,0\,0\,0\,0 \\ 0\,0\,0\,1\,0\,0\,0\,0 \\ 0\,0\,0\,0\,1\,0\,0\,0 \\ 0\,0\,0\,0\,0\,1\,0\,0 \\ 0\,0\,0\,0\,0\,0\,1\,0 \\ 0\,0\,0\,0\,0\,0\,0\,1 \end{pmatrix} \quad 02 = \begin{pmatrix} 0\,1\,0\,0\,0\,0\,0\,0 \\ 0\,0\,1\,0\,0\,0\,0\,0 \\ 0\,0\,0\,1\,0\,0\,0\,0 \\ 1\,0\,0\,0\,1\,0\,0\,0 \\ 1\,0\,0\,0\,0\,1\,0\,0 \\ 0\,0\,0\,0\,0\,0\,1\,0 \\ 1\,0\,0\,0\,0\,0\,0\,1 \\ 1\,0\,0\,0\,0\,0\,0\,0 \end{pmatrix} \quad 03 = \begin{pmatrix} 1\,1\,0\,0\,0\,0\,0\,0 \\ 0\,1\,1\,0\,0\,0\,0\,0 \\ 0\,0\,1\,1\,0\,0\,0\,0 \\ 1\,0\,0\,1\,1\,0\,0\,0 \\ 1\,0\,0\,0\,1\,1\,0\,0 \\ 0\,0\,0\,0\,0\,1\,1\,0 \\ 1\,0\,0\,0\,0\,0\,1\,1 \\ 1\,0\,0\,0\,0\,0\,0\,1 \end{pmatrix}. \tag{3}$$

If we now write $a_0, a_1, \ldots, a_7$ for the rows of A we can write the first row of the 32×32 matrix MA over $\mathbb{F}_2$ as

$$v := (a_1, \quad a_0 \oplus a_1, \quad a_0, \quad a_0).$$

We see now that whether or not the first bit in the set MD' satisfies the $\mathcal{R}$ property relies solely on the rows a_0 and a_1 of the matrix A. As we only need to test matrices A that are not linearly equivalent over $\mathbb{F}_{256}$, we can fix one row of A to a non-zero constant. Let a_0 be fixed. Then we only need to try out all 2^8 possible values for a_2 to see which one gives us the $\mathcal{R}$ property in this bit.

After having determined a_1 (and fixed a_0), we can use the second row of MA to determine a_2 and continue on to determine A uniquely. In each step, we only need to test 2^8 possible values. We can thus split the task of trying of out all 2^{56} candidates for A, to trying out row by row which reduces the complexity to $7 \cdot 2^8 \approx 2^{11}$ steps.

Determining the Secret S-Box. Without assuming anything about the key schedule, we can only determine the secret S-box up to an additive constant before and after the S-box, i.e. $S'(x) \sim a \oplus S(b \oplus x)$ since any additive constants can also be seen as part of the round keys. When not assuming anything about the key schedule, one can for example require that the first byte of the whitening

---

[2] This was indeed the case for all our test runs.

key and the first round key is zero. It is straightforward then to find the correct representative for S out of the 2^{16} options under these constraints. Using knowledge about the key schedule, one can also easily determine the correct variants for the round keys and adjust the representative for the S-box accordingly.

The Complexity of the Attack. The needed data consists of the decryption of 256 Λ-sets which corresponds to a data complexity of 2^{16} chosen ciphertexts. As most of these texts are only used to generate the linear system of equations in the first plaintext byte, most plaintext pairs can be discarded after the corresponding equation has been extracted. The memory complexity is thus $2^{8+8} = 2^{16}$ bytes.

Let us go through the steps to see what the time complexity is. Determining S' up to affine equivalence over $\mathbb{F}_2^8$ requires solving a system of linear equations in 2^8 variables. This requires $2^{3 \cdot 8} = 2^{24}$ steps where each step is comparable to a table lookup. Finding the whitening key requires trying out for each of the 16 key bytes all 2^8 possible solutions with one Λ-set of 2^8 values. It thus takes about $16 \cdot 2^8 \cdot 2^8 = 2^{20}$ table lookups.

To determining S' up to affine equivalence over $\mathbb{F}_{256}$ using the $\mathcal{R}$ property, for each of the seven rows of A that have not been fixed we have to test 2^8 values, each with a Λ sets. Thus the total complexity of this step is $7 \cdot 2^8 \cdot 2^8 \approx 2^{19}$. A step here has about the same complexity as a table lookup.

The complexity of the attack is dominated by solving the linear system of equations, namely 2^{24} steps, which corresponds to 2^{17} encryptions when assuming a complexity of 2^5 table lookups per encryption round. We ran the attack 1000 times on the single core of an Intel Core i7-4600M CPU at 2.90GHz. It found both the correct S-box and the correct key each time and always ran in less than a second (including reading the input data).

3.3   Integral Cryptanalysis on Five Rounds

The attack on four rounds can be extended to five rounds using a technique by Ferguson et al. [6] that allowed to improve the SQUARE attack on six rounds. The underlying idea is to create sets of ciphertexts that form a Λ-set right before the MixColumns step of round 4. Unfortunately, even with key guessing, it is not possible to determine such a set without knowledge of the secret S-box. However, by taking all 2^{32} possible values for four bytes that are in the same column during the MixColumns step of round 4 and keeping all other bytes constant, we can generate a set of ciphertexts that will take all 2^{32} values in that column. This set can now be viewed as the union of 2^{24} Λ -sets (see Fig. 2).

A set of ciphertexts that gives us a Λ-set in the MixColumns step of round 4 will generate a balanced set right after the SubBytes step of round 1. As a sum of balanced sets remains balanced, decrypting our 2^{32} ciphertexts, we get a balanced set of size 2^{32} after the SubBytes step of round 1. This set can now be used to mount the four round attack on five rounds as well.

Just as in the four round version, we use the fact when such a set is balanced, we can, by using 256 of them, create a system of linear equations that can be

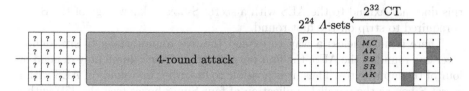

Fig. 2. The 2^{32} ciphertexts take all possible combinations in the blue bytes but constant values in the rest. The state before the MixColumns step in the round before can be seen as the union of 2^{24} Λ-sets as depicted here. It is then possible to apply the 4-round attack again.

solved to find an S-box S' that is an affine equivalent to S over $\mathbb{F}_2^8$. We can use the knowledge of S' again to determine the whitening key up to 256 variants. We can then again generate the corresponding intermediate texts after the first SubBytes step that are affinely equivalent over $\mathbb{F}_2^8$ to the true texts. With these texts we can now determine S up to affine equivalence over $\mathbb{F}_{256}$ by using the $\mathcal{R}$ property. Note that when using the $\mathcal{R}$ property here, we expect the correct set of texts to take in each bit the values 0 and 1 each exactly 2^{31} times as we are now working with the union of 2^{24} Λ-sets. Again to determine S exactly and finding the correct master key is straightforward from this point.

How do the complexities of the attack change as compared to the 4-round variant? As we need 256 sets of ciphertexts, each of size 2^{32}, this leaves us with a data complexity of 2^{40}, an increase by a factor of 2^{24} in comparison to the four round attack. The time complexity of solving the linear system of equations does not change (it is still a system of 256 equations in 256 variables). The complexity of the whitening key recovery increases with the size of the balanced sets, i.e. again by a factor of 2^{24}, leaving us with a complexity of 2^{44} table lookups. Likewise is the complexity of checking the $\mathcal{R}$ property increased by a factor of 2^{24} to a total complexity of 2^{43} steps of the same complexity as a table lookup. This leaves the total time complexity at roughly 2^{45} steps which corresponds to 2^{38} encryptions when assuming a complexity of 2^5 table lookups per encryption round.

The data complexity of 2^{40} chosen ciphertexts corresponds to 18 terabyte of data. But as most of the sets of 2^{32} plaintexts are each only used to generate one linear equation (in the 256 variables), apart from a few (16 suffice), most can be discarded during the generation of the linear system of equations, leaving us with at most 2^{40} bytes that need to be stored in memory at any point in time.

3.4   Integral Cryptanalysis on Six Rounds

The standard way of extending the SQUARE attack to six rounds (in the case of a chosen ciphertext attack) is by guessing four bytes of the whitening key and peeling of the first round of encryption for one byte of intermediate text, thereby increasing the time complexity of the attack by a factor of 2^{32}. Unfortunately, this does not extend to the AES with a secret S-box as knowledge of the S-box is required to strip off the first round.

There is nonetheless a way to extend the five round attack to six rounds. Over one round of the AES, the four output bytes of one column only depend on four of the input bytes. Thus, it is possible to describe two rounds of AES with a secret S-box as the parallel application of four Super-boxes (see also [5]) with a linear transformation before and after. Such a Super-box consists of the parallel application of four S-boxes, a key addition a multiplication of the four bytes with the `MixColumns` matrix, again an application of four S-boxes in parallel and a final key addition.

Just as in the 5-round attack, we can generate sets of texts that are balanced right after the `SubBytes` step in round 2 and we can hence use these texts to generate a system of linear equations that lets us determine the Super-boxes, just as it allowed us to determine the usual S-boxes in the attacks before. Unfortunately, the system of linear equations for one Super-box involves now not 2^8 variables but 2^{32} variables. This means that both the computational complexity as well as the data complexity increase. For the data complexity, when using the round extension as in the five round attack, we need now 2^{32} sets of each 2^{32} texts, leaving us with a data complexity of 2^{64} chosen ciphertexts. Just as with the attack on the normally sized S-box, the set of equations is not of full rank and lets us determine the Super-box only up to $2^{32 \cdot 32 + 32} = 2^{1056}$ affine equivalents – only slightly less when taking the necessary bijectivity of the affine transform into account.

The Super-box that we obtain will thus be of the form

$$A \circ \texttt{SubBytes} \circ \texttt{KeyAddition} \circ \texttt{MixColumns} \circ \texttt{SubBytes} \circ \texttt{KeyAddition}$$

where A is an unknown invertible affine mapping over $\mathbb{F}_2^{32}$ and where the other standard AES steps are truncated to operate on four bytes only. Despite our lack of knowledge of A, this form is already enough to extract from it the secret S-box and the involved key bytes up to 2^{16} variants, i.e. up to two additive constants applied before and after the S-box. After this, it is straightforward to uniquely determine the secret S-box and the key e.g. by guessing the two additive constants and applying standard 6-round SQUARE attack.

If we decrypt a Λ-set with our affinely transformed Super-box, we get a set that is balanced right after the first `SubBytes` step of the Super-box as described in the SASAS paper [1]. Note that it is necessary to assume that A distributes the 8 bits that are being varied in the Λ-set to at least two S-Boxes, an assumption that is true for almost all possible A. At this point we can thus simply apply again the same techniques as we did for the four round attack to determine the secret S-box and the involved key bytes, only that we mount the attack on the affine equivalent of the Super-box now instead of the whole cipher.

What is the complexity of this attack? As already mentioned above, the data complexity is 2^{64} chosen ciphertexts. The time complexity is dominated by the first step of solving the system of 2^{32} linear equations over 2^{32} variables. Using Gaussian elimination, this step consists of 2^{96} operations, each comparable in complexity to a table lookup. Thus, the time complexity corresponds to 2^{90} encryptions when assuming a complexity of 2^5 table lookups per encryption round. The memory complexity of $2^{32} \cdot 2^{32} \cdot 32 = 2^{69}$ bytes is also dominated by the size of the system of equations.

3.5 A Note on Chosen Ciphertext Vs. Chosen Plaintext

Due to the symmetry of the AES regarding encryption and decryption, the attacks described here principally work in both directions. Interestingly though, for the attacks on four and five rounds, the chosen ciphertext variant is considerably more effective than the chosen plaintext attack. This is because the MixColumns matrix is sufficiently sparser than its inverse, creating a difference of 2^{16} in the number of steps when applying the $\mathcal{R}$ property. This changes the time complexities of the 4-round and 5-round attacks to 2^{28} and 2^{54}. As the complexity of the 6-round attack is dominated by the solving of the linear system of equations, it does not make a difference in that attack scenario.

4   Conclusion

In this work, we studied the impact of replacing the S-box in the AES by a secret S-box unknown to the adversary. Despite the expected increase in difficulty of recovering the secret information, we were able to mount efficient attacks based on integral cryptanalysis combined with dedicated techniques.

We were able to show that AES-128 with a secret S-box, reduced to 4 and 5 rounds, is susceptible to attacks with practical complexity that successfully recover both the secret S-box and the key. Furthermore, we have shown an attack on a variant with 6 rounds with a time complexity of 2^{90}, which is much less effort than the time required to do exhaustive search of the key, let alone of the S-box.

Similarly to standard AES, it seems difficult to extend our attacks to more than 6 rounds. Also, the gap between the time complexities of integral attacks on standard AES and the AES with a secret S-box increases dramatically for the attack on 6 rounds. It is an open question whether this complexity can be further reduced.

Acknowledgements. The work in this paper has partially been funded by the Nasjonal sikkerhetsmyndighet (NSM).

A   The AES Key Schedule

In the AES, we think of the round keys as matrices over the Rijndael finite field, just as the state matrix. The first pre-whitening key RK_0 is the n-bit master key itself, so $RK_0 = K$. The key schedule varies slightly across the three AES variants. Here, we describe it for AES-128 and refer to [4] for the other two cases. We consider the 4 columns of the two round keys as $RK_i = (RK_i^0 \| RK_i^1 \| RK_i^2 \| RK_i^3)$ and $RK_{i+1} = (RK_{i+1}^0 \| RK_{i+1}^1 \| RK_{i+1}^2 \| RK_{i+1}^3)$. To derive RK_{i+1} from RK_i, $0 \le i < T$, we do the following

1. Let $RK_{i+1}^j = RK_i^j$ for $j = 0, 1, 2, 3$,
2. Rotate RK_{i+1}^3 such that the byte in the first row is moved to the bottom,
3. Substitute each byte in RK_{i+1}^3 by using the S-box from the SubBytes operation,
4. Update the byte in the first row of RK_{i+1}^3 by adding 02^{i-1} from the Rijndael finite field, and
5. Let $RK_{i+1}^j = RK_{i+1}^j \oplus RK_{i+1}^{j-1 \mod 4}$ for $j = 0, 1, 2, 3$.

This procedure is repeated for $i = 1, \ldots, T$ to obtain the round keys RK_0 to RK_T.

B   Lemma

Let $m \in \mathbb{N}^*$. As $\mathbb{F}_{2^m}$ is an m-dimensional $\mathbb{F}_2$-vector space, its elements can be represented as m-dimensional $\mathbb{F}_2$-vectors. But as the multiplication in $\mathbb{F}_{2^m}$ obeys the distributive law, the multiplication with an element of $\mathbb{F}_{2^m}$ corresponds to a linear mapping from $\mathbb{F}_2^m$ to $\mathbb{F}_2^m$, that is an $m \times m$ matrix over $\mathbb{F}_2$. For an element $a \in \mathbb{F}_{2^m}$, let L_a denote the corresponding $m \times m$ matrix. For $b \in \mathbb{F}_{2^m}$, we then have $a \cdot b = L_a b$.

Lemma 1. *Let a be a primitive element of $\mathbb{F}_{2^m}$. Let B be an $m \times m$ matrix over $\mathbb{F}_2$ which commutes with L_a. Then there exists $b \in \mathbb{F}_{2^m}$ such that $L_b = B$.*

Proof. Let c be any element from $\mathbb{F}_{2^m}^*$. As a is primitive, there exists $k \in \mathbb{N}^*$ such that $c = a^k$ and likewise $L_c = L_a^k$. As B commutes with L_a, by induction B also commutes with L_c. Clearly, B also commutes with L_0, so B commutes with all elements of $\mathbb{F}_{2^m}$.

Let now $b \in \mathbb{F}_{2^m}$ be the image of 1 under B, $b = B1$. We then have for any $c \in \mathbb{F}_{2^m}^*$:

$$Bc = L_1 Bc = L_c L_{c^{-1}} Bc = L_c B L_{c^{-1}} c = L_c B1 = L_c b = c \cdot b = b \cdot c = L_b c.$$

As this is true for any $c \in \mathbb{F}_{2^m}^*$ and clearly also for 0, we have $B = L_b$.   □

References

1. Biryukov, A., Shamir, A.: Structural cryptanalysis of SASAS. In: Pfitzmann, B. (ed.) EUROCRYPT 2001. LNCS, vol. 2045, pp. 394–405. Springer, Heidelberg (2001)
2. Borghoff, J., Knudsen, L.R., Leander, G., Thomsen, S.S.: Cryptanalysis of PRESENT-like ciphers with secret S-boxes. In: Joux, A. (ed.) FSE 2011. LNCS, vol. 6733, pp. 270–289. Springer, Heidelberg (2011)

3. Daemen, J., Knudsen, L.R., Rijmen, V.: The block cipher SQUARE. In: Biham, E. (ed.) FSE 1997. LNCS, vol. 1267, pp. 149–165. Springer, Heidelberg (1997)
4. Daemen, J., Rijmen, V.: The Design of Rijndael: AES - The Advanced Encryption Standard. Information Security and Cryptography. Springer, Heidelberg (2002)
5. Daemen, J., Rijmen, V.: Understanding two-round differentials in AES. In: De Prisco, R., Yung, M. (eds.) SCN 2006. LNCS, vol. 4116, pp. 78–94. Springer, Heidelberg (2006)
6. Ferguson, N., Kelsey, J., Lucks, S., Schneier, B., Stay, M., Wagner, D., Whiting, D.L.: Improved cryptanalysis of rijndael. In: Schneier, B. (ed.) FSE 2000. LNCS, vol. 1978, pp. 213–230. Springer, Heidelberg (2001)
7. Gomathisankaran, M., Lee, R.B.: Maya: A novel block encryption function. In: International Workshop on Coding and Cryptography (2009)
8. Liu, G.-Q., Jin, C.-H., Qi, C.-D.: Improved slender-set linear cryptanalysis. In: Cid, C., Rechberger, C. (eds.) FSE 2014. LNCS, vol. 8540, pp. 431–450. Springer, Heidelberg (2015)
9. Merkle, R.C.: Fast software encryption functions. In: Menezes, A., Vanstone, S.A. (eds.) CRYPTO 1990. LNCS, vol. 537, pp. 476–500. Springer, Heidelberg (1991)
10. National Institute of Standards and Technology. Advanced Encryption Standard. Federal Information Processing Standard (FIPS), Publication 197, U.S. Department of Commerce, Washington D.C., November 2001
11. O'Connor, L.: On the distribution of characteristics in bijective mappings. In: Helleseth, T. (ed.) EUROCRYPT 1993. LNCS, vol. 765, pp. 360–370. Springer, Heidelberg (1994)
12. O'Connor, L.: Properties of linear approximation tables. In: Preneel, B. (ed.) FSE 1994. LNCS, vol. 1008, pp. 131–136. Springer, Heidelberg (1995)
13. Rivain, M., Roche, T.: SCARE of secret ciphers with SPN structures. In: Sako, K., Sarkar, P. (eds.) ASIACRYPT 2013, Part I. LNCS, vol. 8269, pp. 526–544. Springer, Heidelberg (2013)
14. Schneier, B.: Description of a new variable-length key, 64-bit block cipher (Blowfish). In: Anderson, R. (ed.) FSE 1994. LNCS, vol. 809, pp. 191–204. Springer, Heidelberg (1994)
15. Schneier, B., Kelsey, J., Whiting, D., Wagner, D., Hall, C., Ferguson, N.: Twofish: A 128-Bit Block Cipher

Meet-in-the-Middle Attacks and Structural Analysis of Round-Reduced PRINCE

Patrick Derbez$^{(\boxtimes)}$ and Léo Perrin

SnT, University of Luxembourg, Luxembourg City, Luxembourg
{patrick.derbez,leo.perrin}@uni.lu

Abstract. NXP Semiconductors and its academic partners challenged the cryptographic community with finding practical attacks on the block cipher they designed, PRINCE. Instead of trying to attack as many rounds as possible using attacks which are usually impractical despite being faster than brute-force, the challenge invites cryptographers to find practical attacks and encourages them to actually implement them. In this paper, we present new attacks on round-reduced PRINCE including the ones which won the challenge in the 6 and 8-round categories — the highest for which winners were identified. Our first attacks rely on a meet-in-the-middle approach and break up to 10 rounds of the cipher. We also describe heuristic methods we used to find practical SAT-based and differential attacks.

Finally, we also present an analysis of the cycle structure of the internal rounds of PRINCE leading both to a low complexity distinguisher for 4-round PRINCE-core and an alternative representation of the cipher valid in particular contexts and which highlights, in this cases, a poor diffusion.

Keywords: PRINCE · Practical attacks · Meet-in-the-middle · SAT-solver · Statistical analysis

1 Introduction

When tasked with assessing the security of a block cipher, cryptanalysts have now a broad range of tools at their disposal: differential attack [1], linear attack [2], meet-in-the-middle attack [3], etc. The main purpose of a security analysis is usually to identify flaws in the design of a primitive and then to illustrate their gravity through the description of an attack covering as many rounds as possible. However, applicability of said attacks in a realistic situation is usually not the first objective of the cryptanalyst. A simple reason for this is that as our understanding of the design of block ciphers improved, the ease of identifying practical attacks decreased. Furthermore and in accordance with the famous maxim "attacks only get better", an impractical attack submitted at a given time may later be improved.

Patrick Derbez and Léo Perrin are supported by the CORE ACRYPT project from the *Fond National de Recherche* (Luxembourg).

© International Association for Cryptologic Research 2015
G. Leander (Ed.): FSE 2015, LNCS 9054, pp. 190–216, 2015.
DOI: 10.1007/978-3-662-48116-5_10

While impractical attacks provide the academic community with valuable insights into the security provided by different block ciphers, their components, their design strategies, etc., crypanalysis in the industry is more focused on practical attacks. In order to promote this view, the Technical University of Denmark (DTU), NXP Semiconductors and the Ruhr University of Bochum challenged the cryptographic community [4] with finding low data complexity attacks on the block cipher PRINCE [5]. More precisely, they accept attacks requiring only at most 2^{20} chosen plaintexts or 2^{30} known plaintexts. Furthermore, extra rewards (from 1000 to 10000€) are given for attacks on at least 8 rounds which require at most 2^{45} bytes of memory (about 32 Tb) and at most 2^{64} encryptions of the round-reduced variant attacked.

Studying PRINCE in this setting may provide valuable data on multiple accounts. First of all, PRINCE is a lightweight block cipher, meaning that it is intended to be run on processors with little computing power to devote to security related algorithm or on hardware where every logical gate counts. Research on this topic is intense nowadays as the need for such primitives becomes increasingly pressing, see [6] for an extensive review of the algorithms that have been proposed. Second, PRINCE implements a simplified version of the so-called FX construction: encryption under key $(k_0 || k_1)$ consists in xor-ing k_0 to the plaintext, applying a block cipher called PRINCE-core keyed with k_1 and then output the result xor-ed with $L(k_0)$ where L is a simple linear bijection. This strategy allows for a greater key size without the cost of a sophisticated key schedule. However, it is impossible to make a security claim as strong as for a more classical construction. Finally, PRINCE-core has a unique property called α-reflection. If we denote by E_{c,k_1} the encryption under PRINCE-core with subkey k_1, then the corresponding decryption operation is $E_{c,k_1 \oplus \alpha}$ for a constant α. In other words, decryption is merely encryption under a related-key. The consequences of this property have already been studied and, in particular, some values of α different from the one used have been showed to lead to weaker algorithms [7].

PRINCE has already been the subject of several cryptanalysis, notably [8] where the security of the algorithm against multiple attacks was assessed, [7] which investigated the influence of the value of α, [9] which described Meet-in-the-Middle attacks on the block cipher and, finally, [10] proposed the best attack to date in terms of number of rounds attacked. A list of the cryptanalyses of round-reduced PRINCE is provided in Table 1. Attacks working only on PRINCE-core or for modified versions of PRINCE (different α or S-Box) are not shown.

As stated before, most of the attacks usually considered often have impractical complexities. For instance, differential attacks and linear attacks require large amounts of chosen (respectively known) plaintexts, both of which may be impossible to gather to begin with if the algorithm is implemented on a small-device with little computer and, hence, a small throughput. Therefore, we focused our efforts on Meet-in-the-Middle (MitM) attacks, algebraic/logic attack where the fact that a ciphertext is the encryption of a plaintext is encoded as an equation which is fed to a solver and, surprisingly, differential attack for which we found a heuristic method decreasing significantly the data complexity.

Table 1. The best attacks on round-reduced PRINCE in the single-key model.

Description			Complexity		
Reference	Type	Rounds	Data (CP)	Time	Memory
[8]	Integral	4	2^4	2^{64}	2^4
		6	2^{16}	2^{64}	2^6
Section 4	Diff./Logic	4	2^{10}	5s	$\ll 2^{27}$
		6	$2^{14.9}$	$2^{32.9}$	$\ll 2^{27}$
Section 3	MitM	6	2^{16}	$2^{33.7}$	$2^{31.9}$
		8	2^{16}	$2^{50.7}$ (online)	$2^{84.9}$
		8	2^{16}	$2^{65.7}$ (online)	$2^{68.9}$
		10	2^{57}	2^{68} (online)	2^{41}
[9]	MitM	8	2^{53}	2^{60}	2^{30}
		9	2^{57}	2^{64}	$2^{57.3}$
[10]	Multiple diff.	9	$2^{46.89}$	$2^{51.21}$	$2^{52.21}$
		10	$2^{57.94}$	$2^{60.62}$	$2^{61.52}$

Time complexity is measured in encryption units.
Memory complexity is measured in 64-bit blocks.

Our Contribution. We describe different low data complexity attacks on round-reduced PRINCE which we submitted to the PRINCE challenge and which turned out [11] to be the best ones on PRINCE reduced to 6 and 8 rounds. In Sect. 3, we describe our attacks obtained using the meet-in-the-middle technique and we also show a new attack on 10 rounds with practical memory and a time complexity around 2^{68} encryptions. Then, we describe in Sect. 4 how the equation given to a SAT-solver can be modified so as to make an attack on 4 rounds practical, how the power of the filter used to discard wrong pairs in a differential attack can be raised to the power 4 when attacking 6-round PRINCE by considering groups of pairs and, finally, how to attack 6-round PRINCE using a differential attack to recover half of the key and a SAT-solver to recover the other half. We finally present in Sect. 5 some observations about the cycle structure of the internal rounds of PRINCE and how it implies the existence of alternative representations of the cipher highlighting a poor diffusion in some subsets of the input space. While we do not use these to attack PRINCE directly, we show that the size of these subsets remains reasonable and actually find such sets for 4-round PRINCE-core.

2   Specification of PRINCE

2.1   Description of PRINCE

PRINCE is a 64-bit block cipher with a 128-bit key. It is based on a variant of the FX-construction which was proposed by Kilian and Rogaway as a generalization

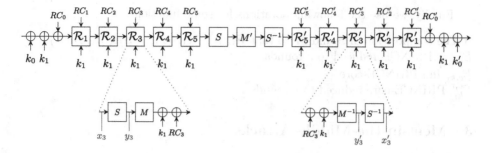

Fig. 1. the PRINCE cipher.

of the DESX scheme. The master key k is split into two 64-bit parts $k = k_0 \parallel k_1$ and k_0 is used to generate a third subkey $k_0' = (k_0 \ggg 1) \oplus (k_0 \gg 63)$. Both k_0 and k_0' are used as pre- and post- whitening keys respectively. The full version of the cipher has 12 rounds and is depicted on Fig. 1.

The encryption is quite similar to the AES and consists of a nibble-based substitution layer S and a linear layer M. The operation M can be divided into a ShiftRows operations and a matrix multiplication M' operating independently on each column but not nibble-oriented. Furthermore the matrix M' is an involution and, combined to the fact that the round constants satisfy the relation $RC_i \oplus RC_i' = \alpha$ where $\alpha =$ C0AC29B7C97C50DD, the decryption process $D_{k_0,k_1,k_0'}$ is equal to the encryption process $E_{k_0',k_1 \oplus \alpha,k_0}$. For further details about PRINCE we refer the reader to [5].

Notations. In the sequel we denote both the plaintext and the ciphertext by p and c respectively. For the first R rounds of $2R$-round PRINCE, we denote the internal state just before (resp. after) the r-th SubNibble layer by x_r (resp. y_r) while for the last R rounds those internal states are denoted by y_r' and x_r' respectively as shown on Fig. 1. Given a collection of messages $\{p^0, \ldots, p^m, \ldots\}$, the notation $x_r^m[i]$ holds for the nibble i of the state x_r of the message p^m. As PRINCE is not fully nibble-oriented we use the notation $x_r[i]_b$ to refer to the bit i of the state x_r and the following relation holds for all $i \in \{0, \ldots, 15\}$:

$$x_r[i] = x_r[4i + 3]_b \parallel x_r[4i + 2]_b \parallel x_r[4i + 1]_b \parallel x_r[4i]_b.$$

					bits														nibbles		
63	62	61	60	47	46	45	44	31	30	29	28	15	14	13	12		15	11	7	3
59	58	57	56	43	42	41	40	27	26	25	24	11	10	9	8		14	10	6	2
55	54	53	52	39	38	37	36	23	22	21	20	7	6	5	4		13	9	5	1
51	50	49	48	35	34	33	32	19	18	17	16	3	2	1	0		12	8	4	0

Fig. 2. Ordering of bits/nibbles in PRINCE.

Finally, we use the following notations for some functions.

R The composition of S and M so that $R(x) = M(S(x)) = SR(M'(S(x)))$.
$E^r_{k_0||k_1}$ PRINCE reduced to r rounds.
E_{c,k_1} full PRINCE-core.
$E^{c,r}_{k_1}$ PRINCE-core reduced to r rounds.

3   Meet-in-the-Middle Attacks

In this section we present both the 6-round attack and the 8-round attack which won the PRINCE Challenge in the chosen-plaintext category together with a new attack on 10 rounds. The aim of the challenge was to find the best attacks using at most 2^{20} chosen plaintexts and thus we decided to follow the strategy used by Demirci and Selçuk on AES in [3], later improved by Dunkelman et al. in [12], Derbez et al. in [13,14] and by Li et al. in [9]. While our 10-round attack does not fit the restriction on the data complexity it shows that this kind of attacks is one of the most powerful on SP-Network.

First we give the definition of an ordered δ-set which is a particular structure of messages used in our attacks.

Definition 1. *Let a δ-set be a set of 16 PRINCE-states that are all different in one state nibble (the active nibble) and all equal in the other state nibble (the inactive nibbles). An ordered δ-set is a δ-set $\{x^0, \ldots, x^{15}\}$ such that the difference in the active nibble between x^0 and x^i is equal to i, for $0 \le i \le 15$.*

In the sequel we consider δ-sets such that nibble 7 is the active one. For such a particular set we made the following observations which are the core of our new attacks.

Observation 1. *Consider the encryption of a collection $\{p^0, p^1, \ldots, p^{15}\}$ of 16 messages through 6-round PRINCE. If the set $\{y_2^0, y_2^1, \ldots, y_2^{15}\}$ is an ordered δ-set then the ordered sequence*

$$\left[y_2'^1[7] \oplus y_2'^0[7], y_2'^2[7] \oplus y_2'^0[7], \ldots, y_2'^{15}[7] \oplus y_2'^0[7] \right]$$

is fully determined by the following 8 nibble parameters:

- $x_3^0[0, 7, 10, 13]$ - $x_3'^0[0, 7, 10, 13]$

Consequently, there are at most $2^{8 \times 4} = 2^{32}$ possible sequences when we consider all the possible choices of keys and ordered δ-sets (out of the $2^{4 \times 15} = 2^{60}$ of the theoretically possible 15-nibble sequences).

Proof. The proof is straightforward. The goal is to propagate the differences from the state y_2 (which are known) to the state nibble $y_2'[7]$. At each intermediate round, each S-box is either a parameter, not required or constant (so output differences are equal to zero).

Observation 2. *Consider the encryption of a collection* $\{p^0, p^1, \ldots, p^{15}\}$ *of 16 messages through 8-round PRINCE. If the set* $\{x_2^0, x_2^1, \ldots, x_2^{15}\}$ *is an ordered* δ*-set then the ordered sequence*

$$[x_2'^1[7] \oplus x_2'^0[7], \ldots, x_2'^{15}[7] \oplus x_2'^0[7], y_2'^1[6] \oplus y_2'^0[6], \ldots, y_2'^{15}[6] \oplus y_2'^0[6]]$$

is fully determined by the following 42 nibble parameters:

- $x_2^0[7]$
- $x_3^0[0, 7, 10, 13]$
- $x_4^0[0..15]$

- $x_4'^0[0..15]$
- $x_3'^0[0, 7, 10, 13]$
- $x_2'^0[7]$

Furthermore, those 42 state nibbles can be directly computed from the full state x_4 *and 4 nibbles of* $M^{-1}(k_1)$*. Consequently, there are at most* $2^{4 \times (16+4)} = 2^{80}$ *possible sequences when we consider all the possible choices of keys and ordered* δ*-sets (out of the* $2^{4 \times 30} = 2^{120}$ *of the theoretically possible 30-nibble sequences).*

Proof. The proof is similar to the one of Observation 1 except the parameters are related. Indeed, from the full state x_4 one can directly compute x_4' as no keys are involved. Then we note that the 4 nibbles $M^{-1}(k_1)[4..7]$ are enough to compute $x_3^0[0, 7, 10, 13]$ from x_4 and $x_3'^0[0, 7, 10, 13]$ from x_4'. Finally, the knowledge of $M^{-1}(k_1)[7]$ allows to compute $x_2^0[7]$ and $x_2'^0[7]$ from $x_3^0[0, 7, 10, 13]$ and $x_3'^0[0, 7, 10, 13]$ respectively.

3.1   6-Round Attack

The 6-round attack is depicted on Fig. 3 and its scenario is straightforward. First the 2^{32} possible sequences given in Observation 1 are computed and stored in a hash table during a preprocessing phase. Then during the online phase, we begin by asking for the encryption of a structure of 2^{16} chosen plaintexts such that nibbles from 4 to 7 take all the possible values while the other ones are constant, and pick one of them denoted p^0. Now the goal of the adversary is to identify an ordered δ-set containing y_2^0. To do so, he has to guess the fives nibbles $x_1^0[4..7]$ and $x_2^0[7]$ and propagate the differences from the state y_2 to the plaintext. Then he gets the corresponding ciphertexts, guess the fives nibbles $x_1'^0[4..7]$ and $x_2'^0[7]$ and propagates the differences from the ciphertexts to $y_2'[7]$. Finally he discards all the guesses which do not lead to a match in the previously built hash table. The probability for a wrong guess to pass the test is $2^{32} \times 2^{-60} = 2^{-28}$ so we expect 2^5 candidates to remain at the end of the attack. The wrong ones can be discarded by replaying the attack with an other choice for p^0 without increasing the overall complexity of the attack.

The data complexity of this attack is 2^{16} chosen plaintexts and the memory requirement is around $2^{32} \times 4 \times 15 \times 2^{-3} \approx 2^{34.9}$ bytes. During the online phase 10 state nibbles are guessed however they can assume only 2^{33} values once the plaintext/ciphertext pair is given. Indeed, the knowledge of the 33 bits

$$\{(k_0 \oplus k_1)[16..27]_b, (k_0' \oplus k_1)[16..27]_b, k_1[28..31]_b, k_0[28..32]_b\},$$

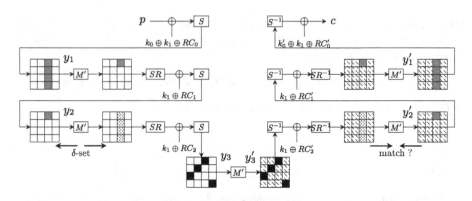

Fig. 3. 6r attack. No difference in white nibbles. Nibbles required in online (resp. offline) phase are in gray (resp. black). Differences in dotted nibbles are known during the offline phase. Hatched nibbles play no role.

is enough to compute all of them from p and c. Thus the time complexity of the online phase is approximately $16 \times 2^{33} \times 40/(6 \times 64) \approx 2^{33.7}$ encryptions.

Key Recovery. At the end of the attack $128 - 33 = 95$ key bits are still missing. To find them the best way is to apply several meet-in-the-middle attacks successively. For instance, one could begin by running the attack depicted on Fig. 12 in Appendix A which has an overall complexity below 2^{28} as most key bits required in the online phase are already known.

3.2 8-Round Attack

The 8-round attack is similar to the one on 6 rounds and is depicted on Fig. 4. It relies on Observation 2 so the memory complexity is around $2^{80} \times 15 \times 8 \times 2^{-3} \approx 2^{83.9}$ bytes. In the online phase, the data complexity remains unchanged to 2^{16} chosen plaintexts but the number of state variable to guess is increased. The identification step requires to guess the four nibbles $x_1^0[4..7]$ and then the nine nibbles $x_1'^0[0..7]$ and $x_2'^0[6]$ are guessed to build the sequence from the ciphertexts. Those 13 nibbles can assume only 2^{49} values once the plaintext/ciphertext pair (p^0, c^0) given as they all can be derived from

$$\{(k_0 \oplus k_1)[16..24, 28..31]_b, (k_0' \oplus k_1)[0..23, 27..31]_b, k_0[25..27]_b, k_1[24..27]_b\}.$$

Thus the time complexity of the online phase is approximately $16 \times 2^{49} \times 52/(8 \times 64) \approx 2^{49.7}$ encryptions and we expect $2^{49} \times 2^{80} \times 2^{-120} = 2^9$ candidates to remain at the end of the attack.

Key Recovery. As for the previous attack, the most efficient way to recover the missing key bits is to perform other attacks. For instance one could run the attack depicted on Fig. 13 (Appendix B) which has the same complexity than the one above since there are approximately 2^9 candidates for the 4 active nibbles of x_1. Then the search space would be small enough to perform an exhaustive search without increasing the overall complexity.

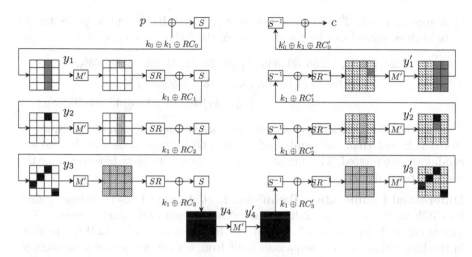

Fig. 4. 8r attack. No difference in white nibbles. Nibbles required in online (resp. offline) phase are in gray (resp. black). Differences in dotted nibbles are known during the offline phase. Hatched nibbles play no role.

Trade-off. It is possible to trade some memory against time without increasing the data complexity by noticing that for a considered structure of 2^{16} plaintexts the 4 active nibbles of x_3 take all the possible values. Thus we can fix them to 0 during the offline phase and save a factor 2^{16} in memory. In the other hand, we now need to run the attack for all the possible choices for p^0 increasing the time complexity by the same factor of 2^{16}.

3.3   10-Round Attack

We now investigate PRINCE reduced to 10 rounds. While we were unable to find an attack requiring less than 2^{20} chosen plaintexts for the PRINCE Challenge, we found one competitive with the actual best known attack. To describe it we first extend the definition of a δ-set as it was done in [13], then we show a meet-in-the-middle attack as the two ones above and finally we apply the differential enumeration technique [12].

δ-set. In [13] Derbez *et al.* shown that the notion of δ-set can be extended to set of states such that some *linear combinations* of state bits are constant. In the sequel we denote by δ-set a set of 16 messages such that $y_2[0..4, 6, 8..12, 14]$ and $M'(y_2)[0..4, 6, 8..12, 14]$ are constant, exploiting the fact that the matrix operating on the columns are not MDS.

10-round Attack. The basis of our attack on 10 rounds is depicted on Fig. 5. The meet-in-the-middle is performed on the four bit-equations described above. The state bytes required as the parameters of the hash table can be computed from the whole state x_5 and 8 nibbles of the equivalent subkey $M^{-1}(k_1)$ and thus approximately 2^{96} 60-bit sequences are stored. In the online phase the 24 state nibbles needed can be computed from the following 66 key bits:

$$\{k_0[0, 20..24, 28..32, 52..56, 60..63]_b, k_1[20..23, 28..31, 52..55, 60..63]_b,$$
$$(k_0 \oplus k_1)[16..19, 24..27, 48..51, 56..59]_b,$$
$$(k_0' \oplus k_1)[16..19, 24..26, 48..51, 56..58]_b\}.$$

Note that this attack does not actually work because the number of sequences stored is higher than the number of possible 60-bit sequences and thus no key candidates are filtered. The aim of the next section is to show how to reduce the memory requirement.

Differential Enumeration Technique. Li et al. applied this technique against PRINCE in [9] and successfully mounted new attacks on 8 and 9 rounds. The idea of this technique originally introduced by Dunkelman *et al.* in [12] is to store in the hash table only the sequences built from a δ-set containing a message p^0 that belongs to a pair (p^0, p^1) following a well-chosen differential characteristic. In our case the truncated differential characteristic is depicted on Fig. 5 assuming a zero difference in hatched nibbles. Thus we expect to store only $2^{96+4-60} = 2^{40}$ sequences in the offline phase. However generating them is not as trivial as for the basic attack. We propose the following procedure which has a time complexity around 2^{72} operations:

1. Consider a pair (p^0, p^1) following the differential characteristic.

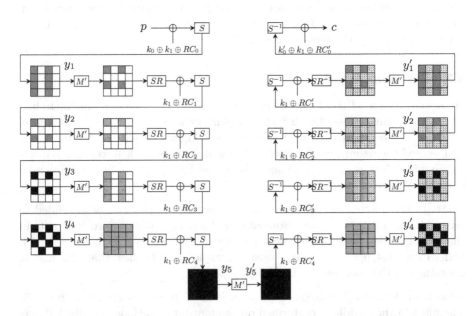

Fig. 5. 10r attack. No difference in white nibbles. Nibbles required in online (resp. offline) phase are in gray (resp. black). Differences in dotted nibbles are known during the offline phase. Hatched nibbles play no role.

2. $S^{-1} \circ M' \circ S$ can be seen as 4 invertible super Sboxes $\S_0, \ldots, \S_3$ operating on 16-bit words. Build 4 hash tables such that one can retrieve (x, y) from $(x \oplus y, S_i(x) \oplus S_i(y))$.

3. Guess the difference in the active nibbles of both y_4 and $y'4$ and retrieve the actual value of x_5 and x'_5 for both messages of the pair.

4. Guess the difference in the two active nibbles of the first column of y_3 and get back the actual values of $y_4[2, 5, 8, 15]$.

5. Combined with the knowledge of x_5 this leads to the knowledge of the four key nibbles $M^{-1}(k_1)[2, 5, 8, 15]$. Use them to partially encrypt x'_5 and check if the difference in the first column of y'_3 is correct.

6. Use $M^{-1}(k_1)[15]$ to partially decrypt y_4 and get the difference in $x_2[15]$ and check its correctness. Do the same for the difference in $x'_2[15]$.

7. Guess the difference in the two active nibbles of the third column of y_3 and get back $M^{-1}(k_1)[0, 7, 11, 13]$.

8. Compute the value of the missing parameters and check whether the pair follows the characteristic or not. If it does then build the 60-bit sequence from p^0 and store it in the hash table.

The complexity of this procedure is dominated by the complexity of steps 4–5 which is 2^{72} simple operations that we estimate to be equivalent to 2^{69} encryptions. Now that the table is built the online phase is quite similar to the one of the offline phase:

1. Ask for a structure of 2^{32} chosen plaintexts and store the ciphertexts in a hash table to identify the pairs that may follows the differential characteristic.

2. For each pair (p^0, p^1):

   (a) Guess the difference in the first column of y_1 and of y_2, deduce the corresponding value of $(k_0 \oplus k_1)[12..15]$ and $k_1[15]$. Store them in a hash table T_0 indexed by $k_1[15]$, $k_0[61..63]_b$.

   (b) Similarly compute $(k'_0 \oplus k_1)[12..15]$ and $k_1[15]$ from the ciphertexts and use T_0 and the linear relations between k_0 and $k'0$ to get back the $2^{2 \times 4 + 2} \cdot 2^{-7} = 2^3$ corresponding values of the key nibbles above. Store those 2^{13} key candidates in a hash table T_1 indexed by $(k_0 \oplus k_1)[12..15]$, $(k'_0 \oplus k_1)[12..15]$ and $k_0[55]_b \oplus k_0[60]_b$ $(= (k_0 \oplus k_1)[55]_b \oplus \ldots \oplus (k_0 \oplus k_1)[60]_b \oplus (k'_0 \oplus k_1)[55]_b \oplus \ldots \oplus (k'_0 \oplus k_1)[59]_b \oplus k_1[60]_b)$.

   (c) Repeat the two steps above but now by guessing the third column of y_2 and use T_1 to obtain the $2^{2 \times 13 - 8 - 8 - 1} = 2^9$ and store them in a hash table T_2 indexed by the difference in y_2. (While the match is on 33 bits, $(k_0 \oplus k_1)[12..15]$ and $(k'_0 \oplus k_1)[12..15]$ only depend on four 4-bit parameters.)

   (d) Repeat the three steps above but now by guessing the third column of y_1 and use T_3 to finally retrieve all the $2^{9+9-8} = 2^{10}$ key candidates.

   (e) For each key candidate identify a δ-set from p^0, build the 60-bit sequence and check whether it belongs to the table constructed in the offline phase. If it does then try the key candidate.

3. Repeat the procedure until the right key is found.

As each structure contains 2^{63} pairs and each of these pairs follows the differential with probability $2^{-28-60} = 2^{-88}$, we need 2^{25} structures on average. Then, for each structure we have to study only $2^{63-32} = 2^{31}$ pairs and for each of them we have to perform $4 \times 2^{13} + 2^{10} \times 2^4$ simple operations estimated to approximately 2^{12} encryptions. Thus this procedure has a the time complexity of $2^{25+31+12} = 2^{68}$ encryptions and requires $2^{25+32} = 2^{57}$ chosen plaintexts. At the end of the attack $2^{66} \times 2^{40} \times 2^{-60} = 2^{46}$ key candidates remain. As 62 key bits are also missing performing an exhaustive search is not a valid option. Instead, the best way to recover the key is to apply several meet-in-the-middle attacks. For instance, we can assume that when a match happens we get back the corresponding values of the red nibbles in Fig. 5 and then deduce step by step each key bits of $M^{-1}(k_1)$ by completing the first and the third columns of y_3' without increasing the overall complexity of the attack.

4   Combining Differential Attack with a SAT-Solver

4.1   Attacking 4-Round PRINCE with a SAT-Solver

Encoding PRINCE as a CNF Formula. The idea is to generate a CNF formula where a set p of boolean variables correspond to the 64 bits of the plaintext, c to the 64 bits of the ciphertext and k to the 128 bits of the key, and such that there exists a unique assignment of the variables satisfying the CNF corresponding to the case $E_k(p) = c$.

Hence, if we generate such a formula, set the variables in p and k to a chosen value and use a SAT-solver to find an assignment satisfying the CNF formula, the variables in c will correspond to the ciphertext. Solving such a formula is easy, an observation which we can relate to the fact that the evaluation of a block cipher has to be "easy" from the point of view of complexity theory.

Another way to use such a formula is to fix the variables in p and in c according to a known plaintext/ciphertext pair, solve the CNF and recover the key from the variables corresponding to it. Unless the number of rounds is very small (at most 3 in the case of PRINCE), solving such a system is impractical. Again, we can relate this observation to the fact that recovering the key given one or several plaintext/ciphertext pair has to be "hard". Our approach consists in using some knowledge about the internal state of the cipher to simplify the task of the SAT-solver and make such a resolution possible for a higher number of rounds.

In order to encode a PRINCE encryption as a CNF formula, we introduce several sets of 64 Boolean variables corresponding to each step of each round: one for the internal state at the beginning of the round (x_r), one for the internal state after going throught the S-Box (y_r), etc. We also use boolean variables corresponding to the key bits.

Our task is then to create a CNF formula connecting these variables in such a way as to ensure that, for instance if $k[0, ..., 63]$ is fixed, it has only one solution where $y_r[0, ..., 63]$ is indeed the image of $x[0, ..., 63]_r$ by S, etc.

In order to encode the linear layer, we use the alternative representation of M' from [10] where it was shown that M' operates on columns of 4-bits independently by first rotating them by a column-dependent number of bit and then xor-ing the hamming weight of the column in each bit. We thus add variables corresponding to the hamming weights of the columns and encode the corresponding xor's as CNF formulas. The SR operation is only a permutation of the bits so we simply set the corresponding bits to be equal.

The encoding of the S-Box is less simple to obtain. In order to find the best one, we chose to look for it directly instead of using the ANF as an intermediate step. Indeed, since the S-Box is 4x4, it is small enough for us to brute-force all clauses[1] involving input and output bits and check if they hold for every input.

Doing this lead us to find 29 clauses with 3 variables. However, they are not sufficient to completely specify the S-Box so we used a greedy algorithm to find the best clauses with 4 variables to add to this encoding. In the end, we have 29 clauses with 3 variables and 9 clauses with 4 variables which are such that the only solutions of the CNF made of all these clauses are all the assignments corresponding to pairs $(x, S(x))$ for all $x \in [0, 15]$.

These clauses with 3 variables can be interpreted as simple implications. For example, if $o[3, ..., 0]_b = S(i[3, ..., 0]_b)$ then the following two clauses hold with probability 1 :

$$\big(i[1]_b \lor o[2]_b \lor o[3]_b\big) \land \big(i[1]_b \lor o[1]_b \lor o[2]_b\big).$$

They are logically equivalent to the following implication:

$$\overline{i[1]_b} \implies \big((o[2]_b \lor o[3]_b) \land (o[1]_b \lor o[2]_b)\big).$$

Differential Over Definition. The approach consisting in using the knowledge from a differential trail to ease the task of a SAT-solver used to attack a cryptographic primitive has been explored in [15] in order to attack MD4 and MD5. The authors of this paper first use heuristic methods to find a high probability differential trail leading to a collision and then use a SAT-solver to find a pair of messages which satisfies this trail. In the same paper, we can find the following observation:

An interesting result of our experiments with SAT solvers is the importance of having a differential path encoded in the formula.

As we shall see, this also holds for block ciphers. Attacking 4 rounds PRINCE-core takes more than 10 h if we simply encode as a CNF that some plaintext are encrypted into known ciphertexts but we can both drastically reduce this time while breaking PRINCE with its whitening keys using *differential over-definition*.

---

[1] A clause is the logical OR of several variables, e.g. $a \lor b$, a, $\overline{a} \lor b \lor \overline{c}$ where $\overline{x}$ is the negation of x.

Definition 2. *We call* Differential Over Definition *(or DOD) the following algorithm which simplifies a CNF formula knowing that the variables correspond to bits of the internal state of an encryption following a certain trail.*
For all pairs of variables in the CNF, proceed as follows:

- *If they are assumed to be equal, replace all occurrences of the first one by the second one.*
- *If they are assumed to be different, replace all occurrences of the first one by the negation of the second one.*

While the idea behind this algorithm is simple, it is necessary for cryptographers to implement it efficiently "by hand". Indeed, the only input of a SAT-solver is a CNF formula, i.e. merely a list of clauses from which deriving what variables are equal to each other without knowledge of the structure of the problem is far from trivial. For instance, it would be necessary for the SAT-solver to "understand" that the set of clauses used to model one S-Box call all correspond to a unique function so that identical inputs lead to identical outputs; all this without having any distinction between the input and output bits. That is why differential over-definition, an easy algorithm for the cryptographer to implement, is a valuable pre-processing step when using a SAT-solver for cryptography leading to gains in time complexity of several orders of magnitude.

This algorithm can be implemented efficiently using a hashtable containing the correspondences between the variables. Once this algorithm has been run, the CNF is over defined: the solution would have been such that the equalities hold anyway but there are less variables and less clauses in the CNF. However, if the pair actually does not follow the trail, the CNF has become unsatisfiable. This is a difference between our work and the one described in [15]: we do not always know before hand if the CNF has a solution. We can think of this as a trade-off between "solving one CNF known to be true" and "solving many over-defined CNF's which may or may not be true": the second approach loses time by requiring several calls to a SAT-solver but these calls take less time thanks to the over-definition.

Such an over definition can be used in different ways.

1. Propagating only the zero differences holding with probability 1 inside a group of 8 encryptions with many zero differences is enough to reduce the time complexity of an attack on 4 rounds from more than 10 h to a few seconds (see below). Furthermore, such a formula is always true.
2. Instead of implementing an algorithm recovering the key from a pair following a particular trail by peeling of layer after layer of encryption in our attack on 6 rounds described in the remainder of this section, we simply re-used the code of our attack on 4 rounds and over-defined the CNF modeling the encryptions of right pairs according to the high probability trail we used.

We implemented the attack described in Algorithm 1 to attack 4-round PRINCE (with its whitening keys) using the SAT-solver Minisat [16] and obtained an average total time of 5.13 s and average time spent solving the CNF of 3.06 s.

The designers of PRINCE did not consider SAT-based attacks but they did investigate algebraic attacks. They manage to attack 4-round PRINCE-core in less than 2 s while our attack requires about 5 s to attack 4-round PRINCE, a cipher which uses twice as much key material.

Algorithm 1. Using Differential over-Definition to enable an attack on 4-round PRINCE.

Query 2^{10} plaintext/ciphertexts where the first 10 bits take all possible values.
Select a subset of 8 plaintext/ciphertext maximizing the number of 0-differences in the output.
Encode the 8 encryptions as a CNF A.
Overdefine A by propagating zero-differences with probability 1.
Use a SAT-solver to retrieve the key bits from A
return $k_0 \| k_1$

4.2 Amplified Differential Trails

Our attacks rely on some differences propagating identically in different pairs. To better describe this, we introduce the following definitions.

Encryption. We call *encryption* a couple plaintext/ciphertext encrypted under a fixed key.

Pair. A *pair* is a set of two encryptions where the plaintexts are separated by a known difference.

Family. A *family* is a group of pairs with a particular structure. They are generated from a single pair $\{(p[0], ..., p[b-1]), (p'[0], ..., p'[b-1])\}$, where $p[i]$ and $p'[i]$ are nibbles. Suppose that the input difference covers the first three nibbles so that $p[3] = p'[3] = c[3], ..., p[b-1] = p'[b-1] = c[b-1]$ for some constants $c[i]$. Then the family corresponding to this pair is made by exchanging some nibbles between the two encryptions in the pair so as to obtain the following pairs:

$$\begin{cases} (p[0], p[1], p[2], c[3], ..., c[b-1]) \\ (p'[0], p'[1], p'[2], c[3], ..., c[b-1]) \end{cases} \quad \begin{cases} (p'[0], p[1], p[2], c[3], ..., c[b-1]) \\ (p[0], p'[1], p'[2], c[3], ..., c[b-1]) \end{cases}$$

$$\begin{cases} (p[0], p'[1], p[2], c[3], ..., c[b-1]) \\ (p'[0], p[1], p'[2], c[3], ..., c[b-1]) \end{cases} \quad \begin{cases} (p[0], p[1], p'[2], c[3], ..., c[b-1]) \\ (p'[0], p'[1], p[2], c[3], ..., c[b-1]) \end{cases}.$$

Overall, if there are n nibble with non-zero differences in the input then a family is made of 2^{n-1} pairs and 2^n encryptions.

In the case of PRINCE, we consider differential trails where the input differences are only over one column and such that all the pairs in a family follow the same trail for the first three rounds. For example, the trails we consider in

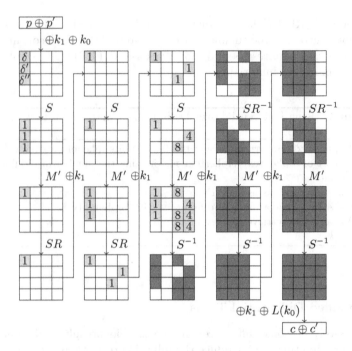

Fig. 6. The 5.5 rounds trail T_1.

this paper (Figs. 6 and 14) are either followed by all the elements in a family or none of them. A similar heuristic is used in [17] to perform a multiset attack on the SASAS structure.

This behaviour comes from the fact that the transition in the trails we study depend only on the transitions occuring during the first round, which are the same in all pairs of a family, and on the actual value of some nibbles to which the difference have not had the time to propagate, which are the same in all encryptions of the structure.

Our Trails. There has already been some differential cryptanalyses of PRINCE, see for example [10], which is the best attack to date, and also [18].

We consider trails which are completely specified during the first 3 rounds and then propagate with probability 1 for 2.5 rounds before having spread to the full internal state. Figure 6 shows a first trail covering 5.5 rounds in this way which we denote T_1. Each array corresponds to the differences between the internal states of two encryptions under 6-round PRINCE and each cell gives the value of the difference: light gray corresponds to a fully specified non-zero value at the nibble level (e.g. a difference of 1), dark gray to an unkown non-zero difference and white to a zero difference. A very similar trail with a probability 2 times smaller, T_2, is given in Fig. 14 (see Appendix C). To compute their probabilities, we use the difference distribution matrix of the S-Box. If we let the input difference be

Table 2. Input differences which might be mapped to a difference of 1 by the S-Box of PRINCE.

Hexadecimal	Binary	Probability
0x1	0001	1/4
0x2	0010	1/8
0x4	0100	1/8
0xb	1011	1/8
0xc	1100	1/4
0xd	1101	1/8

$(1, 1, 1, 0, ..., 0)$, then T_1 has a probability of $2^{-2 \cdot 3} \cdot 2^{-2} \cdot 2^{-2-2-3} = 2^{-15}$ and T_2 has a probability of $2^{-2 \cdot 3} \cdot 2^{-2} \cdot 2^{-2-3-3} = 2^{-16}$.

Querying enough families at random to find one right family for any of these would require $(2^{-15} + 2^{-16})^{-1} = 2^{14.41}$ families with an input difference over 3 nibbles, i.e. $2^{14.41} \cdot 2^3 = 2^{17.41}$ encryptions. However, we can use structures to decrease this complexity.

We note that the input differences which might lead to an output difference of 1 are those listed in Table 2. As we can see, the second bit from the right in little-endian notation is only involved in 0x2 and 0xb which, taken together, only have a probability of 1/4 of leading to a difference of 1. Hence, we use the following structures where b is a bit taking all possible values and c is constant accross the structure:

$$\text{bbcb bbcb bbcb cccc cccc ... cccc.}$$

We found experimentally that such structures contain several[2] right families with probability $2^{-5.9}$ on average when we take into account all possible input differences, i.e. $(\delta, \delta', \delta'', 0, ..., 0)$ where $\delta, \delta', \delta'' \in \{1, 4, c, d\}$. Hence, obtaining at least 2 right families only requires about $2^{9+5.9} = 2^{14.9}$ queries to the encryption oracle on average.

Filtering Right Pairs. Full diffusion has been achieved by the 6-th round. Thus, we guess 16 bits of key material to be able to partially invert the last round on one column. A guess leads to the correct nibble having a zero difference in every pair of the family with probability $2^{-4 \cdot 4} = 2^{-16}$. We repeat this independently over each column and obtain either 64 bits of key material or none at all. Since there are either several right families or none at all in the structures

---

[2] Actually, a structure of size 2^{12} where the first three nibbles take all values contains 64 right families with probability about $2^{-5.9}$. If we reduce these to form the structures of 2^9 plaintext/ciphertext encryptions we described, only some of these 64 families are still present, hence the presence of either 0 or several right families in a structure.

we consider, we only return the key guesses which come from several families as well as the corresponding families.

This is a powerfull filter: while we expect each family from the structure to yield about one 64 bits candidates, the probability to have a collision is very small[3].

4.3   Differential Attacks on 6-Round PRINCE

Pseudo-code describing our attack on 6-round PRINCE is provided in Algorithm 2.

We ran this attack 10 times and found that about $2^{5.75}$ structures were needed on average. The filtering step is the most time consuming: finding a right pair requires about 1h 30 min but the SAT-solver requires about 0.5 s to recover the full key or (rarely) to discard the pair. For this reason, we approximate the complexity of this attack by the complexity of its filtering step. We query $2^{5.9}$ structures of 2^9 encryptions and, for each, encryption, we invert the last round by guessing 2^{16} bits of key material for each of the 2^2 columns. Hence, this attack requires about $2^{5.9+9+16+2} = 2^{32.9}$ partial decryptions and $2^{14.9}$ chosen/plaintexts. Memory complexity is dominated by the SAT-solver but is (well) below 1 Go, i.e. (well) below 2^{27} 64-bits blocks.

5   Structural Analysis of PRINCE

The α-reflection introduced along with PRINCE [5] is the name given to the following property of a block cipher E_k: $E_k^{-1} = E_{k \oplus \alpha}$. In other words there is a constant α such that decryption for a key k is the same operation as encryption under key $k \oplus \alpha$. PRINCE-core implements this property by having a three-parts structure as decribed here:

$$E_{c,k_1} = F_{k_1 \oplus \alpha}^{-1} \circ I \circ F_{k_1},$$

where F_k corresponds to 5 rounds of a classical Substitution-Permutation Network construction and where I is an involution.

Since we are going to study the structure of the cycles of different functions in a fashion similar to the way Biryukov analysed the inner-rounds of some involutional ciphers in [19], we define the *cycle type* of a permutation.

Definition 3. *The cycle type of a permutation π is an (ordered) multiset containing the cycle lengths of the permutation. The cycle type of π is denoted by $\mathcal{L}(\pi)$.*

In what follows, we do not represent the round constants for the sake of simplicity. However, not only do our result hold in their presence but we could actually generalize them to any key schedule preserving the fact that the subkeys of symmetric rounds have a XOR equal to α.

---

[3] Each structure yields $2^{9-3} = 2^6$ families for each of the 4^3 interesting input differences so that we consider the families by groups of 2^{12}. This implies that a collision has a probability of about $\binom{2^{12}}{2} \cdot 2^{-64} \approx 2^{-41}$.

Algorithm 2. Using trails $\mathcal{T}_1, \mathcal{T}_2$ and a SAT-solver to recover the complete key $k_0 \| k_1$ of 6-round PRINCE.

---

while the key has not been retrieved **do**

    Query a structure $\mathcal{S} = \left((p^0, c^0), ..., (p^{2^{12}-1}, c^{2^{12}-1}) \right)$

    $H \leftarrow$ empty hashtable of lists of families indexed by 64-bits integers

    for all families $\mathcal{F}$ in $\mathcal{S}$ **do**

        for all columns of the internal state **do**

            for all 16-bits key guesses k_{16} **do**

                for all pairs in $\mathcal{F}$ **do**

                    Invert key addition for the column using k_{16}

                    Invert S^{-1} for the column

                    Invert M' for the column

                end for

                if the correct nibble has a zero difference in all pairs **then** store k_{16}

            end for

        end for

        Combine all guesses from each column into 64-bits guesses

        for all 64-bits guesses k_{64} append $\mathcal{F}$ to $H[k_{64}]$

    end for

    for all k_{64} among the keys of H **do**

        if $H[k_{64}]$ contains strictly more than 1 element **then**

            for all families $\mathcal{F}$ in $H[k_{64}]$ **do**

                Generate a CNF A encoding all encryptions in $\mathcal{F}$ with same key such

                    that $k_1 + L(k_0) = k_{64}$.

                for all trails $\mathcal{T}$ in $\{\mathcal{T}_1, \mathcal{T}_2\}$ **do**

                    $B \leftarrow DoD(A, \mathcal{T})$

                    if B is satisfiable **then** retrieve $k_0 \| k_1$ from the solution of B and

                    return it

                end for

            end for

        end if

    end for

end while

5.1 Small Cycles in Round-Reduced PRINCE

The central involution is $I = S^{-1} \circ M' \circ S$. Therefore, it is isomorphic to M', a linear involution operating on each column of the internal state independently. It is easy to check experimentally the result given in [7] stating that M' has exactly 2^{32} fixed points, meaning that I also has 2^{32} fixed points. Therefore, I has 2^{32} cycles of length 1 and $2^{63} - 2^{31}$ cycles of length 2.

The cycle type of $I^{\alpha} : x \mapsto I(x) \oplus \alpha$ is more sophisticated but still contains a fair amount of small cycles. After noting that both I and $x \mapsto x \oplus \alpha$ operate on each column of the internal space independently, we denote I_i^{α} the restriction of $x \mapsto I(x) \oplus \alpha$ to column i and I_i that of I. Since each of the I_i^{α}'s operates only on a space of size 2^{16}, it is easy to generate their complete cycle structures independently by searching the whole space. Each I_i^{α} has a cycle type made of

---

Algorithm 3. Generating the cycle type of I^α from those of its columns.

---

for $i \in [0,3]$ **do**
    $\mathcal{L}_i \leftarrow$ List of the cycle length of I_i^α
end for
$\mathcal{L} \leftarrow$ Hashtable indexed by integers
for $(\ell_0, \ell_1, \ell_2, \ell_3) \in \mathcal{L}_0 \times \mathcal{L}_1 \times \mathcal{L}_2 \times \mathcal{L}_3$ **do**
    $\ell \leftarrow \text{lcm}(\ell_0, \ell_1, \ell_2, \ell_3)$
    $\mathcal{L}[\ell] \leftarrow \mathcal{L}[\ell] + \ell^{-1} \cdot \prod_{i=0}^{3} \ell_i$
end for
return $\mathcal{L}$

---

many "small" cycles, the largest having a length of 2844. This is explained by the fact that both I and $x \mapsto x \oplus \alpha$ are involutions and each column of I has exactly 2^8 fixed points. Thus, most of the cycles have a particular structure[4] described in [20] which we recall in Fig. 7. We remark that to each cycle of I_i^α correspond two fixed points of I_i.

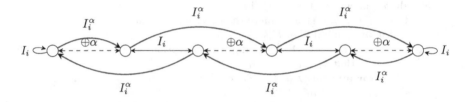

Fig. 7. The structure of a cycle of I_i^α for $i \in [0,3]$.

After generating the cycle type for each I_i^α, we combine them to obtain the cycle type of $x \mapsto I(x) \oplus \alpha$ using Algorithm 3. The cycle type of this function is too complex to be printed completely but some information extracted from it is given in Table 3. If we pick x uniformly at random, the expected length of the cycle it is on is $2^{30.7}$.

Recall that $E_{k_1}^{c,4}$ is the permutation of $\{0,1\}^{64}$ corresponding to an encryption under key k_1 by PRINCE-core reduced to 4 rounds. Then $x \mapsto E_{k_1}^{c,4}(x) \oplus \alpha$ has the same cycle type as I^α due to the cancellation of the last round of one encryption with the first round of the next. Indeed, to each cycle of this function corresponds one of I^α, as illustrated in Fig. 8 where a cycle (x_0, x_1, x_2, x_3) of length 4 of $x \mapsto E_{k_1}^{c,4}$ is represented along with the corresponding cycle of I^α (dashed line).

A first consequence of these observations is the existence of a distinguisher for 4-round PRINCE-core requiring about $2^{27.4}$ adaptatively chosen plaintexts.

---

[4] While there are some cycles which do not have this structure, they are a small minority: for f_0, 256 elements out of 65536 are on such cycles, 64 for f_1, 8 for f_2 and 194 for f_3.

Table 3. Information about the cycle type of I^{α}, where $\ell(x)$ is the length of the cycle on which x is.

Cycle length ℓ	#{cycles of length ℓ}	$P\left[\ell(x) = \ell, x \text{ drawn uniformly}\right]$
1	0	0
2	2^7	2^{-57}
4	$2^{10.25}$	$2^{-53.75}$
8	$2^{15.46}$	$2^{-48.54}$
10080	$2^{33.06}$	$2^{-17.63}$
110880	$2^{31.96}$	$2^{-15.27}$
$\leq 2^{10}$	–	$2^{-22.4}$
$\leq 2^{15}$	–	$2^{-12.4}$
$\leq 2^{24}$	–	$2^{-4.1}$

As stated in Table 2, an element picked at random is on a cycle of length at most 2^{15} with probability $2^{-12.4}$. Therefore, we repeat multiple times the experiment consisting in picking an element x uniformly at random and then check if it is on a cycle of length at most 2^{15} by iterating $x \mapsto E_{k_1}^{c,4}(x) \oplus \alpha$ at most 2^{15}. The experiment is a success if x is on a cycle of length at most 2^{15}. If the permutation is $E_{k_1}^{c,4}$ for some k_1, then its probability of success is $2^{12.4}$ but if the permutation is a random permutation[5], then the probability of success becomes 2^{-49}. We confirmed experimentally the success probability of this experiment for $E_{k_1}^{c,4}$.

A second consequence is the existence of "small" sets of plaintext/ciphertext encryptions where the set of the ciphertexts is the image of the set of the encryptions by a function significantly simpler than a PRINCE encryption. This topic is studied in the next section.

5.2   Simplifications of PRINCE's Representation

The particular cycle types of the round-reduced versions of PRINCE studied above lead to simpler alternative representations of the encryption algorithm.

Consequences of the Cycle Type of I. Suppose that an encryption is such that the input of I is one of the 2^{32} fixed-points of this function. Then the key addition before and after this function cancel each other so that only the addition of α remains. Then, since M is linear, the operations $M^{-1} \circ (\oplus \alpha) \circ M$ become simply the addition of $M^{-1}(\alpha)$. Thus, the 4 center rounds — minus the first and last key addition — become a simple S-Box layer which we denote S'

---

[5] Recall that the probability for x to be on a cycle of length ℓ for a permutation of $[0, N-1]$ is equal to $1/N$. Hence, the probability that the length is smaller than 2^{15} for a permutation of $[0, 2^{64} - 1]$ is $\sum_{\ell=1}^{2^{15}} 2^{-64} = 2^{-49}$.

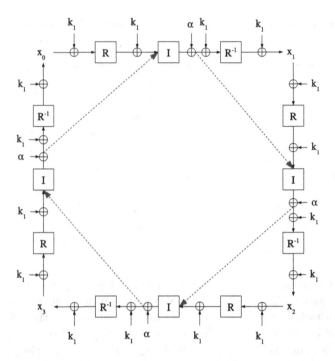

Fig. 8. Correspondance between a cycle of $x \mapsto E_{k_1}^{c,4}(x) \oplus \alpha$ and a cycle of I^α.

and which is defined by

$$S'(x) = S^{-1}\big(S(x) \oplus M^{-1}(\alpha)\big).$$

This simplifying process is summarized in Fig. 9. Note that if $M^{-1}(\alpha)$ has any nibble equal to 0 then the function S' is the identity for this nibble. However, for the value of α chosen by the designers of PRINCE, there is no such nibble.

The simplification goes further. Indeed, since S' operates only at the nibble level, it commutes with the operations SR and SR^{-1} (up to a reordering of the S-Boxes in S'). Therefore, if we add one round before and one round after S',

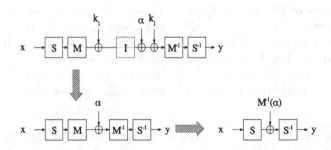

Fig. 9. Simplification of the 4 center-rounds if the input of I is a fixed point.

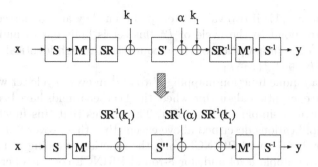

Fig. 10. Simplification of the 6 center-rounds if the input of I is a fixed point.

we can replace $SR^{-1} \circ S' \circ SR$ by S'' where S'' is another S-Box layer. Hence, 6-round of PRINCE operate on each column of the internal state independently: each output bit depends only on 16 bits of the input, 28 bits[6] of k_1 and at most 18 bits of k_0. This simplification is summarized in Fig. 10.

Similar simplifications occur if instead of having a fixed point we have a particular collision between two encryptions. This setting corresponds to the so-called *mirror slide attack* described by Dunkelman *et al.* in [21]. Consider two encryptions (p^0, c^0) and (p^1, c^1) by PRINCE-core as follows

$$c^0 = E_{c,k_1}(p^0) = \left(F_{k_1 \oplus \alpha}^{-1} \circ I \circ F_{k_1}\right)(p^0)$$
$$c^1 = E_{c,k_1}(p^1) = \left(F_{k_1 \oplus \alpha}^{-1} \circ I \circ F_{k_1}\right)(p^1)$$

which are such that $F_{k_1}(p^0) = I\left(F_{k_1}(p^1)\right)$. In this case, we have that

$$c^0 = \left(F_{k_1 \oplus \alpha}^{-1} \circ F_{k_1}\right)(p^1)$$
$$c^1 = \left(F_{k_1 \oplus \alpha}^{-1} \circ F_{k_1}\right)(p^0),$$

where 6 rounds of $F_{k_1 \oplus \alpha}^{-1} \circ F_{k_1}$ can be simplified exactly as described and therefore only operate on each column separately.

In conclusion, if an encryption is such that the input of I is a fixed-point of this function or if two encryptions form a mirror slide pair, then 4 rounds of PRINCE consist simply in 16 parallel operations on each nibble and 6 rounds of PRINCE in 4 parallel operations on each column.

Consequences of the Cycle Type of I^α. Consider a sequence of plaintexts $(p^0, \ldots, p^{\ell-1})$ and their corresponding ciphertexts $(c^0, \ldots, c^{\ell-1})$ such that the input $x_5^i \oplus k_1$ of the sixth round for the plaintext p^i is the image of $x_5^{i-1} \oplus k_1$ by I^α. We call such a sequence a *cycle set* and we give a representation of such

---

[6] In each column, 16 bits from the corresponding column of k_1 are used as well as 16 bits from the corresponding column of $SR^{-1}(k_1)$. Since the top nibble of these two sets is the same, we are left with $32 - 4 = 28$ bits.

a sequence on Fig. 11: if two values are equal then they are connected by a line; red lines correspond to the cycle of I^α this set is built out of and blue lines correspond to the propagation of these equalities through identical operations, namely $x \mapsto k_1 \oplus R^{-1}(x \oplus k_1)$.

There is a unique function mapping p^i to c^{i-1} in every cycle set which corresponds to the encryption algorithm where the 4 center-rounds have been removed and replaced by a simple addition of α. This means that this function undergoes the simplifications described above except that these cover 2 more rounds. In particular, for 6-round PRINCE-core, the function mapping p^i to c^{i-1} only operates at the nibble level and, for 8-round PRINCE-core, it operates at the column level. At least 10 rounds are necessary to obtain full diffusion out of the 12 PRINCE has.

The cycle sets we consider cover the 4 center-rounds of PRINCE but it is possible to generalize this construction to an arbitrary amount of rounds. However, the cycle set sizes are abnormaly small in this case because of the cycle type of I^α. Indeed, a random plaintext/ciphertext pair is in a cycle set of size $2^{30.7}$ and in a cycle set of size smaller than 2^{15} with probability $2^{-12.4}$. In other cases, including *a priori* if we have a cycle covering at least 6 rounds, the expected size of a cycle set is the expected size of the cycle of a random permutation a random element is on, namely 2^{63}.

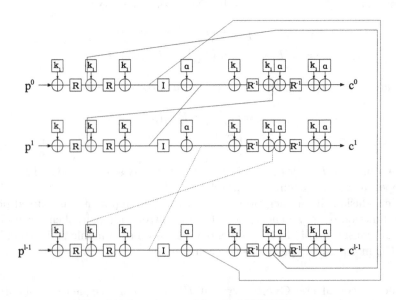

Fig. 11. A cycle set of 6-round PRINCE-core.

Should the cycle sets of PRINCE become identifiable, the security of up to 8 rounds may be compromised as the alternative versions of the cipher we described in this Section are much weaker than the original cipher. Furthermore, since small cycles are not unlikely to be found, the data complexity of such an attack may remain feasible.

6   Conclusion

We looked for practical attacks which would hinder the security provided by round-reduced versions of PRINCE in a realistic framework provided by the designers of this cipher. We found that approaches based on a Meet-in-the-Middle, SAT-based or, surprisingly, differential framework can all lead to practical attacks on up to half of the rounds. We checked our results by actually implementing one of our attacks. As a matter of fact, our attacks were the best submitted to the PRINCE-challenge for 6 and 8 rounds. Furthermore, during our investigations on PRINCE we discovered a new attack on 10 rounds which despite its data complexity of 2^{57} chosen plaintexts has a reasonable complexity and a very (very!) motivated adversary could run it.

We also identified some simplifications of the encryption occurring because of the small cycles of the inner-rounds of this block cipher, thus shedding new light on the consequences of the α-reflection as it is implemented in PRINCE.

Acknowledgement. The authors thank Alex Biryukov for useful discussions about the differential attack on PRINCE. We also thank NXP Semiconductors for organizing the PRINCE challenge and sending us our rewards!

A   The Second 6-Round Attack

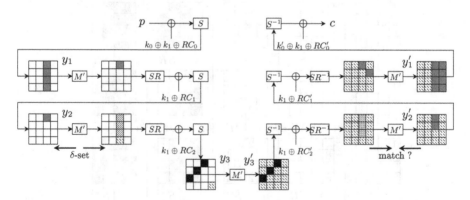

Fig. 12. 6r attack. No difference in white nibbles. Nibbles required in online (resp. offline) phase are in gray (resp. black). Differences in dotted nibbles are known during the offline phase. Hatched nibbles play no role.

B   The Second 8-Round Attack

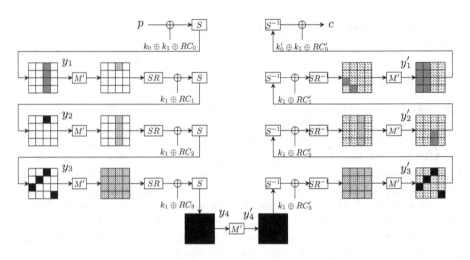

Fig. 13. 8r attack. No difference in white nibbles. Nibbles required in online (resp. offline) phase are in gray (resp. black). Differences in dotted nibbles are known during the offline phase. Hatched nibbles play no role.

C   The Second 5.5 Rounds Trail

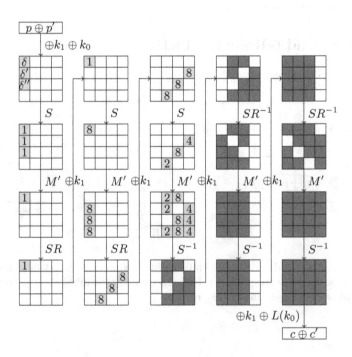

Fig. 14. The second 5.5 rounds trail T_2.

References

1. Biham, E., Shamir, A.: Differential cryptanalysis of DES-like cryptosystems. J. Cryptology **4**(1), 3–72 (1991)
2. Matsui, M.: Linear cryptanalysis method for DES cipher. In: Helleseth, T. (ed.) EUROCRYPT 1993. LNCS, vol. 765, pp. 386–397. Springer, Heidelberg (1994)
3. Demirci, H., Selçuk, A.A.: A meet-in-the-middle attack on 8-round AES. In: Nyberg, K. (ed.) FSE 2008. LNCS, vol. 5086, pp. 116–126. Springer, Heidelberg (2008)
4. Semiconductors, N.: The PRINCE challenge (2014). http://www.emsec.rub.de/research/research_startseite/prince-challenge/
5. Borghoff, J., Canteaut, A., Güneysu, T., Kavun, E.B., Knezevic, M., Knudsen, L.R., Leander, G., Nikov, V., Paar, C., Rechberger, C., Rombouts, P., Thomsen, S.S., Yalçın, T.: PRINCE – a low-latency block cipher for pervasive computing applications. In: Wang, X., Sako, K. (eds.) ASIACRYPT 2012. LNCS, vol. 7658, pp. 208–225. Springer, Heidelberg (2012)
6. Biryukov, A., Perrin, L.: State of the art in lightweight cryptography. http://cryptolux.org/index.php/Lightweight_Cryptography
7. Soleimany, H., Blondeau, C., Yu, X., Wu, W., Nyberg, K., Zhang, H., Zhang, L., Wang, Y.: Reflection cryptanalysis of PRINCE-like ciphers. J. Cryptology. **28**(3), 718–744 (2015). doi:10.1007/s00145-013-9175-4
8. Jean, J., Nikolić, I., Peyrin, T., Wang, L., Wu, S.: Security analysis of PRINCE. In: Moriai, S. (ed.) FSE 2013. LNCS, vol. 8424, pp. 92–111. Springer, Heidelberg (2014)
9. Li, L., Jia, K., Wang, X.: Improved meet-in-the-middle attacks on aes-192 and prince. Cryptology ePrint Archive, Report 2013/573 (2013). http://eprint.iacr.org/
10. Canteaut, A., Fuhr, T., Gilbert, H., Naya-Plasencia, M., Reinhard, J.R.: Multiple differential cryptanalysis of round-reduced PRINCE (full version). Cryptology ePrint Archive, Report 2014/089 (2014). http://eprint.iacr.org/
11. Rechberger, C.: Update on the 10000 euro PRINCE cipher-breaking challenge: results of round-1 (2014). http://crypto.2014.rump.cr.yp.to/d037206eda8f9278cef1ea26cd62e51f.pdf
12. Dunkelman, O., Keller, N., Shamir, A.: Improved single-key attacks on 8-round AES-192 and AES-256. In: Abe, M. (ed.) ASIACRYPT 2010. LNCS, vol. 6477, pp. 158–176. Springer, Heidelberg (2010)
13. Derbez, P., Fouque, P.: Exhausting Demirci-Selçuk meet-in-the-middle attacks against reduced-round AES. In: Fast Software Encryption - 20th International Workshop, FSE 2013, Singapore, 11–13 March 2013, pp. 541–560 (2013). Revised Selected Papers
14. Derbez, P., Fouque, P.-A., Jean, J.: Improved key recovery attacks on reduced-round AES in the single-key setting. In: Johansson, T., Nguyen, P.Q. (eds.) EUROCRYPT 2013. LNCS, vol. 7881, pp. 371–387. Springer, Heidelberg (2013)
15. Mironov, I., Zhang, L.: Applications of SAT solvers to cryptanalysis of hash functions. In: Biere, A., Gomes, C.P. (eds.) SAT 2006. LNCS, vol. 4121, pp. 102–115. Springer, Heidelberg (2006)
16. Eén, N., Sörensson, N.: An extensible SAT-solver. In: Giunchiglia, E., Tacchella, A. (eds.) SAT 2003. LNCS, vol. 2919, pp. 502–518. Springer, Heidelberg (2004)
17. Biryukov, A., Shamir, A.: Structural cryptanalysis of SASAS. In: Pfitzmann, B. (ed.) EUROCRYPT 2001. LNCS, vol. 2045, p. 394. Springer, Heidelberg (2001)

18. Abed, F., List, E., Lucks, S.: On the security of the core of prince against biclique and differential cryptanalysis. Cryptology ePrint Archive, Report 2012/712 (2012). http://eprint.iacr.org/
19. Biryukov, A.: Analysis of involutional ciphers: Khazad and Anubis. In: Johansson, T. (ed.) FSE 2003. LNCS, vol. 2887, pp. 45–53. Springer, Heidelberg (2003)
20. Moore, J.H., Simmons, G.J.: Cycle structure of the DES with weak and semi-weak keys. In: Odlyzko, A.M. (ed.) CRYPTO 1986. LNCS, vol. 263, pp. 9–32. Springer, Heidelberg (1987)
21. Dunkelman, O., Keller, N., Shamir, A.: Minimalism in cryptography: the even-mansour scheme revisited. In: Pointcheval, D., Johansson, T. (eds.) EUROCRYPT 2012. LNCS, vol. 7237, pp. 336–354. Springer, Heidelberg (2012)

Linear Distinguishers in the Key-less Setting: Application to PRESENT

Martin M. Lauridsen[✉] and Christian Rechberger

DTU Compute, Technical University of Denmark, Kgs. Lyngby, Denmark
{mmeh,crec}@dtu.dk

Abstract. The application of the concept of linear cryptanalysis to the domain of key-less primitives is largely an open problem. In this paper we, for the first time, propose a model in which its application is meaningful for distinguishing block ciphers.

Combining our model with ideas from message modification and rebound-like approaches, we initiate a study of cryptographic primitives with respect to this new attack vector and choose the lightweight block cipher PRESENT as an example target. This leads to known-key distinguishers over up to 27 rounds, whereas the best previous result is up to 18 rounds in the chosen-key model.

Keywords: Hash function · Block cipher · Linear cryptanalysis · Distinguisher · PRESENT

1 Introduction

We start off with a simple, clearly undesirable property of a block cipher and generalize it; suppose there is an n-bit block cipher which allows, for a particular known or chosen key, to determine a plaintext, such that the plaintext is the same as the ciphertext. For a good block cipher, accomplishing this should be very unlikely with much less than 2^n trials. It would, for example, allow preimage attacks in fully preimage-secure compression function constructions that use this block cipher.

Now, consider an n-bit block cipher where the key is known or chosen by the attacker and let us focus on a single bit at position i of the plaintext p_i and ciphertext c_i in this setting. We would expect that the equation $p_i = c_i$ holds in exactly half the cases. In fact, any statistically significant deviation from this expectation can be interpreted as a sign of non-randomness in the cipher.

Such an attack would be in the so-called *key-less model*, which covers both the *known-key* and *chosen-key* models, and is hence of relevance if the cipher is used as part of a hash function construction. More generally, it allows to make meaningful statements and differentiate between ciphers beyond what is possible in other models. Should we consider such a cipher as a good building block for a compression function? Not if there would be an alternative cipher with similar implementation characteristics that does not allow for such a distinguisher!

© International Association for Cryptologic Research 2015
G. Leander (Ed.): FSE 2015, LNCS 9054, pp. 217–240, 2015.
DOI: 10.1007/978-3-662-48116-5_11

1.1   Contributions

We discuss the two types of contributions in this paper. One is of a more conceptual/modeling nature, while the other is a concrete cryptanalytic application of the former.

A New Way of Formulating Key-less Distinguishers. The property described in the beginning resembles properties used in linear cryptanalysis to recover secret keys. The problem with the above line of reasoning was that so far there did not exist a meaningful model to properly express the setting. By this, we mean a model which has a proper characterization of the power of generic attackers and a clear distinction as to when a dedicated attack in fact can be considered a valid distinguisher, i.e. outperforms generic attackers. In this paper, after starting off by giving notation and preliminary notions of block ciphers and linear cryptanalysis in Sect. 2, we put in Sect. 3 the above very informal description of a possible demonstration of non-randomness on more rigorous grounds.

The usual requirement for a distinguisher to be valid is, that one must compare the cost of satisfying a specific property, which varies from case to case, for a concrete permutation π, with achieving the same property for an ideal permutation. In our model, we expand on this by posing the problem of determining for a concrete permutation π: (i) a linear relation over π in the form of an input/output mask and (ii) a set of inputs to π, such that the number of inputs satisfying the linear relation is *expected* to deviate from what one expects of an ideal permutation, by a significant amount. A property which should not be attainable for an ideal primitive.

Our proposed key-less linear distinguisher model captures the possibility of distinguishing a cipher using any previous linear cryptanalysis, in the sense that the attacker needs only a linear hull and the probability distribution on the absolute correlation, to perform his analysis. To amplify the distinguisher to either cover more rounds or to need less computation, approaches inspired by message modification [42] and rebound attacks [28,35] are used.

Application to PRESENT. We can find concrete results in the new model in round-reduced versions of the leading lightweight-cipher PRESENT [10] (used in compression function designs advocated e.g. in [11]). In Sect. 4 we describe the relevant aspects of the PRESENT block cipher and give results on linear hulls and keys pertaining to it. Section 5 details the application of the key-less linear distinguisher to PRESENT. We fix a bit position i, devise an algorithm for determining up to $2^{61.97}$ key-dependent plaintexts in a very efficient manner, and study the expected number of plaintext and ciphertext pairs where $p_i = c_i$. What we claim to be able to find is a deviation from the expectation that the equation $p_i = c_i$ is fulfilled with probability $\frac{1}{2}$. Depending on the size of the allowable key-set, this will work for up to 27 rounds of PRESENT. Detailed results are summarized in Table 4, before our conclusions and a discussion of open problems in Sect. 6. We confirm the results with experimental verifications (see Appendix C and [29]).

1.2   Related Work

Linear cryptanalysis, a technique to recover keys in ciphers, was pioneered by Matsui from 1992 on [32,34], with extensions or variants such as multiple linear approximations [5,20], linear hulls [38], multidimensional variants [16], zero-correlations [12] and considerations of a general statistical framework [3,30,37].

The application of linear cryptanalysis to key-less constructions, i.e. in models where the key is either known or chosen by the attacker, is largely an open problem. Sometimes, designs are evaluated with respect to standard linear cryptanalysis [2,31]. Some designers of SHA-3 candidates state properties with respect to this class of attacks (such as linear probability) without ever mentioning specific models. The reason is that there simply was no model, a situation that we address in this paper.

In all cases of linear cryptanalysis applied in a key-less setting, the analysis done is exactly the same as in a setting with a secret key: a linear approximation with a non-zero correlation is presented. The only known exception to us is a linear analysis of Cubehash by Ashur and Dunkelman [2]. There, an 11-round linear approximation with bias 2^{-235} is used to describe a standard distinguisher with 2^{470} queries. Then, inspired by a chosen-plaintext variant of linear cryptanalysis of DES by Knudsen and Mathiassen [23], the authors fix 80 bits of the plaintext input of modular additions, thereby gaining the first round for free, arriving at a 12-round result with a complexity below 2^{512}. This can be seen as a predecessor to our deterministic technique of Sect. 5.2.

The only analysis of PRESENT in a setting without secret keys we know of is by Koyama, Sasaki, and Kunihiro [25]. In their work, differential chosen-key distinguishers (a setting that gives the attacker more freedom than in our known-key model) for up to 18 rounds are obtained.

At its core is a differential rebound attack with an inbound phase of 5 rounds that needs 100 degrees of freedom[1]. In the method we propose, we allow the key to be fixed arbitrarily, and out of the remaining 64 degrees of freedom from the plaintext input more than 61 degrees of freedom remain. Hence our results, that cover more rounds, and use our deterministic phase over 3 rounds that needs only 3 degrees of freedom, compare favorably to this result.

2   Preliminaries

In this section we introduce our notation, give basic definitions and recall known properties related to our analysis throughout the paper.

Notation. For an n-bit block cipher with key space $\mathcal{K}$, let $E : \mathbb{F}_2^n \times \mathcal{K} \to \mathbb{F}_2^n$ and $D : \mathbb{F}_2^n \times \mathcal{K} \to \mathbb{F}_2^n$ denote encryption and decryption functions, respectively. For convenience, we also use the notation that $E_K(x) := E(x, K)$ and $D_K(c) :=$

---

[1] Authors mention that 92 degrees of freedom out of 192 (from key and plaintext input) are left for the outbound phase.

$D(c, K)$. We use $\sharp X$ to denote the size of a set X. For a real number w, $|w|$ denotes the absolute value of w. We let $\mathsf{Perm}(n)$ denote the set of all permutations on n-bit inputs and we let $x \xleftarrow{\$} X$ denote the assignment of x by an element of X chosen uniformly at random. We use $\mathcal{N}(\mu, \sigma^2)$ and $\mathcal{B}(n, p)$ to denote the normal- and binomial distributions respectively. For a distribution D we use $\varPhi(D, x)$ to denote the cumulative distribution function of D at point x. We use the notation that $\mathbf{e}_i$ is a binary string with a 1 in position i and zeroes elsewhere.

In this paper, when we talk about the key-less setting, we implicitly mean adversarial assumptions where the key $K \in \mathcal{K}$ is either known or chosen by the attacker.

Trails and Hulls. In the following, let $F : \mathbb{F}_2^n \to \mathbb{F}_2^n$ be an iterated function of the form $F = F_R \circ \cdots \circ F_1$. We borrow to a large extent the notation from Leander's treatment on linear cryptanalysis [30]. We define a *mask* as a vector $\alpha \in \mathbb{F}_2^n$. For two masks α, β, we denote by $\langle \alpha, \beta \rangle$ the inner product of the two masks:

$$\langle (\alpha_0, \ldots, \alpha_{n-1}), (\beta_0, \ldots, \beta_{n-1}) \rangle := \bigoplus_{i=0}^{n-1} \alpha_i \beta_i.$$

We define an R-round *trail* as an element $(\delta, \alpha_1, \ldots, \alpha_{R-1}, \gamma) \in (\mathbb{F}_2^n)^{R+1}$, where δ and γ are the *input* and *output* masks, respectively. The α_i are called the *intermediate* masks. For a randomly chosen $x \in \mathbb{F}_2^n$, and for $i = 1, \ldots, R$ (letting $\alpha_0 = \delta$ and $\alpha_R = \gamma$), we have

$$\Pr\left[\langle x, \alpha_{i-1} \rangle = \langle F_i(x), \alpha_i \rangle \right] = \frac{1}{2} + \frac{\mathbf{C}_{F_i}(\alpha_{i-1}, \alpha_i)}{2},$$

where $\mathbf{C}_{F_i}(\alpha_{i-1}, \alpha_i)$ is the *correlation* over F_i. The *trail correlation* over F is defined in terms of the $\mathbf{C}_{F_i}$ as

$$\mathbf{C}_F(\delta, \alpha_1, \ldots, \alpha_{R-1}, \gamma) = \mathbf{C}_{F_1}(\delta, \alpha_1) \left(\prod_{i=2}^{R-1} \mathbf{C}_{F_i}(\alpha_{i-1}, \alpha_i) \right) \mathbf{C}_{F_R}(\alpha_{R-1}, \gamma). \quad (1)$$

We say that a trail is *valid* if and only if each constituent correlation of (1) is non-zero.

We define an R-round *linear hull* $\mathsf{LH}_R(\delta, \gamma)$ as the union of all valid linear trails with input mask δ and output mask γ. As such, we use the notation that $t \in \mathsf{LH}_R(\delta, \gamma)$ for an R-round trail t. Note that a linear hull $\mathsf{LH}_R(\delta, \gamma)$ defines an R-round *linear relation* between x and $F(x)$, which we denote $\mathcal{R}_{\delta, \gamma}^F : \mathbb{F}_2^n \to \mathbb{F}_2$, where

$$\mathcal{R}_{\delta, \gamma}^F(x) = \begin{cases} 1 & , \langle x, \delta \rangle = \langle F(x), \gamma \rangle \\ 0 & , \langle x, \delta \rangle \neq \langle F(x), \gamma \rangle \end{cases}.$$

When $\mathcal{R}_{\delta,\gamma}^F(x) = 1$ we say the relation is *satisfied* for input x and otherwise it is not. The *linear hull correlation* [17, Theorem 7.8.1] is given by

$$\mathbf{C}_F(\mathrm{LH}_R(\delta,\gamma)) = \sum_{t \in \mathrm{LH}_R(\delta,\gamma)} \mathbf{C}_F(t)$$

$$= \sum_{t \in \mathrm{LH}_R(\delta,\gamma)} (-1)^{\mathrm{sgn}(t)} \cdot |\mathbf{C}_F(t)|, \quad \mathrm{sgn}(t) = \begin{cases} 0 & , \mathbf{C}_F(t) \geq 0 \\ 1 & , \mathbf{C}_F(t) < 0 \end{cases}.$$

When the trail or hull is understood, we write $\mathbf{C}_F$ for simplicity to mean the correlation of the trail or hull over F. For a block cipher, the value of $\mathrm{sgn}(t)$ for $t \in \mathrm{LH}_R(\delta,\gamma)$ depends on the secret key $K \in \mathcal{K}$, and hence the value of $|\mathbf{C}_F(\mathrm{LH}_R(\delta,\gamma))|$ depends on the difference between the number of trails with $\mathrm{sgn}(t) = 1$ and those with $\mathrm{sgn}(t) = 0$. In this paper, we use the following assumption.

Assumption 1. *For any fixed key $K \in \mathcal{K}$, we assume that for any two trails $t, t' \in LH_R(\delta,\gamma)$, where $t \neq t'$, the signs $\mathrm{sgn}(t)$ and $\mathrm{sgn}(t')$ are independent Bernoulli random variables with $p = \frac{1}{2}$.*

We note that Assumption 1 has been experimentally verified for PRESENT, see e.g. [13,30].

For readers familiar with differential-type attacks in the known-key setting, we offer the following loose analogy. We say that $x \in \mathbb{F}_2^n$ *follows* an R-round trail over F if and only if

$$\langle x, \delta \rangle = \langle F_1(x), \alpha_1 \rangle = \cdots = \langle (F_{R-1} \circ \cdots \circ F_1)(x), \alpha_{R-1} \rangle = \langle F(x), \gamma \rangle.$$

This notion will be used in Sect. 5, when we describe how to use a technique similar to message modification, to extend a presented distinguisher in the key-less setting.

3 Key-less Linear Distinguishers for Block Ciphers

Even though block ciphers have used already for a very long time, either implicitly or explicitly, to construct hash functions, a separate study of the security of block ciphers where the key is either known or under control of the adversary, has started only recently. Knudsen and Rijmen proposed so-called known-key distinguishers [24]. Later Biryukov et al. [8] and Lamberger et al. [27] proposed open- or chosen-key models to evaluate the security of block ciphers.

Even though these models often exhibit a rather contrived looking property, and evade a formally rigorous definition[2] (a property they share with collision attacks), cryptanalysts largely agree that these distinguishers are useful and interesting. Indeed, techniques developed to improve the original known-key distinguishers from [24], such as the rebound attack later led to collision attacks

---

[2] One exception being [1].

on various hash functions [21,27,36]. Also, the findings in the open-key model from [8] were later used to find the first related-key key-recovery attacks on AES-256 and AES-192 [6,7].

3.1   Motivation for Our Distinguisher

Sometimes distinguisher descriptions are merely motivated by the fact that they *can* be formulated, as e.g. the 7-round known-key distinguisher on AES from [24], where byte-level zero-sums are used as a distinguishing property. Another example is the rotational rebound attack on reduced Skein [22], where the existence of "rotational collisions with errors" is defined as a distinguishing property. Sometimes, however, they are better motivated, e.g. by the construction of near-collisions, or the subspace- and limited-birthday distinguishers [19,27,28] that resemble some generalization of the concept of near-collisions.

The distinguisher we propose below comes with a new motivation that stems from preimage attacks on hash functions or compression functions[3]. As an example, consider the compression function construction using a single call to a block cipher in Matyas-Meyer-Oseas mode. The ith message block m_i is compressed by using it as the plaintext input when computing the next chaining value H_{i+1} using H_i as the cipher key, i.e. $H_{i+1} = E_{H_i}(m_i) \oplus m_i$. If an attacker can determine a relation stating that the jth bit of m_i equals the jth bit of $E_{H_i}(m_i)$ with a high probability, then it is likely that the jth bit of H_{i+1} equals zero. In a preimage attack, if the target preimage is zero at position j, this then leads to an advantage over brute-force search.

Motivated by this example, we proceed with our new key-less linear distinguisher model for block ciphers that we will use throughout the paper.

3.2   The Key-less Linear Distinguisher Model

In the following, we give our definition of key-less linear distinguishers. Essentially, the model captures the possibility of distinguishing any block cipher in the key-less setting, given that a linear relation (in the form of a linear hull) of sufficiently high absolute correlation for a reasonable fraction of the key space $\mathcal{K}$, is available. The notions of Definitions 1 and 2 are largely inspired by the recent work of Gilbert on pushing known-key attacks further on the AES [18].

The following definition of α-*separability* formalizes how a linear relation, combined with a set of inputs for a permutation $\pi : \mathbb{F}_2^n \to \mathbb{F}_2^n$, can exhibit a *significant* deviation from the behavior of a random permutation.

Definition 1 (α-separability). *Let $\mathcal{P}$ be a set of permutations from $\mathbb{F}_2^n$ to $\mathbb{F}_2^n$ and let $\pi \in \mathcal{P}$ denote a particular, fixed permutation from $\mathcal{P}$. Let $\mathcal{S} \subseteq \mathbb{F}_2^n$ with size $\mathcal{M}$ and let $\delta, \gamma \in \mathbb{F}_2^n \backslash \{(0, \dots, 0)\}$.*

---

[3] We emphasize here that the application to PRESENT later on in the paper will not be a preimage attack.

Without checking each input, each $x_i \in S$ has an (a priori) associated proba-bility $p_i = \Pr\left[\mathcal{R}^{\pi}_{\delta,\gamma}(x_i) = 1\right]$ that the linear relation is satisfied for that particular input. Let $\mathcal{X} = \sharp\{x \in S \mid \mathcal{R}^{\pi}_{\delta,\gamma}(x) = 1\}$, then $\mathbb{E}\left[\mathcal{X}\right] = \sum_{i=1}^{M} p_i$. We say that the tuple $(\mathcal{P}, \pi, S, \mathcal{R}^{\pi}_{\delta,\gamma})$ is α-separable if and only

$$\Pr\left[\left|\mathbb{E}\left[\mathcal{X}\right] - \frac{\mathcal{M}}{2}\right| \geq \sqrt{\mathcal{M}}\right] \geq \alpha,$$

where the probability is taken over $\pi \in \mathcal{P}$.

Definition 2 ($(T, \mathcal{M}, \alpha)$-intractability). *Let $\mathcal{P}$ be a set of permutations from $\mathbb{F}_2^n$ to $\mathbb{F}_2^n$ and let $\pi \in \mathcal{P}$ denote a particular, fixed permutation from $\mathcal{P}$. Let $S \subseteq \mathbb{F}_2^n$ of size $\mathcal{M}$ and let $\delta, \gamma \in \mathbb{F}_2^n \backslash \{(0, \ldots, 0)\}$. We say that the tuple $(\mathcal{P}, \pi, S, \mathcal{R}^{\pi}_{\delta,\gamma})$ is $(T, \mathcal{M}, \alpha)$-intractable if and only if it is impossible, for any algorithm $\mathcal{A}$ to*

1. *Commit to a choice of $\delta', \gamma' \in \mathbb{F}_2^n \backslash \{(0, \ldots, 0)\}$ and*
2. *When given access to a fixed pair Π, Π^{-1} with $\Pi \xleftarrow{\$} \mathrm{Perm}(n)$, construct a set S' of size $\mathcal{M}$ in time T, s.t. the tuple $(\mathrm{Perm}(n), \Pi, S', \mathcal{R}^{\Pi}_{\delta',\gamma'})$ is α-separable.*

Note 1. For our distinguisher model, the notion of *one time unit* corresponds to a single evaluation of the respective permutation.

With the definition of α-separability and $(T, \mathcal{M}, \alpha)$-intractability in hand, we are ready to formulate our proposed key-less linear distinguisher.

Definition 3 (Key-less linear distinguisher). *Let $E : \mathbb{F}_2^n \times \mathcal{K} \rightarrow \mathbb{F}_2^n$ be a block cipher and let $\mathcal{E}$ to denote the set of permutations due to choices of the key $K \in \mathcal{K}$. Let E_K denote some fixed permutation from $\mathcal{E}$.*

Fix $\delta, \gamma \in \mathbb{F}_2^n \backslash \{(0, \ldots, 0)\}$ and let $\mathcal{A}$ be an algorithm producing in time T a set $S \subseteq \mathbb{F}_2^n$ of size $\mathcal{M}$. Then the tuple $(\mathcal{A}, \mathcal{E}, E_K, S, T, \mathcal{R}^{E_K}_{\delta,\gamma}, \alpha)$ is said to be a key-less linear distinguisher if and only if $(\mathcal{E}, E_K, S, \mathcal{R}^{E_K}_{\delta,\gamma})$ is both α-separable and $(T, \mathcal{M}, \alpha)$-intractable.

Note 2. In all of the definitions above, the fixed linear masks $\delta, \gamma \in \mathbb{F}_2^n \backslash \{(0, \ldots, 0)\}$ are *chosen* by the algorithm $\mathcal{A}$, but the choice *must be made* *before* the production of the input set S commences.

In the context of distinguishing a block cipher, the adversary commits to δ and γ and then obtains access to E_K upon which the production of S in time T begins. The parameter α directly expresses a lower bound on the fraction of the permutations $\pi \in \mathcal{P}$ for which the key-less linear distinguisher is valid. The time T allowed to construct S is a parameter chosen by the adversary.

Analysis. In the following, we analyze and argue that the key-less linear distinguisher is meaningful. First, informally, the notion of α-separability expresses that for a concrete permutation $\pi : \mathbb{F}_2^n \rightarrow \mathbb{F}_2^n$, one can provide a linear relation which captures, for some constructed set of inputs, a *significant non-random* *behavior* in a permutation which is supposed to behave randomly. The *signifi-cant* part is captured by the requirement that the number of inputs satisfying the relation $\mathcal{R}_{\delta,\gamma}^{\pi}$ should deviate from what is expected in the ideal case by at least $\sqrt{\mathcal{M}}$. This reflects the usual requirement in linear cryptanalysis, that the data complexity is inversely proportional to the squared correlation. Second, on top of that, Definition 2 captures the notion that for a random permutation $\Pi \xleftarrow{\$} \mathsf{Perm}(n)$, it should not be possible, in the same amount of time, to pro-vide such a relation with a set of inputs which exhibits the same significant non-random behavior.

With respect to Definition 2, one of the components to analyzing our pro-posed key-less linear distinguisher is to answer the following question: What is the *upper bound* on the probability α' that an algorithm $\mathcal{A}$, when given access to the fixed pair Π and Π^{-1}, can produce in time T a set $\mathcal{S}' \subseteq \mathbb{F}_2^n$ of size $\mathcal{M}$, together with a pre-determined relation $\mathcal{R}_{\delta,\gamma}^{\Pi}$, such that $(\mathsf{Perm}(n), \Pi, \mathcal{S}', \mathcal{R}_{\delta,\gamma}^{\Pi})$ is α'-separable? Our analysis answers this question in the following, and it implic-itly provides a *lower bound* on α for when a concrete permutation $\pi : \mathbb{F}_2^n \to \mathbb{F}_2^n \in \mathcal{P}$ (in the notation of Definitions 1 and 2) can be shown to be $(T, \mathcal{M}, \alpha)$-intractable, for fixed T and $\mathcal{M}$. We begin our analysis with Lemma 1.

Lemma 1. *In the notation of Definition 2, let $\delta', \gamma' \in \mathbb{F}_2^n \setminus \{(0, \ldots, 0)\}$ be fixed, and let then an algorithm $\mathcal{A}$ be given access to Π, Π^{-1}, where $\Pi \xleftarrow{\$} \mathsf{Perm}(n)$. The optimal way for $\mathcal{A}$ to construct $\mathcal{S}' \subseteq \mathbb{F}_2^n$ of size $\mathcal{M}$ in time T is the following:*

1. *Construct an arbitrarily chosen set $\mathcal{Q} \subseteq \mathbb{F}_2^n$ of size T.*
2. *Partition $\mathcal{Q}$ into $\mathcal{Q}_1 = \{x \in \mathcal{Q} \mid \mathcal{R}_{\delta',\gamma'}^{\Pi}(x) = 1\}$ and $\mathcal{Q}_0 = \{x \in \mathcal{Q} \mid \mathcal{R}_{\delta',\gamma'}^{\Pi}(x) = 0\}$ by querying $\Pi(x)$ for all $x \in \mathcal{Q}$.*
3. *Set $\mathcal{S}'$ equal to the larger of the sets $\mathcal{Q}_0$ and $\mathcal{Q}_1$.*
4. *Fill up $\mathcal{S}'$ with arbitrarily chosen inputs from $\mathbb{F}_2^n \setminus \mathcal{Q}$ until $\sharp \mathcal{S}' = \mathcal{M}$.*

Proof. As $\Pi \xleftarrow{\$} \mathsf{Perm}(n)$, the particular choice of $\delta', \gamma' \in \mathbb{F}_2^n \setminus \{(0, \ldots, 0)\}$ does not affect the analysis. The most information $\mathcal{A}$ can learn about Π in time T is to obtain T pairs $(x, \Pi(x))$, as is done when determining $\mathcal{Q}$ and its image under Π. In order to optimally shift the balance of the expected number of inputs of $\mathcal{S}'$ satisfying $\mathcal{R}_{\delta',\gamma'}^{\Pi}$ away from $\mathcal{M}/2$, $\mathcal{A}$ should take the larger of $\mathcal{Q}_1$ and $\mathcal{Q}_0$ and pool it with randomly chosen inputs x for which the value of $\mathcal{R}_{\delta',\gamma'}^{\Pi}(x)$ is not known. □

Continuing our analysis, assuming an algorithm $\mathcal{A}$ constructs $\mathcal{S}'$ as in Lemma 1, we determine an upper bound on the value α' as a function of $\mathcal{M}$ and T, such that the resulting tuple $(\mathsf{Perm}(n), \Pi, \mathcal{S}', \mathcal{R}_{\delta',\gamma'}^{\Pi})$ is α'-separable. We give this result in Theorem 1.

Theorem 1 (Generic success probability). *Let $\mathcal{A}, \Pi, \delta', \gamma', \mathcal{S}'$ and T be as in Lemma 1, where $T \leq 4\sqrt{\mathcal{M}}$, and let $\mathcal{X} := \sharp\{x \in \mathcal{S}' \mid \mathcal{R}_{\delta,\gamma}^{\Pi}(x) = 1\}$. Then*

$$\Pr\left[\left|\mathbb{E}[\mathcal{X}] - \frac{\mathcal{M}}{2}\right| \geq \sqrt{\mathcal{M}}\right] = 2^{-T} \cdot \left[\sum_{k=0}^{T-2\sqrt{\mathcal{M}}} \binom{T}{k} + \sum_{k=2\sqrt{\mathcal{M}}}^{T} \binom{T}{k}\right].$$

Proof. First, note that $\sharp Q_1 \sim \mathcal{B}(T, \frac{1}{2})$. We want to determine the probability that we have $\left| \mathbb{E}[\mathcal{X}] - \frac{M}{2} \right| \geq \sqrt{M}$. The consideration is split into two cases depending on whether or not $\sharp Q_1 \geq T/2$.

Case $\sharp Q_1 \geq T/2$. In this case, we know that at least $\sharp Q_1$ of the M inputs satisfy the relation. Thus, $\mathbb{E}[\mathcal{X}] = \mathbb{E}[Z] + \sharp Q_1$ where $Z \sim \mathcal{B}\left(M - \sharp Q_1, \frac{1}{2}\right)$. Thus, $\mathbb{E}[\mathcal{X}] = \frac{M + \sharp Q_1}{2}$, and the requirement $\left| \mathbb{E}[\mathcal{X}] - \frac{M}{2} \right| \geq \sqrt{M}$ is equivalent to either $\sharp Q_1 \geq 2\sqrt{M}$ or $\sharp Q_1 \leq -2\sqrt{M}$, the latter not being possible as $\sharp Q_1$ is non-negative.

Case $\sharp Q_1 < T/2$. In this case, we know that there are at least $T - \sharp Q_1$ of the M inputs that *do not* satisfy the relation. Thus, $\mathbb{E}[\mathcal{X}] = \mathbb{E}[Z]$ where $Z \sim \mathcal{B}\left(M - T + \sharp Q_1, \frac{1}{2}\right)$. Thus, $\mathbb{E}[\mathcal{X}] = \frac{M - T + \sharp Q_1}{2}$, and the requirement $\left| \mathbb{E}[\mathcal{X}] - \frac{M}{2} \right| \geq \sqrt{M}$ is equivalent to either $\sharp Q_1 \geq T + 2\sqrt{M}$ or $\sharp Q_1 \leq T - 2\sqrt{M}$, the former not being possible as $\sharp Q_1 \leq T$.

In both of the cases considered, there is one event which makes the inequality $\left| \mathbb{E}[\mathcal{X}] - \frac{M}{2} \right| \geq \sqrt{M}$ true. The combined probability of those two events is

$$\Pr\left[\sharp Q_1 \geq 2\sqrt{M} \right] + \Pr\left[\sharp Q_1 \leq T - 2\sqrt{M} \right]$$

$$= 2^{-T} \cdot \left[\sum_{k=0}^{T - 2\sqrt{M}} \binom{T}{k} + \sum_{k=2\sqrt{M}}^{T} \binom{T}{k} \right].$$

From this, the result follows. $\qquad\square$

Note 3. The reason for the requirement $T \leq 4\sqrt{M}$ in the statement of Theorem 1 arises because otherwise the two sums would overlap and add the same terms twice. The probability which is derived as a function of M and T provides a lower bound on α for when, in the notation of Definition 2, a tuple $(\mathcal{P}, \pi, \mathcal{S}, \mathcal{R}_{\delta,\gamma}^{\pi})$ can be (T, M, α)-intractable.

By using the normal approximation of $\sharp Q_1$, i.e. $\sharp Q_1 \sim \mathcal{N}\left(\frac{T}{2}, \frac{T}{4}\right)$, one obtains a very precise and easily-computable approximation of the probability as

$$1 - \Phi\left(\mathcal{N}\left(\frac{T}{2}, \frac{T}{4}\right), 2\sqrt{M} \right) + \Phi\left(\mathcal{N}\left(\frac{T}{2}, \frac{T}{4}\right), T - 2\sqrt{M} \right).$$

Corollary 1. *Let $\mathcal{A}$ be an algorithm which, after a choice of $\delta, \gamma \in \mathbb{F}_2^n \setminus \{(0, \ldots, 0)\}$ is fixed, is given access to some permutation $\pi : \mathbb{F}_2^n \rightarrow \mathbb{F}_2^n \in \mathcal{P}$.*

When $T < 2\sqrt{M}$ and $\mathcal{P} = \mathsf{Perm}(n)$, it is impossible for $\mathcal{A}$ to produce in time T a set $\mathcal{S} \subseteq \mathbb{F}_2^n$ of size M s.t. the tuple $(\mathcal{P}, \pi, \mathcal{S}, \mathcal{R}_{\delta,\gamma}^{\pi})$ is α-separable for any $\alpha > 0$.

On the other hand, when $T \geq 4\sqrt{M}$ and $\mathcal{P} = \mathcal{E}$ (in the notation of Definition 3), then it is impossible for $\mathcal{A}$ to produce in time T a set $\mathcal{S} \subseteq \mathbb{F}_2^n$ of size M s.t. the tuple $(\mathcal{A}, \mathcal{P}, \pi, \mathcal{S}, T, \mathcal{R}_{\delta,\gamma}^{\pi}, \alpha)$ is a key-less linear distinguisher for any $\alpha > 0$.

Proof. The first result follows directly from Theorem 1 when observing that the both sums are zero when $T < 2\sqrt{\mathcal{M}}$. The second result follows from Theorem 1 when observing that the sums equal one when $T = 4\sqrt{\mathcal{M}}$. This makes $(T, \mathcal{M}, \alpha)$-intractability impossible. $\qquad\square$

Note 4. The key-less linear distinguisher specified in Definition 3 does not ask to provide outputs, hence it is not ruled out to give a valid key-less linear distinguisher without pre-computation, i.e. to have $T = 0$. Indeed, one of the concrete attacks we will later show does not need any computations.

Indeed, from Corollary 1 it follows that when no pre-computation is allowed, i.e. when $T = 0$, any algorithm $\mathcal{A}$ producing a set $\mathcal{S} \subseteq \mathbb{F}_2^n$ together with any relation $\delta, \gamma \in \mathbb{F}_2^n \backslash \{(0, \ldots, 0)\}$ for a permutation $E_K \in \mathcal{E}$, yields a key-less linear distinguisher $(\mathcal{A}, \mathcal{E}, E_K, \mathcal{S}, T, \mathcal{R}_{\delta,\gamma}^{E_K}, \alpha)$ for *some* $\alpha > 0$. Note, however, that the parameter α measures how likely such a distinguisher is to work for a specific key. For example, when α is very small, one might have a valid key-less linear distinguisher for many rounds, but for a tiny fraction of the key space. As such, when $T = 0$, such a key-less linear distinguisher is to be taken with a grain of salt, depending on the value α. In the following sections, we always provide together with our distinguishers the parameter α, to make clear the lower bound on the fraction of the key space for which it is valid.

Having analyzed the generic case, we move on to stating in Theorem 2 a necessary condition for when, for a particular fixed $\pi \in \mathcal{P}$ and $\delta, \gamma \in \mathbb{F}_2^n \backslash \{(0, \ldots, 0)\}$, an algorithm $\mathcal{A}$ can construct $\mathcal{S} \subseteq \mathbb{F}_2^n$ of size $\mathcal{M}$ in time T, s.t. the tuple $(\mathcal{P}, \pi, \mathcal{S}, \mathcal{R}_{\delta,\gamma})$ is a α-separable.

Theorem 2. *Let $\pi \in \mathcal{P}$ and fix $\delta, \gamma \in \mathbb{F}_2^n \backslash \{(0, \ldots, 0)\}$. Let $\mathcal{S} \subseteq \mathbb{F}_2^n$ have size $\mathcal{M}$. Then the tuple $(\mathcal{P}, \pi, \mathcal{S}, \mathcal{R}_{\delta,\gamma}^{\pi})$ can be α-separable for $\alpha > 0$ if and only if the absolute correction $|\mathbf{C}_\pi|$ of $\mathcal{R}_{\delta,\gamma}^{\pi}$ satisfies $|\mathbf{C}_\pi| \geq 2/\sqrt{\mathcal{M}}$. Furthermore, the largest α for which α-separability is obtained, is given by $\alpha = \Pr\left[|\mathbf{C}_\pi| \geq 2/\sqrt{\mathcal{M}}\right]$.*

Proof. Let $\mathcal{X} := \{x \in \mathcal{S} \mid \mathcal{R}_{\delta,\gamma}^{\pi}(x) = 1\}$. Then $\mathcal{X} \sim \mathcal{B}\left(\mathcal{M}, \frac{1}{2} + \frac{\mathbf{C}_\pi}{2}\right)$. We have α-separability if and only if $\Pr\left[|\mathbb{E}[\mathcal{X}] - \frac{\mathcal{M}}{2}| \geq \sqrt{\mathcal{M}}\right] \geq \alpha$. Thus, we require either $\mathbb{E}[\mathcal{X}] \geq \frac{\mathcal{M}}{2} + \sqrt{\mathcal{M}}$ or $\mathbb{E}[\mathcal{X}] \leq \frac{\mathcal{M}}{2} - \sqrt{\mathcal{M}}$. Since $\mathbb{E}[\mathcal{X}] = \frac{\mathcal{M}}{2} + \mathcal{M} \cdot \frac{\mathbf{C}_\pi}{2}$, this happens exactly when $|\mathbf{C}_\pi| \geq 2/\sqrt{\mathcal{M}}$. From this, the results follow. $\qquad\square$

4   The Block Cipher PRESENT, Keys and Linear Hulls

PRESENT is a 64-bit iterated block cipher [10] for use in lightweight applications such as RFID tags and wireless sensor networks. Its use in compression function designs is e.g. studied and advocated for in [11]. The key space is $\mathcal{K} = \mathbb{F}_2^\kappa$ with κ either 80 or 128 bits. The respective block ciphers are denoted PRESENT-80 and PRESENT-128. Both ciphers have 31 rounds. The PRESENT key-schedule (see Appendix A for details) produces 32 κ-bit round keys, but only the 64 most significant bits are used in the key addition of each round. We refer to these 64-bit round keys as K_i with $i = 0, \dots, 31$.

The structure of PRESENT is a substitution-permutation network, repeating the round function

$$R_i(x) = P \circ S(x \oplus K_i),$$

where x is the 64-bit state input to round i, S is the parallel application of sixteen identical 4-bit S-boxes and P is a fixed bitwise permutation[4]. The full cipher is composed of 31 applications of the round function followed by addition of a post-whitening key, i.e.

$$E_K = (R_{30} \circ \cdots \circ R_0)(x) \oplus K_{31}.$$

An illustration of a single round of PRESENT is given in Fig. 1. For the specification of the PRESENT S-box and permutation P, see Appendix A.

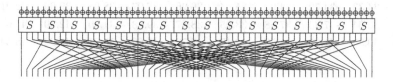

Fig. 1. Top-to-bottom illustration of a single round of PRESENT

4.1   Keys and Linear Hulls in PRESENT

One of the first thorough treatments of linear cryptanalysis on PRESENT is by Ohkuma [39]. This work defines *optimal linear trails* using solely masks of Hamming weight one. Furthermore, 64 *optimal hulls* using these trails are determined, along with the number of trails in each hull.

The absolute correlation for one of Ohkuma's R-round optimal trails t is $|\mathbf{C}_{E_K}(t)| = 2^{-2R}$. Considering a particular R-round optimal hull $\mathrm{LH}_R(\delta, \gamma)$, let T_R^+ (respectively T_R^-) denote the number of trails t in the hull for which $\mathrm{sgn}(t) = 0$ (respectively $\mathrm{sgn}(t) = 1$). We also let $T_R := \sharp\mathrm{LH}_R(\delta, \gamma)$, i.e. $T_R = T_R^+ + T_R^-$. By Assumption 1, for a fixed key $K \in \mathcal{K}$, we have $T_R^+ \sim \mathcal{B}\left(T_R, \frac{1}{2}\right)$, which for sufficiently large T_R is well approximated by $T_R^+ \sim \mathcal{N}\left(\frac{T_R}{2}, \frac{T_R}{4}\right)$. Let $Z = T_R^+ - T_R^- = 2T_R^+ - T_R$. Thus, Z is normally distributed with $\mu = 2 \cdot \frac{T_R}{2} - T_R = 0$ and $\sigma^2 = 2^2 \cdot \frac{T_R}{4} = T_R$, so $Z \sim \mathcal{N}(0, T_R)$. When $|Z| \geq N$, for some N, where $0 \leq N \leq T_R$, the absolute linear hull correlation is

$$|\mathbf{C}_{E_K}| \geq N \cdot 2^{-2R}.$$

Thus, there is a clear trade-off between the lower bound on $|\mathbf{C}_{E_K}|$ and the probability that a randomly chosen $K \in \mathcal{K}$ yields such a lower bound.

---

[4] S and P are called sBoxLayer and pLayer, respectively, in the specification.

For the T_R values, we refer to [39] or Table 6 in Appendix B. For a fixed number of rounds R, using the analysis above, T_R can be used directly to determine (i) a lower bound on $|\mathbf{C}_{E_K}|$ and (ii) the probability that for a random $K \in \mathcal{K}$, this bound is obtained. Table 1 gives, for various probabilities α and number of rounds R the value β such that $\alpha = \Pr\left[|\mathbf{C}_{E_K}| \geq \beta\right]$. Table 7 in Appendix B gives the same data points for $R \in \{1, \ldots, 31\}$.

Table 1. Values $\log_2 \beta$ s.t. $\alpha = \Pr\left[|\mathbf{C}_{E_K}| \geq \beta\right]$ for R-round PRESENT

R	α								
	0.01	0.05	0.10	0.30	0.50	0.70	0.90	0.95	0.99
7	−9.55	−9.94	−10.20	−10.86	−11.48	−12.29	−13.91	−14.91	−17.23
11	−14.74	−15.14	−15.39	−16.06	−16.68	−17.48	−19.10	−20.10	−22.43
16	−21.27	−21.66	−21.92	−22.58	−23.20	−24.01	−25.63	−26.63	−28.95
24	−31.71	−32.11	−32.36	−33.03	−33.65	−34.46	−36.07	−37.07	−39.40
26	−34.33	−34.72	−34.97	−35.64	−36.26	−37.07	−38.68	−39.69	−42.01
28	−36.94	−37.33	−37.58	−38.25	−38.87	−39.68	−41.30	−42.30	−44.62
31	−40.85	−41.25	−41.50	−42.17	−42.79	−43.60	−45.21	−46.22	−48.54

Example 1. For $R = 28$, we have $T_{28} = 45170283840$. Thus, with probability $\alpha = 0.30$, a randomly chosen $K \in \mathcal{K}$ yields that one of Ohkuma's optimal hulls has $|\mathbf{C}_{E_K}| \geq 2^{-38.25}$.

5 Application to PRESENT

In this section we give key-less linear distinguishers on PRESENT for varying parameters; the number of rounds R; the pre-computation time T; the size $\mathcal{M}$ of the set S produced and the lower bound α on the fraction of the key space for which they are valid.

As already hinted in Sect. 4, PRESENT has received some attention in the context of key-recovery attacks, especially with respect to linear cryptanalysis [13,15,30,39] on which our results build. The attack described is completely independent of the key size used, and hence also of the key-schedule.

5.1 Distinguishers with $T = 0$

In this section we present key-less linear distinguishers on PRESENT using the model introduced in Sect. 3. We refer to approach described here as the *probabilistic phase*, which in Sect. 5.2 is combined with a *deterministic phase* to extend the distinguishers for three more rounds.

The distinguishers we present here do not use any pre-computation, i.e. in the notation of the model, we have $T = 0$. Corollary 1 implies in this case that when $|\mathbf{C}_{E_K}| > 0$, the tuple produced by any algorithm $\mathcal{A}$ is always $(T, \mathcal{M}, \alpha)$-intractable for some $\alpha > 0$, and hence a valid distinguisher. The results match those of distinguishers used in key-recovery attacks and are as such of limited interest. We hope the discussion below makes it easier to follow (and appreciate) the real use of the model we introduced, namely for the case described in Sect. 5.2 when we do a some, albeit very little, pre-computation.

In the following, let $\mathcal{R}_{\delta,\gamma}^{E_K}$ be the linear relation used, where $\delta = \gamma = \mathbf{e}_{21}$, which is one of the optimal linear hulls for PRESENT identified by Ohkuma. Also, let $\mathcal{A}$ be an algorithm constructing $\mathcal{S} \subseteq \mathbb{F}_2^n$ by picking $\mathcal{M}$ arbitrary $x \in \mathbb{F}_2^n$. In Table 2 we give, for various $\mathcal{M}$ and number of rounds R, lower bounds α on the fraction of the key space, s.t. $(\mathcal{A}, \mathcal{E}, E_K, \mathcal{S}, T = 0, \mathcal{R}_{\delta,\gamma}^{E_K}, \alpha)$ are key-less linear distinguishers.

Table 2. Lower bounds α on the fraction of the key space $\mathcal{K}$ susceptible to key-less linear distinguishers using $T = 0$ and the specified parameters $\mathcal{M}$ and number of rounds R. A dash indicates that $\alpha < 0.00$.

$\mathcal{M}$	Rounds R													
	10	11	12	13	14	15	16	17	18	19	20	21	22	23
2^{40}	0.96	0.89	0.74	0.41	0.04	-	-	-	-	-	-	-	-	-
2^{44}	0.99	0.97	0.93	0.84	0.61	0.21	-	-	-	-	-	-	-	-
2^{46}	0.99	0.99	0.97	0.92	0.80	0.53	0.12	-	-	-	-	-	-	-
2^{52}	1.00	1.00	1.00	0.99	0.97	0.94	0.85	0.63	0.24	-	-	-	-	-
2^{54}	1.00	1.00	1.00	0.99	0.99	0.97	0.92	0.81	0.55	0.14	-	-	-	-
2^{56}	1.00	1.00	1.00	1.00	0.99	0.98	0.96	0.90	0.77	0.46	0.07	-	-	-
2^{62}	1.00	1.00	1.00	1.00	1.00	1.00	1.00	0.99	0.97	0.93	0.82	0.58	0.17	-
2^{63}	1.00	1.00	1.00	1.00	1.00	1.00	1.00	0.99	0.98	0.95	0.87	0.69	0.33	0.02
2^{64}	1.00	1.00	1.00	1.00	1.00	1.00	1.00	0.99	0.99	0.96	0.91	0.78	0.49	0.09

Note, that the α parameter from Table 2 gives immediately the probability that such an R-round key-less linear distinguisher without pre-computation for PRESENT is valid in practice, for a fixed chosen- or known key $K \in \mathcal{K}$. As examples, we see that with $\mathcal{M} = 2^{40}$, the probability of having a valid key-less linear distinguisher for 13-round PRESENT with a fixed key K is *at least* $\alpha = 0.41$. Another example is a key-less linear distinguisher on 22-round PRESENT which is valid for a fraction of at least $\alpha = 0.33$ of the key space, using $\mathcal{M} = 2^{63}$.

5.2 Extension by Deterministic Phase

Next, we describe how one can use pre-computation to extend the key-less linear distinguishers from Sect. 5.1 to cover three more rounds with no degradation to the valid key space fraction α. In the notation of the model, we now have $T > 0$, which in turn means that $(T, \mathcal{M}, \alpha)$-intractability is no longer granted for free by

Corollary 1, unless below $T < 2\sqrt{M}$. In Appendix D we outline an approach for a deterministic phase over 6 rounds, reminiscent of the rebound approach [28,35], which however has a too-high computational complexity to fit into our model.

We describe in the following the algorithm $\mathcal{A}$ which will construct the set of inputs $\mathcal{S}$. The algorithm we give will construct $\mathcal{S}$ such that each $x \in \mathcal{S}$ is guaranteed to follow the linear trail $\mathcal{T} = (\mathbf{e}_{21}, \mathbf{e}_{21}, \mathbf{e}_{21}, \mathbf{e}_{21})$ over the first three rounds. We remark that this choice of trail is not unique; several others choices are possible, this is but one example. We refer to the approach we describe as the *deterministic phase*.

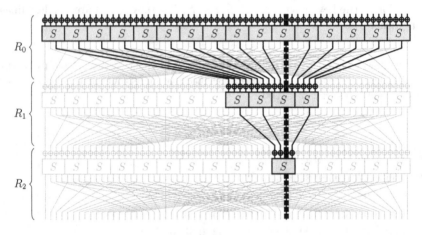

Fig. 2. Construction of $\mathcal{S}$ for 3-round PRESENT using the trail $\mathcal{T} = (\mathbf{e}_{21}, \mathbf{e}_{21}, \mathbf{e}_{21}, \mathbf{e}_{21})$

For notation, in round $r \in \{0, 1, 2\}$, let $S_{r,j}$ denote the jth S-box (counting from right to left) and let $K_{r,j}$ denote the jth least significant bit of the round key K_r, where all indices start from zero. Consider then $S_{2,5}$ which is highlighted in Fig. 2. By inspection, the PRESENT S-box has 10 inputs x which satisfy $\langle x, (0, 0, 1, 0) \rangle = \langle S(x), (0, 0, 1, 0) \rangle$ and hence follow the trail $(\mathbf{e}_{21}, \mathbf{e}_{21})$ over R_2, no matter what the inputs on the other S-boxes are. By adding the key bits $(K_{2,23} \| \cdots \| K_{2,20})$ to each x, we can trace those back through the permutation layer of R_1. For each value of $x \oplus (K_{2,23} \| \cdots \| K_{2,20})$, we now have a particular value on output bit 1 of each of the S-boxes $S_{1,7}, \ldots, S_{1,4}$, as indicated in Fig. 2. By the bijectivity of the S-box, it holds that for each of these S-boxes, half the inputs will give the desired output bit. However, for the S-box $S_{1,5}$ we have the extra requirement that the input bit on position 1 should equal the output bit on position 1, and only 5 inputs have both properties. As such, we can trace each of the ten values for x back through R_1 and also adding the key bits $(K_{1,31} \| \cdots \| K_{1,16})$ to obtain $10 \cdot 8^3 \cdot 5 = 25600$ inputs to $R_2 \circ R_1$ which follow the trail $(\mathbf{e}_{21}, \mathbf{e}_{21}, \mathbf{e}_{21})$ by construction. By tracing each of these values back through R_0 the same way, and adding the full round key K_0, algorithm $\mathcal{A}$ has a construction of the set $\mathcal{S}$ which consists of inputs which follow $\mathcal{T}$ over three rounds with probability 1. Using this approach to constructing $\mathcal{S}$, the size of the set can be *up to* $\mathcal{M} = 25600 \cdot 8^{15} \cdot 5 = 4503599627370496000 \approx 2^{61.97}$. As such, if one should wish to use a smaller $\mathcal{M}$ for the key-less linear distinguisher, this is also possible, simply by leaving out elements in the construction of $\mathcal{S}$.

Table 3. Tight values α such that $(\mathcal{E}, E_K, \mathcal{S}, \mathcal{R}_{\delta,\gamma}^{E_K})$ is α-separable, where E_K is R-round PRESENT for a fixed, known $K \in \mathcal{K}$ (and thus $E_K \in \mathcal{E}$)

Rounds R	18	19	20	21	22	23	24	25	26
α	0.998	0.995	0.988	0.970	0.926	0.819	0.571	0.162	0.001

Consider E_K being R-round PRESENT for a particular fixed $K \in \mathcal{K}$, and thus $E_K \in \mathcal{E}$. Let $\mathcal{A}$ be an algorithm for constructing $\mathcal{S}$ using the 3-round deterministic technique described, with $\mathcal{M} \approx 2^{61.97}$ for one of Ohkuma's optimal linear hull relations $\mathcal{R}_{\delta,\gamma}^{E_K}$. Table 3 gives, for various number of rounds R, the highest possible α s.t. $(\mathcal{E}, E_K, \mathcal{S}, \mathcal{R}_{\delta,\gamma}^{E_K})$ is α-separable as per Definition 1. Of course, in order for the key-less linear distinguisher $(\mathcal{A}, \mathcal{E}, E_K, \mathcal{S}, T, \mathcal{R}_{\delta,\gamma}^{E_K}, \alpha)$ to be valid, it also has to hold that the tuple $(\mathcal{E}, E_K, \mathcal{S}, \mathcal{R}_{\delta,\gamma}^{E_K})$ is $(T, \mathcal{M}, \alpha)$-intractable as per Definition 2, where T is the time required by $\mathcal{A}$ to construct the set $\mathcal{S}$.

In Sect. 5.3, we show that the time T required to construct $\mathcal{S}$ by $\mathcal{A}$ is equivalent to $T = \frac{409641}{16R}$ calls to an R-round PRESENT encryption oracle. As such, we have that $T < 2\sqrt{\mathcal{M}}$, and from Corollary 1, it follows that $(\mathcal{E}, E_K, \mathcal{S}, \mathcal{R}_{\delta,\gamma}^{E_K})$ is $(T, \mathcal{M}, \alpha)$-intractable.

In Appendix C, we give examples of experimental verification of the key-less linear distinguishers presented on 9-round PRESENT. The code for this experimental verification is available as [29].

5.3   Computational Complexity T

In this section we analyze the computational complexity, i.e. the time T required by $\mathcal{A}$ to construct $\mathcal{S}$ in the deterministic phase of Sect. 5.2. In the key-less setting, the attacker has white-box access to the encryption oracle. This is what is exploited by $\mathcal{A}$. In order to measure the time T spent in this phase, we determine the number of S-box lookups performed by $\mathcal{A}$ and then compare this to the number of S-box applications for a full call to the encryption oracle.

Let us consider all S-boxes as being different for generality, as the complexity in this case will certainly upper bound the case where they are all equal. In particular, since the key is known, this allows us to consider the key addition as part of the S-boxes.

The analysis follows the construction of $\mathcal{S}$ by $\mathcal{A}$ itself, starting from R_2 and working its way up (referring again to Fig. 2). To determine the 10 inputs to $S_{2,5}$, $\mathcal{A}$ performs one lookup into this S-box. For each of these 10 values, one bit is traced back to an S-box of R_1, so this adds $10 \cdot 4$ S-box lookups. Finally, $\mathcal{A}$

has 25600 inputs to R_1 for which it traces one bit back to each of the 16 S-boxes of R_0, contributing by $25600 \cdot 16$ S-box lookups.

In total, the number of lookups is $1+10\cdot4+25600\cdot16 = 409641$. Now, comparing to the number of S-box lookups involved with a call to an R-round PRESENT oracle, the number of lookups would be $16R$, not counting key scheduling. As such, we find that the time T spent by $\mathcal{A}$ for constructing $\mathcal{S}$ is $T = \frac{409641}{16R}$.

Memory Complexity. The memory complexity, though not a formal part of the key-less linear distinguisher model, is at a practical level. The storage of the set $\mathcal{S}$ can be encoded efficiently with two lists. In a first list with 4-bit entries of length 256 (128 bytes), we store all possible input values before the first subkey addition. The second list contains 25600 sets of 16 indices to the first list. Even a naïve encoding of this only needs 400kB.

5.4   Overview of Selected Distinguishers and Discussion

Here, we consider key-less linear distinguishers applying the deterministic phase combined with the probabilistic phase, using $\mathcal{M} \leq 2^{61.97}$. Let w_2 and w_1 denote the number of inputs to R_2 and R_1 used by $\mathcal{A}$ in the construction of $\mathcal{S}$. Then $w_2 \leq 10$ and w_1 is constrained by w_2 since $w_1 \leq 8^3 \cdot 5w_2$. Further, $\mathcal{M} \leq 8^{15} \cdot 5w_1$ and the time T required by $\mathcal{A}$ to construct $\mathcal{S}$ is $T = \frac{1+4w_2+16w_1}{16R}$ for R-round PRESENT. Obviously, for a fixed target size $\mathcal{M}$, minimizing w_1 yields the lower time complexity T.

Using these simple observations, we give in Table 4 an overview of selected results for key-less linear distinguishers on R-round PRESENT. We give the size $\mathcal{M}$ of $\mathcal{S} \subseteq \mathbb{F}_2^n$ constructed by $\mathcal{A}$, the time T required to do so, and the parameter α (implicitly, as we give $\alpha \cdot 2^{128}$) for the distinguisher, i.e. the lower bound on the fraction of the key space for which the distinguisher is valid. As such, the table is representative for PRESENT-128. Numbers for PRESENT-80 can be directly determined with the same T and $\alpha \cdot 2^{80}$. Note, however, that for 27-round PRESENT-80 using $\mathcal{M} = 2^{61.97}$, $\alpha \cdot 2^{80} < 0$, so one can distinguish at most 26 rounds of PRESENT-80.

What is evident from Table 4 is, that there is a clear limit to how many rounds can be distinguished using a particular $\mathcal{M}$. This shows in the diagonal line through the table. Another observation is that for a fixed $\mathcal{M}$, there is a clear drop in the fraction of the key space α for which the distinguisher works between R and $R+1$ rounds. For example, with $\mathcal{M} = 2^{61}$, we see a drop from $2^{108.5}$ keys supporting the distinguisher for 26 rounds to just 2^{21} for 27 rounds. What is also apparent is that in all cases, $T \ll 2\sqrt{\mathcal{M}}$, indeed sometimes $T < 1$, so by Corollary 1, $(T, \mathcal{M}, \alpha)$-intractability is for granted.

One thing worth discussion is the time complexity T. This is the time, converted to equivalent calls to an R-round encryption oracle, required by the key-less linear distinguisher algorithm $\mathcal{A}$ to construct the set $\mathcal{S}$. In a scenario where one would verify the distinguisher for a concrete block cipher E_K, i.e. for

Table 4. Overview of parameters for key-less linear distinguishers on PRESENT. The entries give, for each $\mathcal{M}$ and each total number of rounds R a pair $(\log_2 T, \log_2(\alpha \cdot 2^{128}))$ s.t. algorithm $\mathcal{A}$ can construct $\mathcal{S}$ in time T and result in a distinguisher for *at least* a fraction α of the key space. Here, we indicate for PRESENT-128 the number of keys supporting the distinguisher. The equivalent number for PRESENT-80 is obtained as $\alpha \cdot 2^{80}$. A dash indicates that $\alpha \cdot 2^{128} < 0$.

	Rounds R						
$\mathcal{M}$	14	18	22	25	26	27	28
2^{22}	-	-	-	-	-	-	-
2^{25}	-	-	-	-	-	-	-
2^{28}	$(-3.4, 70.9)$	-	-	-	-	-	-
2^{31}	$(-3.4, 119.2)$	-	-	-	-	-	-
2^{34}	$(-3.4, 126.2)$	-	-	-	-	-	-
2^{37}	$(-3.4, 127.5)$	-	-	-	-	-	-
2^{40}	$(-3.4, 127.8)$	$(-3.8, 107.1)$	-	-	-	-	-
2^{43}	$(-3.4, 127.9)$	$(-3.8, 124.3)$	-	-	-	-	-
2^{46}	$(-3.4, 128.0)$	$(-3.8, 127.1)$	-	-	-	-	-
2^{49}	$(-1.7, 128.0)$	$(-2.1, 127.7)$	$(-2.4, 75.1)$	-	-	-	-
2^{52}	$(0.9, 128.0)$	$(0.5, 127.9)$	$(0.3, 119.8)$	-	-	-	-
2^{55}	$(3.9, 128.0)$	$(3.5, 128.0)$	$(3.2, 126.3)$	-	-	-	-
2^{58}	$(6.9, 128.0)$	$(6.5, 128.0)$	$(6.2, 127.5)$	$(6.0, 103.1)$	-	-	-
2^{61}	$(9.9, 128.0)$	$(9.5, 128.0)$	$(9.2, 127.8)$	$(9.0, 123.7)$	$(9.0, 108.5)$	$(8.9, 21.0)$	-
$2^{61.97}$	$(10.8, 128.0)$	$(10.5, 128.0)$	$(10.2, 127.9)$	$(10.0, 125.4)$	$(9.9, 117.1)$	$(9.9, 71.8)$	-

a particular value of K, one would need to determine the value of the random variable $\mathcal{X}$ of Definition 1. What we denote as the *verifying complexity* in this case is dominated by $\mathcal{M}$, because this is the number of inputs to the permutation that needs to be evaluated in order to determine $\mathcal{X}$.

6   Conclusion and Open Problems

In this paper we have formalized the notion of distinguishers for block ciphers using linear cryptanalysis in the key-less setting, i.e. where the block cipher is instantiated with a single known or chosen key.

The introduced key-less statistical distinguisher based on linear cryptanalysis led to a wide variety of results on PRESENT, for example a linear distinguisher of up to 26 and 27 rounds of PRESENT-80 and PRESENT-128, with respective computational complexities of about 2^9 and 2^{10}, and verifying complexities of about 2^{61} and $2^{61.97}$, for both PRESENT variants. The very low computational complexity made a practical verification possible for a reduced number of rounds, but also leaves room for improvements: Is it possible to extend the deterministic phase to cover more rounds while still keeping the work factor below the allowed 2^{30}?

While PRESENT was chosen because it is a relatively high profile cryptanalytic target and the fact that relatively long useful linear hulls exist, we point out that the new distinguisher model is not specifically tailored for it. KATAN, a cipher with a very different round transformation and design philosophy, exhibits linear effects as described in [14] that makes it another interesting target for an application of the techniques introduced in this paper.

More research is needed on the relations between the use of degrees of freedom and the number of rounds that can be sidestepped, e.g. in our deterministic phase. Even though there is no good theoretical understanding of this yet, the literature already contains many data points for differential properties. The linear counterpart seems different and interesting enough to warrant a separate study, see also Appendix D.

The techniques we developed for the presented distinguisher might also have applications to preimage attacks that are inspired by linear cryptanalysis, or at least to somewhat speed-up brute-force preimage search. It will be interesting to see how this approach compares to other such methods [9,41]. Also, the approach naturally and directly applies to permutations, which become an increasingly important primitive in their own right, also due to the popularization of the Sponge [4] construction.

Acknowledgments. We would like to thank Mohamed Ahmed Abdelraheem, Dmitry Khovratovich, Gregor Leander, and Tyge Tiessen for helpful discussions on the paper.

A PRESENT Components

Table 5 gives the 4-bit S-box used in PRESENT. The bit-permutation P is defined s.t. bit i is moved to bit $P(i)$ where

$$P(i) = 16 \cdot (i \bmod 4) + 4 \cdot \left\lfloor \frac{i}{16} \right\rfloor + \left\lfloor \frac{i \bmod 16}{4} \right\rfloor.$$

Algorithms 1 and 2 give pseudo-code for the key-scheduling algorithms for PRESENT-80 and PRESENT-128, respectively.

Table 5. The 4-bit PRESENT S-box in hexadecimal notation

x	0	1	2	3	4	5	6	7	8	9	A	B	C	D	E	F
$S[x]$	C	5	6	B	9	0	A	D	3	E	F	8	4	7	1	2

Algorithm 1. PRESENT-80 key schedule

Data: 80-bit master key K
Result: PRESENT-80 round key array $k_i, 0 \le i \le 31$
for $i \leftarrow 0$ to 31 do

$\quad k_i^\ell \leftarrow [K_{79}\| \dots \|K_{16}];$
$\quad k_i^r \leftarrow [K_{15}\| \dots \|K_0];$
$\quad [K_{79}\|K_{78}\| \dots \|K_1\|K_0] \leftarrow [K_{18}\|K_{17}\| \dots \|K_{20}\|K_{19}];$
$\quad [K_{79}\|K_{78}\|K_{77}\|K_{76}] \leftarrow S[K_{79}\|K_{78}\|K_{77}\|K_{76}];$
$\quad [K_{19}\|K_{18}\|K_{17}\|K_{16}\|K_{15}] \leftarrow [K_{19}\|K_{18}\|K_{17}\|K_{16}\|K_{15}] \oplus (i+1);$

end

Algorithm 2. PRESENT-128 key schedule

Data: 128-bit master key K
Result: PRESENT-128 round key array $k_i, 0 \le i \le 31$
for $i \leftarrow 0$ to 31 do

$\quad k_i^\ell \leftarrow [K_{127}\| \dots \|K_{64}];$
$\quad k_i^r \leftarrow [K_{63}\| \dots \|K_0];$
$\quad [K_{127}\|K_{126}\| \dots \|K_1\|K_0] \leftarrow [K_{66}\|K_{65}\| \dots \|K_{68}\|K_{67}];$
$\quad [K_{127}\|K_{126}\|K_{125}\|K_{124}] \leftarrow S[K_{127}\|K_{126}\|K_{125}\|K_{124}];$
$\quad [K_{123}\|K_{122}\|K_{121}\|K_{120}] \leftarrow S[K_{123}\|K_{122}\|K_{121}\|K_{120}];$
$\quad [K_{66}\|K_{65}\|K_{64}\|K_{63}\|K_{62}] \leftarrow [K_{66}\|K_{65}\|K_{64}\|K_{63}\|K_{62}] \oplus (i+1);$

end

B   Data Pertaining to Correlation Bounding

Table 6 is the one determined by Ohkuma in [39], giving the number of optimal trails in an optimal hull for R rounds with $R \in \{1, \dots, 31\}$. Table 7 gives values $\log_2 \beta$ such that $\Pr\left[|\mathbf{C}_{E_K}| \ge \beta\right] = \alpha$ for various α and number of rounds R.

Table 6. Number of trails T_R in optimal hull for R-round PRESENT, $R \in \{1, \dots, 31\}$

R	T_R	R	T_R	R	T_R	R	T_R
1	1	9	512	17	1140480	25	2517252696
2	1	10	1344	18	2985984	26	6590254272
3	1	11	3528	19	7817472	27	17253512704
4	3	12	9261	20	20466576	28	45170283840
5	9	13	24255	21	53582633	29	118257341400
6	27	14	63525	22	140281323	30	309601747125
7	72	15	166375	23	367261713	31	810547899975
8	192	16	435600	24	961504803		

Table 7. Values $\log_2 \beta$ s.t. $\alpha = \Pr\left[|\mathbf{C}_{E_K}| \geq \beta\right]$ for R-round of PRESENT

R	α												
	0.01	0.05	0.10	0.20	0.30	0.40	0.50	0.60	0.70	0.80	0.90	0.95	0.99
1	−0.63	−1.03	−1.28	−1.64	−1.95	−2.25	−2.57	−2.93	−3.38	−3.98	−4.99	−6.00	−8.32
2	−2.63	−3.03	−3.28	−3.64	−3.95	−4.25	−4.57	−4.93	−5.38	−5.98	−6.99	−8.00	−10.32
3	−4.63	−5.03	−5.28	−5.64	−5.95	−6.25	−6.57	−6.93	−7.38	−7.98	−8.99	−10.00	−12.32
4	−5.84	−6.24	−6.49	−6.85	−7.16	−7.46	−7.78	−8.14	−8.58	−9.19	−10.20	−11.20	−13.53
5	−7.05	−7.44	−7.70	−8.06	−8.36	−8.66	−8.98	−9.35	−9.79	−10.40	−11.41	−12.41	−14.73
6	−8.26	−8.65	−8.90	−9.26	−9.57	−9.87	−10.19	−10.55	−11.00	−11.60	−12.61	−13.62	−15.94
7	−9.55	−9.94	−10.20	−10.56	−10.86	−11.16	−11.48	−11.85	−12.29	−12.90	−13.91	−14.91	−17.23
8	−10.84	−11.24	−11.49	−11.85	−12.16	−12.46	−12.78	−13.14	−13.58	−14.19	−15.20	−16.20	−18.53
9	−12.13	−12.53	−12.78	−13.14	−13.45	−13.75	−14.07	−14.43	−14.88	−15.48	−16.49	−17.50	−19.82
10	−13.44	−13.83	−14.09	−14.45	−14.75	−15.05	−15.37	−15.74	−16.18	−16.78	−17.80	−18.80	−21.12
11	−14.74	−15.14	−15.39	−15.75	−16.06	−16.36	−16.68	−17.04	−17.48	−18.09	−19.10	−20.10	−22.43
12	−16.05	−16.44	−16.69	−17.05	−17.36	−17.66	−17.98	−18.34	−18.79	−19.39	−20.40	−21.41	−23.73
13	−17.35	−17.75	−18.00	−18.36	−18.67	−18.97	−19.29	−19.65	−20.09	−20.70	−21.71	−22.71	−25.04
14	−18.66	−19.05	−19.30	−19.66	−19.97	−20.27	−20.59	−20.95	−21.40	−22.00	−23.01	−24.02	−26.34
15	−19.96	−20.36	−20.61	−20.97	−21.28	−21.58	−21.90	−22.26	−22.70	−23.31	−24.32	−25.32	−27.65
16	−21.27	−21.66	−21.92	−22.28	−22.58	−22.88	−23.20	−23.56	−24.01	−24.61	−25.63	−26.63	−28.95
17	−22.57	−22.97	−23.22	−23.58	−23.89	−24.19	−24.51	−24.87	−25.32	−25.92	−26.93	−27.93	−30.26
18	−23.88	−24.27	−24.53	−24.89	−25.19	−25.49	−25.81	−26.18	−26.62	−27.23	−28.24	−29.24	−31.56
19	−25.19	−25.58	−25.83	−26.19	−26.50	−26.80	−27.12	−27.48	−27.93	−28.53	−29.54	−30.55	−32.87
20	−26.49	−26.89	−27.14	−27.50	−27.80	−28.11	−28.42	−28.79	−29.23	−29.84	−30.85	−31.85	−34.17
21	−27.80	−28.19	−28.44	−28.80	−29.11	−29.41	−29.73	−30.09	−30.54	−31.14	−32.15	−33.16	−35.48
22	−29.10	−29.50	−29.75	−30.11	−30.42	−30.72	−31.04	−31.40	−31.84	−32.45	−33.46	−34.46	−36.79
23	−30.41	−30.80	−31.06	−31.42	−31.72	−32.02	−32.34	−32.71	−33.15	−33.75	−34.77	−35.77	−38.09
24	−31.71	−32.11	−32.36	−32.72	−33.03	−33.33	−33.65	−34.01	−34.46	−35.06	−36.07	−37.07	−39.40
25	−33.02	−33.41	−33.67	−34.03	−34.33	−34.63	−34.95	−35.32	−35.76	−36.37	−37.38	−38.38	−40.70
26	−34.33	−34.72	−34.97	−35.33	−35.64	−35.94	−36.26	−36.62	−37.07	−37.67	−38.68	−39.69	−42.01
27	−35.63	−36.03	−36.28	−36.64	−36.95	−37.25	−37.57	−37.93	−38.37	−38.98	−39.99	−40.99	−43.31
28	−36.94	−37.33	−37.58	−37.94	−38.25	−38.55	−38.87	−39.23	−39.68	−40.28	−41.30	−42.30	−44.62
29	−38.24	−38.64	−38.89	−39.25	−39.56	−39.86	−40.18	−40.54	−40.98	−41.59	−42.60	−43.60	−45.93
30	−39.55	−39.94	−40.20	−40.56	−40.86	−41.16	−41.48	−41.85	−42.29	−42.90	−43.91	−44.91	−47.23
31	−40.85	−41.25	−41.50	−41.86	−42.17	−42.47	−42.79	−43.15	−43.60	−44.20	−45.21	−46.22	−48.54

C Experimental Verification

In this section we describe experiments performed to verify the validity of the proposed key-less linear distinguishers. Concretely, we describe a key-less linear distinguisher $\mathcal{A}$ trying to distinguish 9-round PRESENT (regardless of key size). We let $\mathcal{R}_{\delta,\gamma}^{E_K}$ be the linear relation used in Sect. 5.

We know that to distinguish 9-round PRESENT, we can do a 3-round deterministic phase to construct $\mathcal{S}$ as described in Sect. 5. In this case, the probabilistic phase is 6 rounds. In the following, we give two examples using two different values $\alpha \in \{0.33, 0.75\}$.

For the first example, we have $\alpha = 0.33$. From Theorem 2, we know that to have 0.33-separability, we require that the event $|\mathbf{C}_{E_K}| \geq 2/\sqrt{\mathcal{M}}$ happens with probability (at least) $\alpha = 0.33$. From the analysis of Sect. 4.1, we find that for 6-round PRESENT we have $\Pr\left[|\mathbf{C}_{E_K}| \geq \beta\right] = \alpha$ for $\beta = 2^{-9.66}$. When using the inequality $|\mathbf{C}_{E_K}| \geq 2/\sqrt{\mathcal{M}}$, we find this bound is tight when $\mathcal{M} = 2619369$. As such, $\mathcal{A}$ is an algorithm for constructing an $\mathcal{S}$ of this size in the 3-round deterministic phase described in Sect. 5.2. For this key-less linear distinguisher $\mathcal{A}$, we now have 0.33-separability, because we expect that $\left|\mathbb{E}\left[\mathcal{X}\right] - \frac{\mathcal{M}}{2}\right| \geq \sqrt{\mathcal{M}}$, where $\mathcal{X}$ is the number of inputs satisfying the linear relation.

The experimental part comes now from actually encrypting each $x \in \mathcal{S}$ under a fixed, known key $K \in \mathcal{K}$ using 9-round PRESENT. We then check each $\mathcal{R}_{\delta,\gamma}^{E_K}(x) = 1$ by checking the relation on the input/output pair. For our experiment, we repeated 1000 times the experiment of computing $\mathcal{X}$ for a random key K and the corresponding set $\mathcal{S}$. We found that 389 keys satisfied $\left| \mathbb{E}\left[\mathcal{X}\right] - \frac{\mathcal{M}}{2} \right| \geq \sqrt{\mathcal{M}}$, and as such we see that this fits with $\frac{389}{1000} \geq \alpha = 0.33$.

We repeated the same experiment again with $\alpha = 0.75$. In this case, we found that we require $\mathcal{M} = 24480331$. In the same way, we did 1000 experiments with random keys K and found that 764 keys satisfied $\left| \mathbb{E}\left[\mathcal{X}\right] - \frac{\mathcal{M}}{2} \right| \geq \sqrt{\mathcal{M}}$. Again, this fits with $\frac{764}{1000} \geq \alpha = 0.75$.

D 6-round Deterministic Phase

By combining the 3-round deterministic phase of Sect. 5.2 with another 3 rounds appearing before, it is possible to construct a 6-round deterministic phase, reminiscent of the rebound approach [28, 35] (see Fig. 3). The idea is, that for rounds 3 to 5, the same approach as in Sect. 5.2 is used. Also, the same approach is used, but going in the other direction, for rounds 0 to 2.

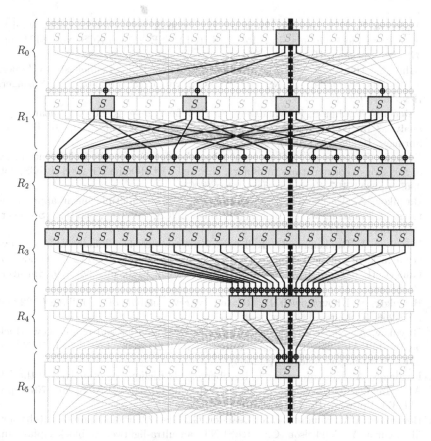

Fig. 3. 6-round deterministic phase for PRESENT using the trail $(e_{21}, e_{21}, e_{21}, e_{21}, e_{21}, e_{21}, e_{21})$

This describes a construction to *independently* obtain (i) a set of *outputs* from round R_2, for which the inputs follow the trail over the *first* three rounds and (ii) a set of *inputs* to R_3 which follow the trail over the *last* three rounds. These two sets meet at the same point: Right around the addition of the round key of round R_3. Thus, one can use said round key to determine a matching between the two sets, to obtain a set which has the desirable property of following the trail over both the top and bottom part. However, as the approaches are independent, there are constraints put on the round key of round R_3 due to both parts, and this loss in degrees of freedom must be taken into account.

While the technique described here is not directly applicable with our model, as it by nature needs to use several different keys to match the two sets, it could potentially be useful in chosen-key models which allow an adversary to make a statement using multiple different keys.

References

1. Andreeva, E., Bogdanov, A., Mennink, B.: Towards understanding the known-key security of block ciphers. In: Moriai, S. (ed.) FSE 2013. LNCS, vol. 8424, pp. 348–366. Springer, Heidelberg (2014)
2. Ashur, T., Dunkelman, O.: Linear analysis of reduced-round cubehash. In: Lopez, J., Tsudik, G. (eds.) ACNS 2011. LNCS, vol. 6715, pp. 462–478. Springer, Heidelberg (2011)
3. Baignères, T., Junod, P., Vaudenay, S.: How far can we go beyond linear cryptanalysis? In: Lee, P.J. (ed.) ASIACRYPT 2004. LNCS, vol. 3329, pp. 432–450. Springer, Heidelberg (2004)
4. Bertoni, G., Daemen, J., Peeters, M., Van Assche, G.: On the indifferentiability of the sponge construction. In: Smart, N.P. (ed.) EUROCRYPT 2008. LNCS, vol. 4965, pp. 181–197. Springer, Heidelberg (2008)
5. Biryukov, A., De Cannière, C., Quisquater, M.: On multiple linear approximations. In: Franklin, M. (ed.) CRYPTO 2004. LNCS, vol. 3152, pp. 1–22. Springer, Heidelberg (2004)
6. Biryukov, A., Dunkelman, O., Keller, N., Khovratovich, D., Shamir, A.: Key recovery attacks of practical complexity on AES-256 variants with up to 10 rounds. In: Gilbert, H. (ed.) EUROCRYPT 2010. LNCS, vol. 6110, pp. 299–319. Springer, Heidelberg (2010)
7. Biryukov, A., Khovratovich, D.: Related-key cryptanalysis of the full AES-192 and AES-256. In: Matsui [33], pp. 1–18
8. Biryukov, A., Khovratovich, D., Nikolić, I.: Distinguisher and related-key attack on the full AES-256. In: Halevi, S. (ed.) CRYPTO 2009. LNCS, vol. 5677, pp. 231–249. Springer, Heidelberg (2009)
9. Bogdanov, A., Khovratovich, D., Rechberger, C.: Biclique cryptanalysis of the full AES. In: Lee, D.H., Wang, X. (eds.) ASIACRYPT 2011. LNCS, vol. 7073, pp. 344–371. Springer, Heidelberg (2011)
10. Bogdanov, A.A., Knudsen, L.R., Leander, G., Paar, C., Poschmann, A., Robshaw, M., Seurin, Y., Vikkelsoe, C.: PRESENT: an ultra-lightweight block cipher. In: Paillier, P., Verbauwhede, I. (eds.) CHES 2007. LNCS, vol. 4727, pp. 450–466. Springer, Heidelberg (2007)

11. Bogdanov, A., Leander, G., Paar, C., Poschmann, A., Robshaw, M.J.B., Seurin, Y.: Hash functions and RFID tags: mind the gap. In: Oswald, E., Rohatgi, P. (eds.) CHES 2008. LNCS, vol. 5154, pp. 283–299. Springer, Heidelberg (2008)

12. Bogdanov, A., Rijmen, V.: Linear hulls with correlation zero and linear cryptanalysis of block ciphers. Des. Codes Cryptogr. **70**(3), 369–383 (2014)

13. Bulygin, S.: More on linear hulls of present-like ciphers and a cryptanalysis of full-round EPCBC-96. IACR Cryptol. ePrint Arch. **2013**, 28 (2013)

14. De Cannière, C., Dunkelman, O., Knežević, M.: KATAN and KTANTAN — a family of small and efficient hardware-oriented block ciphers. In: Clavier, C., Gaj, K. (eds.) CHES 2009. LNCS, vol. 5747, pp. 272–288. Springer, Heidelberg (2009)

15. Cho, J.Y.: Linear cryptanalysis of reduced-round PRESENT. In: Pieprzyk [40], pp. 302–317

16. Cho, J.Y., Hermelin, M., Nyberg, K.: A new technique for multidimensional linear cryptanalysis with applications on reduced round serpent. In: Lee, P.J., Cheon, J.H. (eds.) ICISC 2008. LNCS, vol. 5461, pp. 383–398. Springer, Heidelberg (2009)

17. Daemen, J., Rijmen, V.: The Design of Rijndael: AES - The Advanced Encryption Standard. Information Security and Cryptography. Springer, Heidelberg (2002)

18. Gilbert, H.: A simplified representation of AES. In: Sarkar, P., Iwata, T. (eds.) ASIACRYPT 2014. LNCS, vol. 8873, pp. 200–222. Springer, Heidelberg (2014)

19. Gilbert, H., Peyrin, T.: Super-Sbox cryptanalysis: improved attacks for AES-like permutations. In: Hong, S., Iwata, T. (eds.) FSE 2010. LNCS, vol. 6147, pp. 365–383. Springer, Heidelberg (2010)

20. Kaliski Jr., B.S., Robshaw, M.: Linear cryptanalysis using multiple approximations. In: Desmedt, Y.G. (ed.) CRYPTO 1994. LNCS, vol. 839, pp. 26–39. Springer, Heidelberg (1994)

21. Khovratovich, D., Naya-Plasencia, M., Röck, A., Schläffer, M.: Cryptanalysis of *Luffa* v2 components. In: Biryukov, A., Gong, G., Stinson, D.R. (eds.) SAC 2010. LNCS, vol. 6544, pp. 388–409. Springer, Heidelberg (2011)

22. Khovratovich, D., Nikolić, I., Rechberger, C.: Rotational rebound attacks on reduced skein. In: Abe, M. (ed.) ASIACRYPT 2010. LNCS, vol. 6477, pp. 1–19. Springer, Heidelberg (2010)

23. Knudsen, L.R., Mathiassen, J.E.: A chosen-plaintext linear attack on DES. In: Schneier, B. (ed.) FSE 2000. LNCS, vol. 1978, pp. 262–272. Springer, Heidelberg (2001)

24. Knudsen, L.R., Rijmen, V.: Known-key distinguishers for some block ciphers. In: Kurosawa, K. (ed.) ASIACRYPT 2007. LNCS, vol. 4833, pp. 315–324. Springer, Heidelberg (2007)

25. Koyama, T., Sasaki, Y., Kunihiro, N.: Multi-differential cryptanalysis on reduced DM-PRESENT-80: collisions and other differential properties. In: Kwon et al. [26], pp. 352–367

26. Kwon, T., Lee, M.-K., Kwon, D. (eds.): ICISC 2012. LNCS, vol. 7839. Springer, Heidelberg (2013)

27. Lamberger, M., Mendel, F., Rechberger, C., Rijmen, V., Schläffer, M.: Rebound distinguishers: results on the full whirlpool compression function. In: Matsui [33], pp. 126–143

28. Lamberger, M., Mendel, M., Schläffer, M., Rechberger, C., Rijmen, V.: The rebound attack and subspace distinguishers: application to whirlpool. J. Cryptol. **28**(2), 1–40 (2015)

29. Lauridsen, M.M., Rechberger, C.: Source code for experimental validation. https://github.com/mmeh/present-keyless

30. Leander, G.: On linear hulls, statistical saturation attacks, PRESENT and a cryptanalysis of PUFFIN. In: Paterson, K.G. (ed.) EUROCRYPT 2011. LNCS, vol. 6632, pp. 303–322. Springer, Heidelberg (2011)
31. Li, Y., Ailan, W.: Linear cryptanalysis for the compression function of hamsi-256. In: Proceedings of the 2011 International Conference on Network Computing and Information Security - vol. 01, NCIS 2011, pp. 302–306. IEEE Computer Society, Washington (2011)
32. Matsui, M.: Linear cryptanalysis method for DES cipher. In: Helleseth, T. (ed.) EUROCRYPT 1993. LNCS, vol. 765, pp. 386–397. Springer, Heidelberg (1994)
33. Matsui, M. (ed.): ASIACRYPT 2009. LNCS, vol. 5912. Springer, Heidelberg (2009)
34. Matsui, M., Yamagishi, A.: A new method for known plaintext attack of FEAL cipher. In: Rueppel, R.A. (ed.) EUROCRYPT 1992. LNCS, vol. 658, pp. 81–91. Springer, Heidelberg (1993)
35. Mendel, F., Rechberger, C., Schläffer, M., Thomsen, S.S.: The rebound attack: cryptanalysis of reduced whirlpool and grøstl. In: Dunkelman, O. (ed.) FSE 2009. LNCS, vol. 5665, pp. 260–276. Springer, Heidelberg (2009)
36. Mendel, F., Rechberger, C., Schläffer, M., Thomsen, S.S.: Rebound attacks on the reduced grøstl hash function. In: Pieprzyk [40], pp. 350–365
37. Murphy, S.: The effectiveness of the linear hull effect. J. Math. Cryptol. 6(2), 137–147 (2012)
38. Nyberg, K.: Linear approximation of block ciphers. In: De Santis, A. (ed.) EUROCRYPT 1994. LNCS, vol. 950, pp. 439–444. Springer, Heidelberg (1995)
39. Ohkuma, K.: Weak keys of reduced-round PRESENT for linear cryptanalysis. In: Jacobson Jr., M.J., Rijmen, V., Safavi-Naini, R. (eds.) SAC 2009. LNCS, vol. 5867, pp. 249–265. Springer, Heidelberg (2009)
40. Pieprzyk, J. (ed.): CT-RSA 2010. LNCS, vol. 5985. Springer, Heidelberg (2010)
41. Rechberger, C.: On bruteforce-like cryptanalysis: new meet-in-the-middle attacks in symmetric cryptanalysis. In: Kwon et al. [21], pp. 33–36
42. Wang, X., Yu, H.: How to break MD5 and other hash functions. In: Cramer, R. (ed.) EUROCRYPT 2005. LNCS, vol. 3494, pp. 19–35. Springer, Heidelberg (2005)

Cryptanalysis of Authenticated Encryption Schemes

Differential-Linear Cryptanalysis of ICEPOLE

Tao Huang[✉], Ivan Tjuawinata, and Hongjun Wu

Division of Mathematical Sciences, School of Physical and Mathematical Sciences,
Nanyang Technological University, Singapore, Singapore
{huangtao,wuhj}@ntu.edu.sg, S120015@e.ntu.edu.sg

Abstract. ICEPOLE is a CAESAR candidate with the intermediate level of robustness under nonce misuse circumstances in the original document. In particular, it was claimed that key recovery attack against ICEPOLE is impossible in the case of nonce misuse. ICEPOLE is strong against the differential cryptanalysis and linear cryptanalysis. In this paper, we developed the differential-linear attacks against ICEPOLE when nonce is misused. Our attacks show that the state of ICEPOLE–128 and ICEPOLE–128a can be recovered with data complexity 2^{46} and time complexity 2^{46}; the state of ICEPOLE–256a can be recovered with data complexity 2^{60} and time complexity 2^{60}. For ICEPOLE–128a and ICEPOLE–256a, the secret key is recovered once the state is recovered. We experimentally verified the attacks against ICEPOLE–128 and ICEPOLE–128a.

Keywords: ICEPOLE · Authenticated cipher · CAESAR · Differential-linear cryptanalysis

1 Introduction

ICEPOLE is a new hardware-oriented single-pass authenticated cipher designed by Morawiecki *et al.* It was submitted to the CAESAR competition [14] and published in CHES 2014 [15]. ICEPOLE is designed to be hardware-efficient. It can achieve 41 Gbits/s on the modern FPGA device Virtex 6 which is over 10 times faster than the equivalent implementation of AES-128-GCM [12]. ICE-POLE adopts the well-known duplex construction by Bertoni *et al.* [2] and uses a Keccak-like permutation as its iterative function.

The ICEPOLE family of authenticated ciphers includes three variants: ICEPOLE-128, ICEPOLE– 128a and ICEPOLE–256a. Note that the definition of ICEPOLE–128 has been slightly modified in the CHES 2014 version, which removed the use of secret message number. In this paper, we will follow the version submitted to the CAESAR competition. For the security of ICEPOLE, the designers claim that the confidentiality is the same as the key length, which is 128-bit for ICEPOLE–128 and ICEPOLE–128a and 256-bit for ICEPOLE–256a. The authentication security is 128-bit for all the three variants. In particular, it is mentioned in the document that the internal permutation is strong enough such that *"in the case of nonce reuse the key-recovery attack is not possible"* and the authenticity *"is not threatened by nonce reuse"*.

© International Association for Cryptologic Research 2015
G. Leander (Ed.): FSE 2015, LNCS 9054, pp. 243–263, 2015.
DOI: 10.1007/978-3-662-48116-5_12

In this paper, we apply the differential-linear cryptanalysis to study the security of the permutation of the ICEPOLE family. The differential-linear cryptanalysis is the combination of differential cryptanalysis [5] and linear cryptanalysis [11]. It was introduced by Langford and Hellman in [9] in 1994 to attack the block cipher DES, and later Biham, Dunkelman and Keller gave an enhanced version of this method [3]. This method has been applied to analyze a number of block ciphers such as Serpent [4, 7], CTC2 [8, 10] and SHACAL–2 [16]. Differential-linear attack is also successful in the analysis of certain stream ciphers, *e.g.*, Phelix which involves the message in the state update function [17].

Although the design of authenticated cipher ICEPOLE is different from block ciphers, we manage to exploit the differential-linear property of the permutation when the nonce is reused [1]. We show that under the nonce-reuse assumption, there exists distinguishing attacks on ICEPOLE with both time and data complexity less than 2^{36}. Furthermore, it is possible to recover the 256 bits unknown state of ICEPOLE–128 and ICEPOLE–128a with practical complexity 2^{46}, and recover the 320 bits unknown state of ICEPOLE–256a with complexity 2^{60}. We experimentally verified our results by recovering the state of ICEPOLE–128 using a 64-core server within 10 days. Thus, the security claims of ICEPOLE do not hold under the nonce-reuse circumstances.

Due to the analysis of this paper, the designers have updated the security claims as *"in the case of nonce misuse, the intermediate level of robustness (specified in the documentation) holds only when the SMN is present and respected, namely each message has the corresponding, unique secret message number"* [13]. In the presence of unique SMN, the attack in this paper will no longer work. The reason is that the unique SMN plays the role of the nonce in the initialization, and prevents the differential attack in the message processing.

The rest of this paper is structured as follows: The specification of ICEPOLE is given in Sect. 2. Section 3 describes a differential-linear distinguishing attack on ICEPOLE. Section 4 introduces the state-recovery attack. Section 5 provides our experimental results of the state-recovery attack on ICEPOLE-128. Section 6 concludes the paper.

2   The ICEPOLE Authenticated Cipher

The ICEPOLE family of authenticated ciphers uses three parameters: key length (128 or 256 bits), secret message number (SMN) length (0 or 128 bits) and nonce length (96 or 128 bits). ICEPOLE – 128 has 128-bit secret message number, 128-bit key, and 128-bit nonce. The other two variants, ICEPOLE – 128a and ICEPOLE – 256 a, have no secret message number with 128- and 256-bit secret key respectively. The nonce length for these two variants is 96-bit. We will briefly describe the specification of ICEPOLE authenticated cipher. The full specification can be found in [14]. An overview of ICEPOLE–128 is provided in Fig. 1.

---

[1] Here *nonce* includes the public message number and secret message number. The associated data is set to be identical or empty which is generally allowed.

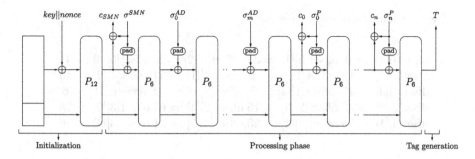

Processing phase   Tag generation

Fig. 1. General scheme of ICEPOLE encryption and authentication (Fig. 1 of [14])

2.1 Notations

The ICEPOLE algorithm has a 1280-bit internal state S. It uses the little-endian convention. The organization of internal state is similar to Keccak [1], which uses a 3-dimension structure. Therefore, the 1280-bit state S can be represented as $S[4][5][64]$, or shortly $S[4][5]$, an array of 64-bit words. For $S[x][y][z]$, it is corresponding to the $64(x + 4y) + z$-th bit of the input. ICEPOLE uses 4×5 *slices*. Each slice has 4 *rows* and 5 *columns*. And $S_{\lfloor n \rfloor}$ denotes the first n bits of the state.

2.2 The ICEPOLE Permutation P

The permutation P is applied iteratively on the ICEPOLE state S during the encryption and authentication. Each permutation is called a *round* or R. The 6– and 12–round of P are represented as P_6 and P_{12} respectively. Each round includes five operations: μ, ρ, π, ψ, and κ.

$$R = \kappa \circ \psi \circ \pi \circ \rho \circ \mu$$

The operations are defined as follows:

μ :
A column vector (Z_0, Z_1, Z_2, Z_3) is multiplied by a constant matrix to produce a vector of four 5-bit words.

$$\begin{bmatrix} 2 & 1 & 1 & 1 \\ 1 & 1 & 18 & 2 \\ 1 & 2 & 1 & 18 \\ 1 & 18 & 2 & 1 \end{bmatrix} \times \begin{bmatrix} Z_0 \\ Z_1 \\ Z_2 \\ Z_3 \end{bmatrix} = \begin{bmatrix} 2Z_0 + Z_1 + Z_2 + Z_3 \\ Z_0 + Z_1 + 18Z_2 + 2Z_3 \\ Z_0 + 2Z_1 + Z_2 + 18Z_3 \\ Z_0 + 18Z_1 + 2Z_2 + Z_3 \end{bmatrix}$$

The operations are done in $GF(2^5)$. The irreducible polynomial $x^5 + x^2 + 1$ is used for the field multiplication. And μ can be efficiently implemented with simple bitwise equations, see Appendix B in [14].

ρ :
The ρ step is the bitwise rotation on each of the 20 64-bit words. It is defined as:

$$\rho(S[x][y]) = S[x][y] \lll \text{offsets}[x][y] \qquad \text{for all}(0 \le x \le 3), (0 \le y \le 4)$$

The rotation offsets are as follows:

$$\text{offset}[0][0] := 0 \quad \text{offset}[0][1] := 36 \quad \text{offset}[0][2] := 3 \quad \text{offset}[0][3] := 41$$
$$\text{offset}[0][4] := 18 \quad \text{offset}[1][0] := 1 \quad \text{offset}[1][1] := 44 \quad \text{offset}[1][2] := 10$$
$$\text{offset}[1][3] := 45 \quad \text{offset}[1][4] := 2 \quad \text{offset}[2][0] := 62 \quad \text{offset}[2][1] := 6$$
$$\text{offset}[2][2] := 43 \quad \text{offset}[2][3] := 15 \quad \text{offset}[2][4] := 61 \quad \text{offset}[3][0] := 28$$
$$\text{offset}[3][1] := 55 \quad \text{offset}[3][2] := 25 \quad \text{offset}[3][3] := 21 \quad \text{offset}[3][4] := 56$$

π :

π reorders the bits within each slice. It maps $S[x][y]$ to $S[x'][y']$ using following rule:

- $x' := (x + y) \mod 4$
- $y' := (((x + y) \mod 4) + y + 1) \mod 5$

ϕ :

ϕ is the S-box layer. ICEPOLE uses following 5-bit S-box:

$$\{ 31, 9, 18, 11, 5, 12, 22, 15, 10, 3, 24, 1, 13, 4, 30, 7,$$
$$20, 21, 6, 23, 17, 16, 2, 19, 26, 27, 8, 25, 29, 28, 14, 0 \}$$

The ϕ applies the 5-bit S-box to all the 256 rows of the state.

κ :

In κ the 64-bit constant is xored with $S[0][0]$. The constants are different for each round and we omit the values here.

2.3   Initialization

First, the state S is initialized with 1280-bit constant:

$$S[0][0] := 0XFF97A42D7F8E6FD4 \quad S[0][1] := 0X90FEE5A0A44647C4$$
$$S[0][2] := 0X8C5BDA0CD6192E76 \quad S[0][3] := 0XAD30A6F71B19059C$$
$$S[0][4] := 0X30935AB7D08FFC64 \quad S[1][0] := 0XEB5AA93F2317D635$$
$$S[1][1] := 0XA9A6E6260D712103 \quad S[1][2] := 0X81A57C16DBCF555F$$
$$S[1][3] := 0X43B831CD0347C826 \quad S[1][4] := 0X01F22F1A11A5569F$$
$$S[2][0] := 0X05E5635A21D9AE61 \quad S[2][1] := 0X64BEFEF28CC970F2$$
$$S[2][2] := 0X613670957BC46611 \quad S[2][3] := 0XB87C5A554FD00ECB$$
$$S[2][4] := 0X8C3EE88A1CCF32C8 \quad S[3][0] := 0X940C7922AE3A2614$$
$$S[3][1] := 0X1841F924A2C509E4 \quad S[3][2] := 0X16F53526E70465C2$$
$$S[3][3] := 0X75F644E97F30A13B \quad S[3][4] := 0XEAF1FF7B5CECA249$$

Then, the key (K) and the *nonce* are XORed to the state. The *nonce* is 128-bit for ICEPOLE–128. And the 96-bit *nonce* for ICEPOLE–128a and ICEPOLE–256a will be padded with 32 zeros to form a 128-bit *nonce*. $nonce_0$ and $nonce_1$ denote two 64-bit words of the padded nonce.

For ICEPOLE–128 and ICEPOLE–128a, K_0 and K_1 denote two 64-bit words of the key,

$$S[0][0] := S[0][0] \oplus K_0$$
$$S[1][0] := S[1][0] \oplus K_1$$
$$S[2][0] := S[2][0] \oplus nonce_0$$
$$S[3][0] := S[3][0] \oplus nonce_1$$

For ICEPOLE–256a, K_0, K_1, K_2 and K_3 denote four 64-bit words of the key,

$$S[0][0] := S[0][0] \oplus K_0$$
$$S[1][0] := S[1][0] \oplus K_1$$
$$S[2][0] := S[2][0] \oplus K_2$$
$$S[3][0] := S[3][0] \oplus K_3$$
$$S[0][1] := S[0][1] \oplus nonce_0$$
$$S[1][1] := S[1][1] \oplus nonce_1$$

After that, the P_{12} permutation is applied to the state S.

2.4   Processing Associated Data and Plaintext

ICEPOLE–128 uses 128-bit secret message number (SMN) σ^{SMN}. It will be processed before associated data and the plaintext. Since ICEPOLE–128a and ICEPOLE–256a do not have SMN, only the associated data σ_i^{AD} and the plaintext σ_i^P will be processed.

For ICEPOLE–128 and ICEPOLE–128a, the length of blocks σ_i^{AD} and σ_i^P is in the range $[0, 1024]$ bits. The blocks will be padded to 1026 bits according to following rule. First, a *frame bit* is appended. It is set to '1' for the last σ^{AD} block and all σ_i^P except the last one. For all other blocks, it is set to '0'. Then, a bit '1' is appended, following by '0's to make the length of padded block be 1026-bit. The number of blocks under a single key is less than 2^{126}.

For ICEPOLE–256a, the associated data and plaintext blocks have length in the range $[0, 960]$. The same padding rule is applied and the padded blocks have length 962-bit. The number of blocks under a single key is less than 2^{62}.

The process of secret message number is as below for ICEPOLE–128:

$$c_{SMN} = S_{\lfloor 128 \rfloor} \oplus \sigma^{SMN}$$
$$\sigma^{SMN} := pad(\sigma^{SMN})$$
$$S_{\lfloor 1026 \rfloor} := S_{\lfloor 1026 \rfloor} \oplus \sigma^{SMN}$$
$$S := P_6(S)$$

The process of associated data and plaintext blocks is as below:

for all blocks σ_i^{AD} {
$$\sigma_i^{AD} := pad(\sigma_i^{AD})$$

$$S_{\lfloor 1026 \rfloor} := S_{\lfloor 1026 \rfloor} \oplus \sigma_i^{AD}$$
$$S := P_6(S)$$

}

for all blocks σ_i^P{

$\quad c_i := S_{\lfloor l \rfloor} \oplus \sigma_i^P$ (l is the length of σ_i^P)

$\quad \sigma_i^P := pad(\sigma_i^P)$

$\quad S_{\lfloor 1026 \rfloor} := S_{\lfloor 1026 \rfloor} \oplus \sigma_i^P$

$\quad S := P_6(S)$

}

2.5 Tag Generation

After the AD and P are processed, the 128-bit tag T is derived: (T_0 and T_1 are two 64-bit words of T).

$$T_0 := S[0][0]$$
$$T_1 := S[0][1]$$

The decryption and verification is trivial and we omit it here.

2.6 Security Goals of ICEPOLE

The main security goals of ICEPOLE are: 128-bit encryption security for ICEPOLE–128 and ICEPOLE–128a; 256-bit encryption security for ICEPOLE–256a; and 128-bit authentication security for all variants.

An important property of ICEPOLE is that the intermediate level of robustness under nonce-misuse circumstance. It claimed that

1. "...in the case of nonce reuse the key-recovery attack is not possible".
2. "Authenticity (integrity) in the duplex construction does not need a nonce requirement, thus is not threatened by nonce reuse".

3   Differential-Linear Distinguishing Attack on ICEPOLE

In [14], the designers have performed initial cryptanalysis on ICEPOLE, including the differential cryptanalysis, linear cryptanalysis and rotational cryptanalysis. In this section, we will revisit the cryptanalysis in [14] and introduce our analysis on ICEPOLE based on the differential-linear cryptanalysis. We would like to emphasize that our attacks only work under the assumption that the *nonce* and *secret message number* can be reused.

The main idea is to query messages with certain input difference and analyze the statistics of the differences of chosen bits (according to the linear mask) in the output. When the XORed differences of the chosen bits have a significant bias from 0.5, the adversary can distinguish the cipher from a random permutation. In [10], Lu studied the implicit assumptions made in [9] and [3] and gave a theorem to compute the probability for the differential-linear distinguisher under the original two assumptions:

1. The involved round functions behave independently.
2. The two inputs $E_0(P)$ and $E_0(P \oplus \alpha)$ of the linear characteristic for E_1 behave as independent inputs with respect to the linear characteristic, where E_0 is the encryption for the differential rounds and E_1 is the encryption for the linear rounds, P is the plaintext and α is the input difference.

Let $\hat{p}$ be the probability that the input of the linear mask has no XORed difference after the differential step while ϵ be the linear characteristic bias for the linear step. The theorem says that the probability that the XORed difference of the output linear mask to be 0 is $\frac{1}{2} + 2(2\hat{p} - 1)\epsilon^2$. In [6], Céline et $al.$ further developed a method on computing the bias which only relies on the independence of the two parts of the cipher.

Hence, when the bias is large enough, it is possible to distinguish it from a random permutation. In the analysis on ICEPOLE, we first divide the encryption P_6 into two parts with equal number of rounds. So the first 3 rounds will be the differential step and the last 3 rounds will be the linear step.

Our task is to find good 3-round differential characteristics and 3-round linear characteristics. Unless otherwise specified, we are discussing the ICEPOLE–128 and ICEPOLE–128a in this section under the nonce-misuse assumption. The ICEPOLE– 256a is similar and we will discuss it later.

3.1 Constructing the Differential Characteristics

In ICEPOLE, S-box is the only non-linear operation, and the maximum differential probability of the S-box is 2^{-2}. The differential probability is largely determined by the number of active S-boxes. Although the designers expected that only 3 % of the difference transitions has the maximum probability 2^{-2}, this probability is not rare in the early rounds. This is because most of the active S-boxes have 1 bit input difference after the diffusion and the differential probability of a single ICEPOLE S-box is 2^{-2} when the input and output differences are identical with weight 1. Those 1-to-1 identical difference transitions are preferred to the 1-to-n ($n \geq 2$) cases even with the same probability as they will propagate to less number of active S-boxes in the next round.

In [14], the designers analyzed the minimum number of active S-boxes using SAT solver and found that the minimum number is 9 for 3 rounds ICEPOLE. There is an intuitive way to construct the differential characteristics reach this lower bound. We can place 1 active S-box in the middle round and let it propagate backward and forward for one round. Then the number of active S-boxes will be in the form of 4–1–4, which reaches the minimum number 9.

However, the above 3 round differential path is not feasible. In fact, only at most 1024 bits(for ICEPOLE–256a, 960 bits) out of the 1280 bits in a state can be affected by the plaintext and are feasible to introduce difference. Thus, we have the following observation on the operation μ.

Observation 1. *For any 20-bit slice, when the output difference is one bit after μ, there is at least one bit input difference at the last column ($S[\cdot][4]$).*

Table 1. The initial differences. Each entry represents a 64-bit word.

(a) D_1

0x0	0x0	0x1	0x0	0x0
0x1	0x0	0x1	0x0	0x0
0x1	0x1	0x1	0x1	0x0
0x0	0x1	0x0	0x0	0x0

(b) D_2

0x0	0x0	0x1	0x0	0x0
0x1	0x1	0x1	0x1	0x0
0x0	0x1	0x0	0x1	0x0
0x1	0x0	0x1	0x0	0x0

(c) D_3

0x1	0x1	0x0	0x0	0x0
0x1	0x0	0x0	0x1	0x0
0x0	0x0	0x0	0x1	0x0
0x1	0x1	0x1	0x0	0x0

(d) D_4

0x0	0x0	0x0	0x0	0x0
0x1	0x0	0x1	0x0	0x0
0x1	0x1	0x1	0x1	0x0
0x0	0x1	0x0	0x1	0x0

(e) D_5

0x0	0x0	0x0	0x0	0x0
0x0	0x1	0x0	0x1	0x0
0x1	0x0	0x1	0x0	0x0
0x1	0x1	0x1	0x1	0x0

This observation can be easily verified by analyzing the inverse operation of μ.

Therefore, when an active S-box is propagated backward, it is likely that a number of active bits will be propagated to the last column of the input state, which is infeasible to introduce. And we programed to verify that it is impossible to find such feasible 4–1–4 differential path.

It implies that for any feasible differential characteristics of ICEPOLE, the minimum number of active S-boxes is 2 in the first round. As a result, we will consider the differential characteristics with two active S-boxes in the first round. The ideal case is that the output difference of each active S-box is only 1-bit. Then after μ, this 1-bit difference in a slice will propagate to 4 bits. So we expect the good differential characteristics will have 8 active S-boxes in round 2 and no more than 32 active S-boxes in round 3.

We searched for good 3-round differential characteristics, and found 5 possible initial differences in Table 1 (the rotated differences on the 64-bit word are not considered here), which can lead to feasible 3-round differential characteristics. We will name them as D_1, D_2, D_3, D_4 and D_5.

The total number of 3-round active S-boxes is 42, which implies that the differential probability is at most 2^{-84}. But in fact, the only requirement is that the input linear mask does not have XORed difference at the beginning of round 4. Hence, a large number of differential characteristics are satisfied. As long as the number of active S-boxes is relatively low (note that 32 is only 1/8 of the total 256 S-boxes), there is a high probability for the differential step.

3.2 Constructing the Linear Characteristic

The bias of an ICEPOLE linear characteristic is determined by the S-boxes involved in the linear characteristic. We use the following method to construct the 3-round linear characteristics.

Take a single bit in both the input and output masks of an S-box in the middle round. Then find related bits in the input of the first round (*input linear mask*) and the output of the third round before S-box (*output linear mask*), assuming that the S-boxes are identical mappings. The rationale here is that the 1-bit identical mappings have a bias $\frac{3}{16}$, it nearly reaches the maximum bias 2^{-2} while keeping the masks low-weight.

Table 2. The linear characteristics, assuming S-boxes are identical mappings

(a) Linear characteristic 1, input linear mask

0x0	0x800000000000000	0x2000000000	0x20000	0x800000000000040
0x40	0x0	0x800000000000000	0x2000020000	0x0
0x0	0x2000000000	0x800000000000000	0x40	0x2000020000
0x0	0x0	0x800002000020000	0x0	0x40

(b) Linear characteristic 1, output linear mask

0x40000	0x1	0x0	0x80000000000	0x0
0x0	0x4	0x0	0x0	0x0
0x0	0x200000	0x2000000000000000	0x0	0x0
0x0	0x0	0x2000000000	0x100000000000000	0x0

(c) Linear characteristic 2, input linear mask

0x120000004000000	0x800000000000000	0x100000000000	0x0	0x0
0x802000000000000	0x4000000	0x800010000000000	0x0	0x100000000000000
0x810000000000000	0x20000000000000	0x0	0x100000000000	0x4000000
0x4000000	0x8100100000000000	0x0	0x0	0x20100000000000

(d) Linear characteristic 2, output linear mask

0x40000	0x1	0x0	0x0	0x0
0x8000	0x4	0x0	0x0	0x0
0x0	0x0	0x2000000000000000	0x0	0x0
0x0	0x400	0x20000000000	0x100000000000000	0x0

The most essential criterion for the input and output masks is low-weight. When the input linear mask has lower weight, the probability that the input linear mask does not have XORed difference after the 3-round differential step will be higher. When the output linear mask has lower weight, less number of active S-boxes in round 6 will be involved in the linear relation.

Two good linear characteristics we found are given in Table 2. They are denoted as L_1 and L_2.

3.3 Observations to Improve the Attack

The following observation will be helpful in the selection of the differential characteristics.

Observation 2. *When the 1024 bits $S[0..3][0..3]$ of an ICEPOLE state S are known, we are able to determine $S[0][2]$, $S[1][3]$, $S[2][4]$, $S[3][0]$, $S[3][2]$ after μ, ρ and π operations are performed on S.*

According to the above observation, we are able to determine the values of certain input bits to the S-boxes in the first round. Thus, we can update the differential tables for the S-boxes with fixed input values.

The following example shows how this will help to improve the differential probability. Suppose the input of an S-box is in the form "$1 * 0 * *$", where the '*'s are the unknown bits and the '1' and '0' are the bits with fixed values, and the input difference is 2, then the output difference is 2 with probability 1, which is larger than the 0.25 in the general case. To get the fixed values, we can manipulate the input bits according to the mask in Table 3.

By setting the bits in $S[0][1]$ selected by the mask $0x800000010$ as '1' and all the other bits selected by the other masks as '0', the two active S-boxes in round 1 will satisfy the above condition on the input values.

Our next observation is about the S-box in the round 6 of P_6.

Table 3. Input mask for the fixed bits in round 1.

0x0	0x800000010	0x200000001	0x0	0x0
0x800000010	0x0	0x0	0x200000001	0x0
0x0	0x800000010	0x0	0x200000001	0x0
0x800000010	0x0	0x800000010	0x200000001	0x0

Observation 3. *When 4 of the 5 bits in the output of an S-box are known, it is possible to recover some of the input bits from the output bits of the S-boxes. Table 4 provides the probability that we can recover a bit at each position of the S-box input.*

Since the ciphertext is generated by XORing the keystream and the plaintext, we can obtain the values of at most 1024 bits in the state after 6 rounds. For ICEPOLE–128 and ICEPOLE–128a, 4 of the 5 bits in the output of all the S-boxes are known. And for ICEPOLE–256a, 4 of the 5 bits for 192 S-boxes and 3 of the 5 bits for 64 S-boxes in the output are known.

Therefore, instead of using the bias of the linear relation in the round 6, we can recover the chosen input bits in round 6 before S-box by enumerating the values of output bits. This can then be used to recover the value of the bit in the linear relation in the output of round 5.

For example, if we consider the output linear mask of L_1, the probability that we can recover the 8 bits can be computed as

$$Pr_{L_1} = (3/4) \times (5/8)^3 \times (1/2)^4 = 2^{-6.45}.$$

And using these 8 bits, we can compute the value of bit $S[1][1][0]$ at the output of round 5.

Similarly, the probability for L_2 is

$$Pr_{L_2} = (3/4)^2 \times (5/8)^3 \times (1/2)^3 = 2^{-5.86}.$$

Table 4. Probability that the input bits can be recovered for an S-box at round 6.

Position	0	1	2	3	4
Probability	$\frac{6}{8}$	$\frac{5}{8}$	$\frac{4}{8}$	$\frac{4}{8}$	$\frac{1}{8}$

Table 5. The difference of state before the first S-box in D_2.

0x0	0x0	0x0		0x0	0x0
0x0	0x0	0x0		0x0	0x0
0x0	0x0	0x0		0x0	0x0
0x0	0x400	0x20000000000		0x0	0x0

3.4 Concatenating the Differential and Linear Characteristics

After the 3-round differential characteristics and 3-round linear characteristics are constructed, we can concatenate them to form 6-round differential-linear characteristics.

First, we choose the initial difference D_2 because the two active S-boxes in round 1 are in the last row which has two known bits. The difference of state before the S-box for D_2 is given in Table 5.

To choose the 3-round linear characteristic, we consider all the possible rotations of the two linear characteristics L_1 and L_2 given in Sect. 3.2. There are 128 possible rotated linear characteristics. The selection of linear characteristic is done experimentally:

1. Randomly pick 1024-bit plaintext blocks pairs with the chosen initial difference D_2 and the fix values (1, 0) for the two known bits at positions 0 and 2 in the round 1 active S-boxes.
2. After 5 rounds, verify whether the XORed difference of the states under the linear characteristic is zero or not. If it is zero, add it to a counter $cntSame$.
3. Repeat the above process, and choose the one with highest bias at $cntSame$ from 0.5.

For D_2 as the initial difference, the highest bias is $2^{-9.2}$ when the linear characteristic L_1 left rotated by 33 bits is used.

We remark that since round independence does not hold in the case of ICE-POLE, the experimental results would be better choices for the biases rather than the theoretical estimation.

From the bias above, we immediately get a distinguishing attack on ICEPOLE.

1. Generate $2^{33.9}$ pairs of two-block plaintext such that the first 1024-bit plaintext block has initial difference D_2 and the fixed values as specified above. All the other bits are random.
2. Use ICEPOLE to encrypt the plaintext blocks and then decide the 1024 bits input and output state of the first P_6. Discard those pairs if the two bits in round 5 output in the linear characteristic L_1 left rotated 33 bits cannot be recovered. Note that for each bit, the probability is $2^{-6.45}$ to recover. So there are 2^{21} pairs left. Then compute the bit at position $S[1][1][33]$ of the output of round 5 using the recovered bits from round 6.
3. Analyze the bias of the XORed difference of those two bits ($S[1][1][33]$). If the bias is larger than $2^{-10.2}$ we conclude that it is the ICEPOLE encryption.

The success probability is computed by using the normal distribution to approximate the binomial distribution of the bias. For ICEPOLE, the bias is a random variable $X \sim N(n(1/2 + 2^{-9.2}), n(1/2 + 2^{-9.2})(1/2 - 2^{-9.2}))$, where n is the number of pairs of the recovered 5 rounds output. When $n = 2^{21}$, the probability that $X \geq 2^{-10.2}$ is 99.3 %. A random permutation, on the other hand, has its bias to be a random variable $Y \sim N(n/2, n/4)$. The value is larger than $2^{-10.5}$ with probability 0.7 %. Hence, we have a very good chance to distinguish the ICEPOLE encryption from a random permutation by using $2^{35.9}$ plaintext blocks (a pair of two-block messages are counted as 4 plaintext blocks), assuming the nonce can be reused.

4   State Recovery Attack on ICEPOLE

In this section, we will use the differential-linear characteristics to launch state recovery attacks on ICEPOLE.

4.1   State Recovery Attacks on ICEPOLE–128 and ICEPOLE–128a

For ICEPOLE–128 and ICEPOLE–128a, there are 256 unknown bits in the state before P_6. They are in the last column of each slice. For convenience, we denote those four 64-bit unknown words in the last column as $\{U_0, U_1, U_2, U_3\}$ according to the row index. We will recover them step by step.

4.1.1   Recovering U_0 and U_3

To recover the unknown bits in the state, we will analyze the input values at the active S-boxes. For D_2, there are two active S-boxes in round 1. One has input difference 2 and the other has input difference 4. We will focus on the one with input difference 4 and denote the five input bits as $b_0, b_1, \ldots, b_4$ according to their positions (b_0 being the least significant bit).

When the two bits of an ICEPOLE S-box are fixed with values $b_0 = 1$ and $b_2 = 0$, there are 8 possible values for the remaining three bits. When the input difference is 4 (at b_2), the output difference have weight 1 only when $b_1 = 1$ and $b_3 = 0$. Intuitively, the lower the weight of the output difference after the first round, the higher the probability that there is no XORed difference at the output linear mask after 5 rounds. Hence, it is possible to relate the input value of the active S-box in round 1 to the bias of XORed output difference in round 5.

We experimentally find the following biases for different values of the input bit b_1 and b_3. Note that we collected 2^{30} data in the experiments to compute the bias and repeated for several time. When the bias is less than 2^{-14}, the experimental results were not very stable, and the average number is listed in the table. In fact, it is not necessary to consider those low biases as only the highest ones could be useful for our analysis.

Note that b_1 is related to an unknown bit in U_3, and b_3 is related to two unknown bits, in U_0 and U_3. So we have following relations:

$$b_1 = U_3^{31} \oplus a_0$$

values	bias (log based 2)
$b_1 = 0, b_3 = 0$	-13.0
$b_1 = 1, b_3 = 0$	-7.3
$b_1 = 0, b_3 = 1$	-13.9
$b_1 = 1, b_3 = 1$	-11.9

and

$$b_3 = U_0^{49} \oplus U_3^{49} \oplus a_1,$$

where U^x is the x-th bit in the 64-bit word U; a_0 and a_1 are constants which can be computed from the 1024-known bits.

We describe the state recovery process given as below:

1. Generate $2^{33.9}$ pairs of two-block plaintext satisfied following requirements. The first block of the plaintext has difference D_2 and each active S-box has fixed values '1' and '0' in bit 0 and 2 respectively. All the other bits are random.
2. Use ICEPOLE to encrypt the plaintext blocks and then decide the 1024 bits input and output state of the first P_6. Discard the pairs if the two bits in round 5 output in the linear characteristic L_1 left rotated 33 bits cannot be recovered. There are 2^{21} pairs left. Then compute the bit at position $S[1][1][33]$ of the output of round 5 using the recovered bits from round 6.
3. If the two bits at the position $S[1][1][33]$ are the same, we compute the values of a_0 and a_1 according to the input and increase the counter for the value of (a_0, a_1) by 1.
4. Suppose the largest counter of (a_0, a_1) takes value $a_0 = v_0$ and $a_1 = v_1$, we guess that $U_3^{31} = v_0 \oplus 1$ and $U_0^{49} \oplus U_3^{49} = v_1$.
5. By rotating the differential-linear characteristic for the other 63 bits, we can recover the two 64-bit unknown words U_0 and U_3.

The success probability of this scheme is equivalent to the probability that a random variable $X \sim N(n(1/2 + 2^{-7.3}), n(1/2 + 2^{-7.3})(1/2 - 2^{-7.3}))$ has value greater than the random variable $Y \sim N(n(1/2 + 2^{-11.9}), n(1/2 + 2^{-11.9})(1/2 - 2^{-11.9}))$. When $n = 2^{19}$, the probability is almost 1. Since we have 2^{21} pairs of input, each of the four choices of b_0 and b_1 will be around 2^{19} pairs.

We remark that here the probability is high enough such that even if the experiment is repeated for 64 times, the success probability is still close to 1.

4.1.2 Recovering U_2

Assuming that U_0 and U_3 have been recovered correctly, we can use similar method to recover U_2. In this case, we use D_1 and L_2 left rotated by 58 bits as the differential-linear characteristic.

The difference of state before the first round S-box for D_1 is given in the Table 6.

Table 6. The difference of state before the first S-box in D_1.

0x0 0x0	0x0 0x0 0x0
0x0 0x4	0x0 0x0 0x0
0x0 0x200000	0x0 0x0 0x0
0x0 0x0	0x0 0x0 0x0

Fixed bits: With the knowledge of U_0 and U_3, we fix bit 0, 2, 3 with the values (1, 0, 0) respectively for the active S-box at the second row. This is to ensure the output difference of this active S-box has weight exactly 1. And we fix bit 0, 4 with the values (1, 1) for the active S-box at the third row. Then, the weight of output difference can be distinguished from the input value of bit 2, which is denoted as b_2.

We experimentally find the following biases for b_2 after 5 rounds. The biases are based on the difference of the output bit at position $S[3][1][58]$.

values	bias (log based 2)
$b_2 = 0$	−11.0
$b_2 = 1$	−15.4

From the active S-box at the third round, it is possible to find following relation:

$$b_2 = U_2^{24} \oplus a,$$

where the constant a can be computed from the known input bits.

The state recovery process process:

1. Generate $2^{36.7}$ pairs of two-block plaintext satisfying following requirements. The first block of the plaintext has difference D_1 and each active S-box has fixed values according to the above paragraph. All the other bits are random.
2. Use ICEPOLE to encrypt the plaintext blocks and then decide the 1024 bits input and output state of the first P_6. Discard the pairs if the two bits in the linear relation (according to L_2 rotated by 58 bits) in the output of round 5 cannot be recovered. There are 2^{25} pairs left. Then compute the bit at position $S[3][1][58]$ of the output of round 5 using the recovered bits from round 6.
3. If the two bits at the position $S[3][1][58]$ are the same, we compute the value of a according to the input and increase the counter for that value by 1.
4. Suppose the largest counter of a take value $a = v$, we guess that $U_1^0 = v$.
5. By rotating the differential-linear characteristic for the other 63 bits, we can recover the 64-bit unknown word U_1.

The estimated success probability is 99.6 % for each bit.

4.1.3   Recovering U_1

At this stage, we assume that U_0, U_2 and U_3 have been recovered correctly. In this case, we select D_3 and L_2 left rotated by 35 bits as the differential-linear characteristic.

The differential of state before the first round S-box for D_3 is given in the Table 7.

Fixed bits: We fix bit 1, 2, 4 with the values $(1, 0, 1)$ for the active S-box at the first row. It is to ensure that the weight of output difference of this active S-box is determined by the value of input bit 3 which is denoted as $b_{0,3}$. And we fix bit 0, 2, 3, 4 with the values $(0, 1, 1, 1)$ for the active S-box at the second row. It is to ensure that the weight of output difference is determined by the value of input bit 1 which is denoted as $b_{1,1}$.

The $b_{0,3}$ and $b_{1,1}$ are related to the unknown bits:

$$b_{0,3} = a_0 \oplus U_1^{12}$$
$$b_{1,1} = a_1 \oplus U_1^{13}$$

where a_0 and a_1 are constants which can be computed from the known input.

We experimentally find the following biases for different values of the input bit $b_{0,3}$ and $b_{1,1}$. The biases are base on the difference of the output bit at position $S[3][1][35]$.

values	bias (log based 2)
$b_{0,3} = 0$, $b_{1,1} = 0$	−11.2
$b_{0,3} = 1$, $b_{1,1} = 0$	−15.2
$b_{0,3} = 0$, $b_{1,1} = 1$	−16.4
$b_{0,3} = 1$, $b_{1,1} = 1$	−14.8

We remark that the biases other than the first row in above table may not be very accurate considering the small bias.

The state recovery process process:

1. Generate $2^{37.7}$ pairs of two-block plaintext satisfied following requirements. The first block of the plaintext has difference D_3 and each active S-box has fixed values according to the above paragraph. All the other bits are random.
2. Use ICEPOLE to encrypt the plaintext blocks and then decide the 1024 bits input and output state of the first P_6. Discard those pairs if the two bits in the linear relation (according to L_2 rotated by 35 bits) in the output of round 5 cannot be recovered. There are 2^{26} pairs left. Then compute the bit at position $S[3][1][35]$ of the output of round 5 using the recovered bits from round 6.
3. If the two bits at the position $S[3][1][35]$ are the same, we compute the value of a_0 and a_1 according to the input and increase the counter for (a_0, a_1) by 1.

4. Suppose the largest counter of (a_0, a_1) take value $a_0 = v_0$ and $a_1 = v_1$, we guess that $U_1^{12} = v_0$ and $U_1^{13} = v_1$.
5. By rotating the differential-linear characteristic for the other 31 even bits less than 64, we can recover the 64-bit unknown word U_1.

Note that in each rotation of the differential-linear characteristic, we are able to recover two consecutive bits, so we only need to test 32 rotations to recover the 64-bit U_1. The estimated success probability is 98.7 % for each bit.

Table 7. The differential of state before the first S-box in D_3.

0x0	0x0	0x80000000000000000	0x0	0x0
0x8000	0x0	0x0	0x0	0x0
0x0	0x0	0x0	0x0	0x0
0x0	0x0	0x0	0x0	0x0

4.1.4   Correcting the Recovered State

In the previous state recovery attack, only the first 128 bits can be correctly recovered with probability almost 1. For the other 128 bits, although the success probability is around 99 %, it is still possible that the state we recovered has some error bits. Whether the state is correct can be easily verified by encrypting some new messages and compare the ciphertext.

We can correct up to 7 error bits with relatively low complexity. To correct i error bits is to choose any i bits from the 128 bits and flip the values. Then test whether the modified unknown state is correct.

Suppose that for the 128 bits U_1 and U_2, the probability that each bit is correct is 0.99, we can compute the probability that the number of error bits is less than 8 as

$$\sum_{i=0}^{7} \binom{128}{i} \times .99^{128-i} \times .01^i = 0.99995.$$

The total number of encryptions to correct up to 7 error bits is $2^{37.5}$, which is negligible to the whole attack.

4.1.5   Summary of the Attack

The data complexity is:

- U_0 and U_3: $2 \times 2 \times 2^{33.9} \times 2^6$. We multiply $2^{33.9}$ by 2 two times due to the fact that we use $2^{33.9}$ pairs of 2-blocks plaintext.
- U_2: $2 \times 2 \times 2^{36.7} \times 2^6$
- U_1: $2 \times 2 \times 2^{37.7} \times 2^5$
- Total: $2^{45.8}$

The time complexity is the $2^{45.8}$ encryptions of the one block plaintext and the possible $2^{37.5}$ encryptions for correction.

The memory cost is mainly on the storage of some counters, which is negligible.

The success rate of this attack is close to 1, and can be adjusted through the number of input messages.

4.2   State Recovery Attack on ICEPOLE–256a

In the case of ICEPOLE–256a, there are 320 unknown bits in the input and output states in the encryption of a block. In addition to the U_0 to U_3 in the previous subsection, we use U_4 to denote the unknown 64-bit word $S[3][3]$.

Different from the ICEPOLE–128 and ICEPOLE–128a, in the last row of the output in ICEPOEL– 256a, there are only 3 known bits instead of 4 known bits. Consequently, it is impossible to recover the input bits given the output bits for that row. To deal with this issue, we have to consider the linear relation of the input mask of the S-box. When the value of the input mask is less than 8, the largest bias is 3/16, but if the value of the input mask is 8, the largest bias is 1/16.

For L_1, there are two mask bits placed in the last row, one is 4 and the other is 8. From the Piling-Up Lemma [11], the bias is $2^{-5.4}$.

For L_2, there are three mask bits placed in the last row, 2, 4, and 8. By Piling up Lemma, the bias is $2^{-6.8}$.

To increase the bias of the last row, we introduce another linear characteristic L_3 (Table 8), which has only 1 bit in the last row of the input mask of round 6 S-box. For L_3, the bias is 3/16 and the probability to recover other bits is $2^{-9.6}$.

To recover the U_4, we use the differential characteristic D_2 with linear characteristic L_1 left rotated 33 bits, same as the recovery of U_0 and U_3. Since the value of $S[3][2]$ is not known, we will only fix the active bits in $S[3][0]$, setting it to 1.

We will find the value of bit 2 in the input of active S-box related to $S[3][1]$ with difference $0x400$. We denote this bit $b_{3,2}$, and we have $b_{3,2} = a \oplus U_4^{33}$, where a is a constant from the known input.

We experimentally find the following biases for the input bit values $b_{3,2}$ after 5 rounds. The biases are base on the difference of the output bit at position $S[1][1][33]$.

values	bias (log based 2)
$b_{3,2} = 0$	-9.2
$b_{3,2} = 1$	-15.3 (negative)

Considering the linear relation of this XORed value to the 4 bits in the two output states, the bias of the XORed difference of the 4 bits becomes 2^{-18} by Piling up lemma. To ensure the high probability of correctly guessing the value, we need around 2^{40} pairs of two-block plaintext. The total data needed is around $2^{58.7}$.

Next, the complexity of recovering the other unknown words need to be amended. We omit the similar attack process and discuss the estimated complexities here.

For U_0 and U_3, the increased bias is $2^{-8.8}$ which needs to be compensated by around $2^{17.6}$ additional messages. Furthermore, some of the bits from the S-box layer in round 6 can directly be recovered from the linear relation, hence increasing the success probability by a factor of 2^4. The total effect is the data complexity becomes $2^{55.5}$.

Table 8. The linear characteristic 3, assuming S-boxes are identical mappings

(a) input linear mask

0x0	0x10000000000000	0x20000	0x82000000000	0x400000000000000
0x410000000000000	0x0	0x80000000000	0x20000	0x2000000000
0x400000000000000	0x10000000000000	0x2000000000	0x80000020000	0x0
0x410000000000000	0x0	0x10000000000000	0x2000020000	0x80000000000

(b) output linear mask

0x40000	0x0	0x0	0x80000000000	0x200000000000
0x8000	0x4	0x0	0x0	0x0
0x8	0x200000	0x0	0x0	0x100000000000
0x0	0x0	0x20000000000	0x0	0x0

For U_2, D_1 with L_3 left rotated 13 bits will be used and for U_1, D_3 with L_1 left rotated 2 bits will be used. The increased bias is roughly $2^{-2.8}$ for both cases (including the increased 5-round bias). And the decreased probability for recovering the values before round 6 S-box has a factor $2^{-7.5}$. Therefore, the total data complexity for recovering each bit is increased by $2^{13.1}$, which is $2^{57.8}$.

Therefore, the total data complexity of the state recovery attack for ICEPOLE–256a is estimated to be $2^{59.8}$, which is less than the constraint 2^{62}.

4.3   Implications of the State Recovery Attacks

For ICEPOLE–128, the state recovery attack implies the failure of encryption security if both the nonce and the secret message number are reused. When an adversary has the full knowledge of a state, he can invert the cipher until the secret message number is injected. Thus, the adversary can decrypt arbitrary plaintext blocks. It also implies a forgery attack on the authentication of plaintext and associated data since the valid tag for any modified associated data or plaintext block can be computed. Since both the key and secret message number are unknown, the adversary cannot recover the key.

Table 9. Number of bits of security when nonce and secret message number can be reused.

	ICEPOLE-128	ICEPOLE-128a	ICEPOLE-256a
Confidentiality for the plaintext	46	46	60
Confidentiality for the secret message number	128	-	-
integrity for the plaintext	46	46	60
Integrity for the associated data	46	46	60
Integrity for the secret message number	46	-	-
Integrity for the public message number	46	46	60

For ICEPOLE–128a and ICEPOLE–256a, the state recovery attack implies the whole security is broken if the nonce is reused. The initialization of ICEPOLE–128a is invertible, so the adversary can directly recover the secret key from the known state. Then both the encryption and authentication are insecure.

Summary of the security of ICEPOLE under our analysis when nonce is reused is given in Table 9.

5   Experimental Results

We experimentally verified the state recovery attack on ICEPOLE–128a. And we managed to recover the 256 unknown bits practically. The experiments used the state after the initialization with all zeros IV and key. The unknowns states are:

$$U_0 = 0x1e7aed5bfaeb535f$$
$$U_1 = 0xe0dcc6422595e5ba$$
$$U_2 = 0x892bf76586876c23$$
$$U_3 = 0x8b2ef3bf50e902f6$$

To recover U_0 and U_3, we run the attack in Sect. 4.1.1 on a server with 64 cores (AMD Opteron(tm) Processor 6276). Instead of checking the constants from input, we used an equivalent method: directly extract the input bits of the active S-box in the first round, and decide whether they are the estimated ones. The number of plaintext pairs we used is 2^{34} for each bit. The attacks takes 15.3 hours and all the 128 bits recovered are correct.

To recover U_2, we run the attack in Sect. 4.1.2 on the server. The number of plaintext pairs we used is 2^{37} for each bit. The attacks takes 3.5 days and all the bits are correct.

To recover U_1, we run the attack in Sect. 4.1.3 on the server. The number of plaintext pairs we used is 2^{38} for each bit. The attacks takes 3.5 days and there is one error bit.

Since the number of error bits is very small, the experiments show that our state recovery attack indeed works for ICEPOLE–128a.

6   Conclusion

In this paper, we analyzed the security of the ICEPOLE family of authenticated ciphers using the differential-linear cryptanalysis when nonce is misused. ICEPOLE is strong against differential cryptanalysis since only part of the input difference is affected by message in the attack (so the best differential attack against the permutation cannot be applied to break ICEPOLE); and ICEPOLE is strong against linear cryptanalysis since only part of the input and output of the permutation are known in the attack (so the best linear attack against the permutation cannot be applied to break ICEPOLE). We successfully developed the differential-linear cryptanalysis against ICEPOLE by bypassing the input/output constraints of ICEPOLE. Our attacks show that the states of all the ICEPOLE variants can be recovered, and the secret key of ICEPOLE–128a and ICEPOLE–256a can also be recovered. The security claims of ICEPOLE do not hold under the nonce misuse circumstances.

From the attacks against ICEPOLE, the lesson we learned is that when we are designing a strong cipher based on a permutation, it is better to consider the best attacks against the permutation in which the input/output can affect the whole state. Furthermore, if the performance of a cipher is improved by considering input/output constraints, the designers should analyze whether the input/output constraints could be bypassed in the attacks.

References

1. Bertoni, G., Daemen, J., Peeters, M., Van Assche, G.: Keccak sponge function family main document. Submission to NIST (Round 2) (2009)
2. Bertoni, G., Daemen, J., Peeters, M., Van Assche, G.: Duplexing the sponge: single-pass authenticated encryption and other applications. In: Miri, A., Vaudenay, S. (eds.) SAC 2011. LNCS, vol. 7118, pp. 320–337. Springer, Heidelberg (2012)
3. Biham, E., Dunkelman, O., Keller, N.: Enhancing differential-linear cryptanalysis. In: Zheng, Y. (ed.) ASIACRYPT 2002. LNCS, vol. 2501, pp. 254–266. Springer, Heidelberg (2002)
4. Biham, E., Dunkelman, O., Keller, N.: Differential-linear cryptanalysis of serpent. In: Johansson, T. (ed.) FSE 2003. LNCS, vol. 2887, pp. 9–21. Springer, Heidelberg (2003)
5. Biham, E., Shamir, A.: Differential cryptanalysis of DES-like cryptosystems. J. Cryptol. 4(1), 3–72 (1991)
6. Blondeau, C., Leander, G., Nyberg, K.: Differential-linear cryptanalysis revisited. In: Cid, C., Rechberger, C. (eds.) FSE 2014. LNCS, vol. 8540, pp. 411–430. Springer, Heidelberg (2015)
7. Dunkelman, O., Indesteege, S., Keller, N.: A differential-linear attack on 12-round serpent. In: Chowdhury, D.R., Rijmen, V., Das, A. (eds.) INDOCRYPT 2008. LNCS, vol. 5365, pp. 308–321. Springer, Heidelberg (2008)
8. Dunkelman, O., Keller, N.: Cryptanalysis of CTC2. In: Fischlin, M. (ed.) CT-RSA 2009. LNCS, vol. 5473, pp. 226–239. Springer, Heidelberg (2009)
9. Langford, S.K., Hellman, M.E.: Differential-linear cryptanalysis. In: Desmedt, Y.G. (ed.) CRYPTO 1994. LNCS, vol. 839, pp. 17–25. Springer, Heidelberg (1994)
10. Lu, J.: A methodology for differential-linear cryptanalysis and its applications. In: Canteaut, A. (ed.) FSE 2012. LNCS, vol. 7549, pp. 69–89. Springer, Heidelberg (2012)
11. Matsui, M.: Linear cryptanalysis method for DES cipher. In: Helleseth, T. (ed.) EUROCRYPT 1993. LNCS, vol. 765, pp. 386–397. Springer, Heidelberg (1994)
12. McGrew, D., Viega, J.: The Galois/Counter Mode of Operation (GCM). http://csrc.nist.gov/CryptoToolkit/modes/proposedmodes/gcm/gcm-spec.pdf
13. Morawiecki, P., Nonce reuse in ICEPOLE, July 2014. http://competitions.cr.yp.to/round1/icepole-misuse.html
14. Morawiecki, P., Gaj, K., Homsirikamol, E., Matusiewicz, K., Pieprzyk, J., Rogawski, M., Srebrny, M., Wójcik, M.: ICEPOLE v1. submission to CAESAR competition. http://competitions.cr.yp.to/round1/icepolev1.pdf

15. Morawiecki, P., Gaj, K., Homsirikamol, E., Matusiewicz, K., Pieprzyk, J., Rogawski, M., Srebrny, M., Wójcik, M.: ICEPOLE: high-speed, hardware-oriented authenticated encryption. In: Batina, L., Robshaw, M. (eds.) CHES 2014. LNCS, vol. 8731, pp. 392–413. Springer, Heidelberg (2014)
16. Shin, Y.S., Kim, J.-S., Kim, G., Hong, S.H., Lee, S.-J.: Differential-linear type attacks on reduced rounds of SHACAL-2. In: Wang, H., Pieprzyk, J., Varadharajan, V. (eds.) ACISP 2004. LNCS, vol. 3108, pp. 110–122. Springer, Heidelberg (2004)
17. Wu, H., Preneel, B.: Differential-linear attacks against the stream cipher phelix. In: Biryukov, A. (ed.) FSE 2007. LNCS, vol. 4593, pp. 87–100. Springer, Heidelberg (2007)

Cryptanalysis of JAMBU

Thomas Peyrin[1], Siang Meng Sim[1] (✉), Lei Wang[1], and Guoyan Zhang[1,2,3] (✉)

[1] Nanyang Technological University, Singapore City, Singapore
{thomas.peyrin,wang.lei}@ntu.edu.sg, ssim011@e.ntu.edu.sg
[2] School of Computer Science and Technology, Shandong University, Jinan, China
[3] Key Laboratory of Cryptologic Technology and Information Security,
Ministry of Education, Shandong University, Jinan, China
guoyanzhang@sdu.edu.cn

Abstract. In this article, we analyse the security of the authenticated encryption mode JAMBU, a submission to the CAESAR competition that remains currently unbroken. We show that the security claims of this candidate regarding its nonce-misuse resistance can be broken. More precisely, we explain a technique to guess in advance a ciphertext block corresponding to a plaintext that has never been queried before (nor its prefix), thus breaking the confidentiality of the scheme when the attacker can make encryption queries with the same nonce. Our attack is very practical as it requires only about 2^{32} encryption queries and computations (instead of the 2^{128} claimed by the designers). Our cryptanalysis has been fully implemented in order to verify our findings. Moreover, due to the small tag length of JAMBU, we show how this attack can be extended in the nonce-respecting scenario to break confidentiality in the adaptive chosen-ciphertext model (IND-CCA2) with 2^{96} computations, with message prefixes not previously queried.

Keywords: JAMBU · Authenticated encryption · Cryptanalysis · Confidentiality · Caesar competition

1 Introduction

Authenticated encryption is a very useful cryptographic primitive that provides both privacy and authenticity when sending data. It is a handy component for many security engineers and protocol designers as it avoids for example the classical threat of a misinterpretation of the privacy-only security provided by a simple encryption mode. The encryption algorithm usually takes as input a plaintext P, some public associated data AD, a public nonce value IV, a secret key K, and it outputs a ciphertext C and a tag value T. Conversely, the decryption algorithm usually takes as input a ciphertext C, a tag value T, some public associated data AD, a public nonce value IV, a secret key K, and outputs either the original plaintext P or an error flag if the authentication process is not valid. Using an encryption scheme for the privacy part and a MAC for the authenticity part is a possible way to obtain authenticated encryption, but the goal of the

© International Association for Cryptologic Research 2015
G. Leander (Ed.): FSE 2015, LNCS 9054, pp. 264–281, 2015.
DOI: 10.1007/978-3-662-48116-5_13

ongoing CAESAR competition [5] is to push to the industry a single primitive providing both properties at the same time, with a single core function, which would potentially permit faster and simpler solutions.

JAMBU is an nonce-based authenticated encryption operating mode proposed by Wu and Huang [14], that can be instantiated with any block cipher. Yet, the submission AES-JAMBU to the CAESAR competition uses AES-128 [6] as internal block cipher. The main advantage of JAMBU mode is its low memory requirement, which places it in the group of lightweight authenticated encryption modes. Indeed, when instantiated with a $2n$-bit block cipher and without counting the memory needed to store the secret key, JAMBU will only require to maintain a $3n$-bit internal state, where classical authenticated encryption modes like OCB [9,11] would require a $6n$-bit internal state or even more. In terms of speed performances, AES-JAMBU is reasonably fast, being about twice slower than AES-CBC [13] (but much slower than OCB since the calls to the internal cipher cannot be parallelized).

The security claims of JAMBU are given in the CAESAR competition submission document [14]. When instantiated with a $2n$-bit block cipher, JAMBU processes plaintext blocks of n bits and eventually outputs an n-bit tag T. When the nonce is not reused, JAMBU is claimed to provide $2n$-bit security for confidentiality and n-bit security for authentication. When the nonce is misused (i.e. several encryptions can be performed with the same nonce), JAMBU is claimed to remain reasonably strong. More precisely, in that scenario, the confidentiality of JAMBU is supposed to be only partially compromised as the authors claim that "*it only leaks the information of the first block or the common prefix of the message*". Regarding authentication in the nonce-misuse scenario, the authors remain vague, only mentioning that "*the integrity of JAMBU will be less secure but not completely compromised*".

Our Contribution. In this article, we first describe a very practical attack on JAMBU that breaks its confidentiality claim in the nonce-misuse scenario. More precisely, with only $2^{n/2}$ encryption queries and computing time (which amounts to 2^{32} for AES-JAMBU), we are able to predict the value of a ciphertext block corresponding to a chosen plaintext whose prefix has never been queried to the encryption oracle before, which invalidates the designers' $2n$-bit security claim.

Our attack works by trying to force a zero-difference on the input of one of the internal block cipher calls of JAMBU. Normally, forcing such a collision on a $2n$-bit value should require 2^n computations, but thanks to a divide-and-conquer technique, we are able to divide this event in two subparts, for a total cost of $2^{n/2}$ computations. Having a collision on one of the internal block cipher calls will render this particular JAMBU round totally linear with regards to differences, and will eventually allow us to predict a ciphertext block for the next round.

Then, because of the rather small tag size of JAMBU, we are able to extend our technique to the more interesting case of a nonce-respecting attacker. More precisely, with $2^{3n/2}$ computations (which amounts to 2^{96} for AES-JAMBU), one can break JAMBU's confidentiality in the adaptive chosen-ciphertext model, with message prefixes not previously queried.

We first describe JAMBU authenticated encryption mode in Sect. 2 and then explain our nonce-misuse scenario attack in Sect. 3, while the nonce-respecting attack will be presented in Sect. 4. Finally, in order to confirm our claims, we have implemented the nonce-misuse attack on AES-JAMBU as detailed in Sect. 5. We remark that our techniques will work independently of the cipher instantiating the JAMBU mode, yet in the rest of this article we will focus on AES-JAMBU for ease of description.

2   The JAMBU Authenticated Encryption Scheme

2.1   Description of JAMBU

JAMBU uses a k-bit secret key K and an n-bit public nonce value IV to authenticate a variable length associated data AD and to encrypt and authenticate a variable length plaintext P. It produces a ciphertext C, which has the same bit length with plaintext, and an n-bit tag T.

The encryption process of JAMBU consists of 5 phases as described below: padding, initialization, processing of the associated data, processing of the plaintext, and finalization/tag generation. The computation structure is illustrated in Figs. 1, 2 and 3, where each line represents an n-bit value. We will represent the $3n$-bit internal state of JAMBU by the variables (S_i, R_i) with $S_i = (U_i, V_i)$, where R_i, U_i and V_i are n-bit values. We will denote by E_K the internal cipher using the secret key K.

Padding. First, the associated data AD is padded with 10* padding: a '1' bit is appended to the data, followed by the least number of '0' bits (possibly none) to make the length of the padded associated data become a multiple of n bits. Then, the same padding method is applied to the plaintext.

Initialization. As depicted in Fig. 1, JAMBU uses an n-bit public nonce value IV to initialize the internal state: $S_0 = E_K(0^n \| IV) \oplus (0^{2n-3} \| 101)$, where $\|$ denotes concatenation, and $R_0 = U_0$.

Processing of the Associated Data. The padded associated data is divided into n-bit blocks, and then processed block by block as described in Fig. 1. Note that a single padded block $1 \| 0^{n-1}$ will be processed in the case of an empty associated data string. We omit the details of this phase since it is irrelevant to our attack. Moreover, in the rest of the article we will only use **empty** AD strings, so we get $S_1 = (U_1, V_1) = E_K(S_0) \oplus (1 \| 0^{2n-2} \| 1)$ and $R_1 = R_0 \oplus U_1$.

Processing of the Plaintext. We denote by p the number of plaintext blocks after padding and $P = (P_1, P_2, \ldots, P_p)$. The plaintext is processed block by block as depicted in Fig. 2. At round i, the internal state is updated with the plaintext block P_i by $S_{i+1} = (U_{i+1}, V_{i+1}) = E_K(S_i) \oplus (P_i \| R_i)$ and $R_{i+1} = R_i \oplus U_{i+1}$. The ciphertext block C_i is then computed with $C_i = P_i \oplus V_{i+1}$.

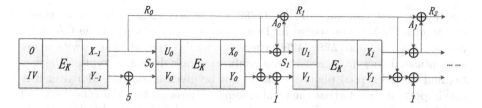

Fig. 1. Initialization and processing of the associated data

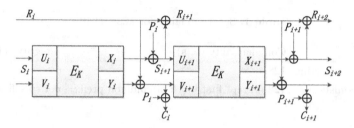

Fig. 2. Processing of the plaintext

Finalization and Tag Generation. When all the plaintext blocks are processed, the final state is (S_{p+1}, R_{p+1}). The authentication tag T is generated with two internal block cipher calls, as depicted in Fig. 3.

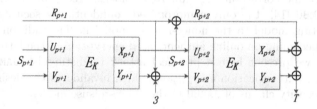

Fig. 3. Finalization and tag generation

2.2 Security Claims

The security claims of JAMBU are given in the CAESAR competition submission document [14]. When the nonce is not reused, JAMBU is claimed to provide $2n$-bit security for confidentiality and n-bit security for authentication. We note that the type of confidentiality security (i.e. IND-CPA, IND-CCA1 or IND-CCA2) is not mentioned by the designers. When the nonce is misused (i.e. several encryptions can be performed with the same nonce), JAMBU is claimed to remain reasonably strong. Namely, in that scenario, the confidentiality of JAMBU is supposed to be only partially compromised as the authors claim that it only leaks the information of the first block or the common prefix of the message. Regarding authentication in the nonce-misuse scenario, the authors remain vague, only mentioning that *"the integrity of* JAMBU *will be less secure but not completely compromised"*. We summarize in Table 1 the security claims of the CAESAR competition candidate AES-JAMBU where $n = 64$. We remark that as with many authenticated encryption schemes, if verification fails during decryption the new tag and the decrypted plaintext should not be given as output. Moreover it is also important to note that the total amount of message material (plaintext and associated data) that can be protected by a single key is limited to 2^{64} bits for AES-JAMBU.

Table 1. Security claims for AES-JAMBU.

	Confidentiality (bits)	Integrity (bits)
nonce-respecting	128	64
nonce-misuse	128 (except first block or common prefix)	not specified

3   Attack on JAMBU in Nonce-Misuse Scenario

In this section, we analyze JAMBU in the nonce-misuse attack model, where a nonce can be used to encrypt multiple plaintexts. In such a model, JAMBU is an *online* authenticated encryption scheme, namely the i-th ciphertext block is produced before the $i + 1$-th plaintext block is read. An inherent property of online authenticated encryption is that common prefix plaintext blocks always produce the same corresponding ciphertext blocks. According to the security claims of JAMBU [14], the only compromised confidentiality security from the nonce-respecting model to the nonce-misuse model is this additional inherent property as becoming an online authenticated encryption in the latter model.

However, we present here a practical attack to distinguish JAMBU from a *random* online authentication encryption, which invalidates the designers' confidentiality security claims of JAMBU in the nonce-misuse model.

3.1   Confidentiality of Online Authenticated Encryption

For an online encryption scheme $(\mathcal{E}_K, \mathcal{D}_K)$ with a key space $\mathcal{K}$, its confidentiality security is usually defined via upper bounding the advantage of all chosen-plaintext distinguishers.[1] We give a brief description as follows, and refer interested readers to [1,7] for the full formal definitions. Let $\mathcal{OAE}$ denote the set of all online authenticated encryption algorithms that have the same block and tag size with $(\mathcal{E}_K, \mathcal{D}_K)$. Let $(\texttt{OEnc}, \texttt{ODec}) \xleftarrow{\$} \mathcal{OAE}$ denote an algorithm randomly selected from $\mathcal{OAE}$. Let $\mathbb{D}$ be a distinguisher that interacts with $\mathcal{E}_K$ or Enc, and outputs one bit. Its advantage is defined as:

$$\mathbf{Adv}_{\mathcal{E}}^{\mathrm{cpa}}(\mathbb{D}) := \Pr\left[K \xleftarrow{\$} \mathcal{K}, \mathbb{D}^{\mathcal{E}_K} \Rightarrow 1\right] - \Pr\left[(\texttt{OEnc}, \texttt{ODec}) \xleftarrow{\$} \mathcal{OAE}, \mathbb{D}^{\texttt{OEnc}} \Rightarrow 1\right].$$

---

[1] It has been proven that an authenticated encryption satisfying both IND-CPA and INT-CTXT security notions is also IND-CCA secure [3,4,8].

Then we define $\mathbf{Adv}_{\mathcal{E}}^{\mathrm{cpa}}(t, q, \sigma, \ell) := \max_{\mathbb{D}} \mathbf{Adv}_{\mathcal{E}}^{\mathrm{cpa}}(\mathbb{D})$, where the maximum takes over all distinguishers that run in time t and make q queries, each of length at most ℓ blocks and of total length at most σ blocks.

3.2 Attack Overview

Our attack is based on an observation that we explain below. JAMBU maintains a $3n$-bit internal state, but uses only one invocation to a $2n$-bit block cipher E_K to update it per plaintext block. Thus, there are always n state bits per round which are not updated through the strong primitive (i.e. the underlying block cipher). More precisely, every round $S_i = (U_i, V_i)$ is input to the block cipher: $(X_i, Y_i) = E_K(S_i)$. On the other hand, R_i is *linearly* injected into the updated state as $V_{i+1} = Y_i \oplus R_i$. Furthermore, if a pair of plaintexts satisfying $\Delta S_i = 0$ is found, then the state differences in two consecutive rounds are linearly related, i.e., $\Delta V_{i+2} = \Delta R_i$, which will be exploited by our cryptanalysis.

Overall, our attack can be divided into three parts. First the attacker will try to build a special difference structure in the internal state by querying the encryption of a fixed message[2] with several different nonces. Then, using this special differential structure, he will try to recover the values of these internal differences and at the same time force a zero-difference on the input of one of the internal cipher calls. Finally, based on this differential structure that is now fully known and controlled, he will be able to distinguish JAMBU from a random online authenticated encryption, and further forge some ciphertext blocks for a message that has never been queried before.

3.3 First Step

For the first step, the attacker picks a random n-bit message block P_1, and asks for the encryption of this message for $2^{n/2}$ distinct nonce values. Since the corresponding ciphertext blocks are also n-bit long, the attacker will have a good chance to observe a collision on the block C_1. We denote IV and IV' the two nonces leading to that collision. One can easily see from Fig. 4 that since no difference is inserted in the block P_1, a collision on C_1 necessarily means that we have a collision on the difference value of the upper branch and lower branch of the internal state (i.e. the difference values in R_1 and in Y_1 are equal). We denote that difference by Δ_R, and we denote the random difference in X_1 by Δ_S. We remark that for this first attack step, we do not need to reuse any nonce value.

3.4 Second Step

In the second step, the goal will be to deduce the value of Δ_S and Δ_R which remain unknown at this moment. In order to achieve this, the attacker will now

---

[2] We note that it is not necessary that the message is fixed. Just for the simplicity of description, we use a fixed message here and in subsequent sections.

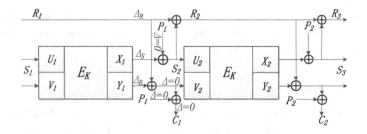

Fig. 4. The first step of the attack.

try to insert a difference in P_1 in a hope that it will be equal to Δ_S. If his choice is right, one can see from Fig. 5 that he will cancel the difference in U_2 and that the difference appearing on the next ciphertext block C_2 (for a plaintext block P_2 without difference) will necessarily be Δ_R. A key observation is that since no difference will be present any more on the input of the incoming block cipher call, the difference on C_2 will remain Δ_R **whatever the choice on the value of P_1.** To summarize, if the attacker adds the difference Δ_S in P_1, then the difference in C_2 will remain the same (i.e. Δ_R) whatever the value of P_1 is. This behavior is what the attacker will use to detect when he makes the right choice for the difference insertion in P_1.

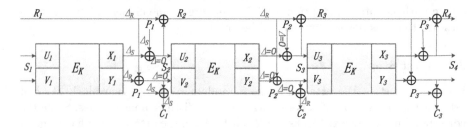

Fig. 5. The second step of the attack.

The detailed procedure to find Δ_S is as follows. Firstly, the attacker constructs two tables as depicted in Fig. 6, each having $2^{n/2}$ three-tuples of one-block plaintexts, such that all pairs created by taking one element from each of these two tables will correspond to all the 2^n possible differences on a n-bit value. More precisely, let $\langle i \rangle$ denote the integer i in a $n/2$-bit binary representation[3]. One table $\mathcal{T}_1$ is $\{\,(\,\langle 0 \rangle \| \langle i \rangle,\ \langle 1 \rangle \| \langle i \rangle,\ \langle 2 \rangle \| \langle i \rangle\,)\,\}$, where i ranges over all $n/2$-bit values.[4] We denote by $(\,\langle 0 \rangle \| \langle i \rangle,\ \langle 1 \rangle \| \langle i \rangle,\ \langle 2 \rangle \| \langle i \rangle\,)$ the i-th element of $\mathcal{T}_1$. The other table $\mathcal{T}_2$ is $\{\,(\,\langle j \rangle \| \langle 0 \rangle,\ \langle 1 \oplus j \rangle \| \langle 0 \rangle,\ \langle 2 \oplus j \rangle \| \langle 0 \rangle\,)\,\}$, where j

---

[3] Typically n is 64, or 128, i.e. even integers.

[4] Note that the attacker can use any three distinct constants other than $\langle 0 \rangle, \langle 1 \rangle$, and $\langle 2 \rangle$ to construct the tables. Here we use these particular constants just for the simplicity of notations.

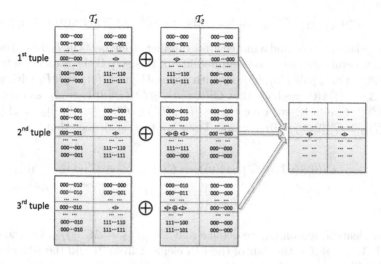

Fig. 6. The tables T_1 and T_2. An example of element pair for difference $\langle j \rangle \| \langle i \rangle$.

ranges over all $n/2$-bit values. Similarly we denote the j-th element of T_2 by $(\langle j \rangle \| \langle 0 \rangle, \langle 1 \oplus j \rangle \| \langle 0 \rangle, \langle 2 \oplus j \rangle \| \langle 0 \rangle)$. The pairwise differences between T_1 and T_2 are $\{ (\langle 0 \rangle \| \langle i \rangle) \oplus (\langle j \rangle \| \langle 0 \rangle) = \langle j \rangle \| \langle i \rangle \}$, where i and j independently range over all $n/2$-bit values. Thus, one can see that it covers all the possible differences of one-block n-bit plaintext. In particular, although each element is a 3-tuple of plaintexts and hence each pair consist of three n-bit differences by XORing the corresponding plaintexts, these differences are all equal, i.e., $(\langle 0 \rangle \| \langle i \rangle) \oplus (\langle j \rangle \| \langle 0 \rangle) = (\langle 1 \rangle \| \langle i \rangle) \oplus (\langle 1 \oplus j \rangle \| \langle 0 \rangle) = (\langle 2 \rangle \| \langle i \rangle) \oplus (\langle 2 \oplus j \rangle \| \langle 0 \rangle)$.

Secondly, the attacker selects a random one-block plaintext P_2. For each element $(\langle 0 \rangle \| \langle i \rangle, \langle 1 \rangle \| \langle i \rangle, \langle 2 \rangle \| \langle i \rangle)$ in table T_1, he uses separately the three plaintext block values as the first block P_1, concatenates them with P_2 as the second block, and makes three encryption queries with the nonce IV to receive the three corresponding ciphertexts. Then, the attacker computes the pairwise differences on the second block of these ciphertexts. In details, let $C[\langle 0 \rangle \| \langle i \rangle]_2$, $C[\langle 1 \rangle \| \langle i \rangle]_2$ and $C[\langle 2 \rangle \| \langle i \rangle]_2$ denote the second ciphertext blocks corresponding to $\langle 0 \rangle \| \langle i \rangle \| P_2$, $\langle 1 \rangle \| \langle i \rangle \| P_2$ and $\langle 2 \rangle \| \langle i \rangle \| P_2$ respectively. The attacker computes the following two n-bit differences and stores them.

$$\Delta C[\langle i \rangle]_1 = C[\langle 1 \rangle \| \langle i \rangle]_2 \oplus C[\langle 0 \rangle \| \langle i \rangle]_2, \quad \Delta C[\langle i \rangle]_2 = C[\langle 2 \rangle \| \langle i \rangle]_2 \oplus C[\langle 0 \rangle \| \langle i \rangle]_2.$$

Similarly, for each element of the second table T_2, the attacker makes encryption queries with the above P_2 as the second block and IV' as the nonce to receive the ciphertexts, and then computes the pairwise differences of the second ciphertext blocks, denoted as $(\Delta C'[\langle i \rangle]_1, \Delta C'[\langle i \rangle]_2)$. Then he matches the differences to previously stored $\{ (\Delta C[\langle i \rangle]_1, \Delta C[\langle i \rangle]_2) \}$. Once a matched pair is found, the attacker computes Δ_R and Δ_S from the corresponding plaintexts and ciphertexts as follows

$$\Delta_R = C[\langle 0 \rangle \| \langle i \rangle]_2 \oplus C'[\langle j \rangle \| \langle 0 \rangle]_2, \quad \Delta_S = (\langle 0 \rangle \| \langle i \rangle) \oplus (\langle j \rangle \| \langle 0 \rangle) = \langle j \rangle \| \langle i \rangle.$$

If the attacker does not find a match after running all elements in T_2, he outputs 0.

Now we evaluate the success probability of this step if the attacker interacts with JAMBU. For a pair $(\langle 0 \rangle \| \langle i \rangle) \| P_2$ with nonce IV and $(\langle j \rangle \| \langle 0 \rangle) \| P_2$ with nonce IV', if $\Delta_S = \langle j \rangle \| \langle i \rangle$, we have that $C[\langle 0 \rangle \| \langle i \rangle]_2 \oplus C'[\langle j \rangle \| \langle 0 \rangle]_2 = \Delta_R$ as explained in Sect. 3.2. Similarly, we have that $C[\langle 1 \rangle \| \langle i \rangle]_2 \oplus C'[\langle 1 \oplus j \rangle \| \langle 0 \rangle]_2 = \Delta_R$ and $C[\langle 2 \rangle \| \langle i \rangle]_2 \oplus C'[\langle 2 \oplus j \rangle \| \langle 0 \rangle]_2 = \Delta_R$. Then, we further deduce that

$$C[\langle 0 \rangle \| \langle i \rangle]_2 \oplus C'[\langle j \rangle \| \langle 0 \rangle]_2 = C[\langle 1 \rangle \| \langle i \rangle]_2 \oplus C'[\langle 1 \oplus j \rangle \| \langle 0 \rangle]_2$$
$$\Rightarrow \quad C[\langle 0 \rangle \| \langle i \rangle]_2 \oplus C[\langle 1 \rangle \| \langle i \rangle]_2 = C'[\langle j \rangle \| \langle 0 \rangle]_2 \oplus C'[\langle 1 \oplus j \rangle \| \langle 0 \rangle]_2$$
$$\Rightarrow \quad \Delta C[\langle i \rangle]_1 = \Delta C'[\langle j \rangle]_1$$

With an identical reasoning, we deduce that $\Delta C[\langle i \rangle]_2 = \Delta C'[\langle j \rangle]_2$. On the other hand, if $\Delta_S \neq \langle j \rangle \| \langle i \rangle$, the pair of the i-th element from T_1 and the j-th element from T_2 will have to satisfy the two n-bit equality conditions randomly, which will happen with probability 2^{-2n}. Since there are in total 2^n such pairs, the probability of faulty positive pairs is negligible. Hence, the attacker gets the correct values of Δ_S and Δ_R with a probability very close to 1.

3.5   Third Step

Finally, in the third and last step, the attacker will choose a random one-block value P_1 such that P_1 and $P_1 \oplus \Delta_S$ have never been queried before as first plaintext block (he can simply keep track of the previously queried P_1 values). Then, he will pick a random value for the second plaintext block P_2 and ask the encryption of the message $(P_1 \| P_2)$ with the nonce IV. He receives ciphertext blocks C_1 and C_2 from the encryption oracle. Then the attacker asks the encryption of another message $(P_1 \oplus \Delta_S \| P_2)$ with the nonce IV', and receives ciphertext blocks C_1' and C_2'. Then he computes $C_2 \oplus C_2'$, and compares it to Δ_R. If $C_2 \oplus C_2' = \Delta_R$ holds, the attacker outputs 1. Otherwise, the attacker outputs 0.

One can easily evaluate the advantage of the attacker. For JAMBU, he will output 1 with a probability equal to 1. On the other hand, for a random authenticated encryption, he outputs 1 with a probability of 2^{-n}. Therefore, the advantage of the attacker is almost 1.

3.6   Attack and Complexity Summary

To summarize, our attack requires in total about $O(2^{n/2})$ encryption queries and computations, and can be divided into three parts:

- **first step** ($2^{n/2}$ encryption queries and computations): the attacker picks a plaintext block P_1 and queries encryption of this block for $2^{n/2}$ distinct nonces. He keeps the nonce pair (IV, IV') that leads to a collision on the ciphertext block C_1.

- **second step** ($O(2^{n/2})$ encryption queries and computations): the attacker picks a random second plaintext block P_2 and a random $n/2$-bit value I and queries the encryption of the $2^{n/2}$ plaintext blocks $P_1 = (0^{n/2}\|I)$ concatenated with P_2 with nonce IV and the encryption of the $2^{n/2}$ plaintext blocks $P_1 = (I\|0^{n/2})$ concatenated with P_2 with nonce IV'. He repeats the process with a few other constant values instead of $0^{n/2}$ in order to improve the filtering, and he eventually deduces the value of Δ_S by checking which difference applied in P_1 leads to the same difference in C_2 whatever is the choice of I. He directly deduces that this difference on C_2 is actually Δ_R.
- **third step** (2 encryption queries and computations): the attacker picks a random value P_1 such that P_1 and $P_1 \oplus \Delta_S$ have never been queried before, and asks the encryption oracle for the ciphertext corresponding to the message $(P_1\|P_2)$ with nonce IV. He receives $(C_1\|C_2)$. Then he queries the encryption of $(P_1 \oplus \Delta_S\|P_2)$ with nonce IV' and receive $(C_1'\|C_2')$. Finally he checks if $C_2' \oplus C_2 = \Delta_R$ holds.

We remark that for JAMBU-AES [14], we have $n = 64$ and thus the confidentiality security is only around 32 bits in the nonce-misuse attack model. Thus, our cryptanalysis invalidates the confidentiality claims of the JAMBU designers.

3.7   Extension to a Plaintext-Recovery Attack

Our distinguishing attack can be extended to a more powerful plaintext-recovery attack in a straightforward way. The setting is as follows. Note that our attack is in the chosen-plaintext model, and hence the attacker requires only the encryption algorithm of JAMBU. In other words he is given access to an encryption oracle of JAMBU instantiated with a randomly selected key that is secret to the attacker. He is allowed to query any plaintext of his own choice and gets the corresponding ciphertext. In the end, the attacker is required to choose a new (nonce, ciphertext) pair[5] and to produce a corresponding plaintext for it. If the plaintext is indeed valid and if the prefix to its last block has never been queried before, then the plaintext-recovery attack is said to succeed (the reason of these restrictions is detailed in the discussion on trivial attacks in Sect. 3.8).

The procedure is as follows and it also has three steps. The first two steps are exactly the same as the first two steps of the distinguishing attack detailed in Sects. 3.3 and 3.4, and we adopt the same notations. In the third and last step, the attacker will choose a random value P_1 such that P_1 and $P_1 \oplus \Delta_S$ have never been queried before as first plaintext block under the nonce IV and IV'. Then, he will pick a random value for the second plaintext block P_2 and ask the encryption of the message $(P_1\|P_2)$ with the nonce IV. He receives ciphertext blocks C_1 and C_2 from the encryption oracle. Since he knows the value of Δ_R and Δ_S, he will be sure that if he applies the difference Δ_S on P_1 with nonce IV', he

---

[5] We note that here the attack is only to analyze processing of plaintext/ciphertex of JAMBU, that is confidentiality of encryption, and hence relaxes the setting such that the attacker is not required to provide the tag for his choice of (nonce, ciphertext) pair.

will get difference Δ_S on C_1 and difference Δ_R on C_2. Therefore, he can predict the plaintext $(P_1 \oplus \Delta_S, P_2 \oplus \Delta_R)$ corresponding to ciphertext $(C_1 \oplus \Delta_S || C_2)$ with nonce IV'. Moreover, it is easy to see that $(C_1 \oplus \Delta_S || C_2)$ is not a prefix of any of previous returned ciphertext of the encryption of JAMBU, since the first ciphertext block is a permutation of the first plaintext block under the same nonce, and since $P_1 \oplus \Delta_S$ has not been queried before as the first plaintext block under IV' to the encryption oracle. One might argue that P_1 is the first plaintext block and this is included in the security exclusions in the JAMBU security claims. However, we have used P_1 for simplicity of description, but the attack remains the same with any amount of random message blocks prepended to P_1.

The complexity of the above plaintext-recovery attacks is also $O(2^{n/2})$ encryption queries and computations. The success probability is almost 1 (we omit the detailed evaluation since it is similar to the distinguishing attack).

3.8   Discussion on Trivial Attacks

Recently, Rogaway claimed a *generic* plaintext-recovery attack on online authenticated encryption in the nonce-misuse setting [10]. His attack adopts divide-and-conquer strategy and recovers the plaintext block by block. In details, the attacker uses the recovered first $i-1$ plaintext blocks as prefix, guesses the i-th plaintext block, and verifies the correctness by sending it to encryption oracle and comparing the received i-th ciphertext block with the i-th target ciphertext block. However, obviously this attack essentially just reveals again the inherent weakness of online authenticated encryption that has been known before and has been also explicitly pointed out by the designer of JAMBU: common prefix plaintext blocks produces the same corresponding ciphertext blocks. In particular, the attacker has to query a plaintext to the encryption oracle, then receive a ciphertext that is exactly the same as the target ciphertext, and then output this plaintext as the correct plaintext. As a comparison, in our plaintext recovery setting, we explicitly exclude such rather trivial attacks by restricting that the last block of the target ciphertext (or plaintext) must not share its prefix with any previously returned ciphertext from the encryption oracle.

One can also think of the following trivial distinguishing attack on JAMBU and several other CAESAR candidates. For an ideal online authenticated encryption as defined in [1,7], the i-th plaintext block should be input to a random permutation to produce the i-th ciphertext block, where the index of the random permutation is determined by the nonce, the associated data and the first $i-1$ plaintext blocks. On the other hand, for JAMBU the i-th plaintext block is simply XORed to an internal state: $C_i = P_i \oplus V_{i+1}$, where the value of V_{i+1} is determined by the nonce, the associated data and the first $i-1$ plaintext blocks. Hence, $\Delta C_i = \Delta P_i$ always holds under the same nonce, the same associated data and the same first $i-1$ plaintext blocks. In details, an attacker queries a nonce IV and a one-block plaintext P_1 to the encryption oracle, and receives a ciphertext C_1. He then queries the same nonce IV and another one-block plaintext P_1' to the encryption, and receives a ciphertext C_1'. If $C_1 \oplus C_1' = P_1 \oplus P_1'$ holds, the attacker outputs 1. Otherwise, he outputs 0. This distinguishing attack can trivially be extended to a plaintext-recovery attack on single-block ciphertexts.

As a comparison, our attacks reveal a specific weakness of JAMBU: when processing plaintext blocks, it uses only one invocation to a small block cipher ($2n$ bits) to update a larger state ($3n$ bits). Such a design choice obviously favours efficiency, but our attacks imply that there is a greater security compromise to pay than originally expected by the JAMBU designers.

4   Attack on JAMBU in Nonce-Respecting Scenario

In this section, we analyse the confidentiality security of JAMBU in the nonce-respecting scenario. JAMBU claims a $2n$-bit confidentiality security (or 128-bit security for AES-JAMBU) in this setting. However, the claim statement does not contain any specification on the attack model considered (IND-CPA, IND-CCA1 or IND-CCA2). Hence, one may wonder if JAMBU can achieve such a confidentiality security level under all (previously known) attack models[6]. We note that the adaptive chosen-ciphertext security (IND-CCA2) of JAMBU can be trivially broken with 2^n queries by reusing messages with common prefixes (see Sect. 4.4). However, our distinguishing attack works with prefixes not previously queried. Furthermore, our method can be extended to a more powerful plaintext-recovery attack.

4.1   Confidentiality Under an Adaptive Chosen-Ciphertext Attack

For an authenticated encryption scheme $(\mathcal{E}_K, \mathcal{D}_K)$ with a key space $\mathcal{K}$, its confidentiality security under adaptive chosen-ciphertext attacks has been defined in [2], usually referred to as IND-CCA2. Here we provide a brief description, and refer interested readers to [2] for the full formal definition. Let $\mathcal{RO}$ denote a random oracle that has the same output bit length as $\mathcal{E}_K$ on every input plaintext. Let $\mathbb{D}$ be a distinguisher that interacts with $(\mathcal{E}_K, \mathcal{D}_K)$ or $(\mathcal{RO}, \mathcal{D}_K)$, and outputs one bit. Its advantage is defined as:

$$\mathbf{Adv}_{\mathcal{E}}^{cca2}(\mathbb{D}) := \Pr\left[K \xleftarrow{\$} \mathcal{K}, \mathbb{D}^{\mathcal{E}_K, \mathcal{D}_K} \Rightarrow 1\right] - \Pr\left[K \xleftarrow{\$} \mathcal{K}, \mathbb{D}^{\mathcal{RO}, \mathcal{D}_K} \Rightarrow 1\right].$$

Then we define $\mathbf{Adv}_{\mathcal{E}}^{cca2}(t, q, \sigma, \ell) := \max_{\mathbb{D}} \mathbf{Adv}_{\mathcal{E}}^{cca}(\mathbb{D})$, where the maximum is taken over all distinguishers that run in time t and makes q queries, each of length at most ℓ blocks and of total length at most σ blocks. The distinguisher must not make two queries with the same nonce to the encryption oracle that is $\mathcal{E}_K$ or $\mathcal{RO}$. Moreover, we assume the distinguisher does not query the outputs from one oracle to the other oracle. Namely, he does not query the received ciphertext from $\mathcal{E}_K$ or $\mathcal{RO}$ to $\mathcal{D}_K$, and does not query the received plaintext from $\mathcal{D}_K$ to $\mathcal{E}_K$ or $\mathcal{RO}$. These assumptions aim at preventing trivial distinguishing attacks.

---

[6] Yet we trivially observe that JAMBU can only achieve 2^n confidentiality security in the IND-CCA3 model [12] (and not the expected 2^{2n}), due to its n-bit tag size.

4.2   Distinguishing Attack

We notice that JAMBU uses an n-bit tag. Therefore, one can always obtain the corresponding plaintext for a ciphertext of his own choice from the decryption oracle by making at most 2^n queries, i.e., by exhaustively guessing the tag value. Based on this observation, we can transform the distinguishing attack in the nonce-misuse setting detailed in Sect. 3 to a distinguishing attack in nonce-respecting setting, with a complexity increase by a factor 2^n and hence with a total complexity of $2^{3n/2}$, which is lower than the $2n$-bit security one might expect.

In details, the attack in the nonce-misuse setting consists of three steps, and the repeating nonces requirement happens in steps 2 and 3. Thus, we will mainly modify these two steps. We adopt the same notation as Sect. 3.

First Step. The procedure is exactly the same as before. For the plaintext P_1, its ciphertext is denoted as C_1 under the nonce IV and as C_1' under the nonce IV'. Then we denote $V[IV]_2 = P_1 \oplus C_1$ and $V[IV']_2 = P_1 \oplus C_1'$.

Second Step. Firstly, the attacker constructs tables T_1 and T_2 as before. Secondly, he selects a random one-block ciphertext block C_2. For each element $(\langle 0 \rangle \| \langle i \rangle, \langle 1 \rangle \| \langle i \rangle, \langle 2 \rangle \| \langle i \rangle)$ in table T_1, he executes a similar procedure to interact with the decryption oracle for each of $\langle 0 \rangle \| \langle i \rangle$, $\langle 1 \rangle \| \langle i \rangle$ and $\langle 2 \rangle \| \langle i \rangle$. Here we use $\langle 0 \rangle \| \langle i \rangle$ as an example to describe this procedure. The attacker computes $V[IV]_2 \oplus (\langle 0 \rangle \| \langle i \rangle)$ as the first ciphertext block, concatenates it with C_2 as the second block, and queries the constructed two-block ciphertext to the decryption oracle with the nonce IV and with a random selected tag value. If the decryption oracle returns a failure symbol $\perp$, the attacker changes the tag to a new value, and makes a decryption query with the same nonce and the same ciphertext. He will repeat such decryption queries by exhaustively trying new tag values until the decryption oracle returns a plaintext instead of $\perp$. In the returned plaintext, it is easy to get that the first block is $\langle 0 \rangle \| \langle i \rangle$, and we denote its second block as $P[\langle 0 \rangle \| \langle i \rangle]_2$. Similarly, we define notations $P[\langle 1 \rangle \| \langle i \rangle]_2$ and $P[\langle 2 \rangle \| \langle i \rangle]_2$ for the second plaintext block corresponding to $\langle 1 \rangle \| \langle i \rangle$ and $\langle 2 \rangle \| \langle i \rangle$ respectively. Once a plaintext obtained, the attacker computes the pairwise differences of the second plaintext blocks as follows:

$$\Delta P[\langle i \rangle]_1 = P[\langle 1 \rangle \| \langle i \rangle]_2 \oplus P[\langle 0 \rangle \| \langle i \rangle]_2, \quad \Delta P[\langle i \rangle]_2 = P[\langle 2 \rangle \| \langle i \rangle]_2 \oplus P[\langle 0 \rangle \| \langle i \rangle]_2.$$

For each element of the other table T_2, the attacker makes similar decryption queries, but using IV' as nonce and $V[IV']_2$ to compute the first ciphertext blocks. We denote the computed pairwise differences of the second plaintext blocks as $(\Delta P'[\langle j \rangle]_1, \Delta P'[\langle j \rangle]_2)$. The attacker matches the differences to previously stored $\{ (\Delta P[\langle i \rangle]_1, \Delta P[\langle i \rangle]_2) \}$. Once a matched pair is found, the attacker computes Δ_R and Δ_S from the corresponding plaintexts and ciphertexts as follows:

$$\Delta_R = P[\langle 0 \rangle \| \langle i \rangle]_2 \oplus P'[\langle j \rangle \| \langle 0 \rangle]_2, \quad \Delta_S = (\langle 0 \rangle \| \langle i \rangle) \oplus (\langle j \rangle \| \langle 0 \rangle) = \langle j \rangle \| \langle i \rangle.$$

If no match is found after trying all elements in T_2, the attacker outputs 0.

Third Step. The attacker selects a random one block C_1 such that C_1 and $C_1 \oplus \Delta_S$ have not been queried before as a first block of ciphertext under the nonces IV and IV'. Then, he selects another random block C_2. Firstly, the attacker makes queries $C_1 \| C_2$ to the decryption oracle with the nonce IV by exhaustively guessing the tag until he receives the plaintext, where the second plaintext block is denoted as P_2. Secondly, the attacker makes queries $C_1 \oplus \Delta_S \| C_2$ to the decryption oracle with the nonce IV' by exhaustively guessing the tag until he receives the plaintext, where the second plaintext block is denoted as P_2'. Finally, he computes $\Delta P_2 = P_2 \oplus P_2'$, and compares it to Δ_R. If $\Delta P_2 = \Delta_R$, the attacker outputs 1. Otherwise, he outputs 0.

The overall complexity is dominated by step 2, which is upper bounded by $O(2^{3n/2})$ (or 2^{96} for AES-JAMBU). The advantage of the distinguisher is almost 1 (we omit the detailed evaluation since it is similar with that of the attacks in previous sections).

4.3 Extension to a Plaintext-Recovery Attack

The plaintext-recovery attack setting is as follows. The attacker is given access to both encryption and decryption oracles of JAMBU instantiated with a randomly selected key that is secret to the attacker. He is allowed to make encryption and decryption queries of his own choice. Note that he must not make two encryption queries with the same nonce. In the end, the attacker is required to choose a nonce and a ciphertext (where the last block of the ciphertext must not have the same prefix than the last blocks of any previously outputted or queried ciphertext under the same nonce) and to produce a corresponding plaintext for it. If the plaintext is indeed valid, the plaintext-recovery attack is said to succeed.

The attack procedure is similar with that of distinguishing attacks from Sect. 4.2. The first two steps are exactly the same, and we adopt the same notations. In the third and last step, the attacker will choose a random one-block value C_1 such that C_1 and $C_1 \oplus \Delta_S$ have never been outputted as the first ciphertext block from the encryption oracle and have never been queried to the decryption oracle as first ciphertext block under the nonce IV and IV'. Then, he will pick a random value for the second plaintext block C_2 and interact with the decryption oracle to receive the plaintext $P_1 \| P_2$ of the ciphertext $(C_1 \| C_2)$ under the nonce IV. Since he knows the value of Δ_R and Δ_S, he will be sure that if he applies the difference Δ_S on P_1 with nonce IV', he will get difference Δ_S on C_1 and difference Δ_R on C_2. Therefore, he can predict the plaintext $(P_1 \oplus \Delta_S, P_2 \oplus \Delta_R)$ corresponding to ciphertext $(C_1 \oplus \Delta_S \| C_2)$ with nonce IV'.

The complexity of the above plaintext-recovery attacks is $O(2^{3n/2})$ encryption queries and computations (or 2^{96} for AES-JAMBU), and its success probability is almost 1 (we omit the detailed evaluation, since it is similar to the distinguishing attack).

4.4 Discussion on Trivial Attacks

In the nonce-respecting scenario, although the attacker cannot make two encryption queries with the same nonce, he is allowed to repeat nonces during the interaction with the decryption oracle. Hence, if he makes more than 2^n decryption queries, he will obtain more than one pair of plaintext and ciphertext under the same nonce. As a result, this leads to several trivial attacks (similar to the trivial attacks on JAMBU in the adaptive chosen-ciphertext attack model described in Sect. 3.8). For example, the attacker can interact with the decryption oracle to receive a plaintext P_1 for nonce IV and a one-block ciphertext C_1, and then interact with the encryption oracle to receive a ciphertext C_1' for a random one-block plaintext P_1' with the same nonce IV. Finally he checks if $P_1 \oplus C_1 = P_1' \oplus C_1'$ holds. We refer to Sect. 3.8 for more discussions on trivial attacks on JAMBU.

5 Implementation of the Attack

We have implemented the attack on AES-JAMBU for the nonce-misuse scenario as described in Sect. 3 and we have verified the special differential structure from Fig. 5. For simplicity, the associated data was set to be empty, and the 128-bit key was set to 0x100f0e0d0c0b0a090807060504030201.

5.1 Results of the Attack

In the first step of the attack, we chose a random 64-bit plaintext P_1 and asked for encryption under different nonce values. With 2^{32} encryption queries, we found a collision on a pair of ciphertexts C_1, C_1' with a pair of nonce values IV, IV' (see Table 2).

Table 2. First step of the attack

K :	01 02 03 04 05 06 07 08 09 0a 0b 0c 0d 0e 0f 10
IV :	b1 ef 89 a0 4e 21 30 bd
IV' :	10 5a 1f 5b 34 49 1e 5c
P_1 :	7f 95 77 ca 09 77 a8 a5
C_1 :	2d 2b 58 18 fa f5 af f1
C_1' :	2d 2b 58 18 fa f5 af f1

With this pair of nonce values, we proceeded to the second step of the attack, P_2 being set to zero for simplicity. We constructed the tables $\mathcal{T}_1$ and $\mathcal{T}_2$ and by matching the differences in the second block of ciphertexts, we obtained the values of Δ_S and Δ_R. Table 3 shows the first tuple of the pair of plaintexts and ciphertexts tables with the matching difference.

Table 3. Second step of the attack

$\langle j \rangle \| \langle 0 \rangle \|$	P_2	: 60 28 6d 74 00 00 00 00 00 00 00 00 00 00 00 00
	$C'[\langle j \rangle \| \langle 0 \rangle]_2$:	af 45 56 9e 26 c6 7e d0
$\langle 0 \rangle \| \langle i \rangle \|$	P_2	: 00 00 00 00 93 47 1e 92 00 00 00 00 00 00 00 00
	$C[\langle 0 \rangle \| \langle i \rangle]_2$:	73 79 44 54 a7 b4 5b 4c
	Δ_S	: 60 28 6d 74 93 47 1e 92
	Δ_R :	dc 3c 12 ca 81 72 25 9c

In the third step, we chose a random 128-bit plaintext $(P_1 \| P_2)$ and asked for its encryption with nonce IV. Upon receiving the ciphertext $(C_1 \| C_2)$, we deduced the ciphertext $(C_1^D \| C_2^D) = (C_1 \oplus \Delta_S \| C_2 \oplus \Delta_R)$ for the plaintext $(P_1 \oplus \Delta_S \| P_2)$ with nonce IV' without querying it to the encryption oracle. Finally, we checked that by asking for the encryption of the plaintext $(P_1 \oplus \Delta_S \| P_2)$ with nonce IV', the ciphertext $(C_1' \| C_2')$ obtained is indeed what we had deduced (as can be seen from Table 4).

Table 4. Third step of the attack

IV	: b1 ef 89 a0 4e 21 30 bd
$P_1 \| P_2$	: 95 d9 43 9e 0b 4d 6d 27 6a ba db 0a 12 f8 13 45
$C_1 \| C_2$	: c7 67 6c 4c f8 cf 6a 73 6b 05 9b c6 fc e6 7a ee
Δ_S	: 60 28 6d 74 93 47 1e 92
Δ_R :	dc 3c 12 ca 81 72 25 9c
$C_1^D \| C_2^D$	: a7 4f 01 38 6b 88 74 e1 b7 39 89 0c 7d 94 5f 72
IV'	: 10 5a 1f 5b 34 49 1e 5c
$P_1 \oplus \Delta_S \| P_2$	: f5 f1 2e ea 98 0a 73 b5 6a ba db 0a 12 f8 13 45
$C_1' \| C_2'$	: a7 4f 01 38 6b 88 74 e1 b7 39 89 0c 7d 94 5f 72

The codes for the attack on AES-JAMBU are included in the supporting document, they are separated in two main codes - Step 1 and Step 2 of the attack, AES-NI is used for running AES-JAMBU.

5.2 Running Time of the Attack

For the first step of the attack, it took about 3.7 h and 36 GB of memory to find a collision. While for the second step of the attack, it took about 8.8 h and 320 GB to find Δ_S and Δ_R.

For the second step of the attack, one can do a trade-off between the computation time and memory requirement. For instance, instead of constructing tables of 2^{32} elements, one can construct tables of 2^{30} (or 2^{28} respectively) elements and the computation time takes about 2.2 h (or 0.5 h respectively) and 80 GB (or 20 GB respectively) of memory. However, in this case, one would have to guess the 2 (or 4 respectively) most significant bits of the difference values i and j. Hence, by repeating the attack procedure 16 times (or 256 times respectively), the value of Δ_S and Δ_R can be recovered by enumerating all the possible most significant bits values.

Conclusion

In this article, we have proposed a cryptanalysis of the confidentiality of JAMBU in both the nonce-misuse and nonce-respecting models. Namely, we have shown that one can break confidentiality in the nonce-misuse scenario with 2^{32} computations and queries, while having access to only the encryption oracle. For the nonce-respecting, we show that our attack can be extended to break confidentiality security of JAMBU with 2^{96} computations and queries in the adaptive chosen-ciphertext attack model, with message prefixes not previously queried.

It would be an interesting future work to study how JAMBU could be patched to resist these attacks. We believe that one simple possibility would be to output P_{i-1} instead of P_i during round i (while keeping the insertion of P_i in the internal state). This would probably prevent our attack since the last block of the distinguishing plaintext/ciphertext pair would have the exact same prefix than the last block of previously queried pairs.

Acknowledgements. The authors would like to thank the JAMBU designers (Hongjun Wu and Tao Huang), Tetsu Iwata and the anonymous referees for their helpful comments. The authors are supported by the Singapore National Research Foundation Fellowship 2012 (NRF-NRFF2012-06).

References

1. Andreeva, E., Bogdanov, A., Luykx, A., Mennink, B., Tischhauser, E., Yasuda, K.: Parallelizable and authenticated online ciphers. In: Sako, K., Sarkar, P. (eds.) ASIACRYPT 2013, Part I. LNCS, vol. 8269, pp. 424–443. Springer, Heidelberg (2013)
2. Bellare, M., Desai, A., Jokipii, E., Rogaway, P.: A concrete security treatment of symmetric encryption. In: 38th Annual Symposium on Foundations of Computer Science, FOCS 1997, Miami Beach, Florida, USA, October 19–22, 1997, pp. 394–403. IEEE Computer Society (1997)
3. Bellare, M., Namprempre, C.: Authenticated encryption: relations among notions and analysis of the generic composition paradigm. In: Okamoto, T. (ed.) ASIACRYPT 2000. LNCS, vol. 1976, pp. 531–545. Springer, Heidelberg (2000)
4. Bellare, M., Namprempre, C.: Authenticated encryption: relations among notions and analysis of the generic composition paradigm. J. Cryptol. **21**(4), 469–491 (2008)
5. Bernstein, D.: CAESAR Competition. http://competitions.cr.yp.to/caesar.html

6. Daemen, J., Rijmen, V.: The Design of Rijndael: AES - The Advanced Encryption Standard. Information Security and Cryptography. Springer, Heidelberg (2002)

7. Fleischmann, E., Forler, C., Lucks, S.: McOE: a family of almost foolproof on-line authenticated encryption schemes. In: Canteaut, A. (ed.) FSE 2012. LNCS, vol. 7549, pp. 196–215. Springer, Heidelberg (2012)

8. Katz, J., Yung, M.: Complete characterization of security notions for probabilistic private-key encryption. In: Yao, F.F., Luks, E.M. (eds.) Proceedings of the Thirty-Second Annual ACM Symposium on Theory of Computing, May 21–23, 2000, pp. 245–254. ACM, Portland (2000)

9. Rogaway, P.: Efficient instantiations of tweakable blockciphers and refinements to modes OCB and PMAC. In: Lee, P.J. (ed.) ASIACRYPT 2004. LNCS, vol. 3329, pp. 16–31. Springer, Heidelberg (2004)

10. Rogaway, P.: Let's not Call It MR (2014). http://web.cs.ucdavis.edu/rogaway/beer.pdf

11. Rogaway, P., Bellare, M., Black, J.: OCB: a block-cipher mode of operation for efficient authenticated encryption. ACM Trans. Inf. Syst. Secur. 6(3), 365–403 (2003)

12. Rogaway, P., Shrimpton, T.: A provable-security treatment of the key-wrap problem. In: Vaudenay, S. (ed.) EUROCRYPT 2006. LNCS, vol. 4004, pp. 373–390. Springer, Heidelberg (2006)

13. Frankel, S., Glenn, R., Kelly, S.: The AES-CBC Cipher Algorithm and Its Use with IPsec. Network Working Group, RFC 3602, September 2003

14. Wu, H., Huang, T.: JAMBU Lightweight Authenticated Encryption Mode and AES-JAMBU (v1). Submitted to the CAESAR competition, March 2014

Related-Key Forgeries for Prøst-OTR

Christoph Dobraunig, Maria Eichlseder$^{(\boxtimes)}$, and Florian Mendel

IAIK, Graz University of Technology, Graz, Austria
maria.eichlseder@iaik.tugraz.at

Abstract. We present a forgery attack on Prøst-OTR in a related-key setting. Prøst is a family of authenticated encryption algorithms proposed as candidates in the currently ongoing CAESAR competition, and Prøst-OTR is one of the three variants of the Prøst design. The attack exploits how the Prøst permutation is used in an Even-Mansour construction in the Feistel-based OTR mode of operation. Given the ciphertext and tag for any two messages under two related keys K and $K \oplus \Delta$ with related nonces, we can forge the ciphertext and tag for a modified message under K. If we can query ciphertexts for chosen messages under $K \oplus \Delta$, we can achieve almost universal forgery for K. The computational complexity is negligible.

Keywords: CAESAR competition · Cryptanalysis · Prøst · Authenticated encryption · Related-key

1 Introduction

Due to the currently ongoing CAESAR competition for authenticated encryption [25], the new favourite toy of the cryptographic community are clearly authenticated ciphers. A significant collective effort will be necessary to judge the 57 submitted candidate ciphers with respect to their security and applicability. The goal of this cryptographic competition is to identify a portfolio of reliable, efficient, secure authenticated encryption algorithms with unique features for different application scenarios. Experience with previous competitions and focused projects like AES, SHA-3, eSTREAM and NESSIE has clearly demonstrated that the joint effort of the community to focus on a particular topic can impressively advance the understanding of the reasearched primitives in a relatively short period of time. Right now, first security analyses of the submitted candidates are necessary to allow the competition committee to judge the first-round candidates adequately, and select the most promising submissions for the next round.

Prøst, designed by Kavun et al. [16], is one of the candidates submitted to the CAESAR competition. It combines a newly designed, efficient permutation, the Prøst permutation, with several modes of operation. The resulting Prøst family of authenticated ciphers consists of three variants: Prøst-COPA, Prøst-OTR, and Prøst-APE, each with its own advantages and features. The Prøst-OTR variant uses the Prøst permutation in a single-key Even-Mansour construction [9,11,12]

© International Association for Cryptologic Research 2015
G. Leander (Ed.): FSE 2015, LNCS 9054, pp. 282–296, 2015.
DOI: 10.1007/978-3-662-48116-5_14

as a block cipher in Minematsu's provably secure, Feistel-based OTR mode of operation [21]. Due to the novelty of the design, previous cryptanalysis results on Prøst itself are limited to the designers' own analysis, published together with the design document [16].

We present a forgery attack on Prøst-OTR in a related-key setting. The scenario is that an attacker is given ciphertexts and tags of two messages: one under the target key K, and one under a related key $K \oplus \Delta$ for some arbitrary Δ. Both keys are secret, but their difference Δ is known to the attacker. The nonces used for encrypting the two messages are also related in a similar way. Then, with negligible computational complexity, the attacker can forge the ciphertext and authentication tag for a third message under the target key K. In fact, depending on the length of the original messages, forgeries for a large number of fake messages can be obtained. In addition, in case the attacker has control over one of the two originally encrypted messages, he can even control the content of the third, forged message.

Our attack is generic and exploits the combination of the OTR mode of operation with an Even-Mansour block cipher construction. It is independent of the used permutation, and thus does not use any particular properties or weaknesses of the Prøst permutation. Consequently, the other members of the Prøst family, Prøst-COPA and Prøst-APE, are not affected or endangered by the attack. However, the attack demonstrates the possible complications of using an Even-Mansour construction as a block cipher in otherwise secure modes of operation. The Even-Mansour approach of creating a block cipher from a pseudorandom permutation by xoring a secret key before and after applying the permutation to the plaintext has been studied extensively [6–9,13,19]. It has been proven secure under different notions of security, with detailed bounds relating the security level with the key length. However, it is inherently susceptible to related-key attacks. The OTR mode of operation allows to "lift" this property to the full encryption and authentication scheme. This unfortunate combination of otherwise secure building blocks shows two things: that the Even-Mansour construction should only be used very cautiously, and that related-key properties are not well covered by the classical security notions, although they can lead to powerful forgery attacks.

Related-key setups are a relatively strong attack setting. Nevertheless, depending on the exact requirements, they are often not entirely far-fetched in practical scenarios. In particular, scenarios where only a known (but arbitrary) difference Δ between any two unknown keys is required, like in our attack, are quite realistic, and occur as side effects of several published protocols. The only limitation the attack imposes on Δ is that it does not affect the least significant bits of the key. For compatibility with the nonce difference, the modified part of the key must not be longer than the nonce length (half the key size in Prøst-OTR).

As an example for related keys in practice, consider the WEP standard [14]. There, the keys for the individual communication links are derived by concatenating (public, random) IVs with the fixed secret WEP key. Clearly, any two keys constructed this way have a publicly known differential relation. Similar scenarios could be imagined in any other network of resource-constrained devices (e.g., of sensor nodes), where individual encryption keys need to be derived in a cheap way from some master secret (e.g., by xoring individual IDs, nonces or challenge values to the key). Despite its inherent susceptibility to birthday attacks, the idea to "xor nonce to key" is also incorporated in several CAESAR candidates, such as AVALANCHE [1] and Calico [24]. Recently, cheap modifications of some master secret have also gained some popularity as a countermeasure to side-channel attacks, termed "fresh re-keying". The rationale is that to avoid differential side-channel attacks, subsequent encryption processes should never use the same key twice, but derive some sort of session keys from the long-term key in a cheap way.

The additional requirement of related nonces is not as strong as the related keys. In many applications, nonces are generated in a very predictable pattern (typically a simple counter as a message sequence number). In some cases, the attacker may even be able to influence the nonce counter: a simple example is by triggering encryptions until the nonce counter arrives at the desired value, or by somehow causing the device to jump the unwanted nonce values. We note that the attack does not require "nonce misuse" in the sense that the attacker requests repeated encryptions under the same nonce.

Related-key attacks [4,17] have been studied extensively, for various ciphers and applications. A prominent example is Biryukov et al.'s related-key attack on AES [5], which makes very strong assumptions about the relations between subkeys. The combination of related keys with related nonces has previously been applied primarily to stream ciphers, in particular in the context of the eSTREAM project. Examples include the key recovery attacks on Grain-v1 and Grain-128 by Lee et al. [20], or the recent analysis of generic chosen-IV attacks with applications to Trivium by Pasalic and Wei [22].

Outline. We first describe the Prøst family of authenticated ciphers and the notational conventions for the remaining document in Sect. 2. In Sect. 3, we derive a first basic related-key attack on Prøst-OTR. In Sect. 4, we propose a few possible improvements to the attack and extended attack scenarios. Finally, in Sect. 5, we conclude with a discussion of the applicability of the Prøst-OTR attack to other authenticated encryption modes.

2   Description of Prøst-OTR-n

2.1   The Prøst Family of Authenticated Ciphers

Prøst is a family of authenticated encryption algorithms. Kavun et al. [16] proposed the cipher family as a candidate in the currently ongoing CAESAR competition [25] for authenticated ciphers. Prøst comes in three flavors: Prøst-COPA, Prøst-OTR and Prøst-APE. All flavors share the same core permutation, the Prøst permutation designed by Kavun et al. [16], but use it in different modes of operation.

Prøst-APE uses the Prøst permutation in Andreeva et al.'s sponge-based APE mode [2]. The other two flavors, Prøst-OTR and Prøst-COPA, use modes of operation that are originally not permutation-based, but block-cipher-based: Andreeva et al.'s COPA mode [3], and Minematsu's OTR mode [21]. In these variants, the Prøst permutation is used in a single-key Even-Mansour construction [9] to provide the required block cipher.

Each of the three flavors is available in two security levels, specified by a parameter $n \in \{128, 256\}$, resulting in a total of six proposed cipher family members. The designers rank the COPA variants as their primary recommendations, the OTR variants second, and the APE variants last.

2.2 Notation

Throughout this paper, we use essentially the same notation as Prøst's designers [16]. Unless noted otherwise, all operations are performed in $\mathbb{F}_{2^{2n}}$ with respect to Prøst's irreducible polynomial, where $n \in \{128, 256\}$ defines the security level. For convenience of notation, elements in $\mathbb{F}_{2^{2n}}$ are often represented interchangeably as elements of $\mathbb{F}_2^{2n}$. We denote addition in $\mathbb{F}_{2^{2n}}$ (xor) by $\oplus$, and multiplication in $\mathbb{F}_{2^{2n}}$ by $\cdot$ (operator omitted where possible). By $N\|10^*$, we mean the n-bit bitstring $N \in \mathbb{F}_2^n$, concatenated with $(1, 0, \ldots, 0) \in \mathbb{F}_2^n$ to get an element in $\mathbb{F}_2^{2n}$. Otherwise, numbers mean integer numbers $\in \mathbb{Z}$ or individual bits $\in \mathbb{F}_2$ when written in roman font $(1, 2, 3, \ldots)$, but elements of $\mathbb{F}_2^{2n}$ in truncated hex notation when written in typewriter font $(\texttt{1}, \texttt{2}, \texttt{3}, \ldots)$; for example, $\texttt{13} = (0, \ldots, 0, 1, 0, 0, 1, 1) \in \mathbb{F}_2^{2n}$. The variable names we use are summarized in Table 1.

Table 1. Notation and variables used throughout this document.

n	Security level
K, K'	$2n$-bit keys (related keys)
N	n-bit nonce
$M = M_0 \cdots M_{2m-1}$	The padded message, split into $2n$-bit blocks
$C = C_0 \cdots C_{2m-1}$	The ciphertext in $2n$-bit blocks
T	n-bit tag
ℓ	Secret counter basis, derived from K and N ($= \delta$ in [16])
P	The Prøst permutation
$\tilde{P}_K$	P Used in single-key Even-Mansour mode as block cipher
Σ	Sum of message blocks, basis for the tag T
Δ	Difference between the related keys K and $K' = K \oplus \Delta$
M', C', T'	Message encrypted under related key K' and nonce
$\widetilde{M}, \widetilde{C}$	Modified message and ciphertext
M^*, C^*, T^*	Attacker's forged message, ciphertext and tag
α, γ	Intermediate values, inputs to P

2.3 Prøst-OTR-n

Prøst-OTR-n uses the block cipher $\tilde{P}_K$, built from the permutation P in a single-key Even-Mansour construction [9], in Minematsu's OTR mode of operation [21]. The result is a nonce-based authenticated encryption scheme with online encryption and decryption that is fully parallelizable [16]. Prøst-OTR-n is proposed in two security levels, $n \in \{128, 256\}$. The security level defines the permutation size $2n$ and block size $2n$, the key size $2n$ and nonce size n, and the tag size n. The claimed security for Prøst-OTR-n is $\frac{n}{2}$ bits (confidentiality and integrity of plaintext and integrity of associated data). No particular claims are made for or against the related-key security of the cipher.

Since our attack does not exploit any particular properties of the Prøst permutation $P : \mathbb{F}_2^{2n} \to \mathbb{F}_2^{2n}$, we do not include the definition of P in this description. The design of the permutation-based block cipher $\tilde{P}_K$, however, is essential for the attack. For a key $K \in \mathbb{F}_2^{2n}$, the block cipher $\tilde{P}_K : \mathbb{F}_2^{2n} \to \mathbb{F}_2^{2n}$ is defined as follows:

$$\tilde{P}_K(x) = K \oplus P(x \oplus K).$$

In OTR, message blocks M_j are encrypted in pairs in 2-round Feistel networks to get the ciphertext blocks C_j. The Feistel round function first adds a counter-like value, then applies the block cipher $\tilde{P}_k$. For the counter-like value, a helper value ℓ is computed in an initialization phase by encrypting the padded nonce $N\|10^*$ under $\tilde{P}_K$. After processing all block pairs, the tag T is finally computed by encrypting a function of the checksum Σ, which is the xor of all odd-indexed message blocks M_{2i+1}. The detailed algorithm is listed in Algorithm 1 and illustrated in Fig. 1. For simplicity, we only describe the mode for empty associated data, and only for padded messages with an even (rather than odd) number of message blocks.

Algorithm 1. Prøst-OTR-n encryption

Input: padded message $M\|01^* = M_0 \cdots M_{2m+1}$, padded nonce $N\|10^*$
Output: ciphertext $C = C_0 \cdots C_{2m+1}$, tag T

$\quad \Sigma \leftarrow 0$
$\quad \ell \leftarrow \tilde{P}_K(N\|10^*)$
$\quad \textbf{for } i = 0, \ldots, m-1 \textbf{ do}$
$\quad\quad C_{2i} \leftarrow \tilde{P}_K(2^{i+2}\ell \oplus M_{2i}) \oplus M_{2i+1}$
$\quad\quad C_{2i+1} \leftarrow \tilde{P}_K(2^{i+2}\ell \oplus \ell \oplus C_{2i}) \oplus M_{2i}$
$\quad\quad \Sigma \leftarrow \Sigma \oplus M_{2i+1}$
$\quad T \leftarrow \mathrm{msb}_n(\tilde{P}_K(3(2^{m+2}\ell \oplus \ell) \oplus \ell \oplus \Sigma))$

---

3 Basic Forgery Attack on Prøst-OTR

In this section, we describe our basic forgery attack on Prøst-OTR. The attack exploits the combination of the OTR mode with the Even-Mansour block cipher construction, and is independent of the concrete permutation P used. We consider a related-key scenario, where encrypted messages of two different keys K and K' can be observed. Both K and K' are secret, but we assume the attacker knows the difference $\Delta = K \oplus K'$ (i.e., $K' = K \oplus \Delta$). In addition, we assume that the attacker can observe encrypted messages for related nonces N, N', such that $\Delta = (N \| 10^*) \oplus (N' \| 10^*)$. Since the last n bits of the padded nonces are identical, this means that the n least significant bits of Δ must be 0.

The basic idea of the proposed forgery attack is to combine information from the encryption of the same message M under the two related keys K, K' to forge a ciphertext and tag for a modified message M^* under one of the two keys, K. More specifically, we will first show how to use the ciphertext from the related key $K' = K \oplus \Delta$ to forge ciphertexts for modified messages under the target key K. Then, we will combine original and forged ciphertexts in a way such that the original tag remains valid for the resulting modified plaintext under K. The attack works for any plaintext of sufficient length (≥ 514 message blocks for Prøst-OTR-128, ≥ 1026 blocks for Prøst-OTR-256).

3.1 Forging the Ciphertext

Assume that the attacker obtains the ciphertext for the same message $M = M_0 \cdots M_{2m-1}$ (from Fig. 1) under a related key $K' = K \oplus \Delta$ and a related nonce $N' \| 10^* = (N \| 10^*) \oplus \Delta$, as illustrated in Fig. 2. Note that since the nonce only has length n (instead of $2n$ like the other values), Δ must only modify the most significant n bits, i.e., $\Delta = \Delta_n \| 0^n$. Then, in the initialization phase illustrated

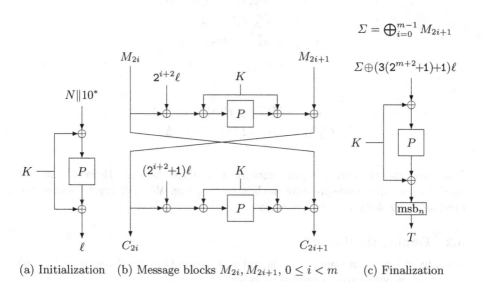

(a) Initialization   (b) Message blocks $M_{2i}, M_{2i+1}, 0 \leq i < m$ (c) Finalization

Fig. 1. Encrypting $2m$ message blocks M_j with Prøst-OTR-n under key K and nonce N. All values are $2n$ bits, with $n \in \{128, 256\}$, except the n-bit tag T.

in Fig. 2a, the differences in K' and N' cancel out right before the call to the permutation P in the initialization. Thus, we receive a related counter value ℓ' with a simple relation to the original ℓ:

$$\begin{aligned}
\ell' &= P_{K'}(N'\|10^*) = K' \oplus P((N'\|10^*) \oplus K') \\
&= K \oplus \Delta \oplus P(K \oplus \Delta \oplus (N\|10^*) \oplus \Delta) \\
&= \ell \oplus \Delta.
\end{aligned}$$

Now consider the encryption of a modified message with message blocks

$$\widetilde{M}_j = M_j \oplus (2^{\lfloor j/2 \rfloor + 2} + 1)\Delta$$

under the original key K and nonce N. As Fig. 3 illustrates, the message differences "cancel out" with the corresponding difference in the ℓ values from the encryption under the related key in Fig. 2. Thus, in both Figs. 2 and 3, the inputs α and γ to the permutations are the same:

$$\begin{aligned}
\alpha &= \widetilde{M}_{2i} \oplus 2^{i+2}\ell \oplus K \\
&= M_{2i} \oplus 2^{i+2}\ell \oplus 2^{i+2}\Delta \oplus \Delta \oplus K, \\
\gamma &= \widetilde{M}_{2i+1} \oplus P(\alpha) \oplus (2^{i+2} + 1)\ell \\
&= M_{2i+1} \oplus P(\alpha) \oplus 2^{i+2}\ell \oplus 2^{i+2}\Delta \oplus \ell \oplus \Delta.
\end{aligned}$$

For this reason, the ciphertext $\widetilde{C}_j$ of the modified message block $\widetilde{M}_j$ under the original key K can be derived from the ciphertexts C'_j of the original message M_j under the related key $K \oplus \Delta$:

$$\begin{aligned}
\widetilde{C}_{2i} &= \widetilde{M}_{2i+1} \oplus P(\alpha) \oplus K \\
&= C'_{2i} \oplus 2^{i+2}\Delta, \\
\widetilde{C}_{2i+1} &= \widetilde{M}_{2i} \oplus P(\gamma) \oplus K \\
&= C'_{2i+1} \oplus 2^{i+2}\Delta,
\end{aligned}$$

since

$$\begin{aligned}
C'_{2i} &= M_{2i+1} \oplus P(\alpha) \oplus K \oplus \Delta, \\
C'_{2i+1} &= M_{2i} \oplus P(\gamma) \oplus K \oplus \Delta.
\end{aligned}$$

Now, we know the correct ciphertexts for a modified message. However, we still need to find the corresponding authentication tag. We will try to re-use the original tag T for our forged message.

3.2   Forging the Tag

For a fixed key K and nonce N, the authentication tag only depends on the xor sum of all message blocks with odd index,

$$\Sigma = \bigoplus_{i=0}^{m-1} M_{2i+1}.$$

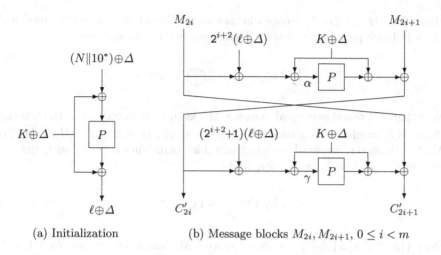

(a) Initialization

(b) Message blocks $M_{2i}, M_{2i+1}, 0 \leq i < m$

Fig. 2. Encrypting the original message blocks M_j under a related key $K \oplus \Delta$ and nonce.

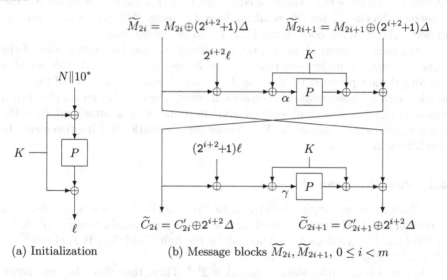

(a) Initialization

(b) Message blocks $\widetilde{M}_{2i}, \widetilde{M}_{2i+1}, 0 \leq i < m$

Fig. 3. Encrypting modified message blocks $\widetilde{M}_j = M_j \oplus (2^{\lfloor j/2 \rfloor + 2} + 1)\Delta$ under the original key K and nonce N.

Thus, if we want to re-use the original tag T for our forged message, we need to make sure that any induced differences cancel out when summing up the message blocks. We want to use original and modified message M and $\widetilde{M}$ to construct the final forged message M^* that satisfies this property.

For each message block pair M^*_{2i}, M^*_{2i+1} of the forged message M^*, we can decide to use either the original message block pair M_{2i}, M_{2i+1}, or the modified blocks $\widetilde{M}_{2i}$, $\widetilde{M}_{2i+1}$. Let λ_i denote whether we use the original ($\lambda_i = 0$) or modified ($\lambda_i = 1$) block pair for $0 \leq i < m$. Then, we get the message sum

$$\Sigma^* = \bigoplus_{i=0}^{m-1} M^*_{2i+1} = \Sigma \oplus \bigoplus_{i=0}^{m-1} \lambda_i(2^{i+2} + 1)\Delta.$$

Note that if Σ would sum up all message blocks (not only every second), then any choice of λ_i would create a successful forgery, since $M_{2i} \oplus M_{2i+1} = \widetilde{M}_{2i} \oplus \widetilde{M}_{2i+1}$. As it is, however, we need to select suitable coefficients $\lambda_i \in \mathbb{F}_2$ such that at least one coefficient λ_{i*} is nonzero and

$$\bigoplus_{i=0}^{m-1} \lambda_i(2^{i+2} + 1)\Delta = 0. \tag{1}$$

Since $\{(2^{i+2} + 1)\Delta\} \subseteq \mathbb{F}_2^{2n}$, a vector space with dimension $2n$, any $2n + 1$ such vectors are linearly dependent, and suitable coefficients λ_i exist. Thus, for any given key difference Δ and known plaintext M with $2m \geq 4n + 2$ message blocks, we can solve this system of equations to find suitable coefficients λ_i. The ciphertext blocks C^* for the resulting forged message M^* can be computed as in Sect. 3.1, while the correct tag $T^* = T$ can be copied from M.

Summarizing, from observing the ciphertext and tag for encryptions of the same message M under two related keys K and $K' = K \oplus \Delta$, the attacker has forged the ciphertext C^* and tag T^* for a different message M^* of the same block length with negligible computational effort. The attacker knows this forged message, but has almost no control over its contents. The attack nonce is the same as the original nonce N. We discuss some remarks and improvements to this attack in Sect. 4.

3.3   Practical Example

For illustration, we apply the attack to Prøst-OTR-128 with $n = 128$. This variant of Prøst-OTR uses a 256-bit key, a 128-bit nonce, and a message blocksize of 256 bits. The irreducible polynomial for the finite field $\mathbb{F}_{2^{2n}}$ is $f(x) = x^{256} \oplus x^{10} \oplus x^5 \oplus x^2 \oplus 1$.

As a simple example, assume that $\Delta = 2^{128}$. Then, the related key and nonce for the target key K and nonce N are

$$K' = K \oplus 2^{128},$$
$$N' = N \oplus 1.$$

Assume that some message M with 514 blocks of 256 bits each was encrypted under K to ciphertext C and tag T, and under K' to C' and T'.

For each block pair (M^*_{2i}, M^*_{2i+1}) of the forged message M^*, we now need to decide whether we copy the original message (M_{2i}, M_{2i+1}) or the modified version $(\widetilde{M}_{2i}, \widetilde{M}_{2i+1})$. Our choice needs to satisfy the coefficient Eq. (1). A solution can easily be found by hand; an example is given in Table 2.

Table 2. A solution for coefficients $\lambda_i = 1$ in Eq. (1) in $\mathbb{F}_{2^{256}}$ with field polynomial $f(x) = x^{256} \oplus x^{10} \oplus x^5 \oplus x^2 \oplus 1$.

Index i	Modifications	
	To plaintext M_{2i}, M_{2i+1} ($\mathbb{F}_{2^{256}}$)	To ciphertext C'_{2i}, C'_{2i+1} (hex)
$i=2$	$(2^4+1)\Delta = 2^{132} + 2^{128}$	$2^4\Delta = 00^{14}\|0010\|00^{16}$
$i=3$	$(2^5+1)\Delta = 2^{133} + 2^{128}$	$2^5\Delta = 00^{14}\|0020\|00^{16}$
$i=5$	$(2^7+1)\Delta = 2^{135} + 2^{128}$	$2^7\Delta = 00^{14}\|0080\|00^{16}$
$i=8$	$(2^{10}+1)\Delta = 2^{138} + 2^{128}$	$2^{10}\Delta = 00^{14}\|0400\|00^{16}$
$i=10$	$(2^{12}+1)\Delta = 2^{140} + 2^{128}$	$2^{12}\Delta = 00^{14}\|1000\|00^{16}$
$i=254$	$(2^{256}+1)\Delta = 2^{138} + 2^{133} + 2^{130}$	$2^{256}\Delta = 00^{14}\|0425\|00^{16}$
$i=256$	$(2^{258}+1)\Delta = 2^{140} + 2^{135} + 2^{132} + 2^{130} + 2^{128}$	$2^{258}\Delta = 00^{14}\|1094\|00^{16}$

For any example message M, we can now forge tag T^* and ciphertext C^* for the modified message M^*, which differs from M in blocks indices $j \in J$:

$$J = \{4, 5, 6, 7, 10, 11, 16, 17, 20, 21, 508, 509, 512, 513\},$$

$$M_j^* = \begin{cases} M_j \oplus (2^{\lfloor \frac{j}{2} \rfloor + 2}+1)\Delta & j \in J, \\ M_j & \text{else;} \end{cases}$$

$$C_j^* = \begin{cases} C_j' \oplus 2^{\lfloor \frac{j}{2} \rfloor + 2}\Delta & j \in J, \\ C_j & \text{else;} \end{cases}$$

$$T^* = T.$$

This example can easily be verified with the reference implementation of Prøst-OTR-128 for any key K, nonce N and message M with ≥ 514 blocks, and the corresponding related values K', N' for $\Delta = 2^{128}$.

4   Remarks and Advanced Attacks

4.1   Remarks on the Message Length

If an attacker carries out the basic attack as in Sect. 3, the modified message may have a slightly modified bit length. This is because the modification can shift the last nonzero bit, which marks the beginning of the message padding. This is not a problem since the message bitlength is not encoded anywhere else in the encryption process – except in the rare case that the last nonzero bit moves to the second-to-last block or earlier, which is not a valid format for the padded plaintext. This can be avoided by not including the last block pair in the modification process.

The attack is also applicable to messages $M = M_0 \cdots M_{2m-1}M_{2m}$ with an odd number of blocks: simply do not include the last block M_{2m} in the modification process, and copy it directly to M_{2m}^*. The same holds true for messages that include associated data A: simply copy the same associated data to the forged message.

4.2   Unknown Messages

The description in Sect. 3 assumes that one and the same message M is encrypted under both keys, K and $K' = K \oplus \Delta$, and that M is known to the attacker. This is, however, not necessarily required. Even without knowing M, the attacker can compute forged ciphertext blocks and the tag. In this case, he will not know the modified message M^*, but only the induced difference $M^* \oplus M$.

Neither is it necessary that the same message M is encrypted under both K and $K \oplus \Delta$. In fact, it is sufficient that the attacker has access to the ciphertexts for any two (not necessarily known, not necessarily equal-length) messages M (under K) and M' (under $K' = K \oplus \Delta$), and knows the difference $M_{2i+1} \oplus M'_{2i+1}$ for at least $2n + 1$ values of i. Let I be the set of indices i with known message differences, with $|I| \geq 2n + 1$. Then, the attacker solves

$$\bigoplus_{i \in I} \lambda_i \left(M_{2i+1} \oplus M'_{2i+1} \oplus (2^{i+2} + 1)\Delta \right) = 0.$$

Again, a non-zero solution for λ exists since the $\geq 2n + 1$ vectors in $\mathbb{F}_2^{2n}$ must be linearly dependent.

The forged message M^* (not known to the attacker, same block length as M), ciphertext C^* and tag T^* are then given by

$$(M_{2i}^*, M_{2i+1}^*) = \begin{cases} (M_{2i}, M_{2i+1}) & i \notin I \vee \lambda_i = 0, \\ (M'_{2i} \oplus (2^{i+2} + 1)\Delta, M'_{2i+1} \oplus (2^{i+2} + 1)\Delta) & i \in I \wedge \lambda_i = 1; \end{cases}$$

$$(C_{2i}^*, C_{2i+1}^*) = \begin{cases} (C_{2i}, C_{2i+1}) & i \notin I \vee \lambda_i = 0, \\ (C'_{2i} \oplus 2^{i+2}\Delta, C'_{2i+1} \oplus 2^{i+2}\Delta) & i \in I \wedge \lambda_i = 1; \end{cases}$$

$$T^* = T.$$

4.3   Multiple Forgeries

As described in Sects. 3 and 4.2, an attacker can forge one message from $4n + 2$ original message blocks. This can be extended to $2^s - 1$ different forgeries from $4n + 2s$ blocks (i.e., $|I| \geq 2n + s$). Then, the homogenous linear system

$$\bigoplus_{i \in I} \lambda_i \left(M_{2i+1} \oplus M'_{2i+1} \oplus (2^{i+2} + 1)\Delta \right) = 0$$

is underdetermined with $\geq 2n + s$ variables for $2n$ equations. Thus, the solution space has dimension $\geq s$, containing $\geq 2^s - 1$ different non-zero solutions for λ.

In the case $M_j = M'_j$, different values λ, λ' produce different plaintexts as long as

$$\max\{i \in I : \lambda_i \neq \lambda'_i\} < \mathrm{ord}(2) - 2,$$

where $\mathrm{ord}(2)$ denotes the multiplicative order of 2 in $\mathbb{F}_{2^{2n}}^*$. For Prøst's irreducible polynomials, $\mathrm{ord}(2) = 2^{256} - 1$ for $n = 128$ and $\mathrm{ord}(2) = 2^{512} - 1$ for $n = 256$. In general, if

$$M_{2i+1} \oplus M'_{2i+1} \oplus (2^{i+2} + 1)\Delta \neq 0 \qquad \forall i \in I,$$

then all different λ produce different forgeries.

4.4   Almost Universal Forgery with Related-Key Queries

Assume that the attacker can query for the encryption of a chosen message under one of the two keys, $K' = K \oplus \Delta$. He wants to forge the ciphertext and tag for a meaningful message M^* (chosen beforehand or provided externally) under the original key K. He can achieve this goal if (a) M^* has an even number of blocks, (b) he has access to the tag T of a known message M with the same number of blocks as M^* under the key K, and (c) he can modify one $2n$-bit block with odd index of M^* (or, alternatively, of M). The attack works as follows:

1. Fix the target message length $|M^*| = 2m$ (in blocks).
2. Obtain tag T for any known message M with $|M| = 2m$ under key K and any nonce N.
3. Fix the preliminary target (challenge) message M^*.
4. Let $j^* = 2i^* + 1$ be the modifiable block of M^*. Modify

$$M^*_{2i^*+1} = M_{2i^*+1} \oplus \bigoplus_{i \neq i^*} M_{2i+1} \oplus M^*_{2i+1}.$$

5. Construct the query message M' as

$$(M'_{2i}, M'_{2i+1}) = (M^*_{2i} \oplus (2^{i+1} \oplus 1)\Delta, M^*_{2i+1} \oplus (2^{i+1} \oplus 1)\Delta) \qquad i = 0, \ldots, m-1.$$

6. Request the ciphertext C' for the query message M' under $K' = K \oplus \Delta$ with nonce $N'\|10^* = (N\|10^*) \oplus \Delta$.
7. The forged ciphertext C^* and tag T^* for message M^* and nonce $N^* = N$ can be computed as

$$(C^*_{2i}, C^*_{2i+1}) = (C'_{2i} \oplus 2^{i+2}\Delta, C'_{2i+1} \oplus 2^{i+2}\Delta) \qquad i = 0, \ldots, m-1,$$
$$T^* = T.$$

This is essentially the same strategy as in Sect. 4.2, except that instead of using fixed M, M' and adapting M^*, we fix M, M^* and adapt M'. To avoid solving the equation system for the correct λ_i (which would require relatively long message lenghts $2m$, and force us to have $M^*_j = M_j$ for many j), we modify one block $M^*_{j^*}$ to make $\forall i : \lambda_i = 1$ a valid solution.

5   Discussion

The core of our attack is the following observation: If an authenticated encryption mode applies the block cipher to variable (controllable) inputs, an attacker can "lift" the inherent related-key weaknesses of the Even-Mansour construction to the entire mode. Then, he can use information from encryptions under a related key to forge ciphertext and tag for the target key.

A question that suggests itself is whether similar attacks are possible on other Prøst modes. In addition, other authenticated encryption modes might display similar problems when combined with an Even-Mansour block cipher.

Prøst-APE does not use the Even-Mansour construction at all, but plugs the permutation into a sponge construction. Thus, the attack is clearly not applicable. Prøst-COPA does use the permutation in an Even-Mansour construction. However, it seems to defy the attack by including $E_K(0)$, the encryption of the value 0, in the definition of the helper value L (which plays a role similar to ℓ in Prøst-OTR). Since a constant instead of the variable nonce N serves as input to the encryption, the input cannot be controlled to produce (differentially) predictable outputs of L. The situation is similar, for example, for the OCB mode of operation [18]: while the message could be used to cancel out differences in the helper counter value, this value is also derived from the encryption $E_K(0)$ of the zero value and thus unpredictable.

On the other hand, other popular modes show significant weaknesses when combined with Even-Mansour ciphers. Of course, unlike Prøst, these modes are usually not recommended for use with an Even-Mansour block cipher, but with AES. Consider, for example, the CCM mode of operation [10,26], an ISO/IEC-standardized combination of CBC-MAC with CTR encryption, as illustrated in Fig. 4. CCM allows a much simpler related-key attack. Assume that an attacker knows the ciphertext (including the tag) $C = C_1 \cdots C_\ell C_{\ell+1}$ of a message $M = M_1 \cdots M_\ell$ under key $K \oplus \Delta$ and padded nonce $(N\|0) \oplus \Delta$ (in the format used as counter input to the CTR encryption). Then, the ciphertext C' for M under key K and padded nonce $N\|0$ is simply

$$ C_i' = \begin{cases} C_i \oplus \Delta & 1 \leq i \leq \ell, \\ C_i & i = \ell+1. \end{cases} $$

As can be observed from Fig. 4, all differences Δ during the CCM computation cancel out either with the nonce difference fed to the Even-Mansour block encryptions $E_{K \oplus \Delta}$, or with neighbouring block cipher calls in the CBC-MAC computation. The final differences at the block cipher outputs from the CTR encryption can simply be added to the ciphertext blocks.

Clearly, the Even-Mansour construction is not well-suited as a general-purpose block cipher construction for all modes of operation. The Prøst-OTR

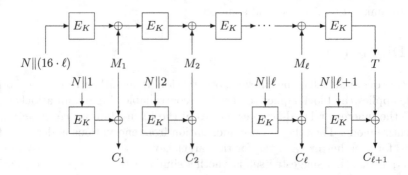

Fig. 4. CCM encryption.

design is an example how even more complex modes can allow some undesirable properties of the Even-Mansour construction to be lifted to the complete authentication mode, in this case to generate related-key forgeries. The rising popularity of sponge modes and permutation-based encryption in general may lead to interesting new observations in this direction.

Finally, we stress again that the presented attack only concerns the OTR variant of Prøst. For this variant, powerful forgery attacks are possible in a related-key setting. The security of the other modes, Prøst-COPA and Prøst-APE, and in particular of the Prøst permutation itself, remains unaffected. It may be possible to tweak OTR to prevent the specific attack, for example by adapting the initialization of ℓ to include $\tilde{P}_K(0)$, similar to COPA and OCB. However, the general interactions of the OTR mode with the single-key Even-Mansour construction remains a reason for concern.

Acknowledgments. The work has been supported in part by the Austrian Science Fund (project P26494-N15) and by the Austrian Research Promotion Agency (FFG) and the Styrian Business Promotion Agency (SFG) under grant number 836628 (SeCoS).

References

1. Alomair, B.: AVALANCHE v1. Submission to the CAESAR competition (2014). http://competitions.cr.yp.to/caesar-submissions.html
2. Andreeva, E., Bilgin, B., Bogdanov, A., Luykx, A., Mennink, B., Mouha, N., Yasuda, K.: APE: authenticated permutation-based encryption for lightweight cryptography. In: Cid, C., Rechberger, C. (eds.) FSE 2014. LNCS, vol. 8540, pp. 168–186. Springer, Heidelberg (2015)
3. Andreeva, E., Bogdanov, A., Luykx, A., Mennink, B., Tischhauser, E., Yasuda, K.: Parallelizable and authenticated online ciphers. In: Sako, K., Sarkar, P. (eds.) ASIACRYPT 2013, Part I. LNCS, vol. 8269, pp. 424–443. Springer, Heidelberg (2013)
4. Biham, E.: New types of cryptanalytic attacks using related keys. In: Helleseth, T. (ed.) EUROCRYPT 1993. LNCS, vol. 765, pp. 398–409. Springer, Heidelberg (1994)
5. Biryukov, A., Khovratovich, D., Nikolić, I.: Distinguisher and related-key attack on the full AES-256. In: Halevi, S. (ed.) CRYPTO 2009. LNCS, vol. 5677, pp. 231–249. Springer, Heidelberg (2009)
6. Biryukov, A., Wagner, D.: Advanced slide attacks. In: Preneel, B. (ed.) EUROCRYPT 2000. LNCS, vol. 1807, pp. 589–606. Springer, Heidelberg (2000)
7. Bogdanov, A., Knudsen, L.R., Leander, G., Standaert, F., Steinberger, J.P., Tischhauser, E.: Key-alternating ciphers in a provable setting: encryption using a small number of public permutations (extended abstract). In: Pointcheval and Johansson [23], pp. 45–62
8. Daemen, J.: Limitations of the Even-Mansour construction. In: Imai et al. [15], pp. 495–498
9. Dunkelman, O., Keller, N., Shamir, A.: Minimalism in cryptography: the Even-Mansour scheme revisited. In: Pointcheval and Johansson [23], pp. 336–354

10. Dworkin, M.J.: SP 800–38C. Recommendation for block cipher modes of operation: The CCM mode for authentication and confidentiality. Technical report, National Institute of Standards & Technology, Gaithersburg, MD, United States (2004)
11. Even, S., Mansour, Y.: A construction of a cipher from a single pseudorandom permutation. In: Imai et al. [15], pp. 210–224
12. Even, S., Mansour, Y.: A construction of a cipher from a single pseudorandom permutation. J. Cryptology 10(3), 151–162 (1997)
13. Gentry, C., Ramzan, Z.: Eliminating random permutation oracles in the Even-Mansour cipher. In: Lee, P.J. (ed.) ASIACRYPT 2004. LNCS, vol. 3329, pp. 32–47. Springer, Heidelberg (2004)
14. IEEE 802.11 working group: IEEE Standard for information technology–Telecommunications and information exchange between systems–Local and metropolitan area networks–Specific requirements–Part 11: Wireless LAN medium access control (MAC) and physical layer (PHY) specifications. IEEE Std 802.11-1997 (1997). http://ieeexplore.ieee.org/servlet/opac?punumber=5258
15. Matsumoto, T., Imai, H., Rivest, R.L. (eds.): ASIACRYPT 1991. LNCS, vol. 739. Springer, Heidelberg (1993)
16. Kavun, E.B., Lauridsen, M.M., Leander, G., Rechberger, C., Schwabe, P., Yalçın, T.: Prøst v1. Submission to the CAESAR competition (2014). http://competitions.cr.yp.to/caesar-submissions.html
17. Knudsen, L.R.: Cryptanalysis of LOKI. In: Imai et al. [15], pp. 22–35
18. Krovetz, T., Rogaway, P.: The OCB authenticated-encryption algorithm. IETF RFC 7253 (2014). http://tools.ietf.org/html/rfc7253
19. Lampe, R., Patarin, J., Seurin, Y.: An asymptotically tight security analysis of the iterated Even-Mansour cipher. In: Wang, X., Sako, K. (eds.) ASIACRYPT 2012. LNCS, vol. 7658, pp. 278–295. Springer, Heidelberg (2012)
20. Lee, Y., Jeong, K., Sung, J., Hong, S.H.: Related-key chosen IV attacks on Grain-v1 and Grain-128. In: Mu, Y., Susilo, W., Seberry, J. (eds.) ACISP 2008. LNCS, vol. 5107, pp. 321–335. Springer, Heidelberg (2008)
21. Minematsu, K.: Parallelizable Rate-1 authenticated encryption from pseudorandom functions. In: Nguyen, P.Q., Oswald, E. (eds.) EUROCRYPT 2014. LNCS, vol. 8441, pp. 275–292. Springer, Heidelberg (2014)
22. Pasalic, E., Wei, Y.: Generic related-key and induced chosen IV attacks using the method of key differentiation. Cryptology ePrint Archive, Report 2013/586 (2013). http://eprint.iacr.org/2013/586
23. Pointcheval, D., Johansson, T. (eds.): EUROCRYPT 2012. LNCS, vol. 7237. Springer, Heidelberg (2012)
24. Taylor, C.: Calico v8. Submission to the CAESAR competition (2014). http://competitions.cr.yp.to/caesar-submissions.html
25. The CAESAR committee: CAESAR: Competition for authenticated encryption: Security, applicability, and robustness (2014). http://competitions.cr.yp.to/caesar.html
26. Whiting, D., Housley, R., Ferguson, N.: Counter with CBC-MAC (CCM). IETF RFC 3610 (2003). http://tools.ietf.org/html/rfc3610

Practical Cryptanalysis of the Open Smart Grid Protocol

Philipp Jovanovic[1(✉)] and Samuel Neves[2]

[1] University of Passau, Passau, Germany
jovanovic@fim.uni-passau.de
[2] University of Coimbra, Coimbra, Portugal
sneves@dei.uc.pt

Abstract. This paper analyses the cryptography used in the Open Smart Grid Protocol (OSGP). The authenticated encryption (AE) scheme deployed by OSGP is a non-standard composition of RC4 and a home-brewed MAC, the "OMA digest".

We present several practical key-recovery attacks against the OMA digest. The first and basic variant can achieve this with a mere 13 queries to an OMA digest oracle and negligible time complexity. A more sophisticated version breaks the OMA digest with only 4 queries and a time complexity of about 2^{25} simple operations. A different approach only requires one arbitrary valid plaintext-tag pair, and recovers the key in an average of 144 *message verification* queries, or one ciphertext-tag pair and 168 *ciphertext verification* queries.

Since the encryption key is derived from the key used by the OMA digest, our attacks break both confidentiality and authenticity of OSGP.

1 Introduction

Authenticated encryption [7] (AE) is the standard technology to protect data that needs to be sent over unsecured communication channels and is deployed in countless applications and protocols, such as (D)TLS, SSH and IPSec. In comparison to regular symmetric encryption schemes, AE not only ensures *privacy* of the data but also guarantees *integrity* and *authenticity*. Unfortunately, failures in the design and implementation of authenticated encryption schemes are a common sight and there are numerous examples. To name just a few (see also [9]):

- Vaudenay's 2002 CBC *padding oracle attack* on MAC-then-encrypt AE modes allows an active adversary to decrypt messages without access to the secret key [30]. This attack stemmed from the authenticity verification leaking whether the decrypted message was adequately padded. Over the years, this strategy has been used quite successfully against TLS [4,10,12,26].
- In 2007, an attack [29] on the Wired Equivalent Privacy (WEP) standard, used in many 802.11 Wi-Fi networks, allowed to recover the secret key within minutes from a few thousand intercepted messages. The attack exploited weaknesses in RC4.

© International Association for Cryptologic Research 2015
G. Leander (Ed.): FSE 2015, LNCS 9054, pp. 297–316, 2015.
DOI: 10.1007/978-3-662-48116-5_15

- In 2009, Albrecht, Paterson, and Watson [2] exploited a flaw in the SSH protocol and its OpenSSH implementation, when coupled with a block cipher in CBC mode. The attack allowed an adversary to recover 14 plaintext bits with probability 2^{-14} or 32 plaintext bits with probability 2^{-18}.
- In 2012, a flaw was uncovered in EAXprime [5], an AE block cipher mode derived from EAX [8], standardized as ANSI C12.22-2008 for Smart Grid applications, and also subject of a forthcoming NIST standard. The flaw facilitates forgery, distinguishing, and message-recovery attacks [25].

In this paper, we investigate another flawed authenticated encryption scheme, which is deployed in the Open Smart Grid Protocol (OSGP) [15]. The latter is an application layer communication protocol for smart grids built on top of the ISO/IEC 14908-1 protocol stack [21], has been developed by the Energy Service Network Association (ESNA), and is a standard of the European Telecommunications Standards Institute (ETSI) since 2012 [1]. According to estimations, OSGP-based smart meters and devices are deployed in over 4 million devices worldwide as of 2015, making OSGP one of the most widely used network protocols for smart grid applications.

Our Results. Table 1 summarises the results of the different attacks on the authenticated encryption scheme of OSGP and also lists the corresponding sections where the attacks are described. While the attacks have various tradeoffs between the number of oracle queries and the computational complexity, each constitutes a complete break of the OSGP AE scheme. We also want to highlight the fact that the attacks from Sect. 3.4 are particularly powerful in the context of the protocol: verification oracles are easy to come across and the attack in its XOR variant does not need to know plaintext at all, since differences can be injected directly into the ciphertext. In other words, this is a practical attack on the AE scheme of OSGP and completely compromises its security.

Related Work. In late 2013, Kursawe and Peters independently analysed OSGP and identified several security flaws, some of which overlap with our own findings [22]. Their work gives a good overview on the various security flaws and shows how they can be exploited to mount some basic attacks on OSGP's cryptographic infrastructure. We, on the other hand, focus on the digest function in more detail and, as a consequence, are able to further move the attacks into practicality. We note that our analysis has been performed solely against the OSGP specification [15] and not against any deployed devices.

Outline. The paper is organised as follows. Section 2 introduces notation and the cryptographic infrastructure used in the Open Smart Grid Protocol. In Sect. 3, we give a detailed analysis of the said AE scheme. We start with some basic attacks that already allow recovery of the entire secret key but are not feasible within the scope of the protocol. Based on that we describe further improvements which eventually allow us to mount fast forgery attacks on the

Table 1. Required number of queries and expected complexity for the attacks of Sect. 3, with varying time-query tradeoff parameter B. The abbreviation KP+ means *known-plaintext with common prefix*, CP denotes *chosen-plaintext*, CC stands for *chosen-ciphertext*, and TG and TV denote *tag-generation* and *tag-verification* oracles, respectively.

Attack	B	Queries	Complexity	Type	Oracle
Section 3.1	1	13	$2^{3.58}$	CP	TG
	2	7	$2^{10.58}$		
	3	5	$2^{18.00}$		
	4	4	$2^{25.58}$		
	5	4	$2^{33.58}$		
	6	3	$2^{41.00}$		
Section 3.2	1	24/13	$2^{10.58}$	KP+/CP	TG
	2	12/7	$2^{17.58}$		
	3	8/5	$2^{25.00}$		
	4	6/4	$2^{32.58}$		
	5	6/4	$2^{40.32}$		
	6	4/3	$2^{48.58}$		
Section 3.4 (XOR)	—	≈ 168	≈ 168	CP/CC	TV
Section 3.4 (Additive)	—	≈ 144	≈ 144	CP	

OSGP AE scheme and furthermore enable recovery of the complete secret key and in this case all within the context of the protocol. Finally, Sect. 4 concludes the paper.

2 Preliminaries

2.1 Notation

An n-bit string x is an element of $\{0,1\}^n$. For $n = 8$ we call x a byte. The size of x in bits is denoted by $|x|$. Concatenation of bit strings is denoted by $\|$. Given a vector of bit strings $(x_0, \ldots, x_{n-1})$, we denote by $x_{i,j}$ the jth bit of the ith word where $0 \leq i \leq n - 1$. When interpreting bit strings as integers we always use little-endian format and denote them in hexadecimal format using `typewriter`. A bit string consisting of n zeros is denoted by 0^n. A cyclic rotation of a bit string x by m bits to the left and right is denoted by $x \lll m$ and $x \ggg m$, respectively. The difference of two bit strings x and x' with respect to XOR is denoted by Δx, whereas a difference with respect to addition modulo 2^n is denoted by $\Delta^{\boxminus} x$.

2.2   The Cryptographic Infrastructure of OSGP

In this paper, we focus solely on OSGP's cryptographic infrastructure, and not on the protocol itself. The high-level structure of OSGP's authenticated encryption (AE) scheme is depicted in Fig. 1.

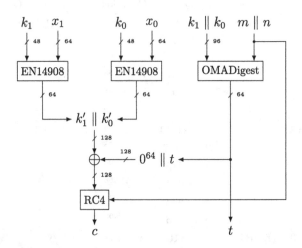

Fig. 1. The OSGP AE scheme. Notation: $x_0 = \{81, 3F, 52, 9A, 7B, E3, 89, BA\}$, $x_1 = \{72, B0, 91, 8D, 44, 05, AA, 57\}$, $k = k_1 \parallel k_0$: Open Media Access Key (OMAK), m : message, n : sequence number, t : authentication tag, $k' = k_1' \parallel k_0'$: Base Encryption Key (BEK), c : ciphertext.

The OSGP AE scheme is based on three algorithms: the EN 14908 algorithm[1], the stream cipher RC4 and the so-called OMA digest, a message authentication code (MAC). These three algorithms are combined in a mixture of the generic composition [7] approaches *MAC-and-encrypt* and *MAC-then-encrypt* to form an authenticated encryption scheme, see again Fig. 1. We note that, while the OMA digest is described in the OSGP specification [15], public information on the EN 14908 algorithm, specified in ISO/IEC 14908-1 [21], is hard to come by. All information on the latter was retrieved from the OSGP specification [15] and the related standard ISO/IEC CD 14543-6-1 [20, p. 232] which, like ISO/IEC 14908-1 and a few other standards [6,19,28], is also a direct descendant of LonTalk [13].

The security of OSGP's AE scheme depends on the 96-bit *Open Media Access Key* (OMAK) $k = k_1 \parallel k_0$ from which all other key material is derived. The OMAK is usually unique to a device but not hardcoded and can be changed, often to be shared with other devices under the same concentrator [15, Sect. 7.1]. Two things are derived from the OMAK: firstly, a so-called *Base Encryption*

---

[1] The OSGP specification describes EN 14908 as an encryption algorithm, but it is clearly nothing of the sort. We therefore only talk about the *EN 14908 algorithm* in this work.

Key (BEK) $k' = k_1' \parallel k_0'$ is computed [15, Sect. 7.3] which is a 128-bit key forming the basis for the RC4 encryption key. The BEK is constructed[2] using the EN 14908 algorithm which appears to have been the basis for the OMA digest but uses smaller 48-bit keys and processes message bytes in reversed order. The EN 14908 algorithm is applied to each of the halves k_0 and k_1 of the OMAK and the two constants $x_0 = \{81, 3F, 52, 9A, 7B, E3, 89, BA\}$ and $x_1 = \{72, B0, 91, 8D, 44, 05, AA, 57\}$. The two 64-bit results are then concatenated to form k', see Fig. 1. Note that the BEK only depends on the OMAK and is thus fixed as long as k remains unchanged.

Secondly, an authentication tag t is produced using the OMA digest on the message m concatenated with a sequence number n and the OMAK k. Let l denote the size of $m \parallel n$ in bytes. The OMA digest starts with its 8-byte internal state $a = (a_0, \ldots, a_7)$ set to zero. First, $m \parallel n$ is zero-padded to a multiple of 144 bytes, meaning

$$m' = m \parallel n \parallel 0^{-l \bmod 144}.$$

Let $m' = m_0' \parallel \cdots \parallel m_{143}'$ denote the first, and possibly only, 144-byte block of the message. The internal state is updated continuously using a nonlinear function $f_{b,c}$ where $b = k_{i \bmod 12, 7-j}$ is a key bit and $c = j$ is the current position in the state. Its specification is as follows:

$$f_{b,c}(x, y, z) = \begin{cases} y + z + (\neg(x + c)) \lll 1 & \text{if } b = 1 \\ y + z - (\neg(x + c)) \ggg 1 & \text{otherwise.} \end{cases}$$

In order to update state element a_j, the function f takes, for $0 \le i \le 17$ and $7 \ge j \ge 0$, two adjacent state elements a_j and $a_{j+1 \bmod 8}$ and a message-byte m_{8i+7-j}' as input, i.e., $a_j = f_{k_{i \bmod 12, 7-j}, j}(a_j, a_{j+1 \bmod 8}, m_{8i+7-j})$, and depending on the value of the key bit $k_{i \bmod 12, 7-j}$ one of the two branches depicted above is evaluated. The next 144-byte message block is processed similarly, with the initial internal state carried over from the previous block. The complete pseudocode of the OMA digest is shown in Algorithm 1 and a visualisation of its innermost loop, where the message bytes are processed, is given in Fig. 2. For the reference implementation we refer to [15, Annex E].

After the tag generation, t is XORed into the lower half of the BEK k' which then produces the final 128-bit RC4 encryption key $k'' = k_1' \parallel (k_0' \oplus t)$, see again Fig. 1. This measure is intended to provide RC4 with ever-changing key material, thus producing a fresh keystream with every new message, since, according to the OSGP specification, the sequence number n, which is appended to m, is continuously increased.

Sequence numbers are shared between sender and receiver in OSGP. The receiver of a message verifies that the correct sequence number was appended

---

[2] The OSGP specification is rather unclear on how the BEK is derived. The presented description is based on our investigations also involving other standards [20, p.232]. The key observation here is that the BEK derived from the OMAK. The concrete realisation is not too important, though, and is only described for the sake of completeness.

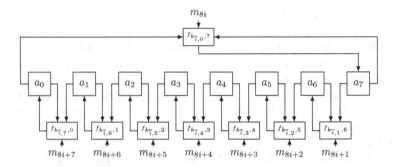

Fig. 2. Data processing (right-to-left) in the OMA digest, with $\bar{\imath} = i \bmod 12$.

Function OMADigest(m,k)
| $a \leftarrow (0,0,0,0,0,0,0,0)$
| $m \leftarrow m \parallel 0^{-|m| \bmod 144}$
| **foreach** 144-*byte block* b *of* m **do**
| | **for** $i \leftarrow 0$ **to** 17 **do**
| | | **for** $j \leftarrow 7$ **to** 0 **do**
| | | | **if** $k_{i \bmod 12, 7-j} = 1$ **then**
| | | | | $a_j \leftarrow a_{(j+1) \bmod 8} + b_{8i+(7-j)} + (\neg(a_j + j)) \lll 1$
| | | | **else** $a_j \leftarrow a_{(j+1) \bmod 8} + b_{8i+(7-j)} - (\neg(a_j + j)) \ggg 1$
| | | **end**
| | **end**
| **end**
| **return** a

Algorithm 1. The OSGP OMA digest.

to the latter. Messages with sequence numbers in the range $\{n, \ldots, n+8\}$ are accepted as valid requests. If a message with sequence number $n-1$ is received, then the recipient does not execute the request but instead re-sends the answer of the (previously executed) request of number $n-1$. Sequence numbers outside of this range trigger an error and the OSGP device replies with a failure code and the correct sequence number. More details on the handling of sequence numbers can be found in [15, Sect. 9.7].

After the setup phase is finished, k'' is used to encrypt $m \parallel n$ via RC4 to obtain the ciphertext c. Finally, $c \parallel t$ is transmitted. Messages $m \parallel n$ processed in OSGP are allowed to have a maximum size of 114 bytes [15, Sect. 9.2]. This complicates some attacks that require up to 136-byte messages. Nevertheless, we will also describe scenarios that respect this message size limit.

3   Analysis

OSGP uses RC4 for encryption without discarding any initial bytes. RC4 has known statistical key- and plaintext-recovery attacks, and these have been shown to be practically feasible [3, 16–18, 27, 29, 31]. However, in this work we do not focus on RC4, but instead on the OMA digest, see Algorithm 1.

The OMA digest algorithm presents multiple flaws. Firstly, it uses a simple zero byte message padding, which results in messages with any number of trailing zeroes sharing the same tag. Secondly, given a tuple (a, m, k) where a is the OMA digest's state or authentication tag, m a message and k the OMAK, the function is fully reversible (see Algorithm 2) which is a very useful property for the attacks presented in Sects. 3.1 and 3.2. Likewise, it is also possible to take an arbitrary internal state, and continue to process it as if to resume a partially digested message. This is depicted in Algorithm 3.

Function OMABackward(a,m,k,n)
> // Assumes $|m| \leq 144$.
> $m \leftarrow m \parallel 0^{-|m| \bmod 144}$
> **for** $l \leftarrow 0$ **to** $n-1$ **do**
> > $i, j \leftarrow \lfloor l/8 \rfloor, l \bmod 8$
> > **if** $k_{(17-i) \bmod 12, 7-j} = 1$ **then** $x \leftarrow (a_j - a_{(j+1) \bmod 8} - m_{143-8i-j}) \ggg 1$
> > **else** $x \leftarrow (a_{(j+1) \bmod 8} + m_{143-8i-j} - a_j) \lll 1$
> > $a_j \leftarrow \neg x - j$
> **end**
> **return** a

Algorithm 2. The "backward" OSGP OMA digest, reverting the internal state back by n message bytes.

Function OMAForward(a,m,k,n)
> /* Essentially Algorithm 1, but start at byte m_n with a known
> state a, and assume $|m| \leq 144$.   */
> $m \leftarrow m \parallel 0^{-|m| \bmod 144}$
> **for** $l \leftarrow n$ **to** 143 **do**
> > $i, j \leftarrow \lfloor l/8 \rfloor, 7 - l \bmod 8$
> > **if** $k_{i \bmod 12, 7-j} = 1$ **then** $a_j \leftarrow a_{(j+1) \bmod 8} + m_{8i+7-j} + (\neg(a_j + j)) \lll 1$
> > **else** $a_j \leftarrow a_{(j+1) \bmod 8} + m_{8i+7-j} - (\neg(a_j + j)) \ggg 1$
> **end**
> **return** a

Algorithm 3. The "forward" OSGP OMA digest, starting with a known initial state and processing message bytes starting at position n.

3.1 Chosen-Plaintext Key Recovery Attacks

Let $a = (a_0, \ldots, a_7)$ denote the 8-byte internal state of the OMA digest. The attacks discussed below use chosen 144-byte messages $m = m_0 \parallel \cdots \parallel m_{143}{}^3$, and exploit differential weaknesses in the OMA digest.

---

[3] For simplicity, we use 144-byte messages throughout this section. Note, however, that the presented attacks use messages which are never longer than 136 bytes.

Bitwise Key Recovery. The first attack recovers the key one bit at a time by differential cryptanalysis. Specifically, we exploit the XOR-differential $(\Delta m_i, \Delta a_j) = (80, 80)$, where Δm_i and Δa_j denote input and output differences, respectively, for $j = 7 - i \bmod 8$. The output difference is obtained immediately after processing message byte m_i (see Algorithm 1) and can be written as

$$f_{k,j}(a_j, a_{j+1 \bmod 8}, m_i \oplus 80)$$
$$= a_{j+1 \bmod 8} + (m_i \oplus 80) \pm (\text{FF} \oplus (a_j + j) \lll r)$$
$$= (a_{j+1 \bmod 8} + m_i \pm (\text{FF} \oplus (a_j + j) \lll r)) \oplus 80$$
$$= f_{k,j}(a_j, a_{j+1 \bmod 8}, m_i) \oplus 80$$

where the rotation offset $r \in \{1, 7\}$ and the $\pm$ operation depend on the value of the key bit $k \in \{0, 1\}$. This differential has probability 1, by well-known differential properties of addition modulo 2^n [23], and propagates cleanly through the state a for the next 8 iterations, resulting in the following difference over the state:

$$\Delta a = (80, 80, 80, 80, 80, 80, 80, 80).$$

The next iteration reveals one key bit. By XOR-linearising the state update function f, the new output difference $\Delta a'_j$ is of the form

$$\Delta a'_j = ((a_{j+1 \bmod 8} \oplus 80) \oplus m_i \oplus (\text{FF} \oplus ((a_j \oplus 80) \oplus j) \lll r)) \oplus$$
$$(a_{j+1 \bmod 8} \oplus m_i \oplus (\text{FF} \oplus (a_j \oplus j) \lll r))$$

where $r \in \{1, 7\}$. As a consequence, we have $\Delta a'_j = 81$, if bit $7 - i \bmod 8$ of $k_{\lfloor i/8 \rfloor \bmod 12}$ is 1, and $\Delta a'_j = \text{C0}$, if the same key bit is 0. While integer addition and XOR behave differently with respect to the propagation of XOR-differences, the *least significant bit* of integer addition and XOR behave identically in this case and can be used to recover the key bit with probability 1.

The above leak, combined with Algorithm 2, can be turned into a chosen-plaintext key-recovery attack retrieving the OMAK k bitwise in at most $96 + 1$ queries. Algorithm 4 describes this attack in full detail. Looking at Fig. 1, we see immediately that the reconstruction of k breaks the complete OSGP AE scheme. In the following, we will explore how the attack can be further improved.

Bytewise Key Recovery. Analysing the above attack more thoroughly, we noticed that we can recover one key byte at a time by injecting the input difference 80 into the message a couple of steps earlier. This reduces the number of queries and the work load of the attack drastically. In other words, we will show how to reconstruct the entire OMAK with only $12 + 1$ chosen-plaintext queries.

Let $k_{i \bmod 12, j}$ denote the jth bit of key byte $i \bmod 12$, for $i = 17, 16, \ldots, 6$ and $j = 0, \ldots, 7$. When injecting the message difference $\Delta m_{8i-8} = 80$ and thereupon processing 16 message bytes, we obtain an XOR-difference of the internal state of the form $\Delta a = (\Delta a_0, \ldots, \Delta a_7) = (\Delta x_0, \ldots, \Delta x_7)$ where Δx_l are arbitrary values for $l = 0, \ldots, 7$. The evolution of the difference propagation in the internal state can be visualised as follows:

```
Function RecoverKey(O)
    // O is an oracle returning a message's OMADigest under key k.
    k ← {0}^{12}
    m ←$ {0..255}^{144}
    a ← O(m)
    for i ← 0 to 11 do
        for j ← 0 to 7 do
            m' ← m
            m'_{136-8i-1-j} ← m'_{136-8i-1-j} ⊕ 80
            a' ← O(m')
            b ← OMABackward(a, m, k, 8i)              // Algorithm 2
            b' ← OMABackward(a', m', k, 8i)           // Algorithm 2
            k_{(17-i) mod 12,7-j} ← (b_{j,0} ⊕ b'_{j,0})
        end
    end
    return k
```

Algorithm 4. Bit-by-bit chosen-plaintext key-recovery attack.

$i = 17,\ldots,6$	Δa_0	Δa_1	Δa_2	Δa_3	Δa_4	Δa_5	Δa_6	Δa_7
$\ldots$	$\ldots$	$\ldots$	$\ldots$	$\ldots$	$\ldots$	$\ldots$	$\ldots$	$\ldots$
m_{8i-9}	00	00	00	00	00	00	00	00
m_{8i-8}	00	00	00	00	00	00	00	80
$\ldots$	$\ldots$	$\ldots$	$\ldots$	$\ldots$	$\ldots$	$\ldots$	$\ldots$	$\ldots$
m_{8i-1}	80	80	80	80	80	80	80	80
m_{8i}	80	80	80	80	80	80	80	Δx_7
m_{8i+1}	80	80	80	80	80	80	Δx_6	Δx_7
$\ldots$	$\ldots$	$\ldots$	$\ldots$	$\ldots$	$\ldots$	$\ldots$	$\ldots$	$\ldots$
m_{8i+7}	Δx_0	Δx_1	Δx_2	Δx_3	Δx_4	Δx_5	Δx_6	Δx_7

By analysing again the XOR-linearisation of the state update function f, one realises that a key byte can be recovered in its entirety by exploiting, as in the case of the bitwise key recovery attack, the information on the key bits stored in the least significant bit of the output differences $\Delta x_0, \ldots, \Delta x_7$. More precisely, key byte $k_{i \bmod 12}$ can be reconstructed as follows:

1. $k_{i \bmod 12,0} = \mathtt{lsb}(\Delta x_7) \oplus \mathtt{lsb}(80)$ 5. $k_{i \bmod 12,4} = \mathtt{lsb}(\Delta x_3) \oplus \mathtt{lsb}(\Delta x_4)$
2. $k_{i \bmod 12,1} = \mathtt{lsb}(\Delta x_6) \oplus \mathtt{lsb}(\Delta x_7)$ 6. $k_{i \bmod 12,5} = \mathtt{lsb}(\Delta x_2) \oplus \mathtt{lsb}(\Delta x_3)$
3. $k_{i \bmod 12,2} = \mathtt{lsb}(\Delta x_5) \oplus \mathtt{lsb}(\Delta x_6)$ 7. $k_{i \bmod 12,6} = \mathtt{lsb}(\Delta x_1) \oplus \mathtt{lsb}(\Delta x_2)$
4. $k_{i \bmod 12,3} = \mathtt{lsb}(\Delta x_4) \oplus \mathtt{lsb}(\Delta x_5)$ 8. $k_{i \bmod 12,7} = \mathtt{lsb}(\Delta x_0) \oplus \mathtt{lsb}(\Delta x_1)$

In order to verify that the above key recovery indeed works, consider the following steps. As we have already seen in the bitwise key recovery attack, the value of $k_{i \bmod 12,0}$ can be read off right away from Δx_7, see step 1 above. The remaining key bits $k_{i \bmod 12,j+1}$, for $j = 0, \ldots, 6$, can be recovered from the XOR-linearisation of f which gives us the relation

$$\Delta x_{6-j} = \Delta x_{7-j} \oplus (\Delta x'_{6-j} \lll r) = \Delta x_{7-j} \oplus (80 \lll r)$$

where Δx_{7-j} and Δx_{6-j} denote output differences and $\Delta x'_{6-j}$ corresponds to the difference before a_{6-j} is updated in the jth step. The latter simply has the value 80 as can be seen in the table on the difference propagation. The above equation can be re-written as

$$\mathrm{lsb}(80 \lll r) = \mathrm{lsb}(\Delta x_{6-j}) \oplus \mathrm{lsb}(\Delta x_{7-j})$$

and since the rotation offset $r \in \{1, 7\}$ depends on $k_{i \bmod 12,j+1}$, the formula above gives us the value of the latter key bit.

Function RecoverKey($\mathcal{O}$)
  // $\mathcal{O}$ is an oracle returning a message's OMADigest under key k.
  $k \leftarrow \{0\}^{12}$
  $m \xleftarrow{\$} \{0..255\}^{144}$
  $a \leftarrow \mathcal{O}(m)$
  for $i \leftarrow 0$ **to** 11 **do**
    $m' \leftarrow m$
    $m'_{136-8i-8} \leftarrow m'_{136-8i-8} \oplus 80$
    $a' \leftarrow \mathcal{O}(m')$
    $b \leftarrow$ OMABackward($a, m, k, 8i$)   // Algorithm 2
    $b' \leftarrow$ OMABackward($a', m', k, 8i$)   // Algorithm 2
    $k_{(17-i) \bmod 12} \leftarrow$ RecoverByte(b, b')
  end
  return k
Function RecoverByte(a, a')
  $x \leftarrow 0$
  $x_0 \leftarrow a_{7,0} \oplus a'_{7,0}$
  for $i \leftarrow 0$ **to** 6 **do** $x_{i+1} \leftarrow a_{6-i,0} \oplus a'_{6-i,0} \oplus a_{7-i,0} \oplus a'_{7-i,0}$
  return x

Algorithm 5. Byte-by-byte chosen-plaintext key-recovery attack.

3.2 Known-Plaintext Key Recovery Attack

The second attack is not differential in nature and requires a weaker attacker. We only assume in the following that the attacker is able to capture plaintexts with a *common prefix* of various lengths. This may be feasible by, e.g., capturing repeated messages with different sequence numbers.

This attack relies uniquely on the OMA digest's invertibility, as seen in Algorithm 2. The basic idea here is to have two messages, m and m' that are equal except in the last r bytes; partially reversing the final state of m by r iterations, then using that state to process the final bytes of m' should only happen when the (guessed) key bits used in those iterations are correct. This does not always happen, but it reduces the keyspace to virtually one or two guesses per key byte. The concrete realisation of the attack is also described in Algorithm 6.

However, due to the slow diffusion of differences already described in Sect. 3.1, to recover r bits of the key one needs more than r iterations back; this is not a problem, though, as long as the key bits corresponding to the common prefix bytes of the message are the same for the forwards and backwards processing of the message. In practice, we have found that $r + 8$ iterations suffice to recover the key with overwhelming probability.

Function RecoverKey($\mathcal{O}$)

  // $\mathcal{O}$ is an oracle returning a message's OMADigest under key k.

  $k \leftarrow \{0\}^{12}$

  $m \xleftarrow{\$} \{0..255\}^{144}$

  $a \leftarrow \mathcal{O}(m)$

  for $i \leftarrow 0$ **to** 11 **do**

    $m' \leftarrow m$

    $m'_{128-8i..|m'|-1} \xleftarrow{\$} \{0..255\}^{|m|-128-8i}$

    $a' \leftarrow \mathcal{O}(m')$

    for $x \leftarrow 0$ **to** 255 **do**

      $k_{(17-i) \bmod 12} \leftarrow x$

      $b \leftarrow$ OMABackward($a, m, k, 8i + 16$)   // Algorithm 2

      $b' \leftarrow$ OMAForward($b, m', k, 128 - 8i$)   // Algorithm 3

      if $a' = b'$ **then**

        | break // May be a false positive; handling omitted.

      end

    end

  end

  return k

Algorithm 6. Byte-by-byte known-plaintext key-recovery attack.

3.3 Optimizing the Attacks

The attacks of Sects. 3.1 and 3.2 have an obvious generalization that trades queries for computation time. This is also a consequence of the OMA digest's reversibility.

Let $B \geq 1$ be the number of key bytes to recover per query; the attack from Sect. 3.2 generalizes trivially to any B, by guessing B adjacent key bytes per query, at an average cost of $\lceil \frac{12}{B} \rceil + 1$ queries and $\lceil \frac{12}{B} \rceil 2^{8B-1}$ operations[4].

The method from Sect. 3.1 also generalizes well to any B, by guessing the last $B - 1$ bytes and recovering the first one by injecting a difference. Its average cost is $\lceil \frac{12}{B} \rceil + 1$ queries and $\lceil \frac{12}{B} \rceil 2^{8(B-1)-1}$ operations. We note that for $B \geq 2$

---

[4] An "operation" here is taken to mean at most the cost of an OMA digest evaluation over a message.

the messages used in either case need not be longer than 113 bytes, bypassing OSGP's restriction on message sizes.

3.4 Forgeries and a Third Key-Recovery Attack

Forgeries in the OMA digest are possible by exploiting the differential properties described in Sect. 3.1. To this end, we first explore XOR differentials and afterwards describe attacks using additive differentials.

Forgeries Using XOR-Differentials. For this attack, we consider input XOR-differences of the shape $(\Delta m_{8i+j}, \Delta m_{8i+j+1}, \Delta m_{8i+j+8}) = (80, 80, \Delta x)$ for $i = 0, \ldots, 17$ and $j = 0, \ldots, 7$. After processing message bytes $m_{8i+j}, m_{8i+j+1}, \ldots, m_{8i+j+7}$, the XOR-differences in the internal state are, up to a rotation, of the form $\Delta a = (80, 00, 00, 00, 00, 00, 00, 00)$. More precisely, after injecting $\Delta m_{8i+j} = 80$, the difference $\Delta m_{8i+j+1} = 80$ is used to prevent the difference of Δm_{8i+j} from spreading to the rest of the state. Creating this stationary difference can be achieved with probability 1. Finally, the difference $\Delta m_{8i+j+8} = \Delta x$ is used to cancel the stationary difference from above thereby creating a forgery. The success of the forgery hinges on whether the formula

$$(m_{8i+j+8} \oplus \Delta x) \pm (\mathsf{FF} \oplus ((a_j \oplus 80) + j) \lll r) = m_{8i+j+8} \pm (\mathsf{FF} \oplus (a_j + j) \lll r)$$

is satisfied. Note that the above formula again includes both possible cases which depend on the value of the key bit $k \in \{0, 1\}$. Using the formulas of Lipmaa and Moriai [23], we can determine the optimal value for Δx with respect to its probability p and the value of the key bit $k_{i+1 \bmod 12, j}$:

$k_{i+1 \bmod 12, j}$		0				1				
Δx	C0	40	01	03	07	0F	1F	3F	7F	FF
$-\log_2 p$	1	1	1	2	3	4	5	6	7	7

Thus, choosing $\Delta x \in \{C0, 40, 01\}$ has a probability of about $1/4$ of creating a valid forgery, assuming a uniformly random key bit.

Forgeries Using Additive Differentials. Injecting additive differences is also useful to get a wider range of possible high-probability differences, since every operation in the OMA digest, with the exception of the cyclic rotation, has additive differential probability 1^5.

Using a similar approach as above, one can inject the additive difference $(\Delta^\boxminus x, -\Delta^\boxminus x, -\Delta^\boxminus y)$ at (m_i, m_{i+1}, m_{i+8}). The success of the forgery here depends on the quality of the approximations

$$\Delta^\boxminus y = ((-a_j - j - 1) \lll 1) - ((-a_j - \Delta^\boxminus x - j - 1) \lll 1)$$

$$\Delta^\boxminus y = -((-a_j - j - 1) \ggg 1) + ((-a_j - \Delta^\boxminus x - j - 1) \ggg 1)$$

---

[5] Note that $\neg x = x \oplus \mathsf{FF} = -x - 1$.

for a_j chosen uniformly at random. Since cyclic rotation is not a deterministic operation with respect to additive differences, one cannot obtain $\Delta^{\boxminus}y$ that works with probability 1. By replacing $((-a_j - \Delta^{\boxminus}x - j - 1) \lll 1)$ by $((-a_j - j - 1) \lll 1) + (-\Delta^{\boxminus}x \lll 1)$, and taking advantage of Daum's results on the interaction of integer addition and rotation [11], we have $\Delta^{\boxminus}y = -((-\Delta^{\boxminus}x \lll 1) - 2\alpha + \beta)$, where (α, β) has, as a function of $\Delta^{\boxminus}x_R = \lfloor (-\Delta^{\boxminus}x)/2 \rfloor$ and $\Delta^{\boxminus}x_L = (-\Delta^{\boxminus}x) \bmod 2^7$, one of the following values of probability p:

(α, β)	p
$(0,0)$	$2^{-8}(2^7 - \Delta^{\boxminus}x_R)(2 + \Delta^{\boxminus}x_L)$
$(0,1)$	$2^{-8}\Delta^{\boxminus}x_R(2 - \Delta^{\boxminus}x_L - 1)$
$(1,0)$	$2^{-8}(2^7 - \Delta^{\boxminus}x_R)\Delta^{\boxminus}x_L$
$(1,1)$	$2^{-8}\Delta^{\boxminus}x_R(\Delta^{\boxminus}x_L + 1)$

Similar remarks apply to the rotation by 7 case. By choosing $\Delta^{\boxminus}x$ carefully, one can maximize the probability of $\Delta^{\boxminus}y$ as well, as also previously exploited by Daum [11]. For instance, choosing the difference $\Delta^{\boxminus}x = $ 02, one obtains $\Delta^{\boxminus}y \in \{$01, FC, 81, FB, FD$\}$, with respective probabilities $\{127/256, 126/256, 1/256, 1/256, 1/256\}$. Therefore, one can expect 2 queries to be sufficient in over $\approx 98\%$ of the time with this method.

Using Forgeries for Key Recovery. Such a high-probability forgery attack, dependent on the value of key bits, gives us yet another attack vector for key recovery. This attack is much simpler than the previous ones, and unlike those it does not need to work "right to left" on the message bytes: given a known plaintext, inject (02, −02, −$\Delta^{\boxminus}y$) and query a verification oracle. If the forged message is validated, recover the key bit corresponding to m_{i+8} by looking up which $\Delta^{\boxminus}y$ corresponds to which key bit. This process can be repeated 96 times to recover the entire key.

Additionally, this attack can work even over ciphertext, by using the XOR-differences (80, 80, Δx) with $\Delta x \in \{$40,C0,01$\}$. The approach here is the same, albeit requiring a few more queries, but it can be applied over unknown ciphertext encrypted with RC4, as is the case with OSGP. The attack thus completely breaks not only the OMA digest, but also the entire cryptographic security of OSGP.

The average number of queries can be reduced by using the following trick: instead of picking a difference at random from the possible set of differences, pick C0 and 40 in order. If none of them results in a forgery, the key bit can only be 1; this results in key recovery in an average of 168 queries. Algorithm 7 illustrates the XOR key-recovery attack on OSGP using this trick, only taking as input a valid ciphertext-tag pair and an oracle that verifies *ciphertexts*.

3.5 Extension of the OSGP Analysis to Other Standards

The EN 14908 algorithm, used in OSGP for key derivation and quite similar to the OMA digest, is also used in other LonTalk-derived standards for authenti-

Function RecoverKey($\mathcal{O}, c, a$)

> // $\mathcal{O}$ is an oracle that returns 1 if (c, a) is a valid OSGP
>   ciphertext-tag pair, 0 otherwise.
> // c, a is a valid OSGP ciphertext-tag pair, i.e., $\mathcal{O}(c, a) = 1$.
> $k \leftarrow \{0\}^{12}$
> for $i \leftarrow 0$ to 95 do
>> $c' \leftarrow c$
>> $c_i' \leftarrow c_i \oplus 80$
>> $c_{i+1}' \leftarrow c_{i+1} \oplus 80$
>> $c_{i+8}' \leftarrow c_{i+8} \oplus \text{C0}$
>> if $\mathcal{O}(c', a) = 1$ then
>>> $k_{\lfloor (i+8)/8 \rfloor \bmod 12, (i+8) \bmod 8} \leftarrow 0$
>>> continue
>>
>> end
>> $c_{i+8}' \leftarrow c_{i+8} \oplus 40$
>> $k_{\lfloor (i+8)/8 \rfloor \bmod 12, (i+8) \bmod 8} \leftarrow 1 - \mathcal{O}(c', a)$
>
> end
> return k

Algorithm 7. Bit-by-bit chosen-ciphertext key-recovery attack, in the context of the OSGP protocol.

cation [6,13,19–21,28]. We found evidence that the foundations of the technology (presumably also including the EN 14908 algorithm) were laid in 1988 [24, p. 3]. LonTalk was estimated to be implemented in over 90 million devices as of 2010 [14]. Given that the EN 14908 algorithm has a 48-bit key, it is already broken by design. That said, the attacks described in the previous sections can be adapted to key recovery attacks on the EN 14908 algorithm—likely present in every other LonTalk-derived standard—in much less than 2^{48} work.

4   Conclusion

We have presented a thorough analysis of the OMA digest specified in OSGP. This function has been found to be extremely weak, and cannot be assumed to provide any authenticity guarantee whatsoever. We described multiple attacks having different levels of applicability in the context of OSGP. The forgery attacks presented in Sect. 3.4 belong to the most powerful and practical, and allow to retrieve the 96-bit secret key in a mere 144 and 168 chosen-plaintext queries to a tag-verification oracle exploiting the very slow propagation of additive and XOR-differences in the OMA digest. We also described how the latter variant can work as a ciphertext-only attack, making it even more devastating. For easier verifiability, we implemented the attacks of Sect. 3 in the Python language; the code is listed in Appendix A.

In summary, the work at hand is another entry in the long list of examples of flawed authenticated encryption schemes, and shows once more how easily a determined attacker can break the security of protocols based on weak cryptography.

Acknowledgments. Our results were fully disclosed to the members of OSGP Alliance, who acknowledged our findings on the OSGP standard, in November 2014. We would like to thank Jean-Philippe Aumasson, Tanja Lange and Ilia Polian for helpful discussions during our work.

A   Proof of Concept

```
import os

def ROT8(x, c):
  return ((x%256 << c%8) | (x%256 >> -c%8)) % 256

def OMADigest(m,k):
  a = [0] * 8
  m = m[:] + [0] * (-len(m) % 144)
  for l in range(0, len(m), 144):
    b = m[l:l+144]
    for i in range(18):
      for j in range(7, -1, -1):
        if (k[i%12] >> (7 - j)) & 1:
          a[j] = (a[(j+1)%8] + b[8*i+7-j] + ROT8(~(a[j] + j), 1)) % 256
        else:
          a[j] = (a[(j+1)%8] + b[8*i+7-j] - ROT8(~(a[j] + j), -1)) % 256
  return a

def EN14908(r, m, k):
  mlen, a = len(m) - 1, r[:]
  while True:
    for i in range(6):
      for j in range(7, -1, -1):
        b = 0 if mlen < 0 else m[mlen]
        mlen -= 1
        if k[i] & (1 << (7 - j)):
          a[j] = a[(j+1)%8] + b + ROT8(~(a[j] + j), 1)
        else:
          a[j] = a[(j+1)%8] + b - ROT8(~(a[j] + j), -1)
    if mlen < 0:
      break
  return a

def RC4Encrypt(X,key):
  def RC4(key, b):
    B,S,i,j,l=[],range(256),0,0,len(key)
    while i < 256:
      j = (j + S[i] + key[i%l]) & 0xff
      S[i], S[j] = S[j], S[i]
      i += 1
    i, j = 1, 0
    while b:
      t = S[i]
      j = (j + S[i]) & 0xff
```

```
            S[i], S[j] = S[j], S[i]
            B += [S[(S[i]+S[j]) & 0xff]]
            b -= 1
            i = (i + 1) & 0xff
        return B
    S = RC4(key,len(X))
    for i in xrange(len(X)):
        X[i] ^= S[i]
    return X

def OSGPKeyDerive(k):
    k1 = EN14908([0x81, 0x3f, 0x52, 0x9a, 0x7b, 0xe3, 0x89, 0xba], [], k)
    k2 = EN14908([0x72, 0xb0, 0x91, 0x8d, 0x44, 0x05, 0xaa, 0x57], [], k)
    return k1 + k2

def OSGPEncrypt(m, k):
    k_ = OSGPKeyDerive(k)
    a  = OMADigest(m, k)
    for i in range(8):
        k_[i] ^= a[i]
    return RC4Encrypt(m, k_) + a

def OSGPDecrypt(c, k):
    assert(len(c) >= 8)
    k_ = k_ = OSGPKeyDerive(k)
    a  = c[-8:]
    for i in range(8):
        k_[i] ^= a[i]
    m = RC4Encrypt(c[:-8], k_)
    return OMADigest(m, k) == a, m

# Test vector
m = [0x02,0x02,0x00,0x30,0x00,
     0x03,0x7f,0x30,0xea,0x6d,
     0x00,0x00,0x00,0x0d,0x00,
     0x20,0x98,0x00,0x31,0xc3,
     0x00,0x08,0x00,0x00,0x00,
     0x00,0x00,0x11]
k = [0xDF] * 12
a = [0xdb, 0xe5, 0xcd, 0xe5, 0x07, 0xb1, 0xcb, 0x3d]
assert(OMADigest(m, k) == a)

def OMABackward(a,m,k,n):
    a, m = a[:], m[:] + [0] * (-len(m) % 144)
    for l in range(n):
        i, j = l // 8, l % 8
        if (k[(17-i)%12] >> (7 - j)) & 1:
            x = ROT8(a[j] - a[(j+1)%8] - m[143-8*i-j], -1)
        else:
            x = ROT8(a[(j+1)%8] + m[143-8*i-j] - a[j], 1)
        a[j] = (~x - j) % 256
    return a

def OMAForward(a,m,k,n):
    a, m = a[:], m[:] + [0] * (-len(m) % 144)
    for l in range(n, 144):
        i, j = l // 8, 7 - l % 8
        if (k[i%12] >> (7 - j)) & 1:
            a[j] = (a[(j+1)%8] + m[8*i+7-j] + ROT8(~(a[j] + j), 1)) % 256
        else:
```

```
      a[j] = (a[(j+1)%8] + m[8*i+7-j] - ROT8(~(a[j] + j), -1)) % 256
  return a

m = map(ord, os.urandom(144))
k = map(ord, os.urandom(12))
a = OMADigest(m, k)
assert( OMAForward([0]*8, m, k, 0) == OMADigest(m,k) )
assert( OMAForward(OMABackward(a,m,k,8),m,k,144-8) == a )

def TagGenOracle(m,init=[True]):
    if init[0]:
        print '[ORACLE] k = ' + str(k)
        init[0] = False
    return OMADigest(m,k)

def TagCheckOracle(m,a):
  return TagGenOracle(m) == a

def OSGPEncryptOracle(m, init=[True]):
  return OSGPEncrypt(m, k)

def OSGPCheckOracle(c):
  ok, _ = OSGPDecrypt(c, k);
  return ok

def Algorithm_4():
  m = map(ord, os.urandom(144))
  a = TagGenOracle(m)
  k = [0] * 12
  for i in range(12):
    for j in range(8):
      m_ = m[:]
      m_[136-8*i-j-1] ^= 0x80
      a_ = TagGenOracle(m_)
      b  = OMABackward(a,m,k,8*i)
      b_ = OMABackward(a_,m_,k,8*i)
      k[(17-i)%12] |= ((b[j] ^ b_[j])&1) << (7 - j)
  return k

print 'Algorithm 4: ' + str(Algorithm_4())

def Algorithm_5():
  def RecoverByte(a, b):
    x = (a[7] ^ b[7]) & 1
    for i in xrange(0,7):
        x |= ((a[6-i] ^ b[6-i] ^ a[7-i] ^ b[7-i]) & 1) << (i+1)
    return x
  k = [0] * 12
  m = map(ord, os.urandom(144))
  a = TagGenOracle(m)
  for i in range(12):
    m_ = m[:]
    m_[136-8*i-8] ^= 0x80
    a_ = TagGenOracle(m_)
    b  = OMABackward(a,m,k,8*i)
    b_ = OMABackward(a_,m_,k,8*i)
    k[(17-i)%12] = RecoverByte(b, b_)
  return k

print 'Algorithm 5: ' + str(Algorithm_5())
```

```python
def Algorithm_6():
  def recurse(m,a,k,i=0):
    if i >= 12:
      a_ = OMADigest(m,k)
      return a_ == a
    m_ = m[:]
    m_[128-8*i:] = map(ord, os.urandom(144-(128-8*i)))
    a_ = TagGenOracle(m_)
    for x in range(256):
      k[(17-i)%12] = x
      b = OMABackward(a, m, k, 8*i + 16)
      b_ = OMAForward(b, m_, k, 128 - 8*i)
      if a_ == b_ and recurse(m,a,k,i+1):
          return True
    return False
  k = [0] * 12
  m = map(ord, os.urandom(144))
  a = TagGenOracle(m)
  recurse(m,a,k)
  return k

print 'Algorithm 6: ' + str(Algorithm_6())


def Algorithm_7():
  k = [0] * 12
  c = OSGPEncryptOracle(map(ord, os.urandom(96+8)))
  for i in range(96):
    c_ = c[:]
    c_[i+0] ^= 0x80
    c_[i+1] ^= 0x80
    c_[i+8] ^= 0xC0
    if OSGPCheckOracle(c_):
      continue
    c_[i+8] = c[i+8] ^ 0x40
    k[((i+8)//8)%12] |= (0 if OSGPCheckOracle(c_) else 1) << ((i+8)%8)
  return k

print 'Algorithm 7: ' + str(Algorithm_7())

# Key-recovery attack from Section 3.4, using additive differences
def Algorithm_8():
  k = [0] * 12
  m = map(ord, os.urandom(96+8))
  a = TagGenOracle(m)
  for i in range(96):
    m_ = m[:]
    m_[i+0] = (m[i+0] + 0x02) % 256
    m_[i+1] = (m[i+1] - 0x02) % 256
    m_[i+8] = (m[i+8] - 0x01) % 256
    if TagCheckOracle(m_, a): continue
    m_[i+8] = (m[i+8] - 0xfc) % 256
    if TagCheckOracle(m_, a):
      k[((i+8)//8)%12] |= 1 << ((i+8)%8)
      continue
    m_[i+8] = (m[i+8] - 0x81) % 256
    k[((i+8)//8)%12] |= (0 if TagCheckOracle(m_, a) else 1) << ((i+8)%8)
  return k

print 'Algorithm 8: ' + str(Algorithm_8())
```

References

1. Approval of OSGP as an ETSI Standard (2012). http://www.etsi.org/news-events/news/382-news-release-18-january-2012
2. Albrecht, M.R., Paterson, K.G., Watson, G.J.: Plaintext recovery attacks against SSH. In: Proceedings of the 2009 30th IEEE Symposium on Security and Privacy, SP 2009, pp. 16–26. IEEE Computer Society (2009)
3. AlFardan, N.J., Bernstein, D.J., Paterson, K.G., Poettering, B., Schuldt, J.C.N.: On the security of RC4 in TLS. In: King, S.T. (ed.) Proceedings of the 22th USENIX Security Symposium, Washington, DC, USA, 14–16 August 2013, pp. 305–320. USENIX Association (2013)
4. AlFardan, N.J., Paterson, K.G.: Lucky thirteen: breaking the TLS and DTLS record protocols. In: 2013 IEEE Symposium on Security and Privacy, SP 2013, Berkeley, CA, USA, 19–22 May 2013, pp. 526–540. IEEE Computer Society (2013). http://ieeexplore.ieee.org/xpl/mostRecentIssue.jsp?punumber=6547086
5. ANSI: Protocol Specification For Interfacing to Data Communication Networks. ANSI C12.22-2008, American National Standards Institute, January 2009
6. ANSI: Control Network Protocol Specification. ANSI/CEA-709.1-C, American National Standards Institute, December 2010
7. Bellare, M., Namprempre, C.: Authenticated encryption: relations among notions and analysis of the generic composition paradigm. In: Okamoto, T. (ed.) ASI-ACRYPT 2000. LNCS, vol. 1976, pp. 531–545. Springer, Heidelberg (2000)
8. Bellare, M., Rogaway, P., Wagner, D.: The EAX mode of operation. In: Roy, B., Meier, W. (eds.) FSE 2004. LNCS, vol. 3017, pp. 389–407. Springer, Heidelberg (2004)
9. Bernstein, D.J.: Cryptographic competitions – Disasters (2014). http://competitions.cr.yp.to/disasters.html. Accessed 27 January 2014
10. Canvel, B., Hiltgen, A.P., Vaudenay, S., Vuagnoux, M.: Password interception in a SSL/TLS channel. In: Boneh, D. (ed.) CRYPTO 2003. LNCS, vol. 2729, pp. 583–599. Springer, Heidelberg (2003)
11. Daum, M.: Cryptanalysis of Hash functions of the MD4-family. Ph.D. thesis, Ruhr University Bochum, May 2005. http://www-brs.ub.ruhr-uni-bochum.de/netahtml/HSS/Diss/DaumMagnus/
12. Duong, T., Rizzo, J.: Here Come The $\oplus$ Ninjas (Unpublished, May 2011)
13. Echelon Corporation: LonTalk Protocol Specification, version 3.0 (1994)
14. Echelon Corporation: 90 Million Energy-Aware LonWorks Devices Worldwide (2010). http://www.businesswire.com/news/home/20100412005544/en/90-Million-Energy-Aware-LonWorks-Devices-Worldwide
15. ETSI: Open Smart Grid Protocol (OSGP). Reference DGS/OSG-001, European Telecommunications Standards Institute, Sophia Antipolis Cedex - France, January 2012. http://www.osgp.org/
16. Fluhrer, S.R., Mantin, I., Shamir, A.: Weaknesses in the key scheduling algorithm of RC4. In: Vaudenay, S., Youssef, A.M. (eds.) SAC 2001. LNCS, vol. 2259, pp. 1–24. Springer, Heidelberg (2001)
17. Fluhrer, S.R., McGrew, D.A.: Statistical analysis of the alleged RC4 keystream generator. In: Schneier, B. (ed.) FSE 2000. LNCS, vol. 1978, pp. 19–30. Springer, Heidelberg (2001)
18. Gupta, S.S., Maitra, S., Paul, G., Sarkar, S.: (Non-)Random sequences from (non-)random permutations - analysis of RC4 stream cipher. J. Cryptology 27(1), 67–108 (2014)

19. IEEE: Draft Standard for Communications Protocol Aboard Passenger Trains. IEEE P1473/D8, July 2010. http://ieeexplore.ieee.org/servlet/opac? punumber=5511471
20. ISO: Information Technology – Interconnection of Information Technology Equipment – Home Electronic System (HES) Architecture – Medium-independent Protocol Based on ANSI/CEA-709.1-B. ISO/IEC CD 14543-6-1:2006, International Organization for Standardization (2006). http://hes-standards.org/doc/ SC25_WG1_N1229.pdf
21. ISO: Information Technology - Control Network Protocol - Part 1: Protocol Stack. ISO/IEC 14908–1:2012, International Organization for Standardization, Geneva, Switzerland (2012)
22. Kursawe, K., Peters, C.: Structural Weaknesses in the Open Smart Grid Protocol. Cryptology ePrint Archive, Report 2015/088 (2015). https://eprint.iacr.org/2015/ 088
23. Lipmaa, H., Moriai, S.: Efficient algorithms for computing differential properties of addition. In: Matsui, M. (ed.) FSE 2001. LNCS, vol. 2355, pp. 336–350. Springer, Heidelberg (2002)
24. LonMark International: LON and BACnet: History and Approach. http://www.lonmark.org/connection/presentations/2012/Q2/Light-Building/ 06+LON+and+BACnet-+History+and-Newron+System.pdf
25. Minematsu, K., Lucks, S., Morita, H., Iwata, T.: Attacks and security proofs of EAX-prime. In: Moriai, S. (ed.) FSE 2013. LNCS, vol. 8424, pp. 327–347. Springer, Heidelberg (2014)
26. Möller, B., Duong, T., Kotowicz, K.: This POODLE Bites: Exploiting The SSL 3.0 Fallback, October 2014. https://www.openssl.org/bodo/ssl-poodle.pdf
27. Sepehrdad, P., Vaudenay, S., Vuagnoux, M.: Discovery and exploitation of new biases in RC4. In: Biryukov, A., Gong, G., Stinson, D.R. (eds.) SAC 2010. LNCS, vol. 6544, pp. 74–91. Springer, Heidelberg (2011)
28. Standardization Administration of China: Control Network LONWORKS Technology Specification – Part 1: Protocol Specification. GB/Z 20177.1-2006 (2006)
29. Tews, E., Weinmann, R.-P., Pyshkin, A.: Breaking 104 bit WEP in less than 60 s. In: Kim, S., Yung, M., Lee, H.-W. (eds.) WISA 2007. LNCS, vol. 4867, pp. 188–202. Springer, Heidelberg (2008)
30. Vaudenay, S.: Security flaws induced by CBC padding - applications to SSL, IPSEC, WTLS. In: Knudsen, L.R. (ed.) EUROCRYPT 2002. LNCS, vol. 2332, pp. 534–546. Springer, Heidelberg (2002)
31. Vaudenay, S., Vuagnoux, M.: Passive–only key recovery attacks on RC4. In: Adams, C., Miri, A., Wiener, M. (eds.) SAC 2007. LNCS, vol. 4876, pp. 344–359. Springer, Heidelberg (2007)

Proofs

Relaxing Full-Codebook Security: A Refined Analysis of Key-Length Extension Schemes

Peter Gaži[1]([✉]), Jooyoung Lee[2], Yannick Seurin[3],
John Steinberger[4], and Stefano Tessaro[5]

[1] IST Austria, Klosterneuburg, Austria
peter.gazi@ist.ac.at
[2] Sejong University, Seoul, Korea
jlee05@sejong.ac.kr
[3] ANSSI, Paris, France
yannick.seurin@m4x.org
[4] Tsinghua University, Beijing, People's Republic of China
jpsteinb@gmail.com
[5] UC Santa Barbara, Santa Barbara, USA
tessaro@cs.ucsb.edu

Abstract. We revisit the security (as a pseudorandom permutation) of cascading-based constructions for block-cipher key-length extension. Previous works typically considered the extreme case where the adversary is given the *entire codebook* of the construction, the only complexity measure being the number q_e of queries to the underlying ideal block cipher, representing adversary's secret-key-independent computation. Here, we initiate a systematic study of the more natural case of an adversary restricted to adaptively learning a number q_c of plaintext/ciphertext pairs that is *less than the entire codebook*. For any such q_c, we aim to determine the highest number of block-cipher queries q_e the adversary can issue without being able to successfully distinguish the construction (under a secret key) from a random permutation.

More concretely, we show the following results for key-length extension schemes using a block cipher with n-bit blocks and κ-bit keys:

- Plain cascades of length $\ell = 2r+1$ are secure whenever $q_c q_e^r \ll 2^{r(\kappa+n)}$, $q_c \ll 2^\kappa$ and $q_e \ll 2^{2\kappa}$. The bound for $r = 1$ also applies to two-key triple encryption (as used within Triple DES).
- The r-round XOR-cascade is secure as long as $q_c q_e^r \ll 2^{r(\kappa+n)}$, matching an attack by Gaži (CRYPTO 2013).
- We fully characterize the security of Gaži and Tessaro's two-call 2XOR construction (EUROCRYPT 2012) for all values of q_c, and note that the addition of a third whitening step strictly increases security for $2^{n/4} \le q_c \le 2^{3/4n}$. We also propose a variant of this construction *without* re-keying and achieving comparable security levels.

Keywords: Block ciphers · Key-length extension · Provable security · Ideal-cipher model

© International Association for Cryptologic Research 2015
G. Leander (Ed.): FSE 2015, LNCS 9054, pp. 319–341, 2015.
DOI: 10.1007/978-3-662-48116-5_16

1   Introduction

1.1   Block Ciphers and Key-Length Extension

Block ciphers (like DES [10] and AES [2]) are the workhorses of cryptography. Most importantly, they constitute the basic building block within several modes of operation for secret-key message encryption and authentication.

Formally, a block cipher with *key length* κ and *block length* n (often referred to as a (κ, n)-*block cipher*) is a family of efficiently computable (and invertible) permutations E_k on the set of n-bit strings indexed by a κ-bit key k. For example, $n = 64$ and $\kappa = 56$ for DES, and $n = 128$ and $\kappa \in \{128, 192, 256\}$ for AES.

BLOCK-CIPHER SECURITY. Most applications assume and require that the underlying block cipher behaves as a *pseudorandom permutation* (PRP), i.e., under a random secret key, it cannot be efficiently distinguished from a uniformly random permutation. To capture this notion, the PRP-security level of a block cipher is defined as the complexity required to distinguish it from a random permutation with non-negligible advantage.

The security level of a block cipher E is inherently limited by its key length κ: Given very few plaintext-ciphertext pairs $(x_i, E_k(x_i))$, a generic brute-force attack can easily recover the secret key k with roughly 2^{κ} evaluations of E. This easily yields a PRP distinguishing attack with the same complexity. Clearly, this attack directly affects legacy designs with short keys, such as DES, for which 2^{56} is well within the boundaries of feasible computation.

KEY-LENGTH EXTENSION AND THE ICM. Nonetheless, legacy designs often remain attractive in niche applications, like e.g. in the financial sector, where DES-based construction are used to encipher PIN numbers due to their short block length (as in the EMV standard [1]). In order to mitigate the effects of the above generic attacks, the well-known *key-length extension* (KLE) problem addresses the following question:

> *"Does there exist a construction* C *transforming any* (κ, n)-*block cipher* E *into a* (κ', n)-*block cipher* C$[E]$ *(for* $\kappa' > \kappa$*), such that* C$[E]$ *is secure against generic attackers (using* E *as a black-box) investing more than* 2^{κ} *effort?"*

Starting with the work of Killian and Rogaway on DESX [16], and followed by a series of subsequent works [5,9,12,14,15,19], KLE has been formalized and studied in the *ideal cipher model* (ICM), where the underlying block cipher is modeled as an *ideal cipher*, i.e., E_k is an independent random permutation for every individual key k. Then, ICM PRP security of a KLE construction C$[E]$ is captured by considering a random experiment where the attacker (also known as a *distinguisher*) issues two types of queries:

- **Block-cipher queries** to evaluate the block cipher $E_k(x)$ and $E_k^{-1}(y)$ for any k, x, and y chosen by the distinguisher.

- **Construction queries** to evaluate on a chosen n-bit input x either the KLE construction $\mathsf{C}[E]_{K'}$ with a uniformly random secret κ'-bit key K', or a uniform random permutation P independent of E. The respective inverses can also be evaluated.

The distinguisher's goal is to decide whether construction queries are answered by the construction or by P, and its power is measured in terms of the number $q_e \leq 2^{n+\kappa}$ of queries of the former type, and the number $q_c \leq 2^n$ of queries of the latter type. Security of C is measured in terms of which values of (q_c, q_e) do not allow distinguishing with non-negligible advantage.

RELAXING FULL-CODEBOOK SECURITY. So far, the security of KLE constructions (with the notable exception of the work of Killian and Rogaway [16]) has been analyzed in the *full-codebook regime*, i.e., where we allow $q_c = 2^n$, and then see how large q_e can be while still retaining pseudorandomness. However, there is often no rational reason to assume that $q_c = 2^n$. Not only this value is usually unreasonably large, but also, we can either easily restrict the number of block cipher evaluations on a certain secret key at the application level (by enforcing re-keying) *or* when using the KLE construction within a certain mode of operation, the security analysis of the latter may simply force security to only hold for smaller q_c anyway (e.g., $q_c \leq 2^{n/2}$ for CBC modes).

In this paper, we relax the unreasonably strong requirement of full-codebook security, and undertake the first in-depth investigation of the security of KLE constructions in the realistic scenario where $q_c \ll 2^n$.

1.2 Plain and Randomized Cascades

Before we turn to our contributions, let us first review previous works on KLE in the full-codebook regime $q_c = 2^n$. A summary of the attainable PRP security levels is given in Appendix A.

CASCADING-BASED KLE. The most natural KLE approach is perhaps *cascading*, generalizing the idea behind triple DES. Formally, the cascade of length ℓ for a (κ, n)-block cipher E is the $(\ell \cdot \kappa, n)$-block cipher which takes an $\ell\kappa$-bit key $\mathsf{mk} = (k_1, \ldots, k_\ell) \in (\{0,1\}^\kappa)^\ell$ and encrypts a plaintext $x \in \{0,1\}^n$ by computing

$$y = \mathsf{CE}_{\mathsf{mk}}[E](x) = E_{k_\ell} \circ E_{k_{\ell-1}} \circ \cdots \circ E_{k_2} \circ E_{k_1}(x).$$

It is well known that the case $\ell = 2$ still allows for a 2^κ-query meet-in-the-middle attack (even though only a smaller distinguishing advantage is achievable for $q_e < 2^\kappa$ as shown by Aiello et al. [3]). For the case $r = 3$ (which generalizes 3DES), Bellare and Rogaway [5] first proved PRP security for $q_e \leq 2^{\kappa+n/2}$. This result was later generalized to arbitrary length ℓ by Gaži and Maurer [14]. Their bound on q_e was however far from tight, and was first improved by Lee [19], and a tight bound (matching an attack by Gaži [12]) was only recently given by Dai, Lee, Mennink, and Steinberger [9].

RANDOMIZED CASCADES. Another approach to key-length extension generalizes the DESX construction, using additional key material to randomize inputs and

Table 1. Overview of our results. Parameters q_c, q_e for which we prove security.

Construction	Security
XCE with r rounds	$q_c q_e^r \ll 2^{r(n+\kappa)}$ (Tight)
2XOR	$q_e \ll \max\{2^{\kappa+n/2}, 2^{\kappa+n-\log(q_c)}\}$ (Tight)
3XOR	$q_c \leq 2^{2/3n} : q_e \ll 2^{\kappa + \frac{4-\log(q_c)}{5}n}$ $\quad$ $q_c \in [2^{\frac{2}{3}n}, 2^{\frac{3}{4}n}] : q_e \ll 2^{\kappa + (2-2\log(q_c))n}$
3XSK	$q_c \leq 2^{2/3n}: q_e \ll 2^{\kappa + \frac{4-\log(q_c)}{5}n}$
CE with $\ell = 2r+1$ rounds	$q_c q_e^r \ll 2^{r(\kappa+n)}, q_c \ll 2^\kappa, q_e \ll 2^{2\kappa}$
Two-key triple encryption	$q_c q_e \ll 2^{\kappa+n}, q_c \ll 2^\kappa, q_e \ll 2^{2\kappa}$

outputs of block-cipher calls. (This technique is often called *whitening*.) For example, the r-round XOR-cascade of a (κ, n)-block cipher E is the $(\kappa + (r + 1)n, n)$-block cipher which, on input key (k, z) (where $z = (z_0, z_1, \ldots, z_r)$ consists of $(r + 1)$ n-bit strings) and message x, returns

$$\mathsf{XCE}[E]((k, z), x) = \oplus_{z_r} \circ E_{\phi_r(k)} \circ \oplus_{z_{r-1}} \circ E_{\phi_{r-1}(k)} \circ \cdots \circ \oplus_{z_1} \circ E_{\phi_1(k)} \circ \oplus_{z_0}(x),$$

where $\oplus_z$ maps x' to $x' \oplus z$, and $\phi_1, \ldots, \phi_r$ are permutations on the κ-bit strings such that $\phi_i(k) \neq \phi_j(k)$ for all k and $i \neq j$. Security bounds for XOR-cascades in the full-codebook regime were proved by Lee [19] and by Gaži [12]. The latter work considered a variant without the last whitening step, and in combination with the result on key-alternating ciphers [8] led to tight bounds.

A simple variant of two-round XOR-cascades, called 2XOR, was studied by Gaži and Tessaro [15], where the third key z_2 is omitted, and $z_0 = z_1$. They prove PRP security for $q_e \leq 2^{\kappa+n/2}$, and that this security level is optimal (for $q_c = 2^n$) with respect to a large class of two-call constructions. We finally emphasize that the work by Killian and Rogaway [16] analyzing DESX (which is the case $r = 1$) is a notable exception to the above restriction to the full-domain regime, and exhibits a smooth security trade-off for any q_c and q_e as long as $q_c \cdot q_e \leq 2^{n+\kappa}$.

1.3 Our Contributions

While tight bounds are known in the full-codebook regime, the landscape is still mostly uncharted when moving to the case $q_c \ll 2^n$. This paper proves lower and upper bounds on the PRP security level of existing and new KLE constructions in the setting where $q_c \ll 2^n$. While a summary of our bounds is given in Table 1, we now discuss our contributions a bit more in detail.

We start with the randomized case:

- **Tight bounds for XOR cascades.** We provide *tight* bounds for XOR-cascades, matching an attack previously given by Gaži [12].
- **Characterizing 2XOR.** We complete the picture of the security of 2XOR for all $q_c \leq 2^n$, showing that $q_e \leq 2^{\kappa+n/2}$ is tight when $q_c \in [2^{n/2}, 2^n]$, and observing that otherwise $q_c \cdot q_e \leq 2^{\kappa+n}$ is necessary and sufficient for $q_c \leq 2^{n/2}$.

- **The 3XOR construction.** We show that adding the whitening key to the output of 2XOR yields a construction—that we name 3XOR—which is always at least as secure as 2XOR and strictly more secure for $2^{n/4} < q_c < 2^{3/4n}$.
- **A two-call construction with no re-keying.** We finally propose a variant of 3XOR (called 3XSK) where both block-cipher calls are with the *same* key, whereas the middle whitening key is a permutation of the original one. The security is comparable to that of 3XOR for $q_c \leq 2^{2/3n}$.

Our results also improve our picture with respect to plain cascading.

- **Odd-length plain cascades.** We prove that cascades of odd length $\ell = 2r+1$ are secure whenever $q_c q_e^r \ll 2^{r(\kappa+n)}$, $q_c \ll 2^\kappa$, and $q_e \ll 2^{2\kappa}$. For κ and n satisfying $\kappa \geq \frac{rn}{r+1}$, this improves on the security bound of Dai *et al.* [9] when $q_c \leq 2^{\frac{rn}{r+1}}$. Moreover, when $\kappa \geq n$, this yields a tight bound (matching Gaži's attack [12]) for *all* parameters (for $\kappa \leq n$, the situation is more involved, see Sect. 5 for a complete discussion).
- **Two-key triple encryption.** We prove a similar bound for two-key triple encryption, where the first and third keys are identical, as in Triple DES.

OVERVIEW OF OUR TECHNIQUES. It turns out that the techniques behind our results are fairly general. We start by defining a general class of KLE constructions called *randomized KLE schemes*, that capture both plain cascades, XOR-cascades and others. Our core technical tool is then a lemma relating the security of a construction from this class to a particular cipher that can be derived from it, called a *sequential cipher*, also introduced here. Such ciphers constitute a generalization of key-alternating ciphers (or KACs, for short), studied in [4,6,17,18,24], and implement a block cipher by invoking a number of permutations in a sequential manner. Our lemma generalizes a previous result by Gaži [12], which only considered the case of KACs but neither our relaxation to randomized KLEs, nor the case without a full codebook.

To instantiate some of our bounds, we provide a generalized analysis of sequential ciphers, extending recent bounds by Chen and Steinberger [8].

1.4 Further Related Works

We note in passing that an orthogonal line of works devoted to cascade-like construction was initiated by Luby and Rackoff [20]. These works study *standard model* security amplification achieved by plain and randomized cascades, and in particular show how, when instantiated with a block cipher which is a weak PRP in the sense of the attacker achieving a large distinguishing advantage, these constructions reduce the best possible advantage with an increasing number of rounds. Increasingly tighter bounds have been given by Maurer and Tessaro [22], and by Tessaro [25]. An information-theoretic version of this question was also studied [21,26].

2   Preliminaries

2.1   Basic Notation and Block Ciphers

In all the following, we fix integers $n, \kappa > 0$, and denote $N = 2^n$ and $K = 2^\kappa$. The set of all permutations on $\{0,1\}^n$ will be denoted $\mathcal{P}_n$. For a set T and an integer $\ell \geq 1$, $(T)_\ell$ denotes the set of all sequences that consist of ℓ distinct elements of T. For integers $1 \leq \ell \leq t$, we will write $(t)_\ell = t(t-1)\cdots(t-\ell+1)$. If $|T| = t$, then $(t)_\ell$ becomes the size of $(T)_\ell$.

A block cipher is a function family $E : \mathcal{K} \times \{0,1\}^n \to \{0,1\}^n$ such that for all $k \in \mathcal{K}$ the mapping $E(k, \cdot)$ is a permutation on $\{0,1\}^n$. We denote by $\mathsf{BC}(\mathcal{K}, n)$ the set of all such block ciphers, shortening to $\mathsf{BC}(\kappa, n)$ when $\mathcal{K} = \{0,1\}^\kappa$. In the ideal-cipher model, a block cipher E is chosen from $\mathsf{BC}(\kappa, n)$ uniformly at random and made available to the participants through oracle queries. It allows for two types of oracle queries $E(k, x)$ and $E^{-1}(k, y)$ for $x, y \in \{0,1\}^n$ and $k \in \{0,1\}^\kappa$.[1] The answer to an inverse query $E^{-1}(k, y)$ is $x \in \{0,1\}^n$ such that $E(k, x) = y$.

For a set $\mathcal{Q} = ((x_1, y_1), \ldots, (x_q, y_q)) \in (\{0,1\}^n \times \{0,1\}^n)^q$ and a permutation $P \in \mathcal{P}_n$, we say that P extends $\mathcal{Q}$, denoted $P \vdash \mathcal{Q}$, if $P(x_i) = y_i$ for $i = 1, \ldots, q$. The *domain* and the *range* of $\mathcal{Q}$ are defined as

$$\mathsf{Dom}(\mathcal{Q}) = \{x \in \{0,1\}^n : (x, y) \in \mathcal{Q}\}, \; \mathsf{Rng}(\mathcal{Q}) = \{y \in \{0,1\}^n : (x, y) \in \mathcal{Q}\}$$

respectively. By an abuse of notation, we will sometimes denote $\mathcal{Q}$ the bijection from $\mathsf{Dom}(\mathcal{Q})$ to $\mathsf{Rng}(\mathcal{Q})$ such that $\mathcal{Q}(x_i) = y_i$ for $i = 1, \ldots, q$. Thus, for another set (bijection) $\mathcal{Q}' \in (\{0,1\}^n \times \{0,1\}^n)^{q'}$, we have

$$\mathsf{Dom}(\mathcal{Q}' \circ \mathcal{Q}) = \{x \in \{0,1\}^n : (x, y) \in \mathcal{Q} \land y \in \mathsf{Dom}(\mathcal{Q}')\}$$
$$\mathsf{Rng}(\mathcal{Q}' \circ \mathcal{Q}) = \{y \in \{0,1\}^n : (x, y) \in \mathcal{Q}' \land x \in \mathsf{Rng}(\mathcal{Q})\}$$

and similar definitions for the composition of more than two bijections. For a set $\mathcal{Q} = ((x_1, k_1, y_1), \ldots, (x_q, k_q, y_q)) \in (\{0,1\}^n \times \{0,1\}^\kappa \times \{0,1\}^n)^q$ and a block cipher $E \in \mathsf{BC}(\kappa, n)$, we say that E extends $\mathcal{Q}$, denoted $E \vdash \mathcal{Q}$, if $E(k_i, x_i) = y_i$ for $i = 1, \ldots, q$.

2.2   Indistinguishability in Idealized Models

In this paper, we consider block ciphers that are built (in a black-box way) on top of an existing primitive F. The primitive F is modeled as an ideal oracle (publicly accessible to the adversary), whose answers follow some probability distribution. Namely, we will consider two slightly different settings: the so-called *KLE-setting* where F will be the ideal cipher E; and the so-called *SC-setting*[2] where F will be a tuple of random permutations $\boldsymbol{P} = (P_1, \ldots, P_m)$. In both settings, we consider

---

[1] We interchangeably use both notations $E(k, x)$ and $E_k(x)$, and similarly $E^{-1}(k, y)$ and $E_k^{-1}(y)$.

[2] This refers to the notion of a *sequential cipher* defined in Sect. 3.1.

a construction C which encrypts a message $x \in \{0,1\}^n$ with some (master) key[3] $mk \in \{0,1\}^{\kappa'}$ by making calls to F, and denote $C[F]$ the resulting block cipher (hence $C[F] \in BC(\kappa', n)$, and $C_{mk}[F]$ is the permutation associated to key mk).

To define security, we consider an adversary (a.k.a. distinguisher) D which interacts with a pair of oracles that we denote generically (P, F). The goal of D is to distinguish whether it is interacting with $(C_{mk}[F], F)$ for some uniformly random key mk (a case we will informally refer to as the "real" world) or with (P, F) where P is a random n-bit permutation independent from F (the "ideal" world). Note that in both worlds the first oracle P is a permutation that can be queried in both directions. The distinguisher's advantage is defined as

$$\mathbf{Adv}_C^{cca}(D) = \left| \Pr\left[D^{C_{mk}[F],F} = 1 \right] - \Pr\left[D^{P,F} = 1 \right] \right|$$

where the first probability is taken over the random choice of mk and the random answers of F, and the second probability is taken over the random choice of P and F. We refer to D's queries to its first and second oracle as *construction* and *primitive* queries, respectively. In the KLE-setting (SC-setting), the primitive queries are sometimes referred to more concretely as block-cipher queries (permutation queries), respectively.

In the KLE-setting, for $q_c, q_e \geq 0$ we define

$$\mathbf{Adv}_C^{cca}(q_c, q_e) = \max_D \mathbf{Adv}_C^{cca}(D)$$

where the maximum is taken over all distinguishers making exactly q_c construction and q_e ideal-cipher queries. Similarly, in the SC-setting, for $q_c, q_p \geq 0$,

$$\mathbf{Adv}_C^{cca}(q_c, q_p) = \max_D \mathbf{Adv}_C^{cca}(D)$$

where the maximum is taken over all distinguishers making exactly q_c construction queries and q_p permutation queries to *each* permutation oracle P_i.

In all the paper, we assume that the distinguisher is computationally unbounded, deterministic, and that it never makes redundant queries (these last two assumptions being *wlog*). In accordance with several recent works on the topic, we are using Patarin's H-coefficients technique [23] in some of our proofs. Our use of the H-coefficients technique will be self-contained, for a more detailed introduction to this method see for example [8].

3   From Randomized KLE Schemes to Sequential Ciphers

In this section we study the relationship of two general classes of constructions that we first define. On one hand, we consider *randomized KLE schemes* that

---

[3] We use the wording *master key* to emphasize that it will usually be used to derive sub-keys for calling the underlying block cipher. We also write $mk = (k, z)$ for key-length extension schemes and $mk = z$ for sequential ciphers (see Sect. 3.1).

generalize both cascades and XOR-cascades,[4] on the other hand we introduce *sequential ciphers* that are in turn a generalization of key-alternating ciphers (whose definition is also provided below). We show that every randomized KLE scheme induces a sequential cipher and the security properties of these two constructions are tightly connected.

3.1 Definitions

RANDOMIZED KLE. Let $n, \kappa > 0$ be some fixed parameters denoting the block- and key-length of the underlying block cipher, respectively. Fix additional parameters $\lambda, r, m > 0$. Let $(\phi_1, \ldots, \phi_m)$ be m permutations of $\{0,1\}^\kappa$ with the property that for any $k \in \{0,1\}^\kappa$, the values $(\phi_1(k), \ldots, \phi_m(k))$ are distinct. (Note that this imposes $m \leq 2^\kappa$.) Let $\sigma : \{1, \ldots, r\} \to \{1, \ldots, m\}$ be a surjective function.[5] For $i = 0, \ldots, r$, let

$$\rho^i : \{0,1\}^\lambda \times \{0,1\}^n \to \{0,1\}^n$$

be a function such that for each $z \in \{0,1\}^\lambda$, $\rho^i(z, \cdot)$ (also denoted $\rho^i_z(\cdot)$) is a permutation on $\{0,1\}^n$.[6]

A *randomized key-length extension scheme* R transforms a block cipher $E \in \mathsf{BC}(\kappa, n)$ into a new block cipher $\mathsf{R}[E] \in \mathsf{BC}(\kappa + \lambda, n)$ specified as follows: for a plaintext $x \in \{0,1\}^n$ and a key $(k, z) \in \{0,1\}^\kappa \times \{0,1\}^\lambda$, the ciphertext is defined as (see Fig. 1)

$$\mathsf{R}[E]((k,z), x) = \rho^r_z \circ E_{k_{\sigma(r)}} \circ \rho^{r-1}_z \circ E_{k_{\sigma(r-1)}} \circ \cdots \circ E_{k_{\sigma(2)}} \circ \rho^1_z \circ E_{k_{\sigma(1)}} \circ \rho^0_z(x) .$$

where we simply write $(k_1, \ldots, k_m) = (\phi_1(k), \ldots, \phi_m(k))$. For a fixed key (k, z), we also denote $\mathsf{R}_{k,z}[E]$ the permutation $x \mapsto \mathsf{R}[E]((k,z), x)$.

SEQUENTIAL CIPHER. With the same primitives σ and $(\rho^0, \ldots, \rho^r)$, a *sequential cipher* S transforms a set of permutations $\boldsymbol{P} = (P_1, \ldots, P_m)$ into a block cipher $\mathsf{S}[\boldsymbol{P}] \in \mathsf{BC}(\lambda, n)$ specified as follows: for a plaintext $x \in \{0,1\}^n$ and a key $z \in \{0,1\}^\lambda$, the ciphertext is defined as (again see Fig. 1)

$$\mathsf{S}[\boldsymbol{P}](z, x) = \rho^r_z \circ P_{\sigma(r)} \circ \rho^{r-1}_z \circ P_{\sigma(r-1)} \circ \cdots \circ P_{\sigma(2)} \circ \rho^1_z \circ P_{\sigma(1)} \circ \rho^0_z(x) .$$

For a fixed key z, we denote $\mathsf{S}_z[\boldsymbol{P}]$ the permutation $x \mapsto \mathsf{S}[\boldsymbol{P}](z, x)$.

---

[4] Our randomized KLE schemes also cover the notion of *sequential constructions* introduced in [12]. Since the latter are KLE schemes, they syntactically differ from the notion of a sequential cipher considered here.

[5] In case this causes confusion, r is the number of rounds, m is the number of distinct keys that are used to call the underlying block cipher, and σ specifies which key is used at each round.

[6] Though each ρ^i is syntactically a block cipher, we prefer to avoid this wording since in most of the paper the ρ^i's will be much simpler than E, the block cipher underlying the key-length extension scheme.

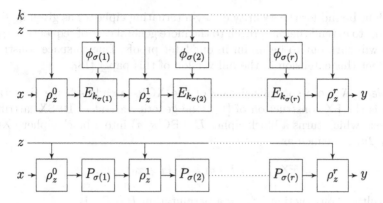

Fig. 1. The randomized key-length extension construction R[E] (top), and its induced sequential cipher $\overline{R}[P]$ (bottom).

3.2 Induced Sequential Ciphers

When the key k is fixed in some key-length extension scheme R, the resulting scheme can be regarded as a sequential cipher with key space $\{0,1\}^\lambda$ using independent random permutations $P_1, \ldots, P_m$ in place of $E_{\phi_1(k)}, \ldots, E_{\phi_m(k)}$ in the ideal cipher model. We formalize this remark as follows.

Definition 1. *Let* R *be a randomized key-length extension scheme defined as above. The* induced sequential cipher *of* R, *denoted* $\overline{R}$, *is a sequential cipher which specifies a block cipher* $\overline{R}[P] \in BC(\lambda, n)$ *from an m-tuple of permutations* $P = (P_1, \ldots, P_m)$ *of* $\{0,1\}^n$ *by replacing each call to* $E(\phi_i(k), \cdot)$, *resp.* $E^{-1}(\phi_i(k), \cdot)$ *when computing* $R_{k,z}[E](x)$ *by a call to* $P_i(\cdot)$, *resp.* $P_i^{-1}(\cdot)$ *in the computation of* $\overline{R}_z[P](x)$.

Example 1. If we let σ be the identity, $\lambda = (r+1)n$ and $\rho^i(z, u) = u \oplus z_i$ for $i = 0, \ldots, r$ where z is split as $z = (z_0, \ldots, z_r) \in (\{0,1\}^n)^{r+1}$, then the resulting randomized KLE and sequential cipher constructions are called an *XOR-cascade scheme* and a *key-alternating cipher (KAC)*, respectively.

More formally, the r-round XOR-cascade construction XCE turns a block cipher $E \in BC(\kappa, n)$ into a new block cipher $XCE[E] \in BC(\kappa + (r+1)n, n)$ as follows. Let $(\phi_1, \ldots, \phi_r)$ be r permutations of $\{0,1\}^\kappa$ with the property that for any $k \in \{0,1\}^\kappa$, the values $(\phi_1(k), \ldots, \phi_r(k))$ are distinct. Then for a plaintext $x \in \{0,1\}^n$ and a key $(k, z) \in \{0,1\}^\kappa \times (\{0,1\}^n)^{r+1}$ with $z = (z_0, \ldots, z_r)$, the ciphertext is defined as (see also Fig. 2):

$$XCE[E]((k,z), x) = \oplus_{z_r} \circ E_{\phi_r(k)} \circ \oplus_{z_{r-1}} \circ E_{\phi_{r-1}(k)} \circ \cdots \circ \oplus_{z_1} \circ E_{\phi_1(k)} \circ \oplus_{z_0}(x),$$

where $\oplus_{z_i}$ denotes the mapping $x \mapsto x \oplus z_i$. Its induced sequential cipher $\overline{XCE}$ is the key-alternating cipher (hence denoted KAC)

$$\overline{XCE}[P](z, x) = KAC[P](z, x) = \oplus_{z_r} \circ P_r \circ \oplus_{z_{r-1}} \circ P_{r-1} \circ \cdots \circ \oplus_{z_1} \circ P_1 \circ \oplus_{z_0}(x).$$

A tight bound for the security of key-alternating ciphers was given in [8]. We show how to extend their approach to the more general case of sequential ciphers, as this will turn out to be useful in our later proofs. Due to space constraints, we present this extension in the full version of this paper [13].

Example 2. A more specialized case of the XOR-cascade scheme (i.e., taking $r = 1$) is the FX construction of [16] (the generic variant of DESX, attributed to Rivest) which turns a block cipher $E \in \mathsf{BC}(\kappa, n)$ into a block cipher $\mathsf{FX}[E] \in \mathsf{BC}(\kappa + 2n, n)$ defined as

$$\mathsf{FX}_{k,(z_0,z_1)}[E](x) = E_k(x \oplus z_0) \oplus z_1.$$

The resulting construction $\overline{\mathsf{FX}}$, for a permutation $P \in \mathcal{P}_n$, is

$$\overline{\mathsf{FX}}_{(z_0,z_1)}[P](x) = P(x \oplus z_0) \oplus z_1,$$

which is exactly the Even-Mansour cipher [11].

3.3   The Reduction

In this section we prove our main lemma that reduces the security of a randomized key-length extension scheme to the security of the corresponding induced sequential cipher. It can be seen as a generalization of [12, Theorem 2] to more general classes of constructions and as well to the setting where the number of construction queries q_c is arbitrary (rather than $q_c = 2^n$).

Lemma 1. *Let R be a randomized key-length extension scheme and let $\overline{\mathsf{R}}$ be its induced sequential cipher. Then for $q_c, q_e, M > 0$, one has*

$$\mathbf{Adv}_{\mathsf{R}}^{\mathrm{cca}}(q_c, q_e) \leq \frac{mq_e}{KM} + \mathbf{Adv}_{\overline{\mathsf{R}}}^{\mathrm{cca}}(q_c, M).$$

Proof. Consider a distinguisher D interacting with (P, E), where E is an ideal cipher and P is either the construction $\mathsf{R}_{k,z}[E]$ for a uniformly random key $(k, z) \in \{0,1\}^\kappa \times \{0,1\}^\lambda$, or a random permutation independent from E. Following the H-coefficients technique [8,23], we summarize all the information gathered by the distinguisher when interacting with the system (P, E) in the *raw query transcript* which is simply the ordered list of queries of D to its oracles together with their answers. From this raw query transcript we can build the *construction query transcript*

$$\mathcal{Q}_C = ((x_1, y_1), \ldots, (x_{q_c}, y_{q_c})),$$

where the i-th pair (x_i, y_i) indicates that the i-th query to the construction/random permutation oracle was either $P(x_i)$ with answer y_i or $P^{-1}(y_i)$ with answer y_i. Similarly, we can build the *ideal cipher query transcript*

$$\mathcal{Q}_E = ((u_1, k_1, v_1), \ldots, (u_{q_e}, k_{q_e}, v_{q_e})),$$

where the i-th triple (u_i, k_i, v_i) indicates that the i-th query to the ideal cipher was either $E(k_i, u_i)$ with answer v_i or $E^{-1}(k_i, v_i)$ with answer u_i. (Since the distinguisher is deterministic, the raw query transcript can unambiguously be reconstructed from the pair $(\mathcal{Q}_C, \mathcal{Q}_E)$.)

Moreover, in the real world, the key k (but not z) is given for free to D at the end of its queries, while in the ideal world (where no such key exists), a dummy key k is drawn uniformly at random and given to D. (This can only *increase* the distinguishing advantage since D can disregard this additional information.) This results in what we simply call the *transcript* $\tau = (\mathcal{Q}_C, \mathcal{Q}_E, k)$ of the attack. We will say that a transcript $\tau = (\mathcal{Q}_C, \mathcal{Q}_E, k)$ is *attainable* if there exists a permutation P and a block cipher E such that the interaction of D with (P, E) yields queries transcripts $(\mathcal{Q}_C, \mathcal{Q}_E)$ (said otherwise, the probability to obtain this transcript in the "ideal" world is non-zero). Finally, we let T_{re}, resp. T_{id} denote the probability distribution of the transcript τ induced by the real world, resp. the ideal world (note that these two probability distributions depend on the distinguisher). By extension, we use the same notation to denote a random variable distributed according to each distribution.

Let D be an optimal distinguisher making q_c construction queries and q_e ideal-cipher queries such that[7]

$$\mathbf{Adv}_R^{\text{cca}}(q_c, q_e) = \mathbf{Adv}_R^{\text{cca}}(D) = \sum_{\tau \in T_1} \Pr[T_{\text{id}} = \tau] - \sum_{\tau \in T_1} \Pr[T_{\text{re}} = \tau]$$

and let T_1 be the set of attainable transcripts $\tau = (\mathcal{Q}_C, \mathcal{Q}_E, k)$ such that the distinguisher outputs 1 when obtaining τ. Given an ideal-cipher queries transcript $\mathcal{Q}_E$, we also define the set of bad keys as

$$\mathsf{Bad}(\mathcal{Q}_E) = \{k \in \{0,1\}^\kappa : |\{(x, y) : (x, k, y) \in \mathcal{Q}_E\}| > M\}.$$

(Hence, a key k is bad if it appears strictly more than M times in $\mathcal{Q}_E$.) We say that an attainable transcript $\tau = (\mathcal{Q}_C, \mathcal{Q}_E, k)$ is *bad* if $\phi_i(k) \in \mathsf{Bad}(\mathcal{Q}_E)$ for some $i = 1, \ldots, m$, and *good* otherwise. We denote resp. T_{bad} and T_{good} the sets of bad and good transcripts (which form a partition of the set of attainable transcripts T). Then we have

$$\begin{aligned}
\mathbf{Adv}_R^{\text{cca}}(D) &= \sum_{\tau \in T_1} \Pr[T_{\text{id}} = \tau] - \sum_{\tau \in T_1} \Pr[T_{\text{re}} = \tau] \\
&\leq \sum_{\tau \in T_{\text{bad}}} \Pr[T_{\text{id}} = \tau] + \sum_{\tau \in T_1 \cap T_{\text{good}}} \Pr[T_{\text{id}} = \tau] - \sum_{\tau \in T_1 \cap T_{\text{good}}} \Pr[T_{\text{re}} = \tau] \quad (1)
\end{aligned}$$

where the inequality follows from the fact that T_{good} and T_{bad} form a partition of the set of attainable transcripts T. We upper bound each summand in turn.

Since in the ideal world the key k is drawn uniformly at random at the end of the interaction of the distinguisher with its oracles, we clearly can bound

---

[7] Without loss of generality, we can assume $\sum_{\tau \in T_1} \Pr[T_{\text{id}} = \tau] \geq \sum_{\tau \in T_1} \Pr[T_{\text{re}} = \tau]$ by slightly modifying D if necessary.

$\sum_{\tau \in \mathcal{T}_{\text{bad}}} \Pr[T_{\text{id}} = \tau] = \Pr[T_{\text{id}} \in \mathcal{T}_{\text{bad}}]$ as

$$\Pr[T_{\text{id}} \in \mathcal{T}_{\text{bad}}] \leq \sum_{i=1}^{m} \Pr[k \leftarrow_{\$} \{0,1\}^{\kappa} : \phi_i(k) \in \mathsf{Bad}(\mathcal{Q}_E)] \leq \frac{mq_e}{KM}, \qquad (2)$$

where the last inequality follows from the fact that each ϕ_i is a permutation (hence $\phi_i(k)$ is uniformly random) and that the size of $\mathsf{Bad}(\mathcal{Q}_E)$ is at most q_e/M by definition.

To upper bound the second term, we consider the following (probabilistic) distinguisher $\overline{\mathsf{D}}$ against construction $\overline{\mathsf{R}}$ (in the random permutation model), which uses D as a subroutine. $\overline{\mathsf{D}}$ has access to $m + 1$ permutation oracles $(P_0, P_1, \ldots, P_m)$, where P_0 is either the construction $\overline{\mathsf{R}}_z[P_1, \ldots, P_m]$ for some random key $z \leftarrow_{\$} \{0,1\}^{\lambda}$, or a random permutation independent from $(P_1, \ldots, P_m)$. At the beginning of the experiment, $\overline{\mathsf{D}}$ draws a key $k \leftarrow_{\$} \{0,1\}^{\kappa}$ uniformly at random. Then, $\overline{\mathsf{D}}$ runs D and answers its queries as follows. First, it relays any construction query from D to its own construction oracle and relays back the corresponding answer to D. When D makes any ideal cipher query for some key $k' \notin \{\phi_1(k), \ldots \phi_m(k)\}$, $\overline{\mathsf{D}}$ simulates a perfectly random permutation associated with k'. If D makes an ideal cipher query for some key $\phi_i(k)$, $i = 1, \ldots, m$, $\overline{\mathsf{D}}$ relays this query to permutation oracle P_i and forwards the corresponding answer to D. However, if D attempts to make more than M queries corresponding to some key $\phi_i(k)$, $i = 1, \ldots, m$, then $\overline{\mathsf{D}}$ aborts and outputs 0. (Hence $\overline{\mathsf{D}}$ always makes at most M queries to each permutation oracle P_i, $i = 1, \ldots, m$.) Otherwise, once D has finished its queries, $\overline{\mathsf{D}}$ forwards k to D (recall that we include k in the transcript) and outputs the same value as D. Clearly, when $\overline{\mathsf{D}}$ is interacting with $(P_0, P_1, \ldots, P_m)$, where P_0 is the construction $\overline{\mathsf{R}}_z[P_1, \ldots, P_m]$ then it is perfectly simulating the real world $(\mathsf{R}_{k,z}[E], E)$ to D, while when $\overline{\mathsf{D}}$ is interacting with $(P_0, P_1, \ldots, P_m)$ where P_0 is independent from $(P_1, \ldots, P_m)$, then it is perfectly simulating the ideal world (P, E) to D. Hence, the distinguishing advantage of $\overline{\mathsf{D}}$ is

$$\mathbf{Adv}_{\overline{\mathsf{R}}}^{\text{cca}}(\overline{\mathsf{D}}) = \left| \sum_{\tau \in \mathcal{T}_1 \cap \mathcal{T}_{\text{good}}} \Pr[T_{\text{re}} = \tau] - \sum_{\tau \in \mathcal{T}_1 \cap \mathcal{T}_{\text{good}}} \Pr[T_{\text{id}} = \tau] \right|. \qquad (3)$$

Since $\overline{\mathsf{D}}$ makes at most q_c queries to its construction and at most M queries to each permutation oracle P_i, $i = 1, \ldots, m$, and since in the information-theoretic setting the advantage of a probabilistic adversary cannot be larger than the one of the best deterministic adversary, one has

$$\mathbf{Adv}_{\overline{\mathsf{R}}}^{\text{cca}}(\overline{\mathsf{D}}) \leq \mathbf{Adv}_{\overline{\mathsf{R}}}^{\text{cca}}(q_c, M). \qquad (4)$$

Combining (1), (2), (3), and (4), we obtain

$$\mathbf{Adv}_{\mathsf{R}}^{\text{cca}}(\mathsf{D}) = \mathbf{Adv}_{\mathsf{R}}^{\text{cca}}(q_c, q_e) \leq \frac{mq_e}{KM} + \mathbf{Adv}_{\overline{\mathsf{R}}}^{\text{cca}}(q_c, M). \qquad \square$$

The following corollary can be easily obtained after optimization of M in Lemma 1 when one has a simple enough upper bound on $\mathbf{Adv}_{\overline{\mathsf{R}}}^{\text{cca}}(q_c, q_p)$.

Corollary 1. *Let* R *be a randomized key-length extension scheme and let* $\overline{\mathsf{R}}$ *be its induced sequential cipher. Assume that*

$$\mathbf{Adv}^{\mathrm{cca}}_{\overline{\mathsf{R}}}(q_c, q_p) \leq A + B\frac{q_c^\alpha q_p^\beta}{N^\gamma},$$

where $A, B, \alpha, \beta, \gamma$ *do not depend on* q_p*, and* $B \geq 1$*,* $\beta \geq 1$*. Then*

$$\mathbf{Adv}^{\mathrm{cca}}_{\overline{\mathsf{R}}}(q_c, q_e) \leq A + mB(\beta + 1)\left(\frac{q_c^\alpha q_e^\beta}{K^\beta N^\gamma}\right)^{\frac{1}{\beta+1}}.$$

4   Randomized Key-Length Extension Schemes

In this section, we derive security bounds for various randomized KLE schemes.

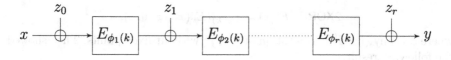

Fig. 2. The XOR-cascade key-length extension scheme XCE[E].

4.1   XOR-Cascades: Tight Bounds

As a first application, we complete the picture of the security of the XOR-cascade key-length extension scheme with independent whitening keys introduced in [12]. We derive a tight security bound for the setting with less than 2^n construction queries. Recall the definition of the r-round XOR-cascade construction XCE given in Sect. 3.2, Example 1.

Lemma 1 shows that the security of the r-round XOR-cascade construction is directly related to the security of the corresponding r-round key-alternating cipher KAC. It was observed in [12] to be related to the security of the $(r - 1)$-round key-alternating cipher, but in hindsight this rather appears as an artifact of the setting $q_c = 2^n$.

Combining our improved result on the security of KAC (following from [8] and given in the full version of this paper [13]) with Lemma 1, we obtain that for any integer M such that $q_c + M \leq N/2$,

$$\mathbf{Adv}^{\mathrm{cca}}_{\mathsf{XCE}}(q_c, q_e) \leq \frac{rq_e}{KM} + 4(r + 2)\left(\frac{rq_c M^r}{(r + 2)N^r}\right)^{\frac{1}{r+1}}.$$

After the optimization of M (by equating the two summands), we arrive at the following theorem.

Theorem 1. *Consider the r-round XOR-cascade construction* XCE. *Then*

$$\mathbf{Adv}_{\mathsf{XCE}}^{\mathrm{cca}}(q_c, q_e) \leq C_r \left(\frac{q_c q_e^r}{K^r N^r} \right)^{\frac{1}{2r+1}},$$

where C_r is a constant that depends only on r, namely

$$C_r = \left(2^{4r+3} \cdot r^{r+1} (r+2)^r \right)^{\frac{1}{2r+1}} \in \mathcal{O}(r).$$

In short, XOR-cascade encryption is secure as long as $q_c q_e^r$ is small compared to $2^{r(\kappa+n)}$. We note that this security bound is matched by a generic attack on sequential constructions given in [12, Theorem 3], since this attack can be easily generalized for arbitrary q_c as observed there.

4.2   2XOR: Tight Bounds

The construction 2XOR was proposed by Gaži and Tessaro [15] to turn a block cipher $E \in \mathsf{BC}(\kappa, n)$ into a new block cipher $\mathsf{2XOR}[E] \in \mathsf{BC}(\kappa + n, n)$ defined as

$$\mathsf{2XOR}_{k,z}[E](x) = E_{\phi(k)}(E_k(x \oplus z) \oplus z),$$

where ϕ is any (fixed) permutation of $\{0,1\}^\kappa$ without fixed points. They showed the following result.

Theorem 2 ([15, Theorem 3]). *For any integer q_e,*

$$\mathbf{Adv}_{\mathsf{2XOR}}^{\mathrm{cca}}(q_c = 2^n, q_e) \leq 4 \cdot \left(\frac{q_e}{2^{\kappa+n/2}} \right)^{\frac{2}{3}}.$$

We describe how to attack 2XOR for any $1 \leq c \leq n/2$ using roughly 2^c construction queries and $2^{\kappa+n-c}$ block-cipher queries.

Theorem 3. *Let $1 \leq c \leq n/2$ and $1 \leq t \leq c$ be integers such that t is even. There exists a distinguisher D which makes at most $q_c = 2^{c+t/2}$ (forward) construction queries and $q_e = 2^{\kappa+n-c+t/2+1}$ ideal cipher queries, and which achieves*

$$\mathbf{Adv}_{\mathsf{2XOR}}^{\mathrm{cca}}(\mathsf{D}) \geq 1 - 2^{\kappa+n-2^t(n-1)}.$$

In particular, for $c = n/2$ and $t = \lfloor \log_2(\kappa/n + 1) \rfloor + 1$, its advantage is negligibly close to 1 (asymptotically in n), and its complexity is $q_c = \mathcal{O}(2^{n/2})$ and $q_e = \mathcal{O}(2^{\kappa+n/2})$ (for κ/n constant).

Proof. Consider the distinguisher D depicted in Fig. 3 (we assume n to be even for simplicity). For its analysis, first note that for any $z \in \{0,1\}^n$, the size of the set V_z determined on line 10 is exactly 2^t, due to the choice of the sets X and U. When D interacts with $(\mathsf{2XOR}_{k,z}[E], E)$, it always outputs 1 since the check on line 11 succeeds for the real key (k, z). In the ideal world (P, E), we can upper-bound the probability that the distinguisher outputs 1 as follows: for each key (k, z), the values $\tilde{v}(k, u)$ and $\tilde{u}(k, x)$ for the 2^t pairs $(x, u) \in V_z$ are independent, so that the probability that the check on line 11 succeeds is exactly $\frac{1}{(2^n)_{2^t}} \leq 2^{-2^t(n-1)}$. By the union bound over the $2^{\kappa+n}$ pairs (k, z), the probability that D returns 1 is at most $2^{\kappa+n-2^t(n-1)}$.   □

Distinguisher $D^{S,E}$:   where $S \in \{2\text{XOR}_{k,z}[E], P\}$

  1: **let** $X := \{x'0^{n-c-t/2} : x' \in \{0,1\}^{c+t/2}\} \subseteq \{0,1\}^n$
  2: **let** $U := \{0^{c-t/2}u' : u' \in \{0,1\}^{n-c+t/2}\} \subseteq \{0,1\}^n$
  3: **for all** $x \in X$ **do**
  4:    **query** $y(x) := S(x)$
  5: **for all** $(k,x) \in \{0,1\}^\kappa \times X$ **do**
  6:    **query** $\tilde{u}(k,x) := E^{-1}_{\phi(k)}(y(x))$
  7: **for all** $(k,u) \in \{0,1\}^\kappa \times U$ **do**
  8:    **query** $\tilde{v}(k,u) := E_k(u)$
  9: **for all** $(k,z) \in \{0,1\}^\kappa \times \{0,1\}^n$ **do**
10:    **let** $V_z := \{(x,u) \in X \times U \mid x \oplus u = z\}$
11:    **if** $\forall (x,u) \in V_z : \tilde{v}(k,u) \oplus \tilde{u}(k,x) = z$ **then**
12:       **return** 1
13: **return** 0

Fig. 3. Distinguisher D for the proof of Theorem 3, attacking the construction 2XOR and parametrized by c, t.

To illustrate that the tradeoff $q_c q_e \leq 2^{\kappa+n}$ imposed by the attack above is tight for $0 \leq \log_2(q_c) \leq n/2$, consider the sequential cipher $\overline{\text{2XOR}}$ induced by 2XOR. By a trivial reduction (simulating its last, independent random permutation), one can show that 2XOR is at least as secure as the Even-Mansour cipher $\overline{\text{FX}}$ described in Example 2 in Sect. 3.2. However, it follows from [11] that $\overline{\text{FX}}$ is secure as long as $q_c q_p \leq 2^n$, which, via $\overline{\text{2XOR}}$ and the application of Lemma 1, implies that 2XOR is secure roughly as long as $q_c q_e \leq 2^{\kappa+n}$. This completes the picture for 2XOR on the interval $0 \leq \log_2(q_c) \leq n/2$. For any $q_c \geq 2^{n/2}$, a tight bound for 2XOR is $q_e = 2^{\kappa+n/2}$ as follows from Theorems 2 and 3, hence the security of 2XOR is now understood for the full spectrum of parameters (q_c, q_e) (see Fig. 5).

4.3 3XOR: Final Whitening Step Helps

It was also argued in [15] that the 2XOR construction has optimal security within a large class of (so-called sequential) two-query constructions in the following sense: They give a generic attack on any construction from this class requiring roughly 2^n construction queries and $2^{\kappa+n/2}$ block-cipher queries, hence matching the security bound from Theorem 2. However, this only shows the optimality of the 2XOR construction (and in particular, no need to add a final XOR step at its end) in the setting where $q_c = 2^n$ is assumed. As we show below, the situation changes as soon as we also consider lower values of q_c. In this general case, adding a third randomization step actually *does improve* security for some range of the parameters (q_c, q_e).

We define the 3XOR construction similarly to the 2XOR construction, but with a final whitening step (see Fig. 4), i.e.,

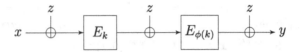

Fig. 4. The 3XOR[E] key-length extension scheme.

$$3\mathrm{XOR}_{k,z}[E](x) = E_{\phi(k)}(E_k(x \oplus z) \oplus z) \oplus z.$$

Note that 3XOR is simply the 2-round XCE construction with identical whitening keys in-between the block-cipher calls. The induced sequential cipher $\overline{\mathrm{3XOR}}$ is hence the 2-round Even-Mansour cipher with independent permutations and identical round keys:

$$\overline{\mathrm{3XOR}}_z[P_1, P_2](x) = P_2(P_1(x \oplus z) \oplus z) \oplus z.$$

The security of this construction was analyzed by Chen *et al.* [7]. We recall their result in the full version of this paper [13]. Combining it with Corollary 1, we obtain the following theorem for the security of the 3XOR construction.

Theorem 4. *Assume that $n \geq 11$, $q_c \geq 9n$, $q_e \geq 9n$, and $2q_c + 2q_e \leq N$. Then the following upper bounds hold:*

(i) When $q_c \leq 2^{\frac{n}{4}}$, one has

$$\mathbf{Adv}^{\mathrm{cca}}_{\mathrm{3XOR}}(q_c, q_e) \leq 24 \left(\frac{q_c q_e}{KN} \right)^{\frac{1}{2}}.$$

(ii) When $2^{\frac{n}{4}} \leq q_c \leq 2^{\frac{2n}{3}}$, one has

$$\mathbf{Adv}^{\mathrm{cca}}_{\mathrm{3XOR}}(q_c, q_e) \leq \frac{6}{N} + 4 \times (13 + 9\sqrt{n}) \left(\frac{q_c^{\frac{1}{5}} q_e}{KN^{\frac{4}{5}}} \right)^{\frac{1}{2}}.$$

(iii) When $2^{\frac{2n}{3}} \leq q_c \leq 2^{\frac{3n}{4}}$, one has

$$\mathbf{Adv}^{\mathrm{cca}}_{\mathrm{3XOR}}(q_c, q_e) \leq \frac{6}{N} + 4 \times (13 + 9\sqrt{n}) \left(\frac{q_c^2 q_e}{KN^2} \right)^{\frac{1}{2}}.$$

(iv) When $q_c \geq 2^{\frac{3n}{4}}$, one has,

$$\mathbf{Adv}^{\mathrm{cca}}_{\mathrm{3XOR}}(q_c, q_e) \leq \frac{1}{eN} + 6n \left(\frac{q_e}{KN^{\frac{1}{2}}} \right)^{\frac{2}{3}}.$$

This security bound is qualitatively similar to the one of 2XOR for $q_c \leq 2^{\frac{n}{4}}$ and $q_c \geq 2^{\frac{3n}{4}}$, but strictly better for $2^{\frac{n}{4}} \leq q_c \leq 2^{\frac{3n}{4}}$ (see Fig. 5). Regarding the tightness of the bound, we note that the general attack against sequential constructions given in [12, Theorem 3] applies to 3XOR, so that for any q_c, the construction is insecure for $q_e \approx 2^{\kappa + n - \frac{1}{2} \log_2 q_c}$. This matches the security bound for the special cases $q_c \approx 1$, $q_c \approx 2^{\frac{2n}{3}}$, and $q_c \approx 2^n$ (see Fig. 5).

In conclusion, our results in Sects. 4.2 and 4.3 show that 3XOR is *always* at least as secure 2XOR for all possible values of q_c, and strictly more secure for $2^{n/4} < q_c < 2^{3n/4}$.

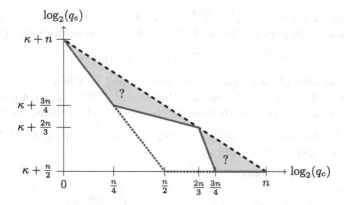

Fig. 5. The security of the 3XOR key-length extension scheme. All parameters below the (red) solid line are secure due to Theorem 4, while all parameters above the (black) dashed line are insecure due to the attack [12]. The status for parameters between these two lines remains unknown. The (blue) dotted line (which merges with the red solid line for $q_c \leq 2^{\frac{n}{4}}$ and $q_c \geq 2^{\frac{3n}{4}}$) also indicates the (tight) security bound for 2XOR (Color figure online).

4.4 3XSK: A 2-Call Construction without Rekeying

A drawback of the 3XOR construction is that the underlying block cipher E is called under two distinct keys. Since rekeying is typically a costly operation for a block cipher, it would be appealing to have a key-length extension construction providing the same level of security as 3XOR, but calling the underlying block cipher E with a single key. We describe such a construction in this section.

Let π be a linear orthomorphism of $\mathbb{F}_2^n$ (a permutation π of $\{0,1\}^n$ is an orthomorphism if $z \mapsto z \oplus \pi(z)$ is also a permutation).[8] We define the 3XSK (*3 XOR, single key*) construction which turns a block cipher $E \in \mathsf{BC}(\kappa, n)$ into a new block cipher $3\mathsf{XSK}[E] \in \mathsf{BC}(\kappa + n, n)$ as follows (see Fig. 6):

$$3\mathsf{XSK}_{k,z}[E](x) = E_k(E_k(x \oplus z) \oplus \pi(z)) \oplus z.$$

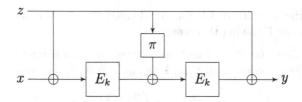

Fig. 6. The 3XSK[E] key-length extension scheme.

---

[8] For example, assuming n even, $\pi : (z_L, z_R) \mapsto (z_R, z_L \oplus z_R)$, where z_L and z_R are respectively the left and right halves of z, is an $\mathbb{F}_2$-linear orthomorphism.

The induced sequential cipher $\overline{\text{3XSK}}$ is exactly the two-round Even-Mansour cipher with a single permutation and the sequence of round keys $(z, \pi(z), z)$,

$$\overline{\text{3XSK}}_z[P](x) = P(P(x \oplus z) \oplus \pi(z)) \oplus z.$$

Again, the security of this construction was studied by Chen et al. [7] and we restate their findings in the full version of this paper [13]. Combining it with Corollary 1, we obtain the following theorem for the security of the 3XSK construction.

Theorem 5. *Assume that* $n \geq 9$, $q_c \geq 9n$, $q_e \geq 9n$, *and* $4q_c + 2q_e \leq N$. *Then the following upper bounds hold:*

(i) *When* $q_c \leq 2^{\frac{n}{3}}$, *one has*

$$\mathbf{Adv}^{\text{cca}}_{\text{3XSK}}(q_c, q_p) \leq \frac{23}{N^{\frac{1}{3}}} + 32 \left(\frac{q_c q_e}{KN} \right)^{\frac{1}{2}}.$$

(ii) *When* $q_c \geq 2^{\frac{n}{3}}$, *one has*

$$\mathbf{Adv}^{\text{cca}}_{\text{3XSK}}(q_c, q_p) \leq \frac{10}{N} + (23 + 6\sqrt{n}) \frac{q_c}{N^{\frac{2}{3}}} + 2 \times (39 + 9\sqrt{n}) \left(\frac{q_e}{KN^{\frac{2}{3}}} \right)^{\frac{1}{2}}.$$

(Note that this bound becomes vacuous for $q_c \geq 2^{\frac{2n}{3}}$.)

This matches the security bound for 2XOR for $q_c < 2^{\frac{n}{3}}$, (and hence the lower bound proven for 3XOR in Sect. 4.3 for $q_c < 2^{\frac{n}{4}}$) while for $2^{\frac{n}{3}} \leq q_c \leq 2^{\frac{2n}{3}}$ it caps at $q_p \approx 2^{\kappa + \frac{2n}{3}}$ (hence it is slightly worse than the security lower bound of 3XOR in that case). The security for q_c larger than $2^{\frac{2n}{3}}$ remains unknown. Note that the attack given in [12] also applies to 3XSK exactly in the same way as to 3XOR, providing an upper bound on its security.

5   Plain Cascade Encryption

In this section, we give another application of Lemma 1, this time to analyze the security of plain cascade encryption in the setting where the number of construction queries is smaller than 2^n. Recall that the ℓ-round cascade encryption using a (κ, n)-block cipher E, denoted $\text{CE}[E]$, takes an $\ell\kappa$-bit key $\mathsf{mk} = (k_1, \ldots, k_\ell) \in (\{0,1\}^\kappa)^\ell$ and encrypts a plaintext $x \in \{0,1\}^n$ by computing

$$y = \text{CE}_{\mathsf{mk}}[E](x) = E_{k_\ell} \circ E_{k_{\ell-1}} \circ \cdots \circ E_{k_2} \circ E_{k_1}(x).$$

We focus on the security of CE for odd length $\ell = 2r + 1$ and our result is summarized in the following theorem.

Theorem 6. *Consider the* ℓ-round cascade encryption CE *where* $\ell = 2r + 1$ *for some* $r \geq 1$. *Then, assuming* $q_c \leq N/4$ *and* $q_e \leq KN/8$, *one has*

$$\mathbf{Adv}^{\text{cca}}_{\text{CE}}(q_c, q_e) \leq \frac{\ell^2}{K} + e^{-n} + r^2(r+1) \left(\frac{3nq_c}{K} \right)^{\frac{1}{2}} +$$

$$\max \left\{ A_r \left(\frac{q_c q_e^r}{K^r N^r} \right)^{\frac{1}{2r+1}}, B_r \left(\frac{nq_e}{K^2} \right)^{\frac{1}{3}} \right\},$$

where $A_r \in \mathcal{O}(r^2)$ and $B_r \in \mathcal{O}(r^{\frac{7}{3}})$ only depend on r, namely

$$A_r = 6r^2(r+1)\left(\frac{2^r}{r^{r+1}(r+1)^{r+1}}\right)^{\frac{1}{2r+1}}, \quad B_r = 6r^2(r+1)\left(\frac{3}{4r(r+1)}\right)^{\frac{1}{3}}.$$

Proof (sketch). From a high-level perspective, the proof consists of the following steps. First, we modify the cascade to use two *independent* ideal ciphers E and E' in an interleaving manner and show that this does not introduce a large distinguishing gap. Second, we need to assume that the block cipher E' used in the odd steps of the cascade is *good* in some well-defined sense and hence we show that the opposite is unlikely (over the randomness of E'). Third, we publish the complete function table of E' (but not the keys being used with it), thus arriving at a randomized KLE scheme of length r. Then we can apply Lemma 1 to reduce its security to the security of the induced sequential cipher. Finally, we analyze the latter directly, using an H-coefficient analysis inspired by [8] that employs the assumption that E' is good. The full proof discussing each of the individual steps in greater detail can be found in the full version of this paper [13].   □

DISCUSSION. In terms of the number of threshold queries, cascade encryption of length $\ell = 2r + 1$ is hence secure when $q_c q_e^r \ll 2^{r(\kappa+n)}$, $q_c \ll 2^\kappa$, and $q_e \ll 2^{2\kappa}$ (asymptotically, ignoring constants). Our bound must be compared with the security result of Dai *et al.* [9], who considered the full-codebook regime $q_c = 2^n$. They showed that, for $\kappa \geq n/(r+1)$ (which is satisfied for virtually any real block cipher we know of), cascade encryption of length $\ell = 2r + 1$ is secure when $q_e \ll 2^{\kappa + \frac{rn}{r+1}}$ (and, obviously, this also holds for any $q_c < 2^n$). Hence, our new bound improves on [9] when $q_c \leq 2^{\frac{rn}{r+1}}$, but only assuming $\kappa \geq \frac{rn}{r+1}$ since otherwise the condition $q_e \ll 2^{2\kappa}$ in our bound becomes more restrictive than Dai *et al.*'s one. This is depicted on Fig. 7. We remark that our bound also applies to cascade encryption of length $2r + 2$, since adding a round cannot decrease security.

TIGHTNESS. As observed in [12], the attack against cascades given there can be adjusted to provide a trade-off between block-cipher and construction queries. This results in an attack against plain cascade of length $\ell = 2r + 1$ that achieves a constant distinguishing advantage as long as $q_c q_e^r \approx 2^{r(\kappa+n)}$ and $q_e \geq 2^\kappa q_c$ (again, ignoring constants). Note that the second condition only comes into play when $q_c \geq 2^{\frac{rn}{r+1}}$, in which case the attack requires $q_e \approx 2^{\kappa + \frac{rn}{r+1}}$ (instead of $q_e \approx 2^{\kappa+n-\frac{1}{r}\log_2 q_c}$). Hence, this matches the bound of [9] for $q_c \geq 2^{\frac{rn}{r+1}}$. When $\kappa \geq n$, this also matches our own new bound for $q_c \leq 2^{\frac{rn}{r+1}}$, yielding a tight bound for all parameters. When $\frac{rn}{r+1} \leq \kappa \leq n$, the attack matches our new bound only for $q_c \geq 2^{r(n-\kappa)}$ since otherwise the security bound caps at $q_e \ll 2^{2\kappa} < 2^{\kappa+n-\frac{1}{r}\log_2 q_c}$. When $\kappa \leq \frac{rn}{r+1}$, there is a provable security gap between this attack and the bound of [9] for any $q_c \leq 2^{\frac{rn}{r+1}}$. This is also summarized on Fig. 7. Again, all this applies to the case of cascade encryption of length $2r + 2$ since Gaži's attack [12] was given for cascades of even length. Note that the case of 3DES ($\kappa = 56$, $n = 64$, and $r = 1$) corresponds to the middle graph.

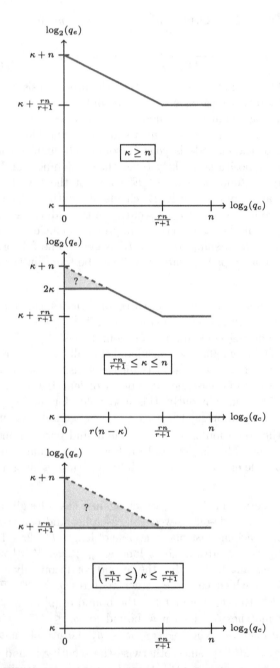

Fig. 7. The security of plain cascade encryption with $2r+1$ or $2r+2$ rounds, depending on κ and n. All parameters below the solid line are secure due either to Theorem 6 or the results of [9]. All parameters above the dashed line are insecure due to the attack of [12]. The status for parameters between these lines remains unknown.

TWO-KEY TRIPLE ENCRYPTION. Let TTE denote a variant of triple encryption where the first and the third keys are identical. So TTE accepts a 2κ-bit key $\mathsf{mk} = (k_1, k_2) \in (\{0,1\}^\kappa)^2$ and encrypts a plaintext $x \in \{0,1\}^n$ by computing $y = \mathsf{TTE}_{\mathsf{mk}}[E](x) = E_{k_1} \circ E_{k_2} \circ E_{k_1}(x)$. We prove the following result.

Theorem 7. *For the two-key triple encryption* TTE, *we have, assuming* $q_c \leq N/4$ *and* $q_e \leq KN/8$,

$$\mathbf{Adv}_{\mathsf{TTE}}^{\mathrm{cca}}(q_c, q_e) \leq e^{-n} + 2 \left(\frac{3nq_c}{K}\right)^{\frac{1}{2}} + 12 \max\left\{\left(\frac{q_c q_e}{2KN}\right)^{\frac{1}{3}}, \left(\frac{3nq_e}{8K^2}\right)^{\frac{1}{3}}\right\}.$$

Proof (sketch). Similar to the analysis of cascade encryption in the proof of Theorem 6, we slightly modify the key-sampling process from **A** to **B**:

A: Choose $\mathsf{mk} \in (\{0,1\}^\kappa)^2$ uniformly at random.
B: Randomly partition $T_1 \cup T_2 = \{0,1\}^\kappa$ so that $|T_1| = |T_2|$, choose $z_1 \in T_1$ and $k_2 \in T_2$ uniformly at random, and then define $\mathsf{mk} = (z_1, k_2)$.

It is easy to show that these two processes have the same probability distribution. The rest of the proof follows exactly the same line of arguments as the proof of Theorem 6 for cascade encryption of length 3. □

Acknowledgment. Peter Gaži was partly funded by the European Research Council under an ERC Starting Grant (259668-PSPC).

Jooyoung Lee was supported by Basic Science Research Program through the National Research Foundation of Korea (NRF) funded by the Ministry of Education (NRF-2013R1A1A2007488).

Yannick Seurin was partially supported by the French National Agency of Research through the BLOC project (contract ANR-11-INS-011).

John Steinberger was funded by National Basic Research Program of China Grant 2011CBA00300, 2011CBA00301, the National Natural Science Foundation of China Grant 61033001, 61361136003, and by the China Ministry of Education grant number 20121088050.

Stefano Tessaro was partially supported by NSF grant CNS-1423566.

A   Overview of Previous Results

The following tables summarize the currently known best bounds for the full-codebook regime where $q_c = 2^n$. For a given ℓ (resp. r), ℓ' (resp. r') is the smallest even integer greater or equal to ℓ (resp. r).

ℓ-Round Plain Cascades		
Ref.	**Max. value of** $\log(q_e)$	**Note**
[5]	$\kappa + \min\{n/2, \kappa/2\}$	$\ell = 3$
[14]	$\kappa + \min\{\kappa(\ell' - 2)/\ell', n/2\}$	
[19]	$\kappa + \min\{\kappa, n\} - 8n/\ell$	
[9]	$\kappa + \min\{\kappa(\ell' - 2)/2, n(\ell' - 2)/\ell'\}$	

r-Round Randomized Cascades		
Ref.	**Max. value of** $\log(q_e)$	**Note**
[16]	$n + \kappa - \log(q_c)$	$r = 1$, FX
[15]	$\kappa + n/2$	$r = 2$, 2XOR
[19]	$\kappa + \min\{\kappa, n\} - 4n/r$	
[12]	$\kappa + \frac{r'-2}{r'}n$	

References

1. EMV Integrated Circuit Card Specification for Payment Systems, Book 2: Security and Key Management, v. 4.2, June 2008
2. Advanced encryption standard (aes). National Institute of Standards and Technology (NIST), FIPS PUB 197, U.S. Department of Commerce, November 2001
3. Aiello, W., Bellare, M., Di Crescenzo, G., Venkatesan, R.: Security amplification by composition: the case of doubly-iterated, ideal ciphers. In: Krawczyk, H. (ed.) CRYPTO 1998. LNCS, vol. 1462, pp. 390–407. Springer, Heidelberg (1998)
4. Andreeva, E., Bogdanov, A., Dodis, Y., Mennink, B., Steinberger, J.P.: On the indifferentiability of key-alternating ciphers. In: Canetti, R., Garay, J.A. (eds.) CRYPTO 2013, Part I. LNCS, vol. 8042, pp. 531–550. Springer, Heidelberg (2013)
5. Bellare, M., Rogaway, P.: The security of triple encryption and a framework for code-based game-playing proofs. In: Vaudenay, S. (ed.) EUROCRYPT 2006. LNCS, vol. 4004, pp. 409–426. Springer, Heidelberg (2006)
6. Bogdanov, A., Knudsen, L.R., Leander, G., Standaert, F.-X., Steinberger, J., Tischhauser, E.: Key-alternating ciphers in a provable setting: encryption using a small number of public permutations - (extended abstract). In: Pointcheval, D., Johansson, T. (eds.) EUROCRYPT 2012. LNCS, vol. 7237, pp. 45–62. Springer, Heidelberg (2012)
7. Chen, S., Lampe, R., Lee, J., Seurin, Y., Steinberger, J.: Minimizing the two-round Even-Mansour cipher. In: Garay, J.A., Gennaro, R. (eds.) CRYPTO 2014, Part I. LNCS, vol. 8616, pp. 39–56. Springer, Heidelberg (2014)
8. Chen, S., Steinberger, J.: Tight security bounds for key-alternating ciphers. In: Nguyen, P.Q., Oswald, E. (eds.) EUROCRYPT 2014. LNCS, vol. 8441, pp. 327–350. Springer, Heidelberg (2014)
9. Dai, Y., Lee, J., Mennink, B., Steinberger, J.: The security of multiple encryption in the ideal cipher model. In: Garay, J.A., Gennaro, R. (eds.) CRYPTO 2014, Part I. LNCS, vol. 8616, pp. 20–38. Springer, Heidelberg (2014)

10. Data encryption standard: National Bureau of Standards, NBS FIPS PUB 46,U.S. Department of Commerce, January 1977
11. Even, S., Mansour, Y.: A construction of a cipher from a single pseudorandom permutation. J. Cryptology **10**(3), 151–162 (1997)
12. Gaži, P.: Plain versus randomized cascading-based key-length extension for block ciphers. In: Canetti, R., Garay, J.A. (eds.) CRYPTO 2013, Part I. LNCS, vol. 8042, pp. 551–570. Springer, Heidelberg (2013)
13. Gaži, P., Lee, J., Seurin, Y., Steinberger, J., Tessaro, S.: Relaxing full-codebook security: a refined analysis of key-length extension schemes. Full version of this paper http://eprint.iacr.org/
14. Gaži, P., Maurer, U.: Cascade encryption revisited. In: Matsui, M. (ed.) ASIACRYPT 2009. LNCS, vol. 5912, pp. 37–51. Springer, Heidelberg (2009)
15. Gaži, P., Tessaro, S.: Efficient and optimally secure key-length extension for block ciphers via randomized cascading. In: Pointcheval, D., Johansson, T. (eds.) EURO-CRYPT 2012. LNCS, vol. 7237, pp. 63–80. Springer, Heidelberg (2012)
16. Kilian, J., Rogaway, P.: How to protect DES against exhaustive key search (an analysis of DESX). J. Cryptology **14**(1), 17–35 (2001)
17. Lampe, R., Patarin, J., Seurin, Y.: An asymptotically tight security analysis of the iterated Even-Mansour cipher. In: Wang, X., Sako, K. (eds.) ASIACRYPT 2012. LNCS, vol. 7658, pp. 278–295. Springer, Heidelberg (2012)
18. Lampe, R., Seurin, Y.: How to construct an ideal cipher from a small set of public permutations. In: Sako, K., Sarkar, P. (eds.) ASIACRYPT 2013, Part I. LNCS, vol. 8269, pp. 444–463. Springer, Heidelberg (2013)
19. Lee, J.: Towards key-length extension with optimal security: cascade encryption and xor-cascade encryption. In: Johansson, T., Nguyen, P.Q. (eds.) EUROCRYPT 2013. LNCS, vol. 7881, pp. 405–425. Springer, Heidelberg (2013)
20. Luby, M., Rackoff, C.: Pseudo-random permutation generators and cryptographic composition. In: Symposium on Theory of Computing - STOC 1986, pp. 356–363. ACM (1986)
21. Maurer, U.M., Pietrzak, K., Renner, R.: Indistinguishability amplification. In: Menezes, A. (ed.) CRYPTO 2007. LNCS, vol. 4622, pp. 130–149. Springer, Heidelberg (2007)
22. Maurer, U.M., Tessaro, S.: Computational indistinguishability amplification: tight product theorems for system composition. In: Halevi, S. (ed.) CRYPTO 2009. LNCS, vol. 5677, pp. 355–373. Springer, Heidelberg (2009)
23. Patarin, J.: The "Coefficients H" technique. In: Avanzi, R.M., Keliher, L., Sica, F. (eds.) SAC 2008. LNCS, vol. 5381, pp. 328–345. Springer, Heidelberg (2009)
24. Steinberger, J.: Improved security bounds for key-alternating ciphers via hellinger distance. Cryptology ePrint Archive, Report 2012/481 (2012). http://eprint.iacr.org/2012/481
25. Tessaro, S.: Security amplification for the cascade of arbitrarily weak PRPs: tight bounds via the interactive hardcore lemma. In: Ishai, Y. (ed.) TCC 2011. LNCS, vol. 6597, pp. 37–54. Springer, Heidelberg (2011)
26. Vaudenay, S.: Adaptive-attack norm for decorrelation and super-pseudorandomness. In: Heys, H.M., Adams, C.M. (eds.) SAC 1999. LNCS, vol. 1758, pp. 49–61. Springer, Heidelberg (2000)

The Related-Key Security of Iterated Even–Mansour Ciphers

Pooya Farshim[1][(✉)] and Gordon Procter[2]

[1] Queen's University Belfast, Belfast, UK
pooya.farshim@gmail.com
[2] Royal Holloway, University of London, Egham, UK
gordon.procter.2011@live.rhul.ac.uk

Abstract. The simplicity and widespread use of blockciphers based on the iterated Even–Mansour (EM) construction has sparked recent interest in the theoretical study of their security. Previous work has established their strong pseudorandom permutation and indifferentiability properties, with some matching lower bounds presented to demonstrate tightness. In this work we initiate the study of the EM ciphers under related-key attacks which, despite extensive prior work on EM ciphers, has received little attention. We show that the simplest one-round EM cipher is strong enough to achieve non-trivial levels of RKA security even under chosen-ciphertext attacks. This class, however, does not include the practically relevant case of offsetting keys by constants. We show that two rounds suffice to reach this level under chosen-plaintext attacks and that three rounds can boost security to resist chosen-ciphertext attacks. We also formalize how indifferentiability relates to RKA security, showing strong positive results despite counterexamples presented for indifferentiability in multi-stage games.

Keywords: Even–Mansour · RKA · Ideal cipher · Indifferentiability

1 Introduction

1.1 Background

Formal analyses of cryptographic protocols often assume that cryptosystems are run on keys that are independently generated and bear no relation to each other. Implicit in this assumption is the premise that user keys are stored in protected areas that are hard to tamper with. Security under *related-key attacks* (RKAs), first identified by Biham and Knudsen [9,10,38], considers a setting where an adversary might be able to disturb user keys by injecting faults [2], and consequently run a cryptosystem on *related* keys. Resilience against RKAs has become a desirable security goal, particularly for blockciphers.

The need for RKA security is further highlighted by the fact that through (improper) design, a higher-level protocol might run a lower-level one on related keys. Prominent examples are the key derivation procedures in standardized

© International Association for Cryptologic Research 2015
G. Leander (Ed.): FSE 2015, LNCS 9054, pp. 342–363, 2015.
DOI: 10.1007/978-3-662-48116-5_17

protocols such as EMV [25] and the 3GPP integrity and confidentiality algorithms [34], where efficiency considerations have led the designers to use a blockcipher under related keys. Similar considerations can arise in the construction of tweakable blockciphers [41], if a blockcipher is called on keys that are offset by xoring tweak values. An RKA-secure primitive can offer security safeguards against such protocol misuse.

Bellare and Kohno (BK) [7] initiated the theoretical treatment of security under related-key attacks and propose definitions for RKA-secure pseudorandom functions (PRFs) and pseudorandom permutations (PRPs). The BK model were subsequently extended by Albrecht et al. [1] to idealized models of computation to account for the possibility that key might be derived in ways that depend on the ideal primitive. Both works prove that the ideal cipher is RKA secure against wide sets of related-key deriving (RKD) functions. Bellare and Cash [5] present an RKA-secure pseudorandom function from standard intractability assumptions and Bellare, Cash, and Miller [6] give a comprehensive treatment of RKA security for various cryptographic primitives, leveraging the RKA resilience of PRGs to construct RKA-secure instances of various other primitives. In this work we are interested in the RKA security of blockciphers.

1.2   The Even–Mansour Ciphers

Key-alternating ciphers were introduced by Daemen and Rijmen [23] with the aim of facilitating a theoretical discussion of the design of AES. The key-alternating cipher has since become a popular paradigm for blockcipher design, with notable examples including AES [22,45], Present [14], LED [32], PRINCE [16], KLEIN [31], and Zorro [30]. Key-alternating ciphers originate in the work of Even and Mansour [26,27], who considered a single round of the construction show in Fig. 1; their motivation was to design the simplest blockcipher possible. This design is closely related to Rivest's DES-X construction, proposed as a means to protect DES against brute-force attacks [36], which itself builds on principles dating back to Shannon [49, p. 713]. In this work, we use the terms 'key-alternating cipher' and 'iterated Even–Mansour cipher' interchangeably.

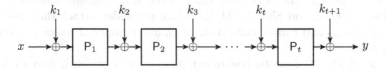

Fig. 1. The t-round iterated Even–Mansour scheme.

PROVABLE SECURITY. Even and Mansour's original analysis [26,27] considers 'cracking' and 'forging' attacks in the random-permutation model and shows that no adversary can predict x given $\mathsf{E}(k,x)$ or $\mathsf{E}(k,x)$ given x with reasonable probability, without making q_1 queries to the permutation and q_{em} to the encryption/decryption oracle, where $q_1 q_{em} \approx 2^n$. The indistinguishability of the Even–Mansour scheme from a random permutation is shown by Kilian and Rogaway [36,37, Theorem 3.1 with $\kappa = 0$] and Lampe, Patarin and Seurin [39, App. Bofthefullversion]. Both works show that an adversary making q_1 and q_{em} queries to the permutation oracle and the encryption/decryption oracles respectively, has a success probability of approximately $q_1 q_{em}/2^{n-1}$. Gentry and Ramzan [29] show that the permutation oracle can be instantiated by a Feistel network with a random oracle without loss of security.

At Eurocrypt 2012, Dunkelman, Keller, and Shamir [24] showed that the Even–Mansour scheme retains the same level of security using only a single key, that is $\mathsf{E}(k,x) = \mathsf{P}(x \oplus k) \oplus k$. Bogdanov et al. [15] show that the t-round Even–Mansour cipher with independent keys and permutations and at least two rounds ($t \geq 2$) provides security up to approximately $2^{2n/3}$ queries but can be broken in $t \cdot 2^{tn/(t+1)}$ queries. Following this work, several papers have moved towards proving a bound that meets this attack [39,50], with Chen and Steinberger [18] able to prove optimal bounds using Patarin's H-coefficient technique [47]. Chen et al. [17] consider two variants of the two-round Even–Mansour scheme: one with independent permutations and identical round keys, the other with identical permutations but a more complex key schedule. In both cases (under certain assumptions about the key schedule), security is maintained up to roughly $2^{2n/3}$ queries.

Maurer, Renner, and Holenstein (MRH) [43] introduce a framework which formalizes what it means for a non-monolithic object to be able to replace another in arbitrary cryptosystems. This framework, know as indifferentiability, has been used to validate the design principle behind many cryptographic constructions, and in particular that of the iterated Even–Mansour constructions. Lampe and Seurin [40] show that the 12-round Even–Mansour cipher using a single key is indifferentiable from the ideal cipher. Andreeva et al. [3] show that a modification of the single-key, 5-round Even–Mansour cipher, where the key is first processed through a random oracle, is indifferentiable from the ideal cipher.

CRYPTANALYSIS. Daemen [21] describes a chosen-plaintext attack that recovers the key of Even–Mansour in approximately $q_1 \approx q_{em} \approx 2^{n/2}$ queries. Biryukov and Wagner [13] are able to give a known-plaintext attack against the Even–Mansour scheme with the same complexity as Daemen's chosen-plaintext attack. Dunkelman, Keller, and Shamir [24] introduce the slidex attack that uses only known plaintexts and can be carried out with any number of queries as long as $q_1 \cdot q_{em} \approx 2^n$.

Mendel et al. [44] describe how to extend Daemen's attack [21] to a related-key version, and are able to recover the keys when all round keys are independent. Bogdanov et al. [15] remark that related-key distinguishing attacks against the iterated Even–Mansour scheme with *independent* round keys "exist trivially," and describe a key-recovery attack, requiring roughly $2^{n/2}$ queries against the two-round Even–Mansour scheme with identical round keys, assuming that an adversary can xor constants into the round key.

Many key-alternating ciphers such as AES [11,12], Present [46], LED [44], and Prince [35] have been analyzed in the related-key model. One of the security claims of the LED blockcipher [32] is a high resistance to related-key attacks, which is justified by giving a lower bound on the number of active S-boxes.

1.3   Contributions

Despite extensive literature on the provable security of iterated Even–Mansour ciphers and (RKA) cryptanalysis of schemes using this design strategy, their formal related-key analysis has received little attention. In this work we initiate the provable RKA security analysis of such key-alternating ciphers. Our results build on the work of Barbosa and Farshim [4] who study the RKA of security of Feistel constructions. They show that by appropriate reuse of keys across the rounds, the 3-round Feistel construction achieves RKA security under chosen-plaintext attacks. With four rounds the authors are able to prove RKA security for chosen-ciphertext attacks. The authors also formalize a random-oracle model transform by Lucks [42] which processes the key via the random oracle before application. Our results are similar and we show that key reuse is also a viable strategy to protect against related-key attacks in key-alternating ciphers. In contrast to the Feistel constructions, key-alternating ciphers operate *intrinsically* in an idealized model of computation, and our analyses draw on techniques used in the formalization of Lucks's heuristic in [4].

We start with the simplest of the key-alternating ciphers, namely the (one-round) EM cipher. We recall that for xor related-key attacks, where an adversary can offset keys by values of its choice, this construction does not provide RKA security [3,15,16,40]. Indeed, it is easy to check that $E((k_1, k_2), x) = E((k_1 \oplus \Delta, k_2), x \oplus \Delta)$, which only holds with negligible probability for the ideal cipher. We term this pattern of adversarial behaviour *offset switching*. One idea to thwart the above attack here would be to enforce key reuse in the construction; although the above equality no longer holds, a close variant still applies:

$$E(k, x) = E(k \oplus \Delta, x \oplus \Delta) \oplus \Delta .$$

Despite this negative result, we show that the minimal EM cipher with key-reuse enjoys a non-trivial level of RKA security (even in the chosen-ciphertext setting). For a set of allowed relate-key queries Φ, we identify a set of sufficient conditions that allow us to argue that $E(\phi(k), x)$ and $E(\phi'(k), x')$ for $\phi, \phi' \in \Phi$ look random and independent from an adversary's point of view. As usual, our conditions impose that the RKD functions have *unpredictable* outputs, as otherwise RKA security is trivially unachievable. (For $\phi(k) = c$, a predictable value, consider an adversary which computes $E(c, 0)$ and compares it $E(\phi(k), 0)$.) Our second condition looks at the generalization of the offset-switching attack above and requires it to be infeasible to find offset claws, i.e., for any pair of functions (ϕ_1, ϕ_2) and any value Δ of adversary's choice, over a random choice of k

$$\phi_1(k) \oplus \phi_2(k) \neq \Delta .$$

This strengthens the standard claw-freeness condition [1,4,7], which corresponds to the $\Delta = 0$ case. In our work, we also consider RKD functions that *depend* on the underlying permutations by placing queries to them. As mentioned above, this is particularly relevant for the Even–Mansour ciphers as they inherently operate in the random-permutation model. We build on previous work in the analysis of such functions [1,4] and formulate adequate restrictions on oracle queries that allow a security proof to be established. Informally, our condition requires that the queries made by ϕ's have empty intersection with the outputs of ϕ's, even with offsets.

The search for xor-RKA security leads us to consider the two-round EM constructions. The first attack discussed above, where the key is offset by a constant, still applies in this setting and once again we consider key reuse. (The two permutations are still independent.) For this cipher, the offset-switching attack no longer applies, which raises the possibility that the two-round Even–Mansour might provide xor-RKA security. We start with chosen-plaintext attacks, formulate three new conditions (analogous to those given for the basic scheme), and prove security under them. These conditions, as before, decouple the queries made to the permutation oracle and allow us to simulate the outer P_2 oracle *forgetfully* in a reduction. We then show that this new set of restrictions are *weak* enough to follow from the standard output-unpredictability and claw-freeness properties. Since xoring with constants is output unpredictable and claw-free [7], the xor-RKA security of the single-key, two-round EM construction follows. Under chosen-ciphertext attacks, however, this construction falls prey to an attack of Andreeva et al. [3] on the indifferentiability of two-round EM (adapted to the RKA setting). For CCA security, we turn to three-round constructions, where we show of the 14 possible way to reuse keys, all but one fall prey to either offset switching attacks or Andreeva et al.'s attack [3]. On the other hand, the three-round construction which uses a single key meets the desired xor-RKA security in the CCA setting.

Dunkelman, Keller, and Shamir [24] consider several variants of the Even–Mansour scheme, such as *addition* Even–Mansour where the xors are replaced with modular additions, and *involution* Even–Mansour, where random permutations are replaced with random involutions. It is reasonable to expect that our results can be modified to also apply to these schemes. Another possible variant of the Even–Mansour scheme is one where the same permutation is used across the rounds [17]; we briefly argue that our proof techniques carry over to this *permutation reuse* setting.

As mentioned above, Lampe and Seurin [40] show that the 12-round EM construction is indifferentiable from the ideal cipher when a single key is used throughout the rounds. Ristenpart, Shacham and Shrimpton [48], on the other hand, point out that indifferentiability does not necessarily guarantee composition in *multi-stage* settings and go on to note that the RKA game is multi-staged. This leaves open the question of whether indifferentiability provides any form of RKA security. We show that if RKD functions query the underlying primitive indirectly *via the construction only*, then composition holds. This level of RKA security is fairly strong as, in our opinion, it is unclear what it menas to *syntactically* changing the RKD functions from those in the ideal setting which have access to the ideal cipher to those which (suddenly) get access to permutations. Our result, in particular, implies that Lampe and Seurin's constructions [40] and Holenstein, Künzler, and Tessaro's 14-round Feistel construction [33] are RKA secure against key offsets in the CCA setting.

Independently and concurrently to this work, Cogliati and Seurin [19, 20] also study the related-key security of iterated EM ciphers. Their Theorem 2 is very similar to our Corollary 3; they analyze more general key schedules and obtain tighter bounds, while our approach deals with a wider range of RKD functions.

2 Preliminaries

NOTATION. We write $x \leftarrow y$ for assigning value y to variable x. We write $x \leftarrow_\$ \mathsf{X}$ for the action of sampling x from a finite set X uniformly at random. If $\mathcal{A}$ is a probabilistic algorithm we write $y \leftarrow_\$ \mathcal{A}(x_1, \ldots, x_n)$ for the action of running $\mathcal{A}$ on inputs $x_1, \ldots, x_n$ with randomly chosen coins, and assigning the results to y. We let $[n] := \{1, \ldots, n\}$, and we denote the bitwise complement of a bit string x by $\bar{x}$.

BLOCKCIPHERS. A (block)cipher is a function $\mathsf{E}: \mathcal{K} \times \mathcal{M} \longrightarrow \mathcal{M}$ such that for every $k \in \mathcal{K}$ the map $\mathsf{E}(k, \cdot)$ is a permutation on $\mathcal{M}$. Such an E uniquely defines its inverse map $\mathsf{D}(k, \cdot)$ for each key k. We write $\mathsf{BC} := (\mathsf{E}, \mathsf{D})$ to denote a blockcipher, which also implicitly defines the cipher's key space $\mathcal{K}$ and message space or domain $\mathcal{M}$. We denote the set of all blockciphers with key space $\mathcal{K}$ and domain $\mathcal{M}$ by $\mathrm{Block}(\mathcal{K}, \mathcal{M})$. The ideal cipher with key space $\mathcal{K}$ and message space $\mathcal{M}$ corresponds to a model of computation where all parties have oracle access to a uniformly chosen random element of $\mathrm{Block}(\mathcal{K}, \mathcal{M})$ in both the forward and backward directions. For a blockcipher $\mathsf{BC} := (\mathsf{E}, \mathsf{D})$, notation $\mathcal{A}^{\mathsf{BC}}$ denotes oracle access to both E and D for $\mathcal{A}$.

PERMUTATIONS. An ideal permutation can be viewed as a blockcipher whose key space contains a single key. In this work, we are interested in building blockciphers with large key spaces from a small number of ideal permutations $\mathsf{P}_1, \ldots, \mathsf{P}_t$ and their inverses. This is equivalent to access to a blockcipher with key space $[t]$, where $\mathsf{P}_i(x) := \mathsf{P}(i, x)$. In order to ease notation, we define a single oracle π, which provides access to all t ideal permutations in both directions. This oracle takes as input (i, x, σ), where $i \in [t]$, $x \in \mathcal{M}$, and $\sigma \in \{+, -\}$ and returns $\mathsf{P}_i(x)$ if $\sigma = +$ and $\mathsf{P}_i^{-1}(x)$ if $\sigma = -$. Slightly abusing notation, we define $\mathsf{P}_i^\sigma(x) := \mathsf{P}^\sigma(i, x) := \pi(i, x, \sigma)$, and assume $\sigma = +$ whenever it is omitted from the superscript. A blockcipher constructed from t ideal permutations π is written $\mathsf{BC}^\pi := (\mathsf{E}^\pi, \mathsf{D}^\pi)$.

RKD FUNCTIONS. A related-key deriving (RKD) function maps keys to keys in some key space $\mathcal{K}$. In this paper, we view RKD functions as circuits that may contain special oracles gates π. An RKD set Φ is a set of RKD functions $\phi^\pi : \mathcal{K} \longrightarrow \mathcal{K}$, where π is an oracle. (The oracle will be instantiated with π as defined above.) Throughout the paper we assume that membership in RKD sets can be efficiently decided.

RKA SECURITY. Following [1, 7], we formalize the RKA security of a blockcipher $\mathsf{BC}^\pi := (\mathsf{E}^\pi, \mathsf{D}^\pi)$ in the (multiple) ideal-permutation model via the game shown in Fig. 2. The RKA game is parametrized by an RKD set Φ which specifies the RKD functions that an adversary is permitted to query during its attack. This game also includes a procedure for oracle π defined above. We define the RKCCA advantage of an adversary $\mathcal{A}$ via

$$\mathbf{Adv}^{\mathsf{rkcca}}_{\mathsf{BC}^\pi, \Phi, t}(\mathcal{A}) := 2 \cdot \Pr\left[\mathsf{RKCCA}_{\mathsf{BC}^\pi, \mathcal{A}, \Phi, t}\right] - 1 \ .$$

The RKCPA game and advantage are defined similarly by considering adversaries that do not make any RKDEC queries (backwards queries to the permutations are still permitted).

$\mathsf{RKCCA}_{\mathsf{BC}^\pi, \mathcal{A}, \Phi, t}$:	$\mathsf{RKEnc}(\phi^\pi, x)$:
$b \leftarrow_\$ \{0,1\}; k \leftarrow_\$ \mathcal{K}$	$k' \leftarrow \phi^\pi(k)$
$(\mathsf{P}, \mathsf{P}^{-1}) \leftarrow_\$ \mathrm{Block}([t], \mathcal{M})$	If $b = 0$ Return $\mathsf{iE}(k', x)$
$(\mathsf{iE}, \mathsf{iD}) \leftarrow_\$ \mathrm{Block}(\mathcal{K}, \mathcal{M})$	Return $\mathsf{E}^\pi(k', x)$
$b' \leftarrow_\$ \mathcal{A}^{\mathrm{RKENC}, \mathrm{RKDEC}, \pi}$	
Return $(b' = b)$	$\mathsf{RKDec}(\phi^\pi, x)$:
	$k' \leftarrow \phi^\pi(k)$
$\pi(i, x, \sigma)$:	If $b = 0$ Return $\mathsf{iD}(k', x)$
Return $\mathsf{P}^\sigma(i, x)$	Return $\mathsf{D}^\pi(k', x)$

Fig. 2. Game defining the Φ-RKCCA security of a blockcipher $\mathsf{BC}^\pi := (\mathsf{E}^\pi, \mathsf{D}^\pi)$ with access to t ideal permutations. An adversary can query the RKENC and RKDEC oracles with a $\phi^\pi \in \Phi$ only. In the RKCPA game the adversary cannot query the RKDEC oracle.

RKA SECURITY OF THE IDEAL CIPHER. Following [7] we define the RKA security of the ideal cipher $\mathsf{IC}' := (\mathsf{iE}', \mathsf{iD}')$ by augmenting the procedures of the above game with those for computing the ideal cipher in both directions, i.e., $(\mathsf{iE}', \mathsf{iD}')$. When working with the ideal cipher, t is often 0, but we consider RKD functions which have oracle access to the ideal procedures iE' and iD' as in [1].

EVEN–MANSOUR CIPHERS. The t-round Even–Mansour (EM) cipher $\mathsf{EM}^\pi := (\mathsf{E}^\pi, \mathsf{D}^\pi)$ with respect to t permutations $\mathsf{P}_1, \ldots, \mathsf{P}_t$ on domain $\{0,1\}^n$ has key space $\mathcal{K} = \{0,1\}^{n(t+1)}$, domain $\mathcal{M} = \{0,1\}^n$, and is defined via

$$\mathsf{E}^\pi((k_1, \ldots, k_{t+1}), x) := \mathsf{P}_t(\cdots \mathsf{P}_2(\mathsf{P}_1(x \oplus k_1) \oplus k_2) \cdots) \oplus k_{t+1} \ ,$$

$$\mathsf{D}^\pi((k_1, \ldots, k_{t+1}), x) := \mathsf{P}_1^{-1}(\cdots \mathsf{P}_{t-1}^{-1}(\mathsf{P}_t^{-1}(x \oplus k_{t+1}) \oplus k_t) \cdots) \oplus k_1 \ .$$

In this work we are interested in EM ciphers where keys are reused in various rounds. Following notation adopted in [4], we denote the EM construction where key k_{i_j} is used before round j by $\mathsf{EM}^\pi[i_1, i_2, \ldots, i_{t+1}]$. We call such key schedules *simple*. Note that $\mathcal{K} = \{0,1\}^{n \cdot |\{i_1, i_2, \ldots, i_{t+1}\}|}$ in these constructions. Of particular interest to us are the $\mathsf{EM}^\pi[1,1]$, $\mathsf{EM}^\pi[1,1,1]$ and $\mathsf{EM}^\pi[1,1,1,1]$ constructions, where a single key is used in all rounds. We emphasize that the round permutations in all these constructions are independently chosen, unless stated otherwise.

3 Indifferentiability and RKA Security

Given the indifferentiability results for the EM and Feistel constructions discussed in the introduction, in this section we study to what extent (if any) an indifferentiable construction can provide resilience against related-key attacks. We start by recalling what it means for a blockcipher construction to be indifferentiable from the ideal cipher [43].

INDIFFERENTIABILITY. Let $\mathsf{BC}^\pi := (\mathsf{E}^\pi, \mathsf{D}^\pi)$ be a blockcipher and let $\mathcal{S}^{\mathsf{IC}}$ be a simulator with oracle access to the ideal cipher having the same key and message spaces as those of BC^π. We define the indifferentiability advantage of a distinguished $\mathcal{D}$ with respect to $\mathcal{S}$ against BC^π via

$$\mathbf{Adv}_{\mathsf{BC}^\pi, t}^{\mathsf{indiff}}(\mathcal{S}, \mathcal{D}) := \Pr\left[\mathcal{D}^{\mathsf{BC}^\pi, \pi}\right] - \Pr\left[\mathcal{D}^{\mathsf{IC}, \mathcal{S}^{\mathsf{IC}}}\right],$$

where the first probability is taken over a random choice of π (as defined in Fig. 2), and the second probability is taken over a random choice of a blockcipher $\mathsf{IC} := (\mathsf{iE}, \mathsf{iD})$. Note that in this definition we require a *universal* simulator that does not depend on the indifferentiability distinguisher. We prove the following theorem in the full version of the paper [28].

Theorem 1. *Let Φ be an RKD set consisting of function ϕ^{OC} having access to a blockcipher oracle OC. Let π be as before, BC^π be a blockcipher construction, and $\mathcal{S}$ be an indifferentiability simulator. Then for any adversary $\mathcal{A}$ against the Φ-RKCCA security of BC^π, where the oracles in the RKD functions are instantiated with BC^π, there are adversaries $\mathcal{D}_1$ and $\mathcal{D}_2$ against the indifferentiability of BC^π, and an adversary $\mathcal{B}$ against the Φ-RKCCA of the ideal cipher, where the oracles in the RKD functions are instantiated with the ideal cipher, such that*

$$\mathbf{Adv}_{\mathsf{BC}^\pi, \Phi, t}^{\mathsf{rkcca}}(\mathcal{A}) \leq \mathbf{Adv}_{\mathsf{BC}^\pi, t}^{\mathsf{indiff}}(\mathcal{S}, \mathcal{D}_1) + \mathbf{Adv}_{\mathsf{BC}^\pi, t}^{\mathsf{indiff}}(\mathcal{S}, \mathcal{D}_2) + \mathbf{Adv}_{\mathsf{IC}, \Phi, t}^{\mathsf{rkcca}}(\mathcal{B}) .$$

CARE WITH COMPOSITION. Ristenpart, Shacham, and Shrimpton [48] show that indifferentiability does *not* always guarantee secure composition in *multi-stage* settings where multiple adversaries can only communicate in restricted ways. The authors then remark that RKA security is multi-staged. To see this, note that the RKA game can be viewed as consisting of two adversaries $\mathcal{A}_1^\pi$ and $\mathcal{A}_2^\pi$ where $\mathcal{A}_1^\pi$ corresponds to the standard RKA adversary $\mathcal{A}^\pi$ and $\mathcal{A}_2^\pi$ is an adversary which has access to the key k, receives an input from $\mathcal{A}_1^\pi$ containing the description of an RKD function ϕ^π and a value x, computes $\phi^\pi(k)$ using its access to π to get

k', and returns $\mathsf{E}^\pi(k', x)$ or $\mathsf{D}^\pi(k', x)$ to $\mathcal{A}_1^\pi$ as needed. With this formalization adversary $\mathcal{A}_2^\pi$ cannot freely communicate with $\mathcal{A}_1^\pi$ as it is restricted to send only encryption and decryption outputs. Our theorem above essentially states that in settings where $\mathcal{A}_2^\pi$ takes the restricted form $\mathcal{A}_2^{\mathsf{BC}^\pi}$ indifferentiability suffices. In our opinion, this restricted access to π suits the RKA security model particularly well. Indeed, when starting in the ideal setting where the RKD functions have access to the ideal cipher, one needs to address how the oracles are instantiated when moved to a construction. A natural way to do this is to simply instantiate the oracles with those of the construction as well (and in this setting, as we show, indifferentiability suffices). Giving the RKD functions direct access to π would constitute a *syntactic* change in the two RKD sets for the ideal cipher and the construction, and it is unclear one should compare RKA security in these settings.

Lampe and Seurin [40, Theorem 2] show that the 12-round $\mathsf{EM}^\pi[1, \cdots, 1]$ construction is indifferentiable from the ideal cipher (with a universal simulator). Bellare and Kohno [7], on the other hand, show that the ideal cipher is $\Phi^\oplus$-RKCCA secure, where

$$\Phi^\oplus := \{k \mapsto k \oplus \Delta : \Delta \in \mathcal{K}\} \ .$$

We therefore obtain as a corollary of the above theorem that the 12-round construction $\mathsf{EM}^\pi[1, \cdots, 1]$ is $\Phi^\oplus$-RKCCA secure. The same conclusion applies to the 14-round Feistel construction of Holenstein, Künzler, and Tessaro [33]. These construction, however, are suboptimal in terms rounds with respect to RKA security. Barbosa and Farshim [4] show that 4 rounds with key reuse suffices for Feistel networks. In the following sections, we study the Even–Mansour ciphers with smaller number of rounds while maintaining RKA security.

4   The RKA Security of $\mathsf{EM}^\pi[1, 1]$

In this section we study RKD sets Φ for which the single-key Even–Mansour construction provides Φ-RKCCA security. Our results are similar to those of Bellare and Kohno [7], Albrecht et al. [1], and Barbosa and Farshim [4] in that we identify a set of restrictions on the RKD set Φ that allow us to establish a security proof. For the one-round construction there are two simple key schedules up to relabeling: $\mathsf{EM}^\pi[1, 1]$ and $\mathsf{EM}^\pi[1, 2]$. Neither of these constructions can provide $\Phi^\oplus$-RKCPA security due to the offset-switching attacks discussed in the introduction. Despite this, we show that the most simple of the EM constructions, $\mathsf{EM}^\pi[1, 1]$, provides a non-trivial level of RKA security. The results of this section will also serve as a warm up to the end goal of achieving strong forms of RKA security, which will encompass key offsets as a special case.

4.1   Restricting RKD Sets

Bellare and Kohno [7] observe that if an adversary is able to choose a $\phi \in \Phi$ that has *predictable* outputs on a randomly chosen key, then Φ-RKCCA security is not achievable. To see this, let ϕ be the constant zero (or any predictable) function. An adversary can simply test if it is interacting with the real or the ideal cipher by enciphering x under the zero key and comparing it to the value it receives from its RKENC oracle on (ϕ, x). This motivates the following definition of unpredictability, adapted to the ideal-permutation model.

OUTPUT UNPREDICTABILITY (OUP). The advantage of an adversary $\mathcal{A}$ against the *output unpredictability* of an RKD set Φ with access to t ideal permutations is defined via

$$\mathbf{Adv}^{\mathsf{oup}}_{\Phi,t}(\mathcal{A}) := \Pr\left[\exists\, (\phi^\pi, c) \in \mathsf{List} : \phi^\pi(k) = c; \mathsf{List} \leftarrow_\$ \mathcal{A}^\pi\right].$$

Here List contains pairs of the form (ϕ^π, c) for $\phi^\pi \in \Phi$ and $c \in \mathcal{K}$, and π is the oracle containing t ideal permutations. The probability is taken over a random choice of $k \leftarrow_\$ \mathcal{K}$, the t random permutations implicit in π, and the coins of the adversary. Note that via a simple guessing argument, this definition can be shown to be equivalent to one where the adversary is required to output a single pair, with a loss of $1/|\mathsf{List}|$ in the reduction.

A second condition that Bellare and Kohno [7] introduce is *claw-freeness*. Roughly speaking, a set Φ has claws if there are two distinct $\phi_1, \phi_2 \in \Phi$ such that $\phi_1(k) = \phi_2(k)$. Although this condition is not in general necessary—given an arbitrary claw there isn't necessarily an attack—it turns out that existence of claws prevent natural approaches to proofs of security. We lift claw-freeness to the ideal-permutation model below.

CLAW-FREENESS (CF). The advantage of an adversary $\mathcal{A}$ against the *claw-freeness* of an RKD set Φ with access to t ideal permutations is defined via

$$\mathbf{Adv}^{\mathsf{cf}}_{\Phi,t}(\mathcal{A}) := \Pr\left[\exists\, (\phi_1^\pi, \phi_2^\pi) \in \mathsf{List} : \phi_1^\pi(k) = \phi_2^\pi(k) \wedge \phi_1^\pi \neq \phi_2^\pi : \mathsf{List} \leftarrow_\$ \mathcal{A}^\pi\right].$$

Here List contains pairs of RKD functions, π is as before, and the probability space is defined similarly to that for output unpredictability. Once again this definition is equivalent to one where List is restricted to be of size one.

Claw-freeness is not a strong enough condition for the one-round EM construction to be RKA secure. Indeed, consider an adversary that queries its encryption oracle with two pairs (ϕ_1, x_1) and (ϕ_2, x_2), possibly with $x_1 \neq x_2$, such that

$$x_1 \oplus \phi_1(k) = x_2 \oplus \phi_2(k).$$

Then the permutation underlying the construction will be queried at the same point and the resulting ciphertexts will differ by $\phi_1(k) \oplus \phi_2(k) = x_1 \oplus x_2$, a predictable value. This observation motivates a strengthening of the claw-freeness property.

XOR CLAW-FREENESS (XCF). The advantage of an adversary $\mathcal{A}$ against the *xor claw-freeness* of an RKD set Φ with access to t ideal permutations is defined via

$$\mathbf{Adv}^{\mathsf{xcf}}_{\Phi,t}(\mathcal{A}) := \Pr\left[\exists\, (\phi_1^\pi, \phi_2^\pi, c) \in \mathsf{List} : \phi_1^\pi(k) \oplus \phi_2^\pi(k) = c \wedge \phi_1^\pi \neq \phi_2^\pi : \mathsf{List} \leftarrow_\$ \mathcal{A}^\pi\right].$$

The variables and probability space are defined similarly to those for claw-freeness.

Xor claw-freeness implies claw-freeness as the latter is a special case with $c = 0$. That claw-freeness is weaker than xor claw-freeness can be seen by considering the set $\Phi^{\oplus}$ corresponding to xoring with constants. This set can be easily shown to be output unpredictable and claw-free [7], but is not xor claw-free as

$$\phi_{\Delta_1}(k) \oplus \phi_{\Delta_2}(k) = \Delta_1 \oplus \Delta_2 \quad \text{where} \quad \phi_\Delta(k) := k \oplus \Delta \ .$$

We also observe that xor claw-freeness of Φ implies that there is at most one $\phi \in \Phi$ which is predictable as any *two* predictable RKD functions can be used to break xor claw-freeness.

Let us now consider oracle access in the RKD functions. Following the attacks identified in [1,4], we consider the oracle-dependent RKD set

$$\Phi := \left\{ id : k \mapsto k, \ \phi^\mathsf{P} : k \mapsto \mathsf{P}(k) \right\} \ .$$

Consider the following Φ-RKCPA adversary against $\mathsf{EM}^\pi[1,1]$. Query $(id, 0)$ and get $y = \mathsf{P}(k) \oplus k$. Query (ϕ^P, y) and get z. Return $(z = 0)$. When interacting with $\mathsf{EM}^\pi[1,1]$ we have that

$$z = \mathsf{E}^\mathsf{P}(\mathsf{P}(k), \mathsf{P}(k) \oplus k) = \mathsf{P}(\mathsf{P}(k) \oplus k \oplus \mathsf{P}(k)) \oplus \mathsf{P}(k) = \mathsf{P}(k) \oplus \mathsf{P}(k) = 0 \ .$$

On the other hand, this identity is true with probability at most $1/(2^n - 1)$ with respect to the ideal cipher. This attack stems from the fact that when answering an RKENC query, π is evaluated at a point already queried by an RKD function. Our final restriction below formalizes what it means for the oracle queries of the RKD function to be disjoint from those of the adversary, including those made implicitly through the encryption or decryption procedures, even up to xoring constants.

XOR QUERY INDEPENDENCE (XQI). The advantage of an adversary $\mathcal{A}$ against the *xor query independence* of an RKD set Φ with access to t ideal permutations is defined via

$$\mathbf{Adv}^{\mathsf{xqi}}_{\Phi,t}(\mathcal{A}) := \Pr\left[\exists (i, \sigma, \phi_1^\pi, \phi_2^\pi, c) \in \mathsf{List} : (i, \phi_1^\pi(k) \oplus c, \sigma) \in \overline{\mathsf{Qry}}[\phi_2^\pi(k)]; \mathsf{List} \leftarrow_\$ \mathcal{A}^\pi \right]$$

where

$$\mathsf{Qry}[\phi^\pi(k)] := \{ (i, x, \sigma) : (i, x, \sigma) \text{ queried to } \pi \text{ by } \phi^\pi(k) \} \ ,$$

$$\overline{\mathsf{Qry}}[k^\pi(k)] := \mathsf{Qry}[\phi^\pi(k)] \cup \{ (i, \pi(i, x, \sigma), -\sigma) : (i, x, \sigma) \in \mathsf{Qry}[\phi^\pi(k)] \} \ .$$

Note that for the EM cipher, restricting the above definition to $i = 1$ suffices. We also define *query independence* [1] as above but demand that $c = 0$.

EXAMPLES. The OUP, XCF, and XQI conditions introduced above do not lead to vacuous RKD sets. As an example of an RKD set which is independent of the permutations consider

$$\Phi^{\mathsf{xu}} := \{ k \mapsto H(k, x) : x \in \mathcal{K}' \} \ ,$$

where H is an xor-universal hash function from $\mathcal{K}$ to $\mathcal{K}$ with key space $\mathcal{K}'$. As a simple instantiation, let $\mathcal{K}' = \{0,1\}^k \setminus 0^k$ and for $k \in \mathcal{K}'$ define $H(k, x) := k \cdot x$, where $\{0,1\}^k$ is interpreted as $\mathrm{GF}(2^k)$ with respect to a fixed irreducible polynomial, and multiplication is defined over $\mathrm{GF}(2^k)$.

As an example of an oracle-dependent RKD set, one can take

$$\Phi := \{k \mapsto \mathsf{P}(k \oplus \Delta) : \Delta \in \mathcal{K}\} \,.$$

4.2 Sufficiency of the Conditions

We now show that if an RKD set Φ meets the output unpredictability, xor claw-freeness and xor query independence properties defined above, then $\mathsf{EM}^\pi[1,1]$ provides Φ-RKCCA security. Throughput the paper we denote the number of queries to various oracles in an attack as follows:

q_i: the number of direct, distinct queries to π with index i made by the adversary $\mathcal{A}$.

q_{em}: the number of distinct queries to the RKENC and (if present) RKDEC oracles by $\mathcal{A}$.

q_i^ϕ: the number of distinct queries to π with index i made by the RKD function ϕ^π.

We call an RKA adversary repeat-free if it does not query its RKENC or RKDEC oracle on a pair (ϕ, x) twice. We call an RKA adversary redundancy-free if it does not query RKENC on (ϕ, x) to get y and then RKDEC on (ϕ, y) to get x, or vice versa. Without loss of generality, we assume that all adversaries in this paper are repeat-free and redundancy-free.

Theorem 2 (Φ-RKCCA *security of* EM^π [1,1]). Let Φ be an RKD set. Then for any adversary $\mathcal{A}$ against the Φ-RKCCA security of $\mathsf{EM}^\pi[1,1]$ with parameters as defined above, there are adversaries $\mathcal{B}_1, \mathcal{B}_2, \mathcal{B}_3$ and $\mathcal{B}_4$ such that

$$\mathbf{Adv}_{\mathsf{EM}^\pi[1,1],\Phi,1}^{\mathrm{rkcca}}(\mathcal{A}) \leq \mathbf{Adv}_{\Phi,1}^{\mathrm{oup}}(\mathcal{B}_1) + \mathbf{Adv}_{\Phi,1}^{\mathrm{xqi}}(\mathcal{B}_2) + \mathbf{Adv}_{\Phi,1}^{\mathrm{xcf}}(\mathcal{B}_3) + \mathbf{Adv}_{\Phi}^{\mathrm{cf}}(\mathcal{B}_4)$$

$$+ \frac{q_{em}(q_1 + \sum_\phi q_1^\phi)}{2^n - (q_1 + \sum_\phi q_1^\phi)} + \frac{2q_{em}^2}{2^n} \,,$$

where $\mathcal{B}_1, \mathcal{B}_2, \mathcal{B}_3$ and $\mathcal{B}_4$ output lists of sizes $2q_1 q_{em}, 2q_{em}^2, q_{em}^2$, and q_{em}^2 respectively and they all make q_1 queries to π.

We give the intuition behind the proof here and leave the details to the full version [28]. The adversary $\mathcal{A}$ in the Φ-RKCCA game is run with respect to the oracles

$$\mathsf{P}(x), \quad \mathsf{P}^{-1}(x), \quad \mathsf{P}(x \oplus \phi^\pi(k)) \oplus \phi^\pi(k), \quad \mathsf{P}^{-1}(x \oplus \phi^\pi(k)) \oplus \phi^\pi(k) \,.$$

Our goal is to make a transition to an environment with the oracles

$$\mathsf{P}(x), \quad \mathsf{P}^{-1}(x), \quad \mathsf{iE}(\phi^\pi(k), x), \quad \mathsf{iD}(\phi^\pi(k), x) \,,$$

where $(\mathsf{iE}, \mathsf{iD})$ denotes the ideal cipher. To this end, we consider two intermediate environments where the last two oracles corresponding to RKENC and RKDEC are handled via a *forgetful* oracle $ that returns uniform strings on each invocation, irrespectively of its inputs. Applying this change to the first environment above gives

$$\mathsf{P}(x), \quad \mathsf{P}^{-1}(x), \quad \$(x \oplus \phi^\pi(k)) \oplus \phi^\pi(k), \quad \$(x \oplus \phi^\pi(k)) \oplus \phi^\pi(k) ,$$

while the second gives

$$\mathsf{P}(x), \quad \mathsf{P}^{-1}(x), \quad \$(\phi^\pi(k), x), \quad \$(\phi^\pi(k), x) ,$$

both of which are identical to the environment $(\mathsf{P}(x), \mathsf{P}^{-1}(x), \$(), \$())$. We will now argue that the above changes alter $\mathcal{A}$'s winning probabilities negligibly, down to the conditions on Φ that we introduced in the previous section.

Let us first look at the change where we replace $\mathsf{iE}(\phi^\pi(k), x)$ and $\mathsf{iD}(\phi^\pi(k), x)$ with $\$(\phi^\pi(k), x)$. We introduce another game and replace the random keyed permutations iE and iD by random keyed *functions* iF and iC:

$$\mathsf{P}(x), \quad \mathsf{P}^{-1}(x), \quad \mathsf{iF}(\phi^\pi(k), x), \quad \mathsf{iC}(\phi^\pi(k), x) .$$

Via (a keyed extension of) the random permutation/random function (RP/RF) switching lemma [8], the environments containing $(\mathsf{iF}, \mathsf{iC})$ and $(\mathsf{iE}, \mathsf{iD})$ can be shown to be indistinguishable up to the birthday bound $q_{em}^2/2^n$. The environments containing $\mathsf{iF}(\phi^\pi(k), x)$ and $\mathsf{iC}(\phi^\pi(k), x)$ and two copies of $\$(\phi^\pi(k), x)$ and can be shown to be identical down to the CF property. Indeed, an inconsistency could arise whenever $(\phi_1^\pi, x_1) \neq (\phi_2^\pi, x_2)$ but $(\phi_1^\pi(k), x_1) = (\phi_2^\pi(k), x_2)$. This means $x_1 = x_2$ and hence we must have that $\phi_1^\pi \neq \phi_2^\pi$. But $\phi_1^\pi(k) = \phi_2^\pi(k)$ and this leads to a break of the claw-freeness.

Let us now look at the changes made when we replace $\mathsf{P}^\pm(x \oplus \phi^\pi(k)) \oplus \phi^\pi(k)$ with $\$(x \oplus \phi^\pi(k)) \oplus \phi^\pi(k)$. We need to consider the points where a forgetful simulation of P or P^{-1} via $ in the last two oracles leads to inconsistencies. Let us define the following six lists.

$\mathsf{List}_{\mathsf{P}}^+ := [(a, \mathsf{P}(a)) : \mathcal{A} \text{ queries } a \text{ to } \mathsf{P}], \mathsf{List}_{\mathsf{P}}^- := [(\mathsf{P}^{-1}(b), b) : \mathcal{A} \text{ queries } b \text{ to } \mathsf{P}^{-1}] ,$

$\mathsf{List}_\phi^+ := [(a, \mathsf{P}(a)) : \phi^\pi(k) \text{ queries } \mathsf{P}(a)], \mathsf{List}_\phi^- := [(\mathsf{P}^{-1}(b), b) : \phi^\pi(k) \text{ queries } \mathsf{P}^{-1}(b)]$

$\mathsf{List}_\$^+ := [(x \oplus \phi^\pi(k), \$(x \oplus \phi^\pi(k))) : \mathcal{A} \text{ queries } (\phi^\pi, x) \text{ to } \mathrm{RKENC}] ,$

$\mathsf{List}_\$^- := [(\$(\phi^\pi(k) \oplus y), \phi^\pi(k) \oplus y) : \mathcal{A} \text{ queries } (\phi^\pi, y) \text{ to } \mathrm{RKDEC}] .$

Let $\mathsf{List}_\star$ be the union of the above lists over all ϕ queried to RKENC or RKDEC. This list encodes the trace of the attack, as in the forgetful environment no queries to P or P^{-1} are made while handling RKENC and RKDEC queries. This trace is consistent with one coming from a permutation unless $\mathsf{List}_\star$ does not respect the permutivity properties, i.e., there are two entries $(a, b), (a', b') \in \mathsf{List}_\star$ such that it is not the case that $(a = a' \iff b = b')$. Note that one of these pairs must be in $\mathsf{List}_\$:= \mathsf{List}_\$^+ \cup \mathsf{List}_\$^-$ as the other oracles are faithfully implemented.

There is an inconsistency on List_* if and only if there is an inconsistency among two lists (one of which is either $\mathsf{List}_\$^+$ or $\mathsf{List}_\$^-$). There are 20 possibilities to consider, including the order that queries are made. We consider first query of a pair being on $\mathsf{List}_\$^+$; the other cases are dealt with symmetrically.

$\mathsf{List}_\$^+$ and $\mathsf{List}_\mathsf{P}^+$: (1) The first component of a pair on $\mathsf{List}_\$^+$—we call this a first entry on $\mathsf{List}_\$^+$—matches a first entry a on $\mathsf{List}_\mathsf{P}^+$. This means that for some query (ϕ^π, x) to RKENC we have that $a = \phi^\pi(k) \oplus x$. This leads to a break of output unpredictability. (2) The second entry on these lists match. More explicitly, we are looking at the probability that $\mathsf{P}(a) = R$, for R the output of $\$$ on a forward query. Here we can assume that R is known and this addresses the adaptivity of choice of a. But even in this case the probability of this event is small as P is a random permutation.

$\mathsf{List}_\$^+$ and $\mathsf{List}_\mathsf{P}^-$: (1) A second entry on $\mathsf{List}_\$^+$ matches a second entry b' on $\mathsf{List}_\mathsf{P}^-$. This means that for some query (ϕ^π, x) to RKENC with output y we have that $b' = \phi^\pi(k) \oplus y$. This leads to a break of output unpredictability. (2) The first entries match on these lists. The argument is similar to case (2) above, but now is for P^{-1}.

$\mathsf{List}_\$^+$ and List_ϕ^+: (1) A first entry on $\mathsf{List}_\$^+$ matches a first entry List_ϕ^+. This means that for some query (ϕ_1^π, x) to RKENC we have that $a = \phi_1^\pi(k) \oplus x$ for a query a of some other ϕ_2^π. This leads to a break of xor query independence. (2) The second entries match on these lists. The argument is as in case (2) of first pair of lists.

$\mathsf{List}_\$^+$ and List_ϕ^-: (1) A second entry on $\mathsf{List}_\$^+$ matches a second entry b' on List_ϕ^-. This means that for some query (ϕ_1^π, x) to RKENC with output y we have that $b' = \phi_1^\pi(k) \oplus y$ for a query b' of some other ϕ_2^π. This leads to a break of xor query independence. (2) The first entries match on these lists. The argument is as in case (2) of the second pair of lists.

$\mathsf{List}_\$^+$ and $\mathsf{List}_\$^+$: Two first entries on $\mathsf{List}_\$^+$ match. This means that for two queries (ϕ_1^π, x_1) and (ϕ_2^π, x_2) to RKENC we have that $\phi_1^\pi(k) \oplus x_1 = \phi_2^\pi(k) \oplus x_2$. Repeat-freeness ensures that $\phi_1 \neq \phi_2$ as otherwise $x_1 = x_2$ as well. This leads to a break of xor claw-freeness. (2) The second entries match on these lists. Since the oracle returns independent random values, this probability can be bounded by the birthday bound.

$\mathsf{List}_\$^+$ and $\mathsf{List}_\$^-$: A second entry on $\mathsf{List}_\$^+$ matches a second entry on $\mathsf{List}_\$^-$. This means that for a queries (ϕ_1^π, x_1) to RKENC with outputs y_1 and (ϕ_2^π, x_2) to RKDEC, we have that $\phi_1^\pi(k) \oplus y_1 = \phi_2^\pi(k) \oplus x_2$. Redundancy-freeness ensures that $\phi_1 \neq \phi_2$ as otherwise x_2 would be an encryption of x_1. This leads to a break of xor claw-freeness. (2) The first entries match on these lists. The probability of this event can be also bounded by the birthday bound.

Hence inconsistencies among any two pairs of lists happen with small probability, and this shows that List_* is also inconsistent with small probability.

5 The Φ-RKCPA Security of $\mathsf{EM}^\pi[1,1,1]$

The theorem established in the previous section does not encompass $\Phi^\oplus$-RKA security as this set is not xor claw-free. In this section, we investigate whether an extra round of iteration can extend RKA security to the $\Phi^\oplus$ set. For the two-round EM constructions, up to relabelling, there are 5 simple key schedules: $[1,1,1]$, $[1,1,2]$, $[1,2,1]$, $[1,2,2]$, and $[1,2,3]$. It is easy to see that offset-switching attacks can be used to attack the $\Phi^\oplus$-RKCPA security of all but the first of these. In the following subsections we study the RKA security of the only remaining construction, $\mathsf{EM}^\pi[1,1,1]$.

5.1 Weakening the Conditions

We start by following a similar proof strategy to that given for $\mathsf{EM}^\pi[1,1]$ and identify a set of restrictions which are strong enough to enable a security proof, yet weak enough to encompass the $\Phi^\oplus$ set. Starting from the CPA environment

$$\pi(i,x,\sigma), \quad \mathsf{P}_2(\mathsf{P}_1(x \oplus \phi^\pi(k)) \oplus \phi^\pi(k)) \oplus \phi^\pi(k) \ ,$$

we simulate the P_2 oracle forgetfully and move to a setting with oracles

$$\pi(i,x,\sigma), \quad \$(\mathsf{P}_1(x \oplus \phi^\pi(k)) \oplus \phi^\pi(k)) \oplus \phi^\pi(k) \quad \equiv \quad \pi(i,x,\sigma), \quad \$() \ .$$

This game can be also be reached from the ideal game $\pi(i,x,\sigma), \mathsf{iE}(\phi^\pi(k),x)$ via an application of the RP/RF switching lemma [8] and the claw-freeness property as in the analysis of $\mathsf{EM}^\pi[1,1]$.

We now analyze the probability that the second environment simulates the first one in an inconsistent way. We look at inconsistencies which arise due to oracles being queried on the same inputs. The first place such an inconsistency might arise is when $\mathcal{A}$ makes an explicit π query $(2, a, +)$ that matches a query made to $\$$, i.e., $\mathsf{P}_1(x \oplus \phi^\pi(k)) \oplus \phi^\pi(k) = a$ for some (ϕ^π, x). Our first condition below addresses this event; we give a slight strengthening of the condition as we will be using it later on.

FIRST-ORDER OUTPUT UNPREDICTABILITY. Let $t \geq 1$. The advantage of an adversary $\mathcal{A}$ against the *first-order output unpredictability* of an RKD set Φ with access to t ideal permutations is defined via

$$\mathbf{Adv}^{\mathrm{oup1}}_{\Phi,t}(\mathcal{A}) := \Pr[\exists (i,\sigma,\phi^\pi,x,c) \in \mathsf{List} \text{ s.t. } \mathsf{P}_i^\sigma(\phi^\pi(k) \oplus x) \oplus \phi^\pi(k) = c : \mathsf{List} \leftarrow^\$ \mathcal{A}^\pi] \ .$$

Oracle π, the probability space, and List are defined analogously to the previous definitions. Note that in the RKCPA setting we do not need to consider inconsistencies resulting from inputs to P_1^{-1} or P_2^{-1} arising through RKDEC queries, and only need to consider $(i,\sigma) = (1,+)$ above.

Inconsistencies arising as a result of two RKENC queries (this oracle places queries to $\$$) lead to the following modification of claw-freeness.

FIRST-ORDER CLAW-FREENESS. Let $t \geq 1$. The advantage of an adversary $\mathcal{A}$ against the *first-order claw-freeness* of an RKD set Φ with access to t ideal permutations is defined via

$$\mathbf{Adv}_{\Phi,t}^{\mathsf{cf1}}(\mathcal{A}) := \Pr[\exists\, (i, \sigma, \phi_1^\pi, x_1, \phi_2^\pi, x_2) \in \mathsf{List}\ \text{s.t.}$$
$$\mathsf{P}_i^\sigma(\phi_1^\pi(k) \oplus x_1) \oplus \phi_1^\pi(k) = \mathsf{P}_i^\sigma(\phi_2^\pi(k) \oplus x_2) \oplus \phi_2^\pi(k) \wedge \phi_1^\pi \neq \phi_2^\pi : \mathsf{List} \leftarrow_{\$} \mathcal{A}^\pi] \;.$$

We now look at inconsistencies in the simulation due to a mismatch in an RKD query to π and a query to \$ made via the RKENC oracle. Since only the second function is forgetfully simulated, we require independence of queries for P_2 only. Once again, in the RKCPA setting, restricting the definition to $(i, \sigma) = (1, +)$ suffices.

FIRST-ORDER QUERY INDEPENDENCE. Let $t \geq 2$. The advantage of an adversary $\mathcal{A}$ against the *first-order query independence* of an RKD set Φ with access to t ideal permutations is defined via

$$\mathbf{Adv}_{\Phi,t}^{\mathsf{qi1}}(\mathcal{A}) := \Pr[\exists(i, \sigma, \phi_1^\pi, x_1, \phi_2^\pi) \in \mathsf{List} : (2, \mathsf{P}_i^\sigma(\phi_1^\pi(k) \oplus x_1) \oplus \phi_1^\pi(k), \pm) \in$$
$$\in \overline{\mathsf{Qry}}[\phi_2^\pi(k)]; \mathsf{List} \leftarrow_{\$} \mathcal{A}^\pi] \;,$$

where, as before,

$$\mathsf{Qry}[\phi^\pi(k)] := \{(i, x, \sigma) : (i, x, \sigma)\ \text{queried to}\ \pi\ \text{by}\ \phi^\pi(k)\}\;,$$
$$\overline{\mathsf{Qry}}[k^\pi(k)] := \mathsf{Qry}[\phi^\pi(k)] \cup \{(i, \pi(i, x, \sigma), -\sigma) : (i, x, \sigma) \in \mathsf{Qry}[\phi^\pi(k)]\}\;.$$

The new set of conditions identified above allow us to carry out a similar proof strategy to that of Theorem 2 and establish the following result. (See the full version [28] for the details of the proof.)

Theorem 3 (Φ-RKCPA *security of* $\mathsf{EM}^\pi[1, 1, 1]$). *Let Φ be an RKD set. Then for any adversary $\mathcal{A}$ against the Φ-RKCPA security of $\mathsf{EM}^\pi[1, 1, 1]$ with parameters as defined before there are $\mathcal{B}_{1a}$ against* OUP1, *$\mathcal{B}_{1b}$ against* OUP, *$\mathcal{B}_{2a}$ against* QI1, *$\mathcal{B}_{2b}$ against* XQI, *$\mathcal{B}_3$ against* CF1, *and $\mathcal{B}_4$ against* CF *such that*

$$\mathbf{Adv}_{\mathsf{EM}^\pi[1,1,1],\Phi,2}^{\mathsf{rkcpa}}(\mathcal{A}) \leq \mathbf{Adv}_{\Phi,2}^{\mathsf{oup1}}(\mathcal{B}_{1a}) + \mathbf{Adv}_{\Phi,2}^{\mathsf{oup}}(\mathcal{B}_{1b}) + \mathbf{Adv}_{\Phi,2}^{\mathsf{qi1}}(\mathcal{B}_{2a}) + \mathbf{Adv}_{\Phi,2}^{\mathsf{xqi}}(\mathcal{B}_{2b})$$
$$+ 2\mathbf{Adv}_{\Phi,2}^{\mathsf{cf1}}(\mathcal{B}_3) + \mathbf{Adv}_{\Phi,2}^{\mathsf{cf}}(\mathcal{B}_4) + \frac{q_{em}(q_2 + \sum_\phi q_2^\phi)}{2^n - (q_2 + \sum_\phi q_2^\phi)} + \frac{2q_{em}^2}{2^n} \;,$$

where $\mathcal{B}_{1a}$ and $\mathcal{B}_{1b}$ output lists of length $q_2 q_{em}$, $\mathcal{B}_{2a}$ and $\mathcal{B}_{2b}$ lists of length q_{em}^2, $\mathcal{B}_3$ a list of length q_{em}^2, and $\mathcal{B}_4$ a list of length at most q_{em}^2.

5.2 $\Phi^\oplus$-RKCPA Security

We show that the restrictions identified above are weak enough so that the offset RKD set $\Phi^\oplus$ can be shown to satisfy them. We start by showing that for oracle-independent sets, Φ is output unpredictable and claw-free if and only if it is first-order output unpredictable and first-order claw-free.

Proposition 1 (OUP $\wedge$ CF $\iff$ OUP1 $\wedge$ CF1). *Let Φ be an oracle-independent RKD set and let $t \geq 1$. Then for any adversary $\mathcal{A}$ against the OUP (resp. CF) game outputting a list of size ℓ and placing q_i permutation queries with index i, there is an adversary $\mathcal{B}_1$ (resp. $\mathcal{B}_2$) outputting a list of size ℓ (resp. ℓ) and placing $q_i + \delta_{1i}\ell$ (resp. q_i) permutation queries with index i such that*

$$\mathbf{Adv}^{\mathsf{oup}}_{\Phi,t}(\mathcal{A}) \leq \mathbf{Adv}^{\mathsf{oup1}}_{\Phi,t}(\mathcal{B}_1) \quad and \quad \mathbf{Adv}^{\mathsf{cf}}_{\Phi,t}(\mathcal{A}) \leq \mathbf{Adv}^{\mathsf{cf1}}_{\Phi,t}(\mathcal{B}_2) .$$

Moreover, for any adversary $\mathcal{A}$ against OUP1 with parameters as before, there is an adversary $\mathcal{B}_1$ against OUP outputting a list of size $\ell \cdot q_\pi := \ell \cdot \sum_i q_i$, where it places q_i permutation queries with index i such that

$$\mathbf{Adv}^{\mathsf{oup1}}_{\Phi,t}(\mathcal{A}) \leq \mathbf{Adv}^{\mathsf{oup}}_{\Phi,t}(\mathcal{B}_1) + \frac{\ell(q_\pi + 1)}{2^n - \ell} .$$

Finally, for any adversary $\mathcal{A}$ against CF1 with parameters as before, there are adversaries $\mathcal{B}_1$ and $\mathcal{B}_2$, where $\mathcal{B}_1$ is as in the previous case, and $\mathcal{B}_2$ outputs a list of size ℓ and makes q_i permutation queries with index i such that

$$\mathbf{Adv}^{\mathsf{cf1}}_{\Phi,t}(\mathcal{A}) \leq \mathbf{Adv}^{\mathsf{oup}}_{\Phi,t}(\mathcal{B}_1) + 2 \cdot \mathbf{Adv}^{\mathsf{cf}}_{\Phi,t}(\mathcal{B}_2) + \frac{\ell}{2^n - \ell} + \frac{\ell}{2^n - 2\ell} .$$

Bellare and Kohno [7] show that the RKD set $\Phi^{\oplus}$ is output unpredictable with advantage $\ell/2^n$ for any adversary outputting a list of size ℓ, and claw-free with advantage 0. The above proposition allow us to conclude that this set is also first-order output unpredictable and first-order claw-free.

Corollary 1. *Let $t \geq 1$ and suppose $\Phi^{\oplus}$ is defined with respect to a key space of size 2^n. Then for any $\mathcal{A}$ outputting a list of at most $\ell \leq 2^n/4$ and making at most q_1 queries to its P_1 oracle,*

$$\mathbf{Adv}^{\mathsf{oup1}}_{\Phi^{\oplus},t}(\mathcal{A}) \leq \frac{\ell \cdot (q_1 + 1)}{2^{n-1}} \quad and \quad \mathbf{Adv}^{\mathsf{cf1}}_{\Phi^{\oplus},t}(\mathcal{A}) \leq \frac{\ell \cdot (q_1 + 2)}{2^{n-1}} .$$

This corollary together with Theorem 3 allow us to establish that $\mathsf{EM}^{\pi}[1,1,1]$ is $\Phi^{\oplus}$-RKCPA secure.

Corollary 2. *For any adversary $\mathcal{A}$ against the $\Phi^{\oplus}$-RKCPA security of $\mathsf{EM}^{\pi}[1,1,1]$ that makes at most q_π queries to its π oracle (of which q_i are to $\pi(i,\cdot,\cdot)$) and at most q_{em} queries to its RKENC oracle, with $q_2 q_{em}, q^2_{em} \leq 2^n/4$, we have*

$$\mathbf{Adv}^{\mathsf{rkcpa}}_{\mathsf{EM}^{\pi}[1,1,1],\Phi^{\oplus},2}(\mathcal{A}) \leq \frac{q_{em}(q_2 + q_{em})(2q_1 + 5)}{2^n} + \frac{q_2 q_{em}}{2^n - q_2} .$$

We remark that via a direct analysis (but at the expense of modularity) the cubic bound above can be tightened to a quadratic one.

REMARK. The above results raises the question if the security proof can be extended to the CCA setting. Adapting an attack due to Andreeva et al. [3] on the indifferentiability of the two-round EM construction to the RKA setting, it can be seen that $\mathsf{EM}^{\pi}[1,1,1]$ is $\Phi^{\oplus}$-RKCCA insecure. Details are given in the full version [28]. This attack also applies if $\mathsf{P}_2 = \mathsf{P}_1$.

6   The Φ-RKCCA Security of $\mathsf{EM}^\pi[1, 1, 1, 1]$

Building on the results of the previous sections, we set out to find a key schedule for the iterated Even–Mansour construction that provides $\Phi^\oplus$-RKCCA security. Our previous results show that at least three rounds are necessary. We start by showing that of the fourteen possible simple key schedules for three-round EM, all but one fall prey to $\Phi^\oplus$-RKCCA attacks. We then show that the remaining $\mathsf{EM}^\pi[1, 1, 1, 1]$ construction does indeed provide $\Phi^\oplus$-RKCCA security.

Up to relabeling, then there are 14 possible key schedules for the three-round Even–Mansour schemes. Of these, 9 are susceptible to offset-switching attacks. These are key schedules where a key appears only in the first or the last round and nowhere else, e.g., $[1, 2, 2, 2]$, $[1, 2, 2, 3]$, or $[1, 2, 2, 1]$. This rules out 9 key schedules. Another 4 can be attacked using Andreeva et al.'s attack [3]. These are the $[1, 1, 2, 1]$, $[1, 2, 1, 1]$, $[1, 1, 2, 2]$, and $[1, 2, 1, 2]$ schedules. Details are given in the full version of the paper [28].

These attacks give a generic 4-query related-key distinguisher for reduced-round LED [32] (8 out of 32 rounds for LED-64 and 16 out of 48 for LED-128). Our results lend support to the designers' claim that LED provides good related-key attack security in spite of the simple key schedule, even though they do not apply directly to LED as the round functions are neither random permutations nor independent.

We now show that $\mathsf{EM}^\pi[1, 1, 1, 1]$ achieves Φ-RKCCA security for sets Φ which include, amongst others, the $\Phi^\oplus$ set. As before, we motivate a number of restrictions on Φ by considering a simulation strategy and analyzing the inconsistencies that could arise. The adversary in the Φ-RKCCA game with respect to the construction has access to π and the oracles

$$\mathsf{P}_3(\mathsf{P}_2(\mathsf{P}_1(x \oplus \phi^\pi(k)) \oplus \phi^\pi(k)) \oplus \phi^\pi(k)) \oplus \phi^\pi(k) \ ,$$

$$\mathsf{P}_1^{-1}(\mathsf{P}_2^{-1}(\mathsf{P}_3^{-1}(x \oplus \phi^\pi(k)) \oplus \phi^\pi(k)) \oplus \phi^\pi(k)) \oplus \phi^\pi(k) \ .$$

Once again we aim to simulate the above two oracles by returning uniformly random values. There are at least two way to perform this:

(a) Simulate the outer permutations in RKENC and RKDEC forgetfully. That is, the P_3 oracle in RKENC and the P_1^{-1} oracle in RKDEC are forgetfully implemented.
(b) Simulate the middle oracles P_2 and P_2^{-1} forgetfully. This will ensure that the inputs to $\mathsf{P}_1^\pm$ and $\mathsf{P}_3^\pm$ are randomized, and hence their outputs will be also random.

The first approach, although in some sense the more natural one, does not work. This is due to the fact that P_1 (resp. P_3) also appear as the first-round permutation in RKENC (resp. RKDEC). An adversary which performs an offset switch can trigger collisions in these oracles without being detected. We therefore adapt the second simulation strategy and for forgetful oracle $\$$ consider

$$\mathsf{P}_3(\$(\mathsf{P}_1(x \oplus \phi^\pi(k)) \oplus \phi^\pi(k)) \oplus \phi^\pi(k)) \oplus \phi^\pi(k) \ ,$$

$$P_1^{-1}(\$(P_3^{-1}(x \oplus \phi^\pi(k)) \oplus \phi^\pi(k)) \oplus \phi^\pi(k)) \oplus \phi^\pi(k) .$$

We now consider inconsistencies, starting with a query collision between π (from a query of $\mathcal{A}$) and $\$$ arising from either the forward or backwards direction. Here we rely on first-order output unpredictability, but note that $(i, \sigma) = (1, +)$ and $(i, \sigma) = (3, -)$ will be critically relied on. Collisions arising between an RKD query to π and a $\$$ query in either direction can be ruled out down to first-order query independence; once again $(i, \sigma) \in \{(1, +), (3, -)\}$ will be used. Finally, the probability that a collision occurs as a result of two queries to $\$$ (due to forward or backward queries) can be bounded by the first-order claw freeness property. As before, inconsistencies also arise due to collisions between the outputs of oracle queries; the probability of this occurring can be bounded information theoretically. Note that here we also rely on independence of queries to the second permutation, but both cases $(i, \sigma) \in \{(1, +), (3, -)\}$ in the definition will be used. We formally prove the following theorem in [28].

Theorem 4 (Φ-RKCCA Security of $\mathsf{EM}^\pi[1,1,1,1]$). *Let Φ be an RKD set. Then for any adversary $\mathcal{A}$ against the Φ-RKCPA security of $\mathsf{EM}^\pi[1,1,1,1]$ with parameters as before, we have adversaries $\mathcal{B}_1$, $\mathcal{B}_2$, $\mathcal{B}_3$, and $\mathcal{B}_4$ such that*

$$\mathbf{Adv}^{\mathrm{rkcca}}_{\mathsf{EM}^\pi[1,1,1,1],\Phi,3}(\mathcal{A}) \leq \mathbf{Adv}^{\mathrm{oup1}}_{\Phi,3}(\mathcal{B}_1) + \mathbf{Adv}^{\mathrm{xqi1}}_{\Phi,3}(\mathcal{B}_2) + 2\mathbf{Adv}^{\mathrm{cf1}}_{\Phi,3}(\mathcal{B}_3)$$

$$+ \mathbf{Adv}^{\mathrm{cf}}_{\Phi,3}(\mathcal{B}_4) + \frac{2q_{em}^2}{2^n} + \frac{2q_{em}(q_2 + \sum_\phi q_2^\phi)}{2^n - (q_2 + \sum_\phi q_2^\phi)} ,$$

where $\mathcal{B}_1$ outputs a list of length $2q_2 q_{em}$, $\mathcal{B}_2$ a list of length $2q_{em}^2$, $\mathcal{B}_3$ a list of length q_{em}^2, and $\mathcal{B}_4$ a list of length at most q_{em}^2.

Corollary 1 together with Theorem 4 allow us to establish that the three-round single-key Even–Manour construction with independent round permutations is $\Phi^\oplus$-RKCCA secure:

Corollary 3. *For any adversary $\mathcal{A}$ against the $\Phi^\oplus$-RKCCA security of $\mathsf{EM}^\pi[1,1,1,1]$ with parameters defined as before. Then*

$$\mathbf{Adv}^{\mathrm{rkcca}}_{\mathsf{EM}^\pi[1,1,1,1],\Phi^\oplus,3}(\mathcal{A}) \leq \frac{2q_{em}(q_2 + q_{em})(2q_1 + 2q_3 + 9)}{2^n} + \frac{2q_{em}q_2}{2^n - q_2} .$$

Once again, via a direct analysis (but at the expense of modularity) the cubic bound above can be tightened to a quadratic one.

Acknowledgments. The authors would like to thank Martijn Stam for discussions on the relation between indifferentiability and RKA security.

References

1. Albrecht, M.R., Farshim, P., Paterson, K.G., Watson, G.J.: On cipher-dependent related-key attacks in the ideal-cipher model. In: Joux, A. (ed.) FSE 2011. LNCS, vol. 6733, pp. 128–145. Springer, Heidelberg (2011)

2. Anderson, R.J., Kuhn, M.G.: Low cost attacks on tamper resistant devices. In: Christianson, B., Lomas, M., Crispo, B., Roe, M. (eds.) Security Protocols 1997. LNCS, vol. 1361, pp. 125–136. Springer, Heidelberg (1998)
3. Andreeva, E., Bogdanov, A., Dodis, Y., Mennink, B., Steinberger, J.P.: On the indifferentiability of key-alternating ciphers. In: Canetti, R., Garay, J.A. (eds.) CRYPTO 2013, Part I. LNCS, vol. 8042, pp. 531–550. Springer, Heidelberg (2013)
4. Barbosa, M., Farshim, P.: The related-key analysis of feistel constructions. In: Cid, C., Rechberger, C. (eds.) FSE 2014. LNCS, vol. 8540, pp. 265–284. Springer, Heidelberg (2015)
5. Bellare, M., Cash, D.: Pseudorandom functions and permutations provably secure against related-key attacks. In: Rabin, T. (ed.) CRYPTO 2010. LNCS, vol. 6223, pp. 666–684. Springer, Heidelberg (2010)
6. Bellare, M., Cash, D., Miller, R.: Cryptography secure against related-key attacks and tampering. In: Lee, D.H., Wang, X. (eds.) ASIACRYPT 2011. LNCS, vol. 7073, pp. 486–503. Springer, Heidelberg (2011)
7. Bellare, M., Kohno, T.: A theoretical treatment of related-key attacks: RKA-PRPs, RKA-PRFs, and applications. In: Biham, E. (ed.) EUROCRYPT 2003. LNCS, vol. 2656, pp. 491–506. Springer, Heidelberg (2003)
8. Bellare, M., Rogaway, P.: The security of triple encryption and a framework for code-based game-playing proofs. In: Vaudenay, S. (ed.) EUROCRYPT 2006. LNCS, vol. 4004, pp. 409–426. Springer, Heidelberg (2006)
9. Biham, E.: New types of cryptanalytic attacks using related keys. J. Cryptology **7**(4), 229–246 (1994)
10. Biham, E.: New types of cryptanalytic attacks using related keys. In: Helleseth, T. (ed.) EUROCRYPT 1993. LNCS, vol. 765, pp. 398–409. Springer, Heidelberg (1994)
11. Biryukov, A., Khovratovich, D.: Related-key cryptanalysis of the full AES-192 and AES-256. In: Matsui, M. (ed.) ASIACRYPT 2009. LNCS, vol. 5912, pp. 1–18. Springer, Heidelberg (2009)
12. Biryukov, A., Khovratovich, D., Nikolić, I.: Distinguisher and related-key attack on the full AES-256. In: Halevi, S. (ed.) CRYPTO 2009. LNCS, vol. 5677, pp. 231–249. Springer, Heidelberg (2009)
13. Biryukov, A., Wagner, D.: Advanced slide attacks. In: Preneel, B. (ed.) EURO-CRYPT 2000. LNCS, vol. 1807, pp. 589–606. Springer, Heidelberg (2000)
14. Bogdanov, A.A., Knudsen, L.R., Leander, G., Paar, C., Poschmann, A., Robshaw, M., Seurin, Y., Vikkelsoe, C.: PRESENT: an ultra-lightweight block cipher. In: Paillier, P., Verbauwhede, I. (eds.) CHES 2007. LNCS, vol. 4727, pp. 450–466. Springer, Heidelberg (2007)
15. Bogdanov, A., Knudsen, L.R., Leander, G., Standaert, F.-X., Steinberger, J., Tischhauser, E.: Key-alternating ciphers in a provable setting: encryption using a small number of public permutations. In: Pointcheval, D., Johansson, T. (eds.) EUROCRYPT 2012. LNCS, vol. 7237, pp. 45–62. Springer, Heidelberg (2012)
16. Borghoff, J., et al.: PRINCE – A low-latency block cipher for pervasive computing applications. In: Wang, X., Sako, K. (eds.) ASIACRYPT 2012. LNCS, vol. 7658, pp. 208–225. Springer, Heidelberg (2012)
17. Chen, S., Lampe, R., Lee, J., Seurin, Y., Steinberger, J.: Minimizing the two-round even-mansour cipher. In: Garay, J.A., Gennaro, R. (eds.) CRYPTO 2014, Part I. LNCS, vol. 8616, pp. 39–56. Springer, Heidelberg (2014)
18. Chen, S., Steinberger, J.: Tight security bounds for key-alternating ciphers. In: Nguyen, P.Q., Oswald, E. (eds.) EUROCRYPT 2014. LNCS, vol. 8441, pp. 327–350. Springer, Heidelberg (2014)

19. Cogliati, B., Seurin, Y.: On the provable security of the iterated even-mansour cipher against related-key and chosen-key attacks. In: Oswald, E., Fischlin, M. (eds.) EUROCRYPT 2015. LNCS, vol. 9056, pp. 584–613. Springer, Heidelberg (2015)

20. Cogliati, B., Seurin, Y.: On the provable security of the iterated Even-Mansour cipher against related-key and chosen-key attacks. Cryptology ePrint Archive, Report 2015/069 (2015). http://eprint.iacr.org/2015/069

21. Daemen, J.: Limitations of the Even-Mansour construction (rump session). In: Imai, H., Rivest, R.L., Matsumoto, T. (eds.) ASIACRYPT 1991. LNCS, vol. 739, pp. 495–498. Springer, Heidelberg (1993)

22. Daemen, J., Rijmen, V.: The block cipher Rijndael. In: Quisquater, J.-J., Schneier, B. (eds.) CARDIS 1998. LNCS, vol. 1820, pp. 277–284. Springer, Berlin Heidelberg (2000)

23. Daemen, J., Rijmen, V.: The wide trail design strategy. In: Honary, B. (ed.) Cryptography and Coding 2001. LNCS, vol. 2260, pp. 222–238. Springer, Heidelberg (2001)

24. Dunkelman, O., Keller, N., Shamir, A.: Minimalism in cryptography: the even-mansour scheme revisited. In: Pointcheval, D., Johansson, T. (eds.) EUROCRYPT 2012. LNCS, vol. 7237, pp. 336–354. Springer, Heidelberg (2012)

25. EMVCo. EMV Integrated Circuit Card Specifications for Payment Systems, Book 2, Security and Key Management, June 2008. Version 4.2

26. Even, S., Mansour, Y.: A construction of a cipher from a single pseudorandom permutation. In: Imai, H., Rivest, R.L., Matsumoto, T. (eds.) ASIACRYPT 1991. LNCS, vol. 739, pp. 210–224. Springer, Heidelberg (1993)

27. Even, S., Mansour, Y.: A construction of a cipher from a single pseudorandom permutation. J. Cryptology 10(3), 151–162 (1997)

28. Farshim, P., Procter, G.: The related-key security of iterated even-mansour ciphers. Cryptology ePrint Archive, Report 2014/953 (2014). http://eprint.iacr.org/2014/953

29. Gentry, C., Ramzan, Z.: Eliminating random permutation oracles in the even-mansour cipher. In: Lee, P.J. (ed.) ASIACRYPT 2004. LNCS, vol. 3329, pp. 32–47. Springer, Heidelberg (2004)

30. Gérard, B., Grosso, V., Naya-Plasencia, M., Standaert, F.-X.: Block ciphers that are easier to mask: how far can we go? In: Bertoni, G., Coron, J.-S. (eds.) CHES 2013. LNCS, vol. 8086, pp. 383–399. Springer, Heidelberg (2013)

31. Gong, Z., Nikova, S., Law, Y.W.: KLEIN: a new family of lightweight block ciphers. In: Juels, A., Paar, C. (eds.) RFIDSec 2011. LNCS, vol. 7055, pp. 1–18. Springer, Heidelberg (2012)

32. Guo, J., Peyrin, T., Poschmann, A., Robshaw, M.: The LED block cipher. In: Preneel, B., Takagi, T. (eds.) CHES 2011. LNCS, vol. 6917, pp. 326–341. Springer, Heidelberg (2011)

33. Holenstein, T., Künzler, R., Tessaro, S.: The equivalence of the random oracle model and the ideal cipher model, revisited. In: Fortnow, L., Vadhan, S.P. (eds.) 43rd ACM STOC, pp. 89–98. ACM Press, June 2011

34. Iwata, T., Kohno, T.: New security proofs for the 3GPP confidentiality and integrity algorithms. In: Roy, B., Meier, W. (eds.) FSE 2004. LNCS, vol. 3017, pp. 427–445. Springer, Heidelberg (2004)

35. Jean, J., Nikolić, I., Peyrin, T., Wang, L., Wu, S.: Security analysis of PRINCE. In: Moriai, S. (ed.) FSE 2013. LNCS, vol. 8424, pp. 92–111. Springer, Heidelberg (2014)

36. Kilian, J., Rogaway, P.: How to protect DES against exhaustive key search. In: Koblitz, N. (ed.) CRYPTO 1996. LNCS, vol. 1109, pp. 252–267. Springer, Heidelberg (1996)

37. Kilian, J., Rogaway, P.: How to protect DES against exhaustive key search (an analysis of DESX). J. Cryptology **14**(1), 17–35 (2001)

38. Knudsen, L.R.: Cryptanalysis of LOKI 91. In: Seberry, J., Zheng, Y. (eds.) AUSCRYPT 1992. LNCS, vol. 718, pp. 196–208. Springer, Heidelberg (1993)

39. Lampe, R., Patarin, J., Seurin, Y.: An asymptotically tight security analysis of the iterated even-mansour cipher. In: Wang, X., Sako, K. (eds.) ASIACRYPT 2012. LNCS, vol. 7658, pp. 278–295. Springer, Heidelberg (2012)

40. Lampe, R., Seurin, Y.: How to construct an ideal cipher from a small set of public permutations. In: Sako, K., Sarkar, P. (eds.) ASIACRYPT 2013, Part I. LNCS, vol. 8269, pp. 444–463. Springer, Heidelberg (2013)

41. Liskov, M., Rivest, R.L., Wagner, D.: Tweakable block ciphers. In: Yung, M. (ed.) CRYPTO 2002. LNCS, vol. 2442, pp. 31–46. Springer, Heidelberg (2002)

42. Lucks, S.: Ciphers secure against related-key attacks. In: Roy, B., Meier, W. (eds.) FSE 2004. LNCS, vol. 3017, pp. 359–370. Springer, Heidelberg (2004)

43. Maurer, U.M., Renner, R.S., Holenstein, C.: Indifferentiability, impossibility results on reductions, and applications to the random oracle methodology. In: Naor, M. (ed.) TCC 2004. LNCS, vol. 2951, pp. 21–39. Springer, Heidelberg (2004)

44. Mendel, F., Rijmen, V., Toz, D., Varıcı, K.: Differential analysis of the LED block cipher. In: Wang, X., Sako, K. (eds.) ASIACRYPT 2012. LNCS, vol. 7658, pp. 190–207. Springer, Heidelberg (2012)

45. National Institute of Standards and Technology. FIPS Publication 197, Announcing the Advanced Encryption Standard (AES) (2001)

46. Özen, O., Varıcı, K., Tezcan, C., Kocair, Ç.: Lightweight block ciphers revisited: cryptanalysis of reduced round PRESENT and HIGHT. In: Boyd, C., González Nieto, J. (eds.) ACISP 2009. LNCS, vol. 5594, pp. 90–107. Springer, Heidelberg (2009)

47. Patarin, J.: The "Coefficients H" technique. In: Avanzi, R.M., Keliher, L., Sica, F. (eds.) SAC 2008. LNCS, vol. 5381, pp. 328–345. Springer, Heidelberg (2009)

48. Ristenpart, T., Shacham, H., Shrimpton, T.: Careful with composition: limitations of the indifferentiability framework. In: Paterson, K.G. (ed.) EUROCRYPT 2011. LNCS, vol. 6632, pp. 487–506. Springer, Heidelberg (2011)

49. Shannon, C.E.: Communication theory of secrecy systems. Bell Syst. Tech. J. **128**(4), 656–715 (1949)

50. Steinberger, J.: Improved security bounds for key-alternating ciphers via hellinger distance. Cryptology ePrint Archive, Report 2012/481 (2012). http://eprint.iacr.org/2012/481

Security of Keyed Sponge Constructions Using a Modular Proof Approach

Elena Andreeva[1]([⊠]), Joan Daemen[2], Bart Mennink[1], and Gilles Van Assche[2]

[1] Department of Electrical Engineering, ESAT/COSIC,
KU Leuven, iMinds, Leuven, Belgium
{elena.andreeva,bart.mennink}@esat.kuleuven.be
[2] STMicroelectronics, Diegem, Belgium
{joan.daemen,gilles.vanassche}@st.com

Abstract. Sponge functions were originally proposed for hashing, but find increasingly more applications in keyed constructions, such as encryption and authentication. Depending on how the key is used we see two main types of keyed sponges in practice: *inner-* and *outer-* keyed. Earlier security bounds, mostly due to the well-known sponge indifferentiability result, guarantee a security level of $c/2$ bits with c the capacity. We reconsider these two keyed sponge versions and derive improved bounds in the classical indistinguishability setting as well as in an extended setting where the adversary targets multiple instances at the same time. For cryptographically significant parameter values, the expected workload for an attacker to be successful in an n-target attack against the outer-keyed sponge is the minimum over $2^k/n$ and $2^c/\mu$ with k the key length and μ the total maximum multiplicity. For the inner-keyed sponge this simplifies to $2^k/\mu$ with maximum security if $k = c$. The multiplicity is a characteristic of the data available to the attacker. It is at most twice the data complexity, but will be much smaller in practically relevant attack scenarios. We take a modular proof approach, and our indistinguishability bounds are the sum of a bound in the PRP model and a bound on the PRP-security of Even-Mansour type block ciphers in the ideal permutation model, where we obtain the latter result by using Patarin's H-coefficient technique.

Keywords: Sponge construction · Keyed sponge · (Authenticated) encryption · Indistinguishability

1 Introduction

Sponge functions are versatile cryptographic primitives that can be used for hashing, but also in a wide range of keyed applications, such as message authentication codes (MAC), stream encryption, authenticated encryption, and pseudo-random sequence generation [5,7,8]. This fact is illustrated by the large number of sponge based candidates in the CAESAR competition for authenticated encryption schemes [12]: Artemia [1], Ascon [15], ICEPOLE [23], Ketje [10],

© International Association for Cryptologic Research 2015
G. Leander (Ed.): FSE 2015, LNCS 9054, pp. 364–384, 2015.
DOI: 10.1007/978-3-662-48116-5_18

Keyak [11], NORX [3], π-Cipher [19], PRIMATEs [2], Prøst [21] and STRIBOB [28]. More recently, Rivest and Schuldt [27] presented an update of the RC4 stream cipher with the name Spritz, also adopting a keyed sponge construction.

The sponge function consists of the application of the sponge construction to a fixed-length permutation (or transformation) f. It is a function that maps an input string of variable length to an output of arbitrary length. The *duplex construction* also makes use of a fixed-length permutation but results in a *stateful object* that can be fed with short input strings and from which short output strings can be extracted [8]. The above mentioned authenticated encryption schemes are for example based on the duplex construction. In [8] Bertoni et al. prove the security of the duplex construction equivalent to the security of the sponge construction, which means that any security result on the sponge construction is automatically valid for the duplex construction.

We can identify two types of keyed sponge functions, both of which we see applied in practice [1–3,10,11,15,19,21,23,25,28,29]. The first type applies the key by taking it as the first part of the sponge input and we call it the *outer-keyed sponge*. The second *inner-keyed sponge* applies the key on the inner part of the initial state, and can be viewed as successive applications of the Even-Mansour [16,17] type block cipher, which in turn calls an unkeyed permutation.

One way to argue security of the keyed sponge constructions is via the indifferentiability result of [6]. This result guarantees that the keyed sponge constructions can replace random oracles in any single-stage cryptographic system [22,26] as long as the total complexity of the adversary is less than $2^{(c+1)/2}$. Bertoni et al. [9] derived an improved bound on the distinguishing advantage against the outer-keyed sponge by separating the total complexity into time and data complexity. However, their proof contains a subtle error: [9, Lemma 1] proves that the keyed sponge output is uniformly and independently distributed if certain conditions are fulfilled, whereas the proof requires uniformity of the *joint* keyed sponge output and queries to f, which does exhibit a bias. Regarding the inner-keyed sponge, Chang et al. considered security of the construction in the so-called standard model in [13]. Central in their reasoning is the clever trick to describe the keyed sponge as the sponge construction calling an Even-Mansour block cipher. Their bound does however not go beyond the generic sponge indifferentiability bound of [6] as their main intention appears to have been to prove security in the standard model rather than the ideal permutation model.

1.1 Our Contribution

We prove bounds on the generic security of both types of keyed sponge constructions in the single-target and multi-target scenarios. In the single-target scenario, we bound the success probability of distinguishing a single instance of the construction from a random oracle for a given attack complexity and providing the adversary with additional access to the underlying permutation f. In the multi-target scenario, the adversary targets multiple instances of the keyed sponge at the same time. In practice, many systems support multiple users using the same algorithm and the adversary may be willing to leverage his resources to break at least one of the users' account. It can be regarded as important to the system provider who wants to avoid losing credibility in such a case. For the multi-target analysis, we introduce a generalized version of indistinguishability security.

Our proofs are performed in two steps. Firstly, considering the keyed sponge constructions to be implicitly based on an underlying block cipher, we derive a bound for the distinguishing advantage of the constructions in the PRP model. Secondly, we deal with the PRP security of the Even-Mansour construction in the ideal permutation model using Patarin's H-coefficient technique [14,24]. This modular proof approach results in compact proofs that are easy to verify.

When estimating the required capacity c to achieve a required security level, the important term in all of the bounds is of the form $\frac{M^2+\mu N}{2^c}$. Here, M is the data complexity, N the time complexity, and μ is the so-called *total maximum multiplicity*. The multiplicity is determined by the keyed sponge outputs available to the adversary and is a function of M. It first appeared in Bertoni et al. [7], and allows us to achieve bounds that significantly improve over the earlier single-target bounds of [9,13]. The multiplicity makes the bound widely applicable, as it allows to take into account the restrictions an adversary faces in a concrete use case. In more detail, in the worst case the multiplicity equals twice the data complexity but in many attack scenarios it is orders of magnitude smaller, leading to a tighter bound. For cryptographically significant parameter values, the dominant term in the bound is the time complexity by divided by $2^c/\mu$. In other words, our bounds imply security beyond the birthday bound on the capacity for all existing keyed sponge based modes.

We remark that a recent work of Jovanovic et al. [20] proved bounds on the distinguishing advantage for keyed sponge based authenticated encryption. Their results are specific for authentication encryption modes applying a keyed sponge construction and explicitly require nonce uniqueness. Moreover, unlike the bounds in this paper, their bound contains a term involving the permutation width making it tight only for large rates. Additionally, our results yield a tight bound whatever the rate, exploiting the multiplicity, which is typically small in the case of unique nonce scenarios (see also Sect. 6). Finally, a concurrent work by Gaži et al. [18] proves tight bounds for the specific case of MACs produced by a keyed sponge, but without generalizing to other applications that require longer output lengths.

1.2 Version History

Gaži, Pietrzak, and Tessaro pointed out that the pre-proceedings version contains an oversight in the analysis of the outer-keyed sponge. Informally, the probability that a distinguisher guesses the key was bounded incorrectly. We have fixed the issue, using a result from Gaži et al. [18]. We refer to the proof of Theorem 6 and the subsequent discussion for more details.

1.3 Outline

The remainder of this paper is organized as follows. In Sect. 2, we provide the definitions of the constructions we use. This is followed by an introduction to the security model of indistinguishability in Sect. 3. In Sect. 4, we prove our bounds for the inner-keyed sponge and in Sect. 5 those for the outer-keyed sponge. Finally, we discuss the implications of our bounds in Sect. 6.

2 Definitions of Constructions

In this section we specify the constructions we address in this paper.

2.1 The Sponge Construction

The sponge construction operates on a state s of b bits, and calls a b-bit permutation f. It takes as input a message $m \in \{0,1\}^*$ and natural number ℓ and outputs a potentially infinite string truncated to the chosen length $\ell \in \mathbb{N}$, denoted $z \in \{0,1\}^\ell$.

We express an evaluation of the sponge function as

$$\text{SPONGE}^f(m, \ell) = z. \tag{1}$$

The sponge function operates as follows. First we apply an injective padding function to the input message m, denoted by $m||\text{pad}[r](|m|)$, with r the rate. This padding rule is required to be injective and the last block is required to be different from 0. Then, we initialize the b bits of the sponge state s to zero. We refer to the first r bits of the state s as the *outer part* $\bar{s}$ and to the last $c = b - r$ bits (c is called the *capacity*) as its *inner part* $\hat{s}$ (think back on ^ as a roof). The padded message is processed by an *absorbing phase* followed by a *squeezing phase*:

Absorbing phase: the r-bit input message blocks are sequentially XORed into the outer part of the state, interleaved with applications of the function f;
Squeezing phase: the bits of the outer part of the state are returned as output blocks, interleaved with applications of the function f, until enough bits are produced.

An illustration is given in Fig. 1 and a formal description is provided in Algorithm 1. The notation $\lfloor x \rfloor_n$ means that the string x is truncated after its first n bits.

2.2 The Even-Mansour Construction

The (single-key) Even-Mansour construction builds a b-bit block cipher from a b-bit permutation and takes a b-bit key [16,17]. It is defined as $f(x \oplus K) \oplus K$. We consider a variant with the first r bits of the key are zero, reducing its effective length to c bits:

$$E_K^f(x) = f(x \oplus (0^r||K)) \oplus (0^r||K). \tag{2}$$

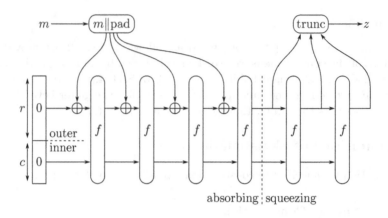

Fig. 1. The sponge construction

Algorithm 1. The sponge construction SPONGE^f

Input: $m \in \{0,1\}^*$, $\ell \in \mathbb{N}$
Output: $z \in \{0,1\}^\ell$
$P = m \| \text{pad}[r](|m|)$
Let $P = m_0 \| m_1 \| \dots \| m_w$ with $|m_i| = r$
$s = 0^b$
for $i = 0$ to w **do**
  $s = s \oplus (m_i \| 0^c)$
  $s = f(s)$
$z = \lfloor s \rfloor_r$
while $|z| < \ell$ **do**
  $s = f(s)$
  $z = z \| \lfloor s \rfloor_r$
return $\lfloor z \rfloor_\ell$

2.3 The Root-Keyed Sponge

As a way to highlight the similarities between the inner- and outer-keyed sponges, which we will define in the next sections, we define a common construction called the *root-keyed sponge*. Basically, it is a variant of the sponge construction where the state is initialized to a key $K \in \{0,1\}^b$ instead of 0^b. The root-keyed sponge RKS_K^f is defined in Algorithm 2.

The root-keyed sponge can be rewritten using the Even-Mansour block cipher. Indeed, we have

$$\text{RKS}_K^f(m, \ell) = \text{RKS}_{\hat{K}\|0^c}^{E_{\hat{K}}^f}(m, \ell), \tag{3}$$

as key additions between subsequent applications of $E_{\hat{K}}^f$ cancel out.

Algorithm 2. The root-keyed sponge construction RKS_K^f

Require: $|K| = b$
Input: $m \in \{0,1\}^*$, $\ell \in \mathbb{N}$
Output: $z \in \{0,1\}^\ell$
$P = m||\text{pad}[r](|m|)$
Let $P = m_0||m_1||\ldots||m_w$ with $|m_i| = r$
$s = K$
for $i = 0$ to w **do**
$\quad s = s \oplus (m_i||0^c)$
$\quad s = f(s)$
$z = \lfloor s \rfloor_r$
while $|z| < \ell$ **do**
$\quad s = f(s)$
$\quad z = z||\lfloor s \rfloor_r$
return $\lfloor z \rfloor_\ell$

2.4 The Inner-Keyed Sponge

The inner-keyed sponge IKS^f is a pseudorandom function (PRF) that was first introduced by Chang et al. [13] (their case EMKSC3). An inner-keyed sponge instance is defined by a permutation f and a key $K \in \{0,1\}^c$ and simply consists of the sponge construction with E_K^f as permutation:

$$\text{IKS}_K^f(m, \ell) = \text{SPONGE}^{E_K^f}(m, \ell). \tag{4}$$

Owing to (3), an equivalent definition of $\text{IKS}_K^f(m, \ell)$ is given by

$$\text{IKS}_K^f(m, \ell) = \text{RKS}_{0^b}^{E_K^f}(m, \ell) = \text{RKS}_{0^r||K}^f(m, \ell). \tag{5}$$

2.5 The Outer-Keyed Sponge

The outer-keyed sponge OKS^f is a PRF construction that was originally introduced by Bertoni et al. [9] as the *keyed sponge*. An outer-keyed sponge instance is defined by a permutation f and a key $K \in \{0,1\}^k$ and simply consists of an evaluation of the sponge construction where the secret key and the message are concatenated:

$$\text{OKS}_K^f(m, \ell) = \text{SPONGE}^f(K||m, \ell). \tag{6}$$

While K may be of any size, we limit our analysis to the case where k is a multiple of the rate r, or $\{0,1\}^k = (\{0,1\}^r)^+$. The outer-keyed sponge can be equivalently described as a function that derives the *root key* $L \in \{0,1\}^b$ from the cipher key $K \in \{0,1\}^k$, followed by the root-keyed sponge with root key L. The root key derivation function $\text{KD}^f(K)$ is defined in Algorithm 3. We obtain:

$$\text{OKS}_K^f(m, \ell) = \text{RKS}_{\text{KD}^f(K)}^f(m, \ell) \overset{(3)}{=} \text{RKS}_{\bar{L}||0^c}^{E_L^f}(m, \ell), \tag{7}$$

Algorithm 3. The root key derivation function $\text{KD}^f(K)$

1: **Input:** $K \in (\{0,1\}^r)^+$
2: **Output:** $s \in \{0,1\}^b$
3: Let $K = K_0 \| K_1 \| \ldots \| K_w$ with $|K_i| = r$
4: $s = 0^b$
5: **for** $i = 0$ to w **do**
6:     $s = s \oplus (K_i \| 0^c)$
7:     $s = f(s)$
8: **return** s

---

with $L = \text{KD}^f(K)$. This alternative description highlights a similarity with the inner-keyed sponge: the only effective difference lies in the presence of the root key derivation function.

3   Security Model

The security analyses in this work are done in the *indistinguishability* framework where one bounds the advantage of an adversary $\mathcal{A}$ in distinguishing a real system from an ideal system. The real system contains one or more specified constructions, while the ideal one consists of ideal functions with the same interface. We explain the high-level idea for the case where $\mathcal{A}$ attacks one instance of a keyed sponge construction.

Suppose $f : \{0,1\}^b \to \{0,1\}^b$ is a permutation and consider a keyed sponge construction $\mathcal{H}_K^f$ based on f and some key $K \in \{0,1\}^k$. Let $\mathcal{RO}$ be a random oracle [4] with the same interface as $\mathcal{H}_K^f$. Adversary $\mathcal{A}$ is given query access to either $\mathcal{H}_K^f$ or $\mathcal{RO}$ and tries to tell both apart. It is also given access to the underlying permutation f, which is modeled by query access. The random oracle is required to output infinitely long strings truncated to a certain length. The function can be defined as $\mathcal{RO} : \{0,1\}^* \times \mathbb{N} \to \{0,1\}^{\mathbb{N}}$ that on input (m, ℓ) outputs $\mathcal{RO}(m, \ell) = \lfloor \mathcal{RO}^{\infty}(m) \rfloor_{\ell}$, where $\mathcal{RO}^{\infty} : \{0,1\}^* \to \{0,1\}^{\infty}$ takes inputs of arbitrary but finite length and returns random infinite strings where each output bit is selected uniformly and independently, for every m.

We similarly consider the PRP security of the Even-Mansour construction E_K^f, where $\mathcal{A}$ is given query access to either this construction or a random permutation $\pi \xleftarrow{\$} \text{Perm}(b)$ with domain and range $\{0,1\}^b$, along with query access to f. We also consider a slightly more advanced notion of kdPRP security, where the root key derivation function KD is applied to K first.

The security proofs of IKS and OKS consist of two steps: the first one reduces the security of the construction to the PRP security (for IKS) or kdPRP security (for OKS) of the Even-Mansour construction. This step does not depend on f and is in fact a standard-model reduction. Next, we investigate the PRP/kdPRP security of Even-Mansour under the assumption that f is a random permutation.

3.1   Counting

We express our bound in terms of the query complexities that model the effort by the adversary. Here we distinguish between keyed sponge *construction* or random oracle queries and *primitive* queries to $f^{\pm}$:

Data or online complexity M: the amount of access to the construction $\mathcal{H}_K^f$ or $\mathcal{RO}$, that in many practical use cases is limited;

Time or offline complexity N: computations requiring no access to the construction, in practical use cases only limited by the computing power and time available to the adversary.

Both M and N are expressed in terms of the number of primitive calls. We include in M only *fresh calls*: a call from $\mathcal{H}_K^f$ to f is not fresh if it has already been made due to a prior query to the construction. In the ideal world a random oracle naturally does not make calls to f, but the data complexity is counted as if it would and as such, it is fully determined by the queries. For N, we assume without loss of generality that the adversary makes no repeated queries.

In our proofs, we use an additional characteristic of the queries called the *total maximum multiplicity* and denote it by μ. Let $\{(s_i, t_i)\}_{i=1}^M$ be the set of M input/output pairs for f made in construction evaluations.

Definition 1 (Multiplicity). *The maximum forward and backward multiplicities are given by*

$$\mu_{\text{fw}} = \max_a \#\{i \in \{1, \ldots, M\} \mid \bar{s}_i = a\} \text{ and}$$
$$\mu_{\text{bw}} = \max_a \#\{i \in \{1, \ldots, M\} \mid \bar{t}_i = a\}.$$

The total maximum multiplicity is given by $\mu = \mu_{\text{fw}} + \mu_{\text{bw}}$.

Note that the total maximum multiplicity μ is the sum of the maximum forward and backward multiplicities while [7] uses the maximum over the forward and backward multiplicities.

3.2   Distinguishing Advantage for Keyed Sponges

We are now ready to give the indistinguishability definition for keyed sponges (the PRP and kdPRP security definitions will be discussed in Sects. 4 and 5). Our definition is broad in the sense that it considers also security against a multi-target attack, where an attacker has access to an array of $n \geq 1$ instances of the keyed sponge or random oracles. We refer to this notion as *joint indistinguishability*. Naturally, joint indistinguishability reduces to plain or regular *indistinguishability* for $n = 1$. The model is illustrated in Fig. 2.

Definition 2 (Joint Distinguishing Advantage). *Let $\mathcal{H}$ be a PRF function based on a permutation $f \in \mathsf{Perm}(b)$. Let $K_1, \ldots, K_n \xleftarrow{\$} \{0, 1\}^k$ be $n \geq 1$ keys*

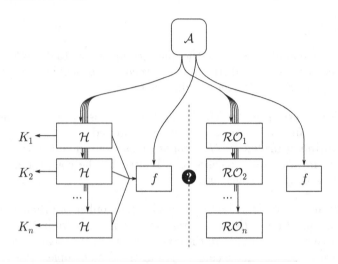

Fig. 2. The keyed sponge distinguishing setup

and $\mathcal{RO}_1, \ldots, \mathcal{RO}_n$ be n independent random oracles with the same interface as $\mathcal{H}_{K_1}, \ldots, \mathcal{H}_{K_n}$. The joint distinguishing advantage of $\mathcal{A}$ is defined as

$$\mathbf{Adv}_{\mathcal{H}}^{\mathrm{ind}[n]}(\mathcal{A}) = \left| \mathrm{Pr}\left(\mathcal{A}^{\mathcal{H}_{K_1}^f, \ldots, \mathcal{H}_{K_n}^f, f} \Rightarrow 1 \right) - \mathrm{Pr}\left(\mathcal{A}^{\mathcal{RO}_1, \ldots, \mathcal{RO}_n, f} \Rightarrow 1 \right) \right|.$$

We use $\mathbf{Adv}_{\mathcal{H}}^{\mathrm{ind}[n]}(M_1, \ldots, M_n, \mu, N)$ to denote the maximum advantage over any adversary with data complexity M_h to the h-th construction oracle ($\mathcal{H}_{K_h}$ or $\mathcal{RO}_h$), time complexity N, and total maximum multiplicity μ.

Note that, as we consider $n \geq 1$ instances of the construction, we have similarly split the online complexity M into $M_1 + \cdots + M_n$. In other words, M gives the online complexity over all n instances.

3.3   Patarin's H-Coefficient Technique

Our proofs partly rely on Patarin's H-coefficient technique [24]. We briefly summarize this technique, and refer to Chen and Steinberger [14] for further discussion.

Consider an information-theoretic adversary $\mathcal{A}$ whose goal is to distinguish two systems X and Y, denoted as

$$\mathbf{Adv}(\mathcal{A}) = \Delta(X; Y),$$

where $\Delta(X; Y)$ denotes the statistical distance between X and Y. Without loss of generality, we can assume $\mathcal{A}$ is a deterministic adversary and will always do so in the following. Indeed, if $\mathcal{A}$ were a randomized adversary, there exists a deterministic adversary $\mathcal{A}'$ with at least the same advantage (namely the one defined by $\mathcal{A}$ and the fixed random tape). We refer to [14] for details. Its interaction with the system X or Y is summarized in a transcript τ. For $Z \in \{X, Y\}$, denote by D_Z the probability distribution of transcripts when interacting with Z. Say that a transcript τ is attainable if it can be obtained from interacting with Y, hence if $\Pr(D_Y = \tau) > 0$, and let $\mathcal{T}$ be the set of all attainable transcripts. The H-coefficient technique states the following [14].

Lemma 1 (H-coefficient Technique). *Consider a fixed deterministic adversary $\mathcal{A}$. Let $\mathcal{T} = \mathcal{T}_{\text{good}} \cup \mathcal{T}_{\text{bad}}$ be a partition of the set of attainable transcripts into "good" and "bad" transcripts. Let ε be such that for all $\tau \in \mathcal{T}_{\text{good}}$:*

$$\frac{\Pr(D_X = \tau)}{\Pr(D_Y = \tau)} \geq 1 - \varepsilon.$$

Then, $\mathbf{Adv}(\mathcal{A}) \leq \varepsilon + \Pr(D_Y \in \mathcal{T}_{\text{bad}})$.

Proofs using Patarin's technique consist of first carefully defining a set of "bad" transcripts $\mathcal{T}_{\text{bad}}$, and then showing that both ε and $\Pr(D_Y \in \mathcal{T}_{\text{bad}})$ are small for this set of bad transcripts.

4 Distinguishing Advantage of the Inner-Keyed Sponge

We bound the distinguishing advantage of the inner-keyed sponge construction in the ideal permutation model. A bound for the case of $n = 1$ is given in Sect. 4.1, and it is generalized to arbitrary n in Sect. 4.2. Both proofs consist of two steps that are both of independent interest. Note that we assume equal key size and capacity in our proofs. If $k < c$, the denominator 2^c in the bounds of Theorems 2 and 4 must be replaced by 2^k.

Before proceeding, we define the notion of PRP security that we will use in the security proof of the inner-keyed sponge to replace $E^f_{K_1}, \ldots, E^f_{K_n}$ with random permutations $\pi_1, \ldots, \pi_n$, in analogy with (4). As multiple instances of E for n different keys are considered, we call this notion *joint PRP security*.

Definition 3 (Joint PRP Advantage). *We define the joint PRP advantage of $\mathcal{A}$ for a given block cipher $E : \{0,1\}^c \times \{0,1\}^b \to \{0,1\}^b$ based on a permutation $f \in \mathsf{Perm}(b)$ as*

$$\mathbf{Adv}_E^{\mathrm{prp}[n]}(\mathcal{A}) = \left| \Pr\left(\mathcal{A}^{E^f_{K_1}, \ldots, E^f_{K_n}, f} \Rightarrow 1 \right) - \Pr\left(\mathcal{A}^{\pi_1, \ldots, \pi_n, f} \Rightarrow 1 \right) \right|.$$

The adversary can make both forward and inverse primitive queries f and f^{-1}, but is restricted to forward construction queries. We use $\mathbf{Adv}_E^{\mathrm{prp}[n]}(M_1, \ldots, M_n, \mu, N)$ to denote the maximum advantage over any adversary with data complexity M_h to the h-th construction oracle ($E^f_{K_h}$ or π_h), time complexity N, and total maximum multiplicity μ.

4.1 Single Target

Theorem 1. *For $\mathrm{IKS}^f_K : \{0,1\}^* \times \mathbb{N} \to \{0,1\}^{\mathbb{N}}$ with $K \xleftarrow{\$} \{0,1\}^c$ and permutation $f \in \mathsf{Perm}(b)$:*

$$\mathbf{Adv}_{\mathrm{IKS}}^{\mathrm{ind}[1]}(M, \mu, N) \leq \frac{M^2}{2^c} + \mathbf{Adv}_E^{\mathrm{prp}[1]}(M, \mu, N).$$

Proof. Using the triangle inequality, we find that for any adversary $\mathcal{A}$:

$$
\begin{aligned}
\mathbf{Adv}_{\mathrm{IKS}}^{\mathrm{ind}[1]}(\mathcal{A}) &\overset{\mathrm{def}}{=} \Delta_{\mathcal{A}}(\mathrm{IKS}_K^f, f; \mathcal{RO}, f) \\
&\overset{(4)}{=} \Delta_{\mathcal{A}}(\mathrm{SPONGE}^{E_K^f}, f; \mathcal{RO}, f) \\
&\leq \Delta_{\mathcal{A}}(\mathrm{SPONGE}^\pi, f; \mathcal{RO}, f) + \Delta_{\mathcal{B}}(E_K^f, f; \pi, f) \\
&= \Delta_{\mathcal{C}}(\mathrm{SPONGE}^\pi, \mathcal{RO}) + \Delta_{\mathcal{B}}(E_K^f, f; \pi, f).
\end{aligned}
$$

Here, $\mathcal{B}$ and $\mathcal{C}$ are adversaries whose joint cost is not above that of $\mathcal{A}$. Concretely, for our cost functions M, N and total maximum multiplicity μ, this means that $\mathcal{B}$ cannot make more than M construction queries with total maximum multiplicity at most μ and at most N primitive queries. Distinguisher $\mathcal{C}$ can make at most M construction queries, and its advantage is covered by the indifferentiability bound proven in [6]. ☐

We now bound the PRP security of the Even-Mansour construction in the ideal permutation model. The proof is a generalization of the security analysis of the Even-Mansour block cipher [16, 17].

Theorem 2. *For E_K^f with $K \overset{\$}{\leftarrow} \{0,1\}^c$ and ideal permutation $f \overset{\$}{\leftarrow} \mathrm{Perm}(b)$ we have*

$$
\mathbf{Adv}_E^{\mathrm{prp}[1]}(M, \mu, N) \leq \frac{\mu N}{2^c}.
$$

Proof. The proof uses Lemma 1. We consider an adversary $\mathcal{A}$ that has access to $X = (E_K^f, f)$ in the real world or $Y = (\pi, f)$ in the ideal world. It can only make forward queries to its oracle $\mathcal{O}_1$, although it can make both forward and backward queries to f. It makes M construction queries with total maximum multiplicity at most μ and at most N primitive queries. The interaction with $\mathcal{O}_1$ is denoted $\tau_1 = \{(s_i, t_i)\}_{i=1}^M$ and the interaction with f is denoted $\tau_f = \{(x_j, y_j)\}_{j=1}^N$. To ease the analysis, we will disclose K at the end of the experiment (in the ideal world, K will simply be a dummy key). The transcripts are thus of the form $\tau = (K, \tau_1, \tau_f)$. We recall that the total maximum multiplicity is μ, which means that

$$
\max_a \#\{(s_i, t_i) \in \tau_1 \mid \bar{s}_i = a\} \leq \mu_{\mathrm{fw}} \text{ and}
$$

$$
\max_a \#\{(s_i, t_i) \in \tau_1 \mid \bar{t}_i = a\} \leq \mu_{\mathrm{bw}},
$$

for some $\mu_{\mathrm{fw}}, \mu_{\mathrm{bw}}$ with $\mu_{\mathrm{fw}} + \mu_{\mathrm{bw}} \leq \mu$.

Definition of good and bad transcripts. We define a transcript τ as *bad* if

$$
\exists (s,t) \in \tau_1, (x,y) \in \tau_f \text{ such that } s \oplus x = 0^r \| K \vee t \oplus y = 0^r \| K. \tag{8}
$$

In the real world a bad transcript implies two calls to f with the same input: one directly from querying the primitive oracle and another one indirectly from querying the construction oracle. In a *good* transcript in the real world, all tuples in (τ_1, τ_f) uniquely define an input-output pair of f. Note also that in the real world the two conditions in (8) are equivalent while in the ideal world they are not.

Bounding the probability of bad transcripts in the ideal world. In the ideal world, (τ_1, τ_f) is a transcript generated independently of the dummy key $K \xleftarrow{\$} \{0,1\}^c$. First consider the first condition of (8). Fix any tuple (x, y) (N choices). By construction, τ_1 contains at most μ_{fw} tuples (s, t) such that $\bar{s} = \bar{x}$. This gives a total of $\mu_{\mathrm{fw}} N$ values $\hat{s} \oplus \hat{x}$, and any could be hit by the randomly generated K. A similar reasoning holds for the second part of (8), resulting in $\mu_{\mathrm{bw}} N$ values. Concluding, $\Pr\left(D_Y \in \mathcal{T}_{\mathrm{bad}}\right) \le \frac{\mu N}{2^c}$, where we use that $\mu = \mu_{\mathrm{fw}} + \mu_{\mathrm{bw}}$.

Bounding the ratio $\Pr\left(D_X = \tau\right) / \Pr\left(D_Y = \tau\right)$ for good transcripts. Consider a good transcript $\tau \in \mathcal{T}_{\mathrm{good}}$. Denote by Ω_X the set of all possible oracles in the real world and by $\mathrm{comp}_X(\tau) \subseteq \Omega_X$ the set of oracles in Ω_X compatible with transcript τ. Note that $|\Omega_X| = 2^c \cdot 2^b!$. Define Ω_Y and $\mathrm{comp}_Y(\tau)$ similarly, where $|\Omega_Y| = 2^c \cdot (2^b!)^2$. The probabilities appearing in Lemma 1 can be computed as follows:

$$\Pr\left(D_X = \tau\right) = \frac{|\mathrm{comp}_X(\tau)|}{|\Omega_X|} \quad \text{and} \quad \Pr\left(D_Y = \tau\right) = \frac{|\mathrm{comp}_Y(\tau)|}{|\Omega_Y|}.$$

Starting with $|\mathrm{comp}_X(\tau)|$, the condition $\tau \in \mathcal{T}_{\mathrm{good}}$ imposes uniqueness of the query tuples in τ, or in other words that any tuple defines exactly one input-output pair of f. As $\tau \cup \tau_f$ consists of $M + N$ tuples, the number of possible functions f compliant with τ is $|\mathrm{comp}_X(\tau)| = (2^b - M - N)!$. For the ideal world, the number of compliant functions π equals $(2^b - M)!$ and the number of compliant oracles f equals $(2^b - N)!$. Therefore,

$$|\mathrm{comp}_Y(\tau)| = (2^b - M)!(2^b - N)! \le (2^b - M - N)!2^b!.$$

We consequently obtain

$$\Pr\left(D_X = \tau\right) = \frac{(2^b - M - N)!}{2^c \cdot 2^b!} = \frac{(2^b - M - N)!2^b!}{2^c \cdot (2^b!)^2}$$

$$\ge \frac{|\mathrm{comp}_Y(\tau)|}{|\Omega_Y|} = \Pr\left(D_Y = \tau\right),$$

and thus $\Pr\left(D_X = \tau\right) / \Pr\left(D_Y = \tau\right) \ge 1$. $\qquad\square$

In the ideal permutation model, the expressions in Theorems 1 and 2 simplify into

$$\mathbf{Adv}_{\mathrm{IKS}}^{\mathrm{ind}[1]}(M, \mu, N) \le \frac{M^2 + \mu N}{2^c}.$$

4.2   Multiple Targets

Theorem 3. *For* $\mathrm{IKS}_K^f : \{0,1\}^* \times \mathbb{N} \to \{0,1\}^{\mathbb{N}}$ *with* $K_1, \ldots, K_n \xleftarrow{\$} \{0,1\}^c$ *and permutation* $f \in \mathrm{Perm}(b)$:

$$\mathbf{Adv}_{\mathrm{IKS}}^{\mathrm{ind}[n]}(M_1, \ldots, M_n, \mu, N) \le \frac{\sum_h M_h^2}{2^c} + \mathbf{Adv}_E^{\mathrm{prp}[n]}(M_1, \ldots, M_n, \mu, N).$$

Proof. A similar reasoning as for Theorems 1, but now using the notion of joint PRP security to replace $E_{K_1}^f, \ldots, E_{K_n}^f$ with n independent random permutations $\pi_1, \ldots, \pi_n$, results in

$$\mathbf{Adv}_{\mathrm{IKS}}^{\mathrm{ind}[n]}(\mathcal{A}) \le \Delta_{\mathcal{C}}(\mathrm{SPONGE}^{\pi_1}, \ldots, \mathrm{SPONGE}^{\pi_n}; \mathcal{RO}_1, \ldots, \mathcal{RO}_n)$$
$$+ \Delta_{\mathcal{B}}(E_{K_1}^f, \ldots, E_{K_n}^f, f; \pi_1, \ldots, \pi_n, f).$$

Here, $\mathcal{B}$ and $\mathcal{C}$ are adversaries whose joint cost is not above that of $\mathcal{A}$, and particularly both make at most M_h h-th construction queries for $h = 1, \ldots, n$. The advantage of $\mathcal{C}$ is in fact the distinguishing bound of n sponges with independent permutations. □

We now bound the joint PRP security of the Even-Mansour construction in the ideal permutation model.

Theorem 4. *For* E_K^f *with* $K_1, \ldots, K_n \xleftarrow{\$} \{0,1\}^c$ *and ideal permutation* $f \xleftarrow{\$} \mathrm{Perm}(b)$ *we have*

$$\mathbf{Adv}_E^{\mathrm{prp}[n]}(M_1, \ldots, M_n, \mu, N) \le \frac{\mu N}{2^c} + \frac{2 \sum_{h \ne h'} M_h M_{h'}}{2^c}.$$

Proof. The proof follows the one of Theorem 2, with the difference that multiple keys are involved. Adversary $\mathcal{A}$ has access to $X = (E_{K_1}^f, \ldots, E_{K_n}^f, f)$ in the real world or $Y = (\pi_1, \ldots, \pi_n, f)$ in the ideal world. The n construction oracles are also denoted $(\mathcal{O}_1, \ldots, \mathcal{O}_n)$. It makes M_h construction queries to $\mathcal{O}_h$ with total maximum multiplicity at most μ (over all $M = M_1 + \cdots + M_n$ construction queries) and at most N primitive queries. The interaction with $\mathcal{O}_h$ (for $h = 1, \ldots, n$) is denoted $\tau_h = \{(s_i, t_i)\}_{i=1}^{M_h}$ and the interaction with f is denoted $\tau_f = \{(x_j, y_j)\}_{j=1}^N$. As before, we will disclose the keys $K_1, \ldots K_n$ at the end of the experiment. The transcripts are thus of the form $\tau = (K_1, \ldots, K_n, \tau_1, \ldots, \tau_n, \tau_f)$.

Definition of good and bad transcripts. We extend the definition of *bad* transcripts from Theorem 2 to multiple keys. Formally, we define a transcript τ as *bad* if one of the following is satisfied:

$$\exists h, (s,t) \in \tau_h, (x,y) \in \tau_f \text{ such that } s \oplus x = 0^r \| K_h \vee t \oplus y = 0^r \| K_h, \quad (9)$$
$$\exists h \ne h', (s,t) \in \tau_h, (s',t') \in \tau_{h'} \text{ such that}$$
$$s \oplus s' = 0^r \| (K_h \oplus K_{h'}) \vee t \oplus t' = 0^r \| (K_h \oplus K_{h'}). \quad (10)$$

The second condition corresponds to colliding calls to f coming from two construction queries with different keys. In the real world, all tuples in a *good* transcript $(\tau_1, \ldots, \tau_n, \tau_f)$ consistently define an input-output pair of f. Note also that in the real world the two conditions in (9) are equivalent, and similarly for the two conditions in (10).

Bounding the probability of bad transcripts in the ideal world. In the ideal world, $(\tau_1, \ldots, \tau_n, \tau_f)$ is a transcript generated independently of the dummy keys $K_1, \ldots, K_n \xleftarrow{\$} \{0,1\}^c$. The proof of Theorem 2 straightforwardly generalizes to show that (9) is set with probability at most $\frac{\mu N}{2^c}$. Here, we use that for any tuple $(x,y) \in \tau_f$, the set $(\tau_1, \ldots, \tau_n)$ of M queries *in total* contains at most μ_{fw} tuples (s,t) such that $\bar{s} = \bar{x}$. A similar exercise is done for (10): for $h \neq h'$, there are at most $2M_h M_{h'}$ values $s \oplus s'$ and $t \oplus t'$ with $(s,t) \in \tau_h$ and $(s',t') \in \tau_{h'}$, and the value $K_h \oplus K_{h'}$ has probability $1/2^c$. Concluding, $\Pr\left(D_Y \in \mathcal{T}_{\mathrm{bad}}\right) \leq \frac{\mu N}{2^c} + \frac{2 \sum_{h \neq h'} M_h M_{h'}}{2^c}$.

Bounding the ratio $\Pr\left(D_X = \tau\right) / \Pr\left(D_Y = \tau\right)$ for good transcripts. As in the proof of Theorem 2, we have $|\Omega_X| = (2^c)^n \cdot 2^b!$ and $|\Omega_Y| = (2^c)^n \cdot (2^b!)^{n+1}$. Also, $|\mathrm{comp}_X(\tau)| = (2^b - M - N)!$ by construction. For the ideal world, the number of compliant functions $\pi_1, \ldots, \pi_n$ equals $\prod_h (2^b - M_h)!$ and the number of compliant oracles f equals $(2^b - N)!$. Therefore,

$$|\mathrm{comp}_Y(\tau)| = \left(\prod_h (2^b - M_h)!\right)(2^b - N)! \leq (2^b - M - N)!(2^b!)^n,$$

and the remainder of the proof follows Theorem 2.   □

In the ideal permutation model, the expressions in Theorems 3 and 4 simplify into

$$\mathbf{Adv}_{\mathrm{IKS}}^{\mathrm{ind}[n]}(M_1, \ldots, M_n, \mu, N) \leq \frac{M^2 + \mu N}{2^c}.$$

We remark that the bound is independent of n, and particularly matches the bound of Sect. 4.1. This is because M is the sum of the complexities $M_1, \ldots, M_n$, and additionally the multiplicity μ is taken over *all* construction queries.

5   Distinguishing Advantage of the Outer-Keyed Sponge

We bound the distinguishing advantage of the outer-keyed sponge construction in the ideal permutation model. A bound for the case of $n = 1$ is given in Sect. 5.1, and it is generalized to arbitrary n in Sect. 5.2. The high-level ideas of the proofs are the same as the ones of Sect. 4. The outer-keyed sponge differs from the inner-keyed sponge by the presence of a key derivation function using f. Therefore, a more involved version of PRP security is needed, where the key derivation L from K is taken into account. We call this notion *joint kdPRP (key derivated PRP) security*. For simplicity, we assume that all keys have equal length, with $v = k/r$ their block length.

Definition 4 (Joint kdPRP Advantage). *We define the joint kdPRP advantage of* $\mathcal{A}$ *for a given block cipher* $E : \{0,1\}^c \times \{0,1\}^b \to \{0,1\}^b$ *based on a permutation* $f \in \mathsf{Perm}(b)$ *as*

$$\mathbf{Adv}_{E,\mathrm{KD}}^{\mathrm{kdprp}[n]}(\mathcal{A}) = \left| \Pr\left(L_1 \leftarrow \mathrm{KD}_{K_1}^f, \ldots, L_n \leftarrow \mathrm{KD}_{K_n}^f; \mathcal{A}^{E_{\hat{L}_1}^f,\ldots,E_{\hat{L}_n}^f,f} \Rightarrow 1 \right) \right.$$

$$\left. - \Pr\left(\mathcal{A}^{\pi_1,\ldots,\pi_n,f} \Rightarrow 1 \right) \right|.$$

The adversary can make both forward and inverse primitive queries f *and* f^{-1}, *but is restricted to forward construction queries. We use* $\mathbf{Adv}_{E,\mathrm{KD}}^{\mathrm{kdprp}[n]}(M_1,\ldots,$ $M_n,\mu,N)$ *to denote the maximum advantage over any adversary with data complexity* M_h *to the* h-*th construction oracle* $(E_{K_h}^f$ *or* $\pi_h)$, *time complexity* N, *and total maximum multiplicity* μ.

Intuitively, permutation f results in a kdPRP secure block cipher if (i) it renders sufficiently secure evaluations of KD and (ii) $E_{\hat{L}_1}^f, \ldots, E_{\hat{L}_n}^f$ are secure Even-Mansour block ciphers. Note that, indeed, Definition 4 generalizes Definition 3 in the same way the OKS_K^f of (7) generalizes over IKS_K^f of (5).

5.1   Single Target

Theorem 5. *For* $\mathrm{OKS}_K^f : \{0,1\}^* \times \mathbb{N} \to \{0,1\}^{\mathbb{N}}$ *with* $K \xleftarrow{\$} \{0,1\}^k$ *and permutation* $f \in \mathsf{Perm}(b)$:

$$\mathbf{Adv}_{\mathrm{OKS}}^{\mathrm{ind}[1]}(M,\mu,N) \leq \frac{M^2}{2^c} + \mathbf{Adv}_{E,\mathrm{KD}}^{\mathrm{kdprp}[1]}(M,\mu,N).$$

Proof. The proof follows the one of Theorem 1 with the difference that now we have $L = \mathrm{KD}^f(K)$, and therefore we bound $\Delta_{\mathcal{B}}(E_{\hat{L}}^f, f; \pi, f) \leq \mathbf{Adv}_{E,\mathrm{KD}}^{\mathrm{kdprp}[1]}(M,\mu,N)$. We note that the initial state $\bar{L}\|0^c$ (cf. (7)) has no influence on the proof, and we can assume it to be disclosed to the adversary. □

We now bound the kdPRP security of the Even-Mansour construction in the ideal permutation model.

Theorem 6. *For* $E_{\hat{L}}^f$ *with* $L = \mathrm{KD}^f(K)$ *for* $K \xleftarrow{\$} \{0,1\}^k$ *and ideal permutation* $f \xleftarrow{\$} \mathsf{Perm}(b)$ *we have*

$$\mathbf{Adv}_{E,\mathrm{KD}}^{\mathrm{kdprp}[1]}(M,\mu,N) \leq \frac{2\mu N}{2^c} + \lambda(N) + \frac{2\left(\frac{k}{r}\right)N}{2^b},$$

where $\lambda(N)$ *is a term bounded in Lemma 2.*

Proof. The proof follows the one of Theorem 2, where now the key generation function KD_K^f needs to be taken into account. Adversary $\mathcal{A}$ has access to $X = (E_{\hat{L}}^f, f)$ in the real world or $Y = (\pi, f)$ in the ideal world. To ease the analysis, we will disclose K at the end of the experiment, *as well as the evalua-tions to f corresponding to the evaluation of* KD^f_K. These evaluations are written as $\kappa = \{(k_j, l_j)\}^v_{j=1}$. In the ideal world, the key K will simply be a dummy key, and κ corresponds to the evaluation of KD^f_K for this dummy key. The transcripts are thus of the form $\tau = (K, \kappa, \tau_1, \tau_f)$. We denote by α the number of distinct elements in κ that are *not* in τ_f:

$$\alpha = |\kappa \backslash \tau_f|.$$

Definition of good and bad transcripts. We extend the definition of *bad* transcripts from Theorem 2 to additionally cover the case κ shows no surprises to $\mathcal{A}$. Formally, we define a transcript τ as *bad* if one of the following is satisfied:

$$(k_v, l_v) \in \tau_f, \tag{11}$$

$$\exists (s, t) \in \tau_1, (x, y) \in \tau_f \text{ such that } s \oplus x = 0^r || \hat{L} \vee t \oplus y = 0^r || \hat{L}. \tag{12}$$

In the real world, all tuples in a *good* transcript (κ, τ_1, τ_f) consistently define an input-output pair of f. Furthermore, all of the pairs defined by (τ_1, τ_f) are unique, but there may be duplicates without contradictions in (κ, τ_f). In fact, this set contains $|\tau_f| + \alpha$ unique tuples.

Bounding the probability of bad transcripts in the ideal world. In the ideal world, (κ, τ_1, τ_f) is a transcript generated independently of the dummy key $K \xleftarrow{\$} \{0, 1\}^c$. By basic probability theory,

$$\begin{aligned}
\Pr(D_Y \in \mathcal{T}_{\mathrm{bad}}) \leq\ & \Pr(D_Y \text{ satisfies } (11)) + \\
& \Pr(D_Y \text{ satisfies } (12) \mid D_Y \text{ does not satisfy } (11)) \\
=\ & \Pr(D_Y \text{ satisfies } (11) \wedge \alpha = 0) + \\
& \Pr(D_Y \text{ satisfies } (11) \wedge \alpha \neq 0) + \\
& \Pr(D_Y \text{ satisfies } (12) \mid D_Y \text{ does not satisfy } (11)).
\end{aligned}$$

We define $\lambda(N) = \Pr(D_Y \text{ satisfies } (11) \wedge \alpha = 0)$, a term which is bounded in Lemma 2. For the second probability, "D_Y satisfies (11) and $\alpha \neq 0$" implies the existence of a maximal index $j \in \{1, \ldots, v-1\}$ such that $(k_j, l_j) \notin \tau_f$ but $(k_{j+1}, l_{j+1}) \in \tau_f$. As the evaluation of f corresponding to (k_j, l_j) is randomly drawn from a set of size at least $2^b - N - \alpha$, the next evaluation $k_{j+1} = l_j \oplus (K_{j+1} || 0^c)$ happens to be in τ_f with probability at most $\frac{N}{2^b - N - \alpha} \leq \frac{2N}{2^b}$, using that $N + \alpha \leq 2^{b-1}$ without loss of generality. Quantification over j gives bound $\frac{2vN}{2^b}$.

Finally, consider the probability that D_Y satisfies (12). Conditioned on the fact that (11) is not satisfied, L is randomly generated from a set of size at least $2^b - N - \alpha$. This particularly means that a given value for $\hat{L}_i$ has probability at most $1/(2^c - (N + \alpha)2^{-r})$. A straightforward generalization of the proof of Theorem 2 shows that the second probability is bound by $\frac{\mu N}{2^c - (N+\alpha)2^{-r}} \leq \frac{2\mu N}{2^c}$, again using that $N + \alpha \leq 2^{b-1}$.

Bounding the ratio $\Pr(D_X = \tau) / \Pr(D_Y = \tau)$ for good transcripts.
We have $|\Omega_X| = 2^k \cdot 2^b!$ and $|\Omega_Y| = 2^k \cdot (2^b!)^2$ as before. Also, $|\mathsf{comp}_X(\tau)| = (2^b - M - N - \alpha)!$ by construction. Similarly, we find

$$|\mathsf{comp}_Y(\tau)| = (2^b - M)!(2^b - N - \alpha)! \leq (2^b - M - N - \alpha)!2^{b!},$$

and the remainder of the proof follows Theorem 2. ☐

In the pre-proceedings version, $\lambda(N)$ was inadvertently bounded by $N/2^k$. A similar event was considered by Gaži et al. [18], and we can use their result. We restate it in Lemma 2.

Lemma 2 (Gaži et al. [18], Lemma 12). *If $k = r$, we have $\lambda(N) \leq \dfrac{N}{2^k}$. Otherwise,*

$$\lambda(N) \leq \min\left\{ \frac{N^2}{2^{c+1}} + \frac{N}{2^k}, \frac{1}{2^b} + \frac{N}{2^{\left(\frac{1}{2} - \frac{\log_2(3b)}{2r} - \frac{1}{r}\right)k}} \right\}.$$

In the ideal permutation model, the expressions in Theorems 5 and 6 simplify into

$$\mathbf{Adv}_{\mathrm{OKS}}^{\mathrm{ind}[1]}(M, \mu, N) \leq \frac{M^2 + 2\mu N}{2^c} + \lambda(N) + \frac{2\left(\frac{k}{r}\right)N}{2^b}.$$

5.2 Multiple Targets

Theorem 7. *For $\mathrm{OKS}_K^f : \{0,1\}^* \times \mathbb{N} \to \{0,1\}^{\mathbb{N}}$ with $K_1, \ldots, K_n \stackrel{\$}{\leftarrow} \{0,1\}^k$ and permutation $f \in \mathsf{Perm}(b)$:*

$$\mathbf{Adv}_{\mathrm{OKS}}^{\mathrm{ind}[n]}(M_1, \ldots, M_n, \mu, N) \leq \frac{\sum_h M_h^2}{2^c} + \mathbf{Adv}_{E,\mathrm{KD}}^{\mathrm{kdprp}[n]}(M_1, \ldots M_n, \mu, N).$$

Proof. The proof is a combination of the ones of Theorems 3 and 5, and therefore omitted. ☐

We now bound the joint kdPRP security of the Even-Mansour construction in the ideal permutation model.

Theorem 8. *For $E_{\hat{L}_h}^f$ with $L_h = \mathrm{KD}^f(K)$ for $K_h \stackrel{\$}{\leftarrow} \{0,1\}^k$ ($h = 1, \ldots, n$) and ideal permutation $f \stackrel{\$}{\leftarrow} \mathsf{Perm}(b)$ we have*

$$\mathbf{Adv}_{E,\mathrm{KD}}^{\mathrm{kdprp}[n]}(M_1, \ldots, M_n, \mu, N)$$
$$\leq \frac{2\mu N}{2^c} + \frac{4\sum_{h \neq h'} M_h M_{h'}}{2^c} + n\lambda(N) + \frac{\binom{n}{2}}{2^k} + \frac{2\left(\frac{k}{r}\right)\left(nN + \binom{n}{2}\right)}{2^b},$$

where $\lambda(N)$ is a term bounded in Lemma 2.

Proof. The proof combines the ones of Theorems 4 and 6, with the difference that multiple derivated keys are involved. Adversary $\mathcal{A}$ has access to $X = (E^f_{\hat{L}_1}, \ldots, E^f_{\hat{L}_n}, f)$ in the real world or $Y = (\pi_1, \ldots, \pi_n, f)$ in the ideal world. As before, we will disclose the keys $K_1, \ldots K_n$ at the end of the experiment, *as well as the evaluations to f corresponding to the evaluations of* $\mathrm{KD}^f_{K_1}, \ldots, \mathrm{KD}^f_{K_n}$. These evaluations are written as $\kappa_h = \{(k_j^{(h)}, l_j^{(h)})\}_{j=1}^v$. The transcripts are thus of the form $\tau = (K_1, \ldots, K_n, \kappa_1, \ldots, \kappa_n, \tau_1, \ldots, \tau_n, \tau_f)$. We denote by α the number of distinct elements in $\cup_h \kappa_h$ that are *not* in τ_f:

$$\alpha = \left| \cup_h \kappa_h \backslash \tau_f \right|.$$

Definition of good and bad transcripts. We extend the definition of *bad* transcripts from Theorem 6 to multiple keys. Formally, we define a transcript τ as *bad* if one of the following is satisfied:

$$\exists h \text{ such that } (k_v^{(h)}, l_v^{(h)}) \in \tau_f, \tag{13}$$

$$\exists h \neq h' \text{ such that } (k_v^{(h)}, l_v^{(h)}) = (k_v^{(h')}, l_v^{(h')}), \tag{14}$$

$$\exists h, (s,t) \in \tau_h, (x,y) \in \tau_f \text{ such that } s \oplus x = 0^r || \hat{L}_h \vee t \oplus y = 0^r || \hat{L}_h, \tag{15}$$

$$\exists h \neq h', (s,t) \in \tau_h, (s',t') \in \tau_{h'} \text{ such that}$$
$$s \oplus s' = 0^r || (\hat{L}_h \oplus \hat{L}_{h'}) \vee t \oplus t' = 0^r || (\hat{L}_h \oplus \hat{L}_{h'}). \tag{16}$$

The only condition different from the ones in Theorems 4 and 6 is (14), which assures that there are no two distinct evaluations of KD that produce the same $\hat{L}$. As before, all query pairs defined by $(\tau_1, \ldots, \tau_n, \tau_f)$ are unique, and $(\kappa_1, \ldots, \kappa_n, \tau_f)$. contains $|\tau_f| + \alpha$ unique query tuples.

Bounding the probability of bad transcripts in the ideal world. In the ideal world, $(\tau_1, \ldots, \tau_n, \tau_f)$ is a transcript generated independently of the dummy keys $K_1, \ldots, K_n \xleftarrow{\$} \{0,1\}^c$. By basic probability theory,

$$\Pr(D_Y \in \mathcal{T}_{\mathrm{bad}}) \leq \Pr(D_Y \text{ satisfies (13)}) +$$
$$\Pr(D_Y \text{ satisfies (15)} \mid D_Y \text{ does not satisfy (13)}) +$$
$$\Pr(D_Y \text{ satisfies (14)}) +$$
$$\Pr(D_Y \text{ satisfies (16)} \mid D_Y \text{ does not satisfy (14)}).$$

Before reasoning generalized to n targets shows that the first two probabilities are bounded by $n\left(\lambda(N) + \frac{2vN}{2^b}\right)$ and $\frac{2\mu N}{2^c}$, respectively. Using that the keys K_h are all randomly drawn from a set of size at least 2^k, the same reasoning directly shows that the third probability is bounded by $\frac{\binom{n}{2}}{2^k} + \frac{2v\binom{n}{2}}{2^b}$. Finally, the fourth probability, that D_Y satisfies (16), can be analyzed slightly differently from the proof of Theorem 4. More formally, as (14) is not satisfied, $\hat{L}_h \oplus \hat{L}_{h'}$ has probability at most $1/(2^c - (N+\alpha)2^{-r})$ for all $h \neq h'$. This leads to a probability upper bound $\frac{4\sum_{h \neq h'} M_h M_{h'}}{2^c}$.

Bounding the ratio $\Pr(D_X = \tau)/\Pr(D_Y = \tau)$ for good transcripts.
The analysis is a direct combination of the proofs of Theorems 4 and 6.   □

In the ideal permutation model, the expressions in Theorems 7 and 8 simplify into

$$\mathbf{Adv}_{\mathrm{OKS}}^{\mathrm{ind}[n]}(M_1, \ldots, M_n, \mu, N) \leq \frac{2M^2 + 2\mu N}{2^c} + n\lambda(N) + \frac{\binom{n}{2}}{2^k} + \frac{2\left(\frac{k}{r}\right)\left(nN + \binom{n}{2}\right)}{2^b}.$$

6   Discussion and Conclusions

Our theorems have implications on *all* keyed-sponge based modes as they impose upper bounds to the success probability for both single-target and multi-target attacks, generic in f. In general, a designer of a cryptographic system has a certain security level in mind, where a security level of s bits implies that it should resist against adversaries with resources for performing an amount of computation equivalent to 2^s executions of f. This security level s determines a lower bound for the choice of the sponge capacity c. The indifferentiability bound of Bertoni et al. [6] gives a bound $\frac{(M+N)^2}{2^{c+1}}$ resulting in the requirement $c \geq 2s - 1$ bits. For attack complexities that are relevant in practice, our success probability bounds are dominated by $\frac{\mu N}{2^c}$, combining the time complexity and the multiplicity. This results in the requirement $c \geq s + \log_2(\mu)$ bits. The designer can use this in its advantage by increasing the rate for higher speed or to take a permutation with smaller width for smaller footprint.

The main advantage of having a dependence on μ in the bound is that it makes its application flexible. The proof in this paper remains generic and independent of any use case scenario by considering an adversary who can perform all kinds of queries. Yet, the way a keyed sponge function is used in a concrete protocol can restrict what the attacker can actually do, and the bound follows depending on how these restrictions affect the multiplicity.

In general, μ depends on the mode of use and on the ability of the adversary, and a designer that cares about efficiency has the challenge to reliably estimate it. In real-world applications, the amount of data that will be available to an adversary can easily be upper bound due to physical, protocol-level or other restrictions, imposing an upper bound to M. As per definition $\mu \leq 2M$ the value of c can be taken $c \geq s + \log_2(M) + 1$.

The bound $\mu \leq 2M$ is actually very pessimistic and virtually never reached. The multiplicity is the sum of two components: the forward multiplicity μ_{fw} and the backward multiplicity μ_{bw}. The latter is determined by the responses of the keyed sponge and even an active attacker has little grip on it. For small rates, it is typically $M2^{-r}$ multiplied by a small constant.

The forward multiplicity, however, can be manipulated in some settings. An example of such a use case is a very liberal mode of use on top of the duplex construction [8]. At each duplexing call, the adversary can choose the input for the next duplexing call to force the outer part to some fixed value and let μ_{fw} approach M. The dominating security term then becomes $\frac{MN}{2^c}$, reducing the requirement to $c \geq s + \log_2(M)$. However, most modes and attack circumstances do not allow the adversary to increase the forward multiplicity μ_{fw} beyond a small multiple of $M2^{-r}$. This is in general the case if the adversary cannot *choose* the outer values. For instance, for sponge based stream ciphers which output a keystream on input of a nonce: if the total number of output blocks is much smaller than $2^{r/2}$, we have $\mu = 2$ with overwhelming probability, reducing the requirement to $c \geq s + 1$. A similar effect occurs in the case of nonce-respecting authenticated encryption scenarios.

Knowing the mode of use and the relevant adversary model, one can often demonstrate an upper bound to the multiplicity. If no sharp bounds can be demonstrated, it may be possible to prove that the multiplicity is only higher than some value μ_{limit} with a very low probability. This probability should then be included in the bound as an additional term.

Acknowledgments. This work was supported in part by the Research Council KU Leuven: GOA TENSE (GOA/11/007). Elena Andreeva and Bart Mennink are Postdoctoral Fellows of the Research Foundation – Flanders (FWO). We thank Peter Gaži, Krzysztof Pietrzak, and Stefano Tessaro for pointing out a flaw in an earlier version of the proof.

References

1. Alizadeh, J., Aref, M., Bagheri, N.: Artemia v1, submission to CAESAR competition (2014)
2. Andreeva, E., Bilgin, B., Bogdanov, A., Luykx, A., Mendel, F., Mennink, B., Mouha, N., Wang, Q., Yasuda, K.: PRIMATEs v1, submission to CAESAR competition (2014)
3. Aumasson, J., Jovanovic, P., Neves, S.: NORX v1, submission to CAESAR competition (2014)
4. Bellare, M., Rogaway, P.: Random oracles are practical: A paradigm for designing efficient protocols. In: Denning, D.E., Pyle, R., Ganesan, R., Sandhu, R.S., Ashby, V. (eds.) ACM CCS 1993, pp. 62–73. ACM (1993)
5. Bertoni, G., Daemen, J., Peeters, M., Van Assche, G.: Sponge functions. In: Ecrypt Hash Workshop 2007, May 2007
6. Bertoni, G., Daemen, J., Peeters, M., Van Assche, G.: On the indifferentiability of the sponge construction. In: Smart, N.P. (ed.) EUROCRYPT 2008. LNCS, vol. 4965, pp. 181–197. Springer, Heidelberg (2008)
7. Bertoni, G., Daemen, J., Peeters, M., Van Assche, G.: Sponge-based pseudorandom number generators. In: Mangard, S., Standaert, F.-X. (eds.) CHES 2010. LNCS, vol. 6225, pp. 33–47. Springer, Heidelberg (2010)
8. Bertoni, G., Daemen, J., Peeters, M., Van Assche, G.: Duplexing the sponge: single-pass authenticated encryption and other applications. In: Miri, A., Vaudenay, S. (eds.) SAC 2011. LNCS, vol. 7118, pp. 320–337. Springer, Heidelberg (2012)
9. Bertoni, G., Daemen, J., Peeters, M., Van Assche, G.: On the security of the keyed sponge construction. In: Symmetric Key Encryption Workshop, February 2011
10. Bertoni, G., Daemen, J., Peeters, M., Van Assche, G., Van Keer, R.: Ketje v1, submission to CAESAR competition (2014)
11. Bertoni, G., Daemen, J., Peeters, M., Van Assche, G., Van Keer, R.: Keyak v1, submission to CAESAR competition (2014)

12. CAESAR: Competition for Authenticated Encryption: Security, Applicability, and Robustness, November 2014. http://competitions.cr.yp.to/caesar.html
13. Chang, D., Dworkin, M., Hong, S., Kelsey, J., Nandi, M.: A keyed sponge construction with pseudorandomness in the standard model. In: NIST SHA-3 Workshop, March 2012
14. Chen, S., Steinberger, J.: Tight security bounds for key-alternating ciphers. In: Nguyen, P.Q., Oswald, E. (eds.) EUROCRYPT 2014. LNCS, vol. 8441, pp. 327–350. Springer, Heidelberg (2014)
15. Dobraunig, C., Eichlseder, M., Mendel, F., Schläffer, M.: Ascon v1, submission to CAESAR competition (2014)
16. Even, S., Mansour, Y.: A construction of a cipher from a single pseudorandom permutation. In: Matsumoto, T., Imai, H., Rivest, R.L. (eds.) ASIACRYPT 1991. LNCS, vol. 739, pp. 210–224. Springer, Heidelberg (1993)
17. Even, S., Mansour, Y.: A construction of a cipher from a single pseudorandom permutation. J. Cryptol. 10(3), 151–162 (1997)
18. Gaži, P., Pietrzak, K., Tessaro, S.: Tight bounds for keyed sponges and truncated CBC. In: Cryptology ePrint Archive, Report 2015/053, 22 January 2015
19. Gligoroski, D., Mihajloska, H., Samardjiska, S., Jacobsen, H., El-Hadedy, M., Jensen, R.: π-Cipher v1, submission to CAESAR competition (2014)
20. Jovanovic, P., Luykx, A., Mennink, B.: Beyond $2^{c/2}$ security in sponge-based authenticated encryption modes. In: Sarkar, P., Iwata, T. (eds.) ASIACRYPT 2014. LNCS, vol. 8873, pp. 85–104. Springer, Heidelberg (2014)
21. Kavun, E., Lauridsen, M., Leander, G., Rechberger, C., Schwabe, P., Yalçın, T.: Prøst v1, submission to CAESAR competition (2014)
22. Maurer, U.M., Renner, R.S., Holenstein, C.: Indifferentiability, impossibility results on reductions, and applications to the random oracle methodology. In: Naor, M. (ed.) TCC 2004. LNCS, vol. 2951, pp. 21–39. Springer, Heidelberg (2004)
23. Morawiecki, P., Gaj, K., Homsirikamol, E., Matusiewicz, K., Pieprzyk, J., Rogawski, M., Srebrny, M., Wójcik, M.: ICEPOLE v1, submission to CAESAR competition (2014)
24. Patarin, J.: The "Coefficients H" technique. In: Avanzi, R.M., Keliher, L., Sica, F. (eds.) SAC 2008. LNCS, vol. 5381, pp. 328–345. Springer, Heidelberg (2009)
25. Perlner, R.: SHA3-based MACs. In: NIST SHA-3 Workshop, August 2014
26. Ristenpart, T., Shacham, H., Shrimpton, T.: Careful with composition: limitations of the indifferentiability framework. In: Paterson, K.G. (ed.) EUROCRYPT 2011. LNCS, vol. 6632, pp. 487–506. Springer, Heidelberg (2011)
27. Rivest, R.L., Schuldt, J.C.N.: Spritz - a spongy RC4-like stream cipher and hash function, October 2014
28. Saarinen, M.: STRIBOB r1, submission to CAESAR competition (2014)
29. Turan, M.S.: Special publication on authenticated encryption. In: NIST SHA-3 Workshop, August 2014

GCM Security Bounds Reconsidered

Yuichi Niwa[1], Keisuke Ohashi[1], Kazuhiko Minematsu[2], and Tetsu Iwata[1](✉)

[1] Nagoya University, Nagoya, Japan
{y_niwa,k_oohasi}@echo.nuee.nagoya-u.ac.jp, iwata@cse.nagoya-u.ac.jp
[2] NEC Corporation, Tokyo, Japan
k-minematsu@ah.jp.nec.com

Abstract. A constant of 2^{22} appears in the security bounds of the Galois/Counter Mode of Operation, GCM. In this paper, we first develop an algorithm to generate nonces that have a high counter-collision probability. We show concrete examples of nonces with the counter-collision probability of about $2^{20.75}/2^{128}$. This shows that the constant in the security bounds, 2^{22}, cannot be made smaller than $2^{19.74}$ if the proof relies on "the sum bound." We next show that it is possible to avoid using the sum bound, leading to improved security bounds of GCM. One of our improvements shows that the constant of 2^{22} can be reduced to 32.

Keywords: GCM · Provable security · Counter-collision · The sum bound

1 Introduction

The Galois/Counter Mode of Operation, GCM, is a widely deployed authenticated encryption scheme. It was designed by McGrew and Viega [18,19] in 2004, and has been adopted by NIST as the recommended blockcipher mode of operation in 2007 [7]. A large number of standards include GCM, e.g., it is included in TLS [29], ISO/IEC [11], NSA Suite B [22], and IEEE 802.1 [10]. A cryptographic competition on authenticated encryption schemes, called CAESAR, has been launched in 2013 [6], and it defines GCM as the benchmark algorithm of the competition. There are a large number of results studying the security of GCM. Ferguson showed a forgery attack against the use of short tags [8]. Joux showed a partial key recovery attack under the nonce-reuse setting [14]. Weak keys of GHASH, a polynomial hash function employed in GCM, was studied by Handschuh and Preneel [9], followed by Saarinen [28], Procter and Cid [24], and Bogdanov [5]. See also [1]. Other results related to GCM include [2,30,31], and Rogaway [26] presented a comprehensive survey on various aspects of GCM.

For the provable security aspect of GCM, the original proposal by McGrew and Viega [18,19] included proofs of the security. Later, Iwata, Ohashi, and Minematsu [12] pointed out a flaw in the proofs of [18,19] with counter examples that invalidate them. They also presented corrected proofs, but the security bounds are larger than the original ones, roughly by a factor of 2^{22}.

© International Association for Cryptologic Research 2015
G. Leander (Ed.): FSE 2015, LNCS 9054, pp. 385–407, 2015.
DOI: 10.1007/978-3-662-48116-5_19

The counter examples invalidate the proofs in [18,19], but they do not exclude the possibility that the original security bounds of [18,19] can still be proved, and in [12], an open question about the possibility of improving the security bounds of [12] was posed, which is the main question we consider in this paper. GCM relies its security on the use of a nonce, and the nonce determines the initial counter value. A collision on counter values, or a counter-collision, leads to an attack on GCM, and the counter-collision probability needs to be small. The crux of [12] is the development of a method to derive an upper bound on the counter-collision probability. [12] showed that the upper bound is obtained by solving a combinatorial problem involving arithmetic additions and xor's, and security bounds are derived by applying the sum bound to the counter-collision probability.

In this paper, we first develop an algorithm to generate nonces that have a high counter-collision probability. The problem is reduced to determining an equation that has as many solutions as possible, and the equation involves an arithmetic addition, finite field multiplications, and xor's. We show that it can be converted into a problem of solving a system of linear equations over GF(2), with a selection process of several constants in a greedy method. As a result, we obtain concrete examples of nonces that have a counter-collision probability of about $2^{20.75}/2^{128} = 2^{-107.25}$, and the results were verified by a program. With the same setting, the upper bound of [12] on the counter-collision probability is about $2^{22.75}/2^{128} = 2^{-105.25}$. This implies that, as long as we follow the proof strategy, in particular the use of the sum bound, the security bounds of [12] are tight within a factor of about 4.

A natural question is then whether it is possible to avoid using the sum bound in the proofs. We next answer this question positively, and we show that the avoidance indeed yields strong security bounds of GCM. We present two types of improvements. The first improvement reduces the constant, 2^{22}, appears in the security bounds in [12], to 32. The new security bounds improve the security bounds in [12] by a factor of 2^{17}, and they show that the security of GCM is actually close to what was originally claimed in [18,19]. Another improvement gives security bounds that are better than the first ones for long data. Specifically, if the average plaintext length to be authenticated and encrypted is longer than about 2 Gbytes, then the second improvement gives a stronger guarantee of security.

We note that the focus of this paper is the general case where a nonce of variable-length is used, while it is known that GCM has strong security bounds if the nonce length is fixed to 96 bits [12].

2   Preliminaries

We write $\{0,1\}^*$ for the set of all finite bit strings, and for an integer $\ell \geq 0$, we write $\{0,1\}^\ell$ for the set of all ℓ-bit strings. For $X \in \{0,1\}^*$, $|X|$ is its length in bits, and $|X|_\ell = \lceil |X|/\ell \rceil$ is its length in ℓ-bit blocks. We write ε for the empty string. For $X, Y \in \{0,1\}^*$, their concatenation is written as $X \parallel Y$,

(X, Y), or XY. The bit string of ℓ zeros is written as $0^\ell \in \{0,1\}^\ell$, and ℓ ones is written as $1^\ell \in \{0,1\}^\ell$. The prefix 0x is used for the hexadecimal notation. For example, 0x28 is 00101000 $\in \{0,1\}^8$. For $X \in \{0,1\}^*$ and an integer ℓ such that $|X| \geq \ell$, $\mathsf{msb}_\ell(X)$ denotes the most significant (the leftmost) ℓ bits of X, and $\mathsf{lsb}_\ell(X)$ denotes the least significant (the rightmost) ℓ bits of X. For $X \in \{0,1\}^*$ such that $|X| = j\ell$ for some integer $j \geq 1$, its partition into ℓ-bit blocks is written as $(X[1], \ldots, X[j]) \xleftarrow{\ell} X$, where $X[1], \ldots, X[j] \in \{0,1\}^\ell$ are unique bit strings that satisfy $X[1] \| \ldots \| X[x] = X$. For integers a and ℓ satisfying $0 \leq a \leq 2^\ell - 1$, we write $\mathsf{str}_\ell(a)$ for the ℓ-bit binary representation of a, i.e., if $a = \mathsf{a}_{\ell-1}2^{\ell-1} + \cdots + \mathsf{a}_1 2 + \mathsf{a}_0$ for $\mathsf{a}_{\ell-1}, \ldots, \mathsf{a}_1, \mathsf{a}_0 \in \{0,1\}$, then $\mathsf{str}_\ell(a) = \mathsf{a}_{\ell-1} \ldots \mathsf{a}_1 \mathsf{a}_0 \in \{0,1\}^\ell$. For $X = \mathsf{x}_{\ell-1} \ldots \mathsf{x}_1 \mathsf{x}_0 \in \{0,1\}^\ell$, let $\mathsf{int}(X)$ be the integer $\mathsf{x}_{\ell-1}2^{\ell-1} + \cdots + \mathsf{x}_1 2 + \mathsf{x}_0$. For a finite set $\mathcal{X}$, we write $\#\mathcal{X}$ for its cardinality, and $X \xleftarrow{\$} \mathcal{X}$ for a procedure of assigning X an element sampled uniformly at random from $\mathcal{X}$.

Throughout this paper, we fix a blockcipher $E : \mathcal{K} \times \{0,1\}^n \to \{0,1\}^n$, where n is its block length in bits, which is fixed to $n = 128$, and $\mathcal{K}$ is a non-empty set of keys. The permutation specified by $K \in \mathcal{K}$ is written as E_K, and $C = E_K(M)$ denotes the ciphertext of a plaintext $M \in \{0,1\}^n$ under the key $K \in \mathcal{K}$. The set of n-bit strings, $\{0,1\}^n$, is also regarded as the finite field with 2^n elements which is written as $\mathrm{GF}(2^n)$. An n-bit string $\mathsf{a}_{n-1} \ldots \mathsf{a}_1 \mathsf{a}_0 \in \{0,1\}^n$ corresponds to a formal polynomial $a(x) = \mathsf{a}_{n-1} + \mathsf{a}_{n-2}x + \cdots + \mathsf{a}_1 x^{n-2} + \mathsf{a}_0 x^{n-1} \in \mathrm{GF}(2)[x]$. The irreducible polynomial used in GCM is $p(x) = 1 + x + x^2 + x^7 + x^{128}$, which is assumed to be the underlying polynomial throughout this paper.

3 Specification of GCM

We follow the description in [12], which follows the specification in [18,19] with minor notational changes. GCM takes two parameters: a blockcipher $E : \mathcal{K} \times \{0,1\}^n \to \{0,1\}^n$ and a tag length τ, where $64 \leq \tau \leq n$. If we use E and τ as parameters, then we write the corresponding GCM as $\mathrm{GCM}[E, \tau]$, and we write GCM-$\mathcal{E}$ for its encryption algorithm and GCM-$\mathcal{D}$ for its decryption algorithm. These algorithms are defined in Fig. 1. In GCM-$\mathcal{E}$ and GCM-$\mathcal{D}$, we use two subroutines defined in Fig. 2. The first one is the counter mode encryption, denoted by CTR, and the other one is the polynomial hash function over $\mathrm{GF}(2^n)$, denoted by GHASH. See Fig. 3 for the overall structure of GCM-$\mathcal{E}$, and Fig. 4 for the subroutines used therein.

The encryption algorithm, GCM-$\mathcal{E}$, takes a key $K \in \mathcal{K}$, a nonce $N \in \{0,1\}^*$, associated data $A \in \{0,1\}^*$, and a plaintext $M \in \{0,1\}^*$ as input, and returns a pair of a ciphertext $C \in \{0,1\}^*$ and a tag $T \in \{0,1\}^\tau$. We require $1 \leq |N| \leq 2^{n/2} - 1$, $0 \leq |A| \leq 2^{n/2} - 1$, and $0 \leq |M| \leq n(2^{32} - 2)$, and it holds that $|C| = |M|$. We write $(C, T) \leftarrow \mathrm{GCM}\text{-}\mathcal{E}_K^{N,A}(M)$. The decryption algorithm, GCM-$\mathcal{D}$, takes a key $K \in \mathcal{K}$, a nonce $N \in \{0,1\}^*$, associated data $A \in \{0,1\}^*$, a ciphertext $C \in \{0,1\}^*$, and a tag $T \in \{0,1\}^\tau$ as input, and returns either a plaintext $M \in \{0,1\}^*$ or the distinguished invalid symbol denoted by $\perp$. We write $M \leftarrow \mathrm{GCM}\text{-}\mathcal{D}_K^{N,A}(C, T)$ or $\perp \leftarrow \mathrm{GCM}\text{-}\mathcal{D}_K^{N,A}(C, T)$.

Algorithm GCM-$\mathcal{E}_K^{N,A}(M)$	Algorithm GCM-$\mathcal{D}_K^{N,A}(C,T)$
1. $L \leftarrow E_K(0^n)$	1. $L \leftarrow E_K(0^n)$
2. if $|N| = 96$ then $I[0] \leftarrow N \,\|\, 0^{31}1$	2. if $|N| = 96$ then $I[0] \leftarrow N \,\|\, 0^{31}1$
3. else $I[0] \leftarrow \mathsf{GHASH}_L(\varepsilon, N)$	3. else $I[0] \leftarrow \mathsf{GHASH}_L(\varepsilon, N)$
4. $m \leftarrow |M|_n$	4. $\widetilde{T}^* \leftarrow E_K(I[0]) \oplus \mathsf{GHASH}_L(A,C)$
5. $S \leftarrow \mathsf{CTR}_K(I[0], m)$	5. $T^* \leftarrow \mathsf{msb}_\tau(\widetilde{T}^*)$
6. $C \leftarrow M \oplus \mathsf{msb}_{|M|}(S)$	6. if $T \neq T^*$ then return $\perp$
7. $\widetilde{T} \leftarrow E_K(I[0]) \oplus \mathsf{GHASH}_L(A,C)$	7. $m \leftarrow |C|_n$
8. $T \leftarrow \mathsf{msb}_\tau(\widetilde{T})$	8. $S \leftarrow \mathsf{CTR}_K(I[0], m)$
9. return (C,T)	9. $M \leftarrow C \oplus \mathsf{msb}_{|C|}(S)$
	10. return M

Fig. 1. Definitions of GCM-$\mathcal{E}_K^{N,A}(M)$ and GCM-$\mathcal{D}_K^{N,A}(C,T)$

Algorithm $\mathsf{CTR}_K(I[0], m)$	Algorithm $\mathsf{GHASH}_L(A,C)$
1. for $j \leftarrow 1$ to m do	1. $a \leftarrow n|A|_n - |A|$
2. $\quad I[j] \leftarrow \mathsf{inc}(I[j-1])$	2. $c \leftarrow n|C|_n - |C|$
3. $\quad S[j] \leftarrow E_K(I[j])$	3. $X \leftarrow A \,\|\, 0^a \,\|\, C \,\|\, 0^c \,\|\, \mathsf{str}_{n/2}(|A|) \,\|\, \mathsf{str}_{n/2}(|C|)$
4. $S \leftarrow (S[1], S[2], \ldots, S[m])$	4. $(X[1], \ldots, X[x]) \xleftarrow{n} X$
5. return S	5. $Y \leftarrow 0^n$
	6. for $j \leftarrow 1$ to x do
	7. $\quad Y \leftarrow L \cdot (Y \oplus X[j])$
	8. return Y

Fig. 2. Definitions of $\mathsf{CTR}_K(I[0], m)$ and $\mathsf{GHASH}_L(A,C)$

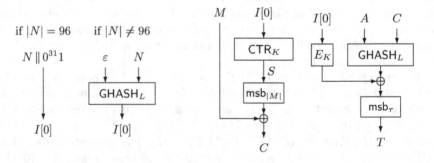

Fig. 3. Overall structure of $(C,T) \leftarrow$ GCM-$\mathcal{E}_K^{N,A}(M)$

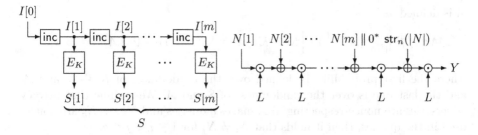

Fig. 4. Subroutines $S \leftarrow \mathsf{CTR}_K(I[0], m)$ and $Y \leftarrow \mathsf{GHASH}_L(A, C)$, where $(A, C) = (\varepsilon, N)$, $N = (N[1], \ldots, N[m])$, $|N[1]| = \cdots = |N[m-1]| = n$, and $1 \leq |N[m]| \leq n$

We use the increment function, denoted by inc, in the definition of CTR. It takes a bit string $X \in \{0,1\}^n$ as input, and we regard the least significant (the rightmost) 32 bits of X as a non-negative integer, and then increment the value by one modulo 2^{32}. That is, we have

$$\mathsf{inc}(X) = \mathsf{msb}_{n-32}(X) \| \mathsf{str}_{32}(\mathsf{int}(\mathsf{lsb}_{32}(X)) + 1 \bmod 2^{32}).$$

For $r \geq 0$, $\mathsf{inc}^r(X)$ means that we apply inc on X for r times, and $\mathsf{inc}^{-r}(X)$ means that we apply the inverse function of inc on X for r times. By convention, we let $\mathsf{inc}^0(X) = X$, and we thus have $I[j] = \mathsf{inc}^j(I[0])$ for $0 \leq j \leq m$ in the 2nd line in the definition of CTR. In the definition of GHASH, the multiplication in the 7th line is over $\mathrm{GF}(2^n)$. We note that when $|N| \neq 96$, we have $\mathsf{GHASH}_L(\varepsilon, N) = X[1] \cdot L^x \oplus \cdots \oplus X[x] \cdot L$, where $X = (X[1], \ldots, X[x]) = N \| 0^{n\lceil N \rceil_n - |N|} \| \mathsf{str}_n(|N|)$.

Let $\mathrm{Perm}(n)$ be the set of all permutations on $\{0,1\}^n$, and we call $P \xleftarrow{\$} \mathrm{Perm}(n)$ a random permutation. Let $\mathrm{GCM}[\mathrm{Perm}(n), \tau]$ be GCM where we use a random permutation P as the blockcipher E_K. We write $\mathrm{GCM}\text{-}\mathcal{E}_P$ for its encryption algorithm and $\mathrm{GCM}\text{-}\mathcal{D}_P$ for its decryption algorithm. Similarly, let $\mathrm{Rand}(n)$ be the set of all functions from $\{0,1\}^n$ to $\{0,1\}^n$, and we call $F \xleftarrow{\$} \mathrm{Rand}(n)$ a random function. Let $\mathrm{GCM}[\mathrm{Rand}(n), \tau]$ be GCM where we use F as E_K. We write $\mathrm{GCM}\text{-}\mathcal{E}_F$ for its encryption algorithm and $\mathrm{GCM}\text{-}\mathcal{D}_F$ for its decryption algorithm.

4   Security Definitions

An adversary is a probabilistic algorithm that has access to one or two oracles. We write $\mathcal{A}^{\mathcal{O}}$ for an adversary $\mathcal{A}$ that has access to an oracle $\mathcal{O}$, and $\mathcal{A}^{\mathcal{O}_1, \mathcal{O}_2}$ for $\mathcal{A}$ that has access to two oracles $\mathcal{O}_1$ and $\mathcal{O}_2$. Following [3,25], we consider privacy and authenticity of GCM.

A privacy adversary $\mathcal{A}$ has access to a GCM encryption oracle or a random-bits oracle. The GCM encryption oracle, which we write Enc_K, takes (N, A, M) as input and returns $(C, T) \leftarrow \mathrm{GCM}\text{-}\mathcal{E}_K^{N,A}(M)$. The random-bits oracle, \$, takes (N, A, M) as input and returns $(C, T) \xleftarrow{\$} \{0,1\}^{|M|+\tau}$. The privacy advantage of

$\mathcal{A}$ is defined as

$$\mathbf{Adv}^{\mathrm{priv}}_{\mathrm{GCM}[E,\tau]}(\mathcal{A}) \overset{\mathrm{def}}{=} \Pr\left[K \overset{\$}{\leftarrow} \mathcal{K} : \mathcal{A}^{\mathsf{Enc}_K(\cdot,\cdot,\cdot)} \Rightarrow 1\right] - \Pr\left[\mathcal{A}^{\$(\cdot,\cdot,\cdot)} \Rightarrow 1\right],$$

where the first probability is defined over the randomness of $K \overset{\$}{\leftarrow} \mathcal{K}$ and $\mathcal{A}$, and the last one is over the randomness of $\$$ and $\mathcal{A}$. We assume that privacy adversaries are nonce-respecting: if $\mathcal{A}$ makes q queries and $N_1 \ldots, N_q$ are nonces used in the queries, then it holds that $N_i \neq N_j$ for $1 \leq i < j \leq q$.

An authenticity adversary $\mathcal{A}$ has access to two oracles, GCM encryption and decryption oracles. The GCM encryption oracle, Enc_K, is described as above. The GCM decryption oracle, Dec_K, takes (N, A, C, T) as input and returns $M \leftarrow \mathrm{GCM}\text{-}\mathcal{D}_K^{N,A}(C,T)$ or $\perp \leftarrow \mathrm{GCM}\text{-}\mathcal{D}_K^{N,A}(C,T)$. The authenticity advantage of $\mathcal{A}$ is defined as

$$\mathbf{Adv}^{\mathrm{auth}}_{\mathrm{GCM}[E,\tau]}(\mathcal{A}) \overset{\mathrm{def}}{=} \Pr\left[K \overset{\$}{\leftarrow} \mathcal{K} : \mathcal{A}^{\mathsf{Enc}_K(\cdot,\cdot,\cdot),\mathsf{Dec}_K(\cdot,\cdot,\cdot,\cdot)} \text{ forges}\right],$$

where the probability is defined over the randomness of $K \overset{\$}{\leftarrow} \mathcal{K}$ and $\mathcal{A}$. If $\mathcal{A}$ makes a query (N, A, M) to Enc_K and receives (C, T), then we assume that $\mathcal{A}$ does not subsequently make a query (N, A, C, T) to Dec_K. We also assume that $\mathcal{A}$ does not repeat a query to Dec_K. We define that $\mathcal{A}$ forges if at least one of the responses from Dec_K is not $\perp$. We assume that authenticity adversaries are nonce-respecting with respect to encryption queries. That is, assume that $\mathcal{A}$ makes q queries to Enc_K and q' queries to Dec_K, where $N_1, \ldots, N_q$ are the nonces used for Enc_K, and $N'_1, \ldots, N'_{q'}$ are the nonces for Dec_K. We assume that $N_i \neq N_j$ holds for $1 \leq i < j \leq q$, but $N_i = N'_j$ may hold for some $1 \leq i \leq q$ and $1 \leq j \leq q'$, and $N'_i = N'_j$ may also hold for some $1 \leq i < j \leq q'$.

5   GCM Security Bounds in [12] Need 881145

5.1   Review of Results in [12]

We first review results from [12]. Consider a privacy adversary $\mathcal{A}$, and suppose that $\mathcal{A}$ makes q queries $(N_1, A_1, M_1), \ldots, (N_q, A_q, M_q)$, where $|N_i|_n = n_i$ and $|M_i|_n = m_i$. Then the total plaintext length is $m_1 + \cdots + m_q$, and the maximum nonce length is $\max\{n_1, \ldots, n_q\}$. The following privacy result was proved.

Proposition 1 [12]. *Let* $\mathrm{Perm}(n)$ *and* τ *be the parameters of* GCM. *Then for any* $\mathcal{A}$ *that makes at most* q *queries, where the total plaintext length is at most* σ *blocks and the maximum nonce length is at most* ℓ_N *blocks,*

$$\mathbf{Adv}^{\mathrm{priv}}_{\mathrm{GCM}[\mathrm{Perm}(n),\tau]}(\mathcal{A}) \leq \frac{0.5(\sigma + q + 1)^2}{2^n} + \frac{2^{22} q(\sigma + q)(\ell_N + 1)}{2^n}. \qquad (1)$$

Suppose that an authenticity adversary $\mathcal{A}$ makes q queries $(N_1, A_1, M_1), \ldots, (N_q, A_q, M_q)$ to Enc_K and q' queries $(N'_1, A'_1, C'_1, T'_1), \ldots, (N'_{q'}, A'_{q'}, C'_{q'}, T'_{q'})$ to Dec_K, where $|N_i|_n = n_i$, $|A_i|_n = a_i$, $|M_i|_n = m_i$, $|N'_i|_n = n'_i$, $|A'_i|_n = a'_i$, and

$|C_i'|_n = m_i'$. Then the total plaintext length is $m_1 + \cdots + m_q$, the maximum nonce length is $\max\{n_1, \ldots, n_q, n_1', \ldots, n_{q'}'\}$, and the maximum input length is $\max\{a_1 + m_1, \ldots, a_q + m_q, a_1' + m_1', \ldots, a_{q'}' + m_{q'}'\}$. The following authenticity result was proved.

Proposition 2 [12]. *Let* $\mathrm{Perm}(n)$ *and* τ *be the parameters of* GCM. *Then for any* $\mathcal{A}$ *that makes at most* q *encryption queries and* q' *decryption queries, where the total plaintext length is at most* σ *blocks, the maximum nonce length is at most* ℓ_N *blocks, and the maximum input length is at most* ℓ_A *blocks,*

$$\mathbf{Adv}_{\mathrm{GCM}[\mathrm{Perm}(n),\tau]}^{\mathrm{auth}}(\mathcal{A}) \leq \frac{0.5(\sigma + q + q' + 1)^2}{2^n}$$

$$+ \frac{2^{22}(q + q')(\sigma + q + 1)(\ell_N + 1)}{2^n} + \frac{q'(\ell_A + 1)}{2^\tau}. \quad (2)$$

We see that a non-small constant, 2^{22}, appears in (1) and (2). In what follows, we recall how the constant was introduced by reviewing the proof of Proposition 1. We first replace a random permutation P with a random function F. We have

$$\mathbf{Adv}_{\mathrm{GCM}[\mathrm{Perm}(n),\tau]}^{\mathrm{priv}}(\mathcal{A}) \leq \mathbf{Adv}_{\mathrm{GCM}[\mathrm{Rand}(n),\tau]}^{\mathrm{priv}}(\mathcal{A}) + \frac{0.5(\sigma + q + 1)^2}{2^n}$$

from the PRP/PRF switching lemma [4].

Now assume that $\mathcal{A}$ makes q queries, and for $1 \leq i \leq q$, let (N_i, A_i, M_i) be the i-th query, where $|M_i|_n = m_i$. Let the initial counter value, $I_i[0]$, be $I_i[0] \leftarrow \mathrm{GHASH}_L(\varepsilon, N_i)$ if $|N_i| \neq 96$, and $I_i[0] \leftarrow N_i \| 0^{31}1$ otherwise. We also let the counter value, $I_i[j]$, be $I_i[j] \leftarrow \mathrm{inc}^j(I_i[0])$ for $1 \leq j \leq m_i$. With this notation, we have the following list of counter values.

$$I_1[0], I_1[1], \ldots, I_1[m_1]$$
$$I_2[0], I_2[1], \ldots, I_2[m_2]$$
$$\vdots \quad\quad\quad\quad\quad (3)$$
$$I_q[0], I_q[1], \ldots, I_q[m_q]$$

At this point, we are ready to define a bad event. We say that the bad event occurs if we have at least one of the following events:

Case (A). $I_i[j] = 0^n$ holds for some (i, j) such that $1 \leq i \leq q$ and $0 \leq j \leq m_i$.
Case (B). $I_i[j] = I_{i'}[j']$ holds for some (i, j, i', j') such that $1 \leq i' < i \leq q$, $0 \leq j' \leq m_{i'}$, and $0 \leq j \leq m_i$.

As analyzed in detail in [13, Appendix D], the absence of the bad event implies that, each time $\mathcal{A}$ makes a query (N_i, A_i, M_i), $\mathcal{A}$ obtains a uniform random string of $|M_i| + \tau$ bits, which in turn implies that the adaptivity of $\mathcal{A}$ does not help and we may fix the q queries $(N_1, A_1, M_1), \ldots, (N_q, A_q, M_q)$ of $\mathcal{A}$. We evaluate the probability of the bad event based on the randomness of L. For simplicity, we write $\Pr_L[\mathsf{E}]$ for $\Pr[L \xleftarrow{\$} \{0,1\}^n : \mathsf{E}]$ for an event E. We have

$$\mathbf{Adv}_{\mathrm{GCM}[\mathrm{Rand}(n),\tau]}^{\mathrm{priv}}(\mathcal{A}) \leq \Pr_L[\text{Case (A) holds}] + \Pr_L[\text{Case (B) holds}]. \quad (4)$$

The first probability is easy to evaluate and we have

$$\Pr_L[\text{Case (A) holds}] \leq \sum_{1 \leq i \leq q, 0 \leq j \leq m_i} \Pr_L[I_i[j] = 0^n] \leq \frac{(\sigma + q)(\ell_N + 1)}{2^n}, \qquad (5)$$

since $\text{inc}^j(I_i[0]) = 0^n$ is a non-trivial equation in L of degree at most $\ell_N + 1$ over $GF(2^n)$ if $|N_i| \neq 96$, and hence the probability is at most $(\ell_N + 1)/2^n$, or we never have the event if $|N_i| = 96$.

The second probability can also be evaluated as the first one by using "the sum bound," and we obtain

$$\Pr_L[\text{Case (B) holds}] \leq \sum_{1 \leq i' < i \leq q, 0 \leq j' \leq m_{i'}, 0 \leq j \leq m_i} \Pr_L[I_i[j] = I_{i'}[j']]. \qquad (6)$$

It remains to evaluate $\Pr_L[I_i[j] = I_{i'}[j']]$ for each (i, j, i', j'), and we have the following four cases to consider: $|N_i| = |N_{i'}| = 96$, $|N_i| \neq 96$ and $|N_{i'}| = 96$, $|N_i| = 96$ and $|N_{i'}| \neq 96$, and $|N_i|, |N_{i'}| \neq 96$.

The case $|N_i| = |N_{i'}| = 96$ is easy to analyze and we have $\Pr_L[I_i[j] = I_{i'}[j']] = 0$. If $|N_i| \neq 96$ and $|N_{i'}| = 96$, then we have $\Pr_L[I_i[j] = I_{i'}[j']] \leq (\ell_N + 1)/2^n$ since $\text{inc}^j(I_i[0]) = \text{inc}^{j'}(I_{i'}[0])$ is a non-trivial equation in L of degree at most $\ell_N + 1$ over $GF(2^n)$. The analysis for the case $|N_i| = 96$ and $|N_{i'}| \neq 96$ is the same as the previous case. The analysis of the last case, $|N_i|, |N_{i'}| \neq 96$, is not simple, and we review the notation used in [12].

For $0 \leq r \leq 2^{32} - 1$ and two distinct nonces N and N' which are not 96 bits, let the counter-collision, denoted by $\text{Coll}_L(r, N, N')$, be the event

$$\text{inc}^r(\text{GHASH}_L(\varepsilon, N)) = \text{GHASH}_L(\varepsilon, N'). \qquad (7)$$

We say $\Pr_L[\text{Coll}_L(r, N, N')]$ a counter-collision probability. Recall that $I_i[j] = I_{i'}[j']$ is equivalent to $\text{inc}^j(I_i[0]) = \text{inc}^{j'}(I_{i'}[0])$, where $I_i[0] \leftarrow \text{GHASH}_L(\varepsilon, N_i)$ and $I_{i'}[0] \leftarrow \text{GHASH}_L(\varepsilon, N_{i'})$, and this can be written as $\text{Coll}_L(r, N, N')$ with $(r, N, N') = (j - j', N_i, N_{i'})$ if $j - j' \geq 0$, and $(r, N, N') = (j' - j, N_{i'}, N_i)$ otherwise.

Now define $\mathbb{Y}_r \subseteq \{0, 1\}^{32}$, for $0 \leq r \leq 2^{32} - 1$, as

$$\mathbb{Y}_r \overset{\text{def}}{=} \{\text{str}_{32}(\text{int}(Y) + r \bmod 2^{32}) \oplus Y \mid Y \in \{0, 1\}^{32}\}, \qquad (8)$$

and write its cardinality as $\alpha_r \overset{\text{def}}{=} \#\mathbb{Y}_r$. We let $\alpha_{\max} \overset{\text{def}}{=} \max\{\alpha_r \mid 0 \leq r \leq 2^{32} - 1\}$. The following result was proved.

Proposition 3 [12]. *For any $0 \leq r \leq 2^{32} - 1$ and two distinct nonces N and N' which are not 96 bits, it holds that $\Pr_L[\text{Coll}_L(r, N, N')] \leq \alpha_r(\ell_N + 1)/2^n$, where $|N|_n, |N'|_n \leq \ell_N$.*

$\mathbb{Y}_r$ can be used to replace the arithmetic addition by r in $\text{inc}^r(X)$ with the xor of some constant. That is, we convert $\text{inc}^r(X)$ into $X \oplus (0^{96} \parallel Y)$ for some

$Y \in \{0,1\}^{32}$, and as argued in [12], $\mathbb{Y}_r$ exhaustively covers all the possible constants, and it must be the case that $Y \in \mathbb{Y}_r$. Note that the constant is of the form $(0^{96} \parallel Y)$ and the most significant 96 bits can be fixed to 0^{96}, as inc has no effect on these bits. For simplicity, for any $Y \in \{0,1\}^{32}$, let $[\![Y]\!] = (0^{96} \parallel Y)$.

In [12], a recursive formula to compute the value of α_r was presented, and the value of $\alpha_{\max}$ was shown to be $\alpha_{\max} = 3524578$, where the equality holds when $r = $ 0x2aaaaaab, 0xaaaaaaab, 0x55555555, and 0xd5555555. We have $3524578 \leq 2^{22}$, and this yields $\mathrm{Pr}_L\left[I_i[j] = I_{i'}[j']\right] \leq 2^{22}(\ell_N + 1)/2^n$ for the last case, which is the source reason why we have this constant in (1) and (2).

A question is if we really need the constant, or if we can make it smaller.

5.2   Case $r = $ 0x55555555

Our approach to the question is to derive the values of r, N, and N' where $\mathrm{Pr}_L[\mathsf{Coll}_L(r, N, N')]$ is large, or equivalently, the equation $\mathsf{Coll}_L(r, N, N')$ has as many solutions (in L) as possible. We now present our main result of this section.

Theorem 1. *There exist $0 \leq r \leq 2^{32} - 1$ and two distinct nonces N and N' such that $|N| = |N'| = 128$ and $\mathrm{Pr}_L[\mathsf{Coll}_L(r, N, N')] \geq 1762290/2^n$.*

Proof. Let $r = $ 0x55555555, and let N and N' be the following values.

$$\begin{cases} N = \text{0x8d44009c dc550100 00000000 00000000} \\ N' = \text{0x5b6dbdd9 f3b151d9 d1bc4145 ecb396ef} \end{cases} \tag{9}$$

Then $\mathsf{Coll}_L(r, N, N')$ is equivalent to

$$\mathsf{inc}^r(U \cdot L^2 \oplus V \cdot L) = U' \cdot L^2 \oplus V \cdot L, \tag{10}$$

where $U = N$, $U' = N'$, and $V = $ 0x00000000 00000000 00000000 00000080. Note that V is the hexadecimal form of $|N| = |N'| = 128$. Now $\mathbb{Y}_r$ consists of $\alpha_{\max}$ constants, and we can list all these constants by listing $\mathsf{str}_{32}(\mathsf{int}(Y) + r \bmod 2^{32}) \oplus Y$ for all $Y \in \{0,1\}^{32}$. Let $\mathbb{Y}_r = \{Y_1, \ldots, Y_{\alpha_{\max}}\}$ be the concrete representation of $\mathbb{Y}_r$. We can solve (in L) the equation $U \cdot L^2 \oplus V \cdot L \oplus [\![Y_\ell]\!] = U' \cdot L^2 \oplus V \cdot L$ for all $Y_\ell \in \mathbb{Y}_r$, which gives us $L = \left[(U \oplus U')^{-1} \cdot [\![Y_\ell]\!]\right]^{1/2}$, and see if this L satisfies (10). We find that 1762290 values of L satisfy (10), which was verified by using a program, and hence we have $\mathrm{Pr}_L[\mathsf{Coll}_L(r, N, N')] \geq 1762290/2^n$. $\square$

With the same value of $r = $ 0x55555555, the values of N and N' in the following list give the same probability.

$$\begin{cases} N = \text{0x215c004e 6e2a8080 00000000 00000000} \\ N' = \text{0xab48deec f9d8a8ec e8de20a2 f659cb77} \end{cases} \tag{11}$$

$$\begin{cases} N = \text{0x1bb000e9 9f71db00 00000000 00000000} \\ N' = \text{0xb0085245 fd3dc69e 9de41b1a 943d314f} \end{cases} \tag{12}$$

$$\begin{cases} N = \text{0x77500027 37154040 00000000 00000000} \\ N' = \text{0xd35a6f76 7cec5476 746f1051 7b2ce5bb} \end{cases} \tag{13}$$

Theorem 1 suggests that, for the particular value of $r = \text{0x55555555}$, there exist N and N' with $\Pr_L[\mathsf{Coll}_L(r, N, N')] \geq 1762290/2^n = 881145(\ell_N + 1)/2^n$, where $|N|_n = |N'|_n = \ell_N = 1$. Specifically, the result shows that the constant, $\alpha_{\max}$, in Proposition 3 for the case $r = \text{0x55555555}$ cannot be made smaller than 881145. Therefore, as long as we make use of the sum bound in (6) to derive the upper bound on $\Pr_L[\text{Case (B) holds}]$, the constants in (1) and (2) cannot be made smaller than 881145. Since $3524578 \leq 2^{21.75}$ and $881145 \geq 2^{19.74}$, we may conclude that (1) and (2) are tight up to a constant factor of about 4 if we use the sum bound. We next present how we have derived the values of N and N' in (9).

5.3 Deriving N and N'

Recall that our goal is to derive r, N, and N' where $\mathsf{Coll}_L(r, N, N')$ defined in (7) has as many solutions in L as possible. We decided to focus on $r = \text{0x55555555}$ since this is one of the four values of r that is potential to have the maximum number of solutions. We also decided to focus on the case $|N| = |N'| = 128$, since even with this restricted length of nonces, we still have about 2^{256} possible search space of N and N'. With the setting, (7) is equivalent to

$$\mathsf{inc}^r(U \cdot L^2 \oplus V \cdot L) = U' \cdot L^2 \oplus V \cdot L, \tag{14}$$

where $r = \text{0x55555555}$ and $V = \text{0x00000000 00000000 00000000 00000080}$ are now fixed, and $U = N$ and $U' = N'$ are the variables we are searching for.

Converting $\mathsf{inc}^r(X)$ *into* $X \oplus [\![Y_\ell]\!]$. As mentioned in the proof of Theorem 1, $\mathbb{Y}_r$ consists of $\alpha_{\max}$ constants, and let $\mathbb{Y}_r = \{Y_1, \dots, Y_{\alpha_{\max}}\}$ be the concrete representation of $\mathbb{Y}_r$. Now instead of directly considering (14), we consider the following simultaneous equation.

$$\begin{cases} \mathsf{inc}^r(U \cdot L^2 \oplus V \cdot L) = U \cdot L^2 \oplus V \cdot L \oplus [\![Y_\ell]\!] & (15) \\ (U \oplus U') \cdot L^2 = [\![Y_\ell]\!] & (16) \end{cases}$$

Equation (15) is the conversion of the arithmetic addition by r in the left hand side of (14) using some constant $Y_\ell \in \mathbb{Y}_r$, and then we obtain (16) by simplifying (14) after the conversion with $Y_\ell \in \mathbb{Y}_r$ used in (15), where the term $V \cdot L$ cancels out. Note that the conversion of (15) is always possible, and (14) holds if and only if (16) holds, and hence (14) is equivalent to (15) and (16) holding for some $Y_\ell \in \mathbb{Y}_r$.

Deriving Conditions on X for $\text{inc}^r(X) = X \oplus [\![Y_\ell]\!]$. Suppose that we fix some Y_ℓ from $\mathbb{Y}_r$, and convert $\text{inc}^r(X)$ into $X \oplus [\![Y_\ell]\!]$. Now we observe that the equality of $\text{inc}^r(X) = X \oplus [\![Y_\ell]\!]$ imposes restrictions on some bits of X. For instance, when $Y_\ell = \text{0x55555555}$, then X must be of the form

$$X = \underbrace{*\cdots**}_{96\text{ bits}}\underbrace{0*0*0*0*0*0*0*0*0*0*0*0*0*0*0*0}_{32\text{ bits}}$$

in binary, where $*$ can be 0 or 1, i.e., if $X = \mathsf{x}_{127}\ldots\mathsf{x}_0$ is the binary representation of X, it must be the case that $\mathsf{x}_{30} = 0 \wedge \mathsf{x}_{28} = 0 \wedge \cdots \wedge \mathsf{x}_0 = 0$. When $Y_\ell = \text{0xefffffff}$, then X must be of the form

$$X = \underbrace{*\cdots**}_{96\text{ bits}}\underbrace{00101010101010101010101010101010}_{32\text{ bits}}$$

in binary. Using $Y_\ell = \text{0x55555555}$ fixes 16 bits of X, and $Y_\ell = \text{0xefffffff}$ fixes 31 bits of X. The condition and the number of bits we have to fix depend on the value of Y_ℓ. We have to fix from 16 to 31 bits of X, and these are two extreme cases that have the minimum number and the maximum number of conditions. On average, around 20 bits are fixed. Let $\mathbb{C}(Y_\ell)$ be the set of conditions to replace $\text{inc}^r(X)$ to $X \oplus [\![Y_\ell]\!]$. We represent $\mathbb{C}(Y_\ell)$ as a column vector

$$\mathbb{C}(Y_\ell) = \begin{bmatrix} \mathsf{x}_{127} \\ \vdots \\ \mathsf{x}_0 \end{bmatrix},$$

where $\mathsf{x}_i \in \{*, 0, 1\}$. Let $\mathbb{I}(Y_\ell)$ be the set of indices with $\mathsf{x}_i \neq *$, i.e., $\mathbb{I}(Y_\ell) = \{i \mid \mathsf{x}_i \neq *\}$. We note that $127, \ldots, 32$ are not in $\mathbb{I}(Y_\ell)$ as $\mathsf{x}_{127}, \ldots, \mathsf{x}_{32}$ are all $*$.

Given Y_ℓ, there are several approaches to write down $\mathbb{C}(Y_\ell)$. For instance, a possible approach is to follow the framework in [21], or to use the tool [15] developed in [16,17]. We present in [23] an algorithm that directly gives us the conditions.

Decomposition into Bits. Let us continue focusing on Y_ℓ from $\mathbb{Y}_r$ that we have fixed. We can solve (16) with respect to L, and we obtain $L = \left[(U \oplus U')^{-1} \cdot [\![Y_\ell]\!]\right]^{1/2} = \left[(U \oplus U')^{-1} \cdot [\![Y_\ell]\!]\right]^{2^{127}}$. Now we consider the argument, $U \cdot L^2 \oplus V \cdot L$, of inc^r of (15). With this L, the argument becomes $U \cdot (U \oplus U')^{-1} \cdot [\![Y_\ell]\!] \oplus V \cdot \left[(U \oplus U')^{-1} \cdot [\![Y_\ell]\!]\right]^{2^{127}}$. At this point, instead of treating U and U' as variables, we let $W = (U \oplus U')^{-1}$ and regard U and W as variables. With this replacement, we have $L = \left[W \cdot [\![Y_\ell]\!]\right]^{2^{127}}$, and the argument becomes

$$U \cdot W \cdot [\![Y_\ell]\!] \oplus V \cdot W^{2^{127}} \cdot [\![Y_\ell]\!]^{2^{127}}. \tag{17}$$

It is well known that a multiplication by a constant and a squaring operation over $\text{GF}(2^n)$ are linear operations in $\text{GF}(2)$, e.g., see [8]. We make an observation that, if we decompose (17) into bits using $U = \mathsf{u}_{127}\ldots\mathsf{u}_0$ and $W = \mathsf{w}_{127}\ldots\mathsf{w}_0$

as variables, then each bit of the first term, $U \cdot W \cdot [\![Y_\ell]\!]$, can be represented by using $u_{127}w_{127}, \ldots, u_{127}w_0, \ldots, u_0w_{127}, \ldots, u_0w_0$, and the second term, $V \cdot W^{2^{127}} \cdot [\![Y_\ell]\!]^{2^{127}}$, can be represented by using $w_{127}, \ldots, w_0$. The first term consists of terms of the form u_iw_j, a total of $128 \times 128 = 16384$ variations, and we replace the term u_iw_j with a monomial s_{128i+j}. Let $z_{127} \ldots z_0$ be the decomposition of (17) into bits. Then we can represent z_i as a linear function of $s_{16383}, \ldots, s_0$ and $w_{127}, \ldots, w_0$. In other words, there is a linear function f_i that describes z_i as

$$z_i = f_i(s_{16383}, \ldots, s_0, w_{127}, \ldots, w_0).$$

Let us define a binary row vector row_i, which is associated to f_i, of length $16384+128$ that lists the coefficients of $s_{16383}, \ldots, s_0, w_{127}, \ldots, w_0$. We can collect them into a $128 \times (16384 + 128)$ binary matrix $\mathbb{M}$ to write

$$\begin{bmatrix} z_{127} \\ \vdots \\ z_0 \end{bmatrix} = \mathbb{M} \cdot \mathbb{S}, \text{ where } \mathbb{M} = \begin{bmatrix} \mathrm{row}_{127} \\ \vdots \\ \mathrm{row}_0 \end{bmatrix} \text{ and } \mathbb{S} \overset{\mathrm{def}}{=} \begin{bmatrix} s_{16383} \\ \vdots \\ s_0 \\ w_{127} \\ \vdots \\ w_0 \end{bmatrix}.$$

$\mathbb{S}$ is the column vector that consists of the variables we are searching for. We note that $\mathbb{M}$ depends on Y_ℓ, and we thus write $\mathbb{M}(Y_\ell)$ to describe the dependency.

Recall that $z_{127} \ldots z_0$ is the decomposition of (17) into bits. The equality of (15) holds if $\mathbb{C}(Y_\ell)$ is satisfied. In other words, we require

$$x_i = f_i(s_{16383}, \ldots, s_0, w_{127}, \ldots, w_0)$$

holds for all $i \in \mathbb{I}(Y_\ell)$.

Deriving U and W. Let us still focus on Y_ℓ from $\mathbb{Y}_r$. For $\mathbb{C}(Y_\ell) = \begin{bmatrix} x_{127} \cdots x_0 \end{bmatrix}^{\mathrm{tr}}$, where $x_i \in \{*, 0, 1\}$ and X^{tr} is the transposition of a row vector X, let $\widetilde{\mathbb{C}}(Y_\ell)$ be a column vector that is obtained from $\mathbb{C}(Y_\ell)$ by removing $*$. Suppose that $\widetilde{\mathbb{C}}(Y_\ell)$ consists of s elements, and let us represent it as $\widetilde{\mathbb{C}}(Y_\ell) = \begin{bmatrix} x_{i_1} \cdots x_{i_s} \end{bmatrix}^{\mathrm{tr}}$. Note that we have $\mathbb{I}(Y_\ell) = \{i_1, \ldots, i_s\}$. Let $\widetilde{\mathbb{M}}(Y_\ell) = \begin{bmatrix} \mathrm{row}_{i_1} \cdots \mathrm{row}_{i_s} \end{bmatrix}^{\mathrm{tr}}$ be a matrix that consists of the relevant s row vectors $\mathrm{row}_{i_1}, \ldots, \mathrm{row}_{i_s}$ of $\mathbb{M}(Y_\ell) = \begin{bmatrix} \mathrm{row}_{127} \cdots \mathrm{row}_0 \end{bmatrix}^{\mathrm{tr}}$. Now we can apply the Gaussian elimination to solve a system of linear equations

$$\widetilde{\mathbb{C}}(Y_\ell) = \widetilde{\mathbb{M}}(Y_\ell) \cdot \mathbb{S} \tag{18}$$

to derive $s_{16383}, \ldots, s_0, w_{127}, \ldots, w_0$, and if we can further derive $u_{127}, \ldots, u_0$ that are consistent with them, then this gives us U and W that have $L = \begin{bmatrix} W \cdot [\![Y_\ell]\!] \end{bmatrix}^{2^{127}}$ as a solution to (15) and (16) .

We next extend this to deal with multiple constants from $\mathbb{Y}_r$. Suppose that we choose j constants $Y_{\ell_1}, \ldots, Y_{\ell_j}$ from $\mathbb{Y}_r$. We combine the conditions of (18) into a single system of linear equations

$$
\begin{bmatrix} \widetilde{\mathbb{C}}(Y_{\ell_1}) \\ \vdots \\ \widetilde{\mathbb{C}}(Y_{\ell_j}) \end{bmatrix} = \begin{bmatrix} \widetilde{\mathbb{M}}(Y_{\ell_1}) \\ \vdots \\ \widetilde{\mathbb{M}}(Y_{\ell_j}) \end{bmatrix} \cdot \mathbb{S}. \tag{19}
$$

If we can derive $s_{16383}, \ldots, s_0, w_{127}, \ldots, w_0$ and $u_{127}, \ldots, u_0$ that are consistent with them, then this gives us U and W that have $L_1 = \left[W \cdot [\![Y_{\ell_1}]\!] \right]^{2^{127}}, \ldots, L_j = \left[W \cdot [\![Y_{\ell_j}]\!] \right]^{2^{127}}$ as j solutions to (15) and (16) .

Our Algorithm. We are now ready to present our algorithm to derive U and W. It turns out that it is not possible to solve (19) if we use all the $\alpha_{\max}$ constants from $\mathbb{Y}_r$. Therefore, we need to choose some of the constants from $\mathbb{Y}_r$, and this turns out to be a non-trivial task. We follow a greedy method and our approach is to list $Y_1, \ldots, Y_{\alpha_{\max}}$ in the increasing order of the number of conditions $\#\mathbb{I}(Y_\ell)$. For the constants with the same number of conditions, we list them in the lexicographic order. Assume that $\mathbb{Y}_r = \{Y_1, \ldots, Y_{\alpha_{\max}}\}$ is listed with this order.

1. First, initialize $\widetilde{\mathbb{C}}$ as an empty binary column vector, and $\widetilde{\mathbb{M}}$ as a binary $0 \times (16384 + 128)$ matrix.
2. Next, execute Steps 3 and 4 for $i = 1$ to $\alpha_{\max}$.
3. Apply the Gaussian elimination to the following system of linear equations and see if it can be solved.

$$
\begin{bmatrix} \widetilde{\mathbb{C}} \\ \widetilde{\mathbb{C}}(Y_i) \end{bmatrix} = \begin{bmatrix} \widetilde{\mathbb{M}} \\ \widetilde{\mathbb{M}}(Y_i) \end{bmatrix} \cdot \mathbb{S} \tag{20}
$$

4. If (20) has a solution, then let $\widetilde{\mathbb{C}} \leftarrow \begin{bmatrix} \widetilde{\mathbb{C}} \\ \widetilde{\mathbb{C}}(Y_i) \end{bmatrix}$ and $\widetilde{\mathbb{M}} \leftarrow \begin{bmatrix} \widetilde{\mathbb{M}} \\ \widetilde{\mathbb{M}}(Y_i) \end{bmatrix}$.
5. Finally, return $\widetilde{\mathbb{C}}$ and $\widetilde{\mathbb{M}}$.

Result. The execution of the algorithm gives us $\widetilde{\mathbb{M}}$ of the form presented in Fig. 5. The matrix is in the row echelon form where the lower left part of the elements are zeros.

We can arbitrarily fix $w_{19}, \ldots, w_0$, and then $w_{57}, \ldots, w_{20}$ are uniquely determined. We then arbitrarily fix $w_{76}, \ldots, w_{58}$, and then $w_{127}, \ldots, w_{77}$ are uniquely determined. At this point, all the bits of $W = w_{127} \ldots w_0$ are fixed, and we substitute them into $s_{128i+j} = u_i w_j$ and see if we can determine $U = u_{127} \ldots u_0$.

It turns out that it is indeed possible if we let $w_{76}, \ldots, w_{58} w_{19}, \ldots, w_0 = 0^{39}$, which gives us $W = $ 0xa288088a 02a88000 00eff100 0e100000, and $N = U$ and $N' = U' = U \oplus W^{-1}$ presented in (9), where the bits of U that can be fixed to any value are fixed to 0. Other results in (11), (12), and (13) are obtained with different values of $w_{76}, \ldots, w_{58} w_{19}, \ldots, w_0$, which are $0^{38}1$ for (11), $0^{37}10$ for (12), and $0^{37}11$ for (13).

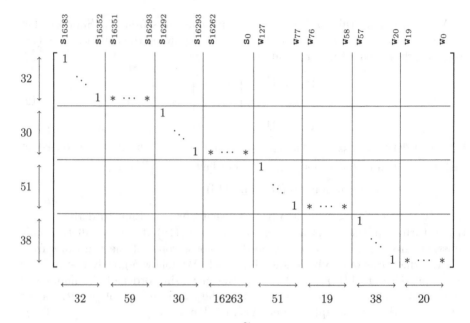

Fig. 5. The output $\widetilde{\mathsf{M}}$ of our algorithm

5.4 Applications to Other Values of r

The algorithm presented in the previous section can be naturally applied to other values of r. We present in Fig. 6 results of applying our algorithm on several values of r. The figure in $\#L$ shows the number of solutions (in L) that we can cover, and this suggests that we have identified N and N' such that $\Pr_L[\mathsf{Coll}_L(r, N, N')] \geq \#L/2^n$. The figure in $\#L/(\ell_N + 1)$ is normalized by dividing $\#L$ with the degree $(\ell_N + 1)$ of the polynomial, and we have $\ell_N = 1$ in our algorithm. The figure in α_r shows the value of α_r, and Proposition 3 states that we have $\Pr_L[\mathsf{Coll}_L(r, N, N')] \leq \alpha_r(\ell_N + 1)/2^n$ for any N and N'.

We see that, for these values of r, our algorithm gives N and N' such that the counter-collision probability is close to the upper bound in Proposition 3, and this suggests that Proposition 3 is tight up to a factor of about 4 to 16 depending on the value of r. However, there are other values of r where our algorithm does not work. We see that for $r = \text{0x2aaaaaab}$ and 0xd5555555, it fails to give N and N' with a high counter-collision probability.

The existence of N and N' with a high counter-collision probability even for several values of r suggests that, if we rely on the sum bound in (6), the constants in security bounds in (1) and (2) cannot be significantly reduced. Now a natural question is whether it is possible to avoid using the sum bound, and if so, whether this leads to improved security bounds. In the next section, we answer these questions positively.

r	$\#L$	$\#L/(\ell_N + 1)$	α_r
0x00000005	17	$2^{3.09}$	$2^{6.48}$
0x00000055	59	$2^{4.88}$	$2^{9.07}$
0x00000555	298	$2^{7.22}$	$2^{11.60}$
0x00005555	1930	$2^{9.91}$	$2^{14.09}$
0x00055555	13115	$2^{12.68}$	$2^{16.49}$
0x00555555	90134	$2^{15.46}$	$2^{18.77}$
0x05555555	667663	$2^{18.35}$	$2^{20.77}$
0x55555555	1762290	$2^{19.75}$	$2^{21.75}$
0x2aaaaaab	35	$2^{4.13}$	$2^{21.75}$
0xaaaaaaab	1762290	$2^{19.75}$	$2^{21.75}$
0xd5555555	35	$2^{4.13}$	$2^{21.75}$

Fig. 6. Summary of application of our algorithm to several values of r

6 Improving GCM Security Bounds

6.1 Avoiding the Sum Bound

For $0 \leq r < r' \leq 2^{32} - 1$ and two distinct nonces N and N' which are not 96 bits, consider deriving the upper bound on $\Pr_L[\mathsf{Coll}_L(r, N, N') \vee \mathsf{Coll}_L(r', N, N')]$, i.e., $\Pr_L\left[\mathsf{inc}^r(I[0]) = I'[0] \vee \mathsf{inc}^{r'}(I[0]) = I'[0]\right]$, where $I[0] \leftarrow \mathsf{GHASH}_L(\varepsilon, N)$ and $I'[0] \leftarrow \mathsf{GHASH}_L(\varepsilon, N')$. The first step is to replace the arithmetic additions by r and r' with the xor of some constants $Y \in \mathbb{Y}_r$ and $Y' \in \mathbb{Y}_{r'}$. We obtain the following upper bound.

$$\Pr_L\left[I[0] \oplus [\![Y]\!] = I'[0] \text{ for some } Y \in \mathbb{Y}_r \vee I[0] \oplus [\![Y']\!] = I'[0] \text{ for some } Y' \in \mathbb{Y}_{r'}\right]$$
(21)

The proof in [12,13] relies on the sum bound, and (6) suggests the use of

$$\sum_{Y \in \mathbb{Y}_r} \Pr_L\left[I[0] \oplus [\![Y]\!] = I'[0]\right] + \sum_{Y' \in \mathbb{Y}_{r'}} \Pr_L\left[I[0] \oplus [\![Y']\!] = I'[0]\right]$$

as the upper bound on (21). We now present the following simple lemma.

Lemma 1. *Fix $0 \leq r < r' \leq 2^{32} - 1$, and consider $Y \in \{0,1\}^{32}$ such that $Y \in \mathbb{Y}_r$ and $Y \in \mathbb{Y}_{r'}$. Then there does not exist $X \in \{0,1\}^n$ that satisfies $\mathsf{inc}^r(X) = X \oplus [\![Y]\!]$ and $\mathsf{inc}^{r'}(X) = X \oplus [\![Y]\!]$ simultaneously.*

Proof. Suppose for a contradiction that there exists $X \in \{0,1\}^n$ that satisfies both $\mathsf{inc}^r(X) = X \oplus [\![Y]\!]$ and $\mathsf{inc}^{r'}(X) = X \oplus [\![Y]\!]$. From $\mathsf{inc}^r(X) = \mathsf{inc}^{r'}(X)$, we have $\mathsf{inc}^{r'-r}(X) = X$. This is a contradiction as $r' - r \not\equiv 0 \bmod 2^{32}$, and hence $\mathsf{lsb}_{32}(\mathsf{inc}^{r'-r}(X))$ and $\mathsf{lsb}_{32}(X)$ cannot take the same value. □

It follows from Lemma 1 that

$$\sum_{Y \in \mathbb{Y}_r} \Pr_L \left[I[0] \oplus [\![Y]\!] = I'[0] \right] + \sum_{Y' \in \mathbb{Y}_{r'} \setminus \mathbb{Y}_r} \Pr_L \left[I[0] \oplus [\![Y']\!] = I'[0] \right] \qquad (22)$$

is also an upper bound on (21). If the cardinality of $\mathbb{Y}_r \cap \mathbb{Y}_{r'}$ is small, then (22) does not seem to give us any improvement. However, it turns out that there is a non-obvious effect of considering the cardinality of $\mathbb{Y}_r \cap \mathbb{Y}_{r'}$, and (22) indeed gives us improved security bounds on GCM.

This observation motivates us to consider another upper bound on (21), which is

$$\sum_{Y \in \mathbb{Y}_r \cup \mathbb{Y}_{r'}} \Pr_L \left[I[0] \oplus [\![Y]\!] = I'[0] \right]. \qquad (23)$$

In what follows, we present improved security bounds of GCM with (22) and (23).

6.2   Towards Improved Security Bounds

Consider an adversary $\mathcal{A}$ in the privacy game. As outlined in Sect. 5.1, we may focus on non-adaptive adversaries and consider the list of counter values in (3). The privacy advantage can be derived as (4), and $\Pr_L$ [Case (A) holds] is obtained as (5). We focus on $\Pr_L$ [Case (B) holds], i.e., we are interested in the probability of having a collision $I_i[j] = I_{i'}[j']$ for some (i, j, i', j'), where $1 \leq i' < i \leq q$, $0 \leq j' \leq m_{i'}$, and $0 \leq j \leq m_i$. For each $2 \leq i \leq q$, we have at most $(m_1 + 1) + (m_2 + 1) + \cdots + (m_{i-1} + 1) + (i-1)m_i$ cases of (j, i', j') to consider. To see this, we observe that for $I_i[0]$, we need to consider

$$I_i[0] \in \{I_{i'}[0], I_{i'}[1], \ldots, I_{i'}[m_{i'}]\} \text{ for some } 1 \leq i' < i, \qquad (24)$$

and thus for $j = 0$, we have $(m_1 + 1) + (m_2 + 1) + \cdots + (m_{i-1} + 1)$ cases of (i', j') to consider. See Fig. 7 (left). For $I_i[1], I_i[2], \ldots, I_i[m_i]$, we consider

$$\begin{aligned}
I_i[1] &\in \{I_1[0], I_2[0], \ldots, I_{i-1}[0]\}, \\
I_i[2] &\in \{I_1[0], I_2[0], \ldots, I_{i-1}[0]\}, \\
&\vdots \\
I_i[m_i] &\in \{I_1[0], I_2[0], \ldots, I_{i-1}[0]\},
\end{aligned} \qquad (25)$$

and we thus have $(i-1)$ cases of (i', j') for each $1 \leq j \leq m_i$. See Fig. 7 (right). We note that we can exclude the cases $I_i[j] = I_{i'}[j']$ for $1 \leq j \leq m_i$, $1 \leq i' < i$, and $1 \leq j' \leq m_{i'}$, as these cases are covered in (24) or in another case of (25).

So far, we have proceeded as was done in [12,13]. Now for $0 \leq a \leq b \leq 2^{32} - 1$ and two distinct nonces N and N' which are not 96 bits, let $\mathsf{Coll}_L([a..b], N, N')$ denote the event

$$\mathsf{inc}^r(\mathsf{GHASH}_L(\varepsilon, N)) = \mathsf{GHASH}_L(\varepsilon, N') \text{ for some } a \leq r \leq b.$$

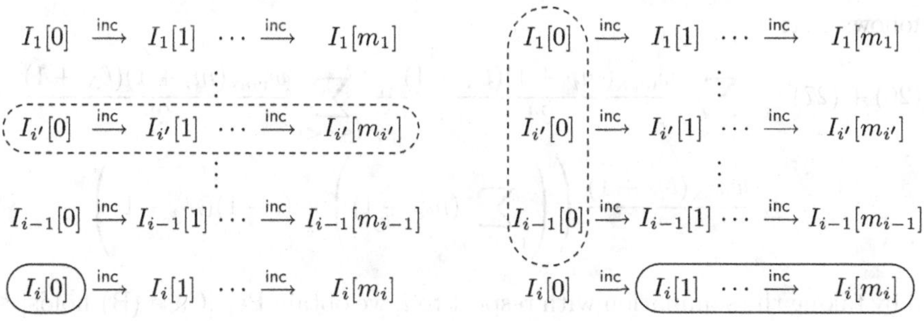

$$I_1[0] \xrightarrow{\text{inc}} I_1[1] \cdots \xrightarrow{\text{inc}} I_1[m_1]$$

$$I_{i'}[0] \xrightarrow{\text{inc}} I_{i'}[1] \cdots \xrightarrow{\text{inc}} I_{i'}[m_{i'}]$$

$$I_{i-1}[0] \xrightarrow{\text{inc}} I_{i-1}[1] \cdots \xrightarrow{\text{inc}} I_{i-1}[m_{i-1}]$$

$$\boxed{I_i[0]} \xrightarrow{\text{inc}} I_i[1] \cdots \xrightarrow{\text{inc}} I_i[m_i]$$

$$I_1[0] \xrightarrow{\text{inc}} I_1[1] \cdots \xrightarrow{\text{inc}} I_1[m_1]$$

$$I_{i'}[0] \xrightarrow{\text{inc}} I_{i'}[1] \cdots \xrightarrow{\text{inc}} I_{i'}[m_{i'}]$$

$$I_{i-1}[0] \xrightarrow{\text{inc}} I_{i-1}[1] \cdots \xrightarrow{\text{inc}} I_{i-1}[m_{i-1}]$$

$$I_i[0] \xrightarrow{\text{inc}} \boxed{I_i[1] \cdots \xrightarrow{\text{inc}} I_i[m_i]}$$

Fig. 7. Cases of (i',j') to consider for $j = 0$ (left) and for $1 \leq j \leq m_i$ (right)

We see that (24) is equivalent to $\text{inc}^0(I_{i'}[0]) = I_i[0] \vee \text{inc}^1(I_{i'}[0]) = I_i[0] \vee \cdots \vee \text{inc}^{m_{i'}}(I_{i'}[0]) = I_i[0]$ for some $1 \leq i' < i$, and the probability can be evaluated as

$$\sum_{1 \leq i' < i} \Pr_L \left[\text{Coll}_L([0..m_{i'}], N_{i'}, N_i) \right]. \tag{26}$$

With respect to (25), we rearrange them as $I_{i'}[0] \in \{I_i[1], I_i[2], \ldots, I_i[m_i]\}$ for some $1 \leq i' < i$. We see that this is equivalent to $\text{inc}^1(I_i[0]) = I_{i'}[0] \vee \text{inc}^2(I_i[0]) = I_{i'}[0] \vee \cdots \vee \text{inc}^{m_i}(I_i[0]) = I_{i'}[0]$ for some $1 \leq i' < i$, and the upper bound on the probability can be evaluated as

$$\sum_{1 \leq i' < i} \Pr_L \left[\text{Coll}_L([1..m_i], N_i, N_{i'}) \right] \leq \sum_{1 \leq i' < i} \Pr_L \left[\text{Coll}_L([0..m_i], N_i, N_{i'}) \right]. \tag{27}$$

6.3 Improving the Security Bounds with (22)

To apply (22) on (26) and (27), we define $\mathbb{W}_r \subseteq \{0,1\}^{32}$, for $0 \leq r \leq 2^{32} - 1$, as

$$\mathbb{W}_0 \stackrel{\text{def}}{=} \mathbb{Y}_0 \text{ and } \mathbb{W}_r \stackrel{\text{def}}{=} \mathbb{Y}_r \setminus (\mathbb{Y}_0 \cup \mathbb{Y}_1 \cup \cdots \cup \mathbb{Y}_{r-1}) \text{ for } r \geq 1.$$

We denote its cardinality as $w_r \stackrel{\text{def}}{=} \#\mathbb{W}_r$ and let $w_{\max} \stackrel{\text{def}}{=} \max\{w_r \mid 0 \leq r \leq 2^{32} - 1\}$. We show the following lemma.

Lemma 2. *For $0 \leq m \leq 2^{32} - 1$ and two distinct nonces N and N' which are not 96 bits, it holds that* $\Pr_L[\text{Coll}_L([0..m], N, N')] \leq w_{\max}(m+1)(\ell_N + 1)/2^n$, *where* $|N|_n, |N'|_n \leq \ell_N$.

Proof. Recall that $\text{Coll}_L([0..m], N, N')$ is the event $\text{inc}^0(I[0]) = I'[0] \vee \text{inc}^1(I[0]) = I'[0] \vee \cdots \vee \text{inc}^m(I[0]) = I'[0]$, and the probability can be evaluated as

$$\sum_{0 \leq r \leq m} \sum_{Y \in \mathbb{Y}_r \setminus (\mathbb{Y}_0 \cup \mathbb{Y}_1 \cup \cdots \cup \mathbb{Y}_{r-1})} \Pr_L \left[I[0] \oplus [Y] = I'[0] \right] \leq \sum_{0 \leq r \leq m} \frac{w_{\max}(\ell_N + 1)}{2^n},$$

since $I[0] \oplus [Y] = I'[0]$ is a non-trivial equation in L over $\text{GF}(2^n)$ of degree at most $\ell_N + 1$. $\square$

It follows that

$$(26) + (27) \le \sum_{1 \le i' < i} \frac{w_{\max}(m_{i'} + 1)(\ell_N + 1)}{2^n} + \sum_{1 \le i' < i} \frac{w_{\max}(m_i + 1)(\ell_N + 1)}{2^n}$$

$$\le \frac{w_{\max}(\ell_N + 1)}{2^n} \left(\left(\sum_{1 \le i' < i} (m_{i'} + 1) \right) + (i - 1)(m_i + 1) \right),$$

and by taking the summation with respect to i, we obtain $\Pr_L$ [Case (B) holds] $\le w_{\max}(q - 1)(\sigma + q)(\ell_N + 1)/2^n$, since

$$\sum_{2 \le i \le q} \left(\left(\sum_{1 \le i' < i} (m_{i'} + 1) \right) + (i - 1)(m_i + 1) \right) \le (q - 1)(\sigma + q).$$

From (5), $\Pr_L$ [Case (A) holds] $+ \Pr_L$ [Case (B) holds] is at most

$$\frac{(\sigma + q)(\ell_N + 1)}{2^n} + \frac{w_{\max}(q - 1)(\sigma + q)(\ell_N + 1)}{2^n} \le \frac{w_{\max}q(\sigma + q)(\ell_N + 1)}{2^n},$$

and it remains to evaluate the value of $w_{\max}$, which is shown in the lemma below.

Lemma 3. $w_{\max} \le 32$.

A proof is presented in Appendix A.

We are now ready to present the improved security bound based on (22).

Theorem 2. *With the same notation as in Proposition 1, we have*

$$\mathbf{Adv}^{\mathrm{priv}}_{\mathrm{GCM[Perm}(n),\tau]}(\mathcal{A}) \le \frac{0.5(\sigma + q + 1)^2}{2^n} + \frac{32q(\sigma + q)(\ell_N + 1)}{2^n}. \tag{28}$$

We have focused on the privacy result, but the authenticity result can also be obtained as follows.

Theorem 3. *With the same notation as in Proposition 2, we have*

$$\mathbf{Adv}^{\mathrm{auth}}_{\mathrm{GCM[Perm}(n),\tau]}(\mathcal{A}) \le \frac{0.5(\sigma + q + q' + 1)^2}{2^n}$$

$$+ \frac{32(q + q')(\sigma + q + 1)(\ell_N + 1)}{2^n} + \frac{q'(\ell_A + 1)}{2^\tau}. \tag{29}$$

Proofs follow the corresponding proofs in [13, Appendix D] for privacy and [13, Appendix E] for authenticity. For privacy, the difference is the analysis of Case (B) in [13, Appendix D], which is presented in this section, and for authenticity, the difference is the analysis of Case (B) and Case (D) in [13, Appendix E], where we can directly apply the analysis of this section.

6.4   Improving the Security Bounds with (23)

To apply (23) on (26) and (27), we define $\mathbb{Z}_r \subseteq \{0,1\}^{32}$, for $0 \leq r \leq 2^{32} - 1$, as

$$\mathbb{Z}_r \overset{\text{def}}{=} \mathbb{Y}_0 \cup \mathbb{Y}_1 \cup \cdots \cup \mathbb{Y}_r,$$

and denote its cardinality as $z_r \overset{\text{def}}{=} \#\mathbb{Z}_r$. We also let $z_{\max} \overset{\text{def}}{=} \max\{z_r \mid 0 \leq r \leq 2^{32} - 1\}$. We show the following lemma.

Lemma 4. *For $0 \leq m \leq 2^{32} - 1$ and two distinct nonces N and N' which are not 96 bits, it holds that $\Pr_L[\mathsf{Coll}_L([0..m], N, N')] \leq z_{\max}(\ell_N + 1)/2^n$, where $|N|_n, |N'|_n \leq \ell_N$.*

Proof. The upper bound on $\Pr_L[\mathsf{Coll}_L([0..m], N, N')]$ can be evaluated as

$$\sum_{Y \in \mathbb{Y}_0 \cup \mathbb{Y}_1 \cdots \cup \mathbb{Y}_m} \Pr_L\left[I[0] \oplus [\![Y]\!] = I'[0]\right] \leq \frac{z_{\max}(\ell_N + 1)}{2^n},$$

since $I[0] \oplus [\![Y]\!] = I'[0]$ is a non-trivial equation of degree at most $\ell_N + 1$. □

It follows that

$$(26) + (27) \leq 2 \sum_{1 \leq i' < i} \frac{z_{\max}(\ell_N + 1)}{2^n} \leq \frac{2(i-1)z_{\max}(\ell_N + 1)}{2^n},$$

and by taking the summation with respect to i, we obtain $\Pr_L[\text{Case (B) holds}] \leq z_{\max}q^2(\ell_N + 1)/2^n$. We use (5) to have

$$\Pr_L[\text{Case (A) holds}] + \Pr_L[\text{Case (B) holds}] \leq \frac{(\sigma + q)(\ell_N + 1)}{2^n} + \frac{z_{\max}q^2(\ell_N + 1)}{2^n},$$

and it remains to evaluate the value of $z_{\max}$, which is stated in the following lemma.

Lemma 5. $z_{\max} \leq 2^{32}$.

We have $\mathbb{Z}_r \subseteq \{0,1\}^{32}$, and hence the lemma follows. We note that the analysis is tight, as $\mathsf{str}_{32}(r)$ is always included in $\mathbb{Y}_r$, and the union $\mathbb{Y}_0 \cup \mathbb{Y}_1 \cup \cdots \cup \mathbb{Y}_{2^{32}-1}$ covers $\{0,1\}^{32}$.

We have the following improved security bound based on (23).

Theorem 4. *With the same notation as in Proposition 1, we have*

$$\mathbf{Adv}^{\text{priv}}_{\text{GCM}[\text{Perm}(n),\tau]}(\mathcal{A}) \leq \frac{0.5(\sigma + q + 1)^2}{2^n} + \frac{(\sigma + q)(\ell_N + 1)}{2^n} + \frac{2^{32}q^2(\ell_N + 1)}{2^n}. \tag{30}$$

The authenticity theorem is given as follows.

Theorem 5. *With the same notation as in Proposition 2, we have*

$$\mathbf{Adv}^{\text{auth}}_{\text{GCM}[\text{Perm}(n),\tau]}(\mathcal{A}) \leq \frac{0.5(\sigma + q + q' + 1)^2}{2^n} + \frac{(\sigma + q + q')(\ell_N + 1)}{2^n}$$

$$+ \frac{2^{32}q(q + q')(\ell_N + 1)}{2^n} + \frac{q'(\ell_A + 1)}{2^\tau}. \tag{31}$$

6.5   Discussions

We present a comparison of the three privacy bounds in (1), (28), and (30). We see that (28) is always smaller than (1), hence we focus on the comparison between (28) and (30). By simplifying (28) $\leq$ (30), we obtain

$$\left(32 - \frac{1}{q}\right)\left(\frac{\sigma}{q} + 1\right) \leq 2^{32}.$$

This suggests that if σ/q, the average block length of each query, is at most $2^{32}/32$ blocks, then (28) is smaller, where $2^{32}/32$ blocks amount to 2 Gbytes from $n = 128$. Similarly, for authenticity, (29) is always better than (2). By simplifying (29) $\leq$ (31), we obtain

$$\frac{\sigma}{q}\left(32 - \frac{1}{q + q'}\right) + \frac{1}{q} + 32 \leq 2^{32}.$$

As with the case of privacy, this suggests that if σ/q is at most $2^{32}/32$ blocks, which is about 2 Gbytes, then (29) gives a better bound than (31).

7   Conclusions

In this paper, we developed an algorithm to generate nonces that have a high counter-collision probability, and showed concrete examples of nonces as the results of our experiments. This implies that, if we use the sum bound in the security proof, then the security bounds of [12] are tight within a factor of about 4. We next showed that it is possible to avoid using the sum bound. We presented improved security bounds of GCM, and one of our security bounds suggests that the security of GCM is close to what was originally claimed by the designers in [18,19].

There are several interesting research directions. With respect to the generation of nonces, it would be interesting to extend our algorithm to handle nonces of different lengths. It would also be interesting to study the security of variants of GCM, including SGCM [27] and MGCM [20].

Acknowledgments. The authors received useful comments from participants of Dagstuhl Seminar 12031 (Symmetric Cryptography), ASK 2012 (Asian Workshop on Symmetric Key Cryptography), Early Symmetric Crypto (ESC) seminar 2013, and "Shin-Akarui-Angou-Benkyou-Kai." In particular, the authors thank Antoine Joux for motivating this work at Dagstuhl Seminar 12031. The work by Tetsu Iwata was supported in part by JSPS KAKENHI, Grant-in-Aid for Scientific Research (B), Grant Number 26280045, and was carried out in part while visiting Nanyang Technological University, Singapore.

A Proof of Lemma 3

Let x and c be integers such that $0 \le x \le 31$ and $0 \le c \le 2^x - 1$. Throughout the proof of Lemma 3, we abuse the notation and regard an integer $0 \le a \le 2^{32} - 1$ and its 32-bit binary representation, $\mathsf{str}_{32}(a)$, identically. For a 32-bit string $a_{31} \ldots a_0$, the i-th bit refers to a_i. We show the proof of Lemma 3 with the following two claims.

Claim. $2^x + c \in \mathbb{Y}_{2^x - c}$.

Proof. We have $2^x + c \in \mathbb{Y}_{2^x - c}$ if there exists $Y \in \{0,1\}^{32}$ that satisfies $Y + (2^x - c) = Y \oplus (2^x + c)$, which is equivalent to $2^x + c = (Y + (2^x - c)) \oplus Y$. Now let $Y \leftarrow \mathsf{str}_{32}(c)$. Then the right hand side is $(c + (2^x - c)) \oplus c$, which is equal to the left hand side from $0 \le c \le 2^x - 1$. Therefore, we have $2^x + c \in \mathbb{Y}_{2^x - c}$. $\quad\square$

Claim. $2^x + c \notin \mathbb{Y}_r$ for $0 \le r < 2^x - c$.

Proof. Let d be an integer such that $c < d \le 2^x$. We show that there does not exist $Y \in \{0,1\}^{32}$ that satisfies $2^x + c = (Y + 2^x - d) \oplus Y$, implying $2^x + c \notin \mathbb{Y}_{2^x - d}$. From $c < d \le 2^x$, we have $2^x + c = 2^x \oplus c$ and $2^x - d = 2^x - 1 - (d - 1) = (2^x - 1) \oplus (d - 1)$.

We first consider the case $d - 1 = c$. We see that the 0-th bit of $2^x + c$ is different from the 0-th bit of $2^x - d$. Therefore, there does not exist Y that satisfies $2^x + c = (Y + 2^x - d) \oplus Y$.

We next consider the case $d - 1 > c$. Let $d' = d - 1$, and let $\mathsf{str}_{32}(c) = c_{31} \ldots c_0$ and $\mathsf{str}_{32}(d') = d'_{31} \ldots d'_0$ be the binary representations of c and d'. Define $\ell \stackrel{\text{def}}{=} \max\{i \mid d'_i \ne c_i\}$. Then we have $d'_\ell = 1$ and $c_\ell = 0$ from $d - 1 > c$. This implies that the ℓ-th bit of $2^x + c$ and the ℓ-th bit of $2^x - d$ are both 0. Now from $d'_{\ell+1} = c_{\ell+1}$ and the fact that the $(\ell+1)$-st bit of 2^x and the $(\ell+1)$-st bit of $2^x - 1$ are different, we necessary have that the $(\ell+1)$-st bit of $2^x + c$ and the $(\ell+1)$-st bit of $2^x - d$ are different. In order the equality of $2^x + c = (Y + 2^x - d) \oplus Y$ to hold, we must have a carry to the $(\ell+1)$-st bit in computing $Y + 2^x - d$. However, it is impossible to have the carry since the ℓ-th bit of $2^x - d$ is 0. Therefore, there does not exist Y that satisfies $2^x + c = (Y + 2^x - d) \oplus Y$. $\quad\square$

The two claims show $2^x + c \in \mathbb{W}_{2^x - c}$. Now any integer between 1 and $2^{32} - 1$ can be uniquely represented in the form of $2^x + c$ for some $0 \le x \le 31$ and $0 \le c \le 2^x - 1$. The uniqueness follows from the fact that, if $(x, c) \ne (x', c')$, then $2^x + c \ne 2^{x'} + c'$. We note that 0 cannot be represented in the form of $2^x + c$, which is an element of $\mathbb{Y}_0$, and is not included in $\mathbb{Y}_r$ for $r \ge 1$, since $0 = (Y + r) \oplus Y$ cannot hold for $r \ge 1$. This implies that $\mathbb{W}_r$ for $r \ge 1$ can be written as $\mathbb{W}_r = \{2^x + c \mid r = 2^x - c, 0 \le x \le 31, 0 \le c \le 2^x - 1\}$. We can specifically list the elements of $\mathbb{W}_r$ as

$$\mathbb{W}_r = \{2^{31} + (2^{31} - 2^x + c), 2^{30} + (2^{30} - 2^x + c), \ldots, 2^{x+1} + (2^{x+1} - 2^x + c), 2^x + c\},$$

where $x = \lceil \log_2 r \rceil$ and $c = r - 2^x$. This proves $\#\mathbb{W}_r = 32 - \lceil \log_2 r \rceil$, and hence we have $w_{\max} \le 32$. $\quad\square$

In [23], we present a small-scale example that supports our claims.

References

1. Abdelraheem, M.A., Beelen, P., Bogdanov, A., Tischhauser, E.: Twisted polynomials and forgery attacks on GCM. In: Oswald, E., Fischlin, M. (eds.) EUROCRYPT 2015, Part I. LNCS, vol. 9056, pp. 762–786. Springer, Heidelberg (2015)
2. Aoki, K., Yasuda, K.: The security and performance of "GCM" when short multiplications are used instead. In: Kutyłowski, M., Yung, M. (eds.) Inscrypt 2012. LNCS, vol. 7763, pp. 225–245. Springer, Heidelberg (2013)
3. Bellare, M., Namprempre, C.: Authenticated encryption: relations among notions and analysis of the generic composition paradigm. J. Cryptology **21**(4), 469–491 (2008)
4. Bellare, M., Rogaway, P.: The security of triple encryption and a framework for code-based game-playing proofs. In: Vaudenay, S. (ed.) EUROCRYPT 2006. LNCS, vol. 4004, pp. 409–426. Springer, Heidelberg (2006)
5. Bogdanov, A.: Challenges and advances in authenticated encryption. Annual Workshop of TCCM-CACR (2014)
6. CAESAR: Competition for Authenticated Encryption: Security, Applicability, and Robustness. http://competitions.cr.yp.to/caesar.html
7. Dworkin, M.: Recommendation for Block Cipher Modes of Operation: Galois/Counter Mode (GCM) and GMAC. NIST Special Publication 800-38D (2007)
8. Ferguson, N.: Authentication Weaknesses in GCM. Public comments to NIST (2005). http://csrc.nist.gov/groups/ST/toolkit/BCM/comments.html
9. Handschuh, H., Preneel, B.: Key-recovery attacks on universal hash function based MAC algorithms. In: Wagner, D. (ed.) CRYPTO 2008. LNCS, vol. 5157, pp. 144–161. Springer, Heidelberg (2008)
10. IEEE Standard for Local and Metropolitan Area Networks Media Access Control (MAC) Security. IEEE Std 802.1AE-2006 (2006)
11. Information Technology – Security Techniques – Authenticated Encryption, ISO/IEC 19772:2009. International Standard ISO/IEC 19772 (2009)
12. Iwata, T., Ohashi, K., Minematsu, K.: Breaking and repairing GCM security proofs. In: Safavi-Naini, R., Canetti, R. (eds.) CRYPTO 2012. LNCS, vol. 7417, pp. 31–49. Springer, Heidelberg (2012)
13. Iwata, T., Ohashi, K., Minematsu, K.: Breaking and Repairing GCM Security Proofs. Cryptology ePrint Archive, Report 2012/438 (2012). http://eprint.iacr.org/
14. Joux, A.: Authentication Failures in NIST version of GCM. Public comments to NIST (2006). http://csrc.nist.gov/groups/ST/toolkit/BCM/comments.html
15. Leurent, G.: ARX Toolkit. http://www.di.ens.fr/~leurent/arxtools.html
16. Leurent, G.: Analysis of differential attacks in ARX constructions. In: Wang, X., Sako, K. (eds.) ASIACRYPT 2012. LNCS, vol. 7658, pp. 226–243. Springer, Heidelberg (2012)
17. Leurent, G.: Construction of differential characteristics in ARX designs application to Skein. In: Canetti, R., Garay, J.A. (eds.) CRYPTO 2013, Part I. LNCS, vol. 8042, pp. 241–258. Springer, Heidelberg (2013)
18. McGrew, D.A., Viega, J.: The security and performance of the Galois/Counter Mode (GCM) of operation. In: Canteaut, A., Viswanathan, K. (eds.) INDOCRYPT 2004. LNCS, vol. 3348, pp. 343–355. Springer, Heidelberg (2004)
19. McGrew, D.A., Viega, J.: The Security and Performance of the Galois/Counter Mode of Operation (Full Version). Cryptology ePrint Archive, Report 2004/193 (2004). http://eprint.iacr.org/

20. Meloni, N., Nègre, C., Hasan, M.A.: High performance GHASH and impacts of a class of unconventional bases. J. Cryptographic Eng. **1**(3), 201–218 (2011)
21. Mouha, N., Velichkov, V., De Cannière, C., Preneel, B.: The differential analysis of S-functions. In: Biryukov, A., Gong, G., Stinson, D.R. (eds.) SAC 2010. LNCS, vol. 6544, pp. 36–56. Springer, Heidelberg (2011)
22. National Security Agency, Internet Protocol Security (IPsec) Minimum Essential Interoperability Requirements, IPMEIR Version 1.0.0 Core (2010). http://www.nsa.gov/ia/programs/suiteb_cryptography/index.shtml
23. Niwa, Y., Ohashi, K., Minematsu, K., Iwata, T.: GCM Security Bounds Reconsidered. Cryptology ePrint Archive, Report 2015/214 (2015). http://eprint.iacr.org/
24. Procter, G., Cid, C.: On weak keys and forgery attacks against polynomial-based MAC schemes. In: Moriai, S. (ed.) FSE 2013. LNCS, vol. 8424, pp. 287–304. Springer, Heidelberg (2014)
25. Rogaway, P.: Authenticated-encryption with associated-data. In: Atluri, V. (ed.) ACM Conference on Computer and Communications Security, CCS 2002. pp. 98–107. ACM (2002)
26. Rogaway, P.: Evaluation of Some Blockcipher Modes of Operation. Investigation Reports on Cryptographic Techniques in FY 2010 (2011). http://www.cryptrec.go.jp/english/
27. Saarinen, M.-J.O.: SGCM: The Sophie Germain Counter Mode. Cryptology ePrint Archive, Report 2011/326 (2011). http://eprint.iacr.org/
28. Saarinen, M.-J.O.: Cycling attacks on GCM, GHASH and other polynomial MACs and hashes. In: Canteaut, A. (ed.) FSE 2012. LNCS, vol. 7549, pp. 216–225. Springer, Heidelberg (2012)
29. Salowey, J., Choudhury, A., McGrew, D.A.: AES Galois Counter Mode (GCM) Cipher Suites for TLS. IETF RFC 5288 (2008)
30. Yap, W., Yeo, S.L., Heng, S., Henricksen, M.: Security analysis of GCM for communication. Secur. Commun. Networks **7**(5), 854–864 (2014)
31. Zhu, B., Tan, Y., Gong, G.: Revisiting MAC forgeries, weak keys and provable security of Galois/Counter Mode of operation. In: Abdalla, M., Nita-Rotaru, C., Dahab, R. (eds.) CANS 2013. LNCS, vol. 8257, pp. 20–38. Springer, Heidelberg (2013)

Design

Boosting OMD for Almost Free Authentication of Associated Data

Reza Reyhanitabar$^{(\boxtimes)}$, Serge Vaudenay, and Damian Vizár

EPFL, Lausanne, Switzerland
{reza.reyhanitabar,serge.vaudenay,damian.vizar}@epfl.ch

Abstract. We propose *pure* OMD (p-OMD) as a new variant of the Offset Merkle-Damgård (OMD) authenticated encryption scheme. Our new scheme inherits all desirable security features of OMD while having a more compact structure and providing higher efficiency. The original OMD scheme, as submitted to the CAESAR competition, couples a single pass of a variant of the Merkle-Damgård (MD) iteration with the counter-based XOR MAC algorithm to provide privacy and authenticity. Our improved p-OMD scheme dispenses with the XOR MAC algorithm and is *purely* based on the MD iteration; hence, the name "pure" OMD. To process a message of ℓ blocks and associated data of a blocks, OMD needs $\ell + a + 2$ calls to the compression function while p-OMD only requires $\max\{\ell, a\} + 2$ calls. Therefore, for a typical case where $\ell \geq a$, p-OMD makes just $\ell + 2$ calls to the compression function; that is, associated data is processed almost freely compared to OMD. We prove the security of p-OMD under the same standard assumption (pseudorandomness of the compression function) as made in OMD; moreover, the security bound for p-OMD is the same as that of OMD, showing that the modifications made to boost the performance are without any loss of security.

Keywords: Authenticated encryption · OMD · Associated data · Performance · CAESAR competition

1 Introduction

An authenticated encryption (AE) scheme provides two complementary data security goals: confidentiality (privacy) and integrity (authenticity). Traditionally, these goals were achieved by combining two cryptographic primitives, a privacy-only encryption scheme and a message authentication code (MAC)—a paradigm known as generic composition (GC) [7,8,20]. The notion of AE, as a desirable symmetric-key primitive in its own right, was introduced in 2000 [7,9,18]. Since then, security notions for AE schemes have been defined and refined [14,23,25–27], together with many dedicated AE designs seeking some advantages over the GC-based schemes.

AE schemes have been studied for over a decade, yet the topic remains a highly active and interesting area of research as evidenced by the currently running CAESAR competition [10]. OMD [12,13] is one of 57 first-round CAESAR

© International Association for Cryptologic Research 2015
G. Leander (Ed.): FSE 2015, LNCS 9054, pp. 411–427, 2015.
DOI: 10.1007/978-3-662-48116-5_20

submissions, among which, at the time of writing this paper, 8 submissions are withdrawn due to major security flaws.

Among the features that OMD possesses, the following two are notably interesting and distinctive: OMD is the only CAESAR submission that is designed (as a mode of operation) based on a compression function [3], and it provides (provably) high security levels (about twice that of the AES-based submissions) when implemented with an off-the-shelf compression function such as those of the standard SHA family [2].

Instantiations of OMD using the compression functions of SHA-256 and SHA-512, called OMD-sha256 and OMD-sha512 respectively, can freely benefit from the widely-deployed optimized implementations of these primitives, e.g. [15,16]; in particular, OMD-sha256 can take advantage of the new Intel SHA Extensions [17].

Motivated by the aforementioned appealing features of OMD, we further investigate the possibility of making algorithmic improvements to the original OMD scheme towards boosting its efficiency, while preserving its security properties. We show that there is a natural way (inspired from the work of [28]) to modify OMD to make it more compact and efficient with respect to processing associated data (AD). Our new variant of OMD—called *pure* OMD (p-OMD)— has the following features:

- **It inherits all desirable security features of OMD.** We prove the security of p-OMD under the same standard assumption (namely, pseudo-randomness of the compression function) as made in OMD. Furthermore, the proven security bounds for p-OMD are the same as those of OMD. This shows that the modifications we made to OMD, to obtain the performance-boosted variant p-OMD, are without sacrificing any security.
- **It has a more compact structure and processing AD is almost free.** The original OMD scheme couples a single pass of the MD iteration—in which the chaining values are xored with specially crafted offsets—with the counter-based XOR MAC algorithm [6] to process a message and its associated data. The p-OMD scheme dispenses with the XOR MAC algorithm and is solely based on the (masked) MD iteration. This is achieved by absorbing the associated data blocks during the core MD path rather than processing them separately by an additional XOR MAC algorithm. To encrypt a message of ℓ blocks having associated data of a blocks, OMD needs $\ell + a + 2$ calls to the compression function while p-OMD only requires $\max\{\ell, a\} + 2$ calls. That is, for a typical case where $\ell \geq a$, p-OMD makes just $\ell + 2$ calls independently of the length of AD.

We note that neither OMD nor p-OMD satisfy the nonce-reuse misuse-resistance notions defined in [14,27]. Misuse-resistant variants of OMD are recently proposed in [21], but in these variants the encryption process is not online and they are less efficient than OMD.

A CORRECTION. In the *preproceedings* version of this paper, we claimed a partial level of robustness to nonce misuse with respect to the authenticity property.

Tomer Ashur and Bart Mennink pointed out [4] that this claim was incorrect; hence, we have removed the claim. This is the revised and corrected version.

ORGANIZATION OF THE PAPER. Notations and preliminary concepts are presented in Sect. 2. Definitions of security notions for AE schemes are reviewed in Sect. 3. Section 4 provides the specification of the p-OMD mode of operation. In Sect. 5, we provide the security analysis of p-OMD. Section 6 provides an experimental performance comparison between p-OMD and OMD.

2 Preliminaries

NOTATIONS. Let $x \xleftarrow{\$} S$ denote choosing an element x from a finite set S uniformly at random. $X \leftarrow Y$ is used for denoting the assignment statement where the value of Y is assigned to X. All strings are binary strings. The empty string is denoted by ε. The set of all strings of length n bits (for some positive integer n) is denoted as $\{0,1\}^n$, the set of all strings whose lengths are upper-bounded by L is denoted by $\{0,1\}^{\leq L}$ and the set of all strings of finite length is denoted by $\{0,1\}^*$. The notations $X\|Y$ and XY both stand for the string obtained by concatenating a string Y to a string X. For an m-bit string $X = X[m-1] \cdots X[0]$ we denote the first (leftmost) bit by $\mathsf{firstbit}(X) = X[m-1]$ and the last (rightmost) bit by $\mathsf{lastbit}(X) = X[0]$. Let $X[i \cdots j] = X[i] \cdots X[j]$ denote a substring of X, for $m - 1 \geq i \geq j \geq 0$; by convention we let $X[i \cdots j] = \varepsilon$ if $i < 0$ and $X[i \cdots j] = X[i \cdots 0]$ if $j < 0$.

For a non-negative integer i let $\langle i \rangle_m$ denote the binary representation of i by an m-bit string. For a bit string $X = X[m-1] \cdots X[0]$, let $\mathsf{str2num}(X) = \sum_{i=0}^{m-1} X[i]2^i$ denote the non-negative integer represented by X. Let $\mathtt{ntz}(i)$ denote the number of trailing zeros (i.e. the number of rightmost bits that are zero) in the binary representation of a positive integer i. Let $1^n 0^m$ denote concatenation of n ones by m zeros.

We let $\mathsf{firstbits}_i(X) = X[m-1 \cdots m-i]$ denote the i leftmost bits and $\mathsf{lastbits}_i(X) = X[i-1 \cdots 0]$ denote the i rightmost bits of X. For two strings $X = X[m-1] \cdots X[0]$ and $Y = Y[n-1] \cdots Y[0]$ of possibly different lengths, let the notation $X \oplus Y$ denote the bitwise xor of $\mathsf{firstbits}_i(X)$ and $\mathsf{firstbits}_i(Y)$ where $i = \min\{m,n\}$. Clearly, if X and Y have the same length then $X \oplus Y$ matches the usual bitwise xor. For any string X, define $X \oplus \varepsilon = \varepsilon \oplus X = \varepsilon$.

The special symbol $\perp$ signifies both that the value of a variable or a function at some input is undefined, and an error. Let $|Z|$ denote the number of elements of Z if Z is a set, and the length of Z in bits if Z is a string. We let $|\varepsilon| = 0$. For $X \in \{0,1\}^*$ let $X_1\|X_2 \cdots \|X_m \xleftarrow{b} X$ denote partitioning X into blocks X_i such that $|X_i| = b$ for $1 \leq i \leq m - 1$ and $|X_m| \leq b$; let $m = |X|_b$ denote length of X in b-bit blocks.

THE FINITE FIELD WITH 2^n ELEMENTS. Let $(GF(2^n), \oplus, .)$ denote the Galois Field with 2^n elements. An element α in $GF(2^n)$ is represented as a formal polynomial $\alpha(X) = \alpha_{n-1}X^{n-1} + \cdots + \alpha_1 X + \alpha_0$ with binary coefficients. We can assign an element $\alpha_i \in GF(2^n)$ to an integer $i \in \{0, \ldots, 2^n - 1\}$ in a natural way, similar applies for α_s and a string $s \in \{0, 1\}^n$. We sometimes refer to the elements of $GF(2^n)$ directly by strings or integers, if the context does not allow ambiguity. The addition "$\oplus$" and multiplication "$\cdot$" of two field elements in $GF(2^n)$ are defined as usual [13]. For $GF(2^{256})$ we use $P_{256}(X) = X^{256} + X^{10} + X^5 + X^2 + 1$, and for $GF(2^{512})$ we use $P_{512}(X) = X^{512} + X^8 + X^5 + X^2 + 1$ as the irreducible polynomials used in the field multiplications.

ADVANTAGE FUNCTION. The insecurity of a scheme Π in regard to a security property xxx is measured using the resource parametrized function $\mathbf{Adv}_{\Pi}^{\text{xxx}}(\mathbf{r}) = max_A \{\mathbf{Adv}_{\Pi}^{\text{xxx}}(A)\}$, where the maximum is taken over all adversaries A which use resources bounded by $\mathbf{r}$.

PSEUDORANDOM FUNCTIONS (PRFS) AND TWEAKABLE PRFS. Let Func $(m, n) = \{f : \{0, 1\}^m \to \{0, 1\}^n\}$ be the set of all functions from m-bit strings to n-bit strings. A random function (RF) R with m-bit input and n-bit output is a function selected uniformly at random from $\text{Func}(m, n)$. We denote this by $R \overset{\$}{\leftarrow} \text{Func}(m, n)$.

Let $\text{Func}^{\mathcal{T}}(m, n)$ be the set of all functions $\left\{\widetilde{f} : \mathcal{T} \times \{0, 1\}^m \to \{0, 1\}^n\right\}$, where $\mathcal{T}$ is a set of tweaks. A tweakable RF with the tweak space $\mathcal{T}$, m-bit input and n-bit output is a map $\widetilde{R} : \mathcal{T} \times \{0, 1\}^m \to \{0, 1\}^n$ selected uniformly at random from $\text{Func}^{\mathcal{T}}(m, n)$; i.e. $\widetilde{R} \overset{\$}{\leftarrow} \text{Func}^{\mathcal{T}}(m, n)$. Clearly, if $\mathcal{T} = \{0, 1\}^t$ then $|\text{Func}^{\mathcal{T}}(m, n)| = |\text{Func}(m + t, n)|$, and hence, $\widetilde{R}$ can be instantiated using a random function R with $(m + t)$-bit input and n-bit output. We use $\widetilde{R}^{\langle T \rangle}(.)$ and $\widetilde{R}(T, .)$ interchangeably, for every $T \in \mathcal{T}$. Notice that each tweak T names a random function $\widetilde{R}^{\langle T \rangle} : \{0, 1\}^m \to \{0, 1\}^n$ and distinct tweaks name distinct (independent) random functions.

Let $F : \mathcal{K} \times \{0, 1\}^m \to \{0, 1\}^n$ be a keyed function and let $\widetilde{F} : \mathcal{K} \times \mathcal{T} \times \{0, 1\}^m \to \{0, 1\}^n$ be a keyed and tweakable function, where the key space $\mathcal{K}$ is some nonempty set. Let $F_K(.) = F(K, .)$ and $\widetilde{F}_K^{\langle T \rangle}(.) = \widetilde{F}(K, T, .)$. Let A be an adversary. Then:

$$\mathbf{Adv}_F^{\text{prf}}(A) = \Pr\left[K \overset{\$}{\leftarrow} \mathcal{K} : A^{F_K(.)} \Rightarrow 1\right] - \Pr\left[R \overset{\$}{\leftarrow} \text{Func}(m, n) : A^{R(.)} \Rightarrow 1\right]$$

$$\mathbf{Adv}_{\widetilde{F}}^{\text{prf}}(A) = \Pr\left[K \overset{\$}{\leftarrow} \mathcal{K} : A^{\widetilde{F}_K^{\langle \cdot \rangle}(.)} \Rightarrow 1\right] - \Pr\left[\widetilde{R} \overset{\$}{\leftarrow} \text{Func}^{\mathcal{T}}(m, n) : A^{\widetilde{R}^{\langle \cdot \rangle}(.)} \Rightarrow 1\right]$$

The resource parametrized advantage functions are defined accordingly, considering that the adversarial resources of interest here are the time complexity (t) of the adversary and the total number of queries (q) asked by the adversary (note that we just consider fixed-input-length functions, so the lengths of queries are fixed and known). We say that F is $(t, q; \epsilon)$-PRF if $\mathbf{Adv}_F^{\text{prf}}(t, q) \leq \epsilon$. We say that $\widetilde{F}$ is $(t, q; \epsilon)$-tweakable PRF if $\mathbf{Adv}_{\widetilde{F}}^{\text{prf}}(t, q) \leq \epsilon$.

3   Security Notions for AEAD

SYNTAX OF AN AEAD SCHEME. A nonce-based authenticated encryption with associated data, AEAD for short, is a symmetric key scheme $\Pi = (\mathcal{K}, \mathcal{E}, \mathcal{D})$. The key space $\mathcal{K}$ is some non-empty finite set. The encryption algorithm $\mathcal{E}$: $\mathcal{K} \times \mathcal{N} \times \mathcal{A} \times \mathcal{M} \to \mathcal{C} \cup \{\bot\}$ takes four arguments, a secret key $K \in \mathcal{K}$, a nonce $N \in \mathcal{N}$, an associated data (a.k.a. header data) $A \in \mathcal{A}$ and a message $M \in \mathcal{M}$, and returns either a ciphertext $\mathbb{C} \in \mathcal{C}$ or a special symbol $\bot$ indicating an error. The decryption algorithm $\mathcal{D} : \mathcal{K} \times \mathcal{N} \times \mathcal{A} \times \mathcal{C} \to \mathcal{M} \cup \{\bot\}$ takes four arguments $(K, N, A, \mathbb{C})$ and either outputs a message $M \in \mathcal{M}$ or an error indicator $\bot$.

For correctness of the scheme, it is required that $\mathcal{D}(K, N, A, \mathbb{C}) = M$ for any $\mathbb{C}$ such that $\mathbb{C} = \mathcal{E}(K, N, A, M)$. It is also assumed that if algorithms $\mathcal{E}$ and $\mathcal{D}$ receive parameter not belonging to their specified domain of arguments they will output $\bot$. We write $\mathcal{E}_K(N, A, M) = \mathcal{E}(K, N, A, M)$ and similarly $\mathcal{D}_K(N, A, \mathbb{C}) = \mathcal{D}(K, N, A, \mathbb{C})$.

We assume that the message and associated data can be any binary string of arbitrary but finite length; i.e. $\mathcal{M} = \{0, 1\}^*$ and $\mathcal{A} = \{0, 1\}^*$, but the key and nonce are some fixed-length binary strings, i.e. $\mathcal{N} = \{0, 1\}^{|N|}$ and $\mathcal{K} = \{0, 1\}^k$, where the positive integers $|N|$ and k are respectively the nonce length and the key length of the scheme in bits. We assume that $|\mathcal{E}_K(N, A, M)| = |M| + \tau$ for some positive fixed constant τ; that is, we will have $\mathbb{C} = C\|\mathsf{Tag}$ where $|C| = |M|$ and $|\mathsf{Tag}| = \tau$. We call C the core ciphertext and Tag the tag.

NONCE RESPECTING ADVERSARIES. Let A be an adversary. We say that A is nonce-respecting if it never repeats a nonce in its *encryption* queries. That is, if A queries the encryption oracle $\mathcal{E}_K(\cdot, \cdot, \cdot)$ on $(N_1, A_1, M_1) \cdots (N_q, A_q, M_q)$ then $N_1, \cdots, N_q$ must be distinct.

PRIVACY NOTION. We adopt the privacy notion called indistinguishability of ciphertext from random bits under CPA (IND$-CPA), which is defined in [26] as a stronger variant of the classical IND-CPA notion [5,7].

Let $\Pi = (\mathcal{K}, \mathcal{E}, \mathcal{D})$ be a nonce-based AEAD scheme. Let A be a nonce-respecting adversary. A is provided with an oracle which can be either a real encryption oracle $\mathcal{E}_K(\cdot, \cdot, \cdot)$ such that on input (N, A, M) returns $\mathbb{C} = \mathcal{E}_K(N, A, M)$, or a fake encryption oracle $\$(\cdot, \cdot, \cdot)$ which on any input (N, A, M) returns $|\mathbb{C}|$ fresh random bits. The advantage of A in mounting a chosen plaintext attack (CPA) against the privacy property of Π is measured as follows:

$$\mathbf{Adv}_{\Pi}^{\mathrm{priv}}(A) = \Pr[K \xleftarrow{\$} \mathcal{K} : A^{\mathcal{E}_K(\cdot, \cdot, \cdot)} \Rightarrow 1] - \Pr[A^{\$(\cdot, \cdot, \cdot)} \Rightarrow 1].$$

AUTHENTICITY NOTION. We adopt the established notion of authenticity, called integrity of ciphertext (INT-CTXT) under CCA attacks. The notion was originally defined in [7] for AE schemes and later revisited to include (authentication of AD in) AEAD schemes in [23].

Let $\Pi = (\mathcal{K}, \mathcal{E}, \mathcal{D})$ be a nonce-based AEAD scheme. Let A be a nonce-respecting adversary. We stress that nonce-respecting is only regarded for the encryption queries; that is, A can repeat nonces during its decryption queries and it can also ask an encryption query with a nonce that was already used in a decryption query. Let A be provided with the encryption oracle $\mathcal{E}_K(\cdot, \cdot, \cdot)$ and the decryption oracle $\mathcal{D}_K(\cdot, \cdot, \cdot)$; that is, we consider adversaries that can mount chosen ciphertext attacks (CCA). We say that A forges if it makes a decryption query $(N, A, \mathbb{C})$ such that $\mathcal{D}_K(N, A, \mathbb{C}) \neq \perp$ and no previous encryption query $\mathcal{E}_K(N, A, M)$ returned $\mathbb{C}$.

$$\mathbf{Adv}_{\Pi}^{\mathrm{auth}}(A) = \Pr[K \xleftarrow{\$} \mathcal{K} : A^{\mathcal{E}_K(\cdot, \cdot, \cdot), \, \mathcal{D}_K(\cdot, \cdot, \cdot)} \text{ forges}].$$

RESOURCE PARAMETERS. Let $(N^1, A^1, M^1) \cdots (N^{q_e}, A^{q_e}, M^{q_e})$ denote the encryption queries and $(N'^1, A'^1, \mathbb{C}'^1) \cdots (N'^{q_v}, A'^{q_v}, \mathbb{C}'^{q_v})$ the decryption queries made by an adversary A. We define the resource parameters of A as $(t, q_e, q_v, \sigma_A, \sigma_M, \sigma_{A'}, \sigma_{\mathbb{C}'}, L_{max})$, where t is the time complexity, q_e and q_v are respectively the total number of encryption queries and decryption queries, L_{max} is the maximum length of each query in bits, $\sigma_A = \sum_{i=1}^{q_e} |A^i|$, $\sigma_M = \sum_{i=1}^{q_e} |M^i|$, $\sigma_{A'} = \sum_{i=1}^{q_v} |A'^i|$ and $\sigma_{\mathbb{C}'} = \sum_{i=1}^{q_v} (|\mathbb{C}'^i| - \tau)$.

The absence of a resource parameter will mean that the parameter is irrelevant in the context and hence omitted.

4   The p-OMD Mode of Operation

p-OMD is a mode of operation that converts a keyed compression function to an AEAD scheme. To instantiate p-OMD, one must first choose and fix a keyed compression function $F : \mathcal{K} \times (\{0,1\}^n \times \{0,1\}^m) \rightarrow \{0,1\}^n$ and a tag length $\tau \leq n$; with the key space $\mathcal{K} = \{0,1\}^k$ and $m \leq n$. Let p-OMD$[F, \tau]$ denote the p-OMD instantiated by fixing F and τ.

If the compression function at hand does not have a dedicated key input per se, as it is the case for standard hash functions, then a keyed compression function with $n + m$ input bits can be obtained from the keyless compression function with $n + b$ input bits by allocating k input bits for the key, such that $b = m + k$. For example, if we use the compression function of SHA-256, we have $n = 256, b = 512$ and setting $k = 256$ will give us a keyed compression function with $m = n = 256$.

DESCRIPTION OF THE MODE. The main design rationale behind p-OMD is the integration of AD processing into the same MD path that processes the message. Figure 1 shows a schematic representation of the encryption algorithm of p-OMD$[F, \tau]$. The decryption algorithm can be straightforwardly derived from the encryption algorithm with the additional verification of the authentication tag at the end of the decryption process. While the overall structure of such design is rather simple, the combined processing of the message and associated data blocks in p-OMD creates several additional possible cases, to be treated and analyzed carefully, compared to the analysis of OMD. Figure 2 provides an algorithmic description.

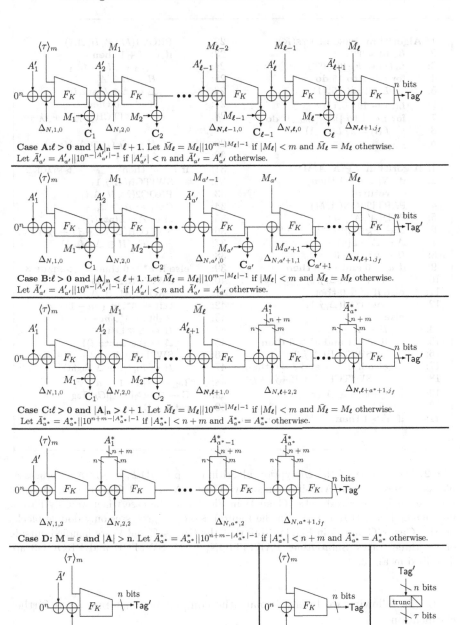

Fig. 1. The encryption process of p-OMD$[F, \tau]$. Refer to Sect. 4 for details. See Sect. 2 for our convention on the notation $X \oplus Y$ for operands of different lengths.

```
 1: Algorithm PRECOMPUTE(K)          22:        PROC1(M, A', H, Δ, i)
 2:    L_*(0) = 0^n                   23:        if i = ℓ + 1 then
 3:    L_*(1) ← F_K(0^n, 0^m)         24:            C_{i-1} ← H ⊕ M_{i-1}
 4:    for i ← 2 to 15 do            25:            H ← H ⊕ A'_i
 5:        L_*(i) = i · L_*(1)        26:            Δ ← Δ ⊕ L(ntz(i))
 6:    L(0) ← 16 · L_*(1)            27:            if a* = 0 then
 7:    for i ← 1 to ⌈log_2(ℓ_{max})⌉ do  28:                SWITCH(Δ, j, 4 + j_A +
 8:        L(i) = 2 · L(i-1)         j_M)
 9:    return                        29:            H ← F_K(H ⊕ Δ, M̄_{i-1})
                                      30:            i ← i + 1
 1: Algorithm ℰ_K(N, A, M)           31:        if ℓ ≥ a' then           ▷ STAGE 2
 2:    if |N| > n - 1 then           32:            SWITCH(Δ, j, 1)
 3:        return ⊥                  33:            PROC2(M, H, Δ, i)
 4:    PARTITION(A, M)               34:            C_{i-1} ← H ⊕ M_{i-1}
 5:    PAD(A', A*, M)                35:            Δ ← Δ ⊕ L(ntz(i))
 6:    Δ ← F_K(N||10^{n-1-|N|}, 0^m) 36:            SWITCH(Δ, j, 6 + j_A + j_M)
 7:    Δ ← Δ ⊕ L(0)                  37:            H ← F_K(H ⊕ Δ, M̄_{i-1})
 8:    H ← 0^n; j ← 0                38:            i ← i + 1
 9:    if a' = 0 and ℓ = 0 then      39:        else if a* > 0 then     ▷ STAGE 3
10:        SWITCH(Δ, j, 3)           40:            SWITCH(Δ, j, 2)
11:    else if a' = 0 then           41:            PROC3(A*, H, Δ, i)
12:        SWITCH(Δ, j, 1)           42:            Left ← A*_{a*}[n + m - 1 ··· m]
13:    else                          43:            Right ← A*_{a*}[m - 1 ··· 0]
14:        H ← H ⊕ A'_1              44:            H ← H ⊕ Left
15:        if a' = 1 and a* > 0 then 45:            Δ ← Δ ⊕ L(ntz(i))
16:            SWITCH(Δ, j, 2)       46:            SWITCH(Δ, j, 12 + j_A + j_M)
17:        else if a' = 1 and ℓ = 0 then  47:            H ← F_K(H ⊕ Δ, Right)
18:            SWITCH(Δ, j, 12+j_A+j_M)   48:    Tag ← H[n - 1 ··· n - τ]
19:        H ← F_K(H ⊕ Δ, ⟨τ⟩_m)     49:    ℂ ← C_1||C_2|| ··· ||C_ℓ||Tag
20:        i ← 2                     50:    return ℂ
21:    if a' > 1 then     ▷ STAGE 1
```

Fig. 2. Description of the encryption algorithm of p-OMD$[F, \tau]$. STAGE 1 processes blocks of message and AD simultaneously (**Cases A, B** and **C** in Fig. 1). STAGE 2 processes only message blocks (**Case B** in Fig. 1 and the case when we only have a message and no AD that is not in the Figure). STAGE 3 processes only double blocks of AD (**Cases C** and **D** in Fig. 1). Note that the **Cases E** and **F** are handled outside of the three stages. Subroutines PARTITION, PAD, SWITCH and PROC1-3 are described in Fig. 3.

In the following we briefly explain the components that may need further clarification.

(1) **Computing** $\Delta_{N,i,j}$. As shown in Fig. 1, before each call to the underlying compression function F, we xor a (key-dependent) masking value $\Delta_{N,i,j}$ to the chaining variable, where N is the nonce, the i component of the index is incremented at each call to the compression function and the j component is changed when needed (according to a pattern that will be detailed shortly). This method is known as the XE method [24] and is used for converting F to a *tweakable* function. There are different plausible ways to compute

1: **Subroutine** PARTITION(A, M)
2: $\quad b \leftarrow n + m$
3: $\quad M_1 || M_2 \cdots M_{\ell-1} || M_\ell \overset{m}{\leftarrow} M$ $\qquad \triangleright$
$\quad (\ell = |M|_m)$
4: $\quad A' \leftarrow A[|A| - 1 \cdots |A| - (\ell+1)n]$
5: $\quad A^* \leftarrow A[|A| - |A'| - 1 \cdots 0]$
6: $\quad A'_1 || A'_2 \cdots A'_{a'-1} || A'_{a'} \overset{n}{\leftarrow} A'$ $\qquad \triangleright$
$\quad (a' = |A'|_n)$
7: $\quad A^*_1 || A^*_2 \cdots A^*_{a^*-1} || A^*_{a^*} \overset{b}{\leftarrow} A^*$ $\qquad \triangleright$
$\quad (a^* = |A^*|_{n+m})$

1: **Subroutine** PAD(A', A^*, M)
2: $\quad$ **if** $|M| \bmod m \neq 0$ **then**
3: $\qquad \bar{M}_\ell \leftarrow M_\ell || 10^{m-|M_\ell|-1}$
4: $\qquad j_M \leftarrow 1$
5: $\quad$ **else**
6: $\qquad \bar{M}_\ell \leftarrow M_\ell$
7: $\qquad j_M \leftarrow 0$
8: $\quad$ **if** $|A'| \bmod n \neq 0$ **then**
9: $\qquad A'_{a'} \leftarrow A'_{a'} || 10^{n-|A'_{a'}|-1}$
10: $\qquad j_A \leftarrow 2$
11: $\quad$ **else if** $|A^*| \bmod n + m \neq 0$ **then**
12: $\qquad A^*_{a^*} \leftarrow A^*_{a^*} || 10^{n+m-|A^*_{a^*}|-1}$
13: $\qquad j_A \leftarrow 2$
14: $\quad$ **else**
15: $\qquad j_A \leftarrow 0$

1: **Subroutine** SWITCH$(\Delta, j, j_{\text{new}})$
2: $\quad \Delta \leftarrow \Delta \oplus L_*(\text{str2num}(\langle j \rangle_4 \oplus$
$\quad \langle j_{\text{new}} \rangle_4))$
3: $\quad j \leftarrow j_{\text{new}}$

1: **Subroutine** PROC1(M, A', H, Δ, i)
2: $\quad r_{\text{stop}} \leftarrow \min\{\ell, a'\}$
3: $\quad$ **for** $r \leftarrow i$ **to** r_{stop} **do**
4: $\qquad C_{r-1} \leftarrow H \oplus M_{r-1}$
5: $\qquad H \leftarrow H \oplus A'_r$
6: $\qquad \Delta \leftarrow \Delta \oplus L(\text{ntz}(r))$
7: $\qquad H \leftarrow F_K(H \oplus \Delta, M_{r-1})$
8: $\quad i \leftarrow r_{\text{stop}} + 1$

1: **Subroutine** PROC2(M, H, Δ, i)
2: $\quad$ **for** $r \leftarrow i$ **to** ℓ **do**
3: $\qquad C_{r-1} \leftarrow H \oplus M_{r-1}$
4: $\qquad \Delta \leftarrow \Delta \oplus L(\text{ntz}(r))$
5: $\qquad H \leftarrow F_K(H \oplus \Delta, M_{r-1})$
6: $\quad i \leftarrow \ell + 1$

1: **Subroutine** PROC3(A^*, H, Δ, i)
2: $\quad$ **for** $r \leftarrow 1$ **to** a^* **do**
3: $\qquad$ Left $\leftarrow A^*_r[n + m - 1 \cdots m]$
4: $\qquad$ Right $\leftarrow A^*_r[m - 1 \cdots 0]$
5: $\qquad H \leftarrow H \oplus$ Left
6: $\qquad \Delta \leftarrow \Delta \oplus L(\text{ntz}(i + r - 1))$
7: $\qquad H \leftarrow F_K(H \oplus \Delta, \text{Right})$
8: $\quad i \leftarrow i + a^* - 1$

Fig. 3. The subroutines used in the encryption algorithm of p-OMD$[F, \tau]$ (Fig. 2)

such masking values (under efficiency and security constraints) [11,19,24]. We adopt the Gray code based method following [19]. In the following, all multiplications (denoted by ".") are in $GF(2^n)$.

(a) PRECOMPUTATION. Let $L_*(0) = 0^n$, $L_*(1) = F_K(0^n, 0^m)$ and $L_*(i) = i \cdot L_*(1)$ for $2 \leq i \leq 15$. Let $L(0) = 16 \cdot L_*(1)$ and $L(j) = 2 \cdot L(j-1)$ for $j \geq 1$. For a fast implementation the values $L_*(i)$ and $L(j)$ can be precomputed and stored in a table for $1 \leq i \leq 15$ and $0 \leq j \leq \lceil \log_2(\ell_{max}) \rceil$, where ℓ_{max} is the bound on the maximum number of blocks in M or A. Alternatively, (if there is a memory restriction) they can be computed on-the-fly. Note that all $L_*(i)$ are linear.

(b) COMPUTATION OF THE MASKING SEQUENCE. The masking values $\Delta_{N,i,j}$ are computed sequentially as follows. Let $\Delta_{N,0,0} = F_K(N || 10^{n-1-|N|}, 0^m)$. For $i \geq 1$ and $j, j' \in \{0, 1, \ldots, 15\}$: $\Delta_{N,i,j} =$

$\Delta_{N,i-1,j'} \oplus L(\texttt{ntz}(i)) \oplus L_* (\texttt{str2num}(\langle j \rangle_4 \oplus \langle j' \rangle_4))$. For details on how we get this compact relation adopting the Gray code based sequence partition method, we refer to Appendix ??.

(2) **Encryption Algorithm:** To encrypt a message $M \in \{0,1\}^*$ with associated data $A \in \{0,1\}^*$ using nonce $N \in \{0,1\}^{|N|}$ and key $K \in \{0,1\}^k$, obtaining a ciphertext $\mathbb{C} = C||\mathsf{Tag} \in \{0,1\}^{|M|+\tau}$, do the following.

(a) PARTITIONING THE MESSAGE AND ASSOCIATED DATA. The partitioning is done by the PARTITION subroutine in Fig. 3. Let $M_1||M_2 \cdots M_{\ell-1}||M_\ell \overset{m}{\leftarrow} M$. Let $A'||A^* \leftarrow A$ where $A' \leftarrow A[|A| - 1 \cdots |A| - (\ell+1)n]$ and $A^* \leftarrow A[|A|-|A'|-1 \cdots 0]$ (refer to the notations in Sect. 2). Let $A'_1||A'_2 \cdots A'_{a'-1}||A'_{a'} \overset{n}{\leftarrow} A'$ and $A_1^*||A_2^* \cdots A_{a^*-1}^*||A_{a^*}^* \overset{n+m}{\longleftarrow} A^*$. The string A' consists of $a' \leq \ell + 1$ n-bit blocks and these blocks will be simply absorbed into the chaining variable during the message encryption. In a typical use case where the associated data is (a header) shorter than the message, we will have $A' = A$ i.e. $A^* = \varepsilon$ (**Case A** and **Case B** in Fig. 1). The string A^* will be non-empty only if $|A| > (\ell+1)n$, in which case, while A^* is being processed, there are no more message blocks to encrypt. To maximize the efficiency, we partition the string A^* into $n + m$-bit blocks so that we can make use of both of the inputs to F (see **Case C** and **Case D** in Fig. 1).

(b) PROCESSING THE MESSAGE AND ASSOCIATED DATA. The message and associated data blocks are processed by the modified MD iteration of the keyed compression functions F as shown in Fig. 1. For every call to F, the n-bit input (chaining variable) is masked by the value $\Delta_{N,i,j}$; where, the N component in the index denotes the nonce; i starts with the value $i = 1$ at the first call to F and is incremented (by one) for every call; the j component is used to separate logical parts in the encryption process as well as different types of input arguments. Appropriate use of the j component is essential for security and facilitates the analysis, as will be described in the following.

(3) **Selection of the j component in the index of the masks $\Delta_{N,i,j}$.** We use different values of j to separate the calls to the masked F in different contexts. Let's classify the calls to the masked F to two types: (1) the final call to F which returns the tag, and (2) the internal calls. We note that in the special case that $M = \varepsilon$ and $|A| \leq n$ there will be only one call to F which returns the tag; hence, it is considered as the final call.

Internal Calls. We use $j \in \{0,1,2\}$ for the internal calls made to the masked F as follows.

For $i = 1$, i.e. the first call to F, the value of j is determined as follows:
- if $\ell > 0$ and $a' > 0$ then let $j = 0$,
- if $\ell > 0$ and $a' = 0$ then let $j = 1$,
- if $\ell = 0$ and $a^* > 0$ then let $j = 2$.

For $1 < i < \ell + 1 + a^*$, depending on the presence of message blocks and AD blocks to be processed at the ith call to the masked F, we have:

- if both an n-bit AD block and an m-bit message block are present then $j = 0$,
- if only an m-bit message block is present (no AD block is processed) then $j = 1$,
- if only an $(n + m)$-bit AD block is present (no message block is processed) then $j = 2$.

Final Call. The final call to F which produces the authentication tag uses $j_f \in \{3, 4, 5, \ldots, 14, 15\}$. If the tag is produced by a call to F with $i \neq 1$, we have three main cases depending on the inputs to the final masked F.

- If both an AD block and a message block are present in the final call (see **Case A** in Fig. 1) then $j_f \in \{4, 5, 6, 7\}$; where, we let $j_f = 4$ if $|M_\ell| = m$ and $|A'_{a'}| = n$; let $j_f = 5$ if $|M_\ell| < m$ and $|A'_{a'}| = n$; let $j_f = 6$ if $|M_\ell| = m$ and $|A'_{a'}| < n$, and otherwise $(|M_\ell| < m$ and $|A'_{a'}| < n)$ let $j_f = 7$.
- If only a message block is present but no AD block is processed in the final call (see **Case B** in Fig. 1) then $j_f \in \{8, 9, 10, 11\}$; where, we let $j_f = 8$ if $|M_\ell| = m$ and $|A'_{a'}| = n$; let $j_f = 9$ if $|M_\ell| < m$ and $|A'_{a'}| = n$; let $j_f = 10$ if $|M_\ell| = m$ and $|A'_{a'}| < n$, and otherwise $(|M_\ell| < m$ and $|A'_{a'}| < n)$ let $j_f = 11$. For the special case where there is no associate data at all, i.e. $A = \varepsilon$, we let $j_f = 8$ if $|M_\ell| = m$ and let $j_f = 9$ if $|M_\ell| < m$.
- If only an AD block is present but no message block is processed in the final call (see **Case C** and **Case D** in Fig. 1) then $j_f \in \{12, 13, 14, 15\}$; where, we let $j_f = 12$ if $|M_\ell| = m$ and $|A^*_{a^*}| = n + m$; let $j_f = 13$ if $|M_\ell| < m$ and $|A^*_{a^*}| = n + m$; let $j_f = 14$ if $|M_\ell| = m$ and $|A^*_{a^*}| < n + m$, and otherwise $(|M_\ell| < m$ and $|A^*_{a^*}| < n + m)$ let $j_f = 15$. For the special case where there is no message at all, i.e. $M = \varepsilon$, let $j_f = 12$ if $|A^*_{a^*}| = n + m$ and let $j_f = 14$ if $|A^*_{a^*}| < n + m$.

For $i = 1$ (meaning that the final call is the same as the first call, which happens if $M = \varepsilon$ AND $|A| \leq n$) we need to apply a special treatment:

- if both $M = A = \varepsilon$ then $j_f = 3$ (**Case F** in Fig. 1),
- if $M = \varepsilon$ and $0 < |A| \leq n$ then we let $j_f = 12$ if $|A| = n$, otherwise, let $j_f = 14$ (**Case E** box in Fig. 1).

Note that there is no variable j_f in Fig. 2 as j_f corresponds to a special use of variable j in the last call to F. Specifically, j_f corresponds to the calls to the SWITCH subroutine that use the value of new j of the form $\text{const} + j_A + j_M$ or the value 3.

(4) **Decryption Algorithm:** The decryption algorithm accepts a ciphertext $\mathbb{C} \in \{0,1\}^*$ together with associated data $A \in \{0,1\}^*$ and nonce $N \in \{0,1\}^{|N|}$, and using key $K \in \{0,1\}^k$ obtains a plaintext $M \in \{0,1\}^*$ or

returns an invalid indication $\perp$. If $|\mathbb{C}| < \tau$ then return $\perp$. Otherwise let C be the first $|\mathbb{C}| - \tau$ bits of $\mathbb{C}$ and Tag be the remaining τ bits. Now, considering that the encryption process of p-OMD is actually an additive stream cipher with an integrated authentication mechanism, the decryption process proceeds the same as the encryption process up until the verification of the tag, which happens at the end of the decryption process where the newly computed tag Tag$'$ is compared with the provided tag Tag. If Tag$' =$ Tag then output M, otherwise output $\perp$.

5   Security Analysis

The security analysis for p-OMD is modular and easy to follow. The high-level structure of the analysis is similar to that of OMD, as expected from the similarities of the algorithms, though the details differ and are more involved. We refer to the full version of this paper [22] for all omitted details.

The proof is divided into three main steps as follows:

Step 1: *Idealization of the p-OMD scheme using a tweakable random function.* We first analyse the security of a generalized variant of p-OMD$[F, \tau]$ where the "masked F" (aimed to instantiate a tweakable function) is replaced by an ideal primitive; namely, a tweakable random function $\widetilde{R}$. This is the major proof step which differs from and is more involved than that of OMD.

Step 2: *Realization of the tweakable random function by a tweakble PRF.* This is a well-known classical method where the (ideal) random function is replaced by a PRF. This proof step is therefore the same as that of OMD.

Step 3: *Instantiation of the tweakable PRF via a PRF.* To make a tweakable PRF out of a PRF, we use the XE method of [24] with the masking sequence generated based on an appropriate adjustment of a canonical Gray code sequence [19, 26]. This step is similar to that of OMD; only the details of the mask generation function differ.

The security bound for p-OMD is given by Theorem 1.

Theorem 1. *Fix $n \geq 1$, $0 \leq \tau \leq n$. Let $F : \mathcal{K} \times (\{0,1\}^n \times \{0,1\}^m) \to \{0,1\}^n$ be a PRF, where the key space $\mathcal{K} = \{0,1\}^k$ for $k \geq 1$ and $1 \leq m \leq n$. We have*

$$\mathbf{Adv}^{\mathrm{priv}}_{\mathrm{p-OMD}[F,\tau]}(t, q_e, \sigma_e, \ell_{max}) \leq \mathbf{Adv}^{\mathrm{prf}}_F(t', 2\sigma_e) + \frac{3\sigma_e^2}{2^n}$$

$$\mathbf{Adv}^{\mathrm{auth}}_{\mathrm{p-OMD}[F,\tau]}(t, q_e, q_v, \sigma, \ell_{max}) \leq \mathbf{Adv}^{\mathrm{prf}}_F(t', 2\sigma) + \frac{3\sigma^2}{2^n} + \frac{q_v \ell_{max}}{2^n} + \frac{q_v}{2^\tau}$$

where q_e and q_v are, respectively, the number of encryption and decryption queries, ℓ_{max} denotes the maximum number of the internal calls to F in an encryption or decryption query, $t' = t + cn\sigma$ for some constant c, and σ_e and σ are the total number of calls to the underlying compression function F in all queries asked by the CPA and CCA adversaries against the privacy and authenticity of the scheme, respectively.

The proof is obtained by combining Lemma 1 in Sect. 5.1 with Lemma 2 in Sect. 5.2 and Lemma 3 in Sect. 5.3.

5.1 Idealization of p-OMD

Let p-$\mathbb{OMD}[\widetilde{R}, \tau]$ be a generalization (idealization) of p-OMD$[F, \tau]$ that uses a tweakable random function $\widetilde{R} : \mathcal{T} \times (\{0,1\}^n \times \{0,1\}^m) \rightarrow \{0,1\}^n$ instead of the masked F. The tweak space $\mathcal{T}$ consists of sixteen mutually exclusive sets of tweaks $\mathcal{T} = \bigcup_{i=0}^{15} \mathcal{N} \times \mathbb{N} \times \{i\}$, where $\mathcal{N} = \{0,1\}^{|N|}$ is the set of nonces and $\mathbb{N}$ is the set of positive integers.

Lemma 1. Let p-$\mathbb{OMD}[\widetilde{R}, \tau]$ be the idealized scheme. Then

$$\mathbf{Adv}^{\mathrm{priv}}_{p\text{-}\mathbb{OMD}[\widetilde{R}, \tau]}(q_e, \sigma_e, \ell_{max}) = 0$$

$$\mathbf{Adv}^{\mathrm{auth}}_{p\text{-}\mathbb{OMD}[\widetilde{R}, \tau]}(q_e, q_v, \sigma, \ell_{max}) \leq \frac{q_v \ell_{max}}{2^n} + \frac{q_v}{2^\tau}$$

where q_e and q_v are, respectively, the number of encryption and decryption queries, ℓ_{max} denotes the maximum number of the internal calls to the underlying tweakable random function $\widetilde{R}$ in an encryption or decryption query, and σ_e and σ are the total number of calls to $\widetilde{R}$ in all queries asked by the CPA and CCA adversaries against the privacy and authenticity of the scheme, respectively.

The proof (and figures depicting p-$\mathbb{OMD}[\widetilde{R}, \tau]$) can be found in the full version of the paper [22].

5.2 Realization of Tweakable RFs with Tweakable PRFs

This is a classical step in which the ideal primitive—tweakable random function $\widetilde{R}$—is replaced with a standard primitive—tweakable PRF $\widetilde{F}$. The security loss induced by this step is stated in the following lemma. See the full version of this paper [22] for the proof.

Lemma 2. Let $\widetilde{R} : \mathcal{T} \times (\{0,1\}^n \times \{0,1\}^m) \rightarrow \{0,1\}^n$ be a tweakable RF and $\widetilde{F} : \mathcal{K} \times \mathcal{T} \times (\{0,1\}^n \times \{0,1\}^m) \rightarrow \{0,1\}^n$ be a tweakable PRF. Then

$$\mathbf{Adv}^{\mathrm{priv}}_{p\text{-}\mathbb{OMD}[\widetilde{F}, \tau]}(t, q_e, \sigma_e, \ell_{max}) \leq \mathbf{Adv}^{\mathrm{priv}}_{p\text{-}\mathbb{OMD}[\widetilde{R}, \tau]}(q_e, \sigma_e, \ell_{max}) + \mathbf{Adv}^{\widetilde{\mathrm{prf}}}_{\widetilde{F}}(t', \sigma_e)$$

$$\mathbf{Adv}^{\mathrm{auth}}_{p\text{-}\mathbb{OMD}[\widetilde{F}, \tau]}(t, q_e, q_v, \sigma, \ell_{max}) \leq \mathbf{Adv}^{\mathrm{auth}}_{p\text{-}\mathbb{OMD}[\widetilde{R}, \tau]}(q_e, q_v, \sigma, \ell_{max}) + \mathbf{Adv}^{\widetilde{\mathrm{prf}}}_{\widetilde{F}}(t'', \sigma)$$

where q_e and q_v are, respectively, the number of encryption and decryption queries, $q = q_e + q_v$, ℓ_{max} denotes the maximum number of the internal calls to F in an encryption or decryption query, $t' = t + cn\sigma_e$ and $t'' = t + c'n\sigma$ for some constants c, c', and σ_e and σ are the total number of calls to the underlying compression function F in all queries asked by the CPA and CCA adversaries against the privacy and authenticity of the scheme, respectively.

5.3   Instantiation of Tweakable PRFs with PRFs

The last step is to instantiate the tweakable PRFs by means of a (keyed) compression function which is assumed to be PRF. Similar to OMD, we use the XE method of [24] as shown in Fig. 4.

The proof and bound for this step follows from that of OMD, which in turn is a straightforward adaptation of the proof of the XE construction in [19]. Lemma 3 states the bound for this transformation. Here, the only aspect which is different between OMD and p-OMD is the way that the masking sequence $\Delta_{N,i,j}$ is computed. It is proved in the full version of this paper [22] that the required security and efficiency properties are satisfied by the specific mask generation scheme of p-OMD, as described in Sect. 4.

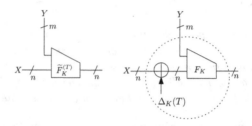

Fig. 4. Building a tweakable PRF $\widetilde{F}_K^{\langle T\rangle}$: $\{0,1\}^n \times \{0,1\}^m \to \{0,1\}^n$ using a PRF $F_K : \{0,1\}^n \times \{0,1\}^m \to \{0,1\}^n$.

Lemma 3. *Let* F : $\mathcal{K} \times (\{0,1\}^n \times \{0,1\}^m) \to \{0,1\}^n$ *be a function family with key space* $\mathcal{K}$. *Let* $\widetilde{F}$: $\mathcal{K} \times \mathcal{T} \times (\{0,1\}^n \times \{0,1\}^m) \to \{0,1\}^n$ *be defined by* $\widetilde{F}_K^{\langle T\rangle}(X,Y) = F_K((X \oplus \Delta_K(T)),Y)$ *for every* $T \in \mathcal{T}, K \in \mathcal{K}, X \in \{0,1\}^n, Y \in \{0,1\}^m$ *and* $\Delta_K(T)$ *is the masking function of p-OMD as defined in Sect. 4. If* F *is PRF then* $\widetilde{F}$ *is tweakable PRF; more precisely*

$$\mathbf{Adv}_{\widetilde{F}}^{\widetilde{\mathrm{prf}}}(t,q) \leq \mathbf{Adv}_F^{\mathrm{prf}}(t',2q) + \frac{3q^2}{2^n}.$$

6   Performance Comparison with OMD

To verify the performance advantage of p-OMD over OMD, with respect to processing associated data, we implemented the two algorithms in software and made some measurements to determine and compare their performance.

The comparison is performed on the x86-64 architecture (Intel Core i7-3632QM, with all measurements carried out on a single core). For OMD, we used the OMD-sha512 instantiation optimised for the AVX1 instruction extension, which achieves the best result according to the CAESAR benchmarking measurements [1]. We made the necessary modifications (as in description of p-OMD) to the same code to obtain our implementation of p-OMD. Both OMD

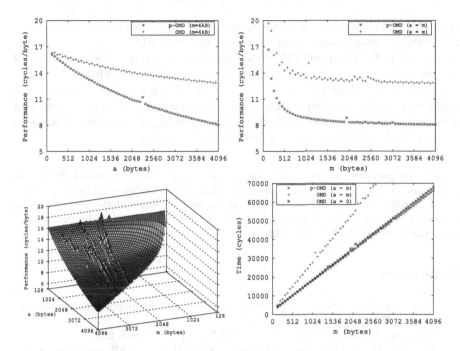

Fig. 5. Performance comparisons between OMD and p-OMD. **Top left**: encryption complexity with fixed message length. **Top right**: encryption complexity with equal message length and AD length. **Bottom right**: comparison of OMD without AD to OMD and p-OMD with AD. **Bottom left**: encryption complexity of p-OMD for varying message and AD lengths.

and p-OMD were instantiated with the same parameters: key length $= 512$, nonce length $= 256$, tag length $= 256$. Both implementations have been built using the gcc compiler and setting the `-Ofast` optimization flag.

We measure the time complexity of the encryption process for varying lengths of message and associated data. For the sake of this section, let m denote the message length and a the AD length in bytes. We measure the encryption time for $m \in \{64, 128, 192, \ldots, 4096\}$ and $a \in \{64, 128, \ldots m\}$ for every value of m. That is, we consider the typical case when AD is at most as long as the message.

For both OMD and p-OMD and for every pair of values m, a, we measure the time of one encryption using the `rdtsc` instruction 200 times to compute the mean time. This is repeated 91 times and the value we take as the result is the median of these 91 mean encryption times. We additionally apply the same procedure to measure time complexity of the encryption of OMD with $m \in \{64, 128, \ldots, 4096\}$ and $a = 0$. The results are shown in Fig. 5.

The top left graph in Fig. 5 shows that the relative complexity of encryption of both OMD and p-OMD decreases as the length of AD increases; however, p-OMD performs better than OMD. The top right graph demonstrates that *if the length of AD is close to the message length* then p-OMD has a clear advantage over OMD. The bottom right graph confirms that the p-OMD provides an almost free authentication of associated data compared to OMD.

For both OMD and p-OMD, these measurements exclude the complexity of the precomputation step in computing $\Delta_{N,i,j}$ (see Sect. 4) which is done only once during the whole lifetime of a key. As an upper bound, we measure the complexity of the precomputation step that is sufficient to encrypt messages with length up to 2^{63} blocks. For OMD the precomputation step takes 5818 cycles while in p-OMD it requires 6863 cycles on average.

Acknowledgments. We would like to thank the anonymous reviewers of FSE 2015 for their constructive comments. We thank Tomer Ashur and Bart Mennink [4] for pointing out a mistaken claim about authenticity under nonce misuse in the preproceedings version of this paper. This work was partially supported by Microsoft Research under MRL Contract No. 2014-006 (DP1061305).

References

1. Implementation notes: amd64, titan0, crypto aead. http://bench.cr.yp.to/web-impl/amd64-titan0-crypto_aead.html
2. Secure Hash Standard (SHS). NIST FIPS PUB 180-4, March 2012
3. Abed, F., Forler, C., Lucks, S.: Classification of the CAESAR candidates. IACR Cryptology ePrint Archive 2014 (2014). http://eprint.iacr.org/2014/792
4. Ashur, T., Mennink, B.: Trivial Nonce-Misusing Attack on Pure OMD. Cryptology ePrint Archive, Report 2015/175 (2015). https://eprint.iacr.org/2015/175.pdf
5. Bellare, M., Desai, A., Jokipii, E., Rogaway, P.: A concrete security treatment of symmetric encryption. In: FOCS 1997, pp. 394–403. IEEE Computer Society (1997)
6. Bellare, M., Guérin, R., Rogaway, P.: XOR MACs: new methods for message authentication using finite pseudorandom functions. In: Coppersmith, D. (ed.) CRYPTO 1995. LNCS, vol. 963, pp. 15–28. Springer, Heidelberg (1995)
7. Bellare, M., Namprempre, C.: Authenticated encryption: relations among notions and analysis of the generic composition paradigm. In: Okamoto, T. (ed.) ASI-ACRYPT 2000. LNCS, vol. 1976, pp. 531–545. Springer, Heidelberg (2000)
8. Bellare, M., Namprempre, C.: Authenticated encryption: relations among notions and analysis of the generic composition paradigm. J. Cryptology **21**(4), 469–491 (2008)
9. Bellare, M., Rogaway, P.: Encode-then-encipher encryption: how to exploit nonces or redundancy in plaintexts for efficient cryptography. In: Okamoto, T. (ed.) ASI-ACRYPT 2000. LNCS, vol. 1976, pp. 317–330. Springer, Heidelberg (2000)
10. Bernstein, D.J.: Cryptographic competitions: CAESAR. http://competitions.cr.yp.to
11. Chakraborty, D., Sarkar, P.: A general construction of tweakable block ciphers and different modes of operations. IEEE Trans. Inf. Theory **54**(5), 1991–2006 (2008)
12. Cogliani, S., Maimut, D., Naccache, D., do Canto, R.P., Reyhanitabar, R., Vaudenay, S., Vizár, D.: Offset Merkle-Damgård (OMD) version 1.0: A CAESAR Proposal, March 2014. http://competitions.cr.yp.to/round1/omdv10.pdf

13. Cogliani, S., Maimuţ, D., Naccache, D., do Canto, R.P., Reyhanitabar, R., Vaudenay, S., Vizár, D.: OMD: a compression function mode of operation for authenticated encryption. In: Joux, A., Youssef, A. (eds.) SAC 2014. LNCS, vol. 8781, pp. 112–128. Springer, Heidelberg (2014)
14. Fleischmann, E., Forler, C., Lucks, S.: McOE: a family of almost foolproof online authenticated encryption schemes. In: Canteaut, A. (ed.) FSE 2012. LNCS, vol. 7549, pp. 196–215. Springer, Heidelberg (2012)
15. Guilford, J., Cote, D., Gopal, V.: Fast SHA512 Implementations on Intel$^{®}$ Architecture Processors, November 2012. http://www.intel.com/content/www/us/en/intelligent-systems/intel-technology/fast-sha512-implementations-ia-processors-paper.html
16. Guilford, J., Yap, K., Gopal, V.: Fast SHA-256 Implementations on Intel$^{®}$ Architecture Processors, May 2012. http://www.intel.com/content/www/us/en/intelligent-systems/intel-technology/sha-256-implementations-paper.html
17. Gulley, S., Gopal, V., Yap, K., Feghali, W., Guilford, J., Wolrich, G.: Intel$^{®}$ SHA Extensions: New Instructions Supporting the Secure Hash Algorithm on Inte$^{®}$ Architecture Processors, July 2013. https://software.intel.com/sites/default/files/article/402097/intel-sha-extensions-white-paper.pdf
18. Katz, J., Yung, M.: Unforgeable encryption and chosen ciphertext secure modes of operation. In: Schneier, B. (ed.) FSE 2000. LNCS, vol. 1978, pp. 284–299. Springer, Heidelberg (2001)
19. Krovetz, T., Rogaway, P.: The software performance of authenticated-encryption modes. In: Joux, A. (ed.) FSE 2011. LNCS, vol. 6733, pp. 306–327. Springer, Heidelberg (2011)
20. Namprempre, C., Rogaway, P., Shrimpton, T.: Reconsidering generic composition. In: Nguyen, P.Q., Oswald, E. (eds.) EUROCRYPT 2014. LNCS, vol. 8441, pp. 257–274. Springer, Heidelberg (2014)
21. Reyhanitabar, R., Vaudenay, S., Vizár, D.: Misuse-resistant variants of the OMD authenticated encryption mode. In: Chow, S.S.M., Liu, J.K., Hui, L.C.K., Yiu, S.M. (eds.) ProvSec 2014. LNCS, vol. 8782, pp. 55–70. Springer, Heidelberg (2014)
22. Reyhanitabar, R., Vaudenay, S., Vizár, D.: Boosting OMD for almost free authentication of associated data (full version). Cryptology ePrint Archive, Report 2015/302 (2015). https://eprint.iacr.org/2015/302.pdf
23. Rogaway, P.: Authenticated-encryption with associated-data. In: ACM Conference on Computer and Communications Security, pp. 98–107 (2002)
24. Rogaway, P.: Efficient instantiations of tweakable blockciphers and refinements to modes OCB and PMAC. In: Lee, P.J. (ed.) ASIACRYPT 2004. LNCS, vol. 3329, pp. 16–31. Springer, Heidelberg (2004)
25. Rogaway, P.: Nonce-based symmetric encryption. In: Roy, B., Meier, W. (eds.) FSE 2004. LNCS, vol. 3017, pp. 348–359. Springer, Heidelberg (2004)
26. Rogaway, P., Bellare, M., Black, J., Krovetz, T.: OCB: a block-cipher mode of operation for efficient authenticated encryption. In: ACM Conference on Computer and Communications Security, pp. 196–205 (2001)
27. Rogaway, P., Shrimpton, T.: A provable-security treatment of the key-wrap problem. In: Vaudenay, S. (ed.) EUROCRYPT 2006. LNCS, vol. 4004, pp. 373–390. Springer, Heidelberg (2006)
28. Yasuda, K.: Boosting Merkle-Damgård hashing for message authentication. In: Kurosawa, K. (ed.) ASIACRYPT 2007. LNCS, vol. 4833, pp. 216–231. Springer, Heidelberg (2007)

Optimally Secure Tweakable Blockciphers

Bart Mennink[1,2](✉)

[1] Department of Electrical Engineering, ESAT/COSIC, KU Leuven,
Leuven, Belgium
bart.mennink@esat.kuleuven.be
[2] iMinds, Leuven, Belgium

Abstract. We consider the generic design of a tweakable blockcipher from one or more evaluations of a classical blockcipher, in such a way that all input and output wires are of size n bits. As a first contribution, we show that any tweakable blockcipher with one primitive call and arbitrary linear pre- and postprocessing functions can be distinguished from an ideal one with an attack complexity of about $2^{n/2}$. Next, we introduce the tweakable blockcipher $\widetilde{F}[1]$. It consists of one multiplication and one blockcipher call with tweak-dependent key, and achieves $2^{2n/3}$ security. Finally, we introduce $\widetilde{F}[2]$, which makes two blockcipher calls, one of which with tweak-dependent key, and achieves optimal 2^n security. Both schemes are more efficient than all existing beyond birthday bound tweakable blockciphers known to date, as long as one blockcipher key renewal is cheaper than one blockcipher evaluation plus one universal hash evaluation.

Keywords: Tweakable blockcipher · Liskov-Rivest-Wagner · Optimal security · Beyond birthday bound

1 Introduction

A blockcipher is a family of permutations indexed via a secret key. Tweakable blockciphers generalize over classical blockciphers by introducing the *tweak* as an additional parameter. More formally, a tweakable blockcipher $\widetilde{E} : \mathcal{K} \times \mathcal{T} \times \mathcal{M} \to \mathcal{M}$ is a family of permutations on $\mathcal{M}$ indexed by a key $k \in \mathcal{K}$ and tweak $t \in \mathcal{T}$. Here, the key input is a secret parameter to guarantee security, while the tweak value is a public parameter with the main purpose to bring flexibility to the cipher. Tweakable blockciphers were formalized by Liskov, Rivest, and Wagner [29] and find a wide spectrum of applications, such as tweakable enciphering schemes [8,13,20–22,34,45,49], authenticated encryption schemes and message authentication codes [2,27,41,42], and online ciphers [2,44].

Example tweakable blockciphers that admit tweaks by design are Schroeppel's Hasty Pudding Cipher [46], Crowley's Mercy [10], and the Threefish cipher used in SHA-3 finalist Skein [14]. Furthermore, Goldenberg et al. [18] demonstrated how to transform a Feistel scheme into a tweakable Feistel scheme that achieves birthday bound security, and Mitsuda and Iwata [35] derived similar

© International Association for Cryptologic Research 2015
G. Leander (Ed.): FSE 2015, LNCS 9054, pp. 428–448, 2015.
DOI: 10.1007/978-3-662-48116-5_21

results for generalized Feistel schemes. Jean et al. [23] considered the problem of tweaking key alternating ciphers by presenting TWEAKEY, a construction that elegantly blends the tweak with the key in the key scheduling algorithm.

A more generic approach is to design a tweakable blockcipher from an ordinary blockcipher (and possibly other cryptographic primitives) in a black-box way. Two such constructions were introduced in Liskov et al.'s original paper. The first construction LRW1 makes two evaluations of an underlying blockcipher E, while the other construction LRW2 is based on a blockcipher E and a universal hash function family H:

$$\text{LRW1}(k, t, m) = E(k, E(k, m) \oplus t), \tag{1}$$

$$\text{LRW2}([k, h], t, m) = E(k, m \oplus h(t)) \oplus h(t), \tag{2}$$

where $h \in H$. These constructions achieve security up to the birthday bound. Related to LRW2 is the XEX construction by Rogaway [41], and extensions of it by Chakraborty and Sarkar [7] and Minematsu [32], which effectively reduces the keyspace to n bits.

Landecker, Shrimpton, and Terashima [27] considered the cascade of two LRW2's:

$$\text{LRW2}[2]([k_1, k_2, h_1, h_2], t, m) = \text{LRW2}([k_2, h_2], t, \text{LRW2}([k_1, h_1], t, m)), \tag{3}$$

and proved it secure up to about $2^{2n/3}$ queries.[1] Lampe and Seurin [26] generalized this approach and considered a cascade of $\rho \geq 1$ evaluations:

$$\text{LRW2}[\rho]([\mathbf{k}, \mathbf{h}], t, m) = \text{LRW2}([k_\rho, h_\rho], t, \cdots \text{LRW2}([k_1, h_1], t, m) \cdots), \tag{4}$$

where $\mathbf{k} = (k_1, \ldots, k_\rho)$ are blockcipher keys and $\mathbf{h} = (h_1, \ldots, h_\rho)$ instantiations of H. Lampe and Seurin proved that for even ρ, this construction is secure up to approximately $2^{\rho n/(\rho+2)}$ queries. Note that this bound only improves over the one of Landecker et al. for $\rho \geq 4$. Lampe and Seurin conjectured that their bound could be improved to $2^{\rho n/(\rho+1)}$. This term approaches the optimal 2^n for increasing ρ, but also the number of primitive calls and the key size increases linearly in ρ.

Tweak-Dependent Keys

Liskov et al. [29] suggested that a change in the tweak should be cheaper than a change in the key. As pointed out by Jean et al. [23], this may seem somewhat counter-intuitive because the adversary has full control over the tweak while it has only limited to no control over the key. They suggest that, in practice, the two inputs should be treated comparably. Additionally, the theoretical quest to derive an (almost) optimally secure tweakable blockcipher complying with this condition lead to an unrestrained increase of primitive calls and of the number of keys.

---

[1] Procter [39] pointed out a flaw in the original proof and suggested a fix. See also the ePrint version of [27].

For example, the tweakable blockcipher $\widetilde{E}(k,t,m) = E(k \oplus t, m)$ is secure up to about $2^{n/2}$ evaluations (in the single-key setting,[2] and if the underlying cipher is sufficiently secure), and thus achieves the same level of security as, for instance, LRW1. If we assume that the underlying cipher E consists of a key scheduling part and a message encryption part (such separation is easily made for key alternating ciphers), each evaluation of $\widetilde{E}$ requires one key scheduling and one message encryption, while each evaluation of LRW1 requires two message encryptions (the key scheduling can be pre-computed). This means that $\widetilde{E}$ is more efficient than LRW1 if the key scheduling part of E is cheaper than its message encryption part.

Minematsu [33] presented a construction of a tweakable blockcipher with tweak-dependent key that achieves beyond birthday bound security. In more detail, he proved that

$$\mathsf{Min}(k,t,m) = E(E(k,t\|0^{n-|t|}), m) \tag{5}$$

is secure up to $\max\{2^{n/2}, 2^{n-|t|}\}$ where $|t|$ denotes the fixed tweak length. Unfortunately, this construction only achieves beyond birthday bound security as long as the tweak is shorter than $n/2$ bits and it can impossibly achieve optimal 2^n security (unless $|t| = 0$). Beyond Minematsu's scheme, no other tweakable blockciphers in this direction are known.[3]

Our Contributions

We investigate the following elementary question. *Can we design an optimally secure tweakable blockcipher $\widetilde{E}$ with n-bit in- and outputs using only a blockcipher E with n-bit in- and outputs?*

We approach this question generically, focusing on the way $\widetilde{E}$ is designed from E, which means that the preprocessing functions that prepare the inputs to the underlying blockcipher may be technically any function as long as the tweakable blockcipher itself is invertible. This also means that the preprocessing functions may utilize another cryptographic primitive (for LRW2 the tweak and message are preprocessed as $(t, m) \mapsto m \oplus h(t)$ for some universal hash function $h \in H$). We will not rely on the potential cryptographic strength of the preprocessing functions: we only make a security assumption on E and assume the mixing functions are efficiently computable.

Formally, security is defined as the information-theoretic indistinguishability of $(\widetilde{E}, E)$ from $(\widetilde{\pi}, E)$, with $\widetilde{\pi}$ an ideal tweakable cipher, E an ideal cipher, and where the distinguisher has forward and inverse query access to both of its oracles. We remark that the same security model is, for instance, oft-employed in the area of key-length extenders [1, 4, 12, 16, 17, 28].

---

[2] In the related-key model we have $\widetilde{E}(k,t,m) = \widetilde{E}(k \oplus \delta, t \oplus \delta, m)$ for any (k,t,m) and any δ [23].

[3] We exclude schemes that use a blockcipher E with a larger key space, such as the tweakable blockcipher $\widetilde{E}(k,t,m) = E(k\|t, m)$ for a blockcipher E with 2n-bit key.

Generic Design. We start with presenting a generic description of a tweakable blockcipher design $\widetilde{E}[\rho]$ for $\rho \geq 1$. It consists of ρ calls to a classical blockcipher E interlaced with arbitrary mixing functions to generate the inputs to primitive calls and to generate the final output of the tweakable cipher. To assure invertibility of $\widetilde{E}[\rho]$, we pose a validity condition on the mixing functions, and only consider mixing functions that comply with this condition. Next, we consider various instances of $\widetilde{E}[\rho]$.

One Blockcipher Call with Linear Mixing. We first focus on the case $\rho = 1$, with the mixing functions being linear mappings over the finite field $\mathrm{GF}(2^n)$, and formally prove that any tweakable blockcipher of this form can be broken in a total complexity of about $2^{n/2}$. The attack covers for instance the tweakable cipher $E(k \oplus t, m)$ discussed before.

One Blockcipher Call with Polynomial Mixing. Next, we allow for mixing functions that involve multiplications, and introduce the tweakable blockcipher $\widetilde{F}[1] : \{0,1\}^n \times \{0,1\}^n \times \{0,1\}^n \rightarrow \{0,1\}^n$ (see also Fig. 1):

$$\widetilde{F}[1](k,t,m) = E(k \oplus t, m \oplus z) \oplus z, \text{ where } z = k \otimes t.$$

We prove that $\widetilde{F}[1]$ is indistinguishable from an ideal tweakable cipher as long as the distinguisher's complexity is at most $2^{2n/3}$. The proof is based on Patarin's H-coefficient technique [38] which has found recent adoption in, among others, generic blockcipher design [9,12] and MAC security [36]. It additionally uses the finite field equivalent of Szemerédi-Trotter theorem [47], a result that was also used by Jetchev et al. [24] in the context of blockcipher based hashing. Informally, this theorem states that if L is a set of lines in a finite field and P a set of two-dimensional points, the number of point-line incidences is at most $\min\{|L|^{1/2}|P| + |L|, |L||P|^{1/2} + |P|\}$. This theorem is applied by viewing construction queries as lines and primitive queries as points.

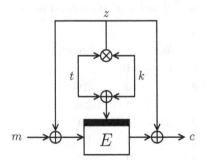

Fig. 1. Tweakable blockcipher $\widetilde{F}[1]$

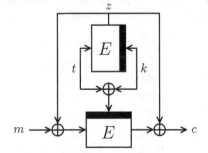

Fig. 2. Tweakable blockcipher $\widetilde{F}[2]$

Two Blockcipher Calls with Linear Mixing. Thirdly, we consider the case $\rho = 2$ and linear mixing functions, and introduce $\widetilde{F}[2] : \{0,1\}^n \times \{0,1\}^n \times \{0,1\}^n \to \{0,1\}^n$ (see also Fig. 2):

$$\widetilde{F}[2](k,t,m) = E(k \oplus t, m \oplus z) \oplus z, \text{ where } z = E(k,t).$$

It differs from $\widetilde{F}[1]$ in that the tweak processing $z = k \otimes t$ is replaced by $E(k,t)$. We remark that PCLMULQDQ and AES are comparably efficient on the latest Intel Haswell processors [19]. Using slightly more involved techniques than for $\widetilde{F}[1]$, we prove that $\widetilde{F}[2]$ is an optimally secure tweakable cipher up to about 2^n queries.

Comparison

A comparison of $\widetilde{F}[1]$ and $\widetilde{F}[2]$ with the state of the art is given in Table 1. It shows that $\widetilde{F}[1]$ and $\widetilde{F}[2]$ compare favorably. For instance, both $\widetilde{F}[1]$ and LRW2[2] achieve $2n/3$-bit security, but the latter uses 2 blockcipher calls and 2 universal hash function calls. This means that $\widetilde{F}[1]$ is more efficient if one key renewal is cheaper than one blockcipher evaluation plus one universal hash evaluation. It additionally uses a key that is four times as small. Similarly, $\widetilde{F}[2]$ achieves optimal security using 2 cipher calls and 1 key renewal. The same bound is asymptotically achieved by LRW2[ρ] for $\rho \to \infty$, but this one requires ρ cipher calls and ρ universal hash calls, and has a key of size $2\rho n$.

On the other hand, $\widetilde{F}[1]$ and $\widetilde{F}[2]$ are proven in the information-theoretic model while the other schemes are analyzed in the complexity-theoretic model. Both schemes require a blockcipher that offers resistance against distinguishers

Table 1. Comparison of $\widetilde{F}[1]$ and $\widetilde{F}[2]$ with existing tweakable blockciphers. Universal hashes in LRW2[ρ] are instantiated as multiplications in the finite field of 2^n elements (see also Sect. 2). Cost is divided into plain E-calls, multiplications or universal hashes $\otimes/h$, and the number of E-calls with tweak-dependent key "tdk". For Min, $|t|$ denotes the fixed size of the tweak. The security bounds on $\widetilde{F}[1]$ and $\widetilde{F}[2]$ are derived in the information-theoretic model.

scheme	security	key	cost			reference
	($\log_2$)	length	E	$\otimes/h$	tdk	
LRW1	$n/2$	n	2	0	0	[29]
LRW2	$n/2$	$2n$	1	1	0	[29]
XEX	$n/2$	n	2	0	0	[41]
LRW2[2]	$2n/3$	$4n$	2	2	0	[27]
LRW2[ρ]	$\rho n/(\rho+2)$	$2\rho n$	ρ	ρ	0	[26]
Min	$\max\{n/2, n-|t|\}$	n	2	0	1	[33]
$\widetilde{F}[1]$	$2n/3$	n	1	1	1	Sect. 4.2
$\widetilde{F}[2]$	n	n	2	0	1	Sect. 5

that may freely choose the tweak that transforms the key input k under XOR. Fortunately, no related-key attacks of this form on the widely used blockciphers such as AES are known: Biryukov et al. [5,6] derived a related-key attack on full AES-192 and AES-256, but using a more complicated and contrived key relation (see also Daemen and Rijmen [11]). We note that the proofs for $\widetilde{F}[1]$ and $\widetilde{F}[2]$ can straightforwardly be transformed to the complexity-theoretic model as long as the underlying blockcipher is related-key secure under XOR in the formalization of Bellare and Kohno [3]. This requires a hybrid proof, where the first step consists of replacing the underlying blockcipher E by an ideal primitive (at the cost of the related-key security of E). This step is, however, relatively loose, which can be seen from the fact that the ideal cipher achieves tight $2^{n/2}$ related-key security under XOR while it yields $2^{2n/3}$ and 2^n security for $\widetilde{F}[1]$ and $\widetilde{F}[2]$ in the information-theoretic model.

Outline

We present the security model in Sect. 2. Our generic tweakable blockcipher design $\widetilde{E}[\rho]$ is given in Sect. 3. In Sect. 4, we consider $\rho = 1$: the impossibility result for linear mixing is given in Sect. 4.1 and our construction $\widetilde{F}[1]$ using polynomial mixing is introduced in Sect. 4.2. Then, in Sect. 5, we consider $\rho = 2$ and present $\widetilde{F}[2]$ based on linear mixing functions. The work is concluded in Sect. 6.

2   Model

By $\{0,1\}^n$ we denote the set of bit strings of length n. Let $\mathrm{GF}(2^n)$ be the field of order 2^n. We identify bit strings from $\{0,1\}^n$ and finite field elements in $\mathrm{GF}(2^n)$. This is done by representing a string $a = a_{n-1}a_{n-2}\cdots a_1 a_0 \in \{0,1\}^n$ as polynomial $a(\mathbf{x}) = a_{n-1}\mathbf{x}^{n-1} + a_{n-2}\mathbf{x}^{n-2} + \cdots + a_1\mathbf{x} + a_0 \in \mathrm{GF}(2^n)$ and vice versa. There is additionally a one-to-one correspondence between $[0, 2^n - 1]$ and $\{0,1\}^n$, by considering $a(2) \in [0, 2^n - 1]$. For $a, b \in \{0,1\}^n$, we define addition $a \oplus b$ as addition of the polynomials $a(\mathbf{x}) + b(\mathbf{x}) \in \mathrm{GF}(2^n)$. Multiplication $a \otimes b$ is defined with respect to the irreducible polynomial $f(\mathbf{x})$ used to represent $\mathrm{GF}(2^n)$: $a(\mathbf{x}) \cdot b(\mathbf{x}) \bmod f(\mathbf{x})$.

If $\mathcal{A}$ is some set, $a \xleftarrow{\$} \mathcal{A}$ denotes the uniformly random drawing of a from $\mathcal{A}$. The size of $\mathcal{A}$ is denoted by $|\mathcal{A}|$.

Distinguishers and Advantages

Throughout this work, a distinguisher $\mathcal{D}$ is a computationally unbounded probabilistic algorithm. It is given query access to one or more oracles $\mathcal{O}$, which means that it can make a certain amount of queries to $\mathcal{O}$ adaptively. After this communication with $\mathcal{O}$, the distinguisher outputs a 0 or a 1. For two different oracles $\mathcal{O}$ and $\mathcal{P}$, we define the advantage of $\mathcal{D}$ in distinguishing both worlds by

$$\mathbf{Adv}(\mathcal{D}) = \left| \mathbf{Pr}\left[\mathcal{D}^{\mathcal{O}} = 1\right] - \mathbf{Pr}\left[\mathcal{D}^{\mathcal{P}} = 1\right] \right|. \tag{6}$$

We use the H-coefficient technique by Patarin [38] and Chen and Steinberger [9]. Consider a fixed deterministic distinguisher trying to distinguish two oracles $\mathcal{O}$ and $\mathcal{P}$, where its advantage function is denoted $\mathbf{Adv}(\mathcal{D})$ as in (6). Denote by X (resp. Y) the probability distribution of views when interacting with $\mathcal{O}$ (resp. $\mathcal{P}$). Let v be a view, i.e., a list of query-response tuples $\mathcal{D}$ may observe while interacting with $\mathcal{O}$ or $\mathcal{P}$. This view is called "attainable" if an interaction with $\mathcal{P}$ could render this view, or formally if $\mathbf{Pr}\,[Y = v] > 0$. We denote by $\mathcal{V}$ the set of attainable views.

Lemma 1 (Patarin's Technique). *Let $\mathcal{D}$ be a deterministic distinguisher. Consider a partition $\mathcal{V} = \mathcal{V}_{\mathrm{good}} \cup \mathcal{V}_{\mathrm{bad}}$ of the set of attainable views. Let $0 \leq \varepsilon \leq 1$ be such that for all $v \in \mathcal{V}_{\mathrm{good}}$,*

$$\frac{\mathbf{Pr}\,[X = v]}{\mathbf{Pr}\,[Y = v]} \geq 1 - \varepsilon. \tag{7}$$

Then, the distinguishing advantage satisfies $\mathbf{Adv}(\mathcal{D}) \leq \varepsilon + \mathbf{Pr}\,[Y \in \mathcal{V}_{\mathrm{bad}}]$.

A proof of this lemma is given in [9]. The idea of the technique is that only few views are significantly more likely to appear in $\mathcal{P}$ than in $\mathcal{O}$. In other words, the ratio (7) is close to 1 for all but a few views: the "bad" views. The definition of "bad" views is sometimes a delicate process, rendering a tradeoff between ε and $\mathbf{Pr}\,[Y \in \mathcal{V}_{\mathrm{bad}}]$. Indeed, a too loose definition of bad views results in a larger second term, while a too tight one renders a larger ε.

Blockciphers and Tweakable Blockciphers

A blockcipher $E : \mathcal{K} \times \mathcal{M} \to \mathcal{M}$ is a mapping such that for every key $k \in \mathcal{K}$, $E_k(\cdot) = E(k, \cdot)$ is a permutation on $\mathcal{M}$. We denote its inverse for fixed k by $E_k^{-1}(\cdot)$. We denote by $\mathsf{BC}(\mathcal{K}, \mathcal{M})$ the set of all such blockciphers.

A tweakable blockcipher $\widetilde{E} : \mathcal{K} \times \mathcal{T} \times \mathcal{M} \to \mathcal{M}$ is a mapping such that for every $k \in \mathcal{K}$ and every tweak $t \in \mathcal{T}$, the function $\widetilde{E}_k(t, \cdot) = \widetilde{E}(k, t, \cdot)$ is a permutation on $\mathcal{M}$. Like before, its inverse is denoted by $\widetilde{E}_k^{-1}(\cdot, \cdot)$. Let $\widetilde{\mathsf{P}}(\mathcal{T}, \mathcal{M})$ be the set of all functions $\widetilde{\pi} : \mathcal{T} \times \mathcal{M} \to \mathcal{M}$ such that for all $t \in \mathcal{T}$, $\widetilde{\pi}(t, \cdot)$ is a permutation on $\mathcal{M}$.

Security of tweakable blockciphers considers a distinguisher $\mathcal{D}$ that has query access to a tweakable blockcipher $\widetilde{E}_k$ for $k \xleftarrow{\$} \mathcal{K}$ or an ideal tweakable permutation $\widetilde{\pi} \xleftarrow{\$} \widetilde{\mathsf{P}}(\mathcal{T}, \mathcal{M})$, and tries to distinguish both worlds. It is typically bounded to have limited resources, such as q queries and τ time. In this work, we focus on modular designs for tweakable blockciphers, where $\widetilde{E}$ uses a blockcipher E as underlying primitive. If we denote by τ_E the time needed for one evaluation of E, the distinguisher can evaluate this underlying cipher at most $r := \tau/\tau_E$ times. We consider E to be perfectly secure and give $\mathcal{D}$ query access to E. More formally, we define the strong tweakable-PRP security of $\widetilde{E}$ based on E as

$$\mathbf{Adv}_{\widetilde{E}}^{\widetilde{\mathrm{sprp}}}(\mathcal{D}) = \left| \mathbf{Pr}\left[\mathcal{D}^{\widetilde{E}_k^{\pm}, E^{\pm}} = 1 \right] - \mathbf{Pr}\left[\mathcal{D}^{\widetilde{\pi}^{\pm}, E^{\pm}} = 1 \right] \right| ,$$

where the probabilities are taken over the random choices of $k \xleftarrow{\$} \mathcal{K}$, $E \xleftarrow{\$}$ $\mathsf{BC}(\mathcal{K}, \mathcal{M})$, and $\widetilde{\pi} \xleftarrow{\$} \widetilde{\mathsf{P}}(\mathcal{T}, \mathcal{M})$, and the random coins of $\mathcal{D}$. Distinguisher $\mathcal{D}$ is bounded to make q queries to its first (construction) oracle and r queries to its second (primitive) oracle.

Universal Hash Functions

A hash function family $H : \mathcal{K} \times \mathcal{X} \to \mathcal{Y}$ is called ε-almost 2-XOR-universal if for all distinct $x, x' \in \mathcal{X}$ and $y \in \mathcal{Y}$, $\mathbf{Pr}\left[h \xleftarrow{\$} \mathcal{K} : H_h(x) \oplus H_h(x') = y \right] \leq \varepsilon$ [25,40]. A well-known universal hash function $H : \{0,1\}^n \times \{0,1\}^n \to \{0,1\}^n$ with $\varepsilon = 2^{-n}$ is defined by multiplication in $\mathrm{GF}(2^n)$: $H_h(x) = h \otimes x$.

3 Generic Design

Here and throughout we consider $\mathcal{K} = \mathcal{T} = \mathcal{M} = \{0,1\}^n$ for some $n \geq 1$. Let $E : \{0,1\}^n \times \{0,1\}^n \to \{0,1\}^n$ be a blockcipher. A generic tweakable blockcipher $\widetilde{E}[\rho] : \{0,1\}^n \times \{0,1\}^n \times \{0,1\}^n \to \{0,1\}^n$ based on $\rho \geq 1$ calls to E can be represented by mappings $A_i : \{0,1\}^{(i+2)n} \to \{0,1\}^n$ for $i = 1, \ldots, \rho + 1$ and $B_i : \{0,1\}^{(i+1)n} \to \{0,1\}^n$ for $i = 1, \ldots, \rho$ as follows:

$$\textbf{procedure } \widetilde{E}[\rho](k, t, m)$$
$$\textbf{for } i = 1, \ldots, \rho \textbf{ do}$$
$$x_i = A_i(k, t, y_1, \ldots, y_{i-1}, m)$$
$$l_i = B_i(k, t, y_1, \ldots, y_{i-1})$$
$$y_i = E(l_i, x_i)$$
$$\textbf{return } c = A_{\rho+1}(k, t, y_1, \ldots, y_\rho, m)$$

The tweakable blockcipher $\widetilde{E}[3]$ making $\rho = 3$ blockcipher calls is depicted in Fig. 3. The design resembles ideas of the permutation based hash function construction described by Rogaway and Steinberger [43] and the blockcipher based hash function construction described by Mennink [31]. However, $\widetilde{E}[\rho]$ is required to be invertible. In other words, on input of k, t, c, $\widetilde{E}[\rho]^{-1}(k, t, c) = m$ should be computable, and we will pose a validity condition on A_i, B_i to guarantee this.

Definition 1 (informal). *The mixing functions A_i for $i = 1, \ldots, \rho + 1$ and B_i for $i = 1, \ldots, \rho$ are valid if there is exactly one function A_{i^*} that processes m, such that the first $i^* - 1$ rounds of $\widetilde{E}[\rho]$ can be computed in forward direction without knowledge of m, the last $\rho - (i^* - 1)$ rounds in inverse direction without knowledge of m, and A_{i^*} can be inverted to obtain m.*

Note that we already require that $B_1, \ldots, B_\rho$ do not get m as input. A formal definition of valid mixing functions is given in Appendix A; this definition is more technical and not strictly needed for a better understanding of the attacks and proofs in this work.

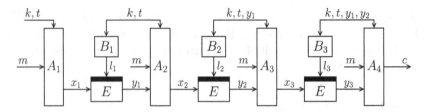

Fig. 3. Tweakable blockcipher $\widetilde{E}[3]$ making three blockcipher evaluations

Apart from the validity condition, the mixing functions could be anything, and may technically even be of the form $A_1(k, t, m) = \mathsf{AES}(k \oplus t, m)$. However, it is reasonable to assume the mixing functions to be sufficiently efficient, and we focus on constructions with polynomial mixing functions.

4   One Blockcipher Call

In Sect. 4.1 we consider $\widetilde{E}[1]$ for any triplet of valid functions A_1, B_1, A_2 that are linear mappings over $\mathrm{GF}(2^n)$, hence only consist of addition and scalar multiplication. We show that any such tweakable cipher can be attacked by an information-theoretic distinguisher in at most $2^{n/2}$ queries, and thus that provable security beyond this bound cannot be achieved. In Sect. 4.2 we allow for mixing functions that consist of a finite field multiplication, and introduce $\widetilde{F}[1]$.

4.1   Linear Mixing

We present an attack on $\widetilde{E}[1]$ for any A_1, B_1, A_2 that comply with the invertibility condition and that are linear.

Proposition 1. *Let $n \geq 1$. Let $\widetilde{E}[1] : \{0,1\}^n \times \{0,1\}^n \times \{0,1\}^n \to \{0,1\}^n$ be a tweakable blockcipher based on valid linear A_1, B_1, A_2. Then, there is a distinguisher $\mathcal{D}$ making at most $2^{n/2+1}$ construction queries and $2^{n/2+1}$ primitive queries, such that*

$$\mathbf{Adv}_{\widetilde{E}[1]}^{\widetilde{\mathrm{sprp}}}(\mathcal{D}) \geq 1 - \frac{1}{2^n} .$$

Proof. The mixing functions are linear, and can be represented by matrices

$$\begin{pmatrix} A_1 \\ B_1 \end{pmatrix} = \begin{pmatrix} a_{11} \; a_{12} \; a_{13} \\ b_{11} \; b_{12} \; 0 \end{pmatrix} \quad \text{and} \quad A_2 = \begin{pmatrix} a_{21} \; a_{22} \; a_{23} \; a_{24} \end{pmatrix} ,$$

where A_1, B_1 are evaluated on (k, t, m) and A_2 on (k, t, y_1, m). Additional conditions apply regarding the validity. Note that we have to distinguish two cases: $i^* = 1$ and $i^* = 2$, and we start with the latter.

Case $i^* = 2$. Validity requires that A_1 is independent of m (hence $a_{13} = 0$) and A_2 is an invertible mapping $m \mapsto c$ for any k, t, y_1 (hence $a_{24} \neq 0$). Distinguisher $\mathcal{D}$ selects an arbitrary t and two arbitrary distinct m, m'. Then, it queries $c \leftarrow \mathcal{O}(t, m)$ and $c' \leftarrow \mathcal{O}(t, m')$, where $\mathcal{O}$ is either $\widetilde{E}[1]$ or $\widetilde{\pi}$. If $c \oplus c' = a_{24}(m \oplus m')$, the distinguisher outputs 1, otherwise it outputs 0. Note that the distinguisher always outputs 1 if it is in the real world: because $a_{13} = 0$, both queries have identical E-calls, and thus $y_1 = y_1'$. Therefore, $c \oplus c' = A_2(0, 0, 0, m \oplus m') = a_{24}(m \oplus m')$. On the other hand, this condition is set in the ideal world with probability $1/2^n$. This gives a distinguisher in 2 construction queries with a success probability of $1 - 1/2^n$.

Case $i^* = 1$. This case is more technical. Validity requires that A_1 is an invertible mapping $m \mapsto x_1$ for any k, t (hence $a_{13} \neq 0$). A_2 is required to be independent of m (hence $a_{24} = 0$) and an invertible mapping $y_1 \mapsto c$ for any k, t (hence $a_{23} \neq 0$). At a high level, we consider a distinguisher $\mathcal{D}$ that queries its construction oracle $\mathcal{O}$ (either $\widetilde{E}[1]$ or $\widetilde{\pi}$) and/or its primitive oracle E, with the goal to find a colliding pair: a construction query (t_i, m_i, c_i) and a primitive evaluation (l_j, x_j, y_j) such that

$$\begin{pmatrix} A_1 \\ B_1 \end{pmatrix} \begin{pmatrix} k \\ t_i \\ m_i \end{pmatrix} = \begin{pmatrix} x_j \\ l_j \end{pmatrix}. \tag{8}$$

In this case, the attacker can verify if $A_2(k, t_i, y_j, m_i) \stackrel{?}{=} c_i$, and output $0/1$ accordingly. Technicalities arise as the key k is unknown and it is not straightforward to find a pair of queries satisfying (8). Additionally, for some A_1, B_1 a different technique has to be employed. We make a further distinction among four cases. The case distinction is made based on the values b_{12}, b_{11}, and a_{11}.

Subcase $b_{12} = 0$. In this case the key input to the blockcipher is $b_{11}k$. The distinguisher selects arbitrary distinct t, t' and an arbitrary m, and sets $m' = m \oplus a_{13}^{-1} a_{12}(t \oplus t')$. Then, it queries $c \leftarrow \mathcal{O}(t, m)$ and $c' \leftarrow \mathcal{O}(t', m')$. If $c \oplus c' = a_{22}(t \oplus t')$, the distinguisher outputs 1, otherwise it outputs 0. The remaining analysis is similar to previous case $i^* = 2$, using that $a_{24} = 0$ and $y_1 = y_1'$ in the real world. This gives a distinguisher in 2 construction queries with a success probability of $1 - 1/2^n$.

Subcase $b_{12} \neq 0$, $b_{11} = a_{11} = 0$. In this case k is not used as input to A_1 and B_1. The distinguisher selects an arbitrary t and arbitrary distinct m, m'. Then, it queries $c \leftarrow \mathcal{O}(t, m)$ and $c' \leftarrow \mathcal{O}(t, m')$. Additionally, it queries $y \leftarrow E(B_1(k, t, m), A_1(k, t, m))$ and $y' \leftarrow E(B_1(k, t, m'), A_1(k, t, m'))$ (which can be queried without knowledge of k as $a_{11} = b_{11} = 0$). If $c \oplus c' = a_{23}(y \oplus y')$, the distinguisher outputs 1, otherwise it outputs 0. The remaining analysis is similar to before. This gives a distinguisher in 2 construction queries and 2 primitive queries with a success probability of $1 - 1/2^n$.

Subcase $b_{12} \neq 0$, $b_{11} \neq 0$. This is the most general subcase. (8) is equivalent to finding a construction query (t_i, m_i, c_i) and a primitive evaluation (l_j, x_j, y_j) such that

$$\begin{pmatrix} 0 & a'_{12} & a_{13} \\ b_{11} & b_{12} & 0 \end{pmatrix} \begin{pmatrix} k \\ t_i \\ m_i \end{pmatrix} = \begin{pmatrix} x_j \oplus b_{11}^{-1}a_{11}l_j \\ l_j \end{pmatrix}, \tag{9}$$

where $a'_{12} = a_{12} \oplus b_{11}^{-1}a_{11}b_{12}$ and where $b_{11}, b_{12}, a_{13} \neq 0$. The distinguisher defines

for $i = 1, \ldots, 2^{n/2}$: $t_i = b_{12}^{-1}(\langle i-1 \rangle_{n/2} \| 0^{n/2})$ and $m_i = a_{13}^{-1}a'_{12}t_i$,
for $j = 1, \ldots, 2^{n/2}$: $l_j = 0^{n/2} \| \langle j-1 \rangle_{n/2}$ and $x_j = b_{11}^{-1}a_{11}l_j$.

Note that these values are selected such that the first equation of (9) holds for any (i, j): it reads $a'_{12}t_i \oplus a'_{12}t_i = 0$. Regarding the second equation, we have $b_{12}\{t_1, \ldots, t_{2^{n/2}}\} \oplus \{l_1, \ldots, l_{2^{n/2}}\} = \{0, 1\}^n$, hence this equation will hold for exactly one $(i^\star, j^\star)$.

For $i = 1, \ldots, 2^{n/2}$, it queries $c_i \leftarrow \mathcal{O}(t_i, m_i)$. For $j = 1, \ldots, 2^{n/2}$, it queries $y_j \leftarrow E(l_j, x_j)$. For every i, j, the distinguisher writes $k_{ij} = b_{11}^{-1}(l_j \oplus b_{12}t_i)$ and verifies if $A_2(k_{ij}, t_i, y_j, m_i) \stackrel{?}{=} c_i$. For any i, j such that this equation holds, the adversary chooses an arbitrary new tweak t'_i and arbitrary message m'_i, sets $x'_j = A_1(k_{ij}, t'_i, m'_i)$ and $l'_j = B_1(k_{ij}, t'_i, m'_i)$, makes construction query $c'_i \leftarrow \mathcal{O}(t'_i, m'_i)$ and primitive query $y'_j \leftarrow E(l'_j, x'_j)$, and verifies if $A_2(k_{ij}, t'_i, y'_j, m'_i) \stackrel{?}{=} c'_i$.

If there is an i, j such that both verifications succeed, the distinguisher outputs 1, otherwise it outputs 0. Recall that in the real world there is exactly one solution $k = k_{i^\star j^\star}$ and both verifications succeed for this key. In the ideal world, the distinguisher outputs 1 if there is a combination of i, j such that both verifications succeed. This happens with probability at most $2^{n/2} \cdot 2^{n/2} \cdot (1/2^n)^2 = 1/2^n$. This gives a distinguisher that makes at most $2^{n/2+1}$ construction queries and $2^{n/2+1}$ primitive queries and succeeds with probability $1 - 1/2^n$.

Subcase $b_{12} \neq 0$, $b_{11} = 0$, $a_{11} \neq 0$. This case is in fact the orthogonal of the previous one. Now, (8) translates to finding a construction query (t_i, m_i, c_i) and a primitive evaluation (l_j, x_j, y_j) such that

$$\begin{pmatrix} a_{11} & a_{12} & a_{13} \\ 0 & b_{12} & 0 \end{pmatrix} \begin{pmatrix} k \\ t_i \\ m_i \end{pmatrix} = \begin{pmatrix} x_j \\ l_j \end{pmatrix}, \tag{10}$$

where $a_{11}, b_{12}, a_{13} \neq 0$. The distinguisher defines

for $i = 1, \ldots, 2^{n/2}$: $t_i = 0^n$ and $m_i = a_{13}^{-1}(\langle i-1 \rangle_{n/2} \| 0^{n/2})$,
for $j = 1, \ldots, 2^{n/2}$: $l_j = 0^n$ and $x_j = 0^{n/2} \| \langle j-1 \rangle_{n/2}$.

Note that the second equation of (10) holds for any (i, j), but there is exactly one combination for which the first equation holds. The remainder of the attack literally follows previous case.   □

The authenticated encryption scheme McOE-X by Fleischmann et al. [15] uses the tweakable blockcipher $\widetilde{E}_{\mathsf{McOE\text{-}X}}(k, t, m) = E(k \oplus t, m)$, and Proposition 1 gives a distinguishing attack in about $2^{n/2}$ queries. In fact, the attack of Mendel et al. [30] on McOE-X uses a generalization of the attack of Proposition 1.

4.2 Polynomial Mixing

We consider the design of a tweakable blockcipher based on one blockcipher call where the mixing functions may consist of a finite field multiplication. Recall the LRW2 tweakable blockcipher of (2) that is based on a 2-XOR-universal hash function h. We make two simplifications: firstly, we instantiate it with the optimally secure 2-XOR-universal hash function $h(x) = h \otimes x$ (see Sect. 2), and secondly, we put $h = k$. This results in the following function $\text{LRW2}' : \{0,1\}^n \times \{0,1\}^n \times \{0,1\}^n \to \{0,1\}^n$:

$$\text{LRW2}'(k,t,m) = E(k, m \oplus z) \oplus z, \text{ where } z = k \otimes t.$$

This function achieves security up to at most $2^{n/2}$ queries [29]. However, it turns out that a significant security gain can be made by making the key input tweak-dependent.

In more detail, we propose the following tweakable cipher $\widetilde{F}[1] : \{0,1\}^n \times \{0,1\}^n \times \{0,1\}^n \to \{0,1\}^n$:

$$\widetilde{F}[1](k,t,m) = E(k \oplus t, m \oplus z) \oplus z, \text{ where } z = k \otimes t.$$

The function is depicted in Fig. 1. In the following theorem, we prove that it achieves $2n/3$-bit security.

Theorem 1. Let $n \geq 1$. Let $\mathcal{D}$ be a distinguisher making at most q construction queries and r primitive queries. Then,

$$\mathbf{Adv}_{\widetilde{F}[1]}^{\text{sprp}}(\mathcal{D}) \leq \frac{2\min\{q^{1/2}r + q, qr^{1/2} + r\}}{2^n}.$$

Equilibrium is achieved for $q = r$, for which $\widetilde{F}[1]$ achieves approximately $2^{2n/3}$ security. Note that the result implies something even stronger: if the online complexity q is at most $2^{n/2}$, the offline complexity r can be up to almost 2^{n-3}. The proof relies on the finite field equivalent of Szemerédi-Trotter theorem [47], which – to our knowledge – was first introduced to cryptography by Jetchev et al. [24].

Lemma 2 (Szemerédi-Trotter Theorem Over Finite Fields). Let $\mathbb{F}$ be a finite field. Let P (resp. L) be a set of points (resp. lines) in $\mathbb{F}^2$. Define $I(P,L) = \{(p, \ell) \in P \times L \mid p \in \ell\}$. Then,

$$|I(P,L)| \leq \min\{|L|^{1/2}|P| + |L|, |L||P|^{1/2} + |P|\}.$$

A proof of this lemma can be found in Tao [48] and Özen [37, Theorem 5.1.5]. (Tao [48] shows that the bound is more or less sharp: put P the set of all points in $\mathbb{F}^2$ and L the set of all lines in $\mathbb{F}^2$. Then, both $|P|$ and $|L|$ are approximately $|\mathbb{F}|^2$ and the number of point-line incidences $I(P,L)$ is about $|\mathbb{F}|^3$.) Using Lemma 2, we are ready to prove Theorem 1.

Proof (Proof of Theorem 1). Let $k \xleftarrow{\$} \{0,1\}^n$, $E \xleftarrow{\$} \mathsf{BC}(\{0,1\}^n, \{0,1\}^n)$, and $\widetilde{\pi} \xleftarrow{\$} \widetilde{\mathsf{P}}(\{0,1\}^n, \{0,1\}^n)$. We consider a computationally unbounded distinguisher $\mathcal{D}$ that has bidirectional access to two oracles: $(\widetilde{F}[1]_k, E)$ in the real world and $(\widetilde{\pi}, E)$ in the ideal world. As $\mathcal{D}$ is computationally unbounded, we can without loss of generality assume that it is deterministic and we apply Lemma 1. The distinguisher makes q queries to $\mathcal{O}_1 \in \{\widetilde{F}[1]_k, \widetilde{\pi}\}$, and these are summarized in a view $v_1 = \{(t_1, m_1, c_1), \ldots, (t_q, m_q, c_q)\}$. Similarly, it makes r queries to $\mathcal{O}_2 = E$, which are summarized in a view $v_2 = \{(l_1, x_1, y_1), \ldots, (l_r, x_r, y_r)\}$. Without loss of generality, we assume that both v_1 and v_2 do not contain duplicate elements. Additionally, we assume that both views are attainable. For v_1, this is the case if and only if for any distinct i, i' such that $t_i = t_{i'}$, we have $m_i \neq m_{i'}$ and $c_i \neq c_{i'}$. The case of v_2 is equivalent.

After $\mathcal{D}$'s interaction with $(\mathcal{O}_1, \mathcal{O}_2)$, but *before* it outputs its decision 0/1, we disclose the key k to the distinguisher. In real world, this is the key used for the game, in the ideal world k will be a fake and freshly drawn key. This is truly without loss of generality, as it only leads to an increase in the distinguishing advantage (the distinguisher can ignore this information, if it wants). The complete view is denoted $v = (v_1, v_2, k)$.

Bad Views. We next present our definition of bad views, followed by an informal explanation. We define by $\mathcal{V}_{\text{bad}}$ the set of all views v such that at least one of the following two conditions holds:

$$\exists\, (t, m, c) \in v_1, (l, x, y) \in v_2 : (k \oplus t, m \oplus k \otimes t) = (l, x), \tag{11a}$$

$$\exists\, (t, m, c) \in v_1, (l, x, y) \in v_2 : (k \oplus t, c \oplus k \otimes t) = (l, y). \tag{11b}$$

Recall the partition $\mathcal{V} = \mathcal{V}_{\text{good}} \cup \mathcal{V}_{\text{bad}}$, implying that any attainable view such that (11) does not hold, is good.

We give a high-level explanation of the definition of bad views. Note that we can implicitly "map" all tuples in v_1 to their corresponding E-evaluation: a tuple $(t, m, c) \in v_1$ corresponds to E-evaluation $(k \oplus t, m \oplus k \otimes t, c \oplus k \otimes t)$, where k is given in v. Intuitively, we want that there are no two tuples in $v_1 \cup v_2$ whose E-evaluations "collide", in the sense that they render the same input to or output of E. Two different tuples from v_2 never collide, by attainability of v. Two different tuples from v_1 also never collide. Indeed, let $(t, m, c), (t', m', c') \in v_1$ be two different tuples. These collide if

$$(k \oplus t, m \oplus k \otimes t) = (k \oplus t', m' \oplus k \otimes t') \text{ or}$$
$$(k \oplus t, c \oplus k \otimes t) = (k \oplus t', c' \oplus k \otimes t'),$$

which is the case if and only if $(t, m) = (t', m')$ or $(t, c) = (t', c')$, impossible due to attainability of v. Finally, collisions between v_1 and v_2 imply (11).

$\mathbf{Pr}[\boldsymbol{Y} \in \mathcal{V}_{\text{bad}}]$. Consider the ideal world $(\widetilde{\pi}, E)$. The key $k \xleftarrow{\$} \{0,1\}^n$ is a dummy key drawn independently of v_1, v_2. Starting with the first bad condition (11a), it is equivalent to

$$\exists\, (t, m, c) \in v_1, (l, x, y) \in v_2 : (k \oplus t, m \oplus (l \oplus t) \otimes t) = (l, x).$$

Note that the second equation is independent of k, it solely depends on the tuples $(t, m, c) \in v_1$ and $(l, x, y) \in v_2$, and we apply Lemma 2. For every $(t, m, c) \in v_1$ we ignore c and represent (t, m) as a line $\ell : y = t \otimes \mathbf{x} \oplus (m \oplus t \otimes t)$ in $\mathrm{GF}(2^n)^2$. For every $(l, x, y) \in v_2$, we ignore y and consider (l, x) as a point $(\mathbf{x}, \mathbf{y})$ in $\mathrm{GF}(2^n)^2$. The number of combinations $(t, m, c) \in v_1$ and $(l, x, y) \in v_2$ such that $m \oplus (l \oplus t) \otimes t = x$ is in fact the number of point-line incidences $I(v_2, v_1)$, which by Lemma 2 is at most $\min\{q^{1/2}r + q, qr^{1/2} + r\} =: f(q, r)$. Any of these tuples fixes one possible value $l \oplus t$. Therefore, there are at most $f(q, r)$ possible keys that could set (11a). A symmetric reasoning applies to (11b). As $k \xleftarrow{\$} \{0, 1\}^n$, we find,

$$\mathbf{Pr}\left[Y \in \mathcal{V}_{\mathrm{bad}}\right] \leq \frac{2\min\{q^{1/2}r + q, qr^{1/2} + r\}}{2^n}.$$

$\mathbf{Pr}[X = v]/\mathbf{Pr}[Y = v]$. Let $v \in \mathcal{V}_{\mathrm{good}}$. For the computation of $\mathbf{Pr}\left[X = v\right]$ and $\mathbf{Pr}\left[Y = v\right]$, it suffices to compute the *fraction of oracles* that could result in view v, for both the real and ideal world. Formally, if we denote by all_X the set of all oracles in the real world, and by $\mathrm{comp}_X(v)$ the fraction of them compatible with v, we find $\mathbf{Pr}\left[X = v\right] = |\mathrm{comp}_X(v)|/|\mathrm{all}_X|$. Similarly for the ideal world.

Note that $|\mathrm{all}_X| = 2^n \cdot (2^n!)^{2^n}$, the number of possible keys k times the number of possible ciphers E. Similarly, $|\mathrm{all}_Y| = 2^n \cdot (2^n!)^{2^n} \cdot (2^n!)^{2^n}$, where the first term now corresponds to the disclosed dummy key. The computation of the number of oracles compatible with v is slightly more involved. We group the tuples in v_1 according to the tweak value and the tuples in v_2 according to the key value. More formally, for $t \in [0, 2^n - 1]$ define $\alpha_t = |\{(t', m', c') \in v_1 \mid t' = t\}|$, and for $l \in [0, 2^n - 1]$ define $\beta_l = |\{(l', x', y') \in v_2 \mid l' = l\}|$. Additionally, denote for $l \in [0, 2^n - 1]$:

$$\gamma_l = \alpha_{k \oplus l} + \beta_l.$$

This definition of γ_l is inspired by the fact that a tuple $(t, m, c) \in v_1$ corresponds to an E-evaluation with key input $l = k \oplus t$.

Using these definitions, we are ready to compute the number of compatible oracles. First consider $\mathrm{comp}_X(v)$. As v is a good view and does not satisfy (11), every query tuple in $v_1 \cup v_2$ defines a unique E-evaluation. This leaves $\prod_{l=0}^{2^n-1}(2^n - \gamma_l)!$ blockciphers $E \in \mathsf{BC}(\{0, 1\}^n, \{0, 1\}^n)$ compliant with (v_1, v_2). Additionally, the key k is uniquely fixed as it is included in v. We find:

$$|\mathrm{comp}_X(v)| = \prod_{l=0}^{2^n-1}(2^n - \gamma_l)!.$$

Next, for the ideal world, a similar reasoning shows that there are $\prod_{t=0}^{2^n-1}(2^n - \alpha_t)!$ tweakable ciphers $\widetilde{\pi} \in \widetilde{\mathsf{P}}(\{0, 1\}^n, \{0, 1\}^n)$ compliant with v_1 and $\prod_{l=0}^{2^n-1}(2^n - \beta_l)!$ blockciphers $E \in \mathsf{BC}(\{0, 1\}^n, \{0, 1\}^n)$ compliant with v_2. We find:

$$|\text{comp}_Y(v)| = \prod_{t=0}^{2^n-1}(2^n - \alpha_t)! \cdot \prod_{l=0}^{2^n-1}(2^n - \beta_l)!$$

$$= \prod_{l=0}^{2^n-1}(2^n - \alpha_{k\oplus l})! \cdot (2^n - \beta_l)! \le (2^n)!^{2^n} \cdot \prod_{l=0}^{2^n-1}(2^n - \gamma_l)!,$$

using that $(2^n - \alpha)! \cdot (2^n - \beta)! \le (2^n - \alpha - \beta)! \cdot 2^n!$ for any $0 \le \alpha, \beta \le 2^n$. Assembling all bounds yields

$$\frac{\mathbf{Pr}\,[X = v]}{\mathbf{Pr}\,[Y = v]} = \frac{|\text{all}_Y| \cdot |\text{comp}_X(v)|}{|\text{all}_X| \cdot |\text{comp}_Y(v)|} \ge \frac{2^n \cdot (2^n!)^{2^n} \cdot (2^n!)^{2^n} \cdot \prod_{l=0}^{2^n-1}(2^n - \gamma_l)!}{2^n \cdot (2^n!)^{2^n} \cdot (2^n)!^{2^n} \cdot \prod_{l=0}^{2^n-1}(2^n - \gamma_l)!} = 1.$$

Lemma 1 thus carries over for $\varepsilon = 0$. □

5 Two Blockcipher Calls

We suggest an alternative to $\widetilde{F}[1]$ based on two blockcipher calls and linear mixing functions A_1, B_1, A_2, B_2, A_3. In more detail, we propose the following tweakable cipher $\widetilde{F}[2] : \{0,1\}^n \times \{0,1\}^n \times \{0,1\}^n \to \{0,1\}^n$:

$$\widetilde{F}[2](k, t, m) = E(k \oplus t, m \oplus z) \oplus z, \text{ where } z = E(k, t).$$

The function is depicted in Fig. 2. $\widetilde{F}[2]$ differs from $\widetilde{F}[1]$ in that the tweak processing $z = k \otimes t$ is replaced by $E(k, t)$. We remark that it is fair to make such transition, as multiplication and AES are comparably expensive on the latest Intel processors. In the following theorem, we prove that $\widetilde{F}[2]$ achieves optimal security.

Theorem 2. *Let $n \ge 1$. Let $\mathcal{D}$ be a distinguisher making at most q construction queries and r primitive queries. Then,*

$$\mathbf{Adv}_{\widetilde{F}[2]}^{\widetilde{\text{sprp}}}(\mathcal{D}) \le \frac{r}{2^n} + \frac{2qr}{(2^n - q)(2^n - r)}.$$

The bound guarantees security of $\widetilde{F}[2]$ up to almost 2^n queries to both the construction and the primitive. In more detail, the bound is at most $1/2$ as long as $q, r \le 2^{n-2}$.

Proof. The proof is in the lines of the one of Theorem 1, but differences arise due to the evaluations of E involved in the transformation of $z = E(k, t)$.

Let $k \xleftarrow{\$} \{0,1\}^n$, $E \xleftarrow{\$} \text{BC}(\{0,1\}^n, \{0,1\}^n)$, and $\widetilde{\pi} \xleftarrow{\$} \widetilde{\mathsf{P}}(\{0,1\}^n, \{0,1\}^n)$. As before, we consider a computationally unbounded, deterministic, distinguisher $\mathcal{D}$ that has bidirectional access to $(\widetilde{F}[2]_k, E)$ in the real world and $(\widetilde{\pi}, E)$ in the ideal world. The distinguisher makes q queries to $\mathcal{O}_1 \in \{\widetilde{F}[2]_k, \widetilde{\pi}\}$, and these are summarized in a view $v_1 = \{(t_1, m_1, c_1), \ldots, (t_q, m_q, c_q)\}$. Similarly, it makes r queries to $\mathcal{O}_2 = E$, which are summarized in $v_2 = \{(l_1, x_1, y_1), \ldots, (l_r, x_r, y_r)\}$.

Again, we assume that both v_1 and v_2 are attainable when interacting with the ideal world and do not contain duplicate elements.

After the $\mathcal{D}$'s interaction with $(\mathcal{O}_1, \mathcal{O}_2)$, but before it outputs its decision $0/1$, we will again disclose the key k (fake k in the ideal world). We *additionally* disclose to the distinguisher all values $z_i = E(k, t_i)$ for $i = 1, \ldots, q$. These will be disclosed in the form of a view $v_z = \{(k, t_1, z_1), \ldots, (k, t_{q'}, z_{q'})\}$, where q' denotes the number of *distinct* tweak values in v_1 (note that, indeed, the same tweak may appear in different tuples of v_1). Again, these disclosures are without loss of generality, as they only lead to an increase in the distinguishing advantage. The complete view is now denoted $v = (v_1, v_2, v_z, k)$.

Bad Views. We define by $\mathcal{V}_{bad}$ the set of all views v such that at least one of the following three conditions holds:

$$\exists\, (l, x, y) \in v_2 : k = l, \tag{12a}$$

$$\exists\, (t, m, c) \in v_1, (l, x, y) \in v_2, (k, t, z) \in v_z : (k \oplus t, m \oplus z) = (l, x), \tag{12b}$$

$$\exists\, (t, m, c) \in v_1, (l, x, y) \in v_2, (k, t, z) \in v_z : (k \oplus t, c \oplus z) = (l, y). \tag{12c}$$

Recall the partition $\mathcal{V} = \mathcal{V}_{good} \cup \mathcal{V}_{bad}$, implying that any attainable view such that (12) does not hold, is good. The bad conditions (12b-12c) match (11a-11b), with the difference that $z = E(k, t)$ is involved. The bad condition (12a) is new and is used to rule out the event that any of the evaluations in v_z already "appears" in v_2 (the condition is slightly stronger, assuring that v_2 does not contain any query for key k).

$\mathbf{Pr}[Y \in \mathcal{V}_{bad}.$ Consider the ideal world $(\widetilde{\pi}, E)$. The key $k \xleftarrow{\$} \{0,1\}^n$ is a dummy key drawn independently of v_1, v_2. Basic probability theory:

$$\mathbf{Pr}\,[(12)] \leq \mathbf{Pr}\,[(12a)] + \mathbf{Pr}\,[(12b) \vee (12c) \mid \neg(12a)]\,.$$

Condition (12a) holds with probability at most $r/2^n$, as there are at most r possible values l, and the key is randomly drawn from $\{0,1\}^n$. Assume (12a) is not set, hence v_2 does not contain any tuple $(k, \cdot, \cdot)$. This particularly means that all values $z_1, \ldots, z_{q'}$ are drawn independently of v_1, v_2. Regarding condition (12b), we have q tuples in v_1 and r tuples v_2. Any combination fixes one possible $(l \oplus t, x \oplus m)$ and also fixes exactly one tuple in v_z. Therefore, there are at most qr possible drawings of (k, z) that could set (12b). A symmetric reasoning applies to (12c). As k is uniformly drawn from a set of size at least $2^n - r$ (condition $\neg$(12a) rules out at most r values), and the corresponding z is drawn from a set of size at least $2^n - q$ (there are at most q values z, all different as E is a blockcipher), we find

$$\mathbf{Pr}\,[(12b) \vee (12c) \mid \neg(12a)] \leq \frac{2qr}{(2^n - q)(2^n - r)}\,.$$

Combining the bounds results in $\mathbf{Pr}\,[Y \in \mathcal{V}_{bad}] \leq \dfrac{r}{2^n} + \dfrac{2qr}{(2^n - q)(2^n - r)}$.

$\Pr[X = v]/\Pr[Y = v]$. The analysis of Theorem 1 carries over verbatim with the difference that we merge $v_2 \cup v_z$. Note that, by our definition of good views, these two sets do not overlap or conflict.   □

The scheme $\widetilde{F}[2]$ is equally expensive as the tweakable blockcipher by Minematsu [33], which also makes two blockcipher calls, one with a tweak-dependent key. On the other hand, it achieves a significantly higher level of security: 2^n versus $2^{\max\{n/2, n-|t|\}}$, where $|t|$ denotes the size of the tweak.

6   Conclusions

We considered the generic design of n-bit tweakable blockciphers *only* based on calls to a classical blockcipher. $\widetilde{F}[1]$ and $\widetilde{F}[2]$ show that good beyond birthday bound security can be achieved quite elegantly. More detailed, the latter construction makes only two blockcipher calls and achieves optimal security.

As suggested in the original formalization of tweakable blockciphers by Liskov et al. [29], tweak renewal should be cheaper than key renewal. To a certain degree, this is a reasonable condition, but once generic constructions such as LRW2[ρ] require more and more primitive calls, it is of theoretical and practical interest to search for alternatives that release this side condition (see also Jean et al. [23]). In fact, $\widetilde{F}[1]$ and $\widetilde{F}[2]$ improve over the state of the art beyond birthday bound solutions, in the key size *and* in the efficiency as long as key renewal is reasonably cheap.

A direction for future research would be to investigate if improved bounds can be derived for $\widetilde{F}[1]$ or any other one-call scheme. Additionally, we note that our schemes are analyzed in the single-key model, and it may be of interest to investigate them under the related-key model where the adversary may influence the key input to the tweakable blockcipher. Finally, it is of interest to derive two-call schemes where the tweak transforms the key input to the underlying blockcipher in a more randomized way (in a similar fashion as Min of (5)).

Acknowledgments. This work was supported in part by the Research Council KU Leuven: GOA TENSE (GOA/11/007). Bart Mennink is a Postdoctoral Fellow of the Research Foundation – Flanders (FWO). The author would like to thank Atul Luykx and the anonymous reviewers of FSE 2015 for their comments and suggestions.

A   Valid Mixing Functions

We propose a formal definition of valid mixing functions, following upon Definition 1.

Definition 2. *Write $x_{\rho+1} := c$. The mixing functions A_i for $i = 1, \ldots, \rho + 1$ and B_i for $i = 1, \ldots, \rho$ are valid if there exists an index $i^* \in \{1, \ldots, \rho + 1\}$ such that*

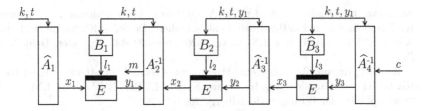

Fig. 4. Inverse of tweakable blockcipher $\widetilde{E}[3]$, where $i^* = 2$

(a) $\forall_{i=1,\ldots,i^*-1}$ there exists a function $\widehat{A}_i$ such that for all $k, t, y_1, \ldots, y_{i-1}, m$:

$$A_i(k, t, y_1, \ldots, y_{i-1}, m) = \widehat{A}_i(k, t, y_1, \ldots, y_{i-1});$$

(b) A_{i^*} is invertible in $m \mapsto x_{i^*}$ for all $k, t, y_1, \ldots, y_{i^*-1};$

(c) $\forall_{i=i^*+1,\ldots,\rho+1}$ there exists a function $\widehat{A}_i$ such that for all $k, t, y_1, \ldots, y_{i-1}, m$:

$$A_i(k, t, y_1, \ldots, y_{i-1}, m) = \widehat{A}_i(k, t, y_1, \ldots, y_{i^*-1}, y_{i-1}),$$

where $\widehat{A}_i$ is furthermore invertible in $y_{i-1} \mapsto x_i$ for all $k, t, y_1, \ldots, y_{i^*-1};$

(d) $\forall_{i=i^*+1,\ldots,\rho}$ there exists a function $\widehat{B}_i$ such that for all $k, t, y_1, \ldots, y_{i-1}$:

$$B_i(k, t, y_1, \ldots, y_{i-1}) = \widehat{B}_i(k, t, y_1, \ldots, y_{i^*-1}).$$

It is straightforward to verify that $\widetilde{E}[\rho]$ is invertible if A_i, B_i are valid mixing functions. Formally, the inverse $\widetilde{E}[\rho]^{-1}$ can be described as follows (for $\rho = 3$ and $i^* = 2$, the inverse $\widetilde{E}[3]^{-1}$ is depicted in Fig. 4):

> **procedure** $\widetilde{E}[\rho]^{-1}(k, t, c)$
> **for** $i = 1, \ldots, i^* - 1$ **do**
> $\quad x_i = \widehat{A}_i(k, t, y_1, \ldots, y_{i-1})$
> $\quad l_i = B_i(k, t, y_1, \ldots, y_{i-1})$
> $\quad y_i = E(l_i, x_i)$
> **for** $i = \rho, \ldots, i^*$ **do**
> $\quad y_i = \widehat{A}_{i+1}^{-1}(k, t, y_1, \ldots, y_{i^*-1}, x_{i+1})$
> $\quad l_i = \widehat{B}_i(k, t, y_1, \ldots, y_{i^*-1})$
> $\quad x_i = E^{-1}(l_i, y_i)$
> **return** $m = A_{i^*}^{-1}(k, t, y_1, \ldots, y_{i^*-1}, x_{i^*})$

References

1. Aiello, W., Bellare, M., Di Crescenzo, G., Venkatesan, R.: Security amplification by composition: the case of doubly-iterated, ideal ciphers. In: Krawczyk, H. (ed.) CRYPTO 1998. LNCS, vol. 1462, pp. 390–407. Springer, Heidelberg (1998)

2. Andreeva, E., Bogdanov, A., Luykx, A., Mennink, B., Tischhauser, E., Yasuda, K.: Parallelizable and authenticated online ciphers. In: Sako, K., Sarkar, P. (eds.) ASIACRYPT 2013, Part I. LNCS, vol. 8269, pp. 424–443. Springer, Heidelberg (2013)

3. Bellare, M., Kohno, T.: A theoretical treatment of related-key attacks: RKA-PRPs, RKA-PRFs, and applications. In: Biham, E. (ed.) EUROCRYPT 2003. LNCS, vol. 2656, pp. 491–506. Springer, Heidelberg (2003)

4. Bellare, M., Rogaway, P.: The security of triple encryption and a framework for code-based game-playing proofs. In: Vaudenay, S. (ed.) EUROCRYPT 2006. LNCS, vol. 4004, pp. 409–426. Springer, Heidelberg (2006)

5. Biryukov, A., Khovratovich, D.: Related-key cryptanalysis of the full AES-192 and AES-256. In: Matsui, M. (ed.) ASIACRYPT 2009. LNCS, vol. 5912, pp. 1–18. Springer, Heidelberg (2009)

6. Biryukov, A., Khovratovich, D., Nikolić, I.: Distinguisher and related-key attack on the full AES-256. In: Halevi, S. (ed.) CRYPTO 2009. LNCS, vol. 5677, pp. 231–249. Springer, Heidelberg (2009)

7. Chakraborty, D., Sarkar, P.: A general construction of tweakable block ciphers and different modes of operations. In: Lipmaa, H., Yung, M., Lin, D. (eds.) Inscrypt 2006. LNCS, vol. 4318, pp. 88–102. Springer, Heidelberg (2006)

8. Chakraborty, D., Sarkar, P.: HCH: a new tweakable enciphering scheme using the hash-counter-hash approach. IEEE Trans. Inf. Theory **54**(4), 1683–1699 (2008)

9. Chen, S., Steinberger, J.: Tight security bounds for key-alternating ciphers. In: Nguyen, P.Q., Oswald, E. (eds.) EUROCRYPT 2014. LNCS, vol. 8441, pp. 327–350. Springer, Heidelberg (2014)

10. Crowley, P.: Mercy: a fast large block cipher for disk sector encryption. In: Schneier, B. (ed.) FSE 2000. LNCS, vol. 1978, pp. 49–63. Springer, Heidelberg (2001)

11. Daemen, J., Rijmen, V.: On the related-key attacks against AES. Proc. Rom. Acad. Ser. A **13**(4), 395–400 (2012)

12. Dai, Y., Lee, J., Mennink, B., Steinberger, J.: The security of multiple encryption in the ideal cipher model. In: Garay, J.A., Gennaro, R. (eds.) CRYPTO 2014, Part I. LNCS, vol. 8616, pp. 20–38. Springer, Heidelberg (2014)

13. Dworkin, M.: NIST SP 800-38E: recommendation for block cipher modes of operation: the XTS-AES mode for confidentiality on storage devices (2010)

14. Ferguson, N., Lucks, S., Schneier, B., Whiting, D., Bellare, M., Kohno, T., Callas, J., Walker, J.: The Skein Hash Function Family (2010). Submission to NIST's SHA-3 competition

15. Fleischmann, E., Forler, C., Lucks, S.: McOE: a family of almost foolproof on-line authenticated encryption schemes. In: Canteaut, A. (ed.) FSE 2012. LNCS, vol. 7549, pp. 196–215. Springer, Heidelberg (2012)

16. Gaži, P.: Plain versus randomized cascading-based key-length extension for block ciphers. In: Canetti, R., Garay, J.A. (eds.) CRYPTO 2013, Part I. LNCS, vol. 8042, pp. 551–570. Springer, Heidelberg (2013)

17. Gaži, P., Maurer, U.: Cascade encryption revisited. In: Matsui, M. (ed.) ASIACRYPT 2009. LNCS, vol. 5912, pp. 37–51. Springer, Heidelberg (2009)

18. Goldenberg, D., Hohenberger, S., Liskov, M., Schwartz, E.C., Seyalioglu, H.: On tweaking luby-rackoff blockciphers. In: Kurosawa, K. (ed.) ASIACRYPT 2007. LNCS, vol. 4833, pp. 342–356. Springer, Heidelberg (2007)

19. Gueron, S.: AES-GCM software performance on the current high end CPUs as a performance baseline for CAESAR competition. In: DIAC 2013 (2013)

20. Halevi, S.: EME*: extending EME to handle arbitrary-length messages with associated data. In: Canteaut, A., Viswanathan, K. (eds.) INDOCRYPT 2004. LNCS, vol. 3348, pp. 315–327. Springer, Heidelberg (2004)
21. Halevi, S., Rogaway, P.: A tweakable enciphering mode. In: Boneh, D. (ed.) CRYPTO 2003. LNCS, vol. 2729, pp. 482–499. Springer, Heidelberg (2003)
22. Halevi, S., Rogaway, P.: A parallelizable enciphering mode. In: Okamoto, T. (ed.) CT-RSA 2004. LNCS, vol. 2964, pp. 292–304. Springer, Heidelberg (2004)
23. Jean, J., Nikolić, I., Peyrin, T.: Tweaks and keys for block ciphers: the TWEAKEY framework. In: Sarkar, P., Iwata, T. (eds.) ASIACRYPT 2014, Part II. LNCS, vol. 8874, pp. 274–288. Springer, Heidelberg (2014)
24. Jetchev, D., Özen, O., Stam, M.: Collisions are not incidental: a compression function exploiting discrete geometry. In: Cramer, R. (ed.) TCC 2012. LNCS, vol. 7194, pp. 303–320. Springer, Heidelberg (2012)
25. Krawczyk, H.: LFSR-based hashing and authentication. In: Desmedt, Y.G. (ed.) CRYPTO 1994. LNCS, vol. 839, pp. 129–139. Springer, Heidelberg (1994)
26. Lampe, R., Seurin, Y.: Tweakable blockciphers with asymptotically optimal security. In: Moriai, S. (ed.) FSE 2013. LNCS, vol. 8424, pp. 133–152. Springer, Heidelberg (2014)
27. Landecker, W., Shrimpton, T., Terashima, R.S.: Tweakable blockciphers with beyond birthday-bound security. In: Safavi-Naini, R., Canetti, R. (eds.) CRYPTO 2012. LNCS, vol. 7417, pp. 14–30. Springer, Heidelberg (2012)
28. Lee, J.: Towards key-length extension with optimal security: cascade encryption and Xor-cascade encryption. In: Johansson, T., Nguyen, P.Q. (eds.) EUROCRYPT 2013. LNCS, vol. 7881, pp. 405–425. Springer, Heidelberg (2013)
29. Liskov, M., Rivest, R.L., Wagner, D.: Tweakable block ciphers. In: Yung, M. (ed.) CRYPTO 2002. LNCS, vol. 2442, pp. 31–46. Springer, Heidelberg (2002)
30. Mendel, F., Mennink, B., Rijmen, V., Tischhauser, E.: A simple key-recovery attack on McOE-X. In: Pieprzyk, J., Sadeghi, A.-R., Manulis, M. (eds.) CANS 2012. LNCS, vol. 7712, pp. 23–31. Springer, Heidelberg (2012)
31. Mennink, B.: Optimal collision security in double block length hashing with single length key. In: Wang, X., Sako, K. (eds.) ASIACRYPT 2012. LNCS, vol. 7658, pp. 526–543. Springer, Heidelberg (2012)
32. Minematsu, K.: Improved security analysis of XEX and LRW modes. In: Biham, E., Youssef, A.M. (eds.) SAC 2006. LNCS, vol. 4356, pp. 96–113. Springer, Heidelberg (2007)
33. Minematsu, K.: Beyond-birthday-bound security based on tweakable block cipher. In: Dunkelman, O. (ed.) FSE 2009. LNCS, vol. 5665, pp. 308–326. Springer, Heidelberg (2009)
34. Minematsu, K., Matsushima, T.: Tweakable enciphering schemes from hash-sum-expansion. In: Srinathan, K., Rangan, C.P., Yung, M. (eds.) INDOCRYPT 2007. LNCS, vol. 4859, pp. 252–267. Springer, Heidelberg (2007)
35. Mitsuda, A., Iwata, T.: Tweakable pseudorandom permutation from generalized feistel structure. In: Baek, J., Bao, F., Chen, K., Lai, X. (eds.) ProvSec 2008. LNCS, vol. 5324, pp. 22–37. Springer, Heidelberg (2008)
36. Mouha, N., Mennink, B., Van Herrewege, A., Watanabe, D., Preneel, B., Verbauwhede, I.: Chaskey: an efficient MAC algorithm for 32-bit microcontrollers. In: Joux, A., Youssef, A. (eds.) SAC 2014. LNCS, vol. 8781, pp. 306–323. Springer, Heidelberg (2014)
37. Özen, O.: Design and analysis of multi-block-length hash functions. Ph.D. thesis, École Polytechnique Fédérale de Lausanne, Lausanne (2012)

38. Patarin, J.: A proof of security in $O(2^n)$ for the Xor of two random permutations. In: Safavi-Naini, R. (ed.) ICITS 2008. LNCS, vol. 5155, pp. 232–248. Springer, Heidelberg (2008)

39. Procter, G.: A note on the CLRW2 tweakable block cipher construction. Cryptology ePrint Archive, Report 2014/111 (2014)

40. Rogaway, P.: Bucket hashing and its application to fast message authentication. In: Coppersmith, D. (ed.) CRYPTO 1995. LNCS, vol. 963, pp. 29–42. Springer, Heidelberg (1995)

41. Rogaway, P.: Efficient instantiations of tweakable blockciphers and refinements to modes OCB and PMAC. In: Lee, P.J. (ed.) ASIACRYPT 2004. LNCS, vol. 3329, pp. 16–31. Springer, Heidelberg (2004)

42. Rogaway, P., Bellare, M., Black, J., Krovetz, T.: OCB: a block-cipher mode of operation for efficient authenticated encryption. In: ACM Conference on Computer and Communications Security, pp. 196–205. New York, ACM (2001)

43. Rogaway, P., Steinberger, J.P.: Security/efficiency tradeoffs for permutation-based hashing. In: Smart, N.P. (ed.) EUROCRYPT 2008. LNCS, vol. 4965, pp. 220–236. Springer, Heidelberg (2008)

44. Rogaway, P., Zhang, H.: Online ciphers from tweakable blockciphers. In: Kiayias, A. (ed.) CT-RSA 2011. LNCS, vol. 6558, pp. 237–249. Springer, Heidelberg (2011)

45. Sarkar, P.: Efficient tweakable enciphering schemes from (block-wise) universal hash functions. IEEE Trans. Inf. Theory **55**(10), 4749–4760 (2009)

46. Schroeppel, R.: The Hasty Pudding Cipher (1998). Submission to NIST's AES competition

47. Szemerédi, E., Trotter Jr., W.T.: Extremal problems in discrete geometry. Combinatorica **3**(3-4), 381–392 (1983)

48. Tao, T.: The Szemerédi-Trotter theorem and the cell decomposition (2009). http://terrytao.wordpress.com/2009/06/12/the-szemeredi-trotter-theorem-and-the-cell-decomposition

49. Wang, P., Feng, D., Wu, W.: HCTR: a variable-input-length enciphering mode. In: Feng, D., Lin, D., Yung, M. (eds.) CISC 2005. LNCS, vol. 3822, pp. 175–188. Springer, Heidelberg (2005)

Lightweight

On Lightweight Stream Ciphers with Shorter Internal States

Frederik Armknecht[(✉)] and Vasily Mikhalev

University of Mannheim, Mannheim, Germany
armknecht@uni-mannheim.de

Abstract. To be resistant against certain time-memory-data-tradeoff (TMDTO) attacks, a common rule of thumb says that the internal state size of a stream cipher should be at least twice the security parameter. As memory gates are usually the most area and power consuming components, this implies a sever limitation with respect to possible lightweight implementations.

In this work, we revisit this rule. We argue that a simple shift in the established design paradigm, namely to involve the fixed secret key not only in the initialization process but in the keystream generation phase as well, enables stream ciphers with smaller area size for two reasons. First, it improves the resistance against the mentioned TMDTO attacks which allows to choose smaller state sizes. Second, one can make use of the fact that storing a *fixed* value (here: the key) requires less area size than realizing a register of the same length. We demonstrate the feasibility of this approach by describing and implementing a concrete stream cipher Sprout which uses significantly less area than comparable existing lightweight stream ciphers.

Keywords: Stream ciphers · Lightweight cryptography · Time-memory-data-tradeoff attacks

1 Introduction

There is a strong and growing need for cryptographic primitives that can be implemented on the devices which have very limited resources such as the area size on the chip, memory, and power consumption. During the last years several lightweight block ciphers, e.g., see [14,15], and stream ciphers [1,6,16,24–26] have been proposed. Stream ciphers usually allow for a higher throughput but require a larger area size compared to block ciphers. The latter is mainly caused by time-memory-data trade-off (TMDTO) attacks which aim to recover the internal state of the stream cipher [5,12,22]. The attack effort is in $O(2^{\sigma/2})$, where σ denotes the size of the internal state of a stream cipher. This results into a rule of thump that for achieving κ-bit security level, the size of internal state should be at least $\sigma = 2 \cdot \kappa$. It means that in order to implement such a cipher at least $2 \cdot \kappa$ memory gates are required which is usually the most area and power-consuming resource.

© International Association for Cryptologic Research 2015
G. Leander (Ed.): FSE 2015, LNCS 9054, pp. 451–470, 2015.
DOI: 10.1007/978-3-662-48116-5_22

Our Contribution. In this work, we investigate an extension in the common design for stream ciphers which allows to realize secure lightweight stream cipher with an area size beyond the trade-off attack bound mentioned above. The core idea is to split the set of internal states into 2^κ equivalence classes such that a TMDTO attack has to consider each of these classes at least once. To achieve this goal, we suggest to involve the key into the update process of the internal state.

Theoretically, the overall approach is still to have a sufficiently large internal state which determines the keystream bits. The main difference though is that part of this state is the secret key itself and not only a state that has been derived from this key. If one considers the case that the key is fixed for the device, one can make use of the fact that storing a fixed key is significantly less area consuming than deploying a register of the same length. In fact, a similar idea has been used in the design of KATAN/KTANTAN [15]. Moreover, the approach may allow for designs where the overall state size is smaller than 2κ.

We demonstrate the feasability of this approach by describing and implementing a concrete stream cipher named Sprout. It builds upon the Grain 128a [1] cipher but uses shorter registers and aims for 80 bit security. We argue that Sprout seems to inherit the strengths of Grain 128a. However, our implementation confirms that Sprout uses significantly less area size than the eStream finalisits of the hardware portfolio and also compares favorably with many lightweight block ciphers (see Table 1 for an overview).

Outline. In Sect. 2, we describe the used model for stream ciphers and recall time-memory-data trade-off attacks. In Sect. 3, we explain our general design

Table 1. Area size of the eStream finalists, lightweight block ciphers and Sprout

Cipher	Area size (GE)	Throughput (Kb/s)*	Logic process	Source
Block ciphers				
PRESENT 80 [14]	1570	200	0.18 μm	[14]
PRESENT 80 [14]	1000	11.4	0.35 μm	[34]
KATAN32 [15]	802	12.5	0.13 μm	[15]
KATAN48 [15]	927	18.8	0.13 μm	[15]
KATAN64 [15]	1054	25.1	0.13 μm	[15]
KTANTAN32 [15]	462	12.5	0.13 μm	[15]
KTANTAN48 [15]	588	18.8	0.13 μm	[15]
KTANTAN64 [15]	688	25.1	0.13 μm	[15]
Stream ciphers				
Mickey [7]	3188	100	0.13 μm	[23]
Trivium [16]	2580	100	0.13 μm	[23]
Grain 80 [26]	1294	100	0.13 μm	[23]
Grain 80 [26]	1162	100	0.18 μm	This work
Sprout	813	100	0.18 μm	This work

*- The throughput is given for the clock frequency of 100 KHz

approach for strengthening stream ciphers against TMDTO attacks. In Sect. 4, we propose a concrete construction following our design approach. Section 5 addresses the security of the proposal. Section 6 concludes the paper.

2 Preliminaries

2.1 Time-Memory-Data-Trade-Off Attacks

Cryptanalysis often boils down to the following question. Given a function F : $\mathcal{N} \rightarrow \mathcal{N}$ and a value y within the image of F, find a preimage of y, i.e., determine a value $x \in \mathcal{N}$ such that $F(x) = y$. To accomplish this goal, two extreme cases are considerable. One approach would be to use brute force search, i.e., randomly pick values $x \in \mathcal{N}$ until $F(x) = y$ does hold. This process would be repeated whenever the attacker aims to invert F. The other extreme approach would be to precompute all possible values beforehand and store them in a large table, i.e., to trade recurring computation effort by memory. This would result into the situation that every subsequent attack is essentially a simple look-up.

In 1980 Hellman [27] suggested a time-memory-trade-off (TMTO) attack which is probabilistic and falls somewhere in between a brute force attack and a precomputation attack. This initiated a long line of research on different trade-off attacks. A typical trade-off attack consists of two phases: the first is the precomputation phase, often called the offline phase, while the second is referred to as the real-time, or on-line phase. In the offline phase, the attacker precomputes a large table (or sets of tables) using the function F he is trying to invert, while in the online phase the attacker captures a function output and checks if this value is located in her tables. If this attack is successful the attacker can learn the value x for which $y = F(x)$. Usually, this type of attacks is evaluated by looking at the following costs:

- $|\mathcal{N}|$ - the size of the search space $\mathcal{N}$.
- T_P - the time effort of the precomputation phase.
- T - the time effort of the online phase.
- M - memory cost of the attack.
- D - number of usable data samples, i.e., outputs of F, during the online phase.

Trade-off attacks usually differ in the relation between these values (often expressed by a trade-off curve) and conditions that need to be met. A further distinctive feature is the concrete attack scenario. Here we are interested into two specific scenarios that we term scenario A and B, respectively, and that we explain below.

In scenario A, an attacker is given *one* image $y \in \mathcal{N}$ and tries to find a preimage under F, that is a value $x \in \mathcal{N}$ such that $F(x) = y$. This scenario-A-attacks represent the most general class of attacks. In Table 2, we list the effort of existing trade-off attacks in scenario A. As one can see, all attacks have in scenario A a precomputation effort which is equivalent to searching the complete search space $\mathcal{N}$. In short, the reason is that a trade-off attack can only be successful if the given image y has been considered during the precomputation phase.

Table 2. Overview of trade-off attacks for scenario A

Work	Trade-off curve	Restrictions	Precomputation time
Hellman [27]	$\|\mathcal{N}\|^2 = TM^2$	$1 \leq T \leq \|\mathcal{N}\|$	$T_P = \|\mathcal{N}\|$
Oeschslin et al. [33]	$\|\mathcal{N}\|^2 = 2TM^2$	$1 \leq T \leq \|\mathcal{N}\|$	$T_P = \|\mathcal{N}\|$
BG [5,22]	$\|\mathcal{N}\| = M$	$T = 1$	$T_P = \|\mathcal{N}\|$
BS [12]	$\|\mathcal{N}\|^2 = TM^2$	$1 \leq T \leq \|\mathcal{N}\|$	$T_P = \|\mathcal{N}\|$
BSW [13]	$\|\mathcal{N}\|^2 = TM^2$	$1 \leq T \leq \|\mathcal{N}\|$	$T_P = \|\mathcal{N}\|$
Barkan et al. [10]	$\|\mathcal{N}\|^2 + \|\mathcal{N}\|M = 2TM^2$	$1 \leq T \leq \mathcal{N}$	$T_P = \|\mathcal{N}\|$
Dunkelman [20]	$\|\mathcal{N}\|^2 = TM^2$	$1 \leq T \leq \|\mathcal{N}\|$	$T_P = \|\mathcal{N}\|$

Table 3. Overview of trade-off attacks for scenario B

Work	Trade-off curve	Restrictions	Precomputation time
BG [5,22]	$\|\mathcal{N}\| = TM$	$1 \leq T \leq D$	$T_P = M$
BS [12]	$\|\mathcal{N}\|^2 = TM^2D^2$	$D^2 \leq T \leq \|\mathcal{N}\|$	$T_P = \|\mathcal{N}\|/D$
BSW [13]	$\|\mathcal{N}\|^2 = TM^2D^2$	$(DR)^2 \leq T$	$T_P = \|\mathcal{N}\|/D$
Barkan et al. [10]	$\|\mathcal{N}\|^2 + \|\mathcal{N}\|D^2M = 2TM^2$	$D^2 \leq T \leq \|\mathcal{N}\|$	$T_P = \|\mathcal{N}\|/D$

This can be relaxed in scenario B. Here, an attacker is given D images $y_1, \ldots, y_D$ of F and the goal is to find a preimage for any of these points, i.e., a value $x_i \in \mathcal{N}$ such that $F(x_i) = y_i$. The main difference is that for a successful attack, it isn't any longer necessary to cover the whole search space $\mathcal{N}$ during the precomputation phase. Instead it is sufficient that at least one of the outputs y_i has been considered. An overview of time-memory-data-trade-off attacks for scenario B is given in Table 3. Note that the parameter R mentioned in the BSW attack stands for the sampling resistance of a stream cipher. In a nutshell, it is connected to the number of special states that can be efficiently enumerated. For example, R can be defined as $2^{-\ell}$ where ℓ is the maximum value for which the direct enumeration of all the special states which generate ℓ zero bits is possible. As the sampling resistance strongly depends on the concrete design, we will not consider it in our general analysis of trade-off attacks.

2.2 Keystream Generators

Description. Stream ciphers are encryption schemes that are dedicatedly designed to efficiently encrypt data streams of arbitrary length. The most common approach for realizing a stream cipher is to design a *keystream generator* (KSG). In a nutshell, a KSG is a finite state machine using an internal state, an update function, and an output function. At the beginning, the internal state is initialized based on a secret key and, optionally, an initial value (IV). Given this, the KSG regularly outputs keystream bits that are computed from the current internal state and updates the internal state. The majority of existing KSGs are covered by the following definition:[1]

Definition 1 (Keystream Generator). *A keystream generator (KSG) comprises three sets, namely*

- *the key space $\mathcal{K} = \mathrm{GF}(2)^\kappa$,*
- *the IV space $\mathcal{IV} = \mathrm{GF}(2)^\nu$,*
- *the state space $\mathcal{S} = \mathrm{GF}(2)^\sigma$,*

and the following three functions

- *an initialization function $\mathsf{Init} : \mathcal{IV} \times \mathcal{K} \to \mathcal{S}$*
- *a bijective[2] update function $\mathsf{Upd} : \mathcal{S} \to \mathcal{S}$*
- *an output function $\mathsf{Out} : \mathcal{S} \to \mathrm{GF}(2)$*

A KSG operates in two phases. In the initialization phase, the KSG takes as input a secret key k and an IV iv and sets the internal state to an initial state $st_0 := \mathsf{Init}(iv, k) \in \mathcal{S}$. Afterwards, the keystream generation phase executes the following operations repeatedly (for $t \geq 0$):

1. *Output the next keystream bit $z_t = \mathsf{Out}(st_t)$*
2. *Update the internal state st_t to $st_{t+1} := \mathsf{Upd}(st_t)$*

In this work, we consider attackers who are given several (possibly many) keystream bits and who aim for computing the remaining keystream. To this end, we assume that the attacker has full control over the IV. This means that the IV is not only known by the attacker but in fact she can choose it. Obviously tradeoff attacks represent a possible threat in this context. We shortly address in the following tradeoff attacks against keystream generators before we discuss our proposed design in the next section.

Trade-Off Attacks Against Keystream Generators.

Recovering the Key. In principle, two different approaches can be considered for applying a trade-off attack, depending on what function the attacker aims to invert. The most obvious approach is to invert the whole cipher. That is one considers the process which takes as input a secret key $k \in \mathcal{K} = \mathrm{GF}(2)^\kappa$ and outputs the first κ keystream bits as a function $F_{\mathsf{KSG}} : \mathrm{GF}(2)^\kappa \to \mathrm{GF}(2)^\kappa$. The search space would be $\mathcal{N} = \mathcal{K} = \mathrm{GF}(2)^\kappa$ in this case. As already explained, trade-off attacks for scenario A would require a precomputation time which is equivalent to exhaustive search in the key space. If we say that a security level

---

[1] As far as we know the only exception is the A2U2 stream cipher [18], which appears to be insecure (see i.e. [2]).

[2] In fact, our discussions can be easily extended to the case of non-invertible update functions. However, assuming reversibility simplifies the explanations and is given for most designs anyhow.

of κ expresses the requirement that a successful attack requires at least once a time effort in $\mathcal{O}(2^\kappa)$, then such attacks do not represent a specific threat.

Observe that although an attacker may have knowledge of significantly more than κ bits, scenario B trade-off attacks are not applicable here (at least not in general). To see why, let $F_{\mathsf{KSG}}^t : \mathrm{GF}(2)^\kappa \to \mathrm{GF}(2)^\kappa$ be the function that takes as input the secret key and outputs the keystream bits for clocks $t, \ldots, t + \kappa - 1$. That is it holds that $F_{\mathsf{KSG}}^0 = F_{\mathsf{KSG}}$ from above. Then, the knowledge of $D + \kappa - 1$ keystream bits translates to knowing images of $F_{\mathsf{KSG}}^0, \ldots, F_{\mathsf{KSG}}^{D-1}$ and in fact, inverting one of these would be sufficient. However, these functions are all different. In particular, any precomputation done for one of these, e.g., F_{KSG}^i, cannot be used for inverting another one, e.g., F_{KSG}^j with $i \neq j$.

Recovering the Internal State. An alternative approach is to invert the output function Out only, that is used in the keystream generation phase. More precisely, let $F_{\mathsf{Out}} : \mathrm{GF}(2)^\sigma \to \mathrm{GF}(2)^\sigma$ be the function that takes the internal state $st_t \in \mathrm{GF}(2)^\sigma$ at some clock t as input and outputs the σ keystream bits $z_t, \ldots, z_{t+\sigma-1}$. The search space would be $\mathcal{N} = \mathcal{S}$. A scenario-A trade-off attack would again require a precomputation time equal to $|\mathcal{N}| = |\mathcal{S}|$ which implies that $\sigma \geq \kappa$ if one aims for a security level of κ.

We come now to the essential part. As each keystream segment $z_t, \ldots, z_{t+\sigma-1}$ is an output of the same function F_{Out} and as the knowledge of one internal state st_t allows to compute all succeeding keystreams bits z_r for $r \geq t$ (and as Upd is assumed to be reversible, the preceeding keystream bits as well), scenario B attacks are suitable. As can be seen from Table 3, each attack would require at least once a time effort of about $\sqrt{|\mathcal{S}|} = 2^{\sigma/2}$. This implies the already mentioned rule of selecting $\sigma \geq 2\kappa$.

3   Our Basic Approach

3.1   Motivation

In this section, we discuss a conceptually simple adaptation of how keystream generators are commonly designed (see Definition 1). The goal is to make stream ciphers more resistant against TMDTO attacks such that shorter internal states can be used. To this end, let us take another look at trade-off attacks. An attacker who is given a part of the keystream aims to find an internal state which allows to compute the remaining keystream. Let $F_{\mathsf{Out}}^{\mathrm{compl.}}$ denote the function that takes as input the initial state and outputs the complete keystream. Here, "complete" refers to the maximum number of keystream bits that are intended by the designer. If no bound is given, then we simply assume that 2^σ keystream bits are produced as this refers to the maximum possible period. From an attacker's point of view, any internal state that allows for reconstructing the keystream is equally good. This brings us to the notion of keystream-equivalent states:

Definition 2 (Keystream-equivalent States). *Consider a KSG with a function* $F_{\mathsf{Out}}^{\mathrm{compl.}}$ *that outputs the complete keystream. Two states* $st, st' \in \mathcal{S}$ *are said* *to be* keystream-equivalent *(in short $st \equiv_{kse} st'$) if there exists an integer $r \geq 0$ such that $F_{Out}^{compl.}(Upd^r(st)) = F_{Out}^{compl.}(st')$. Here,* Upd^r *means the r-times application of* Upd.

Observe that keystream-equivalence is an equivalence relation.[3] For any state $st \in \mathcal{S}$, we denote by $[st]$ its equivalence class, that is

$$[st] = \{st' \in \mathcal{S} | st \equiv_{kse} st'\} \tag{1}$$

To see why this notion is important for analyzing the effectiveness of a TMDTO attack, let us consider an arbitrary KSG with state space $\mathcal{S}$. As any state is member of exactly one equivalence class, the state space can be divided into ℓ distinct equivalence classes:

$$\mathcal{S} = \left[st^{(1)}\right] \dot{\cup} \ldots \dot{\cup} \left[st^{(\ell)}\right] \tag{2}$$

Now assume a TMDTO attacker who is given some keystream (z_t), based on an unknown initial state st_0. Recall that the strategy of a trade-off attack is not to exploit any weaknesses in the concrete design but to efficiently cover a sufficiently large fraction of the search space. In this case if none of the precomputations were done for values in $[st_0]$, the attack cannot be successful unless the online phase searches all equivalence classes that have been ignored during the precomputation phase. This leads to the following observation: a TMDTO attack on the KSG will be a union of TMDTO attacks, one for each equivalence class. That is we have ℓ TMDTO attacks with search spaces $\mathcal{N}_i = \left[st^{(i)}\right]$, $i = 1, \ldots, \ell$, respectively. As each of these attacks has a time effort of at least 1, we get a lower bound of ℓ for the attack effort. Now, if one designs a cipher such that $\ell \geq 2^\kappa$, then one has achieved the required security level against trade-off attacks. This is exactly the idea behind the design approach discussed next.

3.2   The Design Approach

We are now ready to discuss our proposed design. The basic idea is to achieve a splitting of the internal state space in sufficiently many equivalence classes. To achieve this, we divide the internal state into two parts: a variable part that may change over time and a fixed part. For practical reasons the fixed part will be realized by simply re-using the secret key (more on this later). The main difference to a KSG as given in Definition 1, the update function Upd will compute the next variable state from the current variable state *and* the fixed secret key. We call such a construction a KSG with keyed update function, to be defined below. Observe that this definition is in fact covered by definition given in [31].

Definition 3 (Keystream Generator With Keyed Update Function). *A keystream generator (KSG) with* keyed update function *comprises three sets, namely*

---

[3] This is due to the fact that for any state $st \in \mathcal{S}$, the sequence $(Upd^r(st))_{r \geq 0}$ is cyclic and that Upd is reversible by assumption.

- *the key space* $\mathcal{K} = \mathrm{GF}(2)^\kappa$,
- *the IV space* $\mathcal{IV} = \mathrm{GF}(2)^\nu$,
- *the variable state space* $\mathcal{S} = \mathrm{GF}(2)^\sigma$,

and the following three functions

- *an initialization function* $\mathsf{Init} : \mathcal{IV} \times \mathcal{K} \to \mathcal{S}$
- *an update function* $\mathsf{Upd} : \mathcal{K} \times \mathcal{S} \to \mathcal{S}$ *such that* $\mathsf{Upd}_k : \mathcal{S} \to \mathcal{S}$, $\mathsf{Upd}_k(st) :=$ $\mathsf{Upd}(k, st)$, *is bijective for any* $k \in \mathcal{K}$, *and*
- *an output function* $\mathsf{Out} : \mathcal{S} \to \mathrm{GF}(2)$.

The internal state ST *is composed of a variable part* $st \in \mathcal{S}$ *and a fixed part* $k \in \mathcal{K}$. *Initialization and keystream generation work analogously to Definition 1 with the only difference that the state update also depends on the fixed secret key.*

Let us take a look at the minimum time effort for a TMDTO attack against a KSG with keyed update function. We make in the following the assumption that any two different states $ST = (st, k)$ and $ST' = (st', k')$ with $k \neq k'$ never produce the same keystream, that is $F_{\mathsf{Out}}^{\mathrm{compl.}}(ST) \neq_{\mathrm{kse}} F_{\mathsf{Out}}^{\mathrm{compl.}}(ST')$. Hence, we have at least 2^κ different equivalence classes. As the effort grows linearly with the number of equivalence classes, we assume in favor of the attacker that we have exactly 2^κ equivalence classes. This gives a minimum time effort of 2^κ.

Observe that similar techniques are present in stream cipher modes for block ciphers like OFM or CTR. However, as far as we know it has never been discussed for directly designing stream ciphers with increased resistance against TMDTO-attacks. In this context, we think that this approach has two interesting consequences with respect to saving area size in stream cipher implementations:

1. Apparently one can achieve a security level of κ independent of length σ of the variable state. This allows to use a shorter internal state which directly translates to saving area size.[4]
2. For technical reasons, storing a fixed value (here: the key) can be realized with significantly less area size than is necessary for storing a variable value. This effect has been used for example in the construction of the block cipher KTANTAN [15]. It allows for further savings compared to KSGs with an register of length $\geq 2\kappa$.

We use these in the following section for proposing a concrete cipher named Sprout. Our implementations showed that Sprout needs significantly less area size than existing ciphers with comparable security level.

4   The Stream Cipher Sprout

Within this section, we describe and discuss a concrete keystream generator which follows the design strategy presented in the previous section. We start

---

[4] Of course, σ shouldn't be too small. Otherwise, the period of the KSG may become too short and the cipher may also become vulnerable for other attacks like guess-and-determine.

with an overview of the overall structure in Sect. 4.1, give the full specification in Sect. 4.2, explain the design rationale in Sect. 4.3, and present the implementations results in Sect. 4.4. The security of the scheme will be discussed in the next section, i.e., in Sect. 5.

4.1   Overall Structure

The design of Sprout is an adaptation of the basic design used for the Grain family of stream ciphers [1,24–26]. More precisely, we used Grain 128a as the starting point as this is the newest member of the Grain family which overcomes some weaknesses found for previous version. Each Grain cipher is composed of a linear feedback shift register (LFSR), a non-linear feedback shift register (NLFSR), and an output function. The LFSR and NLFSR states represent the internal state which at the beginning are initialized with the key and the IV. The output of the LFSR is fed into the NLFSR to ensure a minimum period with respect to the internal states while the purpose of the NLFSR is to make certain standard attacks like algebraic attacks infeasible. Moreover, several bits are taken from both FSRs as input to the output function. During the initialization phase, the outputs of the output function are fed back into the FSRs, while in the keystream generation phase, they represent the keystream bits.

For Sprout, we adopted this design. That is Sprout likewise uses an LFSR, an NLFSR, and an output function, and these components are connected in a similar way (see Fig. 1). However, several changes have been taken as well. The main differences are:

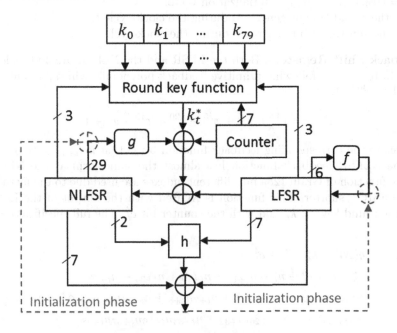

Fig. 1. The structure of Sprout.

Round Key Bits: To involve the secret key into the update function, a round key function has been added. In a nutshell, in each clock it cyclically selects the next key bit and adds it to the state of the NLFSR if the sum of certain LFSR and NLFSR bits is equal to 1. More precisely, it is added to the LFSR output which in turn goes into the NLFSR.

Counter: Like in Grain (or any other stream cipher), we use a counter to determine the number of rounds during the initialization phase. Part of the counter is re-used in Sprout for selecting the current round key bit. In addition, we use one of the counter bits also in the update process. The reason is to avoid situations where shifted keys result into shifted keystreams (and hence violating our assumption that two states with different keys are not keystream-equivalent).

Register Lengths: The sizes of the FSRs have been reduced to 40 bits each. This sums up to 80 bits which is equal to the key length.

4.2   Specifications

We give now the full specification of Sprout. We use the following notation:

- t - the clock-cycle number;
- $L_t = (l_t, l_{t+1}, \cdots, l_{t+39})$ - state of the LFSR during the clock-cycle t.
- $N_t = (n_t, n_{t+1}, \cdots, n_{t+39})$ - state of the NLFSR during the clock-cycle t.
- $C_t = (c_t^0, c_t^1, \cdots, c_t^8)$ - state of the counter during the clock-cycle t.
- $k = (k_0, k_1, \cdots, k_{79})$ - key.
- $iv = (iv_0, iv_1, \cdots, iv_{69})$ - initialization vector.
- k_t^*.- the round key bit generated during the clock-cycle t.
- z_t - the keystream bit generated during the clock-cycle t.

Feedback Shift Registers. Both the LFSR and the NLFSR are 40-bits long. The LFSR uses the following primitive feedback polynomial which guarantees a period of $2^{40} - 1$:

$$P(x) = x^{40} + x^{35} + x^{25} + x^{20} + x^{15} + x^6 + 1 \tag{3}$$

We denote the corresponding feedback function by f, that is $l_{t+40} = f(L_t)$.

The NLFSR feedback function has almost the same form as the NLFSR update function of Grain 128a but different indexes are used due to the fact that the NLFSR is shorter. This function is XORed with the output of the LFSR, with the round key bit k_t^* and with the counter bit c_t^4. The full specification is

$$
\begin{aligned}
n_{t+40} = {}& g(N_t) + k_t^* + l_t + c_t^4 \\
= {}& k_t^* + l_t + c_t^4 + n_t + n_{t+13} + n_{t+19} + n_{t+35} + n_{t+39} \\
& + n_{t+2}n_{t+25} + n_{t+3}n_{t+5} + n_{t+7}n_{t+8} + n_{t+14}n_{t+21} + n_{t+16}n_{t+18} \quad (4) \\
& + n_{t+22}n_{t+24} + n_{t+26}n_{t+32} + n_{t+33}n_{t+36}n_{t+37}n_{t+38} \\
& + n_{t+10}n_{t+11}n_{t+12} + n_{t+27}n_{t+30}n_{t+31}
\end{aligned}
$$

Counter. The 9-bit counter is composed of 2 parts. The first seven bits $(c_t^0 \cdots c_t^6)$ (with c_t^0) indicating the LSB are used to compute the index of the key bit which is selected during the current round. Hence, these bits count from 0 to 79 before being set to zero again. The remaining two bits are only used within the initialization phase to count until $4 \times 80 = 320$.

Round Key Function. The round key function is responsible for making the update function key dependent. At each clock t, the round key function computes one round key bit k_t^* as follows:

$$
\begin{aligned}
k_t^* &= k_t, \ 0 \le t \le 79; \\
k_t^* &= (k_{t \bmod 80}) \cdot (l_{t+4} + l_{t+21} + l_{t+37} + n_{t+9} + n_{t+20} + n_{t+29}), \ t \ge 80;
\end{aligned}
\tag{5}
$$

That is in the first 80 clocks, each key bit is involved exactly once in the update function. Afterwards, the round key function cyclically selects the next key bit and adds it if $l_{t+4} + l_{t+21} + l_{t+37} + n_{t+9} + n_{t+20} + n_{t+29} = 1$. Otherwise the key bit is skipped in this round.

Output Function. The output of the cipher is a nonlinear function which takes several LFSR and NLFSR bits as its input. The nonlinear part of the output function has the form $h(x) = x_0 x_1 + x_2 x_3 + x_4 x_5 + x_6 x_7 + x_0 x_4 x_8$ where $x_0, \cdots, x_8$ corresponds to the state variables: $n_{t+4}, l_{t+6}, l_{t+8}, l_{t+10}, l_{t+32}, l_{t+17}, l_{t+19}, l_{t+23}, n_{t+38}$, respectively. The keystream bit of the cipher is computed as

$$
z_t = h(x) + l_{t+30} + \sum_{j \in B} n_{t+j}
\tag{6}
$$

where $B = \{1, 6, 15, 17, 23, 28, 34\}$.

Initialization Phase. In the initialization phase the 40 NLFSR stages are loaded with the first 40 IV bits, i.e., $n_i = iv_i$ for $0 \le i \le 39$, and the first 30 LFSR stages are loaded with the remaining IV bits, i.e., $l_{i-40} = iv_i$ for $40 \le i \le 69$. To avoid the all-zero state, the last 10 bits of the LFSR are filled with constant values '0' and '1' as follows: $l_{30} = \ldots = l_{38} = 1$ and $l_{39} = 0$. Then, the cipher is clocked 320 times without producing any keystream. Instead the output function is fed back and XORed with the input, both to the LFSR and to the NFSR, i.e., $l_{t+40} = z_t + f(L)$ and $n_{t+40} = z_t + k_t^* + l_t + c_t^4 + g(N_t)$.

Keystream Generation Phase. After 320 clock-cycles the initialization phase is over and the cipher starts operating in accordance with Eqs. (3, 4, 5, 6) generating the keystream.

4.3   Design Rationale

Choice of General Design. As already mentioned, our design adopts the generic idea behind the Grain family. This has been done for several reasons. First of all, our primary goal was to show the feasibility of the approach discussed in Sect. 3. Therefore, we decided against designing a new cipher from scratch (which may have eventually turned out to be vulnerable against other attacks) but rather to build upon an existing established design. To this end, our focus was to pick a stream cipher that is already lightweight, is scalable (at least to some extent), and has undergone already some cryptanalysis.

State Size. Our goal was to show that is possible to develop a secure stream cipher that uses a register of size σ significantly below 2κ. A further goal was however to keep the process of including the key into the update procedure rather simple. While more involved mechanisms are possible in principle, this would come at the cost of an increased area size. However, using a simple key inclusion procedure could make a cipher subject to guess-and-determine attacks, i.e., attacks where the adversary guesses the internal state and tries to derive the key from the keystreams. Therefore, we decided for a conservative choice of $\sigma = \kappa$. This implies that guessing the complete register has the same effort as guessing the key. We leave it as open problem to come up with designs that use a significantly smaller register.

LFSR Update Function. The main reason for involving an LFSR in the Grain family is to ensure a minimum period. Consequently, the feedback polynomial of the LFSR used in Sprout is primitive to guarantee a maximum period of $2^{40} - 1$. A further design criteria was to choose a polynomial with not too few terms in order to increase the resistance of the cipher against correlation attacks.

NLFSR Update Function. The update function of the NLFSR $g(N)$ is XORed with the LFSR output l_t, the round key bit k_t^*, and the counter bit c_t^4. Each of these parts has different purpose and we will discuss them separately.

$g(N)$ is the nonlinear function which has the same form as in Grain 128a, where it was carefully selected in order to resist against different types of attacks [1]. As the used NLFSR is shorter than the one of Grain 128a, different indexes had to be chosen. Nonetheless, the relevant cryptographic properties remained: It is balanced, has a nonlinearity of 267403264, a resiliency of 4, and the set of the best linear approximations is of size 2^{14}. Each of the functions from this set has a bias of $63 \cdot 2^{-15}$ [1]. In fact, because of the involvement of the round key bits we suspect that not all of these properties are still required in Sprout. For example the attacks based on the linear approximations should not work anymore (see Sect. 5). Nonetheless, this function hasn't revealed any unexpected weaknesses over the time why we decided to stick to it.

The LFSR output is XORed with the NLFSR update function the same way as it is done in Grain family so that each of the NLFSR state bits is balanced.

The main goal of using the round key bit is to improve the resistance against TMDTO attacks as explained in Sect. 3.2.

As explained, we aimed for a key involvement procedure that is as simple as possible to save area size. The probably most simple one is to select the key bits cyclically what we consider here (see also the discussion below). However, this would result into the situation that two keys where one is only a shifted version of the other also produce the same keystream (but only shifted). This would clearly violate the basic requirement, namely that two states with different keys are not keystream-equivalent. To avoid this situation, the counter bit c_t^4 is included as well. By doing so, even if one key is just a shifted copy of the other, due to the different counter bits it should not result into the same keystream.

Output Function. The output function has the same form as the one used in Grain 128a. This function has nonlinearity of 61440. The best linear approximation of the nonlinear part h has a bias of 2^5, and there are 2^8 such linear approximations [1].

Round Key Function. The design criteria for the round key function were that over the time, each key bit has been involved into the update function, and that the mechanism is lightweight, i.e. does not consume a lot of area and power. A straightforward approach would be to involve all key bits simultaneously. However, this would require a prohibitively large number of logic gates. Therefore, we decided to involve the key bit by bit, that is at each clock exactly one key bit is involved. In order to make sure that the initial state of both registers depends on all of the key bits after reasonable number of clocks, at first we XOR each of the key bits with the NLFSR update function with the first 80 clocks. Only afterwards the more involved round key function is used.

To avoid situations where some key bits are not (or rarely) selected, we decided that the function goes cyclically through the key bits and always chooses the next key bit. However, to thwart possible guess-then-determine attacks, the key involvement needs to be coupled with the register states somehow (in a preferably simple way). As mentioned above the states of both registers are almost balanced. The idea is that at each clock, a number of register bits are taken and XORed. The currently selected key bit is inserted if and only if the sum of the register bits is equal to 1. In other words, the register bits do not influence which key bit is selected but decide if it is inserted. The advantage is that this requires only a counter and multiplexers. As a counter is required anyway for the initialization phase, one can further save area by simply reusing the counter (what we do). In the concrete realization, we use three bits from the LFSR and NLFSR, each. The three NLFSR bits have been selected in such a way that none of these bits is involved in any other function used in this cipher.

Initialization Phase. The initialization phase is in principle the same as for Grain 128a. For example, fixing some of the LFSR bits is done to avoid that an attacker can simply set the internal state to the all zero state by choosing an appropriate IV. The initialization phase runs 320 clock cycles, which is the same number as in Grain 128a (where 256 clock-cycles are used in the initialization phase and 64 clock-cycles are required for the authentication process). Observe that we use smaller registers though, hence probably even increasing the level of diffusion. That is the number of clock cycles used for the initialization phase is 4 times the state length. This is a stronger ratio than for Grain 80 and Grain 128 where the number of clock cycles is equivalent to the state size.

Naming. The name Sprout has been inspired by two facts. First, it builds upon the Grain cipher which already suggested to choose a plant-related name. Second, the main difference is that we "plant" during the update process key round bits into the middle of the cipher. In some sense, this can be seen as a kind of additional key-related seed that (hopefully) quickly sprouts and expands over the whole state.

4.4 Implementation Results

In order to demonstrate the feasibility of our design, we implemented Sprout and compared the area size with the eStream finalists of portfolio 2 (hardware oriented stream ciphers), being Grain 80 [26], Mickey 2.0 [6], and Trivium [16]. All of them use 80-bits keys.

For the implementation, we used the Cadence RTL Compiler[5] and the technology library UMCL18G212T3 (UMC $0.18\,\mu\text{m}$ process) for synthesis and simulation and aimed for an implementation operating on the clock-frequency of $100\,\text{KHz}$. We stress that in our implementation, we do not consider any area for storing the fixed key. The reason is twofold here. First, storing a fixed value does not require any volatile memory such as flip-flops and can be simply realized by burning it into the device using for example fuses (see [4] for more discussions). Second, other lightweight stream ciphers would, if used on restricted devices such as RFID, likewise require to store the key in non-volatile memory so that when the device is restarted the cipher has to be initialized with the original key. When implementations of stream ciphers are presented, the area required for storing the key is likewise ignored. Observe that the design of KTANTAN [15] likewise is based on the fact that storing fixed keys is less area consuming.

Our implementation of Sprout requires an area size of 813 GEs. In comparison, [23] states implementations of the eStream finalists using $0.13\,\mu\text{m}$ CMOS and the standard cell library. These require for Grain 80 an area size of 1294 GE, for Trivium 2580 GE, and for Mickey v.2 3188 GE. We note that there exist an implementation of Trivium [32] using dynamic logic which requires only 749 GEs. However the lower bound on the clock frequency of this implementation is 1 MHz, which is not achievable in restricted devices [4].

As the choice of the library impacts the area size, for the sake of a fair comparison we made our own implementation of Grain 80 (as it is the most lightweight cipher among the finalists with respect to the area size) using the same technology as has been applied for the Sprout implementation. This gave an implementation of Grain 80 that requires 1162 GE, i.e., being slightly less than the implementation stated in [23] but still being 349 GE larger compared to Sprout.

In general, realizing one register bit requires about 6 GE. Keeping in mind that Grain 80 uses registers of a total length of 160, that Trivium uses a 288 bit state, and that the internal state of Mickey v.2 is 200 bits gives a strong indication that none of these ciphers can be implemented with less than 960 GE.

As explained above, the comparisons are made under the assumption that storing fixed keys can be realized with negligible costs, following [15]. If the key

---

[5] See http://www.cadence.com/products/ld/rtl_compiler/pages/default.aspx.

is stored in registers instead, the size would increase to 1170 GE. As expected there would be no gain in such cases. But even then, we think that the discussed approach has new value as it may allow for new designs with a reduced internal state size (including the key).

5 Security Discussion

In this section we discuss the security of Sprout with respect to key recovery attacks. Due to the relatively short period, coming from the fact that we aim for short internal states, Sprout is subject to distinguishing attacks. Thus, we do not consider these any further and argue that the common use case for a lightweight cipher is not to encrypt extremely large chunks of data. Moreover, as the key is assumed to be fixed, related-key attacks are out of scope as well.

We consider an attack only to be successful if the effort is clearly less than for a brute force attack, i.e. if it is less than 2^κ. Recall that we allow an attacker to freely choose the IV.

Algebraic Attacks. Algebraic attacks against LFSR-based keystream generators were introduced in [17] and became a powerful tool in cryptanalysis of stream ciphers. The goal of such attacks is to construct systems of algebraic equations which describe the operations used in the stream cipher, and to solve these systems for the unknown state variables. The classical algebraic attacks require that the degree of such equations is constant and therefore they usually do not work against the NLFSR-based constructions, where the algebraic degree of describing equations continuously grows. This holds in particular for Sprout.

In [3] an algebraic attack was combined with guess and determine technique in the cryptanalysis of Grain family of stream ciphers. The authors claimed that for Grain 80 and Grain 128 it is possible to construct a system of algebraic equations and to solve it for approximately half of the state-bits, when the other half is guessed. As in total 160 bits are involved in the update process (the registers of total length of 80 bits and the fixed secret key of 80 bits as well), guessing half the bits would result into an effort of at least $2^{80} = 2^\kappa$.

Guess and Determine Attacks. Another potential attack could be a guess and determine attack. Here, an attacker guesses parts of the internal state and/or the key and aims to recover the remaining bits more efficiently. In the following we list some arguments why we do not see an immediate application of such attacks here.

We begin our analysis of the complexity of such attack by assuming that the whole internal state is already known to the attacker who also has access to the output bits. The newly inserted key bit is not used for the output until it propagates to the position n_{t+38}. There it will become part of the monomial $n_{t+4}n_{t+38}l_{t+32}$ of the output function. Even if the attacker knows the other values of the output function, she can only recover this key bit when n_{t+4} and l_{t+32} are both equal to 1. Hence in average only one bit out of four can be recovered in this straightforward way. Observe in addition that before this particular key bit is involved in the output function for the first time, it has been used as linear terms in the NLFSR update function when it was at the position n_{39}. Thus, the key bit influences the state of the NLFSR *before* it could be recovered (which is the case with probability $1/4$ only). Guessing the key bits that cannot be recovered would hence induce an additional effort of $O(2^{3\kappa/4}) = O(2^{60})$.

Moreover, we do not see any straightforward approach for reconstructing the whole internal state with an effort better than guessing. Observe that all but 8 bits of the NLFSR are used in either the update function or the round key function. Therefore, at least these need to be known if an attacker wants to know the next NLFSR state. Moreover, the NLFSR state depends on the LFSR output so that all LFSR bits need to be known as well on the long run. Of course, not all of these bits need to be known exactly. For example a few state bits can be computed directly from the output function (2 bits can be computed before the key bit propagated to the position n_{t+38} and some other register bits can be computed when the round key bits are equal to zero). However, the number of the state bits which can be recovered is relatively small and there are definitely more than 20 state bits which need to be guessed together with in average 60 key bits.

Linear Approximations. In [30] it is explained how to find a time-invariant biased linear relation between the LFSR bits and the keystream bits for Grain family of stream ciphers. This bias depends on the nonlinearity and the resiliency of the NLFSR update and of the output functions.

In the case of Sprout, such a relation would have to include the round key bits as well. However, in this case the mentioned relation will also contain the round key bits which are included non-linearly (if considered as a function of key bits and state bits). Moreover, we use in Sprout functions with the same cryptographic properties as the ones deployed in Grain 128a. These have been selected such that the bias is sufficiently small in order to make these attacks less efficient than exhaustive key search. Therefore we do not expect that they will work against Sprout.

Chosen IV Attacks. In [35] a distinguishing attack on the whole 256 round version of Grain 128 was presented. This indicates that the number of rounds during initialization and/or the nonlinearity of the functions used in Grain 128 are not high enough.

However, the update function of the NLFSR of Grain 128a (and hence of Sprout) was improved with respect to this attack. Moreover, the ratio of the number of rounds during the initialization phase to the state size is also considerably larger in case of Sprout compared to Grain family.

Dynamic Cube Attacks. A dynamic cube attack is (besides of fault attacks) the best publicly known attack against Grain 128 (see [19]). So far, no mechanisms are known to show the resistance against such attacks, especially as these rely on finding "good" cubes by chance. Hence, we cannot exclude that cube attacks may be possible. However, no cube attacks are known so far against

Grain 128a and Sprout uses similar functions. Moreover, the initialization phase is longer which should further strengthen the security of the full cipher.

Time Data Memory Trade-off Attacks. The main conceptual change compared to Grain 128a, namely the involvement of the key bits into the update function, was to increase the security against time data memory trade-off attacks, following the thoughts from Sect. 3.2. To this end, it is important that two different keys always yield states that are not keystream equivalent. Due to the fact that we use the key bit by bit, different keys should influence the keystream generation differently on the long run. However, two keys which are just shifted may result into shifted keystreams. To avoid this we include the counter bit as well. Even if the key is just shifted, due to the different counter values there will be situations where different counter bits are used in the update. The hope is that in the long run, this will ensure that different keys always produce different keystreams. However, as we have no formal proof that this is achieved for Sprout, further analysis needs to be made.

Weak Key-IV Pairs. Recently [36] a distinguishing attack against different versions of Grain was proposed, that exploits the existence of weak Key-IV pairs. These result into the situation that after the initialization phase is over, the LFSR is in the all-zero state. In their attack the number of required keystream bits depends on the best linear approximation for the NFSR update function g. For Grain-128 this results into the case that 2^{86} bits are required to build a distinguisher. In case of Grain 128a (and hence of Sprout as well) the nonlinearity of the NLFSR update function is even higher meaning that even more keystream bits will be required to detect a weak pair. Furthermore, we are aiming for considerably shorter periods of the keystream. As it was mentioned we cannot guarantee that the period is higher than the 2^{40} and therefore do not recommend to produce longer keystreams under the same IV.

Fault Attacks. The systematic study of fault attacks against stream ciphers was done in [28]. Usually, it is assumed that the attacker can flip one random FSR bit (without knowing its position), produce the required number of keystream bits from this faulted internal state, and then compare it with the keystream, which was produced without any faults in internal state. This process of resetting the device and introducing one fault can be done as many times as it is required for the attacker.

All members of the Grain family have been broken using this type of attack [8, 9,11]. However, all these attacks aim to recover the internal state. As elaborated above, knowing the content of the register bits of Sprout does not automatically allow for efficiently recovering the secret key. Moreover, the involvement of the round key bits should make this type of attacks harder.

Side-Channel Attacks. The security of the cryptographic primitives with respect to side-channel attacks depends on the actual implementation. Hence, nothing can be said about the general vulnerability. However, a secure implementation against power-analysis attacks usually leads to a high overhead in the area and power consumption [21] which commonly depends on the number of flip-flops used [29].

Therefore, the resources required for a secure implementation even increase the necessity of developing a stream cipher solutions which require as few flip-flops as possible. Moreover, when less area and power are used to implement the scheme itself, there is more space left in order to implement the necessary countermeasures and still stay feasible in the context of restricted devices.

6 Conclusion

In this work, we discussed a different approach for realizing keystream generators. The core idea is to design a cipher where the set of internal states is split into a large number of equivalence classes such that any trade-off attack has to consider every class at least once. As a concrete approach for realizing this property, we suggest to involve the secret key not only in the initialization process but in the update procedure as well. Although the change is conceptually simple, it may allow to avoid the rule of thumb that the internal state size needs to be at least twice the key length.

Exploiting the fact that storing fixed values is less area consuming than using registers, we were able to present a new stream cipher named Sprout which has a significantly smaller area size. Sprout is considered as a proof of concept to demonstrate the feasibility of this approach. To this end, it exhibits a rather conservative design where the choice of some parameters like the register lengths has been possibly overcautious. We see it as an interesting open question if and to what extend the area size can be further reduced for stream ciphers. At the moment, we do not see any reason why stream ciphers with comparatively short registers shouldn't be possible. Consequently we see this work as a first step towards alternative design approaches that hopefully initiates further research on this question.

Another interesting direction is the following. To thwart TMDTO attacks, it is not necessary to achieve 2^κ equivalence classes. Even if a cipher achieves less than these, it may still be sufficient if the effort for identifying these classes is sufficiently high. In other words, if the effort for finding all equivalence classes times the effort for executing a TMDTO attack is above the effort for exhaustive key search, we are on the safe side.

References

1. Ågren, M., Hell, M., Johansson, T., Meier, W.: Grain-128a: a new version of Grain-128 with optional authentication. Int. J. Wirel. Mob. Comput. 5(1), 48–59 (2011)
2. Abdelraheem, M.A., Borghoff, J., Zenner, E., David, M.: Cryptanalysis of the light-weight cipher A2U2. In: Chen, L. (ed.) IMACC 2011. LNCS, vol. 7089, pp. 375–390. Springer, Heidelberg (2011)
3. Afzal, M., Masood, A.: Algebraic cryptanalysis of a NLFSR based stream cipher. In: 3rd International Conference on Information and Communication Technologies: From Theory to Applications, ICTTA 2008, pp. 1–6. IEEE (2008)

4. Armknecht, F., Hamann, M., Mikhalev, V.: Lightweight authentication protocols on ultra-lightweight RFIDs - myths and facts. In: Workshop on RFID Security - RFIDSec 2014, Oxford, UK, July 2014
5. Babbage, S.: Improved exhaustive search attacks on stream ciphers. In: European Convention on Security and Detection 1995, pp. 161–166. IET (1995)
6. Babbage, S., Dodd, M.: The stream cipher MICKEY 2.0 (2006)
7. Babbage, S., Dodd, M.: The MICKEY stream ciphers. In: Robshaw, M., Billet, O. (eds.) New Stream Cipher Designs. LNCS, vol. 4986, pp. 191–209. Springer, Heidelberg (2008)
8. Banik, S., Maitra, S., Sarkar, S.: A differential fault attack on Grain-128a using MACs. In: Bogdanov, A., Sanadhya, S. (eds.) SPACE 2012. LNCS, vol. 7644, pp. 111–125. Springer, Heidelberg (2012)
9. Banik, S., Maitra, S., Sarkar, S.: A differential fault attack on the Grain family of stream ciphers. In: Prouff, E., Schaumont, P. (eds.) CHES 2012. LNCS, vol. 7428, pp. 122–139. Springer, Heidelberg (2012)
10. Barkan, E., Biham, E., Shamir, A.: Rigorous bounds on cryptanalytic time/memory tradeoffs. In: Dwork, C. (ed.) CRYPTO 2006. LNCS, vol. 4117, pp. 1–21. Springer, Heidelberg (2006)
11. Berzati, A., Canovas, C., Castagnos, G., Debraize, B., Goubin, L., Gouget, A., Paillier, P., Salgado, S.: Fault analysis of grain-128. In: IEEE International Workshop on Hardware-Oriented Security and Trust, HOST 2009, pp. 7–14. IEEE (2009)
12. Biryukov, A., Shamir, A.: Cryptanalytic time/memory/data tradeoffs for stream ciphers. In: Okamoto, T. (ed.) ASIACRYPT 2000. LNCS, vol. 1976, pp. 1–13. Springer, Heidelberg (2000)
13. Biryukov, A., Shamir, A., Wagner, D.: Real time cryptanalysis of A5/1 on a PC. In: Schneier, B. (ed.) FSE 2000. LNCS, vol. 1978, pp. 1–18. Springer, Heidelberg (2001)
14. Bogdanov, A., Knudsen, L.R., Leander, G., Paar, C., Poschmann, A., Robshaw, M.J.B., Seurin, Y., Vikkelsoe, C.: PRESENT: an ultra-lightweight block cipher. In: Paillier, P., Verbauwhede, I. (eds.) CHES 2007. LNCS, vol. 4727, pp. 450–466. Springer, Heidelberg (2007)
15. De Cannière, C., Dunkelman, O., Knežević, M.: KATAN and KTANTAN — a family of small and efficient hardware-oriented block ciphers. In: Clavier, C., Gaj, K. (eds.) CHES 2009. LNCS, vol. 5747, pp. 272–288. Springer, Heidelberg (2009)
16. De Canniere, C., Preneel, B.: Trivium specifications. eSTREAM, ECRYPT Stream Cipher Project (2006)
17. Courtois, N.T., Meier, W.: Algebraic attacks on stream ciphers with linear feedback. In: Biham, E. (ed.) EUROCRYPT 2003. LNCS, vol. 2656, pp. 345–359. Springer, Heidelberg (2003)
18. David, M., Ranasinghe, D.C., Larsen, T.: A2U2: a stream cipher for printed electronics RFID tags. In: 2011 IEEE International Conference on RFID (RFID), pp. 176–183. IEEE (2011)
19. Dinur, I., Güneysu, T., Paar, C., Shamir, A., Zimmermann, R.: An experimentally verified attack on full Grain-128 using dedicated reconfigurable hardware. In: Lee, D.H., Wang, X. (eds.) ASIACRYPT 2011. LNCS, vol. 7073, pp. 327–343. Springer, Heidelberg (2011)
20. Dunkelman, O., Keller, N.: Treatment of the initial value in time-memory-data tradeoff attacks on stream ciphers. Inf. Proces. Lett. **107**(5), 133–137 (2008)
21. Fischer, W., Gammel, B.M., Kniffler, O., Velten, J.: Differential power analysis of stream ciphers. In: Abe, M. (ed.) CT-RSA 2007. LNCS, vol. 4377, pp. 257–270. Springer, Heidelberg (2006)

22. Golić, J.D.: Cryptanalysis of alleged A5 stream cipher. In: Fumy, W. (ed.) EUROCRYPT 1997. LNCS, vol. 1233, pp. 239–255. Springer, Heidelberg (1997)
23. Good, T., Benaissa, M.: Hardware performance of estream phase-III stream cipher candidates. In: Proceedings of Workshop on the State of the Art of Stream Ciphers (SACS 2008) (2008)
24. Hell, M., Johansson, T., Maximov, A., Meier, W.: The Grain family of stream ciphers. In: Robshaw, M., Billet, O. (eds.) New Stream Cipher Designs. LNCS, vol. 4986, pp. 179–190. Springer, Heidelberg (2008)
25. Hell, M., Johansson, T., Meier, W., Maximov, A.: A stream cipher proposal: Grain-128. estream, ecrypt stream cipher project (2006). http://www.ecrypt.eu. org/stream/p3ciphers/grain/Grain128_p3.pdf
26. Hell, M., Johansson, T., Meier, W.: Grain: a stream cipher for constrained environments. Int. J. Wirel. Mob. Comput. $2(1)$, 86–93 (2007)
27. Hellman, M.E.: A cryptanalytic time-memory trade-off. IEEE Trans. Inf. Theory $26(4)$, 401–406 (1980)
28. Hoch, J.J., Shamir, A.: Fault analysis of stream ciphers. In: Joye, M., Quisquater, J.-J. (eds.) CHES 2004. LNCS, vol. 3156, pp. 240–253. Springer, Heidelberg (2004)
29. Mansouri, S.S., Dubrova, E.: An architectural countermeasure against power analysis attacks for FSR-based stream ciphers. In: Schindler, W., Huss, S.A. (eds.) COSADE 2012. LNCS, vol. 7275, pp. 54–68. Springer, Heidelberg (2012)
30. Maximov, A.: Cryptanalysis of the Grain family of stream ciphers. In: Proceedings of the 2006 ACM Symposium on Information, Computer and Communications Security, pp. 283–288. ACM (2006)
31. Menezes, A.J., Vanstone, S.A., Van Oorschot, P.C.: Handbook of Applied Cryptography, 1st edn. CRC Press Inc., Boca Raton (1996)
32. Mentens, N., Genoe, J., Preneel, B., Verbauwhede, I.: A low-cost implementation of Trivium. Preproceedings of SASC 2008, pp. 197–204 (2008)
33. Oechslin, P.: Making a faster cryptanalytic time-memory trade-off. In: Boneh, D. (ed.) CRYPTO 2003. LNCS, vol. 2729, pp. 617–630. Springer, Heidelberg (2003)
34. Rolfes, C., Poschmann, A., Leander, G., Paar, C.: Ultra-lightweight implementations for smart devices – security for 1000 gate equivalents. In: Grimaud, G., Standaert, F.-X. (eds.) CARDIS 2008. LNCS, vol. 5189, pp. 89–103. Springer, Heidelberg (2008)
35. Stankovski, P.: Greedy distinguishers and nonrandomness detectors. In: Gong, G., Gupta, K.C. (eds.) INDOCRYPT 2010. LNCS, vol. 6498, pp. 210–226. Springer, Heidelberg (2010)
36. Zhang, H., Wang, X.: Cryptanalysis of stream cipher Grain family. IACR Cryptology ePrint Archive 2009, 109 (2009)

Lightweight MDS Involution Matrices

Siang Meng Sim[1]([✉]), Khoongming Khoo[2], Frédérique Oggier[1],
and Thomas Peyrin[1]

[1] Nanyang Technological University, Singapore, Singapore
ssim011@e.ntu.edu.sg, {frederique,thomas.peyrin}@ntu.edu.sg
[2] DSO National Laboratories, Singapore, Singapore
kkhoongm@dso.org.sg

Abstract. In this article, we provide new methods to look for lightweight MDS matrices, and in particular involutory ones. By proving many new properties and equivalence classes for various MDS matrices constructions such as circulant, Hadamard, Cauchy and Hadamard-Cauchy, we exhibit new search algorithms that greatly reduce the search space and make lightweight MDS matrices of rather high dimension possible to find. We also explain why the choice of the irreducible polynomial might have a significant impact on the lightweightness, and in contrary to the classical belief, we show that the Hamming weight has no direct impact. Even though we focused our studies on involutory MDS matrices, we also obtained results for non-involutory MDS matrices. Overall, using Hadamard or Hadamard-Cauchy constructions, we provide the (involutory or non-involutory) MDS matrices with the least possible XOR gates for the classical dimensions 4×4, 8×8, 16×16 and 32×32 in $\mathrm{GF}(2^4)$ and $\mathrm{GF}(2^8)$. Compared to the best known matrices, some of our new candidates save up to 50 % on the amount of XOR gates required for an hardware implementation. Finally, our work indicates that involutory MDS matrices are really interesting building blocks for designers as they can be implemented with almost the same number of XOR gates as non-involutory MDS matrices, the latter being usually non-lightweight when the inverse matrix is required.

Keywords: Lightweight cryptography · Hadamard matrix · Cauchy matrix · Involution · MDS

1 Introduction

Most symmetric key primitives, like block ciphers, stream ciphers or hash functions, are usually based on various components that provide confusion and diffusion. Both concepts are very important for the overall security and efficiency of the cryptographic scheme and extensive studies have been conducted to find the best possible building blocks. The goal of diffusion is basically to spread the internal dependencies as much as possible. Several designs use a weak yet fast diffusion layer based on simple XOR, addition and shifting operation, but another trend is to rely on strong linear diffusion matrices, like Maximal Distance

© International Association for Cryptologic Research 2015
G. Leander (Ed.): FSE 2015, LNCS 9054, pp. 471–493, 2015.
DOI: 10.1007/978-3-662-48116-5_23

Separable (MDS) matrices. A typical example is the AES cipher [17], which uses a 4×4 matrix in $GF(2^8)$ to provide diffusion among a vector of 4 bytes. These mathematical objects ensure the designers a perfect diffusion (the underlying linear code meets the Singleton bound), but can be quite heavy to implement. Software performances are usually not so much impacted as memory is not really constrained and table-based implementations directly incorporate the field multiplications in the stored values. However, hardware implementations will usually suffer from an important area requirement due to the Galois field multiplications. The impact will also be visible on the efficiency of software bitslice implementations which basically mimic the hardware computations flow.

Good hardware efficiency has became a major design trend in cryptography, due to the increasing importance of ubiquitous computing. Many lightweight algorithms have recently been proposed, notably block ciphers [9,12,14,19] and hash functions [4,11,18]. The choice of MDS matrices played an important role in the reduction of the area required to provide a certain amount of security. Along with PHOTON hash function [18] was proposed a new type of MDS matrix that can be computed in a serial or recursive manner. This construction greatly reduces the temporary memory (and thus the hardware area) usually required for the computation of the matrix. Such matrices were later used in LED [19] block cipher, or PRIMATEs [1] authenticated encryption scheme, and were further studied and generalized in subsequent articles [2,3,10,28,33]. Even though these serial matrices provide a good way to save area, this naturally comes at the expense of an increased number of cycles to apply the matrix. In general, they are not well suited for round-based or low-latency implementations.

Another interesting property for an MDS matrix to save area is to be involutory. Indeed, in most use cases, encryption and decryption implementations are required and the inverse of the MDS matrix will have to be implemented as well (except for constructions like Feistel networks, where the inverse of the internal function is not needed for decryption). For example, the MDS matrix of AES is quite lightweight for encryption, but not really for decryption[1]. More generally, it is a valuable advantage that one can use *exactly* the same diffusion matrix for encryption and decryption. Some ciphers like ANUBIS [5], KHAZAD [6], ICEBERG [32] or PRINCE [13] even pushed the involution idea a bit further by defining a round function that is almost entirely composed of involution operations, and where the non-involution property of the cipher is mainly provided by the key schedule.

There are several ways to build a MDS matrix [15,20,24,27,29,34], a common method being to use a circulant construction, like for the AES block cipher [17] or the WHIRLPOOL hash function [8]. The obvious benefit of a circulant matrix for hardware implementations is that all of its rows are similar (up to a right shift), and one can trivially reuse the multiplication circuit to save implementation costs. However, it has been proven in [23] that circulant matrices of order 4 can-

---

[1] The serial matrix construction proposed in [18,19] allows an efficient inverse computation if the first coefficient is equal to 1. However, we recall that serial matrices are not well suited for round-based or low-latency implementations.

not be simultaneously MDS and involutory. And very recently Gupta *et al.* [21] proved that circulant MDS involutory matrices do not exist. Finding lightweight matrices that are both MDS and involutory is not an easy task and this topic has attracted attention recently. In [29], the authors consider Vandermonde or Hadamard matrices, while in [15, 20, 34] Cauchy matrices were used. Even if·these constructions allow to build involutory MDS matrices for big matrix dimensions, it is difficult to find the most lightweight candidates as the search space can become really big.

Our Contributions. In this article, we propose a new method to search for lightweight MDS matrices, with an important focus on involutory ones. After having recalled the formula to compute the XOR count, i.e. the amount of XORs required to evaluate one row of the matrix, we show in Sect. 2 that the choice of the irreducible polynomial is important and can have a significant impact on the efficiency, as remarked in [26]. In particular, we show that the best choice is not necessarily a low Hamming weight polynomial as widely believed, but instead one that has a high standard deviation regarding its XOR count. Then, in Sect. 3, we recall some constructions to obtain (involutory) MDS matrices: circulant, Hadamard, Cauchy and Cauchy-Hadamard. In particular, we prove new properties for some of these constructions, which will later help us to find good matrices. In Sect. 4 we prove the existence of equivalent classes for Hadamard matrices and involutory Hadamard-Cauchy matrices and we use these considerations to conceive improved search algorithms of lightweight (involutory) MDS matrices. Our methods can also be relaxed and applied to the search of lightweight non-involutory MDS matrices. In Sect. 5, we quickly describe these new algorithms, providing all the details for lightweight involutory and non-involutory MDS matrices in the full version of this article [31]. These algorithms are significant because they are feasible exhaustive search while the search space of the algorithms described in [15, 20] is too big to be exhausted[2]. Our algorithms guarantee that the matrices found are the lightest according to our metric.

Overall, using Hadamard or Hadamard-Cauchy constructions, we provide the smallest known (involutory or non-involutory) MDS matrices for the classical dimensions 4×4, 8×8, 16×16 and 32×32 in $GF(2^4)$ and $GF(2^8)$. The designers of one of the CAESAR competition candidates, Joltik [22], have used one of the matrices that we have found to build their primitive. All our results are summarized and commented in Sect. 6. Surprisingly, it seems that involutory MDS matrices are not much more expensive than non-involutory MDS ones, the former providing the great advantage of a free inverse implementation as well. We recall that in this article we are not considering serial matrices, as their evaluation either requires many clock cycles (for serial implementations) or an important area (for round-based implementations).

---

[2] The huge search space issue can be reduced if one could search intelligently only among lightweight matrix candidates. However, this is not possible with algorithms from [15, 20] since the matrix coefficients are known only at the end of the matrix generation, and thus one cannot limit the search to lightweight candidates only.

Due to space constraints, all proofs are given in the full version of this article [31].

Notations and Preliminaries. We denote by $\mathrm{GF}(2^r)$ the finite field with 2^r elements, $r \geq 1$. This field is isomorphic to polynomials in $\mathrm{GF}(2)[X]$ modulo an irreducible polynomial $p(X)$ of degree r, meaning that every field element can be seen as a polynomial $\alpha(X)$ with coefficients in $\mathrm{GF}(2)$ and of degree $r - 1$: $\alpha(X) = \sum_{i=0}^{r-1} b_i X^i$, $b_i \in \mathrm{GF}(2)$, $0 \leq i \leq r - 1$. The polynomial $\alpha(X)$ can also naturally be viewed as an r-bit string $(b_{r-1}, b_{r-2}, ..., b_0)$. In the rest of the article, an element α in $\mathrm{GF}(2^r)$ will be seen either as the polynomial $\alpha(X)$, or the r-bit string represented in a hexadecimal representation, which will be prefixed with 0x. For example, in $\mathrm{GF}(2^8)$, the 8-bit string 00101010 corresponds to the polynomial $X^5 + X^3 + X$, written 0x2a in hexadecimal.

The addition operation on $\mathrm{GF}(2^r)$ is simply defined as a bitwise XOR on the coefficients of the polynomial representation of the elements, and does not depend on the choice of the irreducible polynomial $p(X)$. However, for multiplication, one needs to specify the irreducible polynomial $p(X)$ of degree r. We denote this field as $\mathrm{GF}(2^r)/p(X)$, where $p(X)$ can be given in hexadecimal representation[3]. The multiplication of two elements is then the modulo $p(X)$ reduction of the product of the polynomial representations of the two elements.

Finally, we denote by $M[i, j]$ the (i, j) entry of the matrix M, we start the counting from 0, that is $M[0, 0]$ is the entry corresponding to the first row and first column.

2   Analyzing XOR Count According to Different Finite Fields

In this section, we explain the XOR count that we will use as a measure to evaluate the lightweightness of a given matrix. Then, we will analyze the XOR count distribution depending on the finite field and irreducible polynomial considered. Although it is known that finite fields of the same size are isomorphic to each other and it is believed that the security of MDS matrices is not impacted by this choice, looking at the XOR count is a new aspect of finite fields that remains unexplored in cryptography.

2.1   The XOR Count

It is to note that the XOR count is an easy-to-manipulate and simplified metric, but MDS coefficients have often been chosen to lower XOR count, e.g. by having low Hamming weight. As shown in [26], low XOR count is strongly correlated minimization of hardware area.

---

[3] This should not be confused with the explicit construction of finite fields, which is commonly denoted as $\mathrm{GF}(2^r)[X]/(P)$, where (P) is an ideal generated by irreducible polynomial P.

Later in this article, we will study the hardware efficiency of some diffusion matrices and we will search among huge sets of candidates. One of the goals will therefore be to minimize the area required to implement these lightweight matrices, and since they will be implemented with XOR gates (the diffusion layer is linear), we need a way to easily evaluate how many XORs will be required to implement them. We explain our method in this subsection.

In general, it is known that low Hamming weight generally requires lesser hardware resource in implementations, and this is the usual choice criteria for picking a matrix. For example, the coefficients of the AES MDS matrix are 1, 2 and 3, in a hope that this will ensure a lightweight implementation. However, it was shown in [26] that while this heuristic is true in general, it is not always the case. Due to some reduction effects, and depending on the irreducible polynomial defining the computation field, some coefficients with not-so-low Hamming weight might be implemented with very few XORs.

Definition 1. *The XOR count of an element α in the field $\mathrm{GF}(2^r)/p(X)$ is the number of XORs required to implement the multiplication of α with an arbitrary β over $\mathrm{GF}(2^r)/p(X)$.*

For example, let us explain how we compute the XOR count of $\alpha = 3$ over $\mathrm{GF}(2^4)/0\mathrm{x}13$ and $\mathrm{GF}(2^4)/0\mathrm{x}19$. Let (b_3, b_2, b_1, b_0) be the binary representation of an arbitrary element β in the field. For $\mathrm{GF}(2^4)/0\mathrm{x}13$, we have:

$$(0,0,1,1) \cdot (b_3, b_2, b_1, b_0) = (b_2, b_1, b_0 \oplus b_3, b_3) \oplus (b_3, b_2, b_1, b_0)$$
$$= (b_2 \oplus b_3, b_1 \oplus b_2, b_0 \oplus b_1 \oplus b_3, b_0 \oplus b_3),$$

which corresponds to 5 XORs[4]. For $\mathrm{GF}(2^4)/0\mathrm{x}19$, we have:

$$(0,0,1,1) \cdot (b_3, b_2, b_1, b_0) = (b_2 \oplus b_3, b_1, b_0, b_3) \oplus (b_3, b_2, b_1, b_0)$$
$$= (b_2, b_1 \oplus b_2, b_0 \oplus b_1, b_0 \oplus b_3),$$

which corresponds to 3 XORs. One can observe that XOR count is different depending on the finite field defined by the irreducible polynomial.

In order to calculate the number of XORs required to implement an entire row of a matrix, we can use the following formula given in [26]:

$$\text{XOR count for one row of } M = (\gamma_1, \gamma_2, ..., \gamma_k) + (n-1) \cdot r, \tag{1}$$

where γ_i is the XOR count of the i-th entry in the row of M, n being the number of nonzero elements in the row and r the dimension of the finite field.

For example, the first row of the AES diffusion matrix being $(1, 1, 2, 3)$ over the field $\mathrm{GF}(2^8)/0\mathrm{x}11\mathrm{b}$, the XOR count for the first row is $(0+0+3+11)+3\times 8 = 38$ XORs (the matrix being circulant, all rows are equivalent in terms of XOR count).

---

[4] We acknowledge that one can perform the multiplication with 4 XORs as $b_0 \oplus b_3$ appears twice. But that would require additional cycle and extra memory cost which completely outweighed the small saving on the XOR count.

2.2   XOR Count for Different Finite Fields

We programmed a tool that computes the XOR count for every nonzero element over $\mathrm{GF}(2^r)$ for $r = 2, \ldots, 8$ and for all possible irreducible polynomials (all the tables will be given in [31], we provide an extract in Appendix B). By analyzing the outputs of this tool, we could make two observations that are important to understand how the choice of the irreducible polynomial affects the XOR count. Before presenting our observations, we state some terminologies and properties related to reciprocal polynomials in finite fields.

Definition 2. *A reciprocal polynomial* $\frac{1}{p}(X)$ *of a polynomial* $p(X)$ *over* $\mathrm{GF}(2^r)$, *is a polynomial expressed as* $\frac{1}{p}(X) = X^r \cdot p(X^{-1})$. *A reciprocal finite field,* $\mathbf{K} = \mathrm{GF}(2^r)/\frac{1}{p}(X)$, *is a finite field defined by the reciprocal polynomial which defines* $\mathbf{F} = \mathrm{GF}(2^r)/p(X)$.

In other words, a reciprocal polynomial is a polynomial with the order of the coefficients reversed. For example, the reciprocal polynomial of $p(X) = $ 0x11b in $\mathrm{GF}(2^8)$ is $\frac{1}{p}(X) = $ 0x$\frac{1}{11b} = $ 0x1b1. It is also to be noted that the reciprocal polynomial of an irreducible polynomial is also irreducible.

The Total XOR Count. Our first new observation is that even if for an individual element of the field the choice of the irreducible polynomial has an impact on the XOR count, the total sum of the XOR count over all elements in the field is independent of this choice. We state this observation in the following theorem.

Theorem 1. *The total XOR count for a field* $\mathrm{GF}(2^r)$ *is* $r \sum_{i=2}^{r} 2^{i-2}(i-1)$, *where* $r \geq 2$.

From Theorem 1, it seems that there is no clear implication that one irreducible polynomial is strictly better than another, as the mean XOR count is the same for any irreducible polynomial. However, the irreducible polynomials have different distribution of the XOR count among the field elements, that is quantified by the standard deviation. A high standard deviation implies that the distribution of XOR count is very different from the mean, thus there will be more elements with relatively lower/higher XOR count. In general, the order of the finite field is much larger than the order of the MDS matrix and since only a few elements of the field will be used in the MDS matrices, there is a better chance of finding an MDS matrix with lower XOR count.

Hence, our recommendation is to choose the irreducible polynomial with the highest standard deviation regarding the XOR count distribution. From previous example, in $\mathrm{GF}(2^4)$ (XOR count mean equals 4.25 for this field dimension), the irreducible polynomials 0x13 and 0x19 lead to a standard deviation of 2.68, while 0x1f leads to a standard deviation of 1.7075. Therefore, the two first polynomials seem to be a better choice. This observation will allow us to choose the best irreducible polynomial to start with during the searches. We refer to [31] for all the standard deviations according to the irreducible polynomial, here we provide an extract in Appendix B.

We note that the folklore belief was that in order to get lightweight implementations, one should use a low Hamming weight irreducible polynomial. The underlying idea is that with such a polynomial less XORs might be needed when the modular reduction has to be applied during a field multiplication. However, we have shown that this is not necessarily true. Yet, by looking at the data from Appendix B, we remark that the low Hamming weight irreducible polynomials usually have a high standard deviation, which actually validates the folklore belief. We conjecture that this heuristic will be less and less exact when we go to higher and higher order fields.

Matching XOR Count. Our second new observation is that the XOR count distribution implied by a polynomial will be the same compared to the distribution of its reciprocal counterpart. We state this observation in the following theorem.

Theorem 2. *There exists an isomorphic mapping from a primitive $\alpha \in \mathrm{GF}(2^r)/p(X)$ to another primitive $\beta \in \mathrm{GF}(2^r)/\frac{1}{p}(X)$ where the XOR count of α^i and β^i is equal for each $i = \{1, 2, ..., 2^r - 1\}$.*

In Table 4 of Appendix A, we listed all the primitive mapping from a finite field to its reciprocal finite field for all fields $\mathrm{GF}(2^r)$ with $r = 2, \ldots, 8$ and for all possible irreducible polynomials. We give an example to illustrate our theorem. For $\mathrm{GF}(2^4)$, there are three irreducible polynomials: 0x13, 0x19 and 0x1f and the XOR count for the elements are shown in Appendix B. From the binary representation we see that $0x\frac{1}{13} = 0x19$. Consider an isomorphic mapping $\phi : \mathrm{GF}(2^4)/0x13 \rightarrow \mathrm{GF}(2^4)/0x19$ defined as $\phi(2) = 12$, where 2 and 12 are the primitives for the respective finite fields. Table 3 of Appendix A shows that the order of the XOR count is the same.

We remark that for a self-reciprocal irreducible polynomial, for instance 0x1f in $\mathrm{GF}(2^4)$, there also exists an automorphism mapping from a primitive to another primitive with the same order of XOR count (see Appendix A).

Theorem 2 is useful for understanding that we do not need to consider $\mathrm{GF}(2^r)/\frac{1}{p}(X)$ when we are searching for lightweight matrices. As there exists an isomorphic mapping preserving the order of the XOR count, any MDS matrix over $\mathrm{GF}(2^r)/\frac{1}{p}(X)$ can be mapped to an MDS matrix over $\mathrm{GF}(2^r)/p(X)$ while preserving the XOR count. Therefore, it is redundant to search for lightweight MDS matrices over $\mathrm{GF}(2^r)/\frac{1}{p}(X)$ as the lightest MDS matrix can also be found in $\mathrm{GF}(2^r)/p(X)$. This will render our algorithms much more efficient: when using exhaustive search for low XOR count MDS over finite field defined by various irreducible polynomial, one can reduce the search space by almost a factor 2 as the reciprocal polynomials are redundant.

3   Types of MDS Matrices and Properties

In this section, we first recall a few properties of MDS matrices and we then explain various constructions of (involutory) MDS matrices that were used to generate lightweight candidates. Namely, we will study 4 types of diffusion matrices: circulant, Hadamard, Cauchy, and Hadamard-Cauchy. We recall that we do not consider serially computable matrices in this article, like the ones described in [2,3,18,19,28,33], since they are not adapted to round-based implementations. As MDS matrices are widely studied and their properties are commonly known, their definition and properties are given in [31].

3.1   Circulant Matrices

A common way to build an MDS matrix is to start from a circulant matrix, reason being that the probability of finding an MDS matrix would then be higher than a normal square matrix [16].

Definition 3. *A $k \times k$ matrix C is circulant when each row vector is rotated to the right relative to the preceding row vector by one element. The matrix is then fully defined by its first row.*

An interesting property of circulant matrices is that since each row differs from the previous row by a right shift, a user can just implement one row of the matrix multiplication in hardware and reuse the multiplication circuit for subsequent rows by just shifting the input. However in [31], we will show that these matrices are not the best choice.

3.2   Hadamard Matrices

Definition 4. *([20]). A finite field Hadamard (or simply called Hadamard) matrix H is a $k \times k$ matrix, with $k = 2^s$, that can be represented by two other submatrices H_1 and H_2 which are also Hadamard matrices:*

$$H = \begin{pmatrix} H_1 & H_2 \\ H_2 & H_1 \end{pmatrix}.$$

Similarly to [20], in order to represent a Hadamard matrix we use notation $had(h_0, h_1, ..., h_{k-1})$ (with $h_i = H[0, i]$ standing for the entries of the first row of the matrix) where $H[i, j] = h_{i \oplus j}$ and $k = 2^s$. It is clear that a Hadamard matrix is bisymmetric. Indeed, if we define the left and right diagonal reflection transformations as $H_L = T_L(H)$ and $H_R = T_R(H)$ respectively, we have that $H_L[i, j] = H[j, i] = H[i, j]$ and $H_R[i, j] = H[k - 1 - i, k - 1 - j] = H[i, j]$ (the binary representation of $k - 1 = 2^s - 1$ is all 1, hence $k - 1 - i = (k - 1) \oplus i$).

Moreover, by doing the multiplication directly, it is known that if $H = had(h_0, h_1, ..., h_{k-1})$ is a Hadamard matrix, then $H \times H = c^2 \cdot I$, with $c^2 = h_0^2 + h_1^2 + h_2^2 + ... + h_{k-1}^2$. In other words, the product of a Hadamard matrix with itself is a multiple of an identity matrix, where the multiple c^2 is the sum of the square of the elements from the first row.

A direct and crucial corollary to this fact is that a Hadamard matrix over $GF(2^r)$ is involution if the sum of the elements of the first row is equal to 1. Now, it is important to note that if one deals with a Hadamard matrix for which the sum of the first row over $GF(2^r)$ is nonzero, we can very simply make it involutory by dividing it with the sum of its first row.

We will use these considerations to generate low dimension diffusion matrices (order 4 and 8) with an innovative exhaustive search over all the possible Hadamard matrices. We note that, similarity to a circulant matrix, an Hadamard matrix will have the interesting property that each row is a permutation of the first row, therefore allowing to reuse the multiplication circuit to save implementation costs.

3.3 Cauchy Matrices

Definition 5. *A square Cauchy matrix, C, is a $k \times k$ matrix constructed with two disjoint sets of elements from* $GF(2^r)$, $\{\alpha_0, \alpha_1, ..., \alpha_{k-1}\}$ *and* $\{\beta_0, \beta_1, ..., \beta_{k-1}\}$ *such that $C[i, j] = \frac{1}{\alpha_i + \beta_j}$.*

It is known that the determinant of a square Cauchy matrix, C, is given as

$$\det(C) = \frac{\prod_{0 \leq i < j \leq k-1}(\alpha_j - \alpha_i)(\beta_j - \beta_i)}{\prod_{0 \leq i,j \leq k-1}(\alpha_i + \beta_j)}.$$

Since $\alpha_i \neq \alpha_j$, $\beta_i \neq \beta_j$ for all $i, j \in \{0, 1, ..., k-1\}$, a Cauchy matrix is nonsingular. Note that for a Cauchy matrix over $GF(2^r)$, the subtraction is equivalent to addition as the finite field has characteristic 2. As the sets are disjoint, we have $\alpha_i \neq \beta_j$, thus all entries are well-defined and nonzero. In addition, any submatrix of a Cauchy matrix is also a Cauchy matrix as it is equivalent to constructing a smaller Cauchy matrix with subsets of the two disjoint sets. Therefore, a Cauchy matrix is an MDS matrix.

3.4 Hadamard-Cauchy Matrices

The innovative exhaustive search over Hadamard matrices is sufficient to generate low dimension diffusion matrices (order 4 and 8). However, the computation for verifying the MDS property and the exhaustive search space grows exponentially. It eventually becomes impractical to search for higher dimension Hadamard matrices (order 16 or more). Therefore, we use the Hadamard-Cauchy matrix construction, proposed in [20] as an evolution of the involutory MDS Vandermonde matrices [28], that guarantees the matrix to be an involutory MDS matrix.

In [20], the authors proposed a $2^s \times 2^s$ matrix construction that combines both the characteristics of Hadamard and Cauchy matrices. Because it is a Cauchy matrix, a Hadamard-Cauchy matrix is an MDS matrix. And because it is a

Hadamard matrix, it will be involutory when c^2 is equal to 1. Therefore, we can construct a Hadamard-Cauchy matrix and check if the sum of first row is equal to 1 and, if so, we have an MDS and involutory matrix. A detailed discussion on Hadamard-Cauchy matrices is given in [31].

4 Equivalence Classes of Hadamard-Based Matrices

Our methodology for finding lightweight MDS matrices is to perform an innovative exhaustive search and by eventually picking the matrix with the lowest XOR count. Naturally, the main problem to tackle is the huge search space. By exploiting the properties of Hadamard matrices, we found ways to group them in equivalent classes and significantly reduce the search space. In this section, we introduce the equivalence classes of Hadamard matrices and the equivalence classes of involutory Hadamard-Cauchy matrices. It is important to note that these two equivalence classes are rather different as they are defined by very different relations.

4.1 Equivalence Classes of Hadamard Matrices

It is known that a Hadamard matrix can be defined by its first row, and different permutation of the first row results in a different Hadamard matrix with possibly different branch number. In order to find a lightweight MDS involution matrix, it is necessary to have a set of k elements with relatively low XOR count that sum to 1 (to guarantee involution). Moreover, we need all coefficients in the first row to be different. Indeed, if the first row of an Hadamard matrix has 2 or more of the same element, say $H[0, i] = H[0, j]$, where $i, j \in \{0, 1, ..., k-1\}$, then in another row we have $H[i \oplus j, i] = H[i \oplus j, j]$. These 4 entries are the same and thus, H is not MDS.

By permuting the entries we hope to find an MDS involution matrix. However, given k distinct nonzero elements, there are $k!$ ways to permute the first row of the Hadamard matrix, which can quickly become intractable. Therefore, we introduce a relation that relates certain permutations that lead to the same branch number.

Definition 6. *Let H and $H^{(\sigma)}$ be two Hadamard matrices with the same set of entries up to some permutation σ. We say that they are related, $H \sim H^{(\sigma)}$, if every pair of input vectors, $(v, v^{(\sigma)})$ with the same permutation σ, to H and $H^{(\sigma)}$ respectively, have the same set of elements in the output vectors.*

For example, let us consider the following three Hadamard matrices

$$
H = \begin{pmatrix} w & x & y & z \\ x & w & z & y \\ y & z & w & x \\ z & y & x & w \end{pmatrix}, \quad
H^{(\sigma_1)} = \begin{pmatrix} y & z & w & x \\ z & y & x & w \\ w & x & y & z \\ x & w & z & y \end{pmatrix}, \quad
H^{(\sigma_2)} = \begin{pmatrix} w & x & z & y \\ x & w & y & z \\ z & y & w & x \\ y & z & x & w \end{pmatrix},
$$

One can see that $H^{(\sigma_1)}$ is defined by the third row of H, i.e. the rows are shifted by two positions and $\sigma_1 = \{2, 3, 0, 1\}$. Let us consider an arbitrary input vector for H, say $v = (a, b, c, d)$. Then, if we apply the permutation to v, we obtain $v^{(\sigma_1)} = (c, d, a, b)$. We can observe that:

$$v \cdot H = (aw + bx + cy + dz, ax + bw + cz + dy, ay + bz + cw + dx, az + by + cx + dw),$$

$$v^{(\sigma_1)} \cdot H^{(\sigma_1)} = (cy + dz + aw + bx, cz + dy + ax + bw, cw + dx + ay + bz, cx + dw + az + by),$$

It is now easy to see that $v \cdot H = v^{(\sigma_1)} \cdot H^{(\sigma_1)}$. Hence, we say that $H \sim H^{(\sigma_1)}$. Similarily, with $\sigma_2 = \{0, 1, 3, 2\}$, we have $v^{(\sigma_2)} = (a, b, d, c)$ and:

$$v \cdot H = (aw + bx + cy + dz, ax + bw + cz + dy, ay + bz + cw + dx, az + by + cx + dw),$$

$$v^{(\sigma_2)} \cdot H^{(\sigma_2)} = (aw + bx + dz + cy, ax + bw + dy + cz, az + by + dw + cx, ay + bz + dx + cw),$$

and since $v \cdot H$ and $v^{(\sigma_2)} \cdot H^{(\sigma_2)}$ are the same up to the permutation σ_2, we can say that $H \sim H^{(\sigma_2)}$.

Definition 7. *An equivalence class of Hadamard matrices is a set of Hadamard matrices satisfying the equivalence relation $\sim$.*

Proposition 1. *Hadamard matrices in the same equivalence class have the same branch number.*

When searching for an MDS matrix, we can make use of this property to greatly reduce the search space: if one Hadamard matrix in an equivalence class is not MDS, then all other Hadamard matrices in the same equivalence class will not be MDS either. Therefore, it all boils down to analyzing how many and which permutation of the Hadamard matrices belongs to the same equivalence classes. Using the two previous examples σ_1 and σ_2 as building blocks, we generalize them and present two lemmas.

Lemma 1. *Given a Hadamard matrix H, any Hadamard matrix $H^{(\alpha)}$ defined by the $(\alpha + 1)$-th row of H, with $\alpha = 0, 1, 2, ..., k - 1$, is equivalent to H.*

Next, let us consider the other type of permutation. We can see in the example with σ_2 that up to the permutation applied to the Hadamard matrix, input and output vectors are the same. Let $H^{(\sigma)}$, $v^{(\sigma)}$ and $u^{(\sigma)}$ denote the permuted Hadamard matrix, the permuted input vector and its corresponding permuted output vector. We want the permutation to satisfy $u_{\sigma(j)} = u_j^{(\sigma)}$, where $j \in \{0, 1, ..., k - 1\}$. That is the permutation of the output vector of H is the same as the permuted output vector of $H^{(\sigma)}$. Using the definition of the Hadamard matrix, we can rewrite it as

$$\bigoplus_{i=0}^{k-1} v_i h_{i \oplus \sigma(j)} = \bigoplus_{i=0}^{k-1} v_i^{(\sigma)} H^{(\sigma)}[i, j].$$

Using the definition of the permutation and by the fact that it is one-to-one mapping, we can rearrange the XOR order of the terms on the left-hand side and we obtain

$$\bigoplus_{i=0}^{k-1} v_{\sigma(i)} h_{\sigma(i) \oplus \sigma(j)} = \bigoplus_{i=0}^{k-1} v_{\sigma(i)} h_{\sigma(i \oplus j)}.$$

Therefore, we need the permutation to be linear with respect to XOR: $\sigma(i \oplus j) = \sigma(i) \oplus \sigma(j)$. This proves our next lemma.

Lemma 2. *For any linear permutation σ (w.r.t. XOR), the two Hadamard matrices H and $H^{(\sigma)}$ are equivalent.*

We note that the permutations in Lemmas 1 and 2 are disjoint, except for the identity permutation. This is because for the linear permutation σ, it always maps the identity to itself: $\sigma(0) = 0$. Thus, for any linear permutation, the first entry remains unchanged. On the other hand, when choosing another row of H as the first row, the first entry is always different.

With these two lemmas, we can now partition the family of Hadamard matrices into equivalence classes. For Lemma 1, we can easily see that the number of permutation is equal to the order of the Hadamard matrix. However, for Lemma 2 it is not so trivial. Therefore, we have the following lemma.

Lemma 3. *Given a set of 2^s nonzero elements, $S = \{\alpha_0, \alpha_1, ..., \alpha_{2^s-1}\}$, there are $\prod_{i=0}^{s-1}(2^s - 2^i)$ linear permutations w.r.t. XOR operation.*

Theorem 3. *Given a set of 2^s nonzero elements, $S = \{\alpha_0, \alpha_1, ..., \alpha_{2^s-1}\}$, there are $\frac{(2^s-1)!}{\prod_{i=0}^{s-1}(2^s-2^i)}$ equivalence classes of Hadamard matrices of order 2^s defined by the set of elements S.*

For convenience, we call the permutations in Lemmas 1 and 2 the $\mathcal{H}$-permutations. The $\mathcal{H}$-permutations can be described as a sequence of the following types of permutations on the index of the entries:

1. choose $\alpha \in \{0, 1, ..., 2^s - 1\}$, define $\sigma(i) = i \oplus \alpha, \forall i = 0, 1, ..., 2^s - 1$, and
2. fix $\sigma(0) = 0$, in ascending order of the index i, choose the permutation if i is power of 2, otherwise it is defined by the linear permutation (w.r.t. XOR): $\sigma(i \oplus j) = \sigma(i) \oplus \sigma(j)$.

We remark that given a set of 4 nonzero elements, from Theorem 3 we see that there is only 1 equivalence class of Hadamard matrices. This implies that there is no need to permute the entries of the 4×4 Hadamard matrix in hope to find MDS matrix if one of the permutation is not MDS.

With the knowledge of equivalence classes of Hadamard matrices, what we need is an algorithm to pick one representative from each equivalence class and check if it is MDS. The idea is to exhaust all non-$\mathcal{H}$-permutations through selecting the entries in ascending index order. Since the entries in the first column of Hadamard matrix are distinct (otherwise the matrix is not MDS), it is sufficient for us to check the matrices with the first entry (index 0) being the smallest element. This is because for any other matrices with the first entry set as some other element, it is in the same equivalence class as some matrix $H^{(\alpha)}$ where the first entry of $(\alpha + 1)$-th row is the smallest element. For indexes that are powers of 2, select the smallest element from the remaining set. While for the other entries, one can pick any element from the remaining set.

For 8×8 Hadamard matrices for example, the first three entries, α_0, α_1 and α_2 are fixed to be the three smallest elements in ascending order. Next, by Lemma 2, α_3 should be defined by α_1 and α_2 in order to preserve the linear property, thus to "destroy" the linear property and obtain matrices from different equivalence classes, pick an element from the remaining set in ascending order as the fourth entry α_3. After which, α_4 is selected to be the smallest element among the remaining 4 elements and permute the remaining 3 elements to be α_5, α_6 and α_7 respectively. For each of these arrangement of entries, we check if it is MDS (the algorithm can be found in [31]). We terminate the algorithm prematurely once an MDS matrix is found, else we conclude that the given set of elements does not generate an MDS matrix.

It is clear that arranging the entries in this manner will not obtain two Hadamard matrices from the same equivalence class. But one may wonder if it actually does exhaust all the equivalence classes. The answer is yes: Theorem 3 shows that there is a total of 30 equivalence classes for 8×8 Hadamard matrices. On the other hand, from the algorithm described above, we have 5 choices for α_3 and we permute the remaining 3 elements for α_5, α_6 and α_7. Thus, there are 30 Hadamard matrices that we have to check.

4.2   Equivalence Classes of Involutory Hadamard-Cauchy Matrices

Despite having a new technique to reduce the search space, the computation cost for checking the MDS property is still too huge when the order of the Hadamard matrix is larger than 8. Therefore, we use the Hadamard-Cauchy construction for order 16 and 32. Thanks to the Cauchy property, we are ensured that the matrix will be MDS. Hence, the only problem that remains is the huge search space of possible Hadamard-Cauchy matrices. To prevent confusion with Hadamard matrices, we denote Hadamard-Cauchy matrices with K.

First, we restate in Algorithm 1 the technique from [20] to build involutory MDS matrices, with some modifications on the notations for the variables. Although it is not explicitly stated, we can infer from Lemmas 6,7 and Theorem 4 from [20] that all Hadamard-Cauchy matrices can be expressed as an output of Algorithm 1.

Similarly to Hadamard matrices, we denote a Hadamard-Cauchy matrix by its first row of elements as $hc(h_0, h_1, ..., h_{2^s-1})$, with $h_i = K[0, i]$. To summarize the construction of a Hadamard-Cauchy matrix of order 2^s mentioned in Algorithm 1, we pick an ordered set of $s + 1$ linearly independent elements, we call it the basis. We use the first s elements to span an ordered set S of 2^s elements, and add the last element z to all the elements in S. Next, we take the inverse of each of the elements in this new set and we get the first row of the

---

Algorithm 1. Construction of $2^s \times 2^s$ MDS matrix or involutory MDS matrix over $\mathrm{GF}(2^r)/p(X)$.

INPUT: an irreducible polynomial $p(X)$ of $\mathrm{GF}(2^r)$, integers s, r satisfying $s < r$ and $r > 1$, a boolean $B_{involutory}$.

OUTPUT: $2^s \times 2^s$ Hadamard-Cauchy matrix K, where K is involutory if $B_{involutory}$ is set **True**.

  procedure CONSTRUCTH-C$(r, p(X), s, B_{involutory})$
    select s linearly independent elements $x_1, x_2, x_{2^2}, ..., x_{2^{s-1}}$ from $\mathrm{GF}(2^r)$ and construct S, the set of 2^s elements x_i,
        where $\quad x_i \quad = \quad \bigoplus_{t=0}^{s-1} b_t x_{2^t} \quad$ **for all** $\quad i \quad \in \quad [0, 2^s - 1] \quad$ (with $(b_{s-1}, b_{s-2}, ..., b_1, b_0)$ being the binary representation of i)
    select $z \in \mathrm{GF}(2^r) \setminus S$ and construct the set of 2^s elements y_i, where $y_i = z + x_i$ for all $i \in [0, 2^s - 1]$
    initialize an empty array ary_s of size 2^s
    if $(B_{involutory} ==$ **False**$)$ **then**
      $ary\_s[i] = \frac{1}{y_i}$ **for all** $i \in [0, 2^s - 1]$
    else
      $ary\_s[i] = \frac{1}{c \cdot y_i}$ **for all** $i \in [0, 2^s - 1]$, where $c = \bigoplus_{t=0}^{s-1} \frac{1}{z+x_t}$
    end if
    construct the $2^s \times 2^s$ matrix K, where $K[i, j] = ary\_s[i \oplus j]$
    return K
  end procedure

Hadamard-Cauchy matrix. Lastly, we generate the matrix based on the first row in the same manner as an Hadamard matrix.

For example, for an 8×8 Hadamard-Cauchy matrix over $\mathrm{GF}(2^4)/\mathrm{0x13}$, say we choose $x_1 = 1, x_2 = 2, x_4 = 4$, we generate the set $S = \{0, 1, 2, 3, 4, 5, 6, 7\}$, choosing $z = 8$ and taking the inverses in the new set, we get a Hadamard-Cauchy matrix $K = hc(15, 2, 12, 5, 10, 4, 3, 8)$. To make it involution, we multiply each element by the inverse of the sum of the elements. However for this instance the sum is 1, hence K is already an involutory MDS matrix.

One of the main differences between the Hadamard and Hadamard-Cauchy matrices is the choice of entries. While we can choose all the entries for a Hadamard matrix to be lightweight and permute them in search for an MDS candidate, the construction of Hadamard-Cauchy matrix makes it nontrivial to control its entries efficiently. Although in [20] the authors proposed a backward re-construction algorithm that finds a Hadamard-Cauchy matrix with some pre-decided lightweight entries, the number of entries that can be decided beforehand is very limited. For example, for a Hadamard-Cauchy matrix of order 16, the algorithm can only choose 5 lightweight entries, the weight of the other 11 entries is not controlled. The most direct way to find a lightweight Hadamard-Cauchy matrix is to apply Algorithm 1 repeatedly for all possible basis. We introduce now new equivalence classes that will help us to exhaust all possible Hadamard-Cauchy matrices with much lesser memory space and number of iterations.

Definition 8. *Let K_1 and K_2 be two Hadamard-Cauchy matrices, we say they are related, $K_1 \sim_{HC} K_2$, if one can be transformed to the other by either one or both operations on the first row of entries:*

1. multiply by a nonzero scalar, and
2. $\mathcal{H}$-permutation of the entries.

The crucial property of the construction is the independence of the elements in the basis, which is not affected by multiplying a nonzero scalar. Hence, we can convert any Hadamard-Cauchy matrix to an involutory Hadamard-Cauchy matrix by multiplying it with the inverse of the sum of the first row and vice versa. However, permutating the positions of the entries is the tricky part. Indeed, for the Hadamard-Cauchy matrices of order 8 or higher, some permutations destroy the Cauchy property, causing it to be non-MDS. Using our previous 8×8 example, suppose we swap the first two entries, $K' = hc(2, 15, 12, 5, 10, 4, 3, 8)$, it can be verified that it is not MDS. To understand why, we work backwards to find the basis corresponding to K'. Taking the inverse of the entries, we have $\{9, 8, 10, 11, 12, 13, 14, 15\}$. However, there is no basis that satisfies the 8 linear equations for the entries. Thus it is an invalid construction of Hadamard-Cauchy matrix. Therefore, we consider applying the $\mathcal{H}$-permutation on Hadamard-Cauchy matrix. Since it is also a Hadamard matrix, the $\mathcal{H}$-permutation preserves its branch number, thus it is still MDS. So we are left to show that a Hadamard-Cauchy matrix that undergoes $\mathcal{H}$-permutation is still a Hadamard-Cauchy matrix.

Lemma 4. *Given a $2^s \times 2^s$ involutory Hadamard-Cauchy matrix K, there are $2^s \cdot \prod_{i=0}^{s-1}(2^s - 2^i)$ involutory Hadamard-Cauchy matrices that are related to K by the $\mathcal{H}$-permutations of the entries of the first row.*

With that, we can define our equivalence classes of involutory Hadamard-Cauchy matrices.

Definition 9. *An equivalence class of involutory Hadamard-Cauchy matrices is a set of Hadamard-Cauchy matrices satisfying the equivalence relation $\sim_{HC}$.*

In order to count the number of equivalence classes of involutory Hadamard-Cauchy matrices, we use the same technique for proving Theorem 3. To do that, we need to know the total number of Hadamard-Cauchy matrices that can be constructed from the Algorithm 1 for a given finite field.

Lemma 5. *Given two natural numbers s and r, based on Algorithm 1, there are $\prod_{i=0}^{s}(2^r - 2^i)$ many $2^s \times 2^s$ Hadamard-Cauchy matrices over $\mathrm{GF}(2^r)$.*

Theorem 4. *Given two positive integers s and r, there are $\prod_{i=0}^{s-1} \frac{2^{r-1} - 2^i}{2^s - 2^i}$ equivalence classes of involutory Hadamard-Cauchy matrices of order 2^s over $\mathrm{GF}(2^r)$.*

In [15], the authors introduced the notion of compact Cauchy matrices which are defined as Cauchy matrices with exactly 2^s distinct elements. These matrices seem to include Cauchy matrices beyond the class of Hadamard-Cauchy matrices. However, it turns out that the equivalence classes of involutory Hadamard-Cauchy matrices can be extended to compact Cauchy matrices.

Corollary 1. *Any compact Cauchy matrices can be generated from some equivalence class of involutory Hadamard-Cauchy matrices.*

Note that since the permutation of the elements in S and $z + S$ only results in rearrangement of the entries of the compact Cauchy matrix, the XOR count is invariant from Hadamard-Cauchy matrix with the same set of entries.

5   Searching for Involutory MDS and Non-involutory MDS Matrices

Due to space constraints, we have put the new methods we have designed to look for the lightest possible involutory MDS and non-involutory MDS matrices in [31].

More precisely, regarding involutory MDS matrices, using the previous properties and equivalence classes given in Sects. 3 and 4 for several matrix constructions, we have derived algorithms to search for the most lightweight candidate. First, we point out that the circulant construction can not lead to involutory MDS matrices, then we focus on the case of matrices of small dimension using the Hadamard construction. For bigger dimension, we add the Cauchy property to the Hadamard one in order to guarantee that the matrix will be MDS. We recall that, similarity to a circulant matrix, an Hadamard matrix will have the interesting property that each row is a permutation of the first row, therefore allowing to reuse the multiplication circuit to save implementation costs.

Regarding non-involutory MDS matrices, we have extended the involutory MDS matrix search to include non-involutory candidates. For Hadamard construction, we removed the constraint that the sum of the first row elements must be equal to 1. For the Hadamard-Cauchy, we multiply each equivalent classes by a non-zero scalar value. We note that the disadvantage of non-involutory MDS matrices is that their inverse may have a high computation cost. But if the inverse is not required (for example in the case of popular constructions such as a Feistel network, or a CTR encryption mode), non-involution matrices might be lighter than involutory matrices.

6   Results

We first emphasize that although in [15, 20] the authors proposed methods to construct lightweight matrices, the choice of the entries are limited as mentioned in Sect. 4.2. This is due to the nature of the Cauchy matrices where the inverse of the elements are used during the construction, which makes it non-trivial to search for lightweight Cauchy matrices[5]. However, using the concept of equivalence classes, we can exhaust all the matrices and pick the lightest-weight matrix.

---

[5] Using direct construction, there is no clear implication for the choice of the elements α_i and β_j that will generate lightweight entries c_{ij}. On the other hand, every lightweight entry chosen beforehand will greatly restrict the choices for the remaining entries if one wants to maintain two disjoint sets of elements $\{\alpha_i\}$ and $\{\beta_j\}$.

We applied the algorithms of Sect. 5 to construct lightweight MDS involutions over $GF(2^8)$. We list them in the upper half of Table 2 and we can see that they are much lighter than known MDS involutions like the KHAZAD and ANUBIS, previous Hadamard-Cauchy matrices [6,20] and compact Cauchy matrices [15]. In lower half of Table 2, we list the $GF(2^8)$ MDS matrices we found using and show that they are lighter than known MDS matrices like the AES, WHIRLPOOL and WHIRLWIND matrices [7,8,17]. We also compare with the 14 lightweight candidate matrices C_0 to C_{13} for the WHIRLPOOL hash functions suggested during the NESSIE workshop [30, Sect. 6]. Table 2 is comparing our matrices with the ones explicitly provided in the previous articles. Recently, Gupta et $al.$ [21] constructed some circulant matrices that is lightweight for both itself and its inverse. However we do not compare them in our table because their approach minimizes the number of XORs, look-up tables and temporary variables, which might be optimal for software but not for hardware implementations based purely on XOR count.

By Theorem 2 in Sect. 2, we only need to apply the algorithms from Sect. 5 for half the representations of $GF(2^8)$ when searching for optimal lightweight matrices. And as predicted by the discussion after Theorem 1, the lightweight matrices we found in Table 2 do come from $GF(2^8)$ representations with higher standard deviations.

We provide in the first column of the Table 2 the type of the matrices. They can be circulant, Hadamard or Cauchy-Hadamard. The subfield-Hadamard construction is based on the method of [26, Sect. 7.2] which we explain here. Consider the MDS involution $M = had(0x1, 0x4, 0x9, 0xd)$ over $GF(2^4)/0x13$ in the first row of Table 2. Using the method of [26, Sect. 7.2], we can extend it to a MDS involution over $GF(2^8)$ by using two parallel copies of Q. The matrix is formed by writing each input byte x_j as a concatenation of two nibbles $x_j = (x_j^L || x_j^R)$. Then the MDS multiplication is computed on each half $(y_1^L, y_2^L, y_3^L, y_4^L) = M \cdot (x_1^L, x_2^L, x_3^L, x_4^L)$ and $(y_1^R, y_2^R, y_3^R, y_4^R) = M \cdot (x_1^R, x_2^R, x_3^R, x_4^R)$ over $GF(2^4)$. The result is concatenated to form four output bytes (y_1, y_2, y_3, y_4) where $y_j = (y_j^L || y_j^R)$.

We could have concatenated different submatrices and this is done in the WHIRLWIND hash function [7], where the authors concatenated four MDS submatrices over $GF(2^4)$ to form $(M_0|M_1|M_1|M_0)$, an MDS matrix over $GF(2^{16})$. The submatrices are non-involutory Hadamard matrices $M_0 = had(0x5, 0x4, 0xa,$ $0x6, 0x2, 0xd, 0x8, 0x3)$ and $M_1 = (0x5, 0xe, 0x4, 0x7, 0x1, 0x3, 0xf, 0x8)$ defined over $GF(2^4)/0x13$. For fair comparison with our $GF(2^8)$ matrices in Table 2, we consider the corresponding WHIRLWIND-like matrix $(M_0|M_1)$ over $GF(2^8)$ which takes half the resource of the original WHIRLWIND matrix and is also MDS.

The second column of the result tables gives the finite field over which the matrix is defined, while the third column displays the first row of the matrix where the entries are bytes written in hexadecimal notation. The fourth column gives the XOR count to implement the first row of the $n \times n$ matrix. Because all subsequent rows are just permutations of the first row, the XOR count to implement the matrix is just n times this number. For example, to compute the XOR count for implementing $had(0x1, 0x4, 0x9, 0xd)$ over $GF(2^4)/0x13$, we consider the expression for the first row of matrix multiplication $0x1 \cdot x_1 \oplus 0x4 \cdot x_2 \oplus$

$0x9 \cdot x_3 \oplus 0xd \cdot x_4$. From Table 5 of Appendix B, the XOR count of multiplication by $0x1, 0x4, 0x9$ and $0xd$ are $0, 2, 1$ and 3, which gives us a cost of $(0 + 2 + 1 + 3) + 3 \times 4 = 18$ XORs to implement one row of the matrix (the summand 3×4 account for the three XORs summing the four nibbles). For the subfield construction over $GF(2^8)$, we need two copies of the matrix giving a cost of $18 \times 2 = 36$ XORs to implement one row.

We also applied the algorithms that can be found in [31] to find lightweight MDS involution and non-involution matrices of order 4 and 8 over $GF(2^4)$, these matrices are listed in Table 1. By the structure of Hadamard matrix, the first row of an MDS Hadamard matrix must be pairwise distinct. Therefore, there does not exist Hadamard matrix of order larger than 8 over $GF(2^4)$. Due to the smaller dimension of the finite field, the XOR counts of the matrices over $GF(2^4)$ are approximately half of those over $GF(2^8)$.

The application of our work has already been demonstrated in Joltik, a lightweight and hardware-oriented authenticated encryption scheme that uses our lightweight MDS involution matrix of order 4 over $GF(2^4)$ with XOR count as low as 18. On the other hand, the diffusion matrix from Prøst [25] was designed with a goal in mind to minimise the number of XOR operations to perform for implementing it. By Theorem 2 in Sect. 2, we observe that these two matrices are in fact the counterpart of each other in their respective finite fields. Thus, they are essentially the same lightest matrix according to our metric.

We also applied the algorithms from Sect. 5 to find lightweight MDS involution and non-involution matrices of order 4 and 8 over $GF(2^4)$, these matrices are listed in Table 1.

With our work, we can now see that one can use involutory MDS for almost the same price as non-involutory MDS. For example in the upper half of Table 2, the previous 4×4 MDS involution from [20] is about 3 times heavier than the AES matrix[6]; but in this paper, we have used an improved search technique to find an MDS involution lighter than the AES and ANUBIS matrix. Similarly, we have found 8×8 MDS involutions which are much lighter than the KHAZAD involution matrix, and even lighter than lightweight non-involutory MDS matrix like the

Table 1. Comparison of MDS (involution) matrices over $GF(2^4)$

matrix type	finite field	coefficients of the first row	XOR count	reference
4×4 **matrix**				
Involutory Hadamard	$GF(2^4)/0x13$	$(0x1, 0x4, 0x9, 0xd)$	$6 + 3 \times 4 = 18$	Our paper, Joltik [22]
Involutory Hadamard	$GF(2^4)/0x19$	$(0x1, 0x2, 0x6, 0x4)$	$6 + 3 \times 4 = 18$	Prøst [25]
Hadamard	$GF(2^4)/0x13$	$(0x1, 0x2, 0x8, 0x9)$	$5 + 3 \times 4 = 17$	Our paper
8×8 **matrix**				
Involutory Hadamard	$GF(2^4)/0x13$	$(0x2, 0x3, 0x4, 0xc, 0x5, 0xa, 0x8, 0xf)$	$36 + 7 \times 4 = 64$	Our paper
Hadamard	$GF(2^4)/0x13$	$(0x1, 0x2, 0x6, 0x8, 0x9, 0xc, 0xd, 0xa)$	$26 + 7 \times 4 = 54$	Our paper
Hadamard	$GF(2^4)/0x13$	$(0x5, 0x4, 0xa, 0x6, 0x2, 0xd, 0x8, 0x3)$	$33 + 7 \times 4 = 61$	[7]
Hadamard	$GF(2^4)/0x13$	$(0x5, 0xe, 0x4, 0x7, 0x1, 0x3, 0xf, 0x8)$	$39 + 7 \times 4 = 67$	[7]

---

[6] We acknowledge that there are implementations that requires lesser XOR to implement directly the entire circulant AES matrix. However, the small savings obtained on XOR count are completely outweighed by the extra memory cost required for such an implementation in terms of temporary variables.

Table 2. Comparison of MDS Matrices over $GF(2^8)$. The upper table compares the involutory MDS matrices, while the lower table compares the non-involutory MDS matrices (the factor 2 appearing in some of the XOR counts is due to the fact that we have to implement two copies of the matrices)

INVOLUTORY MDS MATRICES

matrix type	finite field	coefficients of the first row	XOR count	reference
4 × 4 matrix				
Subfield-Hadamard	$GF(2^4)/0x13$	$(0x1, 0x4, 0x9, 0xd)$	$2 \times (6 + 3 \times 4) = \mathbf{36}$	Our paper
Hadamard	$GF(2^8)/0x165$	$(0x01, 0x02, 0xb0, 0xb2)$	$16 + 3 \times 8 = \mathbf{40}$	Our paper
Hadamard	$GF(2^8)/0x11d$	$(0x01, 0x02, 0x04, 0x06)$	$22 + 3 \times 8 = \mathbf{46}$	ANUBIS [5]
Compact Cauchy	$GF(2^8)/0x11b$	$(0x01, 0x12, 0x04, 0x16)$	$54 + 3 \times 8 = \mathbf{78}$	[15]
Hadamard-Cauchy	$GF(2^8)/0x11b$	$(0x01, 0x02, 0xfc, 0xfe)$	$74 + 3 \times 8 = \mathbf{98}$	[20]
8 × 8 matrix				
Hadamard	$GF(2^8)/0x1c3$	$(0x01, 0x02, 0x03, 0x91, 0x04, 0x70, 0x05, 0xe1)$	$46 + 7 \times 8 = \mathbf{102}$	Our paper
Subfield-Hadamard	$GF(2^4)/0x13$	$(0x2, 0x3, 0x4, 0xc, 0x5, 0xa, 0x8, 0xf)$	$2 \times (36 + 7 \times 4) = \mathbf{128}$	Our paper
Hadamard	$GF(2^8)/0x11d$	$(0x01, 0x03, 0x04, 0x05, 0x06, 0x08, 0x0b, 0x07)$	$98 + 7 \times 8 = \mathbf{154}$	KHAZAD [6]
Hadamard-Cauchy	$GF(2^8)/0x11b$	$(0x01, 0x02, 0x06, 0x8c, 0x30, 0xfb, 0x87, 0xc4)$	$122 + 7 \times 8 = \mathbf{178}$	[20]
16 × 16 matrix				
Hadamard-Cauchy	$GF(2^8)/0x1c3$	$(0x08, 0x16, 0x8a, 0x01, 0x70, 0x8d, 0x24, 0x76,$ $0xa8, 0x91, 0xad, 0x48, 0x05, 0xb5, 0xaf, 0xf8)$	$258 + 15 \times 8 = \mathbf{378}$	Our paper
Hadamard-Cauchy	$GF(2^8)/0x11b$	$(0x01, 0x03, 0x08, 0xb2, 0x0d, 0x60, 0xe8, 0x1c,$ $0x0f, 0x2c, 0xa2, 0x8b, 0xc9, 0x7a, 0xac, 0x35)$	$338 + 15 \times 8 = \mathbf{458}$	[20]
32 × 32 matrix				
Hadamard-Cauchy	$GF(2^8)/0x165$	$(0xd2, 0x06, 0x05, 0x4d, 0x21, 0xf8, 0x11, 0x62,$ $0x08, 0xd8, 0xe9, 0x28, 0x4b, 0xa6, 0x10, 0x2c,$ $0xa1, 0x49, 0x4c, 0xd1, 0x59, 0xb2, 0x13, 0xa4,$ $0x03, 0xc3, 0x42, 0x79, 0xa0, 0x6f, 0xab, 0x41)$	$610 + 31 \times 8 = \mathbf{858}$	Our paper
Hadamard-Cauchy	$GF(2^8)/0x11b$	$(0x01, 0x02, 0x04, 0x69, 0x07, 0xec, 0xcc, 0x72,$ $0x0b, 0x54, 0x29, 0xbe, 0x74, 0xf9, 0xc4, 0x87,$ $0x0e, 0x47, 0xc2, 0xc3, 0x39, 0x8e, 0x1c, 0x85,$ $0x58, 0x26, 0x1e, 0xaf, 0x68, 0xb6, 0x59, 0x1f)$	$675 + 31 \times 8 = \mathbf{923}$	[20]

NON-INVOLUTORY MDS MATRICES

matrix type	finite field	coefficients of the first row	XOR count	reference
4 × 4 matrix				
Subfield-Hadamard	$GF(2^4)/0x13$	$(0x1, 0x2, 0x8, 0x9)$	$2 \times (5 + 3 \times 4) = \mathbf{34}$	Our paper
Hadamard	$GF(2^8)/0x1c3$	$(0x01, 0x02, 0x04, 0x91)$	$13 + 3 \times 8 = \mathbf{37}$	Our paper
Circulant	$GF(2^8)/0x11b$	$(0x02, 0x03, 0x01, 0x01)$	$14 + 3 \times 8 = \mathbf{38}$	AES [17]
8 × 8 matrix				
Hadamard	$GF(2^8)/0x1c3$	$(0x01, 0x02, 0x03, 0x08, 0x04, 0x91, 0xe1, 0xa9)$	$40 + 7 \times 8 = \mathbf{96}$	Our paper
Circulant	$GF(2^8)/0x11d$	$(0x01, 0x01, 0x04, 0x01, 0x08, 0x05, 0x02, 0x09)$	$49 + 7 \times 8 = \mathbf{105}$	WHIRLPOOL [8]
Subfield-Hadamard	$GF(2^4)/0x13$	$(0x1, 0x2, 0x6, 0x8, 0x9, 0xc, 0xd, 0xa)$	$2 \times (26 + 7 \times 4) = \mathbf{108}$	Our paper
Circulant	$GF(2^8)/0x11d$	WHIRLPOOL-like matrices	between **105 to 117**	[30]
Subfield-Hadamard	$GF(2^4)/0x13$	WHIRLWIND-like matrix	$33 + 39 + 2 \times 7 \times 4 = \mathbf{128}$	[7]
16 × 16 matrix				
Hadamard-Cauchy	$GF(2^8)/0x1c3$	$(0xb1, 0x1c, 0x30, 0x09, 0x08, 0x91, 0x18, 0xe4,$ $0x98, 0x12, 0x70, 0xb5, 0x97, 0x90, 0xa9, 0x5b)$	$232 + 15 \times 8 = \mathbf{352}$	Our paper
32 × 32 matrix				
Hadamard-Cauchy	$GF(2^8)/0x1c3$	$(0xb9, 0x7c, 0x93, 0xbc, 0xbd, 0x26, 0xfa, 0xa9,$ $0x32, 0x31, 0x24, 0xb5, 0xbb, 0x06, 0xa0, 0x44,$ $0x95, 0xb3, 0x0c, 0x1c, 0x07, 0xe5, 0xa4, 0x2e,$ $0x56, 0x4c, 0x55, 0x02, 0x66, 0x39, 0x48, 0x08)$	$596 + 31 \times 8 = \mathbf{844}$	Our paper

WHIRLPOOL matrix. Thus, our method will be useful for future construction of lightweight ciphers based on involutory components like the ANUBIS, KHAZAD, ICEBERG and PRINCE ciphers.

Acknowledgments. The authors would like to thank the anonymous referees for their helpful comments. We also wish to thank Wang HuaXiong for providing useful and valuable suggestions.

A   Primitive Mapping Between Finite Fields

Table 3. Primitive mapping from $GF(2^4)/0x13$ to $GF(2^4)/0x19$

order	0x13 (10011)		0x19 (11001)	
	x	XOR	x	XOR
α	2	1	12	1
α^2	4	2	6	2
α^3	8	3	3	3
α^4	3	5	13	5
α^5	6	5	10	5
α^6	12	5	5	5
α^7	11	6	14	6

order	0x13 (10011)		0x19 (11001)	
	x	XOR	x	XOR
α^8	5	6	7	6
α^9	10	8	15	8
α^{10}	7	9	11	9
α^{11}	14	8	9	8
α^{12}	15	6	8	6
α^{13}	13	3	4	3
α^{14}	9	1	2	1

Table 4. Primitive mapping from finite field to its reciprocal finite field

finite field	$p(X)$	$\frac{1}{p}(X)$	primitive mapping
$GF(2^2)$	0x7	-	$\phi : 2 \mapsto 3$
$GF(2^3)$	0xb	0xd	$\phi : 2 \mapsto 6$
$GF(2^4)$	0x13	0x19	$\phi : 2 \mapsto 12$
	0x1f	-	$\phi : 3 \mapsto 5$
$GF(2^5)$	0x25	0x29	$\phi : 2 \mapsto 20$
	0x3d	0x2f	$\phi : 2 \mapsto 23$
	0x37	0x3b	$\phi : 2 \mapsto 29$
$GF(2^6)$	0x43	0x61	$\phi : 2 \mapsto 48$
	0x57	0x75	$\phi : 3 \mapsto 59$
	0x67	0x73	$\phi : 2 \mapsto 57$
	0x49	-	$\phi : 3 \mapsto 37$
$GF(2^7)$	0x83	0xc1	$\phi : 2 \mapsto 96$
	0xab	0xd5	$\phi : 2 \mapsto 106$
	0x8f	0xf1	$\phi : 2 \mapsto 120$
	0xfd	0xbf	$\phi : 2 \mapsto 95$
	0xb9	0x9d	$\phi : 2 \mapsto 78$
	0x89	0x91	$\phi : 2 \mapsto 72$
	0xe5	0xa7	$\phi : 2 \mapsto 83$
	0xef	0xf7	$\phi : 2 \mapsto 123$
	0xcb	0xd3	$\phi : 2 \mapsto 105$

finite field	$p(X)$	$\frac{1}{p}(X)$	primitive mapping
$GF(2^8)$	0x11d	0x171	$\phi : 2 \mapsto 184$
	0x177	0x1dd	$\phi : 3 \mapsto 239$
	0x1f3	0x19f	$\phi : 6 \mapsto 103$
	0x169	0x12d	$\phi : 2 \mapsto 150$
	0x1bd	0x17b	$\phi : 7 \mapsto 95$
	0x1e7	0x1cf	$\phi : 2 \mapsto 231$
	0x12b	0x1a9	$\phi : 2 \mapsto 212$
	0x1d7	-	$\phi : 7 \mapsto 116$
	0x165	0x14d	$\phi : 2 \mapsto 166$
	0x18b	0x1a3	$\phi : 6 \mapsto 104$
	0x163	0x18d	$\phi : 2 \mapsto 198$
	0x11b	0x1b1	$\phi : 3 \mapsto 217$
	0x13f	0x1f9	$\phi : 3 \mapsto 253$
	0x15f	0x1f5	$\phi : 2 \mapsto 250$
	0x1c3	0x187	$\phi : 2 \mapsto 195$
	0x139	-	$\phi : 3 \mapsto 157$

B   Tables of XOR Count

Table 5. XOR count for $GF(2^2)$, $GF(2^3)$ and $GF(2^4)$

x	$GF(2^2)$	$GF(2^3)$		$GF(2^4)$		
	0x7	0xb	0xd	0x13	0x19	0x1f
0	0	0	0	0	0	0
1	0	0	0	0	0	0
2	1	1	1	1	1	3
3	1	4	2	5	3	5
4	–	2	3	2	3	3
5	–	1	4	6	5	5
6	–	4	1	5	2	6
7	–	3	4	9	6	6
8	–	–	–	3	6	3
9	–	–	–	1	8	5
10	–	–	–	8	5	6
11	–	–	–	6	9	6
12	–	–	–	5	1	6
13	–	–	–	3	5	6
14	–	–	–	8	6	5
15	–	–	–	6	8	3
mean		1.88	1.88	4.25	4.25	4.25
σ		1.4569	1.4569	2.6800	2.6800	1.7075

References

1. Andreeva, E., Bilgin, B., Bogdanov, A., Luykx, A., Mendel, F., Mennink, B., Mouha, N., Wang, Q., Yasuda, K.: PRIMATEs v1. Submission to the CAESAR Competition (2014). http://competitions.cr.yp.to/round1/primatesv1.pdf
2. Augot, D., Finiasz, M.: Direct construction of recursive MDS diffusion layers using shortened BCH codes. In: Cid, C., Rechberger, C. (eds.) FSE 2014. LNCS, vol. 8540, pp. 3–17. Springer, Heidelberg (2015)
3. Augot, D., Finiasz, M.: Exhaustive search for small dimension recursive MDS diffusion layers for block ciphers and hash functions. In: ISIT, pp. 1551–1555 (2013)
4. Aumasson, J.-P., Henzen, L., Meier, W., Naya-Plasencia, M.: QUARK: a lightweight hash. In: Mangard, S., Standaert, F.-X. (eds.) CHES 2010. LNCS, vol. 6225, pp. 1–15. Springer, Heidelberg (2010)
5. Barreto, P., Rijmen, V.: The Anubis Block Cipher. Submission to the NESSIE Project (2000)
6. Barreto, P., Rijmen, V.: The Khazad legacy-level block cipher. In: First Open NESSIE Workshop (2000)
7. Barreto, P., Nikov, V., Nikova, S., Rijmen, V., Tischhauser, E.: Whirlwind a new cryptographic hash function. Des. Codes Crypt. **56**(2–3), 141–162 (2010)
8. Barreto, P., Rijmen, V.: Whirlpool. In: Encyclopedia of Cryptography and Security, 2nd edn. Springer, Heidelberg (2011)

9. Beaulieu, R., Shors, D., Smith, J., Treatman-Clark, S., Weeks, B., Wingers, L.: The SIMON and SPECK Families of Lightweight Block Ciphers. Cryptology ePrint Archive, Report 2013/404 (2013)

10. Berger, T.P.: Construction of recursive MDS diffusion layers from Gabidulin codes. In: Paul, G., Vaudenay, S. (eds.) INDOCRYPT 2013. LNCS, vol. 8250, pp. 274–285. Springer, Heidelberg (2013)

11. Bogdanov, A., Knežević, M., Leander, G., Toz, D., Varıcı, K., Verbauwhede, I.: SPONGENT: a lightweight hash function. In: Preneel, B., Takagi, T. (eds.) CHES 2011. LNCS, vol. 6917, pp. 312–325. Springer, Heidelberg (2011)

12. Bogdanov, A.A., Knudsen, L.R., Leander, G., Paar, C., Poschmann, A., Robshaw, M., Seurin, Y., Vikkelsoe, C.: PRESENT: an ultra-lightweight block cipher. In: Paillier, P., Verbauwhede, I. (eds.) CHES 2007. LNCS, vol. 4727, pp. 450–466. Springer, Heidelberg (2007)

13. Borghoff, J., Canteaut, A., Güneysu, T., Kavun, E.B., Knezevic, M., Knudsen, L.R., Leander, G., Nikov, V., Paar, C., Rechberger, C., Rombouts, P., Thomsen, S.S., Yalçın, T.: PRINCE – a low-latency block cipher for pervasive computing applications. In: Wang, X., Sako, K. (eds.) ASIACRYPT 2012. LNCS, vol. 7658, pp. 208–225. Springer, Heidelberg (2012)

14. De Cannière, C., Dunkelman, O., Knežević, M.: KATAN and KTANTAN — a family of small and efficient hardware-oriented block ciphers. In: Clavier, C., Gaj, K. (eds.) CHES 2009. LNCS, vol. 5747, pp. 272–288. Springer, Heidelberg (2009)

15. Cui, T., Jin, C.I, Kong, Z.: On compact cauchy matrices for substitution-permutation networks. IEEE Trans. Comput. 99(PrePrints), 1 (2014)

16. Daemen, J., Knudsen, L.R., Rijmen, V.: The block cipher SQUARE. In: Biham, E. (ed.) FSE 1997. LNCS, vol. 1267, pp. 149–165. Springer, Heidelberg (1997)

17. Daemen, J., Rijmen, V.: The Design of Rijndael: AES - The Advanced Encryption Standard. Springer, Heidelberg (2002)

18. Guo, J., Peyrin, T., Poschmann, A.: The PHOTON family of lightweight hash functions. In: Rogaway, P. (ed.) CRYPTO 2011. LNCS, vol. 6841, pp. 222–239. Springer, Heidelberg (2011)

19. Guo, J., Peyrin, T., Poschmann, A., Robshaw, M.: The LED block cipher. In: Preneel, B., Takagi, T. (eds.) CHES 2011. LNCS, vol. 6917, pp. 326–341. Springer, Heidelberg (2011)

20. Chand Gupta, K., Ghosh Ray, I.: On constructions of involutory MDS matrices. In: Youssef, A., Nitaj, A., Hassanien, A.E. (eds.) AFRICACRYPT 2013. LNCS, vol. 7918, pp. 43–60. Springer, Heidelberg (2013)

21. Chand Gupta, K., Ghosh Ray, I.: On constructions of circulant MDS matrices for lightweight cryptography. In: Huang, X., Zhou, J. (eds.) ISPEC 2014. LNCS, vol. 8434, pp. 564–576. Springer, Heidelberg (2014)

22. Jean, J., Nikolić, I., Peyrin, T.: Joltik v1.1, 2014. Submission to the CAESAR competition. http://www1.spms.ntu.edu.sg/~syllab/Joltik

23. Nakahara Jr., J., Abraho, I.: A new involutory mds matrix for the aes. I. J Netw. Secur. 9(2), 109–116 (2009)

24. Junod, P., Vaudenay, S.: Perfect diffusion primitives for block ciphers. In: Handschuh, H., Hasan, M.A. (eds.) SAC 2004. LNCS, vol. 3357, pp. 84–99. Springer, Heidelberg (2004)

25. Kavun, E.B., Lauridsen, M.M., Leander, G., Rechberger, C., Schwabe, P., Yalçın, T.: Prøst v1.1, 2014. Submission to the CAESAR competition. http://competitions.cr.yp.to/round1/proestv11.pdf

26. Khoo, K., Peyrin, T., Poschmann, A.Y., Yap, H.: FOAM: searching for hardware-optimal SPN structures and components with a fair comparison. In: Batina, L., Robshaw, M. (eds.) CHES 2014. LNCS, vol. 8731, pp. 433–450. Springer, Heidelberg (2014)

27. Lacan, J., Fimes, J.: Systematic MDS erasure codes based on Vandermonde matrices. IEEE Commun. Lett. **8**(9), 570–572 (2004)

28. Sajadieh, M., Dakhilalian, M., Mala, H., Sepehrdad, P.: Recursive diffusion layers for block ciphers and hash functions. In: Canteaut, A. (ed.) FSE 2012. LNCS, vol. 7549, pp. 385–401. Springer, Heidelberg (2012)

29. Sajadieh, M.I., Dakhilalian, M., Mala, H., Omoomi, B.: On construction of involutory MDS matrices from Vandermonde matrices in GF(2 q). Des. Codes Crypt. **64**(3), 287–308 (2012)

30. Shirai, T., Shibutani, K.: On the diffusion matrix employed in the Whirlpool hashing function. NESSIE Phase 2 Report NES/DOC/EXT/WP5/002/1

31. Sim, S.M., Khoo, K., Oggier, F., Peyrin, T.: Lightweight mds involution matrices. Cryptology ePrint Archive, Report 2015/258 (2015). http://eprint.iacr.org/

32. Standaert, F.-X., Piret, G., Rouvroy, G., Quisquater, J.-J., Legat, J.-D.: ICEBERG : an involutional cipher efficient for block encryption in reconfigurable hardware. In: Roy, B., Meier, W. (eds.) FSE 2004. LNCS, vol. 3017, pp. 279–299. Springer, Heidelberg (2004)

33. Wu, S., Wang, M., Wu, W.: Recursive diffusion layers for (lightweight) block ciphers and hash functions. In: Knudsen, L.R., Wu, H. (eds.) SAC 2012. LNCS, vol. 7707, pp. 355–371. Springer, Heidelberg (2013)

34. Youssef, A.M., Mister, S., Tavares, S.E.: On the design of linear transformations for substitution permutation encryption networks. In: Workshop On Selected Areas in Cryptography, pp. 40–48 (1997)

A New Classification of 4-bit Optimal S-boxes and Its Application to PRESENT, RECTANGLE and SPONGENT

Wentao Zhang[1]($\boxtimes$), Zhenzhen Bao[1], Vincent Rijmen[2]($\boxtimes$), and Meicheng Liu[1]

[1] State Key Laboratory of Information Security,
Institute of Information Engineering, Chinese Academy of Sciences,
Beijing 100093, China
{zhangwentao,baozhenzhen,liumeicheng}@iie.ac.cn
[2] Department of Electrical Engineering ESAT/COSIC and IMinds,
Security Department, KU Leuven, Leuven, Belgium
vincent.rijmen@esat.kuleuven.be

Abstract. In this paper, we present a new classification of 4-bit optimal S-boxes. All optimal 4-bit S-boxes can be classified into 183 different categories, among which we specify 3 platinum categories. Under the design criteria of the PRESENT (or SPONGENT) S-box, there are 8064 different S-boxes up to adding constants before and after an S-box. The 8064 S-boxes belong to 3 different categories, we show that the S-box should be chosen from one out of the 3 categories or other categories for better resistance against linear cryptanalysis. Furthermore, we study in detail how the S-boxes in the 3 platinum categories influence the security of PRESENT, RECTANGLE and SPONGENT$_{88}$ against differential and linear cryptanalysis. Our results show that the S-box selection has a great influence on the security of the schemes. For block ciphers or hash functions with 4-bit S-boxes as confusion layers and bit permutations as diffusion layers, designers can extend the range of S-box selection to the 3 platinum categories and select their S-box very carefully. For PRESENT, RECTANGLE and SPONGENT$_{88}$ respectively, we get a set of potentially best/better S-box candidates from the 3 platinum categories. These potentially best/better S-boxes can be further investigated to see if they can be used to improve the security-performance tradeoff of the 3 cryptographic algorithms.

Keywords: 4-bit S-box · Classification · Block cipher · Hash function · Differential cryptanalysis · Linear cryptanalysis · PRESENT · RECTANGLE · SPONGENT

1 Introduction

S-boxes are widely used in modern block ciphers and hash functions. Substitution-Permutation (SP) and Feistel network are the most common structures. In these structures, S-boxes are usually the only non-linear part. Therefore, S-boxes have

© International Association for Cryptologic Research 2015
G. Leander (Ed.): FSE 2015, LNCS 9054, pp. 494–515, 2015.
DOI: 10.1007/978-3-662-48116-5_24

to be chosen carefully to optimize the security-performance tradeoff. The most common sizes of S-boxes are 8-bit and 4-bit. AES [14] uses an 8-bit S-box, which has influenced many subsequent ciphers; while Serpent [2] and NOEKEON [13] use 4-bit S-boxes. In the past few years, as the need for security in RFID and sensor networks is dramatically increasing, many lightweight constructions have been proposed. Since a 4-bit S-box is usually much more compact in hardware than an 8-bit S-box, many lightweight block ciphers and hash functions use 4-bit S-boxes, such as LED [15], PHOTON [16], PRESENT [10], RECTANGLE [28] and SPONGENT [8].

For 4-bit S-boxes, the optimal values are known with respect to differential and linear cryptanalysis, an S-box attaining these optimal values is called an optimal S-box. In [18], Leander et al. classified all optimal 4-bit S-boxes into 16 affine equivalences; this result can be used to efficiently generate optimal S-boxes fulfilling additional criteria. However, for many constructions, the design criterion of being an optimal S-box is not enough, there are other important properties the designers should take into account. For example, the design criteria of the Serpent S-box require that a 1-bit input difference must cause an output difference of at least two bits.

Given an S-box S, let $CarD1_S$ denote the number of times that a 1-bit input difference causes a 1-bit output difference, and $CarL1_S$ the number of times that a 1-bit input selection pattern causes a 1-bit output selection pattern. We refer to Sect. 2.1 for a precise definition of $CarD1_S$ and $CarL1_S$. For the PRESENT S-box, $CarD1_S = 0$ and $CarL1_S = 8$. In [22], linear hulls were used to mount an attack on 25-round PRESENT. Later, a multidimensional linear attack on 26-round PRESENT was given in [12], which is the best shortcut attack on PRESENT so far. Both of the above attacks use the fact that the value of $CarL1_S$ of the PRESENT S-box is relatively high, i.e., $CarL1_S = 8$, which leads to a significant clustering of linear trails. For comparison, the value of $CarD1_S$ of the PRESENT S-box is zero, the best shortcut differential attack on PRESENT only reaches 18 rounds [26]. It can be seen that, with respect to security margin, there is a big gap between differential cryptanalysis and linear cryptanalysis on PRESENT. More recently, Blondeau and Nyberg [7] showed that there exists a chosen-plaintext truncated differential attack for any known-plaintext multidimensional linear attack, hence, they have successfully derived a truncated differential attack on 26-round PRESENT from the multidimensional linear attack on 26-round PRESENT [12]. From this result, we can learn that a block cipher had better have almost the same security margin against differential-like attacks and linear-like attacks. Now, the questions come up. Is there any optimal S-box satisfying $CarD1_S = 0$ and $CarL1_S = 0$? Is there a better S-box for PRESENT with respect to the security against differential and linear cryptanalysis? These questions are part of motivation of this paper.

SPONGENT is a family of lightweight hash functions based on PRESENT. The internal permutation of each variant uses SP-network with 4-bit S-boxes and a bit permutation. For the SPONGENT S-box, $CarD1_S = 0$ and $CarL1_S = 4$. RECTANGLE is designed with bit-slice technique. RECTANGLE also uses SP-network with 4-bit S-boxes and a bit permutation. For the RECTANGLE S-box,

$CarD1_S = 2$ and $CarL1_S = 2$. Then, one may wonder if the security margin of PRESENT can be improved when replacing its S-box by the SPONGENT or RECTANGLE S-box. Moreover, is the S-box selection of SPONGENT and RECTANGLE optimal with respect to differential and linear cryptanalysis? In this paper, we will partly answer these questions.

1.1   Contributions

In Sect. 3 of this paper, we firstly prove that $CarL1_S \geq 2$ for any optimal S-box. Moreover, if $CarL1_S = 2$, then the S-box must be in 4 (out of 16) affine equivalent classes; if $CarL1_S = 3$, then the S-box must be in 8 (out of 16) affine equivalent classes. We call the subset of optimal S-boxes with the same values of $CarD1_S$ and $CarL1_S$ a Num1-DL category. We show that all optimal 4-bit S-boxes can be classified into 183 different Num1-DL categories. Among all the 183 Num1-DL categories, there are 3 categories with the minimal value of $CarD1_S + CarL1_S$, we call the 3 categories platinum Num1-DL categories.

There are 4 measures to evaluate the security of a cipher against differential and linear cryptanalysis. In Sect. 4, we give a brief discussion on the 4 measures, and show why it is appropriate to use the heuristic measure for the study in this paper.

In Sect. 5, we consider PRESENT and 5 variants of SPONGENT. There are 8064 S-boxes (up to adding constants before and after an S-box, similarly hereinafter) satisfying the design criteria of the PRESENT (or SPONGENT) S-box. The 8064 S-boxes belong to 3 different categories. We show that, for each of the 6 fixed permutation layers, if the S-box comes from 2 out of the 3 categories, then there exists a linear trail with only one active S-box in each round. Hence, for SP-network schemes with the PRESENT or SPONGENT permutation layer, for better resistance against linear cryptanalysis, the S-box should be chosen from 1 out of the 3 categories or other categories.

In Sect. 6, we investigate how the S-boxes in the 3 platinum Num1-DL categories influence the security of PRESENT, RECTANGLE and SPONGENT against differential and linear cryptanalysis. We focus on 64- and 88-bit block length. Consider the following SP-network schemes. For 64-bit block length, the S-box is chosen from the 3 platinum Num1-DL categories, the diffusion layer is either the PRESENT permutation or the RECTANGLE permutation. Thus, there are 6 combinations. Similarly, for 88-bit block length, there are also 6 combinations. For each of these 12 combinations, we use the heuristic measure to evaluate which are the best possible S-box candidates. Our results show that the S-box selection has a significant influence on the security of the 3 primitives. For PRESENT, there are 336 potentially best S-boxes, which does not include the PRESENT S-box. For RECTANGLE, there are 128 potentially best S-boxes, which includes the RECTANGLE S-box. For $SPONGENT_{88}$, we present 4 potentially better S-boxes when considering differential cryptanalysis more important than linear cryptanalysis. We want to point out that these results do not mean any security weakness of PRESENT, RECTANGLE or SPONGENT. However, these results show that there are potentially better S-box selections for PRESENT and SPONGENT, which means, by choosing another S-box, it is possible to improve the hardware/software performance of PRESENT and SPONGENT with a fixed level of security margin. Since any platinum Num1-DL category is not always the best choice, we suggest that designers can extend the range of the S-box selection to the 3 platinum Num1-DL categories and select their S-box carefully, when designing a block cipher or a hash function using 4-bit S-boxes as confusion layer and a bit permutation as diffusion layer.

2   Preliminaries

2.1   Optimal S-box, Affine and PE Equivalence, m-resilient Boolean Function

Given an S-box mapping n bits to m bits $S : F_2^n \to F_2^m$, we call S an $n \times m$ S-box. In this paper, we only concentrate on 4×4 S-boxes.

Let S denote a 4×4 bijective S-box. Let $\triangle I, \triangle O \in F_2^4$, define ND_S $(\triangle I, \triangle O)$ as:

$$ND_S(\triangle I, \triangle O) = \sharp\{x \in F_2^4 | S(x) \oplus S(x \oplus \triangle I) = \triangle O\}.$$

Let $\varGamma I, \varGamma O \in F_2^4$, define the imbalance $Imb_S(\varGamma I, \varGamma O)$ as:

$$Imb_S(\varGamma I, \varGamma O) = |\sharp\{x \in F_2^4 | \varGamma I \cdot x = \varGamma O \cdot S(x)\} - 8|.$$

where "$\cdot$" denotes the inner product on F_2^4.

Define the differential-uniformity of S as:

$$Diff(S) = \max_{\triangle I \neq 0, \triangle O} ND_S(\triangle I, \triangle O)$$

Define the linearity of S as:

$$Lin(S) = \max_{\varGamma I, \varGamma O \neq 0} Imb_S(\varGamma I, \varGamma O)$$

For any bijective 4×4 S-box, $Diff(S) \geq 4$ and $Lin(S) \geq 4$ [18]. An S-box attaining these minima is called an optimal S-box.

Definition 1 ([18]). *Let S be a 4×4 S-box. S is called an **optimal S-box** if it satisfies the 3 conditions:*

1. S is bijective, i.e., $S(x) \neq S(x')$ for any $x \neq x'$.
2. $Diff(S) = 4$.
3. $Lin(S) = 4$.

Let $wt(x)$ denote the Hamming weight of a binary vector x. Define $SetD1_S$ [28] as:

$$SetD1_S = \{(\triangle I, \triangle O) \in F_2^4 \times F_2^4 | wt(\triangle I) = wt(\triangle O) = 1 \text{ and } ND_S(\triangle I, \triangle O) \neq 0\}.$$

Define $SetL1_S$ [28] as:

$$SetL1_S = \{(\varGamma I, \varGamma O) \in F_2^4 \times F_2^4 | wt(\varGamma I) = wt(\varGamma O) = 1 \text{ and } Imb_S(\varGamma I, \varGamma O) \neq 0\}.$$

Let $CarD1_S$ denote the cardinality of $SetD1_S$, and $CarL1_S$ the cardinality of $SetL1_S$.

Definition 2 ([18]). *Two S-boxes S and S' are called **affine equivalent** if there exist two invertible 4×4 matrices A, B over F_2, and constants $a, b \in F_2^4$ such that $S'(x) = B(S(A(x) \oplus a)) \oplus b$.*

Given an S-box S, the values of $Diff(S)$ and $Lin(S)$ both remain unchanged when applying an affine transformation in the domain or co-domain of S [11,21].

Theorem 1 ([18]). *Let S and S' be two affine equivalent S-boxes. If S is an optimal S-box, then S' is an optimal S-box as well.*

According to Theorem 1, all optimal S-boxes can be divided into equivalence classes using affine equivalence relation. All 4×4 optimal S-boxes can be split into only 16 affine equivalence classes [18]. Let $\{G_i, 0 \leq i \leq 15\}$ denote the representatives for the 16 equivalence classes, we refer to [18] for the 16 representatives.

Definition 3 ([18]). *Two S-boxes S and S' are called **permutation-then-XOR equivalent** if there exist two 4×4 permutation matrices P_0, P_1 over F_2, and constants $a, b \in F_2^4$ such that $S'(x) = P_1(S(P_0(x) \oplus a)) \oplus b$. The equivalence is called **PE equivalence**.*

Note that if two S-boxes are PE equivalent, then they must be affine equivalent.

Definition 4. *Let f be a Boolean function $f : F_2^n \to F_2$, define the Walsh Coefficient of f at a as:*

$$f^W(a) = \sum_{x \in F_2^n} (-1)^{f(x) \oplus a \cdot x}.$$

An n-variable Boolean function f is balanced if its output in the truth table contains equal number of 0 and 1. f is balanced if and only if $f^W(0) = 0$.

Definition 5 ([27]). *A Boolean function f is m-resilient if and only if its Walsh Coefficient satisfy $f^W(a) = 0$ for any $0 \leq wt(a) \leq m$.*

For any $b \in F_2^4$, define the corresponding component Boolean function S_b of an S-box S as:

$$S_b : F_2^4 \to F_2, \ S_b(x) = b \cdot S(x).$$

Let $deg(f)$ denote the algebraic degree of the Boolean function f, the algebraic degree is invariant under affine equivalence. Table 1 [18] gives the number of $b \in F_2^4 \setminus \{0\}$ such that $deg(S_b) = 2, 3$ for the 16 representative optimal S-boxes.

Table 1. ([18]) Number of $b \in F_2^4 \setminus \{0\}$ such that $deg(S_b) = 2, 3$

S-box	G_0	G_1	G_2	G_3	G_4	G_5	G_6	G_7	G_8	G_9	G_{10}	G_{11}	G_{12}	G_{13}	G_{14}	G_{15}
$deg(S_b) = 2$	3	3	3	0	0	0	0	0	3	1	1	0	0	0	1	1
$deg(S_b) = 3$	12	12	12	15	15	15	15	15	12	14	14	15	15	15	14	14

2.2 Differential Trail, Difference Propagation, Linear Trail and Linear Propagation

Differential cryptanalysis (DC) [5] and linear cryptanalysis (LC) [19] are among the most powerful techniques available for block ciphers. Let β be a Boolean transformation operating on n-bit vectors that is a sequence of r transformations:

$$\beta = \rho^{(r)} \circ \rho^{(r-1)} \circ \cdots \circ \rho^{(2)} \circ \rho^{(1)}.$$

In this paper, β refers to a key-alternating block cipher [14] or a permutation of a hash function, the round keys (or constants) are added to the state by means of an XOR. Thus, a difference is referred to as an XOR.

A *differential trail* [14] Q over an iterative transformation consists of a sequence of $r + 1$ difference patterns:

$$Q = (q^{(0)}, q^{(1)}, q^{(2)}, \cdots, q^{(r-1)}, q^{(r)}).$$

The probability of a differential step is defined as:

$$Prob(q^{(i-1)}, q^{(i)}) = 2^{-n} \times \sharp\{x \in F_2^n | \rho^{(i)}(x) \oplus \rho^{(i)}(x \oplus q^{(i-1)}) = q^{(i)}\}.$$

Assuming the independence of different steps, the probability of a differential trail Q can be approximated as:

$$Prob(Q) = \prod_i Prob(q^{(i-1)}, q^{(i)}).$$

A *difference propagation* [14] is composed of a set of differential trails, the probability of a difference propagation (a', b') is the sum of the probabilities of all r-round differential trails Q with initial difference a' and terminal difference b':

$$Prob(a', b') = \sum_{q^{(0)}=a', q^{(r)}=b'} Prob(Q) \tag{1}$$

The correlation $C(f, g)$ between two binary Boolean functions $f(a)$ and $g(a)$ is defined as:

$$C(f, g) = 2 \times Prob(f(a) = g(a)) - 1.$$

A *linear trail* [14] U over an iterative transformation consists of a sequence of $r + 1$ selection patterns (also known as linear mask):

$$U = (u^{(0)}, u^{(1)}, u^{(2)}, \cdots, u^{(r-1)}, u^{(r)}).$$

The *correlation contribution* [14] of a linear trail is the product of the correlation of all its steps:

$$Cor(U) = \prod_i C(u^{(i)} \cdot \rho^{(i)}(a), u^{(i-1)} \cdot a). \tag{2}$$

A *linear propagation* is composed of a set of linear trails, the correlation of a linear propagation (u, w) is the sum of the correlation contributions of all r-round linear trails U with initial selection pattern w and final selection pattern u:

$$Cor(u, w) = \sum_{u^{(0)}=w, \, u^{(r)}=u} Cor(U). \tag{3}$$

The square of a correlation (contribution) is called correlation potential. The following theorem gives the expected value of the correlation potential $Cor(u, w)^2$ over all possible values of the expanded key.

Theorem 2 ([14]). *The average correlation potential between an input and an output selection pattern is the sum of the correlation potentials of all linear trails between the input and output selection patterns:*

$$E(Cor_t{}^2) = \sum_i (Cor_i)^2 \tag{4}$$

where Cor_t is the overall correlation, and Cor_i the correlation contribution of a linear trail.

To attack a b-bit block cipher using DC, there must be a predictable difference propagation over all but a few rounds with a probability significantly larger than 2^{-b}. To attack a b-bit block cipher using LC, there must be a predictable linear propagation over all but a few rounds with a correlation potential significantly larger than 2^{-b}.

2.3 An Extension of RECTANGLE - RECTANGLE$_{88}$

Based on the design criteria of RECTANGLE, we present an extension of REC-TANGLE to 88-bit block length, denoted as RECTANGLE$_{88}$. A 88-bit cipher state is pictured as a 4×22 rectangular array of bits. The *SubColumn* is 22 parallel applications of S-boxes to the 22 columns. The *ShiftRow* step is defined as follows: row 0 is not rotated, row 1 is left rotated over 1 bit, row 2 is left rotated over 8 bits, row 3 is left rotated over 17 bits.

3   A New Classification of 4-bit S-boxes

The subset of 4×4 optimal S-boxes with the same values of $CarD1_S$ and $CarL1_S$ is called a category, the following is a formal definition.

Definition 6. *An (nd, nl)-**Num1-DL category** is defined as a subset of all 4×4 optimal S-boxes which satisfy $CarD1_S = nd$ and $CarL1_S = nl$. The category is also called a **Num1-DL category** for short.*

We are especially interested in those categories with low $CarD1_S$ and low $CarL1_S$. It can be easily seen that $0 \leq CarD1_S \leq 16$ and $0 \leq CarL1_S \leq 16$.

Theorem 3. *Let S denote an optimal S-box, then $CarL1_S \geq 2$. In other words, there does not exist an optimal S-box with $CarL1_S = 0$ or $CarL1_S = 1$.*

Proof: Let $x = (x_3, x_2, x_1, x_0)$ and $S(x) = (f_3(x), f_2(x), f_1(x), f_0(x))$, where x_i is the i-th bit of x, and $f_j(x)$ the j-th bit of $S(x)$. Since S is bijective, each Boolean function f_j ($0 \leq j \leq 3$)) is balanced.

Firstly, we show that there exist at least 2 Boolean functions f_{j_1} and f_{j_2} ($0 \leq j_1, j_2 \leq 3$) with algebraic degree 3, equivalently speaking, there exist at most 2 Boolean functions with algebraic degree less than 3. Proof by contradiction. Assume that there exist 3 (or 4) out of the 4 Boolean functions f_j ($j = 0, 1, 2, 3$) with algebraic degree less than 3. Then, for each of the 7 (or 15) non-zero linear combinations of these 3 (or 4) functions, the algebraic degree is also less than 3. However, according to Table 1, for any optimal S-box, there are at most 3 out of the 15 component functions with algebraic degree less than 3, which is a contradiction.

According to Siegenthaler's inequality [25], an n-variable Boolean function with degree $n-1$ is not 1-resilient. Particularly, if the degree of f_j is 3, then there exists $0 \leq i \leq 3$ such that $f_j(x) \oplus x_i$ is not balanced, which means that $(2^i, 2^j) \in SetL1_S$. Since there exist at least 2 functions f_{j_1} and f_{j_2} with algebraic degree 3, we can get that there are at least 2 elements in $SetL1_S$, i.e., $CarL1_S \geq 2$. □

Similar to the proof of Theorem 3, we can prove the following 2 theorems.

Theorem 4. *Let S denote an optimal S-box. If S is affine equivalent to G_9, G_{10}, G_{14} or G_{15}, then $CarL1_S \geq 3$.*

Theorem 5. *Let S denote an optimal S-box. If S is affine equivalent to $G_3, G_4, G_5, G_6, G_7, G_{11}, G_{12}$ or G_{13}, then $CarL1_S \geq 4$.*

According to Theorems 4 and 5, we can get the following corollary.

Corollary 1. *If $CarL1_S = 2$, then S is in the 4 affine equivalence classes corresponding to G_0, G_1, G_2 and G_8; if $CarL1_S = 3$, then S is in the 8 affine equivalence classes corresponding to $G_0, G_1, G_2, G_8, G_9, G_{10}, G_{14}$ and G_{15}.*

Corollary 1 indicates that we can restrict the search of S-boxes with $CarL1_S = 2$ (or $CarL1_S = 3$) within the 4 (or 8) affine equivalence classes. In the following, we present an efficient way which can experimentally classify all 4×4 optimal S-boxes into different categories.

The values of $CarD1_S$ and $CarL1_S$ are not generally invariant under the affine equivalence relation, but the two values are invariant under the PE equivalence relation.

Theorem 6. *Let S and S' be two PE equivalent S-boxes, then $CarD1_S = CarD1_{S'}$ and $CarL1_S = CarL1_{S'}$.*

Every 4×4 optimal S-box can be written as $B(G_i(A(x) \oplus a)) \oplus b$, where G_i ($0 \leq i \leq 15$) is the representative S-box, A and B are two invertible 4×4 matrices over F_2, a and b are two constants over F_2^4. The number of 4×4

invertible matrices is $\prod_{i=0}^{3}(2^4 - 2^i) = 20160$. At the first sight, up to adding constants, we need to consider $16 \times 20160 \times 20160 \approx 2^{32.6}$ S-boxes. However, this number can be decreased greatly.

Lemma 1. *Let M denote a 4×4 matrix over F_2:*

$$M = \begin{pmatrix} a_{03} & a_{02} & a_{01} & a_{00} \\ a_{13} & a_{12} & a_{11} & a_{10} \\ a_{23} & a_{22} & a_{21} & a_{20} \\ a_{33} & a_{32} & a_{31} & a_{30} \end{pmatrix}$$

where $a_{ij} \in F_2$, $0 \le i, j \le 3$. Let $r_i = a_{i3}||a_{i2}||a_{i1}||a_{i0}$ denote the nibble consisting of the 4 bits in the i-th row, a_{i0} is the least significant bit. There are 840 matrices satisfying the following 2 conditions:

1. *invertible.*
2. *$r_0 < r_1 < r_2 < r_3$.*

we call such a matrix a row-increasing matrix.

Proof: Given a 4×4 invertible matrix, there are 24 different matrices obtained by permuting the 4 rows. Among the 24 matrices, only one matrix satisfies $r_0 < r_1 < r_2 < r_3$. Hence there are $20160/24 = 840$ invertible row-increasing matrices. □

According to Lemma 1, every 4×4 optimal S-box is PE equivalent to an S-box with the form $M_1(G_i(M_0^T(x)))$, $0 \le i \le 15$, M_0 and M_1 are two row-increasing matrices. Hence, up to PE equivalence, we only need to consider $16 \times 840 \times 840 = 11289600 \approx 2^{23.43}$ S-boxes. By exhaustively checking all the 11289600 S-boxes, we have the following result.

Result 1. *All optimal 4×4 S-boxes can be split into 183 different Num1-DL categories. Table 2 gives the details, the symbol "$\checkmark$" at position (i, j) means that there exist optimal S-boxes satisfying $CarD1_S = i$ and $CarL1_S = j$. From Table 2, the following facts are of interest:*

1. *No Num1-DL category satisfies that $CarL1_S = 0$ or $CarL1_S = 1$.*
2. *The minimal possible value for $CarD1_S$ is 0. When $CarD1_S = 0$, the minimal possible value for $CarL1_S$ is 4, i.e., the $(0, 4)$-Num1-DL category.*
3. *The minimal possible value for $CarL1_S$ is 2. When $CarL1_S = 2$, the minimal possible value for $CarD1_S$ is 2, i.e., the $(2, 2)$-Num1-DL category.*

Note that the first fact in Result 1 is in accordance with Theorem 3. For each Num1-DL category satisfying $CarD1_S + CarL1_S \le 8$, by checking all the S-boxes (out of 11289600 S-boxes) in this category, we get the following result.

Result 2. *There are 24 Num1-DL categories satisfying $CarD1_S + CarL1_S \le 8$. Table 3 gives the number of PE classes for each of the 24 Num1-DL categories. Moreover, we have the following facts:*

1. *Consider the sum of the values in row 0, there are 20 PE classes satisfying $CarD1_S = 0$.*

Table 2. 183 Num1-DL Categories: marked by ✓

	0	1	2	3	4	5	6	7	8	9	10	11	12	13	14	15	16
0					✓	✓	✓	✓	✓								
1				✓	✓	✓	✓	✓	✓	✓	✓	✓					
2			✓	✓	✓	✓	✓	✓	✓	✓	✓	✓	✓	✓			
3			✓	✓	✓	✓	✓	✓	✓	✓	✓	✓	✓	✓	✓		
4			✓	✓	✓	✓	✓	✓	✓	✓	✓	✓	✓	✓	✓	✓	✓
5			✓	✓	✓	✓	✓	✓	✓	✓	✓	✓	✓	✓	✓	✓	✓
6				✓	✓	✓	✓	✓	✓	✓	✓	✓	✓	✓	✓	✓	✓
7			✓	✓	✓	✓	✓	✓	✓	✓	✓	✓	✓	✓	✓	✓	✓
8				✓	✓	✓	✓	✓	✓	✓	✓	✓	✓	✓	✓	✓	✓
9				✓	✓	✓	✓	✓	✓	✓	✓	✓	✓	✓	✓	✓	✓
10				✓	✓	✓	✓	✓	✓	✓	✓	✓	✓	✓	✓	✓	✓
11				✓	✓	✓	✓	✓	✓	✓	✓	✓	✓	✓	✓	✓	✓
12					✓	✓	✓	✓	✓	✓	✓	✓	✓	✓	✓	✓	✓
13				✓	✓	✓	✓	✓	✓	✓	✓	✓	✓	✓	✓	✓	✓
14					✓	✓	✓	✓	✓	✓	✓	✓	✓	✓	✓	✓	✓
15																✓	✓
16																	

Notes: the leftmost column denotes the 17 possible values of $CarD1_S$ the uppermost row denotes the 17 possible values of $CarL1_S$

Table 3. Number of PE Classes in the 24 Num1-DL Categories satisfying $CarD1_S + CarL1_S \leq 8$

	0	1	2	3	4	5	6	7	8
0					2	2	6	2	8
1				4	26	50	112	113	−
2			4	54	155	290	648	−	−
3			10	116	593	1445	−	−	−
4			9	168	1141	−	−	−	−
5			5	146	−	−	−	−	−

Notes: the leftmost column denotes the possible values of $CarD1_S$ the uppermost row denotes the possible values of $CarL1_S$ "−" denotes the class does not satisfy $CarD1_S + CarL1_S \leq 8$

2. *Restricting* $CarD1_S + CarL1_S \leq 4$, *there are 3 Num1-DL categories:* $(0,4)$-, $(1,3)$-, $(2,2)$-*Num1-DL category. We call these 3 categories* **platinum Num1-DL categories**. *Table 4 lists representative S-boxes for each PE class in each of the 3 platinum Num1-DL categories.*

Table 4. Representative S-boxes for the 3 platinum Num1-DL categories

$(0,4)$-Num1-DL category	0, 11, 12, 5, 6, 1, 9, 10, 3, 14, 15, 8, 13, 4, 2, 7
	0, 12, 13, 10, 5, 11, 14, 7, 15, 6, 2, 1, 3, 8, 9, 4
$(1,3)$-Num1-DL category	0, 12, 9, 7, 6, 1, 15, 2, 3, 11, 4, 14, 13, 8, 10, 5
	0, 12, 9, 7, 15, 2, 6, 1, 3, 11, 4, 14, 10, 5, 13, 8
	0, 11, 8, 5, 15, 12, 3, 6, 14, 4, 7, 9, 2, 1, 13, 10
	0, 13, 4, 11, 7, 14, 9, 2, 6, 10, 3, 5, 8, 1, 15, 12
$(2,2)$-Num1-DL category	0, 13, 8, 2, 14, 11, 7, 5, 15, 6, 3, 12, 4, 1, 9, 10
	0, 11, 14, 1, 10, 7, 13, 4, 6, 12, 9, 15, 5, 8, 3, 2
	0, 11, 6, 9, 12, 5, 3, 14, 13, 7, 8, 4, 2, 10, 15, 1
	0, 14, 9, 5, 15, 8, 10, 7, 3, 11, 6, 12, 4, 1, 13, 2

Note: In each row, the first integer represents the image of 0, the second the image of 1, and so on.

Generally, the S-boxes in a Num1-DL category belong to many affine equivalence classes. For example, $(0,8)$-Num1-DL category includes 8 PE classes, and the 8 PE classes belong to 5 affine equivalence classes. In Result 2, the first fact is in accordance with Fact 4 in [18]. For the $(2,2)$-Num1-DL category, the 4 representative S-boxes are respectively PE equivalent to the 4 representative S-boxes given in [28].

4   Measures for Evaluating the Security Against DC and LC

Kanda et al. [17] classified 4 measures to evaluate the security of a cipher against DC and LC as follows:

1. Precise measure: The maximum probability of difference propagations, and the maximum average correlation potential of linear propagations.
2. Theoretical measure: The upper bound of the maximum probability of difference propagations, and the upper bound of the maximum average correlation potential of linear propagations.
3. Heuristic measure: The maximum probability of differential trails, and the maximum correlation potential of linear trails.
4. Practical measure: The upper bound of the maximum probability of differential trails, and the upper bound of the maximum correlation potential of linear trails.

For many modern ciphers, such as AES and Serpent, it is almost computationally infeasible to perform an evaluation using the precise measure or the
theoretical measure. For ciphers with good diffusion, such as Serpent [2], the
heuristic measure is only effective for a small number of rounds. On the other
hand, many ciphers evaluated with the practical measure are practically secure
against DC and LC, such as AES and NOEKEON, hence the practical measure
is the most common measure.

However, compared with the practical measure, the heuristic measure is more
accurate. If the heuristic measure is feasible for a cipher, then both the cryptanalysts and designers can have a better understanding on the security of the cipher
against DC and LC. Particularly, for PRESENT, RECTANGLE and SPON-
GENT, the heuristic measure is feasible, we will discuss this problem in Sect. 6.2.

Consider the following SP-network schemes. Fix the permutation layer of
PRESENT, RECTANGLE or SPONGENT, the S-box can have many different
choices. Then, for each scheme, we wonder which S-boxes are the best with
respect to DC and LC? In this paper, we mainly concentrate on S-boxes in
the 3 platinum Num1-DL categories. In Sects. 5 and 6, we adopt the heuristic
measure for the study. One may say that, for such schemes, the clustering of
differential/linear trails must not be neglected [6,12,22,26,28], hence it needs to
use the precise (or the theoretical) measure. However, we think that it is still
appropriate to use the heuristic measure for the study. The following gives the
reasons.

The total number of schemes investigated in this paper is 4368 (see Table 5),
it needs an extremely huge computational effort to evaluate the clustering of
differential/linear trails for all the schemes investigated in this paper.

Let rD_p denote the highest number of rounds of an exploitable differential
distinguisher by using the precise measure, and rL_p the highest number of rounds
of an exploitable linear distinguisher by using the precise measure, define $r_p \equiv$
$\max\{rD_p, rL_p\}$. For a fixed permutation, among all the S-box candidates, the
smaller the value of r_p, the better the scheme, because schemes with the minimal
r_p need the least number of rounds to resist against DC and LC. Let rD_h denote
the highest number of rounds of an exploitable differential distinguisher by using
the heuristic measure, and rL_h the highest number of rounds of an exploitable
linear distinguisher by using the heuristic measure, define $r_h \equiv \max\{rD_h, rL_h\}$.
Based on Eqs. (1) and (4), we have $rD_p \geq rD_h$ and $rL_p \geq rL_h$, thus $r_p \geq r_h$. The
smaller the value of $rD_p - rD_h$ ($rL_p - rL_h$), the less the clustering of differential
(linear) trails. Based on the known results on PRESENT, RECTANGLE and
SPONGENT [1,6,12,22,26,28], the difference $rD_p - rD_h$ (or $rL_p - rL_h$) between
the two measures are as follows: For PRESENT against DC, the difference is
$16 - 14 = 2$; for PRESENT against LC, the difference is $24 - 16 = 8$. For
RECTANGLE against DC, the difference is $14 - 14 = 0$; for RECTANGLE
against LC, the difference is $14 - 13 = 1$. For SPONGENT$_{88}$ against LC, the
difference is $23 - 22 = 1$. Based on the above results, we expect that there exist
S-boxes with a small value of both $rD_p - rD_h$ and $rL_p - rL_h$ for each fixed
permutation layer. For such schemes, if r_h reaches the minimal, we expect that
it is very likely that r_p also reaches the minimal. Hence, it is reasonable to make
the following assumption:

Assumption 1. *For each fixed permutation layer, consider the SP-network schemes investigated in this paper. Among those with a minimal value of r_h, there exist some schemes satisfying $rD_p - rD_h \leq 2$ and $rL_p - rL_h \leq 2$.*

By using the heuristic measure, for each combination of a fixed permutation layer and a platinum Num1-DL category, we can discard a large proportion of the S-box candidates and concentrate only on S-boxes with the minimal value of r_h (we will present the results in Sect. 6). We emphasize that this is the first step. For such cipher designs, designers must take differential/linear clustering into consideration. Ideally, designers can make a further selection from the schemes with the minimal value of r_h by selecting an S-box which has the minimal value of $r_p - r_h$. Note that the minimal value of $r_p - r_h$ is not more than 2 under Assumption 1.

5   A Relation of the S-box Selection, the Value of $CarL1_S$ and the Security of PRESENT and SPONGENT

The block length of PRESENT is 64 bits. For SPONGENT [8], the block length of the internal permutation has 5 choices: 88, 136, 176, 240 and 272 bits [1], which are denoted as $SPONGENT_b$ respectively, b is the block length. In this section, we focus on these 6 block lengths.

The design criteria of the PRESENT S-box are as follows:

1. Optimal.
2. $CarD1_S = 0$.
3. For $\Gamma I, \Gamma O \in F_2^4$ such that $wt(\Gamma I) = wt(\Gamma O) = 1$ it holds that Imb_S $(\Gamma I, \Gamma O) = 2$.
4. No fixed point, i.e., $S(x) \neq x$ for any $x \in F_2^4$.

There are 20 PE classes satisfying criteria 1 and 2. Among the 20 PE classes, 14 PE classes satisfy criterion 3. Up to adding constants before and after an S-box, which does not change any of the design criteria 1–3 of the PRESENT S-box and moreover does not change the probability of the best differential trail and the correlation potential of the best linear trail, there are $14 \times 4! \times 4! = 8064$ S-boxes. The 8064 S-boxes belong to 3 different categories. Fix the permutation of PRESENT (or the permutation layer of the SPONGENT internal permutation), we wonder which are the best choices among the 8064 S-boxes.

For the schemes investigated in this section, if the best r-round linear trail has only one active S-box in each round, then its correlation potential is 2^{-4r+4}. Thus, when $r = \frac{b}{4}$, the correlation potential of such a linear trail is 2^{-b+4}, which means there exists a $\frac{b}{4}$-round exploitable linear distinguisher. For $b = 64$ and $b = 88$, our experiments show that there exist some S-boxes such that the correlation potential of the best $\frac{b}{4}$-round linear trail is less than or equal to 2^{-b} (see Tables 7 and 9).

---

[1] The block length of the internal permutation of SPONGENT is extended to 11 different choices in [9]. We do not consider the other 6 choices in this paper.

Algorithm 1

INPUT:
  b: the block length S: an S-box candidate $Perm_b$: the b-bit permutation layer of the block cipher or the hash function
OUTPUT:
  Check if the S-box can result in a linear trail with only one active S-box in each round. If yes, $flag$=1; else $flag$=0.

1. Set $flag$=0. Declare $Init$ as a global variable.
2. Calculate $CarL1_S$ and the $CarL1_S$ pairs $\{(\Gamma I, \Gamma O)\}$ of the set $SetL1_S$.
3. for $\frac{b}{4}$ S-box indexes of $i \in \{0, 1, \cdots, \frac{b}{4} - 1\}$ do
     for $CarL1_S$ pairs $(\Gamma I, \Gamma O) \in SetL1_S$ do
       $\{Init = In = i \times 4 + log_2^{\Gamma I}$; $Out = i \times 4 + log_2^{\Gamma O}$;
       if ($Perm_b[Out] = Init$), then $\{flag$=1; return $flag$ and exit the program$\}$;   //
   a 1-round iterative weak linear trail is found.
         else call **Function loop(2)**; $\}$
4. Return $flag$ and exit the program;

Function loop(r)
$\{$for all pairs $(\Gamma I^*, \Gamma O^*) \in SetL1_S$ satisfying $(Perm_b[Out] \bmod 4 = \Gamma I^*)$ do
   $\{In = Perm_b[Out];$ $Out = \lfloor \frac{In}{4} \rfloor \times 4 + log_2^{\Gamma O^*}$;
     if ($Perm_b[Out] = Init$), then $\{flag = 1;$ return $flag$ and exit the program$\}$;   //
   a r-round iterative weak linear trail is found.
       else if (r < 25), call loop(r+1); $\}$ $\}$

Based on the above discussion, we decide to discard the S-boxes which can result in a linear trail with only one active S-box in each round. Note that a r-round iterative linear trail can be used to construct a r'-round linear trail for any $r' \geq r$. Algorithm 1 is designed to detect if an S-box can result in a r-round iterative linear trail with only one active S-box in each round, note that such a linear trail is connected by the elements in $SetL1_S$. We only check up to 25 rounds for practical reasons (nevertheless, we point out that it can not exclude the possibility that more S-boxes may be discarded if more rounds are checked). Let e_i denote the vector with a single one at position i (counting from zero). Since all of the round input/output selection patterns belong to the set $\{e_i\}$, for simplicity, we use In (Out) to denote the subscript of the input (output) selection pattern of the S-box layer. By running Algorithm 1, we get the following result.

Result 3. *For each of the 6 block lengths, fix the corresponding permutation layer, when combining with the 8064 S-boxes, there are 8064 SP-network schemes. Discard the S-boxes which can result in a linear trail with only one active S-box in each round using Algorithm 1, we have the following facts:*

1. *Table 5 gives the number of the remaining S-boxes, which shows that more than 98.6 percent of the 8064 S-boxes are discarded for each block length.*
2. *For 64-, 88-, 136-, 176- and 240-bit block length, all of the remaining S-boxes belong to the $(0, 4)$-Num1-DL category; for 272-bit block length, there is no S-box left.*

For each of the 6 block lengths, among the 8064 S-boxes, every S-box in $(0, 6)$-Num1-DL and $(0, 8)$-Num1-DL categories can result in a linear trail with only one active S-box in each round. For 272-bit block length, fix the permutation

Table 5. Number of the Remaining S-boxes using Algorithm 1 for the 6 Block Lengths

block length (bits)	64	88	136	176	240	272
number of remaining S-boxes	96	112	32	48	64	0

layer of SPONGENT$_{272}$, for each of the 8064 S-box candidates, there exists a linear trail with only one active S-box in each round. Hence, we get a new design criterion for the S-box of PRESENT-like or SPOGNENT-like schemes.

Design Criterion 1. *For 64-bit (88-, 136-, 176- and 240-bit respectively) block length, fix the permutation layer of PRESENT (the corresponding SPONGENT variant). For better resistance against LC, besides the 4 design criteria for the S-box, designers should add $CarL1_S = 4$ as a new design criterion.*

For 272-bit block length, fix the permutation layer of SPONGENT$_{272}$. For better resistance against LC, designers should change their design criteria $CarD1_S = 0$ and choose an S-box with $CarD1_S \neq 0$.

6 An Investigation of the S-box Selection of PRESENT, RECTANGLE and SPONGENT

Due to the huge computational effort required to run the experiments, we only focus on 64- and 88-bit block lengths in this section. Consider the following SP-network schemes. For 64-bit block length, the S-box is chosen from the 3 platinum Num1-DL categories, the diffusion layer is either the PRESENT or RECTANGLE permutation. Thus, there are 6 combinations. Similarly, for 88-bit block length, there are also 6 combinations. Hence, 12 combinations in total. In Sect. 6.3, we consider both DC and LC for the security of the 12 combinations using the heuristic measure. Since DC is more important than LC for hash functions, in Sect. 6.4, we only consider DC for the 12 combinations.

Definition 7. *Let b denote the block length. For a b-bit block cipher (or permutation of a hash function), let $Prob_r$ denote the probability of the best r-round differential trail, and Cor_r the correlation of the best r-round linear trail. Define r_{min} as*

$$r_{min} = \min_r \{Prob_r \leq 2^{-b} \text{ and } Cor_r{}^2 \leq 2^{-b}\}.$$

In this section, we use the values of r_{min}, $Prob_{r_{min}}$ and $Cor_{r_{min}}$ for a comparative study. Generally speaking, the smaller the value of r_{min}, the better the scheme against DC and LC. For schemes with the same value of r_{min}, the smaller the value of $Prob_{r_{min}}$ (or $Cor_{r_{min}}$), the better the scheme against DC (or LC).

6.1 Influence of S-box Selection and Differential/Linear Trails with One Active S-box per Round

According to Table 4, up to adding constants before and after an S-box, there are 1152, 2304 and 2304 S-boxes in the $(0, 4)$-Num1-DL category, the $(1, 3)$-Num1-DL category and the $(2, 2)$-Num1-DL category respectively. By checking all the

10 platinum representative S-boxes, we get the following result. For any of the investigated schemes, if a r-round linear trail has only one active S-box in each round, then its correlation potential is 2^{-4r+4}; if a r-round differential trail has only one active S-box in each round, then its differential probability is between 2^{-3r} and 2^{-3r+2}.

For each of the 12 combinations, we firstly discard the S-boxes which can result in a differential/linear trail with only one active S-box in each round. For schemes using the PRESENT or SPONGENT$_{88}$ permutation layer, we use Algorithm 1 to perform the filtering, note that Algorithm 1 can be modified a little for the differential case. For schemes using the RECTANGLE or RECTANGLE$_{88}$ permutation, we extend the idea of Algorithm 2 in [28] to perform the filtering, the number of remaining S-boxes only depends on properties of the S-boxes and not on the block length. Table 6 presents our experimental results of the number of remaining S-boxes for the 12 combinations.

In [24], 4 PE classes are specified as "golden" S-boxes. For each of the 4 PE classes, $CarD1_S = 0$ and $CarL1_S = 8$. Fix the RECTANGLE permutation, when combining with these golden S-boxes, we get 2304 SP-network schemes. For each of the 2304 schemes, there exists a linear trail with only one active S-box in each round. Thus, together with Result 3, we get that all of the golden S-boxes are not good choices for the 3 primitives.

Table 6. Number of the Remaining S-boxes for the 12 Combinations

	PRESENT Perm	SPONGENT$_{88}$ Perm	RECTANGLE$_{64}$ Perm /RECTANGLE$_{88}$ Perm
$(0,4)$-Num1-DL	96	112	96
$(1,3)$-Num1-DL	384	592	384
$(2,2)$-Num1-DL	528	640	528

6.2 Search Algorithm for the Best Differential/Linear Trail

Matsui proposed a branch-and-bound search algorithm [20] for determining the best differential/linear trail of DES-like cryptosystems in 1994. Ohta et al. [23] improved Matsui's algorithm by introducing the concept of search pattern to reduce unnecessary search candidates before the search, and applied their algorithm on DES and FEAL. Aoki et al. [3] further improved Ohta's search algorithm by discarding more unnecessary search patterns, and applied their algorithm on FEAL. Based on these 3 previous work, we have written a program for the search of the best differential/linear trails for PRESENT, RECTANGLE and the internal permutation of SPONGENT respectively.

6.3 Experimental Results

In the following, we present our experimental results. The experiments have been performed using 4 computers: 3 with Intel Core i7 (or i5) CPU, and 1 with Intel Xeon E7-2820 (16 cores) CPU. It took us about 4 weeks to do all the experiments.

For each combination, let N denote the number of the remaining S-boxes (see Table 6), the permutation layer is fixed, thus we have N SP-network schemes. Here are some notations:

- R_m: the minimal value of r_{min} among the N schemes
- Num_{R_m}: the number of schemes that the corresponding r_{min} reach the minimum value R_m
- num: the number of schemes with the values $Prob_{R_m}$ and $Cor^2_{R_m}$ in the same row

Tables 7, 8, 9, 10 summarize our experimental results for each fixed permutation. The result in Table 8 is in accordance with that in [28]. From Tables 7, 8, 9, 10, we get the following results:

1. With the PRESENT permutation layer, the values of R_m are the same for the 3 combinations. There are 336 S-boxes (up to adding constants before and after an S-box, similarly hereinafter) such that the value of r_{min} reach the minimum $R_m = 16$.
2. With the RECTANGLE permutation layer, the (1,3)- and (2,2)-Num1-DL categories are better. There are 128 S-boxes such that the value of r_{min} reach the minimum $R_m = 15$. Note that RECTANGLE uses one of these 128 S-boxes.
3. With the SPONGENT$_{88}$ permutation layer, the (1,3)- and (2,2)-Num1-DL categories are better. For the (1,3)-Num1-DL category, $R_m = 19$; for the (2,2)-Num1-DL category, $R_m \leq 19$.
4. With the RECTANGLE$_{88}$ permutation layer, the (2,2)-Num1-DL category is the best. There is only one S-box such that the value of r_{min} reach the minimum $R_m = 17$.

Table 7. Experimental Results With the PRESENT Permutation

category	R_m	Num_{R_m}	$Prob_{R_m}$	$Cor^2_{R_m}$	num
(0, 4)-Num1-DL	16	96	2^{-64}	2^{-64}	96
(1, 3)-Num1-DL	16	192	2^{-70}	2^{-64}	96
			2^{-64}	2^{-64}	96
(2, 2)-Num1-DL	16	48	2^{-68}	2^{-64}	48

In Table 9, for the two combinations marked with "*", we have not finished the experiments for all of the corresponding S-boxes. However, we derived the value of R_m for one combination and a good estimate of R_m for the other, which are enough for us to derive the above results.

Table 8. Experimental Results With the RECTANGLE Permutation

category	R_m	Num_{R_m}	$Prob_{R_m}$	$Cor_{R_m}^2$	num
(0,4)-Num1-DL	16	16	2^{-64}	2^{-80}	16
(1,3)-Num1-DL	15	64	2^{-74}	2^{-66}	16
			2^{-71}	2^{-66}	16
			2^{-65}	2^{-66}	16
			2^{-65}	2^{-64}	16
(2,2)-Num1-DL	15	64	2^{-73}	2^{-64}	8
			2^{-72}	2^{-64}	8
			2^{-69}	2^{-64}	16
			2^{-67}	2^{-66}	8
			2^{-66}	2^{-74}	4
			2^{-66}	2^{-72}	8
			2^{-66}	2^{-70}	4
			2^{-66}	2^{-66}	8

Table 9. Experimental Results With the SPONGENT$_{88}$ Permutation Layer

category	R_m	Num_{R_m}	$Prob_{R_m}$	$Cor_{R_m}^2$	num
(0,4)-Num1-DL	21	8	2^{-118}	2^{-88}	4
			2^{-117}	2^{-88}	4
(1,3)-Num1-DL*	19	?	$\leq 2^{-91}$	2^{-90}	?
(2,2)-Num1-DL*	≤ 19	?	$\leq 2^{-88}$	2^{-90}	?

Table 10. Experimental Results With the RECTANGLE$_{88}$ Permutation

category	R_m	Num_{R_m}	$Prob_{R_m}$	$Cor_{R_m}^2$	num
(0,4)-Num1-DL	22	96	2^{-88}	2^{-118}	84
			2^{-88}	2^{-116}	8
			2^{-88}	2^{-114}	4
(1,3)-Num1-DL	18	56	2^{-93}	2^{-92}	8
			2^{-93}	2^{-88}	10
			2^{-92}	2^{-88}	2
			2^{-91}	2^{-92}	4
			2^{-91}	2^{-90}	2
			2^{-90}	2^{-88}	2
			2^{-88}	2^{-92}	8
			2^{-88}	2^{-90}	6
			2^{-88}	2^{-88}	14
(2,2)-Num1-DL	17	1	2^{-88}	2^{-88}	1

6.4   For Hash Functions - When DC Is More Important Than LC

According to the state-of-art security analysis on hash functions, DC is more important than LC. On the other hand, the permutation (or the compression function) of a hash function is normally required to be pseudo-random, which includes the requirement that there is no effective linear distinguisher. Therefore, we decide to consider the following question: For each of the 12 combinations, when only considering DC for the remaining S-boxes obtained in Sect. 6.1 (see Table 6), what results can we get? At first thought, the (0,4)-Num1-DL category should be the best choice, however, we will show that it is not always the case.

Table 11. Results for the 12 Combinations when only Considering DC

Permutation Layer	category	R_m^D	$Prob_{R_m^D}$
PRESENT	(0, 4)-Num1-DL	16	2^{-64}
Permutation	(1, 3)-Num1-DL	15	2^{-64}
	(2, 2)-Num1-DL	16	2^{-68}
RECTANGLE	(0, 4)-Num1-DL	16	2^{-64}
Permutation	(1, 3)-Num1-DL	14	2^{-69}
	(2, 2)-Num1-DL	14	2^{-68}
SPONGENT$_{88}$	(0, 4)-Num1-DL	17	2^{-94}
Permutation Layer	(1, 3)-Num1-DL*	≤ 18	$\leq 2^{-89}$
	(2, 2)-Num1-DL*	≤ 19	$\leq 2^{-88}$
RECTANGLE $_{88}$	(0, 4)-Num1-DL	22	2^{-88}
Permutation	(1, 3)-Num1-DL	18	2^{-93}
	(2, 2)-Num1-DL	17	2^{-88}

For each scheme, define $r_{min}^D = \min_r \{Prob_r \leq 2^{-b}\}$. For each combination, let R_m^D denote the minimal value of r_{min}^D among the N schemes. Table 11 summarizes our experimental results, and we get the following results:

1. With the PRESENT permutation, the (1,3)-Num1-DL category is the best. The minimal value of r_{min}^D is $R_m^D = 15$.
2. With the RECTANGLE permutation, the (1,3)- and (2,2)-Num1-DL categories are better. The minimal value of r_{min}^D is $R_m^D = 14$.
3. With the SPONGENT$_{88}$ permutation layer, it seems that the (0,4)-Num1-DL category is the best and the minimal value of r_{min}^D is $R_m^D = 17$.
4. With the RECTANGLE$_{88}$ permutation, the (2,2)-Num1-DL category is the best. The minimal value of r_{min}^D is $R_m^D = 17$.

Potentially Better S-boxes for SPONGENT$_{88}$. For SPONGENT$_{88}$, there exists a 17-round differential trail with probability 2^{-86} [4], which is better than the one given by its designers in [9, Table 4]. Moreover, there exists a 22-round linear trail with correlation potential 2^{-84} for SPONGENT$_{88}$ (only one active S-box in each of the 22 rounds).

With the permutation layer of SPONGENT$_{88}$, we found 4 S-boxes in the (0,4)-Num1-DL category such that the probability of the best 17-round differential trail is 2^{-94} and the correlation potential of the best 21-round linear trail is 2^{-88} for each of the 4 schemes. It can be seen that the 4 S-boxes are potentially better than the SPONGENT$_{88}$ S-box with respect to the security against both DC and LC. The 4 S-boxes are listed in Table 12, which can be used for further investigation.

Table 12. 4 Potentially Better S-boxes for SPONGENT$_{88}$

0, 6, 12, 1, 5, 9, 11, 14, 3, 13, 15, 8, 10, 7, 4, 2
0, 6, 5, 8, 10, 13, 15, 1, 12, 9, 11, 7, 3, 14, 4, 2
0, 3, 5, 12, 10, 13, 15, 2, 6, 9, 11, 7, 1, 14, 8, 4
0, 12, 10, 5, 3, 15, 13, 2, 6, 11, 9, 14, 8, 1, 7, 4

6.5 A New Design Criterion

For SP-network schemes with the SPONGENT$_{88}$ permutation layer, when considering both DC and LC, based on the results in Sect. 5 and Table 9, it can be deduced that an S-box with $CarD1_S = 0$ is not an optimal choice, while $(1,3)$- and $(2,2)$- Num1-DL categories are better choices. On the other hand, when considering DC more important than LC, it seems that $(0,4)$-Num1-DL category is the best choice. For SP-network schemes with RECTANGLE-like permutations, based on the results in Tables 7, 8, 9, 10, 11, it seems that the $(2,2)$-Num1-DL category is always an optimal choice. We have the following design criterion.

Design Criterion 2. *For block ciphers (or hash functions) using 4×4 S-boxes as confusion layers and bit permutations as diffusion layers, designers can extend the range of the S-box selection to the 3 platinum Num1-DL categories and select their S-box carefully.*

7 Discussion

Based on our experimental results, there are 336 potentially best S-boxes for PRESENT, 128 potentially best S-boxes for RECTANGLE, and 4 potentially better S-boxes for SPONGENT$_{88}$. To judge if a potentially best (better) S-box is a real best (better) S-box, it needs to investigate the clustering of differential/linear trails. In this respect, the approach used in [1] is of interest, we leave it for further study. The NOEKEON S-box belongs to the $(7,6)$-Num1-DL category. Serpent uses 8 S-boxes, among them, 3 S-boxes belong to the $(0,6)$-Num1-DL category, and the other 5 S-boxes belong to the $(0,8)$-Num1-DL category. It is also interesting to investigate the influence of the 3 platinum Num1-DL categories on the security of NOEKEON and Serpent against DC and LC.

Acknowledgments. We would like to thank anonymous referees for their helpful comments of SAC'2014 and FSE'2015. We also thank Andrey Bogdanov for his helpful discussions which help us to improve the quality of this paper. The main work in this paper was performed while Wentao Zhang was a visitor at KU Leuven. The research presented in this paper is supported by the National Natural Science Foundation of China (No.61379138), the Research Fund KU Leuven (OT/13/071), and the "Strategic Priority Research Program" of the Chinese Academy of Sciences (No.XDA06010701).

References

1. Abdelraheem, M.A.: Estimating the probabilities of low-weight differential and linear approximations on PRESENT-like ciphers. In: Kwon, T., Lee, M.-K., Kwon, D. (eds.) ICISC 2012. LNCS, vol. 7839, pp. 368–382. Springer, Heidelberg (2013)
2. Anderson, R., Biham, E., Knudsen, L.R.: Serpent: A Proposal for the Advanced Encryption Standard. NIST AES proposal (1998)
3. Aoki, K., Kobayashi, K., Moriai, S.: Best differential characteristic search of FEAL. In: Biham, E. (ed.) FSE 1997. LNCS, vol. 1267, pp. 41–53. Springer, Heidelberg (1997)
4. Bao, Z., Zhang, W., Lin, D.: Speeding up the search algorithm for the best differential and best linear trails. In: Lin, D., Yung, M., Zhou, J. (eds.) Inscrypt 2014. LNCS, vol. 8957, pp. 259–285. Springer, Heidelberg (2015)
5. Biham, E., Shamir, A.: Differential cryptanalysis of DES-like cryptosystems. J. Cryptol. **4**(1), 3–72 (1991)
6. Blondeau, C., Gérard, B.: Multiple differential cryptanalysis: theory and practice. In: Joux, A. (ed.) FSE 2011. LNCS, vol. 6733, pp. 35–54. Springer, Heidelberg (2011)
7. Blondeau, C., Nyberg, K.: Links between truncated differential and multidimensional linear properties of block ciphers and underlying attack complexities. In: Nguyen, P.Q., Oswald, E. (eds.) EUROCRYPT 2014. LNCS, vol. 8441, pp. 165–182. Springer, Heidelberg (2014)
8. Bogdanov, A., Knežević, M., Leander, G., Toz, D., Varıcı, K., Verbauwhede, I.: SPONGENT: a lightweight hash function. In: Preneel, B., Takagi, T. (eds.) CHES 2011. LNCS, vol. 6917, pp. 312–325. Springer, Heidelberg (2011)
9. Bogdanov, A., Knezevic, M., Leander, G., Toz, D., Varici, K., Verbauwhede, I.: SPONGENT: the design space of lightweight cryptographic hashing. IEEE Trans. Comput. **62**(10), 2041–2053 (2013)
10. Bogdanov, A.A., Knudsen, L.R., Leander, G., Paar, C., Poschmann, A., Robshaw, M., Seurin, Y., Vikkelsoe, C.: PRESENT: an ultra-lightweight block cipher. In: Paillier, P., Verbauwhede, I. (eds.) CHES 2007. LNCS, vol. 4727, pp. 450–466. Springer, Heidelberg (2007)
11. Carlet, C., Charpin, P., Zinoviev, V.: Codes, bent functions and permutations suitable for DES-like cryptosystems. Des. Codes Crypt. **15**(2), 125–156 (1998)
12. Cho, J.Y.: Linear cryptanalysis of reduced-round PRESENT. In: Pieprzyk, J. (ed.) CT-RSA 2010. LNCS, vol. 5985, pp. 302–317. Springer, Heidelberg (2010)
13. Daemen, J., Peeters, M., Van Assche, G., Rijmen, V.: Nessie Proposal: The Block Cipher Noekeon, Nessie submission (2000). http://gro.noekeon.org/
14. Daemen, J., Rijmen, V.: The Design of Rijndael: AES - The Advanced Encryption Standard. Springer, Heidelberg (2002)

15. Guo, J., Peyrin, T., Poschmann, A., Robshaw, M.: The LED block cipher. In: Preneel, B., Takagi, T. (eds.) CHES 2011. LNCS, vol. 6917, pp. 326–341. Springer, Heidelberg (2011)
16. Guo, J., Peyrin, T., Poschmann, A.: The PHOTON family of lightweight hash functions. In: Rogaway, P. (ed.) CRYPTO 2011. LNCS, vol. 6841, pp. 222–239. Springer, Heidelberg (2011)
17. Kanda, M., Takashima, Y., Matsumoto, T., Aoki, K., Ohta, K.: A strategy for constructing fast round functions with practical security against differential and linear cryptanalysis. In: Tavares, S., Meijer, H. (eds.) SAC 1998. LNCS, vol. 1556, pp. 264–279. Springer, Heidelberg (1999)
18. Leander, G., Poschmann, A.: On the classification of 4 bit S-boxes. In: Carlet, C., Sunar, B. (eds.) WAIFI 2007. LNCS, vol. 4547, pp. 159–176. Springer, Heidelberg (2007)
19. Matsui, M.: Linear cryptanalysis method for DES cipher. In: Helleseth, T. (ed.) EUROCRYPT 1993. LNCS, vol. 765, pp. 386–397. Springer, Heidelberg (1994)
20. Matsui, M.: On correlation between the order of S-boxes and the strength of DES. In: De Santis, A. (ed.) EUROCRYPT 1994. LNCS, vol. 950, pp. 366–375. Springer, Heidelberg (1995)
21. Nyberg, K.: Differentially uniform mappings for cryptography. In: Helleseth, T. (ed.) EUROCRYPT 1993. LNCS, vol. 765, pp. 55–64. Springer, Heidelberg (1994)
22. Ohkuma, K.: Weak keys of reduced-round PRESENT for linear cryptanalysis. In: Jacobson Jr., M.J., Rijmen, V., Safavi-Naini, R. (eds.) SAC 2009. LNCS, vol. 5867, pp. 249–265. Springer, Heidelberg (2009)
23. Ohta, K., Moriai, S., Aoki, K.: Improving the search algorithm for the best linear expression. In: Coppersmith, D. (ed.) CRYPTO 1995. LNCS, vol. 963, pp. 157–170. Springer, Heidelberg (1995)
24. Saarinen, M.-J.O.: Cryptographic analysis of all 4×4-bit S-boxes. In: Miri, A., Vaudenay, S. (eds.) SAC 2011. LNCS, vol. 7118, pp. 118–133. Springer, Heidelberg (2012)
25. Siegenthaler, T.: Correlation-immunity of nonlinear combining functions for cryptographic applications. IEEE Trans. Inf. Theory **30**(5), 776–776 (1984)
26. Wang, M., Sun, Y., Tischhauser, E., Preneel, B.: A model for structure attacks, with applications to PRESENT and Serpent. In: Canteaut, A. (ed.) FSE 2012. LNCS, vol. 7549, pp. 49–68. Springer, Heidelberg (2012)
27. Xiao, G.Z., Massey, J.L.: A spectral characterization of correlation-immune combining functions. IEEE Trans. Inf. Theory **34**(3), 569–571 (1988)
28. Zhang, W., Bao, Z., Lin, D., Rijmen, V., Yang, B., Verbauwhede, I.: RECTANGLE: a bit-slice ultra-lightweight block cipher suitable for multiple platforms. Cryptology ePrint Archive: Report 2014/084. http://eprint.iacr.org/2014/084

Cryptanalysis of Hash Functions
and Stream Ciphers

Rotational Cryptanalysis of ARX Revisited

Dmitry Khovratovich[1](✉), Ivica Nikolić[2], Josef Pieprzyk[3],
Przemysław Sokołowski[4], and Ron Steinfeld[5]

[1] University of Luxembourg, Luxembourg, Luxembourg
dmitry.khovratovich@uni.lu
[2] Nanyang Technological University, Singapore, Singapore
inikolic@ntu.edu.sg
[3] Queensland University of Technology, Brisbane, Australia
josef.pieprzyk@qut.edu.au
[4] Adam Mickiewicz University, Poznan, Poland
przemeks@amu.edu.pl
[5] Monash University, Melbourne, Australia
ron.steinfeld@monash.edu

Abstract. Rotational cryptanalysis is a probabilistic attack applicable
to word oriented designs that use (almost) rotation-invariant constants.
It is believed that the success probability of rotational cryptanalysis
against ciphers and functions based on modular additions, rotations and
XORs, can be computed only by counting the number of additions. We
show that this simple formula is incorrect due to the invalid Markov
cipher assumption used for computing the probability. More precisely,
we show that chained modular additions used in ARX ciphers do not
form a Markov chain with regards to rotational analysis, thus the rotational probability cannot be computed as a simple product of rotational
probabilities of individual modular additions. We provide a precise value
of the probability of such chains and give a new algorithm for computing the rotational probability of ARX ciphers. We use the algorithm to
correct the rotational attacks on BLAKE2 and to provide valid rotational
attacks against the simplified version of Skein.

Keywords: Rotational cryptanalysis · Markov cipher · Markov chain ·
Skein · BLAKE2

1 Introduction

Rotational cryptanalysis, formally introduced in [13], is a probabilistic attack
that follows the evolution of a so-called rotational pair through the rounds of a
function (or a cipher). It targets word-oriented functions and, for a successful
application, it requires all constants used in the functions to preserve their values
after a rotation. Rotational cryptanalysis has been launched against the building
blocks of several hash functions such as BLAKE2 [1,10], Keccak [20], Shabal
[3,23], Skein [13,15,16], SM3 [17], (modified) SIMD and BMW [21], etc.

© International Association for Cryptologic Research 2015
G. Leander (Ed.): FSE 2015, LNCS 9054, pp. 519–536, 2015.
DOI: 10.1007/978-3-662-48116-5_25

The chance of success of probabilistic attacks against a particular cryptographic primitive is computed by finding the probability that inputs and corresponding outputs (produced after application of the primitive) have a specific property that is unexpected for a random permutation/function. For instance, in differential attacks [2], the probability that a pair of plaintexts with a specific difference generates a pair of ciphertexts with another specific difference is unusually high. To compute the probability, one has to investigate the propagation of the input difference through rounds of the cipher. The propagation feature is known as a differential characteristic and its probability is computed as a product of the probabilities of all single-round characteristics. Lai and Massey [18] show that this shortcut in the probability calculation is correct as long as the keys used in the rounds are chosen at random independently and uniformly and the cipher can be modeled as a Markov cipher. This is to say that an iterated cipher can be seen as a sequence of independent rounds, where the round keys are independent and the differential probability of the round functions is independent of the inputs (but not of the input/output difference). Lai and Massey argue that in such a case, the differences after each round (which follows a differential characteristic) can be modeled by a Markov chain. Consequently, the differential probability of each round depends on the input and the output difference only (the differences in previous rounds can be ignored).

The Markov cipher assumption (which results in a Markov chain assumption) is used in practically all differential attacks as well as in other probabilistic attacks. This is despite the fact that the round keys are not independent but are produced from a single master by the key scheduling algorithm. Moreover, some ciphers do not use round keys in every round (after each non-linear operation) – see LED [11] and Zorro [9], for an example of such ciphers. Nevertheless, in practical cryptographic primitives, the role of independent and random round keys is usually replaced by some state words. They introduce sufficient entropy so one can argue that the Markov chain assumption holds. However, exceptions from this rule with respect to differential analysis can be found in the case of ARX or ARX-like primitives – we refer the reader to [4,19,22,24,25] for such examples[1].

Likewise, in the case of rotational cryptanalysis, probabilities are computed under the Markov chain assumption. This makes rotational cryptanalysis exceptionally easy to apply as the rotational probability of a cryptographic primitive is the product of rotational probabilities of all the operations/rounds that are used in the primitive. For instance, in schemes based on modular additions, rotations and XORs (further referred as ARX primitives), only modular addition has rotational probability p_+ smaller than 1. Thus the rotational probability of the whole ARX primitive can be computed easily. If it uses q additions, then the rotational probability is p_+^q. With minor modifications, this formula has been used in rotational cryptanalysis of ARX designs.

---

[1] We are grateful to the reviewers of FSE'15 for pointing out these exceptions.

Our Contribution. We show that in rotational analysis of cryptographic algorithms based on ARX, the Markov chain assumption does not always hold. In particular, we establish that rotational probability of an ARX primitive depends not only on the number of modular additions but also on their positions. In general, the more modular additions are chained (output of the previous additions is the input of the next), the smaller the probability. We work out an explicit formula for the probability of such chained additions and show that the rotational probability of ARX should be computed as the product of the rotational probabilities of modular addition chains. We also reveal that the way the round keys are incorporated into the state, plays a crucial role in calculation of the rotational probability. When round keys are XORed to the state, they might break modular addition chains and thus increase the probability. On the other hand, if they are merged using modular addition, the rotational probability of ARX may be reduced.

Chained modular additions are used in ARX hash functions such as BLAKE2 [1] and Skein [6,7]. Both functions have been successfully attacked using rotational cryptanalysis (in fact, rotational cryptanalysis was officially introduced as a method of analysis on an instance of Skein [13]). The success can be attributed to the lack of constants or to the use of (almost rotational) constants in the designs. We correct the claimed complexity of rotational attacks against BLAKE2 [10]. Our analysis suggests that, due to the aforementioned chains of modular additions, the rotational attacks are applicable only to 7 rounds of BLAKE2 instead of the claimed full 12 rounds in [10]. We also provide analysis of the compression function of Skein. Note, in [13] it is shown that the compression function reduced to 42 rounds is vulnerable to rotational attacks, and further, the attack was extended in [15,16] to include a rebound part, but the rotational part of the attack is still on 42 rounds. We show that due to the structure of addition chains in Skein, the rotational attacks on a version of Skein without any subkey additions, works for 24–28 rounds only (depending on the rotation amount).

The correctness of the results presented in this paper has been experimentally verified on ARX primitives with different state sizes and different numbers of round[2].

2   Differential Cryptanalysis and Markov Ciphers

Differential cryptanalysis, introduced by Biham and Shamir [2], is a probabilistic chosen-plaintext attack. It works against ciphers (and other cryptographic primitives) whose differential properties deviate from those expected by a random cipher. Consider a cipher. We can determine a collection of input (plaintext) differences and the corresponding output (ciphertext) differences. In differential cryptanalysis, we try to identify a pair (α, β), which occurs with a much higher probability than other (possible) pairs, where α is an input (plaintext) difference and β is an output (ciphertext) difference. This property allows to distinguish

---

[2] The results of the experiments are given in the full version of this paper [14].

the cipher from a random permutation and in many cases may lead to secret key recovery (or total cipher break). Finding two differences (α, β) (the pair (α, β) is called a differential) that maximizes the probability is, in fact, the main goal (and the most challenging task) of differential cryptanalysis.

For a chosen plaintext difference, the ciphertext difference can be found by propagating the plaintext difference through the encryption function of the cipher. Most ciphers are iterated, i.e. their encryption function consists of repetitive application of some (possibly weak) non-linear round function $Y = f(X, Z_i)$, where X is a state at the beginning of the round, Z_i is a key used in the round i and Y is an output state. To find β, an initial plaintext difference α is propagated round-by-round and after r rounds (for an r-round cipher), the ciphertext difference β can be obtained. The evolution of differences generated after each round is called a differential characteristic and can be represented by the following sequence $\alpha = \Delta Y(0), \Delta Y(1), \ldots, \Delta Y(r) = \beta$, where $\Delta Y(i)$ is the difference at the output of the ith round.

The efficiency of differential cryptanalysis is tightly related to the probability of differentials (differential characteristics) – the higher the probability the lower the complexity. Lai and Massey [18] put a focus on the probability of differential characteristics and study conditions for differential characteristics to form a Markov chain. Note that a sequence of discrete random variables $v_0, \ldots, v_r$ is a *Markov chain* if, for $0 \leq i < r$,

$$\Pr(v_{i+1} = \beta_{i+1} | v_i = \beta_i, v_{i-1} = \beta_{i-1}, \ldots, v_0 = \beta_0) = \Pr(v_{i+1} = \beta_{i+1} | v_i = \beta_i).$$

They introduce the notion of *Markov cipher* as follows.

Definition 1. *An iterated cipher with round function* $Y = f(X, Z)$ *is a Markov cipher if for all choices of* $\alpha \neq 0, \beta \neq 0$,

$$\Pr(\Delta Y = \beta | \Delta X = \alpha, X = \gamma)$$

is independent of γ *when the round key* Z *is uniformly random, or equivalently, if*

$$\Pr_Z(\Delta Y = \beta | \Delta X = \alpha, X = \gamma) = \Pr_Z(\Delta Y(1) = \beta_1 | \Delta X = \alpha)$$

for all choices of γ.

Their main result is described by the following theorem.

Theorem 1 ([18]). *If an* r-*round iterated cipher is a Markov cipher and the* r *round subkeys are independent and uniformly random, then the sequence of differences* $\Delta Y(0), \Delta Y(1), \ldots, \Delta Y(r)$ *is a Markov chain.*

In other words, the probability of differential characteristics is a product of the probabilities of the single-round characteristics (as they form a Markov chain), as long as *the probabilities of the single-round characteristics do not depend on the value of the input state*, where round keys are independent and uniformly at random (if the cipher is Markov).

It is important to notice that Lai-Massey result does not apply to the cases when round keys are not injected in every round (see LED [11], Zorro [9]) or when they are dependent (this is the case for all modern ciphers as all round keys are produced from a single master key).

However, even in such cases, the probability of a characteristic for the whole cipher is still computed as a product of probabilities of single-round characteristics. The justification is based on the fact (or belief) that a round function introduces enough entropy. The entropy makes the inputs to the next round look completely random thus multiplying the probabilities of single-round characteristics seems to be a valid estimate of the probability of the whole characteristic.

3 Rotational Cryptanalysis and Chained Modular Additions

Rotational cryptanalysis is a probabilistic chosen-plaintext attack. It turns to be an effective cryptanalytical tool against ciphers and hash functions that are based on the three operations: modular additions (denoted as $+$), rotations (denoted as $\lll r$) and XORs (denoted as $\oplus$). Cryptographic algorithms that use the three operations are called ARX primitives. A crucial requirement for rotational cryptanalysis to work effectively is that all constants used in the ARX primitive must preserve their values when rotated[3]. To launch a rotational attack, one starts from a rotational pair of inputs, i.e. two states such that in the first state all words are chosen at random, while the second state is produced by rotating the words of the first state by a fixed amount. If for such input pair (called a rotational pair), the corresponding output pair of the ARX primitive is also rotational, with a probability higher than for a random permutation (or a function), then this property can be used to distinguish the ARX primitive from a random permutation (or a function).

It is claimed in [13] that rotational probabilities of an ARX primitive could be found by multiplying individual rotational probabilities of all the transformations used in the primitive. As ARX is composed of three distinct operations only, the rotational probabilities of addition, rotation and XOR can be computed. Probabilities of the latter two are:

$$\Pr((x \lll r_1) \lll r_2 = (x \lll r_2) \lll r_1) = 1,$$

$$\Pr(x \lll r \oplus y \lll r = (x \oplus y) \lll r) = 1,$$

while rotational probability of modular addition is given by the following lemma.

---

[3] This requirement can be relaxed to some extent and instead of assuming completely rotational constant, one can work with constants that are almost rotational, i.e. the XOR difference between the initial constant and the rotated one gives a word of small Hamming weight.

Lemma 1 (Daum [5]).

$$\Pr((x + y) \lll r = x \lll r + y \lll r) = \frac{1}{4}(1 + 2^{r-n} + 2^{-r} + 2^{-n}).$$

As modular addition only has rotational probability less than one, it is concluded that the theorem given below holds.

Theorem 2 ([13]). *Let q be the number of modular additions in an ARX primitive (that has an arbitrary number of rotations and XORs). Then rotational probability of the ARX primitive is p_+^q, where p_+ is rotational probability of modular addition (which depends on the rotation parameter r and the word size n).*

In other words, to find rotational probability of ARX, one has to count the number of additions q only. If $p_+^q > 2^{-m}$, where m is the state size, then the primitive is susceptible to rotational cryptanalysis. Theorem 2 is true under the (tacit) assumption that an ARX cipher is Markov and round keys are chosen independently and uniformly at random. Note that as in differential cryptanalysis, if round keys are not used in every round, then randomness (required by the Markov chain) must come from the state words, which are updated by the three operations of ARX. Rotations and XORs have rotational probability of 1 and thus are independent of the inputs. The case of modular addition is different. Rotational probability of modular addition is as determined by Lemma 1 as long as inputs are random. The output of modular addition is biased when an input pair is rotational. That is if $(x + y) \lll r = x \lll r + y \lll r$ and $r > 0$, then the value $z = x + y$ is biased. If the output of modular addition is taken as input to another addition, then rotational probability of the second addition may not follow Lemma 1 although Theorem 2 states that this should be irrelevant.

To illustrate the issue, let us focus on two toy ARX primitives given in Fig. 1. Each of them has three inputs a, b, k, two outputs u and w, and uses two modular additions. If the rotation amount r equals 1 and the word size is 64 bits, then by Lemma 1, rotational probability of modular addition is $2^{-1.415}$ and thus by Theorem 2, rotational probability of both of the primitives should be $2^{-2.83}$. Note that for rotation amount of 1, rotational probability of modular addition strongly depends on the value of the most significant bits of the inputs. More precisely, the sum of the most significant bits of the inputs should not be larger than 1.

In the ARX construction on the left of Fig. 1, the two modular additions are chained, i.e. the output of the first is the input to the second. The most significant bit of the word $d = a + b$, when $(a + b) \lll 1 = a \lll 1 + b \lll 1$, is biased towards 1. Therefore, the second modular addition $u = k + d$ has rotational probability smaller than the one given by Lemma 1. As the result, Theorem 2 fails to give the correct probability.

In the ARX on the right of Fig. 1, the two modular additions are separated by rotation. In this case, although the most significant bit of d is still biased towards 1, the rotation moves this bit to a different position, where the mentioned bias is negligible for the computation of the rotational probability. Furthermore,

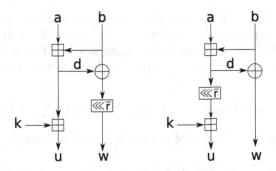

Fig. 1. Two ARX primitives with equal number of additions but different rotational probabilities.

the least significant bit of $d \lll \bar{r}$ becomes a completely random bit and thus the second modular addition $d \lll \bar{r} + k$ has probability given by Lemma 1. Therefore, in this case, Theorem 2 works as expected.

These two examples suggest that rotational probability of ARX cannot be computed simply by counting the number of modular additions. Instead, one has to investigate the relative positions of modular additions, i.e. if they are chained or separated by rotations. In fact, the longer the chain of modular additions, the lower the rotational probability for each consecutive addition. The rotational probability of chained modular additions is given by the following lemma.

Lemma 2 (Chained Modular Additions). *Let $a_1, \ldots, a_k$ be n-bit words chosen at random and let r be a positive integer such that $0 < r < n$. Then*

$$\Pr([(a_1 + a_2) \lll r = a_1 \lll r + a_2 \lll r] \wedge$$
$$\wedge [(a_1 + a_2 + a_3) \lll r = a_1 \lll r + a_2 \lll r + a_3 \lll r] \wedge$$
$$\wedge \ldots$$
$$\wedge [(a_1 + \ldots + a_k) \lll r = a_1 \lll r + \ldots + a_k \lll r]) =$$
$$= \frac{1}{2^{nk}} \binom{k + 2^r - 1}{2^r - 1} \binom{k + 2^{n-r} - 1}{2^{n-r} - 1}$$

Proof. First we consider the rotational probability of addition of l terms:

$$(a_1 + a_2 + \ldots + a_l) \lll r = a_1 \lll r + a_2 \lll r + \ldots + a_l \lll r. \tag{1}$$

Each of the n-bit words a_i can be seen as a concatenation of two words: r-bit word x_i and $(n - r)$-bit word y_i, that is, $a_i = x_i \| y_i, |x_i| = r, |y_i| = n - r$. Then (1) becomes:

$$(x_1 \| y_1 + \ldots + x_l \| y_l) \lll r = (x_1 \| y_1) \lll r + \ldots (x_l \| y_l) \lll r. \tag{2}$$

The terms $(x_i \| y_i) \lll r$ in the right side of (2), after the rotation on r bits, become $(x_i \| y_i) \lll r = y_i \| x_i$, thus (2) can be rewritten as:

$$(x_1 \| y_1 + \ldots + x_l \| y_l) \lll r = y_1 \| x_1 + \ldots y_l \| x_l. \tag{3}$$

The sum $x_1\|y_1 + \ldots + x_l\|y_l$ in the left side of (3) can be expressed as $(x_1 + \ldots + x_l + C_{y_1,\ldots,y_l})\|(y_1 + \ldots + y_l)$, where $C_{y_1,\ldots,y_k}$ is the carry from the sum $y_1 + \ldots + y_l$. Similarly, the sum in the right side of (3) can be expressed as $(y_1 + \ldots + y_l + C_{x_1,\ldots,x_l})\|(x_1 + \ldots + x_l)$. Therefore, after the rotation of the left sum, we obtain:

$$(y_1 + \ldots + y_l)\|(x_1 + \ldots + x_l + C_{y_1,\ldots,y_l}) = (y_1 + \ldots + y_l + C_{x_1,\ldots,x_l})\|(x_1 + \ldots + x_l). \quad (4)$$

If we take into account the size of the words x_i and y_i, from (4) we get:

$$y_1 + \ldots + y_l \equiv y_1 + \ldots + y_l + C_{x_1,\ldots,x_l} \quad (\mathrm{mod}\ 2^{n-r}),$$
$$x_1 + \ldots + x_l + C_{y_1,\ldots,y_l} \equiv x_1 + \ldots x_l \quad (\mathrm{mod}\ 2^r),$$

that is:

$$C_{x_1,\ldots x_l} \equiv 0 \quad (\mathrm{mod}\ 2^{n-r}), \quad C_{y_1,\ldots,y_l} \equiv 0 \quad (\mathrm{mod}\ 2^r). \quad (5)$$

As a result, the rotational probability of l-sum addition is equivalent to the probability that (5) will hold for a random values of $x_i, y_i, i = 1, \ldots, l$.

The probability of chained modular additions given in the Lemma is therefore equivalent to the probability of the following system:

$$C_{x_1,x_2} \equiv 0 \quad (\mathrm{mod}\ 2^{n-r}),\ C_{y_1,y_2} \equiv 0 \quad (\mathrm{mod}\ 2^r)$$
$$C_{x_1,x_2,x_3} \equiv 0 \quad (\mathrm{mod}\ 2^{n-r}),\ C_{y_1,y_2,y_3} \equiv 0 \quad (\mathrm{mod}\ 2^r)$$
$$\ldots$$
$$C_{x_1,\ldots x_k} \equiv 0 \quad (\mathrm{mod}\ 2^{n-r}),\ C_{y_1,\ldots,y_k} \equiv 0 \quad (\mathrm{mod}\ 2^r).$$

Further we will show that the whole system is equivalent to

$$C_{x_1,\ldots x_k} = 0,\ \ C_{y_1,\ldots,y_k} = 0. \quad (6)$$

To do so, we show, by induction on k, that the system of congruences on the left-hand side above, i.e. $C_{x_1,\ldots,x_i} \equiv 0 \pmod{2^{n-r}}$ for all $2 \leq i \leq k$ is equivalent to the equation $C_{x_1,\ldots,x_k} = 0$. The same sequence of reasoning applies to the right hand side of the above system to show that $C_{y_1,\ldots,y_i} \equiv 0 \pmod{2^r}$ for all $2 \leq i \leq k$ is equivalent to the equation $C_{y_1,\ldots y_k} = 0$.

First we deal with the easier reverse direction of the equivalence. Indeed, if $C_{x_1,\ldots x_k} = \lfloor \frac{x_1 + \ldots + x_k}{2^r} \rfloor = 0$ and hence $x_1 + \ldots + x_k < 2^r$, it follows (by positivity of the x_i's) that $x_1 + \ldots x_i < 2^r$ and hence $C_{x_1,\ldots,x_i} = 0$ and also $C_{x_1,\ldots,x_i} \equiv 0 \pmod{2^{n-r}}$ for all $2 \leq i \leq k$, as required for the reverse direction.

We now prove the forward direction of the equivalence by induction on k. For the induction base case, we take $k = 2$. The congruence $C_{x_1,x_2} \equiv 0 \pmod{2^{n-r}}$ is equivalent to $C_{x_1,x_2} = t \cdot 2^{n-r}$ for some non-negative integer t. As the carry of addition of two words cannot be larger than 1, it means that $C_{x_1,x_2} \in \{0,1\}$. If the carry is 1, then from $1 = t \cdot 2^{n-r}$ it follows that $t = 1$ and $2^{n-r} = 1$. However, $r < n$ and thus $2^{n-r} > 1$. Therefore, the carry C_{x_1,x_2} can only equal zero, and thus $C_{x_1,x_2} \equiv 0 \pmod{2^{n-r}}$ is equivalent to $C_{x_1,x_2} = 0$, proving the induction base case $k = 2$.

For the induction step, suppose that for some $k \geq 2$ the congruence system $C_{x_1,\dots,x_i} \equiv 0 \pmod{2^{n-r}}$ for all $2 \leq i \leq k$ implies the equation $C_{x_1,\dots,x_k} = 0$. We show that the congruence system $C_{x_1,\dots,x_i} \equiv 0 \pmod{2^{n-r}}$ for all $2 \leq i \leq k+1$ implies the equation $C_{x_1,\dots,x_{k+1}} = 0$. Indeed, by the induction hypothesis, we have that the first k congruences of the system imply that $C_{x_1,\dots,x_k} = 0$ and hence $x_1 + \dots + x_k < 2^r$, whereas $x_{k+1} < 2^r$, so $x_1 + \dots x_{k+1} < 2^r + 2^r = 2 \cdot 2^r$ and thus $C_{x_1,\dots,x_{k+1}} = \lfloor \frac{x_1 + \dots + x_{k+1}}{2^r} \rfloor \in \{0, 1\}$. Then, similarly as in the base case above, the congruence $C_{x_1,\dots,x_{k+1}} \equiv 0 \pmod{2^{n-r}}$ and the fact that $r < n$ imply that the value of the carry $C_{x_1,\dots,x_{k+1}}$ must be zero, which completes the proof of the induction step. As a result, we have reduced the whole system to the two equations given in (6).

Finally, let us find the probability that (6) holds, when $x_i, y_i, i = 1 \dots, k$ are random r-bit and $(n - r)$-bit words, respectively. Namely, we are looking at

$$\Pr(x_1 + \dots x_k < 2^r \wedge 0 \leq x_i < 2^r) \cdot \Pr(y_1 + \dots y_k < 2^{n-r} \wedge 0 \leq y_i < 2^{n-r}) \quad (7)$$

Note that

$$\Pr(x_1 + \dots x_k < 2^r \wedge 0 \leq x_i < 2^r) = \sum_{j=0}^{2^r - 1} \Pr(x_1 + \dots x_k = j \wedge 0 \leq x_i < 2^r). \quad (8)$$

Furthermore, the terms in the right side of (8) can be evaluated according to the well known combinatorial formula

$$\#\{z_1 + \dots z_k = j \wedge 0 \leq z_i\} = \binom{j + k - 1}{j}, \quad (9)$$

Note that in (9), the condition $0 \leq z_i$ can be replaced with $0 \leq z_i < t$ when $t > j$, as the number of tuples does not increase when $z_i \geq t$ (the sum is always larger than j). Therefore

$$\Pr(z_1 + \dots z_k = j \wedge 0 \leq z_i < t \wedge t > j) = \binom{j + k - 1}{j} t^{-k} \quad (10)$$

and (7) can be expressed as:

$$\Pr(x_1 + \dots x_k < 2^r \wedge 0 \leq x_i < 2^r) \cdot \Pr(y_1 + \dots y_k < 2^{n-r} \wedge 0 \leq y_i < 2^{n-r}) =$$

$$= \sum_{j=0}^{2^r - 1} \binom{j + k - 1}{j} 2^{-rk} \cdot \sum_{j=0}^{2^{n-r} - 1} \binom{j + k - 1}{j} 2^{-(n-r)k} =$$

$$= \frac{1}{2^{nk}} \sum_{j=0}^{2^r - 1} \binom{j + k - 1}{j} \cdot \sum_{j=0}^{2^{n-r} - 1} \binom{j + k - 1}{j}$$

Finally, we use the binomial coefficient formula (for $m, n \in \mathbb{N}$)

$$\sum_{j=0}^{m} \binom{n + j}{j} = \binom{n + m + 1}{m}.$$

and we conclude the proof

$$\Pr([(a_1 + a_2) \lll r = a_1 \lll r + a_2 \lll r] \wedge$$
$$\wedge [(a_1 + a_2 + a_3) \lll r = a_1 \lll r + a_2 \lll r + a_3 \lll r] \wedge$$
$$\wedge \ldots$$
$$\wedge [(a_1 + \ldots + a_k) \lll r = a_1 \lll r + \ldots + a_k \lll r]) =$$

$$\frac{1}{2^{nk}} \sum_{j=0}^{2^r-1} \binom{j+k-1}{j} \cdot \sum_{j=0}^{2^{n-r}-1} \binom{j+k-1}{j} =$$

$$= \frac{1}{2^{nk}} \binom{k + 2^r - 1}{2^r - 1} \binom{k + 2^{n-r} - 1}{2^{n-r} - 1}.$$

$\square$

From the above lemma, we obtain the following important result, which forms the basis for our analysis.

Fact 1. *Chained modular additions do NOT form a Markov chain with respect to rotational differences. Rotational probabilities of chained modular additions cannot be computed as product of probabilities of the individual modular additions.*

We used `GNU Multiple Precision Floating-Point Reliably` library (GNU MPFR) to compute rotational probabilities of chained modular additions according to the results of Lemma 2. Probabilities for 64-bit words, rotation parameters of 1 and 2 and precision of 10000 digits are given in Table 1. For instance, when the rotation parameter is 1 and there are 25 chained modular additions, probability that outputs of these 25 additions are rotational is $2^{-109.6}$. This is to be compared to the claim of Theorem 2, which predicts that probability is $2^{-1.415 \cdot 25} \approx 2^{-35.4}$. We note that we have also computed the rotational probabilities when the rotation amount is greater than 2. The discrepancy is present as well, and it has the tendency to grow – the closer the rotation amount to $n/2$, the larger the discrepancy between the claims of Theorem 2 and of our Lemma 2.

Note that Lemma 2 is used when outputs of all chained additions need to be rotational. This is an important requirement as in ARX, outputs of intermediate modular additions are used as inputs to other operations and are assumed to be rotational. For instance, in Fig. 1, we need d to be rotational, as further it is used in computing the value of w. In contrast, if only the final output of multiple modular additions needs to be rotational, then the rotational probability is computed under different formula (due to space constrains, we omit the formula).

Above it is assumed that only rotations can break the chain of modular additions. We point out that XORs also break such chains as long as the second term of the XOR is a random value. In practice, for ARX algorithms, the chains are broken by both XORs and rotations. Moreover, due to the possibility of XOR to break chains of modular additions, *rotational probability of ARX primitives*

Table 1. The comparison of the rotational probabilities ($\log_2$) of chained modular additions of 64-bit words given by Theorem 2 of [13], and by our Lemma 2.

rotation amount : 1

# of additions	1	2	3	4	5	6	7	8
Theorem 2 [13]	−1.4	−2.8	−4.2	−5.7	−7.1	−8.5	−9.9	−11.3
Lemma 2	−1.4	−3.6	−6.3	−9.3	−12.7	−16.3	−20.1	−24.1
# of additions	9	10	11	12	13	14	15	16
Theorem 2 [13]	−12.7	−14.1	−15.6	−17.0	−18.4	−19.8	−21.2	−22.6
Lemma 2	−28.3	−32.7	−37.1	−41.7	−46.4	−51.3	−56.2	−61.2
# of additions	17	18	19	20	21	22	23	24
Theorem 2 [13]	−24.1	−25.5	−26.9	−28.3	−29.7	−31.1	−32.5	−34.0
Lemma 2	−66.3	−71.4	−76.7	−82.0	−87.4	−92.9	−98.4	−104.0
# of additions	25	26	27	28	29	30	31	32
Theorem 2 [13]	−35.4	−36.8	−38.2	−39.6	−41.0	−42.4	−43.9	−45.3
Lemma 2	−109.6	−115.3	−121.1	−126.9	−132.8	−138.7	−144.6	−150.6

rotation amount : 2

# of additions	1	2	3	4	5	6	7	8
Theorem 2 [13]	−1.7	−3.4	−5.0	−6.7	−8.4	−10.1	−11.7	−13.4
Lemma 2	−1.7	−4.3	−7.5	−11.1	−15.1	−19.4	−23.9	−28.7
# of additions	9	10	11	12	13	14	15	16
Theorem 2 [13]	−15.1	−16.8	−18.4	−20.1	−21.8	−23.5	−25.1	−26.8
Lemma 2	−33.6	−38.7	−44.0	−49.4	−54.9	−60.6	−66.3	−72.2
# of additions	17	18	19	20	21	22	23	24
Theorem 2 [13]	−28.5	−30.2	−31.8	−33.5	−35.2	−36.9	−38.5	−40.2
Lemma 2	−78.1	−84.2	−90.3	−96.5	−102.8	−109.1	−115.5	−122.0
# of additions	25	26	27	28	29	30	31	32
Theorem 2 [13]	−41.9	−43.6	−45.3	−46.9	−48.6	−50.3	−52.0	−53.6
Lemma 2	−128.5	−135.1	−141.8	−148.5	−155.3	−162.1	−169.0	−175.9

highly depends on the way round keys are incorporated into the state, i.e. it is important if round keys are modularly added or XORed to the state. To illustrate this, let us focus on Fig. 2. We have two ARX primitives, each with two modular additions. The difference is that in the ARX on the left of the figure, the round key is modularly added to the state while in the ARX on the right, the round key is XORed to the state. We can see from the figure that in the left ARX the round key does not break the chain of modular additions, while in the right ARX it does. Hence for the left ARX, we have to use Lemma 2 to compute the rotational probability and thus it is much lower.

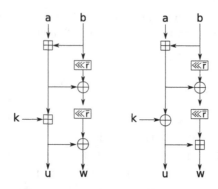

Fig. 2. Two ARX primitives with different incorporations of the subkeys: in the ARX on the left the subkey is modularly added hence does not break the chain of modular additions, while in the ARX on the right the subkey is XORed to the state, thus it breaks the chain.

The correctness of our analysis has been tested using computer simulations. Our tests have confirmed the predicted rotational probabilities – for the details, refer to the full version of this paper [14].

4   Applications

Lemma 2 suggests that the rotational probability of ARX can be computed more accurately if we take into account not only the number of additions used in ARX but also their positions. We cluster the additions into chains and calculate the rotational probability as follows:

1. Find all chains of modular additions (including the ones that are composed of a single additions) in the ARX primitive.
2. For each chain, compute the rotational probability according to Lemma 2.
3. For the entire primitive, calculate the rotational probability as the product of rotational probabilities of chains.

Consider an example of application of the above algorithm to the case of the ARX primitives given in Fig. 1. Our task is to find rotational probabilities of these two primitives when the rotation parameter is 1 (and the word size is 64 bits). The ARX scheme on the left of Fig. 1 has only one chain of two modular additions. Therefore, according to Table 1, the rotational probability of this chain is $2^{-3.6}$. On the other hand, the ARX on the right of Fig. 1, has two chains composed of a single modular addition and thus the rotational probability of this scheme is $2^{-1.4} \cdot 2^{-1.4} = 2^{-2.8}$.

Now we are ready to revisit the existing rotational attacks on the ARX primitives functions.

4.1 Application to Rotational Cryptanalysis of BLAKE2

BLAKE2 [1] is a hash function, which supports 256 and 512-bit outputs. Further on we analyze the version with 512-bit output only but we note that similar analysis applies to the other version too. The compression function of BLAKE2 is based on a permutation $P(V, M)$, where V is a state of sixteen 64-bit words v_i, and M is a message input also composed of sixteen words m_i. The function P consists of 12 identical rounds and each round uses 8 applications of the sub-primitive $G_i(a, b, c, d) = G(a, b, c, d, m_{f(i)}, m_{g(i)})$, where $f(i)$ $g(i)$ implement a permutation on a set of 16 message words. The primitive G is first applied columnwise to 4 columns, and then diagonalwise. The column and diagonal steps are defined, respectively, as:

$$G_0(v_0, v_4, v_8, v_{12}), G_1(v_1, v_5, v_9, v_{13}), G_2(v_2, v_6, v_{10}, v_{14}), G_3(v_3, v_7, v_{11}, v_{15}),$$

$$G_4(v_0, v_5, v_{10}, v_{15}), G_5(v_1, v_6, v_{11}, v_{12}), G(v_2, v_7, v_8, v_{13}), G_7(v_3, v_4, v_9, v_{14}).$$

The function $G(a, b, c, d, m_1, m_2)$ itself works as follows:

$$
\begin{aligned}
&1 : a \leftarrow a + b + m_i && 5 : a \leftarrow a + b + m_j \\
&2 : d \leftarrow (d \oplus a) \ggg 32 && 6 : d \leftarrow (d \oplus a) \ggg 16 \\
&3 : c \leftarrow c + d && 7 : c \leftarrow c + d \\
&4 : b \leftarrow (b \oplus c) \ggg 24 && 8 : b \leftarrow (b \oplus c) \ggg 63
\end{aligned}
$$

Rotational cryptanalysis of the BLAKE2 permutation [10] uses the rotational parameter equal to 1 (in order to increase the probability) and thus rotational probability of addition is around $2^{-1.4}$. Further, it is noted that the function G has 6 modular additions thus the expected rotational probability of G is $2^{-1.4 \cdot 6} = 2^{-8.4}$. The authors also note that the experimental results show that rotational probability is slightly lower or around $2^{-9.1}$. They took this as rotational probability of one application of G and because the whole permutation has 12 rounds, each with 8 calls to G, they conclude that rotational probability of the permutation used in the compression function of BLAKE2 is $2^{-9.1 \cdot 12 \cdot 8} = 2^{-873.6}$. Since this permutation works for 1024 bits, a rotational distinguisher is claimed for the full 12-round permutation.

Our rigorous analysis demonstrates that the actual probability would be far lower due to chaining of modular additions, so the conclusion mentioned above is incorrect. Without the loss of generality, we set all the message words to 0, as this yields the rotational pair of messages delivering the highest rotational probability. Then identify all chained modular additions. Figure 3 shows a round of the permutation, where one can see exactly 8 chains of 4 modular additions each. We can assume the non-chaining inputs of modular additions are independent since they always go through rotations. Therefore, Lemma 2 can be applied. Note that the 8 chains of modular additions continue through the next rounds, totaling $4R$ additions in each chain over R rounds. Consequently, a 7-round permutation (with 8 chains of 28 modular additions each) has rotational probability equal to $(2^{-126.9})^8 = 2^{-1015.2}$ when the rotation amount equal to 1 (see Table 1). Taking more rounds would result in the rotational probability smaller

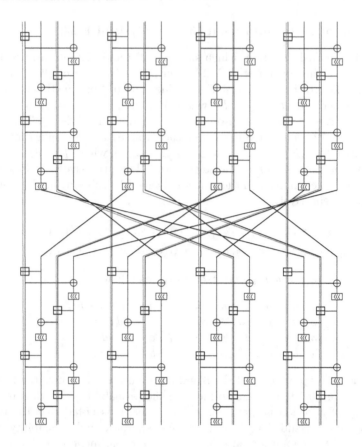

Fig. 3. The 8 chains (denoted in red) of 4 modular additions in one round of the permutation of BLAKE2 (Color figure online).

than 2^{-1024}. Indeed, Table 1 gives the probability of $2^{-132.8}$ for 29 chained modular additions smaller or equal to $2^{-1062.4}$. Hence, a rotational distinguisher for the permutation of BLAKE2 works for up to 7 rounds only, which is smaller than 12 rounds claimed in [10].

4.2   Application to Rotational Cryptanalysis of Skein

Skein [8] is a hash function proposed for the NIST SHA-3 competition, which reached the final round of the competition. At each round the authors proposed some tweaks to the previous version. Here we consider two such versions Skein v1 [6] and Skein v2 [7] and refer to them as Skein, as the attacks [13,16] target them both. In order to stop rotational attacks, the designers changed the key schedule in v3.

We consider the version of Skein with a 512-bit internal state, which we denote by Skein-512. The same analysis applies to other versions. The com-

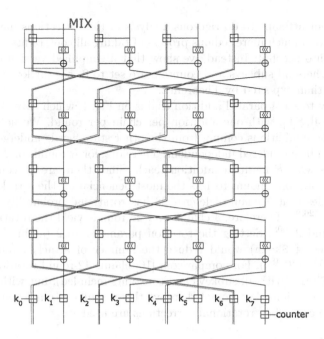

Fig. 4. Four rounds of *Threefish* followed by a subkey addition. In total, *Threefish* uses 18 such four rounds. The rounds use different rotation amounts (Color figure online).

pression function of Skein-512 is based on the block cipher *Threefish*, which is a 72-round ARX scheme with 512-bit state seen as eight 64-bit words. Each round applies 4 parallel MIX functions (Fig. 4), and subkeys (message words) are added every 4 rounds. Subkeys are a bitwise linear function of the master key, the tweak value (not to be confused with the submission tweak), and a round counter.

Skein (and the underlying *Threefish*) was used as a testbed for rotational cryptanalysis [13] due to the rotation-invariant constant 0x555...555 used in the key schedule and a low-weight counter. By setting the rotational amount to 2, 42 rounds were attacked in [13]. Then the attack was combined with the rebound method and extended to 55 rounds in [16]. To deal with the round counter, the authors had to drop the requirement of having rotational property preserved after each round. Instead, using so called rotational errors and corrections, they introduced a disturbance in the internal state and later corrected it in the manner similar to the local collision concept.

The authors also noticed the difference between the theoretical rotational probabilities (Lemma 1) and experimental values. To cope with this problem, they used the experimental value for the 2-round span where the rotational property is required, and a separate value for the local collision part around the subkey injection. Their experiments are well matched with Table 1 and thus are not questioned.

We do not attempt to do rigorous analysis of the corrections method, as it would involve a much more tedious process of taking all constraints and counter properties into account. Instead, we show that a simplified version of the permutation, where all subkeys and counters are set to 0, has far lower rotational probability than expected by Theorem 2.

It is easy to see 4 parallel addition chains on Fig. 4, which cover state words $S[0], S[2], S[4], S[6]$, with one addition per chain per round. We note that the inputs to these additions coming from the other state words undergo rotations and thus can be considered independent. Therefore, for R rounds of *Threefish* we get 4 chains with R modular additions each. Since there are no constants, we can set the rotation amount to 1 as the most beneficial for the attacker. Table 1 clearly implies that a chain of length 28 has rotational probability smaller or equal to $(2^{-126.9})$. Therefore, 4 chains over 28 rounds yield the rotational probability around 2^{-508}. Setting the rotation parameter to 2 (as in the previous cryptanalyses of Skein) would reduce the number of attacked rounds to 24 (as $(2^{-122.0})^4 = 2^{-488}$). For comparison, [16] claims 42-round rotational distinguisher on Skein (with all subkeys and constants included), but with the use of rotational corrections. We cannot disprove these results as our formulas do not apply to the case when rotational corrections are used.

5   Conclusion

We have shown that the rotational probability of ARX depends not only on the number of modular additions, but also on how they are connected. The rotational probability of a chain of modular additions cannot be computed as a product of probabilities of the individual additions. This is because the Markov cipher assumption, used implicitly for computing the probability in such a way, does not hold. Therefore, the chain of additions cannot be a Markov chain with respect to rotational analysis, and thus its probability is lower and is defined by Lemma 2. Our analysis also suggests that the way the subkeys are incorporated into the cipher can influence the rotational probability not only because modular added subkeys simply increase the total number of additions, but because XORed subkeys can break the addition chains and thus can increase the probability.

We have investigated the application of rotational cryptanalysis only to ARX, but we note that our methodology can be used for analysis of rotational attacks on other primitives as well. For instance, the Markov cipher assumption used in the recent rotational attacks on Keccak [20] is valid as in each round of Keccak, there is a very strong diffusion, and, moreover, each of the 25 words goes through a rotation. Therefore the rotational probability in the attacks on Keccak [20] is correct. On the other hand, the assumption used the rotational analysis of NORX [12] is clearly not valid (see Appendix B of [14]) as the diffusion in the rounds of NORX does not introduce sufficient entropy at the inputs of the non-linear operations. Hence, the probability of the rotational analysis of NORX [12] is miscalculated[4].

---

[4] We have confirmed this experimentally as well. The correct probability is lower than the one predicted in [12]. Therefore, as the paper only gives upper bound on

To summarize, the rotational probability of a cryptographic primitive not necessarily equals to the product of the rotational probabilities of the individual operations used in the primitive. Such shortcut in the estimation of probability gives neither upper nor lower bound on the actual probability. The estimation can be used only after confirming that the Markov assumption applies to the primitive. Otherwise, the rotational probability must be computed ad-hoc.

Acknowledgements. The authors would like to thank the anonymous reviewers of FSE'15 for very helpful comments and suggestions. Ivica Nikolić is supported by the Singapore National Research Foundation Fellowship 2012 (NRF-NRFF2012-06). Josef Pieprzyk was supported by Australian Research Council grant DP0987734.

References

1. Aumasson, J.-P., Neves, S., Wilcox-O'Hearn, Z., Winnerlein, C.: BLAKE2: simpler, smaller, fast as MD5. In: Jacobson, M., Locasto, M., Mohassel, P., Safavi-Naini, R. (eds.) ACNS 2013. LNCS, vol. 7954, pp. 119–135. Springer, Heidelberg (2013)
2. Biham, E., Shamir, A.: Differential cryptanalysis of DES-like cryptosystems. J. Cryptology 4(1), 3–72 (1991)
3. Bresson, E., Canteaut, A., Chevallier-Mames, B., Clavier, C., Fuhr, T., Gouget, A., Icart, T., Misarsky, J.-F., Naya-Plasencia, M., Paillier, P., et al.: Shabal, a submission to NISTs cryptographic hash algorithm competition. Submission to NIST (2008)
4. De Cannière, C., Rechberger, C.: Finding SHA-1 characteristics: general results and applications. In: Lai, X., Chen, K. (eds.) ASIACRYPT 2006. LNCS, vol. 4284, pp. 1–20. Springer, Heidelberg (2006)
5. M. Daum. Cryptanalysis of Hash Functions of the MD4-Family. PhD thesis, Ruhr-Universität Bochum, May 2005
6. Ferguson, N., Lucks, S., Schneier, B., Whiting, D., Bellare, M., Kohno, T., Callas, J., Walker, J.: The Skein hash function family. Submission to NIST (Round 1) (2008)
7. Ferguson, N., Lucks, S., Schneier, B., Whiting, D., Bellare, M., Kohno, T., Callas, J., Walker, J.: The Skein hash function family. Submission to NIST (Round 2) (2009)
8. Ferguson, N., Lucks, S., Schneier, B., Whiting, D., Bellare, M., Kohno, T., Callas, J., Walker, J.: The Skein hash function family (2010)
9. Gérard, B., Grosso, V., Naya-Plasencia, M., Standaert, F.-X.: Block Ciphers that are easier to mask: how far can we go? In: Bertoni, G., Coron, J.-S. (eds.) CHES 2013. LNCS, vol. 8086, pp. 383–399. Springer, Heidelberg (2013)
10. Guo, J., Karpman, P., Nikolić, I., Wang, L., Wu, S.: Analysis of BLAKE2. In: Benaloh, J. (ed.) CT-RSA 2014. LNCS, vol. 8366, pp. 402–423. Springer, Switzerland (2014)
11. Guo, J., Peyrin, T., Poschmann, A., Robshaw, M.: The LED block cipher. In: Preneel, B., Takagi, T. (eds.) CHES 2011. LNCS, vol. 6917, pp. 326–341. Springer, Heidelberg (2011)

---

the rotational probability, all the claims of resistance against rotational attacks of NORX still apply.

12. Aumasson, J.-P., Jovanovic, P., Neves, S.: Analysis of NORX: investigating differential and rotational properties. In: Aranha, D.F., Menezes, A. (eds.) LATIN-CRYPT 2014. LNCS, vol. 8895, pp. 306–323. Springer, Heidelberg (2015)
13. Khovratovich, D., Nikolić, I.: Rotational cryptanalysis of ARX. In: Hong, S., Iwata, T. (eds.) FSE 2010. LNCS, vol. 6147, pp. 333–346. Springer, Heidelberg (2010)
14. Khovratovich, D., Nikolić, I., Pieprzyk, J., Sokolowski, P., Steinfeld, R.: Rotational cryptanalysis of ARX revisited. IACR Cryptology ePrint Archive, 2015:95 (2015)
15. Khovratovich, D., Nikolić, I., Rechberger, C.: Rotational rebound attacks on reduced skein. In: Abe, M. (ed.) ASIACRYPT 2010. LNCS, vol. 6477, pp. 1–19. Springer, Heidelberg (2010)
16. Khovratovich, D., Nikolić, I., Rechberger, C.: Rotational rebound attacks on reduced Skein. J. Cryptology **27**(3), 452–479 (2014)
17. Kircanski, A., Shen, Y., Wang, G., Youssef, A.M.: Boomerang and slide-rotational analysis of the SM3 hash function. In: Knudsen, L.R., Wu, H. (eds.) SAC 2012. LNCS, vol. 7707, pp. 304–320. Springer, Heidelberg (2013)
18. Lai, X., Massey, J.L.: Markov ciphers and differential cryptanalysis. In: Davies, D.W. (ed.) EUROCRYPT 1991. LNCS, vol. 547, pp. 17–38. Springer, Heidelberg (1991)
19. Leurent, G.: Analysis of differential attacks in ARX constructions. In: Wang, X., Sako, K. (eds.) ASIACRYPT 2012. LNCS, vol. 7658, pp. 226–243. Springer, Heidelberg (2012)
20. Morawiecki, P., Pieprzyk, J., Srebrny, M.: Rotational cryptanalysis of round-reduced keccak. In: Moriai, S. (ed.) FSE 2013. LNCS, vol. 8424, pp. 241–262. Springer, Heidelberg (2014)
21. Nikolić, I., Pieprzyk, J., Sokołowski, P., Steinfeld, R.: Rotational cryptanalysis of (modified) versions of BMW and SIMD (2010)
22. Stevens, M.: New collision attacks on SHA-1 based on optimal joint local-collision analysis. In: Johansson, T., Nguyen, P.Q. (eds.) EUROCRYPT 2013. LNCS, vol. 7881, pp. 245–261. Springer, Heidelberg (2013)
23. Van Assche, G.: A rotational distinguisher on Shabals keyed permutation and its impact on the security proofs. NIST mailing list (2010)
24. Wang, X., Yin, Y.L., Yu, H.: Finding collisions in the full SHA-1. In: Shoup, V. (ed.) CRYPTO 2005. LNCS, vol. 3621, pp. 17–36. Springer, Heidelberg (2005)
25. Wang, X., Yu, H.: How to break MD5 and other hash functions. In: Cramer, R. (ed.) EUROCRYPT 2005. LNCS, vol. 3494, pp. 19–35. Springer, Heidelberg (2005)

Internal Differential Boomerangs: Practical Analysis of the Round-Reduced Keccak-f Permutation

Jérémy Jean[✉] and Ivica Nikolić

Nanyang Technological University, Singapore, Singapore
{Jjean,INikolic}@ntu.edu.sg

Abstract. We introduce internal differential boomerang distinguisher as a combination of internal differentials and classical boomerang distinguishers. The new boomerangs can be successful against cryptographic primitives having high-probability round-reduced internal differential characteristics. The internal differential technique, which follow the evolution of differences between *parts of* the state, is particularly meaningful for highly symmetric functions like the inner permutation Keccak-f of the hash functions defined in the future SHA-3 standard. We find internal differential and standard characteristics for three to four rounds of Keccak-f, and with the use of the new technique, enhanced with a strong message modification, show practical distinguishers for this permutation. Namely, we need 2^{12} queries to distinguish 7 rounds of the permutation starting from the first round, and approximately 2^{18} queries to distinguish 8 rounds starting from the fourth round. Due to the exceptionally low complexities, all of our results have been completely verified with a computer implementation of the analysis.

Keywords: SHA-3 · Keccak · Internal differential · Boomerang · Practical-complexity distinguisher

1 Introduction

The family of sponge functions Keccak [3] was one of the proposals for the hash function competition organized by NIST [29]. In 2012, Keccak was announced as the winner, and some hash functions from this family will officially become part of the SHA-3 standard [30], to complement the SHA-2 hash standard. As such, Keccak is among the most significant cryptographic primitives to date; its security is therefore of crucial importance.

In the past several years, Keccak has received significant amount of attention from the cryptographic community, both during the competition and after being announced as the winning algorithm. Analyses of round-reduced versions have

---

The authors are supported by the Singapore National Research Foundation Fellowship 2012 (NRF-NRFF2012-06). A long version of this paper is available in [18].

G. Leander (Ed.): FSE 2015, LNCS 9054, pp. 537–556, 2015.
DOI: 10.1007/978-3-662-48116-5_26

been proposed for the hash function, for the underlying permutation, and for various secret-key schemes based on this permutation. So far, the best attacks on the hash function in the standard model reach five rounds [14,15], while in the keyed model reach up to nine rounds [16]. For the underlying permutation, the best analysis in terms of complexity reaches six rounds and requires 2^{11} queries [22], while in terms of number of rounds, the best is eight and requires 2^{491} queries [17].

In this paper, we present distinguishers for round-reduced versions of the permutation Keccak-f used in Keccak based on a new analysis technique called *internal differential boomerang distinguishers*. We stress that we propose distinguishers on the round-reduced permutation: the paper does not target a keyed mode using it, while the technique may encourage follow-up works. From a high-level perspective, this technique resembles classical boomerangs, but in one part of the boomerang it uses internal differentials, which consider differences between *part of* a state, rather than a difference *between* two states. As a result, our boomerang produces *pairs* of state values that have specific input internal and output differences, while classical boomerangs produce *quartets* of inputs.

More precisely, on the one hand, the classical boomerang starts with an input pair that has a specific internal difference, and the corresponding outputs are computed. Then, a second output pair is produced by XORing a specific difference to both output values, and finally, these values are inverted to a second input pair, and it is checked if this pair has the same specific input difference. On the other hand, the internal differential boomerang distinguisher framework depicted in this paper is slightly different than this classical boomerang scenario since it considers *internal* differences, which ultimately produces pairs of inputs rather than quartets. Specifically, an input with particular *internal* difference generates an output to which we apply a specific output difference. The second output is then inverted to a second input, and one checks whether it has the given input *internal* difference.

For both these kinds of boomerangs, the time complexity required to generate either a right quartet or a right pair depends on the probability of the differentials (internal differentials or regular differentials) used in the two parts of the primitive. Furthermore, in internal differential boomerangs, the part of the primitive covered by the internal differential is passed twice, whereas the part covered by the standard differential only once (in classical boomerang, both of the parts are passed twice). Thus, our technique outperforms the classical boomerangs when high-probability internal differentials exist for several rounds of the primitive. We further give an evaluation of the time complexity required to generate right quartets and pairs for both types of boomerangs, and discuss the use of the message modification technique to greatly reduce this complexity when we have the ability to choose bits of intermediate state values.

Interestingly, Dinur et al. [14] collision attacks on Keccak can be seen as an instance of our boomerangs: as they perform only forward queries, their attacks are in fact amplified version of our boomerangs. Thus, the boomerangs presented here can be seen as a generalization of [14].

We distinguish the round-reduced Keccak-f permutation by producing boomerang pairs. First, we find internal differential and standard differential characteristics that are used in the boomerangs. The characteristics span on three to four rounds and, as in some rounds the differences are truncated, have very high probabilities. We combine the characteristics according to the internal differential boomerang, and with the use of an enhanced message modification (which allows to pass deterministically the two low probability rounds in the middle of the boomerang), obtain boomerang pairs with low and practical complexity. We also provide a rigorous bound on the query complexity of producing such boomerang pairs in the case of a random permutation. As this complexity is much higher than what we need for round-reduced Keccak-f, we claim distinguishers.

Our internal characteristics depend on the round constants, thus we give distinguishers on the round-reduced Keccak-f permutation for two different cases: when the permutation starts[1] at round 0, and when it starts at round 3. In the first case, we can distinguish the permutation reduced to 6 rounds with 2^5 queries, and 7 rounds with 2^{13} queries. In the second case, we can distinguish 7 rounds with $2^{10.3}$ queries, and 8 rounds with $2^{18.3}$ queries.

We emphasize that the whole analysis, due to its exceptionally low complexity, has been implemented and successfully verified. We refer the reader to [18] for the outputs produced by our computer experiments. We also stress that our results do not threaten the security of the full-round Keccak-f permutation. A summary of previous analysis of Keccak, along with our new results, are given in Tables 1 and 2.

Application of the Internal Differential Boomerangs. The impact of this kind of boomerangs depends on the analyzed framework. When the subject of analysis is a block cipher, then the impact of the internal differential boomerangs is similar to that of the classical boomerangs, i.e. they immediately lead to distinguishers and possibly can be extended to key recovery attacks. On the other hand, in the framework of hash/compression functions and permutations, their significance depends on the quality of the internal differential and standard differential characteristics used to produce the boomerang pairs. For instance, if the input internal difference complies to the conditions of the input to the hash/compression function and the output difference has a low hamming weight, then an internal differential boomerang pair may lead to near collisions.

The internal differential boomerangs presented further in this paper only apply to the round-reduced Keccak-f permutation, but not to Keccak. This is due to the message modification used in the middle states, which results in inputs that do not comply to the inputs conditions to the sponge construction of Keccak where the values in the capacity part cannot be controlled. Similarly, it prevents applying the distinguishers to other keyed constructions, such

---

[1] Note that while the draft FIPS 202 [30] defines the r-round-reduced versions of Keccak-f as the last r rounds of Keccak-f, this paper allows the reduced permutation to start at any round number.

Table 1. Summary of attacks on Keccak.

Rounds	Complexity	Type	Technique	Reference
2	2^{33}	Collision	Differential	[31]
2	2^{33}	Preimage	Differential	[31]
3	2^{25}	Near-Collision	Differential	[31]
4	2^{221}	Preimage	Rotational	[26]
4	2^{25}	Distinguisher	Differential	[31]
4	practical	Collision	Differential	[15]
4	practical	Collision	Differential	[21]
4	2^{506}	Preimage	Rotational	[26]
5	2^{115}	Collision	Int. differential	[14]
5	2^{35}	Key recovery (MAC)	Cube attack	[16]
5	practical	Near-Collision	Differential	[15]
6	2^{52}	Distinguisher	Differential	[12]
6	2^{36}	Key recovery (Stream)	Cube attack	[16]
8	2^{129}	MAC forgery	Cube attack	[16]
9	2^{256}	Keystream prediction	Cube attack	[16]

Table 2. Distinguishers of reduced-round versions of Keccak-f.

Rounds	Complexity	Type	Technique	Reference
5	2^8	Distinguisher	Rebound	[17]
6	2^5	**Distinguisher**	**Internal Diff. Boomerang**	**Section 4**
6	2^{10}	Distinguisher	Zero-sum	[1,9]
6	2^{11}	Distinguisher	Self-symmetry	[22]
6	2^{32}	Distinguisher	Rebound	[17]
6.5	unknown	Distinguisher	Cube tester	[16]
7	2^{10}	**Distinguisher**[a]	**Internal Diff. Boomerang**	**Section 4**
7	2^{13}	**Distinguisher**	**Internal Diff. Boomerang**	**Section 4**
7	2^{15}	Distinguisher	Zero-sum	[1,9]
7	2^{142}	Distinguisher	Rebound	[17]
8	2^{18}	**Distinguisher**[a]	**Internal Diff. Boomerang**	**Section 4**
8	2^{18}	Distinguisher	Zero-sum	[1,9]
8	2^{491}	Distinguisher	Rebound	[17]
24	2^{1590}	Distinguisher	Zero-sum	[10]

[a]: Start from round 3.

as Keyak [5] and Ketje [4]. Therefore, our internal differential boomerangs only allow to distinguish round-reduced Keccak-f from a random permutation. However, their impact relate to Keccak since it adopts the hermetic sponge strategy as a design philosophy [2]. In its original formulation, this consists of using the sponge construction (providing security against generic attacks) and calling a permutation that should not have any properties (called structural distinguishers) besides having a compact representation. Our results disprove this requirement for the round-reduced Keccak-f by showing a non-random behavior.

2   Description of Keccak-f

In this section, we give a partial description of the hash functions that will be defined in the future SHA-3 standard [30]. In particular, since the results in this paper only deal with the inner permutation (further denoted by Keccak-f), we do not recall the details of the sponge construction. For a complete description of this family of functions, we refer the interested reader to [3,30].

The Keccak-f permutation works on a state of $b = 25 \times 2^l$ bits, where $b \in \{25, 50, 100, 200, 400, 800, 1600\}$, and has $n_r = 12 + 2l$ rounds. We count the rounds starting from zero. The results in this paper consider round-reduced versions of Keccak-$f[1600]$, where the full permutation has $n_r = 24$ rounds. As introduced in [30], we define by Keccak-p a round-reduced version of the Keccak-f permutation, where its $n \geq n_r$ rounds are the n last ones of Keccak-f. In this paper, we leverage the restriction on the starting round number and further introduce the notation Keccak-$p_{i,n}$ to consider the n consecutive rounds of Keccak-$f[1600]$ starting at round i; that is, rounds $i, \ldots, i+n-1$. Using this notation, Keccak-$f[1600]$ would be Keccak-$p_{0,24}$.

Each round of Keccak-$f[b]$ is composed of five steps: the first three (θ, π and ρ, in this order) are linear and further denoted together by $\lambda = \pi \circ \rho \circ \theta$, the fourth step is non-linear and denoted by χ, and the last step ι adds round-dependent constants $RC[i]$, $0 \leq i < n_r$, to break symmetries. Each step applies to different parts of the state, which is seen as a three-dimensional array of bits of dimension $5 \times 5 \times b$. A bit $S[x, y, z]$ in a state S is addressed by its coordinates (x, y, z), $0 \leq (x, y) < 5$ and $0 \leq z < b$. Furthermore, for fixed x, y and z, $S[x, y, \bullet]$ refers to a *lane* of b bits, and $S[\bullet, \bullet, z]$ to a *slice* of 25 bits. We now discuss the details of each of the five steps on a given input state S:

The θ step operates on the slices of the state by performing the following operation at each coordinate (x, y, z):

$$S[x, y, z] \leftarrow S[x, y, z] \oplus \Big(\bigoplus_{y'=0}^{4} a[x-1, y', z] \Big) \oplus \Big(\bigoplus_{y'=0}^{4} a[x+1, y', z-1] \Big).$$

This linear step brings diffusion to the state. For instance, it expands a single bit difference to 11 bits, while the inverse step θ^{-1} expands it to about $b/2$ bits.

The ρ step rotates the bits inside each lane. The rotation constants are independent of the round numbers, and they are different for each of the 25 lanes (refer to [3] for the actual values).

The π **step** operates on each slice independently by permuting the 25 bits. Namely, at each coordinate (x, y, z), it applies:

$$S[x', y', z] \leftarrow S[x, y, z], \quad \text{where:} \quad \begin{pmatrix} x' \\ y' \end{pmatrix} = \begin{pmatrix} 0 & 1 \\ 2 & 3 \end{pmatrix} \begin{pmatrix} x \\ y \end{pmatrix}.$$

This step mixes the lanes and thus brings an additional diffusion to the state.

The χ **step** is the only non-linear operation in a round and it applies the same 5-bit S-Box to each 5-bit row $S[\bullet, y, z]$ of the internal state. In total, $b/5$ independent S-Boxes are applied, that is 320 in the case of Keccak-f[1600]. The S-Box has maximal differential probability 2^{-2}.

The ι **step** XORs the b-bit round-dependent constant $RC[i]$ at round i to the lane $S[0, 0, \bullet]$, $0 \le i < n_r$.

3   The Internal Differential Boomerang Distinguisher

In this section, we introduce a new distinguisher called the *internal differential boomerang distinguisher*. As it combines internal differentials and the boomerang attack, we first give a brief overview of these two strategies, and then present the new technique.

3.1   The Internal Differential Attack

In the internal differential attack [32], the adversary observes the propagation of *the difference between the two halves of the same state* through the rounds of the cryptographic function/permutation. Similar to the case of classical differential analysis, the goal of the adversary is to show that the propagation of some particular internal difference happens with an unusually high probability.

Let F be a permutation, and the n-bit state S is split into two halves S^H and S^L. With this notation, it follows that $|S^H| = |S^L|$ and $S = S^H \| S^L$. The internal difference $\delta(S)$ of the state S is computed as the XOR of its two halves, i.e. $\delta(S) = S^H \oplus S^L$. Then, an internal differential for F is a pair of internal differences (Δ, ∇), and its probability is defined as:

$$\Pr_S \left(\delta(F(S)) = \nabla \,\middle|\, \delta(S) = \Delta \right).$$

In other words, this is the probability that a randomly chosen input state S with an internal difference Δ, after the application of F, will result in an output state with internal difference ∇. Similarly to the standard differential attacks, we can define an internal differential characteristic as the propagation of the internal differences through the rounds of the permutation. Obviously, to each such internal differential characteristic, we can associate a probability that this propagation holds as expected.

3.2   The Boomerang Attack

In classical boomerang attacks [34][2], the permutation F is seen as a composition of two permutations $F = g \circ f$, where each of them covers some rounds at the beginning and at the end of F. Even though a high-probability differential might not exist for F, if high-probability differentials do exist for the two permutations f and g, then one can attack F with the boomerang technique.

Let $\Delta \to \Delta^*$ be a differential for f that holds with a probability p and $\nabla \to \nabla^*$ be a differential for g that holds with a probability q. According to Fig. 1, the adversary starts with a pair of inputs $(P_1, P_2) = (P_1, P_1 \oplus \Delta)$ and, by applying F, produces a pair of corresponding outputs $(C_1, C_2) = (F(P_1), F(P_2))$. Then, the adversary produces a new pair of outputs $(C_3, C_4) = (C_1 \oplus \nabla^*, C_2 \oplus \nabla^*)$. For this pair, the adversary obtains the corresponding pair of inputs $(P_3, P_4) = (F^{-1}(C_3), F^{-1}(C_4))$. The main observation of the boomerang technique is that the difference $P_3 \oplus P_4$ would be Δ with a probability of at least $p^2 q^2$ because:

1. The difference $f(P_1) \oplus f(P_2)$ is Δ^* with probability p.
2. The two differences $g^{-1}(C_1) \oplus g^{-1}(C_3)$ and $g^{-1}(C_2) \oplus g^{-1}(C_4)$ are both ∇ with probability q^2.
3. When 1. and 2. hold, then the difference $g^{-1}(C_3) \oplus g^{-1}(C_4)$ is Δ^* (with probability pq^2), and therefore $f^{-1}(C_3) \oplus f^{-1}(C_4)$ is Δ with probability $p^2 q^2$.

The quartet of states (P_1, P_2, P_3, P_4) fulfilling the conditions $P_1 \oplus P_2 = P_3 \oplus P_4 = \Delta$ and $F(P_1) \oplus F(P_3) = F(P_2) \oplus F(P_4)$ is called a *boomerang quartet*. As shown above, the quartet can be found in time equivalent to $(pq)^{-2}$ queries to the permutations. On the other hand, finding the boomerang quartet in the case of a random permutation requires about 2^n queries. Consequently, the boomerang approach yields a distinguisher for F as soon as the adversary can find the two differentials for f and g such that $(pq)^{-2} < 2^{-n}$, that is $pq > 2^{-n/2}$.

It has been shown in [7,8] that when F is a public permutation, a block cipher in the chosen-key attack framework, or a compression function, then the complexity of producing the boomerang quartet can be reduced with the use of the message modification technique. That is, the adversary can choose particular state words to ensure that some probabilistic differential transitions hold with probability one. Consequently, some rounds can be passed deterministically, so that their probabilities do not contribute towards the total probability $(pq)^2$. The number of such free rounds depends on how efficiently the message modification can be applied. In general, the modification is used in the rounds around the boomerang switch, i.e. the last few rounds of f and the first few rounds of g.

3.3   The Internal Differential Boomerangs

In this section, we show that the internal differential attack can be used in the boomerang setting: we call this combined analysis *the internal differential*

---

[2] The boomerang attack is closely related to higher-order differential techniques [20,23].

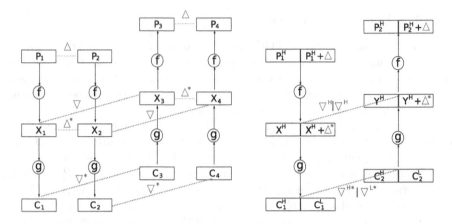

Fig. 1. The classical boomerangs (left). The internal differential boomerangs (right).

boomerangs. Although this new type of analysis shares similarity with the classical boomerangs based on standard differentials, we emphasize that there are a few differences between them. The first difference is in the number of differentials required to achieve the boomerang: the classical boomerang uses four differentials, whereas the internal differential boomerang works with only three. The second difference is in the type of differentials: the classical boomerang can use (almost) any two differentials for f and g, while for the internal differential boomerang, one of the differentials must have a special type.

Let F be a permutation that (similarly to the classical boomerang) is seen as a composition $F = g \circ f$. Let (Δ, Δ^*) be an *internal differential* for f that holds with probability p, and (∇, ∇^*) be a *standard differential* for g that holds with probability q, *where the input difference ∇ has an internal difference of zero*, i.e. $\delta(\nabla) = 0$. Then, the internal differential boomerangs can be described as:

1. Fix a random input P_1 with an internal difference Δ, i.e. $\delta(P_1) = \Delta$.
2. Produce the corresponding output $C_1 = F(P_1)$.
3. Produce another output C_2 such that $C_2 = C_1 \oplus \nabla^*$.
4. Produce the corresponding input $P_2 = F^{-1}(C_2)$.
5. Check if $\delta(P_2) = \Delta$. If it holds, output (P_1, P_2), otherwise go to 1.

The probability that the condition at step 5 holds is at least p^2q. This is based on a reasoning illustrated in Fig. 1. Let $\nabla = \nabla^H \| \nabla^H$ and $\nabla^* = \nabla^{H*} \| \nabla^{L*}$ be the input and the output differences of the standard differential used in the function g. For a random input $P_1 = P_1^H \| (P_1^H \oplus \Delta)$, the output $X = f(P_1)$ will be $X^H \| (X^H \oplus \Delta^*)$ with probability p. Furthermore, for a pair of outputs (C_1, C_2) such that $C_1 \oplus C_2 = \nabla^* = \nabla^{H*} \| \nabla^{L*}$, after the inversion of g, the output pair (X, Y) will satisfy $X \oplus Y = \nabla = \nabla^H \| \nabla^H$ with probability q. Then,

$$Y = X \oplus \nabla = \left[X^H \| (X^H \oplus \Delta^*) \right] \oplus \left[\nabla^H \| \nabla^H \right] = Y^H \| (Y^H \oplus \Delta^*),$$

where $Y^H = X^H \oplus \nabla^H$. Therefore, the internal difference in Y is Δ^*, and after the inversion of f, it will become Δ with probability p. As a result, this algorithm outputs a pair of inputs with probability $p^2 q$. We call such a pair an internal differential boomerang pair.

For a random n-bit permutation F, the pair can be found in around $2^{n/2}$ queries[3] to F. Therefore, the internal differential boomerang yields a distinguisher if $p^2 q > 2^{-n/2}$. Recall that the same condition for the classical boomerangs is $pq > 2^{-n/2}$. Consequently, it is beneficial to use the internal differential boomerang technique over the classical boomerang strategy only if the internal differential for f has a much higher probability than a differential for f.

Given a public permutation (or a compression function) $F = g \circ f$, we can start the internal differential boomerang in any round of f (but not in g), and from there produce the pair of inputs and the pair of outputs. It is usually beneficial to start at the end of f and, with the use of the message modification technique, to pass a few rounds around the boomerang switch for free (deterministically). Then, the formula for the probability of the boomerang becomes $p_*^2 q_*$, where p_* and q_* are the differential probabilities of the non-linear parts of f and g respectively, that are passed probabilistically.

Dinur et al. Collision Attack. In [14], Dinur et al. present a collision attack on reduced variants of Keccak hash function by selecting message blocks in a small subspace[4] such that a high-probability characteristic might map them to a small subspace after a certain number of rounds of Keccak-f. More precisely, they find round-reduced internal characteristics and they extend them for an additional 1.5 round. They call this extension *bounding the size of the output subset* and note that this is possible because the differences are quite sparse and the χ step has a slow diffusion.

We note that Dinur et al. collision attack is in fact based on the internal differential boomerangs presented in this paper. Their internal differential characteristics corresponds to the internal differential part of the boomerang, whereas the aforementioned extension is the standard differential part of the boomerang. Furthermore, Dinur et al. start the attack from the two inputs with specific internal differences and then check if the difference of the two outputs is as expected. This is precisely the variant of the boomerang attack called amplified boomerang [19], where the attacker only makes forward queries. Thus, Dinur et al.'s collision attack succeeds as after the amplification in the middle, the remaining 1.5 rounds are passed according to any standard differential that at the output has no active bits among those that comprise the hash value.

Truncated Differences. We further analyze the case when the input internal difference Δ and the output standard difference ∇^* of the boomerang are not fully determined, but are truncated. Namely, only some bits of these differences

---

[3] In a random permutation, the boomerang will return P_2 with internal difference Δ with a probability $2^{-n/2}$.

[4] A related subspace problem has been discussed in [24].

are determined, whereas the remaining bits can have any value. The lemma given below defines a lower bound on the complexity of finding such boomerang pair in the case of a random permutation. Note, in the lemma, we assume the output difference to be XOR difference, that is, the output difference is produced as an XOR of the two outputs.

Lemma 1. *For a random n-bit permutation π, the query complexity Q of producing an internal differential boomerang pair, with truncated input internal difference Δ determined in n_I bits and truncated XOR output difference ∇^* determined in n_O bits, satisfies:*

$$Q \geq \min(2^{n_I - 2}, 2^{\frac{n_O}{2} - \frac{3}{2}}).$$

Due to space constraints, we refer the interested reader to [18] for the proof of this lemma.

4   Distinguishers for the Round-Reduced Keccak-f Permutation

In this section, we present internal differential boomerang distinguishers on the round-reduced permutation Keccak-$f[1600]$, further denoted Keccak-$p_{i,n}$, where the starting round i and the number of rounds n is specified in the text for each case. In comparison to [30] where all the reduced variants simply called Keccak-p start at the first round, we allow the permutation to start at any number of round.

To describe our results, we first define the two differentials used in the boomerang: the internal differential used in the first rounds, and the standard differential used in the last rounds. Next, we show that a message modification can help to deterministically pass the two rounds that surround the boomerang switch. Finally, we present the actual distinguishers.

4.1   Internal Differential Characteristics

The 1600-bit state S of Keccak is composed of 25 lanes of 64 bits. The internal difference $\delta(S)$ of the state is defined as the XOR difference between the higher 32 bits and the lower 32 bits, for each lane. Hence, the internal difference is composed of 25 words of 32 bits, and can be seen as an 800-bit vector.

Let us scrutinize the behavior of the five round steps in regard to internal differences. The linear step θ may introduce an increase in the hamming weight of the internal difference, by a factor up to 11. The two steps ρ and π only permute the bits in the internal differences, but maintain their hamming weight. The non-linear step χ may increase the hamming weight of the internal difference. For instance, one-bit difference at the input (resp. output) of the S-box, may become a difference in more than 1 bit at the output (resp. input) of the S-box. However, a fixed 1-bit input difference can affect only up to three bits in the output difference, while a fixed 1-bit difference at the output of chi can affect up to 5 bits in the input difference. The ι step that XORs round constants can increase the hamming weight of the internal difference by *at most* the hamming weight of the rounds constant $\delta(RC[i])$, which are very sparse. Indeed, as already noted in [13,15], the round constants used in Keccak-f play a crucial role in the existence of high-probability internal differential characteristics in the inner permutation.

Due to the good diffusion of the round function of Keccak-$f[1600]$, a state with low-weight internal difference can be transformed into a state with a high weight in a matter of a few rounds. To increase the number of rounds covered by the internal differential characteristic, while maintaining a high and practical probability, we use two approaches. First, we start in the middle of the characteristic with zero internal difference and pass one round with probability one. Second, we consider truncated characteristics (or differentials), i.e. the differences are not necessarily fully specified in all bits.

By the first approach, which is often used for constructing standard differential characteristics, the characteristics are built from inside out. First, a low-weight difference in some middle round of the characteristic is fixed, and then, by propagating the difference backwards and forwards, the input and the output differences of the characteristic are obtained. Therefore, the middle rounds of the characteristic have a high probability, while the rounds close to the input and to the output are of low probability. However, the low-probability rounds can be passed for free if we use a message modification or if we consider truncated characteristics, which is in fact the second approach.

The Internal Characteristic $\mathcal{I}_3$. Let us focus on the following 3-round internal differential characteristic $\mathcal{I}_3$, that starts at round 0, and that has been built with the first approach:

$$\begin{bmatrix} 429 \\ 800 \end{bmatrix} \xleftarrow{\lambda^{-1}} \begin{bmatrix} 1 \\ 800 \end{bmatrix} \xleftarrow{\chi^{-1}} \begin{bmatrix} 1 \\ 800 \end{bmatrix} \xleftarrow{\iota_0^{-1}} \begin{bmatrix} 0 \\ 800 \end{bmatrix} \xrightarrow{\lambda, \chi} \begin{bmatrix} 0 \\ 800 \end{bmatrix} \xrightarrow{\iota_1} \begin{bmatrix} 3 \\ 800 \end{bmatrix} \xrightarrow{\lambda} \begin{bmatrix} 33 \\ 800 \end{bmatrix} \xrightarrow{\chi, \iota_2} \begin{bmatrix} ? \\ 800 \end{bmatrix}.$$

$$\underbrace{\hspace{3.5cm}}_{\text{Round 0}} \quad \underbrace{\hspace{3.5cm}}_{\text{Round 1}} \quad \underbrace{\hspace{3.5cm}}_{\text{Round 2}}$$

The states are represented by the column vectors, where the upper number denotes the hamming weight of the internal difference, and the lower number gives the amount of bits in which the internal difference is fully determined. The numbers in **bold** around the χ step of round 1 represent active S-Boxes for that step, which is passed with a probability smaller than one. By ?, we represent an undetermined value.

The characteristic has been built by fixing a zero internal difference at the input of round 1. In the forward direction, there are no active S-Boxes in round 1, and the output difference is defined in all 800 bits after the linear step λ of round 2. The following steps χ and ι_2 produce some differences, but as we show later in Sect. 4.3, the value of this internal difference is irrelevant. In the backward direction, $RC[0]$ of ι_0 introduces only one bit difference, and thus the subsequent χ^{-1} has only one active S-Box. After the inversion of the linear layer, we can fully compute the internal difference at the input of the characteristic, so that each of the 800 bits are fully determined. Therefore, the whole 3-round internal characteristic has 34 active S-Boxes (probability 2^{-68}), and in the first two rounds has only a single active S-Box (probability 2^{-2}).

The Internal Differential $\mathcal{ID}_4$. We can construct a longer characteristic by going backwards one additional round. However, in this round the hamming weight of the internal difference at the input of χ^{-1} would be high (in the above $\mathcal{I}_3$, the weight is 429). To avoid significant reduction of probability, we switch to truncated internal differences. That is, instead of trying to define completely the output difference of this χ^{-1} (that would be obtained with an extremely low probability), we specify the difference only in n_I bits out of 800 bits. The internal difference in each of these n_I specific bits can be either 0 or 1, but the probability of this event must be one. As a result, the probability of the first round of the characteristic would be one.

Once the truncated difference is fixed in n_I bits at the output of χ^{-1}, the remaining three *linear* steps of the round will keep the truncated property: π^{-1} and ρ^{-1} will only permute and rotate the truncated difference and thus at the output of these two steps still it will be defined in n_I bits, while at the output of θ^{-1} the internal difference will belong to a subspace of dimension $800 - n_I$. We note that with a minor modification of Lemma 1, the obtained input internal difference can be used to compare the query complexity to the generic case[5] Therefore, to simplify the presentation of the input internal difference, in the further analysis, we omit the three linear steps of the first round.

The number of bits n_I in which the truncated difference at the output of χ^{-1} is defined with probability one depends on the round constants RC_i. For instance, if we start with round 0, then there is no bits in which the truncated difference is determined, i.e. $n_I = 0$. Only if we start with round 3, the number n_I will be sufficiently large to claim later (according to Lemma 1) that the complexity of producing boomerang pairs for Keccak-$p_{3,n}$ is lower than the generic complexity, with $n \in \{7, 8\}$.

The resulting 4-round internal differential characteristic $\mathcal{I}_4$, that starts at round 3, is defined as:

$$\begin{bmatrix} ? \\ 64 \end{bmatrix} \xleftarrow{\chi^{-1}} \begin{bmatrix} 398 \\ 800 \end{bmatrix} \xleftarrow{\iota_3^{-1}} \begin{bmatrix} 397 \\ 800 \end{bmatrix} \xleftarrow{\lambda^{-1}} \begin{bmatrix} 5 \\ 800 \end{bmatrix} \xleftarrow{\chi^{-1}} \begin{bmatrix} 5 \\ 800 \end{bmatrix} \xleftarrow{\iota_4^{-1}} \begin{bmatrix} 0 \\ 800 \end{bmatrix} \xrightarrow{\lambda,\chi} \begin{bmatrix} 0 \\ 800 \end{bmatrix} \xrightarrow{\iota_5} \begin{bmatrix} 2 \\ 800 \end{bmatrix} \xrightarrow{\lambda} \begin{bmatrix} 22 \\ 800 \end{bmatrix} \xrightarrow{\chi,\iota_2} \begin{bmatrix} ? \\ 800 \end{bmatrix}.$$

$$\underbrace{\hspace{3cm}}_{\text{Round 3}} \quad \underbrace{\hspace{3cm}}_{\text{Round 4}} \quad \underbrace{\hspace{3cm}}_{\text{Round 5}} \quad \underbrace{\hspace{3cm}}_{\text{Round 6}}$$

The characteristic has been built by fixing a zero internal difference at the input of round 5. The forward propagation is similar to $\mathcal{I}_3$. Backwards, after the addition of the constant $RC[4]$, the weight of the internal difference is five. Hence, χ of round 4 has at most five active S-Boxes, that can be passed probabilistically and would result in a state with internal difference of weight five. Then, the linear

---

[5] That is, we use the subspace to claim distinguisher for the permutation. This is in line with our initial intention to show that the round-reduced permutation exhibits non-random properties.

steps λ^{-1} in round 4 and the addition of $RC[3]$ in round 3 increase the weight of the internal difference to 398. *In the following χ^{-1}, we switch to truncated differences.* Although the input difference has a weight of 398 (possibly, all 320 S-Boxes are active), at the output of χ^{-1}, the internal difference is 0 in 55 specific bits, and 1 in 9 other bits. In other words, $n_I = 55 + 9 = 64$ bits of the internal difference are defined deterministically and thus, the probability to pass this χ^{-1} is one. Note, the truncated characteristic in the first round holds with probability one only when moving backwards through the round.

The probability of the truncated internal differential characteristic $\mathcal{I}_4$ can be evaluated as follows: in round 3 the probability is 1, in round 4 there are 5 active S-Boxes, thus the probability is 2^{-10}, in round 6 there are no active S-Boxes, while in round 7 there are 22 active S-Boxes (probability is 2^{-44}). Hence, when going backwards through the rounds, the probability of the whole 4-round characteristic is 2^{-54}. Furthermore, the probability of the first three rounds is 2^{-10}.

Recall that the boomerangs can use differentials instead of characteristics. As the probability of a differential may be higher than the probability of a single characteristic, the complexity of producing boomerang pairs may be reduced. Therefore, let us build a 4-round differential $\mathcal{ID}_4$ by using the same approach as for $\mathcal{I}_4$. That is, for all of the characteristics that belong to $\mathcal{ID}_4$, we start at round 5 with zero internal difference. In the forward direction, we move deterministically through round 5 and at the input of χ in round 6, we have 22 active S-Boxes (i.e. all the characteristics are equally defined in this part of the differential). In the backward direction, all the characteristics are the same up to the input of χ^{-1} of round 4, but the five active S-Boxes in each of the characteristics results in different outputs. Then, for each of the outputs, we move through λ^{-1} of round 4, ι_3, χ^{-1} of round 3, and at the output of χ^{-1}, we check if the truncated difference is defined in the same 64 bits as $\mathcal{I}_4$. Therefore, all the characteristics of the differential $\mathcal{ID}_4$ have the same input truncated difference, and the same difference at the input of χ in round 6 (the output of this χ is irrelevant as before). We found experimentally the probability of $\mathcal{ID}_4$ for the first three rounds to be $2^{-4.6}$. This has to be compared to 2^{-10}, which is the probability of the first three rounds of the characteristic $\mathcal{I}_4$.

4.2 Standard Differential Characteristics

Along with internal differential characteristics, the boomerang technique described in this paper uses standard differential characteristics. Recall that due to the special requirement of our boomerang, the standard characteristic cannot be of any form since it is connected to the two internal characteristics. This constraints the input difference ∇ of the standard characteristics to be symmetric, i.e. $\nabla = \nabla^H || \nabla^H$, or $\delta(\nabla) = \nabla^H \oplus \nabla^H = 0$, Note, the standard characteristic (unlike the internal characteristic) does not depend on the round number, hence further we omit ι_i from the description of the characteristic.

The standard characteristic that we use relies on the already-known concept of parity kernels, which allows to minimize the number of S-Boxes in two consecutive rounds of Keccak-f. This notion has been described in the submission document [3], and has been used in cryptanalytic results [12,22,31]. The behavior is possible due to two observations: first, a state-difference may be invariant of the θ step if there is an even number of active bits in each of the 320 column of the internal state; and second, an active S-Box in χ (or in χ^{-1}) leaves unchanged a 1-bit difference with probability 2^{-2}.

The 4-round standard differential characteristic C_4 that we use in the boomerangs is defined as:

$$\underbrace{\overset{\text{Kernel}}{\xleftarrow{\hspace{3cm}}}}$$

$$\begin{bmatrix} ? \\ 1600 \end{bmatrix} \xleftarrow{\chi^{-1}} \begin{bmatrix} ? \\ 1600 \end{bmatrix} \xleftarrow{\chi^{-1}} \begin{bmatrix} 2+2 \\ 1600 \end{bmatrix} \xrightarrow{\lambda} \begin{bmatrix} 2+2 \\ 1600 \end{bmatrix} \xrightarrow{\chi} \begin{bmatrix} 2+2 \\ 1600 \end{bmatrix} \xrightarrow{\lambda} \begin{bmatrix} 22+22 \\ 1600 \end{bmatrix} \xrightarrow{\chi} \begin{bmatrix} ? \\ 1278 \end{bmatrix} \xrightarrow{\lambda\chi} \begin{bmatrix} ? \\ 118 \end{bmatrix}.$$

$$\underbrace{\hspace{2cm}}_{\text{Round } i} \quad \underbrace{\hspace{2.5cm}}_{\text{Round } i+1} \quad \underbrace{\hspace{2.5cm}}_{\text{Round } i+2} \quad \underbrace{\hspace{2.5cm}}_{\text{Round } i+3}$$

The notations used in the characteristic are the same as before. With "$x+x$", we emphasize that the states are comprised of $2x$ active bits, but the actual difference is symmetric, which implies that there are x active bits in each half of the state, with equal differences.

This differential characteristic has been constructed by selecting a symmetric difference of hamming weight four at the input of round $i+1$ (note, this is the smallest possible weight of a symmetric parity kernel). In the backward direction, the step χ^{-1} has only 4 active S-Boxes, and results in a difference that is irrelevant as we further show in Sect. 4.3. In the forward direction, the selected 4-bit difference acts as a kernel and thus, after the λ step of round $i+1$, results in a 4-bit difference. The same behavior of the following χ step is expected with probability 2^{-8}, so the input difference to round $i+2$ still has a weight of four. The linear step in this round expands the difference to 44 active bits. Then, *we switch to truncated differences.* As a result, the difference in the following χ step is defined in 1278 bits, and after all the steps of round $i+3$, the difference is still deterministically defined in 118 bits (78 zeros and 30 ones).

The differential characteristic C_4 covers four full rounds of the permutation, and holds with probability 2^{-16} in the forward direction since there are a total of 8 active S-Boxes (four in each of the rounds i and $i+1$).

We can define a 3-round differential characteristic C_3, which is basically the same as the first three rounds of C_4, but we start truncating from χ at round $i+1$. That is, in C_3, we begin with 4-bit difference at round $i+1$ and the backward round i is the same as C_4. However, the 4-bit input difference at χ of round $i+1$ results in truncated output difference (with probability 1, instead of 2^{-8}), and after the steps λ and χ of round $i+2$, the truncated difference can still be determined in 1278 bits. Therefore, the probability of C_3 in the forward direction is only 2^{-8} as it has only four active S-Boxes in the first round.

4.3   Message Modification, Matching, and Neutral Bits

In our distinguishers, we start constructing the internal differential boomerang pairs from the middle by fixing some bits of the intermediate states, which allows

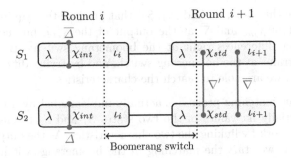

Fig. 2. The boomerang switch: middle of distinguishing structure where the differentials on the two halves of the primitive meet.

to pass low-probability events similarly to the rebound technique [25]. We define in particular the *boomerang switch* as the "middle" where we start constructing the state pairs to be the location where the two internal differential characteristics (or internal differentials) meet with the standard differential characteristic (see Fig. 2). Note that the two surrounding χ steps (denoted χ_{int} in the internal characteristic and χ_{std} in the standard characteristic on Fig. 2) usually have very low differential probabilities. However, since we start in the middle, we can fix partial state values such that these two steps are passed deterministically. Namely, this message modification technique allows to go through these two non-linear steps χ_{int} and χ_{std} without considering their probability.

Freedom Degrees. There are three conditions imposed on the state pair (S_1, S_2) at the boomerang switch: the first two come from the internal differential characteristics, i.e. $\delta(S_1) = \delta(S_2) = \overline{\Delta}$, while the third is from the standard characteristic, i.e. $S_1 \oplus S_2 = \overline{\nabla}$. Therefore, in total, we have 800 bits of freedom; that is, once we fix the first half of S_1, then the second half of S_1 is fully determined, as well as the whole S_2.

The limited degrees of freedom may lead to contradictions. For instance, if there is an active S-Box in the first halves of S_1 and S_2, then the symmetry imposes than such S-Box must also be active in the second halves. If, in addition, these two halves differ in the bits that belong to the S-Boxes (which can occur when there is a non-zero internal difference at these bits), then it may not be possible to fix simultaneously the inputs to the S-Boxes in both of the halves.

Matching. To avoid such contradictions, we first have to make sure that *the internal characteristics and the standard characteristic can be matched*, i.e. there exist two states S_1 and S_2 at the boomerang switch (Fig. 2), that can pass the χ_{int} and χ_{std} steps and that can produce differences as specified by the characteristic. Our extensive computer experiments have shown that if the differences at the boomerang switch are not sparse, then the chance of a match is extremely low[6].

---

[6] This only confirms the fact that for boomerangs (both classical and internal differential), finding the two characteristics for f and g does not guarantee that the boomerang will work – see [28] for more details.

To overcome this issue, we find (S_1, S_2) that produce the required differences $\overline{\Delta}$ at the input of χ_{int} and $\overline{\nabla}$ at the output of the χ_{std}, but not necessarily have the correct differences right at the boomerang switch[7]. By relaxing the difference constraint at the boomerang switch, and by trying different standard characteristics[8], we are able to match the characteristics.

Matching. This matching process is actually implemented by a message modification to partially fix values of the two states S_1 and S_2 to ensure that the boomerang can work by linking the two characteristics. As the output difference of χ_{int} is denser, we start the matching in the boomerang switch right at the output of χ_{int} (see Fig. 2). First, from the fixed output difference $\overline{\nabla}$ of χ_{std}, we produce all possible input differences ∇', which defines the standard difference at the boomerang switch. We propagate each such difference to the output of χ_{int}, and then try to fix the values of all active S-Boxes of χ_{int}. If all the S-Boxes can be fixed, then the matching for χ_{int} is complete. During the matching, the values of some bits of the states S_1 and S_2 are being fixed, but there are still free (non-fixed) bits. We use the freedom of these bits to check if the active S-Boxes of χ_{std} can be passed. If so, then the matching is complete.

Neutral Bits. The above process fixes some bits of S_1 and S_2 but there are more free bits and they can be used as neutral bits [6]. Namely, if S_1 and S_2 have fixed bits according to the matching, then for any value of the free remaining bits, the active S-Boxes of χ_{int} and χ_{std} still produce the required differences.

4.4 Internal Differential Boomerang Distinguishers for Keccak-$p_{i,n}$

We use the internal differential boomerang technique to distinguish the round-reduced Keccak-f permutation. The boomerangs are based on the internal differentials and characteristics from Sect. 4.1, and the standard differential characteristics from Sect. 4.2. To produce a boomerang pair, we start at the boomerang switch, and we first find the values of the fixed bits of S_1 and S_2 according to the message modification, which allows to pass the two rounds that surround the boomerang switch. Then, we randomize the remaining neutral bits of the states and finally, from the two middle states, we produce the corresponding inputs and outputs. If the internal differences of each of the two inputs and the difference of the two outputs are as expected by the boomerang, then we have found the pair. Otherwise, we randomize again the neutral bits and repeat the procedure. An example of the overall description of the 8-round case is given in Fig. 3.

---

[7] This is the reason why we have omitted specifying the differences at the output of the internal characteristics from Sect. 4.1, and at the input of the standard characteristics from Sect. 4.2.

[8] The internal characteristic cannot be changed as its difference propagation is completely defined by the round constants RC_i. On the other hand, there are many different standard characteristics (built upon parity kernels) that hold with the same probability.

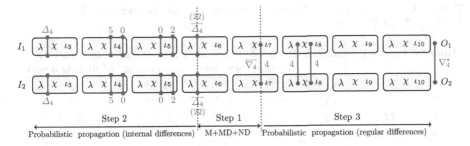

Fig. 3. Example of the internal boomerang distinguisher in the case of Keccak-$p_{3,8}$. In step 1, we first perform the matching (M), then the message modification (MD) and we use neutral bits (ND). We finish the construction of the pair of inputs (I_1, I_2) with the probabilistic propagations in Step 2 and 3.

The query complexity of producing a pair is determined by the differential probability of the characteristics in all the rounds but the middle two[9]. We claim distinguishers for Keccak-$p_{i,n}$ for some (i, n) because the complexity of finding a boomerang pair for Keccak-$p_{i,n}$ is significantly lower compared to the complexity of producing a boomerang pair (with the same conditions on the input and output differences) for a random permutation defined by Lemma 1. In the four boomerangs below, the input internal difference is determined either in 800 bits (when $\mathcal{I}_3$ is used) or in 64 bits (when $\mathcal{ID}_4$ is used), while the output difference is determined either in 1278 bits (when $\mathcal{C}_3$ is used) or in 118 bits (when $\mathcal{C}_4$ is used). Therefore, by Lemma 1, the query complexity of producing a boomerang pair in the case of a random permutation requires at least $2^{57.5}$ queries.

Depending on the starting round i of Keccak-$p_{i,n}$, the boomerang pairs are produced for two cases. First, when the permutation starts at round 0, for the boomerang we use the first internal differential characteristic I_3 given in Sect. 4.1 and the standard characteristics $\mathcal{C}_3$, $\mathcal{C}_4$ given in Sect. 4.2. We can produce the boomerang pair for Keccak-$p_{0,6}$ by using the internal characteristic I_3 and the standard characteristic $\mathcal{C}_3$. As the probability of I_3 without χ_{int} is 2^{-2} and the probability of $\mathcal{C}_3$ without χ_{std} is 1 (recall both of these two χ steps are passed with the message modification), we can produce the boomerang pair with $2 \cdot 2^2 \cdot 2^2 \cdot 1 = 2^5$ queries to the 6-round permutation. Similarly, we can produce boomerang pair for Keccak-$p_{0,7}$ (we combine I_3 with $\mathcal{C}_4$) in $2 \cdot 2^2 \cdot 2^2 \cdot 2^8$ (the additional factor 2^8 is required to pass the 4 active S-boxes in the second round of $\mathcal{C}_4$), or approximately 2^{13} queries to the 7-round permutation.

Then, when the permutation starts at round 3, the boomerang uses the internal differential $\mathcal{ID}_4$ given in Sect. 4.1, and the standard characteristics $\mathcal{C}_3$, $\mathcal{C}_4$ from Sect. 4.2. The boomerang on Keccak-$p_{3,7}$, based on $\mathcal{ID}_4$ and $\mathcal{C}_3$, produces a pair with $2 \cdot 2^{4.6} \cdot 2^{4.6} \cdot 1 = 2^{10.2}$ queries. For Keccak-$p_{3,8}$ (see Fig. 3), the

---

[9] The cost of the message modification can be ignored because it is executed once, but it can be used for producing many boomerang pairs, thus on average it is negligible. The actual cost is around 2^8.

Table 3. The internal differential boomerangs for Keccak-$p_{i,n}$ for $(i,n) \in \{(0,6),(0,7),(3,7),(3,8)\}$.

Rounds	Internal	Standard	Prob. of internal	Prob. of standard	Prob. of the boomerang	Complexity of finding a pair
6	$\mathcal{I}_3$	$\mathcal{C}_3$	2^{-68}	2^{-8}	2^{-140}	2^5
7	$\mathcal{I}_3$	$\mathcal{C}_4$	2^{-68}	2^{-16}	2^{-148}	2^{13}
7	$\mathcal{ID}_4$	$\mathcal{C}_3$	$2^{-48.6}$	2^{-8}	$2^{-105.2}$	$2^{10.2}$
8	$\mathcal{ID}_4$	$\mathcal{C}_4$	$2^{-48.6}$	2^{-16}	$2^{-113.2}$	$2^{18.2}$

boomerang is based on $\mathcal{ID}_4$ and $\mathcal{C}_4$, and for producing a boomerang pair, we need $2 \cdot 2^{4.6} \cdot 2^{4.6} \cdot 2^8 = 2^{18.2}$ queries.

We have checked and confirmed the complexities of the four boomerangs given above. A summary of the distinguishers is given in Table 3.

5   Conclusions

We have presented the internal differential boomerang distinguishers, which are a combination of internal differentials and the boomerang technique. The new boomerangs can be used for cryptanalysis of functions and ciphers that have high-probability internal differentials. We have used the boomerangs to show non-randomness of reduced variants of the permutation Keccak-f. Based on truncated characteristics that hold with exceptionally high probability, and combined with a strong message modification, we have shown how to produce internal differential boomerang pairs for Keccak-f reduced to 6 rounds with only 2^5 queries to the permutation, 7 rounds with 2^{13} queries, and up to 8 rounds with 2^{18} queries.

Our results significantly outperform in terms of practical complexity all the previous cryptanalysis of Keccak-f. We emphasize that the results do not pose threat to the security of the future SHA-3 standard as there is no known way to date to extend the proposed reduced-round permutation distinguishers to the full sponge construction based on the full 24-round Keccak-f permutation. We were unable to extend our distinguishers to larger number of rounds while maintaining practical complexity. On the other hand, we leave as an open problem finding internal differential boomerang distinguishers that cover more rounds and that require theoretical complexity.

References

1. Aumasson, J.P., Meier, W.: Zero-sum distinguishers for reduced Keccak-f and for the core functions of Luffa and Hamsi. rump session of Cryptographic Hardware and Embedded Systems-CHES 2009, 67 (2009)
2. Bertoni, G., Daemen, J., Peeters, M., Assche, G.V.: Cryptographic sponge functions (online)

3. Bertoni, G., Daemen, J., Peeters, M., Assche, G.V.: The Keccak reference (Version 3)
4. Bertoni, G., Daemen, J., Peeters, M., Assche, G.V., Keer, R.V.: Ketje v1. Submitted to the CAESAR competition, March 2014
5. Bertoni, G., Daemen, J., Peeters, M., Assche, G.V., Keer, R.V.: Keyak v1. Submitted to the CAESAR competition, March 2014
6. Biham, E., Chen, R.: Near-collisions of SHA-0. In: Franklin, M. (ed.) CRYPTO 2004. LNCS, vol. 3152, pp. 290–305. Springer, Heidelberg (2004)
7. Biryukov, A., Lamberger, M., Mendel, F., Nikolić, I.: Second-order differential collisions for reduced SHA-256. In: Lee, D.H., Wang, X. (eds.) ASIACRYPT 2011. LNCS, vol. 7073, pp. 270–287. Springer, Heidelberg (2011)
8. Biryukov, A., Nikolić, I., Roy, A.: Boomerang attacks on BLAKE-32. In: Joux, A. (ed.) FSE 2011. LNCS, vol. 6733, pp. 218–237. Springer, Heidelberg (2011)
9. Boura, C., Canteaut, A.: Zero-sum distinguishers for iterated permutations and application to KECCAK-f and Hamsi-256. In: Biryukov, A., Gong, G., Stinson, D.R. (eds.) SAC 2010. LNCS, vol. 6544, pp. 1–17. Springer, Heidelberg (2011)
10. Boura, C., Canteaut, A., De Cannière, C.: Higher-order differential properties of KECCAK and Luffa. In: Joux, A. (ed.) FSE 2011. LNCS, vol. 6733, pp. 252–269. Springer, Heidelberg (2011)
11. Canteaut, A. (ed.): FSE 2012. LNCS, vol. 7549. Springer, Heidelberg (2012)
12. Das, S., Meier, W.: Differential biases in reduced-round Keccak. In: [33], pp. 69–87
13. Dinur, I., Dunkelman, O., Shamir, A.: New attacks on Keccak-224 and Keccak-256. In: [11], pp. 442–461
14. Dinur, I., Dunkelman, O., Shamir, A.: Collision attacks on Up to 5 rounds of SHA-3 using generalized internal differentials. In: [27], pp. 219–240
15. Dinur, I., Dunkelman, O., Shamir, A.: Improved practical attacks on round-reduced Keccak. J. Cryptology 27(2), 183–209 (2014)
16. Dinur, I., Morawiecki, P., Pieprzyk, J., Srebrny, M., Straus, M.: Practical complexity cube attacks on round-reduced Keccak sponge function. IACR Cryptology ePrint Archive 2014, 259 (2014)
17. Duc, A., Guo, J., Peyrin, T., Wei, L.: Unaligned rebound attack: application to Keccak. In: [11], pp. 402–421
18. Jean, J., Nikolic, I.: Internal differential boomerangs: practical analysis of the round-reduced Keccak-f permutation. Cryptology ePrint Archive, Report 2015/244 (2015)
19. Kelsey, J., Kohno, T., Schneier, B.: Amplified boomerang attacks against reduced-round MARS and serpent. In: Schneier, B. (ed.) FSE 2000. LNCS, vol. 1978, pp. 75–93. Springer, Heidelberg (2001)
20. Knudsen, L.R.: Truncated and higher order differentials. In: Preneel, B. (ed.) FSE 1994. LNCS, vol. 1008, pp. 196–211. Springer, Heidelberg (1995)
21. Kölbl, S., Mendel, F., Nad, T., Schläffer, M.: Differential cryptanalysis of Keccak variants. In: Stam, M. (ed.) IMACC 2013. LNCS, vol. 8308, pp. 141–157. Springer, Heidelberg (2013)
22. Kuila, S., Saha, D., Pal, M., Chowdhury, D.R.: Practical aistinguishers against 6-round Keccak-f exploiting self-symmetry. In: [33], pp. 88–108
23. Lai, X.: Higher order derivatives and differential cryptanalysis. In: Blahut, R.E., Costello Jr., D.J., Maurer, U., Mittelholzer, T. (eds.) Communications and Cryptography, pp. 227–233. Springer, New York (1994)
24. Lamberger, M., Mendel, F., Schläffer, M., Rechberger, C., Rijmen, V.: The rebound attack and subspace distinguishers: application to Whirlpool. J. Cryptology 28, 1–40 (2013)

25. Mendel, F., Rechberger, C., Schläffer, M., Thomsen, S.S.: The rebound attack: cryptanalysis of reduced Whirlpool and Grøstl. In: Dunkelman, O. (ed.) FSE 2009. LNCS, vol. 5665, pp. 260–276. Springer, Heidelberg (2009)

26. Morawiecki, P., Pieprzyk, J., Srebrny, M.: Rotational cryptanalysis of round-reduced Keccak. In: [27], pp. 241–262

27. Moriai, S. (ed.): FSE 2013. LNCS, vol. 8424. Springer, Heidelberg (2014)

28. Murphy, S.: The return of the cryptographic boomerang. IEEE Trans. Inf. Theory **57**(4), 2517–2521 (2011)

29. National Institute of Standards and Technology: Cryptographic Hash Algorithm Competition. http://csrc.nist.gov/groups/ST/hash/sha-3/index.html

30. National Institute of Standards and Technology: Draft FIPS 202: SHA-3 Standard: Permutation-Based Hash and Extendable-Output Functions

31. Naya-Plasencia, M., Röck, A., Meier, W.: Practical analysis of reduced-round Keccak. In: Bernstein, D.J., Chatterjee, S. (eds.) INDOCRYPT 2011. LNCS, vol. 7107, pp. 236–254. Springer, Heidelberg (2011)

32. Peyrin, T.: Improved differential attacks for ECHO and Grøstl. In: Rabin, T. (ed.) CRYPTO 2010. LNCS, vol. 6223, pp. 370–392. Springer, Heidelberg (2010)

33. Pointcheval, D., Vergnaud, D. (eds.): AFRICACRYPT. LNCS, vol. 8469. Springer, Heidelberg (2014)

34. Wagner, D.: The boomerang attack. In: Knudsen, L.R. (ed.) FSE 1999. LNCS, vol. 1636, pp. 156–170. Springer, Heidelberg (1999)

New Linear Correlations Related to State Information of RC4 PRGA Using IV in WPA

Ryoma Ito[✉] and Atsuko Miyaji

Japan Advanced Institute of Science and Technology,
1-1 Asahidai, Nomi-shi, Ishikawa 923-1292, Japan
{s1310005,miyaji}@jaist.ac.jp

Abstract. RC4 is a stream cipher designed by Ron Rivest in 1987, and is widely used in various applications. WPA is one of these applications, where TKIP is used for a key generation procedure to avoid weak IV generated by WEP. In FSE 2014, two different attacks against WPA were proposed by Sen Gupta et al. and Paterson et al. Both focused correlations between the keystream bytes and the first 3 bytes of the RC4 key in WPA. In this paper, we focus on linear correlations between *unknown* internal state and the first 3 bytes of the RC4 key in both generic RC4 and WPA, where the first 3 bytes of the RC4 key is *known* in WPA. As a result, we could discover various new linear correlations, and prove these correlations theoretically.

Keywords: RC4 · WPA · Linear correlations

1 Introduction

RC4 is a stream cipher designed by Ron Rivest in 1987, and is widely used in various applications such as Secure Socket Layer/Transport Layer Security (SSL/TLS), Wired Equivalent Privacy (WEP) and Wi-fi Protected Access (WPA), etc. Due to its popularity and simplicity, RC4 has become a hot cryptanalysis target since its specification was made public on the internet in 1994.

WEP is a security protocol for IEEE 802.11 wireless networks, standardized in 1999. Various attacks against WEP, however, have been proposed in [7,16,17] after Fluhrer et al. showed a class of weak IV in 2001 [3], and WEP is considered to be broken completely today. In order to avoid the attack by Fluhrer et al. [3], WEP had been superseded by WPA in 2003. WPA improves a key scheduling procedure known as Temporary Key Integrity Protocol (TKIP) to avoid a class of weak IV generated in WEP. One of characteristic features in TKIP is that the first 3 bytes of the RC4 key $K[0]$, $K[1]$, and $K[2]$ are derived from IV, and then, they are public. The range of $K[1]$ is limited to either $[32, 63]$ or $[96, 127]$ in order to avoid the known WEP attacks by Fluhrer et al. [3].

A. Miyaji—Supported by the project "The Security infrastructure Technology for Integrated Utilization of Big Data" of Japan Science and Technology Agency CREST.

© International Association for Cryptologic Research 2015
G. Leander (Ed.): FSE 2015, LNCS 9054, pp. 557–576, 2015.
DOI: 10.1007/978-3-662-48116-5_27

In FSE 2014, Sen Gupta et al. showed a probability distribution of an addition of the first two bytes of the RC4 key, $K[0] + K[1]$, in detailed, and found that some characteristic features including $K[0] + K[1]$ must be always even [4]. They also showed some linear correlations between the keystream bytes and the first *known* 3 bytes of the RC4 key in WPA. They applied these linear correlations to the existing plaintext recovery attack against SSL/TLS [6] with WPA, and improve its computational complexity required for the attack. In [13], Paterson et al. showed the specific correlations in WPA between the keystream bytes and a combination of IV by a different idea from [4]. They also improved the computational complexity required for the attack against WPA in comparison with the existing attack against SSL/TLS [1].

In this paper, we investigated new linear correlations among four *unknown* values $S_r[i_{r+1}]$, $S_r[j_{r+1}]$, j_{r+1} and t_{r+1} and the first *known* 3 bytes of the RC4 key $K[0]$, $K[1]$, and $K[2]$ in both generic RC4 and WPA. An important differences between ours and previous works [4,13] is to whether analysis target is the internal states or the keystream bytes. The previous works are effective for the plaintext recovery attacks [1,6]. On the other hand, our investigation is effective for the state recovery attacks [2,8,12]. In addition, we also focus on the difference between generic RC4 and WPA, and then, discover that there exist some different correlations between generic RC4 and WPA, which exactly reflect difference of distributions of the first 3 bytes of the RC4 key. Our motivation is to prove these linear correlations theoretically. Some of our proved significant biases are given as follows:

Theorem 1: $\Pr(S_0[i_1] = K[0])_{\text{RC4}} \approx \frac{1}{N}\left(1 - \frac{1}{N}\right)^{N-2}$;

Theorem 2: $\Pr(S_0[i_1] = K[0])_{\text{WPA}} = 0$;

Theorem 3: $\Pr(S_0[i_1] = K[0] - K[1] - 3)$

$$\approx \begin{cases} \frac{2}{N}\alpha_1 + \frac{1}{N}\left(1 - \frac{2}{N}\right)(1 - \alpha_1) & \text{for RC4,} \\ \frac{4}{N}\alpha_1 + \frac{1}{N}\left(1 - \frac{4}{N}\right)(1 - \alpha_1) & \text{for WPA;} \end{cases}$$

Theorem 4: $\Pr(S_0[i_1] = K[0] - K[1] - 1)$

$$\approx \begin{cases} \frac{1}{N}\left(1 + \frac{2}{N}\right)\alpha_1 + \frac{1}{N}\left(1 - \frac{2}{N}\right)(1 - \alpha_1) & \text{for RC4,} \\ \frac{4}{N}\alpha_1 + \frac{1}{N}\left(1 - \frac{4}{N}\right)(1 - \alpha_1) & \text{for WPA;} \end{cases}$$

Theorem 5: $\Pr(S_{255}[i_{256}] = K[0])$

$$\approx \alpha_0\left(1 - \frac{1}{N}\right)^{255} + \frac{1}{N}(1 - \alpha_0)\left(1 - \left(1 - \frac{1}{N}\right)^{255}\right);$$

Theorem 6: $\Pr(S_{255}[i_{256}] = K[1])$

$$\approx \delta\left(1 - \frac{1}{N}\right)^{255} + \frac{1}{N}(1 - \delta)\left(1 - \left(1 - \frac{1}{N}\right)^{255}\right);$$

Theorem 7: $\Pr(S_r[i_{r+1}] = K[0] + K[1] + 1)\,(0 \leq r \leq N)$

$$\approx \begin{cases} \alpha_1 & \text{if } r = 0, \\ \alpha_1\gamma_1 + (1 - \beta_1)\epsilon_2 & \text{if } r = 1, \\ \epsilon_0\left(1 - \frac{1}{N}\right)^{N-1} + \frac{1}{N}(1 - \epsilon_0)\left(1 - \left(1 - \frac{1}{N}\right)^{N-1}\right) & \text{if } r = N - 1, \\ \zeta_1\left(1 - \frac{1}{N}\right)^{N-1} + \frac{1}{N}(1 - \zeta_1)\left(1 - \left(1 - \frac{1}{N}\right)^{N-1}\right) & \text{if } r = N, \\ \zeta_{r+1}\left(1 - \frac{1}{N}\right)^{r-1} + \frac{1}{N}\sum_{x=1}^{r-1}\eta_x\left(1 - \frac{1}{N}\right)^{r-x-1} & \text{otherwise,} \end{cases}$$

where $\alpha_0 = \Pr(S_0[0] = K[0])$, $\alpha_1 = \Pr(S_0[1] = K[0] + K[1] + 1)$, $\beta_1 = \Pr(S_0[S_0[1]] = K[0] + K[1] + 1)$, $\gamma_1 = \Pr(K[0] + K[1] = 1)$, $\delta = \Pr(S_0[0] = K[1])$, $\epsilon_0 = \Pr(S_0[0] = K[0] + K[1] + 1)$, $\zeta_r = \Pr(S_1[r] = K[0] + K[1] + 1)$ and $\eta_r = \Pr(S_r[i_{r+1}] = K[0] + K[1] + 1)$. Both α_0 and α_1 are Roos' biases [15], and β_1 is one of Nested Roos' biases [9].

These newly demonstrated correlations could be added to the known set of biases for $S_r[i_{r+1}]$, $S_r[j_{r+1}]$, j_{r+1} and t_{r+1} for $r \geq 0$ on known key bytes in WPA, and could improve some state recovery attacks against RC4.

This paper is organized as follows: Sect. 2 briefly summarizes notation, RC4 algorithms and key scheduling procedure in WPA. Section 3 presents the previous works on Roos' biases [14,15], Nested Roos' biases [9] and the distribution of $K[0] + K[1]$ in WPA [4]. Section 4 first discusses some linear correlations observed by our experiments, and shows theoretical proofs. Section 5 demonstrates experimental simulations. Section 6 concludes this paper.

2   Preliminary

2.1   Description of RC4

The following notation is used in this paper.

K, l : secret key, the length of secret key (bytes)

r : number of rounds

N : number of arrays in state (typically $N = 256$)

S_r^K : state of KSA after the swap in the r-th round

S_r : state of PRGA after the swap in the r-th round

i, j_r^K : indices of S_r^K for the r-th round

i_r, j_r : indices of S_r for the r-th round

Z_r : one output keystream for the r-th round

t_r : index of Z_r

RC4 consists of two algorithms: Key Scheduling Algorithm (KSA) and Pseudo Random Generation Algorithm (PRGA). KSA generates the state S_N^K from a secret key K of l bytes as described in Algorithm 1. Then, the final state S_N^K in KSA becomes the input of PRGA as S_0. Once the state S_0 is computed, PRGA generates a keystream byte Z_r in each round as described in Algorithm 2. The keystream byte Z_r will be XORed with a plaintext to generate a ciphertext.

2.2   Description of WPA

In order to generate a 16-byte RC4 secret key, WPA uses two key scheduling procedures: a key management scheme and the TKIP, which includes a temporal key hash function [5] to generate RC4 secret key and a message integrity code function to ensure integrity of the message. The key management scheme after the authentication based on IEEE 802.1X generates a 16-byte Temporal Key (TK). Then, the TK, a 6-byte Transmitter Address and a 48-bit IV, which is a sequence counter, are given as the inputs to the temporal key hash function. The temporal key hash function generates the last 13 bytes of the RC4 key. The remaining RC4 key, the first 3 bytes, is computed by the last 16 bits of IV (IV16) as follows:

$$K[0] = (\text{IV16} >> 8) \text{ \& 0xFF},$$
$$K[1] = ((\text{IV16} >> 8) \mid \text{0x20}) \text{ \& 0x7F},$$
$$K[2] = \text{IV16 \& 0xFF}.$$

Note that the range of $K[1]$ is limited to either $[32, 63]$ or $[96, 127]$ in order to avoid the known WEP attack by Fluhrer et al. [3].

Algorithm 1. KSA	Algorithm 2. PRGA
1: **for** $i = 0$ to $N - 1$ **do**	1: $r \leftarrow 0,\ i_0 \leftarrow 0,\ j_0 \leftarrow 0$
2: $S_0^K[i] \leftarrow i$	2: **loop**
3: **end for**	3: $r \leftarrow r + 1,\ i_r \leftarrow i_{r-1} + 1$
4: $j_0^K \leftarrow 0$	4: $j_r \leftarrow j_{r-1} + S_{r-1}[i_r]$
5: **for** $i = 0$ to $N - 1$ **do**	5: Swap($S_{r-1}[i_r], S_{r-1}[j_r]$)
6: $j_{i+1}^K \leftarrow j_i^K + S_i^K[i] + K[i \bmod l]$	6: $t_r \leftarrow S_r[i_r] + S_r[j_r]$
7: Swap($S_i^K[i], S_i^K[j_{i+1}^K]$)	7: **Output:** $Z_r \leftarrow S_r[t_r]$
8: **end for**	8: **end loop**

3   Previous Works

In 1995, Roos' biases [15], correlations between RC4 key bytes and the initial state S_0 of PRGA, are proved in [14] and given as follows:

Proposition 1. [14, Corollary 2]. *In the initial state of PRGA for $0 \le y \le N - 1$, we have*

$$\Pr(S_0[y] = \frac{y(y+1)}{2} + \sum_{x=0}^{y} K[x]) \approx \left(1 - \frac{y}{N}\right) \cdot \left(1 - \frac{1}{N}\right)^{\left[\frac{y(y+1)}{2} + N\right]} + \frac{1}{N}.$$

In FSE 2008, Maitra and Paul showed correlations similar to Roos' biases [9], so called Nested Roos' biases in [10]. Nested Roos' biases are given as follows:

Proposition 2. [9, Theorem 2]. *In the initial state of PRGA for $0 \le y \le 31$, $\Pr(S_0[S_0[y]] = f_y)$ is approximately*

$$\left(\frac{y}{N} + \frac{1}{N}\left(1 - \frac{1}{N}\right)^{2-y} + \left(1 - \frac{y}{N}\right)^2 \left(1 - \frac{1}{N}\right)\right)\left(1 - \frac{1}{N}\right)^{\frac{y(y+1)}{2} + 2N - 4},$$

where $f_y = \frac{y(y+1)}{2} + \sum_{x=0}^{y} K[x]$.

In FSE 2014, Sen Gupta et al. showed that the distribution of $K[0] + K[1]$ has biases from a relation between $K[0]$ and $K[1]$ generated by the temporal key hash function in WPA [4]. This distribution is given as follows:

Proposition 3. [4, Theorem 1] . *For $0 \leq v \leq N - 1$, the distribution of the sum v of $K[0]$ and $K[1]$ generated by the temporal key hash function in WPA is given as follows:*

$$\Pr(K[0] + K[1] = v) = 0 \quad \text{if } v \text{ is odd},$$
$$\Pr(K[0] + K[1] = v) = 0 \quad \text{if } v \text{ is even and } v \in [0, 31] \cup [128, 159],$$
$$\Pr(K[0] + K[1] = v) = 2/256 \text{ if } v \text{ is even and}$$
$$v \in [32, 63] \cup [96, 127] \cup [160, 191] \cup [224, 255],$$
$$\Pr(K[0] + K[1] = v) = 4/256 \text{ if } v \text{ is even and } v \in [64, 95] \cup [192, 223].$$

They also showed that Proposition 3 combining Roos' biases shown in Proposition 1 induced a characteristic bias on the distribution of the initial state $S_0[1]$ of PRGA, which deeply influences on the biases of the first keystream byte Z_1, etc.

4   New Linear Correlations

4.1   Experimental Observation

Let us investigate new correlations of four unknown values $S_r[i_{r+1}]$, $S_r[j_{r+1}]$, j_{r+1} and t_{r+1} for $r \geq 0$. Other linear correlations of the keystream bytes Z_r are investigated in [4]. Let $X_r \in \{S_r[i_{r+1}], S_r[j_{r+1}], j_{r+1}, t_{r+1}\}$, $a, b, c, d \in \{0, \pm1\}$ and $e \in \{0, \pm1, \pm2, \pm3\}$,

$$X_r = a \cdot Z_{r+1} + b \cdot K[0] + c \cdot K[1] + d \cdot K[2] + e. \tag{1}$$

These biases by Eq. (1) can be added to the known set of biases for $S_r[i_{r+1}]$, $S_r[j_{r+1}]$, j_{r+1} and t_{r+1} for $r \geq 0$ on known keys in WPA such as $K[0]$, $K[1]$ and $K[2]$, and may reduce the computational complexity of the existing state recovery attacks against RC4 [2,8,12] especially in WPA.

We have examined all $4 \cdot 3^4 \cdot 7$ equations defined by Eq. (1) in each round with 2^{32} randomly generated 16-byte keys in both generic RC4 and WPA. Some notable experimental results are presented in Tables 1 and 3. Due to lack of space, only the results of correlations with more than 0.0048 or less than 0.0020 in either generic RC4 or WPA are listed. We stress that the case of $S_0[i_1] = K[0]$ in WPA becomes an impossible condition (probability 0), and thus, $S_0[i_1]$ is varied from $[0, N-1] \setminus \{K[0]\}$. Our motivation is to prove these linear correlations theoretically shown in Table 1.

In order to prove the following theorems, we often use Roos' biases (Proposition 1), Nested Roos' biases (Proposition 2) and the probability of $K[0] + K[1] = v$ (Proposition 3), which are denoted by $\alpha_y = \Pr(S_0[y] = \frac{y(y+1)}{2} + \sum_{x=0}^{y} K[x])$, $\beta_y = \Pr(S_0[S_0[y]]) = \frac{y(y+1)}{2} + \sum_{x=0}^{y} K[x])$ and $\gamma_v = \Pr(K[0] + K[1] = v)$, respectively. From uniform randomness of RC4 stream cipher, we assume that the

Table 1. Notable linear correlations in Eq. (1) for both generic RC4 and WPA

X_r	Linear correlations	RC4	WPA	Remarks
	$K[0]$	0.001450	0	Theorems 1 and 2
$S_0[i_1]$	$K[0] - K[1] - 3$	0.005337	0.007848	Theorem 3
	$K[0] - K[1] - 1$	0.003922	0.007877	Theorem 4
$S_{255}[i_{256}]$	$K[0]$	0.137294	0.138047	Theorem 5
	$K[1]$	0.003911	0.037189	Theorem 6
$S_r[i_{r+1}]$	$K[0] + K[1] + 1$	Fig. 1		Theorem 7

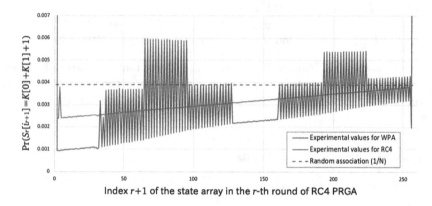

Fig. 1. Observation result of event $(S_r[i_{r+1}] = K[0] + K[1] + 1)$

probability of certain events (e.g. the state information) that we have confirmed experimentally that there are no significant biases is $\frac{1}{N}$ due to random association for the proofs. Furthermore, we assume that the RC4 key is generated uniformly at random in generic RC4.

4.2 Bias in $S_0[i_1]$ for both Generic RC4 and WPA

In this section, we prove Theorems 1–4. Theorems 1 and 2 shows that $S_0[i_1] = K[0]$ holds with low probability and 0 in generic RC4 and WPA, respectively. Theorems 3 and 4 show that both $S_0[i_1] = K[0] - K[1] - 3$ and $K[0] - K[1] - 1$ in WPA hold twice as frequently as probability $\frac{1}{N}$ due to random association. Theorem 3 also shows that event $(S_0[i_1] = K[0] - K[1] - 3)$ provides a case with positive bias in generic RC4.

Theorem 1. *In the initial state of PRGA, we have*

$$\Pr(S_0[i_1] = K[0])_{RC4} \approx \frac{1}{N}\left(1 - \frac{1}{N}\right)^{N-2}.$$

Proof. Figure 2 shows a state transition diagram in the first 2 rounds of KSA. From step 6 in Algorithm 1, both $j_1^K = j_0^K + S_0^K[0] + K[0] = 0 + 0 + K[0] = K[0]$

and $j_2^K = j_1^K + S_1^K[1] + K[1] = K[0] + K[1] + S_1^K[1]$ hold. The probability of event $(S_0[i_1] = K[0])$ can be decomposed in three paths: $K[0] + K[1] = 0$ (Path 1), $K[0] + K[1] = 255$ (Path 2) and $K[0] + K[1] \neq 0, 255$ (Path 3). Both Paths 1 and 2 are further divided into two subpaths: $K[0] = 1$ (Paths 1-1 and 2-1) and $K[0] \neq 1$ (Paths 1-2 and 2-2), respectively. In the following proof, we use $S_0[1]$ instead of $S_0[i_1]$ ($i_1 = 1$) and $S_N^K[1]$ for simplicity.

Path 1-1. Figure 3 shows a state transition diagram in Path 1-1. After the second round of KSA, $S_2^K[1] = K[0]$ always holds since $j_1^K = K[0] = 1$ and $j_2^K = K[0] + K[1] + S_1^K[1] = 0 + 0 = 0$. Furthermore, $S_r^K[1] = S_2^K[1]$ for $3 \leq r \leq N$ if $j_r^K \neq 1$ during the subsequent $N - 2$ rounds, whose probability is $\left(1 - \frac{1}{N}\right)^{N-2}$ approximately. Thus, the probability in Path 1-1 is given as follows:

$$\Pr(S_0[1] = K[0] \mid \text{Path 1-1}) \approx \left(1 - \frac{1}{N}\right)^{N-2}.$$

Path 1-2. Figure 4 shows a state transition diagram in Path 1-2. $S_2^K[0] = K[0]$ always holds since $j_1^K = K[0] \neq 1$ and $j_2^K = (K[0] + K[1]) + S_1^K[1] = 0 + 1 = 1$. Then, event $(S_0[1] = K[0])$ never occurs because $S_r^K[1] \neq K[0]$ always holds for $r \geq 2$. Thus, the probability in Path 1-2 is 0.

Path 2-1. Figure 5 shows a state transition diagram in Path 2-1. $S_2^K[0] = K[0]$ always holds in the same way as Path 1-2. Then, event $(S_0[1] = K[0])$ never occurs. Thus, the probability in Path 2-1 is 0.

Path 2-2. Figure 6 shows a state transition diagram in Path 2-2. $S_2^K[1] = K[0]$ always holds in the same way as Path 1-1. Then, event $(S_0[1] = K[0])$ occurs if $S_r[1] = S_2^K[1]$ for $3 \leq r \leq N$. Thus, the probability in Path 2-2 is given as follows:

$$\Pr(S_0[1] = K[0] \mid \text{Path 2-2}) \approx \left(1 - \frac{1}{N}\right)^{N-2}.$$

Path 3. Figure 2 shows a state transition diagram in Path 3. $S_2^K[0] = K[0]$ always holds in the same way as Paths 1-2 and 2-1. Then, event $(S_0[1] = K[0])$ never occurs. Thus, the probability in Path 3 is 0.

In summary, event $(S_0[i_1] = K[0])$ occurs only in either Paths 1-1 or 2-2. Therefore, we get

$$\Pr(S_0[i_1] = K[0]) = \Pr(S_0[i_1] = K[0] \mid \text{Path 1-1}) \cdot \Pr(\text{Path 1-1})$$
$$+ \Pr(S_0[i_1] = K[0] \mid \text{Path 2-2}) \cdot \Pr(\text{Path 2-2})$$
$$\approx \left(1 - \frac{1}{N}\right)^{N-2} \cdot \frac{1}{N^2} + \left(1 - \frac{1}{N}\right)^{N-2} \cdot \frac{1}{N}\left(1 - \frac{1}{N}\right) = \frac{1}{N}\left(1 - \frac{1}{N}\right)^{N-2}.$$

$\square$

Theorem 2. *In the initial state of PRGA in WPA, we have*

$$\Pr(S_0[i_1] = K[0])_{\text{WPA}} = 0.$$

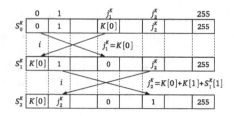

Fig. 2. A state transition diagram in the first 2 rounds of KSA

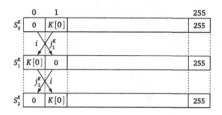

Fig. 3. Path 1-1 in Theorem 1

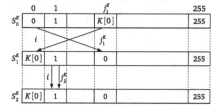

Fig. 4. Path 1-2 in Theorem 1

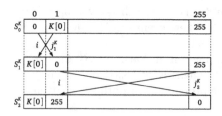

Fig. 5. Path 2-1 in Theorem 1

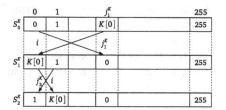

Fig. 6. Path 2-2 in Theorem 1

Proof. Note that event $(S_0[1] = K[0])$ occurs if and only if either $K[0]+K[1] = 0$ or 255, and that Proposition 3 shows that neither $K[0] + K[1] = 0$ nor 255 holds in WPA. Thus, the probability of event $(S_0[1] = K[0])$ in WPA is 0.   □

Theorem 3. *In the initial state of PRGA, we have*

$$\Pr(S_0[i_1] = K[0] - K[1] - 3) \approx \begin{cases} \dfrac{2}{N}\alpha_1 + \dfrac{1}{N}\left(1 - \dfrac{2}{N}\right)(1 - \alpha_1) & \text{for RC4,} \\ \dfrac{4}{N}\alpha_1 + \dfrac{1}{N}\left(1 - \dfrac{4}{N}\right)(1 - \alpha_1) & \text{for WPA.} \end{cases}$$

Proof. The probability of event $(S_0[i_1] = K[0] - K[1] - 3)$ can be decomposed in two paths: $K[1] = 126, 254$ (Path 1) and $K[1] \neq 126, 254$ (Path 2). In the following proof, we use $S_0[1]$ instead of $S_0[i_1]$ $(i_1 = 1)$ for simplicity.

Path 1. In $K[1] = 126, 254$, event $(S_0[1] = K[0] - K[1] - 3)$ occurs if and only if $S_0[1] = K[0] + K[1] + 1$. Thus, the probability in Path 1 is given as follows:

$$\Pr(S_0[1] = K[0] - K[1] - 3 \mid \text{Path 1}) = \alpha_1.$$

Path 2. In $K[1] \neq 126, 254$, event $(S_0[1] = K[0] - K[1] - 3)$ never occurs if $S_0[1] = K[0] + K[1] + 1$. If $S_0[1] \neq K[0] + K[1] + 1$ holds, then we assume that event $(S_0[1] = K[0] - K[1] - 3)$ occurs with probability $\frac{1}{N}$ due to random association. Thus, the probability in Path 2 is given as follows:

$$\Pr(S_0[1] = K[0] - K[1] - 3 \mid \text{Path 2}) \approx \frac{1}{N} \cdot (1 - \alpha_1).$$

In summary, we get

$$
\begin{aligned}
&\Pr(S_0[i_1] = K[0] - K[1] - 3) \\
&= \Pr(S_0[1] = K[0] - K[1] - 3 \mid \text{Path 1}) \cdot \Pr(\text{Path 1}) \\
&\quad + \Pr(S_0[1] = K[0] - K[1] - 3 \mid \text{Path 2}) \cdot \Pr(\text{Path 2}) \\
&\approx \begin{cases} \dfrac{2}{N}\alpha_1 + \dfrac{1}{N}\left(1 - \dfrac{2}{N}\right)(1 - \alpha_1) & \text{for RC4,} \\[3mm] \dfrac{4}{N}\alpha_1 + \dfrac{1}{N}\left(1 - \dfrac{4}{N}\right)(1 - \alpha_1) & \text{for WPA,} \end{cases}
\end{aligned}
$$

where $\alpha_1 = \Pr(S_0[1] = K[0] + K[1] + 1) \approx \left(\frac{N-1}{N}\right)^{N+2} + \frac{1}{N}$. $\qquad \Box$

The probability of $K[1] = 126$ or 254 in generic RC4 is $\frac{1}{N}$ in order to be generated uniformly at random. On the other hand, that of $K[1] = 126$ or 254 in WPA is $\frac{4}{N}$ or 0, respectively. Thus, Theorem 3 reflects the difference of $\Pr(K[1] = 126, 254)$ in both generic RC4 and WPA.

Theorem 4. *In the initial state of PRGA, we have*

$$
\begin{aligned}
&\Pr(S_0[i_1] = K[0] - K[1] - 1) \\
&\approx \begin{cases} \dfrac{1}{N}\left(1 + \dfrac{2}{N}\right)\alpha_1 + \dfrac{1}{N}\left(1 - \dfrac{2}{N}\right)(1 - \alpha_1) & \text{for RC4,} \\[3mm] \dfrac{4}{N}\alpha_1 + \dfrac{1}{N}\left(1 - \dfrac{4}{N}\right)(1 - \alpha_1) & \text{for WPA.} \end{cases}
\end{aligned}
$$

Proof. The probability of event $(S_0[i_1] = K[0] - K[1] - 1)$ can be decomposed in three paths: $K[1] = 127$ (Path 1), $K[1] = 255$ (Path 2) and $K[1] \neq 127, 255$ (Path 3). In the following proof, we use $S_0[1]$ instead of $S_0[i_1]$ ($i_1 = 1$) for simplicity.

Path 1. In $K[1] = 127$, event $(S_0[1] = K[0] - K[1] - 1)$ occurs if and only if $S_0[1] = K[0] + K[1] + 1$. Thus, the probability in Path 1 is given as follows:

$$\Pr(S_0[1] = K[0] - K[1] - 1 \mid \text{Path 1}) = \alpha_1.$$

Path 2. In $K[1] = 255$, event $(S_0[1] = K[0] - K[1] - 1)$ occurs if and only if $S_0[1] = K[0] + K[1] + 1$, and $K[0] + K[1] + 1 = K[0] - K[1] - 1 = K[0]$. Then, from the discussion in Theorem 1, event $(S_0[1] = K[0])$ occurs if and only if either $(K[0] + K[1] = 0 \wedge K[0] = 1)$ or $(K[0] + K[1] = 255 \wedge K[0] \neq 1)$. So, assuming that both $K[1] = 255$ and $S_0[1] = K[0] + K[1] + 1$ hold, event $(S_0[1] = K[0] - K[1] - 1)$ occurs if and only if either $K[0] = 0$ or 1. Thus, the probability in Path 2 is given as follows:

$$\Pr(S_0[1] = K[0] - K[1] - 1 \mid \text{Path 2}) \approx \Pr(K[0] = 0, 1) \cdot \alpha_1.$$

Path 3. In $K[1] \neq 127, 255$, event $(S_0[1] = K[0] - K[1] - 1)$ never occurs if $S_0[1] = K[0] + K[1] + 1$. If $S_0[1] \neq K[0] + K[1] + 1$ holds, then we assume that event $(S_0[1] = K[0] - K[1] - 1)$ occurs with probability $\frac{1}{N}$ due to random association. Thus, the probability in Path 3 is given as follows:

$$\Pr(S_0[1] = K[0] - K[1] - 1 \mid \text{Path 3}) \approx \frac{1}{N} \cdot (1 - \alpha_1).$$

In summary, we get

$$
\begin{aligned}
&\Pr(S_0[i_1] = K[0] - K[1] - 1) \\
&= \Pr(S_0[i_1] = K[0] - K[1] - 1 \mid \text{Path 1}) \cdot \Pr(\text{Path 1}) \\
&\quad + \Pr(S_0[i_1] = K[0] - K[1] - 1 \mid \text{Path 2}) \cdot \Pr(\text{Path 2}) \\
&\quad + \Pr(S_0[i_1] = K[0] - K[1] - 1 \mid \text{Path 3}) \cdot \Pr(\text{Path 3}) \\
&\approx \begin{cases} \frac{1}{N}\left(1 + \frac{2}{N}\right)\alpha_1 + \frac{1}{N}\left(1 - \frac{2}{N}\right)(1 - \alpha_1) & \text{for RC4,} \\ \frac{4}{N}\alpha_1 + \frac{1}{N}\left(1 - \frac{4}{N}\right)(1 - \alpha_1) & \text{for WPA,} \end{cases}
\end{aligned}
$$

where $\alpha_1 = \Pr(S_0[1] = K[0] + K[1] + 1) \approx \left(\frac{N-1}{N}\right)^{N+2} + \frac{1}{N}$.   □

For WPA, Theorems 3 and 4 show that $\Pr(S_0[i_1] = K[0] - K[1] - 3) = \Pr(S_0[i_1] = K[0] - K[1] - 1)$ holds. This is because the probability of $K[1] = 127$ or 255 in WPA is $\frac{4}{N}$ or 0, respectively.

4.3   Biases in $S_{255}[i_{256}]$ for both Generic RC4 and WPA

Theorem 5 shows that $S_{255}[i_{256}] = K[0]$ holds with high probability in both generic RC4 and WPA. On the other hand, Theorem 6 shows $S_{255}[i_{256}] = K[1]$ holds with high probability only in WPA.

Theorem 5. *After the 255-th round of PRGA, we have*

$$\Pr(S_{255}[i_{256}] = K[0]) \approx \alpha_0 \left(1 - \frac{1}{N}\right)^{255} + \frac{1}{N}(1 - \alpha_0)\left(1 - \left(1 - \frac{1}{N}\right)^{255}\right).$$

Proof. The probability of event $(S_{255}[i_{256}] = K[0])$ can be decomposed in two paths: $S_0[0] = K[0]$ (Path 1) and $S_0[0] \neq K[0]$ (Path 2). In the following proof, we use $S_{255}[0]$ instead of $S_{255}[i_{256}]$ ($i_{256} = 0$) for simplicity.

Path 1. In $S_0[0] = K[0]$, event $(S_{255}[0] = K[0])$ occurs if $S_r[0] = S_0[0]$ for $1 \le r \le 255$, whose probability is $\left(1 - \frac{1}{N}\right)^{255}$ approximately. Thus, the probability in Path 1 is given as follows:

$$\Pr(S_{255}[0] = K[0] \mid \text{Path 1}) \approx \left(1 - \frac{1}{N}\right)^{255}.$$

Path 2. In $S_0[0] \ne K[0]$, event $(S_{255}[0] = K[0])$ never occurs if $S_r[0] = S_0[0]$ for $1 \le r \le 255$. Except when $S_r[0] = S_0[0]$ for $1 \le r \le 255$, whose probability is $\left(1 - \left(1 - \frac{1}{N}\right)^{255}\right)$ approximately, we assume that event $(S_{255}[0] = K[0])$ occurs with probability $\frac{1}{N}$ due to random association. Thus, the probability in Path 2 is given as follows:

$$\Pr(S_{255}[0] = K[0] \mid \text{Path 2}) \approx \frac{1}{N}\left(1 - \left(1 - \frac{1}{N}\right)^{255}\right).$$

In summary, we get

$$\Pr(S_{255}[i_{256}] = K[0]) = \Pr(S_{255}[i_{256}] = K[0] \mid \text{Path 1}) \cdot \Pr(\text{Path 1})$$
$$+ \Pr(S_{255}[i_{256}] = K[0] \mid \text{Path 2}) \cdot \Pr(\text{Path 2})$$
$$\approx \alpha_0\left(1 - \frac{1}{N}\right)^{255} + \frac{1}{N}(1 - \alpha_0)\left(1 - \left(1 - \frac{1}{N}\right)^{255}\right),$$

where $\alpha_0 = \Pr(S_0[0] = K[0]) \approx \left(1 - \frac{1}{N}\right)^N + \frac{1}{N}$. $\qquad\square$

Before showing Theorem 6, we will show in Lemma 1 that $S_0[0] = K[1]$ with high probability only in WPA.

Lemma 1. *In the initial state of PRGA, we have*

$$\Pr(S_0[0] = K[1]) \approx \begin{cases} \dfrac{1}{N} - \dfrac{1}{N^2}\left(1 - \alpha_0\right) & \textit{for RC4,} \\[2ex] \dfrac{1}{4}\left(\dfrac{3}{N} + \left(1 - \dfrac{3}{N}\right)\alpha_0\right) & \textit{for WPA.} \end{cases}$$

Proof. The probability of event $(S_0[0] = K[1])$ can be decomposed in two paths: $K[1] = K[0]$ (Path 1) and $K[1] \ne K[0]$ (Path 2).

Path 1. In $K[1] = K[0]$, event $(S_0[0] = K[1])$ occurs if and only if $S_0[0] = K[0]$. Thus, the probability in Path 1 is given as follows:

$$\Pr(S_0[0] = K[1] \mid \text{Path 1}) = \alpha_0.$$

Path 2. In $K[1] \ne K[0]$, event $(S_0[0] = K[1])$ never occurs if $S_0[0] = K[0]$. If $S_0[0] \ne K[0]$, then we assume that event $(S_0[0] = K[1])$ occurs with probability $\frac{1}{N}$ due to random association. Thus, the probability in Path 2 is given as follows:

$$\Pr(S_0[0] = K[1] \mid \text{Path 2}) \approx \frac{1}{N} \cdot (1 - \alpha_0).$$

In summary, we get

$$\Pr(S_0[0] = K[1]) = \Pr(S_0[0] = K[1] \mid \text{Path 1}) \cdot \Pr(\text{Path 1})$$
$$+ \Pr(S_0[0] = K[1] \mid \text{Path 2}) \cdot \Pr(\text{Path 2})$$

$$\approx \begin{cases} \alpha_0 \cdot \dfrac{1}{N} + \dfrac{1}{N}(1 - \alpha_0) \cdot \left(1 - \dfrac{1}{N}\right) = \dfrac{1}{N} - \dfrac{1}{N^2}\left(1 - \alpha_0\right) & \text{for RC4,} \\[3mm] \alpha_0 \cdot \dfrac{1}{4} + \dfrac{1}{N}(1 - \alpha_0) \cdot \dfrac{3}{4} = \dfrac{1}{4}\left(\dfrac{3}{N} + \left(1 - \dfrac{3}{N}\right)\alpha_0\right) & \text{for WPA,} \end{cases}$$

where $\alpha_0 = \Pr(S_0[0] = K[0]) \approx \left(1 - \frac{1}{N}\right)^N + \frac{1}{N}$. $\square$

Lemma 1 reflects that the probability of event $(K[1] = K[0])$ in WPA, $\frac{1}{4}$, is higher than that in generic RC4, $\frac{1}{N}$.

Theorem 6. *After the 255-th round of PRGA, we have*

$$\Pr(S_{255}[i_{256}] = K[1]) \approx \delta\left(1 - \dfrac{1}{N}\right)^{255} + \dfrac{1}{N}(1 - \delta)\left(1 - \left(1 - \dfrac{1}{N}\right)^{255}\right),$$

where δ is $\Pr(S_0[0] = K[1])$ given as Lemma 1.

Proof. The proof itself is similar to Theorem 5, and used the probability of event $(S_0[0] = K[1])$ given as Lemma 1 instead of the probability of event $(S_0[0] = K[0])$. Therefore, we get

$$\Pr(S_{255}[i_{256}] = K[1]) = \Pr(S_{255}[0] = K[1] \mid S_0[0] = K[1]) \cdot \Pr(S_0[0] = K[1])$$
$$+ \Pr(S_{255}[0] = K[1] \mid S_0[0] \neq K[1]) \cdot \Pr(S_0[0] \neq K[1])$$
$$\approx \delta\left(1 - \dfrac{1}{N}\right)^{255} + \dfrac{1}{N}(1 - \delta)\left(1 - \left(1 - \dfrac{1}{N}\right)^{255}\right),$$

where δ is $\Pr(S_0[0] = K[1])$ given as Lemma 1. $\square$

4.4   Bias in $S_r[i_{r+1}]$ $(0 \leq r \leq N)$ for both Generic RC4 and WPA

Theorem 7 shows $\Pr(S_r[i_{r+1}] = K[0] + K[1] + 1)$ for $0 \leq r \leq N$, whose experimental result is listed Fig. 1 in Sect. 4.1. Before showing Theorem 7, Lemmas 2 and 3, distribution of the state in the first 2 rounds of PRGA, are proved.

Lemma 2. *In the initial state of PRGA for $0 \leq x \leq N - 1$, we have*

$$\Pr(S_0[x] = K[0] + K[1] + 1)$$

$$\approx \begin{cases} \left(1 - \dfrac{1}{N}\right)^{N+2} + \dfrac{1}{N} & \textit{if } x=1 \\[3mm] \dfrac{1}{N^2}\left(1 - \dfrac{1}{N}\right)^2 & \textit{if } x=0 \textit{ for WPA} \\[3mm] \dfrac{1}{N}\left(1 - \dfrac{1}{N}\right)\left(\dfrac{1}{N}\left(1 - \dfrac{x+1}{N}\right) + \left(1 - \dfrac{1}{N}\right)^{N-x-2}\right) & \textit{otherwise.} \end{cases}$$

Proof. First, the probability of event $(S_0[1] = K[0] + K[1] + 1)$ follows the result in Proposition 1, that is, $\Pr(S_0[1] = K[0] + K[1] + 1) \approx \left(1 - \frac{1}{N}\right)^{N+2} + \frac{1}{N}$.

Next, the probability of event $(S_0[x] = K[0] + K[1] + 1)$ for $x \in [0, N]\backslash\{1\}$ can be decomposed in two paths: $S_x^K[j_{x+1}^K] = K[0] + K[1] + 1$ (Path 1) and $S_x^K[j_{x+1}^K] \neq K[0] + K[1] + 1$ (Path 2).

Path 1. In $S_x^K[j_{x+1}^K] = K[0] + K[1] + 1$, $S_{x+1}^K[x] = K[0] + K[1] + 1$ always holds due to swap operation. Furthermore, if $S_r^K[x] = S_{x+1}^K[x]$ for $x + 2 \leq r \leq N$, whose probability is $\left(1 - \frac{1}{N}\right)^{N-x-1}$ approximately, then $S_0[x] = K[0] + K[1] + 1$ always holds. Thus, the probability in Path 1 is given as follows:

$$\Pr(S_0[x] = K[0] + K[1] + 1 \mid \text{Path 1}) \approx \left(1 - \frac{1}{N}\right)^{N-x-1}.$$

Path 2. Let y be satisfied with $S_x^K[y] = K[0] + K[1] + 1$. In $S_x^K[j_{x+1}^K] \neq K[0] + K[1] + 1$, $S_{x+1}^K[x] = K[0] + K[1] + 1$ never holds due to swap operation. After the $x + 1$-th round, if $x \geq y$, then event $(S_0[x] \neq K[0] + K[1] + 1)$ occurs because $S_r^K[x] \neq K[0] + K[1] + 1$ always holds for $x + 1 \leq r \leq N$. Else if $x < y$, then we assume that event $(S_0[x] = K[0] + K[1] + 1)$ occurs with probability $\frac{1}{N}$ due to random association, and the probability of $x < y$ is $1 - \frac{x+1}{N}$. In order to be satisfied $x < y$, we further consider $K[0] = 1$, whose probability is $\frac{1}{N}$. If $K[0] \neq 1$, then $S_2^K[1] = K[0] + K[1] + 1$ always holds from the discussion in Theorem 1, and thus, $S_r^K[x] \neq K[0] + K[1] + 1$ holds for $2 \leq r \leq N$. In summary, the probability in Path 2 is given as follows:

$$\Pr(S_0[x] = K[0] + K[1] + 1 \mid \text{Path 2}) = \frac{1}{N^2}\left(1 - \frac{x+1}{N}\right).$$

In summary, we get

$$\Pr(S_0[x] = K[0] + K[1] + 1)$$
$$= \Pr(S_0[x] = K[0] + K[1] + 1 \mid \text{Path 1}) \cdot \Pr(\text{Path 1})$$
$$+ \Pr(S_0[x] = K[0] + K[1] + 1 \mid \text{Path 2}) \cdot \Pr(\text{Path 2})$$
$$\approx \frac{1}{N}\left(1 - \frac{1}{N}\right)\left(\frac{1}{N}\left(1 - \frac{x+1}{N}\right) + \left(1 - \frac{1}{N}\right)^{N-x-2}\right).$$

In the case of $x = 0$ in WPA, event $(S_0[0] = K[0] + K[1] + 1)$ never occurs in $S_0^K[j_1^K] = K[0] + K[1] + 1$ (Path 1) since $S_0^K[j_1^K] = K[0]$ from step 6 in Algorithm 1. Then, $K[1] = 255$ never holds in WPA. Thus, $\Pr(S_0[0] = K[0] + K[1] + 1)$ occurs if and only if Path 2, whose probability is given simply as $\frac{1}{N^2}\left(1 - \frac{1}{N}\right)^2$. $\square$

Lemma 3. *After the first round of PRGA for $0 \leq x \leq N - 1$, we have*

$$\Pr(S_1[x] = K[0] + K[1] + 1) = \begin{cases} \beta_1 & \text{if } x=1 \\ \alpha_1\gamma_{x-1} + (1 - \beta_1)\epsilon_x & \text{otherwise,} \end{cases}$$

where ϵ_x is $\Pr(S_0[x] = K[0] + K[1] + 1)$ given as Lemma 2.

Proof. First, the probability of event $(S_1[1] = K[0] + K[1] + 1)$ follows the result in Proposition 2 because $S_1[1] = S_1[i_1] = S_0[j_1] = S_0[S_0[1]]$ from steps 4 and 5 in Algorithm 2, that is, $\Pr(S_1[1] = K[0] + K[1] + 1) = \beta_1$.

Next, the probability of event $(S_1[x] = K[0] + K[1] + 1)$ for $x \in [0, N-1] \backslash \{1\}$ can be decomposed in two paths: $S_0[1] = K[0] + K[1] + 1$ (Path 1) and $S_0[x] = K[0] + K[1] + 1$ (Path 2).

Path 1. In $S_0[1] = K[0] + K[1] + 1$, if $j_1 = x$, then event $(S_1[x] = K[0] + K[1] + 1)$ always occurs due to swap operation. Although both $S_0[1] = K[0] + K[1] + 1$ and $j_1 = x$ are not independent, both $S_0[1] = K[0] + K[1] + 1$ and $K[0] + K[1] + 1 = x$ become independent by converting $j_1 = x$ into $j_1 = S_0[1] = K[0] + K[1] + 1 = x$. Thus, the probability in Path 1 is given as follows:

$$\Pr(S_1[x] = K[0] + K[1] + 1 \mid \text{Path 1}) = \Pr(K[0] + K[1] = x - 1).$$

Path 2. In $S_0[x] = K[0] + K[1] + 1$, if $j_1 = x$, then event $(S_1[x] = K[0] + K[1] + 1)$ never occurs due to swap operation. If $j_1 \neq x$, then $S_1[x] = S_0[x] = K[0] + K[1] + 1$ always holds, and $S_1[1] \neq K[0] + K[1] + 1$ holds since $S_1[1] = S_0[j_1] \neq S_0[x]$ from swap operation in the first round. So, we assume that both $S_0[x] = K[0] + K[1] + 1$ and $S_1[1] \neq K[0] + K[1] + 1$ are mutually independent. Thus, the probability in Path 2 is given as follows:

$$\Pr(S_1[x] = K[0] + K[1] + 1 \mid \text{Path 2}) = \Pr(S_1[1] \neq K[0] + K[1] + 1).$$

In summary, we get

$$
\begin{aligned}
&\Pr(S_1[x] = K[0] + K[1] + 1) \\
&= \Pr(S_1[x] = K[0] + K[1] + 1 \mid \text{Path 1}) \cdot \Pr(\text{Path 1}) \\
&\quad + \Pr(S_1[x] = K[0] + K[1] + 1 \mid \text{Path 2}) \cdot \Pr(\text{Path 2}) \\
&= \alpha_1 \gamma_{x-1} + (1 - \beta_1)\epsilon_x,
\end{aligned}
$$

where $\alpha_1 = \Pr(S_0[1] = K[0] + K[1] + 1)$, $\beta_1 = \Pr(S_0[S_0[1]] = K[0] + K[1] + 1)$, $\gamma_{x-1} = \Pr(K[0] + K[1] = x - 1)$ and $\epsilon_x = \Pr(S_0[x] = K[0] + K[1] + 1)$ is given as Lemma 2. $\qquad\square$

Theorem 7. *After the r-th round of PRGA for $0 \leq x \leq N$, we have*

$$\Pr(S_r[i_{r+1}] = K[0] + K[1] + 1)$$

$$
\approx
\begin{cases}
\alpha_1 & \text{if } r = 0, \\
\alpha_1 \gamma_1 + (1 - \beta_1)\epsilon_2 & \text{if } r = 1, \\
\epsilon_0 \left(1 - \dfrac{1}{N}\right)^{N-1} + \dfrac{1}{N}(1 - \epsilon_0)\left(1 - \left(1 - \dfrac{1}{N}\right)^{N-1}\right) & \text{if } r = N - 1, \\
\zeta_1 \left(1 - \dfrac{1}{N}\right)^{N-1} + \dfrac{1}{N}(1 - \zeta_1)\left(1 - \left(1 - \dfrac{1}{N}\right)^{N-1}\right) & \text{if } r = N, \\
\zeta_{r+1} \left(1 - \dfrac{1}{N}\right)^{r-1} + \dfrac{1}{N}\displaystyle\sum_{x=1}^{r-1} \eta_x \left(1 - \dfrac{1}{N}\right)^{r-x-1} & \text{otherwise,}
\end{cases}
$$

where ϵ_r is $\Pr(S_0[r] = K[0] + K[1] + 1)$ given as Lemma 2, ζ_r is $\Pr(S_1[r] = K[0] + K[1] + 1)$ given as Lemma 3 and η_r is $\Pr(S_r[i_{r+1}] = K[0] + K[1] + 1)$ given as this theorem.

Proof. First, the probability of events $(S_0[i_1] = K[0] + K[1] + 1)$ and $(S_1[i_2] = K[0] + K[1] + 1)$ follow the result in Lemmas 2 and 3, respectively.

Next, both events $(S_{N-1}[i_N] = K[0] + K[1] + 1)$ and $(S_N[i_{N+1}] = K[0] + K[1] + 1)$ can be proved in the same way as the proof of Theorem 5.

Finally, the probability of event $(S_r[i_{r+1}] = K[0]+K[1]+1)$ for $2 \le r \le N-2$ can be decomposed in two paths: $S_1[i_{r+1}] = K[0] + K[1] + 1$ (Path 1) and $S_x[i_{x+1}] = K[0] + K[1] + 1$ $(1 \le x \le r - 1)$ (Path 2).

Path 1. In $S_1[i_{r+1}] = K[0] + K[1] + 1$, event $(S_r[i_{r+1}] = K[0] + K[1] + 1)$ occurs if $S_y[i_{y+1}] = S_1[i_{r+1}]$ for $2 \le y \le r$, whose probability is $\left(1 - \frac{1}{N}\right)^{r-1}$ approximately. Thus, the probability in Path 1 is given as follows:

$$\Pr(S_r[i_{r+1}] = K[0] + K[1] + 1 \mid \text{Path 1}) \approx \left(1 - \frac{1}{N}\right)^{r-1}.$$

Path 2. In $S_x[i_{x+1}] = K[0] + K[1] + 1$ $(1 \le x \le r - 1)$, if $j_{x+1} = i_{r+1}$, then $S_{x+1}[i_{r+1}] = K[0]+K[1]+1$ always holds due to swap operation. After the $x+1$-th round, event $(S_r[i_{r+1}] = K[0]+K[1]+1)$ occurs if $S_y[i_{y+1}] = S_{x+1}[i_{r+1}]$ for $x + 2 \le y \le r$, whose probability is $\left(1 - \frac{1}{N}\right)^{r-x-1}$ approximately. Thus, the probability in Path 2 is given as follows:

$$\Pr(S_r[i_{r+1}] = K[0] + K[1] + 1 \mid \text{Path 2}) \approx \frac{1}{N}\left(1 - \frac{1}{N}\right)^{r-x-1}.$$

Note that the range of x varies depending on the value of r in Path 2. In summary, we get

$$\Pr(S_r[i_{r+1}] = K[0] + K[1] + 1)$$
$$= \Pr(S_r[i_{r+1}] = K[0] + K[1] + 1 \mid \text{Path 1}) \cdot \Pr(\text{Path 1})$$
$$+ \sum_{x=1}^{r-1} \Pr(S_r[i_{r+1}] = K[0] + K[1] + 1 \mid \text{Path 2}) \cdot \Pr(\text{Path 2})$$
$$\approx \zeta_{r+1}\left(1 - \frac{1}{N}\right)^{r-1} + \frac{1}{N}\sum_{x=1}^{r-1} \eta_x\left(1 - \frac{1}{N}\right)^{r-x-1},$$

where $\zeta_r = \Pr(S_1[r] = K[0]+K[1]+1)$ and $\eta_r = \Pr(S_r[i_{r+1}] = K[0]+K[1]+1)$, which is recursive probability in this theorem.

5   Experimental Results

In order to check the accuracy of notable linear correlations shown in Theorems 1–7, the experiments are conducted using 2^{40} randomly generated keys of 16 bytes in both generic RC4 and WPA, which mean $2^{40}(=N^5)$ trials. Note that $\mathcal{O}(N^3)$ trials are reported to be sufficient to identify the biases with constant probability of success. This is why each correlation has a relative bias with the probability of at least about $\frac{1}{2N}$ with respect to a base event of probability $\frac{1}{N}$ (refer to [11, Theorem 2] in detail). Our experimental environment is as follows: Ubuntu 12.04 machine with 2.6 GHz CPU, 3.8 GiB memory, gcc 4.6.3 compiler and C language. We also evaluate the percentage of relative error ϵ of experimental values compared with theoretical values:

$$\epsilon = \frac{|\text{experimental value} - \text{theoretical value}|}{\text{experimental value}} \times 100\,(\%).$$

Table 2 shows experimental and theoretical values and the percentage of relative errors ϵ, which indicates ϵ is small enough in each case such as $\epsilon \leq 4.589(\%)$. Figure 7 shows comparison between experimental and theoretical values in Theorem 7, and these distributions match on the whole. Therefore, we have convinced that theoretical values closely reflects the experimental values.

Table 2. Comparison between experimental and theoretical values

Results		Experimental value	Theoretical value	$\epsilon(\%)$
Theorem 1		0.001449605	0.001445489	0.284
Theorem 2		0	0	0
Theorem 3 {	for RC4	0.005332558	0.005325263	0.137
	for WPA	0.007823541	0.008182569	4.589
Theorem 4 {	for RC4	0.003922530	0.003898206	0.620
	for WPA	0.007851853	0.008182569	4.212
Theorem 5		0.138038917	0.138325988	0.208
Theorem 6 {	for RC4	0.003909105	0.003893102	0.409
	for WPA	0.037186225	0.037105932	0.216

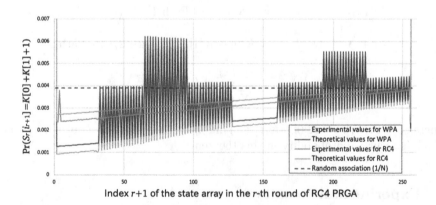

Fig. 7. Comparison between experimental and theoretical values shown in Theorem 7 for both generic RC4 and WPA

6   Conclusion

In this paper, we have focused on the state information and investigated various linear correlations among the *unknown* state information, the first 3 bytes of the RC4 key, and a keystream byte in both generic RC4 and WPA. Particularly, those linear correlations are effective for the state recovery attack since they include the first *known* 3-byte keys (IV-related). As a result, we have discovered more than 150 correlations with positive or negative biases. We have also proved six notable linear correlations theoretically, these are biases in $S_0[i_1]$, $S_{255}[i_{256}]$ and $S_r[i_{r+1}]$ for $0 \leq r \leq N$. For example, we have proved that the probability of $(S_0[i_1] = K[0])$ in WPA is 0 (shown in Theorem 2), and thus, $S_0[i_1]$ is varied from $[0, 255] \setminus K[0]$.

These new linear correlations could contribute to the improvement of the state recovery attack against RC4 especially in WPA. It is still an open problem to prove various linear correlations shown in Table 3 theoretically. It is also given to an open problem to apply newly discovered linear correlations to the state recovery attack.

A   Newly Obtained Linear Correlations

In this part, Table 3 shows notable linear correlations newly discovered by our experiment shown in Sect. 4.1.

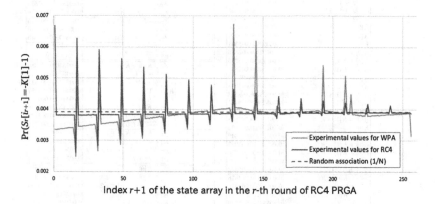

Fig. 8. Experimental result of event $(S_r[i_{r+1}] = -K[1] - 1)$

Table 3. Notable linear correlations in Eq. (1) for both generic RC4 and WPA

X_r	Linear correlations	RC4	WPA
$S_0[i_1]$ ($=j_1$)	$-Z_1+1$	0.007584	0.007660
	$-K[0]-K[1]-K[2]$	0.005361	0.005360
	$-K[0]-K[1]-3$	0.005336	0.008437
	$-K[0]-K[1]+1$	0.005350	0.002600
	$-K[0]-K[1]+3$	0.005331	0.002605
	$-K[0]-1$	0.003823	0.005254
	$-K[0]+2$	0.003902	0.005340
	$-K[0]+K[1]-3$	0.005334	0.005240
	$-K[0]+K[1]-1$	0.005331	0.005229
	$K[1]+1$	0.006765	0.004322
	$K[0]-K[1]+1$	0.005324	0.002221
	$K[0]-K[1]+3$	0.005333	0.002640
	$K[0]+K[1]+K[2]+3$	0.001492	0.001491
	$Z_1-K[0]-K[1]-K[2]-2$	0.005326	0.004753
$S_1[i_2]$	$-Z_2-K[0]+K[1]$	0.003905	0.004957
	$-Z_2-K[0]+K[1]+2$	0.003906	0.004839
	$-Z_2-K[1]+K[2]-3$	0.005314	0.005327
	$-Z_2$	0.007768	0.007791
	$-Z_2+2$	0.007751	0.007749
	$-Z_2+K[1]+K[2]+3$	0.005317	0.005328
	$-Z_2+K[0]-K[1]$	0.003907	0.004958
	$-Z_2+K[0]-K[1]+2$	0.003906	0.004839
	$-K[0]-K[1]-K[2]+1$	0.005348	0.005351
	$-K[0]-K[1]-K[2]+3$	0.005281	0.005290
	$-K[0]-K[1]+3$	0.005329	0.004036
	$-K[0]-K[1]+K[2]-3$	0.005307	0.002491
	$-K[0]-K[1]+K[2]-1$	0.005305	0.008197
	$-K[0]-K[1]+K[2]+1$	0.005317	0.002491
	$-K[0]-K[1]+K[2]+3$	0.005305	0.002474
	$-K[0]+K[2]-2$	0.003904	0.005311
	$-K[0]+K[2]+1$	0.003906	0.005326
	$-K[0]+K[1]-K[2]-3$	0.005293	0.004616
	$-K[0]+K[1]-K[2]-1$	0.005296	0.005885
	$-K[0]+K[1]-K[2]+1$	0.005301	0.005279
	$-K[0]+K[1]-K[2]+3$	0.005300	0.005289
	$-K[0]+K[1]+K[2]-3$	0.005308	0.005322
	$-K[0]+K[1]+K[2]-1$	0.005305	0.005333
	$-K[0]+K[1]+K[2]+1$	0.005306	0.005326
	$-K[0]+K[1]+K[2]+3$	0.005310	0.004261
	$-K[1]-K[2]-3$	0.006748	0.006767
	$-K[2]-1$	0.006127	0.007571
	$-K[2]+1$	0.003915	0.005308
	$-K[2]+3$	0.003904	0.005306
	$K[2]-3$	0.003910	0.005309
	$K[2]-1$	0.003910	0.005321
	$K[2]+1$	0.003909	0.005331
	$K[2]+3$	0.006219	0.003886
	$K[1]+K[2]+3$	0.008157	0.006755
	$K[0]-K[1]-K[2]-1$	0.005309	0.005895
	$K[0]-K[1]-K[2]+1$	0.005302	0.005314
	$K[0]-K[1]-K[2]+3$	0.005308	0.005318
	$K[0]-K[1]+K[2]-3$	0.005295	0.008163
	$K[0]-K[1]+K[2]-1$	0.005290	0.008171
	$K[0]-K[1]+K[2]+1$	0.005309	0.008171
	$K[0]-K[1]+K[2]+3$	0.005310	0.002838
	$K[0]$	0.001455	0.001452
	$K[0]+K[1]-K[2]-3$	0.005312	0.005340
	$K[0]+K[1]-K[2]+1$	0.005291	0.005295
	$K[0]+K[1]-K[2]+3$	0.005304	0.005309
	$Z_2-K[1]-K[2]-3$	0.005323	0.005333
	$Z_2+K[1]+K[2]+3$	0.005322	0.005332
$S_2[i_3]$	$-Z_3-K[0]+K[1]+3$	0.003906	0.004878
	$-Z_3+3$	0.007825	0.007819
	$-Z_3+K[0]-K[1]+3$	0.003907	0.004877
	$-K[0]-K[1]+2$	0.005335	0.005539
	$-K[0]+K[1]+3$	0.003901	0.004983
	$K[0]$	0.001463	0.001458
$S_3[i_4]$	$-K[0]-K[1]-K[2]$	0.005324	0.005325
	$-K[0]-K[1]+3$	0.006721	0.005513
$S_{28}[i_{29}]$	$-Z_{29}-K[0]+K[1]-3$	0.003906	0.004861
$S_{29}[i_{30}]$	$-Z_{30}-K[0]+K[1]-2$	0.003906	0.004863
$S_{30}[i_{31}]$	$-Z_{31}-K[0]+K[1]-1$	0.003907	0.004863
$S_{31}[i_{32}]$	$-Z_{32}-K[0]+K[1]$	0.003906	0.004862
$S_{32}[i_{33}]$	$-Z_{33}-K[0]+K[1]+1$	0.003907	0.004860
$S_{33}[i_{34}]$	$-Z_{34}-K[0]+K[1]+2$	0.003906	0.004860
$S_{34}[i_{35}]$	$-Z_{35}-K[0]+K[1]+3$	0.003907	0.004863
$S_{92}[i_{93}]$	$-Z_{93}+K[0]-K[1]-3$	0.003904	0.004877
$S_{93}[i_{94}]$	$-Z_{94}+K[0]-K[1]-2$	0.003906	0.004877
$S_{94}[i_{95}]$	$-Z_{95}+K[0]-K[1]-1$	0.003907	0.004875

X_r	Linear correlations	RC4	WPA
$S_{95}[i_{96}]$	$-Z_{96}+K[0]-K[1]$	0.003906	0.004878
$S_{96}[i_{97}]$	$-Z_{97}+K[0]-K[1]+1$	0.003906	0.004875
$S_{97}[i_{98}]$	$-Z_{98}+K[0]-K[1]+2$	0.003906	0.004875
$S_{98}[i_{99}]$	$-Z_{99}+K[0]-K[1]+3$	0.003906	0.004875
$S_{124}[i_{125}]$	$-Z_{125}-K[0]+K[1]-3$	0.003908	0.004874
	$-Z_{125}+K[0]+K[1]-3$	0.003906	0.004872
$S_{125}[i_{126}]$	$-Z_{126}-K[0]+K[1]-2$	0.003907	0.004876
	$-Z_{126}+K[0]-K[1]-2$	0.003907	0.004876
$S_{126}[i_{127}]$	$-Z_{127}-K[0]+K[1]-1$	0.003906	0.004874
	$-Z_{127}+K[0]-K[1]-1$	0.003906	0.004876
$S_{127}[i_{128}]$	$-Z_{128}-K[0]+K[1]$	0.003908	0.004875
	$-Z_{128}+K[0]-K[1]$	0.003907	0.004876
$S_{128}[i_{129}]$	$-Z_{129}-K[0]+K[1]+1$	0.003906	0.004875
	$-Z_{129}+K[0]-K[1]+1$	0.003907	0.004875
$S_{129}[i_{130}]$	$-Z_{130}-K[0]+K[1]+2$	0.003906	0.004875
	$-Z_{130}+K[0]-K[1]+2$	0.003906	0.004876
$S_{130}[i_{131}]$	$-Z_{131}-K[0]+K[1]+3$	0.003903	0.004876
	$-Z_{131}+K[0]-K[1]+3$	0.003906	0.004875
$S_{156}[i_{157}]$	$-Z_{157}-K[0]+K[1]-3$	0.003904	0.004876
$S_{157}[i_{158}]$	$-Z_{158}-K[0]+K[1]-2$	0.003906	0.004877
$S_{158}[i_{159}]$	$-Z_{159}-K[0]+K[1]-1$	0.003906	0.004875
$S_{159}[i_{160}]$	$-Z_{160}-K[0]+K[1]$	0.003906	0.004876
$S_{160}[i_{161}]$	$-Z_{161}-K[0]+K[1]+1$	0.003906	0.004876
$S_{161}[i_{162}]$	$-Z_{162}-K[0]+K[1]+2$	0.003907	0.004875
$S_{162}[i_{163}]$	$-Z_{163}-K[0]+K[1]+3$	0.003907	0.004874
$S_{220}[i_{221}]$	$-Z_{221}+K[0]-K[1]-3$	0.003907	0.004860
$S_{221}[i_{222}]$	$-Z_{222}+K[0]-K[1]-2$	0.003907	0.004858
$S_{222}[i_{223}]$	$-Z_{223}+K[0]-K[1]-1$	0.003906	0.004861
$S_{223}[i_{224}]$	$-Z_{224}+K[0]-K[1]$	0.003907	0.004859
$S_{224}[i_{225}]$	$-Z_{225}+K[0]-K[1]+1$	0.003908	0.004861
$S_{225}[i_{226}]$	$-Z_{226}+K[0]-K[1]+2$	0.003907	0.004861
$S_{226}[i_{227}]$	$-Z_{227}+K[0]-K[1]+3$	0.003907	0.004859
$S_{252}[i_{253}]$	$-Z_{253}-K[0]+K[1]-3$	0.003907	0.004876
	$-Z_{253}-3$	0.007813	0.007815
	$-Z_{253}+K[0]-K[1]-3$	0.003906	0.004875
$S_{253}[i_{254}]$	$-Z_{254}-K[0]+K[1]-2$	0.003906	0.004875
	$-Z_{254}-2$	0.007814	0.007812
	$-Z_{254}+K[0]-K[1]-2$	0.003906	0.004875
$S_{254}[i_{255}]$	$-Z_{255}-K[0]+K[1]-1$	0.003905	0.004875
	$-Z_{255}-1$	0.007816	0.007815
	$-Z_{255}+K[0]-K[1]-1$	0.003905	0.004876
$S_{255}[i_{256}]$	$-Z_{256}-K[0]+K[1]$	0.003908	0.004875
	$-Z_{256}$	0.007861	0.007810
	$-Z_{256}+K[0]-K[1]$	0.003909	0.004875
$S_r[i_{r+1}]$	$-K[1]-1$	Fig. 8	
	$K[0]$	Fig. 9	
$S_0[j_1]$	$-Z_1+K[0]+K[1]+1$	0.005330	0.005280
	$-K[0]-K[1]-3$	0.004339	0.005513
	$-K[0]-K[1]+1$	0.005791	0.003417
	$K[1]+1$	0.004933	0.004087
	$K[0]-K[1]-3$	0.004403	0.005342
	$K[0]-K[1]-1$	0.004431	0.005346
	$Z_1-K[0]-K[1]-K[2]-2$	0.005295	0.004726
	$Z_1-K[0]-K[1]-1$	0.005188	0.005115
$S_1[j_2]$	$-Z_2+K[0]+K[1]+1$	0.005316	0.005335
	$-K[0]-K[1]+1$	0.005318	0.005408
	$Z_2-K[0]-K[1]-K[2]-3$	0.005686	0.005694
	$Z_2+K[0]+K[1]+1$	0.005321	0.005344
j_2	$-Z_2+K[0]+K[1]+1$	0.005318	0.005336
	$-Z_2+K[0]+K[1]+3$	0.005302	0.005310
	$-K[0]-K[1]-K[2]+2$	0.005333	0.005856
	$-K[0]-K[1]+K[2]$	0.003919	0.005573
	$-K[0]+K[1]+K[2]$	0.003921	0.005501
	$-K[1]+K[2]-2$	0.003911	0.005479
	$-K[1]+K[2]+3$	0.003899	0.005476
	$K[2]$	0.004428	0.005571
	$K[0]-K[1]+K[2]$	0.003918	0.005618
	$K[0]+K[1]+3$	0.005309	0.003889
t_1	$-Z_1-K[0]-K[1]+1$	0.005251	0.005333
	$-K[0]-K[1]+2$	0.005310	0.003902
	$K[0]$	0.005291	0.004806
	$Z_1-K[0]-K[1]-K[2]-1$	0.006639	0.006094
t_2	$-Z_2-K[0]-K[1]-K[2]+1$	0.005301	0.005306
	$-Z_2+K[0]+K[1]+1$	0.005339	0.005341
	$K[0]+K[1]+1$	0.005317	0.005306
t_3	$K[0]+K[1]+K[2]+3$	0.005297	0.005310
t_r	Z_r	Fig. 10	

See Figs. 8, 9 and 10.

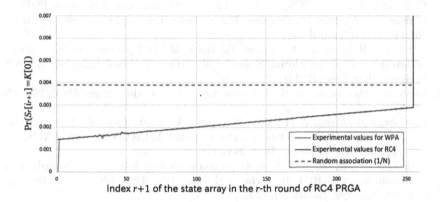

Fig. 9. Experimental result of event $(S_r[i_{r+1}] = K[0])$

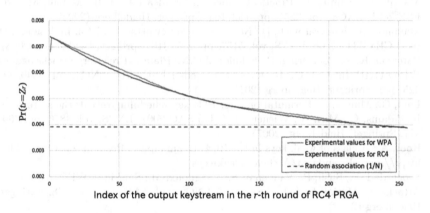

Fig. 10. Experimental result of event $(t_r = Z_r)$

References

1. AlFardan, N.J., Bernstein, D.J., Paterson, K.G., Poettering, B., Schuldt, J.C.N.: On the Security of RC4 in TLS. In: USENIX Security Symposium 2013 (2013)
2. Das, A., Maitra, S., Paul, G., Sarkar, S.: Some combinatorial results towards state recovery attack on RC4. In: Jajodia, S., Mazumdar, C. (eds.) ICISS 2011. LNCS, vol. 7093, pp. 204–214. Springer, Heidelberg (2011)
3. Fluhrer, S.R., Mantin, I., Shamir, A.: Weaknesses in the key scheduling algorithm of RC4. In: Vaudenay, S., Youssef, A.M. (eds.) SAC 2001. LNCS, vol. 2259, pp. 1–24. Springer, Heidelberg (2001)

4. Sen Gupta, S., Maitra, S., Meier, W., Paul, G., Sarkar, S.: Dependence in IV-related bytes of RC4 key enhances vulnerabilities in WPA. In: Cid, C., Rechberger, C. (eds.) FSE 2014. LNCS, vol. 8540, pp. 350–369. Springer, Heidelberg (2015)

5. Housley, R., Whiting, D., Ferguson, N.: Alternate Temporal Key Hash. doc. IEEE 802.11-02/282r2, April 2002

6. Isobe, T., Ohigashi, T., Watanabe, Y., Morii, M.: Full plaintext recovery attack on broadcast RC4. In: Moriai, S. (ed.) FSE 2013. LNCS, vol. 8424, pp. 179–202. Springer, Heidelberg (2014)

7. Klein, A.: Attacks on the RC4 stream cipher. Des. Codes Crypt. 48(3), 269–286 (2008)

8. Knudsen, L.R., Meier, W., Preneel, B., Rijmen, V., Verdoolaege, S.: Analysis methods for (alleged) RC4. In: Ohta, K., Pei, D. (eds.) ASIACRYPT 1998. LNCS, vol. 1514, pp. 327–341. Springer, Heidelberg (1998)

9. Maitra, S., Paul, G.: New form of permutation bias and secret key leakage in keystream bytes of RC4. In: Nyberg, K. (ed.) FSE 2008. LNCS, vol. 5086, pp. 253–269. Springer, Heidelberg (2008)

10. Maitra, S., Paul, G., Sarkar, S., Lehmann, M., Meier, W.: New results on generalization of roos-type biases and related keystreams of RC4. In: Youssef, A., Nitaj, A., Hassanien, A.E. (eds.) AFRICACRYPT 2013. LNCS, vol. 7918, pp. 222–239. Springer, Heidelberg (2013)

11. Mantin, I., Shamir, A.: Practical attack on broadcast RC4. In: Matsui, M. (ed.) FSE 2001. LNCS, vol. 2355, pp. 152–164. Springer, Heidelberg (2002)

12. Maximov, A., Khovratovich, D.: New state recovery attack on RC4. In: Wagner, D. (ed.) CRYPTO 2008. LNCS, vol. 5157, pp. 297–316. Springer, Heidelberg (2008)

13. Paterson, K.G., Poettering, B., Schuldt, J.C.N.: Plaintext recovery attacks against WPA/TKIP. In: Cid, C., Rechberger, C. (eds.) FSE 2014. LNCS, vol. 8540, pp. 325–349. Springer, Heidelberg (2015)

14. Paul, G., Maitra, S.: Permutation after RC4 key scheduling reveals the secret Key. In: Adams, C., Miri, A., Wiener, M. (eds.) SAC 2007. LNCS, vol. 4876, pp. 360–377. Springer, Heidelberg (2007)

15. Roos, A.: A class of weak keys in the RC4 stream cipher. Posts in sci.crypt (1995). http://marcel.wanda.ch/Archive/WeakKeys

16. Sepehrdad, P., Sušil, P., Vaudenay, S., Vuagnoux, M.: Smashing WEP in a Passive Attack. In: Moriai, S. (ed.) FSE 2013. LNCS, vol. 8424, pp. 155–178. Springer, Heidelberg (2014)

17. Teramura, R., Asakura, Y., Ohigashi, T., Kuwakado, H., Morii, M.: Fast WEP-key recovery attack using only encrypted IP packets. IEICE Trans. Fundam. E93–A(1), 164–171 (2010)

Mass Surveillance

A More Cautious Approach to Security Against Mass Surveillance

Jean Paul Degabriele[1] (✉), Pooya Farshim[2], and Bertram Poettering[3]

[1] Royal Holloway, University of London, London, UK
jpdega@gmail.com
[2] Queen's University Belfast, Belfast, UK
[3] Ruhr University Bochum, Bochum, Germany

Abstract. At CRYPTO 2014 Bellare, Paterson, and Rogaway (BPR) presented a formal treatment of symmetric encryption in the light of algorithm substitution attacks (ASAs), which may be employed by 'big brother' entities for the scope of mass surveillance. Roughly speaking, in ASAs big brother may bias ciphertexts to establish a covert channel to leak vital cryptographic information. In this work, we identify a seemingly benign assumption implicit in BPR's treatment and argue that it artificially (and severely) limits big brother's capabilities. We then demonstrate the critical role that this assumption plays by showing that even a slight weakening of it renders the security notion completely unsatisfiable by *any*, possibly deterministic and/or stateful, symmetric encryption scheme. We propose a refined security model to address this shortcoming, and use it to restore the positive result of BPR, but caution that this defense does not stop most other forms of covert-channel attacks.

Keywords: Mass surveillance · Algorithm substitution attack · Symmetric encryption · Covert channel

1 Introduction

In 2013 Edward Snowden shocked the world with revelations of several ongoing surveillance programs targeting citizens worldwide [1,9]. There is now incontestable evidence that national intelligence agencies can go to great lengths to undermine our privacy. The methods employed to attack and infiltrate our communication infrastructure are rather disturbing. Amongst others these include sabotaging Internet routers, wire-tapping international undersea cables, installing backdoors in management front ends of telecom providers, injecting malware in real-time into network packets carrying executable files, and intercepting postal shipping to replace networking hardware.

Some of the revelations concern the domain of cryptography. Somewhat reassuringly, there was no indication that any of the well-established cryptographic primitives and hardness assumptions could be broken by the national intelligence agencies. Instead these agencies resorted to more devious means in order

© International Association for Cryptologic Research 2015
G. Leander (Ed.): FSE 2015, LNCS 9054, pp. 579–598, 2015.
DOI: 10.1007/978-3-662-48116-5_28

to compromise the security of cryptographic protocols. In one particular instance the National Security Agency (NSA) infiltrated and maneuvered cryptographic standardization bodies to recommend a cryptographic primitive which contained a backdoor [15]: The specification of the Dual_EC_DRBG cryptographic random-number generator [2] contains arbitrarily looking parameters for which there exists trapdoor information, known to its creators, that can be used to predict future results from a sufficiently long stretch of output [18]. A recent study [5] explores the practicality of exploiting this vulnerability in TLS. In particular it shows that support of the Extended Random TLS extension [16] (an IETF draft co-authored by an NSA employee) makes the vulnerability much easier to exploit. Furthermore the NSA is known to have made secret payments to vendors in order to include the Dual_EC_DRBG in their products and increase proliferation [11].

Such tactics clearly fall outside of the threat models that we normally assume in cryptography and call for a reconsideration of our most basic assumptions. It is hence natural to ask what other means could be employed by such powerful entities to subvert cryptographic protocols. Recent work by Bellare, Paterson and Rogaway [4] explores the possibility of mass surveillance through *algorithm substitution attacks* (ASA). Consider some type of closed-source software that makes use of a standard symmetric encryption scheme to achieve a certain level of security. In an ASA the standard encryption scheme is substituted with an alternative scheme that the attacker has authored; we call this latter scheme a *subversion*. A successful ASA would allow the adversary, henceforth referred to as *big brother*, to undermine the confidentiality of the data and at the same time circumvent *detection* by its users.

THE RESULTS OF BPR. Bellare, Paterson and Rogaway (BPR) [4] define a formal framework for analyzing ASA resistance of symmetric encryption schemes against a certain class of attacks. Roughly speaking, they define a surveillance model which requires correctly computed (that is, unsubverted) ciphertexts to be indistinguishable from subverted ones from big brother's point of view. BPR also define a dual detection model that requires this property to hold from users' perspective. The detection game is only used for *negative* results. That is, a candidate ASA is considered to be an particularly "deviating one" if it cannot be detected by any efficient procedure. BPR are able to establish a set of positive and negative results within their formalisms. They build on the work of [8] to demonstrate ASAs on specific schemes such as the CTR$ and CBC$ modes of operation. Their negative results culminate with the *biased-ciphertext attack* which can be mounted against any randomized symmetric encryption scheme that uses a sufficient amount of randomness. This attack allows big brother to recover the full keys and plaintexts while enjoying a strong guarantee of undetectability. Biased ciphertexts, therefore, establish a *covert channel* between users and big brother. Thus there is essentially no hope to resist ASAs through probabilistic encryption. Accordingly, BPR turn to stateful deterministic schemes and identify a combinatorial property of such schemes that can be used to formally derive a positive result. Most modern nonce-based schemes [17] can be easily shown to satisfy this property. Put differently,

BPR show that such schemes do not allow covert channels to be established solely using the transmission of ciphertexts.

CONTRIBUTIONS. In this work we revisit the security model proposed by BPR [4] and re-examine its underlying assumptions. Our main critique concerns the notion of *perfect decryptability*, a requirement that every *subversion* must satisfy. Decryptability is introduced as a minimal requirement that a subversion must meet in order to have some chance of avoiding detection. Accordingly, the assumption is that big brother would only consider subversions that satisfy this condition. We argue, however, that this requirement is stronger than what is substantiated by this rationale, and it results in artificially limiting big brother's set of available strategies. Indeed, we show that with a minimal relaxation of the decryptability condition the BPR security notion becomes totally unsatisfiable. More precisely, for *any* symmetric encryption scheme, deterministic or not, we construct a corresponding undetectable subversion that can be triggered to leak information when run on specific inputs known solely by big brother. From a theoretical perspective this shows that the instantiability of the security model crucially depends on this requirement. From a more practical perspective, security in the BPR model simply does not translate to security in practice.

As pointed out in [4], defending against ASAs requires an attempt to detect them. Indeed, the ability to detect an ASA is an important measure of security which should be surfaced by the security model. We observe that here the BPR security definition falls short: Encryption schemes are considered secure as long as subversions can be detected with non-zero probability. This seems to be of little practical value as schemes with a detection probability of 2^{-128}, say, are already deemed secure but are in practice not.

Building on the work of Bellare, Paterson and Rogaway [4] we propose an alternative security definition to address the above limitations. Our model disposes of the perfect decryptability requirement and instead quantifies security via a new detectability notion. In more detail, we start with BPR's surveillance model, and then check how well a candidate user-specific detector can do in distinguishing if a subversion has taken place. Such a detector, besides the user's key, also sees the full transcript of the attack, that is, the messages passed to encryption and the corresponding ciphertexts obtained. Since the detector runs after big brother, our detection strategy is after the fact. (However, if a detector is run "on the fly," the transmission of ciphertexts can be stopped if an anomaly is detected.) This strategy appears to be necessary for detecting the input-triggered subversions discussed above. We quantify security by requiring that any subversion which is undetectable gives big brother limited advantage in surveillance. We re-confirm the relative strength of deterministic stateful schemes compared to randomized ones in the new model, as suggested in [4].

SHORTCOMINGS. Although formal analyses of cryptographic protocols within the provable-security methodology can rule out large classes of attacks, they often fall short of providing security in the real world. Accordingly, our positive results should not be interpreted as providing security in real-world environments either.

Powerful adversarial entities can coerce software vendors and standardization bodies to subvert their products and recommendations. For instance, Snowden's revelations suggest that state agencies have means to subvert many different parts of user hardware, network infrastructure and cryptographic key-generation algorithms, and that they can perform sophisticated side-channel analyses at a distance. Any formal claims of security against such powerful adversaries must come with a model that takes into account these attacks. Indeed, while our models explicitly take into account leakage through biased ciphertext transmission, other forms of covert channels are *not* considered (and most likely exist). On the other hand, a model which incorporates, for instance, hardware subversion might immediately lead to uninstantiability problems (and consequently to non-cryptographic measures against big brother). Our goal here is to take a second step in understanding cryptographic solutions to NSA-like threats. In particular, one benefit of employing the provable-security methodology is that it shifts engineers' attention from primitives' inner details to their security models.

OTHER RELATED WORK. The first systematic analysis of how malicious modification of implemented cryptosystems can weaken their expected security dates back to Simmons [19]. He studied how cryptographic algorithms in black-box implementations can be made to leak information about secret keying material via *subliminal channels*. However, in the considered cases any successful reverse-engineering effort of the manipulated code would be fatal in the sense that, in principle, all affected secrets would be lost universally, (i.e., become known to everybody).

Simmons's approach was refined by Young and Yung in a sequence of works [21–26] under the theme of *Kleptography*, covering mainly primitives in the realm of public-key cryptography (encryption and signature schemes based on RSA and DLP). In their proposals for protocol subversion, a central part of the injected algorithms is the public key of the attacker to which all leakage is 'safely encrypted'. The claim is then that if a successful reverse-engineering eventually reveals the existence of a backdoor, the security of the overall system does not ungracefully collapse, as the attacker's secret key would be held responsibly (by, say, a governmental agency). Kleptographic attacks on RSA systems were also reported by Crépeau and Slakmon [6] who optimized the efficiency of subverted key-generation algorithms by using symmetric techniques. Concerning higher-level protocols, algorithm substitution attacks targeting specifically the SSL/TLS and SSH protocols were reported by Goh et al. [8], and Young and Yung [27].

ASAs and Kleptography can also be considered in the broader context of *covert channels*. In brief, a covert channel allows parties to communicate through unforeseen means in an environment where they are not allowed to communicate. Typically, covert channels are implemented on top of existing network infrastructure (e.g., firewalled TCP/IP networks [13]), but also more exotic mediums such as timing information [20], file storage values [12], and audio links [10]. Finally, observe that in a subliminal channel the communicating parties intentionally modify their algorithms while in ASAs a *third party* does so without users' knowledge.

2 Preliminaries

NOTATION. Unless otherwise stated, an algorithm may be randomized. An adversary is an algorithm. For any algorithm $\mathscr{A}$, $y \leftarrow \mathscr{A}(x_1, x_2, \ldots)$ denotes executing $\mathscr{A}$ with fresh coins on inputs $x_1, x_2, \ldots$ and assigning its output to y. For n, a positive integer, we use $\{0,1\}^n$ to denote the set of all binary strings of length n and $\{0,1\}^*$ to denote the set of all finite binary strings. The empty string is represented by ε. For any two strings x and y, $x \parallel y$ denotes their concatenation and $|x|$ denotes the length of x. For any vector $\mathbf{X}$, we denote by $\mathbf{X}[i]$ its ith component. If S is a finite set then $|S|$ denotes its size, and $y \leftarrow_\$ S$ denotes the process of selecting an element from S uniformly at random and assigning it to y. $\Pr[\, P : E \,]$ denotes the probability of event E occurring after having executed process P. Security definitions are formulated through the code-based game-playing framework.

SYMMETRIC ENCRYPTION. A *symmetric encryption scheme* is a triple $\Pi = (\mathcal{K}, \mathcal{E}, \mathcal{D})$. Associated to Π are the message space $\mathcal{M} \subseteq \{0,1\}^*$ and the associated data space $\mathcal{AD} \subseteq \{0,1\}^*$. The *key space* $\mathcal{K}$ is a non-empty set of strings of some fixed length. The *encryption algorithm* $\mathcal{E}$ may be randomized, stateful, or both. It takes as input the secret key $K \in \mathcal{K}$, a message $M \in \{0,1\}^*$, an associated data $A \in \{0,1\}^*$, and the current encryption state σ to return a ciphertext C or the special symbol $\perp$, together with an updated state. The symbol $\perp$ may be returned for instance if $M \notin \mathcal{M}$ or $A \notin \mathcal{AD}$. The *decryption algorithm* $\mathcal{D}$ is deterministic but may be stateful. It takes as input the secret key K, a ciphertext string $C \in \{0,1\}^*$, an associated data string $A \in \{0,1\}^*$, and the current decryption state ϱ to return the corresponding message M or the special symbol $\perp$, and an updated state. Pairs of ciphertext and associated data that result in $\mathcal{D}$ outputting $\perp$ are called *invalid*.

The encryption and decryption states are always initialized to ε. For either of $\mathcal{E}$ or $\mathcal{D}$, we say that it is a stateless algorithm if for all inputs in $\mathcal{K} \times \{0,1\}^* \times \{0,1\}^* \times \{\varepsilon\}$ the returned updated state is always ε. The scheme Π is said to be stateless if both $\mathcal{E}$ and $\mathcal{D}$ are stateless. We require that for any $M \in \mathcal{M}$ and any $A \in \mathcal{AD}$ it holds that $\{0,1\}^{|M|} \subseteq \mathcal{M}$ and $\{0,1\}^{|A|} \subseteq \mathcal{AD}$.

For any symmetric encryption scheme $\Pi = (\mathcal{K}, \mathcal{E}, \mathcal{D})$, any $\ell \in \mathbb{N}$, any vector $\mathbf{M} = [M_1, \ldots, M_\ell] \in \mathcal{M}^\ell$ and any vector $\mathbf{A} = [A_1, \ldots, A_\ell] \in \mathcal{AD}^\ell$, we write $(\mathbf{C}, \sigma_\ell) \leftarrow \mathcal{E}_K(\mathbf{M}, \mathbf{A}, \varepsilon)$ as shorthand for:

$$(C_1, \sigma_1) \leftarrow \mathcal{E}_K(M_1, A_1, \varepsilon); \ \ldots; \ (C_\ell, \sigma_\ell) \leftarrow \mathcal{E}_K(M_\ell, A_\ell, \sigma_{\ell-1}),$$

where $\mathbf{C} = [C_1, \ldots, C_\ell]$. Similarly we write $(\mathbf{M}', \varrho_\ell) \leftarrow \mathcal{D}_K(\mathbf{C}, \mathbf{A}, \varepsilon)$ to denote the analogous process for decryption.

Definition 1 (Correctness [4]). *A symmetric encryption scheme Π is said to be (q, δ)-correct if for all $\ell \leq q$, all $\mathbf{M} \in \mathcal{M}^\ell$ and all $\mathbf{A} \in \mathcal{AD}^\ell$, it holds that:*

$$\Pr[\, K \leftarrow_\$ \mathcal{K}; (\mathbf{C}, \sigma_\ell) \leftarrow \mathcal{E}_K(\mathbf{M}, \mathbf{A}, \varepsilon); (\mathbf{M}', \varrho_\ell) \leftarrow \mathcal{D}_K(\mathbf{C}, \mathbf{A}, \varepsilon) : \mathbf{M} \neq \mathbf{M}' \,] \leq \delta.$$

Schemes that achieve correctness with $\delta = 0$ for all $q \in \mathbb{N}$ are said to be perfectly correct.

Game IND-CPA$_\Pi^{\mathscr{A}}$	ENC(M_0, M_1, A)
$b \leftarrow_\$ \{0,1\}$	if $|M_0| \neq |M_1|$ then return $\perp$
$\sigma \leftarrow \varepsilon; K \leftarrow_\$ \mathcal{K}$	$(C, \sigma) \leftarrow \mathcal{E}(K, M_b, A, \sigma)$
$b' \leftarrow \mathscr{A}^{\text{ENC}}$	return C
return $(b = b')$	

Fig. 1. Game defining the IND-CPA security of scheme Π against $\mathscr{A}$.

We now recall the standard IND-CPA security notion for symmetric encryption [3].

Definition 2 (Privacy). *Let* $\Pi = (\mathcal{K}, \mathcal{E}, \mathcal{D})$ *be a symmetric encryption scheme and let* $\mathscr{A}$ *be an adversary. Consider the game* IND-CPA$_\Pi^{\mathscr{A}}$ *depicted in Fig. 1. The adversary's advantage is defined as*

$$\mathbf{Adv}_\Pi^{\text{ind-cpa}}(\mathscr{A}) := 2 \cdot \Pr\left[\, \text{IND-CPA}_\Pi^{\mathscr{A}} \,\right] - 1 \,.$$

The scheme Π *is said to be* ϵ-*private if for every practical adversary* $\mathscr{A}$ *its advantage* $\mathbf{Adv}_\Pi^{\text{ind-cpa}}(\mathscr{A})$ *is bounded by* ϵ.

Intuitively, when ϵ is sufficiently small we may simply say that Π is IND-CPA secure.

3   Algorithm Substitution Attacks

In an algorithm substitution attack (ASA), big brother is able to covertly replace the code of an encryption algorithm $\mathcal{E}(K, \ldots)$ (forming part of some wider protocol) with the subverted encryption algorithm $\widetilde{\mathcal{E}}(\widetilde{K}, K, \ldots)$. Here, $\widetilde{\mathcal{E}}$ takes the same inputs as $\mathcal{E}$ together with a subversion key $\widetilde{K}$ which is assumed to be embedded in the code in an obfuscated manner, and hence is inaccessible to users. Intuitively, the subversion key significantly improves big brother's ability to leak information via the ciphertexts without being detected. For instance, it can use $\widetilde{K}$ to encrypt a user's key and use the result as a random-looking IV in the ciphertext. Big brother can later intercept this ciphertext, recover the user's key from the IV, and use it to decrypt the rest of the ciphertexts. In addition allow the operations of $\widetilde{\mathcal{E}}$ to depend on user-specific identification parameter i.

Note that when considering ASAs the concern is not about whether the real encryption scheme contains a backdoor, possibly due to an obscurely generated set of parameters. In fact an inherent assumption in the setting proposed in [4], and in this paper, is that the real encryption scheme $\mathcal{E}$ achieves the required level of security and in particular is free from backdoors. Instead, the question being asked is whether an *implementation* of the real scheme, possibly obfuscated, contains a backdoor and under what circumstances this can be detected.

SUBVERSIONS. For any symmetric encryption scheme $\Pi = (\mathcal{K}, \mathcal{E}, \mathcal{D})$ its subversion is a pair $\widetilde{\Pi} = (\widetilde{\mathcal{K}}, \widetilde{\mathcal{E}})$. The *subversion key space* $\widetilde{\mathcal{K}}$ is a finite non-empty set. The *subverted encryption algorithm* $\widetilde{\mathcal{E}}$ may be randomized, stateful, or both. It takes as input a subversion key $\widetilde{K} \in \widetilde{\mathcal{K}}$, a user's secret key $K \in \mathcal{K}$, a message $M \in \{0,1\}^*$, an associated data string $A \in \{0,1\}^*$, an encryption state σ, and a user identifier i, to return a ciphertext C or the special symbol $\perp$, together with an updated state. The user identifier is considered a public value such as an IP or MAC address unique to each key K; the precise value of i does not matter—it is merely used to label users.

In order for the subversion to be of any use to big brother, there must exist some associated *plaintext-recovery algorithm* which uses the subversion key to recover information from the ciphertexts. In [4] this algorithm was denoted by $\widetilde{\mathcal{D}}$. Its success in recovering the corresponding plaintexts may vary in a number of ways. From the users' standpoint we only concern ourselves to bound this success probability by a small quantity. This is dealt with in the security definitions where any such plaintext-recovery algorithm is implicit in the adversary modeling big brother.

3.1 The Bellare–Paterson–Rogaway Security Model

Bellare, Paterson and Rogaway (BPR) [4] formulate security against ASAs as follows. In addition to the standard security requirements for symmetric encryption they consider two new notions, namely *undetectability* and *surveillance* defined respectively using the DETECT and SURV games shown in Fig. 2.

In DETECT an algorithm $\mathcal{U}$, representing a detection test, is required to distinguish $\mathcal{E}$ from $\widetilde{\mathcal{E}}_{\widetilde{K}}$ when given oracle access to one of these two algorithms. More specifically, a bit b and a subversion key $\widetilde{K}$ are first sampled and $\mathcal{U}$ is then given access to two oracles, KEY and ENC. The game models a multi-user setting and the KEY oracle serves to let user i create a secret key. The ENC oracle takes a message M, associated data A, and a user identifier i and depending on the value of b it returns an encryption under either $\mathcal{E}$ or $\widetilde{\mathcal{E}}_{\widetilde{K}}$. The game ends when $\mathcal{U}$ halts and outputs a bit b' as its guess of bit b. The corresponding advantage is defined as:

$$\mathbf{Adv}_{\Pi, \widetilde{\Pi}}^{\mathrm{det}}(\mathcal{U}) := 2 \cdot \Pr\left[\mathrm{DETECT}_{\Pi, \widetilde{\Pi}}^{\mathcal{U}} \right] - 1.$$

In SURV an adversary $\mathcal{B}$, who does not have access to the users' secret keys but knows the subversion key, is required to distinguish $\mathcal{E}$ from $\widetilde{\mathcal{E}}_{\widetilde{K}}$ when given oracle access to one of these algorithms. The game proceeds by first sampling a bit b and a subversion key $\widetilde{K}$, and then $\mathcal{B}$ is given access to $\widetilde{K}$ and two oracles, KEY and ENC. Oracle KEY only serves to initialize a secret key for specified user i and does not return any value. The ENC oracle takes a message M, associated data A, and a user identifier i, and depending on the value of b it returns an encryption under either $\mathcal{E}$ or $\widetilde{\mathcal{E}}_{\widetilde{K}}$. The game ends when $\mathcal{B}$ halts and outputs a bit b' as its guess of bit b. The corresponding advantage is defined as:

$$\mathbf{Adv}_{\Pi, \widetilde{\Pi}}^{\mathrm{srv}}(\mathcal{B}) := 2 \cdot \Pr\left[\mathrm{SURV}_{\Pi, \widetilde{\Pi}}^{\mathcal{B}} \right] - 1.$$

Game $\text{DETECT}^{\mathscr{U}}_{\Pi,\widetilde{\Pi}}$	Game $\text{SURV}^{\mathscr{B}}_{\Pi,\widetilde{\Pi}}$
$b \leftarrow_\$ \{0,1\}; \widetilde{K} \leftarrow_\$ \widetilde{\mathcal{K}}; b' \leftarrow \mathscr{U}^{\text{KEY,ENC}}$ return $(b = b')$	$b \leftarrow_\$ \{0,1\}; \widetilde{K} \leftarrow_\$ \widetilde{\mathcal{K}}; b' \leftarrow \mathscr{B}^{\text{KEY,ENC}}(\widetilde{K})$ return $(b = b')$
$\underline{\text{KEY}(i)}$	$\underline{\text{KEY}(i)}$
if $K_i = \bot$ then $K_i \leftarrow_\$ \mathcal{K}; \sigma_i \leftarrow \varepsilon$ return K_i	if $K_i = \bot$ then $K_i \leftarrow_\$ \mathcal{K}; \sigma_i \leftarrow \varepsilon$ return ε
$\underline{\text{ENC}(M, A, i)}$	$\underline{\text{ENC}(M, A, i)}$
if $K_i = \bot$ then return $\bot$ if $b = 1$ then $(C, \sigma_i) \leftarrow \mathcal{E}(K_i, M, A, \sigma_i)$ else $(C, \sigma_i) \leftarrow \widetilde{\mathcal{E}}(\widetilde{K}, K_i, M, A, \sigma_i, i)$ return C	if $K_i = \bot$ then return $\bot$ if $b = 1$ then $(C, \sigma_i) \leftarrow \mathcal{E}(K_i, M, A, \sigma_i)$ else $(C, \sigma_i) \leftarrow \widetilde{\mathcal{E}}(\widetilde{K}, K_i, M, A, \sigma_i, i)$ return C

Fig. 2. The DETECT and SURV games from the BPR security model of [4].

In addition to the above two notions, BPR specify the following *decryptability* condition.

Definition 3 (Decryptability). *A subversion* $\widetilde{\Pi} = (\widetilde{\mathcal{K}}, \widetilde{\mathcal{E}})$ *is said to satisfy* (q, δ)-*decryptability with respect to the scheme* $\Pi = (\mathcal{K}, \mathcal{E}, \mathcal{D})$ *if symmetric encryption scheme* $(\widetilde{\mathcal{K}} \times \mathcal{K}, \widetilde{\mathcal{E}}, \mathcal{D}')$ *where* $\mathcal{D}'((\widetilde{K}, K), C, A, \varrho) := \mathcal{D}(K, C, A, \varrho)$ *is* (q, δ)-*correct (for all choices of inputs* i *to* $\widetilde{\mathcal{E}}$).

If $\widetilde{\Pi}$ is $(q, 0)$-decryptable with respect to Π for all $q \in \mathbb{N}$, it is said to be perfectly decryptable. We highlight that BPR requires that any subversion satisfies perfect decryptability. For reasons that will become apparent later we chose to distinguish between (q, δ)-decryptability and perfect decryptability. However BPR do not make this distinction and use the term decryptability to mean perfect decryptability.

OBSERVATIONS. The first thing to note is that the DETECT game is formulated from big brother's point of view who wants his subversion to remain undetected. The notion it yields is that of *undetectability*, and in [4] it is used only for proving *negative* results. For instance BPR use this to show that any randomized encryption scheme can be subverted in an undetectable manner. Concretely, for any randomized scheme Π that uses sufficient amount of randomness there exists a subversion $\widetilde{\Pi}$ such that for all efficient detection tests $\mathscr{U}$ the advantage $\mathbf{Adv}^{\text{det}}_{\Pi,\widetilde{\Pi}}(\mathscr{U})$ is small. Moreover, the subversion $\widetilde{\Pi}$ allows big brother to completely recover the user's key K with overwhelming probability.

Security against surveillance is defined through the SURV game. The requirement here is that big brother, who knows the subversion key $\widetilde{K}$, is unable to tell whether ciphertexts are being produced by the real encryption algorithm $\mathcal{E}$ or the subverted encryption algorithm $\widetilde{\mathcal{E}}_{\widetilde{K}}$. This implicitly ensures that if the real scheme is IND-CPA secure then the subverted scheme still does not reveal to big brother anything about the plaintext. Clearly, without any further restriction on

$\widetilde{\Pi}$ surveillance resilience is not attainable, since for any scheme Π there always exists a trivial subversion $\widetilde{\Pi}$ and an adversary $\mathscr{B}$ which can distinguish the two. (Consider for example the subversion which appends a redundant zero bit to the ciphertexts.) Hence some resistance to detection should hold simultaneously. This is imposed by means of the decryptability condition. More formally, (in [4]) an encryption scheme Π is said to be surveillance secure if for all subversions $\widetilde{\Pi}$ that are perfectly decryptable with respect to Π and all adversaries $\mathscr{B}$ with reasonable resources its advantage $\mathbf{Adv}_{\Pi,\widetilde{\Pi}}^{\mathrm{srv}}(\mathscr{B})$ is small.

3.2 Critique

In [4], although decryptability is formulated as a correctness requirement, it is really used as a notion of *undetectability*. More precisely, it is understood to be the weakest notion of undetectability that big brother can aim for, and failure to meet this notion would certainly lead to his subversion being discovered. In fact, BPR write [4, p. 6].

> This represents the most basic form of resistance to detection, and we will assume any subversion must meet it.

On the other hand the undetectability notion associated to the DETECT game is meant to be a much stronger one. Another excerpt reads [4, p. 7]

> A subversion $\widetilde{\Pi}$ in which this advantage [that is, $\mathbf{Adv}_{\Pi,\widetilde{\Pi}}^{\mathrm{det}}(\mathscr{U})$] is negligible for all practical tests $\mathscr{U}$ is said to be *undetectable* and would be one that evades detection in a powerful way. If such a subversion permitted plaintext recovery, big brother would consider it a very successful one.

This all seems to imply that for any subversion, decryptability is a necessary requirement to avoid detection, and that undetectability is sufficient to yield a strong guarantee of avoiding detection. It is hence natural to expect that undetectability implies decryptability, but as the authors of [4] admit this is not the case. The two notions are in fact incomparable. This is a source of inconsistency, especially when considering that the negative and positive results in [4] are established using measures of undetectability that are incomparable.

The main reason for this discord between decryptability and undetectability is that undetectability allows detection test $\mathscr{U}$ to succeed with negligible probability, whereas (perfect) decryptability requires the test's success probability to be exactly zero. This is unnecessarily strict, as detection tests which succeed only with negligible probability are insignificant and pose no effective threat to big brother. Accordingly it is unrealistic to assume that big brother will only produce subversions that satisfy *perfect* decryptability. Requiring the latter imposes an unnatural restriction on big brother's potential subversion strategies, thereby unjustifiably weakening the security notion.

It would seem that both of the above issues could be easily addressed (at least in part) by letting decryptability admit a small negligible error, that is

$$\text{Algorithm } \widetilde{\mathcal{E}}_{\widetilde{K}}(K, M, A, \sigma, i)$$

$(C, \sigma) \leftarrow \mathcal{E}(K, M, A, \sigma)$
if $\mathbf{R}(\widetilde{K}, K, M, A, \sigma, i) = \mathsf{true}$
  then return $(C \parallel K, \sigma)$
else return (C, σ)

Fig. 3. The encryption algorithm of the subversion $\widetilde{\Pi}$ used in Theorem 1.

requiring (q, δ)-decryptability, for some small δ, instead of perfect decryptability. In particular, one could hope that decryptability would then be implied by undetectability. Unfortunately the situation is not that simple, and a new problem arises. As we demonstrate next, this minor alteration would render the BPR security notion *unsatisfiable* by any symmetric encryption scheme with a reasonably large message space (e.g., if $|\mathcal{M}| \geq |\mathcal{K}|$). More specifically, for any symmetric encryption scheme we can construct a subversion that not only is (q, δ)-decryptable (with negligible δ for any reasonable value q) but is in fact undetectable, and yet there always exists an adversary $\mathcal{B}$ capable of subverting the scheme. This serves to show that the BPR security definition crucially relies on the presupposition that all subversions must satisfy perfect decryptability, and is consequently a rather fragile security definition.

Theorem 1. *Consider a $(1, \delta)$-correct and ϵ-private symmetric encryption scheme $\Pi = (\mathcal{K}, \mathcal{E}, \mathcal{D})$ with message space $\mathcal{M}$ such that $\{0, 1\}^\lambda \subseteq \mathcal{M}$ for some λ (for instance, $\lambda = 128$). For any such scheme there exists a subversion $\widetilde{\Pi} = (\widetilde{\mathcal{K}}, \widetilde{\mathcal{E}})$ that satisfies $(q, q \cdot 2^{-\lambda} + \delta)$-decryptability with respect to Π and $\mathbf{Adv}_{\Pi, \widetilde{\Pi}}^{\mathrm{det}}(\mathcal{U}) \leq q \cdot 2^{-\lambda}$ for all practical detection tests $\mathcal{U}$ making at most q encryption queries. Moreover there exists a corresponding adversary $\mathcal{B}$ such that $\mathbf{Adv}_{\Pi, \widetilde{\Pi}}^{\mathrm{srv}}(\mathcal{B}) \geq 1 - (\epsilon + \delta + 2^{-\lambda})$.*

Proof. The subversion $\widetilde{\Pi} = (\widetilde{\mathcal{K}}, \widetilde{\mathcal{E}})$ is defined by letting $\widetilde{\mathcal{K}} := \{0, 1\}^\lambda$ and $\widetilde{\mathcal{E}}$ be the algorithm depicted in Fig. 3. The predicate $\mathbf{R}(\widetilde{K}, K, M, A, \sigma, i)$ that is used in $\widetilde{\mathcal{E}}$ takes the boolean value true for all tuples where $\widetilde{K} = M$ and the value false otherwise. Hence note that for all inputs where $\widetilde{K} \neq M$ the subverted encryption algorithm $\widetilde{\mathcal{E}}_{\widetilde{K}}$ behaves exactly like the real encryption algorithm $\mathcal{E}$. Let E denote the event that for some $1 \leq j \leq \ell$ it holds that $\widetilde{K} = \mathbf{M}[j]$. Then for all $1 \leq \ell \leq q$ and all message vectors $\mathbf{M} \in \mathcal{M}^\ell$ we have

$$\Pr\left[(\widetilde{K}, K) \leftarrow_{\$} \widetilde{\mathcal{K}} \times \mathcal{K}; (\mathbf{C}, \sigma_\ell) \leftarrow \mathcal{E}_K(\mathbf{M}, \mathbf{A}, \varepsilon); (\mathbf{M}', \varrho_\ell) \leftarrow \mathcal{D}_K(\mathbf{C}, \mathbf{A}, \varepsilon) : \mathbf{M} \neq \mathbf{M}'\right]$$

$$\leq \Pr\left[(\widetilde{K}, K) \leftarrow_{\$} \widetilde{\mathcal{K}} \times \mathcal{K} \mid E\right] + \Pr\Big[(\widetilde{K}, K) \leftarrow_{\$} \widetilde{\mathcal{K}} \times \mathcal{K};$$

$$(\mathbf{C}, \sigma_\ell) \leftarrow \mathcal{E}_K(\mathbf{M}, \mathbf{A}, \varepsilon); (\mathbf{M}', \varrho_\ell) \leftarrow \mathcal{D}_K(\mathbf{C}, \mathbf{A}, \varepsilon) : \mathbf{M} \neq \mathbf{M}' \mid \overline{E}\Big]$$

$$\leq q \cdot 2^{-\lambda} + \delta,$$

where the bound on the second term follows from the δ-correctness of Π. Hence $\widetilde{\Pi}$ satisfies $(q, q \cdot 2^{-\lambda} + \delta)$-decryptability with respect to Π. Since $\mathcal{U}$ is not given any information about $\widetilde{K}$, it is easy to see that for any (even computationally unbounded) detection test $\mathcal{U}$ making at most q queries its advantage $\mathbf{Adv}^{\mathrm{det}}_{\Pi, \widetilde{\Pi}}(\mathcal{U})$ is bounded by $q \cdot 2^{-\lambda}$.

The adversary $\mathcal{B}$, which knows the subversion key, simply queries the pair $(\widetilde{K}, A)$ to its encryption oracle for some $A \in \mathcal{AD}$, and gets in return a ciphertext C^*. It then attempts to parse C^* as $C \parallel K$ and checks whether $\widetilde{K} = \mathcal{D}_K(C, A, \varepsilon)$. If this test succeeds it outputs 0 and otherwise it outputs 1. Note that when the encryption oracle is instantiated with the subversion ($b = 0$), the adversary is guaranteed to guess correctly, i.e., outputs 0, with probability $1 - \delta$ by the correctness of Π. Alternatively when the oracle is instantiated with the real scheme ($b = 1$), it can be shown that the decryption test that $\mathcal{B}$ runs on C^* cannot succeed with probability higher than $\epsilon + 2^{-\lambda}$. Hence, the probability of $\mathcal{B}$ outputting 0 when $b = 1$ is also bounded by this amount. Letting b' denote $\mathcal{B}$'s output and combining the above we have that

$$\mathbf{Adv}^{\mathrm{srv}}_{\Pi, \widetilde{\Pi}}(\mathcal{B}) = \Pr[\,b' = 0 \mid b = 0\,] - \Pr[\,b' = 0 \mid b = 1\,] \qquad (1)$$
$$\geq 1 - \delta - \epsilon - 2^{-\lambda},$$

as desired. It only remains to prove the bound on the second term of Eq. (1). We establish the bound by reducing $\mathcal{B}$ to an IND-CPA adversary $\mathcal{A}$ against Π. The adversary $\mathcal{A}$ starts by picking a subversion key $\widetilde{K}$ uniformly at random and then runs $\mathcal{B}$ on input $\widetilde{K}$. When $\mathcal{B}$ makes its first encryption query (M_0, A), where $M_0 = \widetilde{K}$, $\mathcal{A}$ will sample uniformly at random a second message M_1 of equal length. Then $\mathcal{A}$ submits (M_0, M_1, A) to its own oracle and forwards the ciphertext C^* that the oracle returns to $\mathcal{B}$. At this point $\mathcal{B}$ will halt and $\mathcal{A}$ outputs whatever $\mathcal{B}$ outputs, which we denote by b'. Let d denote the bit in the IND-CPA game indicating which message is being encrypted, then

$$\mathbf{Adv}^{\mathrm{ind-cpa}}_{\Pi}(\mathcal{A}) = 2\Pr[\mathrm{IND\text{-}CPA}^{\mathcal{A}}_{\Pi}] - 1$$
$$= \Pr[\,b' = 0 \mid d = 0\,] - \Pr[\,b' = 0 \mid d = 1\,] \leq \epsilon. \qquad (2)$$

Now note that when C^* corresponds to an encryption of (M_0, A), i.e., $d = 0$, $\mathcal{B}$ gets a perfect simulation of the SURV game with b set to 1. Thus

$$\Pr[\,b' = 0 \mid d = 0\,] = \Pr[\,b' = 0 \mid b = 1\,]. \qquad (3)$$

On the other hand when $d = 1$ the ciphertext C^* is independent of M_0, and hence the decryption test that $\mathcal{B}$ runs cannot be better than guessing the value M_0. Therefore

$$\Pr[\,b' = 0 \mid d = 1\,] \leq 2^{-\lambda}. \qquad (4)$$

Combining Eqs. (2), (3) and (4) we get the desired bound:

$$\Pr[\,b' = 0 \mid b = 1\,] \leq \epsilon + 2^{-\lambda}.$$

INPUT-TRIGGERED SUBVERSIONS. We emphasize that the above subversion applies generically to any practically relevant symmetric encryption scheme, irrespective of whether it is probabilistic or deterministic and whether it maintains a state or not. Additionally, while we present the subversion of Fig. 3 merely as a component of Theorem 1, it actually embodies a powerful subversion strategy[1] for mounting ASAs that are hard to detect. The underlying principle is that a subversion leaks information to big brother only when receiving specific inputs. That is, in order for big brother to exploit his subversion and undermine the privacy of the communication, a trigger needs to be set. On the other hand, without knowledge of this trigger it is practically impossible to distinguish the subversion from the real scheme. In our case the trigger is the set of inputs for which the predicate **R** holds. In practice, **R** can depend on any information that the subverted encryption algorithm may have access to, such as an IP address, a username, or some location information. Such information, in particular network addresses and routing information, can be readily available in the associated data. It is not unreasonable, and is in fact in conformance with the usual approach adopted in cryptography, to assume that big brother may be capable of influencing this information when it needs to intercept a communication. We hence see no basis for excluding such attacks from consideration.

SECURITY GUARANTEES. BPR start from the premise that surveillance security is not possible without requiring some resistance to detection, and they address this by requiring that all subversions satisfy perfect decryptability. Indeed, it seems that the only way of protecting against ASAs is to have a mechanism to detect such attacks. Accordingly, an encryption scheme should be deemed surveillance secure if we have a sufficiently good chance of detecting subversions of that scheme. However, the BPR security notion gives only a very weak guarantee of detecting ASAs. More specifically, we are only guaranteed to detect a subversion with non-zero probability, regardless of how small that may be. In particular, if for a specific scheme there exist subversions which can all be detected with non-zero but only negligible probability, then in the BPR security model this scheme is considered subversion secure. It should be evident however that such a scheme offers no significant resistance to subversion in practice.

Another shortcoming of relying on decryptability as a means of detection is that it does not clearly state what tests one ought to do in order to detect a subversion. Decryption failures may happen for other reasons, and if they occur sporadically they may easily go unnoticed. Secondly, it may not suffice to rely on the decryption algorithm at the receiver's end. For instance, if ciphertexts contain additional information that big brother can exploit but which would result in a decryption failure, big brother could rectify this at the point of interception after having recovered the information he needs. Alternatively big brother may have replaced the decryption algorithm with one that can handle ciphertexts from the subverted encryption algorithm without raising any exceptions. While for an open system like TLS [7] it may be reasonable to assume that big

---

[1] This is akin to a trapdoor. It is a classic technique in computer security to introduce trapdoors in various objects and we certainly do not claim to be the first to do so.

brother is unable to mount an ASA on all of its implementations, on a closed system[2] there is no reason to assume big brother is not able to substitute both the encryption and decryption algorithms.

4   The Proposed Security Model

The analysis of Sect. 3.2 leaves us with an unsatisfactory state of affairs. On the one hand we wish for a more realistic security model, devoid of the perfect decryptability condition. On the other hand we saw that this would allow input-triggered subversions which are generically applicable to any symmetric encryption scheme. This in turn raises the question of whether we have any hope at all of protecting against ASAs. We address these questions by proposing an alternative security model which builds on the ideas of Bellare, Paterson and Rogaway [4].

Our premise is that input-triggered subversions cannot be detected with significant probability through a one-time test, as in the DETECT game. Instead, it seems that the best we can hope for is to detect information leakage from the encryption algorithm from a recorded communication session. That is we are unable to determine whether the encryption algorithm has been substituted or not, since without knowledge of the trigger we have very little chance of detecting this. However we may be able to detect whether big brother is exploiting the subversion and is able to gather information from it, which is what we really care about.

Our approach is to take into consideration all possible subversions that big brother may come up with, without imposing any additional conditions that a subversion must satisfy. Instead we identify a scheme to be subversion resistant, if for all of its possible subversions it is the case that either the subversion leaks no information to big brother, or if it does leak information then we can detect it with high probability. We formalize this by means of a second pair of games $\overline{\text{DETECT}}$ and $\overline{\text{SURV}}$. The game $\overline{\text{SURV}}$ is a single-user version of the SURV game from [4], and can be shown to be equivalent, through a standard hybrid argument, up to a factor equal to the number of users. This serves to specify formally what we intuitively referred to as 'leaking information to big brother'. The $\overline{\text{DETECT}}$ game, on the other hand, differs substantially form the DETECT game of the BPR security model. Most importantly, it is intended for specifying a notion of *detectability* rather than *un*detectability. In $\overline{\text{DETECT}}$, the detection test $\mathscr{U}$ does not get access to an encryption oracle, instead it only gets a transcript of $\mathscr{B}$'s queries to its own oracle. The effectiveness of the detection test $\mathscr{U}$ is quantified by comparing its success in guessing the challenge bit to that of $\mathscr{B}$. This is specified more formally below.

More precisely, the surveillance game starts by picking a bit b uniformly at random, and then generating keys K and $\widetilde{K}$. The adversary is then given access to the subversion key and an encryption oracle but not the key K. Depending on

---

[2] This could be some proprietary application/protocol, for which there exists only one implementation, but which uses a standard (non-proprietary) encryption scheme.

the bit's value the encryption oracle will either return encryptions under scheme Π and the user's key K or encryptions under the subverted scheme (which has access to both keys). The adversary outputs a bit b' as its guess of the challenge bit b. See Fig. 4 (right) for the details. The detection game is an extension of the surveillance game. First $\mathscr{B}$ is run in the same manner as in the surveillance game and a transcript T of its encryption queries is kept. The detection algorithm $\mathscr{U}$ is then given access to this transcript and the user's key. Its goal is to output a bit b'' as its guess of the challenge bit b. See Fig. 4 (left) for the details.

Definition 4 (Subversion resistance). *Let* $\Pi = (\mathcal{K}, \mathcal{E}, \mathcal{D})$ *be an encryption scheme and let* $\widetilde{\Pi} = (\widetilde{\mathcal{K}}, \widetilde{\mathcal{E}})$ *be a subversion of it. For an adversary* $\mathscr{B}$ *and a detection algorithm* $\mathscr{U}$, *define the games* $\overline{\mathrm{SURV}}_{\Pi,\widetilde{\Pi}}^{\mathscr{B}}$ *and* $\overline{\mathrm{DETECT}}_{\Pi,\widetilde{\Pi}}^{\mathscr{B},\mathscr{U}}$ *as depicted in Fig. 4. The surveillance advantage of an adversary* $\mathscr{B}$ *is given by:*

$$\mathbf{Adv}_{\Pi,\widetilde{\Pi}}^{\overline{\mathrm{srv}}}(\mathscr{B}) := 2 \cdot \Pr\left[\overline{\mathrm{SURV}}_{\Pi,\widetilde{\Pi}}^{\mathscr{B}}\right] - 1.$$

The detection advantage of $\mathscr{U}$ *with respect to* $\mathscr{B}$ *is given by:*

$$\mathbf{Adv}_{\Pi,\widetilde{\Pi}}^{\overline{\mathrm{det}}}(\mathscr{B}, \mathscr{U}) := 2 \cdot \Pr\left[\overline{\mathrm{DETECT}}_{\Pi,\widetilde{\Pi}}^{\mathscr{B},\mathscr{U}}\right] - 1.$$

Let $\delta, \epsilon \in [0,1]$. *A pair of algorithms* $(\mathscr{B}, \widetilde{\Pi})$ *is said to be* δ-undetectable with respect to $\mathscr{U}$ *if* $\mathbf{Adv}_{\Pi,\widetilde{\Pi}}^{\overline{\mathrm{det}}}(\mathscr{B}, \mathscr{U}) \leq \delta$. *A pair of algorithms* $(\mathscr{B}, \widetilde{\Pi})$ *is said to be* ϵ-unsubverting if $\mathbf{Adv}_{\Pi,\widetilde{\Pi}}^{\overline{\mathrm{srv}}}(\mathscr{B}) \leq \epsilon$. *A scheme* Π *is said to be* (δ, ϵ)-subversion

Game $\overline{\mathrm{DETECT}}_{\Pi,\widetilde{\Pi}}^{\mathscr{B},\mathscr{U}}$	Game $\overline{\mathrm{SURV}}_{\Pi,\widetilde{\Pi}}^{\mathscr{B}}$
$b \leftarrow\!\!{\scriptstyle\$}\ \{0,1\}; \widetilde{K} \leftarrow\!\!{\scriptstyle\$}\ \widetilde{\mathcal{K}}$ $b' \leftarrow \mathscr{B}^{\mathrm{KEY},\mathrm{ENC}}(\widetilde{K}); b'' \leftarrow \mathscr{U}(T)$ return $(b = b'')$	$b \leftarrow\!\!{\scriptstyle\$}\ \{0,1\}; \widetilde{K} \leftarrow\!\!{\scriptstyle\$}\ \widetilde{\mathcal{K}}$ $b' \leftarrow \mathscr{B}^{\mathrm{KEY},\mathrm{ENC}}(\widetilde{K})$ return $(b = b')$
$\underline{\mathrm{KEY}(i)}$ // called at most once if $K_i = \perp$ then $K_i \leftarrow\!\!{\scriptstyle\$}\ \mathcal{K}; \sigma_i \leftarrow \varepsilon$ $T \leftarrow (K_i, i)$ return ε	$\underline{\mathrm{KEY}(i)}$ // called at most once if $K_i = \perp$ then $K_i \leftarrow\!\!{\scriptstyle\$}\ \mathcal{K}; \sigma_i \leftarrow \varepsilon$ return ε
$\underline{\mathrm{ENC}(M, A, i)}$ if $K_i = \perp$ then return $\perp$ if $b = 1$ then $(C, \sigma_i) \leftarrow \mathcal{E}(K_i, M, A, \sigma_i)$ else $(C, \sigma_i) \leftarrow \widetilde{\mathcal{E}}(\widetilde{K}, K_i, M, A, \sigma_i, i)$ $T \leftarrow T \parallel (M, A, C)$ return C	$\underline{\mathrm{ENC}(M, A, i)}$ if $K_i = \perp$ then return $\perp$ if $b = 1$ then $(C, \sigma_i) \leftarrow \mathcal{E}(K_i, M, A, \sigma_i)$ else $(C, \sigma_i) \leftarrow \widetilde{\mathcal{E}}(\widetilde{K}, K_i, M, A, \sigma_i, i)$ return C

Fig. 4. Games defining the refined single-user security models. Big brother $\mathscr{B}$ can only call the KEY oracle once.

resistant if there is an efficient algorithm $\mathcal{U}$ such that any δ-undetectable $(\mathcal{B}, \widetilde{\Pi})$ is ϵ-unsubverting:

$$\exists \mathcal{U} \; \forall (\mathcal{B}, \widetilde{\Pi}) : \mathbf{Adv}_{\Pi,\widetilde{\Pi}}^{\overline{\det}}(\mathcal{B}, \mathcal{U}) \leq \delta \implies \mathbf{Adv}_{\Pi,\widetilde{\Pi}}^{\overline{\mathrm{srv}}}(\mathcal{B}) \leq \epsilon \,.$$

We say Π is ϵ-subversion resistant iff it is (ϵ, ϵ)-subversion resistant, and that it is subversion resistant iff it is ϵ-subversion resistant for all $\epsilon \in [0, 1]$. Subversion resistance can be equivalently written as

$$\exists \mathcal{U} \; \forall (\mathcal{B}, \widetilde{\Pi}) : \mathbf{Adv}_{\Pi,\widetilde{\Pi}}^{\overline{\mathrm{srv}}}(\mathcal{B}) \leq \mathbf{Adv}_{\Pi,\widetilde{\Pi}}^{\overline{\det}}(\mathcal{B}, \mathcal{U}) \,.$$

Note that a (δ, ϵ)-subversion-resistant scheme is also (δ', ϵ')-subversion resistant if $\delta' \leq \delta$ and $\epsilon' \geq \epsilon$. Furthermore, no scheme can be (δ, ϵ)-subversion resistant for any (δ, ϵ) with $\delta > \epsilon$. Indeed, given such a (δ, ϵ)-subversion-resistant scheme Π and a corresponding detector $\mathcal{U}$ we build a pair $(\widetilde{\Pi}, \mathcal{B})$ such that

$$\mathbf{Adv}_{\Pi,\widetilde{\Pi}}^{\overline{\mathrm{srv}}}(\mathcal{B}) > \epsilon \,,$$

thereby reaching a contradiction. Consider the subverted encryption $\widetilde{\mathcal{E}}_\delta$ which with probability δ runs $\mathcal{E}$ and with probability $(1 - \delta)$ returns a special message $\perp$. Algorithm $\mathcal{B}$ asks for an encryption of a fixed message to get C and returns $(C = \perp)$. Clearly $\mathcal{B}$'s advantage is $\delta > \epsilon$, as required.

This analysis shows that (ϵ, ϵ)-subversion resistance, that is, ϵ-subversion resistance in the terminology of the definition, is the best one can hope for. Note, however, that ϵ-subversion resistance does *not* immediately imply ϵ'-subversion resistance for any $\epsilon' \neq \epsilon$; we would need to have both $\epsilon' \geq \epsilon$ and $\epsilon' \leq \epsilon$. The absolute (that is, non-parameterized) definition of subversion resistance requires all these (potentially incomparable) security measures to hold simultaneously. A corollary of such a statement is that a subversion-resistant scheme is (δ, ϵ)-subversion resistant for all possible values of (δ, ϵ) with $\delta \leq \epsilon$.

For the equivalence of the two formulations of (absolute) subversion resistance observe that the implication in one direction is trivial and in the other follows by taking any

$$\epsilon \in \left(\mathbf{Adv}_{\Pi,\widetilde{\Pi}}^{\overline{\det}}(\mathcal{B}, \mathcal{U}), \mathbf{Adv}_{\Pi,\widetilde{\Pi}}^{\overline{\mathrm{srv}}}(\mathcal{B}) \right]$$

for a contradiction. In a sense, the $\widetilde{\mathcal{E}}_\delta$ subversion above is the best that $\mathcal{B}$ can carry out against subversion-resistant schemes as the final inequality in the definition is sharp for the best possible $\mathcal{U}$ against $\widetilde{\mathcal{E}}_\delta$ and $\mathcal{B}$.

DEFINITIONAL CHOICES. A number of choices have been made in devising the new security definition. Observe that our surveillance game is identical to the single-user version of BPR's original surveillance game in Fig. 2.[3] In particular, it allows big brother to launch $\widetilde{K}$-dependent chosen-plaintext attacks. Our

---

[3] The single-user and multi-user games can be shown equivalent via a standard hybrid argument [4]. Since our detection procedure is also in the single-user setting, we have adopted a single-user surveillance game as well. This choice also translates to a more faithful comparison of concrete advantage terms.

detection game is also single-user and this reflects the fact that users do not need to run a coordinated detection procedure. Detection requires the existence of a strong *universal* detector that depends neither on the subverted algorithm nor on big brother. This is in contrast to BPR's formulation, where detection was used for negative results, and non-universal detectors were also allowed. For detection, as in BPR, we assume explicit knowledge of user keys but do not allow access to the (possibly subverted) encryption procedure or the internal state/randomness of the scheme. Weakening the requirements on the detector only strengthens our positive results. On the other hand, the communicated ciphertexts/messages should be made available to the detector. As we have seen, without this strengthening, resistance against input-triggered subversions is impossible even for multi-user oracle-assisted detectors. We note, however, that our actual detection procedure in Sect. 5 processes ciphertexts one at a time and hence storing only the last computed ciphertext would be sufficient.

5   Subversion Resistance from Unique Ciphertexts

We have not yet determined whether there exist symmetric encryption schemes which satisfy our security definition. In [4] the authors describe a powerful generic attack, termed the *biased-ciphertext attack*, that can be applied to any probabilistic symmetric encryption scheme. Hence any scheme that resists subversion must be deterministic. Bellare, Paterson, and Rogaway identified the *unique ciphertexts* property for symmetric encryption schemes as sufficient to satisfy their notion of surveillance security. We now show that this property is strong enough to also guarantee subversion security in sense of Definition 4. Let us first recall the definition of unique ciphertexts from [4].

Definition 5 (Unique ciphertexts). *A symmetric encryption scheme $\Pi = (\mathcal{K}, \mathcal{E}, \mathcal{D})$ is said to have unique ciphertexts if:*

1. *Π satisfies perfect correctness and,*
2. *for all $\ell \in \mathbb{N}$, all $K \in \mathcal{K}$, all $\mathbf{M} \in \mathcal{M}^\ell$ and all $\mathbf{A} \in \mathcal{AD}^\ell$, there exists exactly one ciphertext vector $\mathbf{C}$ such that:*

$$(\mathbf{M}, \varrho_\ell) \leftarrow \mathcal{D}_K(\mathbf{C}, \mathbf{A}, \varepsilon) \; for \; some \; \varrho_\ell.$$

It follows from Definition 5 that any symmetric encryption scheme that has unique ciphertexts must be deterministic. Note on the other hand that a deterministic encryption scheme does not necessarily have unique ciphertexts. In [4] it is shown how stateful encryption schemes having unique ciphertexts are easily obtained from most nonce-based encryption schemes [17] which are known to satisfy the tidiness property of [14]. The following theorem says that for schemes with unique ciphertexts we are guaranteed to always detect a subversion with the highest possible success rate.

Algorithm $\mathscr{U}(T)$

Parse T as $(K, i) \parallel T'$
$j \leftarrow 1; \mathbf{M} \leftarrow []; \mathbf{A} \leftarrow []; \mathbf{C} \leftarrow []$
for each (M, A, C) in T' do
$\quad \mathbf{M}[j] \leftarrow M, \mathbf{A}[j] \leftarrow A; \mathbf{C}[j] \leftarrow C$
$\quad j \leftarrow j + 1$
$(\mathbf{M}', \varrho_\ell) \leftarrow \mathcal{D}_K(\mathbf{C}, \mathbf{A}, \varepsilon)$
return $(\mathbf{M}' = \mathbf{M})$

Fig. 5. The detection test $\mathscr{U}$ used in Theorem 2.

Theorem 2. *Let* $\Pi = (\mathcal{K}, \mathcal{E}, \mathcal{D})$ *be a symmetric encryption scheme with unique ciphertexts. Then the detection test* $\mathscr{U}$ *of Fig. 5 is such that for all subversions* $\widetilde{\Pi}$ *and all adversaries* $\mathscr{B}$ *we have that*

$$\mathbf{Adv}_{\Pi,\widetilde{\Pi}}^{\overline{\mathrm{srv}}}(\mathscr{B}) \leq \mathbf{Adv}_{\Pi,\widetilde{\Pi}}^{\overline{\mathrm{det}}}(\mathscr{B}, \mathscr{U}).$$

Proof. Fix a subversion $\widetilde{\Pi} = (\widetilde{\mathcal{K}}, \widetilde{\mathcal{E}}, \widetilde{\mathcal{D}})$ and an adversary $\mathscr{B}$. Define

Event E**:** algorithm $\mathscr{B}$ makes a sequence of queries $(\mathbf{M}, \mathbf{A})$ such that the real and subverted encryption algorithms output a different ciphertext sequence, i.e., $\mathcal{E}(K, \mathbf{M}, \mathbf{A}, \varepsilon) \neq \widetilde{\mathcal{E}}(\widetilde{K}, K, \mathbf{M}, \mathbf{A}, \varepsilon, i)$.

Then for any key K, any subversion key $\widetilde{K}$, any subversion $\widetilde{\Pi}$ and any adversary $\mathscr{B}$ the corresponding surveillance advantage can be expressed as:

$$\mathbf{Adv}_{\Pi,\widetilde{\Pi}}^{\overline{\mathrm{srv}}}(\mathscr{B}) = 2\Pr\left[\overline{\mathrm{SURV}}_{\Pi,\widetilde{\Pi}}^{\mathscr{B}} \right] - 1$$
$$= 2\Pr\left[\overline{\mathrm{SURV}}_{\Pi,\widetilde{\Pi}}^{\mathscr{B}} \mid E \right] \Pr[E] + 2\Pr\left[\overline{\mathrm{SURV}}_{\Pi,\widetilde{\Pi}}^{\mathscr{B}} \mid \overline{E} \right] \Pr[\overline{E}] - 1$$

where the probabilities are calculated over the coins of $\mathscr{B}$, the coins of $\widetilde{\mathcal{E}}$, the sampling of the two keys, and bit b. Now if E does *not* occur $\mathscr{B}$ has no information about the bit b in the $\overline{\mathrm{SURV}}$ game, and $\Pr\left[\overline{\mathrm{SURV}}_{\Pi,\widetilde{\Pi}}^{\mathscr{B}} \mid \overline{E} \right] = 1/2$. Hence we may continue

$$= 2\Pr\left[\overline{\mathrm{SURV}}_{\Pi,\widetilde{\Pi}}^{\mathscr{B}} \mid E \right] \Pr[E] + \Pr[\overline{E}] - 1$$
$$\leq \Pr[E].$$

We can expand the detection advantage of $\mathscr{U}$ with respect to $\mathscr{B}$ in a similar manner to obtain:

$$\mathbf{Adv}_{\Pi,\widetilde{\Pi}}^{\overline{\mathrm{det}}}(\mathscr{B}, \mathscr{U}) = 2 \cdot \Pr\left[\overline{\mathrm{DETECT}}_{\Pi,\widetilde{\Pi}}^{\mathscr{B},\mathscr{U}} \mid E \right] \cdot \Pr[E]$$
$$+ 2 \cdot \Pr\left[\overline{\mathrm{DETECT}}_{\Pi,\widetilde{\Pi}}^{\mathscr{B},\mathscr{U}} \mid \overline{E} \right] \cdot \Pr[\overline{E}] - 1.$$

As before, if E does not occur $\mathscr{U}$ has no information about the bit b in the $\overline{\mathrm{DETECT}}$ game and cannot do better than guessing. Moreover, when E occurs, it follows from the construction of $\mathcal{U}$ (see Fig. 5) and the fact that Π has unique ciphertexts that $\mathcal{U}$ can always distinguish the real scheme from a subversion. Thus $\Pr\left[\overline{\text{DETECT}}_{\Pi,\widetilde{\Pi}}^{\mathcal{B},\mathcal{U}} \mid \overline{E}\right] = 1/2$ and $\Pr\left[\overline{\text{DETECT}}_{\Pi,\widetilde{\Pi}}^{\mathcal{B},\mathcal{U}} \mid E\right] = 1$ which yields the desired result:

$$\mathbf{Adv}_{\Pi,\widetilde{\Pi}}^{\overline{\det}}(\mathcal{B}, \mathcal{U}) = \Pr[E] \geq \mathbf{Adv}_{\Pi,\widetilde{\Pi}}^{\overline{\text{srv}}}(\mathcal{B}).$$

6 Concluding Remarks

Through this work we unravelled definitional challenges in modeling resistance against algorithm substitution attacks (ASA), and in the process we proposed a refinement to address some of the shortcomings of the recent model by Bellare, Paterson, and Rogaway (BPR). Within the new model we are able to re-establish that deploying ciphertext-unique encryption schemes can provide a provable (but limited) degree of resistance against adversarial entries who carry out ASAs. These schemes, however, do *not* protect against powerful adversarial entities that are able to manipulate vital components of a system or obtain leakage via means other than simple chosen-plaintext (or ciphertext) attacks. For instance, timing attacks and subversion of hardware modules are realistic (and deployed) attacks that do not fall under our or BPR's model. Characterizing when it is possible to resist against mass surveillance using cryptographic techniques (even in principle) and when this lies beyond the reach of cryptography remains an important issue of real concern.

Acknowledgments. The authors would like to thank Daniel J. Bernstein for many comments on the earlier versions of the paper. J. P. Degabriele and B. Poettering were supported by EPSRC Leadership Fellowship EP/H005455/1. B. Poettering was also supported by a Sofja Kovalevskaja Award of the Alexander von Humboldt Foundation, and the German Federal Ministry for Education and Research.

References

1. Ball, J., Borger, J., Greenwald, G.: Revealed: how US and UK spy agencies defeat internet privacy and security. The Guardian, September 2013. http://www.theguardian.com/world/2013/sep/05/nsa-gchq-encryption-codes-security
2. Barker, E., Kelsey, J.: Recommendation for random number generation using deterministic random bit generators, January 2012. http://csrc.nist.gov/publications/nistpubs/800-90A/SP800-90A.pdf
3. Bellare, M., Desai, A., Jokipii, E., Rogaway, P.: A concrete security treatment of symmetric encryption. In: 38th FOCS, Miami Beach, Florida, 19–22 October, pp. 394–403. IEEE Computer Society Press (1997)
4. Bellare, M., Paterson, K.G., Rogaway, P.: Security of symmetric encryption against mass surveillance. In: Garay, J.A., Gennaro, R. (eds.) CRYPTO 2014, Part I. LNCS, vol. 8616, pp. 1–19. Springer, Heidelberg (2014)

5. Checkoway, S., Niederhagen, R., Everspaugh, A., Green, M., Lange, T., Ristenpart, T., Bernstein, D.J., Maskiewicz, J., Shacham, H., Fredrikson, M.: On the practical exploitability of Dual EC in TLS implementations. In: Fu, K., Jung, J. (eds.) Proceedings of the 23rd USENIX Security Symposium, San Diego, CA, USA, 20–22 August, pp. 319–335. USENIX Association (2014)
6. Crépeau, C., Slakmon, A.: Simple backdoors for RSA key generation. In: Joye, M. (ed.) CT-RSA 2003. LNCS, vol. 2612, pp. 403–416. Springer, Heidelberg (2003)
7. Dierks, T., Rescorla, E.: The Transport Layer Security (TLS) Protocol version 1.2. RFC 5246, August 2008. https://www.ietf.org/rfc/rfc5246.txt
8. Goh, E.-J., Boneh, D., Pinkas, B., Golle, P.: The design and implementation of protocol-based hidden key recovery. In: Boyd, C., Mao, W. (eds.) ISC 2003. LNCS, vol. 2851, pp. 165–179. Springer, Heidelberg (2003)
9. Greenwald, G.: No Place to Hide: Edward Snowden, the NSA and the Surveillance State. Penguin Books Limited (2014)
10. Kirovski, D., Malvar, H.: Robust covert communication over a public audio channel using spread spectrum. In: Moskowitz, I.S. (ed.) IH 2001. LNCS, vol. 2137, pp. 354–368. Springer, Heidelberg (2001)
11. Menn, J.: Exclusive: secret contract tied NSA and security industry pioneer. Reuters, December 2013. http://www.reuters.com/article/2013/12/20/us-usa-security-rsa-idUSBRE9BJ1C220131220
12. Millen, J.K.: 20 years of covert channel modeling and analysis. In: 1999 IEEE Symposium on Security and Privacy, Oakland, California, USA, 9–12 May, pp. 113–114. IEEE Computer Society (1999)
13. Murdoch, S.J., Lewis, S.: Embedding covert channels into TCP/IP. In: Barni, M., Herrera-Joancomartí, J., Katzenbeisser, S., Pérez-González, F. (eds.) IH 2005. LNCS, vol. 3727, pp. 247–261. Springer, Heidelberg (2005)
14. Namprempre, C., Rogaway, P., Shrimpton, T.: Reconsidering generic composition. In: Nguyen, P.Q., Oswald, E. (eds.) EUROCRYPT 2014. LNCS, vol. 8441, pp. 257–274. Springer, Heidelberg (2014)
15. Perlroth, N.: Government announces steps to restore confidence on encryption standards. The New York Times, September 2013. http://bits.blogs.nytimes.com/2013/09/10/government-announces-steps-to-restore-confidence-on-encryption-standards/
16. Rescorla, E., Salter, M.: Extended random values for TLS. Internet Draft, March 2009. https://tools.ietf.org/html/draft-rescorla-tls-extended-random-02
17. Rogaway, P.: Nonce-based symmetric encryption. In: Roy, B., Meier, W. (eds.) FSE 2004. LNCS, vol. 3017, pp. 348–359. Springer, Heidelberg (2004)
18. Shurmow, D., Ferguson, N.: On the possibility of a back door in the NIST SP800-90 Dual EC PRNG. CRYPTO Rump Session (2007). http://rump2007.cr.yp.to/15-shumow.pdf
19. Simmons, G.J.: The prisoners' problem and the subliminal channel. In: Chaum, D. (ed.) CRYPTO 1983, Santa Barbara, USA, pp. 51–67. Plenum Press, New York (1983)
20. Wray, J.C.: An analysis of covert timing channels. In: IEEE Symposium on Security and Privacy, pp. 2–7 (1991)
21. Young, A., Yung, M.: The dark side of "black-box" cryptography, or: should we trust Capstone? In: Koblitz, N. (ed.) CRYPTO 1996. LNCS, vol. 1109, pp. 89–103. Springer, Heidelberg (1996)
22. Young, A., Yung, M.: Kleptography: using cryptography against cryptography. In: Fumy, W. (ed.) EUROCRYPT 1997. LNCS, vol. 1233, pp. 62–74. Springer, Heidelberg (1997)

23. Young, A., Yung, M.: The prevalence of kleptographic attacks on discrete-log based cryptosystems. In: Kaliski Jr., B.S. (ed.) CRYPTO 1997. LNCS, vol. 1294, pp. 264–276. Springer, Heidelberg (1997)
24. Young, A., Yung, M.: Bandwidth-optimal kleptographic attacks. In: Koç, Ç.K., Naccache, D., Paar, C. (eds.) CHES 2001. LNCS, vol. 2162, pp. 235–250. Springer, Heidelberg (2001)
25. Young, A., Yung, M.: Malicious cryptography: kleptographic aspects. In: Menezes, A. (ed.) CT-RSA 2005. LNCS, vol. 3376, pp. 7–18. Springer, Heidelberg (2005)
26. Young, A., Yung, M.: A space efficient backdoor in RSA and its applications. In: Preneel, B., Tavares, S. (eds.) SAC 2005. LNCS, vol. 3897, pp. 128–143. Springer, Heidelberg (2006)
27. Young, A.L., Yung, M.: Space-efficient kleptography without random oracles. In: Furon, T., Cayre, F., Doërr, G., Bas, P. (eds.) IH 2007. LNCS, vol. 4567, pp. 112–129. Springer, Heidelberg (2008)

Author Index

Printed in the United States
By Bookmasters